BEFORE THE LAW

BEFORE THE LAW

An Introduction to the Legal Process

FOURTH EDITION

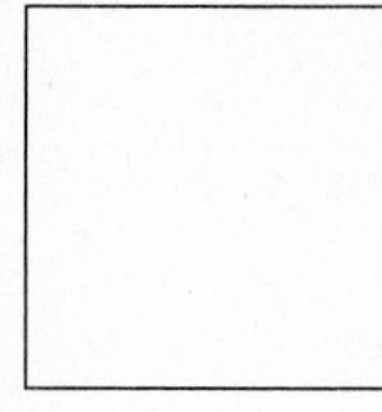

John J. Bonsignore
Ethan Katsh
Peter d'Errico
Ronald M. Pipkin
Stephen Arons
Janet Rifkin

Department of Legal Studies
The University of Massachusetts at Amherst

Houghton Mifflin Company Boston
Dallas □ *Geneva, Illinois*
Palo Alto □ *Princeton, New Jersey*

Cover photograph by Keller and Peet Associates.

Printed in the U.S.A.

Library of Congress Catalog Card Number: 88-83733

ISBN: 0-395-35921-X

ABCDEFGHIJ-B-9543210/89

Contents

Preface

Before the Law: An Introduction to the Legal Process is an introduction to the liberal arts study of law. Its aim is to develop inquisitive, intellectual capacities in the reader. The book contains varied material taken from many sources, ranging from court opinions through sociological, psychological, and anthropological analyses of legal phenomena, to historical and philosophical approaches to law. The book also includes literary views of law in selections from fiction and poetry.

Just as the contents of the book are varied, so are its applications. Although the Table of Contents displays an arrangement primarily oriented toward institutional structures and functions, the materials are susceptible to many other arrangements. A historical or political approach, for example, might result in an entirely different arrangement, perhaps one built to take advantage of current events. A systems approach might focus on legal processes, and a sociological approach on legal actors — with a variety of possible orderings of the readings under either approach. The editors encourage teachers to experiment with the book's contents to take advantage of individual interests and expertise. We hope that the index may facilitate such experimentation.

This fourth edition of *Before the Law* contains a substantially increased array of editorial comment at the start of each chapter and section. Some conclusive comments are also provided. These comments spur the reader to think critically about the selections, to compare selections with one another, and to reflect on larger issues spanning several selections. In keeping with the aim of a broad, nondoctrinaire approach, these comments are written with an eye toward preserving the open-textured quality of the book, while nonetheless guiding and orienting the reader to the existing arrangement of materials. In this way, the themes of the text as a whole are developed without an overly didactic approach.

CHANGES IN THE FOURTH EDITION

In addition to expanded editorial comments, the fourth edition offers a completely new chapter on the rapidly emerging field of nonadversary conflict resolution, with articles and case studies that focus on the essential aspects of this element in American legal culture. Other chapters have been revised, updated, and reorganized to reflect new developments and experience gained in using the previous editions.

Chapter One "An Overview of Legal Theory" provides a survey of some of the major explanations of law and its purposes, and includes illustrative cases and materials for testing these sometimes contradictory versions of legal reality. Chapter Two "The Police" includes new readings on the history of the exclusionary rule, the discretionary powers of police officers, and the role of the police in modern society. Chapter Three "The Legal Profession and the Legal System" has been revised to include a greater emphasis on lawyer-client interactions, the changing gender balance in the legal profession, and the relationships between social hierarchies, legal education, and lawyer specialization. Chapter Four "Juries and Community Participation in the Legal Process" includes substantial new material relating jury nullification to civil disobedience, and adds social science research data on the effect of jury deliberation rules. The materials on jury selection are updated, and a case is included dealing with drug screening as a form of trial without jury. Chapter Five "Conflict Resolution" is the new chapter on dispute resolution. Chapter Six "Images of Law" has been extensively revised to sharpen the focus on rules and reason, and state and society. New material has been added on the relation of law to economic power, and on the role of force involved in law enforcement. A concluding editorial comment draws together the varied materials of the book into an overview of major themes.

DISTINCTIVE FEATURES

One key pedagogical feature of the book is the manner in which the arrangement of readings provokes questioning and discussion and precludes simplistic conclusions to difficult issues. Our intention is to juxtapose selections in such a way as to demonstrate the open-ended quality of law and legal knowledge. There is never any attempt to reduce an area of law to "black letter" answers. Law is demonstrated as a continually changing, multifaceted phenomenon, responding to social, political, and economic forces, and evolving in different ways in different cultures and historical eras.

This thought-provoking quality of the book's editorial structure is reinforced by notes, questions, and short excerpts after each major reading. These provide suggestions for contemplation and discussion, as well as elaborations on particular points. As in previous editions, references for additional reading are provided at the conclusion of each chapter.

In short, this book supports a problem-solving, or inquiry-method, approach to teaching about law. Whether the book is supplemented by films, presentations, or other readings, or is the sole item in the syllabus, *Before the Law* provides the basis for exploring legal issues as a facet of liberal arts education.

ACKNOWLEDGMENTS

We thank students and teachers who have used prior editions of the book for their comments and suggestions toward the present edition. In particular, we thank the following reviewers for their intensive reviews of this edition:

Charles Chastain, *University of Arkansas at Little Rock*

James L. Gibson, *University of Houston*

Christine Harrington, *New York University*

Eugene Hogan, *Western Washington University*

Albert P. Melone, *Southern Illinois University*

John A. Perrotta, *Rhode Island College*

Albert C. Price, *University of Michigan*

Lawrence Rothstein, *University of Rhode Island*

Lee S. Weinberg, *University of Pittsburgh*

We also gratefully acknowledge the continuing strong support of the Department of Legal Studies and the School of Social and Behavioral Sciences at the University of Massachusetts at Amherst, and thank our editors at Houghton Mifflin for their thorough attention to our manuscript.

J.J.B.
E.K.
P.d'E.
R.M.P.
S.A.
J.R.

Introduction

Before the Law: An Introduction to the Legal Process is an unusual textbook. It does not pretend to be the "last word" on the subject. Instead, it raises questions and leaves many topics open-ended. *Before the Law* is not written in linear fashion from beginning to end. Instead, it presents an array of perspectives, any of which may be the start of a discussion leading to other readings.

This book is intended to inspire its readers to think. To this end, the materials and their arrangement are provocative. They criticize accepted ideas, raise questions about values, and provide glimpses into the difficult choices underlying the everyday operation and historical development of the legal system. What one writer or one case may assert is set next to a different assertion by another author or case. The result is that the book reads like a dialogue rather than a monologue. Each selection is presented as part of a discussion, even if its author has written it as though its facts are unquestionable.

The editors of this book regard law as an ongoing process in society. Law itself may speak with the authority of the state, but its meaning and content are as changeable as the political, social, and economic forces of the society. Any reader who comes to this book with expectations of finding legal answers to legal questions — such as "When can the police arrest?" or "What is the liability of the manufacturer for injury to the consumer?" — will probably be disappointed, although there are selections that deal with such specific questions and answers. But the reader who comes to this book hoping to understand the nature and functions of law in society will probably be satisfied. For this is a book in *legal studies,* designed to reach those who are interested in law, with or without a pressing legal problem or the intention to make a career in law.

This book is therefore not simply a legal text. More than being a book *in* law, it is a book *about* law. It is designed to encourage a variety of approaches to the study of law: political, sociological, anthropological, historical, literary, and philosophical. All of these facets are represented in readings throughout the chapters. Some selections are written by famous authors, and many readings come from works by scholars who are recognized as experts in their fields. A few selections are excerpted from popular magazines. The legal materials include court decisions and law review articles. But whatever their sources, the readings are always arranged to present aspects of law in the broad context of culture and history. No legal issue is presented only as a technical rule to be memorized. Rather, each issue is shown as part of a process of law operating in society.

To help you reach for these broad perspectives, we have provided comments before and sometimes after each chapter and section. These editors' comments describe the major themes in the readings, and help orient and guide you. In addition, we have included many notes and questions specifically relating to the selections. These notes include suggestions to prompt discussion and contemplation, and may also provide short excerpts about particular points. We encourage you to use the notes and questions in working with the ideas presented in the main selections.

The comments, notes, and questions provide a basis for you to criticize, understand, and discuss each reading by itself and in conjunction with other readings. It is important to remember, however, that the readings may contain issues other than those pointed out by the editors. Our approach is to provide many starting points and connecting themes, and to prompt your own curiosity and intelligence to be a guide to further inquiry.

A list of Suggested Additional Readings is appended to each chapter. These are meant to be useful to readers who wish to pursue further the major ideas raised in the chapter. Since bibliographical information is provided for each reading in the book, including excerpts in the notes and questions, readers interested in a fuller review of the original sources can look them up at their library. You are encouraged to use the Contents and the Index to seek additional information on a topic, and to find further correlations among selections.

This is the beginning of the book. From here you may go to any other part of it. But first, you may wish to read the Foreword to Chapter One, which follows this Introduction. In the Foreword you will find the source of the book's title in a parable told by a character in a novel by Franz Kafka. The parable itself is written as a teaching about law, about the confusion and contradiction that seems to exist within and around it. We do not know what specific legal question was troubling the man in the story, but we are forced to see the trouble he has in finding a solution to his question.

The Foreword explores the meaning of the parable in a way that demonstrates how this book works: raising questions, suggesting answers, exploring alternatives, and ultimately leaving the final answer open. Like Kafka's protagonist, you may be left with a melancholy feeling after reading this. Perhaps you too would rather have simple answers to the questions you ask about law. On the other hand, you may react to this story as you would to a dream: its logical meaning eludes you, but the power of its imagery inspires much thinking and prods you to further inquiry.

If you are the type of reader who wants to know how the book ends before you really start, you may wish also to look at the Conclusion to Chapter Six. There you will find an overview of the central philosophical themes — about human nature and the nature of society — that run like threads through the fabric of this book. You will not find a conclusion that tells you "who dunnit," but a conclusion that tells you how it is possible to go on with the study of law even when that study is more difficult and troubling than you had expected.

Foreword

Before the Law *Franz Kafka*

"Before the Law stands a doorkeeper on guard. To this doorkeeper there comes a man from the country who begs for admittance to the Law. But the doorkeeper says that he cannot admit the man at the moment. The man, on reflection, asks if he will be allowed, then, to enter later. 'It is possible,' answers the doorkeeper, 'but not at this moment.' Since the door leading into the Law stands open as usual and the doorkeeper steps to one side, the man bends down to peer through the entrance. When the doorkeeper sees that, he laughs and says: 'If you are so strongly tempted, try to get in without my permission. But note that I am powerful. And I am only the lowest doorkeeper. From hall to hall keepers stand at every door, one more powerful than the other. Even the third of these has an aspect that even I cannot bear to look at.' These are difficulties which the man from the country has not expected to meet; the Law, he thinks, should be accessible to every man and at all times, but when he looks more closely at the doorkeeper in his furred robe, with his huge pointed nose and long, thin, Tartar beard, he decides that he had better wait until he gets permission to enter. The doorkeeper gives him a stool and lets him sit down at the side of the door. There he sits waiting for days and years. He makes many attempts to be allowed in and wearies the doorkeeper with his importunity. The doorkeeper often engages him in brief conversation, asking him about his home and about other matters, but the questions are put quite impersonally, as great men put questions, and always conclude with the statement that the man cannot be allowed to enter yet. The man, who has equipped himself with many things for his journey, parts with all he has, however valuable, in the hope of bribing the doorkeeper. The doorkeeper accepts it all, saying, however, as he takes each gift: 'I take this only to keep you from feeling that you have left something undone.' During all these long years the man watches the doorkeeper almost incessantly. He forgets about the other doorkeepers, and this one seems to him the only barrier between himself and the Law. In the first years he curses his evil fate aloud; later, as he grows old, he only mutters to himself. He grows childish, and since in his prolonged watch he has learned to know even the fleas in the doorkeeper's fur collar, he begs the very fleas to help him and to persuade the doorkeeper to change his mind. Finally his eyes grow dim and he does not know whether the world is really darkening around him or whether his eyes are only deceiving him. But in the darkness he can now perceive a radiance that streams immortally from the door of the Law. Now his life is drawing to a close. Before he dies, all that he has experienced during the whole time of his sojourn condenses in his mind into one

---

Franz Kafka (1883–1924) was born in Prague, Czechoslovakia, where he lived and practiced law until his death of tuberculosis. As his diaries reflect, he sometimes found his work as a lawyer incompatible with his art, but there is no doubt that law, from its imposing architecture down to its sometimes overwhelming effects on the average person, permeated all his writings. The parable "Before the Law" was not published during his lifetime; it was part of his unfinished novel, *The Trial*.—ED.

question, which he has never yet put to the doorkeeper. He beckons the doorkeeper, since he can no longer raise his stiffening body. The doorkeeper has to bend far down to hear him, for the difference in size between them has increased very much to the man's disadvantage. 'What do you want to know now?' asks the doorkeeper, 'you are insatiable.' 'Everyone strives to attain the Law,' answers the man, 'how does it come about, then, that in all these years no one has come seeking admittance but me?' The doorkeeper perceives that the man is at the end of his strength and that his hearing is failing, so he bellows in his ear: 'No one but you could gain admittance through this door, since this door was intended only for you. I am now going to shut it.' "

Notes and Questions

1. The parable is both an old and an odd form of education. Parables have been extensively used for instructional purposes in both the Old and New Testaments, not to mention their use in Middle and Far Eastern religions. What makes the parable so rich as a teaching-learning device is our inability to reduce the parable to a single point, message, or slogan. Both teachers and students are left in doubt, even after having studied the parable for some time.

   The parable has other unique features as well. It cannot be dismissed as mere abstraction or as consummate vagueness that leads nowhere. By the time we might be inclined to dismiss the parable, we have become hooked. Our minds struggle to find the meaning that is at once at hand and escaping us. Each line of the parable considered separately is intelligible, but the totality slips away. One more reading might suffice, we think. Well, not quite. Perhaps a third, and so on. We can allow ourselves multiple readings, because the parable is so short and each time through we seem to gain something.

   Before going further, tell what effect the parable produces in you. Are you frustrated, angry, or otherwise disturbed by the story? If so, what lies behind such unwanted feelings?

   What is Kafka telling you about law? Has he drawn a pleasant or an unpleasant picture? In what settings, legal or otherwise, might his lessons be applicable?

☐ Kafka follows the parable of the man from the country and the doorkeeper with a discussion of the parable between a priest and a character named simply K. In doing so, Kafka gives us as much to think about as he resolves. Impishly, but like a great teacher, he both helps us and opens new questions at the same time.

Dialogue Between a Priest and K. *Franz Kafka*

"So the doorkeeper deluded the man," said K. immediately, strongly attracted by the story.

"Don't be too hasty," said the priest, "don't take over an opinion without testing it. I have told you the story in the very words of the scriptures. There's no mention of delusion in it."

"But it's clear enough," said K., "and your first interpretation of it was quite right. The doorkeeper gave the message of salvation to the man only when it could no longer help him."

"He was not asked the question any earlier," said the priest, "and you must consider,

---

too, that he was only a doorkeeper, and as such he fulfilled his duty."

"What makes you think he fulfilled his duty?" asked K. "He didn't fulfill it. His duty might have been to keep all strangers away, but this man, for whom the door was intended, should have been let in."

"You have not enough respect for the written word and you are altering the story," said the priest. "The story contains two important statements made by the doorkeeper about admission to the Law, one at the beginning, the other at the end. The first statement is: that he cannot admit the man at the moment, and the other is: that this door was intended only for the man. But there is no contradiction. The first statement, on the contrary, even implies the second. One could almost say that in suggesting to the man the possibility of future admittance the doorkeeper is exceeding his duty. At that moment his apparent duty is only to refuse admittance, and indeed many commentators are surprised that the suggestion should be made at all, since the doorkeeper appears to be a precisian with a stern regard for duty. He does not once leave his post during these many years, and he does not shut the door until the very last minute; he is conscious of the importance of his office, for he says: 'I am powerful'; he is respectful to his superiors, for he says: 'I am only the lowest doorkeeper'; he is not garrulous, for during all these years he puts only what are called 'impersonal questions'; he is not to be bribed, for he says in accepting a gift: 'I take this only to keep you from feeling that you have left something undone'; where his duty is concerned he is to be moved neither by pity nor rage, for we are told that the man 'wearied the doorkeeper with his importunity'; and finally even his external appearance hints at a pedantic character, the large, pointed nose and the long, thin, black Tartar beard. Could one imagine a more faithful doorkeeper? Yet the doorkeeper has other elements in his character which are likely to advantage anyone seeking admittance and which make it comprehensible enough that he should somewhat exceed his duty in suggesting the possibility of future admittance. For it cannot be denied that he is a little simple-minded and consequently a little conceited. Take the statements he makes about his power and the power of the other doorkeepers and their dreadful aspect which even he cannot bear to see — I hold that these statements may be true enough, but that the way in which he brings them out shows that his perceptions are confused by simpleness of mind and conceit. The commentators note in this connection: 'The right perception of any matter and a misunderstanding of the same matter do not wholly exclude each other.' One must at any rate assume that such simpleness and conceit, however sparingly indicated, are likely to weaken his defense of the door; they are breaches in the character of the doorkeeper. To this must be added the fact that the doorkeeper seems to be a friendly creature by nature, he is by no means always on his official dignity. In the very first moments he allows himself the jest of inviting the man to enter in spite of the strictly maintained veto against entry; then he does not, for instance, send the man away, but gives him, as we are told, a stool and lets him sit down beside the door. The patience with which he endures the man's appeals during so many years, the brief conversations, the acceptance of the gifts, the politeness with which he allows the man to curse loudly in his presence the fate for which he himself is responsible — all this lets us deduce certain motions of sympathy. Not every doorkeeper would have acted thus. And finally, in answer to a gesture of the man's he stoops low down to give him the chance of putting a last question. Nothing but mild impatience — the doorkeeper knows that this is the end of it all — is discernible in the words: 'You are insatiable.' Some push this mode of interpretation even further and hold that these words express a kind of friendly admiration, though not without a hint of condescension. At any rate the figure of the doorkeeper can be said to come out very differently from what you fancied."

"You have studied the story more exactly and for a longer time than I have," said K. They were both silent for a little while. Then K. said: "So you think the man was not deluded?"

"Don't misunderstand me," said the priest, "I am only showing you the various opinions concerning that point. You must not pay too much attention to them. The scriptures are unalterable and the comments often enough merely express the commentator's bewilderment. In this case there even exists an interpretation which claims that the deluded person is really the doorkeeper."

"That's a far-fetched interpretation," said K. "On what is it based?"

"It is based," answered the priest, "on the simple-mindedness of the doorkeeper. The argument is that he does not know the Law from inside, but he knows only the way that leads to it, where he patrols up and down. His ideas of the interior are assumed to be childish, and it is supposed that he himself is afraid of the other guardians whom he holds up as bogies before the man. Indeed, he fears them more than the man does, since the man is determined to enter after hearing about the dreadful guardians of the interior, while the doorkeeper has no desire to enter, at least not so far as we are told. Others again say that he must have been in the interior already, since he is after all engaged in the service of the Law and can only have been appointed from inside. This is countered by arguing that he may have been appointed by a voice calling from the interior, and that anyhow he cannot have been far inside, since the aspect of the third doorkeeper is more than he can endure. Moreover, no indication is given that all these years he ever made any remarks showing a knowledge of the interior except for the one remark about the doorkeepers. He may have been forbidden to do so, but there is no mention of that either. On these grounds the conclusion is reached that he knows nothing about the aspect and significance of the interior, so that he is in a state of delusion. But he is deceived also about his relation to the man from the country, for he is subject to the man and does not know it. He treats the man instead as his own subordinate, as can be recognized from many details that must still be fresh in your mind. But, according to this view of the story, it is just as clearly indicated that he is really subordinated to the man. In the first place, a bondman is always subject to a free man. Now the man from the country is really free, he can go where he likes, it is only the Law that is closed to him, and access to the Law is forbidden him only by one individual, the doorkeeper. When he sits down on the stool by the side of the door and stays there for the rest of his life, he does it of his own free will; in the story there is no mention of any compulsion. But the doorkeeper is bound to his post by his very office, he does not dare strike out into the country, nor apparently may he go into the interior of the Law, even should he wish to. Besides, although he is in the service of the Law, his service is confined to this one entrance; that is to say, he serves only this man for whom alone the entrance is intended. On that ground too he is subject to the man. One must assume that for many years, for as long as it takes a man to grow up to the prime of life, his service was in a sense empty formality, since he had to wait for a man to come, that is to say, someone in the prime of life, and so had to wait a long time before the purpose of his service could be fulfilled, and, moreover, had to wait on the man's pleasure, for the man came of his own free will. But the termination of his service also depends on the man's term of life, so that to the very end he is subject to the man. And it is emphasized throughout that the doorkeeper apparently realizes nothing of all this. That is not in itself remarkable, since according to this interpretation the doorkeeper is deceived in a much more important issue, affecting his very office. At the end, for example, he says regarding the entrance to the Law: 'I am now going to shut it,' but at the beginning of the story we are told that the door leading into the Law stands always open, and if it stands open always, that is to say, at all times, without reference to the life or death of the man, then the doorkeeper is incapable of closing it. There is some difference of opinions about the motive behind the doorkeeper's statement, whether he said he was going to close the door merely for the sake of giving an answer, or to emphasize his devotion to duty, or to bring the man into a state of grief and regret in his last moments. But there is no lack of agreement that the doorkeeper will not be able to shut the door. Many indeed profess to find that he is subordinate to the man even in wisdom, towards the end, at least, for the man sees the radiance that issues from the door of the Law while the doorkeeper in his official position must stand with his back to the door, nor does he say anything to show that he has perceived the change."

"That is well argued," said K., after repeating to himself in a low voice several passages from the priest's exposition. "It is well argued, and I am inclined to agree that the doorkeeper is deluded. But that has not made me abandon my former opinion, since both conclusions are to some extent compatible. Whether the doorkeeper is clear-sighted or deluded does not dispose of the matter. I said the man is deluded. If the doorkeeper is clear-sighted, one might have doubts about that, but if the doorkeeper himself is deluded, then his delusion must of necessity be communicated to the man. That makes the doorkeeper not, indeed, a swindler, but a creature so simple-minded that he ought to be dismissed at once from his office. You mustn't forget that the doorkeeper's delusions do himself no harm but do infinite harm to the man."

"There are objections to that," said the priest. "Many aver that the story confers no right on anyone to pass judgment on the doorkeeper. Whatever he may seem to us, he is yet a servant of the Law; that is, he belongs to the Law and as such is set beyond human judgment. In that case one dare not believe that the doorkeeper is subordinate to the man. Bound as he is by his service, even at the door of the Law, he is incomparably freer than anyone at large in the world. The man is only seeking the Law, the doorkeeper is already attached to it. It is the Law that has placed him at his post; to doubt his integrity is to doubt the Law itself."

"I don't agree with that point of view," said K. shaking his head, "for if one accepts it, one must accept as true everything the doorkeeper says. But you yourself have sufficiently proved how impossible it is to do that."

"No," said the priest, "it is not necessary to accept everything as true, one must only accept it as necessary."

"A melancholy conclusion," said K. "It turns lying into a universal principle."

Notes and Questions

1. Compare your earlier reflections about the parable with the commentaries of the priest and K. Whose come closer to your own?
2. What are the priest and K. arguing about? Who won the argument? Is there a difference between winning an argument and being right?
3. K.'s argument seems to come down to the idea that justice was denied the man from the country. Was justice done, in your judgment?
4. In the dialogue, the priest does most of the talking and K. does very little. (Follow the comments of K. all the way through to see this.) What does this imbalance in the conversation tell you? Does Kafka, the author, speak through the priest or through K.?
5. The priest seems expert and confident, whereas K. appears amateurish and tentative. What effect do these stances have on the ability of either to win the argument or to convince readers of the worth of his contentions?
6. In the parable, the doorkeeper is portrayed as a low-level insider to the law and the man from the country as an outsider. In the discussion, the priest looks more like an insider and K. an outsider. Would either the man from the country or K. have been helped by hiring a lawyer? By having studied law himself?
7. The position of the priest seems to shift as each new question is raised by K. Does the priest's argument get stronger or weaker as he goes along? What about K.'s arguments?
8. The final argument of the priest is that "it is not necessary to accept everything as true, one must only accept it as necessary." What are the implications of this contention? How does K. respond to it? Which position would you endorse?

9. It is sometimes said that bad order may be better than no order at all. Is this true? Which would you prefer? Which would the man from the country prefer?
10. In the encounter between the doorkeeper and the man from the country the rules seem to change as they are made: at first the door is denied the man from the country presumably because he has no right to enter; but later he is told that the door was intended only for him, that it was always his right to enter, in fact, it was his exclusively. Is it possible to have "order" where there are shifting rules?

    However, it could also be said that there is consistency across the entire story. The *rules* may be different, but the *result* stays constant — the man from the country can never enter into the domain of law. If the law never serves him, then for whom is it?
11. With what characters — the man from the country, the doorkeeper, the priest, or K. — should most readers identify? With whom do they *want* to identify? What social roles and positions are represented by these characters?

☐ In the next reading, Kafka answers some of the foregoing questions with an enigma; namely that law is for the few and those associated with the few, but the many do not rebel.

The Problem of Our Laws *Franz Kafka*

Our laws are not generally known; they are kept secret by the small group of nobles who rule us. We are convinced that these ancient laws are scrupulously administered; nevertheless, it is an extremely painful thing to be ruled by laws that one does not know. I am not thinking of possible discrepancies that may arise in the interpretation of the laws, or of the disadvantages involved when only a few and not the whole people are allowed to have a say in their interpretation. These disadvantages are perhaps of no great importance. For the laws are very ancient; their interpretation has been the work of centuries, and has itself doubtless acquired the status of law; and though there is still a possible freedom of interpretation left, it has now become very restricted. Moreover the nobles have obviously no cause to be influenced in their interpretation by personal interests inimical to us, for the laws were made to the advantage of the nobles from the very beginning, they themselves stand above the laws, and that seems to be why the laws were entrusted exclusively into their hands. Of course, there is wisdom in that — who doubts the wisdom of the ancient laws? — but also hardship for us; probably that is unavoidable.

The very existence of these laws, however, is at most a matter of presumption. There is a tradition that they exist and that they are a mystery confided to the nobility, but it is not and cannot be more than a mere tradition sanctioned by age, for the essence of a secret code is that it should remain a mystery. Some of us among the people have attentively scrutinized the doings of the nobility since the earliest times and possess records made by our forefathers —

---

records which we have conscientiously continued — and claim to recognize amid the countless number of facts certain main tendencies which permit of this or that historical formulation; but when in accordance with these scrupulously tested and logically ordered conclusions we seek to orient ourselves somewhat towards the present or the future, everything becomes uncertain, and our work seems only an intellectual game, for perhaps these laws that we are trying to unravel do not exist at all. There is a small party who are actually of this opinion and who try to show that, if any law exists, it can only be this: The Law is whatever the nobles do. This party see everywhere only the arbitrary acts of the nobility, and reject the popular tradition, which according to them possesses only certain trifling and incidental advantages that do not offset its heavy drawbacks, for it gives the people a false, deceptive and over-confident security in confronting coming events. This cannot be gainsaid, but the overwhelming majority of our people account for it by the fact that the tradition is far from complete and must be more fully enquired into, that the material available, prodigious as it looks, is still too meager, and that several centuries will have to pass before it becomes really adequate. This view, so comfortless as far as the present is concerned, is lightened only by the belief that a time will eventually come when the tradition and our research into it will jointly reach their conclusion, and as it were gain a breathing space, when everything will have become clear, the law will belong to the people, and the nobility will vanish. This is not maintained in any spirit of hatred against the nobility; not at all, and by no one. We are more inclined to hate ourselves, because we have not yet shown ourselves worthy of being entrusted with the laws. And that is the real reason why the party which believes that there is no law has remained so small — although its doctrine is in certain ways so attractive, for it unequivocally recognizes the nobility and its right to go on existing.

Actually one can express the problem only in a sort of paradox: Any party which would repudiate, not only all belief in the laws, but the nobility as well, would have the whole people behind it; yet no such party can come into existence, for nobody would dare to repudiate the nobility. We live on this razor edge. A writer once summed the matter up in this way: The sole visible and indubitable law that is imposed upon us is the nobility, and must we ourselves deprive ourselves of that one law?

Notes and Questions

1. According to Kafka, what is the central problem of law and what are the obstacles to its resolution?

2. Where do doorkeepers and lawyers fit into the legal structure as outlined by Kafka?

3. If people were to come to know that law is *of*, *by*, and *for* the nobility, would they necessarily rebel?

4. Kafka says, "We are more inclined to hate ourselves, because we have not yet shown ourselves worthy of being entrusted with the laws." Does this suggest that the problem lies within people and their excessive humility or in the institutions they encounter that inhibit their assertion of autonomy? Put another way, is the problem in the man from the country or in the system symbolized by the doorkeeper?

5. What helps officials of law, like doorkeepers, priests, judges, and lawyers, feel worthy enough to be entrusted with the law? If they felt more like ordinary people, would the problem of law be resolved?

6. In this and in the previous writings, Kafka seems to talk *in circles.* Try to present his central ideas "in a straight line." Imagine, if it helps, explaining Kafka to a roommate who has not read him.

A final selection from Kafka has the virtue of being short, but compact.

Couriers *Franz Kafka*

They were offered the choice between becoming kings or the couriers of kings. The way children would, they all wanted to be couriers. Therefore there are only couriers who hurry about the world, shouting to each other — since there are no kings — messages that have become meaningless. They would like to put an end to this miserable life of theirs but they dare not because of their oaths of service.

Notes and Questions

1. It might be said that this parable calls for strong leadership, since leadership might give meaning to the couriers' messages, which are now meaningless. But how would strong leadership be distinguished from the nobility, which is said to be the integral part of "The Problem of Our Laws"? Are there alternatives to the recommendation of strong leadership?
2. It is also sometimes said that people are "happy" in courier roles and would not abandon them, even if given the opportunity; but Kafka says that couriers lead miserable lives. What are the sources of misery in the courier's life? Are there alternatives to resentful acceptance?
3. In what sense are doorkeepers and lawyers couriers? In what sense are they kings? To whom or to what do they owe their "oaths of service"? Could they revoke their oaths? Should they?
4. You have considered three of Kafka's writings about law. What is Kafka's position on law?

The philosopher Alfred North Whitehead once said that all of Western philosophy was nothing more than footnotes to Plato. It might similarly be said that all discourses on Western law might be nothing more than footnotes to Franz Kafka. If this is true, Kafka's guidance and careful observation might give students all that they will ever need for an understanding of modern legal order.

A Scholar in His Study Watching a Magic Disk. Rembrandt van Rijn: *Faust,* c. 1652. (National Gallery of Art, Washington. Gift of R. Horace Gallatin.)

CHAPTER 1 An Overview of Legal Theory

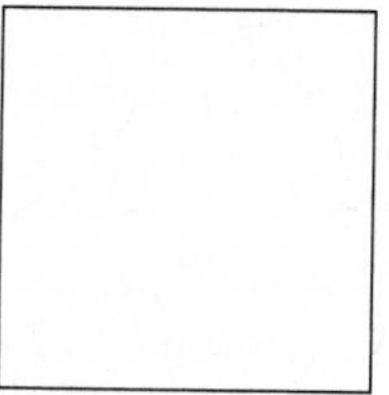

They tell you out at the Law School that the law is a wonderful science — the perfection of reason. 'Tis in fact a hodge-podge of Roman law, Bible texts, canon law, superstitions, scraps of feudalism, crazy fictions, and long dead statutes. Your professors try to bring order out of chaos and make sense where the devil himself couldn't find any.

Ephraim Tutt, *Yankee Lawyer* (1944)

Political philosophies are intellectual and moral creations; they contain high ideals, easy slogans, dubious facts, crude propaganda, sophisticated theories. Their adherents select some facts and ignore others, urge the acceptance of ideals, the inevitability of events, argue with this theory and debunk that one.

C. Wright Mills, *The Marxists* (1962)

All logical systems, East-West, scientific-religious, cyclic or linear, originate in an analysis of the way reality is structured.

Joseph Chilton Pearce, *Crack in the Cosmic Egg* (1982)

Definitions of law are statements of belief akin to political philosophies, articles of faith in religion, or intuition in science. The person who defines has a flash of genius, and the whole legal universe falls momentarily into place. Once a definition is reached, events are shaped to fit the definition, and what is at first only a psychic reality becomes a reality "out there" as well. It is this phenomenon that makes definitions so important and yet so dangerous; they provide concentrated explanations of the legal world but also foreclose possibilities that would disrupt the definition.

Law as a system of thought is only one of many possible structures of reality. As with other systems of thought, model precedes rather than follows data — map often both precedes and supersedes territory itself. Put a different way, conventional wisdom says that we see what exists. Unconventional wisdom says that we see what we are taught to see, or that we see what we instruct ourselves to see, or that we see what *we* let ourselves instruct ourselves to see.

The foregoing may fly in the face of ideas you have about learning. You might think of yourself as wanting to learn and being open to new ideas no matter how startling they might be. Why else would you enroll in a university? But what if the opposite is true, that although you might want to give yourself credit for an abiding desire to learn, you really do not want to learn or want to learn only what you do not have to pay serious attention to, such as studying for a multiple-choice examination? You might be engaging in more and more schooling with less and less effect, encountering no real need to abandon prior hard-won views of the world and possible places in it. The study of law may require you to be both more humble and more brave.

One purpose of an introductory law text is to enrich the ways that people view law and to show that there are alternative ways of looking at law so that you can teach yourself to see alternatives to the existing legal order. The act of teaching and learning should break down stereotypical thinking and also offer constructive possibilities.

What is needed is a reading that shows how models of thinking affect perception. Incoming students, while they say that they know nothing about law and that the lack of knowledge of law is the very reason for their taking an introductory law course, in fact have models of law and expectations that can be traced to television, newspapers, personal experiences, family history, and other sources. This incoming knowledge both interferes with and facilitates new learning. The following reading "Assembly Line" considers the differing arrangements of personal knowledge and the way cultures structure the acquisition and use of knowledge.

Assembly Line *B. Traven*

Mr. E. L. Winthrop of New York was on vacation in the Republic of Mexico. It wasn't long before he realized that this strange and really wild country had not yet been fully and satisfactorily explored by Rotarians and Lions, who are forever conscious of their glorious mission on earth. Therefore, he considered it his duty as a good American citizen to do his part in correcting this oversight.

In search for opportunities to indulge in his new avocation, he left the beaten track and ventured into regions not especially mentioned, and hence not recommended, by travel agents to foreign tourists. So it happened that one day he found himself in a little, quaint Indian village somewhere in the State of Oaxaca.

Walking along the dusty main street of this pueblecito, which knew nothing of pavements, drainage, plumbing, or of any means of artificial light save candles or pine splinters, he met with an Indian squatting on the earthen-floor front porch of a palm hut, a so-called jacalito.

The Indian was busy making little baskets from bast and from all kinds of fibers gathered by him in the immense tropical bush which surrounded the village on all sides. The material used had not only been well prepared for its purpose but was also richly colored with dyes that the basket-maker himself extracted from various native plants, barks, roots and from certain insects by a process known only to him and the members of his family.

His principal business, however, was not producing baskets. He was a peasant who lived on what the small property he possessed — less than fifteen acres of not too fertile soil — would yield, after much sweat and labor and after constantly worrying over the most wanted and best suited distribution of rain, sunshine, and wind and the changing balance of birds and insects beneficial or harmful to his crops. Baskets he made when there was nothing else for him to do in the fields, because he was unable to dawdle. After all, the sale of his baskets, though to a rather limited degree only, added to the small income he received from his little farm.

In spite of being by profession just a plain peasant, it was clearly seen from the small baskets he made that at heart he was an artist, a true and accomplished artist. Each basket looked as if covered all over with the most beautiful sometimes fantastic ornaments, flowers, butterflies, birds, squirrels, antelope, tigers, and a score of other animals of the wilds. Yet, the most amazing thing was that these decorations, all of them symphonies of color, were not painted on the baskets but were instead actually part of the baskets themselves. Bast and fibers dyed in dozens of different colors were so cleverly — one must actually say intrinsically — interwoven that those attractive designs appeared on the inner part of the basket as well as on the outside. Not by painting but by weaving were those highly artistic effects achieved. This performance he accomplished without ever looking at any sketch or pattern. While working on a basket these designs came to light as if by magic, and as long as a basket was not entirely finished one could not perceive what in this case or that the decoration would be like.

People in the market town who bought these baskets would use them for sewing baskets or to decorate tables with or window sills, or to hold little things to keep them from lying around. Women put their jewelry in them or flowers or little dolls. There were in fact a hundred and two ways they might serve certain purposes in a household or in a lady's own room.

Whenever the Indian had finished about twenty of the baskets he took them to town on market day. Sometimes he would already be on his way shortly after midnight because he owned only a burro to ride on, and if the burro had gone astray the day before, as happened frequently, he would have to walk the whole way to town and back again.

At the market he had to pay twenty centavos in taxes to sell his wares. Each basket cost him between twenty and thirty hours of constant work, not counting the time spent gathering bast and fibers, preparing them, making dyes and coloring the bast. All this meant extra time and work. The price he asked for each basket was fifty centavos, the equivalent of about four cents. It seldom happened, however, that a buyer paid outright the full fifty centavos asked — or four reales as the Indian called that money. The prospective buyer started bargaining, telling the Indian that he ought to be ashamed to ask such a sinful price. "Why, the whole dirty thing is nothing but ordinary petate straw which you find in heaps wherever you may look for it; the jungle is packed full of it," the buyer would argue. "Such a little basket, what's it good for anyhow? If I paid you, you thief, ten centavitos for it you should be grateful and kiss my hand. Well, it's your lucky day, I'll be generous this time, I'll pay you twenty, yet not one green centavo more. Take it or run along."

So he sold finally for twenty-five centavos, but then the buyer would say, "Now, what do you think of that? I've got only twenty centavos change on me. What can we do about that? If you can change me a twenty-peso bill, all right, you shall have your twenty-five fierros." Of course, the Indian could not change a twenty-peso bill and so the basket went for twenty centavos.

He had little if any knowledge of the outside world or he would have known that what happened to him was happening every hour of every day to every artist all over the world. That knowledge would perhaps have made him very proud, because he would have realized that he belonged to the little army which is the salt of the earth and which keeps culture, urbanity and beauty for their own sake from passing away.

Often it was not possible for him to sell all the baskets he had brought to market, for people here as elsewhere in the world preferred things made by the millions and each so much like the other that you were unable, even with the help of a magnifying glass, to tell which was which and where was the difference between two of the same kind.

Yet he, this craftsman, had in his life made several hundreds of those exquisite baskets, but so far no two of them had he ever turned out alike in design. Each was an individual piece of art and as different from the other as was a Murillo from a Velásquez.

Naturally he did not want to take those baskets which he could not sell at the market place home with him again if he could help it. In such a case he went peddling his products from door to door where he was treated partly as a beggar and partly as a vagrant apparently looking for an opportunity to steal, and he frequently had to swallow all sorts of insults and nasty remarks.

Then, after a long run, perhaps a woman would finally stop him, take one of the baskets and offer him ten centavos, which price through talks and talks would perhaps go up to fifteen or even to twenty. Nevertheless, in many instances he would actually get no more than just ten centavos, and the buyer, usually a woman, would grasp that little marvel and right before his eyes throw it carelessly upon the nearest table as if to say, "Well, I take that piece of nonsense only for charity's sake. I know my money is wasted. But then, after all, I'm a Christian and I can't see a poor Indian die of hunger since he has come such a long way from his village." This would remind her of something better and she would hold him and say, "Where are you at home anyway, Indito? What's your pueblo? So, from Huehuetonoc? Now, listen here, Indito, can't you bring me next Saturday two or three turkeys from Huehuetonoc? But they must be heavy and fat and very, very cheap or I won't even touch them. If I wish to pay the regular price I don't need you to bring them. Understand? Hop along, now, Indito."

The Indian squatted on the earthen floor in the portico of his hut, attended to his work and showed no special interest in the curiosity of Mr. Winthrop watching him. He acted almost as if he ignored the presence of the American altogether.

"How much that little basket, friend?" Mr. Winthrop asked when he felt that he at least had to say something as not to appear idiotic.

Fifty centavitos, patroncito, my good little lordy, four reales," the Indian answered politely.

"All right, sold," Mr. Winthrop blurted out in a tone and with a wide gesture as if he had bought a whole railroad. And examining his buy he added, "I know already who I'll give that pretty little thing to. She'll kiss me for it, sure. Wonder what she'll use it for?"

He had expected to hear a price of three or even four pesos. The moment he realized that he had judged the value six times too high, he saw right away what great business possibilities this miserable Indian village might offer to a dynamic promoter like himself. Without further delay he started exploring those possibilities. "Suppose, my good friend, I buy ten of these little baskets of yours which, as I might as well admit right here and now, have practically no real use whatsoever. Well, as I was saying, if I buy ten, how much would you then charge me apiece?"

The Indian hesitated for a few seconds, as if making calculations. Finally he said, "If you buy ten I can let you have them for forty-five centavos each, señorito gentleman."

"All right, amigo. And now, let's suppose I buy from you straight away one hundred of these absolutely useless baskets, how much will they cost me each?"

The Indian, never fully looking up to the American standing before him, and hardly taking his eyes off his work, said politely and without the slightest trace of enthusiasm in his voice, "In such a case I might not be quite unwilling to sell each for forty centavitos."

Mr. Winthrop bought sixteen baskets, which was all the Indian had in stock.

After three weeks' stay in the Republic, Mr. Winthrop was convinced that he knew this country perfectly, that he had seen everything and knew all about the inhabitants, their character and their way of life, and that there was nothing left for him to explore. So he returned to good old Nooyorg and felt happy to be once more in a civilized country, as he expressed it to himself.

One day going out for lunch he passed a confectioner's and, looking at the display in the window, he suddenly remembered the little baskets he had bought in that faraway Indian village.

He hurried home and took all the baskets he still had left to one of the best-known candymakers in the city.

"I can offer you here," Mr. Winthrop said to the confectioner, "one of the most artistic and at the same time the most original of boxes, if you wish to call them that. These little baskets would be just right for the most expensive chocolates meant for elegant and high-priced gifts. Just have a good look at them, sir, and let me listen."

The confectioner examined the baskets and found them extraordinarily well suited for a certain line in his business. Never before had there been anything like them for originality, prettiness and good taste. He, however, avoided most carefully showing any sign of enthusiasm, for which there would be time enough once he knew the price and whether he could get a whole load exclusively.

He shrugged his shoulders and said, "Well, I don't know. If you asked me I'd say it isn't quite what I'm after. However, we might give it a try. It depends, of course, on the price. In our business the package mustn't cost more than what's in it."

"Do I hear an offer?" Mr. Winthrop asked.

"Why don't you tell me in round figures how much you want for them? I'm not good in guessing."

"Well, I'll tell you, Mr. Kemple: since I'm the smart guy who discovered these baskets and since I'm the only Jack who knows where to lay his hands on more, I'm selling to the highest bidder, on an exclusive basis, of course. I'm positive you can see it my way, Mr. Kemple."

"Quite so, and may the best man win," the confectioner said. "I'll talk the matter over with my partners. See me tomorrow same time, please, and I'll let you know how far we might be willing to go."

Next day when both gentlemen met again Mr. Kemple said: "Now, to be frank with you, I know art on seeing it, no getting around that. And these baskets are little works of art, they surely are. However, we are no art dealers, you realize that of course. We've no other use for these pretty little things except as fancy packing for our French pralines made by us. We can't pay for them what we might pay considering them pieces of art. After all to us they're only wrappings. Fine wrappings, perhaps, but nevertheless wrappings. You'll see it our way I hope, Mr. —— oh yes, Mr. Winthrop. So, here is our offer, take it or leave it: a dollar and a quarter apiece and not one cent more."

Mr. Winthrop made a gesture as if he had been struck over the head.

The confectioner, misunderstanding this involuntary gesture of Mr. Winthrop, added quickly, "All right, all right, no reason to get excited, no reason at all. Perhaps we can do a trifle better. Let's say one-fifty."

"Make it one-seventy-five," Mr. Winthrop snapped, swallowing his breath while wiping his forehead.

"Sold. One-seventy-five apiece free at port of New York. We pay the customs and you pay the shipping. Right?"

"Sold," Mr. Winthrop said also and the deal was closed.

"There is, of course, one condition," the confectioner explained just when Mr. Winthrop was to leave. "One or two hundred won't do for us. It wouldn't pay the trouble and the advertising. I won't consider less than ten thousand, or one thousand dozens if that sounds better in your ears. And they must come in no less than twelve different patterns well assorted. How about that?"

"I can make it sixty different patterns or designs."

"So much the better. And you're sure you can deliver ten thousand let's say early October?"

"Absolutely," Mr. Winthrop avowed and signed the contract.

Practically all the way back to Mexico, Mr. Winthrop had a notebook in his left hand and a pencil in his right and he was writing figures, long rows of them, to find out exactly how much richer he would be when this business had been put through.

"Now, let's sum up the whole goddamn thing," he muttered to himself. "Damn it, where is that cursed pencil again? I had it right between my fingers. Ah, there it is. Ten thousand he ordered. Well, well, there we got a clean-cut profit of fifteen thousand four hundred and forty genuine dollars. Sweet smackers. Fifteen grand right into papa's pocket. Come to think of it, that Republic isn't so backward after all."

"Buenas tardes, mi amigo, how are you?" he greeted the Indian whom he found squatting in the porch of his jacalito as if he had never moved from his place since Mr. Winthrop had left for New York.

The Indian rose, took off his hat, bowed politely and said in his soft voice, "Be welcome, patroncito. Thank you, I feel fine, thank you. Muy buenas tardes. This house and all I have is at your kind disposal." He bowed once more, moved his right hand in a gesture of greeting and sat down again. But he excused himself for doing so by saying, "Perdóneme, patroncito, I have to take advantage of the daylight, soon it will be night."

"I've got big business for you, my friend," Mr. Winthrop began.

"Good to hear that, señor."

Mr. Winthrop said to himself, "Now, he'll jump up and go wild when he learns what I've got for him." And aloud he said: "Do you think you can make me one thousand of these little baskets?"

"Why not, patroncito? If I can make sixteen, I can make one thousand also."

"That's right, my good man. Can you also make five thousand?"

"Of course, señor. I can make five thousand if I can make one thousand."

"Good. Now, if I should ask you to make me ten thousand, what would you say? And what would be the price of each? You can make ten thousand, can't you?"

"Of course, I can, señor. I can make as many as you wish. You see, I am an expert in this sort of work. No one else in the whole state can make them the way I do."

"That's what I thought and that's exactly why I came to you."

"Thank you for the honor, patroncito."

"Suppose I order you to make me ten thousand of these baskets, how much time do you think you would need to deliver them?"

The Indian, without interrupting his work, cocked his head to one side and then to the other as if he were counting the days or weeks it would cost him to make all these baskets.

After a few minutes he said in a slow voice, "It will take a good long time to make so many baskets, patroncito. You see, the bast and the fibers must be very dry before they can be used properly. Then all during the time they are slowly drying, they must be worked and handled in a very special way so that while drying they won't lose their softness and their flexibility and their natural brilliance. Even when dry they must look fresh. They must never lose their natural properties or they will look just as lifeless and dull as straw. Then while they are drying up I got to get the plants and roots and barks and insects from which I brew the dyes. That takes much time also, believe me. The plants must be gathered when the moon is just right or they won't give the right color. The insects I pick from the plants must also be gathered at the right time and under the right conditions or else they produce no rich colors and are just like dust. But, of course, jefecito, I can make as many of these canastitas as you wish, even as many as three dozens if you want them. Only give me time."

"Three dozens? Three dozens?" Mr. Winthrop yelled, and threw up both arms in desperation. "Three dozens!" he repeated as if he had to say it many times in his own voice so as to understand the real meaning of it, because for a while he thought that he was dreaming. He had expected the Indian to go crazy on hearing that he was to sell ten thousand of his baskets without having to peddle them from door to door and be treated like a dog with a skin disease.

So the American took up the question of price again, by which he hoped to activate the Indian's ambition. "You told me that if I take one hundred baskets you will let me have them for forty centavos apiece. Is that right, my friend?"

"Quite right, jefecito."

"Now," Mr. Winthrop took a deep breath, "now, then, if I ask you to make me one thousand, that is, ten times one hundred baskets, how much will they cost me, each basket?"

That figure was too high for the Indian to grasp. He became slightly confused and for the first time since Mr. Winthrop had arrived he interrupted his work and tried to think it out. Several times he shook his head and looked vaguely around as if for help. Finally he said, "Excuse me, jefecito, little chief, that is by far too much for me to count. Tomorrow, if you will do me the honor, come and see me again and I think I shall have my answer ready for you, patroncito."

When on the next morning Mr. Winthrop came to the hut he found the Indian as usual squatting on the floor under the overhanging palm roof working at his baskets.

"Have you got the price for ten thousand?" he asked the Indian the very moment he saw him, without taking the trouble to say "Good Morning!"

"Si, patroncito, I have the price ready. You may believe me when I say it has cost me much labor and worry to find out the exact price, because, you see, I do not wish to cheat you out of your honest money."

"Skip that, amigo. Come out with the salad. What's the price?" Mr. Winthrop asked nervously.

"The price is well calculated now without any mistake on my side. If I got to make one thousand canastitas each will be three pesos. If I must make five thousand, each will cost nine pesos. And if I have to make ten thousand, in such a case I can't make them for less than fifteen pesos each." Immediately he returned to his work as if he were afraid of losing too much time with such idle talk.

Mr. Winthrop thought that perhaps it was his faulty knowledge of this foreign language that had played a trick on him.

"Did I hear you say fifteen pesos each if I eventually would buy ten thousand?"

"That's exactly and without any mistake what I've said, patroncito," the Indian answered in his soft courteous voice.

"But now, see here, my good man, you can't do this to me. I'm your friend and I want to help you get on your feet."

"Yes, patroncito, I know this and I don't doubt any of your words."

"Now, let's be patient and talk this over quietly as man to man. Didn't you tell me that if I would buy one hundred you would sell each for forty centavos?"

"Si, jefecito, that's what I said. If you buy one hundred you can have them for forty centavos apiece, provided that I have one hundred, which I don't."

"Yes, yes, I see that." Mr. Winthrop felt as if he would go insane any minute now. "Yes, so you said. Only what I can't comprehend is why you cannot sell at the same price if you make me ten thousand. I certainly don't wish to chisel on the price. I am not that kind. Only, well, let's see now, if you can sell for forty centavos at all, be it for twenty or fifty or a hundred, I can't quite get the idea why the price has to jump that high if I buy more than a hundred."

"Bueno, patroncito, what is there so difficult to understand? It's all very simple. One thousand canastitas cost me a hundred times more work than a dozen. Ten thousand cost me so much time and labor that I could never finish them, not even in a hundred years. For a thousand canastitas I need more bast than for a hundred, and I need more little red beetles and more plants and roots and bark for the dyes. It isn't that you just can walk into the bush and pick all the things you need at your heart's desire. One root with the true violet blue may cost me four or five days until I can find one in the jungle. And have you thought how much time it costs and how much hard work to prepare the bast and fibers? What is more, if I must make so many baskets, who then will look after my corn and my beans and my goats and chase for me occasionally a rabbit for meat on Sunday? If I have no corn, then I have no tortillas to eat, and if I grow no beans, where do I get my frijoles from?"

"But since you'll get so much money from me for your baskets you can buy all the corn and beans in the world and more than you need."

"That's what you think, señorito, little lordy. But you see, it is only the corn I grow myself that I am sure of. Of the corn which others may or may not grow, I cannot be sure to feast upon."

"Haven't you got some relatives here in this village who might help you to make baskets for me?" Mr. Winthrop asked hopefully.

"Practically the whole village is related to me somehow or other. Fact is, I got lots of close relatives in this here place."

"Why then can't they cultivate your fields and look after your goats while you make baskets for me? Not only this, they might gather for you the fibers and the colors in the bush and lend you a hand here and there in preparing the material you need for the baskets."

"They might, patroncito, yes, they might. Possible. But then you see who would take care of their fields and cattle if they work for me? And if they help me with the baskets it turns out the same. No one would any longer work his fields properly. In such a case corn and beans would get up so high in price that none of us could buy any and we all would starve to death. Besides, as the price of everything would rise and rise higher still how could I make baskets at forty centavos apiece? A pinch of salt or one green chili would set me back more than I'd collect for one single basket. Now you'll understand, highly estimated caballero and jefecito, why I can't make the baskets any cheaper than fifteen pesos each if I got to make that many."

Mr. Winthrop was hard-boiled, no wonder considering the city he came from. He refused to give up the more than fifteen thousand dollars which at that moment seemed to slip through his fingers like nothing. Being really desperate now, he talked and bargained with the Indian for almost two full hours, trying to make him understand how rich he, the Indian, would become if he would take this greatest opportunity of his life.

The Indian never ceased working on his baskets while he explained his points of view.

"You know, my good man," Mr. Winthrop said, "such a wonderful chance might never again knock on your door, do you realize that? Let me explain to you in ice-cold figures what fortune you might miss if you leave me flat on this deal."

He tore out leaf after leaf from his notebook, covered each with figures and still more figures, and while doing so told the peasant he would be the richest man in the whole district.

The Indian without answering watched with a genuine expression of awe as Mr. Winthrop wrote down these long figures, executing complicated multiplications and divisions and subtractions so rapidly that it seemed to him the greatest miracle he had ever seen.

The American, noting this growing interest in the Indian, misjudged the real significance of it. "There you are, my friend," he said. "That's exactly how rich you're going to be. You'll have a bankroll of exactly four thousand pesos. And to show you that I'm a real friend of yours, I'll throw in a bonus. I'll make it a round five thousand pesos, and all in silver."

The Indian, however, had not for one moment thought of four thousand pesos. Such an amount of money had no meaning to him. He had been interested solely in Mr. Winthrop's ability to write figures so rapidly.

"So, what do you say now? Is it a deal or is it? Say yes and you'll get your advance this very minute."

"As I have explained before, patroncito, the price is fifteen pesos each."

"But, my good man," Mr. Winthrop shouted at the poor Indian in utter despair, "where have you been all this time? On the moon or where? You are still at the same price as before."

"Yes, I know that, jefecito, my little chief," the Indian answered, entirely unconcerned. "It must be the same price because I cannot make any other one. Besides, señor, there's still another thing which perhaps you don't know. You see, my good lordy and caballero, I've to make these canastitas my own way and with my song in them and with bits of my soul woven into them. If I were to make them in great numbers there would no longer be my soul in each, or my songs. Each would look like the other with no difference whatever and such a thing would slowly eat up my heart. Each has to be another song which I hear in the morning when the sun rises and when the birds begin to chirp and the butterflies come and sit down on my baskets so that I may see a new beauty, because, you see, the butterflies like my baskets and the pretty colors on them, that's why they come and sit down, and I can make my canastitas after them. And now, señor jefecito, if you will kindly excuse me, I have wasted much time already, although it was a pleasure and a great honor to hear the talk of such a distinguished caballero like you. But I'm afraid I've to attend to my work now, for day after tomorrow is market day in town and I got to take my baskets there. Thank you, señor, for your visit. Adiós."

And in this way it happened that American garbage cans escaped the fate of being turned into receptacles for empty, torn, and crumpled little multicolored canastitas into which an Indian of Mexico had woven dreams of his soul, throbs of his heart: his unsung poems.

Notes and Questions

1. *A.* Winthrop seems to leave his encounter with the Indian with the same understanding that he had when he arrived. What prevents him from learning from his experience? What hard-won world-view would Winthrop have had to amend, if not discard, if he had taken the Indian seriously?

   B. How does Question *a* relate to the comment in the introductory note to this reading: "model precedes rather than follows data — map often both precedes and supersedes the territory itself"?

   C. What ideas do you already have about legal order? Where do your ideas come from?

   D. Up to this point you have studied parables from Kafka and a short story by Traven. Is this what you expected to find in a law book? What do these expectations about the appropriate materials for law study tell you about your mental model of law?

   E. Return to the parable "Before the Law." What ideas about law did the man from the country have on his arrival at the door? How did his model of law affect his ability to determine his true state of affairs?

2. If the Indian were to be a guest lecturer in a modern economics class, how might his instruction be received?

3. Winthrop and the Indian define life, the world, interpersonal relationships, and economic relationships differently. Can law be a useful institution in such instances of value conflict? Should one reality be adopted and enforced by law?

4. Students generally want to identify with the Indian rather than Winthrop, who is trying to subvert the values and lifestyle of the Indian.

A. What aspects of their lives do you find compelling or repulsive?

B. Have your own interpersonal and institutional encounters been helpful or destructive of what you consider important? Have your values been in jeopardy or are they secure?

5. The story has been called "unrealistic" by many students. What makes it "unrealistic"? What is contemporary realism? Compare the drive toward realism with the desire to identify with the Indian. Also compare it with the following observation by the late Aldous Huxley:

> By the end of the Seventeenth Century, mysticism has lost its old significance . . . and is more than half dead. "Well, what of it," may be asked. "Why shouldn't it die? What use is it when it's alive?" — The answer to these questions is that where there is no vision, the people perish; and that, if those who are the salt of the earth lose their savour, there is nothing to keep that earth disinfected, nothing to prevent it from falling into complete decay. The mystics are channels through which a little knowledge of reality filters down into our human universe of ignorance and illusion. A totally unmystical world would be a world totally blind and insane.*

6. Many students also say that this Indian is "happy." But what signs of suffering do you see in his life? What are the sources of his suffering? Is there a relationship between suffering and personal development?

---

*Aldous Huxley, *Grey Eminence* (1943), p. 98, quoted in C. G. Jung, *Mysterium Coniunctionis, Collected Works* (Princeton, N.J.: Princeton University Press, 1967).

☐ Traven's story, although engaging, nevertheless leaves the question: What has all this to do with law? The answer is "everything" or "nothing," depending on the level at which you are studying the idea of law. If you are interested in the unique ways that culture and disciplined training affect perception, then the story has everything to do with law. If you wish to know about a given system at a given time — about courts, judges, and the like — then the example looks far-fetched.

By looking across a *range* of definitions about law, you can gain more critical insight. Each definition includes the flash of genius of its proponent; each, the element of limited vision caused by exclusion of the unexplainable. Law can be defined as a system of rules and regulations, a cover for the whimsy of officials, a forum for value inquiry, a regime for the resolution of conflict, a power play of elites, or a reflection of popular will. These partial explanations offer promising leads for study. Thinking *across* a field of explanations promotes clearer insight, because competing ideas create tensions and provide a dynamic in law. These tensions create similar conflicts within students of law, who might be inclined to seek *the one best way* to explain law. Yet these tensions make law study a unique educational experience.

The following sections explore some major theoretical explanations of law and process. Because no conversation can proceed for long without discussion of rules, the first section concerns what judges and lawyers do with rules. Section 2 discusses the exercise of official discretion in finding facts, selecting rules, and making decisions. Sections 3 and 4 concern value dilemmas in decision making and the conception of law as a scheme for balancing conflicting interests. Section 5 involves the more radical contention that law is nothing more than a stratagem for preserving the political, social, and economic position of elites. Finally, in Section 6, the role of ordinary people in shaping legal order is examined.

1 LEGAL REASONING

What great king, is the Jewel of the Analytical Powers proclaimed by the Exalted one? Four in number, great king, are the Analytical Powers: Understanding of the Meaning of Words, Understanding of the Doctrine, Grammar and Exegesis, and Readiness in Speaking. Adorned, great king with these Four Analytical Powers, a monk, no matter what manner of assemblage he approaches, whether it be an assemblage of Warriors or an assemblage of Brahmans or an assemblage of householders or an assemblage of religious, approaches confidently, approaches that assemblage untroubled, unafraid, unalarmed, untrembling with no bristling of the hair of the body.

A Buddhist parable

How does a lawyer decide whether a client has a "good" or a "bad" case? Typically, lawyers begin with facts told them by clients and, after other investigation, "apply" the law to the facts and predict a result. Lawyers assume that judges will decide like cases in like manner; that is, when cases involve comparable facts, prior results will be repeated. Two sources of ambiguity arise in conventional legal work: factual ambiguity ("What happened?") and legal ambiguity ("What law might apply to what happened?").

How do lawyers know what the law is? Oliver Wendell Holmes, Jr. (1841–1935), the famous American jurist, observed:

> Take the fundamental question, what constitutes the law? You will find some text writers telling you that it is something different from what is decided by the courts of Massachusetts or England, that it is a system of reason, that it is a deduction from principles or ethics or admitted axioms . . . which may or may not coincide with decisions. But if we take the view of our friend the bad man we shall find that he does not care two straws for the axioms or deductions, but that he does want to know what the Massachusetts or English courts are likely to do in fact. I am much of his mind. The prophecies of what the courts will do in fact, and nothing more pretentious, are what I mean by the law.*

Prophecies about law rest in part on a comparison between cases in question and prior cases that have been decided. Skill in finding similarities

*Oliver Wendell Holmes, "The Path of the Law," *Harvard Law Review,* 10(1897), 457.

and differences among cases is thus a fundamental part of professional law study. In this section the writing of Karl Llewellyn (1893–1962) and a line of cases from North Carolina show what judges and lawyers do with cases.

The Bramble Bush *Karl N. Llewellyn*

First, what is precedent? In the large, disregarding for the moment peculiarities of our law and of legal doctrine — in the large, precedent consists in an official doing over again under similar circumstances substantially what has been done by him or his predecessor before. The foundation, then, of precedent is the official analogue of what, in society at large, we know as folkways, or as institutions, and of what, in the individual, we know as habit. And the things which make for precedent in this broad sense are the same which make for habit and for institutions. It takes time and effort to solve problems. Once you have solved one it seems foolish to reopen it. Indeed, you are likely to be quite impatient with the notion of reopening it. Both inertia and convenience speak for building further on what you have already built; for incorporating the decision once made, *the solution once worked out,* into your operating technique *without reexamination* of what *earlier went into* reaching your solution. From this side you will observe that the urge to precedent will be present in the action of any official, irrespective of whether he wants it, or not; irrespective likewise of whether he thinks it is there, or not. From this angle precedent is but a somewhat dignified name for the *practice* of the officer or of the office. And it should be clear that unless there were such practices it would be hard to know there was an office or an officer. It is further clear that with the institution of written records the background range of the practice of officers is likely to be considerably extended; and even more so is the possible outward range, the possibility of outside imitation. Finally, it is clear that if the written records both exist and are somewhat carefully and continuously consulted, the possibility of change creeping into the practices unannounced is greatly lessened. At this place on the law side the institution of the bar rises into significance. For whereas the courts might make records and keep them, but yet pay small attention to them; or might pay desultory attention; or might even deliberately neglect an inconvenient record if they should later change their minds about that type of case, the lawyer searches the records for convenient cases to support his point, presses upon the court what it has already done before, capitalizes the human drive toward repetition by finding, by making explicit, by urging, the prior cases. . . .

To continue past practices is to provide a new official in his inexperience with the accumulated experience of his predecessors. If he is ignorant, he can learn from them and profit by the knowledge of those who have gone before him. If he is idle he can have their action brought to his attention and profit by their industry. If he is foolish he can profit by their wisdom. If he is biased or corrupt the existence of past practices to compare his action with gives a public check upon his biases and his corruption, limits the frame in which he can indulge them unchallenged. Finally, even though his predecessors may themselves, as they set up the practice, have been idle, ignorant, foolish and biased, yet the knowledge that he will continue what they have done gives a basis from which men may predict the action of the courts; a basis to which they can adjust their expectations and their affairs in advance. To know the law is helpful, even when the law is bad. Hence it is readily

---

From Karl L. Llewellyn, *The Bramble Bush,* pp. 64–69.

understandable that in our system there has grown up first the habit of following precedent, and then the legal norm that precedent is to be followed. The main form that this principle takes we have seen. It is essentially the canon that each case must be decided as one instance under a general rule. This much is common to almost all systems of law. The other canons are to be regarded rather as subsidiary canons that have been built to facilitate working with and reasoning from our past decisions.

Notes and Questions

1. The doctrine of *stare decisis* means that courts will decide like cases in like manner, or that past decisions will be followed. Is there a theory of justice implicit in this doctrine? What are the sources of injustice in such a system?
2. Compare with Llewellyn the following excerpts from Robert Ornstein, *The Psychology of Consciousness* and Aldous Huxley, *The Doors of Perception:*

   Ornstein:

   > The sense organs discard most of the important information reaching us. The brain further limits input, by selectively inhibiting the sensory activity, sending down efferent signals which can modify stimulation even in the receptor itself. Our senses and central nervous system select by responding primarily to changes. We quickly learn to "habituate" to the constancies of the world. Further, we sort the input into categories that depend on transitory needs, language, our past history, our expectations and our cultural biases.*

   Huxley:

   > To make biological survival possible, Mind at Large has to be funneled through the reducing valve of the brain and nervous system. . . . To formulate and express the contents of this reduced awareness man has invented and endlessly elaborated those symbol-systems and implicit philosophies that we call languages. Every individual is at once the beneficiary and the victim of the linguistic tradition into which [s]he has been born — the beneficiary inasmuch as language gives access to the accumulated records of other people's experience, the victim insofar as it confirms . . . the belief that reduced awareness is the only awareness, and as it bedevils [the] sense of reality, so that [s]he is all too apt to take . . . concepts for data, . . . words for actual things. That which, in the language of religion, is called "this world" is the universe of reduced awareness expressed and, as it were, petrified by language.†
3. Return to the story "Assembly Line." Can the theories of Llewellyn, Ornstein, and Huxley explain why Winthrop cannot learn from the Indian?
4. Llewellyn says that it is helpful to know the law even when the law is bad. How is it helpful?
5. Precedent in law becomes more possible by having written records, and so when we think of a precedent system as a general reference to "the past" we should remember that we most often refer to a *written record* of the past. Is there a difference? What is the written record of your life? Does the record adequately encompass your past?
6. Do you use a precedent system in making personal decisions? Does a precedent system operate in your home, in the various classes you attend, at work, in social groups, and so on?

---

*Robert Ornstein, *The Psychology of Consciousness* (San Francisco: Freeman, 1972), p. 43.

†Aldous Huxley, *The Doors of Perception* (New York: Harper & Row, 1954), pp. 22–23.

All the following cases in this section are drawn from reports of the North Carolina Supreme Court. These cases illustrate the doctrine of *stare decisis*.

State v. Pendergrass *2 Dev. & B., N.C. 365 (1837)**

Indictment for assault and battery. The offense consisted of a whipping with a switch, inflicted by defendant, a schoolmistress, upon one of her younger pupils. The switching left marks upon the body of the child, upon which were also found marks apparently made by some blunter instrument than a switch. All of these marks, however, disappeared in a few days. The nature of the charge to the jury appears from the opinion. Verdict was against defendant, who thereupon appealed. . . .

GASTON, J.

It is not easy to state with precision, the power which the law grants to schoolmasters and teachers, with respect to the correction of their pupils. It is analogous to that which belongs to parents, and the authority of the teacher is regarded as a delegation of parental authority. One of the most sacred duties of parents, is to train up and qualify their children, for becoming useful and virtuous members of society; this duty can not be effectually performed without the ability to command obedience, to control stubbornness, to quicken diligence, and to reform bad habits; and to enable him to exercise this salutary sway, he is armed with the power to administer moderate correction, when he shall believe it to be just and necessary. The teacher is the substitute of the parent; is charged in part with the performance of his duties, and in the exercise of these delegated duties, is invested with his power.

The law has not undertaken to prescribe stated punishments for particular offenses, but has contented itself with the general grant of the power of moderate correction, and has confided the graduation of punishments, within the limits of this grant, to the discretion of the teacher. The line which separates moderate correction from immoderate punishment, can only be ascertained by reference to general principles. The welfare of the child is the main purpose for which pain is permitted to be inflicted. Any punishment, therefore, which may seriously endanger life, limbs, or health, or shall disfigure the child, or cause any other permanent injury, may be pronounced in itself immoderate, as not only being unnecessary for, but inconsistent with, the purpose for which correction is authorized. But any correction, however severe, which produces temporary pain only, and no permanent ill, can not be so pronounced, since it may have been necessary for the reformation of the child, and does not injuriously affect its future welfare. We hold, therefore, that it may be laid down as a general rule, that teachers exceed the limits of their authority when they cause lasting mischief; but act within the limits of it, when they inflict temporary pain.

When the correction administered, is not in itself immoderate, and therefore beyond the authority of the teacher, its legality or illegality must depend entirely, we think, on the *qui animo* [the intention] with which it was administered. Within the sphere of his authority, the master is the judge when correction is required, and of the degree of correction necessary; and like all others intrusted with a discretion, he can not be made penally responsible for error of judgment, but only for wickedness of purpose. The best and the wisest of mortals are weak and erring creatures, and in the exercise of functions in which their judgment is to be the guide, can not be rightfully required to engage for more than honesty of purpose, and diligence of exertion.

*Case citations are to volume and page numbers of court reports, in this instance North Carolina reports. — ED.

His judgment must be presumed correct, because he is the judge, and also because of the difficulty of proving the offense, or accumulation of offenses, that called for correction; of showing the peculiar temperament, disposition, and habits, of the individual corrected; and of exhibiting the various milder means, that may have been ineffectually used, before correction was resorted to.

But the master may be punishable when he does not transcend the powers granted, if he grossly abuse them. If he use his authority as a cover for malice, and under pretense of administering correction, gratify his own bad passions, the mask of the judge shall be taken off, and he will stand amenable to justice, as an individual not invested with judicial power.

We believe that these are the rules applicable to the decision of the case before us. If they be, there was error in the instruction given to the jury, that if the child was whipped by the defendant so as to occasion the marks described by the prosecutor, the defendant had exceeded her authority, and was guilty as charged. The marks were all temporary, and in a short time all disappeared. No permanent injury was done to the child. The only appearances that could warrant the belief or suspicion that the correction threatened permanent injury, were the bruises on the neck and the arms; and these, to say the least, were too equivocal to justify the court in assuming that they did threaten such mischief. We think that the instruction on this point should have been, that unless the jury could clearly infer from the evidence, that the correction inflicted had produced, or was in its nature calculated to produce, lasting injury to the child, it did not exceed the limits of the power which had been granted to the defendant. We think also, that the jury should have been further instructed, that however severe the pain inflicted, and however in their judgment it might seem disproportionate to the alleged negligence or offense of so young and tender a child, yet if it did not produce nor threaten lasting mischief, it was their duty to acquit the defendant; unless the facts testified induced a conviction in their minds, that the defendant did not act honestly in the performance of duty, according to her sense of right, but under the pretext of duty, was gratifying malice.

We think that rules less liberal towards teachers, can not be laid down without breaking in upon the authority necessary for preserving discipline, and commanding respect; and that although these rules leave it in their power to commit acts of indiscreet severity, with legal impunity, these indiscretions will probably find their check and correction, in parental affection, and in public opinion; and if they should not, that they must be tolerated as a part of those imperfections and inconveniences, which no human laws can wholly remove or redress.

By Court.

Judgment reversed.

Notes and Questions

1. The *Pendergrass* case follows the pattern of all judicial opinions: Facts are discussed, legal questions are raised, and a rule or rules are applied. Usually courts give some explanation justifying the application of rules to convince readers that the result reached in the case is appropriate. The analysis of cases for facts, issues, rules, and reasons is a central feature in lawyer training. With modest practice, anyone can master this technique and see the strengths and weaknesses of the case method.
2. The court acknowledges that no human law can "wholly remove or redress" certain "imperfections and inconveniences." This is said in support of the delegation of power to teachers, parents, and others given control over the day-to-day lives of children. Do you agree with the court's reluctance to intervene?
3. The court observes that "the best and wisest of mortals may be weak and erring creatures" and that therefore people in authority need room to make mistakes. Would this idea be even more pertinent to the behavior of children?
4. How effective as a limitation on teacher power is parental influence or public opinion? If the court had chosen to

intervene here, would it have dulled parental activism or community outrage?

5. If you were a teacher or a student interested in the law of corporal punishment at the time of the *Pendergrass* case, what would the case tell you? If you were a lawyer giving advice based on the case, would you find the case useful in predicting the outcome of a similar case?

6. The principal reason for the court's decision seems to be the protection of established authority or the maintenance of hierarchical relationships. Is nonhierarchical education thinkable? A powerless teacher? Can law require nonhierarchy? Is law itself inherently hierarchical? If school and the legal order are hierarchical, what are the institutions for training in democratic governance?

Joyner v. Joyner *59 N.C. 322 (1862)*

Petition for divorce. Appeal from an interlocutory order allowing alimony *pendente lite* [during the lawsuit]. The petitioner alleged her marriage with the defendant; that she herself was well-bred and of respectable family, and that her husband was not less than a fair match for her; that her husband had struck her with a horse-whip on one occasion, and with a switch on another, leaving several bruises on her person; and that on several occasions, he had used abusive and insulting language towards her. The petition concluded as set forth in the opinion of the court.

By Court, PEARSON, C. J.

The legislature has deemed it expedient to enlarge the grounds upon which divorces may be obtained; but as a check or restraint on applications for divorces, and to guard against abuses, it is provided that the cause or ground on which the divorce is asked for shall be set forth in the petition "particularly and specially. . . ."

By the rules of pleading in actions at the common law, every allegation of fact must be accompanied by an allegation of "time and place." This rule was adopted in order to insure proper certainty in pleading, but a variance in the *allegata* and *probata* [allegations and proof], that is, a failure to prove the precise time and place, as alleged in the pleading, was held not to be fatal, unless time or place entered into the essence, and made a material part of the fact relied on, in the pleading.

There is nothing on the face of this petition to show us that time was material, or a part of the essence of the alleged cause of divorce, that is, that the blows were inflicted at a time when the wife was in a state of pregnancy, with an intent to cause a miscarriage, and put her life in danger; and there is nothing to show us that the place was a part of the essence of the cause of divorce, that is, that the blows were inflicted in a public place, with an intent to disgrace her, and make her life insupportable — so we are inclined to the opinion that it was not absolutely necessary to state the time and place, or if stated, that a variance in the proof, in respect to time and place, would not be held fatal.

But we are of opinion that it was necessary to state the circumstances under which the blow with the horse-whip, and the blows with the switch, were given; for instance, what was the conduct of the petitioner; what had she done, or said, to induce such violence on the part of the husband? We are informed by the petitioner that she was a woman, "well-bred, and of respectable family, and that her husband was not less than a fair match for her." There is no allegation that he was drunk, nor was there any imputation of unfaithfulness on either side (which is the most common ingredient of applications for divorce), so there was an obvious necessity for some explanation, and the cause of divorce could not be set forth, "particularly and specially," without stating the circumstances which gave rise to the alleged grievances.

It was said on the argument that the fact that a husband on one occasion "struck his wife with a horse-whip, and on another occasion with a switch, leaving several bruises on her person," is of itself a sufficient cause of divorce, and consequently the circumstances which attended the infliction of these injuries are immaterial, and need not be set forth. This presents the question in the case.

The wife must be subject to the husband. Every man must govern his household, and if by reason of an unruly temper, or an unbridled tongue, the wife persistently treats her husband with disrespect, and he submits to it, he not only loses all sense of self-respect, but loses the respect of the other members of his family, without which he cannot expect to govern them, and forfeits the respect of his neighbors. Such have been the incidents of the marriage relation from the beginning of the human race. Unto the woman it is said: "Thy desire shall be to thy husband, and he shall rule over thee": Gen. iii. 16. It follows that the law gives the husband power to use such a degree of force as is necessary to make the wife behave herself and know her place. Why is it, that by the principles of the common law, if a wife slanders or assaults and beats a neighbor, the husband is made to pay for it? Or if the wife commits a criminal offense, less than felony, in the presence of her husband, she is not held responsible? Why is it that the wife cannot make a will disposing of her land, and cannot sell her land without a privy examination, "separate and apart from her husband," in order to see that she did so voluntarily, and without compulsion on the part of her husband? It is for the reason that the law gives this power to the husband over the person of the wife, and has adopted proper safeguards to prevent an abuse of it.

We will not pursue the discussion further. It is not an agreeable subject, and we are not inclined unnecessarily to draw upon ourselves the charge of a want of proper respect for the weaker sex. It is sufficient for our purpose to state that there may be circumstances which will mitigate, excuse, and so far justify the husband in striking the wife "with a horse-whip on one occasion and with a switch on another, leaving several bruises on the person," so as not to give her a right to abandon him, and claim to be divorced. For instance, suppose a husband comes home, and his wife abuses him in the strongest terms — calls him a scoundrel, and repeatedly expresses a wish that he was dead and in torment; and being thus provoked in the *furor brevis* [sudden anger], he strikes her with the horse-whip, which he happens to have in his hands, but is afterwards willing to apologize, and expresses regret for having struck her; or suppose a man and his wife get into a discussion and have a difference of opinion as to a matter of fact, she becomes furious and gives way to her temper, so far as to tell him he lies, and upon being admonished not to repeat the word, nevertheless does so, and the husband taking up a switch, tells her if she repeats it again he will strike her, and after this notice she again repeats the insulting words, and he thereupon strikes her several blows, — these are cases in which, in our opinion, the circumstances attending the act, and giving rise to it, so far justify the conduct of the husband as to take from the wife any ground of divorce for that cause, and authorize the court to dismiss her petition, with the admonition, "If you will amend your manners, you may expect better treatment": See Shelford on Divorce. So that there are circumstances under which a husband may strike his wife with a horse-whip, or may strike her several times with a switch, so hard as to leave marks on her person, and these acts do not furnish sufficient ground for a divorce. It follows that when such acts are alleged as the causes for a divorce, it is necessary in order to comply with the provisions of the statute to state the circumstances attending the acts, and which gave rise to them. . . .

State v. Black *60 N.C. 262 (1864)*

By Court, PEARSON, C. J.

A husband is responsible for the acts of his wife, and he is required to govern his household, and for that purpose the law permits him to use towards his wife such a degree of force as is necessary to control an unruly temper and make her behave herself; and unless some permanent injury be inflicted, or there be an excess of violence, or such a degree of cruelty as shows that it is inflicted to gratify his own bad passions, the law will not invade the domestic forum or go behind the curtain. It prefers to leave the parties to themselves, as the best mode of inducing them to make the matter up and live together as man and wife should.

Certainly the exposure of a scene like that set out in this case can do no good. In respect to the parties, a public exhibition in the courthouse of such quarrels and fights between man and wife widens the breach, makes a reconciliation almost impossible, and encourages insubordination; and in respect to the public, it has a pernicious tendency; so, *pro bono publico* [for the public good], such matters are excluded from the courts, unless there is a permanent injury or excessive violence or cruelty indicating malignity and vindictiveness.

In this case, the wife commenced the quarrel. The husband, in a passion provoked by excessive abuse, pulled her upon the floor by the hair, but restrained himself, did not strike a blow, and she admits he did not choke her, and she continued to abuse him after she got up. Upon this state of facts the jury ought to have been charged in favor of the defendant: *State* v. *Pendergrass,* 2 Dev. & B. 365 [31 Am. Dec. 416]; *Joyner* v. *Joyner,* 6 Jones Eq. 325.

It was insisted by Mr. Winston that, admitting such to be the law when the husband and wife lived together, it did not apply when, as in this case, they were living apart. That may be so when there is a divorce from bed and board, because the law then recognizes and allows the separation, but it can take no notice of a private agreement to live separate. The husband is still responsible for her acts, and the marriage relation and its incidents remain unaffected.

Notes and Questions

1. The court cites the *Pendergrass* and *Joyner* cases as precedent. What are the similarities between those cases and the facts of the *Black* case? The differences?

2. How clear were the prior cases as a guide in the *Black* case? Was the result in *Black* preordained by the earlier cases?

3. In the *Joyner* case, no evidence was given as to who started the fight, whereas in the *Black* case, there was evidence that the wife started it. Is this case, therefore, easier for the court to decide than the *Joyner* case? Which case is the stronger precedent regarding a husband's "right" to chastise his wife?

4. In the *Pendergrass* case, the court said that intervention in the school situation would depend on the *qui animo,* or intentions, of the teacher in punishing. Only for wickedness of purpose would the court find an assault. In the *Black* case, the court spoke of cruelty or the use of force "to gratify his own bad passions." How can these interior states of teachers or husbands be proved?

5. The court indicates in the *Black* case that if the parties make a private agreement to live apart it need not be recognized. Why is the preservation of this agreement less compelling as a public good than the preservation of the privacy of the "domestic forum"?

6. In reading these cases, do you have difficulty in dealing with anything other than whether it is a good idea for teachers to beat students or for husbands to beat their wives? The court does not stay on these larger questions, but instead moves to questions of how, when, and where a beating may take place. The latter questions are more manageable than the ones that first come to mind and can be handled with "less emotion."

What does this approach say about legal analysis? About rules of law? Can a profession, such as law, be based on emotion? What would emotional rules of law look like?

State v. Rhodes *61 N.C. 453 (1868)*

Assault and battery, in which it appeared that the husband struck the wife three blows with a switch about the size of one of his fingers. The other facts are stated in the opinion.

By Court, READE, J.

The violence complained of would, without question, have constituted a battery, if the subject of it had not been the defendant's wife. The question is, how far that fact affects the case.

The courts have been loth to take cognizance of trivial complaints arising out of the domestic relations — such as master and apprentice, teacher and pupil, parent and child, husband and wife. Not because those relations are not subject to the law, but because the evil of publicity would be greater than the evil involved in the trifles complained of, and because they ought to be left to family government. On the civil side of this court, under our divorce laws, such cases have been unavoidable and not infrequent. On the criminal side, there are but two cases reported. In one, the question was whether the wife was a competent witness to prove a battery by the husband upon her, which inflicted no great or permanent injury. It was decided that she was not. In discussing the subject, the court said that the abstract question of the husband's right to whip his wife did not arise: *State* v. *Hussy,* Busb. 123. The other case was one of a slight battery by the husband upon the wife after gross provocation. He was held not to be punishable. In that case, the court said that unless some permanent injury be inflicted, or there be an excess of violence, or such a degree of cruelty as shows that it is inflicted to gratify his own bad passions, the law will not invade the domestic forum, or go behind the curtain: *State* v. *Black,* 1 Winst. 266. Neither of those cases is like the one before us. The first case turned upon the competency of the wife as a witness, and in the second there was a slight battery upon a strong provocation.

In this case no provocation worth the name was proved. The fact found was, that it was "without any provocation except some words which were not recollected by the witness." The words must have been of the slightest import to have made no impression on the memory. We must therefore consider the violence as unprovoked. The question is therefore plainly presented whether the court will allow a conviction of the husband for moderate correction of the wife without provocation.

Our divorce laws do not compel a separation of husband and wife, unless the conduct of the husband be so cruel as to render the wife's condition intolerable or her life burdensome. What sort of conduct on the part of the husband would be allowed to have that effect has been repeatedly considered. And it has not been found easy to lay down any iron rule upon the subject. In some cases it has been held that actual and repeated violence to the person was not sufficient; in others, that insults, indignities, and neglect, without any actual violence, were quite sufficient; — so much does each case depend upon its peculiar surroundings.

We have sought the aid of the experience and wisdom of other times and of other countries.

Blackstone says: "That the husband, by the old law, might give the wife moderate correction; for as he was to answer for her misbehavior, he ought to have the power to control her; but that in the polite reign of Charles the Second this power of correction began to be doubted": 1 Bla. Com. 444. Wharton says that by the ancient common law, the husband possessed the power to chastise his wife; but that the tendency of criminal courts in the present day is to regard the marital relation as no defense to a battery: Crim. Law, secs. 1259, 1260. Chancellor Walworth says of such correction that it is not authorized by the law of any civilized country; not, indeed, meaning that England is not civilized, but referring to the anomalous relics of barbarism which cleave to her jurisprudence: Bishop on Marriage and Divorce, 446, note. The old law of moderate correction has been questioned even in England, and has been repudiated in Ireland and

Scotland. The old rule is approved in Mississippi, but it has met with but little favor elsewhere in the United States: Id. 485. In looking into the discussions of the other states, we find but little uniformity.

From what has been said, it will be seen how much the subject is at sea. And probably it will ever be so; for it will always be influenced by the habits, manners, and condition of every community. Yet it is necessary that we should lay down something as precise and practical as the nature of the subject will admit of for the guidance of our courts.

Our conclusion is, that family government is recognized by law as being as complete in itself as the state government is in itself, and yet subordinate to it; and that we will not interfere with or attempt to control it in favor of either husband or wife, unless in cases where permanent or malicious injury is inflicted or threatened, or the condition of the party is intolerable. For however great are the evils of ill temper, quarrels, and even personal conflicts inflicting only temporary pain, they are not comparable with the evils which would result from raising the curtain and exposing to public curiosity and criticism the nursery and the bed-chamber. Every household has and must have a government of its own, modeled to suit the temper, disposition, and condition of its inmates. Mere ebullitions of passion, impulsive violence, and temporary pain, affection will soon forget and forgive; and each member will find excuse for the other in his own frailties. But when trifles are taken hold of by the public, and the parties are exposed and disgraced, and each endeavors to justify himself or herself by criminating the other, that which ought to be forgotten in a day will be remembered for life.

It is urged in this case that as there was no provocation the violence was of course excessive and malicious; that every one, in whatever relation of life, should be able to purchase immunity from pain by obedience to authority and faithfulness in duty. And it is insisted that in *State* v. *Pendergrass,* 2 Dev. & B. 365 [31 Am. Dec. 416], which was the case of a school-mistress whipping a child, that doctrine is laid down. It is true that it is there said that the master may be punishable even when he does not transcend the powers granted; i.e., when he does not inflict permanent injury, if he grossly abuse his powers, and use them as a cover for his malice. But observe, the language is if he grossly abuse his powers. So that every one would say at once there was no cause for it, and it was purely malicious and cruel. If this be not the rule, then every violence which would amount to an assault upon a stranger would have to be investigated to see whether there was any provocation. And that would contravene what we have said, that we will punish no case of trifling importance. If in every such case we are to hunt for the provocation, how will the proof be supplied? Take the case before us. The witness said there was no provocation except some slight words. But then, who can tell what significance the trifling words may have had to the husband? Who can tell what had happened an hour before, and every hour for a week? To him they may have been sharper than a sword. And so in every case it might be impossible for the court to appreciate what might be offered as an excuse, or no excuse might appear at all, when a complete justification exists. Or suppose the provocation could in every case be known, and the court should undertake to weigh the provocation in every trifling family broil, what would be the standard? Suppose a case coming up to us from a hovel, where neither delicacy of sentiment nor refinement of manners is appreciated or known. The parties themselves would be amazed if they were to be held responsible for rudeness or trifling violence. What do they care for insults and indignities? In such cases, what end would be gained by investigation or punishment? Take a case from the middle class, where modesty and purity have their abode, but nevertheless have not immunity from the frailties of nature, and are sometimes moved by the mysteries of passion. What could be more harassing to them or injurious to society than to draw a crowd around their seclusion? Or take a case the higher ranks, where education and culture have so refined nature that a look cuts like a knife, and a word strikes like a hammer; where the most delicate attention gives pleasure, and the slightest neglect pain; where an indignity is disgrace, and exposure is ruin. Bring all these cases into court side by side, with the same offense charged and the same proof made, and what conceivable charge of the court to the jury would be alike appropriate to all the cases, except that they all have domestic government, which they have formed for themselves, suited to their own peculiar conditions, and that those governments are supreme, and from them there is no appeal, except in cases of great importance requiring the strong arm of the law, and that to those governments they must submit themselves?

It will be observed that the ground upon which we have put this decision is not that the husband has the right to whip his wife much or little, but that we will not interfere with family government in trifling cases. We will no more interfere where the husband whips the wife than where the wife whips the husband, and yet we would hardly be supposed to hold that a wife has a right to whip her husband. We will not inflict upon society the greater evil of raising the curtain upon domestic privacy to punish the lesser evil of trifling violence. Two boys under fourteen years of age fight upon the playground, and yet the courts will take no notice of it, not for the reason that boys have the right to fight, but because the interests of society require that they should be left to the more appropriate discipline of the schoolroom and of home. It is not true that boys have a right to fight; nor is it true that a husband has a right to whip his wife. And if he had, it is not easily seen how the thumb is the standard of size for the instrument which he may use, as some of the old authorities have said, and in deference to which was his honor's charge. A light blow, or many light blows, with a stick larger than the thumb might produce no injury; but a switch half the size might be so used as to produce death. The standard is the effect produced, and not the manner of producing it, or the instrument used.

Because our opinion is not in unison with the decisions of some of the sister states, or with the philosophy of some very respectable law-writers, and could not be in unison with all because of their contrariety, a decent respect for the opinions of others has induced us to be very full in stating the reasons for our conclusion. There is no error. [The husband won.]

Notes and Questions

1. In light of the prior cases in North Carolina, is it fair for the court to say that the subject at issue is "at sea"?

2. Has the court here rejected the common-law rule that a husband may chastise his wife?

3. If the courts will not involve themselves in family quarrels below a certain threshold and it is likely that husbands will be the aggressors in family assaults, has not the court, through a promise of inaction, acknowledged the right of the husband to chastise up to the threshold?

4. If a family is a government, what kind of government is it? What is the relationship between the government of the family and the government of the state? Does the analogy of the family to a government help the court to reach a resolution of the questions before it? Is the court's use of the analogy persuasive to you?

5. What is the status of the "rule of thumb" (that the circumference of the instrument used could be no larger than the circumference of the thumb) after this case?

6. Why does the court cite examples from other countries and other states that seem to differ from its decision? Do these references strengthen or weaken the case as precedent that a husband may chastise his wife?

State v. Mabrey *64 N.C. 592 (1870)*

Assault, tried before WALLS, J., *at Spring Term, 1870, of Halifax.*

The jury found, by a special verdict, that on 7 June, 1869, at the house of the defendant, etc., the latter and his wife had some words and he threatened to leave her; after some very improper language by him, she started off, when he caught her by the left arm and said he would kill her, and drew his knife and struck at her with it, but did not strike her; that he drew back as if to strike again, and his arm was caught by a bystander, whereupon the wife got away and ran about fifteen steps; that the defendant did not pursue her, but told her not to return, if she did he would kill her; that he did not strike her or inflict any personal injury, and that he was a man of violent character, etc., etc.

His Honor thereupon being of opinion that the defendant was not guilty, there was a verdict and judgment accordingly; and the Solicitor for the State appealed.

READE, J.

The facts present a case of savage and dangerous outrage, not to be tolerated in a country of laws and Christianity. We rigidly adhere to the doctrine, in (593) *State* v. *Rhodes*, 61 N.C., 453, and precedent cases in our reports, that the courts will not invade the domestic forum, to take cognizance of trifling cases of violence in family government; but there is no relation which can shield a party who is guilty of malicious outrage or dangerous violence committed or threatened. In *State* v. *Rhodes* the jury had been charged that "the husband had the right to whip his wife with a switch no larger than his thumb." In combating that error the Court said: "A light blow, or many light blows with a stick larger than the thumb, might produce no injury; but a switch half the size might be so used as to produce death. The standard is the *effect produced,* and not the manner of producing it, or the instrument used." Those words were used as applicable to the facts in that case. But on the argument at the bar in this case they were perverted to mean that in any case, no matter what weapon was used or from what motive or intent, unless permanent injury were inflicted, the Court would not interfere; therefore, *here,* although death was threatened and a deadly knife used, yet as it was averted by a bystander, the Court will not interfere. We repudiate any such construction of *State* v. *Rhodes.*

Upon the special verdict there ought to have been judgment against the defendant.

Per Curiam.

Error.

Notes and Questions

1. Judge Reade wrote the opinions in both the *Rhodes* and *Mabry* cases. Are there any words that he wished he had not written in the earlier opinion? Are there any he might have wished he included?
2. What is the combined effect of the *Rhodes* and *Mabrey* cases?

☐ Keep the foregoing cases in mind as you read additional material on precedent from Llewellyn.

The Bramble Bush (continued) *Karl N. Llewellyn*

We turn first to what I may call the orthodox doctrine of precedent, with which, in its essence, you are already familiar. Every case lays down a rule, the rule of the case. The express ratio decidendi is prima facie the rule of the case, since it is the ground upon which the court chose to rest its decision. But a later court can reexamine the case and can invoke the canon that no judge has power to decide what is not before him, can, through examination of the facts or of the procedural issue, narrow the picture of what was actually before the court and can hold that the ruling made requires to be understood as thus restricted. In the extreme form this results in what is known as expressly "confining the case to its particular facts." This rule holds only of redheaded Walpoles in pale magenta Buick cars. And when you find this said of a past case you know that in effect it has been overruled. Only a convention, a somewhat absurd convention, prevents flat overruling in such instances. It seems to be felt as definitely improper to state that the court in a prior case was wrong, peculiarly so if that case was in the same court which is speaking now. It seems to be felt that this would undermine the dogma of the infallibility of courts. So lip service is done to that dogma, while the rule which the prior court laid down is disembowelled. The execution proceeds with due respect, with mandarin courtesy.

Now this orthodox view of the authority of precedent — which I shall call the *strict* view — is but *one of two views* which seem to me wholly contradictory to each other. It is in practice the dogma which is applied to *unwelcome* precedents. It is the recognized, legitimate, honorable technique for whittling precedents away, for making the lawyer, in his argument, and the court, in its decision, free of them. It is a surgeon's knife. . . .

. . . when you turn to the actual operations of the courts, or, indeed, to the arguments of lawyers, you will find a totally different view of precedent at work beside this first one. That I shall call, to give it a name, the *loose view* of precedent. That is the view that a court has decided, and decided authoritatively, *any* point or all points on which it chose to rest a case, or on which it chose, after due argument, to pass. No matter how broad the statement, no matter how unnecessary on the facts or the procedural issues, if that was the rule the court laid down, then that the court has held. . . . In its extreme form this results in thinking and arguing exclusively from *language* that is found in past opinions, and in citing and working with that language wholly without reference to the facts of the case which called the language forth.

Now it is obvious that this is a device not for cutting past opinions away from judges' feet, but for using them as a springboard when they are found convenient. This is a device for *capitalizing welcome precedents.* And both the lawyers and the judges use it so. And judged by the *practice* of the most respected courts, as of the courts of ordinary stature, this doctrine of precedent is like the other, recognized, legitimate, honorable.

What I wish to sink deeper into your minds about the doctrine of precedent, therefore, is that it is two-headed. It is Janus-faced.* That it is not one doctrine, nor one line of doctrine, but two, and two which, *applied at the same time to the same precedent, are contradictory of each other.* That there is one doctrine for getting rid of precedents deemed troublesome and one doctrine for making use of precedents that seem helpful. That these two doctrines exist side by side. That the same lawyer in the same brief, the same judge in the same opinion, may be using the one doctrine, the technically strict one, to cut down half the older cases that he deals with, and using the other doctrine, the loose one, for building with the other half. Until you realize this you do

From Karl L. Llewellyn, *The Bramble Bush*, pp. 64–69.

*Janus was a Roman god with two faces, thus capable of looking in opposite directions simultaneously.

not see how it is possible for law to change and to develop, and yet to stand on the past. . . .

. . . The strict view — that view that cuts the past away — is *hard* to use. An ignorant, an unskilful judge will find it hard to use: the past will bind him. But the skilful judge — he whom we would make free — *is* thus made free. He has the knife in hand; and he can free himself.

Nor, until you see this double aspect of the doctrine-in-action, do you appreciate how little, in detail, you can predict *out of the rules alone;* how much you must turn, for purposes of prediction, to the reactions of the judges to the facts and to the life around them. . . .

. . . The first question is, how much can this case fairly be made to stand for by a later court to whom the precedent is welcome? . . . The second question is, how much is there in this case that cannot be got around, even by a later court that wishes to avoid it?

You have now the tools for arguing from that case as counsel on *either* side of a new case. You turn then to the problem of prediction. Which view will this same court, on a later case on slightly different facts, take: will it choose the narrow or the loose? Which use will be made of this case by one of the other courts whose opinions are before you? Here you will call to your aid the matter of attitude that I have been discussing. Here you will use all that you know of individual judges, or of the trends in specific courts, or, indeed, of the trend in the line of business, or in the situation, or in the times at large — in anything which you may expect to become apparent and important to the court in later cases. But always and always, you will bear in mind that each precedent has not one value, but two, and that the two are wide apart, and that whichever value a later court assigns to it, such assignment will be respectable, traditionally sound, dogmatically correct. Above all, as you turn this information to your own training you will, I hope, come to see that in most doubtful cases the precedents *must* speak ambiguously until the court has made up its mind whether each one of them is welcome or unwelcome. And that the job of persuasion which falls upon you will call, therefore, not only for providing a technical ladder to reach on authority the result that you contend for, but even more, if you are to have *your* use of the precedents made as *you* propose it, the job calls for you, on the facts, to persuade the court your case is sound.

People — and they are curiously many — who think that precedent produces or ever did produce a certainty that did not involve matters of judgment and of persuasion, or who think that what I have described involves improper equivocation by the courts or departure from the courtways of some golden age — such people simply do not know our system of precedent in which they live.

Notes and Questions

1. Llewellyn gives two views of precedent, strict and loose. One point of confusion about his explanation can come from his using the word *strict* in a different way than is customary in constitutional law. In constitutional law, strict construction involves the finding of the intention of the framers of the Constitution and *following* that intention in a contemporary case. As Llewellyn uses the term, a strict view of precedent is used by a judge or lawyer who wishes to *reject* a past case in whole or in part. The strict view thus sometimes contradicts the intentions of the judges in the prior case.
2. Using Llewellyn's explanation, would the lawyer representing the husband in the *Mabrey* case have found the prior cases of *Pendergrass, Joyner, Black,* and *Rhodes* welcome or unwelcome? In part welcome, in part unwelcome? How would the lawyer have presented the facts and rules of the prior cases so as to capitalize on the welcome features and minimize the impact of the unwelcome features. How would the opposition read and interpret the prior cases?
3. Could the judge in *Mabrey* have decided in favor of Mabrey using the precedents available? The judge in fact decided against Mabrey. Does the opinion make a fair application of precedent?
4. Does any of the foregoing material on what judges and lawyers do with cases smack of dishonesty?

5. Assume that the following occurred in North Carolina in 1873: A man came home intoxicated one morning. After complaining to his wife about the food that was around for him to eat, he went out in the yard, cut some switches, and struck her several times with them until he was told to stop by some people who were there. The beating left bruises that lasted two weeks, but did not disable her from her work. She went to the prosecutor and asked what could be done about it. What could he have advised her in light of the prior cases?

State v. Oliver *70 N.C. 60 (1874)*

Indictment for an assault and battery, tried before, MITCHELL, JUDGE, *at Fall Term, 1873, Alexander Superior Court.*

On the trial the jury found the following facts:

Defendant came home intoxicated one morning after breakfast was over; got some raw bacon, said it had skippers on it, and told his wife she [*sic*] would not clean it. He sat down and ate a little, when he threw the coffee cup and pot into the corner of the room and went out; while out he cut two switches, brought them in, and, throwing them on the floor, told his wife that if he whipped her she would leave; that he was going to whip her, for she and her d — d mother had aggravated him near to death. He then struck her five licks with the two switches, which were about four feet long, with the branches on them about half way and some leaves. One of the switches was about half as large as a man's little finger; the other not so large. He had them in both hands, and inflicted bruises on her arm which remained for two weeks, but did not disable her from work.

One of the witnesses swore he struck as hard as he could. Others were present, and after defendant had struck four licks told him to desist. Defendant stopped, saying if they had not been there he would have worn her out.

Upon these facts the Court found defendant guilty and fined him $10. Defendant appealed.

Armfield, for defendant.

Attorney General Hargrove, for the State, called the attention of the Court to the cases of *State* v. *Black,* 60 N.C., 262; *State* v. *Mabrey,* 64 N.C., 592; *State* v. *Rhodes,* 61 N.C., 453; *State* v. *Hussey,* 44 N.C., 123, and *State* v. *Pendergrass,* 19 N.C., 365.

SETTLE, J.

We may assume that the old doctrine that a husband had a right to whip his wife, provided he used a switch no larger than his thumb, is not law in North Carolina. Indeed, the Courts have advanced from that barbarism until they have reached the position that the husband has no right to chastise his wife under any circumstances.

But from motives of public policy, and in order to preserve the sanctity of the domestic circle, the Courts will not listen to trivial complaints.

If no permanent injury has been inflicted, nor malice, cruelty nor dangerous violence shown by the husband, it is better to draw the curtain, shut out the public gaze, and leave the parties to forget and forgive.

No general rule can be applied, but each case must depend upon the circumstances surrounding it.

Without adverting in detail to the facts established by the special verdict in this case, we think that they show both malice and cruelty.

In fact it is difficult to conceive how a man who has promised upon the altar to love, comfort, honor and keep a woman can lay rude and violent hands upon her without having malice and cruelty in his heart.

Let it be certified that the judgment of the Supreme Court is affirmed.

Per curiam.

Judgment affirmed.

Notes and Questions

1. The court had several cases called to its attention, but cited none of them in the opinion. How can this be explained? Could the outcome reached here have been predicted in light of the earlier cases?

2. If Oliver had seen his lawyer shortly before his trial and asked bluntly, "What are my chances?" how might the lawyer have responded?

3. Is an injustice done to Oliver here? Could he say that he had planned his affairs in reliance upon the state of the prior law?

4. Has the court at last solved the problem of family quarreling? Are future cases predictable?

5. Consider the following presentation of time perspectives of a decision maker:

> *Past* (historical or precedent [general sense] oriented): What are the past decisions where the same or equivalent facts, issues, and so forth, have been involved?
> *Present* (existential): To what extent does this case (transaction, event) present dimensions that are unanswerable by reference to the past? To what extent is "the answer" of the past inadequate to meet the "felt needs" of the present?
> *Future* (impact orientation): Will a result contribute to or detract from purposes that the law is designed to serve? Will a result lead to improvement? To a better society?

One or another of these orientations emerges in each of the various North Carolina cases. After relatively smooth sailing with the right of chastisement rule gaining strength and scope, Mabrey uplifts his knife and thereby imposes a need to reconsider carefully the prior law. The impact of a pro-Mabrey result does not look promising; knife play with or without dire effects runs counter to the peace-keeping purposes of law. The pressures of the present and the future on the past forces a reconsideration of the prior law.

What is particularly noteworthy about these cases is that the court makes practically a complete turnabout, without even acknowledging it. In thinking about this odd way in which change is made with all pretenses of stability, one is reminded of the story of the ax that had been in the family for hundreds of years — with two new heads and six new handles!

6. A. After having studied these cases from North Carolina, how is your understanding of precedent and legal reasoning different from someone who has not studied them?

There might be an easy way to test your powers of legal reasoning. Imagine yourself to be a lawyer practicing in North Carolina in 1875 one year after the decision in the *Oliver* case. Assume that either the husband or the wife involved in the following case has consulted you for a professional opinion:

> The husband and his wife had an argument in their home. Two children, both eight years old, were playing where they could see and hear what was going on. One was the child of the couple, the other of a neighbor. The discussion was over finances, the husband's sporadic work, and his drinking, which according to his wife made all their problems worse. The husband insisted that he had not been drinking and that if his wife didn't shut up he would hit her. She continued to shout at him, and he went over to a stack of wood that was piled by the fireplace and picked up a piece of kindling two inches in diameter. He approached his wife with the piece of wood raised up, but when she screamed, he dropped the wood and slapped her with his hand. Her nose started to bleed and her eye later blackened, but there was no sign of injury after five days.

B. How is a lawyer's exploration of the foregoing hypothetical case different from a layperson's? What is the role of legal rules in rendering advice?

7. What do you now see as the essential strengths and weaknesses in legal reasoning? When is legal reasoning preferable to nonlegal reasoning? If thinking like a lawyer involves careful reading of cases and legal reasoning, do you want to think like one?

8. How applicable is the idea of precedent in out-of-court settings, such as the home, among family members, or at school? Are precedents used in those situations? Do strict and loose interpretations of precedents operate? Who gets to "set" precedents in such groups?

   When such questions can be addressed, at least tentatively answered, and acted on, students will have discovered a highly useful aspect of law study and an effective link between law study and other forms of social study.

9. Much has been written about battered women both here and in Great Britain. Government-sponsored research includes *The Silent Victims: Denver's Battered Women,* A Report to the U.S. Commission on Civil Rights (Washington, D.C.: U.S. Commission on Civil Rights, 1977): Mark A. Schulman, *A Survey of Spousal Violence Against Women in Kentucky* (Washington, D.C.: U.S. Government Printing Office, 1980); L. Reidman, *Battered Women in New Hampshire* (Washington, D.C.: U.S. Commission on Civil Rights, 1980); *Federal Response to Domestic Violence* (Washington, D.C.: U.S. Commission on Civil Rights, 1982). See also C. Ewing, *Battered Women Who Kill* (Lexington, Mass.: Lexington Books, 1987); D. Martin, *Battered Wives* (San Francisco: Volcano Press, 1981); W. Glenn, *Campaigns Against Corporal Punishment: Prisoners, Sailors, Women, Children* (Albany: SUNY [State University of New York], 1984).

2 LAW AND OFFICIAL DISCRETION

A crow can pass for a peacock or a nightingale when there is no rivalry and nobody knows the difference.

B. Traven, *Government* (1971)

Law is what is read, not what is written.

Donald Kingsbury, *Courtship Rite* (1981)

If a Hollywood studio were casting for the role of judge in a movie or television series, what would it look for? A man, fiftyish, flowing gray hair — or at least hair graying at the temples — horn-rimmed glasses, mildly imperious but not devoid of compassion, sober, thoughtful, remote, and so on. These images have been perpetuated for so long in popular culture that they take on a life of their own that may mask the realities of the judging process. Popular myths become highly useful to professionals in law: For example, rather than make a frontal assault on judicial wisdom and authority, lawyers often explain that a judge was "forced" to rule in a certain way.

Your study of the mixed doctrines of precedent has already suggested that legal professionals have a range of action and are not necessarily narrowly constrained by prior law. Judges likewise can and must choose courses of action, and are not simply automatons who slavishly follow the pronouncements laid down by their predecessors on the bench. What are some of the factors that lie below the surface of judicial opinions?

Jerome Frank (1889–1957), a teacher, a lawyer, and later a judge, began to expose the realities of judicial process in *Law and the Modern Mind,* which stands as perhaps one of the finest books ever written about U.S. law. There he uncovered dominant popular and professional myths about law and process, probed them psychoanalytically, and recommended changes that he thought would be helpful. Since judges, police, prosecutors, and other decision makers filter the competing notions of law, justice, and process, and control day-to-day outcomes in law, Frank's writing adds a vital link between law in theory and law in practice.

The Judging Process and the Judge's Personality *Jerome Frank*

As the word indicates, the judge in reaching a decision is making a judgment. And if we would understand what goes into the creating of that judgment, we must observe how ordinary men dealing with ordinary affairs arrive at their judgments.

The process of judging, so the psychologists tell us, seldom begins with a premise from which a conclusion is subsequently worked out. Judging begins rather the other way around — with a conclusion more or less vaguely formed; a man ordinarily starts with such a conclusion and afterwards tries to find premises which will substantiate it.[1] If he cannot, to his satisfaction, find proper arguments to link up his conclusion with premises which he finds acceptable, he will, unless he is arbitrary or mad, reject the conclusion and seek another.

In the case of the lawyer who is to present a case to a court, the dominance in his thinking of the conclusion over the premises is moderately obvious. He is a partisan working on behalf of his client. The conclusion is, therefore, not a matter of choice except within narrow limits. He must, that is if he is to be successful, begin with a conclusion which will insure his client's winning the lawsuit. He then assembles the facts in such a fashion that he can work back from this result he desires to some major premise which he thinks the court will be willing to accept. The precedents, rules, principles and standards to which he will call the court's attention constitute this premise.

While "the dominance of the conclusion" in the case of the lawyer is clear, it is less so in the case of the judge. For the respectable and traditional descriptions of the judicial judging process admit no such backward-working explanation. In theory, the judge begins with some rule or principle of law as his premise, applies this premise to the facts, and thus arrives at his decision.

Now, since the judge is a human being and since no human being in his normal thinking processes arrives at decisions (except in dealing with a limited number of simple situations) by the route of any such syllogistic reasoning, it is fair to assume that the judge, merely by putting on the judicial ermine, will not acquire so artificial a method of reasoning. Judicial judgments, like other judgments, doubtless, in most

[1]A convenient analogy is the technique of the author of a detective story.

cases, are worked out backward from conclusions tentatively formulated.

As Jastrow says, "In spite of the fact that the answer in the book happens to be wrong, a considerable portion of the class succeeds in reaching it. . . . The young mathematician will manage to obtain the answer which the book requires, even at the cost of a resort to very unmathematical processes." Courts, in their reasoning, are often singularly like Jastrow's young mathematician. Professor Tulin has made a study which prettily illustrates that fact. While driving at a reckless rate of speed, a man runs over another, causing severe injuries. The driver of the car is drunk at the time. He is indicted for the statutory crime of "assault with intent to kill." The question arises whether his act constitutes that crime or merely the lesser statutory crime of "reckless driving." The courts of several states have held one way, and the courts of several other states have held the other.

The first group maintain that a conviction for assault with intent to kill cannot be sustained in the absence of proof of an actual purpose to inflict death. In the second group of states the courts have said that it was sufficient to constitute such a crime if there was a reckless disregard of the lives of others, such recklessness being said to be the equivalent of actual intent.

With what, then, appears to be the same facts before them, these two groups of courts seem to have sharply divided in their reasoning and in the conclusions at which they have arrived. But upon closer examination it has been revealed by Tulin that, in actual effect, the results arrived at in all these states have been more or less the same. In Georgia, which may be taken as representative of the second group of states, the penalty provided by the statute for reckless driving is far less than that provided, for instance, in Iowa, which is in the first group of states. If, then, a man is indicted in Georgia for reckless driving while drunk, the courts can impose on him only a mild penalty; whereas in Iowa the judge, under an identically worded indictment, can give a stiff sentence. In order to make it possible for the Georgia courts to give a reckless driver virtually the same punishment for the same offense as can be given by an Iowa judge, it is necessary in Georgia to construe the statutory crime of assault with intent to kill so that it will include reckless driving while drunk. If, and only if, the Georgia court so construes the statute can it impose the same penalty under the same facts as could the Iowa courts under the reckless driving statute. On the other hand, if the Iowa court were to construe the Iowa statute as the Georgia court construes the Georgia statute, the punishment of the reckless driver in Iowa would be too severe.

In other words, the courts in these cases began with the results they desired to accomplish: they wanted to give what they considered to be adequate punishment to drunken drivers: their conclusions determined their reasoning.

But the conception that judges work back from conclusions to principles is so heretical that it seldom finds expression.[2] Daily, judges, in connection with their decisions, deliver so-called opinions in which they purport to set forth the bases of their conclusions. Yet you will study these opinions in vain to discover anything remotely resembling a statement of the actual judging process. They are written in conformity with the time-honored theory. They picture the judge applying rules and principles to the facts, that is, taking some rule or principle (usually derived from opinions in earlier cases) as his major premise, employing the facts of the case as the minor premise, and then coming to his judgment by processes of pure reasoning.

Now and again some judge, more clear-witted and outspoken than his fellows, describes (when off the bench) his methods in more

[2]Years ago the writer, just after being admitted to the bar, was shocked when advised by S. S. Gregory, an ex-president of the American Bar Association — a man more than ordinarily aware of legal realities — that "the way to win a case is to make the judge want to decide in your favor and then, and then only, to cite precedents which will justify such a determination. You will almost always find plenty of cases to cite in your favor." All successful lawyers are more or less consciously aware of this technique. But they seldom avow it — even to themselves.

homely terms. Recently Judge Hutcheson essayed such an honest report of the judicial process. He tells us that after canvassing all the available material at his command and duly cogitating on it, he gives his imagination play,

> and brooding over the cause, waits for the feeling, the hunch — that intuitive flash of understanding that makes the jumpspark connection between question and decision and at the point where the path is darkest for the judicial feet, sets its light along the way. . . . In feeling or 'hunching' out his decisions, the judge acts not differently from but precisely as the lawyers do in working on their cases, with only this exception, that the lawyer, in having a predetermined destination in view, — to win the lawsuit for his client — looks for and regards only those hunches which keep him in the path that he has chosen, while the judge, being merely on his way with a roving commission to find the just solution, will follow his hunch wherever it leads him. . . .

And Judge Hutcheson adds:

> I must premise that I speak now of the judgment or decision, the solution itself, as opposed to the apologia for that decision; the decree, as opposed to the logomachy, the effusion of the judge by which the decree is explained or excused. . . . The judge really decides by feeling and not by judgment, by hunching and not by ratiocination, such ratiocination appearing only in the opinion. The vital motivating impulse for the decision is an intuitive sense of what is right or wrong in the particular case; and the astute judge, having so decided, enlists his every faculty and belabors his laggard mind, not only to justify that intuition to himself, but to make it pass muster with his critics. Accordingly, he passes in review all of the rules, principles, legal categories, and concepts which he may find useful, directly or by an analogy so as to select from them those which in his opinion will justify his desired result.

We may accept this as an approximately correct description[3] of how all judges do their thinking. But see the consequences. If the law consists of the decisions of the judges and if those decisions are based on the judge's hunches, then the way in which the judge gets his hunches is the key to the judicial process. Whatever produces the judge's hunches makes the law.

What, then, are the hunch-producers? What are the stimuli which make a judge feel that he should try to justify one conclusion rather than another?

The rules and principles of law are one class of such stimuli.[4] But there are many others, concealed or unrevealed, not frequently considered in discussions of the character or nature of law. To the infrequent extent that these other stimuli have been considered at all, they have been usually referred to as "the political, economic and moral prejudices" of the judge.[5] A moment's reflection would, indeed, induce any

---

[3]. . . A century ago a great American judge, Chancellor Kent, in a personal letter explained his method of arriving at a decision. He first made himself "master of the facts." Then (he wrote) "I saw where justice lay, and the moral sense decided the court half the time; I then sat down to search the authorities. . . . I might once in a while be embarrassed by a technical rule, *but I almost always found principles suited to my view of the case.*". . .

[4]If Hutcheson were to be taken with complete literalness, it would seem that such legal rules, principles and the like are merely for show, materials for window dressing, implements to aid in rationalization. They are that indeed. But although impatience with the orthodox excessive emphasis on the importance of such devices might incline one at times to deny such formulations any real value, it is necessary — and this even Hutcheson would surely admit — to concede them more importance. In part, they help the judge to check up on the propriety of the hunches. They also suggest hunches. . . .

[5]Most of the suggestions that law is a function of the undisclosed attitudes of judges stress the judges' "education," "race," "class," "economic, political and social influences" which "make up a complex environment" of which the judges are not wholly aware but which affect their decisions by influencing their views of "public policy," or "social advantage" or

open-minded person to admit that factors of such character must be operating in the mind of the judge.

But are not those categories — political, economic and moral biases — too gross, too crude, too wide? Since judges are not a distinct race and since their judging processes must be substantially of like kind with those of other men, an analysis of the way in which judges reach their conclusions will be aided by answering the question, What are the hidden factors in the inferences and opinions of ordinary men? The answer surely is that those factors are multitudinous and complicated, depending often on peculiarly individual traits of the persons whose inferences and opinions are to be explained. These uniquely individual factors often are more important causes of judgments than anything which could be described as political, economic, or moral biases.

In the first place, all other biases express themselves in connection with, and as modified by, these idiosyncratic biases. A man's political or economic prejudices are frequently cut across by his affection for or animosity to some particular individual or group, due to some unique experience he has had; or a racial antagonism which he entertains may be deflected in a particular case by a desire to be admired by someone who is devoid of such antagonism.

Second (and in the case of the judge more important), is the consideration that in learning the facts . . . the judge's sympathies and antipathies are likely to be active with respect to the persons of the witness, the attorneys and the parties to the suit. His own past may have created plus or minus reactions to women, or blonde women, or men with beards, or Southerners, or Italians, or Englishmen, or plumbers, or ministers, or college graduates, or Democrats. A certain twang or cough or gesture may start up memories painful or pleasant in the main. Those memories of the judge, while he is listening to a witness with such a twang or cough or gesture, may affect the judge's initial hearing of, or subsequent recollection of, what the witness said, or the weight or credibility which the judge will attach to the witness's testimony.

That the testimony of witnesses is affected by their experiences and temperaments has been often observed. . . .

> Men are prone to see what they want to see.
>
> "It must be admitted that at the present day the testimony of even a truthful witness is much over-rated."
>
> No doubt the eyes of some witnesses are livelier than those of others and the sense of sight may be quickened or diminished by the interest or bias of him who possesses it.
>
> Even where witnesses are upright or honest, their belief is apt to be more or less warped by their partiality or prejudice for or against the parties. It is easy to reason ourselves into a belief in the existence of that which we desire to be true, whereas the facts testified to, and from which the witness deduces his conclusions, might produce a very different impression on the minds of others.
>
> It frequently happens that a person, by long dwelling on a subject, thinks that a

---

their "economic and social philosophies" or "their notions of fair play or what is right and just."

It is to the economic determinists and to the members of the school of "sociological jurisprudence" that we owe much of the recognition of the influence of the economic and political background of judges upon decisions. For this much thanks. But their work has perhaps been done too well. Interested as were these writers in problems of labor law and "public policy" questions, they over-stressed a few of the multitude of unconscious factors and over-simplified the problem.

Much the same is to be said of the views of the "historical school" with respect to the effect of custom on judicial decisions. "Whether a custom will or will not be ratified by the courts depends after all on the courts themselves," says Dickinson. . . . "Whatever forces can be said to influence the growth of the law, they exert that influence only by influencing the judges. . . . Current *mores* . . . are things about which there is room for considerable difference of opinion and . . . when it is a question of their writing themselves into law, the opinion which prevails is the judges' opinion." See Cardozo, "The Nature of the Judicial Process," 174. "In every court there are likely to be as many estimates of the Zeitgeist as there are judges on its bench."

> thing may have happened, and he at last comes to believe that it actually did occur.

The courts have been alive to these grave possibilities of error and have therefore repeatedly declared that it is one of the most important functions of the trial judge, in determining the value and weight of the evidence, to consider the demeanor of the witness.

They have called attention, as of the gravest importance, to such facts as the tone of voice in which a witness's statement is made, the hesitation or readiness with which his answers are given, the look of the witness, his carriage, his evidences of surprise, his gesture, his zeal, his bearing, his expression, his yawns, the use of his eyes, his furtive or meaning glances, or his shrugs, the pitch of his voice, his self-possession or embarrassment, his air of candor or of seeming levity. It is because these circumstances can be manifest only to one who actually hears and sees the witnesses that upper courts have frequently stated that they are hesitant to overturn the decision of the trial judge in a case where the evidence has been based upon oral testimony; for the upper courts have recognized that they have before them only a stenographic or printed report of the testimony, and that such a black and white report cannot reproduce anything but the cold words of the witness. . . .

Strangely enough, it has been little observed that, while the witness is in this sense a judge, *the judge, in a like sense, is a witness.* He is a witness of what is occurring in his courtroom. He must determine what are the facts of the case from what he sees and hears; that is, from the words and gestures and other conduct of the witnesses. And like those who are testifying before him, the judge's determination of the facts is no mechanical art. If the witnesses are subject to lapses of memory or imaginative reconstruction of events, in the same manner the judge is subject to defects in his apprehension of the testimony, so that long before he has come to the point in the case where he must decide what is right or wrong, just or unjust, with reference to the facts of the case as a whole, the trial judge has been engaged in making numerous judgments or inferences as the testimony dribbles in. His beliefs as to what was said by the witnesses and with what truthfulness the witnesses said it, will determine what he believes to be the "facts of the case." If his final decision is based upon a hunch and that hunch is a function of the "facts," then of course what, as a fallible witness of what went on in his courtroom, he believes to be the "facts," will often be of controlling importance. So that the judge's innumerable unique traits, dispositions and habits often get in their work in shaping his decisions not only in his determination of what he thinks fair or just with reference to a given set of facts, but in the very processes by which he becomes convinced what those facts are. . . .

. . . The following is from the reminiscences of a man who has served both as prosecuting attorney and as judge:

> The jockeying for a judge is sometimes almost humorous. Lawyers recognize the peculiarities, previous opinions, leanings, strength and weakness, and likes or dislikes of a particular judge in a particular case. Some years ago one of the bright lawyers of Chicago conferred with me as an assistant state's attorney, to agree on a judge for the trial of a series of cases. We proceeded to go over the list. For the state's attorney, I objected to but one judge of all the twenty-eight Cook County judges, and as I went through the list I would ask him about one or another, "How about this one?" As to the first one I named he said, "No, he decided a case a couple of weeks ago in a way that I didn't like. . . ." As to another, he said, "No, he is not very clear-headed; he is likely to read an editorial by the man who put him on the ticket, and get confused on the law." Of another he said, "No, he might sneer at my witnesses, and I can't get the sneer in the record." To another he objected that "If my clients were found guilty this judge would give them the limit." To still another he said, "No, you can't get him to make a ruling in a case without creating a disturbance in the court room, he is so careful of the Supreme

Court." Again he replied to one, "No, if the state's attorney should happen to sit in the court room I won't get a favorable ruling in the entire case." And so we went along.

One bit of statistical evidence as to the differences between judges is available: A survey was made of the disposition of thousands of minor criminal cases by the several judges of the City Magistrate's Court in New York City during the years 1914 to 1916 with the express purpose of finding to what extent the "personal equation" entered into the administration of justice. It was disclosed that "the magistrates did differ to an amazing degree in their treatment of similar classes of cases." Thus of 546 persons charged with intoxication brought before one judge, he discharged only one and found the others (about 97%) guilty, whereas of the 673 arraigned before another judge, he found 531 (or 79%) not guilty. In disorderly conduct cases, one judge discharged only 18% and another discharged 54%. "In other words, one coming before Magistrate Simons had only 2 chances in 10 of getting off. If he had come before Judge Walsh he would have had more than 5 chances in 10 of getting off." . . . When it came to sentences, the same variations existed. One judge imposed fines on 84% of the persons he found guilty and gave suspended sentences to 7%, while one of his fellows fined 34% and gave suspended sentences to 59%. . . .

But if we determine that the personality of the judge has much to do with law-making, have we done enough? Can we rest content with this mere recognition? Can we stop with the blanket statement that our judicial process at its best will be based upon "the trained intuition of the judges," on the hunches of experienced men? . . .

Just what form a new technique of judging will take, it is too soon to guess. And the same may be said of conjectures as to how long it will be before such a technique can become effective. It would not be wise to be overoptimistic. . . .

. . . What we may hope some day to get from our judges are detailed autobiographies containing the sort of material that is recounted in the autobiographical novel; or opinions annotated, by the judge who writes them, with elaborate explorations of the background factors in his personal experience which swayed him in reaching his conclusions. For in the last push, a judge's decisions are the outcome of his entire life-history. Judges can take to heart the counsel Anatole France gave to the judges of literature:

> All those who deceive themselves into the belief that they put anything but their own personalities into their work are dupes of the most fallacious of illusions. The truth is that we can never get outside ourselves. . . . We are shut up in our own personality as if in a perpetual prison. The best thing for us, it seems to me, is to admit this frightful condition with a good grace, and to confess that we speak of ourselves every time we have not strength enough to remain silent. . . .

. . . The judge's decision is determined by a hunch arrived at long after the event on the basis of his reaction to fallible testimony. It is, in every sense of the word, *ex post facto* [after the fact]. It is fantastic, then, to say that usually men can warrantably act in reliance upon "established law." Their inability to do so may be deplorable. But mature persons must face the truth, however unpleasant.

Why such resistance to the truth? Why has there been little investigation of the actualities of the judging process? If we are right in assuming that the very subject matter of the law activates childish emotional attitudes, we can perhaps find an answer to these questions.

It is a marked characteristic of the young child, writes Piaget, that he does very little thinking about his thinking. He encounters extreme difficulty if asked to give an account of the "how" of his mental processes. He cannot reflect on his own reasoning. If you ask him to state how he reached a conclusion, he is unable to recover his own reasoning processes, but instead invents an artificial account which will somehow seem to lead to the result. He cannot correctly explain what he did to find this result. "Instead of giving a retrospect he starts from the result he has obtained as though he had known it in advance and then gives a more or less elaborate method for finding it again. . . . He starts from his conclusion and argues towards the premises as though he had known from the first whither those premises would lead him."

Once more these difficulties find their explanation in the child's relative unawareness of his self, of his incapacity for dealing with his own thoughts as subjective. For this obtuseness produces in the child an overconfidence in his own ideas, a lack of skepticism as to the subjectivity of his own beliefs. As a consequence, the child is singularly nonintrospective. He has, according to Piaget, no curiosity about the motives that guide his thinking. His whole attitude towards his own thinking is the antithesis of any introspective habit of watching himself think, of alertness in detecting the motives which push him in the direction of any given conclusion. The child, that is, does not take his own motives into account. They are ignored and never considered as a constituent of thinking.

. . . One recalls a dictum of Piaget in talking of the child:

> The less a mind is given to introspection the more it is the victim of the illusion that it knows itself thoroughly.

Notes and Questions

1. Llewellyn, whose work on precedent appears in Section 1, thought that Jerome Frank had overstated the psychological and uncertain in law and had understated the legal and predictable:

> Law . . . is in fact more predictable, and hence more certain than his treatment would indicate. In his very proper enthusiasm for illusion smashing, he paints the illusion as somewhat more illusive than it is. . . . (W)e . . . must recognize that *ways* of deciding, *ways* of thinking, *ways* of sizing up facts 'in terms of legal relevance' are distinctly enough marked in our courts so that we know a lawman, by his judging reactions, from a layman.*

How might Jerome Frank have answered Llewellyn?

2. Does the fact that decisions are made publicly, with lawyers and litigants present, with records and published results that are subject to appeal, present additional limitations on the free flow of psychological forces and intuition? (Students can test these ideas through court visitations.)

3. Frank himself notes that in addition to psychological determinants there are other forces affecting judgment (see Note 5 on pages 30–31). If "environmental forces" take their places alongside psychological ones, what role is left for legal rules in decision making?

4. Using Frank's leads, re-evaluate the cases in Section 1 on wife beating. Can factors of decision besides legal rules be identified?

5. To some, judges would do well to avoid intuition and hunching in decision making and "stick to the law and the facts." Judge Hutcheson, quoted by Frank, found intuition and hunching indispensable to good decision making. What role should these play?

Can intuition be cultivated and improved, or is intuition "just there"? Can intuition peacefully coexist with professionalism and "objectivity"? If any of these elements can be controlled, which ones ought to be?

6. Unlike Llewellyn, Frank believed that for all their professional training and case study, judges make decisions just as ordinary people do, although they have much fancier ways of dressing them up. What do you see to be the political implications of regarding judges as ordinary mortals? For example, could "folk judges" or rotating judges be used instead of law-trained ones? How deeply does Frank's illusion-busting go? Does it undercut professionalism in general, or is it simply designed to produce more

---

*Karl N. Llewellyn, *Jurisprudence* (Chicago: University of Chicago Press, 1962), p. 107. See also Karl N. Llewellyn, *The Common Law Tradition* (Boston: Little, Brown, 1960), pp. 17, 18.

introspection by professionals without putting them out of work?

7. How do you reach decisions? Do you get a flash of intuition or a hunch and rationalize it later, or do you assemble all the pros and cons and only then reach a conclusion? Which sources or methods of decision making do you regard as legitimate and which indefensible?

By what criteria do the people whom you routinely encounter make decisions? Does actual decision making match the officially prescribed ways of making decisions? Would the decision process be different if all people who made decisions were called judges and put on robes?

How does your teacher determine your grades? How are decisions made in your family? Where you work? In your social club? On your athletic team? Can Frank's insights help you understand these settings better and find ways to improve the decision processes used in them?

☐ During the late 1960s, judges became embarrassed by the evident disparities in criminal sentences. A person sentenced in one court might receive dramatically different treatment from a person convicted in another court for the same offense. In an unprecedented development, judges in California and elsewhere convened annually to discuss their sentencing practices. The following case was prepared for discussion at the 1968 California Sentencing Institute.

A Forgery Case *1968 California Sentencing Institute, 77 Cal. Rptr. (Appendix)*

OFFENSE: FORGERY

Defendant cashed a forged check amounting to $145 at a department store. The blank check was taken from the company by which he was formerly employed. There were other checks involved but they were uncharged. Defendant pleaded guilty.

Prior Criminal History

	Auto theft and burglary second	Committed to boys' school
[Five years later]	Drunk driving	One year probation
[Six years later]	Burglary	Six months county jail, one year probation
[Six and one-half years later]	Present offense	

Case History Information This is a 24-year-old man, the third of five children of a Mexican-American working-class family. The father died when defendant was six years of age and thereafter the family was supported by public assistance. He claims he got along well with his mother and the members of his family. However, he asserts they regard him as a "black sheep" because of his difficulties as a youth and as an adult.

Probation officer in Arizona indicates that defendant suffered from rheumatic fever as a child and was overindulged by his mother. He has withdrawn from his family.

Defendant claims high school graduation but verification shows he only completed the ninth grade. His employment record has also been quite spotty. He worked for one year as a warehouse helper and quit because creditors attached his wages. He also has worked as a bus boy.

For the past year and a half subject has been married and one child was born of that union. Wife indicates that marriage has been satisfactory although defendant has difficulty managing finances and friction developed. They have also been plagued by large bills as a result of time payments for furniture and other household goods. Wife had been employed until the time baby was born three months ago.

Subject has a drinking problem which has caused him some difficulty and it has gotten progressively worse in recent years.

Case Evaluation This is a 24-year-old immature man of average intelligence. He gives the appearance of being friendly and likeable but obviously has been unable to accept responsibility. There are a total of eight checks outstanding, amounting to approximately $1,000 worth of purchases in various types of business establishments. He said he would like to have probation so that he could make restitution. His adjustment on probation for the burglary has been marginal and he was placed in a special caseload where the probation officer could furnish intensive supervision. His wife says this simply worried the defendant and may have contributed to his present offense. He appears to have support from his wife, who assumes major responsibility for family stability. The recent birth of his child has created more anxiety for the defendant and he says that this has affected his relationship with his wife.

Notes and Questions

1. The foregoing information is comparable to that which a sentencing judge would receive. On the basis of this report, would you grant probation? Probation with conditions? County jail time? A state prison sentence? Prepare one page giving your decision and your reasons for making it.
2. Now proceed with the opinions of California judges who also considered the case, and compare them with your opinion.

JUDGE SCHOENIG: I would place this man on three years' probation on the condition that he take treatment at DeWitt State Hospital for both alcoholism and emotional problems. Upon his release from the hospital he would be placed under the intensive supervision unit of the probation department and the family would be outpatients at the mental health clinic or Family Service Agency. Work could be secured for him in the food processing plants and deductions would be made from his checks for restitution.

There are other alternatives, of course, which embody the thoughts behind this sentence and that would be first a work furlough program if one was available in the county of sentencing. The same supervision and payroll deduction could be made through the Sheriff's office, but added to the work furlough program would be a continuing period of time under the probation department for proper supervision and outpatient care.

Also to be considered would be the right of the defendant to refuse probation. Since probation has bothered this defendant in the past, he might indicate to the court that the terms of probation are too onerous and refuse same. If such is the case, I would then impose a state prison sentence.

My reasons for the sentence are as follows: In reviewing the case of this 24-year-old Mexican-American, it appears that he does not have a lengthy arrest record and there is no history of violence. His first offense for burglary 2nd degree occurred when he was 16 years of age and he was committed to a boys' school. I assume this was not a State Correctional Institution. Six years later, he was again arrested for burglary and given 6 months in county jail and 1 year probation. His present offense occurred when he was not under probation.

As of this time, this young man is not a confirmed "paper hanger," but merely used this offense as a means to make certain purchases which were evidently for his family. These checks were given as payment in full for various articles that he bought. Inasmuch as we know he has a drinking problem, this undoubtedly is a factor in lowering his will power so that he breaches the rules and regulations set up by society.

His case history indicates that he is an inadequate individual, which has affected his employment and ability to manage his finances. It is also noted that his wife has a certain amount of awareness of his problems. However, I am not in agreement with her statement relative to probation. Her husband's present arrest occurred after he completed his probationary period. The wife is the dominant figure in this family because it appears the husband has refused to face or accept responsibility. I would consider this a further reason for psychiatric help and further, from all indications, this defendant is amenable to such counsel. It would appear that this defendant again needs the intensive supervision of the probation department for the purpose of obtaining professional help for his drinking problem and counselling for him and his wife.

If he were given a straight county jail sentence or committed to state prison, that would defer the treatment that must be implemented to help this man adjust to society and with his family.

I am aware that his previous adjustment on probation was marginal but I am not averse to taking this risk with the defendant when there is some definite goal in mind. If this defendant resided in my jurisdiction, employment could be obtained for him in food processing for the year round with one of the corporate farms in that area. This type of employment would prevent the defendant from handling any money other than his paycheck. Also, the defendant, through the probation department, would be helped in managing his financial obligations, inasmuch as I would order restitution payments on his outstanding checks.

I would recommend outpatient treatment at the mental health facility because of the history of rejection of this defendant by his family and his inability to face problems.

JUDGE COAKLEY: I've had several bad check cases and this is always the type of person you find. What do you do with a fellow who is repeatedly this kind of a customer and yet doesn't have too bad a record otherwise? Well, in any event it's open now for discussion.

JUDGE ROSS A. CARKEET (Tuolumne County): I voted for prison but after doing that I've been thinking that this might be a good case for a Penal Code Sec. 1168 commitment. This guy needs a real good scare. It might do him good to send him to prison and put a recall on him, and see if you want to take him back.

JUDGE D. STERRY FAGAN (Los Angeles County): I gave this man a straight jail sentence. My feeling was that he had a shot at probation and didn't do well. The only reason I would think of probation is that he could make some restitution. His background as presented here is marginal so I feel that it's touch and go between a prison sentence or a county jail sentence. I choose the county jail because of the nonviolence of his criminal activity. I note that . . . his [earlier] crime was burglary and everybody says that now he's changed to a "paper hanger." I also note that the check that was used on this occasion and possibly the other one came from his former employer and I presume that he took them while he was employed there, or he went back and burglarized the place to get the checks after he was terminated. It is highly inferable that he committed a burglary to get the checks and had some knowledge of how they would be passed and what signatures were necessary to pass them.

JUDGE LEONARD M. GINSBURG (Tulare County): I would have sentenced the man to prison on the basis that he's been around the track. He's been in everything from boys' school to apparently ordinary probation on the drunk driving charge, county jail and intensive probation on the burglary. To me, he's reached the point where there's nothing left to do with him and it would be largely on that basis that I believe the protection of society as well as possible rehabilitation of the individual requires this prison sentence.

JUDGE COAKLEY: Dr. Olivier, have you any comments?

DR. OLIVIER: . . . I feel this is a man who hasn't been violent and for whom psychiatry hasn't been tried. I also feel that he's a rather inadequate, dependent guy and . . . I think this fellow would develop a relationship rather easily with a psychotherapist. I don't think prison would do anything at all for him. I think it would increase his dependency and his inadequacy and I think this man would be easily led and if he were to stay in prison very long he would form more identification with the antisocial element. I think he has a lot of problems around his sexual identification and his being a man and if he could stay employed and make restitution, this would be the most ego-enhancing thing that he could do. I think it would well be worth probation on the condition that he obtain psychiatric treatment.

JUDGE HAYDEN: How much treatment do you think would be likely to be developed? Assume he had a service such as yours, how often and how long would you be seeing this man?

DR. OLIVIER: Well, we don't have any kind of standard for length of treatment. If we feel that someone needs a lot of treatment initially to get into a treatment contract then we often recommend our day treatment program where the person can come in eight hours a day, five days a week, for somewhere between two to six weeks. Then, we follow them up with a once a week basis in the out-patient clinic. For a man like this who has been nonviolent and whose latest offense has to do with check forgery, I would think it would be reasonable to start on a once a week basis and I would predict reasonably good results within a matter of six months to a year.

JUDGE GARDINER: I recognize the different kinds of treatment that are available, but I don't see how you come to the conclusion that this fellow hasn't had any treatment. What do you think these other things have been?

DR. OLIVIER: Well, I'm making a distinction between probation where he sees a probation officer periodically and seeing a psychotherapist for a half hour to an hour each and every week with great regularity.

JUDGE GARDINER: There is obviously a tremendous quality difference between the different kinds of people, but must we not recognize the fact that probation officers are giving something which is not unlike psychiatric treatment? Isn't this their objective?

DR. OLIVIER: Well, most of them are not professionally trained. Certainly they can do a great deal of good in a warm human relationship with an individual. That's the vehicle for any professional treatment, but what I'm saying is that this person has not had any kind of intensive psychiatric treatment and I think that we can do more to help him alter his maladapted patterns of life than a probation officer can. But I think the probation officer would play a vital role in helping him to see that he got to sessions and utilized them.

JUDGE J. KELLY STEELE (Kern County): You mentioned several times that this party is nonviolent. Of course, writing checks is a nonviolent offense and he could write them every day and still be considered not violent. On the other hand, you mentioned that it represents an inadequate personality and, of course, an inadequate personality could be shown by crimes of violence as well as crimes of nonviolence. My question is what difference does it make whether he's violent or nonviolent? He might stick a gun in your chest and take the shirt off your back or he might steal your bank account; what difference does it make?

DR. OLIVIER: Well, in the sense that I'm using an inadequate personality, I mean the kind of a guy that isn't very aggressive at all and tends to be passive and, I feel, unlikely to commit violent, aggressive acts. I think that this is the kind of man I would be willing to take a chance on. He hasn't forged checks every day. He had one little spree here and hasn't had a chronic, repetitive pattern at this point and we hope that it wouldn't become one if he had treatment.

JUDGE STEELE: Would you treat a single act of violence differently because of the fact that it is violent?

DR. OLIVIER: Yes, I think society needs more protection from someone who is likely to be violent.

JUDGE SCHAUER: I agree with you, Doctor. I'm not quite ready to give up on this man. He needs one more chance anyway, although I think I'd give him a long term in custody as a condition of probation, such as county jail. I probably would impose a felony on him by suspending an execution of a state prison sentence, but I think I would try probationary supervision with a condition of probation, possibly that he attend Alcoholics Anonymous. I smell in his background here the odor of alcohol and I just wonder what your opinion is in connection with AA as opposed to psychiatric treatment with respect to alcoholism problems.

DR. OLIVIER: Well, I think that could be a very useful adjunct to the program. I think a lot of people that join AA switch a lot of their dependency on alcohol to a dependency on the AA group. It helps them to structure their time in a useful way, they have places to go in the evening but I don't think the goals are exactly the same. I don't see this person as a hard core chronic alcoholic, but nevertheless, I think AA could be a useful adjunct and I don't see it as replacing psychiatric treatment. I think it's interesting that when I recently participated in a Municipal & Justice Court Judges Institute in San Diego one of the judges pointed out that when there were crimes against property, judges tended to be more punitive than in cases of aggression against individuals. Someone who had stolen 50¢ worth of meat from a super market would get a more severe sentence than someone who had threatened his girl friend with a knife, or even injured her and had been assaultive before. I think it's kind of an interesting sidelight of the way society views crimes against property.

JUDGE HAYDEN: You may have gotten a distorted sample, and I would respond to Judge Steele's remarks by saying that I would much rather have a guy hang a thousand dollar bad check on me than take $10 out of my pocket with a gun. I have a different hierarchy of values there.

MR. SHAIN: I want to comment on the discussion at the Institute for Municipal & Justice Court Judges that Dr. Olivier mentioned. The reference that Dr. Olivier had involved discussion of a case in which there was a husband and wife conflict. I think all of us would agree that the violence that emerges from a husband and wife conflict is a far different cry from violence in the more commonly accepted term of assaulting somebody that you don't know. That's the mitigating circumstance in those cases.

DR. OLIVIER: Yes, that is an important point that I had forgotten.

JUDGE DELL: I just don't think it's our function to lock up everybody who is a hazard to property. Now in this case, I would have imposed a felony sentence and as a condition of probation have given the man a maximum period in the county jail with work furlough which we have in Los Angeles County. There are certain crimes that you just have a price tag for. I'd be very reluctant to send a person who is a "paper hanger" to the state prison. I don't think it accomplishes a great deal except to fill up the state prison with people who don't belong there and who learn new crimes. I am concerned about the aspect that Judge Fagan raised, namely, that this is not just a "paper hanger" — this is a burglary and an embezzlement besides which resulted in it. But generally speaking, I don't think a property crime where there is no "bunco" scheme and where it is not very carefully planned to victimize an individual or an institution, should carry a state prison sentence. On the other hand I think that a violent crime is another matter and there we are talking about protecting life and person. I think that's a great deal more important than simply the protection of property.

JUDGE EDWARD P. FOGG (San Bernardino County): I think we've overlooked one fact in this case history that's important to me, at least. This man's employment record had been quite spotty. His record obviously shows that he has had no real occupational training. He isn't fitted to make a good living for his family. Wouldn't state prison and his commitment to the Department of Corrections give the Department an opportunity to offer this man vocational training of some type that would eventually assist in his rehabilitation?

JUDGE SCHOENIG: I thought about that. What bothered me with that is you're giving him a felony rap and saying you're rehabilitating him so that he can get a job. When he comes out he's got a felony rap sheet and who's going to hire him, a Mexican-American with a felony rap? These are all things we have to consider. And I thought about all the other things we were kicking around today. So that bothered me, too. We are a biased society and we might as well face it.

JUDGE HAYDEN: If you have an adequate probation office in your county, which we do not, you should be able to get in much more satisfactory vocational training on probation than he would ever get in a state prison. I think you can examine the history of the state prison's vocational services. Their record is extremely spotty. They, in very few cases, lead to successful continued use of the training received in state prison and there is at least a chance that if you put him on probation and as a condition of probation, make him get a trade, you might make it stick.

JUDGE COAKLEY: Cy, will you come up and give us the results of the poll?

MR. SHAIN: Here is the vote for this case: ⅔ would have committed him to jail with probation; a little more than ¼ would have sent him to prison, about 1 out of 14 would have just given him jail without probation and about 3 percent would have granted him probation using the time that he had already served in jail as fulfilling his incarceration term.

Notes and Questions

1. Using Jerome Frank as a source for criteria, compare the commentaries of the various judges. How would you rank the judges for leniency or severity?
2. As a member of the general public, which judge would you want to decide the case? What does your preference tell you about yourself? About professional perspectives as compared to public perspectives?
3. If you or a member of your family were convicted of a forgery-type offense, which judge would you prefer?
4. Included in the deliberations are the remarks of a psychotherapist, Dr. Olivier. Compare the approaches of the judges with that of the psychotherapist. Would you recommend using one or more psychotherapists, rather than judges, for sentencing decisions?

   Would psychotherapists follow the same decisional sequence that Frank noted about judges?

☐ The following case was also considered by the California judges at the 1968 institute.

A Case of Robbery and Rape

1968 California Sentencing Institute, 77 Cal. Rptr. (Appendix)

OFFENSE: ROBBERY AND RAPE

Defendant offered a ride to a young coed, waiting for a bus, and carrying a heavy bag of freshly washed laundry. She got into the car and upon reaching her residence, he pulled out a gun and ordered her to lie down in the back of the car. He then proceeded to drive to a remote park where he ordered her to hand over her wallet, removing $18, and then ordered her to remove all her clothing. Frightened, she complied, and then defendant proceeded to rape her. She struggled, and defendant choked and beat her severely. He also ordered her to commit an unnatural sex act. After she managed to escape, she reported the offense and defendant's license number to the police. Upon apprehension, defendant admitted offense, and was contrite, blaming recent unemployment for creating feelings of tension and unrest.

Prior Criminal Record

	Petty theft	6 months probation
[One year later]	Present offense	

Case History Information This 23-year-old adult male was the second of four children from a broken home. He was raised by his mother and stepfather, who subsequently divorced. He said his stepfather was quite harsh. He ran away quite often, as a result of which the Illinois juvenile court placed him in a succession of foster homes where he remained from the ages of 11 to 17, at which time he joined the armed forces.

He is a high school graduate, receiving his diploma through correspondence courses while serving in the armed forces. He later attended junior college for a semester but left to work.

He has been married for the past year and his wife is expecting their first child. He asserts that she understands his problem and that she plans to stick by him. His wife indicated that he has had periodic fits of depression, especially during times of unemployment, and also displayed a violent temper, and has beaten her up several times. She indicates that he agreed to see a psychiatrist but they could never afford such treatment. She also feels that her husband harbors considerable inferiority feelings. Defendant had been employed as a production worker in a local plant and prior employers indicate that his work was satisfactory.

He was arrested and convicted of petty theft last year, stealing items from a department store, and placed on probation. He claims it was an impulsive act for which he was sorry.

Military History Subject served three years in the armed service and received a general discharge (under honorable conditions), brought about following his apprehension for "peeping" in nurses' quarters windows while stationed overseas.

Case Evaluation This is a fairly polite, articulate young man, the product of an unsettled background featuring a hostile stepfather and various foster home placements. He has not been able to maintain steady employment and seems to be easily discouraged and lacking in self-confidence. In interview, he reveals a lengthy history of voyeurism. He is aware that he has a serious disorder and was quite eager to discuss his sex problems. Three psychiatrists have interviewed him and disagree regarding his disposition. One would send him to Atascadero,* another would order institutional treatment in a state correctional facility because of the assaultive behavior in the offense and the third would grant him probation under close supervision with psychiatric treatment.

Question

1. What should be done?

---

*A California institution for "mentally disordered sexual offenders." — Ed.

3 Law and Values

My intention was to write it in a cool and detached manner but it came to naught; indignation and pity kept seeping in. This is perhaps just as well, for capital punishment is not merely a problem of statistics and expediency, but also of morality and feeling.

Arthur Koestler, *Reflections on Hanging* (1956)

Even a fairy story — a single fairy story — can call up a normative generalization about the right behavior of mice and pumpkins, and of fairy godmothers and princes. . . .

Karl N. Llewellyn, "The Normative, the Legal and the Law Jobs" (1941)

Studying the relationship of values to any subject matter, including law, is generally out of favor. Scholars in fledgling disciplines are reluctant to delve into such matters lest their colleagues in the hard sciences consider them "prescientific" or just plain soft-headed. This drive for respectability leads to the selection of "manageable" questions for teaching and research.

Part of the reluctance to consider values is traceable to relativism, which takes both crude and sophisticated forms. Relativism — crude form — is captured in such conversation stoppers as "Well, that depends upon your point of view." At times, the refusal to discuss competing points of view takes on similarities to the small-town diplomat who piously proclaims, "There are two topics I never discuss — politics and religion." Underlying such contentions may be a deep fear of exposing oneself to the psychic risks accompanying the exploration of values.

Sophisticated relativism is typified in the academician's contention that all values are situational, that is, depend on time and place. Having concluded thus, instead of relentlessly pursuing a detailed inquiry into the various situations, times, and places and the moralities pertinent to them, some academicians drop inquiry altogether, thereby eliminating wide areas of thought. In addition, it is commonly asserted that research (good research) is (ought to be) value-free. Apart from the nonrecognition that this assertion is itself value-laden — as the parenthetical material indicates — the tenet leads "scholars" to put little psychic investment into their work and aggravates the already excessive antiethical bias that characterizes most schoolwork.

Lawyers are not immune from the pressures of relativism and value freedom. Law students are schooled in the mixed doctrines of precedent and are taught that any side of a case has merit and can be argued with vigor. If they forget that technical arguments are not necessarily *good* arguments, they do not prepare themselves to meet the public demand for improvement of law. As practitioners, their readiness to argue any cause anywhere for any client will at times be of great social benefit, but at its worst can produce a neglect of the value dimensions of law practice. By default, lawyers as a group often simply adopt the values of their clients.

In judicial process, when technique and mere craft predominate, *legalism* results — to the chagrin of all those who encounter the results. Jacques Ellul, a French jurist, observes,

> The judicial element (which becomes principally organization) is no longer charged with pursuing justice or creating law in any way whatsoever. It is charged with applying the laws. This role can be perfectly mechanical. It does not call for a philosopher or a man with a sense of justice. What is needed is a good technician, who understands the principles of the technique, the rules of interpretation, the legal terminology, and the ways of deducing consequences and finding solutions.*

Ellul explains, "Justice is not a thing to be grasped or fixed. If one pursues genuine justice . . . one never knows where one will end. A law created as a function of justice has something unpredictable in it which embarrasses the jurist."† And yet, as he later adds, "Men of law have certain scruples and are unable to eliminate justice from the law completely without the twinges of conscience."‡

Because most contested cases are situational and brim over with questions of value, relativism and value freedom are misplaced maxims with respect to them. Values must be explained, demonstrated where possible or otherwise fully debated if law and legal process are to transcend mere technique. As the dialectic over values unfolds, a socially desirable tension arises between rules and values, pressuring decision makers to integrate the present with the past in anticipation of the future. Llewellyn poignantly describes the dimensions of a contested case:

> The case of trouble . . . is the case of doubt, or is that in which discipline has failed, or is that in which unruly personality is breaking through into new paths of action or of leadership, or is that which an ancient institution is being tried against emergent forces. It is the case of trouble which makes, breaks, twists, or flatly establishes a rule, an institution, an authority. Not all such cases do so. There are also petty rows, the routine of law-stuff which exists among primitives as well as among moderns. For all that, if there be a portion of a society's life in which tensions of the culture come to expression, in which the play of variant urges can be felt and seen, in which emergent power-patterns, ancient security-drives, religion, politics, personality, cross-purposes, and views of justice tangle in the open, that portion of the life will concentrate in the case of trouble or disturbance. Not only the making of new law and the effect of old, but the hold and the thrust of all other vital aspects of the culture, shine clear in the crucible of conflict.§

---

*Jacques Ellul, *The Technological Society* (New York: Random House, 1964), p. 294.

†Ibid., p. 292.

‡Ibid., p. 295.

§From *The Cheyenne Way: Conflict and Case Law in Primitive Jurisprudence*, by Karl N. Llewellyn and E. Adamson Hoebel.

The following case is one of the most remarkable ever to have been heard in either British or American courts. In it, two English seamen were charged with cannibalism of a young sailor with whom they had been shipwrecked on the high seas.

The Queen v. Dudley and Stephens *L.R. 14 Q.B.D. 273 (1884)*

Indictment for the murder of Richard Parker on the high seas within the jurisdiction of the Admiralty.

At the trial before Huddleston, B., . . . the jury, at the suggestion of the learned judge, found the facts of the case in a special verdict, which stated "that on July 5, 1884, the prisoners, Thomas Dudley and Edward Stephens, with one Brooks, all able-bodied English seamen, and the deceased also an English boy, between seventeen and eighteen years of age, the crew of an English yacht, a registered English vessel, were cast away in a storm on the high seas 1600 miles from the Cape of Good Hope, and were compelled to put into an open boat belonging to the said yacht. That in this boat they had no supply of water and no supply of food, except two 1 lb. tins of turnips, and for three days they had nothing else to subsist upon. That on the fourth day they caught a small turtle, upon which they subsisted for a few days, and this was the only food they had up to the twentieth day when the act now in question was committed. That on the twelfth day the remains of the turtle were entirely consumed, and for the next eight days they had nothing to eat. That they had no fresh water, except such rain as they from time to time caught in their oilskin capes. That the boat was drifting on the ocean, and was probably more than 1000 miles away from land. That on the eighteenth day, when they had been seven days without food and five without water, the prisoners spoke to Brooks as to what should be done if no succour came, and suggested that some one should be sacrificed to save the rest, but Brooks dissented, and the boy, to whom they were understood to refer, was not consulted. That on the 24th of July, the day before the act now in question, the prisoner Dudley proposed to Stephens and Brooks that lots should be cast who should be put to death to save the rest, but Brooks refused to consent, and it was not put to the boy, and in point of fact there was no drawing of lots. That on that day the prisoners spoke of their having families, and suggested it would be better to kill the boy that their lives should be saved, and Dudley proposed that if there was no vessel in sight by the morrow morning the boy should be killed. That next day, the 25th of July, no vessel appearing, Dudley told Brooks that he had better go and have a sleep, and made signs to Stephens and Brooks that the boy had better be killed. The prisoner Stephens agreed to the act, but Brooks dissented from it. That the boy was then lying at the bottom of the boat quite helpless, and extremely weakened by famine and by drinking sea water, and unable to make any resistance, nor did he ever assent to his being killed. The prisoner Dudley offered a prayer asking forgiveness for them all if either of them should be tempted to commit a rash act, and that their souls might be saved. That Dudley, with the assent of Stephens, went to the boy and telling him that his time was come, put a knife into his throat and killed him then and there; that the three men fed upon the body and blood of the boy for four days; that on the fourth day after the act had been committed the boat was picked up by a passing vessel, and the prisoners were rescued, still alive, but in the lowest state of prostration. That they were carried to the port of Falmouth, and committed for trial at Exeter. That if the men had not fed upon the body of the boy they would probably not have survived to be picked up and rescued, but would within the four days have died of famine. That the boy, being in a much weaker condition, was likely to have died before them. That at the time of the act in question there was no sail in sight, nor any reasonable prospect of relief. That under these circumstances there appeared to the prisoners every probability that unless they then fed or very soon fed upon the boy or one of themselves they would die of starvation. That there was no appreciable chance of saving life except by killing some one for the others to eat. That assuming any necessity to kill anybody, there was no greater necessity for killing the boy than any of the other three men." But whether upon the whole matter . . . the killing of Richard Parker by Dudley and Stephens be felony and murder the jurors are ignorant, and pray the advice of the Court thereupon, and if upon the whole matter the Court shall be of opinion that the killing of Richard Parker be felony and murder, then the jurors say that Dudley and Stephens were each guilty of felony and murder as alleged in the indictment. . . .

LORD COLERIDGE, C. J.

. . . It was further objected that, according to the decision of the majority of the judges in the *Franconia Case,* there was no jurisdiction in the Court at Exeter to try these prisoners. But in that case the prisoner was a German, who had committed the alleged offence as captain of a German ship; these prisoners were English seamen, the crew of an English yacht, cast away in a storm on the high seas, and escaping from her in an open boat; the opinion of the minority in the *Franconia Case* has been since not only enacted but declared by Parliament to have been always the law; . . . "All offences against property or person committed in or at any place either ashore or afloat, out of her Majesty's dominions by any master seaman or apprentice who at the time when the offence is committed is or within three months previously has been employed in any British ship, shall be deemed to be offences of the same nature respectively, and be inquired of, heard, tried, determined, and adjudged in the same manner and by the same courts and in the same places as if such offences had been committed within the jurisdiction of the Admiralty of England." We are all therefore of opinion that this objection . . . must be overruled.

There remains to be considered the real question in the case — whether killing under the circumstances set forth in the verdict be or be not murder. The contention that it could be anything else was, to the minds of us all, both new and strange, and we stopped the Attorney General in his negative argument in order that we might hear what could be said in support of a proposition which appeared to us to be at once dangerous, immoral, and opposed to all legal principle and analogy. . . . First it is said that it follows from various definitions of murder in books of authority, which definitions imply, if they do not state, the doctrine, that in order to save your own life you may lawfully take away the life of another, when that other is neither attempting nor threatening yours, nor is guilty of any illegal act whatever towards you or any one else. But if these definitions be looked at they will not be found to sustain this contention. The earliest in point of date is the passage cited to us from Bracton, who lived in the reign of Henry III. It was at one time the fashion to discredit Bracton, . . . There is now no such feeling, . . . Sin and crime are spoken of as apparently equally illegal, . . . [I]n the very passage as to necessity, on which reliance has been placed, it is clear that Bracton is speaking of necessity in the ordinary sense — the repelling by violence, violence justified so far as it was necessary for the object, any illegal violence used towards oneself. If, says Bracton, the necessity be "evitabilis, et evadere posset absque occisione, tunc erit reus homicidii" [avoidable and he can escape without harm, then it will be homicide] — words which shew clearly that he is thinking of physical danger from which *escape* may be possible, and that the "inevitabilis necessitas" [unavoidable necessity] of which he speaks as justifying homicide is a necessity of the same nature.

It is, if possible, yet clearer that the doctrine contended for receives no support from the great authority of Lord Hale. It is plain that in his view the necessity which justified homicide is that only which has always been and is now considered a justification. "In all these cases of homicide by necessity," says he, "as in pursuit of a felon, in killing him that assaults to rob, or comes to burn or break a house, or the like, which are in themselves no felony." . . . Again, he says that "the necessity which justifies homicide is of two kinds: (1) the necessity which is of a private nature; (2) the necessity which relates to the public justice and safety. The former is that necessity which obligeth a man to his own defence and safeguard, and this takes in these inquiries: — What may be done for the safeguard of a man's own life;" and then follow three other heads not necessary to pursue. Then Lord Hale proceeds: — "As touching the first of these — viz., homicide in defence of a man's own life, which is usually styled se defendendo." It is not possible to use words more clear to shew that Lord Hale regarded the private necessity which justified, and alone justified, the taking the life of another for the safeguard of one's own to be what is commonly called "self-defence." . . .

But if this could be even doubtful upon Lord Hale's words, Lord Hale himself has made it clear. For in the chapter in which he deals with the exemption created by compulsion or necessity he thus expresses himself: — "If a man be desperately assaulted and in peril of death, and cannot otherwise escape unless, to satisfy his assailant's fury, he will kill an innocent person then present, the fear and actual force will not acquit him of the crime and punishment of murder, if he commit the fact, for he ought rather to die himself than kill an innocent; but if he cannot otherwise save his own life the law permits him in his own defence to kill the assailant, for by the violence of the assault, and the offence committed upon him by the assailant himself, the law of nature, and necessity, hath made him his own protector. . . ."

But, further still, Lord Hale in the following chapter deals with the position . . . , that in a case of extreme necessity, either of hunger or clothing; "theft is no theft, or at least not punishable as theft, as some even of our own lawyers have asserted the same," "But," says Lord Hale, "I take it that here in England, that rule, at least by the laws of England, is false; and therefore, if a person, being under necessity for want of victuals or clothes, shall upon that account clandestinely and animo furandi steal [with intent to steal] another man's goods, it is felony, and a crime by the laws of England punishable with death." . . . If, therefore, Lord Hale is clear — as he is — that extreme necessity of hunger does not justify larceny, what would he have said to the doctrine that it justified murder?

It is satisfactory to find that another great authority, second, probably, only to Lord Hale, speaks with the same unhestitating clearness on this matter. Sir Michael Foster, in the 3rd chapter of his Discourse on Homicide, deals with the subject of "homicide founded in necessity"; and the whole chapter implies, and is insensible unless it does imply, that in the view of Sir Michael Foster "necessity and self-defence" (which he defines as "opposing force to force even to the death") are convertible terms. There is no hint, no trace, of the doctrine now contended for; the whole reasoning of the chapter is entirely inconsistent with it.

In East's Pleas of the Crown (i. 271) the whole chapter on homicide by necessity is taken up with an elaborate discussion of the limits within which necessity in Sir Michael Foster's sense (given above) of self-defence is a justification of or excuse for homicide. There is a short section at the end very generally and very doubtfully expressed, in which the only instance discussed is the well-known one of two shipwrecked men on a plank able to sustain only one of them, and the conclusion is left by Sir Edward East entirely undetermined.

What is true of Sir Edward East is true also of Mr. Sarjeant Hawkins. The whole of his chapter on justifiable homicide assumes that the only justifiable homicide of a private nature is the defence against force of a man's person, house, or goods. In the 26th section we find again the case of the two shipwrecked men and the single plank, with the significant expression from a careful writer, "*It is said* to be justifiable." So, too, Dalton c. 150, clearly considers necessity and self-defence in Sir Michael Foster's sense of that expression, to be convertible terms, though he prints without comment Lord Bacon's instance of the two men on one plank as a quotation from Lord Bacon, adding nothing whatever to it of his own. And there is a remarkable passage at page 339, in which he says that even in the case of a murderous assault upon a man, yet before he may take the life of the man who assaults him even in self-defence, "cuncta prius tentanda" [delay must be attempted]. . . .

Is there, then, any authority for the proposition which has been presented to us? Decided cases there are none. The case of the seven English sailors referred to by the commentator on Grotius and by Puffendorf has been discovered by a gentleman of the Bar, who communicated with my Brother Huddleston, to convey the authority (if it conveys so much) of a single judge of the island of St. Kitts, when that island was possessed partly by France and partly by this country, somewhere about the year 1641. It is mentioned in a medical treatise published at Amsterdam, and is altogether, as authority in an English court, as unsatisfactory as possible. The American case cited by my Brother Stephen in his Digest, from Wharton on Homicide, in which it was decided, correctly indeed, that sailors had no right to throw passengers overboard to save themselves, but on the somewhat strange ground that the proper mode of determining who was to be sacrificed was to vote upon the subject by ballot, can hardly, as my Brother Stephen says, be an authority satisfactory to a court in this country. The observations of Lord Mansfield in the case of *Rex* v. *Stratton and Others*, striking and excellent as they are, were delivered in a political trial, where the question was whether a political necessity had arisen for deposing a Governor of Madras. But they have little application to the case before us, which must be decided on very different considerations.

The one real authority of former time is Lord Bacon, who, . . . lays down the law as follows: — "Necessity carrieth a privilege in itself. Necessity is of three sorts — necessity of conservation of life, necessity of obedience, and necessity of the act of God or of a stranger. First of conservation of life; if a man steal viands to satisfy his present hunger, this is no felony nor larceny. So if divers be in danger of drowning by the casting away of some boat or barge, and one of them get to some plank, or on the boat's side to keep himself above water, and another to save his life thrust him from it, whereby he is drowned, this is neither se defendendo nor by misadventure, but justifiable." On this it is to be observed that Lord Bacon's proposition that stealing to satisfy hunger is no larceny is hardly supported by Staundforde, whom he cites for it, and is expressly contradicted by Lord Hale in the passage already cited. And for the proposition as to the plank or boat, it is said to be derived from the canonists. At any rate he cites no authority for it, and it must stand upon his own. Lord Bacon was great even as a lawyer; but it is permissible to much smaller men, relying upon principle and on the authority of others, the equals and even the superiors of Lord Bacon as lawyers, to question the soundness of his dictum. There are many conceivable states of things in which it might possibly be true, but if Lord Bacon meant to lay down the broad proposition that a man may save his life by killing, if necessary, an innocent and unoffending neighbour, it certainly is not law at the present day.

. . . Neither are we in conflict with any opinion expressed upon the subject by the learned persons who formed the commission for preparing the Criminal Code. They say on this subject: —

"We are certainly not prepared to suggest that necessity should in every case be a justification. We are equally unprepared to suggest that necessity should in no case be a defence; we judge it better to leave such questions to be dealt with when, if ever, they arise in practice by applying the principles of law to the circumstances of the particular case."

It would have been satisfactory to us if these eminent persons could have told us whether the received definitions of legal necessity were in their judgment correct and exhaustive, and if not, in what way they should be amended, but as it is we have, as they say, "to apply the principles of law to the circumstances of this particular case."

Now, except for the purpose of testing how far the conservation of a man's own life is in all cases and under all circumstances, an absolute, unqualified, and paramount duty, we exclude from our consideration all the incidents of war. We are dealing with a case of private homicide, not one imposed upon men in the service of their Sovereign and in the defence of their country. Now it is admitted that the deliberate killing of this unoffending and unresisting boy was clearly murder, unless the killing can be justified by some well-recognized excuse admitted by the law. It is further admitted that there was in this case no such excuse, unless the killing was justified by what has been called "necessity." But the temptation to the act which existed here was not what the law has ever called necessity. Nor is this to be regretted. Though law and morality are not the same, and many things may be immoral which are not necessarily illegal, yet the absolute divorce of law from morality would be of fatal consequence; and such divorce would follow if the temptation to murder in this case were to be held by law an absolute defence of it. It is not so. To preserve one's life is generally speaking a duty, but it may be the plainest and the highest duty to sacrifice it. War is full of instances in which it is a man's duty not to live, but to die. The duty, in case of shipwreck, of a captain to his crew, of the crew to the passengers, of soldiers to women and children, as in the noble case of the *Birkenhead;* these duties impose on men the moral necessity, not of the preservation, but of the sacrifice of their lives for others, from which in no country, least of all, it is to be hoped, in England, will men ever shrink, as indeed, they have not shrunk. It is not correct, therefore, to say that there is any absolute or unqualified necessity to preserve one's life. . . . It would be a very easy and cheap display of commonplace learning to quote from Greek and Latin authors, from Horace, from Juvenal, from Cicero, from Euripides, passage after passage, in which the duty of dying for others has been laid down in glowing and emphatic language as resulting from the principles of heathen ethics; it is enough in a Christian country to remind ourselves of the Great Example whom we profess to follow. It is not needful to point out the awful danger of admitting the principle which has been contended for. Who is to be the judge of this sort of necessity? By what measure is the comparative value of lives to be measured? Is it to be strength, or intellect, or what? It is plain that the principle leaves to him who is to profit by it to determine the necessity which will justify him in deliberately taking another's life to save his own. In this case the weakest, the youngest, the most unresisting, was chosen. Was it more necessary to kill him than one of the grown men? The answer must be "No" —

So spake the Fiend, and with necessity,
The tyrant's plea, excused his devilish deeds.

It is not suggested that in this particular case the deeds were "devilish," but it is quite plain that such a principle once admitted might be made the legal cloak for unbridled passion and atrocious crime. There is no safe path for judges to tread but to ascertain the law to the best of their ability and to declare it according to their judgment; and if in any case the law appears to be too severe on individuals, to leave it to the Sovereign to exercise that prerogative of mercy which the Constitution has intrusted to the hands fittest to dispense it.

It must not be supposed that in refusing to admit temptation to be an excuse for crime it is forgotten how terrible the temptation was; how awful the suffering; how hard in such trials to keep the judgment straight and the conduct pure. We are often compelled to set up standards we cannot reach ourselves, and to lay down rules which we could not ourselves satisfy. But a man has no right to declare temptation to be an excuse, though he might himself have yielded to it, nor allow compassion for the criminal to change or weaken in any manner the legal definition of the crime. It is therefore our duty to declare that the prisoners' act in this case was wilful murder, that the facts as stated in the verdict are no legal justification of the homicide; and to say that in our unanimous opinion the prisoners are upon this special verdict guilty of murder.[1]

[1]My brother Grove furnished me with the following suggestion, too late to be embodied in the judgment but well worth preserving: "If the two accused men were justified in killing Parker, then if not rescued in time, two of the three survivors would be justified in killing the third, and of the two who remained the stronger would be justified in killing the weaker, so that three men might be justifiably killed to give the fourth a chance of surviving." — C.

The court then proceeded to pass sentence of death upon the prisoners.[2]

Notes and Questions

1. Did Coleridge do justice here? How does one judge the quality of judgments? What values are at stake in this case? What good is accomplished by the decision? What harm?
2. Many students, on reading the case, agree with the decision of Coleridge *and* the decision of the queen to commute the sentence to six months. Can one consistently agree with both?
3. What impels Coleridge to rule against the men while at the same time almost inviting the queen to commute the sentence?
4. Coleridge seems afraid — "It is not needful to point out the awful danger of admitting the principle which has been contended for." Is justice done if the basis for a decision is not so much the case at hand but some future case that might come up?
5. How does Coleridge's sense of values affect his treatment of prior cases or other authority? What prior materials were available to him? Could he have written a persuasive contrary opinion based on available authority? Prepare an opinion of acquittal on the ground of necessity, using *only* the material to which Coleridge refers in his opinion.
6. Judge Coleridge states, "We are often compelled to set standards we cannot reach ourselves and to lay down rules which we could not ourselves satisfy." Compare this with the following statement of Oliver Wendell Holmes:

   > It may be the destiny of man that the social instincts shall grow to control his actions absolutely, even in antisocial situations. But they have not done so, and as the rules of law are or should be based on a morality that is generally accepted, no rule of law founded on a theory of absolute unselfishness can be laid down without a breach between law and working beliefs.*

   Which contention should be the predominant value in law?
7. In the previous section on judicial discretion, Jerome Frank described the importance of psychological factors in decision making. Can Coleridge's personal preferences be found in his opinion?
8. Should the attorneys representing either Dudley and Stephens or the Crown be expected to believe in their cases, or is it enough for them to do a craftsmanlike job?
9. Return to Note 5 on pages 30–31. Can the classification of time perspectives presented there be applied to the *Dudley and Stephens* case?
10. Return to the North Carolina cases on school discipline and wife beating. What values are at stake in them? Are they adequately considered by the courts? Compare the results reached in those cases with the quotation from Holmes in Question 6 above.
11. In view of your experiences in this course to date, evaluate the contention that law is or ought to be value-free.
12. *A.* Suppose that the people in the boat had cast lots to see who would be killed to save the rest and who would do the killing. Would you consider the killing in those events justifiable?
    B. According to law, consent to be killed cannot be made. Compare the law about consent with your answer to part *A.*
13. Some jurists have said that procedure is the heart of the law — the *way* a decision is made is more important than *what* decision is made. Evaluate. If Coleridge makes his decision in a judicious way, should we be satisfied?
14. Consider the following from an opinion of Justice William Brennan of the U.S. Supreme Court in a case involving the question of whether the death penalty violates the constitutional provision against cruel and unusual punishment.

---

[2]This sentence was afterwards commuted by the Crown to six months' imprisonment.

*Oliver Wendell Holmes, *The Common Law* (Boston: Little, Brown, 1886), p. 44.

> The basic concept underlying the [Eighth Amendment] is nothing less than the dignity of man. While the state has the power to punish, the Clause stands to assure that this power be exercised within the limits of civilized standards.
>
> Death is truly an awesome punishment. The calculated killing of a human being by the State involves, by its very nature, a denial of the executed person's humanity. . . . When a man is hung, there is an end of our relationship with him. His execution is a way of saying, You are not fit for this world. Take your chances elsewhere.†

15. Consider the following from Justice Harry Blackmun of the U.S. Supreme Court in the famous case of *Roe* v. *Wade* on abortion:

> We forthwith acknowledge our awareness of the sensitive and emotional nature of the abortion controversy, of the vigorous opposing views even among physicians, and of the deep and seemingly absolute convictions that the subject inspires. One's philosophy, one's experiences, one's exposure to the raw edges of human existence, one's religious training, one's attitudes toward life and family and their values, and the moral standards one establishes and seeks to observe, are all likely to influence and to color one's thinking and conclusions about abortion.
>
> In addition, population growth, pollution, poverty, and racial overtones tend to complicate and not to simplify the problem.
>
> Our task, of course, is to resolve the issue by constitutional measurement, free of emotion and predilection.‡

Is it possible to consider the abortion question "free of emotion and predilection"? What is constitutional measurement?

†*Furman* v. *Georgia*, 92 S. Ct. 272 (1972).

‡*Roe* v. *Wade*, 93 S. Ct. 756.

Coleridge's impulse to set standards that he himself might not be able to meet may be traced to a desire to deter killing. Rather than become a moral accomplice to murder, the state stands ready to execute people to assure the sanctity of life. The internal contradiction — taking life to preserve it — has bothered thinking people for a long time, and although the public favors the restoration of the death penalty in the United States (as reflected in public opinion polls), the controversy about the death penalty rages on.

For most people, and perhaps for Coleridge himself, the execution of people sentenced to death remains an abstraction. We may read in a newspaper that a person "has paid his (or her) debt to society." Someone whom we do not know has been executed, by people we do not know and are unlikely to meet, in places we will never see. George Orwell, the famous British writer, enjoyed no such "luxury."

A Hanging *George Orwell*

It was in Burma, a sodden morning of the rains. A sickly light, like yellow tinfoil, was slanting over the high walls into the jail yard. We were waiting outside the condemned cells, a row of sheds fronted with double bars, like small animal cages. Each cell measured about ten feet by ten and was quite bare within except for a plank bed and a pot of drinking water. In some of them brown silent men were squatting at the inner bars, with their blankets draped round them. These were the condemned men, due to be hanged within the next week or two.

One prisoner had been brought out of his cell. He was a Hindu, a puny wisp of a man, with a shaven head and vague liquid eyes. He had a thick, sprouting moustache, absurdly too big for his body, rather like the moustache of a comic man on the films. Six tall Indian warders were guarding him and getting him ready for the gallows. Two of them stood by with rifles and fixed bayonets, while the others handcuffed him, passed a chain through his handcuffs and fixed it to their belts, and lashed his arms tight to his sides. They crowded very close about him, with their hands always on him in a careful, caressing grip, as though all the while feeling him to make sure he was there. It was like men handling a fish which is still alive and may jump back into the water. But he stood quite unresisting, yielding his arms limply to the ropes, as though he hardly noticed what was happening.

Eight o'clock struck and a bugle call, desolately thin in the wet air, floated from the distant barracks. The superintendent of the jail, who was standing apart from the rest of us, moodily prodding the gravel with his stick, raised his head at the sound. He was an army doctor, with a grey toothbrush moustache and a gruff voice. "For God's sake hurry up, Francis," he said irritably. "The man ought to have been dead by this time. Aren't you ready yet?"

Francis, the head jailer, a fat Dravidian in a white drill suit and gold spectacles, waved his black hand. "Yes sir, yes sir," he bubbled. "All iss satisfactorily prepared. The hangman iss waiting. We shall proceed."

"Well, quick march, then. The prisoners can't get their breakfast till this job's over."

We set out for the gallows. Two warders marched on either side of the prisoner, with their rifles at the slope; two others marched close against him, gripping him by arm and shoulder, as though at once pushing and supporting him. The rest of us, magistrates and the like, followed behind. Suddenly, when we had gone ten yards, the procession stopped short without any order or warning. A dreadful thing had happened — a dog, come goodness knows whence, had appeared in the yard. It came bounding among us with a loud volley of barks, and leapt round us wagging its whole body, wild with glee at finding so many human beings together. It was a large woolly dog, half Airedale, half pariah. For a moment it pranced round us, and then, before anyone could stop it, it had made a dash for the prisoner, and jumping up tried to lick his face. Everyone stood aghast, too taken aback even to grab at the dog.

"Who let that bloody brute in here?" said the superintendent angrily. "Catch it, someone!"

A warder, detached from the escort, charged clumsily after the dog, but it danced and gambolled just out of his reach, taking everything as part of the game. A young Eurasian jailer picked up a handful of gravel and tried to stone the dog away, but it dodged the stones and came after us again. Its yaps echoed from the jail walls. The prisoner, in the grasp of the two warders, looked on incuriously, as though this was another formality of the hanging. It was several minutes before someone managed to catch the dog. Then we put my handkerchief through its collar and moved off once more, with the dog still straining and whimpering.

It was about forty yards to the gallows. I watched the bare brown back of the prisoner marching in front of me. He walked clumsily with his bound arms, but quite steadily, with that bobbing gait of the Indian who never straightens his knees. At each step his muscles slid neatly into place, the lock of hair on his scalp danced up and down, his feet printed themselves on the wet gravel. And once, in spite of the men who gripped him by each shoulder, he stepped slightly aside to avoid a puddle on the path.

It is curious, but till that moment I had never realised what it means to destroy a healthy, conscious man. When I saw the prisoner step aside to avoid the puddle, I saw the mystery, the unspeakable wrongness, of cutting a life short when it is in full tide. This man was not dying, he was alive just as we were alive. All the organs of his body were working — bowels digesting food, skin renewing itself, nails growing, tissues forming — all toiling away in solemn foolery. His nails would still be growing when he stood on the drop, when he was falling through the air with a tenth of a second to live. His eyes saw the yellow gravel and the grey walls, and his brain still remembered, foresaw, reasoned — reasoned even about puddles. He and we were a party of men walking together, seeing, hearing, feeling, understanding the same world; and in two minutes, with a sudden snap, one of us would be gone — one mind less, one world less.

The gallows stood in a small yard, separate from the main grounds of the prison, and overgrown with tall prickly weeds. It was a brick erection like three sides of a shed, with planking on top, and above that two beams and a crossbar with the rope dangling. The hangman, a grey-haired convict in the white uniform of the prison, was waiting beside his machine. He greeted us with a servile crouch as we entered. At a word from Francis the two warders, gripping the prisoner more closely than ever, half led, half pushed him to the gallows and helped him clumsily up the ladder. Then the hangman climbed up and fixed the rope round the prisoner's neck.

We stood waiting, five yards away. The warders had formed in a rough circle round the gallows. And then, when the noose was fixed, the prisoner began crying out to his god. It was a high, reiterated cry of "Ram! Ram! Ram! Ram!", not urgent and fearful like a prayer or a cry for help, but steady, rhythmical, almost like the tolling of a bell. The dog answered the sound with a whine. The hangman, still standing on the gallows, produced a small cotton bag like a flour bag and drew it down over the prisoner's face. But the sound, muffled by the cloth, still persisted, over and over again: "Ram! Ram! Ram! Ram! Ram!"

The hangman climbed down and stood ready, holding the lever. Minutes seemed to pass. The steady, muffled cry from the prisoner went on and on, "Ram! Ram! Ram!" never faltering for an instant. The superintendent, his head on his chest, was slowly poking the ground with his stick; perhaps he was counting the cries, allowing the prisoner a fixed number — fifty, perhaps, or a hundred. Everyone had changed colour. The Indians had gone grey like bad coffee, and one or two of the bayonets were wavering. We looked at the lashed, hooded man on the drop, and listened to his cries — each cry another second of life; the same thought was in all our minds: oh, kill him quickly, get it over, stop that abominable noise!

Suddenly the superintendent made up his mind. Throwing up his head he made a swift motion with his stick. "Chalo!" he shouted almost fiercely.

There was a clanking noise, and then dead silence. The prisoner had vanished, and the rope was twisting on itself. I let go of the dog, and it galloped immediately to the back of the gallows; but when it got there it stopped short, barked, and then retreated into a corner of the yard, where it stood among the weeds, looking timorously out at us. We went round the gallows to inspect the prisoner's body. He was dangling with his toes pointed straight downwards, very slowly revolving, as dead as a stone.

The superintendent reached out with his stick and poked the bare body; it oscillated, slightly. "*He's* all right," said the superintendent. He backed out from under the gallows, and blew out a deep breath. The moody look had gone out of his face quite suddenly. He glanced at his wrist-watch. "Eight minutes past eight. Well, that's all for this morning, thank God."

The warders unfixed bayonets and marched away. The dog, sobered and conscious of having misbehaved itself, slipped after them. We walked out of the gallows yard, past the condemned cells with their waiting prisoners, into the big central yard of the prison. The convicts, under the command of warders armed with lathis, were already receiving their breakfast. They squatted in long rows, each man holding a tin pannikin, while two warders with buckets marched round ladling out rice; it seemed quite a homely, jolly scene, after the hanging. An enormous relief had come upon us now that the job was done. One felt an impulse to sing, to break into a run, to snigger. All at once everyone began chattering gaily.

The Eurasian boy walking beside me nodded towards the way we had come, with a knowing smile: "Do you know, sir, our friend (he meant the dead man), when he heard his appeal had been dismissed, he pissed on the floor of his cell. From fright. — Kindly take one of my cigarettes, sir. Do you not admire my new silver case, sir? From the boxwallah, two rupees eight annas. Classy European style."

Several people laughed — at what, nobody seemed certain.

Francis was walking by the superintendent, talking garrulously: "Well, sir, all hass passed off with the utmost satisfactoriness. It wass all finished — flick! like that. It iss not always so — oah, no! I have known cases where the doctor wass obliged to go beneath the gallows and pull the prisoner's legs to ensure decease. Most disagreeable!"

"Wriggling about, eh? That's bad," said the superintendent.

"Ach, sir, it iss worse when they become refractory! One man, I recall, clung to the bars of hiss cage when we went to take him out. You will scarcely credit, sir, that it took six warders to dislodge him, three pulling at each leg. We reasoned with him. 'My dear fellow,' we said, 'think of all the pain and trouble you are causing to us!' But no, he would not listen! Ach, he wass very troublesome!"

I found that I was laughing quite loudly. Everyone was laughing. Even the superintendent grinned in a tolerant way. "You'd better all come out and have a drink," he said quite genially. "I've got a bottle of whisky in the car. We could do with it."

We went through the big double gates of the prison, into the road. "Pulling at his legs!" exclaimed a Burmese magistrate suddenly, and burst into a loud chuckling. We all began laughing again. At that moment Francis's anecdote seemed extraordinarily funny. We all had a drink together, native and European alike, quite amicably. The dead man was a hundred yards away.

Notes and Questions

1. In Section 2, on judging and discretion, there was some discussion of the role of intuition in decisions. Does the vivid description of an execution give rise to certain intuitions or evaluations that require no special philosophizing or gathering of pros and cons? What reactions does Orwell want to excite in his readers? Which of his images are most effective in bringing us closer to the events he wants us to understand?
2. Make a vivid description of an episode that requires evaluation and judgment. Try out your description on a friend to see what effects your description has.
3. Orwell's sense of injustice was aroused by the execution. Interview a friend regarding an episode in which your friend felt that injustice occurred. (Since injustices occur in settings other than formal legal ones or where officials of law are not involved, the episodes need not be "law related.") Compare the episode you gathered with those gathered by other students. Do common themes appear?
4. Orwell does not tell us the offense for which the prisoner was executed. He seems to reach his adverse reaction to the death penalty without needing to know more.

Should he, as a good reporter, have told us the offense so that we might know whether the killing of the man by the state was an unconscious and needless act or a necessary one? Compare this consideration with the claim that people who reject the death penalty fail to consider the victims of an offense.

Must the execution by the state stand on its own?

☐ Orwell was a minor official of the state, a person at the end of the line between the decision to execute a person and the execution itself. Many moral dilemmas are far from officialdom, where each person must make the connection between evaluation and action. Each person has an array of experiences that might be loosely termed *precedents* or *moral habits*. Each has a sphere of action and at least some discretion, to be exercised for better or worse. Each operates in a time, place, and circumstance and draws no consolation from the contention that nothing in general can be said about values, that they depend on the situation.

The next selection is a story of a physician who works among the rural poor of Kentucky. As a professional she has been taught to practice medicine. As a person, she finds that the borders of "her field" give way at every turn and must yield to a need to live life consciously.

Simple Living and Hard Choices *Maureen A. Flannery*

As a family physician in rural Appalachia, I do not confront many of the issues that pervade the literature of contemporary medical ethics. In my county, we do not debate which facilities should have CAT scanners; we are just trying to replace an outmoded x-ray machine so that we can obtain clearer chest films while exposing our patients to less scatter radiation.

Maureen A. Flannery, M.D. is the physician at Berea College Health Service and Medical Director of Mountain Maternal Health League, Berea, Ky. She is clinical instructor in family practice, University of Kentucky College of Medicine, and assistant clinical professor of family practice, University of Louisville School of Medicine. She is also an instructor at the Frontier School of Midwifery and Family Nursing, Hyden, Ky. At the time the article was written, Dr. Flannery was at Homeplace Clinic, Ary, Ky.

Amniocentesis is not much of an issue in my practice. My patients are astonished at the suggestion that they drive three hours to the university medical center to have a risky procedure simply because they are pregnant past the age of thirty-five or forty, because childbearing into these years remains common in Appalachia. Within large families, it is not unexpected that one or two of the children will be "slow" or "strange"; most women reject an invasive test to predict whether a subsequent child might turn out similarly.

For most Appalachian women, abortion is not an option, even in the case of an unplanned and desperately unwanted pregnancy. This is partly because of strong family ties and the value placed on children within the extended mountain family; and perhaps because Appalachian women are resigned to the fact that motherhood is one of the few potentially fulfilling roles available to them in their home communities. The unavailability of abortions, physically and economically, within the region is less of a factor; the unusual woman who elects abortion as a solution to an unwanted pregnancy prefers that the procedure be done far from the gossip of her home community and without the knowledge of the local "welfare office."

I do not see the daughters or sons of women who took DES during pregnancy and are therefore at risk for a rare cancer. The mothers of most of my patients received little, if any, prenatal care, thereby avoiding that particular pharmacologic tragedy. Decisions around "exotic medical lifesaving therapy" and "scarce lifesaving medical resources," to use the jargon of bioethics, are issues only in their general unavailability, sparing me from difficult decisions about the individual allocation of these technologies. . . . When a city friend asked me whether the medical community had criticized my midwife-attended home birth, I responded, "What medical community?"

The ethical issues I face daily are less dramatic than those involved in decisions around critically ill neonates, organ transplants, and brain death; but they are no less difficult to resolve. Some of them are peculiar to practice in a rural and impoverished area; some are shared by practitioners in other poor areas, such as urban slums; many are faced by all primary-care providers. And with the current health budget cuts, ethical issues around allocation of resources are concerns for all health workers.

My definition of medical ethics is simple: it is ordinary ethics applied to the practice of medicine. Medical ethics is what I do when I stop short in the middle of a busy day in the clinic or have difficulty returning to sleep after an early-morning telephone call from the emergency room because I am asking myself, "What ought I to do in this case?" or "What is the right solution to this problem?" — where the answer to my question cannot be found by checking *Medical Letter* or dialing the neonatologist on the medical center hotline.

Sometimes the situation is a new one, like having a member of one of my families with *osteogenesis imperfecta* (a genetic disease in which the bones are abnormally brittle) become pregnant, despite contraceptive and genetic counseling. More often the problem the patient presents is familiar, but something about the patient or the family situation confounds me, calls my assumptions into question, makes me stop and think.

The nature of the situations that present ethical dilemmas are quite different for the family physician than for the specialist. They tend to be personal and unpredictable. As one family doctor described her practice in North Carolina, "I never did specialize in anything except just people and what came along next." I. R. McWhinney's description of the family medicine perspective is useful:

> Family physicians have in common the fact that they obtain fulfillment from personal relations more than from the technical aspects of medicine. Their commitment is to a group of people more than to a body of knowledge. . . . It is difficult for a doctor to commit himself [or herself, throughout] to a person and at the same time to limit his commitment to certain diseases or certain types of problem. . . . the kind of commitment I am speaking of implies that the physician will "stay with" a person whatever his problem may be, and he will do so because his commitment is to people more than to a body of knowledge or a branch of technology. To such a physician, problems become interesting and important not only for their own sake but because they are Mr. Smith's or Mrs. Jones's problem. Very often in such relations there is not even a very clear distinction between a medical problem and a nonmedical one. The patient defines the problem.

For a family physician in a rural area, often the only limit to practice is geographic; everyone within a one- or two-hour driving distance may be the doctor's responsibility. Depending upon the other resources of the area, the physician's commitment may even extend beyond human patients. . . .

Given the general commitment a rural family physician has to the surrounding community, the realities of life for the people nearby largely determine the issues that arise in practice. Survival in rural America involves a unique set of struggles, many of which influence health.

One major factor is *low income*. A disproportionate number of the nation's poor live in rural America. About 25 percent of the U.S. population lives in nonmetropolitan areas, yet the rural population accounts for 40 percent of those people living below the poverty level. Furthermore, of this 40 percent, ethnic minority groups and the elderly make up a significant proportion. Fifty percent of rural Native Americans, 27 percent of rural Hispanics, and 41 percent of rural blacks have incomes below the poverty level, as compared to 11 percent of rural whites. Poverty increases health problems because of its association with poor nutrition, inadequate housing, unsafe living conditions, and inability to purchase health services.

Low income becomes a greater liability when wages are earned in a *hazardous occupation*. According to 1976 Department of Labor statistics, rural Americans represented the majority of workers in those industries that rank first and second in job-related fatalities: mining and agriculture. Despite the well-known health and safety risks of these occupations, they often represent the only available or the only well-paying jobs for rural Americans.

Not only are rural occupations more likely to be low paying and hazardous, these industries generally provide *fewer health benefits* for their employees. Many rural workers cannot get workers' compensation and they are rarely provided with health insurance. In Texas, for instance, workers' compensation is mandatory for all workers except the farmworkers, who constitute the majority of the rural population of the state. Farm workers are rarely provided with health insurance. Employed rural residents in low-benefit industries are often unable to make payments for their health care, generating insufficient revenue for the facilities that provide them services.

A related disadvantage for rural dwellers is a *lower-than-average educational level*, a characteristic that correlates closely with poor usage of health services. Less-educated persons tend not to have had the opportunity to learn about health, hygiene, and preventive measures. Often they are not informed about governmental programs for which they are eligible, programs that might help with some of the costs or remove some of the obstacles to needed health care services.

Rural dwellers tend to have *closer family ties* than city dwellers because of the preservation of traditional values and also because other societal structures upon which a family can depend are limited in rural areas. Divorce is less common than in urban areas; traditional nuclear and/or extended families are the rule. Since 70 percent of rural families have two parents in the home, compared to 39 percent in the inner cities, the rural poor often fail to meet eligibility criteria for governmental insurance programs that were designed to deal with urban poverty, such as Medicaid and Aid to Dependent Children.

The *particular age structure* of rural America affects the health care of its inhabitants. The number of elderly persons and of children under ten is proportionately higher in rural areas. Since women not only constitute the largest number of health care consumers in general, but also live longer than men and bear children, they are disproportionately represented among rural persons in need of health care. Institutions that care for dependent members of society, such as nursing homes and day care centers, are not prevalent in rural areas; nor are they well accepted, since traditional rural families "care for their own."

In addition to these epidemiological characteristics that militate against good health care, many rural areas have a history of *substandard health care providers*. In Appalachia, the most dramatic example is the coal company doctor. In many communities, the first "professional" health provider was a physician brought in by the local coal company to treat all its employees and their families. There was no alternative to the company doc; he was part of the paternalistic monopoly, just like the company store.

Rather than health insurance benefits, workers received free care or else scrip for the company doc's services. Since miners were poorly paid and other health providers were scarce, there was essentially no consumer choice for health care. For a variety of reasons, the coal companies did not attract particularly qualified physicians. And patients saw quite clearly that their doctor's allegiance was to the company management, not to their health. (It was not until the United Mine Workers developed its visionary system of hospitals and clinics in the late 1950s that qualified physicians came in any number to the mountains.) . . .

I became particularly aware of the influence of all these characteristics on the health of rural dwellers this fall when my partner and I taught a self-care course for the patients in our clinic, modifying a curriculum taught in several Kentucky cities. In dealing with our class of twenty layfolk, we came up against the many conditions that hinder outpatients in taking care of themselves — poverty, environmental hazards, dangerous occupations, lack of education, unemployment, socialization into dependence upon "experts," and lack of support for healthy behavior within a society that condones and often encourages self-destructive habits. Trying to modify a curriculum developed for urban middle-class folk to our rural participants made me realize that much of the self-care and holistic health movements does not apply to people who lack control over many of the basic conditions of their lives.

For instance, self-responsibility is a basic concept of the holistic health movement. The notion that individuals are responsible for their health is sometimes extended to assume that people are also responsible for their diseases. Although this idea can be useful for individuals seeking to understand the meaning of their illnesses — particularly illnesses with significant psychological components — much of the popular self-care literature fails to acknowledge that there are some factors over which we have control in our lives and other factors (known and unknown) over which we have little or no control. For the people in our class, the latter often clearly dominated. Black lung victims, for instance, do not create their health problems (unless they also smoke heavily); unhealthy working conditions do. It is wrong to suggest that the victims must change themselves in order to survive; it is the workplace that must be changed. The problem and its treatment are not individual but societal.

Many specifics of the curriculum were as inappropriate to our class as the underlying philosophy. For example, how do you start a jogging regimen when you live up a creekbed, when the nearby public roads have no shoulders and are dominated by overfull and uncovered coal trucks? When "just getting by" occupies most of your time, leaving little for leisure activities, however healthful? And when jogging itself is a foreign concept: in the mountains, anyone who would run for any reason other than to get somewhere — or else to get away from something — is a fool. . . .

Many of the female patients I see tell me that they have come to my office because of "bad nerves"; or else they may use it as a tag-on at the visit's end ("By the way, doc, I've got these bad nerves. . . ."). A doctor who practiced nearby several years ago recorded a number of interviews with "bad nerve" patients in which she explored the origin of the diagnosis and the patient's concept of the nature of the malady. Her discovery was that "bad nerves" was largely an iatrogenic complaint [doctor-created illness]. Asked when they became aware of their bad nerves, patients generally said that they had visited a physician with a somatic complaint, say a headache or a stomach ache, and had been told, "No, you don't have a brain tumor," or "There's no ulcer causing your stomach to hurt," but rather, "What you have is *bad nerves.*" And the treatment in most cases was a prescription for "nerve pills." Patients took this medical diagnosis and its pharmacological treatment very seriously, seeing "bad nerves" as an illness as physical and concrete as a tumor or an ulcer. One woman vividly described her concept of the nerves coursing through her body as "frayed and tarnished" rather than "silvery smooth" as in a fifth-grade health book picture. Another understood the doctor who performed her hysterectomy to say that he saw her nerves "all aquiver" on the operating table, clearly the worst case of "bad nerves" he had witnessed. . . .

A common dilemma I face in my practice is what to do when a woman comes in requesting (and requests unmet soon escalate to demands) drug treatment for her "bad nerves." A thorough history usually confirms the iatrogenic labeling of the "bad nerves" and in addition uncovers a difficult and complex social situation that perpetuates the symptoms. Given a busy practice, a bare-bones staff, and poor human service resources in the area; given that patients who discontinue benzodiazepine tranquilizers after more than four months of regular use have a physiological as well as psychological addiction to overcome; and given that there are no transcendental meditation sessions, yoga or exercise classes, or even competent individual or group therapists within a reasonable driving distance, is it right for me to refuse to refill the patient's Valium, cutting off her way of dulling her responses to the problems of her life? Is it right for me to support her habit? Must a good family physician in a rural area play the roles of counselor, social worker, recreation therapist, and scout leaders as well as doctor? Is it possible for one person, however committed, to handle such multiple and demanding roles?

Another frequent complaint, one so common that it is difficult to get patients to clarify it, is "smothering." In the mountains, "smothering" describes everything from the sudden shortness-of-breath of an acute asthmatic attack to the labored breathing of poor physical condition to the short-windedness of chronic obstructive lung disease. I imagine that the frequency of this description is related to the prevalence of black lung, an occupational disease of enormous significance in our single-industry region. Almost everyone knows a neighbor or relative, retired from years in the coal mines, spending his days bound to his home "breathing machine," coughing into a cut-off milk carton in front of the television set. The image is so familiar that even children pick it up: the other day an asthmatic five-year-old described his problem to me as "smothering." I can't help but think that the image is metaphorical for a group of people as oppressed and accustomed to outside control of their lives, their money, and their land as Appalachians. Is it right for a physician simply to treat "smothering" with epinephrine or aminophylline without attempting to deal with the root causes of the oppression? Must a good rural family physician also be a political activist?

And what do patients' rights mean when dealing with people so oppressed and unassertive that they are reluctant to take any responsibility for the care that they receive? It takes hard work and time to bring such folk to demand any of the rights that they have traditionally signed away, just as their foreparents signed away the mineral rights to the land on which they live. In the midst of a busy practice, it is far easier to lapse into the paternalistic pattern to which patients are accustomed. Must a conscientious rural doc also be a part-time community organizer?

A patient came to me the other day to see whether I could "do something" about the dust accumulation in her parents' home. They live up an isolated holler near the clinic, and the dirt road that once ended at their cabin now provides access to a newly developed strip mine. Huge coal trucks now rumble past day and night — their daughter counted five in the space of an hour. Since her parents are the only inhabitants along the road, the coal company ignores the requirement that it "water" the road several times a day to reduce dust accumulation. My patient was concerned that the particles in the air were exacerbating her father's severe chronic obstructive pulmonary disease, a result of thirty-five years of coal dust exposure in underground mines. And it was certainly affecting the couple's quality of life: her elderly mother, a fastidious housekeeper with an early organic brain syndrome, was wearing herself out in a hopeless situation.

Certainly this is an appropriate problem for a family physician. But how far do I go? Write a letter to the owner of the coal company? Report the violation to the Office of Surface Mining when the owner does not respond? Pursue the matter to the state or federal level when lower officials do not act because they are in league with one of the biggest coal operators in the region? How much time and energy can I consume hassling a nonresponsive bureaucracy to benefit one family? Would it be right for me to do nothing?

. . . [T]he rural physician must constantly ask, how much can one individual do? Can one be a good and ethical physician just by treating symptoms, or must a doctor become deeply involved in addressing the sources of disease in the people she or he cares for? And if a doctor neglects continuing medical education because of political involvements, or "burns out" from the stress of trying to do too much, do the patients and community ultimately benefit or not?

THE WISE OLD WOMAN OF THE VILLAGE

In struggling with the issue of setting limits to commitment, a rural health care provider must deal with a related question: personal survival in a rural community. For a physician in a rural area, there is no boundary between professional and private life. Living among the people whom I serve in a close-knit community, I do not have the luxury of retreating to a suburban lifestyle surrounded by other "young professionals" when I end my day at an inner-city clinic. I am one of a few professionals in my county, and everyone knows where I live, how I spend my days off, and whether I dug up my potatoes before the first frost. . . .

Physicians have traditionally considered their private lives immune to this sort of public scrutiny. Although they have almost unlimited access to patients' minds and bodies, an unwritten ethic of the relationship generally prevents patients from intruding into their doctors' private lives. But is it unreasonable for patients to demand that I connect my public and private lives? To challenge me to be consistent in the values I profess in the clinic and at home? How I spend my time and money, what political convictions I hold — do these not affect my doctoring?

Many urban physicians make a sharp distinction between the people with whom they spend social or after-hours time and those they see as patients. The director of my residency program felt very strongly that a doctor should not accept friends as patients. He believed that confusing friend-friend and doctor-patient relationships created problems for both physician and patient: the blurring made medical judgments more difficult for the physician and detracted from the role of "authority figure" that the physician plays. He also believed in the value of friends who relate to the physician as a person, and who can help him or her escape from medicine after hours. Whatever the merits of that position, a rural physician has little choice in the matter. I would have to drive a long way for friends or my friends would have to travel a long way for their medical care if I followed his advice. Instead, I trust my patient/friends to understand that I need "time off" in order to be there for them as physician/friend.

Given the high visibility of a physician in a small community, anonymity is impossible. From an income disproportionately higher than that of hard-working neighbors to preferential treatment in scheduling a haircut, the "myriad and often subtle privileges of physician status" are striking in a rural community. Should I accept these favors as compensation for the pressing and demanding work I do? Or should I refuse them as elitist and unnecessary? The absence of boundaries between personal and public lives makes it difficult for the rural physician to lead a "well-rounded" life in the sense of an urban or suburban colleague. Yet those of us who are content with our lives as country docs discover ways of dealing with our situations. Mary Howell describes a model that works for me:

> My vision of how I like to work and relate to the people I serve does not correspond to the usual understanding of the professional

role. I have found a different "role model" altogether — that of the wise old woman of the village, the witch healer, who has been privileged to learn from her predecessors and to share with many generations of village folk their experiences as family members, and who can convey what she has distilled (what she "knows") to others so that they too can use that wisdom.

For rural primary health care providers, finding the wisdom to cope with work that specializes only in "people and what comes along next" is often an overwhelming task. How well we seek that wisdom and resolve the everyday ethical issues that arise in our work ultimately determines our effectiveness in helping the people with whom we live and whom we serve.

Notes and Questions

1. The cases in Section 1 on wife beating showed that lawyers and judges use rules of law to convert large questions into small, manageable, and answerable ones. Those cases turned on the permanence of injury, the presence or absence of lethal weapons, or drunkenness rather than on the imponderables of marriage.

Dr. Flannery seems to violate the main tenet of professions: that no question be asked unless it can readily be answered by even the most unenlightened practitioner. For her, problems grow more complex rather than less. Could she behave ethically were she to narrow questions to medical symptoms and the answers found in her black bag? (Is the "black bag" male?)

Did the lawyers and judges in the wife-beating cases behave ethically when they stuck to the law and the facts relevant to the law? Were they duty bound to change the law itself? Or to go beyond the law and help eliminate the root causes of wife abuse?

2. What problems do professionals encounter when they go wherever problems take them? For example:

A. Should Dr. Flannery simply treat black lung or other occupationally related diseases, or must she become active in preventive medicine — mine safety and environmental health?

B. In the case of patients with "bad nerves," should she rewrite prescriptions for addictive tranquilizers (as her medical colleagues might do), or should she take a longer and more burdensome approach that could take her well beyond the field of medicine?

C. Should Dr. Flannery ally herself with activist lawyers, family counselors, or schoolteachers who see that the problems of Appalachia do not fall conveniently within professional specialties?

D. If many problems of Appalachia are subsets of poverty — technically outside everyone's field — what is the appropriate stance for the concerned professional on economic issues?

E. Must the doctor be more than doctor, the lawyer more than lawyer, or the teacher more than teacher to reach the problems that their patients, clients, and students have?

3. What can the "wise old woman" model do for Dr. Flannery that her professional model cannot? Can her "prescription" for ethical activism be transferred to other settings?

4. Dr. Flannery does not seem like a member of the country club set. Must she accept less income than her professional peers if she is to work with the poor?

☐ The previous reading shows that professionals often answer ethical questions on their own. In the following case involving sterilization, law, medicine, and psychiatry must be integrated.

Cook v. State *495 P. 2d 768 Or. (1972)*

FOLEY, J.

This is an appeal from an order of the circuit court which affirmed an order of the State Board of Social Protection after trial . . . in the circuit court.

On May 21, 1971, the State Board of Social Protection entered an order for plaintiff's sterilization based on findings:

> (2) . . . That in the judgment of a majority of the Board the condition of the examinee is such that procreation by the examinee would produce a child or children: . . . (b) who would become neglected or dependent children as a result of the parent's inability by reason of mental illness or mental retardation to provide adequate care.
>
> (3) That in the judgment of the majority of the Board there is no probability that the condition of the examinee investigated and examined will improve to such an extent as to avoid the indicated consequences as set forth in paragraph (2) hereof. . . .

Plaintiff contends that the trial court erred in denying her motion that the state elect between mental retardation and mental illness as the basis for sterilization and that the trial court erred in affirming the Board's order. The remaining assignment of error alleges that ORS 436.070(1)(b) is unconstitutional because it discriminates against indigents in violation of the equal protection provisions of the state and federal constitutions. ORS 436.070 provides:

> (1) The investigation, findings and orders of the board . . . shall be made with the purpose in view of avoiding the procreation of children:
>
> . . . (b) Who would become neglected or dependent children as a result of the parent's inability by reason of mental illness or mental retardation to provide adequate care. . . .

Footnotes have been numbered. — Ed.

Plaintiff is a 17-year-old girl with a history of severe emotional disturbance. At age 13 she was declared a ward of the court and was taken out of her home under circumstances which indicate that she had been physically and sexually abused by her family for some period of time. During the last four years she has been placed in two foster homes, juvenile detention home, F. W. Dammasch State Hospital and Hillcrest School of Oregon. The longest period in any one place was one and one-half years at Dammasch. Her behavior has vacillated between periods of stability that lasted up to three months and aggressive hostility expressed in verbal or physical threats towards others, self-inflicted injury and running away. A petition was filed with the Board of Social Protection[1] after appellant engaged in a series of indiscriminate and impulsive sexual involvements while she was in the hospital.

A psychiatrist who specializes in child guidance has followed plaintiff's care since she became a ward of the court. His uncontradicted testimony was that she would never be able to provide the parental guidance and judgment which a child requires even though she might be able to master the skills necessary to take physical care of herself and a child. He based this conclusion on the girl's lack of emotional control, her consistent low scores in areas of judgment on psychological tests, and the likelihood that she would abuse a child. He said the prognosis is poor because the presence of brain damage makes her condition inherently unstable despite continuous medication. He testified further that both mental illness and mental retardation are contributing factors and are interrelated.

Because of their interrelated nature, plaintiff's condition could not be intelligently

[1]ORS 436.025 provides:

"Any two persons or any person licensed to practice medicine and surgery by the State Board of Medical Examiners may file a petition with the State Board of Social Protection alleging that any other person within the state is within the jurisdiction of the board as provided in subsection (1) of ORS 436.070."

considered without reference to both mental illness and mental retardation. The statute provides for, and the plaintiff was accorded, counsel at public expense, adequate notice and opportunity to be heard. The statute thus satisfies the due process clause. The trial court's denial of the motion to elect was proper. . . .

It is now necessary to determine whether the statute denies plaintiff equal protection of the laws.

In *Buck* v. *Bell* . . . (1927), the United States Supreme Court upheld a Virginia sterilization law. Sterilization was considered beneficial to the patient and to society because it allowed people to be discharged from state institutions, to return to the community, and to become self-supporting.

The only other case involving sterilization laws to come before the United States Supreme Court was *Skinner* v. *Oklahoma* . . . (1942). The purpose of the Oklahoma law was to prevent criminal traits from being inherited by ordering the sterilization of those who had been thrice-convicted of various specified felonies. The law was held unconstitutional as a violation of equal protection because there was no rational basis for distinguishing those felonies which would result in sterilization (one of petitioner's convictions was for chicken stealing) from other felonies which were exempt (embezzlement, for example). The premise that state sterilization laws are constitutional when validly drawn was not disturbed.

The statute with which we are concerned does not discriminate on its face between rich and poor. Plaintiff contends that the statute actually applies only to the poor because a mentally ill or mentally retarded person with money would be able to hire others to care for his child and would never allow the child to become neglected or dependent.[2]

The words "neglected or dependent" are not defined in ORS ch. 436. Plaintiff urges us to interpret both as dependent on state support and to adopt the reasoning in *Smith* v. *Wayne Probate Judge*, . . . (1925). The purpose of the statute in that case was to protect the state from public charges:

> "That he would not be able to support and care for his children, if any, and such children would probably become public charges by reason of his own mental defectiveness." . . .

The Oregon law specifies that the potential offspring would become dependent or neglected as a result of the parent's inability to provide adequate care and is not concerned with the parent's financial status.[3]

The state's concern for the welfare of its citizenry extends to future generations and when there is overwhelming evidence, as there is here, that a potential parent will be unable to provide a proper environment for a child because of his own mental illness or mental retardation, the state has sufficient interest to order sterilization.

Affirmed.

Notes and Questions

1. The court states that due process has been provided under the statute allowing

---

[2]The statute denies the fundamental right of procreation to those who come within its terms. The usual deference given to the judgment of state legislatures does not apply to laws affecting fundamental human rights. . . .

"... [S]trict scrutiny of the classification which a State makes in a sterilization law is essential, lest unwittingly or otherwise invidious discriminations are made against groups or types of individuals in violation of the constitutional guaranty of just and equal laws. . . ." Skinner v. Oklahoma, supra, 316 U.S. at 541, 62 S.Ct. at 1113.

[3]Plaintiff has referred us to the minutes of the House Judiciary Committee, May 17, 1967, and the testimony of one of the principal witnesses who replied, when asked if the legislation was for the welfare of child or parent:

> ". . . Many of these girls can be trained for ordinary housework or simple skills in a community, but if they had the added stress and strain of the responsibility of infants are then unable to function properly. Furthermore, the children become public charges. . . ."

The same witness stated that the children become neglected and "have all sorts of problems." Hearing, Senate Judiciary Committee, May 2, 1967.

sterilization. Due process generally means that the state must go about what it does in a prescribed manner. For example, in the famous case of *in re Gault*, a case involving juvenile proceedings, the U.S. Supreme Court said that due process includes the right to be informed about the nature of charges pending against the juvenile, the right to counsel, the right to confront and cross-examine witnesses, the privilege against self-incrimination, the right to a transcript of proceedings, and a right to appellate review.

Given these protections, does the woman in the *Cook* case have anything to fear?

2. In reading the case, one is struck by at least two areas of vagueness. A first is the language of the statute itself — "the *condition* of the examinee," "adequate care," "no probability of improvement," and so on. A second concerns the group that stands to benefit from the sterilization. The board bears the name Board for Social Protection. Elsewhere the court says that the sterilization will be beneficial to *society*, or that *the state* has a concern that children be raised in a "proper environment." Is it clear enough who is to benefit and what evil is being eradicated? In cases of doubt, should ambiguity be resolved in favor of the individual or the interests of "the state" or "society"?
3. The court says that the statute *on its face* does not discriminate between rich and poor, which probably means that the statute as written is potentially applicable to all people within the state of Oregon.

   OOuht there to be additional tests to determine whether laws are discriminatory?
4. Using Dr. Flannery's eyes (pages 54–60), how does the state's handling of this case look?
5. Is a person who inherits $1 million at birth self-supporting?

4 LAW AND CONFLICTING INTERESTS

> It is the best expedient that can be devised in any government, to secure a steady, upright, and impartial administration of the laws.
>
> *The Federalist*, No. 78

In Greek mythology, Themis was the blindfolded, impartial goddess of justice who carried scales to weigh competing contentions and a sword to enforce her decrees. This powerful metaphor is most extensively developed in the jurisprudence of Roscoe Pound (1870–1964), who observed,

> [W]e all want the earth. We all have a multiplicity of desires and demands which we seek to satisfy. There are very many of us but there is only one earth. The desires of each continually conflict with or overlap those of his neighbors. So there is, as one might say, a great task of social engineering. There is a task of making the goods of existence, the means of satisfying the demands and desires of men living together in a politically organized society, if they cannot satisfy all the claims that men make upon them, at least go round as far as possible. This is what we mean when we say that the end of law is justice. We do not mean justice as an individual virtue.

> We do not mean justice as the ideal relation among men. We mean a regime. We mean such an adjustment of relations and ordering of conduct as will make the goods of existence the means of satisfying human claims to have things and do things, go round as far as possible with the least friction and waste.*

According to Pound, legal systems are designed to determine which of the competing claims to material wealth and life space are to be recognized and secured, and which are to be denied.

How does a legal system provide for the evaluation of claims? Pound suggests that the first way is pragmatic; results that have worked or are likely to work are used. He states, "In the whole development of modern law, courts and lawmakers and law teachers, very likely with no clear theory of what they were doing but guided by a clear instinct of practical purpose, have been at work finding practical adjustments and reconcilings and, if nothing more was possible, practical compromises of conflicting and overlapping interests."† Prior dispositions of trouble provide a start, but fresh conflict may indicate inadequacies in prior solutions.

A second method of evaluation is by reference to what Pound termed *jural postulates,* the goals that all legal orders strive to achieve:

> 1. In civilized society men must be able to assume that others will commit no intentional aggressions upon them.
>
> 2. In civilized society men must be able to assume that they may control for beneficial purposes what they have discovered and appropriated to their own use, what they have created by their own labor, and what they have acquired under the existing social and economic order.
>
> 3. In civilized society men must be able to assume that those with whom they deal in the general intercourse of society will act in good faith and hence
>
> (a) will make good reasonable expectations which their promises or other conduct reasonably create;
>
> (b) will carry out their undertakings according to the expectations which the moral sentiments of the community attaches thereto;
>
> (c) will restore specifically or by equivalent what comes to them by mistake or unanticipated or not fully intended situation whereby they receive at another's expense what they could not reasonably have expected to receive under the circumstances.
>
> 4. In civilized society men must be able to assume that those who are engaged in some course of conduct will act with due care not to cast an unreasonable risk of injury upon others.

---

*From Roscoe Pound, *Social Control Through Law,* pp. 64–65. Copyright © 1942 by Yale University Press. Reprinted by permission of the publisher.

†*Ibid.,* p. 111.

FIGURE 1 Pound's Model of Conflict and the Role of Legal Systems

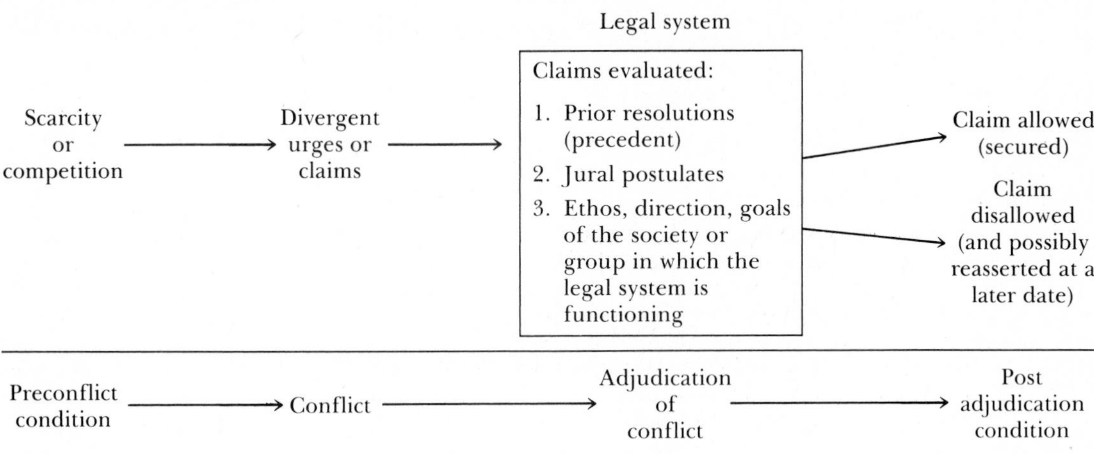

> 5. In civilized society men must be able to assume that those who maintain things likely to get out of hand or to escape and do damage will restrain them or keep them within their proper bounds.‡

A third way that he considered is more diffuse; he suggested that a legal system reflects the overall ethos, directions, and goals of the society in which it functions. In Pound's time, American society was shifting from individualistic-agrarian values to collective, urban-industrial values, and this trend could be noted in legal outcomes. If Pound were alive today, he might be interested in the way that social pressures such as the drive for racial equality, equitable distribution of wealth, ecology, suburbanization, ruralization, and decentralization intrude on legal consciousness and determine legal results. Pound's assumptions about society and the resulting legal order are presented diagrammatically in Figure 1.

Pound thus provided a theory of justice (the reduction of waste); a theory of the source of conflict (scarcity); an explanation of the function of legal systems (the adjudication of competing claims and interests); a theory of change (the reassertion of previously unrecognized claims); and a theory as to the way claims are evaluated (through experience, the jural postulates, and what officials in the legal system perceive as the overall value orientations of the society in which they function).

‡*Ibid.*, pp. 113–115.

Notes and Questions

1. The pervasive underlying assumption in Pound's jurisprudence is that law and legal systems have an exclusively beneficial effect. Given scarcity, competing claims, and so on, people who do legal work try to resolve conflict with a minimum of waste. But compare this view with the following commentary from Laura Nader, a contemporary anthropologist:

   > [S]carcity or perceived scarcity has an effect on how people behave. In terms of law, scarcity of land and other property crucial to subsistence leads people to use forums and procedures that will allow them to win, regardless of what it does to relationships. However, if there is a desire to continue relationships, there is a strong likelihood that compromise will be preferred to a winner-take-all solution. It also appears that the use of penalty or retribution, or at least noncompromise resolutions, is likely to increase where relationships are not important.*

   In light of this quotation, is the resorting to the legal order the sign of a beginning of conflict resolution, or is it the sign of a serious breakdown in human relationships?

   If the use of law is the signal of breakdown, how can law minimize friction and waste?

2. According to Pound, the jural postulates are the aspirations of all peoples at all times. Do you think this is true, or are the jural postulates highly ethnocentric to the West — a unique set of goals rather than cultural universals?

   Are Pound's ideas of contract, property, competition, and aggression aspects of human nature, or are they learned responses in Western culture?

   Could the postulates be rewritten to reflect a different consciousness?

3. In Pound's schema, as partially noted above, courts, judges, and other legal professionals are not part of the problem, but are solely part of the solution to problems. Does this theory make law, the legal order, and functionaries within it look better than they really are? (Use Kafka's parables, the North Carolina cases, the materials in Section 2 on judging, and the cases and materials in Section 3 to illustrate your answer.)

*Laura Nader, "Forums for Justice," *Journal for Social Issues,* 31:152.

The following case drawn from the work of Laura Nader shows the way a court in Mexico attempts to "make a balance" between contending parties.

The Case of the Spoiled Chiles *Laura Nader*

On February 24, 1964, in the town of Ralu'a, District of Villa Alta, State of Oaxaca [Mexico], there arrived at nine thirty before this municipal authority a Mr. Ignacio Andres Zoalage, merchant, fifty-five years of age. He explained the following: "I am coming to make a complaint about the chauffeur of the cream-colored truck that is on the platform, in the middle of which is a bruised basket of chiles weighing forty-seven and a half kilograms." The chauffeur of the cream-colored truck was called; he arrived fifteen minutes later and said that his name was Mario Valdez Herrero, chauffeur of the truck. The Court President asked him whether it was true that he had bruised the basket of chiles, and

From *Law in Culture and Society*, Chicago, Aldine, 1969, p. 74. Reprinted by permission of the author.

he answered: "Actually, I bruised it, but this happened because I don't have anyone to advise me. It is also the truck owner's fault because he ought to let me have a helper. Also, I could not see because the driver's compartment is high. Besides, it is the senor's fault — they put the things they have for sale on the ground, knowing that there is truck traffic."

The Municipal Court President asked Mr. Ignacio Andres: "Why did you put your merchandise down, knowing that the truck would go by?" Mr. Andres answered that there was room for the truck to pass. The chauffeur then said that this was not true, as the space there was at an angle. Mr. Andres said: "Look, Mr. President, the truck came this way, then this way and that way." The Municipal Court President said that it would be most convenient in this case if the chauffeur paid for the damage he had caused, and that the basket of chiles should be brought in, so that an estimate could be made of how much of it had been spoiled.

The plaintiff left and the Municipal Court President ordered the magistrate to have the merchandise brought in. The magistrate returned with the owner, carrying a basket of chiles. They emptied it on the floor. The court magistrate observed the chiles on the floor and put aside the damaged chiles; he then told the President that the quantity ruined was about one and a half kilograms. The Municipal Court President asked the owner of the basket how much he wanted to be paid for the damage. Mr. Andres answered that it was not much — three pesos. The President told the chauffeur that he had to pay three pesos for the damage. Upon this the chauffeur said: "All right, I will go right now for the three pesos." Meanwhile the Municipal Court President reminded the plaintiff to be more careful on the next occasion and to watch where he put his booth — not to put it just anywhere and especially not in front of a truck. Thus this case was closed and the owner walked out with his load of chiles, leaving the damaged merchandise with the municipal authority.

Notes and Questions

1. What is the function of the court in this case?
2. How can the ideas of Pound be applied here?
3. It appears that the court has no interest in the matter beyond getting the dispute settled to the satisfaction of the parties. Is this always the case, or must courts take into account interests that transcend the particular case? Does this case become part of the borderland between truckers and merchants?
4. Do courts sometimes have interests of their own to foster; e.g., rendering consistent results, preserving respect for law, the court, and so forth? In case of a conflict between the interests of the parties and systemic interest, which should yield?
5. Contemporary Americans might marvel at the directness, understandability, and simple justice of the folk court in the *Spoiled Chiles* case. However, Sylvia Forman, in her field work in Ecuador, found that people will behave differently depending on what is in dispute. She found people were most reluctant to compromise in cases when important property, prestige, or access to community power and influence were at stake. Zero-sum strategies are pursued in such instances regardless of the effect of the conflict on social relationships.*

*S. H. Forman, "Law and Conflict in Rural Highland Ecuador," unpublished doctoral dissertation, University of California, Berkeley, 1972.

☐ The *Spoiled Chiles* case suggests the involvement of a court in rudimentary balancing. In the cases that follow on the early judicial response to air pollution, richer dimensions emerge.

Susquehanna Fertilizer Co. v. Malone *20 A.900 73 Md. 268 (1890)*

ROBINSON, J.

This is an action for a nuisance, and the questions to be considered are questions of more than ordinary interest and importance. At the same time, it does not seem to us that there can be any great difficulty as to the principles by which they are governed. The plaintiff is the owner of five dwelling-houses on Eighth avenue, in Canton, one of the suburbs of Baltimore city. The corner house is occupied and kept by the plaintiff as a kind of hotel or public house, and the other houses are occupied by tenants. On the adjoining lot is a large fertilizer factory, owned and operated by the defendant, from which the plaintiff alleges noxious gases escape, which not only cause great physical discomfort to himself and his tenants, but also cause material injury to the property itself. The evidence on the part of the plaintiff shows that this factory is used by the defendant for the manufacture of sulphuric acid and commercial fertilizers; that noxious gases escape therefrom, and are driven by the wind upon the premises of the plaintiff, and of his tenants; that they are so offensive and noxious as to affect the health of the plaintiff's family, and at times to oblige them to leave the table, and even to abandon the house. It further shows that these gases injure, materially, his property, discolor and injure clothing hung out to dry, slime the glass in the windows, and even corrode the tin spouting on the houses. The evidence on the part of the defendant is in direct conflict with the evidence offered by the plaintiff; but still, assuming the facts testified to by plaintiff's witnesses to be true, — and this was a question for the jury, — an actionable injury was done to the plaintiff, for which he was entitled to recover.* No principle is better settled than that where a trade or business is carried on in such a manner as to interfere with the reasonable and comfortable enjoyment by another of his property, or which occasion material injury to the property itself, a wrong is done to the neighboring owner for which an action will lie; and this, too, without regard to the locality where such business is carried on; and this, too, although the business may be a lawful business, and one useful to the public, and although the best and most approved appliances and methods may be used in the conduct and management of the business. . . .

. . . As far back as *Poynton* v. *Gill,* 2 Rolle, Abr. 140, an action, it was held, would lie for melting lead so near the plaintiff's house as to cause actual injury to his property, even though the business was a lawful one, and one needful to the public, "for the defendant," say the court, "ought to carry on his business in waste places and great commons remote from inclosures so that no damage may happen to the owner of adjoining property." And the doctrine thus laid down has been, to this day, the doctrine of every case in which a similar question has arisen.

We cannot agree with the appellant that the court ought to have directed the jury to find whether the place where this factory was located was a convenient and proper place for the carrying on of the appellant's business, and whether such a use of his property was a reasonable use, and if they should so find the verdict must be for the defendant. It may be convenient to the defendant, and it may be convenient to the public, but, in the eye of the law, no place can be convenient for the carrying on of a business which is a nuisance, and which causes substantial injury to the property of another. Nor can any use of one's own land be said to be a reasonable use, which deprives an adjoining owner of the lawful use and enjoyment of his property. . . .

. . . So we take the law to be well settled that, in actions of this kind, the question whether the place where the trade or business is carried on is a proper and convenient place for the purpose, or whether the use by the defendant of his own land is, under the circumstances, a reasonable use, are questions which ought not to be submitted to the finding of the jury. We fully agree that, in actions of this kind, the law does not regard trifling inconveniences;

---

*In this case, money damages. — ED.

that everything must be looked at from a reasonable point of view; that, in determining the question of nuisance in such cases, the locality and all the surrounding circumstances should be taken into consideration; and that, where expensive works have been erected and carried on, which are useful and needful to the public, persons must not stand on extreme rights, and bring actions in respect of every trifling annoyance, otherwise, business could not be carried on in such places. But still, if the result of the trade or business thus carried on is such as to interfere with the physical comfort, by another, of his property, or such as to occasion substantial injury to the property itself, there is wrong to the neighboring owner for which an action will lie. . . .

But then it is said there was a fertilizer factory on the lot on which the appellant's works are now erected, and that this factory was used for the manufacture of sulphuric acid and fertilizers several years before the plaintiff built his house, and that the plaintiff has no right to complain, because he "came to the nuisance." But this constitutes no defense in this action. If the appellant had acquired a prescriptive right, that is to say, a user of the place for 20 years, that would present a different question. But no such right is claimed in this case; and, that being so, the appellant had no right to erect works which would be a nuisance to the adjoining land owned by the plaintiff, and thus measurably control the uses to which the plaintiff's land may in the future be subject. It could not, by the use of its own land, deprive the plaintiff of the lawful use of his property. The question of coming to a nuisance was fully considered in *Bliss* v. *Hall*, 4 Bing. N.C. 183, where, in an action for a nuisance arising from carrying on the business of making candles, the defendant pleaded that he had carried on his business at the same place, in the same manner, and to the same extent, three years before the plaintiff became possessed of his messuage. In sustaining the demurrer to this plea, TINDAL, C. J., says: "That is no answer to the complaint in the declaration, for the plaintiff came to the house he now occupies with all the rights which the common law affords, and one of them is a right to wholesome air. Unless the defendant shows a prescriptive right to carry on his business, the plaintiff is entitled to judgment.". . .

It does not seem to us, therefore, that the defendant has any reason to complain of the several instructions granted by the court. . . . Now, as to the evidence offered in the first exception, it does not seem to us that the fact that $500,000 had been invested in other fertilizer factories in the neighborhood could have any bearing upon the issues before the jury. The defendant had already proved that there was a number of fertilizer factories in the neighborhood, and had offered evidence tending to prove that the nuisance complained of was caused by these factories. Such evidence as this was admissible and proper evidence. But the fact that $500,000 had been invested in other works in the neighborhood could not in any manner affect the plaintiff's right to recover. The only effect of such evidence, it seems to us, would be to show what loss or injury the owners of these factories might sustain if the business carried on by them should be found to be a nuisance. But that was not a question for the consideration of the jury. The law, in cases of this kind, will not undertake to balance the conveniences, or estimate the difference between the injury sustained by the plaintiff and the loss that may result to the defendant from having its trade and business, as now carried on, found to be a nuisance. No one has a right to erect works which are a nuisance to a neighboring owner, and then say he has expended large sums of money in the erection of his works, while the neighboring property is comparatively of little value. The neighboring owner is entitled to the reasonable and comfortable enjoyment of his property, and, if his rights in this respect are invaded, he is entitled to the protection of the law, let the consequences be what they may.

Judgment affirmed.

Question

1. Compare this opinion with the theory of Pound discussed on pages 63–65.

Madison v. Ducktown Sulphur, Copper & Iron Co.

83 S.W. 658, 113 Tenn. 331 (1904)

NEIL, J.

These three cases were instituted separately in the court below, but tried together here. They embrace, in the main, the same facts and the same questions of law, and will be disposed of in a single opinion.

The bills are all based on the ground of nuisance, in that the two companies, in the operation of their plants at and near Ducktown, in Polk county, in the course of reducing copper ore, cause large volumes of smoke to issue from their roast piles, which smoke descends upon the surrounding lands, and injures trees and crops, and renders the homes of complainants less comfortable and their lands less profitable than before. The purpose of all the bills is to enjoin the further operation of these plants; the first bill having been filed against the first-named company, the last bill against the second company, and the intermediate bill against both companies.

The following general facts are applicable to all of the cases:

Prior to 1870 one Rhat began the operation of a copper mine at Ducktown, and worked it for several years. Subsequently it was owned by the Union Consolidated Mining Company, Mr. Rhat's successor. These operations were continued until the year 1879, and were then suspended until 1891. During the latter year the Ducktown Sulphur, Copper & Iron Company commenced operating the properties formerly owned and operated by the Union Consolidated Mining Company, and has continued to operate them ever since. The Pittsburgh & Tennessee Copper Company began operations at Ducktown about the year 1881, and continued until about 1899, when it sold out to the defendant Tennessee Copper Company. The latter began its operations in 1900, and commenced roasting ores in May, 1901. It has continued its works ever since.

Ducktown is in a basin of the mountains of Polk county, in this state, not far from the state line of the states of Georgia and North Carolina. This basin is six or eight miles wide. The complainants are the owners of small farms situated in the mountains around Ducktown.

The method used by the defendants in reducing their copper ores is to place the green ore, broken up, on layers of wood, making large open-air piles, called "roast piles," and these roast piles are ignited for the purpose of expelling from the ore certain foreign matters called "sulphurets." In burning, these roast piles emit large volumes of smoke. This smoke, rising in the air, is carried off by air currents around and over adjoining land.

The lands of the complainants in the first bill, Carter, W. M. Madison and Margaret A. Madison, Verner, and Ballew, lie from two to four miles from the works. The land of Farner, complainant in the last bill, lies six or eight miles away. The distance of McGhee's land is not shown. . . .

These lands are all thin mountain lands, of little agricultural value. Carter's land consists of 80 acres, assessed at $80; Verner's, 89 acres, at $110; Ballew's, 40 acres, at $66; Madison and wife, 43 acres, at $83; W. M. Madison, about 100 acres, at $180; Isaac Farner, 100 acres, at $180. Avery McGee has 75 acres. W. M. Madison has a tract across the Georgia line, and Mrs. Madison also one of 100 acres there. The assessed value of these last three tracts does not appear. All of these lands, however, lie in the same general section of country, and we assume their value to average about the same, in proportion to acreage.

All of the complainants have owned their several tracts since a time anterior to the resumption of the copper industry at Ducktown in 1891. . . .

The general effect produced by the smoke upon the possessions and families of the complainants is as follows, viz.:

Their timber and crop interests have been badly injured, and they have been annoyed and discommoded by the smoke so that the complainants are prevented from using and enjoying their farms and homes as they did prior to the inauguration of these enterprises. The smoke makes it impossible for the owners of farms within the area of the smoke zone to subsist their families thereon with the degree of comfort they enjoyed before. They cannot raise and harvest their customary crops, and their timber is largely destroyed. . . .

There is no finding in either of the cases that the output of smoke by the Ducktown Sulphur, Copper & Iron Company has increased to any extent since 1891, when the business of mining and reducing copper ore was resumed at Ducktown. There is likewise no finding as to this matter in respect of the Tennessee Copper Company since it began roasting ores in May, 1901.

There is a finding that the Ducktown Sulphur, Copper & Iron Company acquired its plant in 1891, and that it has spent several hundred thousand dollars since that time in improving and enlarging the plant.

The Court of Chancery Appeals find that the defendants are conducting and have been conducting their business in a lawful way, without any purpose or desire to injure any of the complainants; that they have been and are pursuing the only known method by which these plants can be operated and their business successfully carried on; that the open-air roast heap is the only method known to the business or to science by means of which copper ore of the character mined by the defendants can be reduced; that the defendants have made every effort to get rid of the smoke and noxious vapors, one of the defendants having spent $200,000 in experiments to this end, but without result.

It is to be inferred from the description of the locality that there is no place more remote to which the operations referred to could be transferred.

It is found, in substance, that, if the injunctive relief sought be granted, the defendants will be compelled to stop operations, and their property will become practically worthless, the immense business conducted by them will cease, and they will be compelled to withdraw from the state. It is a necessary deduction from the foregoing that a great and increasing industry in the state will be destroyed, and all of the valuable copper properties of the state become worthless.

The following facts were also found, viz.:

That the total tax aggregate of Polk County for the year 1903 was $2,585,931.43, of which total the assessments of the defendants amounted to $1,279,533. It is also found that prior to the operations of these companies there lived in the district where these works are located only 200 people, whereas there are now living in this district, almost wholly dependent upon these copper industries, about 12,000 people.

It is also found that one of the defendants, the Tennessee Copper Company, employs upon its pay roll 1,300 men, and that the average pay roll is about $40,000 per month, nearly all of which employes have been drawn from the population of Polk and neighboring counties.

It is further found that one of the defendants, the Tennessee Copper Company, consumes approximately 3,000 tons of coke, 2,800 tons of coal, and 1,000 cords of wood per month, and that it purchases and uses 2,110 car loads of coal, coke, wood, etc., per annum. In the year 1901 it purchased and used approximately 1,100 car loads of cord wood, cross-ties, lumber, and quartz. It was also found that 80 per cent of these supplies were purchased from, and delivered by, the citizens of Polk county. The aggregate paid out for supplies is not stated in the findings of the Court of Chancery Appeals, and cannot be here stated accurately, but certainly the amount is very large; and it seems from the figures stated that one of the defendants alone, the Tennessee Copper Company, pays out annually in wages in Polk county nearly a half million of dollars. The Court of Chancery Appeals finds that the other company employs between 1,100 and 1,200 people, and from this it may be inferred that the company pays out in wages and for supplies annually nearly as much as the Tennessee Copper Company.

It is quite apparent that the two companies pay out annually vast sums of money, which are necessarily of great benefit to the people of the county, and that they are conducting and maintaining an industry upon which a laboring population of from ten to twelve thousand people are practically dependent; and it is found, in substance, by the Court of Chancery Appeals, that, if these industries be suppressed, these thousands of people will have to wander forth to other localities to find shelter and work. . . .

We shall now state the principles which, as we conceive, should control the merits of the controversy involved in the several cases before the court:

While there can be no doubt that the facts stated make out a case of nuisance, for which the complainants in actions at law would be entitled to recover damages, yet the remedy in equity is not a matter of course. Not only must the bill state a proper case, but the right must be clear and the injury must be clearly established, as in doubtful cases the party will be turned over to his legal remedy; and, if there is a reasonable doubt as to the cause of the injury, the benefit of the doubt will be given to the defendant, if his trade is a lawful one, and the injury is not the necessary and natural consequence of the act; and, if the injury can be adequately compensated at law by a judgment for damages, equity will not interfere.

And the equitable remedy by injunction must be applied for with reasonable promptness. . . .

In addition to the principles already announced, the following general propositions seem to be established by the authorities: If the case made out by the pleadings and evidence show with sufficient clearness and certainty grounds for equitable relief it will not be denied because the persons proceeded against are engaged in a lawful business, *Susquehanna Fertilizer Co* v. *Malone,* 73 Md. 268, 282, 20 Atl. 900, or because the works complained of are located in a convenient place, if that place be one wherein an actionable injury is done to another (*Susquehanna Fertilizer Co.* v. *Malone* . . . and . . . cases cited); nor will the existence of another nuisance of a similar character at the same place furnish a ground for denying relief if it appears that the defendant has sensibly contributed to the injury complained of. . . . Nor is it a question of care and skill, but purely one of results.

But there is one other principle which is of controlling influence in this department of the law, and in the light of which the foregoing principle must be weighed and applied. This is that the granting of an injunction is not a matter of absolute right, but rests in the sound discretion of the court, to be determined on a consideration of all of the special circumstances of each case, and the situation and surroundings of the parties, with a view to effect the ends of justice.

A judgment for damages in this class of cases is a matter of absolute right, where injury is shown. A decree for an injunction is a matter of sound legal discretion, to be granted or withheld as that discretion shall dictate, after a full and careful consideration of every element appertaining to the injury.

These propositions will be found to be substantially confirmed and enforced in the following authorities:

In *Powell* v. *Bentley & Gerwig Furniture Co.* (W. Va.) it is said:

"Although a court of equity in such cases follows precedent and goes by rule, as far as it can, yet it follows its own rules, and among them is the one that to abate or restrain in case of nuisance is not a matter of strict right, but of orderly and reasonable discretion, according to the right of the particular case, and hence will refuse relief, and send the party to a court of law, when damages would be a fairer approximation to common justice, because to silence a useful and costly factory is often a matter of serious moment to the state and town as well as to the owner."

In *Clifton Iron Co.* v. *Dye* it is said:

"Counsel have pressed the proposition that mere convenience in the use of its property by the company does not entitle it to pour down upon the appellee's land, and into the stream on his land, the débris from the washers erected by it, and we think the contention is reasonable. But it is not every case of nuisance or continuing trespass which a court of equity will restrain by injunction. In determining this question the court should weigh the injury that may accrue to the one or the other party, and also to the public, by granting or refusing the injunction.

"The court will take notice of the fact that

in the development of the mineral interests of this state, recently made, very large sums of money have been invested. The utilization of these ores, which must be washed before using, necessitates in some measure the placing of sediment where it may flow into streams which constitute the natural drainage of the section where the ore banks are situated. This must cause a deposit of sediment on the lands below, and, while this invasion of the rights of the lower riparian owner may produce injury, entitling him to redress, the great public interests and benefits to flow from the conversion of these ores into pig metal should not be lost sight of. As said by the vice chancellor in *Wood* v. *Sutcliffe,* supra: 'Whenever a court of equity is asked for an injunction in cases of such nature as this [a bill to enjoin the pollution of a stream], it must have regard not only to the dry, strict rights of the plaintiff and defendant, but also to the surrounding circumstances.'"...

A recent statute passed in this state (Acts 1901, p. 246, c. 139) gives legislative expression to the same considerations of duty and public policy which are contained in the foregoing citations. . . .

The act referred to reads as follows:

> An act to amend section 3403 of the Code of Tennessee, 1858 [Shannon's Code, § 5158], and to authorize courts to determine in assessing damages for injuries to real estate, whether the nuisance complained of is a work of public utility and to give to said courts discretionary powers in respect to the abatement of such nuisance.
>
> Section 1. Be it enacted by the General Assembly of the State of Tennessee, that section 3403 of the Code of Tennessee, 1858 [Shannon's Code, § 5158], be so amended as to read as follows: In all suits brought for the recovery of damages resulting from any nuisance and the finding that the matter complained of is a nuisance, the court exercising a sound discretion may immediately upon petition of plaintiff, order or decline to order the nuisance to be abated.
>
> Sec. 2. Be it further enacted, that on the trial of any action for the recovery of damages as above said, either party may show by proof the extent if any of the injury or injuries complained of, and how the alleged nuisance is caused or originates. . . .

It cannot be doubted, therefore, that although the amending acts above copied purport, in terms, to apply to suits brought for the recovery of damages resulting from nuisances, the purpose was to declare the legislative will in respect of the use of the injunctive power in nuisance cases, when sought to be used in effecting final relief, and to ordain that in adminstering this relief the court should exercise a sound discretion, and either "order or decline to order the nuisance to be abated," as such sound discretion should dictate. This act must be regarded as declaring the policy of the state upon the subject referred to. It is perceived from the caption that the Legislature had in view the public utility of enterprises attacked on the ground of nuisance, and authorized the court to grant or withhold the injunction as a wise discretion might suggest or warn.

The question now to be considered is, what is the proper exercise of discretion, under the facts appearing in the present case? Shall the complainants be granted, in the way of damages, the full measure of relief to which their injuries entitle them, or shall we go further, and grant their request to blot out two great mining and manufacturing enterprises, destroy half of the taxable values of a county, and drive more than 10,000 people from their homes? We think there can be no doubt as to what the true answer to this question should be.

In order to protect by injunction several small tracts of land, aggregating in the value less than $1,000, we are asked to destroy other property worth nearly $2,000,000, and wreck two great mining and manufacturing enterprises, that are engaged in work of very great importance, not only to their owners, but to the state, and to the whole country as well, to depopulate a large town, and deprive thousands of working people of their homes and livelihood, and scatter them broadcast. The result would be practically a confiscation of the property of the defendants for the benefit of the complainants — an appropriation without compensation. The defendants cannot reduce their ores in a manner different from that they are now employing, and there is no more remote place to which they can remove. The decree asked for would deprive them of all of their rights. We appreciate the argument based on the fact that the homes of the complainants who live on the small tracts of land referred to are not so comfortable and useful to their owners as they were before they were affected by the smoke complained of, and we are deeply sensible of the truth of the proposition that no man is entitled to any more rights than another on the ground that he has or owns more property than that other. But in a case of conflicting rights, where neither party can enjoy his own without in some measure restricting the liberty of the other in the use of property, the law must make the best arrangement it can between the contending parties, with a view to preserving to each one the largest measure of liberty possible under the circumstances. We see no escape from the conclusion in the present case that the only proper decree is to allow the complainants a reference for the ascertainment of damages, and that the injunction must be denied to them. . . .

Notes and Questions

1. Compare the decision reached here with the decision in *Susquehanna.* Looking back to Llewellyn's theory of welcome and unwelcome precedent, would the court in *Ducktown* have found the *Susquehanna* case helpful or unhelpful in reaching a pro-company result? The court cites *Susquehanna* as precedent; is this a fair reading of the case?
2. How are the competing interests defined and compared in each case?
3. Are different views of what is a good society implicit in each decision?
4. How do inequalities of political, social, and economic status and class affect the weighing of competing interests? Consider the following quote:

   > In practice, legal mythology is primarily directed at obscuring the bitter struggle between social classes, and at articulating in consciousness the view that law is unaligned with any given interest; that it does not arise out of society but is a force superimposed on it to mediate and reconcile its conflicts. In fact, the degree of revolutionary consciousness of a people can often be measured by the degree to which the myth of impartiality of state power is accepted.*

5. How does the *Ducktown* case look in contemporary perspective? What does this say about the process of evaluation of competing claims? What was the "public interest" then? What is the "public interest" today? Who should determine what the public interest is — the private parties to a lawsuit, the court, a state or federal agency, the state legislature, the Congress?

---

*Kenneth Clarke, "Law Is Illegal," in *Radical Lawyers* (New York: Avon, 1971), p. 27.

Georgia v. Tennessee Copper Co. *206 U.S. 236 (1906)*

MR. JUSTICE HOLMES . . .

This is a bill in equity filed in this court by the State of Georgia, in pursuance of a resolution of the legislature and by direction of the Governor of the State, to enjoin the Defendant Copper Companies from discharging noxious gas from their works in Tennessee over the plaintiff's territory. It alleges that in consequence of such a discharge a wholesale destruction of forests, orchards and crops is going on, and other injuries are done and threatened in five counties of the State. It alleges also a vain application to the State of Tennessee for relief. A preliminary injunction was denied, but, as there was ground to fear that great and irreparable damage might be done, an early day was fixed for the final hearing and the parties were given leave, if so minded, to try the case on affidavits. This has been done without objection, and, although the method would be unsatisfactory if our decision turned on any nice question of fact, in the view we take we think it unlikely that either party has suffered harm.

The case has been argued largely as if it were one between two private parties; but it is not. The very elements that would be relied upon in a suit between fellow-citizens as a ground for equitable relief are wanting here. The State owns very little of the territory alleged to be affected, and the damage to it capable of estimate in money, possibly, at least, is small. This is a suit by a State for an injury to it in its capacity of *quasi*-sovereign. In that capacity the State has an interest independent of and behind the titles of its citizens, in all the earth and air within its domain. It has the last word as to whether its mountains shall be stripped of their forests and its inhabitants shall breathe pure air. It might have to pay individuals before it could utter that word, but with it remains the final power. The alleged damage to the State as a private owner is merely a makeweight, and we may lay on one side the dispute as to whether the destruction of forests has led to the gullying of its roads.

. . . When the States by their union made the forcible abatement of outside nuisances impossible to each, they did not thereby agree to submit to whatever might be done. They did not renounce the possibility of making reasonable demands on the ground of their still remaining *quasi*-sovereign interests. . . .

Some peculiarities necessarily mark a suit of this kind. If the State has a case at all, it is somewhat more certainly entitled to specific relief than a private party might be. It is not lightly to be required to give up *quasi*-sovereign rights for pay; and, apart from the difficulty of valuing such rights in money, if that be its choice it may insist that an infraction of them shall be stopped. The States by entering the Union did not sink to the position of private owners subject to one system of private law. This court has not quite the same freedom to balance the harm that will be done by an injunction against that of which the plaintiff complains, that it would have in deciding between two subjects of a single political power. Without excluding the considerations that equity always takes into account, we cannot give the weight that was given them in argument to a comparison between the damage threatened to the plaintiff and the calamity of a possible stop to the defendants' business, the question of health, the character of the forests as a first or second growth, the commercial possibility or impossibility of reducing the fumes to sulphuric acid, the special adaptation of the business to the place.

It is a fair and reasonable demand on the part of a sovereign that the air over its territory should not be polluted on a great scale by sulphurous acid gas, that the forests on its mountains, be they better or worse, and whatever domestic destruction they have suffered, should not be further destroyed or threatened by the act of persons beyond its control, that the crops and orchards on its hills should not be endangered from the same source. If any such demand is to be enforced this must be, notwithstanding the hesitation that we might feel if the suit were between private parties, and the doubt whether for the injuries which they might be suffering to their property they should not be left to an action at law.

The proof requires but a few words. It is not denied that the defendants generate in their works near the Georgia line large quantities of sulphur dioxide which becomes sulphurous acid by its mixture with the air. It hardly is denied and cannot be denied with success that this gas often is carred by the wind great distances and over great tracts of Georgia land. On the evidence the pollution of the air and the magnitude of that pollution are not open to dispute. Without any attempt to go into details immaterial to the suit, it is proper to add that we are satisfied by a preponderance of evidence that the sulphurous fumes cause and threaten damage on so considerable a scale to the forests and vegetable life, if not to health, within the plaintiff State as to make out a case within the requirements of *Missouri* v. *Illinois,* 200 U.S. 496. Whether Georgia by insisting upon this claim is doing more harm than good to her own citizens is for her to determine. The possible disaster to those outside the State must be accepted as a consequence of her standing upon her extreme rights. . . .

If the State of Georgia adheres to its determination, there is no alternative to issuing an injunction, after allowing a reasonable time to the defendants to complete the structures that they now are building, and the efforts that they are making, to stop the fumes. The plaintiff may submit a form of decree on the coming in of this court in October next.

Injunction to issue.

MR. JUSTICE HARLAN, *concurring.*

The State of Georgia is, in my opinion, entitled to the general relief sought by its bill, and, therefore, I concur in the result. With some things, however, contained in the opinion, or to be implied from its language, I do not concur. When the Constitution gave this court original jurisdiction in cases "in which a State shall be a party," it was not intended, I think, to authorize the court to apply in its behalf, any principle or rule of equity that would not be applied, under the same facts, in suits wholly between private parties. If this was a suit between private parties, and if under the evidence, a court of equity would not give the plaintiff an injunction, then it ought not to grant relief, under like circumstances, to the plaintiff, because it happens to be a State possessing some powers of sovereignty. Georgia is entitled to the relief sought, not because it is a State, but because it is a *party* which has established its right to such relief by proof. The opinion, if I do not mistake its scope, proceeds largely upon the ground that this court, sitting in this case as a court of equity, owes some special duty to Georgia as a State, although it is a party, while under the same facts, it would not owe any such duty to the plaintiff, if an individual.

Notes and Questions

1. In *Diamond* v. *General Motors* (20 Cal. App. 3d 374, 97 Cal. Rptr. 639, 1971), a class action was brought on behalf of all the residents of Los Angeles County against 293 corporations engaged in automobile manufacture, refining and distributing oil products, generating energy, transportation for damages, and injunctive relief for air pollution. Their suit was dismissed, and they appealed. In their brief on appeal, the plaintiffs argued,

   > This lawsuit was prompted by the steady deterioration of the air supply of Los Angeles County, and the lack of any significant response by the executive and legislative branches of various levels of government. Legislative tinkering with ineffective laws, illusory, periodic bureaucratic reorganizations, and industry controlled administrators have led to drastic increases in discomfort, disease, and death. More and more, legal scholars have concluded that judicial intervention is necessary and proper.

   Later they contended,

   > The defendants who ask this Court to defer to the legislative and executive branches of the government are the same persons who continue to corrupt the system with their lobbying, influence peddling, and campaign contributions. Defendants do not come into court with clean hands. This honorable Court is the only institution which they cannot contaminate. If there is to be a solution to this environmental tragedy, it will have to come from the judiciary.

   The court upheld the dismissal, stating,

   > Once it is acknowledged that a superior court cannot, by decree, abolish air pollution, it is appropriate to face some demonstrable realities of the problem which plaintiff is asking the court to solve. We do not deal with a simple dispute between those who breathe the air and those who contaminate it. The need for controls is not

in question. The issue is not "shall we," but "what kind, how much, how soon."

Both the United States Congress and the California Legislature have decided that the discharge of air contaminants must be controlled. Legislative enactments have provided for administrative machinery at the federal, state and local levels. These agencies conduct research, hold public hearings, and, upon the knowledge thereby acquired, set and revise the allowable limits for the discharge of the various kinds of contaminants. The statutory systems provide means for enforcement of the standards through license revocation, civil injunctions and criminal prosecution.

Plaintiff's brief makes it clear that his case is not based upon violation of any existing air pollution control law or regulation. His position is that the present system of statutes and administrative rules is inadequate, and that the enforcement machinery is ineffective. Plaintiff is simply asking the court to do what the elected representatives of the people have not done: adopt stricter standards over the discharge of air contaminants in this country, and enforce them with the contempt power of the court.

It is indisputable that there exists, within the community, a substantial difference of opinion as to what changes in industrial processes should be required and how soon, what new technology is feasible, what reduction in the volume of goods and services should result and what increase in production costs for the sake of cleaner air will be acceptable. These issues are debated in the political arena and are being resolved by the action of those elected to serve in the legislative and executive branches of government.

We assume, for the purposes of this decision, that notwithstanding the existing administrative machinery, anyone claiming to have sustained personal injury or property damage caused by an unreasonable discharge of contaminants into the atmosphere by one or more of the defendants could state a cause of action for his damages and for injunctive relief. But the class action attempted by plaintiff, as the purported representative of every resident of the county, is a wholly different kind of suit. The objective, which plaintiff envisions to justify his class action, is judicial regulation of the processes, products and volume of business of the major industries of the county.

It was entirely reasonable for the trial court to conclude from the face of the pleading that such an undertaking was beyond its effective capability.

How does the court anticipate that the varying interests in environmental questions will be accommodated? Is this expectation reasonable? Desirable?

☐ In the *Diamond* case, the action was brought through the courts of California. In the following case, the state of Ohio took the question of the pollution of Lake Erie to the top of the legal order, by bringing an action against alleged polluters in the U.S. Supreme Court — a procedure comparable to the one used in the case of *Georgia* v. *Tennessee Copper.*

Ohio v. Wyandotte Chemicals Corp. *401 U.S. 494 (1971)*

MR. JUSTICE HARLAN . . .

Ohio seeks to invoke this Court's original jurisdiction. . . .

The action, for abatement of a nuisance, is brought on behalf of the State and its citizens, and names as defendants Wyandotte Chemicals Corp. (Wyandotte), Dow Chemical Co. (Dow America), and Dow Chemical Company of Canada, Ltd. (Dow Canada). Wyandotte is incorporated in Michigan and maintains its principal office and place of business there. Dow America is incorporated in Delaware, has its principal office and place of business in Michigan, and owns all the stock of Dow Canada. Dow Canada is incorporated, and does business, in Ontario. A majority of Dow Canada's directors are residents of the United States.

The complaint alleges that Dow Canada and Wyandotte have each dumped mercury into streams whose courses ultimately reach Lake Erie, thus contaminating and polluting that lake's waters, vegetation, fish, and wildlife, and that Dow America is jointly responsible for the acts of its foreign subsidiary. Assuming the State's ability to prove these assertions, Ohio seeks a decree: (1) declaring the introduction of mercury into Lake Erie's tributaries a public nuisance; (2) perpetually enjoining these defendants from introducing mercury into Lake Erie or its tributaries; (3) requiring defendants either to remove the mercury from Lake Erie or to pay the costs of its removal into a fund to be administered by Ohio and used only for that purpose; (4) directing defendants to pay Ohio monetary damages for the harm done to Lake Erie, its fish, wildlife, and vegetation, and the citizens and inhabitants of Ohio. . . .

I

That we have jurisdiction seems clear enough. Beyond doubt, the complaint on its face reveals the existence of a genuine "case or controversy" between one State and citizens of another, as well as a foreign subject. . . .

. . . [T]he evolution of this Court's responsibilities in the American legal system has brought matters to a point where much would be sacrificed, and little gained, by our exercising original jurisdiction over issues bottomed on local law. This Court's paramount responsibilities to the national system lie almost without exception in the domain of federal law. As the impact on the social structure of federal common, statutory, and constitutional law has expanded, our attention has necessarily been drawn more and more to such matters. We have no claim to special competence in dealing with the numerous conflicts between States and nonresident individuals that raise no serious issues of federal law. . . .

Thus, we think it apparent that we must recognize "the need [for] the exercise of a sound discretion in order to protect this Court from an abuse of the opportunity to resort to its original jurisdiction in the enforcement by States of claims against citizens of other States.". . .

II

In applying this analysis to the facts here presented, we believe that the wiser course is to deny Ohio's motion for leave to file its complaint. . . .

In essence, the State has charged Dow Canada and Wyandotte with the commission of acts, albeit beyond Ohio's territorial boundaries, that have produced and, it is said, continue to produce disastrous effects within Ohio's own domain. While this Court, and doubtless Canadian courts, if called upon to assess the validity of any decree rendered against either Dow Canada or Wyandotte, would be alert to ascertain whether the judgment rested upon an evenhanded application of justice, it is unlikely that we would totally deny Ohio's competence to act if the allegations made here are proved true. . . .

Our reasons for thinking that, as a practical matter, it would be inappropriate for this Court to attempt to adjudicate the issues Ohio seeks to present are several. History reveals that the course of this Court's prior efforts to settle disputes regarding interstate air and water pollution has been anything but smooth.

The difficulties that ordinarily beset such cases are severely compounded by the particular setting in which this controversy has reached us. For example, the parties have informed us without contradiction, that a number of official bodies are already actively involved in regulating the conduct complained of here. A Michigan circuit court has enjoined Wyandotte from operating its mercury cell process without judicial authorization. The company is, moreover, currently utilizing a recycling process specifically approved by the Michigan Water Resources Commission and remains subject to the continued scrutiny of that agency. Dow Canada reports monthly to the Ontario Water Resources Commission on its compliance with the commission's order prohibiting the company from passing any mercury into the environment.

Additionally, Ohio and Michigan are both participants in the Lake Erie Enforcement Conference, convened a year ago by the Secretary of the Interior pursuant to the Federal Water Pollution Control Act. . . . The Conference is studying all forms and sources of pollution, including mercury, infecting Lake Erie. The purpose of this Conference is to provide a basis for concerted remedial action by the States or, if progress in that regard is not rapidly made, for corrective proceedings initiated by the Federal Government. . . . And the International Joint Commission, established by the Boundary Waters Treaty of 1909 between the United States and Canada, . . . issued on January 14, 1971, a comprehensive report, the culmination of a six-year study carried out at the request of the contracting parties, concerning the contamination of Lake Erie. That document makes specific recommendations for joint programs to abate these environmental hazards and recommends that the IJC be given authority to supervise and coordinate this effort.

In view of all this, granting Ohio's motion for leave to file would, in effect, commit this Court's resources to the task of trying to settle a small piece of a much larger problem that many competent adjudicatory and conciliatory bodies are actively grappling with on a more practical basis.

The nature of the case Ohio brings here is equally disconcerting. It can fairly be said that what is in dispute is not so much the law as the facts. And the factfinding process we are asked to undertake is, to say the least, formidable. We already know, just from what has been placed before us on this motion, that Lake Erie suffers from several sources of pollution other than mercury; that the scientific conclusion that mercury is a serious water pollutant is a novel one; that whether and to what extent the existence of mercury in natural waters can safely or reasonably be tolerated is a question for which there is presently no firm answer: and that virtually no published research is available describing how one might extract mercury that is in fact contaminating water. Indeed, Ohio is raising factual questions that are essentially ones of first impression to the scientists. The notion that appellate judges, even with the assistance of a most competent Special Master, might appropriately undertake at this time to unravel these complexities is, to say the least, unrealistic. Nor would it suffice to impose on Ohio an unusually high standard of proof. That might serve to mitigate our personal difficulties in seeking a just result that comports with sound judicial administration, but would not lessen the complexity of the task of preparing responsibly to exercise our judgment, or the serious drain on the resources of this Court it would entail. Other factual complexities abound. For example, the Department of the Interior has stated that eight American companies are discharging, or have discharged, mercury into Lake Erie or its tributaries. We would, then, need to assess the business practices and relative culpability of each to frame appropriate relief as to the one now before us.

Finally, in what has been said it is vitally important to stress that we are not called upon by this lawsuit to resolve difficult or important problems of federal law and that nothing in Ohio's complaint distinguishes it from any one of a host of such actions that might, with equal justification, be commenced in this Court. Thus, entertaining this complaint not only would fail to serve those responsibilities we are principally charged with, but could well pave the way for putting this Court into a quandary whereby we must opt either to pick and choose arbitrarily among similarly situated litigants or to devote truly enormous portions of our energies to such matters. . . .

III

What has been said here cannot, of course, be taken as denigrating in the slightest the public importance of the underlying problem Ohio would have us tackle. Reversing the increasing contamination of our environment is manifestly a matter of fundamental import and utmost urgency. What is dealt with above are only considerations respecting the appropriate role this

Court can assume in efforts to eradicate such environmental blights. We mean only to suggest that our competence is necessarily limited, not that our concern should be kept within narrow bounds. . . .

Motion denied.

MR. JUSTICE DOUGLAS, *dissenting.*

The complaint in this case presents basically a classic type of case congenial to our original jurisdiction. It is to abate a public nuisance. Such was the claim of Georgia against a Tennessee company which was discharging noxious gas across the border into Georgia. Georgia v. Tennessee Copper Co., . . . The Court said:

> "It is a fair and reasonable demand on the part of a sovereign that the air over its territory should not be polluted on a great scale by sulphurous acid gas, that the forests on its mountains, be they better or worse, and whatever domestic destruction they have suffered, should not be further destroyed or threatened by the act of persons beyond its control, that the crops and orchards on its hills should not be endangered from the same source." . . .

Dumping of sewage in an interstate stream, Missouri v. Illinois, . . . or towing garbage to sea only to have the tides carry it to a State's beaches, New Jersey v. New York City, . . . have presented analogous situations which the Court has entertained in suits invoking our original jurisdiction. The pollution of Lake Erie or its tributaries by the discharge of mercury or compounds thereof, if proved, certainly creates a public nuisance of a seriousness and magnitude which a State by our historic standards may prosecute or pursue as *parens patriae.*

The suit is not precluded by the Boundary Waters Treaty of 1909 . . . [It] does not evince a purpose on the part of the national governments of the United States and Canada to exclude their States and Provinces from seeking other remedies for water pollution. Indeed, Congress in later addressing itself to water pollution in the Federal Water Pollution Control Act, . . . said in § 1(c):

> "Nothing in this chapter shall be construed as impairing or in any manner affecting any right or jurisdiction of the States with respect to the waters *(including boundary waters)* of such States." (Emphasis added.)

This litigation, as it unfolds, will, of course, implicate much federal law. The case will deal with an important portion of the federal domain — the navigable streams and the navigable inland waters which are under the sovereignty of the Federal Government. It has been clear since Pollard's Lessee v. Hagan, . . . decided in 1845, that navigable waters were subject to federal control. . . .

Congress has enacted numerous laws reaching that domain. One of the most pervasive is the Rivers and Harbors Act of 1899, . . . which was before us in United States v. Republic Steel Corp. . . . In that case we read § 13 of the 1899 Act . . . which forbids discharge of "any refuse matter of any kind or description whatever other than that flowing from streets and sewers and passing therefrom in a liquid state" as including particles in suspension. . . .

In the 1930's fish and wildlife legislation was enacted granting the Secretary of the Interior various heads of jurisdiction over the effects on fish and wildlife of "domestic sewage, mine, petroleum, and industrial wastes, erosion silt, and other polluting substances." . . .

The Federal Water Pollution Control Act, as amended, 33 U.S.C. § 1151 (1970 ed.), gives broad powers to the Secretary to take action respecting water pollution on complaints of States, and other procedures to secure federal abatement of the pollution. *Ibid.* The National Environmental Policy Act of 1969, . . . gives elaborate ecological directions to federal agencies and supplies procedures for their enforcement.

On December 23, 1970, the President issued an Executive Order which correlates the duties of the Corps of Engineers and the Administrator of the new Environmental Protection Agency under the foregoing statutes. . . .

Yet the federal scheme is not preemptive of state action. Section 1(b) of the Water Pollution Control Act declares that the policy of Congress is "to recognize, preserve, and protect the primary responsibilities and rights of the States in preventing and controlling water pollution." . . . Section 10 provides that except where the Attorney General has actually obtained a court order of pollution abatement on behalf of the United States, "State and interstate action to abate pollution of *** navigable waters *** shall not *** be displaced by Federal enforcement action." . . .

The new Environmental Quality Improvement Act of 1970, . . . while stating the general policy of Congress in protecting the environment, also states: "The primary responsibility for implementing this policy rests with State and local governments." 42 U.S.C. § 4371 (b) (2) (1970 ed.).

There is much complaint that in spite of the arsenal of federal power little is being done. That, of course, is not our problem. But it is our concern that state action is not pre-empted by federal law. Under existing federal law, the States do indeed have primary responsibility for setting water quality standards; the federal agency only sets water quality standards for a State if the State defaults. . . .

There is not a word in federal law that bars state action. . . .

Much is made of the burdens and perplexities of these original actions. Some are complex, notably those involving water rights.

The drainage of Lake Michigan with the attendant lowering of water levels, affecting Canadian as well as United States interests, came to us in an original suit. . . .

The apportionment of the waters of the Colorado between Arizona and California was a massive undertaking entailing a searching analysis. . . .

The apportionment of the waters of the North Platte River among Colorado, Wyoming, and Nebraska came to us in an original action. . . .

But the practice has been to appoint a Special Master which we certainly would do in this case. We could also appoint — or authorize the Special Master to retain — a panel of scientific advisers. The problems in this case are simple compared with those in the water cases discussed above. It is now known that metallic mercury deposited in water is often transformed into a dangerous chemical. This lawsuit would determine primarily the extent, if any, to which the defendants are contributing to that contamination at the present time. It would determine, secondarily, the remedies within reach — the importance of mercury in the particular manufacturing processes, the alternative processes available, the need for a remedy against a specified polluter as contrasted to a basin-wide regulation, and the like.

The problem, though clothed in chemical secrecies, can be exposed by the experts. It would indeed be one of the simplest problems yet posed in the category of cases under the head of our original jurisdiction.

The Department of Justice in a detailed brief tells us there are no barriers in federal law to our assumption of jurisdiction. I can think of no case of more transcending public importance than this one.

Notes and Questions

1. The U.S. Supreme Court has said a number of things to the state of Ohio: that it has other and more important business to attend to and cannot undertake fact finding and the determination of remedies; that the companies have already come under the scrutiny of the states of Michigan and Ohio and the province of Ontario and that the Court's taking the case would deal with only one dimension of a larger problem; and finally that whatever relief Ohio needs can be secured through its own court system.

   Compare these contentions with those of the dissent. Also compare the reasoning of the Court in *Wyandotte* with the reasoning of the *Diamond* case that appears in the notes preceding the case.

   Has the Supreme Court adequately weighed the competing interests and minimized friction and waste, which Pound observed to be the central functions of law in adjudicating controversies?

2. The *Diamond* and *Wyandotte* cases demonstrate that as a pollution problem becomes more intense and affects wider geographical areas the elimination of the problem through court, legislative, or administrative action becomes correspondingly difficult. If solutions are sought locally through court action, as was the case in *Diamond,* the inclination may be to buck the problem to political or administrative agencies. If relief is sought at the top, as was the case in *Wyandotte,* the question may be referred to either lower or still higher authorities. Where there are to be independent efforts at all levels and branches of government or through consortia of governments, even across national boundaries, there is a risk that everyone acting will mean that no one acts or that the pollution question will be confounded by competing power structures and policies, the only constant across all the activity being the passage of time and the persistence of pollution.

The foregoing lament on the ineffectiveness of environmental protection antedates deregulation under Ronald Reagan's administration, the resignation of lawyers in protest over the abandonment of zealous enforcement of the EPA, and the resignations and criminal convictions of those appointees charged with carrying out Congressional mandates on the environment.

3. For additional discussion of the contemporary difficulties in moving against intransigent polluting corportions, see Arthur D. Wolfe and Fred J. Naffziger, *Legal Perspectives of American Business Associations* (Columbus, Ohio: Grid, 1977), pp. 650ff. The case involved efforts by environmental groups, the states of Minnesota, Michigan, and Wisconsin, and the U.S. government to stop the dumping into Lake Superior of tailings from taconite mining operations by the Reserve Mining Company, a wholly owned subsidiary of Armco Steel and Republic Steel.

5 LAW, STATUS, WEALTH, AND POWER

When leaving his surgery on the morning of April 16 Dr. Bernard Rieux felt something soft under his foot. It was a dead rat lying in the middle of the landing. On the spur of the moment he kicked it to one side and without giving it further thought, continued on his way downstairs. Only when he stepped forth into the street did it occur to him that a dead rat had no business to be on his landing.

Albert Camus, *The Plague*

The preservation of power is a vital necessity for the powerful, since it is their power which provides their sustenance; but they have to preserve it both against their rivals and against their inferiors, and these latter cannot do otherwise than try to rid themselves of dangerous masters; for, through a vicious circle, the master produces fear in the slave by the very fact that he is afraid of him, and vice versa; and the same is true as between rival powers.

Simone Weil, *Oppression and Liberty* (1973)

If you're strong, you don't have to say thank you.

Fenna Lee Bonsignore, age four

Max Weber, German lawyer and sociologist, defined law as *coercive* order, an order that has the potential backing of the full force of the state. He thus distinguished law from other norms such as custom, ethics, and religion, which have different sanctions like the cold shoulder, internal guilt, or the threat of eternal damnation. Elsewhere, he observed that a society has two basic ways of providing rewards to its membership — honor (status) and economic return (wealth, class). A troublesome question arises when law and social rewards are considered together: Is the legal system used to perpetuate prevailing patterns in the allocation of status and wealth?

This is an unpleasant question in U.S. law since our society is said to be classless and each citizen is deemed equal before the law. Notable jurists like Holmes, Llewellyn, and Pound rarely develop the power dimension in law perhaps because it is almost unthinkable that law and legal process may do no more than reinforce social and economic positionings; it is more comfortable to think of law as impartial or as a balancing process, than as a means to accomplish the wishes of a few well-placed elites.

And yet a number of concrete instances can be explained in no other way. Certain rules of law inhibit the raising of large questions that cut to the quick of the social, political, and economic order. Despite the furor over the fighting of an undeclared war in Vietnam, the courts refused to consider the legality of the war, on the ground that a political rather than a legal question was involved. For this reason the courts refused for many years to consider the legality of legislative districting, although historical districts were obviously biased in favor of rural areas at the expense of urban areas. In addition, disputes involving housing, welfare, employment, and other areas that have wide impact are channeled into discrete confines so that contesting parties do not see themselves as representatives of a large group of persons who have a similar interest in redressing parallel grievances about control of property or the allocation of power.

Beyond the dampening of threats to the status quo by rules that inhibit legal action, the powerful spend large sums of money and energy to keep the law favorable. Most notable is the growth of PACs [political action committees] and other forms of influence peddling at the state and national levels, but also significant are the resources devoted to win contested cases that threaten. Most of the law of contract and property has been shaped to perpetuate existing power and property relationships. Not surprisingly, fine print, which is almost always inimical to the interests of the poor and low-income wage earners — to say nothing of people in small businesses or the general public — becomes the currency of the powerful. It is the powerful who furnish the documentation for most transactions, and it is they who benefit from the documents. Insurance policies, promissory notes, mortgages, conditional sales contracts, leases, and other papers that people are expected to sign are as often instruments of domination as they are evidence of an evenly bargained deal. Courts typically do not look behind the documentation to discover the economic realities of a transaction.

Other examples can readily be found. For decades, it has been known that laws "regulating" corporations have been shaped to meet managerial and financial interests rather than the needs of the ordinary shareholder or the public generally. Taxation, which is theoretically progressive in nature and should over time be a force for greater equality in income and wealth, has tended in exactly the opposite direction, leading one writer to characterize the preferential treatment of the rich as a "great Treasury raid" (perhaps an inapt metaphor, since the money never made it to the U.S. Treasury). As the materials of the next section will demonstrate, the disenchantment of the average taxpayer with an unfair national taxing system has contributed to the appearance of an underground economy and greater tax dodging. Administrative agencies covering activities like public utilities, communication, transportation, and other vital services are often as much directed by the businesses to be controlled as by public officials acting independently.

Criminal law and enforcement has always been a highly visible demonstration of the importance of wealth, status, and power in affecting legal outcomes. Gentlemanly offenses like business tax evasion, abuse of expense accounts, antitrust violations, and embezzlement have often been treated differently from poor people's offenses such as theft, burglary, and purse snatching. It is expected that discretion will be exercised by police and prosecutors so that people who are not "criminals" will be saved from the opprobrium that accompanies arrest, the criminal process, and jail or prison. Watergate, which led to criminal convictions of many high officials of the Nixon administration, was an unusual and distinctly small exception to the rule of preferential treatment. And even after Watergate, President Nixon was given a handsome pension and a personal staff at government expense. Like other Watergate "ex-cons" who returned to the public eye after serving token sentences, Nixon published his memoirs, engaged in television interviews, and was consulted on affairs of state as if he had never needed a presidential pardon to save him from criminal prosecution.

After a relatively scandal-free Carter administration, the Reagan administration added numerous cases of corruption and illegality in high places. These included perjury to congressional committees investigating the Environmental Protection Agency; conflicts of interest and influence peddling by former White House assistants, and violations of congressional prohibitions on aid to the Contras in Honduras (via arms sales to Iran and through numbered Swiss bank accounts). Although some were asked to resign from office and others were convicted, the net effect of these cases looked to some observers like differential treatment according to the social class and political connections of the offenders.

The following material examines some of the many faces of status, wealth, class, and power as they affect the making and application of law.

Streich v. General Motors Corp. *126 N.E. 2d 389 5. Ill. App. 2d 485 (1955)*

McCORMICK, J. . . .

. . . The complaint was filed in an action for damages occasioned by the defendant's alleged wrongful cancellation of a contract. . . .

A motion to dismiss the complaint was filed by the defendant, in which, among other things, it was alleged that purchase order No. 11925 shows on its face that the plaintiff need not make or deliver, and that the defendant need not buy, any air magnet valves as therein identified, except when and as specified in written releases issued by the defendant. . . .

The trial court . . . dismissed the suit. . . .

There were three exhibits attached to the complaint. Purchase Order No. 11925 provided that it was a purchase order for air magnet valves, drawing 8024271 Rev. A, at a price of $13.50 net each. On the face of the purchase order it was provided:

> This Purchase Order is issued to cover shipments of this part, to be received by us from September 1, 1948, to August 31, 1949, as released and scheduled on our series 48 "Purchase Order release and Shipping Schedule" No. 478412 attached and all subsequent Purchase Order releases.
>
> The total quantity covered by this Purchase Order will always be included in the amount shown under "Total Released" on the latest "Purchase Order Release and Shipping Schedule."

This order was dated April 19, 1948. It provided that the order, including the terms and conditions on the face and reverse side, constitute "the complete and final agreement between Buyer and Seller and no other agreement in any way modifying any of said terms and conditions will be binding upon Buyer unless made in writing and signed by Buyer's authorized representative."

On the reverse side are twenty-three provisions, among which are the following:

> The contract resulting from the acceptance of this order is to be construed according to the laws of the state. . . . This contract is nonassignable by Seller.
>
> Deliveries are to be made both in quantities and at times specified in schedules furnished by Buyer. Buyer will have no liability for payment for material or items delivered to Buyer which are in excess of quantities specified in the delivery schedules. Buyer may from time to time change delivery schedules or direct temporary suspension of scheduled shipments.
>
> Buyer reserves the right to cancel all or any of the undelivered portion of this order if Seller does not make deliveries as specified in the schedules, or if Seller breaches any of the terms hereof including the warranties of Seller.
>
> Unless otherwise herein agreed, Seller at its own expense shall furnish, keep in good condition and replace when necessary all dies, tools, gauges, fixtures and patterns necessary for the production of the material ordered. . . . Buyer has the option, however, to take possession of and title to any dies, tools, gauges, fixtures and patterns that are special for the production of the material covered by this order and shall pay to Seller the unamortized cost thereof; provided, however, that this option shall not apply if the material hereby ordered is the standard product of Seller or if a substantial quantity of like material is being sold by Seller to others. . . .

It is the contention of the plaintiff, Frank Streich, hereafter referred to as "seller," that the defendant, General Motors Corporation, hereafter referred to as the "buyer," had entered into a binding contract to purchase all the requirements of the buyer from September 1, 1948, through August 31, 1949, from the seller, and that, while the amount of the requirements was not specified, parol evidence [oral agreements] might be properly introduced to show what the requirements were. . . .

. . . The promise of the seller to furnish

identified items at a stated price is merely an offer and cannot become a contract until the buyer issues a release or order for a designated number of items. Until this action is taken the buyer has made no promise to do anything, and either party may withdraw. The promise is illusory, and the chimerical contract vanishes. "An agreement to sell to another such of the seller's goods, wares, and merchandise as the other might from time to time desire to purchase is lacking in mutuality because it does not bind the buyer to purchase any of the goods of the seller, as such matter is left wholly at the option or pleasure of the buyer." . . .

. . . The agreement in question is an adaptation of what was termed an "open end contract," which was used extensively by the federal government during the late war. However, it was used only in cases where the commodities dealt with were staples and either in the possession of or easily accessible to the seller. In this case the use of the contract is shifted and extended to cover commodities which must be manufactured before they are available for sale. According to the admitted statements in the complaint, special tools had to be manufactured in order to produce the item herein involved. The seller here, misled by the many and detailed provisions contained in purchase order No. 11925 and ordinarily applicable to an enforceable bilateral contract, undoubtedly, as he alleged in his complaint, did go to considerable expense in providing tools and machines, only to find that by the accepted agreement the buyer had promised to do absolutely nothing. A statement of expectation creates no duty. Courts are not clothed with the power to make contracts for parties, nor can they, under the guise of interpretation, supply provisions actually lacking or impose obligations not actually assumed.

. . . The seller also argues the fact that he has alleged in his complaint he was advised by the defendant it would release approximately 1,600 units for shipment under the said purchase order. The written purchase order 11925 contains a provision that the terms and conditions thereof are the complete and final agreement between the buyer and the seller. . . .

> In *Sterling-Midland Coal Co. v. Great Lakes Coal [& Coke] Co.*, 334 Ill. 281, at page 290, 165 N.E. 793, at page 797, wherein the Supreme Court in passing upon a contract similar to this one, said: "If a written contract purports on its face to be a complete expression of the whole agreement, it is to be presumed that the parties introduced into it every material item and term, and parol evidence is not admissible to add another term to the agreement about which the contract is silent. . . . The clause of the contract . . . expressly negatives the fact that there are any understandings, whether arising by implication of law or otherwise, between the parties, as to the subject-matter of the contract — i.e., as to the coal itself which is the subject-matter of the contract. This clause of the contract is just as binding upon the parties as any other clause, and the municipal and Appellate Courts had no right to disregard it."

In the instant case the seller argues that the suit should not be dismissed because if the case were tried he should be permitted to introduce parol evidence for the purpose of showing an agreement on the part of the buyer to purchase approximately 1,600 valves. The formal agreement contained in purchase order 11925 purports to be a final and complete agreement. A provision therein contained so recites. Parol evidence of this character would vary and contradict the terms of the agreement, and such evidence is inadmissible.

Professor Fuller, discussing insurance and correspondence school contracts, says:

> One often has the impression of a kind of running battle between draftsmen and the courts, with much shifting of ground on the part of both.
>
> Back of this development lies a problem that touches the basic philosophy of contract

> law. The law of contracts is founded generally on the principle that it is the business of the courts to interpret and enforce the agreements that the parties have negotiated. This theory confronts the social reality that in many cases no real negotiations take place, and the terms of the contract are in fact set by the will of one party alone. This situation may arise where one party is indifferent or ignorant, or it may result from a superiority of bargaining power on one side. In such situations, there seems to be emerging a principle of law not yet frankly acknowledged which might be phrased something as follows: where one party to a contract has the power to dictate its terms, the terms of the contract are subject to judicial review, and may be modified by the court if they are unduly harsh. [Fuller, Basic Contract Law, p. 260.]

The courts have many times passed on cases involving insurance contracts, which in many respects are similar to the agreement in this case. Concerning such cases it has been said:

> The history of the cases is, very largely, the history of a struggle between the insurance companies and the courts. . . . The courts, endeavoring to compel fair play, but trammelled and often thwarted by the stringent terms of the contracts, have devised doctrines and asserted principles which are sometimes more creditable to the ingenuity and subtlety of the judges than easily harmonized with decisions rendered, under less violent bias, in other departments of the law.

The agreement contained in purchase order No. 11925 was artfully prepared. It contains, in print so fine as to be scarcely legible, more than twenty-three clauses, most of which are applicable to bilateral contracts. It has all the indicia of a binding and enforceable contract, but it was not a binding and enforceable contract because the promise was defective. Behind the glittering facade is a void. This agreement was made in the higher echelons of business, overshadowed by the aura of business ethics. To say the least, the agreement was deceptive. In a more subterranean atmosphere and between persons of lower ethical standards it might, without any strain on the language, be denominated by a less deterged appellation.

Nevertheless, as the law is today, on the pleadings in the instant case, the trial court could do nothing but sustain the motion to dismiss the complaint. The judgment of the Circuit Court is affirmed.

Judgment affirmed.

Notes and Questions

1. The judge seems to be saying at the end of his opinion that the results is legally correct, but ethically wrong. What rules of law kept him from reaching the opposite conclusion? What interests stand to benefit most from such rules of law?
2. Some of the provisions of the purchase order are set out in the opinion. Who drew them up? Who stands to benefit from them? Why would a person disadvantaged under a proposed agreement sign it? What does that person's signature indicate?
3. Which interests in society stand to benefit most from rules of law that require strict interpretation of contracts and limit the court from going beyond the documentation?
4. The court states that the parties here had an agreement, but no contract. What is the difference? Would most people think that there is a difference?
5. Sometimes agreements are compared to private governments set up to accomplish a result. What kind of government was established by the parties here?
6. In the 1972 issue of Martindale Hubbell (a directory of lawyers), Robert J. Gorman, counsel to Streich, is shown to be a solo practitioner. Pope and Ballard, attorneys for General Motors, is a firm with forty-eight lawyers in Chicago and eleven in Washington, D.C. While it must be conceded

that a legal David can slay a Goliath with a well-placed stone, the figures demonstrate that there can be gross differences in the availability of legal resources in contested cases. Under U.S. practice, parties must pay for their own lawyers whether they win or lose (unless a contrary provision is written into the agreement!).

7. At the most General Motors stood to pay $23,600 to Streich. So why all the commotion and high-priced legal talent?

8. Streich is regarded as having his own personal lawsuit against General Motors. Suppose that he could find other suppliers to General Motors who were in situations similar to his. Would it be appropriate for them to gather their claims and other grievances in one lawsuit? Should a party to a particular lawsuit be able to demonstrate General Motors' contracting and cancellation practices across a number of contracts?

The State *V. I. Lenin*

In primitive society, when people lived in small family groups and were still at the lower stages of development, in a condition approximating to savagery — an epoch from which modern, civilized human society is separated by several thousands of years — there were yet no signs of the existence of a state. We find the predominance of custom, authority, respect, the power enjoyed by the elders of the clan; we find this power sometimes accorded to women — the position of women then was not like the downtrodden and oppressed condition of women today — but nowhere do we find a special *category* of people who are set apart to rule others and, for the sake and purpose of rule, systematically and permanently to wield a certain apparatus of coercion, an apparatus of violence, such as is represented at the present time, as you all realize, by the armed detachments of troops, the prisons and the other means of subjugating the will of others by force — all that which constitutes the essence of the state.

If we abstract ourselves from the so-called religious teachings, subtleties, philosophical arguments and the various opinions advanced by bourgeois scholars, if we abstract ourselves from these and try to get at the real essence of the matter, we shall find that the state really does amount to such an apparatus of rule separated out from human society. When there appears such a special group of men who are occupied with ruling and nothing else, and who in order to rule need a special apparatus of coercion and of subjugating the will of others by force — prisons, special detachments of men, armies, etc. — then there appears the state.

. . . History shows that the state as a special apparatus for coercing people arose only wherever and whenever there appeared a division of society into classes, that is, a division into groups of people some of whom are permanently in a position to appropriate the labour of others, where some people exploit others.

And this division of society into classes must always be clearly borne in mind as a fundamental fact of history. The development of all human societies for thousands of years, in all countries without exception, reveals a general conformity to law, a regularity and consistency in this development; so that at first we had a society without classes — the original patriarchal, primitive society, in which there were no aristocrats; then we had a society based on slavery — a slaveowning society. The whole of modern civilized Europe has passed through this stage — slavery ruled supreme two thousand years ago. The vast majority of peoples of the other parts of the world also passed through this

---

From V. I. Lenin, *The State* (Peking: Foreign Languages Press, 1965).

stage. Among the less developed peoples traces of slavery survive to this day; you will find the institution of slavery in Africa, for example, at the present time. Slaveowners and slaves were the first important class divisions. The former group not only owned all the means of production — the land and the implements, however primitive they may have been in those times — but also owned people. This group was known as slaveowners, while those who laboured and supplied labour for others were known as slaves.

This form was followed in history by another — feudalism. In the great majority of countries slavery in the course of its development evolved into serfdom. The fundamental division of society was now into feudal landlords and peasant serfs. The form of relations between people changed. The slaveowners had regarded the slaves as their property; the law had confirmed this view and regarded the slave as a chattel completely owned by the slaveowner. As far as the peasant serf was concerned, class oppression and dependence remained, but it was not considered that the feudal landlord owned the peasants as chattels, but that he was only entitled to their labour and to compel them to perform certain services. In practice, as you know, serfdom, especially in Russia, where it survived longest of all and assumed the grossest forms, in no way differed from slavery.

Further, with the development of trade, the appearance of the world market and the development of money circulation, a new class arose within feudal society — the capitalist class. From the commodity, the exchange of commodities and the rise of the power of money, there arose the power of capital. During the eighteenth century — or rather, from the end of the eighteenth century and during the nineteenth century — revolutions took place all over the world. Feudalism was eliminated in all the countries of Western Europe. This took place latest of all in Russia. In 1861 a radical change took place in Russia as well, as a consequence of which one form of society was replaced by another — feudalism was replaced by capitalism, under which division into classes remained, as well as various traces and relics of serfdom, but in which the division into classes fundamentally assumed a new form.

The owners of capital, the owners of the land, the owners of the mills and factories in all capitalist countries constituted and still constitute an insignificant minority of the population who have complete command of the labour of the whole people, and, consequently, command, oppress and exploit the whole mass of labourers, the majority of whom are proletarians, wage workers, that procure their livelihood in the process of production only by the sale of their own workers' hands, their labour power. With the transition to capitalism, the peasants, who were already disunited and downtrodden in feudal times, were converted partly (the majority) into proletarians, and partly (the minority) into wealthy peasants who themselves hired workers and who constituted a rural bourgeoisie.

This fundamental fact — the transition of society from primitive forms of slavery to serfdom and finally to capitalism — you must always bear in mind, for only by remembering this fundamental fact, only by inserting all political doctrines into this fundamental framework will you be able properly to appraise these doctrines and understand what they refer to; for each of these great periods in the history of mankind — slaveowning, feudal and capitalist — embraces scores and hundreds of centuries and presents such a mass of political forms, such a variety of political doctrines, opinions and revolutions, that this extreme diversity and immense variety can be understood — especially in connection with the political, philosophical and other doctrines of bourgeois scholars and politicians — only by firmly holding, as to a guiding thread, to this division of society into classes, this change in the forms of class rule, and from this standpoint examining all social questions — economic, political, spiritual, religious, etc.

. . . People are divided into ruled, and into specialists in ruling, those who rise above society and are called rulers, representatives of the state. This apparatus, this group of peole who rule others, always takes possession of a certain apparatus of coercion, of physical force, irrespective of whether this violence over people is expressed in the primitive club, or, in the epoch of slavery, in more perfected types of weapons, or in the firearms which appeared in the Middle Ages, or, finally, in modern weapons, which in the twentieth century are marvels of technique and are entirely based on the latest achievements of modern technology. The methods of violence changed, but whenever there was a state there existed in every society a group of persons who ruled, who commanded, who dominated and who in order to maintain their power possessed an apparatus of physical coercion, an apparatus of violence, with those weapons which corresponded to the technical level of the given epoch. And by examining these general phenomena, by asking ourselves why no state existed when there were no classes, when there were no exploiters and exploited, and why it arose when classes arose — only in this way shall we find a definite answer to the question of the essence of the state and its significance.

Notes and Questions

1. How could the case of *Streich* v. *General Motors* be explained by reference to Lenin's historical analysis?
2. E. B. Pashukanis, a Soviet legal philosopher, argued that it has been in the area of criminal law where class antagonisms have reached their highest intensity. People accused of crime are transformed by the system into "juridic objects," enabling lawmakers to intrude more roughly upon their personalities and, through the accused people so transformed, impose class domination. According to him, the standard of justification of criminal law as being vital to the protection of the safety of the community conceals reality, since the true role of criminal law, from feudalism through industrialism, has been nothing more than the preservation of hierarchy, privilege, and property.*

   Return to the case of the check forger in Section 2. Using Lenin and Pashukanis, reexamine the case and the judges' deliberations.
3. When sentencing convicted offenders, judges apply sentencing criteria to determine whether a person should get probation, local jail time, or a prison term. Sentencing factors include prior criminal record, age, intelligence, educational background, family and marital status, church record, military experience, work history, and neighborhood environment.† These factors are used by judges to predict probation success.

   Do sentencing criteria discriminate against lower class offenders? Are the factors relevant in determining sentences the same as those denoting "success" in society? To what extent does the achievement of success in society result from the prior achievement of status, wealth, and power by one's family?
4. Return to the case of *Cook* v. *State* in Section 3, and review the questions following that case. Has any of the material you have read since then altered your answers to those questions? How?

---

*Hugh W. Babb, tr. *Soviet Legal Philosophy* (1951), pp. 206–207, 211–213.

†See, e.g., 1965 California Sentencing Institute 45 Cal. Rptr. (Appendix).

☐ The organization of plantation slavery in the antebellum South is the subject of the next excerpt.

From Day Clean to First Dark *Kenneth Stampp*

One summer afternoon in 1854, a traveler in Mississippi caught a vivid picture of a gang of field-hands returning to their toil after a thundershower. "First came, led by an old driver carrying a whip, forty of the largest and strongest women I ever saw together; they were all in a simple uniform dress of a bluish check stuff, the skirts reaching little below the knee; their legs and feet were bare; they carried themselves loftily, each having a hoe over the shoulder, and walking with a free, powerful swing, like chasseurs on the march." Then came the plow-hands with their mules, "the cavalry, thirty strong, mostly men, but a few of them women. . . . A lean and vigilant white overseer, on a brisk pony, brought up the rear." In this procession were the chief components of the plantation's production machinery — the regimented laborers whom slavery was expected to provide.

Slavery was above all a labor system. Wherever in the South the master lived, however many slaves he owned, it was his bondsmen's productive capacity that he generally valued most. And to the problem of organizing and exploiting their labor with maximum efficiency he devoted much of his attention.

On small agricultural units — and the great majority of them were small — the organization was simple: the masters usually gave close personal supervision to the unspecialized labor of a few slaves. Most of these masters could not afford merely to act as managers; and many of them were obliged to enter the fields with their bondsmen and drive a plow or wield a hoe. Farmers who worked alongside their slaves could be found throughout the South. The son of a small slaveholder in the South Carolina Low Country remembered that his mother ran a spinning wheel, wove cloth, did her own cooking, and milked the cows, while his father plowed, drove the wagon, and made shoes. In the Upper South, as a contemporary student of southern society observed, it was not unusual to see "the sturdy yeoman and his sons working in company of their negroes." One could hear "the axe of master and man falling with alternate strokes" and watch "the negroes and their masters ploughing side by side."

Masters who had at their command as few as a half dozen field-hands, however, were tempted to improve their social status by withdrawing from the fields and devoting most of their time to managerial functions. Lacking skilled craftsmen in their small slave forces, they still found it necessary to perform certain specialized tasks such as carpentering and repairing tools; and in an emergency (a crop rarely went from spring planting to fall harvesting without a crisis of some kind) they temporarily forgot their pride. If some of the land needed to be replanted, if a crop was "in the grass" — i.e., overgrown with weeds — after a long spell of wet weather, or if illness created a shortage of plowhands, a master often had to choose between losing his crop and pitching in with his slaves. Cotton farmers who did not do ordinary field work helped with the picking in the fall, for that was a time when the labor force was seldom adequate.

But most slaves never saw their masters toiling in the fields, because most did not live on farms of the size where such intimate relationships and unspecialized economic functions existed. The great majority of bondsmen belonged to those whose holdings were large enough to enable them to escape routine farm labor. Even the slaves in the more modest holdings did not always work with their masters on small farms. Some of them worked in the cities. Others belonged to overseers and hence labored on the plantations. Still others belonged to the children or grandchildren of large planters and were used on the family estates. Hence the normal relationship between field-hands and their

---

masters was not that of fellow workers but of labor and management. . . .

The substantial farmers and small planters who owned from ten to thirty slaves had at their disposal enough field-hands to make the problems of organization and supervision more complex. Members of this class usually handled these problems themselves without the aid of an overseer — unless they operated more than one farm or combined farming with some other business or profession. In such cases the owner often required his overseer to work in the field as well as to manage the slaves. . . .

The planters who owned more than thirty slaves were the ones who achieved maximum efficiency, the most complex economic organization, and the highest degree of specialization within their labor forces. Slightly less than half of the slaves belonged to the approximately twenty-five thousand masters operating plantations of these dimensions. Planters in this group who did not use overseers were as rare as the smaller slaveholders who did. In 1860 the number of Southerners who were employed as overseers about equalled the number of plantations with more than thirty slaves.

The planter who hired a full-time overseer limited his direction of routine crop cultivation to periodic inspections of the fields and concentrated upon problems of marketing, finance, and general plantation administration. Being free from the need to give constant attention to his labor force, he enjoyed greater leisure and was able to absent himself from the plantation more or less at his discretion. He employed his overseer on a year-to-year basis, usually by a written contract which could be terminated at the will of either party. The planter paid his overseer an annual salary ranging all the way from $100 to $1200, in addition to furnishing a house, an allowance of corn and pork, and a slave servant.

A prudent planter defined the overseer's duties in a detailed set of written instructions. Each planter had his own peculiar notions about the proper way to manage an estate, but his instructions tended to follow a somewhat standardized pattern. A Mississippian generalized about the overseer's responsibilities in a way that almost any planter would have endorsed: "The Overseer will never be expected to work in the field, but he must always be with the hands when not otherwise engaged in the Employers business and must do every thing that is required of him, provided it is directly or indirectly connected with the planting or other pecuniary interest of the Employer." Specific instructions related to the care and control of the slaves, the amount and kinds of labor to be performed, the care of plantation tools and livestock, and the behavior and activities of the overseer himself. The owner often required his overseer to keep a daily record of general plantation activities and to make regular oral or written reports. In short, he expected the overseer to be an efficient general manager and a careful guardian of his employer's property. . . .

In working the slave force the overseer generally made use of one or more slave drivers. If there were several of them one was designated head driver and acted almost as a sub-overseer. Sometimes the drivers were required to work and thus to set the pace for the rest of the slaves; sometimes they were exempted from labor and urged the gangs on by word or whip. A South Carolina rice planter defined their duties in his plantation rules: "Drivers are, under the Overseer, to maintain discipline and order on the place. They are to be responsible for the quiet of the negro-houses, for the proper performance of tasks, for bringing out the people early in the morning, and generally for the immediate inspection of such things as the Overseer only generally superintends." Planters thus called upon trusted slaves to become part of the plantation's command hierarchy. A Georgia planter described the efficient managerial system that existed on his estate:

> Every evening the drivers . . . make a report to the overseer in my presence of the employment of their respective hands. The drivers report . . . the quantity and kind of work they have done, and the field in which it is done. . . . These reports . . . are copied into the "Journal of Plantation Work," which

> forms a minute and daily record of the occupation and quantity of work done by the different gangs. After the reports are received, the work for the following day is arranged, and the head driver is directed what is to be done, and the manner in which it is to be executed. He distributes the orders to the sub-drivers and others: — the sub-drivers to the hands composing the gangs.
>
> As the quantity of land in each field is accurately known, a constant check is had on the fidelity of the reports as to the quantity of work done. It only remains, by a daily inspection, to see that all operations have been well performed.

On a plantation containing more than thirty slaves there was always considerable labor specialization, the amount depending upon its size. The minimum was a clear distinction between household servants and field-hands, the latter in turn being divided into plow and hoe gangs. On the larger plantations some slaves devoted their full time to such occupations as ditching, tending livestock, driving wagons, and cultivating vegetable gardens. Here, too, there were substantial numbers of skilled slave artisans, and a high degree of specialization among household servants. In addition, each of the southern staples demanded its own kinds of specialists. These agricultural enterprises, with their business directors, production managers, labor foremen, and skilled and unskilled workers, approached the organizational complexity of modern factories. Though agriculture was not yet mechanized, the large plantations were to a considerable extent "factories in the fields."

Notes and Questions

1. Lenin contended that the modern organization replicates the formal arrangements of slavery and feudalism. Therefore, it is more than an exercise in antiquarianism or the study of the roots of modern racism that impels the investigation of slavery. In order to appraise current conditions, modern students need to know the extent to which form persists while surfaces change.

Non-Marxists have also sometimes endorsed the idea that there are constants across organizational history. Max Weber, a German sociologist and lawyer, traced the evolution of organizations from charismatic types (led by dynamic and visionary leaders who had compelling personal qualities) to routine forms where systems are established and goals are pursued by elaborate divisions of labor and specialization. The routine form does not completely displace the charismatic form, but actually builds upon it — the antique army with provisional leadership, willingly followed, influences the arrangement of peacetime affairs. Later, the expectation that leaders be dazzling or earn respect of their followers gets lost, but the leader-follower notion is retained. Over time, hierarchies become permanent and not dependent upon the consent of underlings.*

What contemporary questions are suggested by the investigation of slavery? Can modern-day roles be placed in the paradigm of masters, overseers, drivers, and slaves? What is the connection between role and rule, the relationship between position in organization and determination of the direction and activities of organizations, and what is done to noncooperative participants? Over centuries, has there been progress, or no change, or decline in the distribution of power and wealth? And lastly, how does the form of organizations affect the achievement of the central democratic values of liberty and equality?

2. The position of the driver under slavery was especially difficult. He was vital to the success of the plantation, for he was responsible for the maintenance of production and discipline, and yet as a black slave, he was disqualified from full status; thus, he must have suffered serious crises of conscience. To do well in the master's eyes and gain material success and a measure of

---

*See, generally, Hans Gerth and C. Wright Mills, *From Max Weber* (New York: Oxford University Press, 1946); Frederick Thayer, *An End to Hierarchy and Competition* (New York: Watts, 1981).

status would help the master prosper, thereby contributing to the perpetuation of slavery and the profound indignities experienced by both the driver and his brethren. As a person of influence, the driver could beneficially affect the day-to-day lives of his fellow slaves, but winning battles could mean the loss of the war.

The unenviable position of the driver typifies those in the middle ranks of many organizations. They are neither in positions of appreciable wealth and power nor at the lower levels where their kin loyalties and origins lay. To make gains, they inevitably suffer losses.

What modern-day parallels do you see to the driver-slave relationship? What difficulties would there be for slavery or for the modern organization were there no such relationships?

Compare the position of the driver with the position of the doorkeeper in Kafka's parable "Before the Law."

3. A. Were you to find yourself in a culture and economy with only four organizational positions — master, overseer, driver, or slave — which position would you prefer? Before jumping to the conclusion that the answer is obvious, consider the nature of each role and how you would be able to act and be expected to act in each.

B. If you were not able to exercise your preference, but instead were assigned a position by lot or by birth, how would this affect your thinking?

C. In the modern organization with top, middle, and bottom levels, where would you prefer to be? How would your thinking about organizations be affected if roles were assigned rather than being subject to your preference? How does the relative scarcity of upper-level positions affect your thinking about the way organizations should be designed?

4. What did law have to do with slavery? Students might think that since slavery was and is inherently unjust there could have been no relationship between law and slavery — the system would keep quiet about it, so to speak. The contrary was the case. Summaries of cases dealing with slavery fill five volumes, and every slave state had numerous statutes dealing with the subject.† This substantial body of law demonstrates conclusively that legal order was indispensable to the maintenance and nurturance of slavery.

But what made law so vital to the system? Pre-eminently important was the definition of slaves as personal property to be used, traded, put up as collateral for loans, and inherited at death. A second critical aspect of law involved the delegation of power over the slave to the masters and their appointees, meaning that the day-to-day governance and discipline on plantations were of no concern to the courts. In addition to being property, slaves were considered persons for purposes of criminal law so that the police power of the state could be invoked at critical times in aid of masters whose slaves got out of control. Under law, slavery was a system of property and delegated power, with state power available in times of emergency.

5. Slaves naturally did not willingly subject themselves to bondage. At the plantation level where the law decreed that slavery relationships be fought out on a daily basis, slaves used a variety of tactics to undo master-overseer power. Since the slave was simultaneously a valuable property, a source of labor, and an "object" requiring constant discipline, there were limits on the physical abuse that could be inflicted on a slave. A dead slave was valueless for sale or labor.

Beginning with this outside limit, slaves engaged in a full range of tactics that led one master to characterize them as a "troublesome property." Common tactics were work slow-downs, feigning of illness or ineptitude, shoddy workmanship, the playing off of masters against overseers, thefts from masters, arson on crops and buildings, assaults and murders of masters and overseers, and running away. These tactics limited the otherwise complete control by masters and were vital ingredients in daily working arrangements.

There are still countless situations when as

---

†Helen Catterall, ed., *Judicial Cases* (Westport, Conn.: Greenwood, 1926).

a matter of formal rule "all the power" is held by one or a few persons over others "who have no power." What do people who are in powerless situations do to preserve a measure of their autonomy and dignity? Compare these actions with the tactics of the slaves on plantations. Are these challenges to power a form of lawmaking?

We follow the cotton northward to Lowell, Massachusetts, which in the 1850s was the center of the New England textile industry. Most of the factory "hands" were women, who were recruited first from the farms of the area and later from successive groups of immigrants — Irish, French-Canadians, and southern Europeans. The following case arose in the same period as the preceding excerpt on slavery and shows the early organization of the textile industry.

Thornton and Wife v. The Suffolk Manufacturing Company

64 Mass. 376 (1852)

Action of contract for the breach of an agreement under which the female plaintiff, Catherine Cassidy, before her marriage, worked in the manufactory of the defendants, at Lowell.

This agreement and breach were alleged . . . that the female plaintiff went to work for the defendants under the agreement that if she faithfully performed her duties in their employ for the term of at least twelve months, at the expiration of such period, upon giving a fortnight's notice, she would be entitled to leave, and to receive from them "a line," or honorable discharge, by means of which she might obtain employment in the other mills in Lowell. It was also alleged that there was an agreement among the several manufacturing companies in Lowell, that if an operative did not receive such "line" or honorable discharge, he could not afterwards obtain employment in any other of the mills in Lowell. It was also alleged that the female plaintiff faithfully performed services for the defendants for more than twelve months, and became thereby entitled to such discharge, or "line," upon giving a fortnight's notice of her intention to leave, and working for that period; but that the defendants, regardless of their contract, wrongfully discharged her without such "line," and thereby deprived her of work in any other mill in Lowell.

At the trial in this court before FLETCHER, J., the plaintiffs called Alexander P. Wright. He testified: "I am agent of the Lowell (carpet) company; have been so for about twenty-three years; am generally acquainted with the rules and customs of the Lowell companies. I know of no certain agreement between companies to require a 'line'; I believe the custom is to require a 'line' wherever an operative has been previously employed in other mills in Lowell, or not to hire them. Our company requires it; never have known of hiring an operative when they have been discharged from another company without a line, if it was known; the invariable custom is to give a line if there is no objection to the conduct of the help from the overseer; never have known any difference for twenty-three years that I have been here; if the help work properly it is usual to give a line; there may be cases of opposition on the part of the overseers, but this is usually for cause. I never have known an overseer to refuse arbitrarily, but always for cause shown; if help work a year, and give a fortnight's notice, they are entitled to a 'line'; this is a general custom, and understood by all concerned; so far as I know, the help hire with knowledge of this custom; if a line is refused by the overseers they apply to me. I should say improper conduct is the only cause of refusal; if the overseer refuses a line, he makes his statement to me. I should say bad temper, producing disturbance in [the] room, would be sufficient cause of discharge; any such conduct as would render the hand unserviceable elsewhere, such as insulting the overseer, trying to get other hands discontented. I know of no right in operatives to demand a line; this line is like a recommendation to a servant in a family; the regulation paper is the substance of the contract. I should suppose it optional with the overseer whether he gave a line or not; . . .

John B. McAlvin testified: "I have been paymaster on the Suffolk for eighteen years; have the books of the company in my hands; it appears from this book that the plaintiff came to work for the company, May 29, 1848, and was discharged, July 19, 1849; the entry is, 'discharged for improper conduct.' I know the handwriting of John Clark; this paper handed me is in his handwriting; it is one of the blanks furnished by the Suffolk Company to their overseers, filled up by Mr. Clark, as follows: 'Suffolk Dressing Room, No. 3. Catherine Cassidy, has worked since pay-day, thirteen days; pay her for warping nineteen beams, at 22c. per beam, $6.08. John C. Clark, overseer. Discharged for improper conduct, July 18, 1849. She has worked in this room ——— months. She leaves with notice.' If the blank is filled up, namely, has worked here *twelve* months, and leaves with notice, I should give a line, but should generally ask the overseer; giving her a line would be a compliance with the rules of the Suffolk company, if she worked twelve months and left with notice; if she leaves with notice, it would be a compliance with rules to give her a line, but of late years I have usually asked the overseer, if there is any objection to her having a line. . . .

. . . The rule further is to give notice to all other companies when a hand has been discharged without a line, so such hand may not be employed, but this is not always done; seldom send a notice or receive one; I can't say whether one was sent or not in the plaintiff's case. Soon after she left, she came to me with another woman; brought me this bill, (the one signed by Clark,) and demanded a line; I told her I could not give her a line. If the bill comes from the overseer in this form, by the rules, I cannot give a line or honorable discharge. I told her to go to the overseer, and she went out as if to go to see him. If the hand comes with a bill in the form of this one we do not give a line; it is our usual practice not to give a line without seeing the overseer, to see if there are objections. I know of no other contract with the hands than that contained in the regulation paper mentioned. My business is paymaster, I have nothing to do with hiring or discharging hands, this is done by the overseers. The help go to the overseer and make their engagements with him as to what price they are to have, and how they are to be employed, and then come to the counting-room and get the regulation paper; . . .

James Montague testified: "I have lived in Lowell twelve years; have known the female plaintiff four years; she has worked in the mill since I knew her; she lived next door to me with her mother; her father was dead; she has worked with the Suffolk Company; after she was discharged she requested me to go to the company and get an honorable discharge for her. I called on Mr. Clark, her overseer, to give her a discharge or a line so she could get work in the other factories in Lowell, as she had a crippled mother dependent on her. He said he would not give her an honorable discharge, or a line, though she might come back and work there. This is the discharge I showed to Mr. Clark; I told him I thought it a rather hard discharge. I told him how hard it was for her and her mother; and, after some talk, he said he would go and see Mr. Wright, the agent, and it might be arranged. We went to see Mr. Wright; I told him the same I had told Mr. Clark. Wright said that he would not give her a line, but that she might come back; assured her that she was a very good girl, there was nothing against her. This was in October, 1849. I then told Mr. Wright I thought there would be some trouble about it, that she would prosecute; he said he would spend $5,000 rather than change the line he had given her, and I left."

William Markland testified: "I am overseer

in Lowell Company; have been so five years, but have been employed there ten years. The female plaintiff applied to me for work in our company, August 2, 1849; got work, and worked six and three-fourth days at that time; she left because she could not get a line from the Suffolk Company, the last place where she worked; she could not give me a line so as to have a regulation paper from our company; she appeared to do well so far as I could see, and I was satisfied with her. She began to learn to weave; this was new business to her, and could at first earn at it only fifty cents per day; a good weaver can earn from seventy-five to eighty cents per day. I don't know as there is any specified rule, but it is necessary, as I understand it, to have a line before a hand can get work who has worked in Lowell before. If they work twelve months, and give a fortnight's notice, they are entitled to a line, as I consider it; this has always been my practice; I have never done any other way. I hired myself with this understanding when I came to work for the company. I hire my own help with this understanding. I have twenty-two men, four boys, and one hundred and thirty-five girls under me; they are frequently changing; the operatives all understand this rule about a line so far as I know. After she left, because she could not get a line, she came back December 31, 1849, and brought a line from the Merrimack Company; I then employed her for thirteen months; she was an average good weaver, and did an average quantity of work; she made about eighty cents per day; I can't tell exactly how much. I found her a fair hand and had no difficulty with her. I suppose it is a matter of discretion with the overseer whether he will give a line; it is so with me; but I never refused one without a cause; disobedience is sufficient."

Homer Bartlett testified: "I have been employed as agent and treasurer of the Massachusetts Mills, since 1839. Am now treasurer. I know the rules of the Massachusetts Mills. I know the general rules amongst companies of Lowell. . . . If a girl works a year and fulfills all her duties, and asks for a line, I should give it to her; I never refused one under these circumstances; this is well understood amongst the operatives in Lowell; some new ones from the country may not understand it. I suppose the rule to be the same on all the corporations in Lowell. If a girl should treat her overseer with disrespect, should neglect her work, create insubordination, or in any other way be guilty of misconduct, this would deprive her of a line. . . .

Bridget Gaiten testified: "After the female plaintiff was discharged from the Suffolk, I went with her to the Boott Mills to get work; she engaged work with the overseer, and went to the counting-room to get her regulation paper, and they asked her for her line; she showed them the one she had; they said that would not do, she must go to the Suffolk and get a line. I went with her to the paymaster, and she asked him for a line; he said he could not give one, she must get one from her overseer. We went to the overseer, and he said that he would not do any thing about it; it was left at the counting-room; she did not get a line, and came away."

The plaintiffs here rested their case, and at the suggestion of the presiding judge, the case was withdrawn from the jury, and reported to the whole court for their opinion upon the matter of law. . . .

SHAW, C. J.

In this action, brought by Catharine Cassidy, whilst sole, we see no ground on which the plaintiffs can recover, as upon a contract. The ground relied on is, that in consideration of services, the employer engages that if the operative remains in the service a certain time, he will give her an honorable discharge; or in other words, that her service and conduct have been good and satisfactory. Were such a contract made in express terms, intended to be absolute, it seems to us that it would be bad in law, as plainly contrary to good morals and public policy. Such a discharge is a certificate of a fact; but if the fact is otherwise, if the conduct of the operative has not been satisfactory, it would be the certificate of a falsehood, tending to mislead and not to inform other employers. Besides; if such a custom were general, such a discharge would be utterly useless to other employers and utterly worthless to the receiver. It could give other employers no information, upon which they could rely. To avoid such illegality, it must be taken with some limitation and qualification, to wit, that the conduct of the operative has been such in all respects, including not only skill and industry in the employment, but conduct in point of morals, temper, language, and deportment, and the like, so that a certificate of good character would be true. Then it stands upon the same footing with the custom which governs most respectable persons in society, upon the termination of the employment of a servant, to give him a certificate of good character, if entitled to it. In such case, it is for the employer to give or withhold such certificate, according to his own conviction of the truth, arising from his own personal knowledge, or from other sources. It is the state of the employer's mind, his belief of the good character of the servant, or the contrary, which other employers desire to know, and have a right to know. It must therefore necessarily depend upon the employer's own determination, when so applied to for a certificate, whether with a just regard to truth and honesty, he can certify to the good character or not. If an assurance of an employer on engaging a servant, that at the end of the time he will give him a certificate of good character, if he should then think him entitled to it, could in any respect be deemed a contract, and not the promise of an ordinary act of courtesy, it would be no breach of such contract, to aver and prove that the servant, after the termination of the service, demanded such certificate, and was refused it. . . .

[The corporation] could only know the truth of the facts, of such good conduct and behavior, by the report of the superintendent under whom such operative may have been employed. He alone may know the facts and be able to state them. Should they certify to good character without, or against such report, they might certify to a falsehood, and only mislead those who should rely upon such certificate. This certainly they cannot be legally obliged to do. When therefore the overseer certifies that the operative is discharged for impropriety, as in the present case, this evidence must be conclusive with the corporation, because they can have no other to justify them in giving a certificate.

It is said by way of objection to this, that an overseer may arbitrarily refuse to certify a good character, or falsely certify a bad one. This is possible, and if he does it capriciously, or without cause, it is extremely dishonorable and wrong, and would tend soon to impair his own reputation and standing for honesty and uprightness. Still, when an appeal is necessarily made to a man's own personal knowledge, judgment, and conscience, his decision must be presumed to be according to the truth, and conclusive. . . .

The fact, that on account of the peculiar situation of the various companies in Lowell, in relation to each other, the common interest they have in maintaining their discipline, the certificate of good character is of so much more importance to the servant, than elsewhere, can make no difference to the servant, in regard to his rights. In the same proportion in which it is important to the servant out of employ, to hold a certificate of good character and honorable discharge, it is important to corporations, their agents and servants, and all interested in them, to be cautious and conscientious, in giving such discharges and recommendations, when they are honestly deserved, and in withholding them when they are not.

The court are of opinion, that upon the evidence adduced, a jury would not have been warranted in finding a verdict for the plaintiffs. . . .

Notes and Questions

1. In the textile industry, the owners appointed agents who in turn named overseers to direct the factory workers. Compare the organization of large southern plantations with the organization of cotton textile factories.
2. If a person wanted to leave a factory in Lowell, what inhibitions would she or he have had? Can quitting a job in a factory in Lowell be compared to a slave's running away?

3. Compare the judge's reasoning in the *Thornton* case with the commentary in an 1823 case from North Carolina:

   With the services and labours of a slave the law has nothing to do; they are the master's by the law; the government and control of them being exclusively to him. Nor will the law interfere upon the ground that the state's rights and not the master's have been violated.

   In establishing slavery then, the law vested in the master the absolute and uncontrolled right to the services of the slave, and the means of enforcing those services follow as necessary consequences; nor will the law weigh with the most scrupulous niceties his acts in relation thereto.*

**State* v. *Read* 9, N.C. 365 (1823). Quoted in Mark Tushnet, *The American Law of Slavery* (Princeton, N.J.: Princeton University Press, 1981).

4. The court leaves fairness in the terms of a worker's departure to the discretion of the overseer "who alone may know the facts and be able to state them." The limitation on arbitrariness comes from the overseer's desire to protect his own reputation for honesty. Compare this limitation with those placed on schoolteachers in punishing children and on husbands in chastising wives as reported in the early North Carolina cases in Section 1.
5. The court "takes the case away from the jury" and rules that a jury could have no legal basis to find for the plaintiff employee. Do you think a jury's deliberations would have been helpful in the case? Which would the company prefer as decision maker in the case, a judge or a jury? Which would Ms. Cassidy have preferred?
6. What large questions seemed to be riding on the outcome of the case? What would impel the agent of the company to say that he was willing to spend $5,000 on the defense of a case involving a weaver who earned $3 to $5 a week?

Until the emergence of organized labor and collective bargaining, workers like Catherine Cassidy were expected to bargain individually with employers to set the terms and conditions of their employment. From the mid-nineteenth century until the 1930s, there was no legal support of unions and collective action, which led Samuel Gompers (the first president of the AFL) to pray, "God save labor from the courts." Decades of discriminatory uses of the antitrust laws and the labour injunction, to say nothing of the use of police, state militias, and the U.S. army, had led him to conclude that no law at all would be preferable to the anti-labor law that had inhibited the development of organized labor from the outset.

During the Great Depression, Congress softened the law affecting organized labor and collective bargaining. Whether the resulting National Labor Relations Act of 1935 (the Wagner Act) was passed out of a desire to head off more radical activism by labor or out of a genuine interest in bringing about greater mutuality has long been debated by labor historians. But most agree that the Wagner Act marked a significant shift in national labor policy.

At the center of the act were provisions to secure the free choice of workers regarding unions and union representatives, to mandate collective bargaining, and to protect collective action in the form of strikes, boycotts, and picketing. The National Labor Relations Board (NLRB) was created to be the first point of adjudication of disputes between labor and management.

One of the main areas of conflict under the Wagner Act and subsequent labor legislation concerned the scope of collective bargaining. About what subjects did the law require labor and management to bargain? The law stated that bargaining was to take place over "wages, hours, and other terms and conditions of employment." If the phrase were given a broad interpretation, literally anything might find its way into a collective bargaining agreement, for example, the purposes and scope of the business, what products or services would be made or furnished, the manner of making or furnishing them, to whom they would go and at what prices, and the formula for sharing the proceeds from their sale. If given a narrow interpretation — how much money and for how long, and matters close to money and time — owner-manager discretion would remain virtually unaffected by congressionally mandated bargaining. There would in the latter case be definite limits upon the gains that workers could make through the formation of unions and collective bargaining.

In 1964 the U.S. Supreme Court rendered a decision that has had a profound impact on the range of collective bargaining and on whether the congressional intentions of bringing about labor peace through the rule of law can be realized. On the surface the case of *Fibreboard Paper Products Corp. v. NLRB* would not have looked momentous enough to shape the next twenty years of labor law. A union work force had done the maintenance at a manufacturing plant in California, but when the time for renewal of the contract came up, the employer refused to bargain with the employees saying that because of its plans to use an outside contractor to perform maintenance services, bargaining would be "pointless."

After all the rounds of administrative and lower court decisions, the U.S. Supreme Court had before it the question of whether the Wagner Act required an employer to bargain with a union before "contracting out" to an outside firm the work that had been done previously by its own employees. The Court ruled for the union, out of an impulse to promote collective bargaining and reduce "industrial strife," noting that the work still had to be performed and that the employer was in effect substituting an outside work force for the one previously under contract.

Justice Stewart agreed with the decision, but saw far-reaching implications to a broad interpretation of Wagner Act language — "wages, hours and other terms and conditions of employment."

Fibreboard Paper Products Corp. v. NLRB *379 U.S. 204 (1964)*

MR. JUSTICE STEWART, . . . *concurring:*

Viewed broadly, the question before us stirs large issues. The Court purports to limit its decision to "the facts of this case." But the Court's opinion radiates implications of such disturbing breadth that I am persuaded to file this separate statement of my own views.

Section 8(a) (5) of the National Labor Relations Act, as amended, makes it an unfair labor practice for an employer to "refuse to bargain collectively with the representatives of his employees." Collective bargaining is defined in § 8(d) as:

> "the performance of the mutual obligation of the employer and the representative of the employees to meet at reasonable times and confer in good faith with respect to wages, hours, and other terms and conditions of employment."

The question posed is whether the particular decision sought to be made unilaterally by the employer in this case is a subject of mandatory collective bargaining within the statutory phrase "terms and conditions of employment." That is all the Court decides. The Court most assuredly does not decide that every managerial decision which necessarily terminates an individual's employment is subject to the duty to bargain. . . . Within the narrow limitations implicit in the specific facts of this case, I agree with the Court's decision.

Fibreboard had performed its maintenance work at its Emeryville manufacturing plant through its own employees, who were represented by a local of the United Steelworkers. Estimating that some $225,000 could be saved annually by dispensing with internal maintenance, the company contracted out this work, informing the union that there would be no point in negotiating a new contract since the employees in the bargaining unit had been replaced by employees of the independent contractor, Fluor. Maintenance work continued to be performed within the plant, with the work ultimately supervised by the company's officials and "functioning as an integral part" of the company. Fluor was paid the cost of operations plus $2,250 monthly. The savings in costs anticipated from the arrangement derived largely from the elimination of fringe benefits, adjustments in work scheduling, enforcement of stricter work quotas, and close supervision of the new personnel. Under the cost-plus arrangement, Fibreboard remained responsible for whatever maintenance costs were actually incurred. On these facts, I would agree that the employer had a duty to bargain collectively concerning the replacement of his internal maintenance staff by employees of the independent contractor.

The basic question is whether the employer failed to "confer in good faith with respect to *** terms and conditions of employment" in unilaterally deciding to subcontract this work. This question goes to the scope of the employer's duty in the absence of a collective bargaining agreement. . . .

The phrase "conditions of employment" is no doubt susceptible of diverse interpretations. At the extreme, the phrase could be construed to apply to any subject which is insisted upon as a prerequisite for continued employment. Such an interpretation, which would in effect place the compulsion of the Board behind any and all bargaining demands, would be contrary to the intent of Congress, as reflected in this legislative history. Yet there are passages in the Court's opinion today which suggest just such an expansive interpretation, for the Court's opinion seems to imply that any issue which may reasonably divide an employer and his employees must be the subject of compulsory collective bargaining.

Only a narrower concept of "conditions of employment" will serve the statutory purpose of delineating a limited category of issues which are subject to the duty to bargain collectively. Seeking to effect this purpose, at least seven circuits have interpreted the statutory language to exclude various kinds of management decisions from the scope of the duty to bargain. In common parlance, the conditions of a person's employment are most obviously the various physical dimensions of his working environment. What one's hours are to be, what amount of work is expected during those hours, what periods of relief are available, what safety practices are observed, would all seem conditions of one's employment. There are other less tangible but no less important characteristics of a person's employment which might also be deemed "conditions" — most prominently the characteristic involved in this case, the security of one's employment. On one view of the matter, it can be argued that the question whether there is to be a job is not a condition of employment; the question is not one of imposing conditions on employment, but the more fundamental question whether there is to be employment at all. However, it is clear that the Board and the courts have on numerous occasions recognized that union demands for provisions limiting an employer's power to discharge employees are mandatorily bargainable. Thus, freedom from discriminatory discharge, seniority rights, the imposition of a compulsory retirement age, have been recognized as subjects upon which an employer must bargain, although all of these concern the very existence of the employment itself.

While employment security has thus properly been recognized in various circumstances as a condition of employment, it surely does not follow that every decision which may affect job security is a subject of compulsory collective bargaining. Many decisions made by management affect the job security of employees. Decisions concerning the volume and kind of advertising expenditures, product design, the manner of financing, and sales, all may bear upon the security of the workers' jobs. Yet it is hardly conceivable that such decisions so involve "conditions of employment" that they must be negotiated with the employees' bargaining representative.

In many of these areas the impact of a particular management decision upon job security may be extremely indirect and uncertain, and this alone may be sufficient reason to conclude that such decisions are not "with respect to *** conditions of employment." Yet there are other areas where decisions by management may quite clearly imperil job security, or indeed terminate employment entirely. An enterprise may decide to invest in labor-saving machinery. Another may resolve to liquidate its assets and go out of business. Nothing the Court holds today should be understood as imposing a duty to bargain collectively regarding such managerial decisions, which lie at the core of entrepreneurial control. Decisions concerning the commitment of investment capital and the basic scope of the enterprise are not in themselves primarily about conditions of employment, though the effect of the decision may be necessarily to terminate employment. If, as I think clear, the purpose of § 8(d) is to describe a limited area subject to the duty of collective bargaining, those management decisions which are fundamental to the basic direction of a corporate enterprise or which impinge only indirectly upon employment security should be excluded from that area. . . .

This kind of subcontracting falls short of such larger entrepreneurial questions as what shall be produced, how capital shall be invested in fixed assets, or what the basic scope of the enterprise shall be. In my view, the Court's decision in this case has nothing to do with whether any aspects of those larger issues could under any circumstances be considered subjects of compulsory collective bargaining under the present law.

I am fully aware that in this era of automation and onrushing technological change, no problems in the domestic economy are of greater concern than those involving job security and employment stability. Because of the potentially cruel impact upon the lives and fortunes of the working men and women of the Nation, these problems have understandably engaged the solicitous attention of government, of responsible private business, and particularly of organized labor. It is possible that in meeting these problems Congress may eventually decide to give organized labor or government a far heavier hand in controlling what until now have been considered the prerogatives of private business management. That path would mark a sharp departure from the traditional principles of a free enterprise economy. Whether we should follow it is, within constitutional limitations, for Congress to choose. But it is a path which Congress certainly did not choose when it enacted the Taft-Hartley Act.

Notes and Questions

1. The following hypothetical case shows how important it is to define the scope of mandatory collective bargaining:

> Erewhon College in Eupeka, after a prolonged student strike, recognized a union of students for collective bargaining regarding "grades, credits, and other terms and conditions of education."
>
> The students have elected a bargaining committee which is to meet with a committee of the college chosen from faculty and administrators. The committee must decide what they would want to appear in a collective agreement with the school. Erewhon students have expressed interest in a number of issues; grading and alternative grading systems, such as pass-fail courses and credit versus no-grade courses; flexible grading for courses of differing degree of difficulty (science students are convinced that their teachers mark harder); requirements for majors and for graduation, especially required writing courses, foreign languages and science courses; the ratio of teaching assistants to full-time faculty; class size and the admission to classes that have been closed because of oversubscription; the selection and retention of faculty and administrators; and a better placement service.

What are the possible interpretations of the phrase "grades, credits and other terms and conditions of education"? How should the phrase be interpreted?

Compare the language on the scope of educational bargaining with the language of the NLRA, "wages, hours, and other terms and conditions of employment."

☐ The union won the battle in *Fibreboard* over subcontracting but lost the war over the scope of mandatory bargaining. Justice Stewart's allocation of the "larger entrepreneurial questions" to the prerogatives of owner-managers has become the center of bargaining law.

Plant closings and partial terminations of businesses became increasingly visible areas of conflict between workers and corporations, as corporations moved more operations overseas or sharply curtailed activity in the severe recession (depression) of the early 1980s. Can workers do anything about the security of their employment through the collective bargaining process? The U.S. Supreme Court in 1981 had before it a case where a union contended that an employer had a duty to collectively bargain regarding the termination of a major contract with a customer, which would have led to large layoffs.

First National Maintenance Corp. v. NLRB

452 U.S. 666, 101 S.Ct. 2573 (1981)

JUSTICE BLACKMUN *delivered the opinion of the Court.*

Must an employer, under its duty to bargain in good faith "with respect to wages, hours, and other terms and conditions of employment," . . . negotiate with the certified representative of its employees over its decision to close a part of its business? In this case, the National Labor Relations Board (Board) imposed such a duty on petitioner with respect to its decision to terminate a contract with a customer, and the United States Court of Appeals, although differing over the appropriate rationale, enforced its order.

I

Petitioner, First National Maintenance Corporation (FNM), is a New York corporation engaged in the business of providing housekeeping, cleaning, maintenance, and related services for commercial customers in the New York City area. It supplies each of its customers, at the customer's premises, contracted-for labor force and supervision in return for reimbursement of its labor costs (gross salaries, FICA and FUTA taxes, and insurance) and payment of a set fee. It contracts for and hires personnel separately for each customer, and it does not transfer employees between locations.

During the spring of 1977, petitioner was performing maintenance work for the Greenpark Care Center, a nursing home in Brooklyn. Its written agreement dated April 28, 1976, with Greenpark specified that Greenpark "shall furnish all tools, equiptment [*sic*], materials, and supplies," and would pay petitioner weekly "the sum of five hundred dollars plus the gross weekly payroll and fringe benefits." . . . Its weekly fee, however, had been reduced to $250 effective November 1, 1976. . . . The contract prohibited Greenpark from hiring any of petitioner's employees during the term of the contract and for 90 days thereafter. . . . Petitioner employed approximately 35 workers in its Greenpark operation.

Petitioner's business relationship with Greenpark, seemingly, was not very remunerative or smooth. In March 1977, Greenpark gave petitioner the 30 days' written notice of cancellation specified by the contract, because of "lack of efficiency." . . . This cancellation did not become effective, for FNM's work continued after the expiration of that 30-day period. Petitioner, however, became aware that it was losing money at Greenpark. On June 30, by telephone, it asked that its weekly fee be restored at the $500 figure and, on July 6, it informed Greenpark in writing that it would discontinue its operations there on August 1 unless the increase were granted. . . . By telegram on July 25, petitioner gave final notice of termination. . . .

While FNM was experiencing these difficulties, District 1199, National Union of Hospital and Health Care Employees, Retail, Wholesale and Department Store Union, AFL-CIO (union), was conducting an organization campaign among petitioner's Greenpark employees. On March 31, 1977, at a Board-conducted election, a majority of the employees selected the union as their bargaining agent. On July 12, the union's vice president, Edward Wecker, wrote petitioner, notifying it of the certification and of the union's right to bargain, and stating: "We look forward to meeting with you or your representative for that purpose. Please advise when it will be convenient." . . . Petitioner neither responded nor sought to consult with the union.

On July 28, petitioner notified its Greenpark employees that they would be discharged three days later. Wecker immediately telephoned petitioner's secretary-treasurer, Leonard Marsh, to request a delay for the purpose of bargaining. Marsh refused the offer to bargain and told Wecker that the termination of the Greenpark operation was purely a matter of money, and final, and that the 30 days' notice

---

Footnotes deleted. — ED.

provision of the Greenpark contract made staying on beyond August 1 prohibitively expensive. . . . Wecker discussed the matter with Greenpark's management that same day, but was unable to obtain a waiver of the notice provision. . . . Greenpark also was unwilling itself to hire the FNM employees because of the contract's 90-day limitation on hiring. . . . With nothing but perfunctory further discussion, petitioner on July 31 discontinued its Greenpark operation and discharged the employees. . . .

II

A fundamental aim of the National Labor Relations Act is the establishment and maintenance of industrial peace to preserve the flow of interstate commerce. *NLRB* v. *Jones & Laughlin Steel Corp.*, . . . Central to achievement of this purpose is the promotion of collective bargaining as a method of defusing and channeling conflict between labor and management. § 1 of the Act, as amended, 29 U.S.C. § 151. Congress ensured that collective bargaining would go forward by creating the Board and giving it the power to condemn as unfair labor practices certain conduct by unions and employers that it deemed deleterious to the process, including the refusal "to bargain collectively.". . .

Although parties are free to bargain about any legal subject, Congress has limited the mandate or duty to bargain to matters of "wages, hours, and other terms and conditions of employment." A unilateral change as to a subject within this category violates the statutory duty to bargain and is subject to the Board's remedial order. *NLRB v. Katz*. . . . Conversely, both employer and union may bargain to impasse over these matters and use the economic weapons at their disposal to attempt to secure their respective aims. *NLRB v. American National Ins. Co.* . . . Congress deliberately left the words "wages, hours, and other terms and conditions of employment" without further definition, for it did not intend to deprive the Board of the power further to define those terms in light of specific industrial practices.

Nonetheless, in establishing what issues must be submitted to the process of bargaining, Congress had no expectation that the elected union representative would become an equal partner in the running of the business enterprise in which the union's members are employed. Despite the deliberate open-endedness of the statutory language, there is an undeniable limit to the subjects about which bargaining must take place:

> "Section 8(a) of the Act, of course, does not immutably fix a list of subjects for mandatory bargaining. . . . But it does establish a limitation against which proposed topics must be measured. In general terms, the limitation includes only issues that settle an aspect of the relationship between the employer and the employees.". . .

Some management decisions, such as choice of advertising and promotion, product type and design, and financing arrangements, have only an indirect and attenuated impact on the employment relationship. See *Fibreboard*, . . . (Stewart, J., concurring). Other management decisions, such as the order of succession of layoffs and recalls, production quotas, and work rules, are almost exclusively "an aspect of the relationship" between employer and employee. *Chemical Workers*, . . . The present case concerns a third type of management decision, one that had a direct impact on employment, since jobs were inexorably eliminated by the termination, but had as its focus only the economic profitability of the contract with Greenpark, a concern under these facts wholly apart from the employment relationship. This decision, involving a change in the scope and direction of the enterprise, is akin to the decision whether to be in business at all, "not in [itself] primarily about conditions of employment, though the effect of the decision may be necessarily to terminate employment." *Fibreboard*, . . . At the same time, this decision touches on a matter of central and pressing concern to the union and its member employees: the possibility of continued employment and the retention of the employees' very jobs. . . .

Petitioner contends it had no duty to

bargain about its decision to terminate its operations at Greenpark. This contention requires that we determine whether the decision itself should be considered part of petitioner's retained freedom to manage its affairs unrelated to employment. The aim of labeling a matter a mandatory subject of bargaining, rather than simply permitting, but not requiring, bargaining, is to "promote the fundamental purpose of the Act by bringing a problem of vital concern to labor and management within the framework established by Congress as most conducive to industrial peace," *Fibreboard,* . . . The concept of mandatory bargaining is premised on the belief that collective discussions backed by the parties' economic weapons will result in decisions that are better for both management and labor and for society as a whole. . . . This will be true, however, only if the subject proposed for discussion is amenable to resolution through the bargaining process. Management must be free from the constraints of the bargaining process to the extent essential for the running of a profitable business. It also must have some degree of certainty beforehand as to when it may proceed to reach decisions without fear of later evaluations labeling its conduct an unfair labor practice. Congress did not explicitly state what issues of mutual concern to union and management it intended to exclude from mandatory bargaining. Nonetheless, in view of an employer's need for unencumbered decisionmaking, bargaining over management decisions that have a substantial impact on the continued availability of employment should be required only if the benefit, for labor-management relations and the collective-bargaining process, outweighs the burden placed on the conduct of the business.

The Court in *Fibreboard* implicitly engaged in this analysis with regard to a decision to subcontract for maintenance work previously done by unit employees. . . .

> "The Company's decision to contract out the maintenance work did not alter the Company's basic operation. The maintenance work still had to be performed in the plant. No capital investment was contemplated; the Company merely replaced existing employees with those of an independent contractor to do the same work under similar conditions of employment. Therefore, to require the employer to bargain about the matter would not significantly abridge his freedom to manage the business." . . .

The Court also emphasized that a desire to reduce labor costs, which it considered a matter "peculiarly suitable for resolution within the collective bargaining framework," . . . was at the base of the employer's decision to subcontract. . . .

III

A Both union and management regard control of the decision to shut down an operation with the utmost seriousness. As has been noted, however, the Act is not intended to serve either party's individual interest, but to foster in a neutral manner a system in which the conflict between these interests may be resolved. It seems particularly important, therefore, to consider whether requiring bargaining over this sort of decision will advance the neutral purposes of the Act.

A union's interest in participating in the decision to close a particular facility or part of an employer's operations springs from its legitimate concern over job security. The Court has observed: "The words of [§ 8(d)] . . . plainly cover termination of employment which . . . necessarily results" from closing an operation. *Fibreboard,* . . . The union's practical purpose in participating, however, will be largely uniform: it will seek to delay or halt the closing. No doubt it will be impelled, in seeking these ends, to offer concessions, information, and alternatives that might be helpful to management or forestall or prevent the termination of jobs. It is unlikely, however, that requiring bargaining over the decision itself, as well as its effects, will augment this flow of information and suggestions. There is no dispute that the union must be given a significant opportunity to bargain about these matters of job security as part of the "effects" bargaining mandated by § 8(a)(5). . . . And, under § 8(a)(5), bargaining over the effects of a decision must be conducted in a meaningful manner and at a meaningful time, and the Board may impose sanctions to insure its adequacy. A union, by pursuing such bargaining rights, may achieve valuable concessions from an employer engaged in a partial closing. It also may secure in contract negotiations provisions implementing rights to notice, information, and fair bargaining. . . .

Moreover, the union's legitimate interest in fair dealing is protected by § 8(a)(3), which prohibits partial closings motivated by antiunion animus, when done to gain an unfair advantage. *Textile Workers* v. *Darlington Co.*, . . . Under § 8(a)(3) the Board may inquire into the motivations behind a partial closing. An employer may not simply shut down part of its business and mask its desire to weaken and circumvent the union by labeling its decision "purely economic."

Thus, although the union has a natural concern that a partial closing decision not be hastily or unnecessarily entered into, it has some control over the effects of the decision and indirectly may ensure that the decision itself is deliberately considered. It also has direct protection against a partial closing decision that is motivated by an intent to harm a union.

Management's interest in whether it should discuss a decision of this kind is much more complex and varies with the particular circumstances. If labor costs are an important factor in a failing operation and the decision to close, management will have an incentive to confer voluntarily with the union to seek concessions that may make continuing the business profitable. . . . (UAW agreement with Chrysler Corp. to make concessions on wages and fringe benefits). At other times, management may have great need for speed, flexibility, and secrecy in meeting business opportunities and exigencies. It may face significant tax or securities consequences that hinge on confidentiality, the timing of a plant closing, or a reorganization of the corporate structure. The publicity incident to the normal process of bargaining may injure the possibility of a successful transition or increase the economic damage to the business. The employer also may have no feasible alternative to the closing, and even good-faith bargaining over it may both be futile and cause the employer additional loss.

There is an important difference, also, between permitted bargaining and mandated bargaining. Labeling this type of decision mandatory could afford a union a powerful tool for achieving delay, a power that might be used to thwart management's intentions in a manner unrelated to any feasible solution the union might propose. . . .

While evidence of current labor practice is only an indication of what is feasible through collective bargaining, and not a binding guide, . . . that evidence supports the apparent imbalance weighing against mandatory bargaining. We note that provisions giving unions a right to participate in the decisionmaking process concerning alteration of the scope of an enterprise appear to be relatively rare. Provisions concerning notice and "effects" bargaining are more prevalent. . . . (charting provisions giving interplant transfer and relocation allowances; advance notice of layoffs, shutdowns, and technological changes; and wage-employment guarantees; no separate tables on decision-bargaining, presumably due to rarity). . . .

Further, the presumption analysis adopted by the Court of Appeals seems ill-suited to advance harmonious relations between employer and employee. An employer would have difficulty determining beforehand whether it was faced with a situation requiring bargaining or one that involved economic necessity sufficiently compelling to obviate the duty to bargain. If it should decide to risk not bargaining, it might be faced ultimately with harsh remedies forcing it to pay large amounts of backpay to employees who likely would have been discharged regardless of bargaining, or even to consider reopening a failing operation. . . . A union, too, would have difficulty determining the limits of its prerogatives, whether and when it could use its economic powers to try to alter an employer's decision, or whether, in doing so, it would trigger sanctions from the Board. . . .

We conclude that the harm likely to be done to an employer's need to operate freely in deciding whether to shut down part of its business purely for economic reasons outweighs the incremental benefit that might be gained through the union's participation in making the decision, and we hold that the decision itself is *not* part of § 8(d)'s "terms and conditions," . . . over which Congress has mandated bargaining.

B In order to illustrate the limits of our holding, we turn again to the specific facts of this case. First, we note that when petitioner decided to terminate its Greenpark contract, it had no intention to replace the discharged employees or to move that operation elsewhere. Petitioner's sole purpose was to reduce its economic loss, and the union made no claim of antiunion animus. . . . Further, the union was not selected as the bargaining representative or certified until well after petitioner's economic difficulties at Greenpark had begun. We thus are not faced with an employer's abrogation of ongoing negotiations or an existing bargaining agreement. Finally, while petitioner's business enterprise did not involve the investment of large amounts of capital in single locations, we do not believe that the absence of "significant investment or withdrawal of capital," . . . is crucial. The decision to halt work at this specific location represented a significant change in petitioner's operations, a change not unlike opening a new line of business or going out of business entirely.

The judgment of the Court of Appeals, accordingly, is reversed. . . .

JUSTICE BRENNAN, *with whom* JUSTICE MARSHALL *joins, dissenting.*

. . . As the Court today admits, the decision to close an operation "touches on a matter of central and pressing concern to the union and its member employees." . . . Moreover, as the Court today further concedes, Congress deliberately left the words "terms and conditions of employment" indefinite, so that the NLRB would be able to give content to those terms in light of changing industrial conditions. . . . In the exercise of its congressionally delegated authority and accumulated expertise, the Board has determined that an employer's decision to close part of its operations affects the "terms and conditions of employment" within the meaning of the Act, and is thus a mandatory subject for collective bargaining. *Ozark Trailers, Inc.*, . . . Nonetheless, the Court today declines to defer to the Board's decision on this sensitive question of industrial relations, and on the basis of pure speculation reverses the judgment of the Board and of the Court of Appeals. I respectfully dissent.

The Court bases its decision on a balancing test. It states that "bargaining over management decisions that have a substantial impact on the continued availability of employment should be required only if the benefit, for labor-management relations and the collective-bargaining process, outweighs the burden placed on the conduct of the business." . . . I cannot agree with this test, because it takes into account only the interests of *management;* it fails to consider the legitimate employment interests of the workers and their union. . . . (balancing of interests of workers in retaining their jobs against interests of employers in maintaining unhindered control over corporate direction). This one-sided approach hardly serves "to foster in a neutral manner" a system for resolution of these serious, two-sided controversies. . . .

Even if the Court's statement of the test were accurate, I could not join in its application, which is based solely on speculation. Apparently, the Court concludes that the benefit to labor-management relations and the collective-bargaining process from negotiation over partial closings is minimal, but it provides no evidence to that effect. The Court acknowledges that the union might be able to offer concessions, information, and alternatives that might obviate or forestall the closing, but it then asserts that "[i]t is unlikely, however, that requiring bargaining over the decision . . . will augment this flow of information and suggestions." . . . Recent experience, however, suggests the contrary. Most conspicuous, perhaps, were the negotiations between Chrysler Corporation and the United Auto Workers, which led to significant adjustments in compensation and benefits, contributing to Chrysler's ability to remain afloat. . . . Even where labor costs are not the direct cause of a company's financial difficulties, employee concessions can often enable the company to continue in operation — if the employees have the opportunity to offer such concessions.

The Court further presumes that management's need for "speed, flexibility, and secrecy" in making partial closing decisions would be frustrated by a requirement to bargain. . . . In some cases the Court might be correct. In others, however, the decision will be made openly and deliberately, and considerations of "speed, flexibility, and secrecy" will be inapposite. Indeed, in view of management's admitted duty to bargain over the effects of a closing, . . . it is difficult to understand why additional bargaining over the closing itself would necessarily unduly delay or publicize the decision.

I am not in a position to judge whether mandatory bargaining over partial closings *in all cases* is consistent with our national labor policy, and neither is the Court. The primary responsibility to determine the scope of the statutory duty to bargain has been entrusted to the NLRB, which should not be reversed by the courts merely because they might prefer another view of the statute. . . . I therefore agree with the Court of Appeals that employers presumptively have a duty to bargain over a decision to close an operation, and that this presumption can be rebutted by a showing that bargaining would be futile, that the closing was due to emergency financial circumstances, or that, for some other reason, bargaining would not further the purposes of the National Labor Relations Act. . . .

Notes and Questions

1. The Court ruled that in general companies need not bargain about the *decision* to totally or partially close a portion of its business when there is economic justification for it, but it must bargain over the *effects* of the decision. How does this distinction between *the decision* and *effects* of the decision affect workers?
2. Should the phrase "wages, hours and other terms and conditions of employment" be broad enough to include bargaining about total or partial plant closings?
3. If there is to be no "equal partnership" between unions and managers, what is the relationship to be? Without equality, what are the prospects of bringing about labor peace through collective bargaining?
4. After the *Fibreboard* and *First National Maintenance* decisions, is it fair to say that the more important a question is to worker welfare, the less likely it is to be considered by the courts as a mandatory subject for collective bargaining?
5. Given the limits of collective bargaining, what is the future role of unions? Since only 25 percent of the work force of the United States is unionized (apart from France, the lowest percentage in the industrialized world), what is the role of nonunion workers in setting the terms and conditions of their employment? How is their position different from that of Catherine Cassidy described in the case of *Thornton* v. *Suffolk Manufacturing*?
6. Return to the contention that early organizational forms appear under different guises at a later time. What perennial themes do you see being replayed through the conflict over the scope of collective bargaining?
7. In a slightly earlier case, *Yeshiva* v. *NLRB*, the U.S. Supreme Court had before it the question of whether teachers in a private university could unionize. The Court ruled that they could not, because supervisory personnel are excluded from statutes permitting unionization and collective bargaining. The Court contrasted faculty with workers in industry, stating that collective bargaining "was intended to accommodate the type of management-employee relations that prevail in the

pyramidal hierarchies of private industries." In short, university professors are too unlike work forces at the bottom of industrial organizations, and their privileged position made unionization inapt. Although the decision was about teachers, it said as much about the organizational place of "ordinary" workers in industry.

Local 1330, United Steelworkers v. U.S. Steel

631 F.2d 1264 (1980)

EDWARDS, CHIEF JUDGE.

This appeal represents a cry for help from steelworkers and townspeople in the City of Youngstown, Ohio who are distressed by the prospective impact upon their lives and their city of the closing of two large steel mills. These two mills were built and have been operated by the United States Steel Corporation since the turn of the century. The Ohio Works began producing in 1901; the McDonald Works in 1918. The District Court which heard this cause of action found that as of the notice of closing, the two plants employed 3,500 employees.

The leading plaintiffs are two labor organizations, Locals 1330 and 1307 of the United Steelworkers of America. This union has had a collective bargaining contract with the United States Steel Corporation for many years. These local unions represent production and maintenance employees at the Ohio and McDonald Works, respectively.

In the background of this litigation is the obsolescence of the two plants concerned, occasioned both by the age of the facilities and machinery involved and by the changes in technology and marketing in steelmaking in the years intervening since the early nineteen hundreds.

For all of the years United States Steel has been operating in Youngstown, it has been a dominant factor in the lives of its thousands of employees and their families, and in the life of the city itself. The contemplated abrupt departure of United States Steel from Youngstown will, of course, have direct impact on 3,500 workers and their families. It will doubtless mean a devastating blow to them, to the business community and to the City of Youngstown itself. While we cannot read the future of Youngstown from this record, what the record does indicate clearly is that we deal with an economic tragedy of major proportion to Youngstown and Ohio's Mahoning Valley. As the District Judge who heard this case put the matter:

> Everything that has happened in the Mahoning Valley has been happening for many years because of steel. Schools have been built, roads have been built. Expansion that has taken place is because of steel. And to accommodate that industry, lives and destinies of the inhabitants of that community were based and planned on the basis of that institution: Steel.

In the face of this tragedy, the steelworker local unions, the Congressman from this district, and the Attorney General of Ohio have sued United States Steel Corporation, asking the federal courts to order the United States Steel Corporation to keep the two plants at issue in operation. Alternatively, if they could not legally prevail on that issue, they have sought intervention of the courts by injunction to require the United States Steel Corporation to sell the two plants to the plaintiffs under an as yet tentative plan of purchase and operation by a community corporation and to restrain the piecemeal sale or dismantling of the plants until such a proposal could be brought to fruition.

Defendant United States Steel Corporation answered plaintiff's complaints, claiming that the plants were unprofitable and could not be made otherwise due to obsolescence and change in technology, markets, and transportation. The company also asserts an absolute right to make a business decision to discharge its former employees and abandon Youngstown. It states that there is no law in either the State of Ohio or the United States of America which provides either legal or equitable remedy for plaintiffs.

The District Judge, after originally restraining the corporation from ceasing operations as it had announced it would, and after advancing the case for prompt hearing, entered a formal opinion holding that the plants had become unprofitable and denying all relief. We believe the dispositive paragraphs . . . are the following:

> This Court has spent many hours searching for a way to cut to the heart of the economic reality — that obsolescence and market forces demand the close of the Mahoning Valley plants, and yet the lives of 3500 workers and their families and the supporting Youngstown community cannot be dismissed as inconsequential. United States Steel should not be permitted to leave the Youngstown area devastated after drawing from the lifeblood of the community for so many years.
>
> Unfortunately, the mechanism to reach this ideal settlement, to recognize this new property right, is not now in existence in the code of laws of our nation.
>
> * * *
>
> This Court is mindful of the efforts taken by the workers to increase productivity, and has applauded these efforts in the preceding paragraphs. In view of the fact, however, that this Court has found that no contract or enforceable promise was entered into by the company and that, additionally, there is clear evidence to support the company's decision that the plants were not profitable, the various acts of forebearance taken by the plaintiffs do not give them the basis for relief against defendant. . . .

I. THE CAUSE OF ACTION . . .

The primary issue in this case is a claim on the part of the steel worker plaintiffs that United States Steel made proposals to the plaintiffs and/or the membership of the plaintiffs to the general effect that if the workers at the two steel plants concerned put forth their best efforts in terms of productivity and thereby rendered the two plants "profitable," the plants would then not be closed. It is clear that this claimed contract does not rest upon any formal written document, either authorized or signed by the parties to this lawsuit.

Plaintiffs themselves recognize that they cannot rely upon any formal contract law. Nonetheless, in this section we shall discuss relationships between the parties which plaintiffs have not raised in order to place their issues in proper context.

As noted above, the steelworkers have a formal collective bargaining contract with the U.S. Steel Corporation. In this record there is no indication that there ever was any formal negotiation or amendment of that contract in relation to the issues of this case. Further, there is no indication in this record that the contract alleged in this complaint could be the subject for arbitration under Section 8(A)(2) of the Steelworkers Agreement of August 1, 1977:

> The Board shall have jurisdiction and authority only to interpret, apply, or determine compliance with the provisions of this Agreement and such local working conditions as may hereafter be in effect in the plants of the Company, insofar as shall be necessary to the determination of grievances appealed to the Board. The Board shall not have jurisdiction or authority to add to, detract from, or alter in any way the provisions of this Agreement.

Nor is there any indication in this appellate record that the claimed contract ever was made a subject for arbitration. . . .

The collective bargaining agreement applicable in this period also contains three sections which management asserts bear directly upon its claim of unilateral right to close any plant. . . .

> *Section 3 — Management*
>
> The Company retains the exclusive rights to manage the business and plants and to direct the working forces. The Company, in the exercise of its rights, shall observe the provisions of this Agreement.
>
> The rights to manage the business and plants and to direct the working forces include the right to hire, suspend or discharge for proper cause, or transfer and the right to relieve employees from duty because of lack of work or for other legitimate reasons.

More directly applicable to the present case is Section 16 entitled "Severance Allowance." . . .

> *Section 16 — Severance Allowance*
>
> A. Conditions of Allowance
>
> When, in the sole judgment of the Company, it decides to close permanently a plant or discontinue permanently a department of a plant or substantial portion thereof and terminate the employment of individuals, an employee whose employment is terminated either directly or indirectly as a result thereof because he was not entitled to other employment with the Company. . . . shall be entitled to a severance allowance. . . .
>
> B. Eligibility
>
> Such an employee to be eligible for a severance allowance shall have accumulated three or more years of continuous Company service. . . .
>
> 1. In lieu of severance allowance, the Company may offer an eligible employee a job, in at least the same job class for which he is qualified, in the same general locality. The employee shall have the option of either accepting such new employment or requesting his severance allowance. . . .
>
> C. Scale of Allowance
>
> An eligible individual shall receive severance allowance based upon the following weeks for the corresponding continuous Company service.
>
> | *Continuous Company Service* | *Weeks of Severance Allowance* |
> |---|---|
> | 3 years but less than 5 years | 4 |
> | 5 years but less than 7 years | 6 |
> | 7 years but less than 10 years | 7 |
> | 10 years or more | 8 |
>
> . . . .
>
> G. Payment of Allowance
>
> Payment shall be made in a lump sum at the time of termination. Acceptance of severance allowance shall terminate employment. . . .

The contract from which we have been quoting is dated August 1, 1977, and provides for termination 60 days after written notice by either party, "but in any event shall not terminate earlier than August 1, 1980.". . .

We are unable to construe any claims set forth in the instant litigation as being based upon any language contained in this collective bargaining agreement. Indeed, plaintiffs make no claim in this case that the United States Steel Corporation has violated the provisions of this section (or any section) of the collective bargaining agreement.

The defendant company also claims that plaintiffs' reliance upon any oral contract is defeated by Section 2-B of the contract entitled "Local Working Conditions." Paragraph 5 thereof provides:

> No local working condition shall hereafter be established or agreed to which changes or modifies any of the provisions of this Agreement, except as it is approved in writing by an International Officer of the Union and the Personnel Services Executive of the Company.

It is clear that the approvals called for in the just quoted paragraph never occurred. . . .

The District Judge's rejection of any formal

legal contract claims was clearly mandated by both state and federal contract law. The lack of such features as a written document, authorization by the corporate Board of Directors and the Executive Boards of the steelworkers' national and local bodies . . . demonstrate that the minimum features of a formal legal contract are missing.

Appellant's principal argument in this appeal is, however, that the District Court should have found a contract based upon the equitable doctrine of promissory estoppel. . . .

II. PROMISSORY ESTOPPEL

The doctrine of promissory estoppel recognizes the possibility of the formation of a contract by action or forbearance. . . . Restatement (Second) of Contracts §90 (1932) states:

> A promise which the promisor should reasonably expect to induce action or forbearance of a definite and substantial character on the part of the promisee and which does induce such action or forbearance is binding if injustice can be avoided only by enforcement of the promise. . . .

Thus, appellants' contract claim depends essentially upon oral statements and newspaper releases concerning the efforts of the company to secure increased productivity by enlisting the help of the workers of the plant and upon the employee responses thereto. The representations as set forth in the steelworkers' complaint include many oral statements made over the "hotline" employed by management in the plants to advise U.S. Steel employees of company policy. They began in the Fall of 1977 in the midst of much public speculation that the Ohio and McDonald works at Youngstown were to be closed. . . .

. . . Plaintiffs' second amended complaint states the promises as follows:

"a. After a visit to the Ohio and McDonald Works by David Roderick, then President of Defendant United States Steel, in August 1977, William Ashton, then Superintendent of the Youngstown District for Defendant, on September 1, 1977, made the following statement over the intra-company or 'hot line' telephone to Defendant's Youngstown employees:

> "Hello, this is Bill Ashton.
>
> In response to many rumors, I want to tell you that there are no immediate plans to permanently shut down either the Ohio Works or McDonald Mills.
>
> However, steps will have to be taken to improve these plants' profitability. These steps, which have been and are currently under study, will require the suspension and consolidation of some operations in the months ahead.
>
> Ohio Works and McDonald Mills are faced with very serious profit problems caused by a combination of heavy imports of foreign steel, higher energy costs, higher taxes and, of course, environmental expenditures.
>
> The continued operation of these plants is absolutely dependent upon their being profit-makers.
>
> In the months ahead, we will be calling for the full support of each and every one of you. Your cooperation and assistance is absolutely necessary if our facilities are to continue to operate." . . .

"c. On or about January 3, 1978, Edgar Speer, then Chairman of the Board of United States Steel, was asked by a NEW YORK TIMES reporter whether at some point the Ohio and McDonald Works would have to be closed, and answered, 'Yup.' . . .

". . . [O]n January 4, 1978, William Kirwan, Superintendent of the Youngstown District for Defendant, made the following statements on the 'hot line':

> "Hello, this is Bill Kirwan talking, and I want to set the record straight on what you read in the paper concerning our facilities. Mr. Speer's comments yesterday, are essentially the same as the announcement made last September when the Company said there were *no immediate* plans to shut

> down the Youngstown operations. At that time United States Steel said that continued operation in Youngstown would depend on the plant's ability to become profitable. Since that time some progress *has* been made in reducing our losses. With your help, this effort will continue and if and when there will be a phase-out depends on the plant's profitability, but no time table has been set. I intend to give this my best effort and I am confident you will too."
> "(Emphasis in original.) . . .

"g. At an undetermined date during the winter of 1977–78, J. Hepplewhite, an agent of Defendant, stated on the 'hot line':

> "The future of our continued operations at Youngstown is dependent upon our ability to be a profit maker. To achieve this end each of us must accept the challenge to be innovative and continue to produce quality products for our customers."

"h. On or about April 7, 1978, Mr. Kirwan stated on the 'hot line':

> "Hello, this is Bill Kirwan.
>
> I want to share the good news with all of you.
>
> In the month of March, for the first [time] in a long long time, the Youngstown Works earned a profit for the United States Steel Corporation.
>
> We didn't make a bundle, and we are still in the hole for the year, but this is the first indication that the changes in our operations, and our attitudes are turning the place around.
>
> While one month's profits doesn't solve our problems, it sure shows U.S. Steel, our customers and our families that the goal set for us *is* attainable.
>
> We got the orders and the opportunity to make April even a better month. Keep up the momentum — our future is what we make it."
>
> "(Emphasis in original.)

"i. On or about April 17, 1978, Mr. Kirwan stated to the press about the Youngstown District facilities, 'We'll be doing business here for some time to come.'

"j. On or about April 17, 1978, Mr. Walthius stated to the press about the Youngstown District facilities:

> "Company management has repeatedly said that the works will stay open if they become profitable. Well, now they are profitable."

"k. On November 8, 1978, Mr. Kirwan stated on the 'hot line':

> "Hello, this is Bill Kirwan.
>
> As you already know, by the grapevine, the chopper was in yesterday with the top executives of Eastern Steel. Visits are being made to all the plants to discuss problems facing us in 1979. On the basis of your performance so far this year our outlook is pretty good. . . .
>
> Improved productivity is almost entirely up to you. I am asking each of you to consider how you may help in keeping Youngstown the going plant it is today."

"l. On December 21, 1978, Mr. Kirwan stated on the 'hot line':

> "Hello, this is Bill Kirwan.
>
> You will recall that early in 1978 we initiated significant changes in our operations in order to make Youngstown Works profitable and once again a viable plant. Our efforts took many turns, but we have attained our 1978 goal which was 'survival' and now we embark on the 1979 goal which is 'revival.'
>
> I want to express my thanks to every man and woman employed at McDonald Mills and the Ohio Works for your efforts and contributions to this success. Ed Speer has always said that Youngstown Works has the best bunch of steelworkers in the business. I couldn't say it any better myself. . . ."

"n. On or about May 2, 1979, Mr. Kirwan stated to the press about the Youngstown District facilities:

> "Ten years down the road that may be different, maybe even three years. . . . But we currently have an operation here that's been going profitably since the early part of 1978. . . ."

"o. On or about June 5, 1979, the press attributed to Mr. Kirwan the statement that the Youngstown District finished 1978 in the black and even managed to win a profitability contest against U.S. Steel's much-newer plant in Baytown, Texas, which produces many of the same kinds of products.

"p. On or about June 18, 1979, David Roderick, Chairman of the Board of United States Steel, stated to the press and on ABC television:

> "Simply stated, we have no plans for shutting down our Youngstown operation.
>
> Only two things would result in a Youngstown shutdown: [massive expenditures to meet environmental requirements of [sic] [or?] an unproductive plant operation.]
>
> The Youngstown plant is profitable. We're operating in the black there." . . .

> [The union then listed many issues that had arisen due to the responses and actions taken in order to make the plants profitable. These issues ranged from reduction of janitorial service, nonmaintenance of equipment, and not insisting on safety measures.]

"b. Because of Defendant's promise and in detrimental reliance thereon, Defendant Youngstown employees immediately began to work harder and to increase their productivity. The results were evident as early as October 1977, when, for the first time in 1977 according to the method of accounting employed by Defendant, the Youngstown District made a monthly profit. Defendant's Manager of Accounting for the Youngstown District reported:

> "In October, Youngstown made a *profit* of $34. The importance of this profit can only properly be comprehended if the odds against it, at this level of operations, are clearly understood. The break-even point on October's fixed expenses of $3828 ($3178 Fixed and $650 SG & A) is 74,400 tons. . . . October's shipments of 51,283 tons were 23,100 tons below the break-even point, and therefore, only extraordinary performance variance achievements from hot metal through primary rolling drove the actual variable cost. . . . to $273 per ton below the Standard variable cost of $297. . . .
>
> ". . . The Ohio Works variance is the most favorable variance performance achieved since May, 1975. . . .
>
> ". . . If Youngstown is judged strictly on its own fixed expense, October's profit would have been $1,408, and the year to date loss would be reduced from the Profit Contribution reports' $19,421 to $4,947."
>
> "(Emphasis in original.)

"c. In further illustration of the action and forbearance induced by Defendant's promise, in detrimental reliance thereon, on March 8, 1978 Mr. Kirwan stated on the 'hot line':

> "The Ohio Works is hosting the Corporation's Steel Producing Conference on March 9th and 10th. Representatives from other U.S. Steel Plants will be here to discuss new steel producing projects and to look at our operations. Many improvements have been made to our Open Hearth and through *the outstanding efforts of our personnel, Youngstown's productivity gains are second to none. . . .*"
>
> "(Emphasis added.)

"d. . . . [O]n May 12, 1978 Mr. Kirwan stated on the 'hot line':

> "Hello, this is Bill Kirwan.
>
> Congratulations! For the second month in a row, I am happy to report that, due to your outstanding performances, Youngstown

> Works has, again, been a profitable steel plant.
>
> In April the Blast Furnace Department set a new monthly record and the crews on # 51 Open Hearth did the same. All of you kept on top of your individual assignments and the result is most gratifying. . . ."

"e. In further illustration of the action and forbearance induced by Defendant's promise, in detrimental reliance thereon, on June 1, 1978 Norm Waite, an agent of Defendant, stated on the 'hot line':

> "Hello, this is Norm Waite.
>
> I'm very happy to report that for the second month in a row my crew in the Blast Furnace Department has set a monthly production record. This has been accomplished primarily through an improvement in the burden and some innovative operating techniques on their part.
>
> . . . We're trying everything to keep Youngstown District and U.S. Steel profitable." . . .

"g. Because of Defendant's promise and in detrimental reliance thereon, Plaintiff Locals agreed to combine into one seniority list the machinists at the Ohio and McDonald Works. This negotiated understanding was embodied in a "Special Seniority Agreement Covering Craftsman Of McDonald Mills Machine Shop," signed by Charles L. Richards, Superintendent-Employee Relations for Defendant, and Marvin Weinstock, Staff Representative, United Steelworkers of America, and dated December 14, 1978. A similar understanding was negotiated for Boiler Shop employees in the two mills. . . .

"i. . . . [O]n or about June 5, 1979 Mr. Kirwan stated to the press that anxiety about the future of the Youngstown District had generated what he termed 'a nonadversarial relationship' between management and the work force.

"j. Because of Defendant's promise and in detrimental reliance thereon, in August 1979 President Reno DePietro of Plaintiff Local 1307 and grievance committeeman Michael Mignogna met with David Houck, an agent of Defendant, to consider how to improve the profitability of the 12 mill at the McDonald Works. Defendant shut down the 12 mill so that DiPietro and Mignogna could meet the crews in the company conference room. De Pietro and Mignogna relayed the message from management that if the mills could be kept profitable, they would stay open, and urged the men to work more efficiently. The men told their union representatives about problems in the 12 mill which impeded their work. In September 1979, DePietro and Mignogna met with Will McCorckle and George Benkey, agents of Defendant to discuss the status of the 12 mill. Benkey reported that attitudes were better and production was up. . . .

[The union contended that it gave up valuable contractual rights regarding layoffs, rescheduling of workers, and work rules.]

"n. Action and forbearance as described, *supra,* was continuously induced by Defendant through social occasions sponsored by Youngstown District management. In May 1979, newly elected officers of Plaintiff Locals and Youngstown District supervisors were convened at the Mahoning County Country Club, 700 E. Liberty Street, Girard, Ohio, for an affair known as 'A Beer With The Boss.' Mr. Kirwan addressed the group. He described planned improvements in the Sinter Plant and the installation of a new coiler in the 18 mill. He predicted a steel shortage in the mid-1980's and an opportunity at that time for the Youngstown District to make the capital investment needed for long term viability. In answer to a question from President Vasquez of Plaintiff Local 1330, Mr. Kirwan stated that the investment he had in mind was $250 million for electric furnaces and a continuous caster at the McDonald Works. He also stated that the mills were presently profitable and that the men should keep up their good work. In September 1979, Burning Yard employees were invited to dinner at Sokol Center Restaurant, 850 E. Midlothian Avenue, Youngstown, Ohio, where Mr. Kirwan and Mr. Tkatch congratulated them and told them they had saved their jobs.

"12. Also in detrimental reliance on Defendant's promise, individual Plaintiffs, or some of them, gave up opportunities to take other employment and committed themselves to major, long-term expenditures such as the purchase of homes. By way of illustration:

> "a. LeRoy Benson, 455 Utah Avenue, McDonald, Ohio 44437, the first-named individual Plaintiff, had been in the mill ten years as of June 1979. Since his pension became vested at that time he considered whether to seek other employment. His foreman, Thomas Augustine, advised him not to do so because he had a secure future with United States Steel. Accordingly, Mr. Benson gave up the idea of seeking work elsewhere, bought a car in July 1979, and on October 28, 1979 bought a home.
>
> "b. Frank Georges, R.D. 2, Hillsville Road, Lowelville, Ohio 44436, another individual Plaintiff, bought a new home on November 27, 1979, and heard the news of Defendant's shutdown announcement on the car radio as he drove home from the bank.
>
> "c. Michael Meser, 810 New York Avenue, McDonald, Ohio 44437, another individual Plaintiff, spent considerable time deciding where to send his son Mickey to college. After hearing David Roderick's statement on TV in June 1979, . . . Mr. Meser decided on Hiram College where tuition was $2,000 a year rather than Youngstown State University where Mickey could have gone tuition free. On the strength of Mr. Roderick's assurance Mr. Meser also decided to buy a new car which he had not done since 1956. On November 21, 1979, he took out a $4,000 loan from the employee credit union." . . .

As we read this lengthy record, and as the District Judge read it, it does not contain any factual dispute over the allegations as to company statements or the responsive actions of steelworkers in relation thereto. It is beyond argument that the local management of U.S. Steel's Youngstown plants engaged in a major campaign to enlist employee participation in an all-out effort to make these two plants profitable in order to prevent their being closed. It is equally obvious that the employees responded wholeheartedly.

The District Judge, however, rejected the promissory estoppel contract theory on three grounds. The first ground was that none of the statements made by officers and employees of the company constituted a definite promise to continue operation of the plants if they did become profitable. The second ground was that the statements relied upon by plaintiffs were made by employees and public relations officers of the company and not be company officers. The third ground was a finding of fact that "The condition precedent of the alleged contract and promise — profitability of the Youngstown facilities — was never fulfilled. . . ."

. . .

The District Judge's findings on profitability bear quotation in full:

> There is a second, independent ground for denying relief under the contract and detrimental reliance theories, and that is the failure of the condition precedent to defendant's liability — the profitability of the Mahoning Valley plants.
>
> Plaintiffs attempted to demonstrate profitability by defining minimum profitability as the "gross profit margin," which William R. Roesch, President and Chief Operating Officer of United States Steel, described as "the revenues minus the variable costs of performing the operation to produce the product." He admitted that "technically, if you are losing money at the gross margin operation, there is no way to make that operation profitable." Plaintiffs then turned to their exhibits 32 through 37, which were summary sheets of operating profitability for the Youngstown facilities for 1977, 1978, 1979, and 1980. These exhibits revealed that the gross profit margin for 1977 was $24,899,000.00, that for 1978 was $41,770,000.00, that for 1979 was $32,571,000.00 and that the projected gross profit margin for 1980, as of November 20, 1979, was $32,396,000.00.

These figures do indicate that at the variable-cost margin, the plant was, in a sense, profitable. It should be remembered, however, that even with the projected $32,396,000.00 gross profit margin projected for 1980, the *over-all* projection for the year was a loss of $9,387,000.00. This suggests that with a different definition of profit, especially one that would include fixed costs, the outcome of an accounting analysis could be made to be nonprofitability. Mr. Roesch testified that the gross profit margin "does not represent the profit of the operation," nor does it represent that the operation is necessarily profitable considered as a whole. He explained that "[t]here are other factors involved because, once you have the gross margin, you have to subtract the depreciation for the equipment which was involved and depreciate it over a period of time; you have to subtract the selling expenses which are necessary; and you have to subtract the administrative charges, the taxes, and so forth." He also explained that, because of the integrated system of the national corporation, many of the unseen costs of the Youngstown Works were absorbed by other plants and operations in the steel company. Mr. Roesch testified that it was primarily the obsolescence of the plant facilities that made the plant unprofitable.

The testimony of David Roderick, Chairman of the Board of Directors and Chief Executive Officer of United States Steel, confirmed Mr. Roesch's opinion. In answer to the question "And through the end of October, 1979, Youngstown [sic] the performance of that year was in the area of about the break even, was it not?" Mr. Roderick replied ". . . the actual number was about a $300 thousand loss, as of the end of October, cumulative for the year. And further, as I recall, they had lost money three out of the four months preceding it." Further, Mr. Roderick explained the opinion of the Board of Directors on the trend of the loss in this way:

> Well, what I really mean by an irreversible loss is based on our best judgment, or my best judgment, the loss would be incurred and there was nothing the plant could do to avoid that loss, that the market was working negatively and that it was our projection that the plant would lose money in five out of six months of the second half, that the loss for the year would be quite substantial in 1979, and with all the facts that we could see on the horizon for 1980, plus the actual performance for the second half of 1979, we felt there was no way that the loss trend could be reversed for the calendar year of 1980.

This Court is loath to exchange its own view of the parameters of profitability for that of the corporation. It is clear that there is little argument as to the production figures for the Youngstown mills — the controversy surrounds the interpretation of those figures. Plaintiffs read the figures in light of a gross profit margin analysis of minimum profitability. Defendant sees capital expenditure, fixed costs and technical obsolescence as essential ingredients of the notion of profitability. Perhaps if this Court were being asked to interpret the word "profit" in a written contract between plaintiffs and defendant, some choice would have to be made. Given the oral nature of the alleged promises in the case at bar and the obvious ambiguity of the statements made, this Court finds that there is a very reasonable basis on which it can be said that Youngstown facilities were not profitable. Further, plaintiffs have made no showing of bad faith on the part of the Board of Directors in the Board's determination of profitability, nor have they given any grounds to suggest that defendant's definition of profitability is an unrealistic or unreasonable one. The condition precedent of the alleged contract and promise — profitability of the Youngstown facilities — was never fulfilled, and the actions in contract and for detrimental reliance cannot be found for plaintiffs. . . .

. . . The plaintiffs wish to employ the direct costs of operating the two plants, compared to the total selling price of their products. The difference, they contend, is "profit." This formula would eliminate such charges as corporate purchasing and sales expense allocable to the Youngstown plants, and allocable corporate management expenses including, but not limited to marketing, engineering, auditing, accounting, advertising. Obviously, any multiplant corporation could quickly go bankrupt if such a definition of profit was employed generally and over any period of time.

Plaintiffs-appellants point out, however, that this version of Youngstown profitability was employed by the Youngstown management in setting a goal for its employees and in statements which described achieving that goal. . . .

[Appeal ct. agrees to the disallowance of the steelworkers argument.]

III. THE COMMUNITY PROPERTY CLAIM

At a pretrial hearing of this case on February 28, 1980, the District Judge made a statement at some length about the relationship between the parties to this case and the public interest involved therein. He said:

> Everything that has happened in the Mahoning Valley has been happening for many years because of steel. Schools have been built, roads have been built. Expansion that has taken place is because of steel. And to accommodate that industry, lives and destinies of the inhabitants of that community were based and planned on the basis of that institution: Steel.
>
> * * *
>
> We are talking about an institution, a large corporate institution that is virtually the reason for the existence of that segment of this nation [Youngstown]. Without it, that segment of this nation perhaps suffers, instantly and severely. Whether it becomes a ghost town or not, I don't know. I am not aware of its capability for adapting.
>
> * * *
>
> But what has happened over the years between U.S. Steel, Youngstown and the inhabitants? Hasn't something come out of that relationship, something that out of which — not reaching for a case on property law or a series of cases but looking at the law as a whole, the Constitution, the whole body of law, not only contract law, but tort, corporations, agency, negotiable instruments — . . . and then sitting back and reflecting on what it seeks to do, and that is to adjust human relationships in keeping with the whole spirit and foundation of the American system of law, to preserve property rights.
>
> * * *
>
> It would seem to me that when we take a look at the whole body of American law and the principles we attempt to come out with — and although a legislature has not pronounced any laws with respect to such a property right, that is not to suggest that there will not be a need for such a law in the future dealing with similar situations — *it seems to me that a property right has arisen from this lengthy, long-established relationship between United States Steel, the steel industry as an institution, the community in Youngstown, the people in Mahoning County and the Mahoning Valley in having given and devoted their lives to this industry.* Perhaps not a property right to the extent that can be remedied by compelling U.S. Steel to remain in Youngstown. But *I think the law can recognize the property right to the extent that U.S. Steel cannot leave that Mahoning Valley and the Youngstown area in a state of waste, that it cannot completely abandon its obligation to that community, because certain vested rights have arisen out of this long relationship and institution.*

Subsequently thereto, steelworkers' complaint was amended . . . asserting as follows:

> 52. A property right has arisen from the long-established relation between the community of the 19th Congressional District and Plaintiffs, on the one hand, and Defendant on the other hand, which this Court can enforce.

> 53. This right, in the nature of an easement, requires that Defendant:
> a. Assist in the preservation of the institution of steel in that community;
> b. Figure into its cost of withdrawing and closing the Ohio and McDonald Works the cost of rehabilitating the community and the workers;
> c. Be restrained from leaving the Mahoning Valley in a state of waste and from abandoning its obligation to that community.

This court has examined these allegations with care and with great sympathy for the community interest reflected therein. Our problem in dealing with plaintiffs' fourth cause of action is one of authority. Neither in brief nor oral argument have plaintiffs pointed to any constitutional provision contained in either the Constitution of the United States or the Constitution of the State of Ohio, nor any law enacted by the United States Congress or the Legislature of Ohio, nor any case decided by the courts of either of these jurisdictions which would convey authority to this court to require the United States Steel Corporation to continue operations in Youngstown which its officers and Board of Directors had decided to discontinue on the basis of unprofitability.

This court has in fact dealt with this specific issue in *Charland* v. *Norge Division, Borg-Warner Corp.* . . . The case was, as appellants point out, substantially different from the present complaint in that there was a single individual plaintiff involved. He was, however, one of many Norge employees who had been thrown out of work by the removal of the Norge Muskegon Heights plant to Fort Smith, Arkansas. As is true in this case, there was a union contractual agreement for very limited severance pay. The union at the Norge plant is Muskegon Heights had succeeded in negotiating some severance pay and "very limited removal rights to Fort Smith." Appellant Charland refused to accept the union-negotiated removal agreement. We recite his position as follows:

> Appellant . . . tells us, in effect, I worked 30 years for defendant Norge. At the end I am thrown out of a job unless I move hundreds of miles to another city and start as a new employee behind hundreds of local residents and without either accumulated seniority or pension rights. In the alternative if I sign a complete release of all rights arising out of my job, I get $1,500. This is fundamentally unfair. And it is a deprivation of my property rights in my job in violation of Article V of the United States Constitution. . . .

This court's response to Charland's claims bears repetition here:

> Article V of the Constitution, of course, makes no mention of employment. But it (and the Fourteenth Amendment) does prohibit deprivation of property without due process of law. Thus appellant's assumption submits the fundamental question of whether or not there is a legally recognizable property right in a job which has been held for something approaching a lifetime.
>
> The claim presented by this appellant brings sharply into focus such problems as unemployment crises, the mobility of capital, technological change and the right of an industrial owner to go out of business. . . . Thus far federal law has sought to protect the human values to which appellant calls our attention by means of such legislation as unemployment compensation, . . . and social security laws, . . . These statutes afford limited financial protection to the individual worker, but they assume his loss of employment.
>
> Whatever the future may bring, neither by statute nor by court decision has appellant's claimed property right been recognized to date in this country. . . .

Appellants, however, cite and rely upon a decision of the Supreme Court of the United States, *Munn v. Illinois*, . . . claiming "that a corporation affected by the public interest, which seeks to take action injurious to that interest, may be restrained from doing so by the equitable powers of a court of law." This case does represent a fundamental statement of the power of the legislative branch of government over private business and private property. It pertained to the question as to whether or not the General Assembly of Illinois could, within the federal commerce clause and the due process clause of the Federal Constitution, "Fix by law the maximum of charges for the storage of grain in warehouses at Chicago and other places in the State having not less than one hundred thousand inhabitants." Justice Waite held that no federal constitutional principle was violated by the state legislative enactment.

The case is undoubtedly important precedent establishing power on the part of state legislatures to regulate private property (particularly public utilities) in the public interest. It cannot, however, properly be cited for holding that federal courts have such legislative power in their own hands.

We recognize that plaintiffs rely upon one sentence: "So, too, in matters which do affect the public interest, and as to which legislative control may be exercised, if there are no statutory regulations upon the subject, the courts must determine what is reasonable. The controlling fact is the power to regulate at all. If that exists, the right to establish the maximum of charge, as one of the means of regulation, is implied." . . . This dictum was laid down in connection with an enterprise which the court treated as essentially a public utility. We find no ground to extend it to assert judicial power to order a steel manufacturing corporation to continue the operation of two plants which it (and a District Court on competent evidence) have found to be unprofitable.

The problem of plant closing and plant removal from one section of the country to another is by no means new in American history. The former mill towns of New England, with their empty textile factory buildings, are monuments to the migration of textile manufacturers to the South, without hindrance from the Congress of the United States, from the legislatures of the states concerned, or, for that matter, from the courts of the land.

In the view of this court, formulation of public policy on the great issues involved in plant closings and removals is clearly the responsibility of the legislatures of the states or of the Congress of the United States. . . .

We find no legal basis for judicial relief as to appellants' fourth cause of action.

IV. THE ANTITRUST CLAIM

Finally, appellants contend that the United States Steel Corporation has violated federal antitrust laws, 15 U.S.C. § 1 *et seq.* (1976). The essence of the antitrust complaint is that defendant United States Steel Corporation has refused to sell to the plaintiffs the Ohio and McDonald works which it seeks to abandon. Plaintiffs claim defendant has thus "exercised monopoly power" for the purpose of preventing a potential competitor from entering the steel market.

> Steelworkers' reply brief contends that:
>
> U.S. Steel has now four times refused to deal with Steelworkers: first, when Chairman of the Board Roderick stated on January 31, 1980, in response to a question about Steelworkers' hope of buying the Youngstown Works, that the company would not sell to a subsidized competitor; second, when a representative of U.S. Steel's Realty Division told Steelworkers on February 14, 1980, that the property was not for sale to them; third, when Mr. Roderick testified to the same effect, and fourth, when Mr. Roderick formally communicated this position to Steelworkers by letter of April 18, 1980 . . .

Steelworkers also contend on this issue that they have been denied their day in court on their antitrust claim.

Out of perhaps an excess of caution, we

vacate the District Court judgment dismissing appellants' antitrust claim. We agree with the District Judge that as of the date of his order dismissing this aspect of the complaint, he did not have before him any binding offer to purchase the Youngstown plants of United States Steel. Appellants contend, however, that they were caught by surprise by the District Judge's sudden demand for their antitrust proofs or in lieu thereof a complete offer to prove the existence or early prospect of such an offer. They also argue, in effect, that the District Judge did not take into account their contention that the antitrust violation they charge against United States Steel — the public announcement by its President of a flat refusal to sell to any "subsidized" purchasers — helped make impossible the formulation of such an offer.

United States Steel's implied claim that it can, consistent with federal antitrust laws, refuse to do business with a corporation which has been aided, directly or indirectly by the United States government through the operation of duly adopted law, is unique in this court's experience. Nor has our research served to date to disclose any legal precedent for such a position. The ramifications of this refusal would be far-reaching. Could United States Steel, in the event the Chrysler Corporation sought to manufacture some portion of its own steel needs, refuse to sell steel to that corporation because of the massive aid which the federal government has seen fit to supply to Chrysler? These questions are not ones which this court is in a position to answer on this record. The issue as to whether or not there has been a flat refusal to deal with plaintiffs on the basis alleged should be the subject of trial testimony. The antitrust issue which we perceive as arguable should be the subject of briefing, argument and trial court decision before consideration by this court.

Summary judgment in antitrust matters is not favored absent a clarity of fact and law not apparent here. . . .

The judgment previously entered by the District Court is affirmed in all respects except as to plaintiffs-appellants' antitrust claim. . . .

APPENDIX A

Congressional Record: Proceedings and Debates of the 96th Congress, First Session . . . July 31, 1979 . . . (Senate)

By MR. RIEGLE:

S. 1608. A bill to require business concerns which undertake changes of operations to give notice to the Secretary of Labor, and to affected labor organizations, employees, and local governments; to require business concerns to provide assistance to employees who suffer an employment loss caused by changes of operations; to authorize the Secretary of Labor to provide assistance to such business concerns, and to such affected employees and local governments, and for other purposes; to the Committee on Labor and Human Resources.

[This bill was not passed. — Ed.]

Notes and Questions

1. As you read the communications made by management to the steelworkers, do you believe that U.S. Steel made promises that would induce reliance by the workers? If not creating a legally enforceable obligation, was the company accepting an ethical duty? What would either a legal or ethical duty have required?
2. There is a dispute in the case about profits and when an operation is profitable. The first test, adopted by U.S. Steel and accepted by the court, is that a plant is profitable when all costs that can be fairly attributable to that plant have been met.

   The steelworkers' union made a different argument, based on the idea that it may be profitable to operate a plant so long as the variable costs are met; i.e., once a plant is in place, it may pay to operate that plant so long as the costs that would not be saved by shutting down — current wages, for example — are met. Revenues beyond such costs would amount to a partial return on fixed investments, which would be totally lost were production to be terminated.

   Should the court have presumed that the

company's financial conclusions were correct, or should it have made its own determinations, such as a consideration of the argument by the union that it is economical to operate plants for whole or partial return of sunk costs?

3. Does a worker have a property right to a job? When a worker says "my job," what does he or she mean? Does a company owe older workers anything beyond severance pay and vested pensions? Does a company owe anything to a community where it has been located for a long time?

   When a company is operating, does it expect local government, schools, and the community to be helpful and to render concrete services to it? What does it owe in return, besides taxes?

4. What made U.S. Steel so reluctant to sell a business that by its own expert judgment was beyond chances of profitability? Should antitrust laws reach this foreclosure of potential competition?

5. For a decade, the U.S. Congress had a number of proposals on plant closings and the flight of capital to the Third World. Legislation provided federal assistance to workers whose jobs are lost through international competition, and in 1988, after a veto by President Reagan, Congress finally passed a trade bill containing a requirement specifying that employers give 60 days' notice of a plant closing. The decision to operate or close a plant has been otherwise unaffected by this legislation.

6. After having read something about the organization of plantation slavery; early industry; the scope of collective bargaining, and the efforts of work forces to affect plant closings and runaway corporations; what can you say about the relationships of law to power, economy, and organization?

6 LAW AND POPULAR WILL

The Chief Magistrate derives all of his authority from the people.

Abraham Lincoln, First Inaugural Address (1861)

. . . that this nation, under God, shall have a new birth of freedom — and that government of the people, by the people and for the people shall not perish from the earth.

Abraham Lincoln, Gettysburg Address (1863)

The people united, can never be defeated.

Kent State (1977)

In a period when alienation from virtually all institutions is proceeding swiftly, one begins to wonder when people might wake up and shake government and law off their backs. Those voters who have faith enough to cast periodic ballots labor under no illusion that their voting makes a grand difference. At most, it is often designed to "throw the bums out" rather than to usher in more compelling government or law.

There might have been less alienation in the nineteenth century when scholars took an interest in tracing the origin of law and the evolution of legal institutions. They believed that law evolved out of the customary practices of people. At first, practices occurred and unarticulated sentiments were felt in a group of people. There was no consciousness that certain activities were the *right* ones or the *only* ones that would be tolerated. After a time, and particularly on occasions of deviance from prior practice, *a* way of acting or behaving became *the* way of acting and behaving; what previously was customary had now become law.

Readers of the early literature are left with the idea that there is an organic connection between law and custom. Law grows out of custom, or in other words, custom contains embryonic law, practice on its way to becoming perfect — as soon as the appropriate level of consciousness has been reached. The materials on the Cheyenne that appear in this section suggest that the organic connection between the exercise of authority and custom is not wholly inaccurate, as did the case of the *Spoiled Chiles,* which appeared in Section 4.

As society grows larger and more specialized, people feel less correspondence between their understandings and the institutions around them. Whereas a Cheyenne might know intimately much of "the law" of the tribe, it is highly unlikely that in modern America citizens would know, let along agree with, much of the law that could touch their lives. Understandably, the expression "Can *they* do that?" displaces "This is how *we* handle situations like that"; hierarchy, bewilderment, resentment, and fear replace mutuality, understanding, voluntary compliance, and love.

Stanley Diamond, a contemporary anthropologist who rejects the earlier theory of the congenial relationship between custom and law describes the relationship as follows:

> Efforts to legislate conscience by external political power are the antithesis of custom; customary behavior comprises precisely those aspects of social behavior which are traditional, moral and religious, which are in short, conventional and nonlegal. Put another way, custom is social morality. The relationship between custom and law is basically one of contradiction, not continuity.*

For Diamond, then, the advent of law is a sign of social breakdown rather than a mark of heightened consciousness and civility. Life under law becomes less liveable for the average person.

There are numerous difficulties in charting the relationship between law and popular will. Who are *the* people whose will is expressed or frustrated by the creation and operation of law? *The* people may mean a numerical majority, an influential elite, the poor, the middle class once referred to as the "silent majority," blacks and minorities, women, white Anglo-Saxon Protestant males, the young, the aged, and so on. Although

---

*Stanley Diamond, "The Rule of Law versus the Order of Custom," in *In Search of the Primitive* (New Brunswick, N.J.: Transaction Books, 1974).

popular sentiments may be shared among these groups on many questions, there will be large differences.

How does popular will get expressed? By voting? Street protest? Boycotts? "Public interest" groups? PACs? Fancy lobbyists? What is the link between tactics and legal action and outcomes? Is activism designed to get law made or unmade? Do people want better law, more law, less bad law, or no law at all?

The difficulties in making a coherent statement on the relationship between people and law might make it tempting to scrap the inquiry altogether, or limit the explanation to "simple" societies. However, there are too many occasions of tension between people and their institutions for the question to be abandoned. In the North Carolina cases on wife beating, the courts — unless mindless and diabolical — must have had some feel for the probable reception of their decisions, however chauvinistic their decisions look from today's perspectives. Similarly in the *Ducktown Sulphur* case, the court might have been afraid that the closing of the plant would cause a local furor, by the elite and the nonelite alike.

Although the influence of ordinary people on law has been sporadic and diffuse, there have been notable instances of popular pressure. In the nineteenth century, Populism took the form of advocating soft money for the repayment of debt, opposing the power of railroads, and pressing for the recognition of labor unions and collective bargaining. Not surprisingly, people who have sought changes in the status quo — from farmers to Wobblies to suffragists — have found themselves on the wrong side of law. As an example, during the first seven years of the Sherman Antitrust Act — an act supposedly designed to curb the power of large business — the federal courts found twelve violations of the act by labor and only one by business!

The last thirty years have been marked by black activism, resistance to the Vietnam War, farmers' strikes for parity, the women's movement, gay rights initiatives, antinuclear protests, and, more recently, a fundamentalist Christian revolt against pornography, abortion, and the prohibition of school prayer.

In the 1980s, economic questions crowded out earlier causes of popular unrest. Many workers were permanently laid off by a changing economy and the flight of capital and industry abroad for higher profits. Small businesses, especially in home building, experienced the highest rate of bankruptcies since the Great Depression. Farmers on prime land, with the best cash crops in a hungry world, found themselves caught in a cost-price squeeze that took many of them out of farming.

When people assert themselves, they are usually regarded as crazies or revolutionaries, or both. To the extent that challenges to authority disrupt the prevailing order, activists are at least provisional anarchists, and a reading from an early anarchist, Peter Kropotkin, on law and authority continues to have contemporary relevance. Following Kropotkin, one fascinating dimension of the struggle between people and government appears — the taxpayer, the IRS, and the "underground economy."

But first, how did custom-law-government work in so-called simple societies?

The Cheyenne Way *Karl N. Llewellyn and E. Adamson Hoebel*

THE TRIBAL OSTRACISM AND REINSTATEMENT OF STICKS EVERYTHING UNDER HIS BELT

Once, at a time when all the Cheyenne tribe was gathered together, Sticks Everything Under His Belt went out hunting buffalo alone. "I am hunting for myself," he told the people. He was implying that the rules against individual hunting did not apply to him because he was declaring himself out of the tribe — a man on his own.

All the soldier chiefs and all the tribal chiefs met in a big lodge to decide what to do in this case, since such a thing had never happened before. This was the ruling they made: no one could help Sticks Everything Under His Belt in any way, no one could give him smoke, no one could talk to him. They were cutting him off from the tribe. The chiefs declared that if anyone helped him in any way that person would have to give a Sun Dance.

When the camp moved, Sticks Everything Under His Belt moved with it, but the people would not recognize him. He was left alone and it went to his heart, so he took one of his horses (he had many) and rode out to the hilltops to mourn.

His sister's husband was a chief in the camp. This brother-in-law felt sorry for him out there mourning, with no more friends. At last he took pity on his poor brother-in-law; at last he spoke to his wife, "I feel sorry for your poor brother out there and now I am going to do something for him. Cook up all those tongues we have! Prepare a good feast!"

Then he invited the chiefs to his lodge and sent for his brother-in-law to come in. This was after several years had passed, not months.

When the chiefs had assembled, the brother-in-law spoke. "Several years ago you passed a ruling that no one could help this man. Whoever should do so you said would have to give a Sun Dance. Now is the time to take pity on him. I am going to give a Sun Dance to bring him back in. I beg you to let him come back to the tribe, for he has suffered long enough. This Sun Dance will be a great one. I declare that every chief and all the soldiers must join in. Now I put it up to you. Shall we let my brother-in-law smoke before we eat, or after?"

The chiefs all answered in accord, "Ha-ho, ha-ho [thank you, thank you]. We are very glad you are going to bring back this man. However, let him remember that he will be bound by whatever rules the soldiers lay down for the tribe. He may not say he is outside of them. He has been out of the tribe for a long time. If he remembers these things, he may come back."

Then they asked Sticks Everything Under His Belt whether he wanted to smoke before or after they had eaten. Without hesitation he replied, "Before," because he had craved tobacco so badly that he had split his pipe stem to suck the brown gum inside of it.

The lodge was not big enough to hold all the chiefs who had come to decide this thing, so they threw open the door, and those who could not get in sat in a circle outside. Then they filled a big pipe and when it was lighted they gave it to Sticks Everything Under His Belt. It was so

From *The Cheyenne Way: Conflict and Case Law in Primitive Jurisprudence*, by Karl N. Llewellyn and E. Adamson Hoebel.

long since he had had tobacco that he gulped in the smoke and fell over in a faint. As he lay there the smoke came out of his anus, he was so empty. The chiefs waited silently for him to come to again and then the pipe was passed around the circle.

When all had smoked, Sticks Everything Under His Belt talked. "From now on I am going to run with the tribe. Everything the people say, I shall stay right by it. My brother-in-law has done a great thing. He is going to punish himself in the Sun Dance to bring me back. He won't do it alone, for I am going in, too."

After a while the people were getting ready for the Sun Dance. One of the soldiers began to get worried because he had an ugly growth on his body which he did not want to reveal to the people. He was a good-looking young man named Black Horse. Black Horse went to the head chiefs asking them to let him sacrifice himself alone on the hilltops as long as the Sun Dance was in progress.

"We have nothing to say to that," they told him. "Go to the pledger. This is his Sun Dance."

Black Horse went to the brother-in-law of Sticks Everything Under His Belt, who was a brother-in-law to him as well. "Brother-in-law," he begged, "I want to be excused from going into the lodge. Can't you let me go into the hills to sacrifice myself as long as you are in there, to make my own bed?"

"No," he was rebuffed, "you know my rule is that all must be there."

"Well, brother-in-law, won't it be all right if I set up a pole on the hill and hang myself to it through my breasts? I shall hang there for the duration of the dance."

This brother-in-law of his answered him in these words. "Why didn't you take that up when all the chiefs were in the lodge? I have agreed with them that everyone must be in the lodge. I don't want to change the rule. I won't give you permission to go outside."

Then Black Horse replied, "You will not make the rules my way. Now I am going to put in a rule for everybody. Everyone in there has to swing from the pole as I do."

"No," countered the brother-in-law. "That was not mentioned in the meeting. If you want to swing from the pole, that is all right, but no one else has to unless he wishes to."

When they had the Sun Dance everyone had a good time. Black Horse was the only one on the pole, and there were so many in the lodge that there was not room enough for all to dance. Some just had to sit around inside the lodge. Though they did not dance, they starved themselves for four days. This dance took place near Sheridan, Wyoming, seven years before Custer. I was only a year old at that time, but what I have said here was told by Elk River and others. We call this place "Where the Chiefs Starved Themselves."

CRIES YIA EYA BANISHED FOR THE MURDER OF CHIEF EAGLE

Cries Yia Eya had been gone from the camp for three years because he had killed Chief Eagle in a whiskey brawl. The chiefs had ordered him away for his murder, so we did not see anything of him for that time. Then one day he came back, leading a horse packed with bundles of old-time tobacco. He stopped outside the camp and sent a messenger in with the horse and tobacco who was to say to the chiefs for him, "I am begging to come home."

The chiefs all got together for a meeting, and the soldier societies were told to convene, for there was an important matter to be considered. The tobacco was divided up and chiefs' messengers were sent out to invite the soldier chiefs to come to the lodge of the tribal council, for the big chiefs wanted to talk to them. "Here is the tobacco that that man sent in," they told the soldier chiefs. "Now we want you soldiers to decide if you think we should accept his request. If you decide that we should let him return, then it is up to you to convince his family that it is all right." (The relatives of Chief Eagle had told everybody that they would kill Cries Yia Eya on sight if they ever found him. "If we set eyes on him, he'll never make another track," they had vowed.) The soldier chiefs took the tobacco and went out to gather their troops. Each society met in its own separate lodge to talk among themselves, but the society servants kept passing back and forth between their different lodges to report on the trend of the discussion in the different companies.

At last one man said, "I think it is all right. I believe the stink has blown from him. Let him return!" This view was passed around, and this is the view that won out among the soldiers. Then the father of Chief Eagle was sent for and asked whether he would accept the decision. "Soldiers," he replied, "I shall listen to you. Let him return! But if that man comes back, I want never to hear his voice raised against another person. If he does, we come together. As far as that stuff of his is concerned, I want nothing that belonged to him. Take this share you have set aside for me and give it to someone else."

Cries Yia Eya had always been a mean man, disliked by everyone, but he had been a fierce fighter against the enemies. After he came back to the camp, however, he was always good to the people.

WHEN WALKING RABBIT RAISED A PROBLEM

A war party was organizing. Walking Rabbit approached the leader with a question. "Is it true that you have declared we must all go afoot? If so, I would like to be able to lead a horse to pack my mocassins and possibles." The leader gave him an answer. "There is a reason for my ruling. I want no horses, that it may be easier for us to conceal our movements. However, you may bring one horse." Then Walking Rabbit asked for instructions concerning the location of the first and second nights' camps, for he would start late and overtake the party.

Walking Rabbit's sweetheart had been married only recently to another. "My husband is not the man I thought he was," she told her former suitor. So Walking Rabbit took her to join the war party. [The Cheyennes have a phrase for the single man who marries a one-time married woman — "putting on the old mocassin."] In this way, it turned out that the "mocassin" he was packing was a big woman.

When they saw this woman there, the warriors got excited. The party turned into the hills and stopped. The leader opened his pipe. The leader's pipe was always filled before they left the camp, but it was not smoked until the enemy was seen or their tracks reported. Now the leader spoke. "When we take a woman with us it is usually known in the camp. Here is a man who has sneaked off with another's wife. Now what is going to happen?" That is what they were talking about.

The leader declared, "The only thing this man can do is return and make a settlement with the husband. Then he may follow us up."

One warrior was for aiding Walking Rabbit. "Why can't we let him stay?" was his proposal. "If we take any horses, we can give them to her husband." That was rejected.

The decision was that he had to go back. "If you had told us you wanted her so badly, we might have waited for you to settle for her. Then we could have taken her the right way. If you really want to go to war with us, you will be able to overtake us. We are afoot."

Then three or four warriors spoke up, each promising Walking Rabbit a horse to send to the husband. Everyone gave one or two arrows to be sent as well.

In the meantime Walking Rabbit's father had fixed it up with the aggrieved husband. Since he and his wife were incompatible, he was willing to release her. When Walking Rabbit came in and told his father the story of the soldiers' action, the father said, "Just let that stand. The thing is fixed. When those fighters come back they may want to give to the girl's parents. You go back after your party." But Walking Rabbit preferred to stay at home.

When Walking Rabbit did not go out, his closest relatives raised a big tipi. When they heard of the approach of the returning war party, everything was in readiness.

The warriors came charging in, shooting; they had taken many horses. The first coupcounters were in the van. Walking Rabbit's father had a right to harangue; he was a crier. "Don't go to your homes! Don't go to your own lodges! Come here to the lodge of Walking Rabbit, your friend!"

When they were all in this lodge the old man entered and told them his story. "I had this thing all settled before my son returned. You have sent arrows and promised horses. Now I have kept this girl here pending your return. I shall send her back to her parents with presents. I have waited to see what you are going to do."

The leader replied for his followers. "Yes, we will help you. We promised to help your son. When you send her back, we'll send presents with her. The men who had promised horses went out to get them. Others gave captured horses.

Sending her back with these presents was giving wedding gifts. Her relatives got them all. They gathered up their goods to send back. The war party was called together once more; to them this stuff was given. It was a great thing for the people to talk about. It was the first and last time a woman was sent home on enemy horses the day they came in.

Questions

1. What was the law in these cases?
2. What was the relationship between the exercise of tribal authority and the popular sentiments of the Cheyenne?
3. Was a precedent system operating here?
4. What values were at stake in the cases?
5. How were the varying positions or interests delineated, recognized, and secured?
6. Did the Cheyenne equivalent of the person on the street have anything to complain about regarding the way trouble was handled or the outcomes reached?

The Cheyenne could find correspondence between their personal beliefs and the exercise of tribal authority, but modern Americans may frequently feel that there is no accord between themselves and the institutions they come "under." Today the "system" and "law" are "out there" — potentially menacing, remote creations. Lincoln could speak comfortably of government "*of, by,* and *for* the people," but Americans today might think of government as *of, by,* and *for* someone else. Yet, like Kafka's commoners, they might be inclined to blame troubles on "personal problems" rather than structural failures. To think and act otherwise would be both psychically and socially disruptive.

Peter Kropotkin (1842–1921) was not so shy in speaking about law and authority, when he openly declared that most people would be better off if law were eliminated.

Law and Authority *Peter Kropotkin*

I

We are so perverted by an education which from infancy seeks to kill in us the spirit of revolt, and to develop that of submission to authority; we are so perverted by this existence under the ferrule of a law, which regulates every event in life — our birth, our education, our development, our love, our friendship — that, if this state of things continues, we shall lose all initiative, all habit of thinking for ourselves. Our society seems no longer able to understand that it is possible to exist otherwise than under the reign of law, elaborated by a representative government and administered by a handful of

From *Kropotkin's Revolutionary Pamphlets,* ed. by Roger N. Baldwin (Vanguard Press, 1927).

rulers. And even when it has gone so far as to emancipate itself from the thralldom, its first care has been to reconstitute it immediately. "The Year I of Liberty" has never lasted more than a day, for after proclaiming it men put themselves the very next morning under the yoke of law and authority.

Indeed, for some thousands of years, those who govern us have done nothing but ring the changes upon "Respect for law, obedience to authority." This is the moral atmosphere in which parents bring up their children, and school only serves to confirm the impression. Cleverly assorted scraps of spurious science are inculcated upon the children to prove necessity of law; obedience to the law is made a religion; moral goodness and the law of the masters are fused into one and the same divinity. The historical hero of the schoolroom is the man who obeys the law, and defends it against rebels.

Later when we enter upon public life, society and literature, impressing us day by day and hour by hour as the water-drop hollows the stone, continue to inculcate the same prejudice. Books of history, of political science, of social economy, are stuffed with this respect for law. Even the physical sciences have been pressed into the service by introducing artificial modes of expression, borrowed from theology and arbitrary power, into knowledge which is purely the result of observation. Thus our intelligence is successfully befogged, and always to maintain our respect for law. The same work is done by newspapers. They have not an article which does not preach respect for law, even where the third page proves every day the imbecility of that law, and shows how it is dragged through every variety of mud and filth by those charged with its administration. Servility before the law has become a virtue, and I doubt if there was ever even a revolutionist who did not begin in his youth as the defender of law against what are generally called "abuses," although these last are inevitable consequences of the law itself. . . .

The confused mass of rules of conduct called law, which has been bequeathed to us by slavery, serfdom, feudalism, and royalty, has taken the place of those stone monsters, before whom human victims used to be immolated, and whom slavish savages dared not even touch lest they should be slain by the thunderbolts of heaven.

This new worship has been established with especial success since the rise to supreme power of the middle class — since the great French Revolution. Under the ancient régime, men spoke little of laws; . . . Obedience to the good pleasure of the king and his lackeys was compulsory on pain of hanging or imprisonment. But during and after the revolutions, when the lawyers rose to power, they did their best to strengthen the principle upon which their ascendancy depended. The middle class at once accepted it as a dyke to dam up the popular torrent. The priestly crew hastened to sanctify it, to save their bark from foundering amid the breakers. Finally the people received it as an improvement upon the arbitrary authority and violence of the past.

To understand this, we must transport ourselves in imagination into the eighteenth century. Our hearts must have ached at the story of the atrocities committed by the all-powerful nobles of that time upon the men and women of the people before we can understand what must have been the magic influence upon the peasant's mind of the words, "Equality before the law, obedience to the law without distinction of birth or fortune." He who until then had been treated more cruelly than a beast, he who had never had any rights, he who had never obtained justice against the most revolting actions on the part of a noble, unless in revenge he killed him and was hanged — he saw himself recognized by this maxim, at least in theory, at least with regard to his personal rights, as the equal of his lord. Whatever this law might be, it promised to affect lord and peasant alike; it proclaimed the equality of rich and poor before the judge. The promise was a lie, and to-day we know it; but at that period it was an advance, a homage to justice, as hypocrisy is a homage rendered to truth. This is the reason that when the saviors of the menaced middle class . . . proclaimed "respect for law, the same for every man," the people accepted the compromise; for their revolutionary impetus had already spent its force in the contest with a foe whose ranks drew closer day by day; they bowed their neck beneath the yoke of law to save themselves from the arbitrary power of their lords.

The middle class has ever since continued to make the most of this maxim, which with another principle, that of representative government, sums up the whole philosophy of the bourgeois age, the nineteenth century. It has preached this doctrine in its schools, it has propagated it in its writings, it has moulded its art and science to the same purpose, it has thrust its beliefs into every hole and corner — like a pious Englishwoman, who slips tracts under the door — and it has done all this so successfully that today we behold the issue in the detestable fact that men who long for freedom begin the attempt to obtain it by entreating their masters to be kind enough to protect them by modifying the laws which these masters themselves have created!

But times and tempers are changed. Rebels are everywhere to be found who no longer wish to obey the law without knowing whence it comes, what are its uses, and whither arises the obligation to submit to it, and the reverence with which it is encompassed. The rebels of our day are criticizing the very foundations of society which have hitherto been held sacred, and first and foremost amongst them that fetish, law.

The critics analyze the sources of law, and find there either a god, product of the terrors of the savage, and stupid, paltry and malicious as the priests who vouch for its supernatural origin, or else, bloodshed, conquest by fire and sword. They study the characteristics of law, and instead of perpetual growth corresponding to that of the human race, they find its distinctive trait to be immobility, a tendency to crystallize what should be modified and developed day by day. They ask how law has been maintained, and in its service they see the atrocities of Byzantinism, the cruelties of the Inquisition, the tortures of the middle ages, living flesh torn by the lash of the executioner, chains, clubs, axes, and gloomy dungeons of prisons, agony, curses and tears. In our own days they see, as before, the axe, the cord, the rifle, the prison; on the one hand, the brutalized prisoner, reduced to the condition of a caged beast by the debasement of his whole moral being, and on the other, the judge, stripped of every feeling which does honor to human nature, living like a visionary in a world of legal fictions, revelling in the infliction of imprisonment and death, without even suspecting, in the cold malignity of his madness, the abyss of degradation into which he has himself fallen before the eyes of those whom he condemns.

They see a race of law-makers legislating without knowing what their laws are about; today voting a law on the sanitation of towns, without the faintest notion of hygiene, tomorrow making regulations for the armament of troops, without so much as understanding a gun; making laws about teaching and education without ever having given a lesson of any sort, or even an honest education to their own children; legislating at random in all directions, but never forgetting the penalties to be meted out to ragamuffins, the prison and the galleys, which are to be the portion of men a thousand times less immoral than these legislators themselves.

Finally, they see the jailer on the way to lose all human feeling, the detective trained as a blood-hound, the police spy despising himself; "informing," metamorphosed into a virtue; corruption, erected into a system; all the vices, all the evil qualities of mankind countenanced and cultivated to insure the triumph of law.

All this we see, and, therefore, instead of inanely repeating the old formula, "Respect the law," we say, "Despise law and all its attributes!" In place of the cowardly phrase, "Obey the law," our cry is "Revolt against all laws!"

Only compare the misdeeds accomplished in the name of each law with the good it has been able to effect, and weigh carefully both good and evil, and you will see if we are right.

II

Relatively speaking, law is a product of modern times. For ages and ages mankind lived without any written law, even that graved in symbols upon the entrance stones of a temple. During that period, human relations were simply regulated by customs, habits and usages, made sacred by constant repetition, and acquired by each person in childhood, exactly as he learned how to obtain his food by hunting, cattlerearing, or agriculture. . . .

Every tribe has its own manners and customs; customary law, as the jurists say. It has social habits, and that suffices to maintain cordial relations between the inhabitants of the village, the members of the tribe or community. Even amongst ourselves — the "civilized" nations — when we leave large towns, and go into the country, we see that there the mutual relations of the inhabitants are still regulated according to ancient and generally accepted customs, and not according to the written law of the legislators. The peasants of Russia, Italy and Spain, and even of a large part of France and England, have no conception of written law, It only meddles with their lives to regulate their relations with the State. As to relations between themselves, though these are sometimes very complex, they are simply regulated according to ancient custom. Formerly, this was the case with mankind in general.

Two distinctly marked currents of custom are revealed by analysis of the usages of primitive people.

As man does not live in a solitary state, habits and feelings develop within him which are useful for the preservation of society and the propagation of the race. Without social feelings and usages, life in common would have been absolutely impossible. It is not law which has established them; they are anterior to all law. Neither is it religion which has ordained them; they are anterior to all religions. They are found amongst all animals living in society. They are spontaneously developed by the very nature of things, like those habits in animals which men call instinct. They spring from a process of evolution, which is useful, and, indeed, necessary, to keep society together in the struggle it is forced to maintain for existence. Savages end by no longer eating one another because they find it in the long run more advantageous to devote themselves to some sort of cultivation than to enjoy the pleasure of feasting upon the flesh of an aged relative once a year. Many travelers have depicted the manners of absolutely independent tribes, where laws and chiefs are unknown, but where the members of the tribe have given up stabbing one another in every dispute, because the habit of living in society has ended by developing certain feelings of fraternity and oneness of interest, and they prefer appealing to a third person to settle their differences. The hospitality of primitive peoples, respect for human life, the sense of reciprocal obligation, compassion for the weak, courage, extending even to the sacrifice of self for others which is first learnt for the sake of children and friends, and later for that of members of the same community — all these qualities are developed in man anterior to all law, independently of all religion, as in the case of the social animals. Such feelings and practices are the inevitable results of social life. Without being, as say priests and metaphysicians, inherent in man, such qualities are the consequence of life in common.

But side by side with these customs, necessary to the life of societies and the preservation of the race, other desires, other passions, and therefore other habits and customs, are evolved in human association. The desire to dominate others and impose one's own will upon them; the desire to seize upon the products of the labor of a neighboring tribe; the desire to surround oneself with comforts without producing anything, while slaves provide their master with the means of procuring every sort of pleasure and luxury — these selfish, personal desires give rise to another current of habits and customs. The priest and the warrior, the charlatan who makes a profit out of superstition, and after freeing himself from the fear of the devil cultivates it in others; and the bully, who procures the invasion and pillage of his neighbors that he may return laden with booty and followed by slaves. These two, hand in hand, have succeeded in imposing upon primitive society customs advantageous to both of them, but tending to perpetuate their domination of the masses. Profiting by the indolence, the fears, the inertia of the crowd, and thanks to the continual repetition of the same acts, they have permanently established customs which have become a solid basis for their own domination.

For this purpose, they would have made use, in the first place, of that tendency to run in a groove, so highly developed in mankind. In children and all savages it attains striking proportions, and it may also be observed in animals. Man, when he is at all superstitious, is always afraid to introduce any sort of change into existing conditions; he generally venerates what is ancient. "Our fathers did so and so; they got on pretty well; they brought you up; they were not unhappy; do the same!" the old say to the young every time the latter wish to alter things. The unknown frightens them, they prefer to cling to the past even when the past represents poverty, oppression and slavery.

It may even be said that the more miserable a man is, the more he dreads every sort of change, lest it may make him more wretched still. Some ray of hope, a few scraps of comfort, must penetrate his gloomy abode before he can begin to desire better things, to criticize the old ways of living, and prepare to imperil them for the sake of bringing about a change. So long as he is not imbued with hope, so long as he is not freed from the tutelage of those who utilize his superstition and his fears, he prefers remaining in his former position. . . .

The spirit of routine, originating in superstition, indolence, and cowardice, has in all times been the mainstay of oppression. In primitive human societies it was cleverly turned to account by priests and military chiefs. They perpetuated customs useful only to themselves, and succeeded in imposing them on the whole tribe. So long as this conservative spirit could be exploited so as to assure the chief in his encroachments upon individual liberty, so long as the only inequalities between men were the work of nature, and these were not increased a hundred-fold by the concentration of power and wealth, there was no need for law and the formidable paraphernalia of tribunals and ever-augmenting penalties to enforce it.

But as society became more and more divided into two hostile classes, one seeking to establish its domination, the other struggling to escape, the strife began. Now the conqueror was in a hurry to secure the results of his actions in a permanent form, he tried to place them beyond question, to make them holy and venerable by every means in his power. Law made its appearance under the sanction of the priest, and the warrior's club was placed at its service. Its office was to render immutable such customs as were to the advantage of the dominant minority. Military authority undertook to ensure obedience. This new function was a fresh guarantee to the power of the warrior; now he had not only mere brute force at his service; he was the defender of law.

If law, however, presented nothing but a collection of prescriptions serviceable to rulers, it would find some difficulty in insuring acceptance and obedience. Well, the legislators confounded in one code the two currents of custom of which we have just been speaking, the maxims which represent principles of morality and social union wrought out as a result of life in common, and the mandates which are meant to ensure external existence to inequality. Customs, absolutely essential to the very being of society, are, in the code, cleverly intermingled with usages imposed by the ruling caste, and both claim equal respect from the crowd. "Do not kill," says the code, and hastens to add, "And pay tithes to the priest." "Do not steal," says the code, and immediately after, "He who refuses to pay taxes, shall have his hand struck off."

Such was law; and it has maintained its two-fold character to this day. Its origin is the desire of the ruling class to give permanence to customs imposed by themselves for their own advantage. Its character is the skilful commingling of customs useful to society, customs which have no need of law to insure respect, with other customs useful only to rulers, injurious to the mass of the people, and maintained only by the fear of punishment.

Like individual capital, which was born of fraud and violence, and developed under the auspices of authority, law has no title to the respect of men. Born of violence and superstition, and established in the interests of consumer, priest and rich exploiter, it must be utterly destroyed on the day when the people desire to break their chains. . . .

Notes and Questions

1. Compare with Kropotkin the saying "Obedience to law is freedom."
2. The promise of equality after the French Revolution must have looked especially appealing to those who had suffered under the old regime of royalty and nobility. Should people have rejected the promise of more equality through the rule of law, on the ground that other tyrannies would creep in with the institutions that were said to be necessary to preserve equality?

   If it would have been prudent to reject postrevolutionary law, how would the gains of the revolution have been consolidated, or is the idea of consolidation itself an illusion?
3. Kropotkin argues that law has a mixed character, that is, something to hold the interest of average people and preserve the legitimacy of law-as-a-whole while providing substantial gains to a minority. Could the desirable elements of law be retained while preferential elements are purged, or is the whole institution of law inherently flawed?
4. Could there be a society where there are no leaders? Or where every person is a leader with no followers? Would it be possible to have a society in which all people agreed with Kropotkin? While skeptical about the prospects of peace through law, Kropotkin did have great faith in the development of voluntary relationships of mutual aid. How would the people involved in voluntary relationships have settled their differences?
5. In the society ordered through custom, Kropotkin states that upon occasions of dispute people "prefer appealing to a third party to settle their differences." Would such reference of disputes to third parties give rise to law? To a hierarchy with people who settle differences between disputants being in a preferred place? Should good anarchists reject third-party intervention in disputes?
6. According to Kropotkin, the relationship of law to custom entails the incorporation into law practices of *both* equality and domination. Compare this view of Kropotkin with the observations by Stanley Diamond found in the introduction to this section.
7. Kropotkin argues that people who make laws about health know nothing of hygiene, those who legislate about education know nothing of teaching, and so on. Would he advocate the transferring of questions from law to scientists and other experts? Would experts come to rule the inexpert? Should they be in authority, or are they just as unfit to rule as are bourgeois lawyers? If lawyers and other experts cannot rule without tyrannizing, who can?
8. What is the relationship between anarchy and democracy?
9. In previous sections of the text, questions of school discipline, marital conflict, criminal law violations, pollution, and labor have come to the courts. Did the operation of law have beneficial effects in those instances, or would people have been just as well off, and possibly better off, if there were no law?
10. Kropotkin encourages the study of sources of law, who made it, who benefits from it, and what its effects are. Examine a rule of law of the state or the place where you live, work, or go to school. Try to find the source of the rule and its effects, and explore what your life would be like were the rule eliminated.
11. Make an inventory of newspaper articles relating to state law or institutional rules and policies. Assess whether the writers are calling for more law, less law, or different law. How anarchical does your inventory suggest people to be?

Taxation — and current antipathies to taxation — may comprise a large and growing exception to the general belief that law should be unswervingly obeyed. In the early 1980s, news about the underground economy — which can be loosely defined as any activity that produces money or valuable exchanges that people do not let the government know about — appeared with such regularity in all media that it would seem that only a fool would line up to pay full taxes. But wriggling out of taxes seems to be as old as the country itself, when one recalls the difficulties of the English in extracting taxes from the Colonies and the revolutionists' claim that Britain could not collect taxes legitimately.

The end of the Revolutionary War did not end hostility to taxes. Knowing popular attitudes, the new government prudently imposed taxes as temporary measures to be withdrawn as soon as particular exigencies, most notably the financing of wars, had passed. It is not a little remarkable, even making allowances for inflation, that over the first ten years of tax collection, the government collected only a small fraction of what the IRS now collects in a single day! Until the Civil War, taxes were not continually levied, and only after 1860 was there a permanent commissioner of internal revenue.

Contemporary commentators do not speak as much of revolution or anarchy as they do of "tensions between the taxpayer and the IRS." Behind the polite talk lies the fact that all taxpayers are going to some lengths to escape taxation. For the small timers, there is the effort to "skim cash," get "off the books," or to barter services or goods to escape taxation. For the bigger timers, there are tax conferences where, far from the cash-skimming set, prestigious tax advisers gather to figure out the latest ways to arrange their clients' affairs so as to minimize taxes. At one such conference, six reasons were listed as to why taxpayers felt more and more inclined to err in their own favor:

> 1. Inflation. — Inflation has had an enormous impact on taxpayer attitudes. Rising monetary incomes have pushed many taxpayers into high marginal tax brackets. These individuals do not feel rich, and in fact are not, but are nevertheless paying what appear to them to be shockingly high amounts of tax.
>
> 2. Economic slow-down, ranging to recession. — If a taxpayer is concerned about his job or personal financial security, his attitude toward complying with the tax system may well be negatively affected.
>
> 3. Complexity of the tax law. — . . . A first type is the complexity of the tax law and regulations themselves. A second type is the complexity of properly filling in the required tax forms and returns. A final type of complexity is the record-keeping requirements. . . .
>
> 4. A pervasive feeling that the other guy is getting away with something.

5. A generalized disrespect for the political process and governmental agencies. . . .

6. A feeling of anxiety and despair, relating to the perceived decline of the United States in the world economy and a world leadership role.*

People who are left of center politically might add a seventh reason why the government cannot be trusted with money, namely, the use of more and more revenue and debt to finance an unwanted arms buildup and unjustified intervention by the United States into the affairs of other countries.

While there can be substantial debate about this or other explanations of the IRS's difficulty in finding willing taxpayers, one conclusion seems inescapable: people of all persuasions find ample reasons for nonpayment of all the taxes the government wants, ranging from home economics to international perspectives. Such thinking makes many Americans anarchists, at least in the privacy of their homes or in other secret sanctuaries where they conduct their "underground economies" or do their "tax planning." If successful, their sometimes quiet and personal actions would ultimately starve the government to death. These arguments say nothing of corporations, the artificial persons who seem to be even more anarchically inclined than real people when it comes to minimizing taxes.

The subject of taxation is so complex that it could require a lifetime of study (most of it highly motivated). In the remainder of this section, some of the main lines of conflict between the IRS and ordinary taxpayers can be outlined, beginning with congressional hearings on the tax protester movement.

**Taxes* magazine, December 1980, p. 816.

IRS Response to the Illegal Tax Protester Movement

U.S. House of Representative Hearings (1981)

Washington, D.C. . . .

MR. ROSENTHAL [Representative Benjamin S. Rosenthal]: The committee will be in order.

Today's hearing into IRS response to the illegal tax protester movement continues the. . . examination of various aspects of the underground economy. We are here to assess the adequacy of IRS performance in the tax protest area and to determine the protest movement's impact on our self-assessment tax system.

We are concerned by reports that between 1978 and 1980 the number of illegal tax protester returns identified by IRS increased 156 percent. We are also concerned by an IRS study which concludes that the number of illegal tax protesters cannot be accurately estimated and

---

Hearings, U.S. House of Representatives, Committee on Government Operations, "IRS Response to the Illegal Tax Protester Movement," 97th Congress, 1st Session, 1981.

that the movement has the potential of undermining voluntary compliance with the tax laws.

This subcommittee's longstanding interest in efficient tax administration is premised on a belief that our self-assessment tax system is jeopardized when any segment of our population can successfully evade payment of its fair share of taxes. It is for this reason that the IRS must deal swiftly and effectively with the illegal tax protester movement.

Our first witness is William Anderson, Director, General Government Division of the General Accounting Office.

MR. ANDERSON: Our testimony deals with the results of our review of the Internal Revenue Service's efforts to detect and deter illegal tax protesters. Our review was based primarily on a random sample of 167 cases projected to a universe of 3,870 cases identified as protesters in 1978 and 1979. . . .

IRS defines an illegal tax protester as "a person who advocates and/or participates in a scheme with a broad exposure that results in an illegal underpayment of taxes." The protest movement has grown significantly in the past few years. Although it is but a part of the subterranean economy, it alone poses a threat to our Nation's voluntary compliance tax system. To counter this threat, IRS has taken some important actions including the establishment of a nationwide program to detect and deter protesters and a related program to identify persons who file false form W–4's* to evade taxes. As a result, IRS has had some important successes including convictions of major illegal protest leaders. . . .

The exact extent and makeup of the illegal tax protest movement are unknown. The best available data on the number of illegal tax protesters are probably those compiled by IRS on the basis of tax returns identified primarily by IRS 10 service centers as being filed by protesters.

. . . IRS identified about 7,100 protest returns in calendar year 1978 when it first began collecting data, and about 18,200 protest returns in calendar year 1980 — an increase of about 156 percent. . . .

[I]llegal protester activity continues to be heaviest in the West and Southwest where it started in the 1920's, accounting for about 54 percent in just Ogden and Fresno. However, it is intensifying across the country and had the largest percentage increase in the Northeast.

Over the years, illegal tax protesters have developed various complex and sophisticated schemes to evade or reduce their taxes, and the courts have denied the legality of many schemes. However, . . . the constitutional, family estate trust, and church-related schemes have been most popular in recent years. Together these schemes comprised about 80 percent of all protest returns identified by IRS in 1980. Since 1974, the filing of a false form W–4, . . . has become a more common scheme and is often used by illegal protesters in conjunction with another scheme. . . .

IRS does not generate periodic profile statistics on the characteristics of illegal tax protesters or on the amount of taxes involved in these protests. However, based on our random sample the largest number of cases in the three districts involved protesters who were nonprofessional wage earners, had incomes between $15,000 and $50,000, and on the average owed about $3,700 more in taxes when IRS made adjustments.

Although IRS data on the illegal tax movement is the best available, its figures overall are understated because of problems in the identification procedures. . . . Nevertheless, the data is sufficient in our opinion to show that the movement is growing.

In recent years because of the growth of the protest movement IRS has taken some positive steps to deal with the problem nationally. The most significant of these was its establishment in November 1978, of its priority illegal tax protester program, which was designed primarily to

---

*The W–4 form, filed by employees, shows the number of exemptions they claim. The overstatement of exemptions means that the employer will withhold less or nothing from paychecks. At the end of the year, owing money, the taxpayer might become a nonfiler. — ED.

identify and control protester returns and documents. . . .

In April 1980 IRS initiated another program — the questionable form W–4 program — to identify illegal tax protesters as well as other persons who file false income withholding certificates to evade taxes. Under this program, employers are required to submit to IRS at least quarterly form W–4's on which employees claim 10 or more withholding exemptions or complete exemption from withholding. . . .

IRS procedures for detecting illegal protesters are limited primarily to identifying those who choose to file a protest return or otherwise notify IRS of their protest. Those who are silent about why they are cheating, IRS really does not know whether they are a tax protester or not. Moreover, weaknesses in IRS procedures allow certain protesters who do file a return or other document to elude detection. Thus, IRS information on the extent of the protest problem is understated and its understanding of the nature and the makeup of the problem is limited.

"Silent protesters" who do not file returns are the most difficult to detect. Neither we nor IRS know how many nonfilers, including those IRS identifies nationally as part of its nonfiler program, would meet IRS official definition of an illegal tax protester. However, since protest leaders encourage nonfiling, it seems reasonable that some nonfilers are also protesters. . . .

Although not all persons who file false W–4's are illegal tax protesters, IRS may realize a significant increase in the number of protesters identified through its new questionable form W–4 program. The volume of questionable form W–4's received since the program began and those requiring followup have both greatly exceeded IRS' initial estimates.

. . . IRS estimated that in the program's first year about 1 million W–4's meeting the filing criteria would be received from employers. It further estimated that processing these documents would produce 30,000 questionable W–4's requiring followup. However, in the first 6 months of the program, IRS received about 687,000 documents filed by employers which yielded over 143,000 forms for followup rather than the 30,000 that IRS had estimated. The chances are good that IRS will eventually identify some of these as having been filed by illegal tax protesters. . . .

[C]ertain aspects of the program could cause IRS problems in its dealings with illegal tax protesters identified only through the W–4 program. The first aspect involves the long time lag between when a person submits a form W–4 to his or her employer and when IRS notifies the employer to disregard that form W–4. . . .

Once IRS identifies illegal tax protesters, it has not been as timely and effective as it could be in bringing them into compliance. Cases are often delayed during many phases of the enforcement process for extensive periods, sometimes by the protester and other times by IRS. . . .

About 84 percent of the 2,280 open cases had been open for a year or more and about 41 percent had been open 2 or more years. Most of the open cases were still in the Examination Division and had been there 1 or more years; therefore, taxes had not been assessed. . . .

Many delays in bringing protesters into compliance were caused by the fact that they were generally uncooperative and took advantage of the tax administration system to prolong IRS' inquiry. . . .

IRS itself also contributed to delays due to, one, difficulties in locating tax returns and assembling other tax information from its files; two, competing priorities and heavy caseloads; and, three, the need to do additional work in developing cases. One overriding cause has been that rather than establishing special procedures for protester cases, IRS chose to handle them within its regular compliance system, a system designed to deal with generally cooperative and compliant taxpayers. More importantly, the program suffers from a lack of authoritative management, direction and attention at all organizational levels within IRS. . . .

Of equal concern are the constraints on the resources of the Justice Department and the Federal court system, which must get involved in criminal and civil litigation against protesters. Because of the threat posed by the protest movement, it is essential that IRS have a planned approach so that it has a basis for assigning its resources to and expediting those cases which will have the most deterrent effect on the protester problem. The plan would also provide a basis for measuring program results and making appropriate changes. . . .

Although the number of known protesters in comparison to the taxpaying population is not overwhelming, the protest movement is growing. It remains a threat to our Nation's voluntary compliance tax system because of the visibility of tax protest leaders and their sales approach. Therefore, it is essential that IRS demonstrate to protesters and to the taxpaying public that it can and will aggressively pursue protest cases to a timely conclusion. Otherwise, protesters will continue to file protest returns or become nonfilers, and presently compliant taxpayers will possibly become protesters. . . .

MR. ROSENTHAL: . . . can somebody explain to us what those so-called schemes are?

MR. ANDERSON: The first one, which accounts for by far the most of the protesters that IRS is concerned with . . . these are people that would send in a return with zeros all over it and [claim the] fifth amendment. . . .

The family estate trust is a scheme that is being sold apparently by a number of tax advisors across the country, whereby an individual will establish a family trust, transfer all assets and income into it, and pay their living expenses and assert that the living expenses, the money being withdrawn, are expenses of the trust. IRS . . . is rather successful in getting corrected returns from these people who frequently were misled citizens rather than overt tax protesters of the type that we associate with the phrase generally. . . .

The church-related schemes are schemes that have been promoted to avoid taxation on the basis of two different types of schemes: first, a vow of poverty scheme whereby all of the income of the person is offset for tax reporting purposes. A ministry is in effect established and we have a family church. . . .

There are other instances where, as you know, up to 50 percent of contributions can be provided to a church and they will establish a family church and so report in that regard. IRS has a couple of landmark cases in the criminal court on this right now, has been successful. On the civil side they have had 25 successes, I think is their most recent figure on it.

In any event, though, this is the most difficult for IRS . . . trying to make that distinction between what is a legitimate church and what is something else, whatever you would call it. It is difficult even for IRS to identify them because in listing contributions to charitable institutions on the return you are not required to identify the church that you gave it to, for example. You do not have to say that it was a Methodist church or the Catholic church or whatever, and so IRS is even at a disadvantage there in trying to identify whether it is what they term a "nontraditional" church.

They did do a study in the Western region, 8,740 returns that showed 40 percent or more of adjusted gross income going to church-related contributions. When they finally worked through that pile they came down to 192 returns, I believe, that went to nontraditional churches and hence, you might say, gave cause for further inquiry. . . .

Those are the principal ones, accounting for 80 percent. I would like to drop down if I could and tell a little bit about the false form W–4's which have had quite a bit of press in the last 6 months or so, primarily as a result of a situation up in Flint, Mich., involving a number of employees of General Motors Corp., . . . as well as another situation involving a number of employees of a construction company. . . .

When you start a job, you are required to provide the employer with a W–4 so that he will know how much Federal taxes to take out of your pay each week. Well, across the country in a number of locations — it is like a contagion, it will start and it will spread out — people have found that by the very simple fact of filling out a form W–4 and showing 80 exemptions, they do not need to pay Federal income taxes any more, at least none will be withheld from their pay. They can even claim total exemption. . . .

IRS considers that these people are protesters because they are not paying the taxes that are due the Federal Government, that you and

I and most honest folks across this country. . . . "Protesters" perhaps is one word that could be used to characterize them; perhaps "cheaters" is another word that could be used equally as well. . . .

[W]hen IRS became aware of the problem — it just sprang up since 1974 and seemed to be spreading across the country — they did put a program into effect which requires employers quarterly to report to IRS any W–4's they have received that claim 10 or more withholding allowances or claim total exemption from taxes.

They will then match that against information in their files to find out whether the person, for example, had a tax liability the previous year. If they get a match like that they will go back to the employer and say, "Disregard that W–4 that employee submitted. You will withhold as though that was a single person."

Now the importance of getting to these people is that once they have paid no taxes, they can choose not to file a return at the end of the year. Now even if IRS catches them through its various matching processes, they still had the use of the Government's money for an extended period of time, and the Government's ability to get the money . . . without going to court is again uncertain.

MR. CONYERS [Representative John Conyers, Jr.]: Now, Mr. Anderson, how many so-called "tax protesters" have been convicted in the last few years?

MR. ANDERSON: The figure that I have seen is about 260, I believe, sir, in the last 30 months. . . .

MR. CONYERS: Now how does that compare with the number of persons convicted for having participated in other illegal tax schemes, like tax straddles, abusive tax shelters, and the like?

MR. HARRIS: We do not have that information offhand, sir, but we could submit it for the record.

[The material referred to follows:]

> During the last 30 months, IRS and Justice had 89 prosecutions and 10 convictions relating to tax shelters.

MR. CONYERS: Well, then, what are you comparing this conviction rate against?

MR. ANDERSON: We are comparing it against the number of tax protesters that IRS has identified, sit. I guess it shows that in terms of the number that are identified, the number that are actually brought to justice — if you accept the fact that they are doing something illegal or improper — is not too large.

MR. CONYERS: Well, if you do not know how many other people are being prosecuted and convicted for tax avoidance,* then what are you matching this conviction rate against? You said you thought it was low; they ought to be doing more. Maybe they ought to be doing more in some other areas but you do not even have any yardstick against which to make the measurement. . . . Now you say that this definition of tax protester — what is a "tax protester"?

MR. ANDERSON: . . . This is IRS definition: "A person who advocates and/or participates in a scheme with a broad exposure that results in the illegal underpayment of taxes."

MR. CONYERS: Is a tax straddler a tax protester?

MR. HARRIS: No, sir, not according to IRS, they would not be considered a protester.

MR. CONYERS: Why not? What is the difference? . . . Well, he has the same, identical intent, doesn't he? Well, the difference is obvious. It is a rich guy deciding to cheat in his taxes against a poor guy. That is the difference. The intention is the same. The tax protester does not rip off as many bucks.

Did you examine, while you were making this study, the validity of that definition?

MR. ANDERSON: It seemed like a reasonable definition at the time we did the work, sir.

---

*Tax lawyers distinguish between tax avoidance and tax evasion. Tax avoidance minimizes tax liability through recognized loopholes in the tax law, whereas tax evasion involves the nonpayment of taxes for which there is no legally recognized excuse. Tax protesters are regarded as tax evaders rather than tax avoiders. — ED.

MR. CONYERS: Well, do you know comparatively how much money we are losing through abusive tax shelters and tax straddlers, as against what is lost through tax protesters?

MR. ANDERSON: I am sure that it is considerably more than IRS has been able to associate with illegal protesters, with those illegal protesters that it has identified. However, that number as I pointed out is probably vastly understated. . . .

MR. CONYERS: Well, I have heard about $5 billion are lost in tax straddling and abusive tax shelter schemes but millions more in other related types of activity. In other words, the point is that there are far more serious kinds of cheating going on —

MR. ANDERSON: Absolutely.

MR. CONYERS [continuing]: But you have not said that anywhere in your long, long summary statement. For 45 minutes here we have been listening to this and there has been no comparison whatsoever being made to the other forms of cheating. Why aren't the rich who cheat the subject of as much IRS attention as the largely working class so-called tax protesters?

MR. ANDERSON: We were asked to address the tax protester program in particular. I guess that I feel, I sense that you are understating the importance of tax protesters. IRS considers that this is an important problem because the U.S. tax system depends on voluntary compliance. Now trying to beat the system is one thing but the concern is that this could spread to otherwise honest taxpayers, and that is why they attach so much importance to it.

MR. CONYERS: OK. You said that several times, and I would like to close my discussion with you on that point. Has it occurred to you that perhaps merely swift and effective prosecution may not change this one bit, and that there may be something more serious underlying this protest movement than whether or not the GAO or the IRS or the Feds will crack down on these working people? Has it occurred to you that they might be challenging an unfair system in a nonviolent way? . . . [Y]ou have not even once suggested that there may be some other, underlying reason than that people want to keep some money in their pockets and beat Uncle Sam. These might happen to be patriotic Americans. They might happen to be people that are not trying to overthrow the Government but they might be trying to tell lunkheads like me and you that there is a message out there that we ought to deal with. . . . [Y]ou kept talking that the whole Government could fall if the movement spreads, and you do not make one serious analysis or suggestion about its underlying causes except mention of deterrents, just as in our criminal justice system the assumption is that the more people you punish and the longer you throw them in the slammer, that somehow they will commit less crime. Yet we get precisely the same result, more crime.

MR. ANDERSON: To me the law is the law, sir, and that is why most Americans adhere to it. . . .

MR. WILLIAMS: Isn't the difference between what my colleague has just talked about the fact that the courts have already ruled on these schemes and found them illegal? Isn't that the difference?

MR. ANDERSON: That is correct, sir.

MR. WILLIAMS: That is not the case with other tax abuses.

MR. ANDERSON: That is correct, sir. . . . That is correct, loopholes.

Notes and Questions

1. At the close of the hearing, there is a sharp debate between Conyers and Anderson over the difference between wage earner schemes and the "tax planning" of the rich. If the rich can use tax straddles (used by commodity traders to escape the taxation of gains) and tax shelters (used to avoid taxes altogether or to defer them to a later date), then why should wage earners not be able to escape full taxation of their incomes by creating their own loopholes? Why should the taxes on wages be the vital link in "voluntary compliance with the tax laws"

when other forms of income are not so considered?

If wage earners have become hostile to the inequities of taxation, their hostilities are grounded in legal realities. In his best-selling book *The Rich and the Super Rich,** Ferdinand Lundberg gave the following overview of how tax laws affect the ability to get and stay rich:

1. [T]he propertied elite with the connivance of a malleable, deferential Congress deals itself very substantial continuing tax advantages at the expense of the vast majority of the population.
2. [T]he national tax burden is largely shouldered absolutely and relatively by the politically illiterate nonmanagerial labor force rather than by big property owners or by the upper echelon corporate executives.
3. [T]he resultant tax structure is such that it intensifies the abject and growing poverty of 25 to 35% of the population.

His appraisal was written before the tax changes of 1982, which skewed tax laws still further in the direction he outlined!

2. Who pays what portion of the federal taxes in the United States? A report published by the Congress† disclosed that there have been a number of long-term changes in the sources of federal revenues. A greater portion now comes from the individual income tax and the payroll tax (for Social Security) and less from the corporate income tax. From 1952 to 1981, personal taxes went from 42 percent to 48 percent and payroll taxes from 10 percent to 30 percent, while corporate taxation declined from 32 percent to 10 percent. The relative decline in corporate taxation was attributable to the investment credit and more liberal cost recovery formulas.

It is difficult to assess the relative tax burdens within the personal income tax structure across classes of taxpayers because of the way that the government gathers and compiles its data. An economist would consider income of whatever type and from whatever source and compare it to the tax bill to determine the tax burden. Instead, the government uses *adjusted gross income,* which is the creature of the preferential tax system itself and seriously distorts the true income of tax-paying classes. Income from tax-exempt securities, capital gains, and amounts paid to retirement accounts and for business expenses were not included in the adjusted gross income figure, making the tax bill a higher percentage of "income" than it would otherwise be. For ordinary taxpayers, economic income will approximate adjusted gross income, but this would not be true for higher-income taxpayers who derive less of their income from wages and salaries and more from professional fees, interest, dividends, and capital gains. The use of the adjusted gross income figure makes the personal income tax structure look more progressive than it actually is.

Another study, done by the Treasury Department‡ considered tax breaks by level of adjusted gross income and concluded that the 4.4 percent of taxpayers who earn more than $50,000 get one third of the tax breaks examined. This taxpaying class received $52 billion; they got $4.3 billion of the $4.6 billion of tax-exempt security income, 73 percent of the tax savings on income earned overseas, 63 percent of the reduced tax liability on capital gains, and 50 percent of the deduction for charitable contributions.

3. As the congressional conferees indicated, tax protesting is but a small corner of the "underground," "subterranean," or "irregular economy." The IRS did a study§ that showed that for 1976 unreported income amounted to $135 billion, $95 billion from legal sources, and $40 billion from illegal sources such as drugs, gambling, and prostitution (see Table 1). (The IRS did not include barter and did not cover thefts and embezzlements from business, thought to run $25 billion for 1976.)

---

*New York: Bantam, 1969.

†U.S. Senate, Committee on Finance, "Incidence of the Federal Tax Burden," 97th Congress, 2nd Sess., 1982.

‡U.S. Congress, Joint Economic Committee, December 1982.

§Department of the Treasury, IRS Estimate of Unreported Income, 1979.

TABLE 1 Reported and Nonreported Income, by Type

Legal Source of Income	*1976 Reportable*	*Reported*	*Percent Reported*	*Percent Unreported*
Self-employment	93–99 (billions)	60	60–64	36–40
Wages and salaries	902–908	881	97–98	2–3
Interest	54–58	49	84–90	10–16
Dividends	27–30	25	84–92	8–16
Rents and royalties	9–12	7	50–65	35–50
Pensions, etc.	31–33	27	84–88	12–16
Capital gains	9–10	7	70–75	25–30

Source: Hearings, U.S. House of Representatives, Committee on Ways and Means, "The Underground Economy," 96th Congress, 1st Session, 1979.

Peter Gutmann, an economist whose article on the subject|| inspired a number of economic studies and a series of government hearings, gave a higher but "conservative" estimate of the size of the underground economy: $176 billion for 1976, or 10 percent of GNP. He believed that a higher figure of 13 percent or 14 percent could be defended.# Using Gutmann's estimates for selected years subsequent to 1976 (Table 2), some alarming totals are reached:

TABLE 2 The Underground Economy (Estimates Based on the GNP)

Year	*GNP (in billions)*	*10 percent*	*14 percent*
1977	$1,991	$199	$278
1979	2,508	251	251
1981	3,053	305	427
1983	3,406	341	476
1985	3,998	400	559

Source: GNP figures from *Statistical Abstract of the United States* (Washington, D.C.: U.S. Government Printing Office, 1987).

Gutmann's estimate of $250 billion for the year 1976 would have meant a loss of revenue of $50 billion at tax rates of 20 percent, about 10 percent of all taxes collected that year.

4. The IRS experiences its greatest success in collecting taxes at the source through wage withholding. When the IRS depends upon self-reporting, as it does for other forms of income, its success drops of dramatically; see Table 1. Thus the government misses the reporting of only 2 to 3 percent when the income is subject to withholding, but 35 to 50 percent of rent and royalty income. Until tax changes in 1982, only wages were subject to withholding, but federal deficits were becoming so large that to ferret out more income information, the administration tried to make interest and dividend income subject to withholding at 10 percent. However, these measures were repealed before going into effect, largely through the efforts of the banking lobby. The much publicized "working off the books" or "for cash only" falls within the category of self-employment where it is estimated that only 60 percent of income received is reported.

||Peter Gutmann, "The Subterranean Economy," *Financial Analysts' Journal*, December 1977.

#Hearings, U.S. Congress, Joint Economic Committee, "The Underground Economy," 96th Congress, 1st Sess., 1979, 23.

About the only way that a wage earner subject to withholding can escape taxes is by filing a false W–4 form and overstating exemptions. When the government collects no taxes in the first place, it is unlikely to collect them at all because taxpayers who owe all or most of their taxes either do not file returns or file protest returns. The next case illustrates the handling of the small number of cases that reach the criminal courts.

United States v. Carlson *617 F.2d 518 (1980)*

WALLACE, CIRCUIT JUDGE:

Carlson was convicted of willful failure to file income tax returns in violation of 26 U.S.C. § 7203. On appeal he seeks reversal by claiming that his failure to file proper returns constituted a valid exercise of his Fifth Amendment privilege against self-incrimination. We affirm the conviction.

I

Carlson, a factory worker, earned $9,346.21 in 1974 and $13,053.53 in 1975. Although he had filed complete tax returns for previous years, Carlson did not do so for 1974 and 1975. Instead, as part of a tax protest movement, he utilized the following tax-evasion scheme for each of those years. In 1974, Carlson claimed 99 withholding exemptions on the withholding tax form (form W–4) that he submitted to his employer, although he was not married and had no dependents. This form W–4 remained effective through 1975, and resulted in no federal income taxes being withheld from Carlson's wages in either 1974 or 1975. Carlson thereafter asserted the Fifth Amendment on his 1974 and 1975 year-end tax returns (form 1040) in lieu of providing any information from which his tax liability could be calculated. He appended to the 1974 return tax protest material claiming that federal reserve notes were unconstitutional, that he therefore had not received enough constitutionally valid money to require filing a tax return, and that all rules promulgated by the Secretary of the Treasury were also unconstitutional.

The result of Carlson's submission of the false withholding form and his subsequent assertion of the Fifth Amendment in his year-end returns was that Carlson paid no federal income taxes for 1974 or 1975. Carlson claims that he validly asserted the Fifth Amendment to avoid incriminating himself for having previously filed the false withholding forms. After hearing all of the evidence, however, the district judge, sitting without a jury, found that Carlson "did not have a good-faith claim or reasonable ground for [asserting the] privilege, as he was a tax protestor and his activities and his actions and methods of submitting his returns were those of a tax protestor only." He held, therefore, that Carlson's Fifth Amendment claim did not constitute defense to his prosecution, pursuant to section 7203, for failure to file a tax return.

II

This case presents a question of first impression: can the privilege against self-incrimination constitute a defense to a section 7203 prosecution when it is asserted to avoid incrimination for a past violation of income tax laws? . . .

We have recently considered the validity of a Fifth Amendment assertion made in a tax return to avoid self-incrimination for non-tax-law violations. *United States* v. *Neff* . . . (1980). We held that the validity of such an assertion should be assessed in light of the following factors: whether the privilege was asserted at the time of filing the return and in response to specific

Some footnotes have been omitted.

questions contained therein, whether the taxpayer was faced with a real and appreciable danger of self-incrimination, and whether he had reasonable cause to believe that an honest response to the questions would provide a link in the chain of evidence needed to prosecute him for a crime. Moreover, we determined that the trial judge is to ascertain the potentially incriminatory nature of elicited responses by examining the questions, their setting, and the peculiarities of the case, with the burden of showing their hidden danger falling upon the taxpayer should the trial judge find the questions to be innocuous. . . .

An examination of the facts of this case reveals that Carlson did assert the privilege at the time he filed his return, and did so while facing a real and appreciable hazard of prosecution for having previously filed a false withholding form.[1] In addition, there is little doubt that a truthfully completed tax return, stating his gross income, the lack of federal income taxes actually withheld, and the true number of available deductions would have provided "'a lead or clue' to evidence having a tendency to incriminate" Carlson. . . . It is equally certain that a trial judge examining these facts would find a substantial threat of incrimination. Thus, it appears that Carlson satisfies those indicia of validity previously considered by us in cases where the privilege has been asserted to avoid self-incrimination other than under the tax laws.

When the privilege is asserted to avoid incrimination for past tax crimes, however, additional complications arise. If Carlson's assertion of the privilege were valid, it would license a form of conduct that would undermine the entire system of personal income tax collection. The essence of Carlson's plan was to claim 99 withholding exemptions so that no federal income tax would be withheld by his employer, and then to assert the Fifth Amendment privilege in lieu of a properly completed tax return, thus attempting to avoid both prosecution for the false withholding claim and payment of required income taxes. The widespread use of such a scheme would emasculate the present system of revenue collection which, by virtue of its scope alone, necessarily depends upon personal reporting by wage earners.[2] We are thus confronted with the collision of two critical interests: the privilege against self-incrimination, and the need for public revenue collection by a process necessarily reliant on self-reporting.

To decide which of these two interests prevails, we follow Supreme Court guidance:

> Tension between the State's demand for disclosures and the protection of the right against self-incrimination is likely to give rise to serious questions. Inevitably these must be resolved in terms of balancing the public need on the one hand, and the individual claim to constitutional protections on the other; neither interest can be treated lightly.

. . . We approach this balancing task with care, for we believe that fundamental constitutional protections, such as the privilege against self-incrimination, may be limited only for the most substantial of reasons. . . . The Supreme Court has stated that "the privilege has never been given the full scope which the values it helps to protect suggest," . . . but it has also persistently instructed that the privilege "must be accorded liberal construction in favor of the right it was intended to secure." . . . In balancing Carlson's assertion of the privilege against the governmental interest in revenue collection, we conclude that there are two factors we should consider: the history and purposes of the privilege, and the character and urgency of the countervailing public interests. . . .

The history of the privilege against self-incrimination predates its enshrinement within the Bill of Rights. . . . It initially arose in response to procedures whereby the ecclesiastical courts of England would compel one against

[1]The government concedes that Carlson could have been prosecuted under 26 U.S.C. § 7205 for filing a false withholding form.

[2]Because withholding forms are filed only with the employer, 26 U.S.C. § 3402(f)(2), false forms are not readily detected by the Internal Revenue Service. This problem is compounded when the taxpayer successfully refuses to provide the IRS with information normally received in a tax return.

whom no charge had been made to incriminate himself in response to broad, incrimination-seeking questions. . . . The privilege, which had been recognized to some extent in colonial America, . . . and which had been incorporated into the constitutions of several states prior to ratification of the federal Constitution, . . . was adopted by the drafters of the Bill of Rights "not only [as] an answer to numerous instances of colonial misrule but [as] a shield against 'the evils that lurk[ed] in the shadows of a new and untried sovereignty.'" . . .

As history illustrates, the primary purpose of the privilege is protective.

> The ancient privilege of a witness against being compelled to incriminate himself is precious to free men as a shield against high-handed and arrogant inquisitorial practices. It has survived centuries of controversies, periodically kindled by popular impatience that its protection sometimes allows the guilty to escape punishment. But it has endured as a wise and necessary protection of the individual against arbitrary power, and the price of occasional failures of justice is paid in the larger interest of general personal security.

. . . Stated differently, the privilege is an effort to "comply with the prevailing ethic that the individual is sovereign and that proper rules of battle between government and individual require that the individual not be bothered for less than good reason and not be conscripted by his opponent to defeat himself. . . ." . . .

In the case before us, Carlson has attempted to take advantage of the privilege's protective capacity to further a calculated effort to avoid the payment of taxes. Although it is true that Carlson actually seeks protection against self-incrimination for his prior tax crime, he does so only as part of an overall plan to evade taxes. The first step of that plan — submitting a false withholding form to his employer — was concealed from the Service by assertion of the Fifth Amendment on Carlson's year-end returns; and the very act of asserting the Fifth Amendment also effectuated the second step of the plan — failing to file meaningful returns that would divulge both his prior misstatement and his overall year-end tax liabilities. In other words, the Fifth Amendment was the linchpin of Carlson's plan to evade the payment of taxes. He used the privilege more as a sword than as a shield. . . . The history and purpose of the privilege do not, in light of such circumstances, weigh heavily in favor of extending its coverage to Carlson.

At the same time, the character and urgency of the public interest in raising revenue through self-reporting weighs heavily against affording the privilege to Carlson. The federal government's power to raise revenue is its lifeblood. Were taxpayers permitted to employ Carlson's scheme, they could avoid filing completed tax returns and thereby severely impair the government's ability to determine tax liability. Such frustration of the self-reporting system would force the Internal Revenue Service either to investigate each citizen's claimed and permissible withholding exemptions in an effort to prosecute for each separate filing of a false withholding claim, or to bear the burden of investigating and calculating from scratch each citizen's tax liability in order to assess the appropriate amount of income tax. Needless to say, either alternative would be inordinately burdensome if not impossible.

Another factor in our weighing process is that the requirement of filing an annual income tax return is primarily designed to facilitate revenue collection, not criminal prosecution. "[T]he questions in the income tax return [are] neutral on their face and directed at the public at large." . . . For this reason, refusal to file any return at all has never been protectable by a taxpayer's privilege against self-incrimination. *United States* v. *Sullivan* (1927). . . .

After weighing the appropriate factors, we conclude that the purpose and history of the privilege against self-incrimination do not compel protection of Carlson's actions, and that the character and urgency of the opposing revenue interests require that his scheme not be permitted. We therefore hold that an individual who seeks to frustrate the tax laws by claiming too many withholding exemptions, with an eye to covering that crime and evading the tax return requirement by assertion of the Fifth Amendment, is not entitled to the amendment's protection. . . .

Notes and Questions

1. This case creates a number of inconsistencies between the tax laws and other criminal laws. It is well settled that a person accused of crime can remain silent and refuse to cooperate in the state's making of a case before, during, and after trial. Defendants do not have "to take the stand" during criminal trials, even though what they might say could be highly useful in determining guilt. Where there is no evidence from the accused, the state is expected to make its case through its own investigation, and if it is more troublesome, the trouble is said to be the reasonable price of freedom.

   Trace the arguments that the court uses to distinguish violations of tax laws from other criminal cases. Are you satisfied that there is a difference between tax evasion and other crimes?
2. The court argues that the national interest in collecting revenue must be balanced against constitutional privileges. Would there not be a compelling state interest in all cases where constitutional privileges might be applicable? For example, would the community interest in safety affect constitutional privileges in murder and assault cases? Would the interest in property undo the constitutional law as it might apply in theft cases?
3. The *Carlson* case is one of many of roughly the same type. Tax protesters, often representing themselves, advance ingenious arguments based on the Constitution, the tax laws, or criminal procedure, only to have the courts reject them in the interest of securing the mainstay of the national revenue system — taxes on wages.

   A sample of the creativity brought to this battle can be found in the case of *U.S.* v. *Buras* (633 F.2d 1356, 1981), where the taxpayer made the argument that wages do not constitute income since the worker experiences no gain or profit through them. Like soil being eroded or a mine playing out, worker energies are exhausted through work and wages maintain but do not advance the worker. This argument, like so many others in a whole line of tax protester cases, was summarily dismissed.

   The best defense in a tax case resides neither in the Constitution nor in the intricacies of tax law and procedure but rather in the numbers of cases that must be processed through the IRS and the Justice Department. Were it simply a matter of finding enough laws on the books, there would be no substantial problem in eliminating the underground economy.

   A further illustration of the no-nonsense approach in wage cases can be found by comparing the disposition of criminal cases involving doctors and laborers; see Table 1. Many explanations can be offered for the more lenient disposition in cases involving doctors: more effective counsel in sentencing negotiations; sentencing factors like prior record; the status of the offender (higher-status offenders may be believed to have "suffered enough" through the loss of community prestige); but also quite possibly a deep-seated bias in the tax system when wage earners defect from the ranks of faithful taxpayers.

TABLE 1 *Tax Evasion Prosecutions, First Half 1978*

	Indicted	*Percent*	*Convicted*	*Percent*	*Sentenced to Prison*	*Percent*
Doctors	29	100	22	76	4	14
Laborers	75	100	65	87	29	39

Source: Hearings, U.S. Congress, Joint Economic Committee, "The Underground Economy," 96th Congress, 1st Session, 1979.

Tax protesting has long been practiced by religious groups opposed either to the intervention of government generally or to expenditures for war. In the early 1980s, a new wave of tax protesting arose regarding U.S. military involvement in Latin America and the shift in the national budget from social services to the military. The following case from the Vietnam era shows the main lines of conflict.

United States v. Catlett *584 F.2d 864 (1978)*

VAN OOSTERHOUT, J.

On October 25, 1977, Richard Ralston Catlett was charged in a three-count information, . . . with having willfully and knowingly failed to file his income tax returns for the calendar years 1971, 1972 and 1973 in violation of 26 U.S.C. § 7203. Defendant filed a motion to dismiss the information on the basis that the criminal prosecution against him constituted selective prosecution in violation of the Fifth and Fourteenth Amendments and further violated his first amendment rights of free speech, free exercise of religion and right of petition. He also moved to compel production by the government of certain documents for inspection . . . to substantiate his claim. . . .

Defendant Catlett is a 68 year old Quaker who runs a health food store in Columbia, Missouri. He has long been an active and public protester of certain policies of the U.S. Government, particularly with respect to its engaging in war and expending government funds for military related activities. He has travelled to Washington, D.C., to protest the Vietnam War, and in 1967 he organized the Student Action Center in his Columbia home as headquarters for the peace movement there. Catlett and his protests have received widespread publicity and notoriety. One facet of his protests has been his failure to file income tax returns. According to the defendant, he has refused to pay income taxes since the late 1940's. Apparently, Catlett first came to the attention of the Internal Revenue Service prior to the initiation of these criminal charges by reason of his prior failure to pay income taxes for the calendar years 1969 and 1970. The I.R.S. pursued civil remedies against Catlett which ultimately culminated in a takeover of his store by the I.R.S. until he raised over $4300 for payment of back taxes. Catlett once again continued his refusal to file income tax returns. Thereafter, this criminal prosecution was brought charging him with willfully and knowingly failing to file income tax returns for the calendar years 1971, 1972 and 1973.

Defendant Catlett's primary contention on appeal is that the district court erred in denying him discovery and a hearing or *in camera* inspection of requested government documents in order to substantiate his allegation of selective prosecution. However, a mere allegation of selective prosecution by the defendant does not require the government to disclose the contents of its files. . . .

. . . [A] defendant must first demonstrate that he has been singled out for prosecution while others similarly situated have not been prosecuted for conduct similar to that for which he was prosecuted. Second, the defendant must demonstrate that the government's discriminatory selection of him for prosecution was based upon an impermissible ground, such as race, religion or his exercise of his first amendment right to free speech. . . .

Defendant contends that he was selected for criminal prosecution based on a governmental policy which penalizes him for the exercise of his first amendment rights. He concedes that the government has the option to pursue civil or criminal remedies against persons who fail to file income tax returns. However, defendant

Some footnotes have been omitted.

claims that the government has established a policy which makes a clear distinction and an invidious discrimination between two classes of "nonfilers." The first class includes protestors whose alleged failure to file is in conformance with a personal, moral or religious belief but is little publicized. The government allegedly proceeds with civil remedies to recover unpaid taxes from members of this class. The second class includes "those protestors who are alleged to have failed to file because of objections to government policies of spending public funds for war activities and *whose protests and objections have been widely publicized.*" The government allegedly prosecutes members of the second class under the criminal statutes. Defendant Catlett, an admitted protestor of government military expenditure policies whose protests have "received widespread publicity and notoriety," contends that the decision to pursue criminal prosecution against him was the result of this policy.

As evidence of the alleged impermissible governmental purpose, defendant appended to his motion to dismiss a copy of I.R.S. Manual Supplement 95G–50 which is set out in pertinent part in [note 1 below].[1] This document directs a selective approach as the most effective and efficient means of deterring the widespread use of tax noncompliance as a means of protest. . . . The document also calls for a quarterly report including a brief narrative summary of tax protest trends and "sensitive case reports" as provided in IRM 9551. Defendant contends that this governmental policy is evidenced by an examination of these and other documents he requested in his motion to produce.[2]

---

[1]"We are concerned about the continuing publicity of taxpayers' admitted failures to comply with the Federal tax laws as a means of protest. Our concern is because the publicity of seemingly successful tax violations, regardless of motive, causes erosion of public confidence in our tax system, with a resultant adverse impact on voluntary compliance.

"Much of the "tax protest" publicity in recent years has focused on those protesting American military involvement in Southeast Asia.

* * *

"Nationally, the Intelligence Division has taken or is taking action against many violators who achieved self-promoted prominence as tax protestors. We believe the publicity attending these enforcement actions has done much to deter others from embarking on similar courses of illegal action.

* * *

"Our objective is to deter the widespread use of tax noncompliance as a means of protest. We believe a selective approach, rather than a large scale national project, is the most effective and efficient way to achieve this objective. Therefore, primary emphasis will be placed on the identification and investigation of cases in which prosecution will result in the maximum contribution to this objective. These cases will normally be those involving flagrant violations and those involving violations by individuals who have achieved notoriety as tax protestors. Such cases usually provide a vehicle for extensive news coverage which alerts a large segment of the taxpaying public to the consequences of noncompliance. The publicity aspects, of course, require a close working relationship with the public information officers.

"It is neither our intention nor desire to suppress dissent or to persecute individuals because they are critical of, or are identified with groups critical of, the tax system or government policies. Our sole purpose is to further the total Service objective of encouraging and achieving the highest possible degree of voluntary compliance with the tax laws by enforcing statutory sanctions. Therefore, the existing criteria for evaluating information items and selecting cases for criminal investigation must be scrupulously observed, with special emphasis on the high impact cases mentioned above."

[2]The defendant's motion to produce documents sought:

(1) Any and all internal revenue memoranda of the Internal Revenue Service referring to the defendant as a prominent or notorious tax protestor or recommending criminal prosecution of defendant because of his allegedly being a notorious protestor.

(2) Any and all similar internal memoranda of the Justice Department.

(3) All quarterly Regional Narrative Reports of Intelligence operations (IRM 9562) since September 30, 1973, and all "Sensitive Case Reports" as provided in IRM 9551 (as further identified in IRS Manual Supplement 95G–50).

(4) All summaries of successful cases in the tax protest area disseminated by the IRS, as referred to in the above IRS Manual Supplement.

(5) The correspondence from the IRS to the Justice Department recommending criminal prosecution of defendant.

(6) The correspondence from the Justice Department to the District Attorney for the Western District of Missouri directing the filing of criminal charges against defendant.

Assuming that such a governmental policy was applied to the defendant, and further taking as true all of defendant's allegations, we conclude that he has failed to establish a *prima facie* case of purposeful discrimination. While the decision to prosecute an individual cannot be made in retaliation for his exercise of his first amendment right to protest government war and tax policies, the prosecution of those protestors who publicly and with attendant publicity assert an alleged personal privilege not to pay taxes as part of their protest is not selection on an impermissible basis.

In *United States* v. *Swanson,* . . . this court upheld a selective program of investigation and prosecution of accountants, attorneys, and other professionals who customarily gave tax advice to others and who should have been knowledgeable about their tax responsibilities. More recently, . . . we upheld the conviction of a former Minnesota state representative for failure to file income tax returns in violation of 26 U.S.C. § 7203. Ojala had publicly announced at a news conference his refusal to file income tax returns because of his opposition to military activities of the United States in Vietnam. He was promptly investigated, indicted and convicted. Ojala claimed that the decision to prosecute him was made in reprisal for his exercise of his first amendment right to speak out against the war. . . . We noted that selection for prosecution based in part upon the potential deterrent effect on others serves a legitimate interest in promoting more general compliance with the tax laws. Since the government lacks the means to investigate and prosecute every suspected violation of the tax laws, it makes good sense to prosecute those who will receive, or are likely to receive, the attention of the media. . . .

Defendant's theory is *not* that he has been singled out for prosecution solely because he has protested the war and tax policies of the government. Rather, he objects to his prosecution only on the basis that he was selected due to the *publicity* his protests have received. The decision to prosecute, therefore, rests upon the amount of publicity one's protests receive, not upon the exercise of one's first amendment right to free speech. Such a decision is not based upon an impermissible ground but rather serves a legitimate governmental interest in promoting public compliance with the tax laws. . . .

☐ Tax changes came fast and furiously during the Reagan administration. First there was the Economic Recovery and Tax Act of 1980, which promised that tax reductions and favorable tax treatment to corporations and high-income taxpayers would increase saving and investment. These in turn would stimulate employment, increase tax revenues, and enable the government to balance the budget while cutting taxes. The best of all worlds would result: lower taxes, fuller employment, more revenue, without inflation.

Pretty much the opposite occurred. Investment remained flat or declined, and unemployment and business failures reached the highest levels since the Great Depression. Inflation slowed, not through the austerity of the federal government, which ran historically high deficits, but through the lower level of economic activity and lower oil prices.

Precipitated by unprecedented deficits, more tax law changes were made through the Tax Equity and Fiscal Responsibility Act of 1982. The equity was to come from closing some of the more flagrant loopholes created by the 1980 law as well as through a war on the underground economy and tax protesting. It was argued that if there were less "tax chiseling," the government's fiscal problems would be solved and the growing disenchantment of law-abiding taxpayers would abate.

The method that the government chose to employ was to pit computerization and cross-reporting against the ability of taxpayers to hide income. By matching one reporting source against another, it would be known whether a given taxpayer was reporting and reporting accurately. Independent contractors and waitresses, with ready ability to hide income, would be discovered through those who deducted payments to them on their own returns as a business expense, or through restaurant reports of gross sales, a percentage of which could measure tip income.

Those who aided and abetted underground economizers and protestors were also targeted. At latest reckoning, the underground economy is still very large, but no completely accurate statistics are available on its exact magnitude.

In the years following the furor over the underground economy and tax protesting, the emphasis shifted back to high-income taxpayers and tax shelters. Using the partnership business form, wealthier taxpayers could defer income to a later year, convert income taxable at ordinary rates to capital gains taxable at lower rates, or generate paper losses that could be used to offset income from other sources. In 1984, the IRS had some 330,000 cases in audit (almost twice the 1979 level) that involved tax shelters, and one-third of the 63,000-case backlog of the Tax Court concerned them. Losses in tax revenues were estimated at $7.5 billion for 1983 and 43 percent of taxpayers with incomes of $200,000 or more reported partnership losses. (For comparison, for taxpayers with incomes between $10 and $20 thousand, only 0.6 percent report such losses.)*

Some very large individual taxpayers — some among the *Forbes Magazine* $400,000,000 Club — paid no taxes at all, and Robert McIntyre of Citizens for Tax Justice observed that no real-estate developer of any consequence paid income taxes.

The virtual nonpayment of taxes by most of America's largest corporations also received publicity. General Electric, a large defense contractor that benefited substantially from increased military spending, earned $6.5 billion between 1981 and 1983 and paid no taxes. In fact, by a quirky provision of the 1980 tax changes, GE was able to get $283 million out of the government while cutting domestic investment by 15 percent. GE's tax strategizing was particularly flagrant, but not exceptional among corporate giants.

The answer was still another tax law change — the Tax Reform Act of 1986 — declared by President Reagan to be a "revolutionary" answer

---

*U.S. Congress, Joint Committee on Taxation, "Tax Reform Proposals: Tax Shelters," August 1985.

to an "un-American" tax system. (His role in creating what had become un-American was not made altogether clear.) This time, income was not to trickle down to the less fortunate by leaving untaxed resources in the hands of the wealthy. Everyone and every business was to pay, at reduced overall rates with fewer deductions, if necessary through minimum taxes where a taxpayer could otherwise entirely escape them.

Some skeptics, from Missouri and elsewhere, had questions. Would income taxation, which from its inception more than 70 years ago has had no perceptible effect in equalizing relative shares of income and wealth, suddenly become a force for equality? And how could it be that Robert Packwood, the voice for tax fairness on the Senate Finance Committee, would receive $7 million in campaign contributions, $1 million of them from PACs (political action committees) — the highest amount for any incumbent senator in 1986? It simply was too early for people disaffected with tax law to proclaim Kropotkin's prophecies dead.

CONCLUSION

This chapter has introduced some of the major explanations of law. Most of these themes recur in later chapters, and you will have numerous opportunities to see their worth in a variety of contexts. Each explanation — law as rules, discretion, value conflict, a balance of competing interests, a power play, or the voice of the people — tends to drive competing contenders from attention. But law resembles a field of forces rather than one force operating for all time, and more is gained through surveying an array of perspectives than through focusing on a single vision.

The strengths and weaknesses of alternative explanations can be put succinctly. Rule lovers drive toward certainty only to be brought up short by difficulties of interpretation and vagaries of fact. Students of discretion find choice everywhere but neglect constraint, not only from rules but also from the pressures of context. Those inclined toward the study of values advanced and retarded by law often become philosopher kings without territory who must settle for a running dialogue with the less thoughtful who nevertheless have power. Legal professionals who see themselves as balancing conflict and minimizing waste fail to see that involvement is never neutral and that they may be creating as much or more waste than they hoped to arrest. Power theorists can raise the current contradictions, but they rarely tell what can be done next, leaving their adherents waiting patiently for a spontaneous revolution. Neopopulists, seeking a demise of hierarchy and endemic alienation, sometimes overlook the less desirable aspects of popular will and the reasons earlier institutions failed.

The contradictory elements emerging from the study of different perspectives about law can leave people so confused that they assume the role of Kafka's commoners — aware that life can be miserable but in need of a more definitive clincher before attempting to work their way out of their misery. Nothing could be a more undesirable outcome from a broad-based study of law. After study, one must choose a best course of action rather than flounder among the pros and cons. To do otherwise simply perpetuates the status quo. The confusion we experience differs from unalloyed relativism where anything goes and power settles everything.

Clearly some understandings about law are more conducive to maintaining the status quo, whereas others support the need for profound change if not revolution. Judges and lawyers can be proud and the citizenry thankful if legal officials with prudent discretion apply legitimate rules to advance agreed-on values and alleviate conflict. But what if the Marxists and anarchists are right and law enacts power and privilege while leaving most people on the outside looking in? If they are reading the contemporary system correctly, then law study becomes part of the documentation of the decline of the American dream of equality and freedom and a painful prelude to transforming activism.

Suggested Additional Readings

Introduction to Law

Auerbach, Carl, et al. *The Legal Process.* San Francisco: Chandler, 1961.

Berman, Harold, and Greiner, William. *The Nature and Functions of Law.* Mineola, N.Y.: Foundation Press, 1966.

Schur, Edwin. *Law and Society.* New York: Random House, 1968.

Legal Reasoning

Cardozo, Benjamin. *The Nature of the Judicial Process.* New Haven, Conn.: Yale University Press, 1921.

Levi, Edward. *An Introduction to Legal Reasoning.* Chicago: University of Chicago Press, 1949.

Llewellyn, Karl. *The Bramble Bush.* New York: Oceana Publications, 1930.

Zelermyer, William. *The Process of Legal Reasoning.* Englewood Cliffs, N.J.: Prentice-Hall, 1963.

Law and Official Discretion

Arnold, Thurman. *The Symbols of Government.* New Haven, Conn.: Yale University Press, 1935.

Frank, Jerome. *Law and the Modern Mind.* New York: Anchor Books, 1930.

———. *Courts on Trial.* Princeton, N.J.: Princeton University Press, 1949.

Noonan, John. *Persons and Masks of the Law.* New York: Farrar, Straus & Giroux, 1976.

Law and Values

Berry, Wendell. *The Unsettling of America.* New York: Avon Books, 1978.

Cahn, Edmond. *The Moral Decision.* Bloomington: Indiana University Press, 1955.

———. *The Sense of Injustice.* Bloomington: Indiana University Press, 1964.

Ellul, Jacques. *The Technological Society.* New York: Random House, 1964.

Piaget, Jean. *The Moral Judgement of the Child.* New York: Free Press, 1965.

Rawls, John. *A Theory of Justice.* Cambridge, Mass.: Harvard University Press, 1971.

Shklar, Judith. *Legalism.* Cambridge, Mass.: Harvard University Press, 1964.

Thompson, William. *At the Edge of History.* New York: Harper & Row, 1971.

Law and Conflicting Interests

Coser, Lewis. *The Functions of Social Conflict.* New York: Free Press, 1956.

Ehrlich, Eugen. *Fundamental Principles of the Sociology of Law.* Translated by W. Moll. New York: Russell & Russell, 1962.

Pound, Roscoe. *Social Control Through Law.* New Haven, Conn.: Yale University Press, 1942.

Summers, Robert. *Law: Its Nature, Functions and Limits.* Englewood Cliffs, N.J.: Prentice-Hall, 1972.

Wigdor, David. *Roscoe Pound.* Westport, Conn.: Greenwood Press, 1974.

Law, Status, Wealth, and Power

Babb, Hugh, trans. *Soviet Legal Philosophy.* Cambridge, Mass.: Harvard University Press, 1951.

Balbus, Isaac. *The Dialectics of Legal Repression.* New Brunswick, N.J.: Transaction, 1973.

Bankowski, Zenon, and Mungham, Geoff. *Images of Law.* London: Routledge & Kegan Paul, 1976.

Black, Jonathan, ed. *Radical Lawyers.* New York: Avon Books, 1971.

Bluestone, Barry, *et al. Deindustrialization of America.* New York: Basic Books, 1982.

Cain, Maureen, and Hunt, Alan. *Marx and Engels on Law.* London: Academic Press, 1979.

Genovese, Eugene. *Roll Jordan Roll.* New York: Pantheon, 1974.

Kirchheimer, Otto. *Political Justice.* Princeton, N.J.: Princeton University Press, 1961.

Lefcourt, Robert. *Law Against the People.* New York: Random House, 1971.

Mills, C. Wright. *The Power Elite.* New York: Oxford University Press, 1957.

Quinney, Richard. *Class, State & Crime.* New York: McKay, 1977.

Weber, Max. *On Law in Economy and Society.* Translated with introduction by Max Rheinstein et al. Cambridge, Mass.: Harvard University Press, 1954.

Law and Popular Will

Baldwin, Roger, ed. *Kropotkin's Revolutionary Pamphlets.* New York: Vanguard, 1927.

Bohannan, Paul, ed. *Law and Warfare.* Garden City, N.Y.: Natural History Press, 1967.

Bookchin, Murray. *The Ecology of Freedom.* Palo Alto, Calif.: Cheshire, 1982.

Guerin, Daniel. *Anarchism from Theory to Practice.* New York: Monthly Review Press, 1970.

Llewellyn, Karl, and Hoebel, E. Adamson. *The Cheyenne Way.* Norman: University of Oklahoma Press, 1941.

Maine, Henry. *Ancient Law.* London: Oxford University Press, 1931.

Martin, James J. *Men Against the State.* Colorado Springs: Myles, 1970.

Nader, Laura, ed. *Law in Culture and Society.* Chicago: Aldine, 1969.

Savigny, Fredrick. *Of the Vocation of Our Age for Legislation and Jurisprudence.* Translated by A. Hayward, London: Littlewood, 1831.

Tönnies, Ferdinand. *Community and Society.* Edited and translated by Charles P. Loomis. New York: Harper & Row, 1963.

Ward, Colin. *Anarchy in Action.* New York: Harper & Row, 1973.

Woodcock, George. *Anarchism.* New York: New American Library, 1962.

Police Court. (The Bettmann Archive, Inc.)

CHAPTER 7 The Police

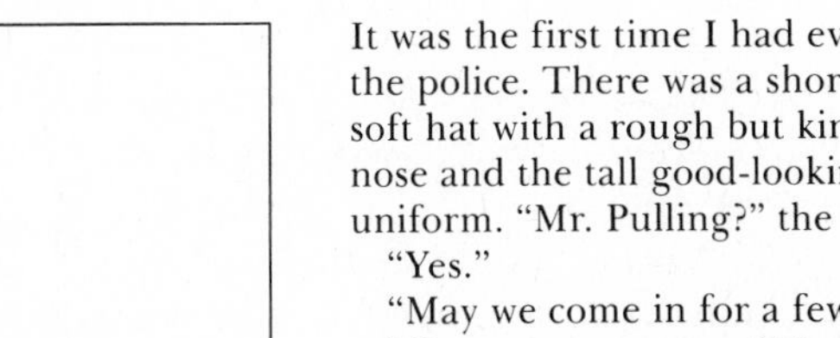

It was the first time I had ever been called on by the police. There was a short middle-aged man in a soft hat with a rough but kindly face and a broken nose and the tall good-looking young man in uniform. "Mr. Pulling?" the detective asked.

"Yes."

"May we come in for a few moments?"

"Have you a warrant?" I asked.

"Oh no, no, it hasn't come to that. We just want to have a word or two with you." I wanted to say something about the Gestapo, but I thought it wiser not. I led them into the dining-room, but I didn't ask them to sit down. The detective showed me an identity card and I read on it that he was Detective-Sergeant Sparrow, John.

"You know a man called Wordsworth, Mr. Pulling?"

"Yes, he's a friend of my aunt's."

"Did you receive a package from him in the street yesterday?"

"I certainly did."

"Would you have any objection to our examining the package, Mr. Pulling?"

"I most certainly would."

"You know, sir, we could easily have obtained a search warrant but we want to do things delicately. . . ."

Graham Greene, *Travels with My Aunt* (1969)

A policeman's lot is not a happy one.

Gilbert and Sullivan, *The Pirates of Penzance*

In the stereotypical frontier town, the sheriff — not the judge, as in Gilbert and Sullivan — would have sung, "I am the law." Indeed, he was even referred to as a *lawman.* To many people, the police officer still not only symbolizes the law, but *is* the law. As the first quote above reveals, a person may often feel that the law is not what a judge says it is, but rather what the police officer says it is.

One source of such a feeling is the power that the police have. In other parts of this book, the discretionary powers of district attorneys, judges, and even juries are discussed. It should not be surprising to find that the police, who are an integral part of the same system, hold much the same power. The readings in this chapter raise many issues that may have occurred to you when you read the introductory epigraphs. For example, how do the police affect the law, and how does the law affect them? Should police have any discretion about when to act? What controls are there over police discretion? What are the functions of the police? What do they do? What should they be doing?

The following account was written by George Orwell, a brilliant essayist and journalist, most widely known as the author of the novels *1984* and *Animal Farm.* The story is about Orwell's service in Southeast Asia as a policeman in Burma when it was under British rule, and presents an intriguing, first-person account about the use of power and authority and how decisions are made and carried out. Orwell's experience in Burma probably influenced his thinking on the themes of freedom and totalitarian rule that he explored in his famous novels.

Shooting an Elephant *George Orwell*

In Moulmein, in Lower Burma, I was hated by large numbers of people — the only time in my life that I have been important enough for this to happen to me. I was sub-divisional police officer of the town, and in an aimless, petty kind of way anti-European feeling was very bitter. No one had the guts to raise a riot, but if a European woman went through the bazaars alone somebody would probably spit betel juice over her dress. As a police officer I was an obvious target and was baited whenever it seemed safe to do so. When a nimble Burman tripped me up on the football field and the referee (another Burman) looked the other way, the crowd yelled with hideous laughter. This happened more than once. In the end the sneering yellow faces of young men that met me everywhere, the insults hooted after me when I was at a safe distance, got badly on my nerves. The young Buddhist priests were the worst of all. There were several thousands of them in the town and none of them seemed to have anything to do except stand on street corners and jeer at Europeans.

All this was perplexing and upsetting. For at that time I had already made up my mind that imperialism was an evil thing and the sooner I chucked up my job and got out of it the better. Theoretically — and secretly, of course — I was all for the Burmese and all against their oppressors, the British. As for the job I was doing, I hated it more bitterly than I can perhaps make clear. In a job like that you see the dirty work of Empire at close quarters. The wretched prisoners huddling in the stinking cages of the lock-ups, the grey, cowed faces of the long-term convicts, the scarred buttocks of the men who had been flogged with bamboos — all these oppressed me with an intolerable sense of guilt. But I could get nothing into perspective. I was young and ill-educated and I had had to think

---

out my problems in the utter silence that is imposed on every Englishman in the East. I did not even know that the British Empire is dying, still less did I know that it is a great deal better than the younger empires that are going to supplant it. All I knew was that I was stuck between my hatred of the empire I served and my rage against the evil-spirited little beasts who tried to make my job impossible. With one part of my mind I thought of the British Raj as an unbreakable tyranny, as something clamped down, in *saecula saeculorum* [forever], upon the will of prostrate peoples; with another part I thought that the greatest joy in the world would be to drive a bayonet into a Buddhist priest's guts. Feelings like these are the normal by-products of imperialism; ask any Anglo-Indian official, if you can catch him off duty.

One day something happened which in a round-about way was enlightening. It was a tiny incident in itself, but it gave me a better glimpse than I had had before of the real nature of imperialism — the real motives for which despotic governments act. Early one morning the subinspector at a police station the other end of the town rang me up on the 'phone and said that an elephant was ravaging the bazaar. Would I please come and do something about it? I did not know what I could do, but I wanted to see what was happening and I got on to a pony and started out. I took my rifle, an old .44 Winchester and much too small to kill an elephant, but I thought the noise might be useful *in terrorem* [as a warning]. Various Burmans stopped me on the way and told me about the elephant's doings. It was not, of course, a wild elephant, but a tame one which had gone "must." It had been chained up, as tame elephants always are when their attack of "must" is due, but on the previous night it had broken its chain and escaped. Its mahout, the only person who could manage it when it was in that state, had set out in pursuit, but had taken the wrong direction and was now twelve hours' journey away, and in the morning the elephant had suddenly reappeared in the town. The Burmese population had no weapons and were quite helpless against it. It had already destroyed somebody's bamboo hut, killed a cow and raided some fruit-stalls and devoured the stock; also it had met the municipal rubbish van and, when the driver jumped out and took to his heels, had turned the van over and inflicted violences upon it.

The Burmese subinspector and some Indian constables were waiting for me in the quarter where the elephant had been seen. It was a very poor quarter, a labyrinth of squalid bamboo huts, thatched with palm-leaf, winding all over a steep hillside. I remember that it was a cloudy, stuffy morning at the beginning of the rains. We began questioning the people as to where the elephant had gone and, as usual, failed to get any definite information. That is invariably the case in the East; a story always sounds clear enough at a distance, but the nearer you get to the scene of events the vaguer it becomes. Some of the peple said that the elephant had gone in one direction, some said that he had gone in another, some professed not even to have heard of any elephant. I had almost made up my mind that the whole story was a pack of lies, when we heard yells a little distance away. There was a loud, scandalized cry of "Go away, child! Go away this instant!" and an old woman with a switch in her hand came round the corner of a hut, violently shooing away a crowd of naked children. Some more women followed, clicking their tongues and exclaiming; evidently there was something that the children ought not to have seen. I rounded the hut and saw a man's dead body sprawling in the mud. He was an Indian, a black Dravidian coolie, almost naked, and he could not have been dead many minutes. The people said that the elephant had come suddenly upon him round the corner of the hut, caught him with its trunk, put its foot on his back and ground him into the earth. This was the rainy season and the ground was soft, and his face had scored a trench a foot deep and a couple of yards long. He was lying on his belly with arms crucified and head sharply twisted to one side. His face was coated with mud, the eyes wide open, the teeth bared and grinning with an expression of unendurable agony. (Never tell me, by the way, that the dead look peaceful. Most of the corpses I have seen looked devilish.) The friction of the great beast's foot had stripped the skin from his back as neatly as one skins a rabbit. As soon as I saw the dead man I sent an orderly to a friend's house nearby to borrow an elephant rifle. I had already sent back the pony, not wanting it to go mad with fright and throw me if it smelt the elephant.

The orderly came back in a few minutes with a rifle and five cartridges, and meanwhile some Burmans had arrived and told us that the elephant was in the paddy fields below, only a few hundred yards away. As I started forward practically the whole population of the quarter flocked out of the houses and followed me. They had seen the rifle and were all shouting excitedly that I was going to shoot the elephant. They had not shown much interest in the elephant when he was merely ravaging their homes, but it was different now that he was going to be shot. It was a bit of fun to them, as it would be to an English crowd; besides they wanted the meat. It made me vaguely uneasy. I had no intention of shooting the elephant — I had merely sent for the rifle to defend myself if necessary — and it is always unnerving to have a crowd following you. I marched down the hill, looking and feeling a fool, with the rifle over my shoulder and an evergrowing army of people jostling at my heels. At the bottom, when you got away from the huts, there was a metalled road and beyond that a miry waste of paddy fields a thousand yards across, not yet ploughed but soggy from the first rains and dotted with coarse grass. The elephant was standing eight yards from the road, his left side towards us. He took not the slightest notice of the crowd's approach. He was tearing up bunches of grass, beating them against his knees to clean them and stuffing them into his mouth.

I had halted on the road. As soon as I saw the elephant I knew with perfect certainty that I ought not to shoot him. It is a serious matter to shoot a working elephant — it is comparable to destroying a huge and costly piece of machinery — and obviously one ought not to do it if it can possibly be avoided. And at that distance, peacefully eating, the elephant looked no more dangerous than a cow. I thought then and I think now that his attack of "must" was already passing off; in which case he would merely wander harmlessly about until the mahout came back and caught him. Moreover, I did not in the least want to shoot him. I decided that I would watch him for a little while to make sure that he did not turn savage again, and then go home.

But at that moment I glanced round at the crowd that had followed me. It was an immense crowd, two thousand at the least and growing every minute. It blocked the road for a long distance on either side. I looked at the sea of yellow faces above the garish clothes — faces all happy and excited over this bit of fun, all certain that the elephant was going to be shot. They were watching me as they would watch a conjurer about to perform a trick. They did not like me, but with the magical rifle in my hands I was momentarily worth watching. And suddenly I realized that I should have to shoot the elephant after all. The people expected it of me and I had got to do it; I could feel their two thousand wills pressing me forward, irresistibly. And it was at this moment, as I stood there with the rifle in my hands, that I first grasped the hollowness, the futility of the white man's dominion in the East. Here was I, the white man with his gun, standing in front of the unarmed native crowd — seemingly the leading actor of the piece; but in reality I was only an absurd puppet pushed to and fro by the will of those yellow faces behind. I perceived in this moment that when the white man turns tyrant it is his own freedom that he destroys. He becomes a sort of hollow, posing dummy, the conventionalized figure of a sahib. For it is the condition of his rule that he shall spend his life in trying to impress the "natives," and so in every crisis he has got to do what the "natives" expect of him. He wears a mask, and his face grows to fit it. I had got to shoot the elephant. I had committed myself to doing it when I sent for the rifle. A sahib has got to act like a sahib; he has got to appear resolute, to know his own mind and do definite things. To come all that way, rifle in hand, with two thousand people marching at my heels, and then to trail feebly away, having done nothing — no, that was impossible. The crowd would laugh at me. And my whole life, every white man's life in the East, was one long struggle not to be laughed at.

But I did not want to shoot the elephant. I watched him beating his bunch of grass against his knees, with that preoccupied grandmotherly air that elephants have. It seemed to me that it would be murder to shoot him. At that age I was not squeamish about killing animals, but I had never shot an elephant and never wanted to. (Somehow it always seems worse to kill a *large* animal.) Besides, there was the beast's owner to be considered. Alive, the elephant was worth at least a hundred pounds; dead, he would only be worth the value of his tusks, five pounds, possibly. But I had got to act quickly. I turned to some experienced-looking Burmans who had been there when we arrived, and asked them how the elephant had been behaving. They all said the same thing: he took no notice of you if you left him alone, but he might charge if you went too close to him.

It was perfectly clear to me what I ought to do. I ought to walk up to within, say, twenty-five yards of the elephant and test his behavior. If he charged, I could shoot; if he took no notice of me, it would be safe to leave him until the mahout came back. But also I knew that I was going to do no such thing. I was a poor shot with a rifle and the ground was soft mud into which one would sink at every step. If the elephant charged and I missed him, I should have about as much chance as a toad under a steamroller. But even then I was not thinking particularly of my own skin, only of the watchful yellow faces behind. For at that moment, with the crowd watching me, I was not afraid in the ordinary sense, as I would have been if I had been alone. A white man mustn't be frighted in front of "natives"; and so, in general, he isn't frightened. The sole thought in my mind was that if anything went wrong those two thousand Burmans would see me pursued, caught, trampled on and reduced to a grinning corpse like that Indian up the hill. And if that happened it was quite probable that some of them would laugh. That would never do. There was only one alternative. I shoved the cartridges into the magazine and lay down on the road to get a better aim.

The crowd grew very still, and a deep, low, happy sigh, as of people who see the theatre curtain go up at last, breathed from innumerable throats. They were going to have their bit of fun after all. The rifle was a beautiful German thing with cross-hair sights. I did not then know that in shooting an elephant one would shoot to cut an imaginary bar running from ear-hole to ear-hole. I ought, therefore, as the elephant was sideways on, to have aimed straight at his ear-hole; actually I aimed several inches in front of this, thinking the brain would be further forward.

When I pulled the trigger I did not hear the bang or feel the kick — one never does when a shot goes home — but I heard the devilish roar of glee that went up from the crowd. In that instant, in too short a time, one would have thought, even for the bullet to get there, a mysterious terrible change had come over the elephant. He neither stirred nor fell, but every line of his body had altered. He looked suddenly stricken, shrunken, immensely old, as though the frightful impact of the bullet had paralysed him without knocking him down. At last, after what seemed a long time — it might have been five seconds, I dare say — he sagged flabbily to his knees. His mouth slobbered. An enormous senility seemed to have settled upon him. One could have imagined him thousands of years old. I fired again into the same spot. At the second shot he did not collapse but climbed with desperate slowness to his feet and stood weakly upright, with legs sagging and head drooping. I fired a third time. That was the shot that did for him. You could see the agony of it jolt his whole body and knock the last remnant of strength from his legs. But in falling he seemed for a moment to rise, for as his hind legs collapsed beneath him he seemed to tower upward like a huge rock toppling, his trunk reaching skywards like a tree. He trumpeted, for the first and only time. And then down he came, his belly towards me, with a crash that seemed to shake the ground even where I lay.

I got up. The Burmans were already racing past me across the mud. It was obvious that the elephant would never rise again, but he was not dead. He was breathing very rhythmically with long rattling gasps, his great mound of a side painfully rising and falling. His mouth was wide open — I could see far down into caverns of pale pink throat. I waited a long time for him to die, but his breathing did not weaken. Finally I fired my two remaining shots into the spot where I thought his heart must be. The thick blood welled out of him like red velvet, but still he did not die. His body did not even jerk when the shots hit him, the tortured breathing continued without a pause. He was dying, very slowly and in great agony, but in some world remote from me where not even a bullet could damage him further. I felt that I had got to put an end to that dreadful noise. It seemed dreadful to see the great beast lying there, powerless to move and yet powerless to die, and not even to be able to finish him. I sent back for my small rifle and poured shot after shot into his heart and down his throat. They seemed to make no impression. The tortured gasps continued as steadily as the ticking of a clock.

In the end I could not stand it any longer and went away. I heard later that it took him half an hour to die. Burmans were bringing dahs and baskets even before I left, and I was told they had stripped his body almost to the bones by the afternoon.

Afterwards, of course, there were endless discussions about the shooting of the elephant. The owner was furious, but he was only an Indian and could do nothing. Besides, legally I had done the right thing, for a mad elephant has to be killed, like a mad dog, if its owner fails to control it. Among the Europeans opinion was divided. The older men said I was right, the younger men said it was a damn shame to shoot an elephant for killing a coolie, because an elephant was worth more than any damn Coringhee coolie. And afterwards I was very glad that the coolie had been killed; it put me legally in the right and it gave me a sufficient pretext for shooting the elephant. I often wondered whether any of the others grasped that I had done it solely to avoid looking a fool.

1 A CITIZEN'S PERSPECTIVE

> If law is not made more than a policeman's nightstick, American society will be destroyed.
> Arthur J. Goldberg

Orwell's description of a police officer's decision, although it occurs in a remote time and place, suggests many important themes of contemporary significance and is an appropriate introduction for this chapter. The enforcement of law is not an automatic process. The police officer is not part of a mechanistic system in which the law is always clear and can be easily and predictably applied. Rather, the police officer — like the law itself, as described in Chapter 1 — is influenced by a variety of social, economic, and political factors. Although the uniform worn by police officers often suggests cool impersonality, a close examination shows that the police officer works at the center of a "hot," confused storm of conflicting emotions and constraints.

Orwell's essay illustrates the paradox of police power. To the Burmese citizen, it seems obvious that the police officer, carrying an elephant gun and representing colonial power, also has much power. Yet Orwell himself feels almost powerless, pushed willy-nilly by the crowd. This difference in perception continues to produce police-citizen misunderstanding and antagonism.

In the following reading, Charles Reich, a former professor at the Yale Law School, graphically describes his feelings about his own confrontations with the police. He also explains some elements of the police role in society and suggests how to find an acceptable balance between the need for social order and predictable rules, and the competing need for flexibility and individual freedom. Subsequent readings and cases in this chapter explore other perspectives on this issue, on what role the U.S. Supreme Court should play in controlling police power, and on what alternatives to the present structure and composition of police forces are available.

Police Questioning of Law Abiding Citizens *Charles A. Reich*

For a member of one of the most staid occupations, I have had a disturbing number of encounters with the police. I can count nine or ten times that I have been stopped and questioned in the past few years — almost enough to qualify me as an adjunct member of the Mafia. Most recently, when the officer told me he had the right to stop anyone any place any time — and for no reason — I decided I had better write an article. Let me describe some of my adventures.

My problem is that I like to walk. In Chevy Chase, Maryland, a tree-lined suburb that smells of honeysuckle on spring nights, a police car swooped down on me about eleven at night. The officer wanted me to identify myself: where did I live, where was I going. He was not looking for anyone in particular; just on patrol. In Santa Barbara, California, where I had gone to give a paper on conservation, I was stopped on Main Street, about ten blocks from where I was staying. I was looking for a restaurant, a search which I was allowed to continue after giving a satisfactory explanation of my presence. In Belmont, Massachusetts, I was halted two blocks from my brother's house. I admit that it was *very* early morning. But my small niece had been up. In New Haven, about eleven at night, I was stopped a half mile from my own residence. Since this was home territory, and since the officers had summoned me off the sidewalk without even getting out of their patrol car, I protested. This was the only time that the police implied they were actually looking for someone — a prowler, they said. Two more patrol cars and a sergeant arrived as I continued to stand my ground on the sidewalk. After ten minutes' discussion we all dispersed. In Long Lake, New York, an Adirondack vacation town, a state policeman stopped me on the main street about ten at night. I was walking on the sidewalk. He demanded I tell my age, occupation, and reason for being out on the street, and that I produce some identification. When I told him I had none, he was ready to arrest me — for walking on the wrong side of the street, or for vagrancy, he said. I pointed out that my family has owned a house at Long Lake for sixty

---

Reprinted by permission of The Yale Law Journal Company, the author, and Fred B. Rothman & Company from *The Yale Law Journal Company,* Vol. 75, pp. 1161–1172.

years — and that there was no sidewalk on the other side of the street.

I should add that I have been stopped many times without cause while driving a car. It has happened in New York State, in Massachusetts, and as far away as Oregon; always in broad daylight; each time I asked why I had been flagged down with siren and flashing light; each time at first no answer was given; only when I was dismissed did the officer say "just checking." In each case the officer wanted not only to see my license, but also to know where I was going, where I was coming from, and my business. In all of my experiences, I have never been arrested, never told that I was committing an offense, and never told that I answered a particular description.

These circumstances define the problem that I wish to discuss. In this article, I am not concerned with police investigations after a crime has been reported, or with circumstances which suggest that the individual who has been stopped may be doing something illegal. My problem is this: no crime has been reported, no suspect has been described, there is no visible sign of an offense, there is nothing whatever to direct police attention to this particular individual. I am concerned with what is called *preventive* police work.

Although the experiences I have had are in themselves trivial, the increasing preventive activities of the police present an issue of first importance. What happens when the person stopped is a Negro, or poor, or frightened? What intrusions upon privacy, what affronts to dignity, occur? How much discretion do the police have to invent an offense for anyone who objects to being questioned? May the police establish a regular routine of requiring pedestrians to carry identification and explain their presence, or of requiring motorists to stop and tell where they are going? I do not have answers, but I have some questions. Let us focus on the moment of contact between the citizen and the police.

The first issue that troubles me is whether the police have any power at all to stop a law abiding person on a public street. Of course any individual has a right to approach any other individual — to ask him the time, to ask him how to find the Yale Divinity School, or to ask his opinion about foreign policy. But it is not quite the same when the police stop someone. There is authority in the approach of the police, and command in their tone. I can ignore the ordinary person, but can I ignore the police? Police officers tell me that they have a *right* to stop anyone in a public place, without having a reason. I think I have a *right* not to be stopped. So far as I know, reported court decisions do not supply us with an answer.

The next issue is what questions the police may ask. Name? Address? Occupation? Age? Marital status? Explanation of presence and destination? Documentary proof of identity? Many people might have no objection to giving out any or all of these facts about themselves. But I have a strong sense that however innocuous the facts may be, some things are nobody's business. I do not particularly like to be probed, and I like it much less when the probing is official. I certainly do not think that every police officer has a roving commission to satisfy his curiosity about anyone he sees on the street.

Closely related to questioning is the issue of the individual's replies. May he refuse to answer? May he demand to know the identity of the officer? May he demand to know why he is being stopped? May he lie to the officer about his age, or why he is out on the street? May he turn and go on his way? I submit that very few people know what their rights are under such circumstances. I do not even know how to find out.

The next issue is what *actions* the officer may take if the individual attempts to claim some rights. May the officer detain him? Frisk him? Search him? Take him to the police station? Hold him there for questioning? Here the law does supply an answer in general terms, for we know that arrests and searches can be made only upon probable cause. But concrete answers really depend upon what we conclude about the right to stop and to ask questions.

The last issue is what remedies are available to the citizen to test out the law in the circumstances I have described. There is always the right to defend against any criminal charge that may result. There is always a tort action for false arrest. Perhaps in some extreme circumstances there might be grounds for an action under one the civil rights statutes, or for an injunction against a continuing police practice. But these remedies are often costly, time-consuming, and ultimately unsuccessful. No one effectively "polices the police."

The questions that I have raised are difficult, but they should be faced. Let me suggest some of the fundamental issues that are at stake in these small encounters.

1. TONE

On one occasion when a patrol car flagged me down for a "routine check" on Route 2 near Boston, the officer, after ascertaining my name by looking at my driver's license, said "What were you doing in Boston, Charlie?" And he continued quite deliberately to address me in that fashion. The incident happened a couple of years ago, so that I do not think he mistook me for a teenager. On several of the other occasions I have mentioned, I was either called by my first name or addressed in a way that was intentionally familiar. Nor am I unique in having such experiences. My brother, a psychiatrist, his wife, and a lady friend, also a psychiatrist, were driving through Keene, New Hampshire early on a Sunday evening after a weekend in Vermont. A policeman stopped them — for no reason. He made all of them get out of the car and stand in the rain. He called my brother by his first name. After looking at identification papers belonging to their friend, he said, in a tone that carried insult, "What kind of a doctor are you, Ellie?"

I have read that when Negroes complain of "police brutality" in areas like the Watts section of Los Angeles, they are as much concerned with verbal tone as with physical violence. And this is understandable; incidents like those described cause a sense of injury to the person in a direct, visceral sense. Members of a minority group are likely to be especially sensitive to such address. There is something deeply offensive in familiarity which is deliberately used by a person in authority for the purpose of causing humiliation.

The crucial importance of tone may be demonstrated by a simple test: Imagine that in any of the ten incidents I have related, the officer said "Mr." or "Sir" or "excuse me" as I would do when addressing a stranger. The average person's response would be quite different; perhaps I would not even be writing this article. I am not so unrealistic as to suppose that every encounter with the police can leave the ego unbruised, nor do I suggest that the police should practice obsequious manners. But we are dealing with the chief point of personal contact between the individual citizen and the law, and what is at stake is the respect and dignity due to each individual from his government. It is no small matter.

2. DISCRIMINATION

Although I have based much of what I have said so far on personal experience, it is not for myself that I write. For what is but a rare occurrence in my life may be a much more significant part of the lives of minority groups and of the poor. I suspect that the police are far more likely to stop a Negro than a white man; far more likely to question a shabbily dressed man than one in an expensive suit. I imagine that the tone of the questioning is different. I can get away with asking a policeman what right he has to stop me; could a Negro safely do this? Of course the crime statistics show that the crime rate is higher among Negroes and among the poor, but that is just what worries me — that statistics and appearances will be held against individuals, and that the police in their contacts with the populace will treat some group differently from others. It is a form of discrimination which is particularly baleful because it is so hard to prove and so hard to correct. And it is a form of discrimination which must deeply affect the attitudes of minority groups toward the police and government. It is the raw material of alienation and rebellion.

There is one minority group that deserves special mention in connection with police questioning — youth; in particular, teenagers. This is a group easily identified and easily harassed. It is a group with a special need for privacy in public, since they have insufficient privacy at home. It is a group acutely conscious of its dignity and resentful of authority. The boy humiliated by a police officer in front of others must surely feel his whole self threatened.

I recall one story told by a college freshman in California: police officers stopped a whole group of college boys and girls on their way by car to a picnic. The officers questioned everyone with an infuriating slowness, insisting that the boys call them "Sir" and finally making everyone sit and wait for a long time. No charges of any kind were made, and finally the group was granted permission to go on its way.

Youth present a problem in every community, and many adults are ready to wish their responsibilities on the police. If the police are not scrupulous in their contacts with youth, the effect may be to aggravate just the cynicism, alienation and resentment which are already the sources of trouble. Here the use of authority to stop and question is likely to inflict direct harm to society in terms of a lasting disrespect for law.

3. DISCRETIONARY LAWS

Discrimination and tone in questioning are important problems only because the questioner has authority. It seems to be customary in the retail automobile business to call everyone by his first name; if a buyer finds it annoying, he can lower his offer for the car. If the questioner is a government man but not a policeman, we are still in the realm of annoyance rather than a great issue; one can always talk back, or lodge a complaint. It is the police officer's power to *arrest* that makes his mode of address a matter of concern. That power raises the important question of discretionary laws.

The police officer who stopped me in Long Lake, New York told me that he could arrest me on any of three or four charges if he chose to. He mentioned vagrancy and walking on the wrong side of the road; he might also have mentioned disorderly conduct, refusal to obey an order, loitering and perhaps the catchall notion of "suspicion" used in some jurisdictions. Laws on the subject of vagrancy and disorderly conduct are so broad and so vague that a policeman has almost unlimited discretion; walking down the street might indeed come within the literal definition of vagrancy. It is small comfort that the person arrested for vagrancy might eventually be found innocent by a court. The source of an officer's power is not so much the possibility that he can subject a person to arrest, delay, a night in jail, frantic calls to relatives and lawyers, the expense and trouble of a trial, and the undeniable uncertainty about whether a local magistrate's court might, in fact, convict. No one who refuses to "cooperate" with the police can be certain that the policeman will not arrest him. The motorist is still more vulnerable; he can always be charged with having faulty equipment or an obstructed window, or with careless driving, and his license can be revoked in some states even if he is not convicted of any charge. For either the pedestrian or the motorist, arrest, no matter how unjustified, can have lasting consequences. Many application, employment, and security forms ask whether the "subject" has ever been *arrested.* And for most people, custody and jail can be a severe and disturbing shock.

My present concern is not with these discretionary laws as such. They present a separate issue which should be of major concern to lawyers. My point here is that this virtually unlimited sanction lurks behind the policeman's questions and the citizen's answers; it makes me think twice before I tell a policeman that my reason for going for a walk is none of his business.

4. INSTITUTIONALIZING THE QUESTIONING PROCESS

So long as police questioning remains genuinely casual and occasional, the problems it presents are comparatively limited. But when such a practice becomes accepted in theory, it tends to be made part of regular routine. We now have a number of police practices which are essentially institutionalizations of, or extrapolations from, the questioning process.

Most of these practices have grown up around the automobile. In Connecticut, the state police set up roadblocks and stop whole lines of cars in order to check drivers' licenses and registrations. Connecticut also uses roadblocks on holidays to check all drivers for signs of drinking. And near the New York border, Connecticut police have regularly placed roadblocks to stop teenage drivers to see if they have been drinking in New York State, where the minimum age is lower. Some states also use roadblocks to check for equipment such as faulty brakes and worn tires. Several years ago, I discovered that at toll booths on the Connecticut Turnpike and the New York State Thruway cameras were used to take photographs of vehicles passing through. The Acting Counsel of the New York State Thruway Authority wrote me that such photographic records were used to determine "if vehicles are being properly classified by our toll collectors." "With respect to the question of authority for making such records, if thereby you mean statutory authority, we need none. . . ."

5. UNCHECKED AUTHORITY

Police questioning carries with it the inherent danger of any unchecked, unreviewable authority. What safeguards exist to prevent authority from being used as the instrument of malice, revenge, or even crime? Is it safe to incur a policeman's anger? In one case that reached the federal courts, a motorist in Colorado was stopped at a police roadblock for a "routine check of his car and driver's license." He exchanged "rather harsh words" with one patrolman. On a later date, this patrolman spotted the motorist, followed him for six miles, and then stopped him, accusing him of failing to dim his lights. The man had misplaced his driver's license and had tried earlier that day to get a duplicate, but the office was closed. The patrolman said he was going to arrest the motorist. After further words, the patrolman wrenched the motorist's arm, hit the unresisting man on the head, shoulders, hands and wrists with a blackjack, handcuffed him, and took him to jail. His clothing and other belongings were taken from him, and he was offered no medical attention for his injuries until late that evening. After spending the night in jail, the motorist found he now was charged with drunken driving, and bail was set at $1,000. He was sent back to jail and told he must stay there unless he pleaded guilty. He said he would lose his job if he did not get out of jail by Monday, but the justice insisted that he plead guilty. Finally he did, and the justice allowed the patrolman to tell his version of the incident but refused to hear the motorist's version. The man was fined $355, given a 90-day suspended jail sentence, and lost his driver's license for one year. Prior to the arraignment, the justice of the peace and the patrolman conferred, and the justice was heard to say if the motorist pleaded innocent "he would make it rough enough on him for him to change his plea." The man was 40 years old, married with five children, had been arrested only once before in his life, had worked as a miner in Leadville for the same company for 14 years, had contracted silicosis during that time, and had he lost his job he would have been unable to secure employment with another company. He paid a lawyer $661 in an effort to appeal his case, lost one day's earnings, and had to pay a fee to get his car back. The federal court eventually held that he was entitled to damages under the Civil Rights statutes for arbitrary misuse of official power. *Stringer* v. *Dilger,* 313 F.2d 536 (10th Cir. 1963).

I cite this case as an officially reported instance of what *can* happen. Police are human, and there is a very real possibility that a person who stands on his rights one day may find the same officer "out to get him" another day. Moreover, we have all too much evidence that talking back to a police officer can produce violence and perhaps serious injury to the individual, particularly if he is a Negro or an outcast. And as was previously noted, an ensuing arrest can set off a chain reaction of disasters, very rarely compensated by a successful damage suit. . . .

6. CONSTITUTIONAL RIGHTS AND PRIVACY

In the encounter between citizen and police officer, certain major constitutional principles are at stake. Among these are rights deriving from the Fourth Amendment's protection against unreasonable searches and seizures, and the Fifth Amendment's guarantee of due process of law. I shall not attempt a definition of these rights here, but will point out how in a general sense these values are threatened.

There is a very real danger of erosion of rights through failure to challenge possible invasions. If the average person is intimidated by an encounter with the police, if remedies for abuses are relatively unusable, it is likely that the constitutionality of police practices will go untested. Thus there are few cases on the validity of police roadblocks, although the practice is common. There are even fewer cases on the questioning of pedestrians who are not suspected of crime. With the constitutionality of these practices unsettled and a matter of debate and uncertainty among lawyers, the community, worried about crime, may readily accept whatever the police say is necessary. After all, what is "reasonable" in a constitutional sense rests to some degree on what is thought "necessary." Thus constitutional protections are likely to be abandoned by default. The First Amendment remains healthy because possible invasions of it can usually be challenged in a civilized, scholarly way in a dignified appellate court. Constitutional rights that must be defended, if at all, on a lonely street, on a highway at night, in a police station or before a justice of the peace are always in trouble.

In addition to the values specifically protected by the constitution, there is the more general right of privacy, recently recognized by the Supreme Court, but yet only gradually emerging as an accepted legal principle. In our society privacy and anonymity are increasingly hard pressed. Many police officers seem to think that everyone should carry identification papers to be produced on demand, a requirement which is common in Europe. Such requirements are at war with the notion that one should be able to go out, for an hour or for a month, and merge into the anonymity of a new street or a new city.

How shall we begin to develop guidelines for encounters between the police and the law abiding citizen? . . .

The broad outline of a set of rules for the police can be suggested briefly.

(1) The police should not be allowed to stop anyone unless something particular about him, as distinguished from the mass of people, gives cause to believe that he has committed a crime.

(2) When a person is stopped, the officer should identify himself, and explain, with particularity, his reasons for stopping the person.

(3) The person may be questioned, but the person cannot be required to answer. He may be asked, but not required, to produce identification.

(4) The officer must conduct himself in a manner that would be proper in ordinary business relationships between equals.

(5) The officer may search a person only if he reasonably believes that he (the officer) is in danger, or if he has probable cause in the constitutional sense.

(6) If the person stopped desires to continue on his way, the officer may not detain him unless he has probable cause to arrest him for a crime.

These guidelines are a beginning: there is much room for working out details, but almost any rules will have the virtue of some certainty in an area where unlimited uncertainty now exists. Perhaps such instructions might be effectively enforced by a civilian police review board which could provide the sort of sanctions and remedies that the courts are unable to provide.

Perhaps this article sounds as if I have something against police officers — as if I do not appreciate the difficulties and dangers they face, the impossible demands upon them, and how well most of them perform their duty. But this is not my meaning. My meaning is that everyone, including the police, must live under rules. All organizations, and all officials, get out of hand if they do not have rules to guide them, if they do not do their work within limits.

I should add that while I believe that prevention is a far more desirable way of controlling crime than apprehension and punishment, I do not think that prevention is primarily a job for the police. Highway safety is more a function of better engineering of cars and roads, and better training of those who drive. Neighborhood safety is to a large extent a function of social conditions. Just as I do not believe that any amount of harsh punishment will significantly diminish crime, so I do not believe that any amount of surveillance will succeed.

We live in a society that is increasingly concerned with safety, but we give little thought to the price of safety. Suppose we had electric eyes and computers which could catch *every* traffic violation, *every* miscalculation of income tax, *every* instance of shoplifting. Would this really be the good society? Let me quote a letter to the New York Times on the subject of lifeguarding at public swimming places. The letter-writer protests that bathers, even good swimmers, are shepherded into small areas. "By such tactics the guards convert the great ocean into a wading pool and treat all bathers like children." The writer continues that at Cape May, he found that in a perfectly calm ocean bathers were rarely allowed beyond their depth, and were not even allowed to swim parallel to the shore beyond the lifeguard's station; the lifeguards mostly devoted themselves "to the castigation of bathers recalcitrant in obeying the whistle's orders." The letter ends, "I think, however, that in a free society I should be allowed to face my own dangers and challenges as long as I do not directly endanger others."

Overemphasis on safety also makes a great deal of hypocrisy and avoidance of responsibility. I think particularly of the attempts to put a stop to teenage drinking — an effort to make teenagers conform to standards adults do not themselves observe and an effort to secure a surface appearance of the rightness of things to cover up the profound wrongness within. Some of the most extreme examples of police surveillance are likely to be found in just those neat suburban communities which push all turmoil down into some invisible place, where it is left to fester unseen.

But I have a larger point to make. I fully recognize that safety is important and that safety requires measures. But other qualities also require measures: I mean independence, boldness, creativity, high spirits. In a society that presses toward sameness and safeness these all too perishable qualities must be given some help — they must be fostered and nourished. Otherwise their seed will fall upon asphalt and concrete, and die. The good society must have its hiding places — its protected crannies for the soul. Under the pitiless eye of safety the soul will wither. If I choose to get in my car and drive somewhere, it seems to me that where I am coming from, and where I am going, are nobody's business; I know of no law that requires me to have either a purpose or a destination. If I choose to take an evening walk to see if Andromeda has come up on schedule, I think I am entitled to look for the distant light of Almach and Mirach without finding myself staring into the blinding beam of a police flashlight.

Notes and Questions

1. What functions of the police is Reich describing? Are these functions legitimate?
2. What is Reich willing to sacrifice in order to achieve a more secure society? What is he *not* willing to sacrifice? What liberties are you willing to give up to achieve this goal?
3. Would you mind being in one of many cars being stopped at a roadblock? Would you feel any different if you were the only one stopped and questioned? If there is a difference, how do you explain it?
4. What criteria would you use if you had to decide whether or not the police should be allowed to demand personal identification?
5. Is Reich arguing that police should have no discretion? Is such a system possible?
6. The meaning of "preventive police work" may be confusing because the goal of preventive police work is not simply to prevent crimes from occurring. Rather, it is often designed to catch law violators whose criminal actions have not been reported to the police. For example, the police may know statistically that a certain percentage of cars on an interstate highway will be stolen vehicles. Preventive police work thus may consist of stopping every car and asking for proof of purchase.

   Such practices conflict with the general rule that individuals should be free to go where they want and do what they want unless something special leads a police officer to believe they have committed a crime. In legal terms, the police must normally have "probable cause" to believe that an individual has done some illegal act before the citizen may be stopped. The policy behind the law is to protect a person's freedom, liberty, and privacy unless there is a good reason to believe that that person has infringed on someone else's rights. Understanding this policy, do you believe that Reich is being unreasonable? Are we demanding too high a price from night walkers? To answer this question, it is necessary to determine what the price is to the individual who is stopped. Is it simply inconvenience? Or is it an invasion of privacy, the "right to be let alone," a fundamental freedom? Is losing one's privacy too high a price to pay for additional security? Should we be more reluctant to invade people's privacy than to cause them inconvenience?

These are not easy questions, and the answers are made even more difficult by the fact that the same act may invade someone's privacy as well as cause inconvenience. For example, having one's briefcase searched at the library exit or at the airplane boarding ramp are both inconveniences and invasions of privacy. Although some people have threatened to contest the constitutionality of airport searches, most people do not find the practice repugnant. Do you think this is because the fear of hijackings is high, or because we have simply become accustomed to the practice? Could we become more accepting of street searches if it became "safer" to walk the streets? This question is particularly relevant today because technology is available that would reduce some crime, make the streets safer, and cause us little inconvenience. The only price to be paid would be loss of privacy and anonymity. Closed-circuit television cameras, for example, are now installed on some streets and on some public buildings. Is this practice any different from the replacement of bank guards with television cameras? Does it make a difference whether the camera is on the street or inside a building? Whether the state or a private corporation installs the camera? Why should privacy be protected?

7. If the use of hidden television cameras does not seem too troublesome, consider the issue of drug testing. Should testing of all prospective employees for drug use be allowed? Should mandatory AIDS testing of persons before marriage be permitted? In 1986, the U.S. Customs Service began requiring that employees who sought promotion into certain positions be tested for drugs. The practice was challenged in court and the District Court held it unconstitutional and a violation of the Fourth Amendment (*National Treasury Employees Union* v. *Von Raab,* 649 F.Supp. 380, 1986).When this decision was appealed, the Court of Appeals reversed and declared that such practices were not unconstitutional (*National Treasury Employees Union* v. *Von Raab,* 816 F.2d 170, 1987). (See also *Capua* v. *Plainfield,* Chapter 4.)

☐ In 1979, the U.S. Supreme Court finally had an opportunity to decide a case involving the issue raised by Charles Reich. Is a citizen who is not suspected of any criminal act required to respond to police questions? How broad is the right to be free of police interference and the right to remain silent? These questions were answered in the following Supreme Court opinion.

Brown v. Texas *99 S. Ct. 2637 (1979)*

MR. CHIEF JUSTICE BURGER *delivered the opinion of the Court. . . .*

I

At 12:45 in the afternoon of December 9, 1977, Officers Venegas and Sotelo of the El Paso Police Department were cruising in a patrol car. They observed appellant [Brown] and another man walking in opposite directions away from one another in an alley. Although the two men were a few feet apart when they were first seen, Officer Venegas later testified that both officers believed the two had been together or were about to meet until the patrol car appeared.

The car entered the alley, and Officer Venegas got out and asked appellant to identify himself and explain what he was doing there. The other man was not questioned or detained. The officer testified that he stopped appellant because the situation "looked suspicious and we had never seen that subject in that area before." The area of El Paso where appellant was stopped has a high incidence of drug traffic. However, the officers did not claim to suspect appellant of any specific misconduct, nor did they have any reason to believe that he was armed.

Appellant refused to identify himself and angrily asserted that the officers had no right to stop him. Officer Venegas replied that he was in a "high drug problem area"; Officer Sotelo then "frisked" appellant, but found nothing.

When appellant continued to refuse to identify himself, he was arrested for violation of Texas Penal Code Ann. § 38.02(a) (1974), which makes it a criminal act for a person to refuse to give his name and address to an officer "who has lawfully stopped him and requested the information."[1] Following the arrest the officers searched appellant; nothing untoward was found.

While being taken to the El Paso County Jail appellant identified himself. Nonetheless, he was held in custody and charged with violating § 38.02(a). When he was booked he was routinely searched a third time. Appellant was convicted in the El Paso Municipal Court and fined $20 plus court costs for violation of § 38.02. He then exercised his right under Texas law to a trial *de novo* [anew] in the El Paso County Court. There, he moved to set aside the information on the ground that § 38.02(a) of the Texas Penal Code violated the First, Fourth, and Fifth Amendments and was unconstitutionally vague in violation of the Fourteenth Amendment. The motion was denied. Appellant waived a jury, and the court convicted him and imposed a fine of $45 plus court costs. . . .

II

When the officers detained appellant for the purpose of requiring him to identify himself, they performed a seizure of his person subject to the requirements of the Fourth Amendment. In convicting appellant, the County Court necessarily found as a matter of fact that the officers "lawfully stopped" appellant. The Fourth Amendment, of course, "applies to all seizures of the person, including seizures that involve only a brief detention short of traditional arrest." *Davis v. Mississippi,* 394 U.S. 721, 89 S.Ct. 1394, 22 L.Ed.2d 676 (1969); *Terry v. Ohio,* 392 U.S. 1, 16–19, 88 S.Ct. 1868, 1877, 20 L.Ed.2d 889 (1968). "'[W]henever a police officer accosts an individual and restrains his freedom to walk away, he has "seized" that person,' *id.,* at 16, 88 S.Ct., at 1877, and the Fourth Amendment requires that the seizure be 'reasonable.'" *United States v. Brignoni-Ponce,* 422 U.S. 873, 878, 95 S.Ct. 2574, 2578, 45 L.Ed.2d 607 (1975).

The reasonableness of seizures that are less

Some case citations have been omitted. One footnote has also been omitted. — ED.

[1]The entire section reads as follows:

"§ 38.02 Failure to Identify as Witness

"(a) A person commits an offense if he intentionally refuses to report or gives a false report of his name and residence address to a peace officer who has lawfully stopped him and requested the information."

intrusive than a traditional arrest, depends "'on a balance between the public interest and the individual's right to personal security free from arbitrary interference by law officers.'" *Pennsylvania v. Mimms,* 434 U.S. 106, 109, 98 S.Ct. 330, 332, 54 L.Ed.2d 331 (1977); *United States v. Brignoni-Ponce, supra,* 422 U.S., at 878, 95 S.Ct., at 2578. Consideration of the constitutionality of such seizures involves a weighing of the gravity of the public concerns served by the seizure, the degree to which the seizure advances the public interest, and the severity of the interference with individual liberty.

A central concern in balancing these competing considerations in a variety of settings has been to assure that an individual's reasonable expectation of privacy is not subject to arbitrary invasions solely at the unfettered discretion of officers in the field. To this end, the Fourth Amendment requires that a seizure must be based on specific, objective facts indicating that society's legitimate interests require the seizure of the particular individual, or that the seizure must be carried out pursuant to a plan embodying explicit, neutral limitations on the conduct of individual officers.

The State does not contend that appellant was stopped pursuant to a practice embodying neutral criteria, but rather maintains that the officers were justified in stopping appellant because they had a "reasonable, articulable suspicion that a crime had just been, was being, or was about to be committed." We have recognized that in some circumstances an officer may detain a suspect briefly for questioning although he does not have "probable cause" to believe that the suspect is involved in criminal activity, as is required for a traditional arrest. . . . However, we have required the officers to have a reasonable suspicion, based on objective facts, that the individual is involved in criminal activity. . . .

The flaw in the State's case is that none of the circumstances preceding the officers' detention of appellant justified a reasonable suspicion that he was involved in criminal conduct. Officer Venegas testified at appellant's trial that the situation in the alley "looked suspicious," but he was unable to point to any facts supporting that conclusion.[2] There is no indication in the record that it was unusual for people to be in the alley. The fact that appellant was in a neighborhood frequented by drug users, standing alone, is not a basis for concluding that appellant himself was engaged in criminal conduct. In short, the appellant's activity was no different from the activity of other pedestrians in that neighborhood. When pressed, Officer Venegas acknowledged that the only reason he stopped appellant was to ascertain his identity. The record suggests an understandable desire to assert a police presence; however, that purpose does not negate Fourth Amendment guarantees.

In the absence of any basis for suspecting appellant of misconduct, the balance between the public interest and appellant's right to personal security and privacy tilts in favor of freedom from police interference. The Texas statute under which appellant was stopped and required to identify himself is designed to advance a weighty social objective in large metropolitan centers: prevention of crime. But even assuming that purpose is served to some degree by stopping and demanding identification from an individual without any specific basis for believing he is involved in criminal activity, the guarantees of the Fourth Amendment do not allow it. When such a stop is not based on objective criteria, the risk of arbitrary and abusive police practices exceeds tolerable limits.

The application of Tex. Penal Code Ann., Tit. 8, § 38.02 (1974), to detain appellant and require him to identify himself violated the Fourth Amendment because the officers lacked any reasonable suspicion to believe appellant was engaged or had engaged in criminal conduct. Accordingly, appellant may not be pun-

[2]This situation is to be distinguished from the observations of a trained, experienced police officer who is able to perceive and articulate meaning in given conduct which would be wholly innocent to the untrained observer. See *United States* v. *Brignoni-Ponce,* 422 U.S. 873, 884–885, 95 S.Ct. 2574, 2582, 45 L.Ed.2d 607 (1975); *Christensen* v. *United States,* 104 U.S. App.D.C. 35, 36, 259 F.2d 192, 193 (1958).

ished for refusing to identify himself, and the conviction is

Reversed.

APPENDIX TO OPINION OF THE COURT

THE COURT: . . . What do you think about if you stop a person lawfully, and then if he doesn't want to talk to you, you put him in jail for committing a crime.

MR. PATTON [Prosecutor]: Well first of all, I would question the Defendant's statement in his motion that the First Amendment gives an individual the right to silence.

THE COURT: . . . I'm asking you why should the State put you in jail because you don't want to say anything.

MR. PATTON: Well, I think there's certain interests that have to be viewed.

THE COURT: Okay, I'd like you to tell me what those are.

MR. PATTON: Well, the Governmental interest to maintain the safety and security of the society and the citizens to live in the society, and there are certainly strong Governmental interests in that direction and because of that, these interests outweigh the interests of an individual for a certain amount of intrusion upon his personal liberty. I think these Governmental interests outweigh the individual's interests in this respect, as far as simply asking an individual for his name and address under the proper circumstances.

THE COURT: But why should it be a crime to not answer?

MR. PATTON: Again, I can only contend that if an answer is not given, it tends to disrupt.

THE COURT: What does it disrupt?

MR. PATTON: I think it tends to disrupt the goal of this society to maintain security over its citizens to make sure they are secure in their . . . homes.

THE COURT: How does that secure anybody by forcing them, under penalty of being prosecuted, to giving their name and address, even though they are lawfully stopped?

MR. PATTON: Well I, you know under the circumstances in which some individuals would be lawfully stopped, it's presumed that perhaps this individual is up to something, and the officer is doing his duty simply to find out the individual's name and address, and to determine what exactly is going on.

THE COURT: I'm not questioning, I'm not asking whether the officer shouldn't ask questions. I'm sure they should ask everything they possibly could find out. *What I'm asking is what's the State's interest in putting a man in jail because he doesn't want to answer something.* I realize lots of times an officer will give a defendant a *Miranda* warning which means a defendant doesn't have to make a statement. Lots of defendants go ahead and confess, which is fine if they want to do that. But if they don't confess, you can't put them in jail, can you, for refusing to confess to a crime? [Emphasis added.]

Notes and Questions

1. If Brown had been driving an automobile, should the police have been allowed to stop him and check his license and registration? In *Delaware* v. *Prouse*, 99 S.Ct. 1391 (1979), the U.S. Supreme Court ruled that cars may not be stopped simply to check whether the driver has a proper license and registration.
2. If his behavior had been "suspicious" but not illegal, could Brown have been questioned?

The questions above are considered in Section 2's cases. The fact that *all* participants in the legal process exercise discretion is a central theme of this book. Many citizens, however, find it difficult to accept the fact that judges, prosecutors, jurors, and police all have discretion. They cling, in Judge Jerome Frank's words, to the "myth of certainty," to the belief that law is predictable and certain (see Frank's reading in Chapter 1). They see the mere existence of discretion as negating law. The following excerpt analyzes why discretion is an inevitable component of the system.

Once discretion is recognized, the most important question becomes how discretion may be exercised most equitably. As Professor Kenneth Davis wrote,

> Engraved in stone on the Department of Justice Building in Washington, on the Pennsylvania Avenue side where swarms of bureaucrats and others pass by, are these five words: "Where law ends tyranny begins."
>
> I think that in our system of government, where law ends tyranny need not begin. Where law ends, discretion begins, and the exercise of discretion may mean either beneficence or tyranny, either justice or injustice, either reasonableness or arbitrariness.*

*Kenneth Davis, *Discretionary Justice* (Baton Rouge: Louisiana State University Press, 1969), p. 3.

Selective Enforcement *Carl B. Klockars*

If visitors from another planet, anxious to learn our ways, asked us to explain how our police behave, perhaps the most unhelpful thing we could do would be to hand them a copy of our legal code and say "Our police enforce these laws." What would make this bit of bad advice so terribly unhelpful is its failure to recognize the enormous range of police discretion, which, far more than legal codes, shapes the way our police behave. . . .

WHY POLICE DISCRETION?

If this book were about doctors, lawyers, judges, scholars, or scientists, or even if it were simply about police detectives, it is extremely unlikely that there would be anywhere in it a section entitled "Why Medical (or Legal or Judicial or Scholarly or Scientific or Investigative) Discretion?" There would not be such a section not only because everyone already knows that all these professionals routinely exercise discretion but also because everyone thinks that the fact that they do exercise discretion is a good and necessary thing.

Things are, of course, quite different when the question turns to police. Only within the past 20 years have we really learned how widely discretionary police behavior can be, is, and has to be. Yet, even today, many police agencies minimize or deny the existence of their enormous powers of discretion, many politicians behave toward police as if they had very little discretion at all, and most citizens are under the impression that the job of police is simply to enforce the law. They have a number of good reasons for doing so.

Full-Enforcement Statutes Most states have some form of "full-enforcement statute," a law providing that police shall enforce *all* laws. These full-enforcement statutes themselves are rarely enforced, but they clearly make it the duty of police to enforce *every* law relating to the safety of persons or property. Although there is some debate in legal circles on the question, in states with full-enforcement statutes it appears that selective enforcement of the law is illegal by statute.

Separation of Powers The vast majority of states, in imitation of the federal government, separate the powers of government into three separate and distinct branches: the executive, the legislative, and the judicial. As every grade-school civics text explains, the power of each separate branch is limited and each branch's rights and duties are kept distinct from those of the others in order that a system of checks and balances be preserved. Selective enforcement of the law, by which I mean a police decision *not* to enforce a law that the legislative branch has passed, usurps the legislature's rights and violates the principle of separation of governmental powers. In the words of one critic of selective enforcement, "The police . . . purpose is to enforce prohibitions articulated by the legislature. We do not say to police: 'Here is the problem. Deal with it.' We say: 'Here is a detailed code. Enforce it.'" . . .

A Government of Laws At the heart of the "separation of powers" objection to police discretion is the contention that ours is a government of laws, not men. Under a government of laws the police should not be allowed to make what amounts to their own laws, amend laws that have already been made, or decide that some people should have certain laws enforced on them while allowing others to violate the same laws with impunity. The whole idea of police enjoying such broad discretionary powers seems to open the door to arbitrariness, favoritism, and discrimination. . . . In light of these three strong objections to the whole idea of police discretion in selective enforcement, it might seem to be a good idea to try to eliminate it entirely. But before you jump to that conclusion you should consider the counterarguments. If you have ever been stopped for a traffic violation and managed to talk your way out of getting a ticket — or think you should have been able to — you might be inclined to appreciate that at least on some occasions, police discretion might be a good thing. . . .

ENFORCING THE LAW . . .

In making the case for police discretion in selective enforcement it will be helpful to examine a law that is familiar, simple, and unambiguous. Why? Because such a law will permit me to demonstrate that even the most simple, familiar, straightforward, and unambiguous of laws requires selective enforcement. The law I would like to consider specifies that on a given stretch of road no motorist may travel legally in excess of 35 miles per hour. What law could be more familiar, simple, or unambiguous than that?

Now, let's see what you could say to a reasonable police officer who clocks you doing 50 miles per hour in a 35 mile per hour zone to get out of being cited when there [is] all the legal evidence necessary for the officer to do so? I can think of at least ten good excuses under the following heading:

"WHERE'S THE FIRE?": THE OVERREACH OF THE LAW

(1) I am a volunteer fireman responding to a fire alarm.
(2) I am a volunteer ambulance driver responding to a call.
(3) I am an undercover cop tailing the car ahead which you did not stop.
(4) My wife just called and told me to rush home. She is starting to have her baby.
(5) I am having a baby.
(6) I am on my way to the hospital. There has been an accident. My child was hurt.
(7) I am on my way home. I left for work a short while ago, but halfway there I remembered that I left a steam iron burning on the kitchen table.
(8) I am on my way home. I left for work a

short while ago, but halfway there I discovered I have a serious case of diarrhea.

(9) I am a school crossing guard. I am late for work because I just had a flat tire. If I don't get to my post right away, the children will try to cross a dangerous intersection by themselves.

(10) I am part of a funeral entourage on its way to the cemetery. I do not know the way to get there and a few blocks back I got separated. Unless I catch up I will miss the burial.

Many other excuses of this type are possible. But what you should understand about those listed above is that each of them makes a somewhat different kind of claim that the 35 mph speed limit law is written so broadly that it includes all kinds of situations that should be exempt from it. Each claims in a different way that the law as written *overreaches:* It includes cases that it ought to exempt. Furthermore, considering the range and variety of exemptions that just these ten excuses claim, I think you will appreciate that no traffic law could be written in such a way as to anticipate all of the possible reasonable exemptions to it. But the point of this example goes beyond traffic law. Simply stated, it is that every law has the property of overreach, whether it provides penalties for traveling in excess of 35 mph on a given stretch of road, gambling, assault, burglary, robbery, or the killing of another human being. Police exercise discretion in the selective enforcement of all of these and every other law because it is in the very nature of all law to criminalize more than it intends.

"I'M SORRY, OFFICER, I'LL NEVER DO IT AGAIN.": THE PURPOSE OF THE LAW

In addition to the fact that police discretion exists because the law overreaches and cannot be written so as to anticipate every reasonable exception to it, police discretion also exists because the law as written has a purpose that may, under certain circumstances, be amply served by not enforcing it. Consider the following appeals, apologies, and explanations from motorists clocked at 50 in a 35 mph zone:

(1) I'm sorry, officer. I've just come from my mother's funeral and I'm still kind of upset. I just didn't check my speedometer.

(2) I'm sorry, officer. I just got fired from my job. I don't know how I'm going to support my family. Please don't give me a ticket. I don't know how I'd get the money to pay it.

(3) I'm sorry, officer. I've never in my life been stopped before. I think I'm going to faint. (*Thud*)

(4) I'm sorry, officer, but the kids were yelling in one ear and my wife was hollering in the other, and I just didn't notice the limit dropped to 35.

(5) I'm sorry, officer. I've been driving for 25 years and I've never even received a parking ticket before. In fact, I teach the driver education class at Central High School. Could you please give me a break? If I get a ticket for speeding, I'll be the laughing stock of the whole school. I could even lose my job. Please officer, just this once. . . .

"WHY AREN'T YOU OUT CATCHING RAPISTS AND MURDERERS?": THE QUESTION OF PRIORITIES

Caught dead to rights and without any believable claim that the law overreaches or would be better served by nonenforcement in their case, traffic law violators often resort to challenging police priorities in enforcing laws. Every policeman of any experience has heard some violator claim that instead of arresting him the policeman should be out arresting some more serious offender. The claim will not get you out of a ticket, but it raises one of the most telling arguments in demonstrating the necessity of selective enforcement.

The fact is that police resources are limited. A choice to enforce one type of law — be it traffic, vice, burglary, robbery, rape, or murder — usually involves diverting resources from the enforcement of laws of another type. The more specialized a police agency becomes, the more it is divided up into units that work on only one type of problem, the more obvious are the agency's enforcement priorities. In and of itself the fact that police resources are limited forces police to make selective enforcement policies whether they openly admit them or not. . . .

Having said this much about police discretion in selective enforcement in terms of familiar, simple, and unambiguous traffic law, let's return to the three objections to discretionary enforcement with which this section began.

Full Enforcement First there was the issue of the full-enforcement statutes and their requirement that police enforce all laws. By now you should understand that this requirement is (a) impossible because police do not have the resources to do it; (b) unjust because all law overreaches and criminalizes more than it should, (c) unwise because all just purposes of the law can sometimes be served adequately by not enforcing it; and (d) not to be taken seriously because legislatures know full well as they enact them that a great many laws will not be enforced unless there is active special interest in their enforcement.

Separation of Powers Second there was the issue of the separation of governmental powers and the argument that selective enforcement usurps the rights of the legislature to make or amend law. By now you should understand that a statement like "We do not say to police, 'Here is a problem. Deal with it.' We say 'Here is a detailed code. Enforce it.'" embodies an abominable misunderstanding of the relationship between the police, the legislative branch of government, and the law. Day in and day out, if police do anything they deal with problems, some of which are more important than others, some of which can be helped by enforcing the law as the legislature wrote it, and others of which cannot. . . . Despite the fact that it is fashionable to talk about police as "law enforcement" officers (and police often identify themselves in that way), it should be clear by now that that is neither what they are nor what we expect them to be. The police are not a "law enforcement" agency; they are a "regulatory" agency. They regulate relationships between citizens and between citizens and institutions. What's more, by and large they do so reactively — when someone requests their help because things have gotten out of hand.

A Government of Laws Third and finally there was the problem of "a government of laws, not men" and the invitations to arbitrariness, favoritism, and discrimination that selective enforcement presents. By now you should realize that "a government of laws, not men" would probably be no better than "a government of men, not laws." The simple fact is that good government requires both. If we cannot write a law specifying that on a certain stretch of road no motorist shall travel in excess of 35 mph without having to rely on a substantial measure of police discretion for its fair enforcement, we should understand that no society — and especially not one as complex as ours — can be governed by mere law.

Notes and Questions

1. How might a society make sure that discretionary powers will not be used unjustly?
2. What is the difference between discretion and unchecked power? How can one determine whether in a particular instance a police officer is exercising discretion or unchecked power?
3. What does the phrase "law and order" mean to you? Is discretionary power compatible with achieving "law and order"?
4. In what ways are a police officer's duties similar to a judge's?
5. What discretion does your teacher have? Does she or he have too much discretion? What limits, if any, are there on his or her powers? Are there comparable limitations on police discretion?
6. Consider the following findings of one sociological study:

   Our observations . . . show that officers decided not to make arrests of one or more suspects for 43 percent of all felonies and 52 percent of all misdemeanors judged by observers as situations where an arrest could have been made on probable cause.

Something other than probable cause is required, then, for the officer to make an arrest.

For the police, that something else is a *moral belief* that the law should be enforced and the violation sanctioned by the criminal justice system. The line officer usually reaches that decision by conducting an investigation to establish probable cause and by conducting a "trial" to determine who is guilty. His decision, therefore, is in an important sense judicial. This judicial determination will be influenced, as it is in the courts, by the deference and demeanor of the suspect, argument as to mitigating circumstances, complainant preferences for justice, and the willingness of the complainant to participate in seeing that it is done. All in all, an officer not only satisfies probable cause but also concludes after his careful evaluation that the suspect is guilty and arrest is therefore just.*

7. Does requiring police officers to justify their actions before a civilian review board take away the officers' discretion?

*Albert Reiss, *The Police and the Public* (New Haven, Conn.: Yale University Press, 1971), p. 134.

2 LEGAL PERSPECTIVES ON POLICE-CITIZEN ENCOUNTERS

Our instincts and our reasons all revolt at the idea of permitting the police to use their custody of a person for the purpose of coercing a confession, regardless of whether that confession be truthful or not. On the other hand, reason and experience tell us that in the vast majority of cases when people are asked about a crime about which they know something, they are willing to and they do tell the police what they know. If this were not so, law enforcement would be almost impossible. Is it in the public interest to make it more and more difficult for the police to solve crimes by undue restriction of their right to question and unreasonable limitation of the time allowed to check and investigate? Can the police be given this power without undue risk of its abuse?

Edward J. Lumbard, "The Administration of Criminal Justice: Some Problems and their Resolution," *American Bar Association Journal* (1963).

As Charles Reich's reading noted, and as most citizens know very well themselves, it is generally advisable to be at least polite when dealing with the police, because the police have a great deal of power. What, we might ask, has the U.S. Supreme Court done to limit this power? What could it do? What do the "handcuffs on the police" consist of?

The first two cases in this section raise many questions regarding the relationship between U.S. Supreme Court rulings and police behavior. Unlike the decision in *Brown* v. *Texas,* the Court in these two cases permits the police to invade the privacy of citizens. In the majority opinion in the first case, *Terry* v. *State of Ohio,* former Chief Justice Warren explicitly acknowledges the difficulty of controlling police power through court decisions. The opinion also shows us what some judges perceive the police officer's perspective to be. The second case, *Pennsylvania* v. *Mimms,* was decided ten years after *Terry.* It again confronts the problem of regulating police-citizen encounters and shows how one choice was made between the police and citizen perspectives. The last case in this section considers the practice of setting up police roadblocks and invasions of privacy without a search warrant.

Terry v. State of Ohio *392 U.S. 1 (1968)*

MR. CHIEF JUSTICE WARREN *delivered the opinion of the Court.*

This case presents serious questions concerning the role of the Fourth Amendment in the confrontation on the street between the citizen and the policeman investigating suspicious circumstances.

Petitioner Terry was convicted of carrying a concealed weapon and sentenced to the statutorily prescribed term of one to three years in the penitentiary. Following the denial of a pretrial motion to suppress, the prosecution introduced in evidence two revolvers and a number of bullets seized from Terry and a codefendant, Richard Chilton, by Cleveland Police Detective Martin McFadden. At the hearing on the motion to suppress this evidence, Officer McFadden testified that while he was patrolling in plain clothes in downtown Cleveland at approximately 2:30 in the afternoon of October 31, 1963, his attention was attracted by two men, Chilton and Terry, standing on the corner of Huron Road and Euclid Avenue. He had never seen the two men before, and he was unable to say precisely what first drew his eye to them. However, he testified that he had been a policeman for 39 years and a detective for 35 and that he had been assigned to patrol this vicinity of downtown Cleveland for shoplifters and pickpockets for 30 years. He explained that he had developed routine habits of observation over the years and that he would "stand and watch people or walk and watch people at many intervals of the day." He added: "Now, in this case when I looked over they didn't look right to me at the time."

His interest aroused, Officer McFadden took up a post of observation in the entrance to a store 300 to 400 feet away from the two men. "I get more purpose to watch them when I seen their movements," he testified. He saw one of the men leave the other one and walk southwest on Huron Road, past some stores. The man paused for a moment and looked in a store window, then walked on a short distance, turned around and walked back toward the corner, pausing once again to look in the same store window. He rejoined his companion at the corner, and the two conferred briefly. Then the second man went through the same series of motions, strolling down Huron Road, looking in the same window, walking on a short distance, turning back, peering in the store window again, and returning to confer with the first man at the corner. The two men repeated this ritual alternately between five and six times apiece — in all, roughly a dozen trips. At one point, while the two were standing together on the corner, a third man approached them and engaged them briefly in conversation. This man then left the two others and walked west on Euclid Avenue. Chilton and Terry resumed their measured pacing, peering and conferring. After this had gone on for 10 to 12 minutes, the two men walked off together, heading west on Euclid Avenue, following the path taken earlier by the third man.

By this time Officer McFadden had become thoroughly suspicious. He testified that after observing their elaborately casual and oft-repeated reconnaissance of the store window on Huron Road, he suspected the two men of "casing a job, a stick-up," and that he considered it his duty as a police officer to investigate further. He added that he feared "they may have a gun." Thus, Officer McFadden followed Chilton and

---

Footnotes and some case citations have been omitted. — Ed.

Terry and saw them stop in front of Zucker's store to talk to the same man who had conferred with them earlier on the street corner. Deciding that the situation was ripe for direct action, Officer McFadden approached the three men, identified himself as a police officer and asked for their names. At this point his knowledge was confined to what he had observed. He was not acquainted with any of the three men by name or by sight, and he had received no information concerning them from any other source. When the men "mumbled something" in response to his inquiries, Officer McFadden grabbed petitioner Terry, spun him around so that they were facing the other two, with Terry between McFadden and the others, and patted down the outside of his clothing. In the left breast pocket of Terry's overcoat Officer McFadden felt a pistol. He reached inside the overcoat pocket, but was unable to remove the gun. At this point, keeping Terry between himself and the others, the officer ordered all three men to enter Zucker's store. As they went in, he removed Terry's overcoat completely, removed a .38-caliber revolver from the pocket and ordered all three men to face the wall with their hands raised. Officer McFadden proceeded to pat down the outer clothing of Chilton and the third man, Katz. He discovered another revolver in the outer pocket of Chilton's overcoat, but no weapons were found on Katz. The officer testified that he only patted the men down to see whether they had weapons, and that he did not put his hands beneath the outer garments of either Terry or Chilton until he felt their guns. So far as appears from the record, he never placed his hands beneath Katz' outer garments. Officer McFadden seized Chilton's gun, asked the proprietor of the store to call a police wagon, and took all three men to the station, where Chilton and Terry were formally charged with carrying concealed weapons.

On the motion to suppress the guns the prosecution took the position that they had been seized following a search incident to a lawful arrest. The trial court rejected this theory, stating that it "would be stretching the facts beyond reasonable comprehension" to find that Officer McFadden had had probable cause to arrest the men before he patted them down for weapons. However, the court denied the defendants' motion on the ground that Officer McFadden, on the basis of his experience, "had reasonable cause to believe . . . that the defendants were conducting themselves suspiciously, and some interrogation should be made of their action." Purely for his own protection, the court held, the officer had the right to pat down the outer clothing of these men, who he had reasonable cause to believe might be armed. The court distinguished between an investigatory "stop" and an arrest, and between a "frisk" of the outer clothing for weapons and a full-blown search for evidence of crime. The frisk, it held, was essential to the proper performance of the officer's investigatory duties, for without it "the answer to the police officer may be a bullet, and a loaded pistol discovered during the frisk is admissible."

After the court denied their motion to suppress, Chilton and Terry waived jury trial and pleaded not guilty. The court adjudged them guilty, and the Court of Appeals for the Eighth Judicial District, Cuyahoga County, affirmed. *State* v. *Terry,* 5 Ohio App.2d 122, 214 N.E.2d 114 (1966). The Supreme Court of Ohio dismissed their appeal on the ground that no "substantial constitutional question" was involved. We granted certiorari, 387 U.S. 929, 87 S.Ct. 2050, 18 L.Ed.2d 989 (1967), to determine whether the admission of the revolvers in evidence violated petitioner's rights under the Fourth Amendment, made applicable to the States by the Fourteenth. *Mapp* v. *Ohio,* 376 U.S. 643, 81 S.Ct. 1684, 6 L.Ed.2d 1081 (1961). We affirm the conviction.

The Fourth Amendment provides that "the right of the people to be secure in their persons, houses, papers, and effects, against unreasonable searches and seizures, shall not be violated. . . ." We have recently held that "the Fourth Amendment protects people, not places," *Katz* v. *United States,* 389 U.S. 347, 351, 88 S.Ct. 507, 511, 19 L.Ed.2d 576 (1967), and wherever an individual may harbor a reasonable "expectation of privacy," id., at 361, 88 S.Ct. at 507 (Mr. Justice Harlan, concurring), he is entitled to be free from unreasonable governmental intrusion. . . . Unquestionably petitioner was entitled to the protection of the Fourth Amendment as he walked down the street in Cleveland. The question is whether in all the circumstances of this on-the-street encounter, his right to personal security was violated by an unreasonable search and seizure. . . .

On the one hand, it is frequently argued that in dealing with the rapidly unfolding and often dangerous situations on city streets the police are in need of an escalating set of flexible responses, graduated in relation to the amount of information they possess. For this purpose it is urged that distinctions should be made between a "stop" and an "arrest" (or a "seizure" of a person), and between a "frisk" and a "search." Thus, it is argued, the police should be allowed to "stop" a person and detain him briefly for questioning upon suspicion that he may be connected with criminal activity. Upon suspicion that the person may be armed, the police should have the power to "frisk" him for weapons. If the "stop" and the "frisk" give rise to probable cause to believe that the suspect has committed a crime, then the police should be empowered to make a formal "arrest," and a full incident "search" of the person. This scheme is justified in part upon the notion that a "stop" and a "frisk" amount to a mere "minor inconvenience and petty indignity," which can properly be imposed upon the citizen in the interest of effective law enforcement on the basis of a police officer's suspicion.

On the other side the argument is made that the authority of the police must be strictly circumscribed by the law of arrest and search as it has developed to date in the traditional jurisprudence of the Fourth Amendment. . . . The heart of the Fourth Amendment, the argument runs, is a severe requirement of specific justification for any intrusion upon protected personal security, coupled with a highly developed system of judicial controls to enforce upon the agents of the State the commands of the Constitution. Acquiescence by the courts in the compulsion inherent in the field interrogation practices at issue here, it is urged, would constitute an abdication of judicial control over, and indeed an encouragement of, substantial interference with liberty and personal security by police officers whose judgment is necessarily colored by their primary involvement in "the often competitive enterprise of ferreting out crime." *Johnson* v. *United States,* 33 U.S. 10, 14, 68 S.Ct. 367, 369, 92 L.Ed. 436 (1948). This, it is argued, can only serve to exacerbate police-community tensions in the crowded centers of our Nation's cities.

. . . The State has characterized the issue here as "the right of a police officer . . . to make an on-the-street stop, interrogate and pat down for weapons (known in street vernacular as 'stop and frisk')." But this is only partly accurate. For the issue is not the abstract propriety of the police conduct, but the admissibility against petitioner of the evidence uncovered by the search and seizure. Ever since its inception, the rule excluding evidence seized in violation of the Fourth Amendment has been recognized as a principal mode of discouraging lawless police conduct. Thus its major thrust is a deterrent one, and experience has taught that it is the only effective deterrent to police misconduct in the criminal context, and that without it the constitutional guarantee against unreasonable searches and seizures would be a mere "form of words." The rule also serves another vital function — "the imperative of judicial integrity. . . ."

The exclusionary rule has its limitations, however, as a tool of judicial control. . . . In some contexts the rule is ineffective as a deterrent. Street encounters between citizens and police officers are incredibly rich in diversity. They range from wholly friendly exchanges of pleasantries or mutually useful information to hostile confrontations of armed men involving arrests, or injuries, or loss of life. Moreover, hostile confrontations are not all of a piece. Some of them begin in a friendly enough manner, only to take a different turn upon the injection of some unexpected element into the conversation. Encounters are initiated by the police for a wide variety of purposes, some of which are wholly unrelated to a desire to prosecute for crime. Doubtless some police "field interrogation" conduct violates the Fourth Amendment. But a stern refusal by this Court to condone such activity does not necessarily render it responsive to the exclusionary rule. Regardless of how effective the rule may be where obtaining convictions is an important objective of the police, it is powerless to deter invasions of constitutionally guaranteed rights where the police either have no interest in prosecuting or are willing to forgo successful prosecution in the interest of serving some other goal.

Proper adjudication of cases in which the exclusionary rule is invoked demands a constant awareness of these limitations. The wholesale harassment by certain elements of the police community, of which minority groups, particularly Negroes, frequently complain, will not be stopped by the exclusion of any evidence from any criminal trial. Yet a rigid and unthinking application of the exclusionary rule, in futile protest against practices which it can never be used effectively to control, may exact a high toll in human injury and frustration of efforts to prevent crime. No judicial opinion can comprehend the protean variety of the street encounter, and we can only judge the facts of the case before us. Nothing we say today is to be taken as indicating approval of police conduct outside the legitimate investigative sphere. Under our decision, courts still retain their traditional responsibility to guard against police conduct which is overbearing or harassing, or which trenches upon personal security without the objective evidentiary justification which the Constitution requires. When such conduct is identified, it must be condemned by the judiciary and its fruits must be excluded from evidence in criminal trials. . . .

. . . [W]e cannot blind ourselves to the need for law enforcement officers to protect themselves and other prospective victims of violence in situations where they may lack probable cause for an arrest. When an officer is justified in believing that the individual whose suspicious behavior he is investigating at close range is armed and presently dangerous to the officer or to others, it would appear to be clearly unreasonable to deny the officer the power to take necessary measures to determine whether the person is in fact carrying a weapon and to neutralize the threat of physical harm. . . .

Our evaluation of the proper balance that has to be struck in this type of case leads us to conclude that there must be a narrowly drawn authority to permit a reasonable search for weapons for the protection of the police officer, where he has reason to believe that he is dealing with an armed and dangerous individual, regardless of whether he has probable cause to arrest the individual for a crime. The officer need not be absolutely certain that the individual is armed; the issue is whether a reasonably prudent man in the circumstances would be warranted in the belief that his safety or that of others was in danger. And in determining whether the officer acted reasonably in such circumstances, due weight must be given, not to his inchoate and unparticularized suspicion or "hunch," but to the specific reasonable inferences which he is entitled to draw from the facts in light of his experience.

We must now examine the conduct of Officer McFadden in this case to determine whether his search and seizure of petitioner were reasonable, both at their inception and as conducted. He had observed Terry, together with Chilton and another man, acting in a manner he took to be preface to a "stick-up." We think on the facts and circumstances Officer McFadden detailed before the trial judge a reasonably prudent man would have been warranted in believing petitioner was armed and thus presented a threat to the officer's safety while he was investigating his suspicious behavior. The actions of Terry and Chilton were consistent with McFadden's hypothesis that these men were contemplating a daylight robbery — which, it is reasonable to assume, would be likely to involve the use of weapons — and nothing in their conduct from the time he first noticed them until the time he confronted them and identified himself as a police officer gave him sufficient reason to negate that hypothesis. Although the trio had departed the original scene, there was nothing to indicate abandonment of an intent to commit a robbery at some point. Thus, when Officer McFadden approached the three men gathered before the display window at Zucker's store he had observed enough to make it quite reasonable to fear that they were armed; and nothing in their response to his hailing them, identifying himself as a police officer, and asking their names served to dispel that reasonable belief. We cannot say his decision at that point to seize Terry and pat his clothing for weapons was the product of a volatile or inventive imagination, or was undertaken simply as an act of harassment; the record evidences the tempered act of a policeman who in the course of an investigation had to make a quick decision as to how to protect himself and others from possible danger, and took limited steps to do so. . . .

. . . The sole justification of the search in the present situation is the protection of the police officer and others nearby, and it must therefore be confined in scope to an intrusion reasonably designed to discover guns, knives, clubs, or other hidden instruments for the assault of the police officer. The scope of the search in this case presents no serious problem in light of these standards. Officer McFadden patted down the outer clothing of petitioner and his two companions. He did not place his hands in their pockets or under the outer surface of their garments until he had felt weapons, and then he merely reached for and removed the guns. He never did invade Katz' person beyond the outer surfaces of his clothes, since he discovered nothing in his pat-down which might have been a weapon. Officer McFadden confined his search strictly to what was minimally necessary to learn whether the men were armed and to disarm them once he discovered the weapons. He did not conduct a general exploratory search for whatever evidence of criminal activity he might find.

We conclude that the revolver seized from Terry was properly admitted in evidence against him. At the time he seized petitioner and searched him for weapons, Officer McFadden had reasonable grounds to believe that petitioner was armed and dangerous, and it was necessary for the protection of himself and others to take swift measures to discover the true facts and neutralize the threat of harm if it materialized. The policeman carefully restricted his search to what was appropriate to the discovery of the particular items which he sought. Each case of this sort will, of course, have to be decided on its own facts. We merely hold today that where a police officer observes unusual conduct which leads him reasonably to conclude in light of his experience that criminal activity may be afoot and that the persons with whom he is dealing may be armed and presently dangerous, where in the course of investigating this behavior he identifies himself as a policeman and makes reasonable inquiries, and where nothing in the initial stages of the encounter serves to dispel his reasonable fear for his own or others' safety, he is entitled for the protection of himself and others in the area to conduct a carefully limited search of the outer clothing of such persons in an attempt to discover weapons which might be used to assault him. Such a search is a reasonable search under the Fourth Amendment and any weapons seized may properly be introduced in evidence against the person from whom they were taken.

Affirmed.

[Concurring opinion of MR. JUSTICE HARLAN has been omitted. — ED.]

MR. JUSTICE DOUGLAS, *dissenting*.

I agree that petitioner was "seized" within the meaning of the Fourth Amendment. I also agree that frisking petitioner and his companions for guns was a "search." But it is a mystery how that "search" and that "seizure" can be constitutional by Fourth Amendment standards, unless there was "probable cause" to believe that (1) a crime had been committed or (2) a crime was in the process of being committed or (3) a crime was about to be committed.

The opinion of the Court disclaims the existence of "probable cause." If loitering were in issue and that was the offense charged, there would be "probable cause" shown. But the crime here is carrying concealed weapons; and there is no basis for concluding that the officer had "probable cause" for believing that that crime was being committed. Had a warrant been sought, a magistrate would, therefore, have been unauthorized to issue one, for he can act only if there is a showing of "probable cause." We hold today that the police have greater authority to make a "seizure" and conduct a "search" than a judge has to authorize such action. We have said precisely the opposite over and over again.

In other words, police officers up to today have been permitted to effect arrests or searches without warrants only when the facts within their personal knowledge would satisfy the constitutional standard of *probable cause.* At the time of their "seizure" without a warrant they must possess facts concerning the person arrested that would have satisfied a magistrate that "probable cause" was indeed present. The term "probable cause" rings a bell of certainty that is not sounded by phrases such as "reasonable suspicion." Moreover, the meaning of "probable cause" is deeply imbedded in our constitutional history. As we stated in *Henry* v. *United States,* 361 U.S. 98, 100–102, 80 S.Ct. 168, 170:

> The requirement of probable cause has roots that are deep in our history. The general warrant, in which the name of the person to be arrested was left blank, and the writs of assistance, against which James Otis inveighed, both perpetuated the oppressive practice of allowing the police to arrest and search on suspicion. Police control took the place of judicial control, since no showing of "probable cause" before a magistrate was required. . . .
>
> That philosophy [rebelling against these practices] later was reflected in the Fourth Amendment. And as the early American decisions both before and immediately after its adoption show, common rumor or report, suspicion, or even "strong reason to suspect" was not adequate to support a warrant for arrest. And that principle has survived to this day. . . .

. . . To give the police greater power than a magistrate is to take a long step down the totalitarian path. Perhaps such a step is desirable to cope with modern forms of lawlessness. But if it is taken, it should be the deliberate choice of the people through a constitutional amendment. . . .

There have been powerful hydraulic pressures throughout our history that bear heavily on the Court to water down constitutional guarantees and give the police the upper hand. That hydraulic pressure has probably never been greater than it is today.

Yet if the individual is no longer to be sovereign, if the police can pick him up whenever they do not like the cut of his jib, if they can "seize" and "search" him in their discretion, we enter a new regime. The decision to enter it should be made only after a full debate by the people of this country.

Notes and Questions

1. Why did Chief Justice Warren say that the exclusionary rule is not very effective in regulating police actions in which arrest is not the police officer's aim?

2. The famous decisions of the Warren court concerning police officers [e.g., *Miranda* v. *Arizona,* 384 U.S. 436 (1966), *Escobedo* v. *Illinois,* 378 U.S. 478 (1964), *Mapp* v. *Ohio,* 367 U.S. 643 (1961)] all involved cases in which the defendant had been convicted after trial. What role can the U.S. Supreme Court play in the vast majority of cases in which defendants plead guilty and do not have a trial?

3. The Burger court's most predictable decisions were probably those relating to police searches, and almost all those decisions permitted questionable searches that revealed criminal conduct. From 1972 to 1977, the Court decided twenty-five cases involving the legality of police searches. In twenty-two of these cases, the Court sustained the search as valid. One indicator of the radical change in Fourth Amendment law that occurred in these cases is that in twenty of the cases, the Court reversed lower court rulings that the searches had been unconstitutional.

In another four cases decided between 1972 and 1977, the Court severely limited the right of searched people to invoke the exclusionary rule, which prohibits illegally seized evidence from being introduced at a hearing. Because of these rulings, evidence seized illegally may be used against a defendant in a civil case or a grand jury proceeding, although it still may not be admitted into evidence in a criminal trial. In three of these four cases, the Court reversed lower court decisions that had allowed the citizen to invoke the exclusionary rule in noncriminal trial situations.

More recently, of twenty-three search-and-seizure cases decided by the U.S. Supreme Court between 1983 and 1987, nineteen of the searches were held to be valid.

4. In *Terry*, do you think that McFadden acted properly?
5. If you had been in McFadden's place, what would you have done?
6. Was his fear that Terry and Chilton had guns justifiable?
7. How much do you think McFadden's fear of violence motivated his behavior?
8. If police officers are more afraid of attack than are other citizens, how can the judge, when determining the reasonableness of the officer's perception, evaluate the "specific reasonable inferences which he is entitled to draw from the facts in light of his experience"? (page 182) Under this test, would it be permissible for police officers to stop and frisk blacks more often than whites? Youths more often than the elderly? Men more often than women?
9. Why does Douglas believe that "probable cause" is a more meaningful concept than "reasonable suspicion"?

Commonwealth of Pennsylvania v. Harry Mimms *98 S.Ct. 330 (1977)*

Per Curiam.

Petitioner Commonwealth seeks review of a judgment of the Supreme Court of Pennsylvania reversing petitioner's conviction for carrying a concealed deadly weapon and a firearm without a license. That court reversed the conviction because it held that respondent's "revolver was seized in a manner which violated the Fourth Amendment to the Constitution of the United States." Because we disagree with this conclusion, we grant the Commonwealth's petition for certiorari and reverse the judgment of the Supreme Court of Pennsylvania.

The facts are not in dispute. While on routine patrol, two Philadelphia police officers observed respondent Harry Mimms driving an automobile with an expired license plate. The officers stopped the vehicle for the purpose of issuing a traffic summons. One of the officers approached and asked respondent to step out of the car and produce his owner's card and operator's license. Respondent alighted, whereupon the officer noticed a large bulge under respondent's sports jacket. Fearing that the bulge might be a weapon, the officer frisked respondent and discovered in his waistband a .38-caliber revolver loaded with five rounds of ammunition. The other occupant of the car was also carrying a .32-caliber revolver. Respondent was immediately arrested and subsequently indicted for carrying a concealed deadly weapon and for unlawfully carrying a firearm without a license. His motion to suppress the revolver was denied, and after a trial at which the revolver was introduced into evidence respondent was convicted on both counts.

The Supreme Court of Pennsylvania reversed respondent's conviction, however, holding that the revolver should have been suppressed because it was seized contrary to the guarantees contained in the Fourth and Fourteenth Amendments to the United States Constitution.[1] The Pennsylvania court did not doubt

---

Some footnotes have been omitted. — Ed.

[1]Commonwealth v. Mimms, 471 Pa. 546, 548, 370 A.2d 1157, 1158 (1977). Three judges dissented on the federal constitutional issue.

that the officers acted reasonably in stopping the car. It was also willing to assume, *arguendo,* that the limited search for weapons was proper once the officer observed the bulge under respondent's coat. But the court nonetheless thought the search constitutionally infirm because the officer's order to respondent to get out of the car was an impermissible "seizure." This was so because the officer could not point to "objective observable facts to support a suspicion that criminal activity was afoot or that the occupants of the vehicle posed a threat to police safety." Since this unconstitutional intrusion led directly to observance of the bulge and to the subsequent "pat down," the revolver was the fruit of an unconstitutional search, and in the view of the Supreme Court of Pennsylvania, should have been suppressed.

We do not agree with this conclusion. The touchstone of our analysis under the Fourth Amendment is always "the reasonableness in all the circumstances of the particular governmental invasion of a citizen's personal security." *Terry* v. *Ohio,* 392 U.S. 1, 19, 88 S.Ct. 1868, 1878, 20 L.Ed.2d 889 (1968). Reasonableness, of course, depends "on a balance between the public interest, and the individual's right to personal security free from arbitrary interference by law officers." *United States* v. *Brignoni-Ponce,* 422 U.S. 873, 878, 95 S.Ct. 2574, 45 L.Ed.2d 607 (1975).

In this case, unlike *Terry* v. *Ohio,* there is no question about the propriety of the initial restrictions on respondent's freedom of movement. Respondent was driving an automobile with expired license tags in violation of the Pennsylvania Motor Vehicle Code. Deferring for a moment the legality of the "frisk" once the bulge had been observed, we need presently deal only with the narrow question of whether the order to get out of the car, issued after the driver was lawfully detained, was reasonable and thus permissible under the Fourth Amendment. This inquiry must therefore focus not on the intrusion resulting from the request to stop the vehicle or from the later "pat-down," but on the incremental intrusion resulting from the request to get out of the car once the vehicle was lawfully stopped.

Placing the question in this narrowed frame, we look first to that side of the balance which bears the officer's interest in taking the action that he did. The State freely concedes the officer had no reason to suspect foul play from the particular driver at the time of the stop, there having been nothing unusual or suspicious about his behavior. It was apparently his practice to order all drivers out of their vehicles as a matter of course whenever they had been stopped for a traffic violation. The State argues that this practice was adopted as a precautionary measure to afford a degree of protection to the officer and that it may be justified on that ground. Establishing a face-to-face confrontation diminishes the possibility, otherwise substantial, that the driver can make unobserved movements; this, in turn, reduces the likelihood that the officer will be the victim of an assault.[2]

We think it too plain for argument that the State's proffered justification — the safety of the officer — is both legitimate and weighty. "Certainly it would be unreasonable to require that police officers take unnecessary risks in the performance of their duties." *Terry* v. *Ohio,* supra. 392 U.S. at 23, 88 S.Ct. at 1881. And we have specifically recognized the inordinate risk confronting an officer as he approaches a person seated in an automobile. "'According to one study, approximately 30% of police shootings occurred when a police officer approached a suspect seated in an automobile.'" Bristow, "Police Officer Shootings — A Tactical Evaluation," 54 Crim.L.C. & P.S. 93 (1963). — *Adams* v. *Williams,* 407 U.S. 143, 148 n. 3, 92 S.Ct. 1921, 1924, 32 L.Ed.2d 612 (1972). We are aware that not all these assaults occur when issuing traffic summons, but we have before expressly de-

[2]The State does not, and need not, go so far as to suggest that an officer may frisk the occupants of any car stopped for a traffic violation. Rather, it only argues that it is permissible to order the driver out of the car. In this particular case, argues the State, once the driver alighted, the officer had independent reason to suspect criminal activity and present danger and it was upon this basis, and not the mere fact that respondent had committed a traffic violation, that he conducted the search.

clined to accept the argument that traffic violations necessarily involve less danger to officers than other types of confrontations. *United States* v. *Robinson,* 414 U.S. 218, 234, 94 S.Ct. 467, 38 L.Ed.2d 427 (1973). Indeed, it appears "that a significant percentage of murders of police officers occurs when the officers are making traffic stops." *Id.,* at 234, n. 5, 94 S.Ct. at 476.

The hazard of accidental injury from passing traffic to an officer standing on the driver's side of the vehicle may also be appreciable in some situations. Rather than conversing while standing exposed to moving traffic, the officer prudently may prefer to ask the driver of the vehicle to step out of the car and off onto the shoulder of the road where the inquiry may be pursued with greater safety to both.

Against this important interest we are asked to weigh the intrusion into the driver's personal liberty occasioned not by the initial stop of the vehicle, which was admittedly justified, but by the order to get out of the car. We think this additional intrusion can only be described as *de minimis.* The driver is being asked to expose to view very little more of his person than is already exposed. The police have already lawfully decided that the driver shall be briefly detained; the only question is whether he shall spend that period sitting in the driver's seat of his car or standing alongside it. Not only is the insistence of the police on the latter choice not a "serious intrusion upon the sanctity of the person," but it hardly rises to the level of a "'petty indignity.'" *Terry* v. *Ohio,* supra, 392 U.S. at 17, 88 S.Ct. at 1877. What is at most a mere inconvenience cannot prevail when balanced against legitimate concerns for the officer's safety.[3]

There remains the second question of the propriety of the search once the bulge in the jacket was observed. We have as little doubt on this point as on the first; the answer is controlled by *Terry* v. *Ohio,* supra. In that case we thought the officer justified in conducting a limited search for weapons once he had reasonably concluded that the person whom he had legitimately stopped might be armed and presently dangerous. Under the standard enunciated in that case — whether "the facts available to the officer at the moment of the seizure or the search 'warrant a man of reasonable caution in the belief' that the action taken was appropriate"[4] — there is little question the officer was justified. The bulge in the jacket permitted the officer to conclude that Mimms was armed and thus posed a serious and present danger to the safety of the officer. In these circumstances, any man of "reasonable caution" would likely have conducted the "pat-down."

MR. JUSTICE MARSHALL, *dissenting.*

I join my Brother Stevens' dissenting opinion, but I write separately to emphasize the extent to which the Court today departs from the teachings of *Terry* v. *Ohio,* 392 U.S. 1, 88 S.Ct. 1868, 20 L.Ed.2d 889 (1968).

In *Terry* the policeman who detained and "frisked" the petitioner had for 30 years been patrolling the area in downtown Cleveland where the incident occurred. His experience led him to watch petitioner and a companion carefully, for a long period of time, as they individually and repeatedly looked in a store window and then conferred together. Suspecting that the two men might be "'casing'" the store for a "'stick-up'" and that they might have guns, the officer followed them as they walked away and joined a third man with whom they had earlier conferred. At this point the officer approached the men and asked for their names. When they "'mumbled something'" in response, the officer grabbed petitioner, spun him around to face the other two, and "patted down" his clothing. This frisk led to the discovery of a pistol and to petitioner's subsequent weapons conviction. . . .

[3]Contrary to the suggestion in the dissent of our Brother Stevens . . . , we do not hold today "that whenever an officer has an occasion to speak with the driver of a vehicle, he may also order the driver out of the car." We hold only that once a motor vehicle has been lawfully detained for a traffic violation the police officers may order the driver to get out of the vehicle without violating the Fourth Amendment's proscription of unreasonable searches and seizures.

[4]Terry v. Ohio, 392 U.S. 1, 21–22, 88 S.Ct. 1868, 1880, 20 L.Ed.2d 889 (1963).

The "stop and frisk" in *Terry* was thus justified by the probability, not only that a crime was about to be committed, but also that the crime "would be likely to involve the use of weapons." *Id.,* at 28, 88 S.Ct., at 1883. The Court confined its holding to situations in which the officer believes "that the persons with whom he is dealing may be armed and presently dangerous" and "fear[s] for his own or others' safety." *Id.,* at 30, 88 S.Ct., at 1884. . . .

In the instant case, the officer did not have even the slightest hint, prior to ordering respondent out of the car, that respondent might have a gun. As the Court notes, "the officer had no reason to suspect foul play." The car was stopped for the most routine of police procedures, the issuance of a summons for an expired license plate. Yet the Court holds that, once the officer had made this routine stop, he was justified in imposing the additional intrusion of ordering respondent out of the car, regardless of whether there was any individualized reason to fear respondent.

Such a result cannot be explained by *Terry,* which limited the nature of the intrusion by reference to the reason for the stop. The Court held that "the officer's action [must be] reasonably related in scope to the circumstances which justified the interference in the first place." 392 U.S., at 20, 88 S.Ct., at 1879. In *Terry* there was an obvious connection emphasized by the Court, *id.,* at 28–30, 88 S.Ct., at 1883–1884, between the officer's suspicion that an armed robbery was being planned and his frisk for weapons. In the instant case, "the circumstances which justified the interference in the first place" was an expired license plate. There is simply no relation at all between that circumstance and the order to step out of the car. . . .

MR. JUSTICE STEVENS, *with whom* MR. JUSTICE BRENNAN *and* MR. JUSTICE MARSHALL *join, dissenting.*

Ten years ago in *Terry* v. *Ohio,* 392 U.S. 1, 88 S.Ct. 1868, 20 L.Ed.2d 889, the Court held that "probable cause" was not required to justify every seizure of the person by a police officer. That case was decided after six months of deliberation following full argument and unusually elaborate briefing. The approval in *Terry* of a lesser standard for certain limited situations represented a major development in Fourth Amendment jurisprudence.

Today, without argument, the Court adopts still another — and even lesser — standard of justification for a major category of police seizures. More important, it appears to abandon "the central teaching of this Court's Fourth Amendment jurisprudence" — which has ordinarily required individualized inquiry into the particular facts justifying every police intrusion — in favor of a general rule covering countless situations. . . .

This case illustrates two ways in which haste can introduce a new element of confusion into an already complex set of rules. First, the Court has based its legal ruling on a factual assumption about police safety that is dubious at best; second, the Court has created an entirely new legal standard of justification for intrusions on the liberty of the citizen.

Without any attempt to differentiate among the multitude of varying situations in which an officer may approach a person seated in an automobile, the Court characterizes the officer's risk as "inordinate" on the basis of this statement:

> According to one study, approximately 30% of police shootings occurred when a police officer approached a suspect seated in an automobile. Bristow, "Police Officer Shootings — A Tactical Evaluation," 54 Crim.L.C. & P.S. 93 (1963). — *Adams v. Williams,* 407 U.S. 143, 148 n. 3, 92 S.Ct. 1921, 1924, 32 L.Ed.2d 612 (1972). . . .

That statement does not fairly characterize the study to which it refers. Moreover, the study does not indicate that police officers can minimize the risk of being shot by ordering drivers stopped for routine traffic violations out of their cars. The study reviewed 110 selected police shootings that occurred in 1959, 1960, and 1961. In 35 of those cases, "officers were attempting to investigate, control, or pursue suspects who were in automobiles."[5] Within the group of 35 cases, there were examples of officers who "were shot through the windshield or car body while their vehicle was moving"; examples in which "the officer was shot while dismounting from his vehicle or while approaching the suspect's vehicle"; and, apparently, instances in which the officer was shot by a passenger in the vehicle. *Ibid.*

In only 28 of the 35 cases was the location of the suspect who shot the officer verified. In 12 of those cases the suspect was seated behind the wheel of the car, but that figure seems to include cases in which the shooting occurred before the officer had an opportunity to order the suspect to get out. In nine cases the suspect was outside the car talking to the officer when the shooting occurred.

These figures tell us very little about the risk associated with the routine traffic stop;[6] and they lend no support to the Court's assumption that ordering the routine traffic offender out of his car significantly enhances the officer's safety. Arguably, such an order could actually aggravate the officer's danger because the fear of a search might cause a serious offender to take desperate action that would be unnecessary if he remained in the vehicle while being ticketed. Whatever the reason, it is significant that some experts in this area of human behavior strongly recommend that the police officer "never allow the violator to get out of the car. . . ."

Obviously, it is not my purpose to express an opinion on the safest procedure to be followed in making traffic arrests or to imply that the arresting officer faces no significant hazard, even in the apparently routine situation. I do submit, however, that no matter how hard we try we cannot totally eliminate the danger associated with law enforcement, and that, before adopting a nationwide rule, we should give further consideration to the infinite variety of situations in which today's holding may be applied.

The Court cannot seriously believe that the risk to the arresting officer is so universal that his safety is *always* a reasonable justification for ordering a driver out of his car. The commuter on his way home to dinner, the parent driving children to school, the tourist circling the Capitol, or the family on a Sunday afternoon outing hardly pose the same threat as a driver curbed after a high-speed chase through a high-crime area late at night. Nor is it universally true that the driver's interest in remaining in the car is negligible. A woman stopped at night may fear for her own safety; a person in poor health may object to standing in the cold or rain; another who left home in haste to drive children or spouse to school or train may not be fully dressed; an elderly driver who presents no possible threat of violence may regard the police command as nothing more than an arrogant and unnecessary display of authority. Whether viewed from the standpoint of the officer's interest in his own safety, or of the citizen's interest in not being required to obey an arbitrary command, it is perfectly obvious that the millions of traffic stops that occur every year are not fungible.

Until today the law applicable to seizures of a person has required individualized inquiry into the reason for each intrusion, or some comparable guarantee against arbitrary harassment. A factual demonstration of probable cause is required to justify an arrest; an articulable reason to suspect criminal activity and possible violence is needed to justify a stop and frisk. But to eliminate any requirement that an officer be able to explain the reasons for his actions signals an abandonment of effective judicial supervision of this kind of seizure and leaves police discretion

---

[5]*Ibid.* Since 35 is 32% of 110, presumably this is the basis for the "30%" figure used in the Court's statement. As the text indicates, however, not all of these cases involved police officers approaching a parked vehicle. Whether any of the incidents involved routine traffic offenses, such as driving with an expired license tag, is not indicated in the study.

[6]Over the past 10 years, more than 1,000 police officers have been murdered. Federal Bureau of Investigations, Uniform Crime Reports 289 (1977). Approximately 10% of those killings, or about 11 each year, occurred during "traffic pursuits and stops," but it is not clear how many of those pursuits and stops involved offenses such as reckless or high speed driving, rather than offenses such as driving on an expired license, or how often the shootings could have been avoided by ordering the driver to dismount.

utterly without limits. Some citizens will be subjected to this minor indignity while others — perhaps those with more expensive cars, or different bumper stickers, or different-colored skin — may escape it entirely. . . .

I am not yet persuaded that the interest in police safety requires the adoption of a standard any more lenient than that permitted by *Terry* v. *Ohio.* In this case the offense might well have gone undetected if respondent had not been ordered out of his car, but there is no reason to assume that he otherwise would have shot the officer. Indeed, there has been no showing of which I am aware that the *Terry* standard will not provide the police with a sufficient basis to take appropriate protective measures whenever there is any real basis for concern. When that concern does exist, they should be able to frisk a violator, but I question the need to eliminate the requirement of an articulable justification in each case and to authorize the indiscriminate invasion of the liberty of every citizen stopped for a traffic violation, no matter how petty.

Notes and Questions

1. What do these decisions tell police who find a gun on someone they search, about what they should say in court?
2. Should the police have the right to carry out routine weapon checks of the general public as a protection against the danger of concealed weapons?
3. The majority opinion in the *Mimms* case describes being ordered to get out of the car as a *de minimis* intrusion into a driver's liberty. How do you think Charles Reich would describe it?
4. Consider the following suggestions* to police officers on whom to select for field interrogation:

   A. Be suspicious. This is a healthy police attitude, but it should be controlled and not too obvious.

   B. Look for the unusual.
      1. Persons who do not "belong" where they are observed.
      2. Automobiles which do not "look right."
      3. Business opened at odd hours, or not according to routine or custom.

   C. Subjects who should be subjected to field interrogations.
      1. Suspicious persons known to the officer from previous arrests, field interrogations, and observations.
      2. Emaciated appearing alcoholics and narcotics users who invariably turn to crime to pay for cost of habit.
      3. Person who fits description of wanted suspect as described by radio, teletype, daily bulletins.
      4. Any person observed in the immediate vicinity of a crime very recently committed or reported as "in progress."
      5. Known trouble-makers near large gatherings.
      6. Persons who attempt to avoid or evade the officer.
      7. Exaggerated unconcern over contact with the officer.
      8. Visibly "rattled" when near the policeman.
      9. Unescorted women or young girls in public places, particularly at night in such places as cafes, bars, bus and train depots, or street corners.

   [Eleven additional categories of persons followed.]

   What do these criteria suggest to the police officer about the value of respecting an individual's freedom except where "probable cause" exists?
5. The "reasonableness" standard has recently been accepted by the U.S. Supreme Court in school searches. Teachers and administrators may search students when it is reasonable, even if no probable cause exists. Because of the school's "need to maintain an environment in which learning can take place," the Court held that searches are lawful when there are reasonable grounds for suspecting that the search will turn up evidence that the student has violated or is violating either the law or the rules of the school." *New Jersey* v. *T.L.O.*, 105 S.Ct. 733, 745 (1985).

---

*From Thomas F. Adams, "Field Interrogation," *Police,* March–April 1963, p. 28.

People v. John *453 N.Y.S. 2d 160, 56 N.Y. 2d 482 (1982)*

WACHTLER, JUDGE. [*Giving the opinion of the Court*]

In response to a series of burglaries committed in a remote rural region, the local police stopped vehicles traveling in the area. The stops were conducted in a uniform, nonarbitrary and nondiscriminatory manner for the purpose of ascertaining the identity of the occupants and obtaining information regarding the criminal activity. The question on this appeal is whether these stops violate the constitutional proscription against unreasonable searches and seizures.

On December 19, 1978 the New York State Police discovered that approximately 40 burglaries of vacant summer homes had occurred in the sparsely populated area of Sullivan County's Anawanda-Tennanah Lake region. Investigator Connors began surveillance of the area on December 21 with the expressed intent of stopping all of the vehicles that he found and interviewing all people in the general vicinity of the lake.

At about 9:30 p.m. on the same day, defendant Stephen CC.'s automobile was stopped by Connors' unmarked parked police cruiser and two other police vehicles.

In response to a demand for his driving license and automobile registration, defendant Stephen CC. exited from the car to produce the requested documents. Connors then looked inside the open car door with his flashlight and observed a rifle case protruding from under the front seat as well as several flashlights lying on the floor of the vehicle. Connors seized the rifle case, opened it and discovered that it contained a pellet gun. One of the officers recalled that a pellet gun had been reported stolen from one of the nearby cottages.

Defendant Stephen CC., when asked where he obtained the gun, responded that he bought it from a friend along with a pair of audio speakers which were in the trunk. He could not, however, remember the name of the friend who had sold him the items. Since speakers had also been reported stolen from one of the burglarized cottages, the trunk was opened without Stephen CC.'s consent and the speakers were seized. The other three passengers in the car, including defendant John BB., responded to interrogation regarding their activities in the area with conflicting statements.

Both defendants were taken to police headquarters, waived their rights, and confessed to the commission of several burglaries. After being indicted on multiple counts of burglary in the second degree . . . defendants moved to suppress their confessions and the evidence seized from Stephen CC.'s vehicle on the ground that the initial stop of the vehicle was not grounded upon reasonable suspicion of current criminal activity and was therefore unconstitutional. Following denial of that motion defendants pleaded guilty to four counts of attempted burglary in the second degree . . . and were adjudicated youthful offenders. The Appellate Division, 81 A.D.2d 188, 440 N.Y.S.2d 387, upheld the validity of the roving roadblock and affirmed the judgment of the court below. We agree with the Appellate Division's determination that the procedure employed by the police was constitutionally permissible and therefore affirm.

The defendants are correct in their contention that the Constitutions, both Federal and State, protect an individual from unreasonable searches or seizures conducted by law enforcement officials. And although not every encounter of an inquisitorial nature rises to the level of a seizure within the meaning of the constitutional language, it cannot be disputed that the stop of Stephen CC.'s automobile was at least a limited seizure subject to constitutional limitations. (*Delaware v. Prouse,* 440 U.S. 648, 99 S.Ct. 1391, 59 L.Ed.2d 660; *People v. Ingle,* 36 N.Y.2d 413, 369 N.Y.S.2d 67, 330 N.E.2d 39).

The question then is whether the stop of the defendants was the type of unreasonable seizure prohibited by the Constitution. While this proscription generally forbids any unwarranted intrusion into the private affairs or conduct of any individual, we have noted that there is no

---

Some footnotes and case citations have been omitted. — ED.

absolute right to be free from all official inquisitorial interference however minimally intrusive (*People v. De Bour,* 40 N.Y.2d 210, 386 N.Y.S.2d 375, 352 N.E.2d 562). The indefiniteness of the term "unreasonable" militates against the construction of a general rule of universal application for determining the validity of official intrusions of this nature. Rather, the facts of each case much be examined and the essential inquiry is whether the police conduct may be characterized as reasonable, which in turn requires a balancing of the State's interest in the inquiry at issue against the individual's interest in being free from governmental interference (*Delaware v. Prouse,* 440 U.S. 648, 99 S.Ct. 1391, 59 L.Ed.2d 660, *supra; People v. De Bour,* 40 N.Y.2d 210, 386 N.Y.S.2d 375, 352 N.E.2d 562, *supra*).

We recognize that the obvious impact of stopping the progress of an automobile is more intrusive than the minimal intrusion involved in stopping a pedestrian (*People v. De Bour, supra;* cf. *People v. Cantor,* 36 N.Y.2d 106, 365 N.Y.S.2d 509, 324 N.E.2d 872). But this does not mean that the broad range of factors relevant for the purpose of constitutional examination can never be analyzed in a manner which leads to the ultimate conclusion that the State may stop an automobile and question the occupants for legitimate reasons.

The evidence as developed at the suppression hearing establishes that the determination of the police to stop Stephen CC.'s vehicle was made pursuant to a nonarbitrary, nondiscriminatory and uniform procedure, involving the stop of all vehicles located in the heavily burglarized area, in order to facilitate the concededly legitimate function of acquiring information regarding the recent burglaries. The remote, sparsely populated area subject to surveillance was too large to permit any meaningful utilization of traditional investigative procedures, and the roving patrol was limited to stopping vehicles located in the region in which there had been a large number of burglaries. Under these circumstances the momentary inconvenience inevitable in this police confrontation cannot be said to be unreasonable.

The record before us demonstrates that the stop of Stephen CC.'s vehicle was not undertaken with an intent to harass and was based on much more than the mere whim, caprice, or idle curiosity of government officials. Although not controlling, the elimination of the element of arbitrariness has been identified time and again as a critical factor in determining the reasonableness of official investigative activity of an intrusive nature. For this reason, too, the cases relied on by defendants, involving official intrusion of a random and discriminatory nature are inappropriate. In fact, in *United States v. Martinez-Fuerte,* 428 U.S. 543, 96 S.Ct. 3074, 49 L.Ed.2d 1116, *supra,* the Supreme Court held that nonrandom checkpoint border stops do not violate the Fourth Amendment because they present no potential for unlimited interference with the use of the highways subject only to the unbridled discretion of government officials. For similar reasons we hold that the Fourth Amendment does not prohibit the police from employing a roving roadblock in a uniform and nondiscriminatory manner in a sparsely populated area in which there has been a recent series of burglaries.

Defendants also contend that even if the initial stop and request for information were proper, the subsequent seizure of the pellet gun and speakers was prohibited. This claim is without merit. The rifle case was in plain view and Investigator Connors acted reasonably in seizing the case and examining its contents for the protection of himself and the other officers. The pellet gun was then identified as potential contraband and this fact, combined with the conflicting explanations offered by the occupants of the vehicle and Stephen CC.'s own statements about the speakers, also known to be reported stolen, supplied the necessary exigency and probable cause to believe that the vehicle contained additional contraband, thereby justifying the warrantless opening of the vehicle's trunk compartment.

We have reviewed the various other contentions raised by defendants on appeal and find that they, too, are without merit.

Accordingly, the order of the Appellate Division should be affirmed.

MEYER, JUDGE *(dissenting)*.

The concept that the need to obtain information concerning numerous recent burglaries in a rural area authorizes an individual police officer to stop every vehicle in the area, without information about or observation of the vehicle or its occupants which gives rise to reasonable suspicion of criminal activity involving it or them, is so inconsistent with prior precedent under both the Federal and the State Constitutions, that I cannot accept it. As is apparent from the failure of the majority to make any reference to the conduct of defendants or the vehicle prior to the conceded seizure of the vehicle and its repeated reference to a nonarbitrary, nondiscriminatory and uniform procedure for stopping all vehicles, the majority's ruling leaves to the unconstrained discretion of the officer in the field (provided only that he takes the same action with respect to every vehicle) action which has heretofore been acceptable only after judicial issuance of an area warrant or the administrative adoption of standards, guidelines or procedures promulgated by higher governmental officials than the police officer in the field, or by an exigency, such as the immediate necessity to blockade an area against the escape of a kidnapper with his victim. I, therefore, respectfully dissent.

Clear from the testimony of Troopers Connors and Greaves is that Connors' "plan" was to stop every vehicle in the area in order to inquire of any occupant who he was and what he was doing in the area, to see if he might be the burglar or have been a witness to any of the burglaries. *Brown v. Texas,* 443 U.S. 47, 52, 99 S.Ct. 2637, 2641, 61 L.Ed.2d 357 flatly held that as to an individual whose activity was no different than that of others in the neighborhood, a stop the purpose of which was to ascertain identity and for which the officers lacked reasonable suspicion to believe the person stopped to be engaged or have been engaged in criminal conduct violated the Fourth Amendment . . . notwithstanding that the neighborhood was one frequented by drug users. . . .

The procedure followed in the present case was not a nonarbitrary, nondiscriminatory, uniform highway traffic procedure. It was, by the majority's concession clearly a seizure, rather than a stop, and was justified neither by any emergency, nor reasonable suspicion concerning defendants, nor a judicially issued warrant nor an administratively approved checkpoint plan. It was, therefore, unconstitutional.

The order of the Appellate Division should be reversed, the convictions vacated, the evidence and statements suppressed and the indictment dismissed.

COOKE, C. J., *and* JASEN, GABRIELLI *and* JONES, J. J., *concur with* WACHTLER, J.

MEYER, J., *dissents and votes to reverse in a separate opinion in which* FUCHSBERG, J., *concurs.*

Order affirmed.

Notes and Questions

1. In May 1983, the U.S. Supreme Court decided the case of *Kolender* v. *Lawson* (103 S.Ct. 1855, 1983). Lawson, like Charles Reich, liked to walk at night in residential areas. Between March 1975 and January 1977, he was arrested fifteen times under a California law that required suspicious persons who were stopped by the police to provide "credible and reliable" identification. Since what was "credible and reliable" was not defined by any clear standard but was to be decided by the police officer, the Supreme Court overturned Lawson's conviction and ruled that the law was unconstitutional. It left open the possibility that a less vague statute that required responding to a police demand for identification might be upheld even when a *Terry*-type frisk revealed no weapon.

3 LEGAL PERSPECTIVES ON THE EXCLUSIONARY RULE

> Our decision, founded on reason and truth, gives to the individual no more than that which the Constitution guarantees him, to the police officer no less than that to which honest law enforcement is entitled, and, to the courts, that judicial integrity so necessary in the true administration of justice.
>
> Justice Tom Clark, *Mapp* v. *Ohio* (1961)

What should happen if the police conduct an illegal search and, as a result, discover incriminating evidence? According to the exclusionary rule, such evidence may not be introduced at a trial or be considered by a jury in considering guilt or innocence. The exclusion of evidence from consideration at the trial was the goal of the defense lawyers in the cases you just read. If no other evidence of guilt exists, the defendant will go free. If there is enough *other* evidence of guilt, however, the defendant may still be convicted.

The exclusionary rule is almost seventy years old and is still surrounded by controversy. It is not required by the Constitution nor mentioned in it. Rather, courts have imposed it because they felt that it was the most workable and feasible way to deter illegal police conduct and maintain an honest system of law enforcement.

A description of the facts in the landmark case of *Mapp* v. *Ohio* precedes the following discussion of the exclusionary rule. Judicial opinions typically do not allow the reader any insight into the feelings and perspectives of the parties to a case. In the following chapter from their book about the Constitution, Professors Fred Friendly and Martha Elliot provide a rare view of the citizen-police confrontation that ultimately led the Supreme Court to declare that the exclusionary rule applies to the states as well as to federal officials.

In subsequent readings, Federal Court of Appeals Judge Malcolm Wilkey asserts that society can no longer bear the costs that the rule brings, that guilty persons escape prosecution because of it, and that illegal police conduct is not deterred. Political scientist Bradley Canon, on the other hand, argues that Judge Wilkey is incorrect in claiming that the rule does not deter the police.

A Knock at the Door: How the Supreme Court Created a Rule to Enforce the Fourth Amendment

Fred W. Friendly and Martha J. H. Elliot

It was an unseasonably raw May morning in Cleveland. Police Sergeant Carl Delau, home from a party and "a little drunk," had just fallen asleep when the phone rang at 2:30 A.M. Don King, an alleged numbers racketeer, who would later become the prominent promoter of championship boxing bouts, was on the other end of the line. "Sergeant, they just bombed my house," King excitedly reported.

"Donald, how do you know?" Delau asked in a sleepy daze.

"Well," King said, "I can look out and I don't have a front porch; I don't have a front wall."

When in response to Delau's next question, King said he had not yet called the police, Delau phoned in the report. In a few minutes, his phone rang again. This time a police dispatcher told him to "get your pants on. There is a big bomb in there."

That call was the beginning of the Cleveland police's investigation of the bombing of King's house. It was also the beginning of a Supreme Court case that would have constitutional repercussions in every police station in America. For *Mapp* v. *Ohio,* as the case would be known, would establish throughout the land the Fourth Amendment right against unreasonable search and seizure. Yet the case began as a test of obscenity law.

THE SEARCH AND SEIZURE

Three days later, on May 23, 1957, Sergeant Delau received a phone tip that a person connected with the bombing was hiding out at 14705 Milverton Road. He and his two partners drove over to the two-family house; it happened to be the home of Dollree Mapp.

Miss Mapp, as she likes to be called, still bristles with hostility when she talks about the Cleveland cops; Delau, who was a vice squad officer, himself borders on the obscene when he describes her as "a foxy girl" with "a swagger about her that was just as calm as can be and just as jibe as can be and just as flippant as can be." Now in her fifties, Dollree Mapp is still a handsome, verbal woman, who has all the charisma and body English of a knockout. Married for a short time to boxer Jimmy Bivans, who during World War II briefly held the light heavyweight boxing championship, Miss Mapp had been, according to columnist Walter Winchell, the fiancée of light heavyweight champion Archie Moore.

When the three plainclothesmen arrived at the Mapp house about 1:30 that afternoon, they noted the bombing suspect's car parked outside, "so we sat there and waited for a long time," remembers Delau. "And he was not leaving. . . . I said, well, how would it look if we made an inquiry. They might just say, 'Hiya, come right in.' But I knew Dollree Mapp, and I figured it would be a little different than that." He was right.

More than two decades after the ensuing search and arrest, Dollree Mapp and the now-retired Sergeant Delau give surprisingly similar versions of the episode. Delau and the patrolmen, Michael Haney and Thomas Devers, knocked on the side door of the house. Miss Mapp poked her head out of the upstairs window and asked what they wanted. The police responded that they wanted to make a search, but the visibly annoyed Miss Mapp said she would not open the door before calling her lawyer. A few minutes later she was back, refusing to admit them and insisting that they first obtain a search warrant.

Delau and company returned to their car to radio in, asking that another officer get a search warrant while they watched the house. At about 4:30 they returned to the side door, this time accompanied by a half-dozen uniformed colleagues. Once again they asked Miss Mapp to consent to the search, claiming to have a warrant, and once again she leaned out the window and defiantly shouted, "Nooo."

This time the police broke a pane of glass, unlatched the door, and barreled into the stairwell that led up to Miss Mapp's apartment. Observing all this from her second-floor perch, she marched downstairs and met the officers on the landing between floors.

"I said, 'Hold it. Where's the warrant?'" Miss Mapp recalls. "And he [Delau] held up the piece of paper. . . ."

In Miss Mapp's bedroom, the police confiscated some "obscene" materials: "pictures of both male and female nude models with all their organs totally undressed," some pencil sketches of nudes, and four books, *London Stage Affairs, Affairs of a Troubadour, Memoirs of a Hotel Man,* and *Little Darlings.* Then the police went to the basement of the house and confiscated some policy paraphernalia (betting materials). At the time, Miss Mapp claimed that all of the contraband belonged to a former roomer, Morris Jones, whose belongings she was storing, although she now admits that the sketches were hers. Meanwhile, the bombing suspect, Virgil Ogiltree, was finally found in the first-floor apartment. Miss Mapp was arrested and charged for possession of the betting equipment and the obscene materials.

The charge for possession of the policy paraphernalia was a misdemeanor, and she was tried and acquitted in police court. Possession of obscene material was a felony under a recently amended Ohio statute.

It was not until September 1958 that Miss Mapp went on trial for "unlawfully and knowingly having in her possession certain lewd and lascivious books, pictures, and photographs . . . being so indecent and immoral . . . that some would be offensive to the Court and improper to be placed in the records thereof." By that time, the search warrant had mysteriously disappeared. Miss Mapp pleaded not guilty, and her lawyer, Alexander L. Kearns, moved to have the evidence suppressed on the grounds that the officers were required to obtain a warrant before conducting a search. It is important to note that even if the warrant could have been produced, it would not have mentioned the obscene materials. The police were empowered only to look for the bombing suspect and policy paraphernalia. However, Judge Donald F. Lybarger overruled the motion to suppress the evidence. . . .

Despite the "missing" search warrant and after only 20 minutes of deliberation, the jury found Dollree Mapp guilty as charged, and she was sentenced to serve one to seven years in the Ohio State Reformatory for Women. After a friend posted her bail, Dollree Mapp appealed.

THE CONSTITUTIONAL ISSUES

Underlying Dollree Mapp's conviction were two constitutional questions, involving the First and Fourth Amendments. First, was the Ohio obscenity statute constitutional? And, second, was the search of her house an unreasonable search and seizure, and if so, was the evidence (i.e., the books, pictures, and pencil drawings) therefore not admissible in court?

The First Amendment Although the United States Supreme Court had made it clear in *Near, DeJonge,* and other cases that the First Amendment protections for free speech and press were enforceable against the states, the Court had also asserted that those protections were not absolute. In *Near,* Chief Justice Hughes had listed some of the exceptions, including obscenity:

> No one would question but that a government might prevent actual obstruction to its recruiting service or the publication of the sailing dates of transports or the number and location of troops. *On similar grounds, the primary requirements of decency may be enforced against obscene publications.* The security of the community life may be protected against incitements to acts of violence and the overthrow by force of orderly government.

In 1957, the Court had expanded its views on obscenity in *Roth* v. *United States.* In that case Samuel Roth had been convicted of four counts of using the United States mails to advertise and distribute obscene materials. Speaking for the majority in upholding Roth's conviction, Justice William Brennan declared that "this Court has always assumed that obscenity is not protected by the freedoms of speech and press. . . . [T]he unconditional phrasing of the First Amendment was not intended to protect every utterance." Although "All ideas having even the slightest redeeming social importance — unorthodox ideas, controversial ideas, even ideas hateful to the prevailing climate of opinion — have the full protection of the guaranties," Brennan continued, "obscenity [is] utterly without redeeming social importance." And Brennan defined obscenity as "material which deals with sex in a manner appealing to prurient interest." He qualified that by saying the work should be considered as a whole, not just in terms of specific passages. He also said that "sex" and "obscenity" are not synonymous. The portrayal of sex "in art, literature and scientific works, is not itself sufficient reason to deny material the constitutional protection. . . ."

Dollree Mapp's lawyers had never argued that the material found in her home was not obscene. The constitutional question that would eventually arise was whether the Ohio obscenity statute was overly broad. For, according to the judge's charge, even if the jury believed that the books belonged to her roomer, she was guilty of possession because she knew the obscenity was in her home. And "knowing possession" of obscene material — even holding it, packed away, for another person — was a felony.

The Fourth Amendment and the Exclusionary Rule The other question was far more complicated. It had to do with the guarantee spelled out in the Fourth Amendment:

> The right of the people to be secure in their houses, papers and effects, against unreasonable searches and seizures, shall not be violated and no warrants shall issue, but upon probable cause, supported by oath or affirmation, and particularly describing the place to be searched, and the persons or things to be seized at the time.

In Dollree Mapp's case the matter of the warrant was at issue. Even if, as the police claimed, there had been a warrant, it did not list "obscene materials" as one of the things to be searched for.

In conjunction with the Fourth Amendment was a judge-made rule known as the "exclusionary rule," which prohibited illegally obtained evidence from being admitted in federal court. Former Supreme Court Justice Potter Stewart has described this rule as having been "jerry-built" — that is, in its development it was "a little bit like a roller coaster track constructed while the roller coaster sped along, with each new piece of track attached hastily and imperfectly to the one before it, just in time to prevent the roller coaster from crashing, but without the opportunity to measure the curves and dips preceding it or to contemplate the twists and turns that inevitably lay ahead."

The development of the Fourth Amendment and the exclusionary rule traces to English and colonial history. The framers of the Bill of Rights were opposed to the use of "general warrants" by the British crown. These documents, which did not list specific persons and were issued without probable cause, were used to aid in the apprehension and prosecution of critics of the crown. Once issued, the warrants were good for the life of the monarch. . . .

Almost a century elapsed between the ratification of the Constitution and the Supreme Court's justification of the exclusion of evidence on constitutional grounds, in *Boyd* v. *United States* in 1886. E. A. Boyd and Sons was involved in a forfeiture proceeding for importing from Liverpool, England, 35 cases of plate glass in violation of the federal import and revenue laws. In order to prove the case, the government needed the company's invoices. Although Boyd eventually produced the records, he objected, charging that his Fourth (search and seizure) and Fifth (self-incrimination) Amendment rights had been violated. After losing the forfeiture case, Boyd appealed to the United States Supreme Court.

The high court's opinion, written by Justice Joseph Bradley and joined by six other justices, added a new dimension to the Fourth Amendment by reading it in conjunction with the Fifth. It was, Bradley said, a case in which "the Fourth and Fifth Amendments run almost into each other." The government was seeking not contraband, but private papers protected by the Fourth Amendment. Bradley concluded, "[W]e have been unable to perceive that the seizure of a man's private books and papers to be used in evidence against him is substantially different from compelling him to be a witness against himself." Thus admitting the invoices into evidence was a double violation of Boyd's constitutional rights. The invoices could not be introduced, and a new trial was ordered.

The emergence of the exclusionary rule came in 1914, when a Kansas City Express Company employee, Fremont Weeks, was convicted in a federal court of using the mails to conduct an illegal lottery. The evidence used against him had been obtained when the police acquired a key to his home and took incriminating papers. Weeks then sued for return of his personal property.

In the United States Supreme Court, Justice William R. Day ruled that the property must be returned and that because of Weeks' Fifth Amendment rights the government could not enter the papers as evidence at the trial. Thus, a federal rule of evidence formally was written: The federal government could not produce books and papers that it had illegally seized and could not subpoena.

After *Weeks,* the exclusionary rule began to impact upon other areas and was eventually enlarged to include contraband as well as personal papers. A few states voluntarily adopted the rule, but it was not without its critics. In 1926, Judge Benjamin Cardozo (then a member of the New York State Court of Appeals and eventually a justice on the United States Supreme Court) wrote in a dissenting opinion in *People* v. *Defore*: "There has been no blinking the consequences. The criminal is to go free because the constable has blundered."

Nonetheless, until 1948, the Fourth Amendment only applied to federal searches and seizures. Then came *Wolf* v. *Colorado.* In that 1948 abortion conviction case, the Court had a chance to decide whether the Fourth Amendment and its extension, the exclusionary rule, were mandated in state proceedings via the Fourteenth Amendment's due process clause.

In 1944, Julius A. Wolf, a reputable Denver physician, had been tried for conspiring to perform an illegal abortion on Mildred Cairo. He and his co-defendant had pleaded not guilty. In their trial, the district attorney attempted to introduce into evidence Dr. Wolf's appointment book, which had been obtained without a search warrant. The defense then claimed that the appointment book linking Dr. Wolf to Mildred Cairo's abortion had been obtained illegally in violation of Colorado's own version of the Fourth Amendment. The trial judge overruled the objection, and the evidence was admitted. Wolf was convicted and sentenced to 15 months to 5 years. After Wolf's sentence was confirmed by the state supreme court, the high court agreed to hear his case in March 1948.

Justice Felix Frankfurter began his eloquent opinion for the majority by insisting that a police search without a judge's specifically worded warrant was a violation of human rights:

> A knock at the door, whether by day or by night as a prelude to a search, without authority of law but solely on the authority of the police, did not need the commentary of recent history to be condemned as inconsistent with the conception of human rights enshrined in the history and the basic constitutional documents of English-speaking peoples.

So, illegal searches, whether by federal, state, or city police, were now unconstitutional. Under the court's decision the Fourth Amendment protections were now enforceable upon the states because they were "implicit in the concept of ordered liberty." However, Frankfurter and five of his brethren refused to require the states to institute the exclusionary rule. It was not, they reasoned, the only remedy for disciplining the "blundering constable"; the states were free to adopt any one of a number of effective remedies to rectify wrongful searches and seizures. A suit against the offending officer or a charge of criminal trespass might be acceptable alternatives to the exclusion of tainted evidence. In their minds, the exclusionary rule was not inextricably bound to the Fourth Amendment, because the Constitution did not dictate a specific remedy. It didn't matter *how* the states enforced the Fourth Amendment — as long as they did enforce it.

The dissenters — Justices Douglas, Murphy, and Rutledge — scoffed at the idea of other remedies as unrealistic. Justice Murphy wrote, "Alternatives are deceptive. . . . there is but one alternative to the rule of exclusion. That is no sanction [against illegal searches] at all."

OHIO'S RULES

Like Colorado, Ohio was one of the states that had not adopted the exclusionary rule. In fact, although an Ohio statute required warrants, they were seldom used because of a 1936 case, *State* v. *Lindway*. . . .

. . . [T]his case had established for Ohio what became known as the Lindway rule: In a criminal prosecution, evidence obtained by an unlawful search was admissible if pertinent to the main issue of the case.

DOLLREE MAPP APPEALS . . .

It looked as if Dollree Mapp would have to go to prison; the cost of taking her case to the United States Supreme Court was beyond her means. But a friend came to her rescue and put up the money, nearly $8,000, to appeal. After granting *certiorari,* the court scheduled the argument for March 29, 1961.

Three cases were scheduled for hearing before the Court on that Wednesday in March, but the arguments in *Mapp* v. *Ohio* were unusually long — two hours — and took up most of the afternoon. As the nine justices filed in at noon, sitting in the back of the courtroom was Dollree Mapp, who had flown in from Ohio to hear her case argued. As Justice Stewart recalls, the overwhelming portion of the oral arguments that he heard that day were devoted to the issue of the constitutionality of the Ohio statute.

With all the bravado of a Clarence Darrow and the inflection of W. C. Fields, Alexander L. Kearns, Miss Mapp's lawyer, began by reciting in detail the facts in the case: the police inquiry, the breaking of glass, the retrieving of the "warrant," and the extensive search of Miss Mapp's home. Ignoring the constitutional precedents, he emphasized that the obscene material had belonged to a roomer, not to his client, and that the Ohio Supreme Court had accepted this fact and yet had upheld her conviction.

Finally, seemingly bored with the factual recitation, Justice Felix Frankfurter interrupted, asking Kearns, "May I trouble you to tell us what do you deem to be the questions that are open before this court?" He explained that he couldn't tell if the question of search and seizure and the adequacy of evidence were issues to be considered.

Kearns, a bit flustered, replied that search and seizure *was* at issue and began to explain the *Lindway* case. In his mind, because the Ohio legislature had enacted a statute in 1955 that required officers to obtain warrants and ensure Fourth Amendment rights, the *Lindway* case had, in effect, been overturned by the legislature. But Frankfurter, seemingly uninterested in Kearns's explanation, interrupted again, "Are you asking us to overrule the Wolf case in the court? I notice it isn't cited in your brief." Even more unsettled, Kearns shrugged off the comment by saying that he thought the state would have cited the case and that he was not asking the court to reconsider *Wolf* (the case that said the states do not have to adopt the exclusionary rule).

However, Kearns's unfamiliarity with *Wolf* did not close the question. For the first time in history, the Court had granted argument time to the Civil Liberties Union, which had become involved in the case because of the important constitutional issues. Bernard Berkman, the attorney for the Ohio Civil Liberties Union, began his presentation by referring back to Frankfurter's question and stipulating:

> The American Civil Liberties Union and its Ohio affiliate . . . [are] very clear as to the question directed toward the appellant that we are asking this court to reconsider *Wolf* v. *Colorado* and to find that evidence that is unlawfully and illegally obtained should not be permitted into a state proceeding and its production is a violation of the federal constitution's Fourth Amendment and the Fourteenth Amendment. We have no hesitancy in asking the court to reconsider it because we think that it is a necessary part of due process.

Berkman then addressed the First Amendment issue. He explained that the principal reason for his appearance was to "urge the unconstitutionality of the Ohio obscenity law." He told the justices that inasmuch as that statute made mere possession a crime, "if a normal adult has an obscene book in his possession without any criminal intent whatsoever, he has committed a felony." He continued, "As we see it, the central issue in considering the validity of this statute is this: is this an area in which the individual has a right to be let alone to be free of government restraint?"

According to Berkman and the ACLU, even though the realm of morals was a proper area for legislative enactments, "such enactments must . . . not be arbitrary or excessive. Furthermore they must not infringe upon paramount individual rights, particularly where similar legislative result may be achieved by other, less drastic measures. We submit that interposing a policeman between a normal adult and his library is not a proper means of accomplishing what otherwise might be a valid legislative purpose." He concluded, "The statute is unconstitutional."

That question of the relationship between a person and his library was one that fascinated Justice Felix Frankfurter. Shortly after Gertrude Bauer Mahon, assistant prosecutor for Cuyahoga County, began her argument, Frankfurter stopped to question her on that point:

> FRANKFURTER: Let me see if I understand — it [the law] means any book on my shelves, any of my shelves, . . . found to be obscene, constitutes a possession. He does nothing but have it on his shelf . . .
>
> MAHON: A knowing possession under this statute, a knowing possession of obscenity is prohibited by this statute. . . . I would say it extends to anybody who had . . .
>
> FRANKFURTER: On his book shelf, merely a part of his library. He's a bibliophile and he collects first editions, not for the content, but because they are first editions. Any book on his shelf — my shelf — which I know to be obscene in content, a matter of great indifference to me because I'm interested in the fact that it was published in 1527. That makes me . . . a violator of this statute. Is that correct?
>
> MAHON: I would say so, your Honor. Any collection of obscenity would be . . .
>
> *(Laughter in courtroom.)*
>
> FRANKFURTER: Mark Twain had one of the biggest collections, and I could tell you now where it is, but it's outside your jurisdiction.
>
> *(Laughter in courtroom.)*
>
> But . . . you said that the purpose of this — the aim of this statute is to prevent circulation, dissemination. Now, having it on a shelf isn't disseminating it, quite the opposite. There are no more miserly people in world than bibliophiles.

Mrs. Mahon then tried to explain that anyone who had possession would have the opportunity to circulate the material, but Frankfurter countered with the fact that there had been no charge that Dollree Mapp had attempted to circulate the books and pictures.

Later, Frankfurter returned to the same issue, asking if the state had made any examination of the libraries of the universities in Ohio. Mrs. Mahon tried to avoid the question by asserting that she would find it hard to believe that any of those libraries possessed any obscene books, but that "if any of those libraries had the obscene books and pictures and the hand-penciled drawings that are to be found to be exhibits in this case, then somebody should be arrested. [Laughter.]"

Mrs. Mahon concluded by saying the state of Ohio had a right to rely on the Court's decision in the *Wolf* case and in the *Roth* case, and that the trial court had a right to rely on the *Lindway* decision: "We feel that [the Fourth Amendment's] constitutional provision does not cancel out evidence of a criminal offense."

At the conference following the argument "a majority of the Justices agreed that the Ohio statute violated the First and Fourteenth Amendments." What happened after Justice Tom Clark was assigned to write the opinion is really a matter of speculation. Justice Potter Stewart has given one explanation: "I have always suspected that the members of the soon-to-be *Mapp* majority had met in what I affectionately call a 'rump caucus' to discuss a different basis for the decision. But regardless of how they reached their decision five Justices of the Court concluded that Dollree Mapp's conviction had to be reversed because evidence seized in an illegal search had to be excluded from state trials as well as federal ones. *Wolf* v. *Colorado* was to be overruled."

Dollree Mapp had gone home after the oral arguments uncertain of her fate. But, as she tells it, immediately after the hearing, she had gone up to one of the bailiffs and asked, "'How long before I can expect a decision?' And he said, 'Oh, months, months, months.' . . . And I said, . . . 'You should call me. Really you should call me collect.' He said, 'Well, you know they only come down on Monday.' . . . And every Monday I waited and every Monday he called. That thirteenth Monday, he called and he said, 'Dollree, you don't have to go to jail. It's all over.' That's the way he said it to me. That's all I heard."

Miss Mapp didn't care *why* she didn't have to go to jail, just that she didn't. She admits that she had never even heard of the exclusionary rule prior to that time. But thousands of law enforcement officials had heard of the rule, and the Court's findings would have enormous impact on every law enforcement official in the nation.

Speaking for a 5-to-4 majority, Justice Clark declared that "all evidence obtained by searches and seizures in violation of the Constitution is, by that same authority, inadmissable in a state court." He reasoned that without the exclusionary rule, the Fourth Amendment guarantees would be "'a form of words,' valueless and undeserving of mention in perpetual character of inestimable human liberty." The conclusion that the exclusionary rule is an integral part of the Fourth Amendment, he wrote, "is not only the logical dictate of prior cases, but it also makes very good sense. There is no war between the Constitution and common sense." . . .

The exclusionary rule is now invoked every day in courts of all sizes and jurisdictions. However, the number of cases in which it frees the criminal is slight. Less than 1 percent of federal cases are not prosecuted because the evidence is inadmissible. The limits of the rule are continually being tested and challenged in the United States Supreme Court. Some politicians, lawyers, and jurists continue to argue that it has been stretched too far, allowing the criminal to go free simply because "the constable has blundered." Others hold it up as a unique American symbol of equal justice under law. Thus the debate is far from over. Chief Justice Burger has suggested that civil suits for damages against the offending officers might be a plausible compromise. Others have proposed a "good faith doctrine," which would give judges the discretion to decide whether the police's conduct was within the bounds of reasonable search and seizure. When and where the exclusionary rule's roller-coaster ride ends is a matter which the Court may decide the next time a Dollree Mapp comes along.[1]

---

[1]In 1973 Dollree Mapp was convicted of drug possession in New York City. Under the state's newly enacted "Rockefeller laws," Miss Mapp was sentenced to serve 20 years to life at the Bedford Hills correctional facility. After spending 9 years, 4 months, and 17 days in prison, she was paroled and her sentence was commuted. She now works on Long Island as a legal aide for prison inmates. Miss Mapp still maintains her innocence of the drug charge and has petitioned state officials for a full pardon.

Why Suppress Valid Evidence? *Malcolm Richard Wilkey*

Among nations of the civilized world we are unique in two respects: (1) We suffer the most extraordinary crime rate with firearms, (2) in criminal prosecutions, by a rule of evidence which exists in no other country, we exclude the most trustworthy and convincing evidence.

These two aberrations are not unconnected. In fact, the "exclusionary rule" has made unenforceable the gun control laws we have and will make ineffective any stricter controls which may be devised. Its fetters particularly paralyze police efforts to prevent, detect and punish street crimes involving not only weapons but narcotics.

What is this "exclusionary rule" that permits a professional criminal to swagger down the street with a handgun bulging in his hip pocket, immune to police search and seizure? It is not required by the Constitution. The Fourth Amendment only forbids "unreasonable searches and seizures." The exclusionary rule is a judge-made rule of evidence which bars "the use of evidence secured through an illegal search and seizure."

When it was adopted in 1914 it was applied only to evidence seized by federal agents and offered in federal courts. In 1960 it was broadened to bar in federal courts evidence originally seized by state police, over which the federal government had no control. Finally, the ban was extended in 1961 to evidence seized by state officials and offered in state courts.

Four out of literally tens of thousands of cases illustrate its application. In *United States v. Robinson (1973)*, Robinson was arrested for driving with a forged driver's license. He was searched and a packet containing heroin was found.

The court of appeals held Robinson's search illegal, and, applying the exclusionary rule, suppressed the heroin evidence illegally seized. The Supreme Court reversed, holding the evidence was obtained by a legal search and therefore the exclusionary rule did not apply.

In *United States v. Montgomery (1977)*, two police officers patrolling a residential neighborhood observed Montgomery driving as if he were "sizing up" the area. A stop for identification revealed Montgomery had an arrest warrant outstanding. A protective search turned up a .38 caliber bullet, a magnum revolver loaded with six rounds and a sawed-off shotgun with shells.

WRITING A DISSENT

The court of appeals reversed the conviction, holding that no probable cause existed for stopping Montgomery, hence all evidence was the product of an illegal search. The exclusionary rule mandated suppression of evidence about the loaded revolver and sawed-off shotgun, which was essential to conviction.

(It is well to cite here my own involvement: I wrote the dissent in our court of appeals 5–4 decision in *Robinson* and our dissenting position was upheld in the Supreme Court. I dissented in the 2–1 decision of our court in *Montgomery* in which time for seeking *certiorari* has now expired.)

In *Brewer v. Williams (1977)*, a prisoner charged with murder of a 10-year-old girl was subtly induced to take police officers to the site of the body. The Supreme Court held 5–4 that: The prisoner's Sixth Amendment right to counsel was violated (*Robinson* and *Montgomery* involved Fourth Amendment illegal searches and seizures), the confession was thus illegally obtained, the evidence of location of the victim's body was thus tainted because it was derived from the illegal confession, therefore, the exclusionary rule barred evidence of the prisoner's statements and the location of the body.

Also in 1977, the conviction of a New York doctor who pled guilty to sexual abuse was reversed and eyewitness testimony suppressed.

After complaints of sexual misconduct against the doctor during gynecological examinations of patients under anesthetic gas, a policewoman posing as a patient visited the doctor's offices. At the same time a male investigator was outside to protect her. He peered through the heavily curtained windows and saw the doctor commit sex acts on another patient.

The court of appeals held the search (observation) illegal, suppressing the investigator's eyewitness testimony under the exclusionary rule, thus eliminating any possibility of conviction.

The legal argument in these cases is whether the police had a valid basis, *i.e.*, "probable cause," for their action. Where to draw the line between "reasonable" and "unreasonable" under the Fourth Amendment is one issue. Whether evidence should automatically be excluded as a result of an illegal search is quite another, and is the issue addressed here. At present no court but the Supreme Court has any choice on the latter.

The impact of the exclusionary rule is that the most valid, conclusive and factual evidence is excluded from the jury. This rule produces a distortion of the truth. Irrefutable facts of decisive importance are forever barred.

In exclusionary rule cases involving material evidence there is never any question of reliability. Reliability is in question, for example, with a coerced confession or a faulty lineup for identification. Exclusion of evidence is then proper, because the evidence is inherently unreliable. But when a pistol or narcotics is found on a person the legality of the search cannot impair the truth of the physical evidence.

Then why the exclusionary rule? The justification is purely theoretical: Excluding evidence will punish the officers committing the illegal act and thus deter policemen from repetition. As Justice Cardozo predicted in 1926, in describing the complete irrationality of the exclusionary rule, "The criminal is to go free because the constable has blundered. . . . A room is searched against the law, and the body of a murdered man is found. . . . The privacy of the home has been infringed, and the murderer goes free."

SHUNNED BY OTHER COUNTRIES

If the exclusionary rule had merit, surely at least one other country since 1914 would have followed our example. All have shunned it. The rule in all other countries — in England, Canada, Germany, Israel, for example — is that relevant evidence is admitted, whether obtained legally or illegally.

The exclusionary rule has been devastating to gun control laws. Unless a police officer has "probable cause" to make a reasonable search, nothing found during the search — no sawed-off shotgun, automatic pistol or submachine gun — can be introduced as evidence. Therefore, since it is virtually impossible to be convicted in the U.S. of carrying a weapon illegally, American criminals do carry guns and use them. Since police know they carry and use them, they engage in far more searches and seizures than in the countries mentioned above, and some of those searches and seizures are blatantly illegal.

Thus under the exclusionary rule, Americans have the worst of it both ways: The public is harassed more by both criminals and police than citizens of many other countries.

The only excuse offered for this irrational rule is that there is "no effective alternative" to make the police obey the law. But other civilized countries control their police by disciplinary measures against errant policemen, not by freeing the criminal. Judging by the results in England and Canada, among others, disciplinary measures work very well.

But there are other alternatives to disciplinary measures. Every prosecution in which an illegal search is claimed might be followed by a minitrial of the accused officer, at the conclusion of which the same judge who heard the evidence at the principal trial would mete out deserved punishment for any proven infraction.

Unlike the exclusionary rule, this would not free the convicted criminal, but it would provide a deterrent against officers violating constitutional rights. And in instances not resulting in prosecution, offended citizens could be given a right to sue the governmental entity by which the individual officer is employed.

Handguns — crimes by handguns — are one of our gravest problems. No laws on gun control will work if the laws cannot be effectively enforced. No gun control law can be enforced with the unique American exclusionary rule keeping out the most reliable evidence necessary for conviction.

There are proven workable alternatives to the exclusionary rule. Either the Supreme Court (which created it) or Congress can abolish it, and surely one or the other will do so.

The Exclusionary Rule: Have Critics Proven That It Doesn't Deter Police? *Bradley Canon*

Judge Malcolm Wilkey attacks the exclusionary rule in search and seizure in terms of both logic and experience. I will leave the logical arguments to others; my purpose here is to evaluate his claims that experience proves that the rule is socially costly and that it fails to achieve its purpose of securing police compliance with the Fourth Amendment.

According to Wilkey a variety of crimes would be significantly curtailed if the rule did not exist: gambling, narcotics, prostitution, armed robbery and concealed weapons.[1] No evidence, however, is offered in support of this assertion. Indeed, it is hard to see even a logical connection between the rule and the incidence of some of the crimes. Armed robbery is certainly far more a product of a society whose public policy (the only one in the civilized world, I might add) allows almost unrestricted access to weapons rather than the legal inability of the police to search for guns in the few minutes before the crime occurs.

Moreover, the exclusionary rule in no way prevents the police from confiscating concealed weapons. The real problem is not that criminals walk down the streets with bulging automatics in their coats or submachine guns thinly covered by blankets. The problem is that the weapons are well hidden and the police often do not know whom to search. Though reading Dick Tracy may suggest otherwise, criminals do not come in malformed, misshapen sizes rendering them easily identifiable to the police. Getting rid of the exclusionary rule would not alter the situation very much (unless, of course, the police adopted a policy of searching *everyone* randomly — in which case we would truly be living in a police state).

THE IMPACT OF MAPP

Indeed, taking Wilkey's argument to its logical conclusion, one would have to believe that we lived in a rather crime-free society before *Mapp v. Ohio* in 1961. This of course is hardly the case. It was in the 1920's and 1930's, not the 1970's that Dillinger, Capone and other gangsters walked the streets carrying violin cases. It was in the 1950's, not the 1970's, when organized crime's involvement in gambling became so notorious that the Kefauver Committee made headlines for months investigating it. I argue not that there is less crime today than there was before *Mapp*, but Judge Wilkey's assertion that the incidence of crime is *related to* the exclusionary rule fails to withstand even the most modest scrutiny.

From *Judicature*, Volume 62, Number 8, March 1979. Used by permission of the author. (Most footnotes omitted.)

[1]Malcolm Richard Wilkey, "The Exclusionary Rule: Why Suppress Valid Evidence?" 62 *Judicature* 215 (November 1978).

In this vein, in fact, I find it amazing that Wilkey imputes to criminals a detailed knowledge of the law of search and seizure. ("Criminals," he writes, "know the difficulties of the police in making a valid search which will stand up under challenge at trial.") No evidence is offered that criminals are so learned in the law and it seems quite anomalous to assume so, considering that search and seizure law is so confusing or uncertain that the nation's most prominent jurists and legal scholars have described it as a "quagmire," a "no man's land" and a "course of true law [that] has not run smooth."

Ironically, Chief Justice Burger, a staunch opponent of the exclusionary rule, argues that one of its disadvantages is that *policemen* do not understand the intricacies of search and seizure law and thus often make mistakes in search situations. He may well be right on this point, but if so Judge Wilkey's imputation seems all the more surprising. It takes more credulity than I have to believe that the basic problem is one of "smart crooks" and "dumb cops."

A DIFFERENTIAL IMPACT

My main concern with Judge Wilkey's article, however, is not a fear that readers will be taken in by his exaggerated or unsound claims about the responsibility of the exclusionary rule for the high incidence of crime nowadays. Most readers, I am confident, have sufficient judgment to discount such claims. My concern, rather, is that they will accept the judge's assertion that empirical studies demonstrate that the rule is ineffective in deterring police violations of the Fourth Amendment. After all, they might reason, Wilkey is not reporting his own observations or conclusions here, but is merely citing studies carried out by others.

The problem is that Judge Wilkey's treatment of these studies leaves much to be desired. It seems that he relies in large part on the summaries of these studies and conclusions drawn from them by Professor Steven Schlesinger in his recent monograph on the rule. Schlesinger is quite open in his hostility to the exclusionary rule and, unfortunately, this has led him to misinterpret some studies and downplay others. Moreover, additional evidence has become available after Schlesinger's work was published.

When the totality of the evidence is examined more fully and more dispassionately, it does not support the Wilkey-Schlesinger conclusion that the rule is inefficacious in curbing illegal police searches. Neither, I should make it clear, does the evidence support the opposite conclusion — that the rule deters police illegalities nearly 100 per cent of the time. Put shortly, the rule has a differential impact depending upon time and place.

REPLICATING THE OAKS' STUDY

Let us take a hard look at the empirical evidence. Wilkey argues that Dallin Oaks' study is the "most comprehensive study ever undertaken" on the subject. But Oaks' own research is devoted chiefly to drawing inferences about police behavior in Cincinnati from arrest records in search and seizure type crimes (largely gambling, narcotics, and weapons offenses) in the five or six years before and after *Mapp.* It is a careful study and there is little doubt that the rule had only minimal impact on police behavior in Cincinnati immediately following *Mapp.* But it can hardly be considered comprehensive.

Few would be so bold as to join Judge Wilkey in claiming that police behavior in one city 15 years ago is representative of police behavior throughout the United States in 1978. Oaks himself freely admits that his study "obviously falls short of an empirical substantiation or refutation of the deterrent effect of the exclusionary rule." Indeed, Wilkey puts words in Oaks' mouth when he tells us that "Oaks concluded" that the exclusionary rule is a failure; Oaks took pains to note that this assertion "is an argument, not a conclusion."

Working on a Ford Foundation grant in 1972–73, I replicated Oaks' Cincinnati study for 19 other American cities. Statistical techniques were used to eliminate arbitrary judgments and control for alternate explanations. In nine of the cities, there was a statistically significant decrease in arrests in all or most search and seizure crimes following *Mapp,* while in the other 10 the impact was minimal or absent.

Seemingly the exclusionary rule can and does have a very real, although hardly universal deterrent, effect on the police. The rule's impact, I concluded, depended much on such factors as degree of professional training prevailing in a department, policies of chiefs of police and squad commanders, the attitudes of mayors, city councils and other officials, etc. There simply was no singular response (or non-response) pattern to the exclusionary rule in the five or six years after *Mapp.*

OTHER STUDIES

Schlesinger also briefly discusses Michael Ban's study of the use of search warrants in Cincinnati and Boston and the Columbia Law School study of narcotics arrests in Manhattan following *Mapp.* Ban found the annual use of search warrants rose from virtually zero to over 100 in Cincinnati while in Boston it went from about 100 to nearly 1,000. He argued the Cincinnati figures are too low to represent whole-hearted compliance with the Fourth Amendment — a conclusion that dovetails well with Oaks' Cincinnati findings. On the other hand, Ban concedes the Boston figures imply considerable if begrudging police compliance.

The Columbia study noted a dramatic decline in narcotics arrests in premises but only a slight decline of street arrests. The authors conclude that *Mapp* inhibited police from illegal invasion of homes, etc., but not from street searches. They also speculate that this was partly due to the vice squad's (which conducts raids on premises) greater awareness of the decision and its implications. Again, these studies demonstrate the differential impact of the exclusionary rule; they hardly lend support to Judge Wilkey's claims that the empirical evidence shows the rule to be a "total failure in its primary task of deterring illegal police activity."

The data involved in the above studies have one common feature: they come from the period immediately following the *Mapp* decision. However, in evaluating the exclusionary rule with an eye toward a public policy decision of retention, modification or abrogation, we must be interested in its present rather than its past impact on police behavior. Unless we can be reasonably sure that the impact reported in the early 1960's persists without great change into the present, the value of the above studies is quite limited. And while the data are thin and inferences tenuous, there is some reason to believe that the rule has become more effective than it was in the early 1960's.

A RECENT SURVEY

In 1973 I sent questionnaires to police departments, prosecutors and public defenders in all American cities with populations of more than 100,000. I asked whether their current search and seizure practices differed from those prevalent in 1967 and, if so, how. Responses came from over half the cities and clearly indicated that in most of them police compliance with the Fourth Amendment increased significantly over the six-year period.

- Four-fifths of them reported the use of search warrants was more than 50 per cent greater than the 1967 level and 35 per cent of the cities reported an increase of more than 100 per cent.
- Nearly two-thirds of the departments reported more restrictive policies pertaining to searches accompanying an arrest than they espoused six years earlier. 18 per cent reported a stricter policy regarding searches of automobiles.
- Moreover, while comparison with 1967 figures showed only modest change, 50 per cent of the cities reported that motions to suppress evidence were granted less than 10 per cent of the time and in 63 per cent it was reported that charges were "rarely" dropped because of illegal seizure of the evidence.

Even in the absence of the above data, one could reasonably surmise on the basis of impact patterns reported for other Supreme Court criminal justice decisions that the exclusionary rule is more effective now than it was in the immediate post-*Mapp* years. The controversial *Miranda* decision, for instance, received only spotty compliance by police departments in the two or three years after its promulgation. More recently, however, it seems to be effective in controlling police behavior — and even has won the approval of many officers. And immediately following *In re Gault,* compliance was a hit and miss affair; many juvenile judges did not seem to know that such a decision had even been made. Again, a decade's time has permitted the word to circulate and eroded resistance.

Experience tells us that sudden and dramatic changes in policy such as occurred with the *Mapp* decision do not produce alteration in behavior overnight. Information about Supreme Court decisions is particularly poorly disseminated, often easily misunderstood and sometimes ignored in deference to habit or convenience. But eventually the word is spread; young, professionally trained recruits infuse the ranks; old-timers become a vanishing breed. It is not certain, of course, that police search and seizure behavior has followed this scenario, but it is certainly a plausible hypothesis.

SPIOTTO'S STUDY

The only other empirical evidence Judge Wilkey discusses is James Spiotto's study comparing results of a study of motions to suppress [evidence] in search and seizure crimes in the Chicago Municipal Court in 1950 with those in 1969 and 1971. Wilkey makes much of the findings and quotes Spiotto as follows:

> over a twenty year period in Chicago, the proportional number of motions to suppress evidence [in narcotics and weapons cases] allegedly obtained illegally increased significantly. This is the opposite result of what would be expected if the rule had been efficacious in deterring police misconduct.

This is an amazing conclusion. Spiotto is utterly unaware that Illinois adopted the exclusionary rule in 1924 — some 37 years before *Mapp.* (Besides being a legal researcher, Spiotto is an Illinois resident, so it is not easy to explain this monumental error.) Thus the court was governed by the rule in 1951 as well as in 1969 and 1971 and the *Mapp* decision would have no legal impact on its receptivity to motions to suppress.

It could be argued — although it is not a point made by either Spiotto or Wilkey — that *Mapp* had an impact even in those states which had previously adopted the rule because federal civil liberties decisions have a greater visibility than those made by states or because police officers have reason to believe that state judges do not take such decisions seriously while federal judges do. This may be true in some jurisdictions, but it is obviously not the case in Chicago. Its court was clearly enforcing the exclusionary rule prior to *Mapp*; the 1950 study shows that 98 per cent of all motions to suppress were granted.

Even if Illinois had not adopted the rule long before *Mapp,* Spiotto's conclusion about the rule's inefficacy would be flawed. After all, if there were no exclusionary rule, there would be no point in defendants moving to suppress evidence (such motions would obviously be denied) and consequently there would be few such motions filed and none granted. Thus it would be perfectly natural that the proportion of such motions granted would rise dramatically after the *Mapp* decision when judges would be constitutionally obligated to consider them seriously and grant those with merit. The "significant increase" Spiotto reports would tell us nothing about the impact of the rule on police conduct; it would speak only of the perfectly obvious impact of the rule on the conduct of *defense attorneys.*

Finally, it might be argued that regardless of when the exclusionary rule was adopted, the percentage of motions to suppress is much too high — running 69 per cent in 1950 and in the 30 per cent to 35 per cent range in the 1969–71 period — and that this in itself is damning evidence of the rule's ineffectiveness. Chicago, however, is not a very typical city in this respect.

As previously noted, in three-fifths of large American cities, 10 per cent or fewer of such motions are granted and in only a handful were over 25 per cent of such motions granted. Indeed, Chicago police are reputed to enforce the vice laws in a manner which insures that motions to suppress will be successful. Thus they have their cake and eat it too by appearing to engage in vigorous enforcement activity and yet refraining from seriously endangering the continued existence of organized vice.

CONCLUSION

In summary, Spiotto's study of motions to suppress sheds no light at all on the efficacy of the exclusionary rule. It is highly unfortunate that both Professor Schlesinger and Judge Wilkey place so much reliance on it. The endorsement of the badly flawed study by persons in such positions lends it undeserving credibility among readers unfamiliar with the subject. That Wilkey and Schlesinger rely on Spiotto's so-called conclusions so eagerly is (especially in Schlesinger's case, as he is a social scientist presumably experienced in the analysis of data) yet another attestation to the ever present human tendency to grasp at any straw in order to promote values and beliefs already adopted.

None of the above is meant to suggest that the exclusionary rule is or inevitably will be largely effective in securing police compliance with the Fourth Amendment. What it is, simply, is a refutation of repeated assertions and implications that the rule is ineffective in deterring police misconduct. Existing data at the present time make it impossible to establish empirically a universal "yes, it works" or a "no, it doesn't work" conclusion — or even anything approximating such a conclusion.

Judge Wilkey, Professor Schlesinger and others have every right to disagree with the exclusionary rule; certainly there are reasoned arguments which can be advanced against it independent of an empirical one. But what they do not have a right to do is to disseminate a myth that empirical studies show that the issue has been resolved negatively. To the degree that empirical studies of its impact bear on the decision to retain, modify or abandon the rule, the public — and the decision-makers — are entitled to facts, not myths.

Notes and Questions

1. Consider the following:

> More than fifty years have passed since the Supreme Court decided the *Weeks* case, barring the use in federal prosecutions of evidence obtained in violation of the Fourth Amendment, and the *Silverthorne* case, invoking what has come to be known as the "fruit of the poisonous tree" doctrine. The justices who decided those cases would, I think, be quite surprised to learn that some day the value of the exclusionary rule would be measured by — and the very life of the rule might depend on — an empirical evaluation of its efficacy in deterring police misconduct.
>
> The dissenters in *United States* v. *Calandra*, 414 U.S. 338, 357 (1974), were, I think, plainly right when they maintained that "uppermost in the minds of the framers of the [exclusionary] rule" was not "the rule's possible deterrent effect," but "the twin goals of enabling the judiciary to avoid the taint of partnership in official lawlessness and of assuring the people [that] the government would not profit from its lawless behavior, thus minimizing the risk of seriously undermining popular trust in government.*

2. Judge Wilkey is not the only federal judge opposed to the exclusionary rule. The most famous critic is former Chief Justice Burger. In a dissenting opinion in 1972, Burger wrote the following:

> Although I would hesitate to abandon it until some meaningful substitute is developed, the history of the suppression doctrine demonstrates that it is both conceptually sterile and practically ineffective in accomplishing its stated

*Yale Kamisar, "Is the Exclusionary Rule an Illogical or Unnatural Interpretation of the Fourth Amendment?" *Judicature*, 62 (August 1968):67.

objective (*Bivens* v. *Six Unknown Named Agents of the Federal Bureau of Narcotics,* 403 U.S. 388, 1972).

Justice Burger's opposition to the rule did not lead to an overturning of *Mapp* or *Weeks.* During the past fifteen years, however, the Court considered the rule in a substantial number of cases, and restricted its scope. Thus, the rule can still be invoked by a defendant at a criminal trial, but not at a grand jury proceeding; in a *habeas corpus* proceeding by a state prisoner (see *Stone* v. *Powell,* 428 U.S. 465, 1976), when the illegal search is conducted on someone other than the defendant (see *United States* v. *Payner,* 447 U.S. 727, 1980); or when a defective warrant has been obtained in "good faith." *United States* v. *Leon,* 104 S.Ct. 3405 (1984); *Massachusetts* v. *Shepard,* 104 S.Ct. 3424 (1984). The Burger and Rehnquist Courts have generally been lenient in upholding police law enforcement practices, and the policy of limiting the defendant's opportunities for invoking the exclusionary rule seems likely to continue. This is an effective approach for those opposed to the exclusionary rule, particularly when one considers the fact that most cases are plea bargained and do not get to trial where the police search could be scrutinized by a judge.

THE MEDIA PERSPECTIVE

The squad was a shock. It was absurd. Really. It was like a raft in the middle of a tidal wave, and people trying to bail. The *mobs* of complainants, thinking something could be done to help them. You know, expecting television detectives who'll run out and find the attacker and bring him to justice. Man, I saw complainants get *educated.* Burglary victims. They all wanted to know why the detectives weren't over at their apartments dusting for prints. "He came in the door. He came in the window. There must be fingerprints. Get the fingerprints." They didn't believe it when you told them you needed all ten for identification. And that anyway the burglar was probably some junkie with no address. They looked at you like you were contradicting twenty years of television.

James Mills, *Report to the Commissioner* (1972)

Throughout history, once a ruling class has established its rule, the primary function of its cultural media has been the legitimization and maintenance of its authority. Folk tales and other traditional dramatic teaching stories have always reinforced established authority, teaching that when society's rules are broken, retribution is visited upon the violators. The importance of the existing social order is always implicit in such stories.

George Gerbner and Larry Gross, "The Scary World of TV's Heavy Viewer," *Psychology Today* (1976)

☐ For most people, information about the police comes not from personal experiences but from television and newspapers. As Harvard Law School professor Alan Dershowitz has written, "Popular culture — TV, movies, newspapers and magazines — often has a greater impact on people's behavior than the law itself. Indeed, most Americans learn their law not from dusty statute books, but from the manner in which cases are treated in the media. (Even my students sometimes confuse the rulings of Judge Wapner and the verdicts reached by juries on 'L.A. Law' with the precedents of real courts.)" The question of whether one can obtain an accurate vision of reality and of law from the mass media is not new. Thomas Jefferson, for example, once wrote of his concern for "his fellow citizens, who, reading newspapers, live and die in the belief, that they have known something of what has been passing in the world in their time."* The popularity of television today makes this issue much more important than it has ever been. In a relatively short period of time, television has become a major educational and social force in the United States. The introduction of television has caused "the most rapid change in popular communications and culture the human race has ever experienced."† The typical adult spends more time watching television than doing anything else, except for working and sleeping.‡ By the time of high school graduation, a teenager will have spent an average of 15,000 hours in front of the television set, compared with 12,000 hours spent in school. For most people, television is the primary source of information. The number of television sets in the United States is nearly twice the total daily circulation of newspapers.

Some of the most popular television dramas have focused on the police. Each of these programs is watched by approximately 25 million people. Millions more watch these programs overseas (dubbed into other languages), where they are among the most popular programs. Characterized by violent beginnings, car chases, violent middles, more chases, and violent endings, the shows may also be a major source of "information" about law.

In August 1982, one of the featured speakers at the annual meeting of the American Bar Association was the actress Veronica Hamel. She plays a public defender on the television series *Hill Street Blues,* and her appearance at the meeting shows how fine a line there is between television reality and what actually happens in the legal system. "One can turn off the television set," says sociologist Rose Goldsen, "but one cannot turn off the television environment."§

**The Writings of Thomas Jefferson,* Vol. 9, p. 73 (P. L. Ford, ed., 1892–1899), cited in Harry Kranz, "The Presidency v. The Press — Who Is Right?" *Human Rights,* 2, No. 1 (March 1972), p. 29.

†Ben Bagdikian, *The Information Machines* (New York: Harper & Row, 1971), p. 182.

‡Tony Schwartz, *The Responsive Chord* (Garden City, N.Y.: Anchor Press/Doubleday, 1973), p. 52.

§Rose Goldsen, *The Show and Tell Machine* (New York, Dial Press, 1977), p. xi.

Television, the Law, and the Police

Stephen Arons and Ethan Katsh

In TV crime shows, the real star is the action: high-speed, twisting car chases; rooftop shoot-outs; and scenes in which supercops crash through locked doors and slap suspects around before finally making the collar.

The trouble with this passion for "action" is that it has a way of doing violence to the very law and order the police are sworn to uphold. Here, for instance, is TV detective Bert d'Angelo:

D'ANGELO: "What do I know about the law? I'm not a lawyer, I'm a cop."

INSPECTOR KELLER: "It's your job to enforce it."

D'ANGELO: "It's my job to protect people from the mugger, the rapist, the armed robber, and the killer. People like Joey, like my partner Mickey, did the law help them? Did the law stop that killer? All the laws in the world won't stop one man with a gun. It's going to take me or somebody like me. And you know what? I'll do it any way I can."

INSPECTOR KELLER: "You're a dangerous man, Bert."

D'ANGELO: "That's right. You'd better be damn glad I'm on your side."

Today, *Bert d'Angelo* is off the air. It would be encouraging if we could report that the series was scratched because the average TV buff was fed up with having his 26 hours of weekly viewing time dominated by attitudes like D'Angelo's. But one look at the hard-nosed, antilaw crime series that are still running convinces us that public revulsion against lawlessness had nothing to do with the show's demise. Take, as a case in point, this scene from *Kojak*:

The police laboratory reports that particles of tin and lead with traces of red paint were found on the soles of a murdered person's shoes. Kojak theorizes that the murdered person had stepped on a red tin soldier in a collection owned by a doctor of whom Kojak is suspicious, but the detective has insufficient evidence to arrest or search. The following discussion then takes place in Kojak's office:

CAPTAIN McNEIL: "Theo, could you get your hands on one of those broken soldiers to send it to the lab?"

KOJAK: [*To another detective.*] "C'mon, Crocker, I'll do the talking and you swipe the soldier."

No doubt scenes like this can be viewed as nothing more than good, slambang entertainment. But there is more here than meets the casual eye. The image of police on television has been changing, and the change has political significance.

During the Vietnam War years, the police earned themselves a bad image. Newscasts regularly showed helmeted riot police clubbing student protesters or gassing antiwar demonstrators. The effect was one of public disapproval. Today even the most blatantly illegal and unconstitutional behavior of police officers is glorified by an endless stream of television police dramas. The result, we believe, is that what started off as merely fictional entertainment has now begun to have the political effect of "softening up" public opinion and making it more accepting of such police conduct.

All of this very much includes our courts. Over the past few years . . . [t]he Court has been legalizing outrageous police conduct, enacting into law principles much like those projected in the TV crime shows. Those principles include the notions that the end justifies the means, that the state is always right, and that violence is perfectly acceptable when resorted to by the right people.

We are not suggesting here a one-to-one causal relationship between TV crime shows and Supreme Court decisions. And yet, one wonders. In a recent Supreme Court brief by

---

Originally published in *Saturday Review's* March 19, 1977 issue under the title of "How TV Cops Flout the Law."

the state of Iowa, in which the state attempted to undercut a defendant's access to his attorney during police questioning, the following statement appeared: "What is really wrong with tricking a man into telling the truth? That is one of the goals of a good Perry Mason-type cross-examination." In any case, we would say that these crime shows and the recent decisions of the Supreme Court are both modifying and responding to a body of public opinion that is increasingly permissive about the flouting of our laws by law enforcers themselves.

These dark conclusions of ours are not based on guesswork. They arise from our decision, several years ago, to monitor TV police shows and analyze them from the point of view of constitutional law. We undertook this study because we'd read an article in *The Wall Street Journal* that extolled TV police thrillers as morality plays that "encourage belief in moral values, in law, in government institutions." This encomium didn't seem to square at all with what we'd been seeing on the tube, so we decided to check the matter for ourselves. . . .

During a one-and-a-half-year period, from the fall of 1974 to the spring of 1976, we videotaped the various TV police shows, viewing and reviewing them as if they were hypothetical court cases. We were looking for the image of law projected by the shows occupying so much of prime time, looking to see whether the behavior legitimized by television drama is the same as that required by the Constitution that the man on the beat is sworn to uphold and protect. We were thinking seriously about these essentially foolish shows because their incessantly repeated episodes are the average person's main contact with police work, and his or her primary exposure to the conflict between individual privacy and police logic. If television had indeed joined the courts, schools, and political institutions as a teacher of values, we wanted to know what was being taught.

The following typical scenes are gleaned from a statistically random sample of television police dramas screened during the course of the study. In reading these passages, one might keep in mind these words from the Bill of Rights:

> The right of the people to be secure in their persons, houses, papers, and effects, against unreasonable searches and seizures, shall not be violated. . . .
>
> — U.S. Constitution, Amendment IV

Bumper Morgan, the "Blue Knight," is on the trail of jewelry store thieves and has been told that one of the persons he is looking for is in Room 330 of the Riverside Hotel. As the next scene opens, Morgan is at the hotel desk looking through the guest register:

CLERK: "I assume you have a warrant for that, Morgan."

MORGAN: "Yes, size 13EEE. . . . Give me the key."

CLERK: "I'm going to testify that it was an illegal entry."

MORGAN: "You do that."

POLICE LT.: [*Later, at the police station.*] "Well, I've got to hand it to you, Bumper. That was damn good work."

Sergeant Friday [*Jack Webb in a "Dragnet" rerun*] *has just taken a suspect's photograph from her roommate, Sara, and is continuing his search for information about the absent girl:*

FRIDAY: "Do you have any samples of her handwriting?"

SARA: "Yes, the book by the phone. That's her address book."

FRIDAY: "We'll have to take this along with us, too. It'll be returned."

SARA: "But what do I tell Mary if she notices her picture and address book are gone?"

FRIDAY: "What time do you expect her today?"

SARA: "Right after work, about five."

FRIDAY: "All right. These'll be back by four P.M. Now, we'd appreciate it if you wouldn't say anything about it until we've completed our investigation."

SARA: "Oh, don't worry. I don't want to make things any worse than they are. I just know Mary isn't guilty. She's too nice."

FRIDAY: "Well, if she's that nice, she *isn't* guilty, and if she's guilty, she's not that nice."

These scenes are typical of the nonchalance with which some constitutional rights are obliterated on TV. We found the same fate in store for the right to counsel and the right against self-incrimination. In 15 randomly selected prime-time police programs televised during one week in March 1976, we found 43 separate scenes in which serious questions could be raised about the propriety of the police action. They stacked up as follows:

Clear constitutional violations	Omissions of constitutional rights	Police brutality and harassment
21	7	15

. . . The 21 "clear constitutional violations" occurred during scenes in which people were interrogated without being informed of their rights; in which evidence was taken without a warrant; or in which another form of illegal search was conducted. In the "omissions" scenes, we were unable to judge from the context whether a person's rights were being violated or whether he had waived his rights. (For example, there were scenes in which a person was being interrogated in a police station without a lawyer being present. The arrest, however, had never been shown. Therefore, what appeared to be an invasion of the suspect's rights might have resulted from a decision by the suspect to answer questions in spite of his right to remain silent.) The "police brutality and harassment" category consisted of a variety of improper, but perhaps not unconstitutional, police actions. Police officers trying to get information from various people on the street frequently obtained it by force. For example, Bumper Morgan, the Blue Knight, is by no means as chivalrous as some of his legendary namesakes:

MORGAN: *Standing across the street from a shoeshine stand.*] "Hey, Tully, come here a minute."

TULLY: "You got something to say, come over here, my man." [*Morgan crosses the street, throws Tully against the wall, and grabs him by his shirt lapels.*]

TULLY: "Hey, man, wait a minute, what's going on here?"

MORGAN: "Let me fill you out on a couple of things, my man. First of all, I ain't your man and secondly, when you see this badge, you'll call me officer and you'll do it nice and polite. You got that?"

TULLY: [*Shaken again by Morgan.*] "Sure, sure."

MORGAN: "Now where's the stuff?"

TULLY: "What are you talking about? What stuff?"

MORGAN: [*Shakes Tully again.*] "The stones from Harry's."

TULLY: "I ain't been to Harry's, man."

MORGAN: [*Shakes Tully again.*] "Listen. You know what you are doing now? You are insulting my intelligence."

TULLY: "I haven't done anything. Who said I did something?"

MORGAN: "I said it was you. You calling me a liar? That's called contempt of cop. Now you're really making me mad." [*Morgan angrily shakes him again.*]

TULLY: "All right . . . all right . . . all right. Hey, it was this chick. She's a hooker. Her name is Linda. Now let me go and I'll find her for you."

MORGAN: "Linda, huh, yeah. I know her." [*Morgan's demeanor changes and, exuding friendliness, he straightens out Tully's shirt, pats him, and walks away.*]

TULLY: [*Angrily.*] "I'm making a complaint on this, too."

MORGAN: "What? I just asked you a question."

Such TV abuses of constitutional rights and basic political values are not new, but they do seem to have increased dramatically shortly after the election of Richard Nixon on a hard-line, law-and-order platform. Albert Tedesco, a researcher on the communications faculty of Drexel University in Philadelphia, found that the number of law enforcement characters on television increased from 80 in 1969 to 168 in 1971. At the same time, the number of characters who were lawyers or other legal professionals decreased from 25 to 18. More significant are Tedesco's findings on illegal searches and the absence of counsel for suspects. In an average week's viewing during the period from 1969 to 1971, the number of instances in which police failed to secure search warrants, when that would have been appropriate, rose from 21 to 62. During the same period, the number of times per week the police failed to advise suspects of their right to counsel upon arrest rose from 13 to 32. Tedesco is still analyzing much of his data, but he claims to see an emerging correlation between television content and the political values of the early Nixon reign.

Beyond the statistics lie the qualitative impressions we gained from our immersion in the shows we covered in our own study. The overall image the shows project is clearly one that is alien to the Constitution. The facts would horrify the average judge if they were brought into court as real cases. Hardly a single viewing hour passes without an illegal search, or a confession obtained by coercion, or the failure to provide counsel. Warrants are not sought or issued, and hardly any mention is made of notifying suspects of their rights against self-incrimination. Scores of citizens uninvolved in the crime under investigation are roughed up, shaken down, or harassed — by police. Homes, offices, and cars are broken into regularly — by police. With a sixth sense that only scriptwriters can generate, every such invasion of personal privacy turns up the real, and usually demented, criminal, or is justified because the victim was probably guilty of some crime anyway. Honest, law-abiding citizens are miraculously never hurt by these methods. There are no trials, no plea bargains, no defense, no argument about illegal police conduct affecting the guilty, the innocent, or the society as a whole. . . .

There is an ironic inconsistency in this fast-action fairyland. The Television Broadcasters Code, a sanitized version of middle-American morality that is supposed to fend off congressional regulation of artistic expression on the tube, states that "the treatment of criminal activities should always convey their social and human effects." Crime is not supposed to pay, and on television, at least, we can be sure that it won't. But what about all the crimes committed by our video police in the process of catching their criminal counterparts? The television producers' answer is that people with badges shouldn't be treated the same way as everyone else. You can tell by the color of their hats or their horses that these people have only the noblest of aims; and they never miss. Besides, as Bert d'Angelo knew, law can't stop crime; and as TV producers know, handcuffing the police with the Bill of Rights would make for dull viewing.

One television screenwriter, discussing his own experiences, sees the same images inside the TV industry as viewers see from the outside: "The message we're getting is that authority is never wrong. The desired image is of a paternalistic 'great society' in which all law enforcement agents are properly motivated and their opponents are hippies, crazies, and un-American weirdos. It is clearly not good to criticize the institutions of the country."

This authoritarian attitude — possibly the product of a fear that only repression can prevent the world order from crumbling — comes from all corners: from producers, studios, and network executives. Like the television signal itself, the message that the status quo must be protected at all costs seems simply to be "in the air." David Rintels, president of the Writers Guild of America West, says there are no written rules and rarely any clear commands from those who own and operate commercial television, but that the prevailing values are clear to everyone in the industry. The world's most effective salesman of laundry detergent and hemorrhoid ointment is selling political ideology, too. And on television, by Rintels's lights, "make-believe makes belief."

We have asked ourselves whether the repeated images in which illegal police conduct is ignored or pays off on television are softening up the public about individual freedom. As we have discovered in showing videotape clips from our study to university students, many people are unaware of the police violations they see on the screen until after considerable discussion. It may not be a very great leap from this dim awareness of constitutional rights to the failure to recognize or react to constitutional violations perpetrated by police in everyday life. If the examples of police conduct we see on TV fail to make us more aware of the clash between civil liberties and police logic, and if crime-show violations of the Constitution always turn out to be a good thing, then these TV morality plays may amount to nothing more than reactionary propaganda.

There is a clear contradiction between what common sense and the Constitution permit flesh-and-blood police to do and what scriptwriters let TV cops get away with. This contradiction seems destined to be resolved before too long. Most of the illegal TV police activities we discovered in our study are still, a year later, violations of the Constitution. But over the past few years the Supreme Court has been moving so steadily to the right on police and civil liberties issues that the gaps between the Court and the television may be all but erased by the next TV season.

Many of the personal freedoms that the police lobby views as "technicalities," and that the producers think would make such dull television viewing, seem lately to have escaped the consciousness of both the broadcasters and the judiciary. A single, uncontradictory image of acceptable police behavior is being fashioned by both institutions; and the Constitution and the public's welfare are having little effect on it. If we follow some of these recent decisions of the Supreme Court, we can imagine what the television cop shows of the future may be like — shows in which all the police behavior will be legal and neither the courts nor the citizenry will be offended. Herewith, several of these decisions, in each case followed by the sort of TV crime show that the decision might logically inspire:

CASE ONE: In 1974, the Supreme Court ruled in *Gustafson* v. *Florida* [and *United States* v. *Robinson* — ED.] that a police officer making even a minor custodial arrest was not violating a citizen's privacy by conducting a complete search of the citizen's person, even though the officer lacked either a warrant or probable cause to make the search.

TV SHOW ONE: A bank robbery has reportedly been committed by two men with long hair. After a frustrating search for other clues, the police decide simply to search everywhere for the money. Since searches without probable cause are generally unacceptable to the courts, but since almost everyone spends some time in his car daily and has a broken taillight or commits some minor traffic offense, over the next three days the police make traffic arrests of every long-haired male in town. Lots of contraband is turned up, personal grudges are acted out, and the town is generally "cleaned up," but no money is found. Under the pressure of prosecution for drug possession, however, one person reveals information leading to the bank robbers. The dragnet idea is commended as being generally useful.

CASE TWO: In 1976, the Supreme Court ruled in *Hampton* v. *U.S.* that police setting up a defendant are not guilty of entrapping him, nor have they conducted themselves so outrageously as to violate his due process rights, as long as the defendant "was predisposed to commit the crime."

The police in this case supplied narcotics to the defendant and also bought the narcotics from him.

TV SHOW TWO: Several police on the city force discover that searches of citizens (such as those in *Show One*) have yielded narcotics that do not have to be turned in as evidence if no charges are filed against the defendant. This leaves several officers with large stores of heroin, which they begin peddling on the sly (in plain clothes and disguises) to supplement their meager incomes. One street pusher with a grudge catches on to the scam and tries to contact federal agents to expose the city police. Before he can do this, the police get wind of it and set him up, selling him one pound of heroin as usual, but buying it from him in small packages a few hours later as undercover agents. The buyer is then arrested by the police and charged with selling narcotics. Claims that the police were running an illegal dope ring are met with statements that this was a ruse to catch pushers and that the defendant was a known pusher. The defendant is convicted and the police go on with their business.

CASE THREE: In 1976, the Supreme Court ruled in *Paul* v. *Davis* that the police did not violate a citizen's privacy or his due process rights when they publicly circulated a flyer with his name and picture under the title "Active Shoplifters." The citizen had never been convicted of shoplifting, but had been detained as a shoplifter by a store detective two years earlier. No charges had ever been placed against him. While the majority opinion condoned this police tactic, Justice Brennan dissented: "The Court today holds that police officials acting in their official capacities as law enforcers may on their own initiative, and without trial, constitutionally condemn innocent individuals as criminals and thereby brand them with one of the most stigmatizing and debilitating labels in our society."

TV SHOW THREE: At this point, the Court's steady progress in strengthening the forces of law and order by legalizing crimes by police officers overtakes television police dramas. As television values and judicial values merge, the definitions of crime and freedom are reversed, and a brave new fiction emerges in the public mind: More freedom for police reduces crime. *Show Three* may appear on the networks, in the courts, or on the street.

One may wonder whether the Court shares with television the blindness to individual liberty that is the easy byproduct of a single-minded devotion to stopping crime. One may wonder, too, whether the public consciousness is pushed in unhealthy directions by either of these great norm-molding institutions, or whether in court and on television we simply get what we want, as the market researchers would say.

The line between television logic, police logic, and judicial logic is becoming all but indiscernible. The ideological tension between security and liberty seems to have diminished, very much to the disadvantage of liberty. For television, the challenge is how to give sane, constitutional values access to the TV crime scene. Meanwhile, sad to say, our study of television police dramas indicates that a very dubious type of police logic is in clear control of the airwaves.

Notes and Questions

1. Police dramas on TV misrepresent the nature of police work as well as the nature of constitutional rights. Consider the following:

> The society which TV police shows imply is possible has the police as our primary protectors and saviors from criminals. This image actually does a disservice to both citizens and the real police. Citizens come to expect the police to reduce the crime rate. They hold the police primarily responsible if the crime rate goes up. Policemen, who then become the object of criticism, respond by attacking the "handcuffs" placed on them by the Supreme Court. The TV image which increases the status of police thus creates an impossible task and leads to unwarranted criticism of or insensitivity to the very values which protect innocent persons from police-state activities.
>
> There is an interesting experiment one

can do when watching a television police show. Concentrate on the information the police officer has. Disregard the information communicated to the viewer which the police officer does not know. The errorless identification of criminals by TV police will then be seen to be both miraculous and illegal. We cannot and should not expect the same from local police officers. As an antidote to the message communicated by these programs, consider the following facts:

1. The best estimates are that at least half the crimes committed are never reported to the police. Even Kojak could not solve these crimes. He would not know whom or what to begin looking for.

2. Persons who are caught by the police rarely are convicted of the main crime they are arrested for. Plea bargaining usually results in a reduction of charges. In New York City, for example, 80% of the persons arrested for felonies in 1974 pleaded guilty to misdemeanors.

3. The recidivism rate for persons who are released from prison is so high that even if the police could catch everyone who committed a crime, a serious problem would remain. A major part of the problem is the criminal justice system itself.

The point to be understood is that crime is caused by many complex and interrelated factors. Police shows end happily with arrest but in real life this is only the starting point in what one judge has called "America's only working railroad."*

2. The uniform message presented by police programs seems to be systematically created and not merely the result of coincidence. A 1971 survey of the Writers Guild of America revealed that of those who responded:

> Eighty-six (86) percent have found, from personal experience, that censorship exists in television. Many state, further, that they have never written a script, no matter how innocent, that has not been censored.
>
> Eighty-one (81) percent believe that television is presenting a distorted picture of what is happening in this country today — politically, economically, and racially.
>
> Only eight (8) percent believe that current television programming is "in the public interest, convenience and necessity," as required by the Federal Communications Act of 1934, Title 47, U.S. Code, Secs. 307a, 307d.†

The kind of content control exercised over scriptwriters for police programs was graphically illustrated by David Rintels, president of the Writers Guild of America-West, in testimony before the Senate Subcommittee on Constitutional Rights several years ago. Mr. Rintels stated that,

> I was asked to write another episode of "The FBI" on a subject of my choice, at about the time, five or six years ago, when the four little black girls were killed by the bomb in the Birmingham Church. It had been announced that the FBI was involving itself in the case and I told the producer I wanted to write a fictional account of it. He checked with the sponsor, the Ford Motor Company, and with the FBI — every proposed show is cleared sequentially through the producing company, Quinn Martin; the Federal Bureau of Investigation; the network, ABC; and the sponsor, Ford; and any of the four can veto any show for any reason, which it need not disclose — and reported back that they would be delighted to have me write about a Church bombing subject only to these stipulations: The Church must be in the North, there could be no Negroes involved, and the bombing could have nothing at all to do with civil rights. After I said I wouldn't write that program, I asked if I could do a show on police brutality, also in the news at that time; certainly, the answer came back, as long as the charge was trumped up, the policeman vindicated, and the man who brought the specious charge prosecuted.‡

---

*Ethan Katsh and Stephen Arons, "Television, the Law, and the Police," *Wall Street Journal,* July 22, 1975, p. 16. Reprinted by permission of *Wall Street Journal,*

†*Hearings on Freedom of the Press Before the Subcommittee on Constitutional Rights of the Senate Committee on the Judiciary,* 92nd Cong. 1st and 2nd sessions, at 522 (1972).

‡Ibid., at 525.

3. Steven Stark has argued that there is a relationship between public attitudes about the police and portrayals of the police on television. He has written,

> In television's history, when the police rose in TV esteem, lawyers fell correspondingly. . . . In eras when the police are popular, criminal lawyers — foils of law enforcement — tend not to be. . . .
>
> It is thus no coincidence that recent polls continue to document the elevated status of the police. According to one survey, approximately seventy-two percent of the public has a "very favorable" image of the police, a marked difference from just twenty-five years ago. Another tally found that local police are now more highly thought of than the American Medical Association, Congress, the press, or the Supreme Court, not to mention lawyers. In a 1985 Gallup Poll, forty-seven percent of the public rated the honesty and ethical standards of the police as "very high" or "high," a rise of ten percent in just eight years. Meanwhile, in the same period, those rating lawyers "low" or "very low" rose from twenty-six percent to thirty percent. Other polls yielded similar results. Thus, the transformation of public opinion about the police is now virtually complete. In one generation, the police have gone from scapegoats to heroes, while the esteem and popularity of lawyers seems to have traveled roughly in the opposite direction. This reversal in public sentiment is not surprising in light of the fact that crime shows have portrayed the police as the public's guardian against criminals, while portraying lawyers — usually public defenders — as criminals' guardians against the criminal justice system.§

§Reprinted from the *University of Miami Law Review*, 42 U. Miami L. Rev. 229 (1987) (which holds copyright on this article). (Footnotes omitted.)

5 A SOCIETAL PERSPECTIVE

Nations carve their police systems in their own likeness.

P. J. Stead

28. No constable or other bailiff of ours shall take anyone's grain or other chattels without immediately paying for them in money. . . .
29. No constable shall require any knight to give money in place of his ward of a castle. . . .
30. No sheriff or bailiff of ours or any one else shall take horses or wagons of any free man for carrying purposes except on the permission of that free man. . . .
38. No bailiff for the future shall place any one to his law on his simple affirmation without credible witnesses brought for this purpose. . . .
45. We will not make justiciars, constables, sheriffs, or bailiffs except of such as know the law of the realm and are well inclined to observe it.

Magna Carta

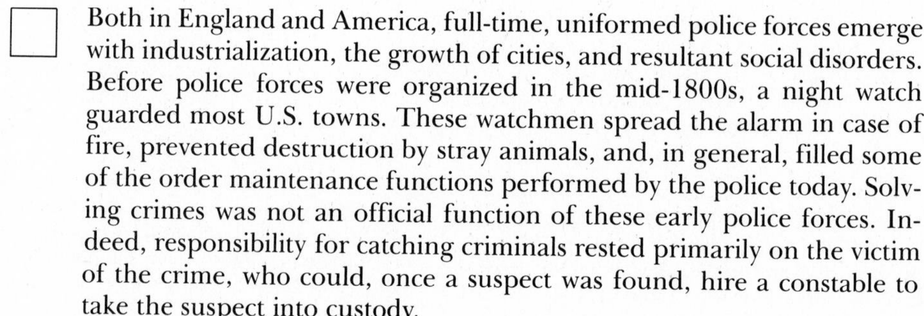

Both in England and America, full-time, uniformed police forces emerge with industrialization, the growth of cities, and resultant social disorders. Before police forces were organized in the mid-1800s, a night watch guarded most U.S. towns. These watchmen spread the alarm in case of fire, prevented destruction by stray animals, and, in general, filled some of the order maintenance functions performed by the police today. Solving crimes was not an official function of these early police forces. Indeed, responsibility for catching criminals rested primarily on the victim of the crime, who could, once a suspect was found, hire a constable to take the suspect into custody.

In the early 1800s, riots and gang wars made it clear that the system was inadequate. As one historian has written,

> New York City was alleged to be the most crime-ridden city in the world, with Philadelphia, Baltimore and Cincinnati not far behind. . . . Gangs of youthful rowdies in the larger cities . . . threatened to destroy the American reputation for respect for law. . . . Before their boisterous demonstrations the crude police forces of the day were often helpless.*

In 1838, therefore,

> Boston created a day police force to supplement the nightwatch, and other cities soon followed its lead. Crime, cities were finding, was no respecter of daylight. There were certain inherent difficulties, however, in these early two-shift police systems. Keen rivalries existed between the day and night shifts, and separate administrations supervised each shift. Recognizing the evils of separate police forces, the New York Legislature passed a law in 1844 that authorized creating the first unified day and night police, thus abolishing its nightwatch system. Ten years later Boston consolidated its nightwatch with the day police.
>
> Following the New York model, other cities developed their own unified police forces during the next decade. By the 1870s the Nation's largest cities had full-time police forces. And by the early 1900s there were few cities of consequence without such unified forces. These forces gradually came under the control of a chief or commissioner, often appointed by the mayor, sometimes with the consent of the city council and sometimes elected by the people.†

The following readings provide several additional perspectives on how the police both reflect and affect a society. In the first reading, Mark H. Moore and George L. Kelling argue for an increased community orientation by the police and for less emphasis on the crime-fighting or law enforcement function. The second selection presents a much more radical analysis of the police role in contemporary U.S. society, arguing that they reflect the values and needs of the economic system. The third reading describes the Japanese police, who operate very differently from U.S. police forces.

It will quickly become evident to you that these selections present very different, and often contradictory, views on the role that the police should play in society. The readings share, however, an important message: any discussion of the police should consider the nature of the society in which the police function.

---

*Arthur Charles Cole, "The Irrepressible Conflict, 1859–1865," *A History of American Life,* vol. 8, Arthur M. Schlesinger, Sr., and Dixon Ryan Fox, eds. (New York: Macmillan, 1934), pp. 154–155.

†President's Commission on Law Enforcement and Administration of Justice, *Task Force Report: The Police* (Washington, D.C.: U.S. Government Printing Office, 1967), p. 5.

"To Serve and Protect": Learning from Police History

Mark H. Moore and George L. Kelling

Over the last three decades, American police departments have pursued a strategy of policing that narrowed their goals to "crime fighting," relied heavily on cars and radios to create a sense of police omnipresence, and found its justification in politically neutral professional competence. The traditional tasks of the constable — maintaining public order, regulating economic activity, and providing emergency services — have been deemphasized, and those of the professional "crime fighter" have increased. Joe Friday's polite but frosty professionalism ("Just the facts, Ma'am") is a perfect expression of the modern image.

In many ways, this strategy has been remarkably successful. Thirty years ago, the idea that the police could arrive at a crime scene anywhere in a large city in less than five minutes would have been idle dreaming, yet we now have that capability. Similarly, the idea that the police would have moved out from under the shadow of political influence and flagrant abuses of individual rights would also have seemed unrealistic, yet most people now think of the police as much more honest and professional than in the past. In fact, in many ways the current strategy of policing is the apotheosis of a reform spirit that has guided police executives for over eighty years.

It is ironic, then, that precisely at the moment of its greatest triumph, the limits of this strategy have also become apparent. The concrete experience of citizens exposed to this strategy of policing is different from what the reformers had imagined. Officers stare suspiciously at the community from automobiles, careen through city streets with sirens wailing, and arrive at a "crime scene" to comfort the victim of an offense that occurred twenty minutes earlier. They reject citizen requests for simple assistance so that they can get back "in service" — that is, back to the business of staring at the community from their cars. No wonder so many citizens find the police unresponsive. Officers treat problems which citizens take seriously — unsafe parks, loud neighbors — as unimportant. And when a group of citizens wants to talk about current police policies and procedures, they are met by a "community relations specialist" or, at best, a precinct patrol commander, neither of whom can respond to their problems without calling headquarters.

This situation would not be so bad if the police were succeeding in their crime-fighting role. But the fact of the matter is that they are not. Crime rates continue to increase, and the chance that a violent crime among strangers will be solved to the satisfaction of the police (let alone the prosecutors and the courts) is still less than 20 percent. The reason for this poor performance, research now tells us, is that the police get less help than they need from victims and witnesses in the community. . . .

PRIVATE AND PUBLIC POLICING

It is easy to forget that publicly-supported police agencies were only recently created in the United States. Throughout the colonial period and up until the mid-nineteenth century, everyday policing was performed by night watchmen who also lit lamps, reported fires, managed runaway animals, and stood ready to help in family emergencies. Their role as "crime fighters" was restricted to raising a general alarm whenever they saw criminal misconduct — an event that must have been rare, given the small numbers of watchmen and the haphazard methods of patrol. Apprehension of the fleeing felons then depended on vigorous pursuit by private citizens. The investigation of past criminal offenses also depended on private initiative. When sufficient evidence was gathered, a victim could enlist the aid of a constable to regain his property

---

Reprinted with permission of the authors from: *The Public Interest,* No. 70 (Winter 1983), pp. 49–64. © 1983 by National Affairs, Inc. (Footnotes omitted.)

or make an arrest, but the constable would ordinarily rely on the victim to locate the suspect.

By the 1840s, this informal arrangement became insufficient to deal with the increasing lawlessness of American cities, so city governments began experimenting with new forms of policing. The most important model for these changes was England, which was also debating about and experimenting with new forms of policing. The old English system, which had served as the model for the American, also placed heavy reliance on private individuals for crime prevention, apprehension, and investigation; beyond that, there was only a loose network of publicly supported watchmen, constables, and courts. Publicly supported policing was, however, supplemented by commercial "thief catching" firms, the "Bow Street Runners" being the most famous. These firms depended on informants and undercover operations, as well as more traditional investigative techniques. While these methods seemed to give commercial firms a competitive advantage in solving crime, the potential for corruption and abuses was quite high. (Some of their success seems to have depended on arranging for the crimes to occur in the first place!)

Despite the traditional authority of the constables, and the vitality and ingenuity of private commercial policing, the English forces of public order tottered before the social challenges of the 1830s. As in the United States, the problem lay in the growing cities, where authorities not only had to cope with street crime, but also with riots, demonstrations, and increasing assaults on public decency (i.e., drunkenness and "juvenile delinquency"). And the street lights still had to be lit.

Much as the American "crime wave" and riots of the 1960s led to the creation of federal commissions and independent research centers to study the prevention of crime, the English social disturbances of the early-nineteenth century led to a fundamental reevaluation of policing. Jeremy Bentham and Patrick Colquhoun proposed a form of "preventative policing" and drafted legislation mandating the regular supervision of known criminals, people in "dangerous" occupations (e.g., minstrels), and even specific ethnic groups (e.g., Jews). The English also looked across the Channel at the "continental model" of policing based on informants and covert surveillance rather than overt patrols.

In the end, neither "detective policing," as suggested by the Bow Street Runners and the French, nor "preventative policing," as conceived by Colquhoun, was adopted as a strategy for English policing in the mid-1800s. Instead, Parliament chose a model of policing based on the success of the Thames River Police. Originally established as an experiment funded privately by insurance companies to reduce property losses, the Thames River Police were so successful that they became the first police organization in England to be financed entirely by public revenues. Publicly supported policing was then mandated throughout England in 1829 by the Metropolitan Police Act, and the Metropolitan Police began patroling the streets of London shortly thereafter. . . .

The transformation of British policing in the early-nineteenth century had a tremendous impact on American thinking and practice. New York City established a municipal police force based on the British model in 1845, followed quickly by Boston and Philadelphia; by 1855, cities as far west as Milwaukee had police departments. As in England, these departments consisted of overt, reactive patrol forces capable of operating in large or small units. And because the forces were accessible to citizens at all hours, they retained their constabulary functions, providing emergency service as well as controlling crime and maintaining public order. . . .

By the end of the 1800s the police became a favorite target of reformers in the Progressive movement, who despised both the established power of the political machines and the "disorder" that characterized those parts of the cities where police had stopped enforcing vice laws. Ending the "corruption" of the police became a central feature of the Progressive program, as was the transfer of social welfare functions from the police to the new social work professionals. The Progressive conception of the police was one radically different from the practices which had developed over the previous century, and consisted of several significant departures: The police were to become a highly disciplined, paramilitary organization independent of local political parties; to ensure that independence, the force would be organized along functional rather than geographic lines; personnel procedures would be strictly meritocratic rather than political; and police duties would be limited to the strict enforcement of existing laws. . . .

Several other developments reinforced the notion of police officer as "crime fighter." One was the improvement of communication and transportation technologies. With cars, telephones, and radios, all of which became widely available to the police in the 1940s and 1950s, it seemed that an omnipresent patrol force could be created. Moreover, the new technology complemented the objective of creating centralized, tightly disciplined police organizations. The second influence was the development of the Uniform Crime Reports which publish rates of homicide, rape, robbery, aggravated assault, burglary, larceny, and motor vehicle theft for every city in the country. These data inevitably became important indicators of police performance, and encouraged police administrators to focus on these crimes as the most important targets of police work.

The net result of these recent developments — cars, radios, and statistics — has been a new reform strategy that resembles the old in its commitment to equal enforcement of the laws and its emphasis on a disciplined police bureaucracy, but differs in that it focuses narrowly on property crimes and violent crimes rather than the enforcement of all laws — especially those regarding public order and economic regulation. To a great extent, the professionalized "crime fighting" strategy of policing that emerged after World War II is the current dominant police strategy. Its explicit goal is the control of crime, not maintaining public order or providing constabulary services. It depends on even-handed, non-intrusive enforcement of the laws, but only those laws with widespread public support. Its basic mode of operation includes motorized patrol, rapid responses to calls for service, and retrospective investigation of offenses, not high-profile foot patrol or "preventative policing."

THE CONSEQUENCES OF REFORM

By now, the goal of "professionalizing" police forces — of making them conform to the reform strategy — has become an orthodoxy. Police executives, experts on policing, the police themselves, even mayors and legal philosophers, are all eager to trade constables and cops on the beat for professional crime fighters — to transform their "street corner politicians" into Joe Fridays and then into SWAT teams. The irony is that this orthodoxy has become powerful in shaping police aspirations and practices at about the same time that embarrassing weaknesses are beginning to appear.

It is now clear, for example, that there is a limit to the deployment of police resources (squad cars, rapid-response police teams, investigators) beyond which the rate of violent crime is very insensitive. The most recent research convincingly establishes three points. First, neither crime nor fear of crime are importantly affected by major changes in the number of officers patrolling in marked cars. Apparently, within broad ranges, neither criminals nor citizens can tell whether an area is heavily or superficially patrolled when the patrolling is done in cars. Second, rapid responses to calls for service do not dramatically increase the apprehension of criminals. The reason is that citizens do not call the police until long after a crime has been completed, and the attacker has fled the scene. Given these delays, even instantaneous police responses would do little good. Third, police investigators are unable to solve crimes without major assistance from victims and witnesses. Indeed, unless they can identify the offender, chances are overwhelming that the crime will not be solved. On the other hand, if citizens can identify the offender, it is difficult to see what modern detectives add to what the local constables used to do. And, at any rate, the capacity of the police to solve crimes — particularly those involving violence among strangers — remains shockingly low. Fewer than 20 percent of robberies are solved, and an even smaller fraction of burglaries. All this suggests that the orthodox police strategy provides neither general deterrence, nor successful apprehension of individual offenders.

Besides running up against limits to professionalized crime fighting, it is now clear that contemporary police strategies ignore a large number of tasks which the police have traditionally performed. There are no streetlamps to light anymore, but there are a large number of constabulary functions — maintaining order in public places (parks, buses, subway platforms), resolving marital disputes, disciplining noncriminal but harmful juvenile behavior, preventing public drug and alcohol use — which no other public organizations have taken up since they were abandoned by the police. These jobs simply are not done, and what is worse, they have come to be seen as illegitimate functions of *any* public body or private citizen. The role of modern legal philosophy is very important here, for it has been most responsible for making many of these once implicitly-sanctioned practices explicitly illegal for the police, and without that implicit support individual private citizens have become unwilling to take matters into their own hands.

The bitter irony of this development is that it is probably these constabulary functions, properly performed, that make people feel safer in their neighborhoods than a drop in the "crime rate" as measured in the Uniform Crime Reports. Seeing a cop on the beat, allowing one's children to play unsupervised in the park, not being offered drugs on the street, taking the bus or subway late at night without being approached by vagrants — all these things probably make citizens feel safer than a drop in average police response time from five to three minutes. The sort of infringements on public order we are describing are often "unlawful," but they are not serious crime. As a result, the police neglect these offenses and escape the charge of discriminatory enforcement. Yet such offenses may matter more to citizen security than relatively rare "crime" as the police now define it. . . .

REFORMING THE REFORMS

If there is anything to be learned from the relatively short history of the American police it is that, whatever the real benefits of professionalization (e.g., reduced corruption, due process, serious police training), the reforms have ignored, even attacked, some features that once made the police powerful institutions in maintaining a sense of community security. Of course, it would be hopelessly romantic to think that modern police could immediately reclaim an intimate relationship with well defined communities in today's cities, or resume their broad social functions. And, indeed, there is much in the modern conception and operations of police departments that is worth preserving.

But still, within bounds, it may now be possible for imaginative police executives and those who supervise their operations to make changes that could reclaim some of the old virtues while sacrificing little of value in the modern reforms. We offer ideas in four distinct areas: police dealings with private self-defense efforts; scope of police responsibility; police deployment; and the organizational structure of the force. In each case, the proposals are designed to link the police more surely to the communities in which they now operate.

Private and Public Enforcement Private citizens inevitably play an important role in controlling crime. By limiting their exposure to risk, investing in locks and guns, banding together to patrol their own streets, or financing a private security force, private citizens affect the overall level of crime, and the distribution of the benefits and burdens of policing. Police strategists should encourage those private mobilizations, provide guidance and technical assistance, and position the police as back-ups to private efforts.

To a degree, of course, police forces now do this. They pass out police whistles, urge people to mark their property so that it can be more easily identified when stolen, help to organize block watches, and set up emergency call systems tied to rapid responses to calls to service. Yet, apart from responding to calls for service, one has the feeling that the police do not really take such activities seriously; and when the private efforts become powerful, the police often attack them as a danger to liberty (though their greater concern might well be the economic security that comes from monopolizing crime control efforts).

Nowhere is this ambivalence more obvious than in the general response to the growth of the Guardian Angels, a private paramilitary group that began in New York City and spread across the country. Many consider the Guardian Angels a useful auxiliary patrol force that reminds private citizens of their public responsibilities, and dignifies the young men and women who join; opponents (often including the police) see the Angels as vigilantes threatening the rights of citizens with undisciplined enforcement. Neither view is quite appropriate. Those who welcome the Angels as a novelty forget that private policing was the only form of policing for centuries, and that the creation of a public police force was conceived as a great reform.

Those who think of the Angels as dangerous vigilantes forget the value of private crime-control efforts, and the crucial difference between vigilantes and responsible citizens playing their traditional role in crime control. The Guardian Angels limit their functions to deterrence and, occasionally, apprehension; they neither judge guilt nor mete out punishment. And the Angels do not take offense or intervene easily; they respond only to serious crimes that they observe. In so doing, they assume nothing more than the rights and responsibilities of good democratic citizens. It is somewhat ironic that the appearance of several thousand Guardian Angels attracts such great public interest and worry, when the emergence of a *commercial* private security force numbering in the millions has attracted almost no notice at all. . . .

The Scope of Police Responsibility If the police are going to ask for more help from their communities, it seems likely that they will have to produce more of what communities want. As we have seen, police agencies have narrowed their purposes to combatting serious crime. This narrowing is applauded by a general citizenry that thinks "serious crime" is what it fears, by legal philosophers who think the enduring social interest in non-intrusive and fair policing can best be served by focusing attention on a few serious and visible crimes, by professional police administrators who want to allocate scarce resources to the most urgent areas, and by the police themselves who prefer the imagery of "combatting bad guys" to the more complex, mundane tasks. This is a strategic error. The error comes not in emphasizing the importance of controlling violent crime — no one looking at U.S. crime statistics could possibly propose not taking violent crime seriously — but rather in imagining that effective control can be gained simply by complaining about court decisions that "handcuff" the police. More effective control of violent crime depends on an increased willingness on the part of communities to help the police identify and prosecute offenders, but the police miss many opportunities to establish closer relationships with the community, relationships that would encourage such assistance.

Take, for example, the current police response to victims of violent crime. When a violent crime occurs, the police dispatch a patrol car. The officer takes a statement from the victim and identifies witnesses; occasionally an arrest is made at the scene. The officer disappears, and the case is turned over to a detective who may, or may not, interview the victim. The offender is taken to court and often released on bail. The terrified victim may well be intimidated by the offender, yet when he or she calls the police, the call is given a low priority. Neither the arresting officer nor the detective is likely to hear of, or allay, the victim's fear. Surely there is more that can be done by the police to reassure victims: They could be given a name and number of another to call, and the police might even arrange to visit periodically, in unusual cases, or to stake out the home of the victim. Note that the *police* should do this, not some social work agency. Police involvement is important, not only because they have a plausible capacity to protect, but also because they can simultaneously earn credit with the community and strengthen their case against the offender.

In a similar vein, the police could take more seriously their responsibilities to maintain public order. If, as an accumulating body of evidence suggests, it is public disorder and incivility — not violent crime — that increases fear, and if the police wish to reassure citizens, they must maintain public order — in parks, on busy street corners, at bus stops — as well as fight crime. Similarly, commercial regulation such as traffic and parking control, which is now performed mechanically, should be explicitly organized to support local commerce. Finally, police departments should *welcome* their role in providing emergency services — coping with traffic accidents, fires, health emergencies, domestic disputes, etc. Officers will inevitably perform these services, so they might as well incorporate them in their mission, perform them well, and get credit for them. After all, it is an important and popular function which the police typically do well.

DEPLOYMENT AND ORGANIZATION

Deployment Current police deployment strategy is based heavily on overt, reactive patrol: About 60 percent of the resources of most police departments are committed to patrol, and most of that to uniformed officers riding the streets in clearly marked cars. In addition, most police departments devote 10 percent of the resources to a detective unit engaged in retrospective investigations of criminal offenses. The rest of the resources are devoted to other tasks such as vice squads, juvenile units, narcotics division, and so on.

This strategy is consistent with a focus on serious crime and a strong interest in even-handed, non-intrusive policing. The capacity of patrol to thwart crimes through general deterrence, and their capacity to respond quickly to calls for service, are assumed to control crime; when deterrence fails and the police force arrives too late to catch the offender, the detectives take over to solve the crime. The enforcement effort is even-handed because patrol surveillance is general, and because anyone, for the price of a phone call, can claim services. And modern policing is non-intrusive in that intensive investigation begins only after a crime has been committed and focuses narrowly on the solution of that crime. Thus, the decision made in the mid-1800s to make public policing a patrol and detective activity, rather than a system of preventive policing, carries on until today: The police skim the surface of social life.

Given the success of this deployment in protecting important social values, it is not surprising that it has been widely utilized. Still, this deployment has internal contradictions as a crime-fighting strategy, to say nothing of the limitations as a device to draw the community into a closer relationship with the police. One basic contradiction has already been noted: In the vast, anonymous cities of today, this deployment apparently fails to deter crime or apprehend offenders. A second difficulty is that once an overt patrol force is made available to citizens at the price of a phone call, officers will be involved in much more than crime fighting. The commitment to "accessibility" then conspires to defeat the narrow focus on crime fighting: We end up with police forces that invite more citizens' requests than can be handled, then frustrate them by failing to take some calls seriously, and finally fail to control crime.

It is now time for police executives to reconsider their deployment strategies. The enormous investment in telephones, radios, and cars that now allow the police to respond to crime calls in under five minutes (often with more than one car) has bought little crime control, no greater sense of security, and has prevented the police from taking order maintenance and service functions seriously. To the extent that victim services, order maintenance, and a general community presence are valuable not only in themselves, but also as devices for strengthening crime control and building the police as a popular community institution, it is crucial that police executives get some of their officers out of cars and away from dispatchers at least some of the time. Some recent evidence suggests that foot patrol *does* promote a sense of security, and also reduces calls for service. Apparently cops on the beat can deal effectively with many citizen complaints.

For "crime fighting," other tactics may be appropriate and effective. Special decoys or stake-outs targeted at muggers and robbers may be more effective in controlling such offenses than random patrol. Similarly, if current evidence about the large number of offenses committed by a small number of offenders turns out to be correct, it may make sense for the police to develop intelligence systems for "street crimes" similar to those used in combatting organized crime and narcotics traffic. It is even possible that expanded use of informants would be possible. Obviously these methods are more intrusive and proactive than the current deployment, but they may be tolerable if they prove to be effective, and if they enjoy the support of local communities.

Departmental Organization Most police departments are currently organized along functional lines: There is a patrol division, a narcotics bureau, a youth division and so on. This structure is consistent with many reform ambitions: It allows for convenient reallocation of resources across the city to respond to changing circumstances; it promotes the development of specialized expertise; and, most importantly, it strengthens the control police chiefs have over their subordinates. The alternative scheme is to organize along geographic lines, giving area commanders responsibility for all police operations within a given geographic area. This geographic organization would also make the police department policy-making and operations more accessible to citizens in the community because the area commander would have both the interest and the capacity to respond to local requests.

Geographic organization was the traditional form attacked by the reformers because precinct-level politicians had become too powerful and had bent the police to their corrupt purposes. It was preferable, the reformers thought, to organize in a way that moved power towards the chief (and those who influenced him) rather than leave it in the hands of precinct captains vulnerable to local political machines. The functional organization served these purposes; but there was a price to be paid. Local community groups such as PTA's, merchants associations, block associations, churches, and individual citizens frightened by crimes — all no longer organized in political machines — now have no one to turn to in the local precinct. There is the precinct commander, but his direct authority typically extends only to the patrol division, and he feels more responsible to those "downtown" than the citizens of the community. There may also be a "community relations officer," but his authority usually extends nowhere. It is no wonder, then, that citizens who have interests and problems different from those of the city as a whole feel abandoned by the police. If police executives wish to cultivate stronger political support from local neighborhoods, they should consider a more geographic division of responsibilities, shifting more power to local precinct commanders, or even to lower levels in the department such as lieutenants or sergeants who could serve as leaders for "team policing" units. Again, the point is that the police must become more visible and active in neighborhood affairs.

A POST-DRAGNET ERA?

Police strategies do not exist in a vacuum. They are shaped by important legal, political, and attitudinal factors, as well as by local resources and capabilities, all factors which now sustain the modern conception of policing. So there may be little leeway for modern police executives. But the modern conception of policing *is* in serious trouble, and a review of the nature of that trouble against the background of the American history of policing gives a clear direction to police forces that wish to improve their performance as crime fighters *and* public servants.

The two fundamental features of a new police strategy must be these: that the role of private citizens in the control of crime and maintenance of public order be established and encouraged, not derided and thwarted, and that the police become more active, accessible participants in community affairs. The police will have to do little to encourage citizens to participate in community policing, for Americans are well practiced at undertaking private, voluntary efforts; all they need to know is that the police force welcomes and supports such activity. Being more visible and accessible is slightly more difficult, but hiring more "community relations" specialists is surely *not* the answer. Instead, the police must get out of their cars, and spend more time in public spaces such as parks and plazas, confronting and assisting citizens with their private troubles. This is mundane, prosaic work but it probably beats driving around in cars waiting for a radio call. Citizens would surely feel safer and, perhaps, might even be safer. . . .

Notes and Questions

1. How do you think Charles Reich would react to Moore and Kelling's proposals?
2. What is the function and responsibility of the police? Consider the following:

> Basing their opinions, perhaps, on the Western, the detective story, and the "cops and robbers" saga, Americans tend to see police officers as spending most of their time in investigating felons and arresting them, often after a gun battle. In fact, most officers can serve for years without using their guns, except for practice, and their arrests of felons, or even serious misdemeanants, are not very frequent. Except for detectives, who usually constitute only a small portion of an urban police department, most officers do not even spend a substantial portion of their time in investigation.
>
> Most officers spend their time doing routine patrol. This patrol is interrupted frequently or occasionally, depending on the character of the area, by events requiring their presence. These events are likely to consist of a fight, which may include use of a knife or other weapon, between spouses, relatives, or friends; a party which is noisy and disturbing the neighborhood; a group of youngsters congregating on a street corner and bothering passers-by; a drunk lying on the sidewalk; or a person who is lost.
>
> These situations require delicate judgments about how the officer should handle the situation. He has a variety of possible methods from which to choose. For example, after a fight, the officer can often make an arrest for assault as a felony or misdemeanor — the line between the two is extremely imprecise; order one or both persons to leave the scene on threat of being arrested; refer one or both persons to a social agency for help; or himself attempt to settle the matter. Similarly, a group of youngsters who are congregating can be arrested for loitering or another minor crime; warned to move on upon threat of arrest; or influenced to leave or behave themselves by friendly advice from an officer who has previously earned their respect.
>
> The point is that the situations in which police officers most frequently find themselves do not require the expert aim of a marksman, the cunningness of a private eye, or the toughness of a stereotyped Irish policeman. Instead, they demand knowledge of human beings and the personal, as opposed to official, authority to influence people without the use or even threat of force.
>
> These characteristics are not commonly found in police officers because police departments do not consider these values as paramount. As a result, persons with these abilities are not attracted to police work nor rewarded by promotion or other incentive if they happen to enter a department.
>
> The image of police officers must be radically changed to consider them as a part of the broad category of occupations which deal with people who are sometimes difficult to handle. Others with similar problems include teachers, gang workers, recreation workers, and parole, probation, and correctional officers. If police work were seen in this light, individuals who were more sympathetic to human beings, and less prejudiced on racial and other grounds, would enter police work because they wanted to help human beings, instead of young men who are looking for excitement and the opportunity to exercise authority. However, just as gang work generally requires persons with above-average physical abilities in order to deal with delinquents, so police officers must have the physical bearing needed to deal with

delinquents and other hostile persons without constantly using force.*

Professor James Q. Wilson has described these two broad police functions as "order maintenance" and "law enforcement." The first category would include helping public drunks, responding to family quarrels, dealing with noisy teenagers, keeping traffic moving around accidents, and so on. The latter category would include responding to reports of burglaries and the like. The difference, he points out,

> . . . between order maintenance and law enforcement is not simply the difference between "little stuff" and "real crime" or between misdemeanors and felonies. The distinction is fundamental to the police role, for the two functions involve quite dissimilar police actions and judgments. Order maintenance arises out of a dispute among citizens who accuse each other of being at fault; law enforcement arises out of the victimization of an innocent party by a person whose guilt must be proved. Handling a disorderly situation requires the officer to make a judgment about what constitutes an appropriate standard of behavior; law enforcement requires him only to compare a person's behavior with a clear legal standard. Murder or theft is defined, unambiguously, by statutes; public peace is not. Order maintenance rarely leads to an arrest; law enforcement (if the suspect can be found) typically does.†

Thus, police discretion results not simply from the inadequate resources of police departments or the need to consider the circumstances of individual cases. Discretion also occurs because the order maintenance function requires some police response other than arrest.

3. At what point might "order maintenance" be considered an antilegal concept? In a critique of Moore and Kelling, Carl Klockars writes

> What order maintenance means is police assumption of an active role in the suppression of a whole range of citizen behaviors that community respectables find disruptive, annoying, or offensive even though those behaviors violate no laws. To one degree or another police everywhere engage in activity of this type, but in order to give it the priority he believes it deserves, Kelling advises police agencies to take a series of steps to encourage it. These steps include adopting foot patrol wherever population density permits it, deemphasizing police response to telephone requests for service, abandoning law and professional expertise as the primary bases for the legitimacy of police action. . . . Order maintenance policing is policing that involves overenforcing, underenforcing, and selectively enforcing laws, as well as taking actions wholly without legal basis or authority for purposes unrecognized by written codes of law.‡

---

*Reprinted from "The Role of the Police" by Bruce J. Terris in volume no. 374 of *The Annals* of The American Academy of Political and Social Science, © 1967, by The American Academy of Political and Social Science. All rights reserved, pp. 67–68.

†James Q. Wilson, "What Makes a Better Policeman," *Atlantic Monthly* 223 (March 1969): p. 131.

‡Carl Klockars, "Order Maintenance, the Quality of Urban Life, and Police: A Different Line of Argument," in William Geller, ed., *Police Leadership in America* (New York: Praeger, 1985), pp. 309–321.

The Iron Fist and the Velvet Glove

Center for Research on Criminal Justice

During the past ten years, the police have taken on an unprecedented importance in the U.S. In the past, the police forces in this country were, for the most part, fragmented and scattered in many different levels and jurisdictions, uncoordinated with each other, without central planning or comprehensive strategies. Relatively little money was spent on strengthening local police forces and little attention was given to developing new concepts and techniques of police practice. In the 1960's all this began to change.

First, there has been a rapid growth in the sheer number of police in this country and in the amount of funds generated to support them. According to one estimate, the total number of Federal, State, and local police officers increased from 339,000 in 1967 to about 445,000 in 1974. In some areas, the increase has been even more dramatic. For example, in California the number of authorized police personnel has been increasing at a rate of 5–6 percent annually, while the overall population is increasing at about 2.5 percent a year. In California in 1960, there were about 22,000 police officers; in 1972, there were almost 52,000, and it has been estimated that there will be 180,000 by the year 2000. Government spending on the police, too, has been rising significantly. The rate of spending on criminal justice *generally* has been increasing for about twenty years, and increasing more rapidly in the last decade. In 1955, government spending on the criminal justice system amounted to about one-half of one percent of the U.S. Gross National Product (GNP); in 1965 the rate had risen to two-thirds of one percent. By 1971, government spending on criminal justice was about one percent of GNP, and the rate of increase since 1966 was about five times as great as it was in the previous decade. Over $10.5 billion was spent on criminal justice, at all levels of government, in 1971. In 1974, the figure reached over $14 billion, over $8 billion of which went for the police alone.

Even more significant than this increase in the size and fiscal importance of the police is the growing sophistication and increasing centralization of the U.S. police system over the last ten years. For the first time, the Federal government has become deeply involved in the police system, mainly through the creation of the massive Federal Law Enforcement Assistance Administration (LEAA), devoted primarily to standardizing and centralizing the police and other criminal justice agencies, and to funding the development of new and increasingly sophisticated police strategies. At the same time, the 1960's saw the rise of a whole "police-industrial complex," a rapidly growing industry that took technical developments originally created for overseas warfare or for the space program and, backed by government funds, applied them to the problems of domestic "order" in the United States.

In addition to the rise of new, sophisticated technologies, another striking development in the U.S. police apparatus during the sixties was the growth of new strategies of community penetration and "citizen participation" that sought to integrate people in the process of policing and to secure the legitimacy of the police system itself. Along with this has been a dramatic increase in the money and attention given to various kinds of "police education" programs and other efforts designed to give a new "professional" look to the police. The federal government in the early 1970's began spending about $20 million annually on police education in the universities, colleges, and even high schools, and today over 750 colleges and universities offer degrees or courses in "police science" or "criminal justice." On the other side of the coin, the police have developed a variety of new "tough" specialized units — special antiriot and tactical patrol forces, "special weapons" teams, and highly sophisticated intelligence units. And the growth and spread of the U.S. police apparatus has not stopped at the national boundaries; since the sixties, the United States has been actively exporting its police concepts, technologies, and personnel to the far corners of the American empire. Finally, the government effort to beef up and streamline the police system has been matched by an equally dramatic increase in the number of private police, security guards, and private corporations engaged in producing and selling all kinds of complicated security hardware and services.

The new emphasis on the police is also reflected in popular culture in the United States. Today there are so many television shows dealing with the police that it is hard to keep up with them, and movies with some kind of police theme dominate the neighborhood theaters.

What happened to cause this sudden growth in the size and significance of the police? Most importantly, the 1960's and early '70's have been a time of great crisis for American capitalism — not the first crisis the U.S. capitalist system has undergone, but one of the most severe. The crisis has had many different aspects, economic, social, and political, but in terms of the growth of the police, the most important is the erosion of the popular acceptance of the corporate system and of the political power that supports it, both at home and abroad. During the last ten years, this crisis in legitimacy has been manifested in many ways — not only in the widespread resistance and rebellion in the Third World, student, and White working-class communities, but in the rapidly and steadily rising rates of street crime. The combined rates of the seven "serious" crimes as defined by the F.B.I. (murder, rape, robbery, burglary, aggravated assault, larceny, and auto theft) rose by 158 percent between 1960 and 1971. Crime became a central preoccupation and fear for many people during this period, and emerged as a crucial political issue of the sixties. It became especially critical in the "inner cities," where by the early seventies one person in every five was being victimized by some form of serious crime each year.

The new emphasis on strengthening and streamlining the police is one of the most important responses of the American government to the widespread challenge to its legitimacy. It goes along with other, similar attempts to refurbish the "correctional" system, to harness the public schools more tightly to corporate values and interests, and to rationalize the "mental health" and welfare systems in the face of the growing disintegration of the "consensus" that was supposed to exist in the U.S. in the 1940's and '50's. How successful the state is in developing such means of integration and repression will depend on how effectively we are able to resist that development.

THE ROLE OF THE POLICE

Why are we so concerned about the growth of the police in the first place? Why don't we welcome it as a step toward a safer and more decent society?

The answer lies in our basic view of the functions that the police perform in the U.S. today, and have performed throughout U.S. history. Although the actual role of the police at any given time — like the role of the state in general or advanced capitalist societies — is complex and should not be oversimplified, it is clear that the police have *primarily* served to enforce the class, racial, sexual, and cultural oppression that has been an integral part of the development of capitalism in the U.S. As long as this function remains, any strengthening of the powers of the police, any movement toward greater efficiency or sophistication in their methods, must be seen as inherently contrary to the interests and needs of the majority of people in this country, and in other countries where the U.S. police system penetrates.

Our position is very different from that of most people who write about the police. Whether "liberal" or "conservative," most commentators on the police share a common assumption: they all take the existence of the police for granted. They assume that any modern society necessarily has to have a large and ever-present body of people whose purpose is to use coercion and force on other people. "Conservatives" usually point to such things as the decline in respect for authority, the breakdown of traditional values or of family discipline, as the source of the need for the police, who are seen as a "thin blue line" holding back the forces of evil and destruction that lurk just beneath the surface of civilization. This view is often found within police departments (and was promoted for decades by the F.B.I. under J. Edgar Hoover) and in many popular movie and T.V. portrayals of the police. A more "liberal" approach — increasingly evident among academic and professional police reformers — sees the need for police in the growing complexity and diversity of modern urban society. Liberal commentators often point to social and economic conditions — especially poverty and unemployment — as factors underlying the crime and social disorder that make the police necessary. But these conditions are usually accepted, in the liberal view, as either inevitable or as problems that can only be solved in the "long run." In the meantime, we have to accept the basic role of the police for the indefinite future, although we can do something about correcting police abuses and inefficiency. A classic example of this kind of thinking can be found in the (1967) Report of the President's Crime Commission, a standard source for modern liberal platitudes about the police. The Commission recognized that "the police did not create and cannot resolve the social conditions that stimulate crime" and went so far as to acknowledge that "the economy is not geared to provide (criminals) with jobs." But the Commission did not go on to examine in detail the particular conditions that cause crime, or how these conditions are related to the most basic structures of the U.S. economy. It did not ask, for example, why the economy has not been able to provide enough jobs throughout the entire twentieth century. The larger social and economic issues were raised, but then conveniently dropped, and the rest of the Report deals with ways of improving the functional capacity of the criminal justice system.

To accept the basic role of the police in this way is to accept the system of social, political, and economic relations that role supports. Behind both the liberal and conservative views of the police there is a basic pessimism about the possibilities for human liberation and cooperation, a pessimism that we do not share. We believe that a society that must be held together by constant force or the threat of force is an oppressive society, and we do not believe that oppression is inevitable. Around us there are examples of societies that have done much to eliminate the sources of exploitation and suffering that generate crime. A main premise of our approach to the police, then, is that we believe things *can* be different; that we can build a society without grinding poverty, ill-health, mutual exploitation and fear — and, therefore, without a vast, repressive police apparatus.

How do the present police enforce the oppressive social and personal relations of capitalist society? There are two different, but related, ways in which this is accomplished.

(1) The laws that define what is and what is not "crime" — and thus what is or is not a concern of the police — have been primarily defined in U.S. history by and for the people who benefit most from the capitalist system;

(2) Even within the inherently one-sided system of laws the police have been used *selectively,* enforcing *some* of the laws against *some* kinds of people, while allowing other laws to fall into disuse and letting other kinds of law-breakers go free, or nearly free.

(1) The Definition of Crime The most violent and socially harmful acts in the history of the U.S. have been carried out by the government and the wealthy rulers of the corporate economy. Whether measured in human lives or dollars, these acts constitute the most severe crimes of all, though they are not labelled as such in the criminal codes. The overwhelming number of killings in the 1960's were committed by the U.S. armed forces in Southeast Asia. The largest thefts in U.S. history were carried out by the U.S. government against the lands of Mexicans and the various Native American tribes. The most brutal kidnapping since Blacks were forced into slavery was carried out by the U.S. government, against the Japanese-Americans in the 1940's, when they were stripped of their belongings and held in camps during World War II. Perhaps most importantly, the process of getting rich off the labor of other people, far from being considered a crime, is the basis of normal economic life in the U.S., and people who do it successfully have great prestige and power.

Historically, the *main* function of the police has been to protect the property and well-being of those who benefit most from an economy based on the extraction of private profit. The police were created primarily in response to rioting and disorder directed against oppressive working and living conditions in the emerging industrial cities. . . . They were used consistently to put down striking workers in the industrial conflicts of the late 19th and early 20th centuries. The police did not shoot or beat the corporate executives of Carnegie Steel, the Pullman Company, or the Pennsylvania Railroad who subjected their workers to long hours, physical danger, and low pay; instead, they shot and beat the workers who protested against that exploitation. In the 1960's, the police did not arrest the men who planned and directed the U.S. aggression in Southeast Asia; they arrested the people who protested against that aggression. And in the ghetto revolts of Harlem, Watts, and Newark, the police did not use tear gas and shotguns on slumlords or on merchants who sold shoddy and overpriced goods; they used them on the Black people who rebelled against that victimization.

All of this is often conveniently forgotten in discussions of the police. It adds up to the simple fact that the police were not created to serve "society" or "the people," but to serve *some* parts of society and *some* people at the expense of others. Sometimes, this means that things like racism, sexism, economic exploitation, or military aggression are defined as worthy rather than criminal. In other cases, something more subtle happens. Many of the most socially and personally damaging acts that *are* forbidden in U.S. law are handled as "civil" rather than "criminal" issues. This is often true, for example, for such things as denying people jobs on the grounds of sex or race, or violating safety or anti-pollution regulations. Generally, the executives of corporations and other institutions that violate these laws are not visited by armed police, handcuffed and thrown in patrol wagons, and taken to jail. Instead, a long, drawn out, and expensive process of litigation takes place, during which "business as usual" goes on as before. This distinction, like the basic definition of crime, is not natural or inevitable, but reflects the social priorities and sources of political power in a society built on private profit.

(2) Selective Enforcement Even when the actions of the wealthy and powerful are defined as criminal and detected, the penalties they face are usually relatively mild and rarely applied in practice. Offenses such as embezzlement, fraud, tax fraud, and forgery resulted in a loss of $1.73 billion in 1965. In the same year, robbery, burglary, auto theft, and larceny resulted in a loss of $690 million — less than half as much. Although the "crime in the suites" represented much more stolen wealth, it was much less severely punished. Less than 20 percent of those convicted of tax fraud in 1969 (which averaged $190,000) served prison terms, and these terms averaged only 9 months. At the same time, over 90 percent of those convicted of robbery were sentenced to prison, where they served an average of 52 months.

Alongside this systematic leniency toward white-collar or corporate offenders, there is considerable evidence showing that underneath the formal structure of the criminal law there is an unofficial but systematic pattern of selective use of the police to coerce and intimidate oppressed people. Studies of police street practices consistently show that the police use their discretion to arrest more often against working-class people than others. For example, middle-class youth are much more likely to be let off with a reprimand for many kinds of crimes, while working-class youth are far more likely to be formally arrested and charged, for the same kinds of offenses. More dramatically, it has been shown that the police systematically use their ultimate weapon, deadly force, much more often against Black people than against Whites. A recent study found that between 1960 and 1968, 51 percent of the people killed by police were

Black in a country where Blacks make up something over 10 percent of the population. The police response to the crime of rape is another example of this pattern, for although rape — unlike most expressions of sexism — is considered in law as a serious crime, it is typically dealt with in ways that serve to degrade and further victimize women and to enforce oppressive and stereotypical conceptions of women's role. In these and other ways too numerous to mention here, the routine operation of the police creates an informal system of criminal law that, even more than the formal one, is designed to support the fundamentally oppressive social relations of capitalism. It should be emphasized that this is not just a question of easily correctible police "abuses." The selective use of the police has been a systematic and constant feature of the whole pattern of "social control" in the U.S., and its consistency shows how tightly it is tied in to the repressive needs of the system as a whole.

DEALING WITH CRIME

Even though we believe that the most dangerous criminals sit in corporate and government offices, we recognize that the more conventional kinds of crime — "street" crimes — are a real problem which must be confronted. In the U.S., people are faced every day with the danger of theft or personal violence. This is especially true of poor people. Most street crimes are committed by the poor against the poor — particularly against poor Third World people. Blacks are four times as likely to be robbed as Whites; Black women are four times as likely to be raped as White women. In general, people who live in inner cities are three times more likely to be victimized by major crime than those who live in the suburbs. The fear of crime is a demoralizing and oppressive fact of life for many people. Because of this, many people believe that the police should be encouraged and supported, since they at least provide *some* protection against this type of crime. We understand this attitude, but we believe it is fundamentally mistaken.

The reasons why there is so much street crime in the U.S. are complex, but they are rooted in the material deprivations and personal alienation and misery that capitalism produces. No "war on crime" can provide a truly enduring solution to the problem of crime unless it directly attacks the sources of that misery and alienation. Strengthening the existing police does not do this; but only helps to strengthen the system that generates crime in the first place. This isn't to say that beefing up the police might not reduce some kinds of crime; obviously, flooding the society with more and better-equipped police — putting a cop on every corner — could have some effect on rates of crime. But this kind of "solution" would not touch the underlying roots of crime, and could only be done at a tremendous cost in social and personal values.

To deal with crime by strengthening the police is to accept the inevitability of crime and the permanence of the oppressive social system that breeds it. We believe that real solutions to the problem of crime must begin by challenging that system itself: by moving toward programs that take power away from that system and its rulers, and transfer it to the people it now oppresses. Alternative approaches to crime must be of a kind that increase the consciousness of oppressed people and extend their ability to control their own lives. They must be linked to the broader movement to totally transform the economic and political institutions of U.S. society — the movement to build socialism in this country. In this way, the fight against crime and for a safer and more decent life can be joined with the larger struggle against the real crimes of racism, sexism, and exploitation at home and abroad.

SOME CAUTIONS

It's important to emphasize that although we believe that crime is deeply bound up with the nature of capitalist society, we are not suggesting that capitalism is responsible for *all* crime or that crime will necessarily magically disappear when capitalism does. The picture is a little more complicated than that. From what we know about crime in socialist societies, for example, it's clear that crime has not altogether disappeared in them; but it's also clear that many kinds of crime — including theft, drug use, and crimes of personal violence — have strikingly decreased, and are likely to decrease even more in the future, as the traces of earlier, oppressive relationships are gradually obliterated. It is also obvious that crime appears differently in different capitalist societies. The U.S. has much higher rates of crime than most other "developed" capitalist countries, for example Sweden, Switzerland, or England. This means that it isn't really possible to predict exactly how much or what kinds of crime will be present in a society simply by knowing that it is capitalist. To understand the specific extent and pattern of crime in any actual capitalist system, it has to be seen as a historically unique society with its own special conditions and traditions. In the U.S., for example, the historical patterns of racism and the internal colonization of Third World people are crucially connected to the types and amount of crime in this country, and have to be considered equally with the capitalist nature of the system in understanding them. Because capitalist development in the U.S. has depended heavily on the special exploitation of Third World people both here and overseas, the special oppression of Third World people is a fact of life of American capitalism, and it contributes strongly to the especially high rates of crime (as well as of disease, infant mortality, and other symptoms of oppression) in the U.S. as opposed to some other capitalist countries. Recognizing this, though, does not mean that it is any less true that we must end capitalism in order to end crime; it simply means that ending capitalism must also mean ending racism (and all other forms of human exploitation and domination) as well. In other words, the understanding that capitalism creates conditions that are likely to lead to crime is just the *beginning* of an analysis of crime and the police in the U.S., not the end of it.

Jammed Tokyo's Crime Rate Is Far Below New York's

Sydney H. Schanberg

People in Tokyo rarely cross the street against a red light. They do not scrawl graffiti on subway walls. And they do not commit many murders either.

Indeed, the world's most populous city — 11.6 million people — has the lowest crime rate. Tokyo had 196 murders last year; New York, with a population of almost eight million, had 1,680 — nearly nine times as many.

That Japan's capital is the least crime-troubled of any big city in the world is in itself not news. Tourist brochures regularly make the same point: "Even on dark, lonely streets in the dead of night, you need not be afraid of lurking shadows."

But seldom does anyone here try to explain why, for law and order is a condition of life the Japanese have come to take for granted.

Though the "why" is not some Oriental mystery, neither is it simple to explain, for it involves a mixture of social and legal factors that go to the heart of the national character.

Consider a few of them: The gun-control and drug laws are severe, and they are enforced by an efficient police force. Public respect for law and authority is traditionally strong. Arrest is a deep disgrace both for oneself and for one's family. The level of education is high. Unemployment is low. The country is ethnically and culturally homogeneous, with virtually no racial strains.

Finally, the Japanese, living close together on an isolated and densely populated island group, have developed an ability to deal with stresses and an adaptability to others, as well as a sense of obligation not to trespass on the lives of their neighbors.

"In Japan most people agree on what is right and what is wrong," said a young businessman who had just returned from several years in the United States. "In America different groups have different ideas about right and wrong."

Not surprisingly, the people proudest about Tokyo's low crime rate are the metropolitan police. "We sent two men to New York last year to study crime there," said Inspector Junzo Hirooka, chief of the crime prevention section. "They found crime so high that even they were afraid of walking around at night."

The Tokyo police are especially fond of contrasting their crime level with that of New York, where murderers and muggers lead a more active life. Other things being equal, New York — which, in fact, is not the most crime-ridden of American cities — ought to have less crime. But as the statistics demonstrate — and the 42,420 Tokyo policemen are as proud of their statistical accuracy as they are of their crime rate — other things are clearly not equal.

New York, with a 31,000-man police force, had 72,750 reported robberies last year; Tokyo had 361. New York had 3,735 reported rapes, Tokyo 426. New York had 38,148 reported assaults, Tokyo 17,171. New York had 82,731 reported auto thefts, Tokyo 3,550. New York reported 22,843 drug crimes, Tokyo 1,283. And so on.

In brief, while cities in Europe and the United States have seen their crime rates double and more over the last decade, crime in Tokyo has not increased. In the category of major crimes the rate has actually dropped despite steady population growth.

Are the Japanese less criminally inclined than other urbanized people, or are the Japanese police simply more effective in controlling and preventing crime?

Probably some of both — although the police are more visible and easier to explain than the intricacies of Japanese psychology. They are also one of the few vehicles through which an outsider can get a glimpse of that psychology at work.

The Tokyo police are recruited from all over the country in a search for the best men — which gives them added prestige in a nation where prestige is important. Here, the neighborhood policeman is known respectfully as O-Mawari-San — Mr. Walkaround.

He earns about $6,000 a year [in 1974] after three years' service, compared with the $16,000 of a New York policeman with the same experience. And he does walk around, for there are many more foot patrolmen here than in New York. Sprinkled every few blocks throughout the city are koban, or police booths, manned by one to a dozen or so men, who patrol their neighborhoods constantly. There are 1,242 such booths, which vary in size depending on population and crime rate.

Every koban policeman has responsibility, on the average, for about 150 households, each of which he is required to visit at least twice a year. Moreover, he must provide his headquarters with data on the occupants of each household and what they do for a living.

There is also a voluntary civilian crime-prevention organization, set up under police aegis, with an unpaid block captain for every 30 households; the purpose is to encourage cooperation with the police and the speedy reporting of crimes and traffic accidents by use of the police emergency telephone number, 110.

In these ways — and through patrol cars and a modern communications system, with a computerized control room at headquarters — the police cover virtually every square foot of territory and usually know as much about each resident as any nosy neighbor in a small American town.

This helps explain the high arrest rate. It also provides occasional surprises for residents. The other day an American businessman living here received a call from his O-Mawari-San, who reminded him that his dog was due for its rabies shot.

The police are unusual in other ways. Their restraint impressed an American reporter who spent a night on the streets with them in

Kabukicho, the neighborhood in the bustling Shinjuku district with the worst crime rate in the city. A district of garish and often sleazy bars, cabarets, coffee shops and amusement parlors, it used to be thick with organized criminal gangs, but has been somewhat cleaned up.

As the policemen walked through the neon-bathed alleys in pairs — in most other areas they patrol alone — drunken revelers would occasionally toss wisecracks at them. The policemen never gave them a glance.

They approached a man who had parked illegally on a sidewalk and asked for his license and registration. His tone was rude and arrogant. They asked why he had parked illegally. He retorted that he did not know the traffic regulations "because I have been in jail for two years and just got out."

Unfazed by his disrespectful attitude, the policemen simply called back to the koban on their walkie-talkie to check his papers. Once they had established his identity, his previous record and the validity of his present address, they returned the papers and sent him on his way.

Policemen get no bonus, financial or otherwise, for making a lot of arrests for minor offenses. There also seems to be no adversary relationship between the average citizen and the policeman — he is not the enemy.

Police energies seem directed mainly at winning the neighborhood's confidence and checking serious crime. Drunks, for example, are not treated as criminals. Even if one is abusive and in falling-down condition, the police will merely carry him to the koban, put him in a corner where he can sleep it off and send him home in the morning — giving him careful directions in case he is lost.

Policemen rarely draw their pistols; the rules on firearms are rigid and strictly circumscribed. Force of any kind is to be used only when absolutely necessary.

So strict is the precept that when the special riot policemen, who do not carry arms, become too vigorous in pushing against demonstrators with their metal shields, their chief, behind them, will rap them on their plastic riot helmets with his baton — a command to get hold of themselves and show more restraint.

"Our policemen have self-control — they do not get carried away by emotion," said Takashi Miyatami, a sergeant at the Kabukicho police booth, who has a long scar from the bridge of his nose to his chin — a legacy from a student's rock in a riot in Yokosuka eight years ago.

He said he bore no grudge against students for injuring him. "It is simply my professional duty to deal with left-wing students and restrict them," he added blandly.

The man in the police booth affords a closeup of how the force works. At the other end of the elaborate communications network is the central control room at headquarters, which is one of the best places to monitor Tokyo crime. There, television sets, computers, tape decks, radiophoto machines, alarm buzzers, telephones and flashing lights are awesomely arrayed against the criminal.

The officer in charge reels off for the visitor more of the department's ever-handy statistics. There have been 823 calls from citizens and policemen since last midnight. There were 140,757 calls about traffic accidents last year. The average response time between a citizen's call and the arrival of a police car is 3 minutes 40 seconds.

The alarm buzzer rings. A citizen is calling to report that a neighbor is waving a long knife; no one has been injured yet. A radio car is dispatched.

The officer goes back to ticking off more statistics, but the buzzer goes again. This time it is a report of two missing teen-agers quickly followed by a report that some demonstrating workers have shifted the route of their protest march.

There is only one thing that does not quite fit in this gargantuan room dedicated to transistor technology — everyone has to wear slippers. Maybe it's a venerated tradition, the visitor thinks, a touching contrast. Just the opposite: It's more worship of the machine. The officer in charge explains that shoes bring in dust and dust is bad for the machines.

Notes and Questions

1. Why should the Japanese police be called police? Consider the following:

 Many kobans post scorecards outside listing yesterday's frightening traffic toll, others post photos or drawings of suspects wanted by police. Inside, it isn't unusual to be greeted by a photo of the revered Mt. Fuji or by a delightful floral display. Despite Tokyo's urban sprawl and heavy pollution, Japanese have a unique appreciation for beauty and aesthetic touches. This is said to reflect the influence of Confucianism. In any event Tokyo police recruits — required to demonstrate skill in judo, kendo, and other martial arts — may be the only policemen in the world whose curriculum includes flower arrangement, music appreciation and the tea ceremony. . . .

 Like the Japanese approach to so much else, the concepts of Japanese justice and law are based on conciliation and compromise. Indeed, the oldest written code in Japan, Prince Shotoku's historic 17 maxims established almost 1,400 years ago, begins, "Concord is to be honored." Today, local police stations provide conciliation rooms where elders seek to reconcile warring parties. Laymen participate widely in judicial proceedings to mediate civil and domestic disputes. After an active night in any of Tokyo's 28,000 drinking establishments, which form an integral part of Japan's social and business milieu, obstreperous drunks are made to sleep it off in special foam rubber padded detention centers — and are punished by having to listen to tape recordings of their previous night's ranting and raving.*

2. How do you think Charles Reich would feel about the Japanese police?
3. The cultural differences reflected in policing patterns are also evident in the differing number of lawyers in Japan and the United States and in the number of lawsuits in each country. Consider the following:

 Government figures show that in 1979 about 160,000 civil suits were filed in Japan, while the comparable total in the United States was several million.

 There are about half a million lawyers in the United States, compared with just over 10,000 in Japan, which has half the population of the United States.

 The lack of litigiousness in Japan is often cited as an economic advantage. The Japanese, it is said, do not spend much time, money or energy suing each other but, instead, concentrate on outproducing other nations.

 That Japan is a relatively suit-free society is generally attributed to its cohesive culture, with its heritage of shunning open confrontation.

 In his recent book, "The Litigious Society," Jethro K. Lieberman, a journalist who is a graduate of Harvard Law School, writes: "Litigiousness is not a legal but a social phenomenon. It is born of a breakdown in community, a breakdown that exacerbates and is exacerbated by the growth of law. But until there is a consensus on fundamental principles, the trust that is essential to a self-ordering community cannot be."

 To a remarkable degree, the requisite consensus on fundamental principles exists in Japan.

 Legal practices and habits also reflect a society's values, according to Carl J. Green, a Washington lawyer and a senior research fellow at the Harvard Law School specializing in the Japanese legal system. In Japan, Mr. Green says, the harmony of community is valued most and people go to court only as a last resort.

 In the United States, by contrast, the rights of the individual are given priority and the courtroom is a key forum in which the conflicting claims of individuals are arbitrated. "We would be unhappy with the Japanese system," Mr. Green said.†

---

*Edwin McDowell, "Tokyo, Where Law Means Order," *Wall Street Journal,* November 29, 1973. Reprinted by permission of the Wall Street Journal © 1973 Dow Jones & Co., Inc. All Rights Reserved.

†*New York Times,* March 10, 1982. Copyright © 1982 by The New York Times Company. Reprinted by permission.

4. For an argument that the Japanese are less litigious because their court system is highly inefficient, see Cynthia Mayer, "Japan: Behind the Myth of Japanese Justice," *American Lawyer* (July–August 1984):113.

Suggested Additional Readings

A Civilian Perspective

Brown, Michael. *Working the Street.* New York: Russell Sage, 1981.

Davis, Kenneth. *Police Discretion.* St. Paul, Minn.: West, 1975.

Kafka, Franz. *The Trial,* trans. by Willa Muir and Edwin Muir. New York: Knopf, 1937.

Malamud, Bernard. *The Fixer.* New York: Farrar, Straus & Giroux, 1966.

LaFave, Wayne. *Arrest: The Decision to Take a Suspect into Custody.* Boston: Little, Brown, 1965.

Muir, William Ker. *Police: Streetcorner Politicians.* Chicago: University of Chicago Press, 1977.

Packer, Herbert. "Two Models of the Criminal Process." *University of Pennsylvania Law Review* 113 (1964):1.

Symposium, "Discretion in Law Enforcement." *Law and Contemporary Problems* 47 (1984):1–312.

Williams, Gregory H. *The Law and Politics of Police Discretion.* Westport, Conn.: Greenwood Press, 1984.

Zimbardo, Philip. "The Psychology of Police Confessions." *Psychology Today,* 1 (June 1967).

Legal Perspectives

Amsterdam, Anthony. "Perspectives on the Fourth Amendment." *Minnesota Law Review* 58 (1974):349.

Canon, Bradley. "The Exclusionary Rule: A Conservative Argument for Its Retention." *South Texas Law Journal* 23 (1982):559.

Kamisar, Yale. "The Fourth Amendment in an Age of Drug and AIDS Testing." *New York Times Magazine,* September 13, 1987.

Schlesinger, Steven. *Exclusionary Injustice.* New York: M. Dekker, 1977.

Stewart, Potter. "The Road to *Mapp* v. *Ohio* and Beyond: The Origins, Development and Future of the Exclusionary Rule in Search and Seizure Cases." *Columbia Law Review* 83 (1983):1365.

Sutton, Paul. "The Fourth Amendment in Action: An Empirical View of the Search Warrant Process." *Criminal Law Bulletin* 22 (1986):405.

"Symposium on Testing for Drug Use in the American Workplace." *Nova Law Review* 11 (1987):291–824.

The Media Perspective

Arnold, Thurman. *The Symbols of Government.* New Haven, Conn.: Yale University Press, 1935.

Carlson, James. *Prime Time Law Enforcement.* New York: Praeger, 1985.

Chase, Anthony. "Lawyers and Popular Culture: A Review of Mass Media Portrayals of American Attorneys." *American Bar Foundation Research Journal* 281 (1986):1986.

Gerbner, George, and Gross, Larry. "The Scary World of TV's Heavy Viewer." *Psychology Today* 9 (April 1976):89.

McLuhan, Marshall. *Understanding Media.* New York: McGraw-Hill, 1964.

Mander, Jerry. *Four Arguments for the Elimination of Television.* New York: William Morrow, 1978.

Mankiewicz, Frank, and Swerdlow, Joel. *Remote Control.* New York: Quadrangle, 1978.

Papke, David. *Framing the Criminal: Crime, Cultural Work and the Loss of Critical Perspective, 1830–1900.* Hamden, Conn.: Archon, 1987.

Schwartz, Tony. *The Responsive Chord.* New York: Doubleday, 1973.

A Societal Perspective

Bayley, David. *The Police and Political Development in India.* Princeton, N.J.: Princeton University Press, 1961.

———. *Forces of Order: Police Behavior in Japan and in the United States.* Berkeley: University of California Press, 1976.

———. *Patterns of Policing: A Comparative International Analysis.* New Brunswick, N.J.: Rutgers University Press, 1985.

Bittner, Egon. *The Functions of the Police in Modern Society.* Cambridge, Mass.: Oelgeschlager, Gunn & Hain, 1980.

Fogelson, Robert. *Big-City Police.* Cambridge, Mass.: Harvard University Press, 1979.

Goldstein, Herman. *Policing a Free Society.* Cambridge, Mass.: Ballinger, 1977.

Hersey, John. *The Algiers Motel Incident.* New York: Knopf, 1968.

Klockars, Carl, ed. *Thinking About Crime: Contemporary Readings.* New York: McGraw-Hill, 1983.

Manning, Peter. *Police Work: The Social Organization of Policing.* Cambridge, Mass.: M.I.T. Press, 1977.

Parker, L. Craig. *The Japanese Police System Today: An American Perspective.* Tokyo: Kodansha International, 1984.

Robinson, Cyril, and Scaglion, Richard. "The Origin and Evolution of the Police Function in Society." *Law and Society Review* 21 (1987):109.

Wilson, James Q., and Kelling, George. "Broken Windows." *Atlantic Monthly* 249 (March 1982):29–38.

"Arming for the Fray," Nineteenth-Century British Barrister. (Harvard Law Art Collection)

CHAPTER 3 The Legal Profession and the Legal System

Woe unto you also, ye lawyers, for ye lade men with burdens grievous to be borne, and ye yourselves touch not the burdens with one of your fingers.

New Testament (Luke 11:46)

Could the ambivalence toward law . . . be related to the possibility that the lawyer must do things the community regards as necessary — but still disapproves of? Hence is the lawyer something of a scapegoat? Now to be sure this does not distinguish lawyers from prostitutes, politicians, prison wardens, some debtors and many other occupational groups. What does distinguish lawyers in the role is that they are feared and disliked — but needed — because of their matter-of-factness, their sense of relevance, their refusal to be impressed by magical solutions to peoples' problems.

David Riesman, *Individualism Reconsidered* (1954)

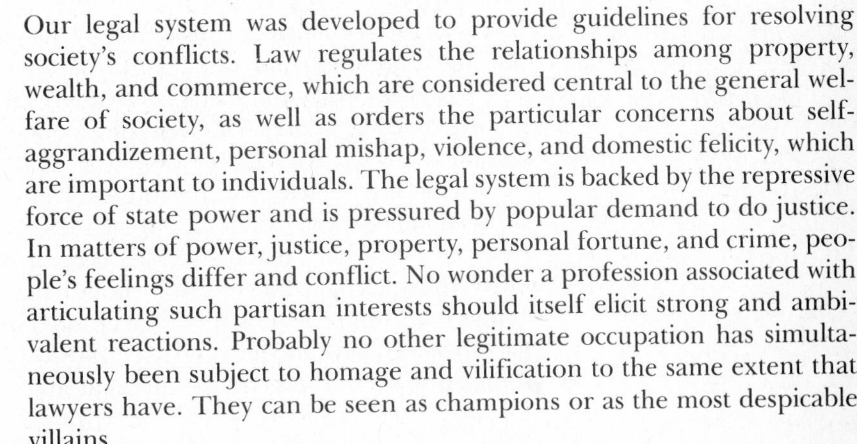

Our legal system was developed to provide guidelines for resolving society's conflicts. Law regulates the relationships among property, wealth, and commerce, which are considered central to the general welfare of society, as well as orders the particular concerns about self-aggrandizement, personal mishap, violence, and domestic felicity, which are important to individuals. The legal system is backed by the repressive force of state power and is pressured by popular demand to do justice. In matters of power, justice, property, personal fortune, and crime, people's feelings differ and conflict. No wonder a profession associated with articulating such partisan interests should itself elicit strong and ambivalent reactions. Probably no other legitimate occupation has simultaneously been subject to homage and vilification to the same extent that lawyers have. They can be seen as champions or as the most despicable villains.

This chapter focuses closely on the legal profession: its role in society; the organization, development, and education of legal novices; lawyers' relationship to clients and the meaning of advocacy; the nature of legal practice; the possible significance of gender as more women enter the profession; and, lastly, the interrelationship of legal practice, client type, and development of law.

The readings in Section 1 strike several themes that carry through the chapter: the relationship of lawyers to sources of power; the role lawyers play in maintaining democratic institutions and social stability; and the forces that divide the profession and challenge its independence from the private interests of its clients.

Section 2 deals with the initiation of students into the legal profession — law school. Themes from the first section are developed further, showing how people of ordinary origins take on the lawyer's habits of mind and social posture that Tocqueville called aristocratic, and how novice lawyers are trained to accept the hierarchies in this stratified profession.

Section 3 concerns lawyers in court and the adversary process. The central question involves the nature and meaning of client representation. What are the limits of advocacy? How much loyalty does a lawyer owe a client? What about truth? What kind of justice can there be without truth? What kind of society permits justice without truth?

Section 4 carries the themes of the preceding sections into empirical studies of legal practice. The interplay in criminal practice of plea bargaining with client's needs and court's goals provides insights about advocacy. A divorce lawyer's office offers a contrasting setting for exploring how lawyers negotiate a legal definition of a client's grievances. Also considered here is the question of legal practice and gender. Some feminists have argued that advocacy and legal problem-solving by women may produce less conflict and a healthier form of dispute resolution than has been encouraged by the adversary process. And, lastly, the issue of lawyers and social reform is considered in the context of the assertion that the "haves" always come out ahead.

Law as a profession has recently enjoyed unprecedented popularity among college students. Demographic data presented in Section 1 of the chapter show dramatic increases in the profession's size over the past two decades. Many reasons for this interest continue to hold sway. The legal profession is expected to continue its incredible growth into the twenty-first century. Many readers of this book are probably themselves seriously considering whether they should seek to become lawyers. This chapter aims to provide a theoretical understanding of the place of lawyers in society and the legal system, and to provoke conversations about some issues in the practice of law that are important for all citizens to discuss. Readers may also wish to use those conversations to project themselves into imagined situations of legal practice in order to answer questions about their own values and aspirations.

---

1 THE PROFESSION OF LAW

[The lawyer's] profession enables him to *serve the State.* As well as any other, better than any other profession or business or sphere, more directly, more palpably, it enables and commands him to perform certain grand and difficult and indispensable duties of patriotism, — certain grand, difficult and indispensable duties to our endeared and common native land. . . . [Service to the state raises the profession] from a mere calling by which bread, fame, and social place may be earned, to a function by which the republic may be served. It raises it from a dexterous art and a subtle and flexible science, — from a cunning logic, a gilded rhetoric, and an ambitious learning, wearing the purple robe of the sophists, and letting itself to hire, — to the dignity of almost a department of government, — an instrumentality of the State for the well-being and conservation of the State.

Rufus Choate, "The Position and Functions of the American Bar, as an Element of Conservatism in the State," Address delivered before the Harvard Law School (1845)

It is true that vast power has been lodged in the legal profession, but that certainly does not justify the complaint that lawyers have too much power. . . . What is unfortunate . . . is not the grant of power to the bar but the failure of the profession to make plain to people the reasons for the grant and its meanings.

Albert P. Blaustein and Charles O. Porter, *The American Lawyer* (1954)

[T]he law is a hustle.

Florynce Kennedy, "The Whorehouse Theory of Law," in Robert Lefcourt, ed., *Law Against the People* (1971)

The tension in American society between lawyers and other social elements is as old as the country itself. In 1640, when the Massachusetts Bay Colony founded its short-lived utopia in the New World, like Plato's Republic it had no room for lawyers. That men by legal training should defend with equal tenacity the cause of the righteous and the sinner, the aggrieved and those who injure, the interests of society and the evils of its most pernicious elements, was completely unacceptable to the Puritan moral community.

Nor were lawyers welcomed elsewhere in the colonies. In Virginia, the landed aristocracy jealously guarded its governing powers from the intrusion of lawyers by restricting the practice of law to the most petty circumstances. In New York, first under the Dutch and later the English occupation, the practice of law was permitted, but with licensure and fee regulation imposed by the dominant merchant and land-holding class.

For the first seventy years after the settlement of Pennsylvania, no lawyers practiced in that colony. The hostility of Quakers to the tyranny of English law and their religious antipathy to the lawyer's occupation that was preoccupied with conflict and social strife was carried over to their frontier society.

The absence of lawyers did not mean that the colonies were lawless nor did the hostility toward lawyers prevent "law-jobs" — to use Llewellyn's term — from being done. Acting for others as legal advocates, counselors, and advisors were a plethora of clergymen, laymen court clerks and justices, traders and merchants, sheriffs, and a class called *pettifoggers,* who had the gift of clever penmanship or sharp oratory. In addition, frontier self-sufficiency often included knowing enough law to get by. For the greater part of the seventeenth century the American colonies used a legal system without lawyers.

The demand for a trained bar came with the first stages of urban growth and increasing commercialism at the close of the seventeenth century. Earlier reticence toward the encouragement of a professional lawyer class succumbed to the immediate legal needs of a growing country.

In the fifty years before the Revolutionary War, the bar flourished in the colonies. Many prosperous Southern families sent sons to England to be trained in law at the Inns of Court. In the North, the more typical path was by apprenticeship to a successful attorney after having attended Harvard, Yale, Dartmouth, or one of the other colleges for gentlemen. By the time of the Revolution, the majority of lawyers in the colonies were college educated; the practice of law by laymen was at a minimum; and the licensure requirements were tightly controlled by the legal elite.

Twenty-five of the fifty-two signers of the Declaration of Independence were lawyers. But the Revolutionary War decimated the bar. Consistent with their conservative views, many lawyers, including some of the most prominent, had aligned themselves with the interests of the state and king. Most were forced to flee when the legal government toppled. Massachusetts lost nearly a third of its lawyers to the Tory cause.

After the Revolution, the popular antilawyer sentiment, submerged during most of the century, resurfaced when the chief law business became cleaning up the war's legal debris: collecting debts, imprisoning intractable debtors, foreclosing mortgages, assisting the collection of ruinous taxes, and litigating the cases of returning Tories and English creditors. In 1787, Daniel Shays led an army of farmers out of the hills of Massachusetts in the country's first antilawyer riot.

In the early nineteenth century, under the influence of Jeffersonian — later Jacksonian — persuasions, state legislatures began dismantling the restrictive licensure requirements for practice of law by which the bar had been garrisoned from "the common man." Individual omnicompetence was the prevailing view. That anyone could be a lawyer was supported by the national principles of equality and democracy, by the American repudiation of class privileges associated with European societies, and by the demonstrated self-sufficiency of life on the frontier. In most states admission to legal practice became a right of citizenship, not of education or social position. The era of easy access to a lawyer's license for socially mobile aspirants began. The bar lost, for a century, its traditional power of self-regulation and its position of gatekeeper to the profession.

Americans of this period were ambivalent as to what the place of law and lawyers in society should be. On the one hand, the U.S. Supreme Court, constitutionally an equal branch in the governmental triumvirate, was considered too insignificant to merit special space in the Capitol Building built in Washington. From 1801 to 1860, the highest court in the land "was driven, like a poor-paying tenant, from one abode to another: from the marshal's office to the clerks' office, to the Law Library in the basement, to the clerk's home on Pennsylvania Avenue, thence to the North Wing of the Capitol Building, then back to the Law Library, then to the old Senate Chamber, then to the District of Columbia Committee Room, then to the Judiciary Committee Room, and finally back to the Senate Chamber."* The justices were made to ride judicial circuits, spending as much as six months of the year traveling the muddy backroads of the country.

The legislative loosening of licensure requirements was meant to depreciate the status of the legal profession. However, simultaneously, this act recognized the importance of law and the profession for the society. With the opening of the profession to those who were not well-born, people assumed that the ranks of lawyers would include representation of interests from all segments of society. Thus, the bar would be democratic; law would be democratic.

Into this milieu, in 1831, arrived a young French lawyer, Alexis de Tocqueville — one of history's most extraordinarily perceptive tourists. His official mission was to study U.S. prison reform. His personal mission was to satisfy himself — and report to his countrymen — whether this new experiment in democracy could succeed. He saw the antagonism between populism and lawyers' elitism, between a fundamental faith in the common man and a claim for the legitimacy of authority, and

---

*Drew Pearson and Robert S. Allen, *The Nine Old Men* (New York: Doubleday, Doren, 1937), p. 7.

between a "tyranny of the masses" and the restraint required for the maintenance of democratic institutions. He concluded that lawyers have a special role in this democracy. His analysis is not only historically interesting; it frames the issues still surrounding the legal profession today.

The Temper of the Legal Profession in the United States

Alexis de Tocqueville

In visiting the Americans and studying their laws, we perceive that the authority they have entrusted to members of the legal profession, and the influence that these individuals exercise in the government, are the most powerful existing security against the excesses of democracy. This effect seems to me to result from a general cause, which it is useful to investigate, as it may be reproduced elsewhere. . . .

Men who have made a special study of the laws derive from this occupation certain habits of order, a taste for formalities, and a kind of instinctive regard for the regular connection of ideas, which naturally render them very hostile to the revolutionary spirit and the unreflecting passions of the multitude.

The special information that lawyers derive from their studies ensures them a separate rank in society, and they constitute a sort of privileged body in the scale of intellect. This notion of their superiority perpetually recurs to them in the practice of their profession: they are the masters of a science which is necessary, but which is not very generally known; they serve as arbiters between the citizens; and the habit of directing to their purpose the blind passions of parties in litigation inspires them with a certain contempt for the judgment of the multitude. Add to this that they naturally constitute *a body*; not by any previous understanding, or by an agreement that directs them to a common end; but the analogy of their studies and the uniformity of their methods connect their minds as a common interest might unite their endeavors.

Some of the tastes and the habits of the aristocracy may consequently be discovered in the characters of lawyers. They participate in the same instinctive love of order and formalities; and they entertain the same repugnance to the actions of the multitude, and the same secret contempt of the government of the people. I do not mean to say that the natural propensities of lawyers are sufficiently strong to sway them irresistibly; for they, like most other men, are governed by their private interests, and especially by the interests of the moment.

In a state of society in which the members of the legal profession cannot hold that rank in the political world which they enjoy in private life, we may rest assured that they will be the foremost agents of revolution. . . .

I am in like manner inclined to believe that a monarch will always be able to convert legal practitioners into the most serviceable instruments of his authority. There is a far greater affinity between this class of persons and the executive power than there is between them and the people, though they have often aided to overturn the former; just as there is a greater natural affinity between the nobles and the monarch than between the nobles and the people, although the higher orders of society have often, in concert with the lower classes, resisted the prerogative of the crown.

Lawyers are attached to public order beyond every other consideration, and the best se-

---

curity of public order is authority. It must not be forgotten, also, that if they prize freedom much, they generally value legality still more: they are less afraid of tyranny than of arbitrary power; and, provided the legislature undertakes of itself to deprive men of their independence, they are not dissatisfied.

I am therefore convinced that the prince who, in presence of an encroaching democracy, should endeavor to impair the judicial authority in his dominions, and to diminish the political influence of lawyers, would commit a great mistake: he would let slip the substance of authority to grasp the shadow. He would act more wisely in introducing lawyers into the government; and if he entrusted despotism to them under the form of violence, perhaps he would find it again in their hands under the external features of justice and law.

The government of democracy is favorable to the political power of lawyers; for when the wealthy, the noble, and the prince are excluded from the government, the lawyers take possession of it, in their own right, as it were, since they are the only men of information and sagacity, beyond the sphere of the people, who can be the object of the popular choice. If, then, they are led by their tastes towards the aristocracy and the prince, they are brought in contact with the people by their interests. They like the government of democracy without participating in its propensities and without imitating its weaknesses; whence they derive a two-fold authority from it and over it. The people in democratic states do not mistrust the members of the legal profession, because it is known that they are interested to serve the popular cause; and the people listen to them without irritation, because they do not attribute to them any sinister designs. The lawyers do not, indeed, wish to overthrow the institutions of democracy, but they constantly endeavor to turn it away from its real direction by means that are foreign to its nature. Lawyers belong to the people by birth and interest, and to the aristocracy by habit and taste; they may be looked upon as the connecting link between the two great classes of society.

The profession of the law is the only aristocratic element that can be amalgamated without violence with the natural elements of democracy and be advantageously and permanently combined with them. I am not ignorant of the defects inherent in the character of this body of men; but without this admixture of lawyer-like sobriety with the democratic principle, I question whether democratic institutions could long be maintained; and I cannot believe that a republic could hope to exist at the present time if the influence of lawyers in public business did not increase in proportion to the power of the people.

This aristocratic character, which I hold to be common to the legal profession, is much more distinctly marked in the United States and in England than in any other country. This proceeds not only from the legal studies of the English and American lawyers, but from the nature of the law and the position which these interpreters of it occupy in the two countries. The English and the Americans have retained the law of precedents; that is to say, they continue to found their legal opinions and the decisions of their courts upon the opinions and decisions of their predecessors. In the mind of an English or American lawyer a taste and a reverence for what is old is almost always united with a love of regular and lawful proceedings.

This predisposition has another effect upon the character of the legal profession and upon the general course of society. The English and American lawyers investigate what has been done; the French advocate inquires what should have been done; the former produce precedents, the latter reasons. A French observer is surprised to hear how often an English or an American lawyer quotes the opinions of others and how little he alludes to his own, while the reverse occurs in France. There the most trifling litigation is never conducted without the introduction of an entire system of ideas peculiar to the counsel employed; and the fundamental principles of law are discussed in order to obtain a rod of land by the decision of the court. This abnegation of his own opinion and this implicit deference to the opinion of his forefathers, which are common to the English and American lawyer, this servitude of thought which he is obliged to profess, necessarily gives him more timid habits and more conservative inclinations in England and America than in France.

The French codes are often difficult to comprehend, but they can be read by everyone; nothing, on the other hand, can be more obscure and strange to the uninitiated than a legislation founded upon precedents. The absolute need of legal aid that is felt in England and the United States, and the high opinion that is entertained of the ability of the legal profession, tend to separate it more and more from the people and to erect it into a distinct class. The French lawyer is simply a man extensively acquainted with the statutes of his country; but the English or American lawyer resembles the hierophants of Egypt, for like them he is the sole interpreter of an occult science. . . .

In America there are no nobles or literary men, and the people are apt to mistrust the wealthy; lawyers consequently form the highest political class and the most cultivated portion of society. They have therefore nothing to gain by innovation, which adds a conservative interest to their natural taste for public order. If I were asked where I place the American aristocracy, I should reply without hesitation that it is not among the rich, who are united by no common tie, but that it occupies the judicial bench and the bar.

The more we reflect upon all that occurs in the United States, the more we shall be persuaded that the lawyers, as a body, form the most powerful, if not the only, counterpoise to the democratic element. In that country we easily perceive how the legal profession is qualified by its attributes, and even by its faults, to neutralize the vices inherent in popular government. When the American people are intoxicated by passion or carried away by the impetuosity of their ideas, they are checked and stopped by the almost invisible influence of their legal counselors. These secretly oppose their aristocratic propensities to the nation's democratic instincts, their superstitious attachment to what is old to its love of novelty, their narrow views to its immense designs, and their habitual procrastination to its ardent impatience. . . .

The influence of legal habits extends beyond the precise limits I have pointed out. Scarcely any political question arises in the United States that is not resolved, sooner or later, into a judicial question. Hence all parties are obliged to borrow, in their daily controversies, the ideas, and even the language, peculiar to judicial proceedings. As most public men are or have been legal practitioners, they introduce the customs and technicalities of their profession into the management of public affairs. The jury extends this habit to all classes. The language of the law thus becomes, in some measure, a vulgar tongue; the spirit of law, which is produced in the schools and courts of justice, gradually penetrates beyond their walls into the bosom of society, where it descends to the lowest classes, so that at last the whole people contract the habits and the tastes of the judicial magistrate. The lawyers of the United States form a party which is but little feared and scarcely perceived, which has no badge peculiar to itself, which adapts itself with great flexibility to the exigencies of the time and accommodates itself without resistance to all the movements of the social body. But this party extends over the whole community and penetrates into all the classes which compose it; it acts upon the country imperceptibly, but finally fashions it to suit its own purposes.

Notes and Questions

1. Tocqueville described lawyers as all having a taste for formalism, a dislike for arbitrary power, conservative, harboring a contempt for the judgment of the masses, and a natural affinity with sources of power. How do lawyers acquire these attributes? Some argue that such changes occur during education for the law. In what ways do these qualities contribute to the profession's function in maintaining democratic institutions?
2. Tocqueville wants us to understand the legal profession in the role of power broker. Contrast the following views:

   It should need no emphasis that the lawyer is today, even when not himself a "maker" of policy, the one indispensable advisor of every responsible policy-maker of our society — whether we speak of the head of a government department of agency, of the executive of a corporation or labor union, of the secretary of a trade or other private association, or even of the humble independent enterpriser or professional man. As such an advisor the lawyer, when informing the policy-maker of what he can or cannot *legally* do, is, as policy-makers often complain, in an unassailably strategic position to influence, if not create, policy.*

A profession attains and maintains its position by virtue of the protection and patronage of some elite segment of society which has been persuaded that there is some special value in its work. Its position is thus secured by the political and economic influence of the elite which sponsors it. . . .

If the source of the special position of the profession is granted, then it follows that professions are occupations unique to high civilizations, for there it is common to find not only full-time specialists but also elites with organized control over large populations. Further, the work of the chosen occupation is unlikely to have been signaled out if it did not represent or express some of the important beliefs or values of that elite. . . .†

Can lawyers be both brokers and servitors of power? What does Tocqueville suggest?

3. Tocqueville states that lawyers "are less afraid of tyranny than of arbitrary power" and that they can turn despotism into "the external features of justice and law." What do these ideas imply in the context of a democratic society?

4. One of Tocqueville's themes, that the legal profession serves the state as an agent of social control, has many contemporary advocates. Much of the evidence for this view comes from the analysis of poverty law practice, where clients are powerless, controlled by their lawyers, and usually have their grievances given short shrift by the legal system. Maureen Cain, however, has argued that the idea of lawyers as controllers misses the fact that most clients are *not* working-class people.‡ Rather, except for the restricted case of criminal law practice, lawyers' clients are primarily middle- or upper-class individuals (or their organizations), who are themselves the primary beneficiaries of state power in capitalist society. By her interpretation, lawyers *do* — as Tocqueville and many contemporary theorists have noted — translate the grievances of clients into other terms. But it is not a translation intended to repress the desires and interests of clients; rather, it merely converts these claims into the universalistic discourse of law where middle- and upper-class values and interests are sustained. Thus for most clients in law the interests of state, class, and client coincide.

If this view is accepted, does it answer Questions 2 and 3?

5. What is Tocqueville's view of the assumption of individual omnicompetence — that all persons are capable of being lawyers regardless of education or social station? In contemporary times, is there an assumption of omnicompetence for law-trained persons?

6. Tocqueville predicted that in the United States law would become a "vulgar tongue" of the people — the language and concepts of law would pervade all institutions and daily interactions in the society. Has the prediction been borne out?

*Harold Lasswell and Myres McDougal, "Legal Education and Public Policy," *Yale Law Journal* 52 (1943): 208–209.

†Eliot Freidson, *Profession of Medicine* (New York: Dodd, Mead, 1970), pp. 72–73.

‡Maureen Cain, "The General Practice Lawyer and the Client: Towards a Radical Reconception," in Robert Dingwall and Philip Lewis, eds., *The Sociology of the Professions: Lawyers, Doctors and Others* (London: Macmillan, 1983), pp. 106–131.

In the 1870s lawyers began forming bar associations. At first they were intended merely to promote social intercourse among the legal elite. Beginning in the 1920s, they took on the objectives of a guild. Bar associations pressed the state legislatures and courts to empower them with the right to determine who could be lawyers. Stricter educational and bar admission requirements were thereafter imposed by law, replacing the previous permissive ones — the ideology of the people's omnicompetence was supplanted by the ideology of the expert. Again the legal profession became self-defining and self-regulating.

For a century the lawyer had been second only to the captain of industry as the hero of the popular rags-to-riches myths. The profession had been open and had grown. According to the best estimates, in 1850 there were about 22,000 lawyers in the country, 60,000 in 1880, 114,000 in 1900, and 220,000 in 1950. The great majority of lawyers were sons of merchants and clerks; many were foreign-born or the children of immigrants. The image of the profession had become intimately tied to the American dream — that a person with little capital could acquire wealth, status, and social prestige by intelligence and hard work. Today, although access to legal practice has become much narrower than a century ago, the same image of the profession has adhered.

This period was also a time of transformation in the nature of lawyering and the legal profession. The most prestigious and highly paid practices of law moved from the courtroom to the offices of Wall Street (and its other city equivalents). The profession became socially heterogeneous, stratified, and internally organized by the relationships of its practitioners to that awesome entity newly created by lawyers — the economic megalith called "the corporation." The transition and consequences are well described by C. Wright Mills.

Lawyers *C. Wright Mills*

Both Tocqueville, near the beginning of the nineteenth century, and Bryce, near the end, thought the American lawyers' prestige was very high; in fact, they believed lawyers, as Willard Hurst puts it, to be a sort of ersatz aristocracy. Yet there has always been an ambiguity about the popular image of lawyers — they are honorable but they are also sharp. A code of professional ethics, it should be recalled, was not adopted by the American Bar Association until 1908, and even then did not really deal with the Bar's social responsibility.

Before the ascendancy of the large corporation, skill and eloquence in advocacy selected nineteenth-century leaders of the bar; reputations and wealth were created and maintained in the courts, of which the lawyer was an officer. He was an agent of the law, handling the general interests of society, as fixed and allowed in the law; his day's tasks were as varied as human activity and experience itself. An opinion leader,

---

a man whose recommendations to the community counted, who handled obligations and rights of intimate family and life problems, the liberty and property of all who had them, the lawyer personally pointed out the course of the law and counseled his client against the pitfalls of illegality. Deferred to by his client, he carefully displayed the dignity he claimed to embody. Rewarded for apparent honesty, carrying an ethical halo, held to be fit material for high statesmanship, the lawyer upheld public service and was professionally above business motives.

But the skills and character of a profession shift, externally, as the function of the profession changes with the nature of its clients' interests, and internally, as the rewards of the profession are given to new kinds of success. The function of the law has been to shape the legal framework for the new economy of the big corporation, with the split of ownership and control and the increased monopoly of economic power. The framework for this new business system has been shaped out of a legal system rooted in the landed property of the small entrepreneur, and has been adapted to commercial, industrial, and then investment economies. In the shift, the public has become for the lawyer what the public has been for the lawyer's chief client — an object of profit rather than of obligation.

There is one lawyer for approximately 750 persons in the United States but this lawyer does not serve equally each of these 750. In rural districts and small cities, there is one lawyer for approximately every 1200, in big cities one for every 400 or 500. More directly, people with little or no money are largely unable to hire lawyers. Not persons, not unorganized publics of small investors, propertyless workers, consumers, but a thin upper crust and financial interests are what lawyers serve. Their income, a better income today than that received by any other professional group except doctors, comes from a very small upper income level of the population and from institutions.

In fulfilling his function the successful lawyer has created his office in the image of the corporations he has come to serve and defend. Because of the increased load of the law business and the concentration of successful practice, the law office has grown in size beyond anything dreamed of by the nineteenth-century solicitor. Such centralization of legal talent, in order that it may bear more closely upon the central functions of the law, means that many individual practitioners are kept on the fringes, while others become salaried agents of those who are at the top. As the new business system becomes specialized, with distinct sections and particular legal problems of its own, so do lawyers become experts in distinct sections and particular problems, pushing the interests of these sections rather than standing outside the business system and serving a law which co-ordinates the parts of a society.

In the shadow of the large corporation, the leading lawyer is selected for skill in the sure fix and the easy out-of-court settlement. He has become a groomed personality whose professional success is linked to a law office, the success of which in turn is linked to the troubles of the big corporation and contact with those outside the office. He is a high legal strategist for high finance and its profitable reorganizations, handling the affairs of a cluster of banks and the companies in their sphere in the cheapest way possible, making the most of his outside opportunities as an aide to big management that whistles him up by telephone; impersonally teaching the financiers how to do what they want within the law, advising on the chances they are taking and how best to cover themselves. The complications of modern corporate business and its dominance in modern society, A. A. Berle Jr. has brilliantly shown, have made the lawyer 'an intellectual jobber and contractor in business matters,' of all sorts. More than a consultant and counselor to large business, the lawyer is its servant, its champion, its ready apologist, and is full of its sensitivity. Around the modern corporation, the lawyer has erected the legal framework for the managerial demiurge.

As big capitalist enterprise came into social and economic dominance the chance to climb to the top ranks without initial large capital declined. But the law 'remained one of the careers through which a man could attain influence and wealth even without having capital at the start.'

With law as background, the lawyer has often become a businessman himself, a proprietor of high acumen, good training, many contacts, and sound judgment. In his own right, he has also become the proprietor and general manager of a factory of law, with forty lawyers trained by Harvard, Yale, Columbia, and two hundred clerks, secretaries, and investigators to assist him. He competes with other law factories in pecuniary skills and impersonal loyalties, in turning out the standardized document and the subtle fix on a mass production basis. Such offices must carry a huge overhead; they must, therefore, obtain a steady flow of business; they therefore become adjuncts 'to the great commercial and investment banks.' They appear less in court than as 'financial experts and draftsmen of financial papers.'

The big money in law goes to some three or four hundred metropolitan law factories specializing in corporation law and constituting the brains of the corporate system. These law factories, as Ferdinand Lundberg has called them, are bureaucracies of middle size. Perhaps the largest has about seventy-five lawyers, with an appropriate staff of office workers.

The top men are chosen as are film stars, for their glamour. Behind them, the front men, stand men with technical abilities, as in Hollywood, looking out for the main chance and sometimes finding it, but working for a small salary. Below the partners are associates who are salaried lawyers, each usually working in a specialized department: general practice, litigation, trusts, probate, real estate, taxation. Below them are the clerk-apprentices in the law, then the investigators, bookkeepers, stenographers, and clerks. In special instances there are certified accountants and investment consultants, tax experts, engineers, lobbyists, also ranged in rank. For every partner there may be two salaried lawyer assistants, for every lawyer two or three office workers. A partnership of 20 lawyers may thus have some 40 associates and 120 office workers. Such offices, geared to quantity and speed of advice, must be highly organized and impersonally administered. High overhead — including oriental rugs and antique desks, panelled walls and huge leather libraries — often accounts for 30 per cent of the fees charged; the office must earn steadily, and the work be systematically ordered in the way of the managerial demiurge everywhere. Under the supervision of one of the partners, the office manager, sometimes a lawyer who seldom practices law, must see that production lines and organization run smoothly. Efficiency experts are called in to check up on the most effective operations for given tasks. In some offices each salaried lawyer, like a mechanic in a big auto repair shop, is required to account for his time, in order that fees may be assigned to given cases and the practice kept moving.

Each department, in turn, has its subdivisions: specialization is often intense. Teams of three lawyers or so, usually including one partner, work for only one important client or on one type of problem. Some lawyers spend all their time writing briefs, others answer only constitutional questions; some deal in Federal Trade Commission actions, others only with the rulings of the Interstate Commerce Commission.

Much of the work is impersonal, vitiating the professional precept that lawyer and client should maintain a personal relationship. Personal intercourse between the members of the profession and between lawyers and clients, calls upon each other on matters of business, have been replaced by hurried telephone conversations, limited to the business at hand, entirely eliminating the personal quality. An opponent may be absolutely unknown, except over the telephone: you know the sound of his voice, but if you were to meet him on the street, you would be unable to recognize him. In the earlier days, a comparatively intimate acquaintance might have been formed even with an opponent. Once a meeting in a lawyer's office with a client not only was agreeable, but had a tendency to begin and cement a personal relationship. It now frequently happens that, although a lawyer may be actively employed for a client, personal intercourse does not occur.

Under this specialization, the young salaried lawyer does not by his experience round out into a man adept at all branches of law; indeed, his experience may specifically unfit him for general practice. The big office, it is said within the bar, often draws its ideas from the young men fresh from the preferred law schools, whom the big offices 'rush,' like fraternity men seeking pledges. Certainly the mass of the work is done by these able young men, while their product goes out under the names of the senior partners.

The young lawyer, just out of law school, fresh from matching wits with law professors and bar examiners, lacks one thing important for successful practice — contacts. Not only knowledge of trade secrets, but the number of contacts, is the fruit of what is called experience in modern business professions. The young men may labor and provide many of the ideas for the produce that goes out under the older man's name, but the older man is the business-getter: through his contacts, Karl Llewellyn has observed, he can attract more orders than he or twenty like him can supply. The measure of such a man is the volume of business he can produce; he creates the job for the young salaried lawyers, then puts his label on the product. He accumulates his reputation outside the office from the success of the young men, themselves striving for admittance to partnership, which comes after each has picked up enough contacts that are too large and dangerous to allow him to be kept within the salaried brackets. In the meantime he sweats, and in the meantime, the new law-school graduates are available every year, making a market with depressed salaries, further shut out by those new young men who have already inherited through their families a name that is of front-office caliber. The powerful connection, the strategic marriage, the gilt-edged social life, these are the obvious means of success.

Not only does the law factory serve the corporate system, but the lawyers of the factory infiltrate that system. At the top they sit on the Boards of Directors of banks and railroads, manufacturing concerns, and leading educational institutions. The firm of Sullivan and Cromwell, one of the largest law factories, holds 65 directorships. Below the directors, staff lawyers may be vice presidents of the corporation, other lawyers may be on annual retainers, giving the corporation a proprietary right to the lawyer as a moral agent. Of the corporation, for the corporation, by the corporation. Listening in on every major directors' meeting, phrasing public statements on all problems, the omnipresent legal mind, an officer of the court, assists the corporation, protects it, cares for its interests.

As annex to the big finance, the law factory is in politics on a national scale, but its interest in politics is usually only a means of realizing its clients' economic interests. Yet the lawyer who is successful in politics in his own right is all the more important and useful to his former clients, to whose fold he often returns after a political interlude. In corporation law firms one finds former senators and representatives, cabinet officers, federal prosecutors, state and federal tax officials, ambassadors and ministers, and others who have been acquainted with the inside workings of the upper levels of the government. High government officials, cabinet officers, ambassadors, and judges are often drawn directly from the corporation law offices, the partners of which welcome the opportunity to be of national service. Since the Civil War, the corporation law firms have contributed many justices to the United States Supreme Court; at present the majority of its members are former corporation lawyers. Lawyers have been in politics since the constitutional period but today the lawyers from law factories work less as political heroes in the sunlight than as fixers and lobbyists in the shade. When the TNEC investigations were going on, lawyers for the big corporations took up one entire hotel in Washington, D.C.

There are also, of course, political law firms, smaller than the law factories, which draw their clients from the political world and regularly enter that world themselves. For it is through politics that the lawyer may attain a position on the bench. Usually these political law offices have only local political interests. Whereas corporate law factories are usually headed by men of Anglo-Scotch stock, these political offices, mainly in the northeast and in big cities, where politics often centers on immigrant levels, are frequently staffed by Irish, Polish, Jewish, Italian Americans. The opportunism of these smaller firms may make them appear tolerant and liberal, and certainly many of the partners in them are up from the ranks.

The lawyer uses political office as a link in a legal career, and the politician uses legal training and law practice as links in a political career. Skills of pleading and bargaining are transferable to politics; moreover, in exercising them as a lawyer, there is a chance to obtain politically relevant publicity. The lawyer is occupationally and financially mobile: more easily than most men, he can earn a living and still give time to politics. So it is not surprising that 42 per cent of the members of Congress in 1914, 1920, and 1926 and of state governors in 1920 and 1924 had been prosecuting attorneys; and of these, Raymond Moley has calculated, 94 per cent had held this office first or second in their political careers. Between 1790 and 1930, Willard Hurst has computed, two-thirds of the Presidents and of the U.S. Senate, and about half of the House of Representatives were lawyers.

Below the corporation law offices and the political firms are middle-sized law offices, containing from 3 to 20 partners and few, if any, associates. These offices, especially in small towns, are rooted in the local affairs of their business communities, dividing their time between local politics and the practice of local litigations. Finally, at the bottom of the legal pyramid is the genuine entrepreneur of law, the individual practitioner who handles the legal affairs of individuals and small businesses. At the lower fringe of this stratum, in the big cities especially, are those lawyers who live 'dangerously close to the criminal class.' The hierarchical structure of the legal profession is thus not confined inside the big offices; it is characteristic of the profession as a whole, within various cities as well as nationally.

In most cities, the legal work of banks and local industries, of large estates and well-to-do families, is divided among a few leading law firms, whose members sit on the boards of local banks and companies, who lead church, college, and charity affairs. They perpetuate themselves by carefully selecting the most likely young men available and by nepotism, sons of relatives, of partners, and of big clients being given marked preference over strangers, local graduates of local law schools over outside ones. In St. Paul, Minnesota, for example, graduates of Princeton or Yale often take their law work in St. Paul Law School, rather than in the University of Minnesota, in order to become acquainted with members of the local bar who act as instructors. Below these leading firms, the small firms and individual practitioners get the business that is left over; occasional cases for well-to-do citizens, the plaintiff's damage suit, criminal defense cases, divorce work. Below all these groups are the lumpen-bourgeoisie of the law profession. Usually products of local schools, they haunt the courts for pickups; large in number, small in income, living in the interstices of the legal-business system, besieging the larger office for jobs, competing among themselves, from time to time making irritating inroads into the middle-sized firms, lowering the dignity of the profession's higher members by competing for retainers instead of conferring a favor by accepting a case. Even as top men toady to big corporation chieftains, men on the bottom assiduously chase ambulances and cajole the injured.

Among the difficulties that have arisen for lawyers since 1929 is the fact that laymen are invading many fields that were long considered the lawyers' domain. Drafting of deeds and mortgages has been taken over by real-estate men; various service organizations have taken over taxation difficulties, automobile accidents, and conditional sales; workmen's compensation now takes care of many industrial accidents. There has also been a declining use of courts and litigation methods of settling controversies, caused by the public desire for speedy settlements. Traditional litigation is giving way to a system of administrative adjudication in which the lawyer has an equal footing with the layman. Members of the legal profession are slowly losing their monopoly of political careers, as men trained in such disciplines as economics increasingly find their way into higher government offices.

Yet, despite the displacement of individual practitioner by legal factory, law has remained enticing to many young men. Thousands every year graduate from law schools.

Notes and Questions

1. Tocqueville argued that a force internal to the legal profession gives it cohesion and autonomy from the claims of its clientele. This force is a traditional conception of professions — conditions of employment are established by the worker (in this case, the lawyer) rather than the employer. How does Mills challenge this conception?

2. Large corporate law firms have grown exponentially in the years since the 1950s. At the time Mills wrote, the largest firms in the country were about seventy-five lawyers, and all located in New York City. In 1988, the Chicago-headquartered firm of Baker & McKenzie was the first to break the thousand-lawyer mark. The firm has branch offices in several U.S. cities, Europe, and in such far-flung places as Bangkok, Melbourne, and Rio de Janeiro. The second largest firm has over eight hundred lawyers; firms with three hundred to five hundred lawyers have become increasingly common. This expansion in firm size has been tied to the recent tremendous growth in the size of corporations and the world economy.

Firms are not only larger but have expanded to encompass a wide range of expertise through elaborated divisions of labor. This development has made increasingly possible the practice of what Marc Galanter has labeled "mega-law" — a doomsday level of litigation, legal warfare between financial behemoths brought into the nuclear age:

> Investment of massive amounts of time, relentless investigation, exhaustive research and lavish deployment of expensive experts imposes on the other side corresponding expenditures, endless delays, and costly disruptions of their normal operations. If not everything is an open question, sufficient investment can make almost any matter sufficiently problematic that it takes considerable money and time to lay it to rest. Pursued in multiple forums, with brazen insistence on extracting the last measure of formal entitlement, and offering little hope of respite — such litigation raises the bluster and stratagem of ordinary litigation to lethal proportions. Litigation in the mega-law mode is distinctive in the way that mobile high technology warfare between superpowers differs from the set piece battles of an earlier day.*

3. Jerome Carlin's study, *Lawyers on Their Own*,† is the classic analysis of lawyers at the "bottom" of the bar. The following excerpt is from an interview Carlin had with a young lawyer who was just breaking into practice. It not only gives the flavor and pathos of that work but the essence of the reason it has endured as well.

> INTERVIEWER: What is the nature of your practice?
>
> RESPONDENT: [Looking through his clients' file folders piled on top of his desk and in the drawers] I do all the subrogation work for an insurance company. I have 300 files in the drawer. There's supposed to be $3,000 worth of claims there; a third is mine, but most are uncollectable. It's a lot of work for the income involved.
>
> INTERVIEWER: How did you get these cases?
>
> RESPONDENT: My brother-in-law's brother knows an attorney who has a half interest in the insurance company. [Continuing through his files:]
>
> Hardware store — collections.
>
> A real estate deal for my milkman.
>
> A will and trust matter for my sister-in-law's neighbor's mother.
>
> My sister-in-law's aunt — personal injury.
>
> This is for my sister-in-law's mother. I will do some estate planning — draw up a will and have some shares of stock transferred.
>
> A case for —— [lawyer for whom he works in the office]. The owner of a trailer claims a faulty installation, a suit for damages.
>
> —— [Other lawyer in the office] was in an auto accident.

---

*From Marc Galanter, "Mega-Law and Mega-Lawyering in the Contemporary United States," in Robert Dingwall and Philip Lewis, eds., *The Sociology of the Professions: Lawyers, Doctors and Others* (London: Macmillan, 1983), p. 163.

†From *Lawyers on Their Own: A Study of Individual Practitioners in Chicago* by Jerome E. Carlin. Copyright © 1962 by Rutgers, The State University. Reprinted with permission of Rutgers University Press.

> My brother-in-law was in an auto accident.
>
> I bought a washer and dryer at an appliance store. I asked them if they had any work for me. They gave me a few matters. I hope to get them for a retainer client. If only I had a few small retainers then I'd be okay. Otherwise, its very sporadic.
>
> Personal injury for my wife's aunt — auto accident.
>
> Personal injury for a friend.
>
> Personal injury for a friend — adulterated food.
>
> Here's my star client — I've thrown her out a hundred times. I'm handling a bunch of things for her. She's not satisfied with a tuck-pointing job in one of her buildings; I called him up and got him to agree to a compromise. Personal property tax for a shoe store she owns. Default judgment against a shoe store; I'll have that vacated. Her son and daughter-in-law got sick from a bad pizza. A precinct captain broke a window in her building; I know him and he'll fix it. I haven't got any fees from her yet. They'll start coming in soon, though.
>
> An immigration matter — I referred it to another attorney and I'm splitting a fee on it.
>
> That's the extent of my practice now.

In his first year out of law school Ronald earned $3,000 from the practice of law. In addition, he made a little over $1,000 as a telephone solicitor for a storm window concern. The first month of the second year he made $50, and in the second, $400. He has a wife and two children, and is having difficulty paying his bills.

> It's really touch and go. I don't know whether I'll make it. I may have to give up the practice. . . . I could make a lot more doing something else. I was offered $10,000 at the lumber yard, and I had a $7,500 offer from the Illinois Commerce Commission.
>
> INTERVIEWER: Why haven't you taken either of them?
>
> RESPONDENT: I don't know. I ask myself that. That's what we talk about — my friends and I — three of my cronies and I — we have coffee every morning and talk about our practice and our problems. If you're a salesman, it doesn't sound so good. It's a matter of pride or ego. I like the law, but it's not a burning thing in my life — I *must* be a lawyer. If I quit now I'd be admitting defeat. I'd be ashamed. . . . It's a nice profession, nice clean work, a respected profession. If I could get some income it would be a good life. You can get away when you want to play golf, and you're your own boss, that appeals to me. And if people ask you what you're doing it's nice to tell them I'm a lawyer, and not a clerk in a store. And my dad gets satisfaction from the fact that I'm a lawyer.

Compare the role of "contacts" in the personal service sector of legal practice as shown in the Carlin excerpt with that noted by Mills in the corporate service sector. How does this comparison help explain the importance of social variables in the stratification of the bar?

4. Typically, those who note the stratification of the legal profession distinguish lawyers in very different kinds of practices. Consider the hierarchies noted in the following description of the criminal defense bar by one of its members:

> Many judges who handle civil cases regard criminal trials as emotionally distasteful and intellectually unchallenging. Those judges who handle criminal cases often regard criminal lawyers with contempt and suspicion. Many of the highest paid criminal lawyers regard the rest of the criminal bar as incompetent. White-collar criminal lawyers regard the rest of the criminal bar as lower-class shysters. Most of the criminal bar regard Mafia lawyers as co-conspirators with their clients. Mafia lawyers regard public defenders who defend muggers as threats to society. Movement lawyers regard lawyers who don't love their clients as "whores." Large and medium-sized law firms don't do any criminal work because they consider it unseemly and their prestigious clients wouldn't want to share a roster or waiting room with the average rapist. Most lawyers

regard movement lawyers as pretentious and self-righteous. The general practitioner who handles only an occasional criminal case will take great pains to point out to any one who will listen, "I usually don't do this kind of work." And the public, for the most part, regards the lawyer who defends criminals as a crook.‡

‡Seymour Wishman, *Confessions of a Criminal Lawyer* (Baltimore: Penguin Books, 1981), pp. 55–56.

☐ During the past two decades, as noted, the U.S. legal profession has had explosive growth. A number of explanations have been offered for it: the acceleration in the country's economy creating greater demand for legal services; the bulky passage (like a rat into a snake) of the "baby boom" generation into the work force; the massive shift of women from traditional occupational roles into the professions; the affinity of law with many objectives of idealistic contemporary political movements — e.g., civil rights, the women's movement, gay rights, and children's rights; and, at least for a time, the "yuppies'" perception that law was where the action is.

Barbara Curran provides a demographic snapshot of the legal profession as it looks now.

American Lawyers in the 1980s: A Profession in Transition

Barbara A. Curran

Between 1951 and the beginning of 1984, the lawyer population in the United States increased by 427,600 or almost 200 percent. . . . The rate of growth exceeded that of the general population, as evidenced by the decline in the population to lawyer ratio. While one out of every 695 people was a lawyer in 1951, by 1984 one in every 364 people was a lawyer. . . .

The influx of large numbers of young lawyers into the profession, particularly since 1970, materially altered its composition with respect to the age and experience of its membership. The median age of lawyers dropped from forty-six years in 1960 to thirty-nine years in 1980. Lawyers under thirty-six made up 24 percent of the lawyer population in 1960 and 39 percent in 1980. . . .

The rate of growth of the female lawyer population since the late 1960s has substantially exceeded that of males. In each year from 1951 to 1968, approximately 3 percent of new admittees were women. In 1969, the proportion rose to 4 percent and has been increasing ever since. It is estimated that during 1983, 34 percent of new admittees were women. Particularly noteworthy is the fact that as the rate of female bar admissions continued to climb throughout the 1970s and into the 1980s, the rate of male admissions began to level off. . . . [T]he number of men admitted to the bar during each year from 1974 through 1983 did not change significantly, but the number of women admitted increased throughout the entire period.

The overall effect of the rapid growth in female bar admissions in the 1970s and 1980s is reflected in the substantially greater

 (Footnotes omitted and tables renumbered.)

TABLE 1 ***Distribution of Private Practitioners by Practice Setting (1980)***

Practice Setting	*Number*	*Percent of Private Practitioners (N = 370,111)*	*Percent of All Lawyers (N = 542,205)*
Solo practice	179,923	48.6	33.2
2-lawyer firm	32,509	8.8	6.0
3-lawyer firm	22,635	6.1	4.2
4-lawyer firm	16,233	4.4	3.0
5-lawyer firm	11,574	3.1	2.1
6–10-lawyer firm	33,377	9.0	6.2
11–20-lawyer firm	24,130	6.5	4.5
21–50-lawyer firm	22,529	6.1	4.2
50+-lawyer firm	27,200	7.3	5.0
Total	370,111	100.0	68.3

representation of women among lawyers in the 1980s. . . . [W]omen lawyers were less than 3 percent of the lawyer population during the entire period from 1951 through 1970 but 8.1 percent in 1980 and almost 13 percent in 1984.

In the years between 1970 and 1980, the female lawyer population increased by over 300 percent compared with only 44 percent for male lawyers. As a result, women lawyers were substantially younger than men in 1980 (median ages were thirty-two and forty, respectively). Lawyers admitted since 1970 comprised 77 percent of the 1980 female lawyer population but only 39 percent of the male lawyer population.

THE EMPLOYMENT OF LAWYERS

In 1980, the majority of lawyers (68.3%) were actively engaged in the private practice of law. . . . Approximately equal proportions were working for private industry (10.1%) and in government (9.3%). About 4 percent were employed in the judiciary and another 4 percent were employees of educational institutions, legal aid and public defender programs, private associations such as unions and trade associations, or other special interest organizations. The remaining 5.3 percent were retired or otherwise inactive.

The distribution of lawyers by type of employment has changed over time. . . . The proportion of lawyers in private practice declined from 72 percent in 1960 to 68 percent by 1980. During the same period, the proportion engaged in all other types of employment increased from 24 percent to 27 percent, while retired and inactive lawyers remained at or near 5 percent over the years.

Lawyers in Private Practice The decline between 1960 and 1980 in the proportion of lawyers in private practice reflects a slower growth rate in this sector of the lawyer population compared to others and not an absence of growth. Indeed, there were approximately 130,000 more private practitioners in 1980 than in 1970, even though they remained a constant proportion of all lawyers. Moreover, the growth rate of the private practitioner population substantially exceeded that of the general population, as evidenced by the drop in the population to private practitioner ratio from 870 in 1960 to 612 in 1980. . . .

Almost two-thirds of all private practitioners practiced law either alone or in association with one or two other lawyers. Although the proportion of private practitioners engaged in solo practice has declined over the years, nearly one-half of all private practitioners in 1980 continued to practice alone (see Table 1). . . .

Although firm practice often is associated with large firms, in fact only a small proportion of firm lawyers work in such settings. In 1980, 29 percent of firm practitioners were in firms of two or three lawyers, about 44 percent were in firms of two to five lawyers, and three-quarters practiced in firms of twenty lawyers or less. . . .

In 1980, almost one-quarter of lawyers in firm practice were associates, an increase over the figures for 1960 (20%) and 1970 (21%). Associates were concentrated in larger firms; only about 19 percent were in firms of five or fewer lawyers (see Table 2). . . .

TABLE 2 Distribution of Associates by Firm Size (1980) (in percent)

Firm Size	*Associates (N = 45,908)*
2-lawyer firm	3.3
3-lawyer firm	5.0
4-lawyer firm	5.6
5-lawyer firm	5.0
6–10-lawyer firm	18.0
11–20-lawyer firm	15.9
21–50-lawyer firm	18.2
50+-lawyer firm	29.1

Lawyers in the Judiciary The number of lawyers in the judiciary more than doubled between 1960 and 1980. Most of this growth occurred after 1970. In absolute numbers, the larger increase was at the state and local level. Relatively, however, the federal judiciary had the higher growth rate, as lawyers in the federal judiciary increased from 7 percent of all lawyers in the judiciary in 1960 to 14 percent in 1980. . . .

Lawyers in Government Although the proportion of the lawyer population employed in government has remained about the same over the years, the total numbers of lawyers in both the federal and state and local governments have increased since 1960. The rate of increase after 1970 was greater at the state and local level. . . .

Although lawyers were employed in almost every department and agency of the federal government in 1980, the largest share (18%) was, predictably, in the Department of Justice. The Department of Justice, together with the Internal Revenue Service, the Department of Defense (including the armed services), the Department of Health and Human Services, the National Labor Relations Board, and Congress, employed 51 percent of all lawyers in federal government. . . . Of the 20,132 lawyers in federal government, 11,869 (59%) were located in the Washington, D.C., area.

The single largest group of lawyers in state and local government were employed in city, county, or district prosecuting attorneys' offices. The second largest group consisted of lawyers working for state attorneys general. These two groups comprised 55 percent of all lawyers in state or local government. . . .

Lawyers in Private Industry In 1980, 10 percent of all lawyers were employed in private industry. Although this proportion was somewhat higher in 1970 (11 percent of all lawyers), the total number working in industry grew from just under 40,000 in 1970 to almost 55,000 by 1980. . . . [A]lmost half (49.1%) of the lawyers in private industry in 1980 were employed by Fortune 500 companies or by one of the Fortune 50 companies in selected industries. Among the other 50.9 percent of lawyers in industry, the largest portion (15.2%) were in insurance and banking.

Some companies employed only one lawyer, others more than two hundred. Slightly less than one-third (30.5%) of industry lawyers worked for companies with one to three lawyers; slightly more than one-third (37.1%) worked for companies with four to fifty lawyers; and the balance (32.4%) were employed by companies with more than fifty lawyers. . . .

Lawyers in Other Employment Employed lawyers who were not in private practice and not employed in the judiciary, government, or private industry made up 3.5 percent of the lawyer population. This group consisted of lawyers who were employees of private associations and special interest groups (0.8%), legal aid (0.9%) and public defender programs (0.6%), and educational institutions (1.2%). In the last category, 68 percent were employed in law schools and the rest at the college and graduate level and in elementary and secondary education. . . .

THE EMPLOYMENT OF WOMEN LAWYERS

In 1980, there were 44,185 women lawyers, comprising 8 percent of the total lawyer population of 542,205. Over three-quarters of these women (33,825) entered the profession in the years of 1971–79. While the number of men entering the profession during the same period was substantially greater (195,359), 1971–79 male admittees constituted a relatively smaller proportion (39.2%) of the total male lawyer population in 1980 (see Table 3).

TABLE 3 Distribution of Male and Female Lawyer Populations by Admission Cohort (1980) (in percent)

Admission Cohort	*Male Lawyers (N = 498,010)**	*Female Lawyers (N = 44,183)**
1975–79	23.0	62.7
1971–74	16.2	14.1
1961–70	22.7	9.0
1951–60	16.0	5.1
Pre-1951	22.0	9.1

*Date of bar admission was not available for 10 males and 2 females in the 1980 lawyer population.

. . . [W]omen lawyers were less likely to engage in private practice and more likely to be in other employment than men lawyers. Only 55.7 percent of women lawyers were private practitioners compared to 69.4 percent of men. For women, government was the second most frequently selected employment setting, followed by private industry. For men, the order was reversed. The proportion of women in legal aid and public defense, although small (less than 5%), was much greater than that of men (1.2%).

The 1980 employment distribution for women lawyers reveals relative underrepresentation in some employment settings and overrepresentation in others. . . . [W]omen lawyers were underrepresented in the primary setting in which lawyers are employed, namely, private practice. While they were 8.1 percent of the total lawyer population in 1980, they accounted for 6.6 percent of private practitioners. Except for state and local judiciary and private industry, women lawyers were overrepresented in all other employment settings.

Women lawyers in private practice were more likely to be solo practitioners or to work in very large firms than were men. . . . On the other hand, women were less likely than men to practice in small and intermediate-sized firms. . . .

That female firm practitioners were overrepresented among associates in 1980 is reflected in the fact that 14.8 percent of all associates were women . . . while less than 2 percent of lawyers not identified as associates (in firms with designated associates) were women, and only 4 percent of lawyers in firms with no associates were women. . . .

FUTURE GROWTH OF THE LEGAL PROFESSION

If annual admissions to the bar were to remain at the level of the early 1980s, the lawyer population would reach three-quarters of a million before 1990 and one million a decade later. The lawyer population will continued to grow in size at a somewhat slower rate even if new admissions decline because mortalities will remain low in relation to admissions until the substantial number of young lawyers who entered the profession in the 1970s and early 1980s begin to reach ages associated with high mortality rates. Until then, new admission rates would have to drop by at least half for the size of the legal profession to stabilize, let alone decline. As mortalities continue to reduce the size of the pre-1971 admission cohorts in which women are heavily underrepresented, the overall proportion of women in the profession may be expected to continually increase throughout the 1980s and into the 1990s — unless in those years there is a precipitous decline in the number of female admissions in relation to male admissions. Only the maturation of the 1971–79 admission cohort will reveal whether some of the differences observed in 1980 employment patterns between this group and pre-1971 admittees, particularly in the case of women lawyers, are simply differences associated with normal career development or presage further, and fundamental, shifts in lawyer employment.

Notes and Questions

1. Curran's study reports national trends for the legal profession. The distributions, however, are highly skewed by geographical region. For example, 40 percent of the lawyers in the country are found in five states: California, New York, Texas, Illinois, and Pennsylvania. Jurisdictions with the highest lawyer-to-population ratio are District of Columbia, 1 lawyer for every 25 persons: New York, 1 to 280; Alaska, 1 to 297; Massachusetts, 1 to 309; and Colorado, 1 to 334. Nationwide, there is 1 lawyer for every 418 persons. By the year 2000 it is estimated there will be 1 million lawyers; the ratio will then be 1 for 300 persons.

What are the implications of this trend for society? Is it likely to mean less or more law–society conflict? What might Tocqueville have said about the trend?

2. As Curran noted, the two most dramatic changes in the legal profession over the past two decades has been the tremendous increase in the number of women attorneys and the substantial decrease in the average age of the bar. As of 1987, almost 75 percent of female lawyers, and almost 50 percent of male lawyers, were under the age of 40.

3. Of course, a significant contribution to the growth of the profession is the widely held perception that lawyers make a great deal of money. Surveys of lawyers' salaries tend to support that view: In 1987, according to the American Bar Association, the average lawyer's income was $101,455 and the median was $65,995. The average lawyer's net worth was $512,300; the median net worth was $227,410. The difference between the average and median is a consequence of a small proportion having very high salaries relative to the rest. Much of the difference is related to the age distribution of lawyers. From a survey during this period in New England, lawyers 4 years out of law school had an average salary of $40,000; those 11 years out averaged $62,000; sixteen years out, $80,000; and those 26 years and over averaged $100,000.*

According to the Federal Reserve Board, in 1987 only 2 percent of all U.S. families earned more than $100,000 a year. Lawyers and accountants (lawyers were not surveyed separately), make up 1 percent of the nation's population, but constitute 12 percent of the wealthiest families.

*Michael Matza, "The Paths Most Traveled By," *Student Lawyer,* 16 (May 1987): 41.

☐ Contemporary social scientific scholarship on the legal profession has begun to examine closely the nature of differentiation among lawyers. As Mills and Curran discussed, lawyers are distinguished from each other by practicing in different types of settings and by having different clienteles. However, these differences are not simply a consequence of diverse interests and expertise. Rather, also significant are those distinctions that reflect the larger society — religion, ethnicity, race, social class background, gender, and educational pedigrees. These traits of lawyers, which would seem unrelated to professional merit, have great importance not only for the distribution of lawyers across practice settings but also for the fields of law practice, as well.

John P. Heinz and Edward O. Laumann describe the nature of social differentiation and hierarchies in the legal profession from their extensive study of the Chicago bar. They begin with the unusual and seemingly upside-down hypothesis that the subject matter of legal work determines who will perform it. This logic makes sense, because legal subject matter serves as a conduit for the client's interests.

The Legal Profession: Client Interests, Professional Roles, and Social Hierarchies *John P. Heinz and Edward O. Laumann*

We present data on a large random sample drawn from the full range and variety of the legal profession in a major American city. The sample appears to be a reasonably representative cross section of the population. As part of a larger study of the legal profession and the organized bar, our staff personally interviewed 777 lawyers with offices in the city of Chicago and gathered information about the nature of the respondents' legal practice and clients, the respondents' personal and social characteristics, their attitudes toward major social and legal issues, and their membership and participation in the various bar associations.

I. DIFFERENTIATION OF THE LEGAL PROFESSION: THE VARIABLES

The fields of law differ in their substantive doctrines, in their characteristic tasks, in the settings in which the fields are practiced, and in the social origins of their practitioners. But we hypothesize that these differences are secondary to yet another variable: the type of client served. We suggest that differences between clients profoundly influence many of the other types of differentiation among the fields — that the legal profession is, to a great degree, externally oriented, and in consequence is shaped and structured by its clients.

Many of the recognized fields of law correspond to bodies of doctrine generally regarded as distinct legal subjects and taught as separate courses in law school — *e.g.*, crimes, real estate, commercial transactions, personal injury, tax, labor, corporations, antitrust, and securities. But the practicing bar commonly distinguishes between two sides of many of these doctrinal areas, sides that serve adverse clients — *e.g.*, criminal defense versus prosecution, personal-injury plaintiffs' work versus personal-injury defense, labor law on the union side versus the management side, and so on. Other fields divide into parts that, though not necessarily adverse, are nonetheless distinct. Corporate tax planning differs from personal income tax work, real estate development work from home-mortgage preparation and title searching, and corporate litigation from a "general trial" practice that may encompass bits of divorce, commercial, personal-injury or even criminal work. As these examples make clear, lawyers are accustomed to think in terms of categories of work that distinguish, within broader doctrinal areas, fields or sub-fields defined by the types of clients served. One of the objectives of our research, therefore, was to ascertain the extent to which the operational definitions of the customary categories of legal work — which may, themselves, influence the structure of the profession — are determined by corresponding

Abridged from *Michigan Law Review*, Volume 76, June 1978, pp. 1111–1142 (footnotes omitted). Reprinted by permission of *Michigan Law Review* and the author.

categories of client-types rather than by doctrinal categories or other systematic theory.

The needs of a particular client or type of client often dictate the character and the diversity or homogeneity of the work of a lawyer or a law firm. The practitioner who serves a neighborhood's small businesses will often also handle the personal income tax returns of the owners of those businesses, will file their divorces, and will settle their automobile accident claims. The large firm that deals with a corporation's antitrust problems is also likely to handle its real estate acquisitions, its securities issues, and its corporate tax returns. But a lawyer who represents labor unions in one case is unlikely to represent management in another, and in this country a lawyer may not both prosecute and defend criminal cases simultaneously (though many young prosecutors later become defense lawyers). Broadly, the tendency of lawyers' work to address congeries of problems associated with particular types of clients organizes the profession into types of lawyers: those serving corporations, and those serving individuals and individuals' small businesses. Fields within each of these broad sectors of the legal profession have more in common — on a whole range of social variables — than do fields from different sectors.

The referral systems through which lawyers find clients or clients find lawyers may also structure the relationships among the fields of law. Patent lawyers, for example, may maintain close ties with counsel for corporations likely to invent patentable products, and lawyers specializing in commercial litigation may seek contact with office lawyers who represent commercial enterprises, while criminal defense lawyers may cultivate court clerks or prison wardens. The shared interest of lawyers and clients in an uninterrupted supply of each other creates mechanisms to insure this supply, and these mechanisms tend to bring together otherwise disparate fields of law, as the examples demonstrate. By contrast, other types of lawyers — criminal prosecutors, for example — may not need to seek clients, and this deprives those fields of one incentive for decreasing their social isolation from professional colleagues in other fields of practice.

Similarly, referral networks among graduates of particular law schools may bind together some fields and separate others. To the extent that practitioners of the most elite forms of corporate law graduated from the same few law schools, while personal injury or criminal lawyers studied at less prestigious, "local" law schools, "old school tie" networks may lengthen the social distance between these types of practice. This phenomenon is part of a more general tendency toward equal-status contact. That is, lawyers in fields that enjoy similar levels of prestige within the profession are more likely to associate with one another than are lawyers from fields with widely differing prestige.

Obviously, these mechanisms reinforce one another. Practitioners in fields concerned with corporate clients' legal problems probably recruit at the same law schools, participate in the same client-referral networks, and share similar prestige within the profession. The tendency of all these factors will be the same: to forge relationships among the fields of corporate-law practice and to separate them from noncorporate fields.

Characteristics more intrinsic to the practice of the various fields of law may also contribute to the degree of their social differentiation. Similarities in the legal doctrines, statutes, or regulatory schemes dealt with by two fields might, thus, beget a kinship that would increase social proximity. So might their general modes of analysis or the strategic problems they characteristically address. Some fields of law, for example, involve "symbol manipulation," and others "people persuasion." The former category might include preparing securities-registration statements or similarly complex, technical documents; divorce, criminal, or personal injury work might fall into the latter category.

This distinction relates, of course, to the more general differentiation of the types of tasks performed. The practitioners in some fields are nearly always in court or preparing for it, while other fields consist almost exclusively of office practice. And, within both litigation and office practice, further fundamental distinctions may be drawn. Within litigation, important distinctions of status and task type exist between state court and federal court litigation and between trial and appellate work. Within office practice, lawyers in some fields primarily advise clients (on possible tax or antitrust consequences of alternative courses of action, for example, or on techniques of real estate acquisition). Lawyers in other fields, such as matrimonial law, devote much time and energy to the emotional needs of clients, to personal counseling, or to smoothing ruffled feathers. Lawyers in still other fields characteristically spend considerable time drafting legal documents such as wills, trust agreements, debentures, or contracts. To the extent that these distinct tasks call for distinct skills, the mobility of lawyers among fields requiring dissimilar skills is inhibited. The likelihood that a lawyer will do a substantial amount of work in two fields of law is, of course, one measure of the social distance between the fields. Once that probability passes a certain point, we would say that no social or behavioral distinction exists between the two fields and that any distinction between them is purely conceptual or doctrinal.

For similar reasons, the fields of law that deal with statutory or regulatory codes may be more insular than those that work primarily with older common law. Every lawyer learns the basic principles of the common law in law school and, thus, may accept a simple tort or contract case even though he principally attends to some other field. By contrast, lawyers may be less confident of their skills, or less willing to invest the time necessary to acquire them, in fields such as broadcast regulation or labor law, and there may be less tendency to accept the occasional case in that kind of field. Much of the innovation in regulatory law, with the consequent growth of multi-volume codes, has occurred at the federal level, spawning entirely new specialties in federal regulatory law. Because these new fields share some common elements or common skills (and also because of the types of clients, the networks among clients and lawyers, and the differences between federal and state procedural rules), the distinction between federal practice and state practice also tends to create social distance among the fields — federal law tends to involve larger, corporate clients and to enjoy higher prestige within the profession.

Finally, fields of law that process large numbers of individual clients through the state courts are socially distant from the fields that often require several man-years of lawyers' time on each case (antitrust work, for example). But a fundamental socioeconomic difference corresponds to this difference among the fields. High-volume cases and the lawyers who handle them are unlikely to resemble the processing or the processors of "unique" legal problems, but the discovery of a unique issue is likely to be a function of the amount of time that lawyers devote to a case, and thus of the amount of money that the client spends on lawyers. If the stakes are high, the problems can become very complex; if the client lacks money, his problems are likely to be routine.

Service to the individual client is often repetitious and therefore dull. Although a divorce, a limb wasted by an automobile accident or by medical malpractice, a home-mortgage foreclosure, a sanity hearing, a criminal charge, a lost job, or an adoption or child-custody proceeding may all involve anxiety and suffering for the client, the specialized lawyer often finds them routine. The intellectual challenges they present will usually not be great. Since the law is a "learned profession," we may expect the profession to value and respect intellectual acuity and effort and to assign prestige within the profession to the intellectually demanding fields. Because clients with deep pockets create the complex work, the value placed on intellectual challenge will tend to lead lawyers into the service of a socioeconomic elite. In this respect, the legal profession differs from medicine. An exotic medical problem may afflict rich or poor (though such a problem is no doubt more likely to be detected in the well-to-do), and prestige within the medical profession may not, therefore, correspond so closely to the wealth of patients. Even poor people can have prestigious diseases.

One could posit a great many legal professions, perhaps dozens, and to some degree real distinctions separate all these types of lawyers. But one fundamental difference accounts for much of the variation within the legal profession: the difference between lawyers who represent large organizations (corporations, labor unions, or governments) and those who represent individuals or individuals' small businesses. Let us proceed, then, to the data that lead us to that conclusion.

II. MEASUREMENT OF THE CATEGORIES

Differentiation within the legal profession has occurred despite official endorsement of a holistic conception of the profession. Unlike the medical profession, which formally recognizes and certifies many specialities, the legal profession enshrines the myth of the omnicompetent practitioner. With only minor and recent exceptions, the profession's ethical rules forbid lawyers to represent themselves as specialists except in three small, abstruse fields: patents, trademarks, and admiralty. Nonetheless, many distinct fields of legal work clearly exist, and we began our research by categorizing those fields.

In compiling the list of thirty fields of legal work that we presented to our lawyer-respondents, we consulted the literature and sought to employ categories that would be familiar to lawyers. The list, therefore, consisted of labels that practicing lawyers commonly use to describe recognized legal specialities or types of practice. We decided to use fairly fine-grained categories and to combine them later if our sample contained too few respondents in any specialty to permit separate analysis of it.

We asked each respondent to indicate whether he devoted less than five percent, five to twenty-five percent, twenty-five to fifty percent, or more than fifty percent of his professional time to each of the thirty types of work. The respondents who reported that they devoted twenty-five percent or more of their professional time to a field are the practitioners whose responses were used in computing the characteristics of the fields that are reported here. For example, we derived the attributes of "securities" law and of its practitioners from the responses of lawyers who estimated that they spend at least a quarter of their legal effort on securities law. . . .

. . . Figure 1 depicts the relationships among the fields of law, representing them as points in two-dimensional space and accounting for their positions on a number of variables. Fields with similar profiles lie in close proximity (that is, share a region of Euclidean space); those with greater differences on the variables lie at greater distances from one another.

The twelve variables used in this analysis are:

1. Business clients (mean percentage of income received from clients who are businesses rather than persons).
2. Client volume (median number of clients in the past year).
3. Client stability (mean percentage of clients represented for three years or more).
4. Lawyer referrals of clients (mean percentage of clients obtained through referrals from other lawyers).
5. Choice of clients (percentage of practitioners indicating "wide latitude in selecting" clients).
6. Technical procedures versus negotiating and advising (percentage of practitioners indicating their work involves "highly technical procedures rather than skills in negotiation and advising clients").
7. Litigation in state courts (median number of state court appearances per month).
8. Size of practice organizations (median number of lawyers in the firm or other organization in which practitioners work).
9. Government employment (percentage of practitioners employed by federal, state, or local government).
10. "Local" law school (percentage of practitioners who attended any of four "local" law schools in Chicago).
11. High-status Protestants (percentage of practitioners who state a preference for one of the "Type-I" Protestant denominations).

FIGURE 1 Multidimensional Scalogram Analysis of Twenty-Five Fields of Law on Twelve Selected Variables

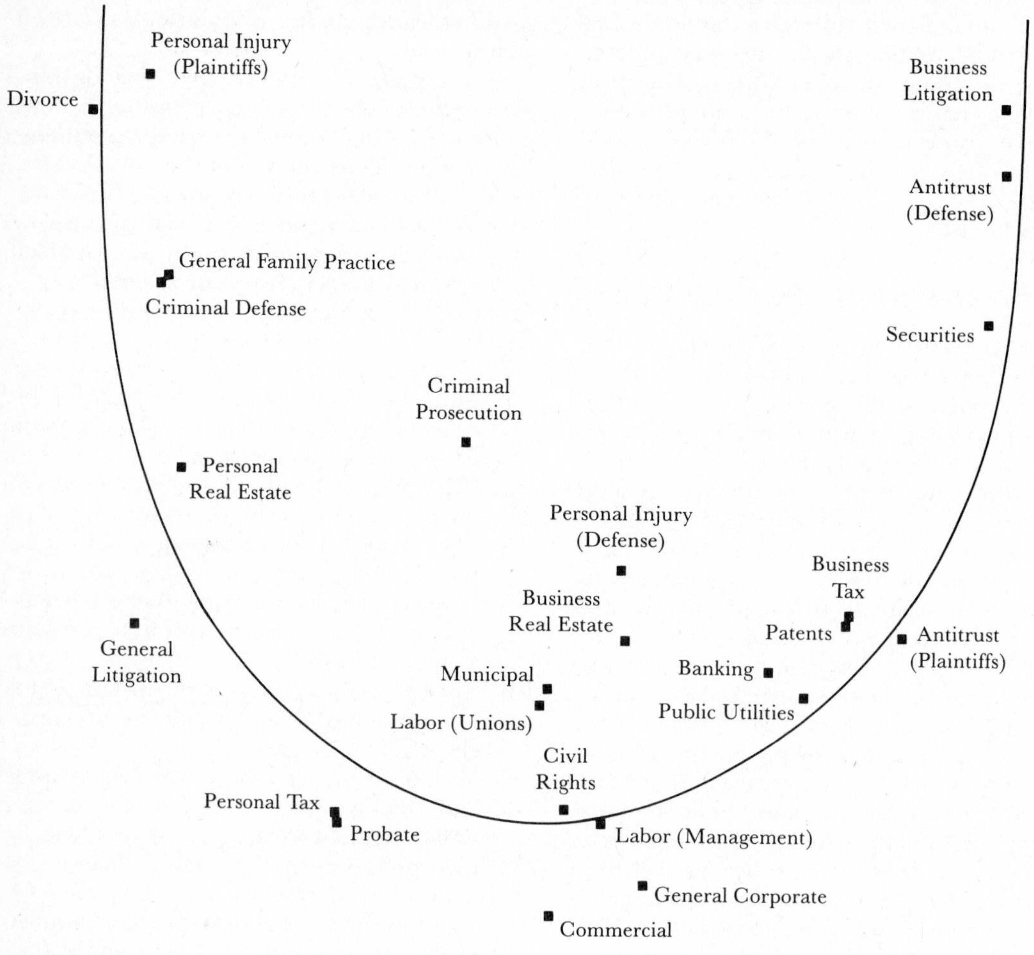

12. Jewish origin (percentage of practitioners who report either Jewish religion or ethnicity). . . .

. . . Thus, the twelve variables include one client-type variable, two concerning the nature of the lawyer-client relationship, two on sources of clients, two task types, two types of practice organizations, one law school type, and two ethnicity variables. Finally, and perhaps most importantly, we required that the variables chosen have substantive significance. There is a persuasive case that each of the variables used might have important influence on the social distances among the fields. Those arguments have, in fact, already been summarized in Part I.

As we see from the figure, the relationships among the fields form a U-shaped structure. The fields that serve corporate clients lie to the right; fields that serve persons rather than corporations lie to the left. Fields that serve either a mixture of the two or special sorts of corporations such as governments or labor unions fall toward the middle. If one draws a vertical line just to the left of the point representing criminal prosecution, we find that, with the sole exception of civil rights, all of the fields to the right of that line belong to our corporate sector and all of the fields to the left to the personal sector. The reader will recall that only one of the twelve variables used in the multidimensional scalogram analysis explicitly measures type of client — though, as we have already noted and argued, client volume and stability relate to these distinctions, and some of the other variables correlate with client type.

The vertical dimension of the structure reflects the differences between litigation and office practice. The fields with higher rates of court appearances tend to be higher in the space; those that litigate less tend to be located lower. Other general patterns in the structure are perhaps less striking, but they are surely discernible. The fields with higher percentages of practitioners reporting a free choice of clients lie outside the U, while those with less client choice are found in the inner rim of the U-structure. The median size of the law firm or other practice organization increases as one moves from the upper left counterclockwise around the U. Client volume and the percentage of practitioners who attended a "local" law school both move in the opposite direction, increasing as one proceeds clockwise around the U. The percentage of stable clients generally increases as one moves toward the bottom of the figure. From previously reported research, we know that the most prestigious fields of law are at the upper right of the U and the lowest are at the upper left; prestige decreases in a generally orderly clockwise fashion. . . .

. . . A small cluster of high status fields representing the largest corporations lies at the upper right of the U. Moving clockwise, we then encounter a group of fields dealing with administrative law, particularly with federal regulatory agencies. These include patents and public utilities . . . and banking, business tax, and antitrust plaintiffs' work. . . . The work for larger business corporations appears to be concentrated higher on the right side of the U, and the size of the businesses represented decreases as one moves down. . . . Criminal prosecution, obviously sui generis, is off by itself. Though criminal prosecutors represent a corporate client, the substance of their work and perhaps the networks of relationships among practitioners move criminal prosecution away from the corporate fields and toward the "personal plight" group. Returning to the rim of the U, and still proceeding clockwise, we next find the four fields of the"personal business" group. Of these, the two that deal most with the transmission of wealth and thus with wealthier personal clients — probate and personal tax — lie nearest the corporate fields. Finally, at the upper left of the U, we find four of the five fields of the "personal plight" group. The fifth, civil rights, is a special case. Because half of its practitioners are full-time government employees, we could in fact define civil rights work as a governmental function and place the field in the "political" group of the corporate sector, which is about where it appears in the figure.

These findings suggest that even though the measures used to determine the characteristics of the fields of law (principally, the twenty-five percent time criterion) generate rather weak or contaminated categories, the variables display a consistent structure based primarily on the nature of the clients served by the fields. Because particular types of clients are frequently associated with corresponding types of legal issues, however, it is often difficult to determine whether some aspect of the structure of the fields of law is more plausibly attributed to the nature of the clients served or to the knowledge or skills used in the fields. . . .

To attempt to distinguish the independent effects of client type and of knowledge base on the structure of the fields would, in such circumstances, be not only difficult but artificial and misleading. We should, instead, appreciate that the two are inextricably entwined and then seek to understand their relationship and how the legal and social systems produced it. . . .

Again, therefore, we conclude that the most plausible interpretation of the findings is that the nature of the clients served by the fields primarily determines the fields' social structure. If correct, this reading of the data raises an important question: given the tendency of the profession's structure to respond to interests and demands of clients — that is, of parties external to the profession — how much autonomy does the legal profession enjoy in defining professional roles, in determining which lawyers will perform which services for which clients, and in organizing the delivery of those services? . . .

VI. CONCLUSION

A crucial issue in the study of any profession is this: To what extent does the profession manifest client interests (or, perhaps, the interests of others outside the profession) and to what extent does it reflect its own concerns, interests, or values? Common lore says that lawyers are "hired guns," that within the vague limits of "professional responsibility" they do their clients' bidding. But the lore also holds that some forces or agencies within the legal profession serve to unify it, to give it a sense of identity or coherence. Thus, the bar associations, the law schools, or the court-appointed boards that control lawyer discipline and admission to the bar may be thought to create or enforce norms and values that originate within the profession. How accurate is the lore? Or, to put the same question in a manner that more clearly restates the research issue posed at the beginning of this paragraph, what balance does the legal profession strike between competing intra-professional and extra-professional interests?

As our statement of the question implies, the issue is one of degree. Every profession reflects to some extent the economic, social, and ideological interests of its clients. All the professions also reflect norms and values of the professionals *qua* professionals — tenets that spring from the profession's own interests, ideology, and socialization process. To varying degrees and in varying ways in the different professions, the professionals sometimes speak for themselves and at other times advocate the interests of persons or groups outside the profession. Beyond their "hired gun" role (but by no means unrelated to it), lawyers and other professionals may adopt their clients' views and, thus advocate client interests because they have accepted them as their own. A cancer specialist may campaign for the control of environmental carcinogens even though a successful campaign might reduce the number of his patients. A tax lawyer may seek to simplify the tax code even though simplicity would reduce the demand for his professional advice. (If our study is correct, however, a lawyer is not likely to advocate the abolition of a tax shelter if that would conflict with his client's interests.) Though we did not attempt it, one way to assess the relative importance to a profession of internal and external interests might be to examine the frequency with which the professionals advocate each sort of interest.

Professions may reflect this co-existence of interests, however, in a more subtle, but perhaps more fundamental manner. The interests may affect the social structure of the profession itself — they will influence the organization of the bar into groups or fields, the distribution of lawyers from different social origins among those groups, and the patterns of relationships among the lawyers. External influences that may shape the legal profession's social structure include the interests of clients and the baggage that the professionals bring with them into the profession. The attitudes and behavior of professionals as professionals are, no doubt, affected by their other roles — as spouses, parents, churchmen, Daughters of the American Revolution, or Sons of Italy (*i.e.*, as clansmen or Klansmen). The early socialization of professionals may also be relevant to their professions, as may their commitments to religious, political, or social values.

But what is the relevance of our findings to these issues, and what are their implications for the profession? Our findings suggest that the second piece of lore is wrong. Bar associations, law schools, and court agencies appear to accomplish little social integration of the profession. Even the organized bar functions less as an interest group than as a forum within which interest groups compete for power. Unless some coalition within the bar can mobilize powerful constituencies, often from outside the bar, and can thus impose its will on the profession as a whole, the profession is unlikely to take a definite stand on a consequential issue. The legal profession can and does take definite stands, however, on issues that lack moment for most of the profession and most of its clients, and the organized bar often delegates such decisions to the concerned subgroup within the profession. In sum, the profession is so riven by conflict — reflecting the conflicting interests of its clients — that the bar can reach a consensus only on inconsequential issues or on symbolic issues that permit the profession's differences to be "papered-over."

The data that we have collected and analyzed suggest that the legal profession is highly differentiated, that that differentiation is systematically structured, and that that structure is determined largely by the impact of client interests. As we noted above, autonomy is said to be one of the characteristics that distinguishes the professions from other occupations.

Except to the extent that lawyers' clients are lawyers themselves (corporate house counsel, for instance), the dominance of the profession by its clients deprives lawyers of this autonomy. If nonprofessionals control the work of lawyers and thus determine the profession's social organization, the profession will lack the power to draw the boundaries that separate lawyers' work from that of other occupations (to define "unauthorized practice of law"), to set standards of professional conduct, and thus to control the course of the profession. In sum, the influence of client interests may threaten the profession's coherence and identity. If clients' interests rather than professional norms determine the attitudes and behavior of lawyers, the profession will tend to fragment — the social integration of the profession will suffer. . . . [W]e believe that our research provides substantial evidence that sharp, systematically structured divisions exist within the profession.

Notes and Questions

1. Heinz and Laumann's study discloses the tight parallel between social stratification in the legal profession and in the larger society. Access to law school, and therefore ultimately the legal profession, is now mediated by the Law School Admission Test (LSAT). This "objectified" assessment of aptitude for law study has been believed to filter out social distinctions so that entry into the profession becomes solely meritocratic. Some research suggests, however, that the process has *not* been freed of social bias:

> A 1973 ETS [Education Testing Service] study by Franklin Evans and Donald Rock . . . analyzed the scores and backgrounds of incoming students at eight law schools. The LSAT distinguished not only rich and poor, but also rich and middle class. Students of "high" socioeconomic status had a mean LSAT score about forty points higher than those of "average" background who in turn ranked higher than the "low" status students by about thirty points.
>
> Evans and Rock also found scores to be related to an aspect of the candidate's personality, their test anxiety. . . . When the effects of social class and anxiety were combined, the impact was considerable: low-income people with high test anxiety received an average LSAT of 505; high income people with low anxiety averaged 622.*

Ronald Pipkin reported that even when students' LSAT scores, college grade-point averages, and quality of undergraduate college attended were comparable, social factors influenced the allocation of students to law schools of differing status. With seven law schools classified in three categories of prestige and quality (I being highest), Pipkin found:

---

*Allan Nairn and Associates, *The Reign of ETS* (Washington, D.C.: The Ralph Nader Report on the Educational Testing Service, 1980), pp. 222–223.

> Within the same levels of academic background, women were about forty percent less likely than men to attend a school in stratum I versus stratum II or stratum III. Catholics were forty-eight percent less likely than Protestants and sixty-four percent less likely than Jews to attend a school in stratum I versus stratum II. . . . Those of the highest socio-economic class were forty to sixty percent more likely than students from the other three social groups to attend a school in stratum I instead of a school in stratum II or stratum III. In other words, the "inside tracks" to stratum I schools were largely awarded to those with the highest academic qualifications from high-status colleges. However, once the field was thereby narrowed, the advantages went to males from the highest social class backgrounds who were Jewish or Protestant.†

On the point that the status of law school attended has a strong effect on the status of law practice, Frances Kahn Zemans and Victor G. Rosenblum found in their study of the practicing bar in Chicago (*The Making of a Public Profession* [Chicago: American Bar Foundation, 1981]) that 73 percent of all lawyers in Chicago's largest law firms (over fifty members) were graduates of only twelve national law schools — Harvard, Yale, Columbia, Chicago, Michigan, Northwestern, Georgetown, New York University, Pennsylvania, Stanford, Virginia, and Wisconsin — only two of which were located in Chicago. In contrast, solo practitioners came primarily from four local law schools — Loyola, IIT-Kent, DePaul, and John Marshall.

2. In Heinz and Laumann's view, the structure of the legal profession is determined by its relationship with those who purchase its services. Yet the legal profession is often called a *public* profession, by which is meant that collectively lawyers first serve the public good — they are the keepers of the society's laws and institutions of justice. Can the idea of a public service profession be maintained if Heinz and Laumann are correct?
3. Heinz and Laumann seem to assume the relationship of lawyers to clients is merely one of satisfying clients' needs. Contrast that assumption to the common public view that "[l]awyers . . . create the circumstances under which their knowledge and skill are needed. . . ."‡ What does it means for the lawyer-client relationship if clients see lawyers as *causing* their problems? What might Tocqueville have said about this idea?

†Ronald Pipkin, study referenced in "Entropy and Skewness in the Allocation of Students to Law Schools," *Washington University Law Quarterly* 59, no. 3(1981).

‡Gordon Horobin, "Professional Mystery: The Maintenance of Charisma in General Medical Practice," In Robert Dingwall and Philip Lewis, eds., *The Sociology of the Professions: Lawyers, Doctors and Others* (London: Macmillan, 1983), p. 94.

2 THE EDUCATION OF LAWYERS

You are sitting, let us say, in a class in Contracts, or Personal Property, or Domestic Relations. John Smith in the third row is reciting on a case, and has got the facts confused, or he has misread the Restatement section in the footnote. A dozen hands are up, and a dozen eager faces reflect the desire to close in for the kill. The professor delays the moment of slaughter and deliberately passes over the volunteer matadors in order to call on Dick Jones in the tenth row. The professor knows from previous experience that he can count on Jones not only to set Smith right, but to introduce a new misconception that will transfer the error to a still deeper level of confusion. Jones performs according to expectation. More hands go up as more of the class come to share the illumination, taking it either from an inner flame or from the whispered coachings of neighbors. The whole discussion is lively and stimulating; everyone is put on his mettle and seeks to show his best capacities.

Lon L. Fuller, "On Teaching Law," *Stanford Law Review* (1950)

Students learn from the emotional content of the law curriculum that they ought to distrust their own deepest moral sensibilities; that they ought to avoid global moral and political inquiry (because it is dangerous, simplistic, and unlawyerlike); that they ought to revere hierarchy; and that manipulating vulnerable people is an acceptable form of professional behavior.

Karl E. Klare, "The Law-School Curriculum in the 1980s: What's Left?" *Journal of Legal Education* (1982)

Law schools are the gatekeepers for the legal profession. For those who aspire to be lawyers but are financially unresourceful or academically uncompetitive, like Kafka's guard, law schools are the barrier to law. To those aspirants allowed to pass, law schools are the profession's initiation — a rite of passage all lawyers share, a basis of community.

The purpose of law school is to change people, to make them different because of the experience — to transform them from laypeople into novice lawyers. Law school provides them with some competence in legal rules and legal problem solving. It instills in them a nascent self-concept as a professional, a commitment to the values of the calling, and a claim to that elusive and esoteric style of reasoning called "thinking like a lawyer."

Many issues have been raised about the quality, substance, and effects of legal education. People have challenged whether this education actually teaches students how to practice law (would you allow a doctor to operate on you if you knew his or her only training was reading books on surgery?), and whether it is morally numbing (Watergate and all that) or unnecessarily harsh (a world of Professor Kingsfields from Jay Osborne's *Paper Chase*).

The readings here are directed toward some of those issues. But the major themes explore the ways in which law school education inculcates in the lawyer novitiate the profession's values and sustains the profession's hierarchies.

The Trouble with Law School *Scott Turow*

The professor stands in the center of the room, and the students — one hundred of them or more — are seated in tiers that rise steeply above him. Suddenly, the professor will call out a name, chosen at random from the seating chart he has before him. "Mr. Jones," the professor will say, "state the case."

Slowly, Jones will describe the facts and issues of a dispute that has come before an appeals court somewhere in the English-speaking countries, usually in the United States. At moments, the professor will interrupt Jones, pressing the student to make his answers clearer, his reasoning more precise. Just how was the contract breached? What part of the agreement was most essential to the court in reaching its findings? Often the professor will add remarks of his own. Then he will choose another student, Ms. Green. She will be asked to state the next case, and, more important, to compare it with the case Jones described. In what ways are the facts and results of the two cases similar? In what ways are they distinct? What consistent principles seem to emerge in the comparison? And in their seats the other students will sit, intent, listening to these dialogues. Now and then, a few of the others will venture questions or comments of their own. But for the most part, they will answer only in their own minds the questions Jones and Green are asked. They will make occasional notes. They will feel acutely anxious every time the professor returns to the seating chart to select a new student to interrogate. They are learning the law.

For a hundred years it has been this way for American law students: the professorial inquisitions called "the Socratic method," the deduction of legal principles from a tireless comparison of case after case. There are variations from the pattern I describe, often significant ones; but since the case and Socratic methods were first developed in the 1870s at Harvard Law School, under the guidance of Dean Christopher Columbus Langdell, the pedagogy of American law schools has remained remarkably uniform and fixed. Today, the methods of Dean Langdell predominate at virtually every law school in the country — no less so at Harvard, where they were initially practiced, and where I entered as a first-year law student in the fall of 1975.

Traditionally, the first year of legal education is the most dramatic of law school's three years. The curriculum of the first year has become as well established in the past century as the teaching methods. Nearly all of the 40,000 young Americans who begin their legal educations every fall are required, as I was, to take what are generally thought of as the basic subjects — contracts, torts, property, the criminal law, and civil procedure. And for all of them, the effects of that education are thought to be equally predictable and far-reaching. It is during the first year that law students learn to read a case, to frame a legal argument, to distinguish between seemingly undistinguishable ideas; then that you begin to absorb the mysterious language of the law, full of words like "estoppel" and "replevin." It is during the first year, according to a saying, that a law student learns "to think like a lawyer," to develop the habits of mind and world perspective that will stay with him or her throughout a legal career.

For me my first year of law school at Harvard was a time of extraordinary intellectual excitement. But it was also a period when I came to recognize and regret many of the shortcomings of the peculiar educational system that has been so long employed in preparing young Americans for the bar. Certainly doubts about legal education are not original with me. For about a decade now, law students and young lawyers have been raising questions about the way in which they were trained, and the complaints that my classmates and I made were more or less the same as those that have been heard for years: that law classes are too large — they keep tuition low but leave students feeling anonymous and lonely; that the professors are too remote — brilliant men and women but often startlingly aloof; that Socratic inquisition, which comes without warning and forces students to perform before their peers, is anxiety-provoking and sometimes brutal in its results.

But the most serious and persistent criticism I heard was less specific, since it seemed to call into question the aims of legal education itself. By the middle of my first term of law school, I'd begun to hear from classmates (and feel myself) strong objections to the process of learning to think like a lawyer.

The first complaints began after about a month of school. Nicky Morris, the young professor who taught us civil procedure, had spoken in class about the education we were undergoing.

"Right now," he told us, "you have probably begun to recognize that going to law school involves learning a lot of legal rules, and you'll find pretty quickly that there's quite a premium placed on mastering the rules and knowing how to apply them. But in learning rules, don't feel like you've got to forsake a sense of moral scrutiny. The law in almost all its phases is a reflection of competing value systems. Don't feel because you're learning the rule, you've necessarily taken on the values that produced the rule in the first place."

The remark struck a number of my classmates, and as we left class for lunch, I talked about what Nicky had said with one of them, Gina Spitz. Gina came on as the last of the tough cookies. She'd just graduated from Barnard and she was full of the bristle of New York City. She was big, fiesty, outspoken and glitteringly bright. But Nicky's words had touched her in a way that left her sounding plaintive.

"They're making me different," she said, referring to our professors. "They're turning me into someone else, someone I don't want to be. I have the feeling all the time that I'm being indoctrinated."

As I listened to Gina that day, and judging from other remarks, I decided that she'd articulated feelings that seemed to have become common to many of the first-year students. On the one hand, the problem was as simple as the way Morris had put it. Some of us felt we were being forced to identify with rules and social notions with which we didn't really agree. In Contracts, for instance, it had already become clear that our professor, Rudolph Perini, was an ardent free-market exponent. Perini quickly succeeded in showing us that many of the traditional contract rules reflected free-market assumptions. When he threw the floor open for comment about whether those free-market rules were desirable or not, many students were reluctant to contest him. Perini was fearsome in debate and a renowned expert on contract law, and as a result many of us felt that we had no choice but to accept the logic of what Perini was saying, to take it as the law we would live and work with.

But there was a subtler difficulty in our education, one that went to the basis of legal thinking itself, and became especially apparent in class. We were learning more than a process of analysis or a set of rules. In our discussions with the professors, as they questioned us and picked at what we said, we were also being tacitly instructed in the strategies of legal argument, in putting what had been analyzed back together in a way that would make our contentions persuasive to a court. We all quickly saw that this kind of argument was supposed to be reasoned, consistent, progressive in its logic. Nothing was taken for granted; nothing was proven just because it was strongly felt. All of our teachers tried to impress upon us that you did not sway a judge with emotional declarations of faith. Nicky Morris often derided responses as "sentimental goo," and Perini on more than one occasion quickly dispatched those students who tried to argue by asserting supposedly irreducible principles.

Why, Perini asked one day, was the right to bargain and form contracts granted all adults, rather than a select group within the society?

Because that was fundamental, one student suggested, basic: all persons are created equal.

"Oh *are* they?" Perini asked. "Did you create them, Mr. Vivian? Have you taken a survey?"

"I believe it," Vivian answered.

"Well, hooray," said Perini, "that proves a great deal. How do you *justify* that, Mr. Vivian?"

The demand that we examine and justify our opinions was not always easily fulfilled. Many of the deepest beliefs often seemed inarticulable in their foundations, or sometimes contradictory to other strongly felt principles. I found that frequently. I thought, for example, that wealth should be widely distributed, but there were many instances presented in class that involved taking from the poor, where I felt that property rights should be regarded as absolute.

Yet with relative speed we all seemed to gain skill in reconciling and justifying our positions. In the fourth week of the term, Professor Bertram Mann, our criminal-law teacher, promoted a class debate on various schemes for regulating prostitution, and I noticed the differences in style of argument from similar sessions we'd had earlier in the year. Students now spoke about crime statistics and patterns of violence in areas where prostitution occurred. They pointed to evidence and avoided emotional appeals and arguments based on the depth and longevity of their feelings.

But to students like Gina, the process that had produced this kind of change was frightening.

"I don't care if Bertram Mann doesn't want to know how I *feel* about prostitution," she said at lunch that day. "I *feel* a lot of things about prostitution and they have everything to do with the way I *think* about prostitution. I don't want to become the kind of person who tries to pretend that my feelings have nothing to do with my opinions. It's not *bad* to feel things."

The deepest fear among us seemed to be the one Gina expressed — that, somehow, deep personal changes were being forced upon us by the process of legal education. More and more often as the year wore on, I would hear comments from classmates to the effect that we were being limited, harmed by the education, forced to substitute dry reason for emotion, to cultivate opinions that were "rational" but had no roots in the experience, the life we'd had before. We were being cut away from ourselves, we felt. And thus, more and more often I would scrutinize myself for the signs of those unwanted changes. On occasion I would find them.

At home, for instance, my wife, Annette, told me that I had started to "lawyer" her when we quarreled, badgering and cross-examining her much as the professors did students in class. And there seemed to me other habits to be wary of. It was a grimly literal, linear, step-by-step process of thought that we were learning. The kind of highly structured problem-solving method taught in each class, that business of sorting through the initial details of a case and then moving outward toward the broadest implications, was an immensely useful technical skill, but I feared it would calcify my approach to other subjects. And besides rigidity, there was a sort of mood to legal thinking that I found plainly unattractive.

"Legal thinking is nasty," I said to Gina at one point in our conversation, and I began to think later I'd hit on a substantial truth. Thinking like a lawyer involved being suspicious and distrustful. You re-evaluated statements, inferred from silences, looked for loopholes and ambiguities. You did everything but take a statement at face value.

So on one hand you believed nothing. And on the other, for the sake of logical consistency, and to preserve long-established rules, you would accept the most ridiculous fictions — that a corporation was a person, that an apartment tenant was renting land and not a dwelling.

In time I began to recognize that all of

these smaller complaints about rigidity, emotional suffocation, the tortured logic of the law were part of a more fundamental phenomenon in the law itself. Law is at war with ambiguity, with uncertainty. In the courtroom, the adversary system — plaintiff against defendant — guarantees that someone will always win, someone lose. No matter if justice is evenly with each side, no matter if the issues are indefinite and obscure, the rule of law will be declared. The law and the arbitrary certainty of some of its results are no doubt indispensable for the secure operation of a society where there is ceaseless conflict requiring resolution.

But a lot of those attitudes toward certainty seem to rub off on the institutions of legal education, which show a similar seeking after sureness and definition, a desire to subdue the random element. The structure of classroom relations is an example, with all power and control vested in the professor. Yet it is hardly clear that the need that supports the customs of the courtroom is present in class. Not even the law can abolish the fundamental unclearness of many human situations, but in the law schools there is precious little effort to address the degree to which human choice is arbitrary. We are taught instead that there is always a reason, always a rationale, always an argument. And too much of that amounts to a tacit tutoring of students in strategies for avoiding, for ignoring, for somehow subverting the unquantifiable, the inexact, the emotionally charged, those things that still pass in my mind under the label "human." Eventually, I came to regard that kind of schooling not merely as objectionable, but even as inappropriate in light of the ultimate purposes of legal education — the fact that as future lawyers, my classmates and I were training to become the persons on whom this society rests the chief responsibility for making and doing justice.

Notes and Questions

1. Law school teaching uses two techniques, the Socratic dialogue and the case method. In this pedagogic combination a teacher intensively interrogates individual students concerning the facts and principles presumed to be operative in an appellate opinion. The method is intended to accomplish two goals. The first is informational: instruction in the substantive rules of discrete bodies of law. The second is to develop in the student a cognitive restructuring for the style of analysis generally called "thinking like a lawyer." In that analysis, a student is trained to account for the factual minutiae as well as for the legal issues determined by the court to be at the core of the dispute, that may allow an intelligent prediction of what another court would do with a similar set of facts. The technique is learner-centered: students are closely questioned and the teacher often takes their responses to further direct the dialogue.

   One student described the dialogue from the student's perspective as follows:

   > Even knowing all the answers affords scant protection against the awful moment when you are plucked from the sea of faces and forced to perform. As you sit drowning in adrenaline, rational thought becomes impossible. Facts are forgotten or jumbled together. Basic principles of coherent sentence structure and logical argument are irretrievably lost. Answers that would be brilliant in any other context fall flat. Creativity is strictly taboo. Each response must be carefully tailored to the demands of the question. Too complete an answer can be as damaging as none at all. Law professors jump at each opportunity for sarcasm or outright cruelty. It's not that they are sadistic. They're simply indifferent. It doesn't matter that some students cry or vomit or pass out in class. How else will they learn?*

   This teaching method has been at the center of much criticism of law education. Paul Savoy, in a frequently cited article, compared the pedagogy to game playing:

   > The Socratic method . . . consists largely of a set of "games," the most popular of which is "Corner." . . . The objective in each case is to drive the student into a corner by refuting any position he takes. In being

*Victoria Steinberg, "Why I Quit Law School," *College Digest* (Spring 1982): 7A.

> presented with . . . a Socratic question, the student is cast on the horns of a dilemma: he is made to feel that there is some answer he must find, but in seeking it out, he begins to despair of finding it because everything he says is rejected as wrong. . . .
>
> A variation of the game of "Corner" is "One-Up":
>
> Student: "Do you think that custodial interrogation in the absence of counsel is a violation of the dignity of the individual?"
>
> Teacher: "What do you mean by 'dignity'?" . . .
>
> Then there is the familiar "chamber of horrors" gambit — the logical paradigm of which is the *reductio ad absurdum* argument — or what I prefer to call the game of "Now I've Got You, You Son-of-a-Bitch." By the time a law student reaches his second year, he knows the game and either stops playing it, plays along cynically, or initiates the counter-game of "Wooden Leg" ("What can you expect of a 'dumb' student like me"). . . . Another popular pastime of professors that often passes for Socratic dialogue is the game of "Guess What I'm Thinking"; the student counter-game is "Mindreading I, II or III," depending on the number of previous courses the student has had with the professor.†

Andrew Watson, a psychiatrist and law professor, sees the pedagogy of law education as causing students to lose their willingness to care about other people:

> It is my contention that law school education explicitly shapes the character development of law students in certain ways which are detrimental to efficient professional performance. The character adaptation is necessary in order to resolve and escape the tensions of the classroom. The principle [*sic*] characterological development change is to become "unemotional." In addition to being told that this is a desirable attribute to develop, it is also a reaction to classroom anxiety. . . . Marked stoicism and emotional unresponsiveness may be regarded as characterological defenses against underlying emotions. Intellectual means in the form of cynicism about the human aspect of the lawyer's role may also be used to accomplish this purpose. This cynicism is a kind of characterological defense which enables a person to avoid the necessity of caring about people with its intrinsic capacity to stir up anxiety.‡

Robert Nagel§ provides the common justification of the Socratic method:

> Many students see their teachers as a self-selected group of the meanest of the legal profession, a group that seems to get a personal thrill out of brow beating students. Every reasonable answer begets just another question, and it is frustrating and embarrassing to be put on the spot. But to conclude, because of such feelings, that the teacher is trying to hurt is for the student to confuse his personal reactions with the motive of the professor. It is to ignore the teacher as a person in his own right, with his own objectives. The teacher's aim is to enable the student to respond under pressure, even in situations where at first the student thinks he has no response. The objective is to encourage the student to think and communicate even more precisely and effectively than he thought he could. Law students are in training to be professional advocates and counselors. For a professional, arguments cannot be merely adequate or normal or bright. Lawyers are paid to be always clear and sometimes moving and brilliant in their communications; they must meet this professional obligation even when they feel embarrassed, even when they are distracted, even when at first they think they have no response.

Alan Stone, a psychiatrist and law teacher,

†Paul Savoy, "Toward a New Politics of Legal Education," *Yale Law Journal* 79 (1970): 457–459.

‡Andrew Watson, "The Quest for Professional Competence: Psychological Aspects of Legal Education," *University of Cincinnati Law Review* 37 (1968): 131.

§Robert F. Nagel, "Invisible Teachers: A Comment on Perceptions in the Classroom," *Journal of Legal Education* 32 (1982): 359. Reprinted by permission of the author.

responded to law education's critics as follows:

> Despite its admitted potential for destructive interaction, Socratic dialogue also has enormous value in channeling group emotions into structural academic inquiry. As individuals vie for status during the period when a group evolves into a coherent entity the entire gamut of intense feelings and personal motivations, including a certain amount of free floating hostility, is inevitably generated. . . . What the Socratic technique can do at its best is to channel the inevitable hostility into the academic inquiry. Most professors do not allow one student to become the constant target, nor do they accept the role of target themselves; rather, the ritual has evolved such that hopefully a student's ideas rather than the student are the impersonal target; at worst, a number of students in turn will be the focus. . . . Its functional value is, however, that group hostility is controlled, and the class knows that the teacher's authority — in this context his capacity to control group hostility and other emotional excesses — is unquestioned.‖

Lastly, from another section of Scott Turow's book, a student's remark:

> At moments during the year, it sometimes appeared to me that my female classmates were not themselves entirely comfortable with the open aggression that law and law school demanded. In class, they tended to be retiring. . . . Moreover, if I could believe Gina, many of the women were sometimes even more uncomfortable than the men when they were called on.
>
> "I know how this sounds," she told me once, "but a lot of the women say the same thing. When I get called on, I really think about rape. It's sudden. You're exposed. You can't move. You can't say no. And there's this man who's in control, telling you exactly what to do. Maybe that's melodramatic," she said, "but for me, a lot of the stuff in class shows up all kinds of male/female power relations that I've sort of been training myself to resent."#

That the Socratic dialogue provokes anxiety, hostility, and aggression seems to be generally agreed on. Savoy's analogy to game playing and Watson's observation that students are encouraged to become unemotional suggests an important part of law training is to develop in novice lawyers a sense of detachment from the emotion-laden fray. Stone and the student focused on the domination by the law teacher as authority figure, suggesting that another aspect of the training is to enforce a respect for authoritative power. What are the implications of such training for the roles these new lawyers are ultimately to fill? Should the nonprofessional population — both lawyers' clients and members of society generally — be concerned about the psychological aspects of law education?

2. The process of taking on professional attitudes and identity, called professional socialization by sociologists, can be traumatic. The following is a quote from a first-year law student:

> In my two and a half months here I have felt myself deteriorate mentally, emotionally and spiritually. My high level of self-confidence and self-pride that I carried with me is gone. For the first time in any academic or intellectual phases of my life I feel completely inadequate and find myself losing sleep. I am unable to communicate with former friends of mine from college who are not in law school. Law school has made me a miserable person and the worst thing about it is that I can sense it happening. I had quite a creative talent when I came here; I feel I have lost it. I had quite a flair with the subject matter of my undergraduate major. I find it inapplicable now. It is necessary that I am doing this to myself? How much longer will I last? Does anybody in this law school care?**

‖Alan Stone, "Legal Education on the Couch," *Harvard Law Review* 85 (1971): 412–413.

#Selections from *One L* by Scott Turow. Copyright © 1977 by Scott Turow. Reprinted by permission of Farrar, Straus and Giroux, Inc.

**Ronald M. Pipkin, "Legal Education: The Consumers' Perspective," *American Bar Foundation Research Journal* 1976, no. 4 (1976): 1191.

This experience is largely a phenomenon of the first year in law school. The intensity of the experience diminishes as students adopt the accepted style of thinking, develop coping devices (academic ploys as suggested by Savoy, or psychological defenses as Watson noted), and class rank becomes established through the first battery of examinations.

3. Wilbert Moore, a well-known sociologist of professions, has developed a theory of professional training called "punishment-centered socialization," which casts law school education in a somewhat different light. He notes that suffering is a prominent component in the training of all developed professions. The training includes hazing, demands that are "unpleasant and even hazardous to . . . good standing," and "challenging and painful experiences." These experiences are shared with other initiates "who thus have a sort of fellowship of suffering."

He concludes that occupational identity and commitment are proportional to the degree that initiates are compelled to suffer, have a realistic fear of failure, have acceptable role models available, and develop collective bonds based on hardships.††

In Moore's view, the greater the amount of suffering and mortification in professional preparation, the more likely students are to take on the proffered professional identities and values. Even if this analysis correctly describes the collective experience of students in law school, the reader should not be left with the impression that all students suffer the education, do not find excitement, or have traumatic anxieties. The degree of personal turmoil for any individual is likely tied to the resistance of that person's "home culture" and its distance from the institutionally accepted culture.

††See Wilbert E. Moore, *The Professions: Roles and Rules* (New York: Russell Sage Foundation, 1970), pp. 76–79.

☐ The readings from Mills and from Heinz and Laumann have provided a view of the legal profession as fragmented by client constituency and hierarchically structured by the social and educational backgrounds of lawyers. But how did lawyers move into these strata and practices? How is the hierarchy in the legal profession reproduced over time? Legal education is a generalist's education, covering both of Heinz and Laumann's legal hemispheres with some comprehensiveness. Law schools may be distinguished from each other by the academic qualifications of their students, but there is little difference in their curricula. Elite law schools offer courses in family and criminal law, and local law schools offer courses in corporate financing and international law (even though few, if any, of their respective graduates are likely ever to practice in these areas). Given a law education curriculum that seems to hold the whole panoply of professional careers open, what role, if any, do law schools play in reproducing the profession's hierarchy? In the following reading, Duncan Kennedy, a controversial member of the Harvard Law School faculty, suggests some answers.

Legal Education and the Reproduction of Hierarchy *Duncan Kennedy*

One can distinguish in a rough way between two aspects of legal education as a reproducer of hierarchy. A lot of what happens is the inculcation through the formal curriculum and the classroom experience of a set of political attitudes toward the economy and society in general, toward law, and toward the possibilities of life in the profession. These have a general ideological significance, and they have an impact on the lives even of law students who never practice law. Then there is a complicated set of institutional practices that orient students to willing participation in the specialized hierarchical roles of lawyers. In order to understand these, one must have at least a rough conception of what the world of practice is like.

Students begin to absorb the more general ideological message before they have much in the way of a conception of life after law school, so I will describe this formal aspect of the educational process first. I will then try to sketch in the realities of professional life that students gradually learn about in the second and third year, before describing the way in which the institutional practices of law schools bear on those realities. . . .

THE FORMAL CURRICULUM: LEGAL RULES AND LEGAL REASONING

The intellectual core of the ideology is the distinction between law and policy. Teachers convince students that legal reasoning exists, and is different from policy analysis, by bullying them into accepting as valid in particular cases arguments about legal correctness that are circular, questionbegging, incoherent, or so vague as to be meaningless. Sometimes these are just arguments from authority, with the validity of the authoritative premise put outside discussion by professorial fiat. Sometimes they are policy arguments (security of transaction, business certainty) that are treated in a particular situation as though they were rules that everyone accepts, but that will be ignored in the next case when they would suggest that the decision was wrong. Sometimes they are exercises in formal logic that wouldn't stand up for a minute in a discussion between equals. . . .

Within a given subfield, the teacher is likely to treat cases in three different ways. There are the cases that present and justify the basic rules and basic ideas of the field. These are treated as cursory exercises in legal logic. Then there are cases that are anomalous — sometimes they are "outdated," sometimes "wrongly decided" because they don't follow the supposed inner logic of the area. There won't be many of these, but they are important because their treatment persuades students that the technique of legal reasoning is at least minimally independent of the results reached by particular judges, is capable of criticizing as well as legitimating.

Finally, there will be an equally small number of peripheral or "cutting edge" cases the teacher sees as raising policy issues about growth or change in the law. Whereas in discussing the first two kinds of cases the teacher behaves in an authoritarian way supposedly based on his objective knowledge of the technique of legal reasoning, here everything is different. Because we are dealing with "value judgments" that have "political" overtones, the discussion will be much more free-wheeling. Rather than every student comment being right or wrong, all student comments get pluralist acceptance, and the teacher will reveal himself to be either a liberal or a conservative, rather than merely a legal technician.

The curriculum as a whole has a rather similar structure. It is not really a random assortment of tubs on their own bottoms, a forest of tubs. First, there are contracts, torts, property, criminal law and civil procedure. The rules in these courses are the ground-rules of late nineteenth century laissez-faire capitalism. Teachers teach them as though they had an

---

Abridged from *Legal Education and the Reproduction of Hierarchy: A Polemic Against the System* (Cambridge, Mass.: Afar, 1983). Reprinted with permission of the author.

inner logic, as an exercise in legal reasoning with policy (e.g., promissory estoppel in the contracts course) playing a relatively minor role.

Then there are second and third year courses that expound the moderate reformist program of the New Deal and the administrative structure of the modern regulatory state (with passing reference to the racial egalitarianism of the Warren Court). These courses are more policy oriented than first year courses, and also much more ad hoc. Teachers teach students that limited interference with the market makes sense, and is as authoritatively grounded in statutes as the ground rules of laissez faire are grounded in natural law. But each problem is discrete, enormously complicated, and understood in a way that guarantees the practical impotence of the reform program.

Finally, there are peripheral subjects, like legal philosophy or legal history, legal process, clinical legal education. These are presented as not truly relevant to the "hard" objective, serious, rigorous analytic core of law. They are a kind of playground or a finishing school for learning the social art of self-presentation as a lawyer.

This whole body of implicit messages is nonsense. Legal reasoning is not distinct, *as a method for reaching correct results,* from ethical and political discourse in general (i.e., from policy analysis). It is true that there is a distinctive lawyers' body of knowledge of the rules in force. It is true that there are distinctive lawyers' argumentative techniques for spotting gaps, conflicts and ambiguities in the rules, for arguing broad and narrow holdings of cases, and for generating pro and con policy arguments. But these are *only* argumentative techniques. There is never a "correct legal solution" that is other than the correct ethical and political solution to that legal problem.

Put another way, everything taught, except the formal rules themselves and the argumentative techniques for manipulating them, is policy and nothing more. It follows that the classroom distinction between the unproblematic legal case and the policy oriented case is a mere artifact: each could as well be taught in the opposite way. And the curricular distinction between the "nature" of contract law as highly legal and technical by contrast, say, with environmental law, is equally a mystification.

These errors have a bias in favor of the center-liberal program of limited reform of the market economy and pro forma gestures toward racial and sexual equality. The bias arises because law school teaching makes the choice of hierarchy and domination, which is implicit in the adoption of the rules of property, contract and tort, look as though it flows from legal reasoning, rather than from politics and economics. The bias is reenforced when the center-liberal reformist program of regulation is presented as equally authoritative, but somehow more policy oriented, and therefore less fundamental. . . .

INCAPACITATION FOR ALTERNATIVE PRACTICE

Law schools channel their students into jobs in the hierarchy of the bar according to their own standing in the hierarchy of schools. Students confronted with the choice of what to do after they graduate experience themselves as largely helpless: they have no "real" alternative to taking a job in one of the conventional firms that hires from their school. Partly, faculties generate this sense of student helplessness by propagating myths about the character of the different kinds of practice. They extol the forms that are accessible to their students; they subtly denigrate or express envy about the jobs that will be beyond their students' reach; they dismiss as ethically and socially suspect the jobs their students won't have to take.

As for any form of work outside the established system — for example, legal services for the poor, and neighborhood law practice — they convey to students that, although morally exalted, the work is hopelessly dull and unchallenging, and that the possibilities of reaching a standard of living appropriate to a lawyer are slim or non-existent. These messages are just nonsense — the rationalizations of law teachers who long [to move] upward, fear status degradation, and above all hate the idea of risk. Legal services practice, for example, is far more intellectually stimulating and demanding, even with a high case load, than most of what corporate lawyers do. It is also more fun.

Beyond this dimension of professional mythology, law schools act in more concrete ways to guarantee that their students will fit themselves into their appropriate niches in the existing system of practice. First, the actual content of what is taught in a given school will incapacitate students from any other form of practice than that allotted graduates of that institution. This looks superficially like a rational adaptation to the needs of the market, but it is in fact almost entirely unnecessary. Law schools teach so little, and that so incompetently, that they cannot, as now constituted, prepare students for more than one career at the bar. But the reason for this is that they embed skills training in mystificatory nonsense, and devote most of their teaching time to transmitting masses of ill-digested rules. A more rational system would emphasize the way to learn law, rather than rules, and skills rather than answers. Student capacities would be more equal as a result, but students would also be much more flexible in what they could do in practice.

A second incapacitating device is the teaching of doctrine in isolation from practice skills. Students who have no practice skills tend to exaggerate how difficult it is to acquire them. There is a distinct lawyers' mystique of the irrelevance of the "theoretical" material learned in school, and of the crucial importance of abilities that cannot be known or developed until one is out in the "real world," "on the firing line" and "in the trenches." Students have little alternative to getting training in this dimension of things after law school. If you have any choice in the matter, it will seem impractical to think about setting up your own law firm, and only a little less impractical to go to a small or political or unconventional firm rather than to one of those that offers the standard package of post-graduate education. Law schools are wholly responsible for this situation. They could quite easily revamp their curricula so that any student who wanted it would have a meaningful choice between independence and servility.

A third form of incapacitation is more subtle. Law school, as an extension of the educational system as a whole, teaches students that they are weak, lazy, incompetent and insecure. And it also teaches them that if they are fortunate, and willing to accept dependency, large institutions will take care of them almost no matter what. The terms of the bargain are relatively clear. The institution will set limited, cognizable tasks, and specify minimum requirements in their performance. The student/associate has no other responsibilities than performance of those tasks. The institution takes care of all the contingencies of life, both within the law (supervision and back up from other firm members; firm resources and prestige to bail you out if you make a mistake) and in private life (firms offer money, but also long term job security and delicious benefits packages aimed to reduce risks of disaster). In exchange, you renounce any claim to control your work setting or the actual content of what you do, and agree to show the appropriate form of deference to those above you and condescension to those below.

By comparison, the alternatives are risky. Law school does not train you to run a small law business, to realistically assess the outcome of a complex process involving many different actors, or to enjoy the feeling of independence and moral integrity that comes of creating your own job to serve your own goals. It tries to persuade you that you are barely competent to perform the much more limited roles it allows you, and strongly suggests that it is more prudent to kiss the lash than to strike out on your own.

HIERARCHIES OF THE LEGAL PROFESSION

Throughout their legal education, students are engaged in reconceiving themselves and the legal profession. Partly this is an affair of knowledge. Students find out things about the bar and about themselves that they didn't know before, and the process has a direction — it is a process of loss, of possibilities foreclosed. Knowledge of professional life renders irrelevant capacities you have but will not be allowed to use. Newly discovered incapacities of the self make it impossible to play roles it was easy to fantasize as a college student.

To begin with, there is the fact that most law jobs, and almost all the jobs at the top of the hierarchy, consist of providing marginally important services to businesses in their dealings among themselves and with consumers and stray victims. Of the remaining jobs, the great majority involve trying to get money out of the business community in the form of compensation for injuries to individuals, or of arranging the private affairs of middle class or upper class people. The total number of jobs that directly serve the public interest is small, and the number of jobs that integrate law and left political action is tiny. The notion that lawyers as a group work at a profession which is intrinsically involved with justice, or that lawyers are at least on the front lines of class struggle, is one of the things that allows left students to resolve their ambivalence enough to go to law school. But in fact the profession is mainly engaged in greasing the wheels of the economy.

A second crucial piece of information is that this is partly drudge work, partly puzzle solving (with the narcotically fascinating and morally vacuous quality of, say, bridge), and partly a macho battle of wills in which all that counts is winning. Most of this work has no discernible moral spin to it, let alone a political spin. It is not that it is "evil," it is that it is socially inconsequential, even when you look at it in terms of the profession as a whole rather than in terms of individual lawyers. It is fulfilling to help people achieve their objectives (theirs, not yours), to exercise one's skills, to make money and be respected. That's it.

As dreams of pursuing careers that would be unambiguously good begin to fade, it becomes important that lawyers submit to hierarchy in concrete ways, as well as in the more abstract way of abandoning their hope of integrating their jobs and their politics. One will drudge, solve puzzles and fight the battle of wills in a law firm.

Many students have a clear sense of the hierarchical role of lawyers in society, but little sense of just how stratified is the bar itself. Getting into law school, or getting into an elite law school seems to parachute them beyond the land of struggle into a realm of assured superiority. They discover some of how wrong this is through the admissions process, which firmly establishes that law schools exist on a scale of rank which has its ambiguities but is unequivocal in its rejections. But it is still a shock that what your background is, where you went to law school, and how well you did seem to make an enormous difference to where you can get a job, what the actual content of your job will be, and what you can reasonably look forward to in the way of professional advancement over your whole career.

Law firms are ranked just as law schools are (with the same ambiguity and the same near finality). The lawyers in the "top" firms make more money, exercise more power and have more prestige than lawyers in the next rank, these lawyers lord it over those below them, and so forth to the bottom. The top firms have top clients, work in the top courts, have top office conditions, do more "challenging" work, and are less subject to all kinds of minor pains and humiliations than those lower down. . . .

The hierarchy of firms is based in part on the general class, sexual and racial structure of American society. There are lower middle class, middle class and upper middle class lawyers, and because they congregate in groups *mainly* according to class criteria, there are lower middle, middle and upper middle class law firms. In some, lawyers wear leisure suits, in others, three piece worsted suits. In some there are photographs of lawyers' sailboats on the office walls along with the diplomas; in others there are reproductions of seascapes bought by wives to brighten things up. There are regional accents, but also class accents; fancy colleges and unfancy colleges. There are few blacks anywhere to be seen. Women are underrepresented in the top firms; within those firms, they tend to do legal jobs with relatively low prestige (trusts and estates rather than litigation). In general, the legal universe just reproduces the society around it: most people live in homogeneous enclaves within which they rigidly observe the rituals and guard the prerogatives of their station, while vigorously denying that the concept of station has any relevance to their lives.

The hierarchy of firms is also in part a professional hierarchy. Lawyers in top firms went to higher ranked law schools and got better grades than lawyers in the next-to-top, and so through gradations to the bottom. Within the bar, it is possible to distinguish oneself as a technically terrific lawyer and move up a notch or two, or to be *such* a bad lawyer one is disgraced and tumbled a rung or two down.

At first glance, it might appear that there would be a constant tension between the demands of the two hierarchies, since there is no reason to believe that professional merit is distributed other than randomly with regard to class, sex or race. But there are practices within the system that work to minimize or altogether eliminate any such tension. The first is that the class/sex/race system gets hold of people long before the professional one, and *creates* them in such a way that they will, with some legitimating exceptions, appear to deserve on professional grounds the position that is in fact based on other things. Your chances of ending up at a "top" law school are directly proportional to your status at birth.

Second, people who are able to succeed according to existing professional criteria learn that they must also put themselves through a process of assimilation that has nothing to do with professionalism. Law schools are finishing schools as well as trade schools, where everyone learns to act more or less according to the behavioral criteria of the rung of the profession they hope to enter. There are children of lower middle class parents at Yale, but the student culture is relentlessly upper middle class. There are children of working class parents at Boston College, but the student culture mixes only lower middle and middle class styles. The result of the initial stacking of the system combined with the norm of upward assimilation is that the class/sex/race hierarchy controls the professional hierarchy rather than being disrupted by it.

Law firms offer security and training only in exchange for complicity in various further forms of hierarchy. The first of these is internal to the firm. There is the generational hierarchy of lawyers, and the sharp occupational hierarchy that separates the lawyers from the secretaries and the secretaries from messengers and maintenance people. The pecking order conditions all of working life. Young lawyers are no more free to disown their hierarchical superiority to the staff than to cast off deference and dependence on partners. It is almost as bad to treat your secretary like a partner as to do the reverse, and no one smiles on a perverse rejection of the rewards and reassurances (flexible hours and expense accounts, for example) that go along with your particular place in the scheme of things.

A second hierarchy is that of the judicial system, in which judges play the role of tin gods, exacting an extraordinary servility from their court personnel and the lawyers and litigants who appear before them. Judges are free to treat, and often do treat those who come before them with a degree of personal arrogance, a sense of entitlement to arbitrariness, and an insistence on deference that provide an extreme model of everything that is wrong with legal hierarchy.

Lawyers are complicit in this behavior: they expect it, and even enjoy the purity of the experience — the absolute character of the submission demanded, with its suggestion of playing a game which is really and truly for keeps. Beyond that, the judicial system is based on the same extreme specialization of function and differentiation of capacities as the hierarchy of the bar and the internal hierarchy of particular firms. All of this deforms the very idea of justice, rendering it at once impersonal, inaccessible to ordinary human understanding and ordinary human practice, and intensely personal, since everything depends, most of the time, on the crotchets and whims of petty dictators.

The third hierarchy relates lawyers to their clients. It works differently for different firms, according to their rank in the hierarchy of the bar. Top firms deal with the managers of large corporations. They engage with them on the basis of an implicit deal: the lawyers accept, even participate enthusiastically in the self-interested, or immoral, or downright criminal behavior of the client, in return for client acquiescence in the charging of ludicrous fees for work that is mainly elementary or mindless, and vastly swollen by conventions of over-research and over-writing. Within their assigned province, the lawyers behave as though they possessed the knowledge of the Delphic oracle.

At the lower levels of the hierarchy, there are different patterns of domination, mainly involving lawyers making decisions for clients, where the client was perfectly capable of deciding on his own or her own, in ways that make things easy for the lawyer, or profitable, or correspond to the lawyer's own morality or preferences. As in corporate law, the whole thing is based on excluding clients from knowledge they would need to decide on their own, while at the same time mystifying that knowledge. But in many lawyer/client encounters below the top level, that is also social inequality between the parties, with the lawyer of higher social class than the client, and this hierarchy reenforces and is reenforced by the professional one.

The final hierarchy that concerns us is the general social arrangement in which lawyers are treated — even in a country with a long tradition of anti-lawyer polemicizing — as among the elite of the nation. Partly this is simply a reflection of the fact that many lawyers come from the upper middle class to start with. But it has some small basis in the usefulness of lawyers' skills and lawyers' knowledge in the actual operation of legislative and executive politics, and some small basis in the real importance and value of the legal profession as an expression both of commitment to truth and to helping people. On this foundation, lawyers have managed to erect a massive edifice of social prestige and material over-reward. At each level of the class system, lawyers are granted a measure of deference and a measure of power altogether disproportionate to their objective merit. In their group activities, but also in their individual social lives, they tend to exploit this deference and to accentuate it by emphasizing the arcane character of what they know and do.

The legal hierarchies I have been describing have three features in common. First, the people involved in each of them have roles, and the roles require different activities and draw on different capacities. There are partners, associates, secretaries and janitors. There are corporate lawyers, business litigation lawyers, real estate lawyers, small time personal injury lawyers. There are lawyers and mere lay people. Second, if we look at each hierarchy as a joint enterprise within which people are producing things, participants playing different roles receive unequal rewards, and exercise unequal degrees of power, both over production decisions and over the organization and style of the workplace. This is most obviously true in the highly organized, oligarchical world of the individual firm, but also true of the bar taken as a unit, and of the hierarchical relations of the profession to its clients and to society at large.

Third, each hierarchy operates within a cultural framework that gives a meaning to the differences in activities and capacities, and to the inequality of power and reward. The meaning is that the whole arrangement is based on the natural differences between people, with respect to talent and energy, that it serves the social function of maximizing the quantity and quality of legal services to society, and that it is therefore just. Hierarchy reflects desert. The parties signify their participation in this universe of shared meanings (whether or not they really believe in it) through deferential or imperious behavior towards others, and by "explaining" what is going on in its terms. "Why do some firms make so much more than others, year after year?" "Well, the best firms can charge higher prices than the less good firms. Since they can charge more, they can hire the best law students, so they make even more money. And so on."

Besides having common features (differentiation of activities and capacities, inequality of power and reward, meritocratic legitimating ideology), the hierarchies are related to one another in a functional way. Internally hierarchical firms are the building blocks of the hierarchy of firms, and it is the bar as a whole that is in a hierarchical relation to society at large. The structure of the parts reproduces the structure of the whole, or vice versa, depending on how you look at it. Individuals are to firms as firms are to the bar as the bar is to society. . . .

THE CONTRIBUTION OF LEGAL EDUCATION TO THE HIERARCHIES OF THE BAR

The relationship between legal education and legal hierarchy is complex, and I think it's worth going into in some detail because it offers insight into the issue of how hierarchy works in general. I want to distinguish three different ways in which one can see legal education as a causal factor in the persistence of hierarchy within the bar.

The Analogy Effect The first of these is the simplest and the weakest — it might be called the analogy effect. Legal education has an internal structure very much like that of the bar. Each law school has its arrangement of professors, assistant professors, students and staff, roughly analogous to the internal arrangement of a law firm. Law schools themselves are ranked, with differences in what they teach, how they teach it, how much power they have in the field of legal education, and what rewards their faculties receive. Within the world of legal education, there is a legitimating ideology which explains and justifies these rankings in terms of natural differences in capacities, social utility and fairness. There are patterns of deference through which people signify their participation in this world of shared meanings, as anyone who has attended a meeting of the Association of American Law Schools can testify. . . .

Legal Ideology as an "Input" A second way in which legal education relates to legal hierarchy after law school arises from its specialized character as education. Law teachers are constantly involved in explaining how the world works, and also in formulating notions of how it should work. As it presently operates, legal education is like education in general in that it propagates the message that things are the way they are because it is best, or close to best that they should be that way. In others words, the legal education system produces ideology. Ideology is one of its "inputs" into the rest of the social system. Since the bar is part of the social system, it benefits from this legitimating contribution.

I am not here speaking of anything law schools teach about law practice, but about their general message about the legal rules in force. Law schools, as we saw above, do more than teach these rules. They also teach why they are a good thing, and that they are there because they are a good thing. These rules provide the framework within which social actors create all the hierarchies of our society, including the hierarchies of the bar. If the rules were different — for example, if all bosses were legally obligated to spend part of every day on their own typing, or if secretaries had a legal right to education for upward job mobility — the hierarchies would be different too. In so much as legal education legitimates the rules in force, it legitimates the consequences, in terms of the division of labor and inequality of power and reward, that flow from the rules. By teaching law students that the rules are groovy, law teachers also teach them that they are entitled to the six figure salaries they will earn in corporate law practice, just as doctors and business managers are entitled to theirs.

Within its general ideological message, legal education has some particular things to say to lawyers — namely, that what they do is more than just a craft, like, say carpentry. What they do is "legal reasoning." Law schools are largely (though not exclusively) responsible for persuading lawyers and the lay public that lawyers do more than exercise the skills I described in the section on the curriculum. So they are also at least partly responsible for the hierarchical relations that lawyers manage to erect on that shadowy foundation. The mystique of legal reasoning reenforces all these hierarchies because it makes it seem that people who have gone to law school are privy to secrets that are loaded with social value.

The actual capacities of lawyers — knowledge of rule systems, of issue spotting, case analysis and pro/con policy argument — have real social value; they are difficult to acquire; and one can't practice law effectively without them. But they are nowhere near as inaccessible as they are made to seem by the mystique of legal education. By mystifying them, law schools make it seem necessary to restrict them to a small group, presumed to be super-talented. That, in turn, makes it seem necessary to divide the labor in the joint enterprise of providing legal services so that most of the participants (secretaries, paralegals, office assistants, court clerks, janitors, marshalls, and so on) are firmly and permanently excluded from doing the things that are most challenging and rewarding within the overall activity. Once they have devalued everyone else on "professional" grounds, it also seems natural for those who have gone to law school to specialize in the most desirable tasks, while controlling the whole show and reaping the lion's share of the rewards.

The Hierarchical Structuring of the Group of Prospective Lawyers The third way in which legal education contributes causally to the hierarchies of the bar is by structuring the population of potential lawyers so that it will seem natural, efficient and fair that they should incorporate themselves into the existing hierarchy of law firms without much changing it. To grasp this, imagine that by some bizarre chance all the lawyers in the country decided to create a bar of roughly equal firms, in place of the existing hierarchy. Such a program would have many things in its way, even supposing the decision to pursue it was unanimous, including the influence by analogy of all the other hierarchies of our society, and the ideological messages about existing legal arrangements, and about the nature of legal reasoning, that the schools now propagate.

But the program of equalization would also have to contend with the fact that law school graduates enter practice as a group already structured hierarchically. They already have different capacities, different values and expectations, and different visions of what law practice should be. There is more to it than difference: they are unequal, in many though by no means all respects, before they have even begun.

The internal structure of the group corresponds roughly to the structure of the bar: some prospective lawyers are prepared for elite practice, others for small time solo practice. The whole group tends most of the time to believe that these differences among themselves, these inequalities, flow from individual characteristics, from their personal virtues and vices, talents and energies.

Notes and Questions

1. Both Turow and Kennedy make the point that political values are often fused with the learning of legal dogma. Ralph Nader wrote of this process, "Students are conditioned to react to questions and issues which they have no rule in forming or stimulating. Such teaching *forms* have been crucial in perpetuating the status quo in teaching *content.* For decades, the law school curriculum reflected with remarkable fidelity the commercial demands of law firm practice."*

Another critic of law education suggests that the reliance of the case method on appellate opinions, which are elicited primarily by those who are sufficiently affluent to pursue costly appeals, biases the instruction:

> The emphasis placed on the study of appellate decisions omits consideration of the actual problem of trial work, such as the prejudices of judges and juries, the deals which are made in criminal courts, or the political focus affecting various classes of interested parties, such as tenants. This coincides with the insistence of many law schools that emphasis be placed on a supposedly value-free theoretical approach to law. In practice this means that law students draw only from theory heavily tinged with corporate values. They will thus be able to offer solutions for corporate

---

*Ralph Nader, "Law Schools and Law Firms," *New Republic* (October 11, 1969): p. 21.

problems, but not for the problems posed by injustices in the judicial system or other injustices caused by corporate interests."†

If this criticism is taken seriously, what kind of measures should be considered to control or balance such political messages in law training? What interests should society have in this matter?

†David N. Rockwell, "The Education of the Capitalist Lawyer: The Law School," in Robert Lefcourt, ed., *Law Against the People* (New York: Vintage Books, 1971), p. 97.

2. Kennedy says that people generally accept the idea that hierarchies express the net value of each individual's worth, and thus they also accept not only other people's unequal relationship to themselves, but also their own location in unequal systems. How does this proposition align with Heinz and Laumann's explanation of hierarchies in legal practice?

3 LAWYERS AND THE ADVERSARY PROCESS

Lawyers are not savages. They are basically decent, concerned, well-educated citizens. Their sense of moral outrage can be extracted if the subject is man's capacity for cruelty and brutality. They would be first in line to suggest corrections aimed at curbing our more base instincts. If the subject is war or discrimination or starvation or the rape of the planet or our medieval prison system, they are in the forefront of reform. Yet change the focus, ask them about litigation or trial practice, and their sense of moral outrage goes only as far as the villainy of their current adversary. They often greet the subject with a cynicism worthy of Machiavelli.

Abraham P. Ordover, "The Lawyer as Liar," *American Journal of Trial Advocacy* (1979)

From the moment I left on the trip until I returned, every penny I spent, even for the newspaper, was charged to the client's account. Every quarter I handed a shoeshine man or dollar I put down for a drink was not my own money. And if anyone thinks this was great, I would like to point out one fact. Every motion I made, every word I uttered, every thought I had was also not my own. It belonged to somebody else.

Charles Reich, *The Sorcerer of Bolinas Reef* (1976)

[T]he adversary ethic is an inadequate aspiration for a community, and it is a pernicious moral principle. As an idea about power in the community, it depends not on goodness but on force and therefore reaches only the small, desperate residues of the community's life. As a moral principle it depends on the idea that one person should be able to buy the loyalty of another and often poisons the hope that people can grow together.

Thomas L. Shaffer, *On Being a Christian and a Lawyer* (1982)

The feature of the U.S. legal system most central to its definition, operation, and character is its theory that conflict resolution is best achieved in an adversary process. The assumptions in the theory are: (1) that the primary responsibility for articulating the sides in a dispute is best left to those most closely affected by it; (2) the biases of self-interest necessarily produced by forcing partisan dialogue between disputants can best be offset by having it take place in a neutral forum before impartial arbiters; and (3) that the conflict and dialogue can be constrained by a system of universalistic procedural and substantive rules (that is, law) that sets forth the interests of the state in the outcome of disputes. The ultimate objective in the adversary process — winning a case — is realized when the state is enticed into joining the side of one disputant against the other.

Thus, in the adversary process, disputants are expected to marshall and present the best (that is, self-serving) arguments and evidence they can. Lawyers act as advocates for their clients in this process. In court, they stand in the place of their clients. Their credentials, skills, special knowledge, influence, and even their personalities are for rent. As noted earlier, lawyers are sometimes said to be modern-day "hired guns." The readings in this section call into question the meaning of advocacy, the relationship between lawyer and client, the neutrality of the law, and gender assumptions in the adversary system.

The Ethics of Advocacy *Charles P. Curtis*

I

I want first of all to put advocacy in its proper setting. It is a special case of vicarious conduct. A lawyer devotes his life and career to acting for other people. So too does the priest, and in another way the banker. The banker handles other people's money. The priest handles other people's spiritual aspirations. A lawyer handles other people's troubles.

But there is a difference. The loyalty of a priest or clergyman runs, not to the particular parishioner whose joys or troubles he is busy with, but to his church; and the banker looks to his bank. It is the church or the bank, not he, but he on its behalf, who serves the communicant or the borrower. Their loyalties run in a different direction than a lawyer's.

So too when a lawyer works for the government. His loyalties hang on a superior peg, like the priest's or the clergyman's. For it is fiction to say that he only has the government for his client. The government is too big. It absorbs him. He is part of it.

Likewise with the general counsel for a corporation. His identification with his client is all but complete. Taft in some lectures at the Albany Law School,[1] referring to work in the legal department of a corporation, said, "Such employment leads to a lawyer's becoming nothing more than an officer of the corporation as closely identified with it as if he was the president, the secretary or the treasurer,"[2] Indeed, he usually is a director or a vice-president.

Not so the lawyer in private practice. His loyalty runs to his client. He has no other master. Not the court? you ask. Does not the court take the same position as the church or the bank? Is not the lawyer an officer of the court? Doesn't the court have first claim on his loyalty? No, in a paradoxical way. The lawyer's official duty, required of him indeed by the court, is to devote himself to the client. The court comes second by the court's, that is the law's, own command. . . .

. . . How far must a lawyer accompany his client and turn his back on the court? . . .

The person for whom you are acting very

[1]The Hubbard Lectures in May 1914.

[2]Cheatham, *Cases and Materials on the Legal Profession* 60 (1938).

reasonably expects you to treat him better than you do other people, which is just another way of saying that you owe him a higher standard of conduct than you owe to others. This goes back a long way. It is the pre-platonic ethics which Socrates had disposed of at the very outset of the *Republic*; that is that justice consists of doing good to your friends and harm to your enemies. A lawyer, therefore, insensibly finds himself treating his client better than others; and therefore others worse than his client. A lawyer, or a trustee, or anyone acting for another, has lower standards of conduct toward outsiders than he has toward his client or his beneficiaries or his patrons against the outsiders. He is required to treat outsiders as if they were barbarians and enemies. The more good faith and devotion the lawyer owes to his client, the less he owes to others when he is acting for his client. It is as if a man had only so much virtue, and the more he gives to one, the less he has available for anyone else. The upshot is that a man whose business it is to act for others finds himself, in his dealings on his client's behalf with outsiders, acting on a lower standard than he would if he were acting for himself, and lower, too, than any standard his client himself would be willing to act on, lower, in fact, than anyone on his own.

You devote yourself to the interests of another at the peril of yourself. Vicarious action tempts a man too far from himself. Men will do for others what they are not willing to do for themselves — noble as well as ignoble things. What I want to do now is to illustrate this in the practice of law by a number of perplexing situations. They raise ethical problems, but none of them, I think, has a simple right or wrong answer, and I know of no canons of ethics or morals which lead to any answer. How could there be when the cause of the perplexity is the difference between acting for another and acting for yourself? . . .

II

A lawyer is called on the telephone by a former client who is unfortunately at the time a fugitive from justice. The police want him and he wants advice. The lawyer goes to where his client is, hears the whole story, and advises him to surrender. Finally he succeeds in persuading him that this is the best thing to do and they make an appointment to go to police headquarters. Meanwhile the client is to have two days to wind up his affairs and make his farewells. When the lawyer gets back to his office, a police inspector is waiting for him, and asks him whether his client is in town and where he is. Here are questions which the police have every right to ask of anybody, and even a little hesitation in this unfortunate lawyer's denials will reveal enough to betray his client. Of course he lies.

And why not? The relation between a lawyer and his client is one of the intimate relations. You would lie for your wife. You would lie for your child. There are others with whom you are intimate enough, close enough, to lie for them when you would not lie for yourself. At what point do you stop lying for them? I don't know and you are not sure.

To every one of us come occasions when we don't want to tell the truth, not all of it, certainly not all of it at once, when we want to be something less than candid, a little disingenuous. Indeed, to be candid with ourselves, there are times when we deliberately and more or less justifiably undertake to tell something else or something different. Complete candor to anyone but ourselves is a virtue that belongs to the saints, to the secure, and to the very courageous. Even when we do want to tell the truth, all of it, ultimately, we see no reason why we should not take our own time, tell it as skillfully and as gracefully as we can, and most of us doubt our own ability to do this as well by ourselves and for ourselves as another could do it for us. So we go to a lawyer. He will make a better fist of it than we can.

I don't see why we should not come out roundly and say that one of the functions of a lawyer is to lie for his client; and on rare occasions, as I think I have shown, I believe it is. Happily they are few and far between, only when his duty gets him into a corner or puts him on the spot. Day in, day out, a lawyer can be as truthful as anyone. But not ingenuous.

A lawyer is required to be disingenuous. He is required to make statements as well as arguments which he does not believe in. But the further his statements descend toward the particular, the more truthful he may be, indeed must be, because no one appreciates the significance of the particular better than a lawyer. In the higher brackets of generality, he has to be freed from his own beliefs and prejudices, for they are irrelevant, unless they are pressed into service for the client. But his insincerity does not extend to the particular, except, of course, particulars which do not belong to him, but are his client's secrets. Barring these, when he is talking for his client, a lawyer is absolved from veracity down to a certain point of particularity. And he must never lose the reputation of lacking veracity, because his freedom from the strict bonds of veracity and of the law are the two chief assets of the profession.

I have said that a lawyer may not lie to the court. But it may be a lawyer's duty not to speak. Let me give you a case from the autobiography of one of the most distinguished and most conscientious lawyers I or any other man has ever known, Samuel Williston. In his autobiography, *Life and Law,* he tells of one of his early cases. His client was sued in some financial matter. The details of the claim are not important. Williston, of course, at once got his client's letter file and went through it painstakingly, sorting, arranging, and collating it. The letters, we may well believe, told the whole story, as they usually do in such a case. Trial approached, but the plaintiff's lawyers did not either demand to see the correspondence, nor ask for their production. "They did not demand their production and we did not feel bound to disclose them."[3] At the close of the trial, "In the course of his remarks the Chief Justice stated as one reason for his decision a supposed fact which I knew to be unfounded. I had in front of me a letter that showed his error. Though I have no doubt of the propriety of my behavior in keeping silent, I was somewhat uncomfortable at the time."

This was a letter, a piece of evidence, a fact. Suppose it had been a rule of law. Suppose the Chief Justice had equally mistakenly given as a reason for his decision some statute or regulation which Williston knew had been repealed or amended, and it was not a letter but a copy of the new statute which he had in front of him. Williston would have interrupted the Chief Justice and drawn his attention to it. This is sometimes debated, but it is beyond dispute that this would have been Williston's duty, and there is no doubt at all that he would have performed it as scrupulously as he respected his duty to his client. . . .

III

"I must be cruel only to be kind," said Hamlet, on his way to his mother. And so likewise a lawyer has to tell himself strange things on his way to court. But they are strange only to those who do not distinguish between truth and justice. Justice is something larger and more intimate than truth. Truth is only one of the ingredients of justice. Its whole is the satisfaction of those concerned. It is to that end that each attorney must say the best, and only the best, of his own case.

This is not the method we have used in other endeavors, with not only more, but with conspicuous success. But the law has other things than success to think about. It must give the losing party, and his friends and his sympathizers, as much satisfaction as any loser can expect. At least the most has been said for him. The whole has been shaken out into the sun, and everyone concerned is given a feeling akin to the feeling of security which you get when you have told yourself the worst before you make a decision. The administration of justice is no more designed to elicit the truth than the scientific approach is designed to extract justice from the atom.

Advocacy requires a lawyer to start with something to be proved, and this is as true of facts as it is of propositions of law. When he goes to interview a witness as well as when he goes to the law library, he goes to get something. He will waste a lot of time if he goes with an open mind.

[3] Williston, *Life and Law* 271 (1940).

He must, of course, first formulate the issue in his mind, but he does this only to make it the easier to find what lies on his side of the issue. He fixes on the conclusion which will best serve his client's interests, and then he sets out to persuade others to agree.

The problem presented to a lawyer when he is asked to defend a man he knows is guilty or to take a case he knows is bad is perplexing only to the laymen. Brandeis said, "As a practical matter, I think the lawyer is not often harassed by this problem, partly because he is apt to believe at the time in most of the cases that he actually tries, and partly because he either abandons or settles a large number of those he does not believe in."[4]

It is profoundly true that the first person a lawyer persuades is himself. A practicing lawyer will soon detect in himself a perfectly astonishing amount of sincerity. Bt the time he has even sketched out his brief, however skeptically he started, he finds himself believing more and more in what it says, until he has to hark back to his original opinion in order to orient himself. And later, when he starts arguing the case before the court, his belief is total, and he is quite sincere about it. You cannot very well keep your tongue in your cheek while you are talking. He believes what he is saying in a way that will later astonish himself as much as now it does others.

Not that he cares how much we are astonished. What he does care is whether we are persuaded, and he is aware that an unsound argument can do much worse than fall flat. For it may carry the implication that he has no better one. He will not want to make it unless he really has no better.

IV

The classical solution to a lawyer taking a case he knows is bad is Dr. Johnson's. It is perfectly simple and quite specious. Boswell asked Johnson whether as a moralist Johnson did not think that the practice of the law, in some degree, hurt the nice feeling of honesty.

"What do you think," said Boswell, "of supporting a cause which you know to be bad?"

Johnson answered, "Sir, you do not know it to be good or bad till the Judge determines it. I have said that you are to state facts fairly; so that your thinking, or what you call knowing, a cause to be bad, must be from reasoning, must be from your supposing your arguments to be weak and inconclusive. But, Sir, that is not enough. An argument which does not convince yourself, may convince the Judge to whom you urge it: and it it does convince him, why, then, Sir, you are wrong, and he is right."

Dr. Johnson ignored the fact that it is the lawyer's job to know how good or how bad his case is. It is his peculiar function to find out. Dr. Johnson's answer is sound only in cases where the problem does not arise.

A lawyer knows very well whether his client is guilty. It is not the lawyer, but the law, that does not know whether his case is good or bad. The law does not know, because it is trying to find out, and so the law wanted everyone defended and every debatable case tried. Therefore the law makes it easy for a lawyer to take a case, whether or not he thinks other people think it bad. It is particularly important that it be made as easy as possible for a lawyer to take a case that other people regard as bad.

We want to make it as easy as we can for a lawyer to take a bad case, and one of the ways the bar helps go about it is the canon of ethics which says, "It is improper for a lawyer to assert in argument his personal belief in his client's innocence or in the justice of his cause." It is called improper just so that the lawyer may feel that he does not have to. This, I think, must be its only purpose, for it is honored in no other way. . . .

No, there is nothing unethical in taking a bad case or defending the guilty or advocating what you don't believe in. It is ethically neutral. It's a free choice. There is a Daumier drawing of a lawyer arguing, a very demure young

---

[4]Brandeis, *The Opportunity in the Law, 39 Am. L. Rev.* 561 (1905).

woman sitting near him, and a small boy beside her sucking a lollypop. The caption says, "He defends the widow and the orphan, unless he is attacking the orphan and the widow." And for every lawyer whose conscience may be pricked, there is another whose virtue is tickled. Every case has two sides, and for every lawyer on the wrong side, there's another on the right side.

I am not being cynical. We are not dealing with the morals which govern a man acting for himself, but with the ethics of advocacy. We are talking about the special moral code which governs a man who is acting for another. Lawyers in their practice — how they behave elsewhere does not concern us — put off more and more of our common morals the farther they go in a profession which treats right and wrong, vice and virtue, on such equal terms. Some lawyers find nothing to take its place. There are others who put on new and shining raiment. . . .

I have talked perhaps too lovingly about the practice of the law. I have spoke unsparingly, as I would to another lawyer. In a way the practice of the law is like free speech. It defends what we hate as well as what we most love. I don't know any other career that offers ampler opportunity for both the enjoyment of virtue and the exercise of vice, or, if you please, the exercise of virtue and the enjoyment of vice, except possibly the ancient rituals which were performed in some temples by vestal virgins, in others by sacred prostitutes.

V

Let us now go back and reconsider, and perhaps reconstruct, in the light of my examples and our discussion, this "entire devotion" which a lawyer owes to his client.

The fact is, the "entire devotion" is not entire. The full discharge of a lawyer's duty to his client requires him to withhold something. If a lawyer is entirely devoted to his client, his client receives something less than he has a right to expect. For, if a man devotes the whole of himself to another, he mutilates or diminishes himself, and the other receives the devotion of so much the less. This is no paradox, but a simple calculus of the spirit.

There is authority for such detachment. It is not Christian. Nor is the practice of law a characteristically Christian pursuit. The practice of law is vicarious, not altruistic, and the lawyer must go back of Christianity to Stoicism for the vicarious detachment which will permit him to serve his client.

E. R. Bevan, in his *Stoics and Sceptics*,[5] summarized the Stoic faith as follows: "The Wise Man was not to concern himself with his brethren . . . he was only to serve them. Benevolence he was to have, as much of it as you can conceive; but there was one thing he must not have, and that was love. . . . He must do everything which it is possible for him to do, shrink from no extreme of physical pain, in order to help, to comfort, to guide his fellow men, but whether he succeeds or not must be a matter of pure indifference to him. If he has done his best to help you and failed, he will be perfectly satisfied with having done his best. The fact that you are no better off for his exertions will not matter to him at all. Pity, in the sense of a painful emotion caused by the sight of other men's suffering, is actually a vice. . . . In the service of his fellow men he must be prepared to sacrifice his life; but there is one thing he must never sacrifice: his own eternal calm.". . .

The Stoics gave us a counsel of perfection, but it is none the less valid. If a lawyer is to be the best lawyer he is capable of being, and discharge his "entire duty" to his clients, here in the Stoic sage is his exemplar. Here in Stoicism is his philosophy. Let him be a Christian if he choose outside the practice of the law, but in his relations with his clients, let him be a Stoic, for the better Stoic, the better lawyer.

A lawyer should treat his cases like a vivid novel, and identify himself with his client as he does with the hero or the heroine in the plot. Then he will work with "the zest that most people feel under their concern when they assist at existing emergencies, not actually their own; or

---

[5]As quoted in 6 Toynbee, *A Study of History,* 146–47 (1939).

join in facing crises that are grave, but for somebody else. . . ."[6]

How is a lawyer to secure this detachment? There are two ways of doing it, two devices, and all lawyers, almost all, are familiar with one or the other of them.

One way is to treat the whole thing as a game. I am not talking about the sporting theory of justice. I am talking about a lawyer's personal relations with his client and the necessity of detaching himself from his client. Never blame a lawyer for treating litigation as a game, however much you may blame the judge. The lawyer is detaching himself. A man who has devoted his life to taking on other people's troubles, would be swamped by them if he were to adopt them as his own. He must stay on the upland of his own personality, not only to protect himself, but to give his client the very thing that his client came for. . . .

The other way is a sense of craftsmanship. Perhaps it comes to the same thing, but I think not quite. There is a satisfaction in playing a game the best you can, as there is in doing anything else as well as you can, which is quite distinct from making a good score. . . .

A Lawyer may have to treat the practice of law as if it were a game, but if he can rely on craftsmanship, it may become an art. . . .

. . . I wonder if there is anything more exalted than the intense pleasure of doing a job as well as you can irrespective of its usefulness or even of its purpose. At least it's a comfort.

I have compared the lawyer to the banker who handles other people's money and to the priest who handles other people's spiritual aspirations. Let me go further. Compare the lawyer with the poet whose speech goes to the heart of things. "Yet he is that one especially who speaks civilly to Nature as a second person and in some sense is the patron of the world. Though more than any he stands in the midst of Nature, yet more than any he can stand aloof from her."[7]

[6] Cozzens, *Guard of Honor* 479 (1948).

[7] VII Writings of Henry David Thoreau, 289 (1906).

Notes and Questions

1. Curtis asserts that lawyers who work for government or corporations are absorbed by their clients. Should such lawyers have no obligations to the public beyond those of their employers? Consider the following from the ethical code for lawyers in federal government employment:

> *Federal Ethics Consideration 8–2*
>
> The situation of the federal lawyer which may give rise to special considerations, not applicable to lawyers generally, includes certain limitations on complete freedom of action in matters relating to Canon 8. [Canon 8 of the American Bar Association Code of Professional Responsibility states, "A Lawyer Should Assist in Improving the Legal System."] For example, a lawyer in the Office of the Chief Counsel of the Internal Revenue Service may reasonably be expected to abide, without public criticism, with certain policies or rulings closely allied to his sphere of responsibility even if he disagrees with the position taken by the agency. But even if involved personally in the process of formulating policy or ruling there may be rare occasions when his conscience compels him publicly to attack a decision which is contrary to his professional, ethical or moral judgment. In that event, however, he should be prepared to resign before doing so, and he is not free to abuse professional confidence reposed in him in the process leading to the decision.*

2. The lawyers' code of professional ethics sets forth a number of ethical standards that are meant to assure clients of their lawyers' competent, confidential, and zealous counsel. Should society have any interest in the lawyer-client relationship so long as the lawyer is ethical?

3. In a case in Lake Pleasant, New York, two lawyers appointed to defend a man charged with murder were told by their client of two other murders that, unknown to police, he had committed. The lawyers, following the

*Federal Bar Association, *Federal Ethical Considerations* (Washington, D.C.: FBA, adopted November 17, 1973).

client's directions, discovered the bodies in an abandoned mine shaft and photographed them. They did not, however, inform the police until several months later, after their client confessed to those killings. In addition, the parents of one victim had approached one of the lawyers seeking information about their missing daughter. The attorney denied having any information.

Monroe Freedman, a law school dean and prominent writer on legal ethics, wrote of this case,

> The adversary system, within which the lawyer functions, contemplates that the lawyer frequently will learn from the client information that is highly incriminating and may even learn, as in the Lake Pleasant case, that the client has in fact committed serious crimes. In such a case, if the attorney were required to divulge that information, the obligation of confidentiality would be destroyed, and with it, the adversary system itself.†

Should there be any limits to a lawyer's advocacy?

4. The final draft of the *Model Rules of Professional Conduct* of the American Bar Association contains the following rules:

Rule 1.2(d)	A lawyer shall not counsel or assist a client in conduct that the lawyer knows is criminal or fraudulent . . . ;
Rule 1.6(b)(1)	A lawyer may reveal such information to the extent the lawyer reasonably believes necessary to prevent the client from committing a criminal or fraudulent act that the lawyer reasonably believes is likely to result in death or substantial bodily harm, or in substantial injury to the financial interests or property of another . . . ;

and discussion:

> the lawyer may learn that a client intends prospective conduct that is criminal or fraudulent. Inaction by the lawyer is not a violation of Rule 1.2(d), except in the limited circumstances where failure to act constitutes assisting the client. . . . However, the lawyer's knowledge of the client's purpose may enable the lawyer to prevent commission of the prospective crime or fraud. If the prospective crime or fraud is likely to result in substantial injury, the lawyer may feel a moral obligation to take preventive action. When the threatened injury is grave, such as homicide or serious bodily injury, the lawyer may have an obligation under tort or criminal law to take reasonable preventive measures. Whether the lawyer's concern is based on moral or legal consideration, the interest in preventing the harm may be more compelling than the interest in preserving confidentiality of information relating to the client. As stated in paragraph (b)(1), the lawyer has professional discretion to reveal information in order to prevent substantial harm likely to result from a client's criminal or fraudulent act.‡

A distinction is made between the obligation under the professional rules, a violation of which could result in a loss of license to practice, and moral and legal obligations. Why? Do these rules and interpretation support Curtis's ethics of advocacy? Do they support Freedman's argument on behalf of the lawyers in the Lake Pleasant case? If a lawyer who was employed by the government believed that the government was intending to violate the law in ways that would cause substantial injury to taxpayers, what guidance would these rules provide for that lawyer?

5. Curtis claims that lawyers must be understood as playing a game. Lawyer and novelist Louis Auchincloss also uses the metaphor of game playing when his character in *Diary of a Yuppie,* Attorney Robert Service, describes the morality of the 1980s:

> The trouble with you and Blakelock is that neither of you has the remotest

†Monroe, H. Freedman, *Lawyers' Ethics in an Adversary System* (Indianapolis, Ind.: Bobbs-Merrill, 1975), p. 5.

‡*Model Rules of Professional Conduct* (Chicago: American Bar Association, 1983), pp. 4, 7.

> understanding of the moral climate in which we live today. It's all a game, but a game with very strict rules. You have to stay meticulously within the law; the least misstep, if caught, involves an instant penalty. But there is no particular moral opprobrium in incurring a penalty, any more than there is being offside in football. A man who is found to have bought or sold stock on inside information, or misrepresented his assets in a loan application, or put his girl friend on the company payroll, is not "looked down on," except by sentimentalists. He's simply been caught, that's all. Even the public understands that. Watergate showed it. You break the rules, pay the penalty and go back to the game.§

Does Curtis's perspective necessarily lead a lawyer to the kind of cynical understanding of moral action described by Service? What about Watergate?

§Louis Auchincloss, *Diary of a Yuppie* (New York: St. Martin's Press, 1986), pp. 26–27.

☐ The courtroom is not merely a field upon which personal grievances are settled by rhetorical combat. It is not a closed scene in which only the parties to the dispute have an interest. Adjudication is a process of state governance. The court represents the government and, less directly, the society. Judgments of the court are backed by state power. Adjudication is imbued with the public interest.

The "Fight" Theory versus the "Truth" Theory *Jerome Frank*

I

When we say that present-day trial methods are "rational," presumably we mean this: The men who compose our trial courts, judges and juries, in each law-suit conduct an intelligent inquiry into all the practically available evidence, in order to ascertain, as near as may be, the truth about the facts of that suit. That might be called the "investigatory" or "truth" method of trying cases. Such a method can yield no more than a guess, nevertheless an educated guess.

The success of such a method is conditioned by at least these two factors: (1) The judicial inquirers, trial judges or juries, may not obtain all the important evidence. (2) The judicial inquirers may not be competent to conduct such an inquiry. Let us, for the time being, assume that the second condition is met — i.e., that we have competent inquirers — and ask whether we so conduct trials as to satisfy the first condition, i.e., the procuring of all the practically available important evidence.

The answer to that question casts doubt on whether our trial courts do use the "investigatory" or "truth" method. Our mode of trials is commonly known as "contentious" or "adversary." It is based on what I would call the "fight" theory, a theory which derives from the origin of trials as substitutes for private out-of-court brawls.

Many lawyers maintain that the "fight" theory and the "truth" theory coincide. They think that the best way for a court to discover the facts in a suit is to have each side strive as hard as it can, in a keenly partisan spirit, to bring to the court's attention the evidence favorable to that side. Macaulay said that we obtain the fairest decision "when two men argue, as unfairly as possible, on opposite sides," for then "it is certain

From Jerome Frank, *Courts on Trial: Myth and Reality in American Justice*. Excerpt, pp. 80–102, reprinted with permission of Princeton University Press.

that no important consideration will altogether escape notice."

Unquestionably that view contains a core of good sense. The zealously partisan lawyers sometimes do bring into court evidence which, in a dispassionate inquiry, might be overlooked. Apart from the fact element of the case, the opposed lawyers also illuminate for the court niceties of the legal rules which the judge might otherwise not perceive. The "fight" theory, therefore, has invaluable qualities with which we cannot afford to dispense.

But frequently the partisanship of the opposing lawyers blocks the uncovering of vital evidence or leads to a presentation of vital testimony in a way that distorts it. I shall attempt to show you that we have allowed the fighting spirit to become dangerously excessive.

II

This is perhaps most obvious in the handling of witnesses. Suppose a trial were fundamentally a truth-inquiry. Then, recognizing the inherent fallibilities of witnesses, we would do all we could to remove the causes of their errors when testifying. Recognizing also the importance of witnesses' demeanor as clues to their reliability, we would do our best to make sure that they testify in circumstances most conducive to a revealing observation of that demeanor by the trial judge or jury. In our contentious trial practice, we do almost the exact opposite.

No businessman, before deciding to build a new plant, no general before launching an attack, would think of obtaining information on which to base his judgment by putting his informants through the bewildering experience of witnesses at a trial. "The novelty of the situation," wrote a judge, "the agitation and hurry which accompanies it, the cajolery or intimidation to which the witness may be subjected, the want of questions calculated to excite those recollections which might clear up every difficulty, and the confusion of cross-examination . . . may give rise to important errors and omissions." "In the court they stand as strangers," wrote another judge of witnesses, "surrounded with unfamiliar circumstances giving rise to an embarrassment known only to themselves."

In a book by Henry Taft (brother of Chief Justice Taft, and himself a distinguished lawyer) we are told: "Counsel and court find it necessary through examination and instruction to induce a witness to abandon for an hour or two his habitual method of thought and expression, and conform to the rigid ceremonialism of court procedure. It is not strange that frequently truthful witnesses are . . . misunderstood, that they nervously react in such a way as to create the impression that they are either evading or intentionally falsifying. It is interesting to account for some of the things that witnesses do under such circumstances. An honest witness testifies on direct examination. He answers questions promptly and candidly and makes a good impression. On cross-examination, his attitude changes. He suspects that traps are being laid for him. He hesitates; he ponders the answer to a simple question; he seems to 'spar' for time by asking that questions be repeated; perhaps he protests that counsel is not fair; he may even appeal to the court for protection. Altogether the contrast with his attitude on direct examination is obvious; and he creates the impression that he is evading or withholding," Yet on testimony thus elicited courts every day reach decisions affecting the lives and fortunes of citizens.

What is the role of the lawyers in bringing the evidence before the trial court? As you may learn by reading any one of a dozen or more handbooks on how to try a law-suit, an experienced lawyer uses all sorts of stratagems to minimize the effect on the judge or jury of testimony disadvantageous to his client, even when the lawyer has no doubt of the accuracy and honesty of that testimony. The lawyer considers it his duty to create a false impression, if he can, of any witness who gives such testimony. If such a witness happens to be timid, frightened by the unfamiliarity of court-room ways, the lawyer, in his cross-examination, plays on that weakness, in order to confuse the witness and make it appear that he is concealing significant facts. Longenecker, in his book *Hints On*

The Trial of a Law Suit (a book endorsed by the great Wigmore), in writing of the "truthful, honest, over-cautious" witness, tells how "a skilful advocate by a rapid cross-examination may ruin the testimony of such a witness." The author does not even hint any disapproval of that accomplishment. Longenecker's and other similar books recommend that a lawyer try to prod an irritable but honest "adverse" witness into displaying his undesirable characteristics in their most unpleasant form, in order to discredit him with the judge or jury. "You may," writes Harris, "sometimes destroy the effect of an adverse witness by making him appear more hostile than he really is. You may make him exaggerate or unsay something and say it again." Taft says that a clever cross-examiner, dealing with an honest but egotistic witness, will "deftly tempt the witness to indulge in his propensity for exaggeration, so as to make him 'hang himself.' And thus," adds Taft, "it may happen that not only is the value of his testimony lost, but the side which produces him suffers for seeking aid from such a source" — although, I would add, that may be the only source of evidence of a fact on which the decision will turn. . . .

The lawyer not only seeks to discredit adverse witnesses but also to hide the defects of witnesses who testify favorably to his client. If, when interviewing such a witness before trial, the lawyer notes that the witness has mannerisms, demeanor-traits, which might discredit him, the lawyer teaches him how to cover up those traits when testifying: He educates the irritable witness to conceal his irritability, the cocksure witness to subdue his cocksureness. In that way, the trial court is denied the benefit of observing the witness's actual normal demeanor, and thus prevented from sizing up the witness accurately.

Lawyers freely boast of their success with these tactics. They boast also of such devices as these: If an "adverse," honest witness, on cross-examination, makes seemingly inconsistent statements, the cross-examiner tries to keep the witness from explaining away the apparent inconsistencies. "When," writes Tracy, counseling trial lawyers, in a much-praised book, "by your cross-examination, you have caught the witness in an inconsistency, the next question that will immediately come to your lips is, 'Now, let's hear you explain.' Don't ask it, for he may explain and, if he does, your point will have been lost. If you have conducted your cross-examination properly (which includes interestingly), the jury will have seen the inconsistency and it will have made the proper impression on their minds. If, on re-direct examination the witness does explain, the explanation will have come later in the case and at the request of the counsel who originally called the witness and the jury will be much more likely to look askance at the explanation than if it were made during your cross-examination." Tracy adds, "Be careful in your questions on cross-examination not to open the door that you have every reason to wish kept closed." That is, don't let in any reliable evidence, hurtful to your side, which would help the trial court to arrive at the truth. . . .

Nor, usually, will a lawyer concede the existence of any facts if they are inimical to his client and he thinks they cannot be proved by his adversary. If, to the lawyer's knowledge, a witness has testified inaccurately but favorably to the lawyer's client, the lawyer will attempt to hinder cross-examination that would expose the inaccuracy. He puts in testimony which surprises his adversary who, caught unawares, has not time to seek out, interview, and summon witnesses who would rebut the surprise testimony. "Of course," said a trial lawyer in a bar association lecture in 1946, "surprise elements should be hoarded. Your opponent should not be educated as to matters concerning which you believe he is still in the dark. Obviously, the traps should not be uncovered. Indeed, you may cast a few more leaves over them so that your adversary will step more boldly on the low ground believing it is solid."

These, and other like techniques, you will find unashamedly described in the many manuals on trial tactics written by and for eminently reputable trial lawyers. The purpose of these tactics — often effective — is to prevent the trial judge or jury from correctly evaluating the truthworthiness of witnesses and to shut out evidence the trial court ought to receive in order to approximate the truth.

In short, the lawyer aims at victory, at winning in the fight, not at aiding the court to discover the facts. He does not want the trial court to reach a sound educated guess, if it is likely to be contrary to his client's interest. Our present trial method is thus the equivalent of throwing pepper in the eyes of a surgeon when he is performing an operation. . . .

III

That brings me to a point which the fighting theory obscures. A court's decision is not a mere private affair. It culminates in a court order which is one of the most solemn of governmental acts. Not only is a court an agency of government, but remember that its order, if not voluntarily obeyed, will bring into action the police, the sheriff, even the army. What a court orders, then, is no light matter. The court represents the government, organized society, in action.

Such an order a court is not supposed to make unless there exist some facts which bring into operation a legal rule. Now any government officer, other than a judge, if authorized to do an act for the government only if certain facts exist, will be considered irresponsible if he so acts without a governmental investigation. For instance, if an official is empowered to pay money to a veteran suffering from some specified ailment, the official, if he does his duty, will not rely solely on the applicant's statement that he has such an ailment. The government officer insists on a governmental check-up of the evidence. Do courts so conduct themselves?

In criminal cases they seem to, after a fashion. In such cases, there is some recognition that so important a governmental act as a court decision against a defendant should not occur without someone, on behalf of the government itself, seeing to it that the decision is justified by the actual facts so far as they can be discovered with reasonable diligence. For, in theory at least, usually before a criminal action is begun, an official investigation has been conducted which reveals data sufficient to warrant bringing the defendant to trial. In some jurisdictions, indigent defendants charged with crime are represented by a publicly-paid official, a Public Defender. . . . And the responsibility of government for mistakes of fact in criminal cases, resulting in erroneous court judgments, is recognized in those jurisdictions in which the government compensates an innocent convicted person if it is subsequently shown that he was convicted through such a mistake.

In civil cases (non-criminal cases), on the whole a strikingly different attitude prevails. Although, no less than a criminal suit, a court's order is a grave governmental act, yet, in civil cases, the government usually accepts no similar responsibilities, even in theory. Such a suit is still in the ancient tradition of "self help." The court usually relies almost entirely on such evidence as one or the other of the private parties to the suit is (a) able to, and (b) chooses to, offer. Lack of skill or diligence of the lawyer for one of those parties, or that party's want of enough funds to finance a pre-trial investigation necessary to obtain evidence, may have the result, as I explained, that crucial available evidence is not offered in court. No government official has the duty to discover, and bring to court, evidence, no matter how important, not offered by the parties.

In short, the theory is that, in most civil suits, the government, through its courts, should make orders which the government will enforce, although those court-orders may not be justified by the actual facts, and although, by reasonable diligence, the government, had it investigated, might have discovered evidence — at variance with the evidence presented — coming closer to the actual facts.

Yet the consequence of a court decision in a civil suit, based upon the court's mistaken view of the actual facts, may be as grave as a criminal judgment which convicts an innocent person. If, because of such an erroneous decision, a man loses his job or his savings and becomes utterly impoverished, he may be in almost as serious a plight as if he had been jailed. His poverty may make him a public charge. It may lead to the delinquency of his children, who may thus become criminals and go to jail. Yet in no jurisdiction is a man compensated by the government for serious injury to him caused by a judgment against him in a non-criminal case, even if later it is shown that the judgment was founded upon perjured or mistaken testimony.

I suggest that there is something fundamentally wrong in our legal system in this respect. If a man's pocket is picked, the government brings a criminal suit, and accepts responsibility for its prosecution. If a man loses his life's savings through a breach of contract, the government accepts no such responsibility. Shouldn't the government perhaps assume some of the burden of enforcing what we call "private rights"? . . .

IV

Suppose, that, in a crude "primitive" society, A claims that B took A's pig. If that is true, B violated a well-settled tribal rule. But B denies that he took the pig. A attacks B and kills him. Does A's killing of B prove that B was wrong about the facts? Does that killing constitute the enforcement of the tribal rule? Now suppose somewhat the same sort of dispute in the U.S.A. A sues B, claiming that by fraud and deceit, B got A's pig. A legal rule says that if B did those acts, then A has a legal right to get back the pig or its money value. If A wins that suit, does the decision in his favor constitute the enforcement of that legal rule, even if A won through perjured testimony or because the trial court erroneously believed an honest but mistaken witness?

A lawyer friend of mine, to whom I put this question, replied, "Yes, in theory. In theory, the facts as found must be assumed to be true." His answer does not satisfy me. That we must accept the facts found by a trial court does not mean that a rule against fraud is really enforced when a court holds a man liable for a fraud he did not commit. My friend is saying, in effect, that, even were it true that the courts misfound the facts in 90% of all cases, still the courts would be enforcing the rules.

The conclusion does not bother the hardened cynic. "In the long run," one may imagine him saying, "what is the difference whether courts make many mistakes in fact-finding, and, as a result, render erroneous decisions — as long as the public generally doesn't learn of those mistakes? . . . [I]f a noncriminal legal rule is of a desirable kind — for instance, a rule concerning the duty of a trustee to the beneficiaries of a trust — why bother whether, in particular lawsuits, the courts, through failure to discover the actual facts, apply it to persons who haven't violated it? Public respect for that rule, and its infiltration into community habits, will come just as well from its misapplications as from its correction applications — if only the public doesn't learn of its misapplications. If you call it injustice to punish the innocent or mistakenly to enter money judgments against men who have done no legal wrongs, then I answer that effectively concealed instances of injustice are not only harmless but socially beneficial. They serve as useful examples. Don't get squeamish about such mistakes." I doubt whether any reader will agree with the cynic.

V

No one can doubt that the invention of courts, which preserve the peace by settling disputes, marked a great step forward in human progress. But are we to be so satisfied with this forward step that we will rest content with it? Should not a modern civilized society ask more of its courts than that they stop peace-disrupting brawls? The basic aim of the courts in our society should, I think, be the just settlement of particular disputes, the just decision of specific lawsuits.

The just settlement of disputes demands a legal system in which the courts can and do strive tirelessly to get as close as is humanly possible to the actual facts of specific court-room controversies. Court-house justice is, I repeat, done at retail, not at wholesale. The trial court's job of fact-finding in each particular case therefore looms up as one of the most important jobs in modern court-house government. With no lack of deep admiration and respect for our many able trial judges, I must say that that job is not as well done as it could and should be.

Notes and Questions

1. Curtis commented that "the administration of justice is no more designed to elicit the truth than the scientific approach is designed to extract justice from the atom." Would Judge Frank agree? How can there be justice without truth?
2. How would Frank be likely to view the following quote?

   Justice as a professional aspiration is corrupting the extent that the culture of justice finds it hard to say that a lawyer's life is ministry and that that ministry aims beyond justice to compassion and hope. Compassion is the heart of counseling, and counseling is what lawyers do most of the time. Lawyers do not, most of the time, "dispense" or "administer" or serve justice; they serve people who know and who want to know how to live together. The professional culture's proclaimed concern with justice, became justice is often irrelevant to this enterprise, makes compassion more rather than less difficult, and, therefore, the professional culture makes things worse. The practice of hope in a lawyer's professional life involves the use of knowledge and intellectual skill as an expression of truth; but exclusive concern with justice in the professional culture often comes out expressing itself in terms of coercion, rather than truth, and in that way, too, professional culture makes things worse. Justice is an important professional virtue, no doubt, but it is not an adequate aspiration for the life the average lawyer leads.*

3. In criminal cases, the state is a party to the legal dispute. Does this fact explain why the government may be more diligent in searching for truth in such cases than in civil cases between private parties? If the court were to conduct its own truth-seeking inquiries to settle private disputes, would it jeopardize its own status as impartial arbiter? If so, how could that outcome be avoided?
4. What is Frank's view of the interests of the state and society in private litigation? Does he suggest a role for lawyers different from that put forth by Curtis?

*Thomas L. Shaffer, *On Being a Christian and a Lawyer* (Provo, Utah: Brigham Young University Press, 1982), p. 162.

The following lawyer's story is offered as an example for the discussion of the ethics of advocacy and the "fight" theory versus the "truth" theory.

The Criminal Lawyer's "Different Mission": Reflections on the "Right" to Present a False Case *Harry I. Subin*

About fifteen years ago I represented a man charged with rape and robbery. The victim's account was as follows: Returning from work in the early morning hours, she was accosted by a man who pointed a gun at her and took a watch from her wrist. He told her to go with him to a nearby lot, where he ordered her to lie down on the ground and disrobe. When she complained that the ground was hurting her, he took her to his apartment, located across the street. During the next hour there, he had intercourse with her. Ultimately, he said that they had to leave to avoid being discovered by the woman with whom he lived. The complainant responded that since he had gotten what he wanted, he should give her back her watch. He said that he would.

As the two left the apartment, he said he

Abridged and footnotes renumbered from *Georgetown Journal of Legal Ethics,* Volume 1 (1987), pp. 125–136. Reprinted with permission.

was going to get a car. Before leaving the building, however, he went to the apartment next door, leaving her to wait in the hallway. When asked why she waited, she said that she was still hoping for the return of her watch, which was a valued gift, apparently from her boyfriend.

She never did get the watch. When they left the building, the man told her to wait on the street while he got the car. At that point she went to a nearby police precinct and reported the incident. She gave a full description of the assailant that matched my client. She also accurately described the inside of his apartment. Later, in response to a note left at his apartment by the police, my client came to the precinct, and the complainant identified him. My client was released at that time but was arrested soon thereafter at his apartment, where a gun was found.[1] No watch was recovered.

My client was formally charged, at which point I entered the case. At our initial interview and those that followed it, he insisted that he had nothing whatever to do with the crime and had never even seen the woman before.[2] He stated that he had been in several places during the night in question: visiting his aunt earlier in the evening, then traveling to a bar in New Jersey, where he was during the critical hours. He gave the name of a man there who would corroborate this. He said that he arrived home early the next morning and met a friend. He stated that he had no idea how this woman had come to know things about him such as what the apartment looked like, that he lived with a woman, and that he was a musician, or how she could identify him. He said that he had no reason to rape anyone, since he already had a woman, and that in any event he was recovering from surgery for an old gun shot wound and could not engage in intercourse. He said he would not be so stupid as to bring a woman he had robbed and was going to rape into his own apartment.

I felt there was some strength to these arguments, and that there were questionable aspects to the complainant's story. In particular, it seemed strange that a man intending rape would be as solicitous of the victim's comfort as the woman said her assailant was at the playground. It also seemed that a person who had just been raped would flee when she had the chance to, and in any case would not be primarily concerned with the return of her watch. On balance, however, I suspected that my client was not telling me the truth. I thought the complaining witness could not possibly have known what she knew about him and his apartment, if she had not had any contact with him. True, someone else could have posed as him, and used his apartment. My client, however, could suggest no one who could have done so.[3] Moreover, that hypothesis did not explain the complainant's accurate description of him to the police. Although the identification procedure used by the police, a one person "show up," was suggestive, the woman had ample opportunity to observe her assailant during the extended incident. I could not believe that the complainant had selected my client randomly to accuse falsely of rape. By both her and my client's admission, the two had not had any previous association.

That my client was probably lying to me had two possible explanations. First, he might have been lying because he was guilty and did not see any particular advantage to himself in admitting it to me. It is embarrassing to admit that one has committed a crime, particularly one of this nature. Moreover, my client might well have feared to tell me the truth. He might have believed that I would tell others what he said, or, at the very least, that I might not be enthusiastic about representing him.

He also might have lied not because he was guilty of the offense, but because he thought the concocted story was the best one under the circumstances. The sexual encounter may have taken place voluntarily, but the woman

[1]The woman was not able to make a positive identification of the gun as the weapon used in the incident.

[2]A student working on the case with me photographed the complainant on the street. My client stated that he could not identify her.

[3]The woman had indicated that her assailant opened the door with a key. There was no evidence of a forced entry.

complained to the police because she was very angry at my client for refusing to return the valued wrist watch, perhaps not stolen, but left, in my client's apartment. My client may not have been able to admit this, because he had other needs that took precedence over the particular legal one that brought him to me. For example, the client might have felt compelled to deny any involvement in the incident because to admit to having had a sexual encounter might have jeopardized his relationship with the woman with whom he lived. Likewise, he might have decided to "play lawyer," and put forward what he believed to be his best defense. Not understanding the heavy burden of proof on the state in criminal cases, he might have thought that any version of the facts that showed that he had contact with the woman would be fatal because it would simply be a case of her word against his.

I discussed all of these matters with the client on several occasions. Judging him a man of intelligence, with no signs of mental abnormality, I became convinced that he understood both the seriousness of his situation, and that his exculpation did not depend upon maintaining his initial story. In ensuring that he did understand that, in fact, I came close enough to suggesting the "right" answers to make me a little nervous about the line between subornation of perjury and careful witness preparation, known in the trade as "horseshedding." In the end, however, he held to his original account.

At this point the case was in equipoise for me. I had my suspicions about both the complainant's and the client's version of what had occurred, and I supposed a jury would as well. That problem was theirs, however, not mine. All I had to do was present my client's version of what occurred in the best way that I could.

Or was that all that was required? Committed to the adversarial spirit . . . , I decided that it was not. The "different mission" took me beyond the task of presenting my client's position in a legally correct and persuasive manner, to trying to untrack the state's case in any lawful way that occurred to me, regardless of the facts.

With that mission in mind, I concluded that it would be too risky to have the defendant simply take the stand and tell his story, even if it were true. Unless we could create an iron-clad alibi, which seemed unlikely given the strength of the complainant's identification, I thought it was much safer to attack the complainant's story, even if it were true. I felt, however, that since my client had persisted in his original story I was obligated to investigate the alibi defense, although I was fairly certain that I would not use it. My students and I therefore interviewed everyone he mentioned, traveled and timed the route he said he had followed, and attempted to find witnesses who may have seen someone else at the apartment. We discovered nothing helpful. The witness my client identified as being at the bar in New Jersey could not corroborate the client's presence there. The times the client gave were consistent with his presence at the place of the crime when the victim claimed it took place. The client's aunt verified that he had been with her, but much earlier in the evening.

Because the alibi defense was apparently hopeless, I returned to the original strategy of attempting to undermine the complainant's version of the facts. I demanded a preliminary hearing, in which the complainant would have to testify under oath to the events in question. Her version as precisely as I have described it, and she told it in an objective manner that, far from seeming contrived, convinced me that she was telling the truth. She seemed a person who, if not at home with the meanness of the streets, was resigned to it. To me that explained why she was able to react in what I perceived to be a nonstereotypical manner to the ugly events in which she had been involved.

I explained to my client that we had failed to corroborate his alibi, and that the complainant appeared to be a credible witness. I said that in my view the jury would not believe the alibi, and that if we could not obtain any other information, it might be appropriate to think about a guilty plea, which would at least limit his exposure to punishment. The case, then in the middle of the aimless drift towards resolution that typifies New York's criminal justice system, was left at that.

Some time later, however, my client called me and told me that he had new evidence; his aunt, he said, would testify that he had been with her at the time in question. I was incredulous. I reminded him that at no time during our earlier conversations had he indicated what was plainly a crucial piece of information, despite my not too subtle explanation of the elements of an alibi defense. I told him that when the aunt was initially interviewed with great care on this point, she stated that he was not with her at the time of the crime. Ultimately, I told him that I thought he was lying, and that in my view even if the jury heard the aunt's testimony, they would not believe it.

Whether it was during that session or later that the client admitted his guilt I do not recall. I do recall wondering whether, now that I knew the truth, that should make a difference in the way in which the case was handled. I certainly wished that I did not know it and began to understand, psychologically if not ethically, lawyers who do not want to know their clients' stories.

I did not pause very long to ponder the problem, however, because I concluded that knowing the truth in fact did not make a difference to my defense strategy, other than to put me on notice as to when I might be suborning perjury. Because the mission of the defense attorney was to defeat the prosecution's case, what I knew actually happened was not important otherwise. What did matter was whether a version of the "facts" could be presented that would make a jury doubt the client's guilt.

Viewed in this way, my problem was not that my client's story was false, but that it was not credible, and could not be made to appear so by legal means. To win, we would therefore have to come up with a better theory than the alibi, avoiding perjury in the process. Thus, the defense would have to be made out without the client testifying, since it would be a crime for him to assert a fabricated exculpatory theory under oath. This was not a serious problem, however, because it would not only be possible to prevail without the defendant's testimony, but it would probably be easier to do so. Not everyone is capable of lying successfully on the witness stand, and I did not have the sense that my client would be very good at it.

There were two possible defenses that could be fabricated. The first was mistaken identity. We could argue that the opportunity of the victim to observe the defendant at the time of the original encounter was limited, since it had occurred on a dark street. The woman could be made out to have been in great emotional distress during the incident.[4] Expert testimony would have to be adduced to show the hazards of eyewitness identification. We could demonstrate that an unreliable identification procedure had been used at the precinct. On the other hand, given that the complainant had spent considerable time with the assailant and had led the police back to the defendant's apartment, it seemed doubtful that the mistaken identification ploy would be successful.

The second alternative, consent, was clearly preferable. It would negate the charge of rape and undermine the robbery case.[5] To prevail, all we would have to do would be to raise a reasonable doubt as to whether he had compelled the woman to have sex with him. The doubt would be based on the scenario that the woman and the defendant met, and she voluntarily returned to his apartment. Her watch, the object of the alleged robbery, was either left there by mistake or, perhaps better, was never there at all.

The consent defense could be made out entirely through cross-examination of the complainant, coupled with argument to the jury about her lack of credibility on the issue of force. I could emphasize the parts of her story that sounded the most curious, such as the defendant's solicitude in taking his victim back to his apartment, and her waiting for her watch when she could have gone immediately to the nearby

---

[4]This would be one of those safe areas in cross-examination, where the witness was damned no matter what she answered. If she testified that she was distressed, it would make my point that she was making an unreliable identification; if she testified that she was calm, no one would believe her. . . .

[5]Consent is a defense to a charge of rape. *E.g.*, N.Y. Penal Law § 130.05 (McKinney 1975 & Supp. 1987). While consent is not a defense to a robbery charge, N.Y. Penal Law §§ 160.00-.15 (McKinney 1975 & Supp. 1987), if the complainant could be made out to be a liar about the rape, there was a good chance that the jury would not believe her about the stolen watch either.

precinct that she went to later. I could point to her inability to identify the gun she claimed was used (although it was the one actually used), that the allegedly stolen watch was never found, there was no sign of physical violence, and no one heard screaming or any other signs of a struggle. I could also argue as my client had that even if he were reckless enough to rob and rape a woman across the street from his apartment, he would not be so foolish as to bring the victim there. I considered investigating the complainant's background, to take advantage of the right, unencumbered at the time, to impeach her on the basis of her prior unchastity.[6] I did not pursue this, however, because to me this device, although lawful, was fundamentally wrong. No doubt in that respect I lacked zeal, perhaps punishably so.

Even without assassinating this woman's character, however, I could argue that this was simply a case of a casual tryst that went awry. The defendant would not have to prove whether the complainant made the false charge to account for her whereabouts that evening, or to explain what happened to her missing watch. If the jury had reason to doubt the complainant's charges it would be bound to acquit the defendant.

How all of this would have played out at trial cannot be known. Predictably, the case dragged on so long that the prosecutor was forced to offer the unrefusable plea of possession of a gun. As I look back, however, I wonder how I could justify doing what I was planning to do had the case been tried. I was prepared to stand before the jury posing as an officer of the court in search of the truth, while trying to fool the jurors into believing a wholly fabricated story, i.e., that the woman had consented, when in fact she had been forced at gunpoint to have sex with the defendant. I was also prepared to demand an acquittal because the state had not met its burden of proof when, if it had not, it would have been because I made the truth look like a lie. If there is any redeeming social value in permitting an attorney to do such things, I frankly cannot discern it.

Others have discerned it, however, and while they have been criticized, they seem clearly to represent the majority view. They rely on either of two theories. The first is that the lawyer cannot possibly be sufficiently certain of the truth to impose his or her view of it on the client's case. The second is that the defense attorney need not be concerned with the truth even if he or she does know it. Both are misguided.

[6]When this case arose it was common practice to impeach the complainant in rape cases by eliciting details of her prior sexual activities. Subsequently the rules of evidence were amended to require a specific showing of relevance to the facts of the case. N.Y. Crim. Proc. Law § 60.42 (McKinney 1981 & Supp. 1987).

Notes and Questions

1. When legal authorities debate the "truth" theory versus the "fight" theory, most take the side of the latter. In *United States* v. *Wade* (388 U.S. 218, 1967) Justice Byron White wrote,

   > Law enforcement officers have the obligation to convict the guilty and to make sure they do not convict the innocent. They must be dedicated to making the criminal trial a procedure for the ascertainment of the true facts surrounding the commission of the crime. To this extent, our so-called adversary system is not adversary at all; nor should it be. But defense counsel has no comparable obligation to ascertain or present the truth. . . . He must be and is interested in preventing the conviction of the innocent, but . . . we also insist that he defend his client whether he is innocent or guilty. . . . Our interest in not convicting the innocent permits counsel to put the State to its proof, to put the State's case in the worst possible light, regardless of what he thinks or knows to be the truth. . . . [A]s part of the duty imposed on the most honorable defense counsel, we countenance or require conduct which in many instances has little if any, relation to the search for truth.

2. Criminal law examples are typically used to support the "fight" theory. These examples usually invoke rights given to citizens by the U.S. Constitution to inhibit the ready use of

state force. What happens to the "fight" theory when civil disputes are the example — for example, in divorce, contract disputes, and negligence cases? What about cases of administrative regulation, such as pollution controls, product safety and labeling, workplace safety, antimonopoly regulations, consumer protection, insider stock trading, and campaign contribution regulations? Is zealous legal advocacy as appropriate here as when a defendant's life or liberty is at stake? What might adoption of the "truth" theory in these areas do to the adversary process? What would be the lawyer's role?

4 LAWYERS AND LEGAL PRACTICE

[T]he function of law is not so much to guide society, as to comfort it. . . . Though the notion of a "rule of law" may be the moral background of revolt, it ordinarily operates to induce acceptance of things as they are. It does this by creating a realm somewhere within the mystical haze beyond the courts, where all our dreams of justice in an unjust world come true. . . . From a practical point of view it is the greatest instrument of social stability because it recognizes every one of the yearnings of the underprivileged, and gives them a forum in which those yearnings can achieve official approval without involving any particular action which might joggle the existing pyramid of power.

Thurman Arnold, *The Symbols of Government* (1935)

Consider the dilemma of one who supplies rare legal skills to people unusually disadvantaged in protecting their rights. Employing an exceptional ability, the altruist wins an apparently hopeless case for an unpopular indigent. Heroically vindicating the rule of law against heavy odds, his triumph at once earns a celebration of self and justifies dismay for the legality of a system that implements rights on such unpredictable, extraordinary contingencies.

Jack Katz, *Poor People's Lawyers in Transition* (1982)

☐ The readings in the preceding section have dealt with issues of advocacy in the legal process largely as abstract, professional and ethical problems involving the appropriate construction of the lawyer's role. Their focus is more normative than empirical. What do lawyers do about issues of advocacy in day-to-day practice? In this section, four readings are offered on this question. The first two are empirical studies of legal practice — one in criminal court, the other in a divorce lawyer's office. The third raises significant questions about whether a lawyer's gender may affect his or her orientation to advocacy and legal problem solving, and calls for speculation on the effects that may come from the large-scale infusion of women into the legal profession. The concluding reading ties in the issues of advocacy with client type and professional hierarchy to suggest that the combination actually shapes law and bends it to the interests of society's more powerful elements. With this reading the focus on lawyers is brought full circle to Tocqueville.

The Practice of Law as Confidence Game *Abraham S. Blumberg*

The overwhelming majority of convictions in criminal cases (usually over 90 per cent) are not the product of a combative, trial-by-jury process at all, but instead merely involve the sentencing of the individual after a negotiated, bargained-for plea of guilty has been entered. Although more recently the overzealous role of police and prosecutors in producing pretrial confessions and admissions has achieved a good deal of notoriety, scant attention has been paid to the organizational structure and personnel of the criminal court itself. Indeed, the extremely high conviction rate produced without the features of an adversary trial in our courts would tend to suggest that the "trial" becomes a perfunctory reiteration and validation of the pretrial interrogation and investigation.

The institutional setting of the court defines a role for the defense counsel in a criminal case radically different from the one traditionally depicted. Sociologists and others have focused their attention on the deprivations and social disabilities of such variables as race, ethnicity, and social class as being the source of an accused person's defeat in a criminal court. Largely overlooked is the variable of the court organization itself, which possesses a thrust, purpose, and direction of its own. It is grounded in pragmatic values, bureaucratic priorities, and administrative instruments. These exalt maximum production and the particularistic career designs of organizational incumbents, whose occupational and career commitments tend to generate a set of priorities. These priorities exert a higher claim than the stated ideological goals of "due process of law," and are often inconsistent with them.

Organizational goals and discipline impose a set of demands and conditions of practice on the respective professions in the criminal court, to which they respond by abandoning their ideological and professional commitments to the accused client in the service of these higher claims of the court organization. All court personnel, including the accused's own lawyer, tend to be coopted to become agent-mediators who help the accused redefine his situation and restructure his perceptions concomitant with a plea of guilty.

Of all the occupational roles in the court the only private individual who is officially recognized as having a special status and concomitant obligations is the lawyer. His legal status is that of "an officer of the court" and he is held to a standard of ethical performance and duty to his client as well as to the court. This obligation is thought to be far higher than that expected of ordinary individuals occupying the various occupational statuses in the court community. However, lawyers, whether privately retained or of the legal-aid, public defender variety, have close and continuing relations with the prosecuting office and the court itself through discreet relations with the judges via their law secretaries or "confidential" assistants. Indeed, lines of communication, influence and contact with those offices, as well as with the Office of the Clerk of the court, Probation Division, and with the press, are essential to present and prospective requirements of criminal law practice. Similarly, the subtle involvement of the press and other mass media in the court's organizational network is not readily discernible to the casual observer. Accused persons come and go in the court system schema, but the structure and its occupational incumbents remain to carry on their respective career, occupational and organizational enterprises. The individual stridencies, tensions, and conflicts a given accused person's case may present to all the participants are overcome, because the formal and informal relations of all the groups in the court setting require it. The probability of continued future relations and interaction must be preserved at all costs.

This is particularly true of the "lawyer regulars" *i.e.,* those defense lawyers, who by virtue of their continuous appearances in behalf of defendants, tend to represent the bulk of a crimi-

---

Abraham S. Blumberg, "The Practice of Law as Confidence Game," from *Law and Society Review,* Volume 1:2. Reprinted by permission of the Law and Society Association.

nal court's non-indigent case workload, and those lawyers who are not "regulars," who appear almost casually in behalf of an occasional client. Some of the "lawyer regulars" are highly visible as one moves about the major urban centers of the nation, their offices line the back streets of the courthouses, at times sharing space with bondsmen. Their political "visibility" in terms of local club house ties, reaching into the judge's chambers and prosecutor's office, are also deemed essential to successful practitioners. Previous research has indicated that the "lawyer regulars" make no effort to conceal their dependence upon police, bondsmen, jail personnel. Nor do they conceal the necessity for maintaining intimate relations with all levels of personnel in the court setting as a means of obtaining, maintaining, and building their practice. These informal relations are the *sine qua non* not only of retaining a practice, but also in the negotiation of pleas and sentences.

The client, then, is a secondary figure in the court system as in certain other bureaucratic settings. He becomes a means to other ends of the organization's incumbents. He may present doubts, contingencies, and pressures which challenge existing informal arrangements or disrupt them; but these tend to be resolved in favor of the continuance of the organization and its relations as before. There is a greater community of interest among all the principal organizational structures and their incumbents than exists elsewhere in other settings. The accused's lawyer has far greater professional, economic, intellectual and other ties to the various elements of the court system than he does to his own client. In short, the court is a closed community.

This is more than just the case of the usual "secrets" of bureaucracy which are fanatically defended from an outside view. Even all elements of the press are zealously determined to report on that which will not offend the board of judges, the prosecutor, probation, legal-aid, or other officials, in return for privileges and courtesies granted in the past and to be granted in the future. Rather than any view of the matter in terms of some variation of a "conspiracy" hypothesis, the simple explanation is one of an ongoing system handling delicate tensions, managing the trauma produced by law enforcement and administration, and requiring almost pathological distrust of "outsiders" bordering on group paranoia.

The hostile attitude toward "outsiders" is in large measure engendered by a defensiveness itself produced by the inherent deficiencies of assembly line justice, so characteristic of our major criminal courts. Intolerably large caseloads of defendants which must be disposed of in an organizational context of limited resources and personnel, potentially subject the participants in the court community to harsh scrutiny from appellate courts, and other public and private sources of condemnation. As a consequence, an almost irreconcilable conflict is posed in terms of intense pressures to process large numbers of cases on the one hand, and the stringent ideological and legal requirements of "due process of law," on the other hand. A rather tenuous resolution of the dilemma has emerged in the shape of a large variety of bureaucratically ordained and controlled "work crimes," short cuts, deviations, and outright rule violations adopted as court practice in order to meet production norms. Fearfully anticipating criticism on ethical as well as legal grounds, all the significant participants in the court's social structure are bound into an organized system of complicity. This consists of a work arrangement in which the patterned, covert, informal breaches, and evasions of "due process" are institutionalized, but are, nevertheless, denied to exist.

These institutionalized evasions will be found to occur to some degree, in all criminal courts. Their nature, scope, and complexity are largely determined by the size of the court, and the character of the community in which it is located, *e.g.*, whether it is a large, urban institution, or a relatively small rural county court. In addition, idiosyncratic, local conditions may contribute to a unique flavor in the character and quality of the criminal law's administration in a particular community. However, in most instances a variety of strategems are employed — some subtle, some crude, in effectively disposing of what are often too large caseloads. A wide variety of coercive devices are employed against an accused-client, couched in a depersonalized, instrumental, bureaucratic version of due process of law, and which are in reality a perfunctory obeisance to the ideology of due process. These include some very explicit pressures which are exerted in some measure by all court personnel, including judges, to plead guilty and avoid trial. In many instances the sanction of a potentially harsh sentence is utilized as the visible alternative to pleading guilty, in the case of recalcitrants. Probation and psychiatric reports are "tailored" to organizational needs, or are at least responsive to the court organization's requirements for the refurbishment of a defendant's social biography, consonant with his new status. A resourceful judge can, through his subtle domination of the proceedings, impose his will on the final outcome of a trial. Stenographers and clerks, in their function as record keepers, are on occasion pressed into service in support of a judicial need to "rewrite" the record of a courtroom event. Bail practices are usually employed for purposes other than simply assuring a defendant's presence on the date of a hearing in connection with his case. Too often, the discretionary power as to bail is part of the arsenal of weapons available to collapse the resistance of an accused person. The foregoing is a most cursory examination of some of the more prominent "short cuts" available to any court organization. There are numerous other procedural strategies constituting due process deviations, which tend to become the work style artifacts of a court's personnel. Thus, only court "regulars" who are "bound in" are really accepted; others are treated routinely and in almost a coldly correct manner.

The defense attorneys, therefore, whether of the legal-aid, public defender variety, or privately retained, although operating in terms of pressures specific to their respective role and organizational obligations, ultimately are concerned with strategies which tend to lead to a plea. It is the rational, impersonal elements involving economies of time, labor, expense and a superior commitment of the defense counsel to these rationalistic values of maximum production of court organization that prevail, in his relationship with a client. The lawyer "regulars" are frequently former staff members of the prosecutor's office and utilize the prestige, know-how and contacts of their former affiliation as part of their stock in trade. Close and continuing relations between the lawyer "regular" and his former colleagues in the prosecutor's office generally overshadow the relationship between the regular and his client. The continuing colleagueship of supposedly adversary counsel rests on real professional and organizational needs of a *quid pro quo,* which goes beyond the limits of an accommodation or *modus vivendi* one might ordinarily expect under the circumstances of an otherwise seemingly adversary relationship. Indeed, the adversary features which are manifest are for the most part muted and exist even in their attenuated form largely for external consumption. The principals, lawyer and assistant district attorney, rely upon one another's cooperation for their continued professional existence, and so the bargaining between them tends usually to be "reasonable" rather than fierce.

FEE COLLECTION AND FIXING

The real key to understanding the role of defense counsel in a criminal case is to be found in the area of the fixing of the fee to be charged and its collection. The problem of fixing and collecting the fee tends to influence to a significant degree the criminal court process itself, and not just the relationship of the lawyer and his client. In essence, a lawyer-client "confidence game" is played. A true confidence game is unlike the case of the emperor's new clothes wherein that monarch's nakedness was a result of inordinate gullibility and credulity. In a genuine confidence game, the perpetrator manipulates the basic dishonesty of his partner, the victim or mark, toward his own (the confidence operator's) ends. Thus, "the victim of a con scheme must have some larceny in his heart."

Legal service lends itself particularly well to confidence games. Usually, a plumber will be able to demonstrate empirically that he has performed a service by clearing up the stuffed drain, repairing the leaky faucet or pipe — and therefore merits his fee. He has rendered, when summoned, a visible, tangible boon for his client in return for the requested fee. A physician, who has not performed some visible surgery or otherwise engaged in some readily discernible procedure in connection with a patient, may be deemed by the patient to have "done nothing" for him. As a consequence, medical practitioners may simply prescribe or administer by injection a placebo to overcome a patient's potential reluctance or dissatisfaction in paying a requested fee, "for nothing."

In the practice of law there is a special problem in this regard, no matter what the level of the practitioner or his place in the hierarchy of prestige. Much legal work is intangible either because it is simply a few words of advice, some preventive action, a telephone call, negotiation of some kind, a form filled out and filed, a hurried conference with another attorney or an official of a government agency, a letter or opinion written, or a countless variety of seemingly innocuous, and even prosaic procedures and actions. These are the basic activities, apart from any possible court appearance, of almost all lawyers, at all levels of practice. Much of the activity is not in the nature of the exercise of the traditional, precise professional skills of the attorney such as library research and oral argument in connection with appellate briefs, court motions, trial work, drafting of opinions, memoranda, contracts, and other complex documents and agreements. Instead, much legal activity, whether it is at the lowest or highest "white shoe" law firm levels, is of the brokerage, agent, sales representative, lobbyist type of activity, in which the lawyer acts for some one else in pursuing the latter's interests and designs. The service is intangible. . . .

Although the fee at times amounts to what the traffic and the conscience of the lawyer will bear, one further observation must be made with regard to the size of the fee and its collection. The defendant in a criminal case and the material gain he may have acquired during the course of his illicit activities are soon parted. Not infrequently the ill gotten fruits of the various modes of larceny are sequestered by a defense lawyer in payment of his fee. Inexorably, the amount of the fee is a function of the dollar value of the crime committed, and is frequently set with meticulous precision at a sum which bears an uncanny relationship to that of the net proceeds of the particular offense involved. On occasion, defendants have been known to commit additional offenses while at liberty on bail, in order to secure the requisite funds with which to meet their obligations for payment of legal fees. Defense lawyers condition even the most obtuse clients to recognize that there is a firm interconnection between fee payment and the zealous exercise of professional expertise, secret knowledge, and organizational "connections" in their behalf. Lawyers, therefore, seek to keep their clients in a proper state of tension, and to arouse in them the precise edge of anxiety which is calculated to encourage prompt fee payment. Consequently, the client attitude in the relationship between defense counsel and an accused is in many instances a precarious admixture of hostility, mistrust, dependence, and sycophancy. By keeping his client's anxieties aroused to the proper pitch, and establishing a seemingly causal relationship between a requested fee and the accused's ultimate extrication from his onerous difficulties, the lawyer will have established the necessary preliminary groundwork to assure a minimum of haggling over the fee and its eventual payment.

In varying degrees, as a consequence, all law practice involves a manipulation of the client and a stage management of the lawyer-client relationship so that at least an *appearance* of help and service will be forthcoming. This is accomplished in a variety of ways, often exercised in combination with each other. At the outset, the lawyer-professional employs with suitable variation a measure of sales-puff which may range from an air of unbounding selfconfidence, adequacy, and dominion over events, to that of complete arrogance. This will be supplemented by the affectation of a studied, faultless mode of personal attire. In the larger firms, the furnishings and office trappings will serve as the backdrop to help in impression management and client intimidation. In all firms, solo or large scale, an access to secret knowledge, and to the seats of power and influence is inferred, or presumed to a varying degree as the basic vendible commodity of the practitioners.

The lack of visible end product offers a special complication in the course of the professional life of the criminal court lawyer with respect to his fee and in his relations with his client. The plain fact is that an accused in a criminal case always "loses" even when he has been exonerated by an acquittal, discharge, or dismissal of his case. The hostility of an accused which follows as a consequence of his arrest, incarceration, possible loss of job, expense and other traumas connected with his case is directed, by means of displacement, toward his lawyer. It is in this sense that it may be said that a criminal lawyer never really "wins" a case. The really satisfied client is rare, since in the very nature of the situation even an accused's vindication leaves him with some degree of dissatisfaction and hostility. It is this state of affairs that makes for a lawyer-client relationship in the criminal court which tends to be a somewhat exaggerated version of the usual lawyer-client confidence game.

At the outset, because there are great risks of nonpayment of the fee, due to the impecuniousness of his clients, and the fact that a man who is sentenced to jail may be a singularly unappreciative client, the criminal lawyer collects his fee *in advance*. Often, because the lawyer and the accused both have questionable designs of their own upon each other, the confidence game can be played. The criminal lawyer must serve three major functions, or stated another way, he must solve three problems. First, he must arrange for his fee; second, he must prepare and then, if necessary, "cool out" his client in case of defeat (a highly likely contingency); third, he must satisfy the court organization that he has performed adequately in the process of negotiating the plea, so as to preclude the possibility of any sort of embarrassing incident which may serve to invite "outside" scrutiny.

In assuring the attainment of one of his primary objectives, his fee, the criminal lawyer will very often enter into negotiations with the accused's kin, including collateral relatives. In many instances, the accused himself is unable to pay any sort of fee or anything more than a token fee. It then becomes important to involve as many of the accused's kin as possible in the situation. This is especially so if the attorney hopes to collect a significant part of a proposed substantial fee. It is not uncommon for several relatives to contribute toward the fee. The larger the group, the greater the possibility that the lawyer will collect a sizable fee by getting contributions from each.

. . . Should the case go to trial, the fee will be proportionately larger, depending upon the length of the trial. But the larger the fee the lawyer wishes to exact, the more impressive his performance must be, in terms of his stage managed image as a personage of great influence and power in the court organization. Court personnel are keenly aware of the extent to which a lawyer's stock in trade involves the precarious stage management of an image which goes beyond the usual professional flamboyance, and for this reason alone the lawyer is "bound in" to the authority system of the court's organizational discipline. Therefore, to some extent, court personnel will aid the lawyer in the creation and maintenance of that impression. There is a tacit commitment to the lawyer by the court organization, apart from formal etiquette, to aid him in this. Such augmentation of the lawyer's stage managed image as this affords, is the partial basis for the *quid pro quo* which exists between the lawyer and the court organization. It tends to serve as the continuing basis for the higher loyalty of the lawyer to the organization; his relationship with his client, in contrast, is transient, ephemeral and often superficial.

DEFENSE LAWYER AS DOUBLE AGENT

The lawyer has often been accused of stirring up unnecessary litigation, especially in the field of negligence. He is said to acquire a vested interest in a cause of action or claim which was initially his client's. The strong incentive of possible fee motivates the lawyer to promote litigation which would otherwise never have developed. However, the criminal lawyer develops a vested interest of an entirely different nature in his client's case: to limit its scope and duration rather than do battle. Only in this way can a case be "profitable." Thus, he enlists the aid of relatives not only to assure payment of his fee, but he will also rely on these persons to help him in his agent-mediator role of convincing the accused to plead guilty, and ultimately to help in "cooling out" the accused if necessary.

It is at this point that an accused-defendant may experience his first sense of "betrayal." While he had perhaps perceived the police and prosecutor to be adversaries, or possibly even the judge, the accused is wholly unprepared for his counsel's role performance as an agent-mediator. In the same vein, it is even less likely to occur to an accused that members of his own family or other kin may become agents, albeit at the behest and urging of the other agents or mediators, acting on the principle that they are in reality helping an accused negotiate the best possible plea arrangement under the circumstances. Usually, it will be the lawyer who will activate next of kin in this role, his ostensible motive being to arrange for his fee. But soon latent and unstated motives will assert themselves, with entreaties by counsel to the accused's next of kin, to appeal to the accused to "help himself" by pleading. *Gemeinschaft* sentiments are to this extent exploited by a defense lawyer (or even at times by a district attorney) to achieve specific secular ends, that is, of concluding a particular matter with all possible dispatch.

The fee is often collected in stages, each installment usually payable prior to a necessary court appearance required during the course of an accused's career journey. At each stage, in his interviews and communications with the accused, or in addition, with members of his family, if they are helping with the fee payment, the lawyer employs an air of professional confidence and "inside-dopesterism" in order to assuage anxieties on all sides. He makes the necessary bland assurances, and in effect manipulates his client, who is usually willing to do and say the things, true or not, which will help his attorney extricate him. Since the dimensions of what he is essentially selling, organizational influence and expertise, are not technically and precisely measurable, the lawyer can make extravagant claims of influence and secret knowledge with impunity. Thus, lawyers frequently claim to have inside knowledge in connection with information in the hands of the D.A., police, probation officials or to have access to these functionaries. Factually, they often do, and need only to exaggerate the nature of their relationships with them to obtain the desired effective impression upon the client. But, as in the genuine confidence game, the victim who has participated is loath to do anything which will upset the lesser plea which his lawyer has "conned" him into accepting.

In effect, in his role as double agent, the criminal lawyer performs an extremely vital and delicate mission for the court organization and the accused. Both principals are anxious to terminate the litigation with a minimum of expense and damage to each other. There is no other personage or role incumbent in the total court structure more strategically located, who by training and in terms of his own requirements, is more ideally suited to do so than the lawyer. In recognition of this, judges will cooperate with attorneys in many important ways. For example, they will adjourn the case of an accused in jail awaiting plea for sentence if the attorney requests such action. While explicitly this may be done for some innocuous and seemingly valid reason, the tact purpose is that pressure is being applied by the attorney for the collection of his fee, which he knows will probably not be forthcoming if the case is concluded. Judges are aware of this tactic on the part of lawyers, who, by requesting an adjournment, keep an accused incarcerated awhile longer as a not too subtle method of dunning a client for payment. However, the judges will go along with this, on the ground that important ends are being served. Often, the only end served is to protect a lawyer's fee.

The judge will help an accused's lawyer in still another way. He will lend the official aura of his office and courtroom so that a lawyer can stage manage an impression of an "all out" performance for the accused in justification of his fee. The judge and other court personnel will serve as a backdrop for a scene charged with dramatic fire, in which the accused's lawyer makes a stirring appeal in his behalf. With a show of restrained passion, the lawyer will intone the virtues of the accused and recite the social deprivations which have reduced him to his present state. The speech varies somewhat, depending on whether the accused has been convicted after trial or has pleaded guilty. In the main, however, the incongruity, superficiality, and ritualistic character of the total performance is underscored by a visibly impassive, almost bored reaction on the part of the judge and other members of the court retinue.

Afterward, there is a hearty exchange of pleasantries between the lawyer and the district attorney, wholly out of context in terms of the supposed adversary nature of the preceding events. The fiery passion in defense of his client is gone, and the lawyers for both sides resume their offstage relations, chatting amiably and perhaps including the judge in their restrained banter. No other aspect of their visible conduct so effectively serves to put even a casual observer on notice, that these individuals have claims upon each other. These seemingly innocuous actions are indicative of continuing organizational and informal relations, which, in their intricacy and depth, range far beyond any priorities or claims a particular defendant may have.

Criminal law practice is a unique form of private law practice since it really only appears to be private practice. Actually it is bureaucratic practice, because of the legal practitioner's enmeshment in the authority, discipline, and perspectives of the court organization. Private practice, supposedly, in a professional sense, involves the maintenance of an organized, disciplined body of knowledge and learning; the individual practitioners are imbued with a spirit of autonomy and service, the earning of a livelihood being incidental. In the sense that the lawyer in the criminal court serves as a double agent, serving higher organizational rather than professional ends, he may be deemed to be engaged in bureaucratic rather than private practice. To some extent the lawyer-client "confidence game," in addition to its other functions, serves to conceal this fact. . . .

Notes and Questions

1. Curtis said that clients benefit from the detachment of lawyers when lawyers treat litigation as a game. How is this "detachment game" similar to the confidence game?
2. The criminal justice system is frequently criticized for being cumbersome and slow. If Blumberg's observations are true, would more courts, judges, and lawyers necessarily speed up the process, as typically suggested?
3. Consider the following excerpt from a study of criminal defendants:

   > They tended to see the individuals and institutions which apprehended and punished them — police officers, prosecutors, public defenders, judges — as essentially playing games not much different from the games they played themselves. They perceived the behavior of law enforcement officials as being essentially the same as the behavior of law violators — conning, manipulating, lying, using power and resources rather than applying principles of justice. . . .
   >
   > For many of the men, the game-like nature of the system extended even to their relationship to their lawyer. In particular most of those who were represented by public defenders thought their major adversary in the bargaining process to be not the prosecutor or the judge, but rather their own attorney, for he was the man with whom they had to bargain. They saw him as the surrogate of the prosecutor — a member of "their little syndicate" — rather than as their own representative.*

   A confidence game can work only if the victim is unaware of the consequences of the game. Who is getting conned in Blumberg's confidence game? Is it the client? Is it the larger society?

---

*Jonathan D. Casper, "Did You Have a Lawyer When You Went to Court? No, I Had a Public Defender," *Yale Review of Law and Social Action* 1 (Spring 1974): 4–9.

Blumberg's study took place in an atypical legal practice setting — the New York City criminal courts. Given certain elements in the study — the big-city legal system, criminal law, low-status lawyers, and poor defendants — generalizations based on his findings and analysis may not be applicable to legal practice and lawyers in other settings, such as small towns, civil law, high-status lawyers, and affluent clients.

Sarat and Felstiner's study probes that idea and also introduces a number of new points for discussion of the lawyer-client relationship. The study was conducted over thirty-three months in two small-town sites, one in Massachusetts and the other in California. The researchers followed one side of forty divorce cases, from the time of first lawyer-client interview until the divorce was final. They sat in during lawyer-client office conferences, attended court and mediation hearings and trials, and continuously interviewed the lawyers and clients during the process of each case. The following is a report from one portion of their study.

Law and Strategy in the Divorce Lawyer's Office

Austin Sarat and William L. F. Felstiner

The lawyer involved in this case graduated from one of the country's top-ranked law schools. He was forty years old at the time of the conference and had practiced for fourteen years. His father was a prominent physician in a neighboring city. The lawyer had spent four years as a public defender after law school and had been in private practice for ten years. He considers himself a trial lawyer and states that he was drawn to divorce work because of the opportunity it provides for trial work. He is married and has never been divorced.

The client and her husband were in their late thirties and had no children. Their marriage had been stormy, involving both substantial separations and infidelity by the husband. Both had graduate degrees and worked full-time; financial support was not an issue. They owned a house, bank stocks, several limited partnerships in real estate, his retirement benefits and personal property. The house was their major asset. It was an unconventional building to which the husband was especially attached. Housing in the area is very expensive. This divorce was the client's second; there were no children in the first marriage either. She had received extensive psychological counseling prior to and during the case which we observed.

The parties in this divorce initially tried to dissolve their marriage by engaging a mediator and did not at the time individually consult lawyers. The mediator was an established divorce lawyer with substantial experience in divorce mediation. At the first substantive session, the mediator stated that he did not think that further progress could be made if both the spouses

Austin Sarat and William F. Felstiner, "Law and Strategy in the Divorce Lawyer's Office," from *Law and Society Review,* Volume 20:1. Reprinted by permission of the Law and Society Association. (Most footnotes omitted.)

continued to live in the house. Although she considered it to be a major sacrifice, the wife said that she had moved out of the house to facilitate mediation after her husband absolutely refused to leave. Thereafter, she visited the house occasionally, primarily to check on plants and pets. The client reported that she was careful to warn her husband when she intended to visit.

Over time, however, this arrangement upset her husband. Rather than raise the problem at a mediation session, he hired a lawyer and secured an *ex parte* order restraining the client from entering the property at any time for any reason. The husband had previously characterized the lawyer that he hired as "the meanest son-of-a-bitch in town." The restraining order ended any prospects for mediation and the client, on the advice of the mediator and another lawyer, hired the lawyer involved in the conference.

Subsequently, a hearing about the propriety of the *ex parte* order was held by a second judge. The issues at this hearing were whether the order should be governed by a general or a divorce-specific injunction statute, what status quo the order was intended to maintain, and whether the husband's attempt to secure the order violated a moral obligation undertaken when the client agreed to move out of the house. The second judge decided against the client on the first two issues, but left consideration of the bad faith question open to further argument. The client's therapist attended the hearing and the lawyer-client conference that immediately followed. At that conference the therapist stressed that contesting the restraining order further might not be in the client's long-term interest even if it corrected the legal wrong.

The conference analyzed in this paper followed the meeting attended by the therapist and was the seventh of twelve that occurred during the course of the case. It took place in the lawyer's office five weeks after the first meeting between lawyer and client. Its two phases, interrupted for several hours at midday, lasted a total of about two hours.

The people referred to in this conference are:[1]

Lawyer	Peter Edmunds
Client	Jane Carroll
Spouse	Norb
Spouse's lawyer	Paul Foster

THE LEGAL PROCESS OF DIVORCE

Clients look to lawyers to explain how the legal system works and to interpret the actions and decisions of legal officials. Despite their lack of knowledge about and contact with the law, clients are likely to have some general notions that the law works as a formally rational legal order, one that is rule governed, impersonal, impartial, predictable, and relatively error free. How do lawyers respond to this picture? In this conference we are interested in the image of the legal process that the lawyer presents. Does he subscribe to the formalist image or does he present the kind of picture that would be drawn by a legal realist, one in which rules are of limited relevance, impersonality gives way to communities of interest shaped by the needs of ongoing relationships, routinization provides the only predictability, and errors are frequently made but seldom acknowledged? Or does he present some mix of the two images or a set of messages different from both?

In this conference the lawyer presents the legal process of divorce largely in response to questions or remarks by the client. In many conferences clients ask for an explanation of some aspect of the legal system's procedures or rules. In this conference the client repeatedly inquires about both. While most of her questions concern the details of her own case, several are general. Thus, she invites her lawyer to explain the way that the legal process operates as well as to justify its operation in her case. At no point does the lawyer deliver a monologue on how it works. Instead his comments are interspersed in the discussion of major substantive issues, particu-

[1]Fictional names have been assigned to all the participants and places.

larly concerning what to do about the restraining order and how to proceed with settlement negotiations. Throughout the conference the client persists in focusing on the restraining order until finally she asks:

CLIENT: How often does a case like this come along — a restraining order of this nature?

LAWYER: Very common.

CLIENT: It's a very common thing. So how many other people are getting the same kind of treatment I am? With what, I presume, is very sloppily handled orders that are passed out.

LAWYER: Yeah, you know, I talked, I did talk to someone in the know — I won't go any further than that — who said that this one could have been signed purely by accident. I mean, that the judge could have — if he looked at it now — said, I would not sign that, knowing what it was, and it could have been signed by accident, and I said, well, then how does that happen? And he said, well, you've got all this stuff going; you come back to your office, and there's a stack of documents that need signatures. He says, you can do one of two things: you can postpone signing them until you have time, but then it may be the end of the day; the clerk's office is closing, and people who really need this stuff aren't going to get the orders, because there's someone else that needs your attention, so you go through them, and one of the main things you look for is the law firm or lawyer who is proposing them. And you tend to rely on them.

The lawyer thus states that a legal order of immense consequence to this woman may have been handled in a way that in several respects is inconsistent with the formalist image of a rational system: It may have been signed by accident. Moreover, the lawyer claims that he has received this information from "someone in the know," someone he refuses to identify. By this refusal, he implies that the information was given improperly, in breach of confidence. Furthermore, the lawyer's description of how judges handle court orders suggests a high level of inattention and routinization. Judges sign orders without reading them to satisfy "people who really need this stuff." While the judge is said to ignore the substance of the order, he does pay attention to the lawyer or law firm who requests it. The legal process is thereby portrayed as responding more to reputation than to substantive merit. Thus, the client is introduced to a system that is hurried, routinized, personalistic, and accident prone.

Throughout this conference, the theme of the importance of insider status and access within the local legal system is reinforced by references to the lawyer's personal situation. . . .

The lawyer later claims that he knows one of the judges involved in this client's case well enough to tell him off in private ("I'll tell you when this is over, I'm going to take it to John Hancock and I don't think he'll ever do it again") and that he supported the other's campaign for office. These references suggest that a lawyer's capacity to protect his client's interests depends in part on his special access to the system's functionaries who will react to who he is rather than what he represents. We found this emphasis on insider status, reputation, and local connections repeatedly in the cases that we observed. The lawyer in this case and other lawyers we studied generally presented themselves as well-connected insiders, valuable because they are known and respected rather than because they are expert legal technicians.

The kind of familiarity with the way the system works that insiders possess is all the more important in divorce cases because the divorce process is extremely difficult to explain even to acute outsiders.

CLIENT: Tell me just the mechanics of this, Peter. What exactly is an interlocutory?

LAWYER: You should know. It's your right to know. But whether or not I'm going to be able to explain this to you is questionable. . . . It's a very . . . It's sort of simple in practice, but it's very confusing to explain. I've got an awful lot of really smart people who've — who I haven't represented — who've asked me after the divorce is over, now what the hell was the interlocutory judgment?

The communications that we have been discussing are, for the most part, explicit. The message is in the message. But there is also a way in which the language forms that the lawyer employs to describe the legal process communicate something about that process itself. Although this lawyer is articulate and knowledgeable, his reactions to many of the client's questions are nevertheless circuitous and confusing. Interviews with clients, as well as our observations, suggest that this failing is common. Instead of direct description, lawyers frequently use analogies that seem to obscure more than they reveal. This practice, of course, may be seen as a simple problem of communication. Yet it also suggests that law and legal process are themselves so dense and erratic that they pose a formidable barrier even to well educated and intelligent laypeople. . . .

Moving from the restraining order to the question of how a settlement could be reached, the client asks why her lawyer did not acknowledge to the other side what he had shared with her, namely that a court battle might end in defeat. In response the lawyer might simply have said that it is poor strategy in a negotiation to tell the other side that you recognize that you may lose. Instead he says:

LAWYER: Okay. I'll do it in my usual convoluted way, using lots of analogies and examples. When you write to . . . when a lawyer writes to an insurance company, representing a person who's been injured in an automobile accident, usually the first demand is somewhat higher than what we actually expect to get out of the case. I always explain that to clients. I explain it very, very carefully. I don't like to write letters of any substance without my client getting a copy of it, and inevitably, I will send a copy of it to my client with another letter explaining, "This is for settlement purposes. Please do not think that your case, which I evaluate at $10,000, is really worth $35,000." And then months later when I finally get the offer to settle for $10,000, I will convey it to my client, and they'll say, well, I've been thinking about this, and I think that you're right; it really was worth $35,000. I then am in a terrible position of having to talk my own client down from a number that I created in the first place and that I tried to support and convince them — of course, they wanted to be convinced, so it was easy — that's the difference between a letter that you send to your adversary and a letter that you, or than what you communicate to your client. They're two different kinds of communications. I truly, I mean, where I am is that I . . . The way I evaluate the case is the way I did when Irene was here. This is an objective evaluation for your use, and there is this tension and conflict in every representation. You have hired me to represent your interests. I do that in two fashions. One, I tell you the way I truly see the picture, and then I try to advance your cause as aggressively as I can. Sometimes — almost always — those are inconsistent. I mean, the actions, the words, and so forth are inconsistent.

. . . The lawyer's point is the hypocrisy of orthodox settlement negotiations. Even if warned, he claims, clients are likely to confuse demands and values. That is their error. In the legal process words and goals, expressed objectives and real objectives, are usually "inconsistent."

Not only is the legal process inconsistent, but it cannot be counted on to protect fundamental rights or deal in a principled way with the important matters that come before it. Thus, the lawyer validates the client's expressed belief that her rights are neither absolute nor secure in the legal process.

CLIENT: I just really cannot quite believe this, you know. Part of me is still incredulous. I'm . . . It's . . . It's nothing else than property rights. I don't even have the rights of a landlord, to go to a home that I own 50 percent of, to make sure it's not being destroyed. I don't understand that.

[Long pause.] I always thought that, in some way or another, if one's human rights were not protected, one's property rights were.

LAWYER: No. . . .

Later in the conference the relationship of law to values like fairness and justice is discussed more explicitly. At that point the client muses about her goals and hopes about the legal process of divorce.

CLIENT: Well, I mean, I'm a liberal. Right? A liberal dream is that you will find social justice, and so here was this statement that it was possible to fight injustice, and you were going to protect me from horrible things like judicial abuse. So that's, uh, it was really nice.

To the client, "justice" demands that the error of the restraining order be righted. For the lawyer that kind of justice simply gets in the way of what for him is the real business of divorce: to reach a property settlement, not to right wrongs or vindicate justice. There is, if you will, a particular kind of justice that the law provides, but it is not broad enough to include the kind that the client seeks. For her justice requires some compensation, or at least an acknowledgment that she has "been treated unjustly." When she finally gets the lawyer to speak in terms of justice, he admits that it cannot be secured through the legal process.

CLIENT: But as you say, if you want justice in this society, you look somewhere other than the court. I believe that's what you were saying to Bob.

LAWYER: Yeah, that's what I said. Ultimate justice, that is.

Legal justice is thus juxtaposed to ultimate justice. The person seeking such a final accounting is clearly out of place in a system that focuses much more narrowly. To fit into the system the client must reduce her conception of justice to what the law can provide. But perhaps the language of justice serves, for this client, a purpose that is neither as abstract nor as disinterested as her language suggests. This client identifies justice solely with the vindication of her own position. She never refers to a more general standard. Thus the failure of law to provide justice is, for her, a failure to validate her position. The language of justice also serves to bolster her image of herself as an innocent, rather gracious, victim of an evil husband and his untrustworthy lawyer. Tendencies toward self-exculpation and blaming are quite common in the divorces in our sample, although the use of the language of justice toward such ends is not. This language also serves to exert moral pressure on this lawyer to validate the client's sense of herself even as he attempts to explain the limits of the legal process.

In total, the lawyer's description of the legal process involves an open acknowledgment of human frailties, contradictions between appearance and reality, carelessness, incoherence, accident, and built-in limitations. The picture presented is both cynical and probably considered by the lawyer to be realistic. . . .

TO FIGHT OR TO SETTLE? . . .

While many clients think of the legal process as an arena for a full adversarial contest, most divorce disputes are not resolved in this manner. Although not all lawyers are equally dedicated to reaching negotiated agreements, most of those we observed advised their clients to try to settle the full range of issues in the case. This is not to say that these divorces were free of conflict, for the negotiations themselves were often quite contentious. Although some of our lawyers occasionally advised clients to ask for more than the client had originally contemplated or to refuse to concede on a major issue when the client was inclined to do so, most seemed to believe that it is generally better to settle than contest divorce disputes. Thus, we are interested in the ways in which lawyers get their clients to see settlement as the preferred alternative.

The conference we are examining revolves around two major issues: (1) whether to ignore or contest the restraining order; and (2) what position to take concerning disposition of the family residence. Much of the conference is devoted to discussing the restraining order — its origins, morality, and legality; the prospects for dissolving it; the lawyer's stake in contesting it; and the client's emotional reaction to it. Substantively the order is not as important as the house itself, which received much less attention and generated much less controversy. Both issues, however, force the lawyer and client to decide whether they will retain control of the case by engaging in negotiations or cede control to the court for hearing and decision. The lawyer definitely favors negotiations.

LAWYER: Okay. What I would like your permission to do then is to meet with Foster, see if I can come up with or negotiate a settlement with him that, before he leaves . . . I leave his office or he leaves my office, he says, we've got something here that I can recommend to my client, and I can say, I've got something here that I can recommend to my client. My feeling is, Jane, that if we reach that point, both lawyers are prepared to make a recommendation on settlement to their respective clients, if either of the clients, either you or Norb, find something terribly disagreeable with the proposal that we have, the lawyers have come to between themselves, then the case just either can't be settled or it's not ripe for settlement. But we would have given it the best shot. But I wouldn't . . . as you know, I'm very concerned about wasting a lot of time and energy trying to settle a case where two previous attempts have been dismally unsuccessful.

The major ingredient of this settlement system is the primacy of the lawyers. They produce the deals while the clients are limited to initial instructions and after-the-fact ratification. The phrase "we would have given it our best shot" is crucial. The "we" seems to refer to the lawyers. Indeed, their efforts could come to nothing if either client backs out at the last minute. The settlement process as described thus has two dimensions — a lawyer to lawyer phase, in which an arrangement is worked out, and a lawyers versus clients phase, in which the opposing lawyers join together to sell the deal to their clients. . . . If the clients do not accept the settlement as a package, the only alternative is to go to trial. Furthermore if the professionals are content with the agreement they have devised, dissatisfied clients not only have nothing to contribute but also had perhaps better seek psychotherapy. . . .

THE LEGAL CONSTRUCTION OF THE CLIENT

To get clients in divorce cases to move toward accepting settlement as well as to carry out the terms of such agreements, lawyers may have to try to cool them out when they are at least partially inclined toward contest. In divorce as in criminal cases, the lawyer must help redefine the client's orientation toward the legal process. . . . In the criminal case this means that lawyers must help the client come to terms with dropping the pretense of innocence; in divorce work this means that lawyers must help their clients view the emotional process of dissolving an intimate relationship in instrumental terms. In both instances, lawyers and clients struggle, although rarely explicitly, with the issue of what part of the client's personality is relevant to the legal process. Thus, the discussion of whether to fight or settle is more than a conversation about the most appropriate way to dispose of the case. Contained within the discourse about negotiation is the construction of a legal picture of the client, a picture through which a self acceptable to the legal process is negotiated and validated. . . . This construction is necessary because the legal process will not or cannot deal with many aspects of the disputes that are brought to it. Legal professionals behave as if it were natural and inevitable that a litigant's problems be divided up in the manner that the legal process prescribes. . . . Lawyers thus legitimate some parts of human experience and deny the relevance of others, but they do not explicitly state what is required of the client. Rather, the approved form of the legal self is built up from a set of oppositions and priorities among these oppositions.

The negotiation of the legal self in this case begins by focusing on the relative importance of emotions engaged by the legal process and the symbolic aspects of the divorce as opposed to its financial and material dimensions. . . .

Throughout this conference the lawyer stresses the need for two parallel separations: the separation of the emotional issues from the legal and the separation of the client and her husband.

CLIENT: I mean, I don't want to fight and I do want to fight, right? That's exactly what it comes down to.

LAWYER: Yeah, you're ambiguous.

CLIENT: Oh, boy, am I ever. And I have to live with it.

LAWYER: That's right. I'd say the ambiguity goes even deeper than the issue of fighting and not fighting. It's how . . . The ambiguity is what Irene talked about and that is — it's the real hard one — it's terminating the entire relationship. You do and you don't, and the termination . . . I mean, you're angry; you're pissed off. You've said that. And are you ready to call a halt to the anger and I'm not so sure that that's humanly possible. Can your rational mind say, okay, Jane, there has been enough anger expended on this; it is time to get on with your life. If you are able to do that, great. But I don't know.

As the lawyer sees it, the client will only be able to make an adequate arrangement with her husband when she can contemplate their relationship unemotionally. As the client sees it, the second separation seems impossible if the first is carried out. She cannot become free of her husband if she thinks about legal problems in material terms only — if she fails to take her feelings into account she will continue to be affected by them. Thus, the program the lawyer presents to the client appropriates her marriage to the realm of property and defines her connection to her husband exclusively in those terms. She, on the other hand, sees property issues embedded in a broader context. The client speaks about the separation of the emotional and financial issues as being difficult to effect because it is unnatural. The market does not exhaust her realm of values, and she has difficulty assigning governing priority to it. Yet this is what the lawyer indicates the law requires.

Nevertheless, the separation of emotional and economic matters may benefit the client. While it does exact an emotional toll, concentrating on the instrumental, tangible aspects of the divorce may produce a more satisfactory disposition than focusing on the emotional concerns. The lawyer may be trying to explain to his client that in the long run she is going to be more interested in the economics of the settlement than in the vindication of her immediate emotional needs. In his view, legal justice, although narrow, is justice nonetheless, and his job is to secure for her the best that can be achieved given the legal process as he knows it.

Putting emotional matters aside may also serve the interests of lawyers untrained in dealing with emotional problems and unwilling to find ways to cope with them. It allows lawyers to sidestep what is clearly one of the most difficult and least rewarding aspects of divorce practice. In so doing they are able to avoid assuming a sense of responsibility for the human consequences of being unresponsive to emotion. In this conference, for example, the lawyer suggests that the legal process works best for those who can control their emotions and concentrate on the instrumental, the calculating, the pecuniary. The client's uncertainty about the possibility of such a separation of issues is met by a certainty expressed by the lawyer. But the lawyer's certainty is not that the client can effect the required separation but rather that the separation is an imperative of the legal process without which the system cannot efficiently deliver its goods. Having expressed this imperative, the lawyer is thus relieved of any responsibility for helping his client to come to terms with the anger and frustration that condition her feelings about property issues. Ultimately, it seems that the client gets the message. As she says, "The extraneous factors, which are every bit as important as the rest of it, are not going to be paid attention to at all."

CONCLUSION

Lawyer-client interaction involves attempts to negotiate acceptable resolutions of problems in which lawyers and clients usually have different agendas, expectations, and senses of justice. As in any negotiation, the parties possess different information and have different needs to fulfill. Clients know their histories and goals, lawyers must learn about them. Lawyers know the law and the legal process, clients must find out about them. Every conference is thus to some extent competitive: Each of the participants sets out to fulfill their own agenda and generally only provides what the other wants on demand. . . .

Lawyer-Client Interaction: The Lawyer's Perspective Clients bring to their encounters with lawyers an expectation that the justice system will impartially sort the facts in dispute to provide a deductive reading of the "truth." They expect the legal process to take their problems seriously, and they usually seek vindication of the positions that they have adopted. They expect the legal process to follow its own rules, to proceed in an orderly manner, and to be fair and error free. . . . [M]ost litigants begin with a fairly strong belief in "formal justice." By the time a problem has become serious enough to warrant bringing it to a lawyer and mobilizing the legal process, "the grievant wants vindication, protection of his or her rights, an advocate to help in the battle or a third party who will uncover the 'truth' and declare the other party wrong. Observations suggest that courts rarely provide this . . . but inexperienced plaintiffs do not know this." . . .

To some extent, it is the job of lawyers to bring these expectations and images of law and legal justice closer to the reality that they have experienced. For them legal justice is situational and outcomes are often unpredictable. The legal process provides an arena where compromises are explored, settlements are reached, and, if money is at issue, assets are divided. Lawyers are intimately familiar with the human dimensions of the legal process. They know that in most instances the process is not rule governed, that there is widespread use of discretion, and that decisions are influenced by matters extraneous to legal doctrine. Moreover, they believe that most clients cannot afford or would not want to pay the cost of a full adversarial contest. They may conclude, therefore, based on experience, that the client who demands vindication today will want both a larger financial settlement and a smaller lawyer's bill tomorrow. . . .

Lawyer-Client Interaction: The Client's Perspective Because divorce clients may not direct their litigation does not mean that they play no part in it. Because clients may acquiesce in the end to the lawyer's agenda does not mean that they do not make demands on their lawyer during the process. Clients may insist that lawyers attend to issues beyond those that are technically relevant and with which lawyers do not feel particularly comfortable; they may persist in bringing these matters into the conversation even after lawyers think that they have been settled. Clients may, in addition, resist recommendations that a lawyer believes are obviously in the client's interest. They may press lawyers to explain and justify advice given, actions taken, and results produced. Finally, clients may insist that lawyers interpret and account for the actions of others, particularly their spouse, their spouse's lawyer, and judges, and that lawyers justify these actions in light of the client's sense of what is appropriate and fair. In these ways, clients transform the agendas of lawyers as well as their preferred professional style.

This conference allowed the client to express her frustrations with a legal process that refused to protect her "rights." . . .

In addition, the conference provided the client with an opportunity to work through conflicting goals: She did not want to capitulate to her husband but she did want to put an end to the fighting between them. Like many of the clients we have observed, she is uncertain about what she really wants. The wisdom of a negotiated settlement is clear to the lawyer, but for her it is fraught with ambiguity and difficulty. . . .

The Consequences of the Two Perspectives The competing perspectives of lawyer and client and the manner in which they are articulated establish the boundaries within which the strategy and tactics of divorce litigation develop. When the client feels betrayed and victimized, the lawyer may have to spend a significant amount of time and energy in selling negotiation as the means of resolving the case. This effort may affect the timing as well as the style and success of settlement efforts. . . .

Moreover, when divorce clients demand to know about the legal rules that will be applied, the probabilities of achieving various results, the costs they will incur, the pace at which various things will happen, and the roles that different actors will play, there are no standard answers that lawyers can give. What the client is asking for is a distillation of the lawyer's experience as it is relevant to cases like hers. What the lawyer can provide is not a *corpus juris* learned in law school or available in any texts but rather a personal view of how the legal system actually works in the community in which he is practicing.

The lawyer's emphasis on the uncertain and personalistic nature of that process may have three effects. First, the extent to which the lawyer's picture of the legal system is at variance with the image that the client brings to her contact with the law may help to explain the common finding that experience with the legal process often results in dissatisfaction and a lower level of respect for law, regardless of substantive outcome. . . . Clients are brought face-to-face with the law's shortcomings by the testimony of their own lawyers . . . as well as by the results that they experience.

Second, this characterization of the legal process may increase the client's dependence on the lawyer. People in the midst of divorce frequently feel a reduced sense of control over their lives. Their former lover and friend has become an enemy. They cannot live where and as they did, they must relate to their children in new ways, they may face new jobs and major economic threats, and their relations with family and friends may be strained, sometimes to the breaking point. When lawyers then introduce clients to an uncontrollable and unpredictable legal system, their sense of reduced control over their lives may become even stronger. They are, in essence, further threatened by a system that they had expected would reintroduce structure and predictability into their lives. In this situation, the lawyer's services become more essential and the lawyer himself more indispensable. . . .

Finally, the lawyer's emphasis on the client's need to separate emotional and instrumental issues may help to construct or reflect a vision of law in which particular parts of the self are valued while others are denied or left for others to validate. In the legal realm, lawyers insist that the rational and instrumental are to govern. While this lawyer clearly recognizes the human consequence of this opposition and hierarchy, he never questions it but instead treats it as both necessary and inevitable. . . . Throughout this conference the lawyer encourages the client to be clear headed and to grant priority to monetary issues. By defining the ultimate goal as the resolution to the case and resolution in terms of the division of property, and by seeking to exclude the emotional focus that the client continues to provide, he expresses the indifference of the law to those parts of the self that might be most salient at the time of the divorce. The legal process of divorce becomes at best a distraction, at worst an additional trauma. By the end of the conference both lawyer and client speak in terms of a divided self, she, if only briefly, to fight against it or at least to express her ambivalence, he to do its bidding in the name of a system that is unchanging and unchangeable. . . .

Notes and Questions

1. How does Sarat and Felstiner's understanding of the adversary process compare to that of Curtis, Frank, or Blumberg? Does the lawyer in the divorce case seem to embrace either the "truth" theory or the "fight" theory in his approach to this case and client? What about the lawyer's paternalistic attitudes toward the client — are they justified? Does he know best? About what does he know best?
2. The divorce lawyer tries to draw the client into understanding a distinction between legal justice and ultimate justice. Why isn't ultimate justice a possible legal outcome here? If the client cannot be satisfied with anything less that ultimate justice, is that a failure of the law or of the lawyer?
3. As discussed by Sarat and Felstiner, much of the negotiation described in this study revolves around seemingly contradictory understandings of the lawyer and the client concerning the nature of law and legal process. The client assumes clarity and predictability; the lawyer assumes uncertainty and unpredictability. Under these circumstances, what is the basis of the lawyer's authority as an expert?

☐ As noted in Curran's demographic study, the legal profession has always been a male preserve. Only in the past decade have women lawyers begun to move beyond their token status. Some feminist scholars argue that male control has caused law and its practice to be permeated with masculine values; among them are adversariness, paternalism, conflict, intimidation, suppression of emotions, and domination of the weak. The prevalent images of the legal trial as gladiatorial combat, knightly jousts, or gunfighter showdowns have only masculine referents. Certainly, many readings in this text about lawyers, police, and judges could provide examples of male values and virtues. However, as women become a greater proportion of lawyers, feminine values — such as nurturance, healing, cooperation, and release of emotion — are expected by some to carry deeply into law and legal practice, ultimately transforming both. The metaphor of the law as male is a challenging image. However, even if that idea is accepted, the questions remain, will women change law and lawyering, as some feminists hope? — or, conversely, will women be changed by these institutions? The following reading provides some background for this speculation and debate.

Portia in a Different Voice: Speculations on a Women's Lawyering Process *Carrie Menkel-Meadow*

INTRODUCTION

As a scholar of the legal profession, I have asked whether the increased presence of women in the legal profession might lead to alternative ways of seeing what lawyers do and how they do it. Will it be simply that more lawyers are women, or will the legal profession be transformed by the women who practice law? In recent years, two developments in feminist scholarship have offered insights which promise to shed some light on that question. This essay explores some of the potential applications to law of these two developments in feminist scholarship stated as speculative hypotheses for further study.

The first of these developments in feminist scholarship is the self-conscious observation of how women's entry into formerly male-dominated fields has changed both the knowledge base of the field and the methodology by which knowledge is acquired. Since our knowledge of how lawyers behave and of how the legal system functions is based almost exclusively on male subjects of study, our understanding of what it means to be and act like a lawyer may be misleadingly based on a male norm. We need to broaden our inquiry to include the new participants in the profession so that we can discover whether our present understandings are accurate. With more women lawyers available for study we may learn first, whether women perform lawyering tasks in ways different from men; second, whether our descriptions of what lawyers do may have to change to reflect different goals or task orientations; and third, whether the increased presence of women in the profession may have broad institutional effects. Current studies of gender differences in other fields offer a powerful heuristic for application to our understanding of the lawyering process.

Abridged from *Berkeley Women's Law Journal,* Volume 1, No. 1 (Fall, 1985), pp. 39–63 (footnotes omitted). Reprinted by permission.

The second development is a body of theoretical and empirical research in psychology and sociology. This research has postulated that women grow up in the world with a more relational and affiliational concept of self than do men. This concept of self has important implications for the values that women develop and for the actions that are derived from those values. This research is controversial and is generating criticism from many different quarters. I am not unsympathetic to some of the criticism, which in part reflects a growing maturity and differentiation in feminist scholarship.

I find persuasive, though not unproblematic, the notion that values, consciousness, attributes, and behavior are gendered, *i.e.,* that some are identified as belonging to women and others to men. The attachment of gender labels is a product of both present empirical research and social process. Thus, we may label the quality of caring a female quality, but note its presence in many men. Further, a man who exhibits many feminine qualities may be perceived as feminine, *e.g.* "He's too sensitive to be a good trial lawyer," or alternatively, an assertive woman may be met with remarks such as, "She's as sharp as any of the men on the team." Attributing behavior characteristics to a particular gender is problematic, because even as we observe such generalizations to be valid in many cases, we risk perpetuating the conventional stereotypes that prevent us from seeing the qualities as qualities without their gendered context.

The process is one that most feminists deplore because what is labeled female or feminine typically is treated as inferior, and is subordinated to what is labeled male or masculine. This is particularly true if the context in which they are found is one, such as the practice of law, which has itself traditionally been labeled male. For the purpose of this essay I assume that gender differences exist as they have been documented by such writers as Simone de Beauvoir, Carol Gilligan, Nancy Chodorow, Jean Baker

Miller, Anne Schaef and others, and will leave to others the important inquiry into the origins of these differences, be they biological, sociological, political, or some combination of these. My perspective on this issue is that as long as such differences exist, studies of the world — here the legal profession — that fail to take into account women's experience of that world are incomplete, and prevent us from having a greater repertoire of societal as well as individual choices.

An important part of this inquiry is whether it is yet possible to see if women conduct themselves as lawyers differently from men. I have commented elsewhere that just because there are increasing numbers of women in the practice and teaching of law, we do not yet know whether women will transform the practice or themselves when they are found in sufficient numbers. Social research has indicated that those in token numbers may feel strong pressure to conform to the already existing norms of the workplace and to minimize, rather than emphasize, whatever differences exist. Thus, when we look at women who are lawyers in 1985, we may be studying those women who have been successful in assimilating to male norms. Although there is already some evidence of Portia-like dissatisfaction with the present male voice, more women lawyers may be necessary to form a critical mass that will give full expression to a women's voice in law (whether expressed exclusively by women or with men in another voice.) . . .

A DIFFERENT VOICE: PSYCHOLOGICAL THEORIES ABOUT WOMEN

Several recent studies and books in psychological development have traced the implications of gender differences in psychological development for personality, moral development, child rearing, and ultimately, the very structure of major social institutions. The common theme that unites this body of work by psychologists such as Chodorow, Dinnerstein, Miller, Schaef, and most recently, Gilligan, is that women experience themselves through connections and relationships to others while men see themselves as separately identified individuals. In the view of Dinnerstein and Chodorow, these differences are the result of a childrearing system which is based on mothering, so that growing up is a process of identification and connection for a girl and separation and individuation for a boy. Miller and Schaef, working as psychologists, heard women express values different from men's: vulnerability instead of strength, and responsiveness instead of independence. Noddings and Gilligan, both professors of education, observed values of caring, responsiveness and relatedness in women, while they found values of principle, rights and universalism in men. These observations and hypotheses led to the conclusion that women tend to see themselves as affiliated and related to others, while men are more likely to see themselves as separate, individualized, and different from (m)other. Although each of these writers came at their inquiry with different questions, their findings and theories are strikingly similar.

Because Carol Gilligan's work is the most recent entry into this stream of research, and because it has already served as a powerful heuristic for legal studies, I will explore, mostly by speculative analogy rather than by suggesting a possibly fallacious direct relationship, how, from a women's different voice in moral development, we might infer a women's different voice in legal processes.

In her book, *In a Different Voice: Psychological Theory and Women's Development,* Gilligan observes that much of what has been written about human psychological development has been based on studies of male subjects exclusively. As a consequence, girls and women have either not been described, or they are said to have "failed" to develop on measurement scales based on male norms. Just as Gilligan has observed that studies of human psychological development have been centered on males, feminists have observed the law to be based on male values and behaviors. As Frances Olsen notes:

> Law is supposed to be rational, objective, abstract and principled, like men; it is not supposed to be irrational, subjective, contextualized or personalized like women. The social, political and intellectual practices that constitute "law" were for many years carried out almost exclusively by men. Given that women were long excluded from the practice of law, it should not be surprising that the traits associated with women are not greatly valued by law. Moreover, in a kind of vicious cycle, the "maleness" of law was used as a justification for excluding women from practicing law. While the number of women in law has been rapidly increasing, the field continues to be heavily male dominated.

This phenomenon has also been noted by the sociologist Cynthia Fuchs Epstein, who observed that because white middle-aged men have been the demographic norm of "lawyer" for so long, we come to identify the characteristics of white middle-aged maleness as necessary for lawyering. We do not consider what the qualities of being a lawyer are independent of their identification with the male gender. Thus, with males as the only source of our descriptions of lawyers, what is normal, good or true is identified solely with how men behave in law, a close parallel to Gilligan's conclusions in the area of moral development.

The male-derived model of moral reasoning and psychological development described by Gilligan values hierarchical thinking based on the logic of reasoning from abstract, universal principles. Gilligan measures her findings against the work of her colleague, Lawrence Kohlberg. His theory of moral development comprised of six "universal" stages is based on a study of eighty-four *boys* from childhood through adulthood. Gilligan explains that when Kohlberg's model is applied to women, they tend to score at stage three, a stage characterized by seeing morality as a question of interpersonal relations and caring for and pleasing others. In looking at moral judgments and hearing the "women's voice," Gilligan discovered that:

> [w]hen one begins with the study of women and derives developmental constructs from their lives, the outline of a moral conception different from that described by Freud, Piaget, or Kohlberg begins to emerge and informs a different description of development. In this conception, the moral problem arises from conflicting responsibilities rather than from competing rights and requires for its resolution a mode of thinking that is contextual and narrative rather than formal and abstract.

An example drawn from Gilligan's work best illustrates the duality of girls' and boys' moral development. In one of the three studies on which her book is based, a group of children are asked to solve Heinz's dilemma, a hypothetical moral reasoning problem used by Kohlberg to rate moral development on his six-stage scale. The dilemma is that Heinz's wife is dying of cancer and requires a drug which the local pharmacist has priced beyond Heinz's means. The question is posed: should Heinz steal the drug?

To illustrate and explain the differences between the ways boys and girls approached this problem, Gilligan quotes from two members of her sample, Jake and Amy. Jake, an eleven-year-old boy, sees the problem as one of "balancing rights," like a judge who must make a decision or a mathematician who must solve an algebraic equation. Life is worth more than property, therefore Heinz should steal the drug. For Amy, an eleven-year-old girl, the problem is different. Like a "bad" law student she "fights the hypo"; she wants to know more facts: Have Heinz and the druggist explored other possibilities, like a loan or credit transaction? Why couldn't Heinz and the druggist simply sit down and talk it out so that the druggist would come to see the importance of Heinz's wife's life? In Gilligan's terms, Jake explores the Heinz dilemma with "the logic of justice" while Amy uses the "ethic of care." Amy scores lower on the Kohlberg scale because she sees the problem rooted in the persons involved rather than in the larger universal issues posed by the dilemma.

In conventional terms Jake would make a good lawyer because he spots the legal issues of excuse and justification, balances the rights, and reaches a decision, while considering implicitly, if not explicitly, the precedential effect of his decision. But as Gilligan argues, and as I develop more fully below, Amy's approach is also plausible and legitimate, both as a style of moral reasoning and as a style of lawyering. Amy seeks to keep the people engaged; she holds the needs of the parties and their relationships constant and hopes to satisfy them all (as in negotiation), rather than selecting a winner (as in a lawsuit). If one must be hurt, she attempts to find a resolution that will hurt least the one who can least bear the hurt. (Is she engaged in a "deep pocket" policy analysis?) She looked beyond the "immediate lawsuit" to see how the "judgment" will affect the parties. If Heinz steals the drug and goes to jail, who will take care of his wife? Furthermore, Amy is concerned with *how* the dilemma is resolved: the process by which the parties communicate may be crucial to the outcome. (Amy cares as much about procedure as about substance.) And she is being a good lawyer when she inquires whether all of the facts have been discovered and considered.

The point here is not that Amy's method of moral reasoning is better than Jake's, nor that she is a better lawyer than Jake. (Some have read Gilligan to argue that the women's voice is better. I don't read her that way.) The point is that Amy does some things differently from Jake when she resolves this dilemma, and these things have useful analogies to lawyering and may not have been sufficiently credited as useful lawyering skills. Jake and Amy have something to learn from one another.

Thus, although a "choice of rights" conception (life vs. property) of solving human problems may be important, it is not the only or the best way. Responsibilities to self and to others may be equally important in measuring moral, as well as legal decision making, but have thus far been largely ignored. For example, a lawyer who feels responsible for the decisions she makes with her client may be more inclined to think about how those decisions will hurt other people and how the lawyer and client feel about making such decisions. (Amy thinks about Heinz, the druggist, and Heinz's wife at all times in reaching her decision; Jake makes a choice in abstract terms without worrying as much about the people it affects.)

In tracing through the sources of these different approaches to moral reasoning, Gilligan's analysis tracks that of Chodorow, Dinnerstein and Noddings. Men, who have had to separate from their differently gendered mother in order to grow, tend to see moral dilemmas as problems of separateness and individual rights, problems in which choices must be made and priorities must be ordered. Women, who need not completely separate from their same gendered mother in order to grow, see the world in terms of connections and relationships. "While women thus try to change the rules in order to preserve relationships, men, in abiding by these rules, depict relationships as easily replaced." Where men see danger in too much connection or intimacy, in being engulfed and losing their own identity, women see danger in the loss of connection, in not having an identity through caring for others and by being abandoned and isolated.

Both Gilligan and Noddings see differences in the ethics men and women derive from their different experiences of the world. Men focus on universal abstract principles like justice, equality and fairness so that their world is safe, predictable and constant. Women solve problems by seeking to understand the context and relationships involved and understand that universal rules may be impossible.

The two different voices Gilligan describes articulate two different developmental processes. To the extent that we all have both of these voices within us and they are not exclusively gender based, a mature person will develop the ability to consider the implications of both an abstract rights analysis and a contextualized responsibilities analysis. For women, this kind of mature emotional and intellectual synthesis may require taking greater account of self and less account of the other; for men, the process may be the reverse. Such an integration will not resolve all issues of personal development. Those who seek interdependence will not necessarily find if by the individualistic integration and reciprocity of reasoning styles proposed above. And if this integration fosters equality between the sexes, there still remains the problem of equity. As one of Gilligan's subjects observed: "People have real emotional needs to be attached to something and equality doesn't give you attachment. Equality fractures society and places on every person the burden of standing on his own two feet." The different paths toward mature moral development for men and women may give us more than one road to take to the same place, or we may find that there is more than one interesting place to go.

II. THE DIFFERENT VOICES OF LAWYERING

What does moral or psychological development have to do with the law? Gilligan's observations about male-female differences in moral reasoning may have a great deal to suggest about how the legal system is structured, how law is practiced and made, and how we reason and use law in making decisions. I will speculate about each of these below but will focus primarily on the implications of these insights for the lawyering process.

Two sets of questions illustrate how we might think about the impact of two voices on our legal system as presently constituted and as it might be transformed. First, how has the exclusion, or at least the devaluation, of women's voices affected the choices made in the values underlying our current legal structures? When we value "objectivity," or a "right" answer, or a single winner, are we valuing male goals of victory, exclusion, clarity, predictability? What would our legal system look like if women had not been excluded from participating in its creation? What values would women express in creating the laws and institutions of a legal system? How would they differ from what we see now? How might the different male and female voices join together to create an integrated legal system? Second, can we glimpse enclaves of another set of values within some existing legal structures? Is the judge "male," the jury "female?" Is the search for facts a feminine search for context and the search for legal principles a masculine search for certainty and abstract rules? If could be argued that no functional system could be either wholly masculine or wholly feminine, that there is a tendency for one set of characteristics in a system to mitigate the excesses of the other. Thus, the harshness of law produced the flexibility of equity, and conversely, the abuse of flexibility gave rise to rules of law to limit discretion. In this sense, the legal system could be seen to encompass both male and female voices already. Yet, even though our present legal structures may reflect elements of both sets of values, there is a tendency for the male-dominated or male-created forms and values to control. Thus, equity begins to develop its own harsh rules of law and universalistic regulations applied to discretionary decisions, undermining the flexibility that discretion is supposed to protect. Because men have, in fact, dominated by controlling the legal system, the women's voice in law may be present, but in a male form.

These two sets of questions explore a central issue, which is whether, to the extent that there are value choices to be made in the legal system, those choices will be differently made and with different results when the people who make decisions include a greater representation of women among their numbers. Some may prefer to see these different values as not necessarily taking gendered forms — I do. But even if the choices of values are not themselves gendered, it may be that women will favor one set of values over another in sufficient numbers, or with sufficient intensity, to change the balance at times. Although existing structures give a glimpse of what the legal system could look like, we cannot yet know what the consequences of women's participation in the legal system will be — some fear the women's voice will simply be added on and be drowned out by the louder male voice; others fear an androgynous, univoiced world with no interesting differences.

Perhaps by examining these issues in their concrete forms we can see how Portia's different voice might expand our understanding of the lawyering process. I will explore some of the tasks of the lawyer and skills that lawyers employ, and the larger adversarial system in which lawyering is embedded. The rules with which lawyers practice, which until recently have been articulated almost exclusively with male voices, will be examined so we can begin to speculate about how a woman's voice might affect the ethical rules which govern the profession and the substantive principles of the law. It is my hope that this preliminary review will spark more thorough and comprehensive research.

III. THE ADVOCACY-ADVERSARIAL MODEL

The basic structure of our legal system is premised on the adversarial model, which involves two advocates who present their cases to a disinterested third party who listens to evidence and argument and declares one party a winner. In this simplified description of the Anglo-American model of litigation, we can identify some of the basic concepts and values which underlie this choice of arrangements: advocacy, persuasion, hierarchy, competition, and binary results (win/lose). The conduct of litigation is relatively similar (not coincidentally, I suspect) to a sporting event — there are rules, a referee, an object to the game, and a winner is declared after the play is over. As I have argued elsewhere, this conception of the dispute resolution process is applied more broadly than just in the conventional courtroom. The adversarial model affects the way in which lawyers advise their clients ("get as much as you can"), negotiate disputes ("we can really get them on that") and plan transactions ("let's be sure to draft this to your advantage"). All of these activities in lawyering assume competition over the same limited and equally valued items (usually money) and assume that success is measured by maximizing individual gain. Would Gilligan's Amy create a different model?

By returning to Heinz's dilemma we see some hints about what Amy might do. Instead of concluding that a choice must be made between life and property, in resolving the conflict between parties as Jakes does, Amy sees no need to hierarchically order the claims. Instead, she tries to account for all the parties' needs, and searches for a way to find a solution that satisfies the needs of both. In her view, Heinz should be able to obtain the drug for his wife and the pharmacist should still receive payment. So Amy suggests a loan, a credit arrangement, or a discussion of other ways to structure the transaction. In short, she won't play by the adversarial rules. She searches outside the system for a way to solve the problem, trying to keep both parties in mind. Her methods substantiate Gilligan's observations that women will try to change the rules to preserve the relationships.

Furthermore, in addition to looking for more substantive solutions to the problem (i.e., not accepting the binary win/lose conception of the problem), Amy also wants to change the process. Amy sees no reason why she must act as a neutral arbiter of a dispute and make a decision based only on the information she has. She "belie[ves] in communication as the mode of conflict resolution and [is convinced] that the solution to the dilemma will follow from its compelling representation. . . ." If the parties talk directly to each other, they will be more likely to appreciate the importance of each other's needs. Thus, she believes direct communication, rather than third party mediated debate, might solve the problem, recognizing that two apparently conflicting positions can both be simultaneously legitimate, and there need not be a single victor.

The notion that women might have more difficulty with full-commitment-to-one-side model of the adversary system is graphically illustrated by Hilary, one of the women lawyers in Gilligan's study. This lawyer finds herself in one of the classic moral dilemmas of the adversary system: she sees that her opponent has failed to make use of a document that is helpful to his case and harmful to hers. In deciding not to tell him about the document because of what she sees as her "professional vulnerability" in the male adversary system, she concludes that "the adversary system of justice impedes not only the supposed search for truth (the conventional criticism), but also *the expression of concern for the person on the other side.*" Gilligan describes Hilary's tension between her concept of rights (learned through legal training) and her female ethic of care as a sign of her socialization in the male world of lawyering. Thus, the advocacy model, with its commitment to one-sided advocacy, seems somehow contrary to "apprehending the reality of the other" which lawyers like Hilary experience. Even the continental inquisitorial model, frequently offered as an alternative to the adversarial model, includes most of these elements of the male system — hierarchy, advocacy, competition and binary results.

So what kind of legal system would Amy and Hilary create if left to their own devices? They might look for ways to alter the harshness of win/lose results; they might alter the rules of the game (or make it less like a game); and they might alter the very structures and forms themselves. Thus, in a sense Amy and Hilary's approach can already be found in some of the current alternatives to the adversary model such as mediation. Much of the current interest in alternative dispute resolution is an attempt to modify the harshness of the adversarial process and expand the kinds of solutions available, in order to respond better to the varied needs of the parties. Amy's desire to engage the parties in direct communication with each other is reflected in mediation models where the parties talk directly to each other and forge their own solutions. The work of Gilligan and Noddings, demonstrating an ethic of care and a heightened sense of empathy in women, suggests that women lawyers may be particularly interested in mediation as an alternative to litigation as a method of resolving disputes.

Even within the present adversarial model, Amy and Hilary might, in their concern for others, want to provide for a broader conception of interested parties, permitting participation by those who might be affected by the dispute (an ethic of inclusion). In addition, like judges who increasingly are managing more of the details of their cases, Amy and Hilary might seek a more active role in settlement processes and rely less on court-ordered relief. Amy and Hilary might look for other ways to construct their lawsuits and remedies in much the same way as courts of equity mitigated the harshness of the law courts' very limited array of remedies by expanding the conception of what was possible.

The process and rules of the adversary system itself might look different if there were more female voices in the legal profession. If Amy is less likely than Jake to make assertive, rights-based statements, is she less likely to adapt to the male-created advocacy mode? In my experience as a trial lawyer, I observed that some women had difficulty with the "macho" ethic of the courtroom battle. Even those who did successfully adapt to the male model often confronted a dilemma because women were less likely to be perceived as behaving properly when engaged in strong adversarial conduct. It is important to be "strong" in the courtroom, according to the stereotypic conception of appropriate trial behavior. The woman who conforms to the female stereotype by being "soft" or "weak" is a bad trial lawyer; but if a woman is "tough" or "strong" in the courtroom, she is seen as acting inappropriately for a woman. Note, however, that this stereotyping is contextual: the same woman acting as a "strong" or "tough" mother with difficult children would be praised for that conduct. Women's strength is approved of with the proviso that it be exerted in appropriately female spheres.

Amy and Hilary might create a different form of advocacy, one resembling a "conversation" with the fact finder, relying on the creation of a relationship with the jury for its effectiveness, rather than on persuasive intimidation. There is some anecdotal evidence that this is happening already. Recently, several women prosecutors described their styles of trial advocacy as the creation of a personal relationship with the jury in which they urge the jurors to examine their own perceptions and values and encourage them to think for themselves, rather than "buying" the arguments of one of the advocates. This is a conception of the relationship between the lawyer and the fact-finder which is based on trust and mutual respect rather than on dramatics, intimidation and power, the male mode in which these women had been trained and which they found unsatisfactory.

In sum, the growing strength of women's voice in the legal profession may change the adversarial system into a more cooperative, less war-like system of communication between disputants in which solutions are mutually agreed upon rather than dictated by an outsider, won by the victor, and imposed upon the loser. Some seeds of change may already be found in existing alternatives to the litigation model, such as mediation. It remains to be seen what further changes Portia's voice may make.

REFERENCES

Chodorow, Nancy. *The Reproduction of Mothering* (1978).

De Beauvoir, Simone. *The Second Sex* (1953).

Dinnerstein, D. *The Mermaid and the Minotaur* (1978).

Epstein, Cynthia Fuchs. *Woman's Place: Options and Limits in Professional Careers* (1970).

Gilligan, Carol. *In a Different Voice: Psychological Theory and Women's Development* (1982).

Kohlberg, Lawrence. *The Philosophy of Moral Development* (1981).

Maccoby, Eleanor, and Jacklin, C. *The Psychology of Sex Difference* (1974).

Miller, Jean Baker. *Toward a New Psychology of Women* (1976).

Noddings, N. *Caring: A Feminine Approach to Ethics and Moral Education* (1974).

Olsen, Frances. "The Sex of Law." Unpublished manuscript.

Schaef, Anne. *Women's Reality* (1981).

Notes and Questions

1. So far the evidence to support the idea that women and men lawyers differ in their ability to be adversarial is inconclusive. Part of the difficulty in proving the fact lies in the way the theory's proponents understand the concepts of masculine and feminine. Rather than discrete categories tied to gender — e.g., males are masculine and females are feminine — the terms are said to describe the opposite ends of a set of continua on which gender varies. In other words, women have masculine qualities and men have feminine qualities. Of course, in general women have more feminine qualities than do men and men have more masculine qualities than do women. But for individuals the intermix of these qualities varies. Thus, it could be that most women attracted to law (or who have the capacity to survive the rigors of the Law School Admission Test, law school admission, three years of legal education, and the bar exam) have a greater portion of masculine qualities than the general population of women. Or it could be that legal education and law practice represses the feminine qualities in women (and men) and stimulates the masculine qualities. Some support for this idea is provided in a study by E. R. Robert and M. F. Winter.* The authors wrote,

> Examining the traits that had a significant effect upon women's GPA, it is apparent that successful female law students showed fairly consistent cross-sex identification; they described themselves in terms usually applied to males, and . . . rejected more feminine characterizations. . . .

If it is true that masculine qualities are privileged in legal practice then what are the implications of the great infusion of women into law for these women, for male lawyers, for the legal profession in general, for law, and for society?

2. Heinz and Laumann's study did not include female lawyers because at the time there were too few to sample. Given Menkel-Meadow's characterization of women as caring, responsive, and connected, which of the two sectors of legal practice — corporate or personal plight — is most likely to appeal

*"Sex-Role and Success in Law School," *Journal of Legal Education,* 29, no. 3 (September 1978): 449–458.

to women? What is likely to be the reception to these qualities among male attorneys in that sector? Among clients in that sector? Would it matter whether clients were men, women, or organizations? What would likely happen if women were to become dominant in the sector least receptive to these qualities? Would problem-solving styles change? Would clients be likely to prefer the change?

3. Would it have made a difference if the lawyer in the Sarat and Felstiner study had been a woman?

The final article in this chapter is offered to interweave the strands of understanding developed through the reading of Tocqueville, Mills, Heinz and Laumann, Kennedy, Curtis, Blumberg, Sarat and Felstiner, and the others into a complex tapestry of clients, lawyers, and law. While Galanter's specific concern is the limits of legal reform, his analysis helps summarize and recapitulate the themes of the legal profession's function in society, the implications of its hierarchies, and its absorption of the interests of clients and the legal system.

Why the "Haves" Come Out Ahead: Speculations on the Limits of Legal Change *Marc Galanter*

For purposes of this analysis, let us think of the legal system as comprised of these elements:

A body of authoritative normative learning — for short, *rules*

A set of institutional facilities within which the normative learning is applied to specific cases — for short, *courts*

A body of persons with specialized skill in the above — for short, *lawyers*

Persons or groups with claims they might make to the courts in reference to the rules, etc. — for short, *parties*

Let us also make the following assumptions about the society and the legal system:

It is a society in which actors with different amounts of wealth and power are constantly in competitive or partially cooperative relationships in which they have opposing interests.

This society has a legal system in which a wide range of disputes and conflicts are settled by court-like agencies which purport to apply pre-existing general norms impartially (that is, unaffected by the identity of the parties).

The rules and the procedures of these institutions are complex; wherever possible disputing units employ specialized intermediaries in dealing with them.

The rules applied by the courts are in part worked out in the process of adjudication (courts devise interstitial rules, combine diverse rules, and apply old rules to new situations). There is a living tradition of such rule-work and a system of communication such that the outcomes in some of the adjudicated cases affect the outcome in classes of future adjudicated cases.

Resources on the institutional side are insufficient for timely full-dress adjudication in every case, so that parties are permitted or even encouraged to forego bringing cases and to "settle" cases, — that is, to bargain to a mutually acceptable outcome.

There are several levels of agencies, with

Marc Galanter, "Why the 'Haves' Come Out Ahead: Speculations on the Limits of Legal Change," from *Law and Society Review,* Volume 9:1. Reprinted by permission of the Law and Society Association.

"higher" agencies announcing (making, interpreting) rules and other "lower" agencies assigned the responsibility of enforcing (implementing, applying) these rules. (Although there is some overlap of function in both theory and practice, I shall treat them as distinct and refer to them as "peak" and "field level" agencies.)

Not all the rules propounded by "peak" agencies are effective at the "field level," due to imperfections in communication, shortages of resources, skill, understanding commitment and so forth. (Effectiveness at the field level will be referred to as "penetration.")

I. A TYPOLOGY OF PARTIES

Most analyses of the legal system start at the rules end and work down through institutional facilities to see what effect the rules have on the parties. I would like to reverse that procedure and look through the other end of the telescope. Let's think about the different kinds of parties and the effect these differences might have on the way the system works.

Because of differences in their size, differences in the state of the law, and differences in their resources, some of the actors in the society have many occasions to utilize the courts (in the broad sense) to make (or defend) claims; others do so only rarely. We might divide our actors into those claimants who have only occasional recourse to the courts (one-shotters or OS) and repeat players (RP) who are engaged in many similar litigations over time. The spouse in a divorce case, the auto-injury claimant, the criminal accused are OSs; the insurance company, the prosecutor, the finance company are RPs. Obviously this is an oversimplification; there are intermediate cases such as the professional criminal. So we ought to think of OS-RP as a continuum rather than as a dichotomous pair. Typically, the RP is a larger unit and the stakes in any given case are smaller (relative to total worth). OSs are usually smaller units and the stakes represented by the tangible outcome of the case may be high relative to total worth, as in the case of injury victim or the criminal accused). Or, the OS may suffer from the opposite problem: his claims may be so small and unmanageable (the shortweighted consumer or the holder of performing rights) that the cost of enforcing them outruns any promise of benefit.

Let us refine our notion of the RP into an "ideal type" if you will — a unit which has had and anticipates repeated litigation, which has low stakes in the outcome of any one case, and which has the resources to pursue its long-run interests. (This does not include every real-world repeat player; that most common repeat player, the alcoholic derelict, enjoys few of the advantages that may accrue to the RP [see below]. His resources are too few to bargain in the short run or take heed of the long run.) An OS, on the other hand, is a unit whose claims are too large (relative to his size) or too small (relative to the cost of remedies) to be managed routinely and rationally.

We would expect an RP to play the litigation game differently form an OS. Let us consider some of his advantages:

(1) RPs, having done it before, have advance intelligence; they are able to structure the next transaction and build a record. It is the RP who writes the form contract, requires the security deposit, and the like.

(2) RPs develop expertise and have ready access to specialists. They enjoy economies of scale and have low start-up costs for any case.

(3) RPs have opportunities to develop facilitative informal relations with institutional incumbents.

(4) The RP must establish and maintain credibility as a combatant. His interest in his "bargaining reputation" serves as a resource to establish "commitment" to his bargaining positions. With no bargaining reputation to maintain, the OS has more difficulty in convincingly committing himself in bargaining.

(5) RPs can play the odds. The larger the matter at issue looms for OS, the more likely

he is to adopt a minimax strategy (minimize the probability of maximum loss). Assuming that the stakes are relatively smaller for RPs, they can adopt strategies calculated to maximize gain over a long series of cases, even where this involves the risk of maximum loss in some cases.

(6) RPs can play for rules as well as immediate gains. First, it pays an RP to expend resources in influencing the making of the relevant rules by such methods as lobbying. (And his accumulated expertise enables him to do this persuasively.)

(7) RPs can also play for rules in litigation itself, whereas an OS is unlikely to. That is, there is a difference in what they regard as a favorable outcome. Because his stakes in the immediate outcome are high and because by definition OS is unconcerned with the outcome of similar litigation in the future, OS will have little interest in that element of the outcome which might influence the disposition of the decision-maker next time around. For the RP, on the other hand, anything that will favorably influence the outcomes of future cases is a worthwhile result. The larger the stake for any player and the lower the probability of repeat play, the less likely that he will be concerned with the rules which govern future cases of the same kind. Consider two parents contesting the custody of their only child, the prizefighter vs. the IRS for tax arrears, the convict facing the death penalty. On the other hand, the player with small stakes in the present case and the prospect of a series of similar cases (the IRS, the adoption agency, the prosecutor) may be more interested in the state of the law.

Thus, if we analyze the outcomes of a case into a tangible component and a rule component, we may expect that in case 1, OS will attempt to maximize tangible gain. But if RP is interested in maximizing his tangible gain in a series of cases 1 . . . *n*, he may be willing to trade off tangible gain in any one case for rule gain (or to minimize rule loss.) We assumed that the institutional facilities for litigation were overloaded and settlements were prevalent. We would then expect RPs to "settle" cases where they expected unfavorable rule outcomes. Since they expect to litigate again, RPs can select to adjudicate (or appeal) those cases which they regard as most likely to produce favorable rules. On the other hand, OSs should be willing to trade off the possibility of making "good law" for tangible gain. Thus, we would expect the body of "precedent" cases — that is, cases capable of influencing the outcome of future cases — to be relatively skewed toward those favorable to RP.

Of course it is not suggested that the strategic configuration of the parties is the sole or major determinant of rule-development. Rule-development is shaped by a relatively autonomous learned tradition, by the impingement of intellectual currents from outside, by the preferences and prudences of the decision-makers. But courts are passive and these factors operate only when the process is triggered by parties. The point here is merely to note the superior opportunities of the RP to trigger promising cases and prevent the triggering of unpromising ones. It is not incompatible with a course of rule-development favoring OSs (or, as indicated below, with OSs failing to get the benefit of those favorable new rules).

In stipulating that RPs can play for rules, I do not mean to imply that RPs pursue rule-gain as such. If we recall that not all rules penetrate (i.e., become effectively applied at the field level) we come to some additional advantages of RPs.

(8) RPs, by virtue of experience and expertise, are more likely to be able to discern which rules are likely to "penetrate" and which are likely to remain merely symbolic commitments. RPs may be able to concentrate their resources on rule-changes that are likely to make a tangible difference. They can trade off symbolic defeats for tangible gains.

> (9) Since penetration depends in part on the resources of the parties (knowledge, attentiveness, expert services, money), RPs are more likely to be able to invest the matching resources necessary to secure the penetration of rules favorable to them.

It is not suggested that RPs are to be equated with "haves" (in terms of power, wealth and status) or OSs with "have-nots." In the American setting most RPs are larger, richer and more powerful than are most OSs, so these categories overlap, but there are obvious exceptions. RPs may be "have-nots" (alcoholic derelicts) or may act as champions of "have-nots" (as government does from time to time); OSs such as criminal defendants may be wealthy. What this analysis does is to define a position of advantage in the configuration of contending parties and indicate how those with other advantages tend to occupy this position of advantage and to have their other advantages reinforced and augmented thereby. This position of advantage is one of the ways in which a legal system formally neutral as between "haves" and "have-nots" may perpetuate and augment the advantages of the former. . . .

We may think of litigation as typically involving various combinations of OSs and RPs. We can then construct a matrix such as Figure 1 and fill in the boxes with some well-known if only approximate American examples. (We ignore for the moment that the terms OS and RP represent ends of a continuum, rather than a dichotomous pair.)

On the basis of our incomplete and unsystematic examples, let us conjecture a bit about the content of these boxes:

Box I: OS vs. OS The most numerous occupants of this box are divorces and insanity hearings. Most (over 90 per cent of divorces, for example) are uncontested. A large portion of these are really pseudo-litigation, that is, a settlement is worked out between the parties and ratified in the guise of adjudication. When we get real litigation in Box I, it is often between parties who have some intimate tie with one another, fighting over some unsharable good, often with overtones of "spite" and "irrationality." Courts are resorted to where an ongoing relationship is ruptured; they have little to do with the routine patterning of activity. The law is invoked *ad hoc* and instrumentally by the parties. There may be a strong interest in vindication, but neither party is likely to have much interest in the long-term state of the law (of, for instance, custody or nuisance). There are few appeals, few test cases, little expenditure of resources on rule-development. Legal doctrine is likely to remain remote from everyday practice and from popular attitudes.

Box II: RP vs. OS The great bulk of litigation is found in this box — indeed every really numerous kind except personal injury cases, insanity hearings, and divorces. The law is used for routine processing of claims by parties for whom the making of such claims is a regular business activity. Often the cases here take the form of stereotyped mass processing with little of the individuated attention of full-dress adjudication. Even greater numbers of cases are settled "informally" with settlement keyed to possible litigation outcome (discounted by risk, cost, delay).

The state of the law is of interest to the RP, though not to the OS defendants. Insofar as the law is favorable to the RP it is "followed" closely in practice (subject to discount for RP's transaction costs). Transactions are built to fit the rules by creditors, police, draft boards and other RPs. Rules favoring OSs may be less readily applicable, since OSs do not ordinarily plan the underlying transaction, or less meticulously observed in practice, since OSs are unlikely to be as ready or able as RPs to invest in insuring their penetration to the field level.

Box III: OS vs. RP All of these are rather infrequent types except for personal injury cases which are distinctive in that free entry to the arena is provided by the contingent fee. In auto injury claims, litigation is routinized and settle-

FIGURE 1 A Taxonomy of Litigation by Strategic Configuration of Parties

Defendant \ *Initiator, Claimant*	ONE-SHOTTER	REPEAT PLAYER
ONE-SHOTTER	Parent v. Parent (Custody) Spouse v. Spouse (Divorce) Family v. Family Member (Insanity Commitment) Family v. Family (Inheritance) Neighbor v. Neighbor Partner vs. Partner OS vs OS I	Prosecutor v. Accused Finance Co. v. Debtor Landlord v. Tenant I.R.S. v. Taxpayer Condemnor v. Property Owner RP vs OS II
REPEAT PLAYER	Welfare Client v. Agency Auto Dealer v. Manufacturer Injury Victim v. Insurance Company Tenant v. Landlord Bankrupt Consumer v. Creditors Defamed v. Publisher OS vs RP III	Union v. Company Movie Distributor v. Censorship Board Developer v. Suburban Municipality Purchaser v. Supplier Regulatory Agency v. Firms of Regulated Industry RP vs RP IV

ment is closely geared to possible litigation outcome. Outside the personal injury area, litigation in Box III is not routine. It usually represents the attempt of some OS to invoke outside help to create leverage on an organization with which he has been having dealings but is now at the point of divorce (for example, the discharged employee or the cancelled franchisee). The OS claimant generally has little interest in the state of the law; the RP defendant, however, is greatly interested.

BOX IV: RP vs. RP Let us consider the general case first and then several special cases. We might expect that there would be little litigation in Box IV, because to the extent that two RPs play with each other repeatedly, the expectation of continued mutually beneficial interaction would give rise to informal bilateral controls. This seems borne out by studies of dealings among businessmen and in labor relations. Official agencies are invoked by unions trying to get established and by management tying to prevent them from getting established, more rarely in dealings between bargaining partners. Units with mutually beneficial relations do not adjust their differences in courts. Where they rely on third parties in dispute-resolution, it is likely to take a form (such as arbitration or a domestic tribunal) detached from official sanctions and applying domestic rather than official rules.

However, there are several special cases. First, there are those RPs who seek not furtherance of tangible interests, but vindication of fundamental cultural commitments. An example would be the organizations which sponsor much church-state litigation. Where RPs are contending about value differences (who is right) rather than interest conflicts (who gets what) there is less tendency to settle and less basis for developing a private system of dispute settlement.

Second, government is a special kind of RP. Informal controls depend upon the ultimate sanction of withdrawal and refusal to continue beneficial relations. To the extent that withdrawal of further association is not possible in dealing with government, the scope of informal controls is correspondingly limited. The development of informal relations between regulatory agencies and regulated firms is well known. And the regulated may have sanctions other than withdrawal which they can apply; for instance, they may threaten political opposition. But the more inclusive the unit of government, the less effective the withdrawal sanction and the greater the likelihood that a party will attempt to invoke outside allies by litigation even while sustaining the ongoing relationship. This applies also to monopolies, units which share the government's relative immunity to withdrawal sanctions. RPs in monopolistic relationships will occasionally invoke formal controls to show prowess, to give credibility to threats, and to provide satisfactions for other audiences. Thus we would expect litigation by and against government to be more frequent than in other RP vs. RP situations. There is a second reason for expecting more litigation when government is a party. That is, that the notion of "gain" (policy as well as monetary) is often more contingent and problematic for governmental units than for other parties, such as businesses or organized interest groups. In some cases courts may, by proffering authoritative interpretations of public policy, redefine an agency's notion of gain. Hence government parties may be more willing to externalize decisions to the courts. And opponents may have more incentive to litigate against government in the hope of securing a shift in its goals.

A somewhat different kind of special case is present where plaintiff and defendant are both RPs but do not deal with each other repeatedly (two insurance companies, for example.) In the government/monopoly case, the parties were so inextricably bound together that the force of informal controls was limited; here they are not sufficiently bound to each other to give informal controls their bite; there is nothing to withdraw from! The large one-time deal that falls through, the marginal enterprise — these are staple sources of litigation.

Where there is litigation in the RP vs. RP situation, we might expect that there would be heavy expenditure on rule-development, many appeals, and rapid and elaborate development of the doctrinal law. Since the parties can invest to secure implementation of favorable rules, we would expect practice to be closely articulated to the resulting rules.

On the basis of these preliminary guesses, we can sketch a general profile of litigation and the factors associated with it. The great bulk of litigation is found in Box II; much less in Box III. Most of the litigation in these Boxes is mass routine processing of disputes between parties who are strangers (not in mutually beneficial continuing relations) or divorced — and between whom there is a disparity in size. One party is a bureaucratically organized "professional" (in the sense of doing it for a living) who enjoys strategic advantages. Informal controls between the parties are tenuous or ineffective; their relationship is likely to be established and defined by official rules; in litigation, these rules are discounted by transaction costs and manipulation selectively to the advantage of the parties. On the other hand, in Boxes I and IV, we have more infrequent but more individualized litigation between parties of the same general magnitude, among whom there are or were continuing multi-stranded relationships with attendant informal controls. Litigation appears when the relationship loses its future value; when its "monopolistic" character deprives informal controls of sufficient leverage and the parties invoke outside allies to modify it; and when the parties seek to vindicate conflicting values.

FIGURE 2 A Typology of Legal Specialists

		Lawyer	
	SPECIALIZED BY PARTY	SPECIALIZED BY FIELD AND PARTY	SPECIALIZED BY FIELD
Client RP	"House Counsel" or General Counsel for Bank, Insurance Co., etc. Corporation Counsel for Government Unit	Prosecutor Personal Injury Defendant Staff Counsel for NAACP Tax Labor/Management Collections	Patent
Client OS	"Poverty Lawyers" Legal Aid	Criminal Defense Personal Injury Plaintiff	Bankruptcy Divorce

II. LAWYERS

What happens when we introduce lawyers? Parties who have lawyers do better. Lawyers are themselves RPs. Does their presence equalize the parties, dispelling the advantage of the RP client? Or does the existence of lawyers amplify the advantage of the RP client? We might assume that RPs (tending to be larger units) who can buy legal services more steadily, in larger quantities, in bulk (by retainer) and at higher rates, would get services of better quality. They would have better information (especially where restrictions on information about legal services are present). Not only would the RP get more talent to begin with, but he would on the whole get greater continuity, better record-keeping, more anticipatory or preventive work, more experience and specialized skill in pertinent areas, and more control over counsel.

One might expect that just how much the legal services factor would accentuate the RP advantage would be related to the way in which the profession was organized. The more members of the profession were identified with their clients (i.e., the less they were held aloof from clients by their loyalty to courts or an autonomous guild) the more the imbalance would be accentuated. The more close and enduring the lawyer-client relationship, the more the primary loyalty of lawyers is to clients rather than to courts or guild, the more telling the advantages of accumulated expertise and guidance in overall strategy.

What about the specialization of the bar? Might we not expect the existence of specialization to offset RP advantages by providing OS with a specialist who in pursuit of his own career goals would be interested in outcomes that would be advantageous to a whole class of OSs? Does the specialist become the functional equivalent of the RP? We may divide specialists into (1) those specialized by field of law (patent, divorce, etc.), (2) those specialized by the kind of party represented (for example, house counsel), and (3) those specialized by both field of law and "side" or party (personal injury plaintiff, criminal defense, labor). Divorce lawyers do not specialize in husbands or wives, nor real-estate lawyers and tax lawyers and stockholders-derivate-suit lawyers do specialize not only in the field of law but in representing one side. Such specialists may represent RPs or OSs. Figure 2 provides some well-known examples of different kinds of specialists.

Most specializations cater to the needs of particular kinds of RPs. Those specialists who service OSs have some distinctive features:

First, they tend to make up the "lower echelons" of the legal profession. Compared to the lawyers who provide services to RPs, lawyers in these specialties tend to be drawn from lower socio-economic origins, to have attended local, proprietary or part-time law schools, to practice alone rather than in large firms, and to possess low prestige within the profession. (Of course the correlation is far from perfect; some lawyers who represent OSs do not have these characteristics and some represented RPs do. However, on the whole the difference in professional standing is massive).

Second, specialists who service OSs tend to have problems of mobilizing a clientele (because of the low state of information among OSs) and encounter "ethical" barriers imposed by the profession which forbids solicitation, advertising, referral fees, advances to clients, and so forth.

Third, the episodic and isolated nature of the relationship with particular OS clients tends to elicit a stereotyped and uncreative brand of legal services. Carlin and Howard (1965:385) observe that:

> The quality of service rendered poorer clients is . . . affected by the non-repeating character of the matters they typically bring to lawyers (such as divorce, criminal, personal injury): this combined with the small fees encourages a mass processing of cases. As a result, only a limited amount of time and interest is usually expended on any one case — there is little or no incentive to treat it except as an isolated piece of legal business. Moreover, there is ordinarily no desire to go much beyond the case as the client presents it, and such cases are only accepted when there is a clear-cut cause of action; i.e., when they fit into convenient legal categories and promise a fairly certain return.

Fourth, while they are themselves RPs, these specialists have problems in developing optimizing strategies. What might be good strategy for an insurance company lawyer or prosecutor — trading off some cases for gains on others — is branded unethical when done by a criminal defense or personal injury plaintiff lawyer. It is not permissible for him to play his series of OSs as if they constituted a single RP.

Conversely, the demands of routine and orderly handling of a whole series of OSs may constrain the lawyer form maximizing advantage for any individual OS. Rosenthal (1970:172) shows that "for all but the largest [personal injury] claims an attorney loses money by thoroughly preparing a case and not settling it early."

For the lawyer who services OSs, with his transient clientele, his permanent "client" is the forum, the opposite party, or the intermediary who supplies clients. Consider, for example, the dependence of the criminal defense lawyer on maintaining cooperative relations with the various members of the "criminal court community." Similarly, Carlin notes that among metropolitan individual practitioners whose clientele consists of OSs, there is a deformation of loyalty toward the intermediary.

> In the case of those lawyers specializing in personal injury, local tax, collections, criminal, and to some extent divorce work, the relationship with the client . . . is generally mediated by a broker or business supplier who may be either another lawyer or a layman. In these fields of practice the lawyer is principally concerned with pleasing the broker or winning his approval, more so than he is with satisfying the individual client. The source of business generally counts for more than the client, especially where the client is unlikely to return or to send in other clients. The client is then expendable: he can be exploited to the full. Under these conditions, when a lawyer receives a client . . . he has not so much gained a client as a piece of business, and his attitude is often that of handling a particular piece of merchandise or of developing a volume of a certain kind of merchandise.

The existence of a specialized bar on the OS side should overcome the gap in expertise, allow some economies of scale, provide for bargaining commitment and personal familiarity. But this is short of overcoming the fundamental strategic advantages of RPs — their capacity to structure the transaction, play the odds, and influence rule-development and enforcement policy.

Specialized lawyers may, by virtue of their identification with parties, become lobbyists, moral entrepreneurs, proponents of reforms on the parties' behalf. But lawyers have a cross-cutting interest in preserving complexity and mystique so that client contact with this area of law is rendered problematic. Lawyers should not be expected to be proponents of reforms which are optimum from the point of view of the clients taken alone. Rather, we would expect them to seek to optimize the clients' position without diminishing that of lawyers. Therefore, specialized lawyers have an interest in a framework which keeps recovery (or whatever) problematic at the same time that they favor changes which improve their clients' position within this framework. (Consider the lobbying efforts of personal injury plaintiffs and defense lawyers.) Considerations of interest are likely to be fused with ideological commitments: the lawyers' preference for complex and finely-tuned bodies of rules, for adversary proceedings, for individualized case-by-case decision-making. Just as the culture of the client population affects strategic position, so does the professional culture of the lawyers.

III. INSTITUTIONAL FACILITIES

We see then that the strategic advantages of the RP may be augmented by advantages in the distribution of legal services. Both are related to the advantages conferred by the basic features of the institutional facilities for the handling of claims: passivity and overload.

These institutions are passive, first, in the sense that Black refers to as "reactive" — they must be mobilized by the claimant — giving advantage to the claimant with information, ability to surmount cost barriers, and skill to navigate restrictive procedural requirements. They are passive in a further sense that once in the door the burden is on each party to proceed with his case. The presiding official acts as umpire, while the development of the case, collection of evidence and presentation of proof are left to the initiative and resources of the parties. Parties are treated as if they were equally endowed with economic resources, investigative opportunities and legal skills. . . . Where, as is usually the case, they are not, the broader the delegation to the parties, the greater the advantage conferred on the wealthier, more experienced and better organized party.

The advantages conferred by institutional passivity are accentuated by the chronic overload which typically characterizes these institutions. Typically there are far more claims than there are institutional resources for full dress adjudication of each. In several ways overload creates pressures on claimants to settle rather than to adjudicate:

(a) by causing delay (thereby discounting the value of recovery);
(b) by raising costs (of keeping the case alive);
(c) by inducing institutional incumbents to place a high value on clearing dockets, discouraging full-dress adjudication in favor of bargaining, stereotyping and routine processing;
(d) by inducing the forum to adopt restrictive rules to discourage litigation.

Thus, overload increases the cost and risk of adjudicating and shields existing rules from challenge, diminishing opportunities for rule-change. This tends to favor the beneficiaries of existing rules.

Second, by increasing the difficulty of challenging going practice, overload also benefits those who reap advantage from the neglect (or systematic violation) of rules which favor their adversaries.

Third, overload tends to protect the possessor — the party who has the money or goods — against the claimant. For the most part, this amounts to favoring RPs over OSs, since RPs typically can structure transactions to put themselves in the possessor position.

Finally, the overload situation means that there are more commitments in the formal system than there are resources to honor them — more rights and rules "on the books" than can be vindicated or enforced. There are, then, questions of priorities in the allocation of resources. We would expect judges, police, administrators and other managers of limited institutional facilities to be responsive to the more organized, attentive and influential of their constituents. Again, these tend to be RPs.

Thus, overloaded and passive institutional facilities provide the setting in which the RP advantages in strategic position and legal services can have full play.

IV. RULES

We assume here that rules tend to favor older, culturally dominant interests. This is not meant to imply that the rules are explicitly designed to favor these interests, but rather that those groups which have become dominant have successfully articulated their operations to preexisting rules. To the extent that rules are even-handed or favor the "have-nots," the limited resources for their implementation will be allocated, I have argued, so as to give greater effect to those rules which protect and promote the tangible interests of organized and influential groups. Furthermore, the requirements of due process, with their barriers or protections against precipitate action, naturally tend to protect the possessor or holder against the claimant. Finally, the rules are sufficiently complex and problematic (or capable of being problematic if sufficient resources are expended to make them so) that differences in the quantity and quality of legal services will affect capacity to derive advantages from the rules.

Thus, we arrive at Figure 3 which summarizes why the "haves" tend to come out ahead. It points to layers of advantages enjoyed by different (but largely overlapping) classes of "haves" — advantages which interlock, reinforcing and shielding one another. . . .

V. IMPLICATIONS FOR REFORM: THE ROLE OF LAWYERS

We have discussed the way in which the architecture of the legal system tends to confer interlocking advantages on overlapping groups whom we have called the "haves." To what extent might reforms of the legal system dispel these advantages? Reforms will always be less total than the utopian ones envisioned above. Reformers will have limited resources to deploy and they will always be faced with the necessity of choosing which uses of those resources are most productive of equalizing change. What does our analysis suggest about strategies and priorities?

Our analysis suggests that change at the level of substantive rules is not likely in itself to be determinative of redistributive outcomes. Rule change is in itself likely to have little effect because the system is so constructed that changes in the rules can be filtered out unless accompanied by changes at other levels. In a setting of overloaded institutional facilities, inadequate costly legal services, and unorganized parties, beneficiaries may lack the resources to secure implementation; or an RP may restructure the transaction to escape the thrust of the new rule. . . . Favorable rules are not necessarily (and possibly not typically) in short supply to "have-nots;" certainly less so than any of the other resources needed to play the litigation game. Programs of equalizing reform which focus on rule-change can be readily absorbed without any change in power relations. The system has the capacity to change a great deal at the level of rules without corresponding changes in everyday patterns of practice or distribution of tangible advantages. . . . Indeed rule-change may become a symbolic substitute for redistribution of advantages. . . .

The low potency of substantive rule-change is especially the case with rule-changes procured from courts. That courts can sometimes be induced to propound rule-changes that legislatures would not make points to the limitations as well as the possibilities of court-produced change. With their relative insulation from retaliation by antagonistic interests, courts may

FIGURE 3 Why the "Haves" Tend to Come Out Ahead

Element	*Advantages*	*Enjoyed by*
Parties	• ability to structure transaction • specialized expertise, economies of scale • long-term strategy • ability to play for rules • bargaining credibility • ability to invest in penetration	• repeat players large, professional[a]
Legal Services	• skill, specialization, continuity	• organized, professional,[a] wealthy
Institutional Facilities	• passivity • cost and delay barriers • favorable priorities	• wealthy, experienced, organized • holders, possessors • beneficiaries of existing rules • organized, attentive
Rules	• favorable rules • due process barriers	• older, culturally dominant • holders, possessors

[a]in the simple sense of "doing it for a living"

more easily propound new rules which depart from prevailing power relations. But such rules require even greater inputs of other resources to secure effective implementation. And courts have less capacity than other rule-makers to create institutional facilities and re-allocate resources to secure implementation of new rules. Litigation then is unlikely to shape decisively the distribution of power in society. It may serve to secure or solidify symbolic commitments. It is vital tactically in securing temporary advantage or protection, providing leverage for organization and articulation of interests and conferring (or withholding) the mantle of legitimacy. The more divided the other holders of power, the greater the redistributive potential of this symbolic/tactical role.

Our analysis suggests that breaking the interlocked advantages of the "haves" requires attention not only to the level of rules, but also to institutional facilities, legal services and organization of parties. It suggests that litigating and lobbying have to be complemented by interest organizing, provisions of services and invention of new forms of institutional facilities.

The thrust of our analysis is that changes at the level of parties are most likely to generate changes at other levels. If rules are the most abundant resource for reformers, parties capable of pursuing long-range strategies are the rarest. The presence of such parties can generate effective demand for high grade legal services — continuous, expert, and oriented to the long run — and pressure for institutional reforms and favorable rules. This suggests that we can roughly surmise the relative strategic priority of various rule-changes. Rule changes which relate directly to the strategic position of the parties by facilitating organization, increasing the supply of legal services (where these in turn provide a focus for articulating and organizing common interests) and increasing the costs of opponents — for instance authorization of class action suits, award of attorney's fees and costs, award of provisional remedies — these are the most powerful fulcrum for change. The intensity of the opposition to class action legislation and autonomous reform-oriented legal services . . . indicates the "haves" own estimation of the relative strategic impact of the several levels.

The contribution of the lawyer to redistributive social change, then, depends upon the organization and culture of the legal profession. We have surmised that court-produced substantive rule-change is unlikely in itself to be a determinative element in producing tangible redistribution of benefits. The leverage provided by litigation depends on its strategic combination with inputs at other levels. The question then is whether the organization of the profession permits lawyers to develop and employ skills at these other levels. The more that lawyers view themselves exclusively as courtroom advocates, the less their willingness to undertake new tasks and form enduring alliances with clients and operate in forms other than courts, the less likely they are to serve as agents of redistributive change. Paradoxically, those legal professionals most open to accentuating the advantages of the "haves" (by allowing themselves to be "captured" by recurrent clients) may be most able to become (or have room for, more likely) agents of change, precisely because they provide more license for identification with clients and their "causes" and have a less strict definition of what are properly professional activities.

REFERENCES

Carlin, Jerome E. (1966) *Lawyers' Ethics: A Survey of the New York City Bar.* New York: Russell Sage Foundation.

———. (1962) *Lawyers on Their Own: A Study of Individual Practitioners in Chicago.* New Brunswick: Rutgers University Press.

Carlin, Jerome E., and Jan Howard (1965) "Legal Representation and Class Justice," 12 *U.C.L.A. Law Review* 381.

Rosenthal, Douglas E. (1970) *Client Participation in Professional Decision: the Lawyer-Client Relationship in Personal Injury Cases.* Unpublished dissertation, Yale University.

Notes and Questions

1. Consider the following two quotes as complements to Galanter's analysis:

> Through the individual incident or transaction, law makes individuals the basic unit of any case. Class actions exist in civil law, but numerous and growing restrictions frustrate attempts to reach basic issues. The persons who are normally engaged in legal controversy are separated out from the mass of people by the legal process and made to look special; and each case is made to appear different from others . . . social struggles and political movements are splintered into their individual components and prevented from making any stronger or more collective statements than might be made by any of the individuals involved. Yet often, the only way a judge or jury might understand motivations behind a particular act is through its collective statement.*

> Legal thought can generate equally plausible rights justifications for almost any result. Moreover, the discourse of rights imposes constraints on those who use it that make it almost impossible for it to function effectively as a tool of radical transformation. Rights are by their nature "formal," meaning that they secure to individuals legal protection for arbitrariness — to speak of rights is precisely not to speak of justice between social classes, races, or sexes. Rights discourse, moreover, simply presupposes or takes for granted that the world is and

---

*Kenneth Cloke, "The Economic Basis of Law and State," in Robert Lefcourt, ed., *Law Against the People* (New York: Random House, 1971), p. 69.

should be divided between a state sector that enforces rights and a private world of "civil society" in which atomized individuals pursue their diverse goals.†

2. At the conclusion of the article, Galanter makes the somewhat ironic argument that lawyers for have-nots must give up what they think it means to be a lawyer in order to really help their clients. Lawyer Steven Wexler stated it this way:

> Lawyers are taught to believe, and have a three-year investment in believing, that what they have learned in law school was hard to learn, and that they are somehow special for having learned it. It is difficult for a lawyer to commit himself to believing that poor people can learn the law and be effective advocates; but until he believes that, a lawyer will create dependency instead of strength for his clients, and add to rather than reduce their plight. . . .
>
> The poses that the . . . lawyer adopts in order to be able to talk to his clients are called his professional bearing or manner; it is very important that a poor people's lawyer drop that professional bearing. He must realize that what makes him a lawyer are accidents of birth and interest, and those accidents have not made him something special; they have only given him the opportunity to help someone else.‡

Why is this advice necessary? Are lawyers for the have-nots in a different position vis-à-vis their clients than lawyers for haves? What do Heinz and Laumann and Mills offer to the discussion of this topic?

3. Others have argued that a focus on individual cases with high caseloads rather than class actions with low caseloads does not necessarily preclude law reform efforts. For example,

> [O]ne of the basic forces for social change in the law is a high caseload. If the volume is very heavy, there is of course a distinct drawback in that it forces the lawyer to give less thorough attention to the details of each individual case, but a large caseload has great advantages if it can be harnessed and used to effect change.
>
> The fact is that, if the Welfare Department buys out an individual case, we are precluded from getting a principle of law changed, but if we give them one thousand cases to buy out, that law has been effectively changed whether or not the law as written is changed. . . . The value of a heavy caseload is that it allows you to populate the legal process. It allows you to apply unremitting pressure on the agency you are dealing with.§

4. Reconsider Kafka's parable of the man from the country and the doorkeeper before the law. Does Galanter's analysis provide some insight into the meaning of the parable? How about the dialogue between the priest and K? Did the fact that K was an OS player shape that dialogue?

---

†Duncan Kennedy, "Legal Education and the Reproduction of Hierarchy," *Journal of Legal Education* 32, no. 4 (1982): 591, 598.

‡Steven Wexler, "Practicing Law for Poor People," *Yale Law Review* 79(1970): 1049.

§Harold J. Rothwax, "The Law as an Instrument of Social Change," in Harold H. Weissman, ed., *Justice and the Law in the Mobilization for Youth Experience* (New York: Association Press, 1969), p. 140.

Suggested Additional Readings

Abel, Richard L., and Lewis, Philip S., eds. *Lawyers in Society Vol. I: The Common Law World.* Berkeley: University of California Press, 1988.

Abramson, Jill, and Franklin, Barbara. *Where They Are Now: The Story of the Women of Harvard Law 1974.* Garden City, N.J.: Doubleday, 1986.

Auerbach, Jerome. *Unequal Justice.* New York: Oxford University Press, 1976.

Carlin, Jerome E. *Lawyers on Their Own.* New Brunswick, N.J.: Rutgers University Press, 1962.

Halliday, Terence C. *Beyond Monopology: Lawyers, State Crises, and Professional Empowerment.* Chicago: University of Chicago Press, 1987.

Heinz, John P., and Laumann, Edward O. *Chicago Lawyers: The Social Structure of the Bar.* New York: Basic Books, 1983.

Katz, Jack. *Poor People's Lawyers in Transistion.* New Brunswick, N.J.: Rutgers University Press, 1982.

Morello, Karen Berger. *The Invisible Bar: The Women Lawyer in America: 1638 to the Present.* New York: Random House, 1986.

Nelson, Robert L. *Partners with Power: Social Transformation of the Large Law Firm.* Berkeley: University of California Press, 1988.

Spangler, Eve. *Lawyers for Hire: Salaried Professionals at Work.* New Haven, Conn.: Yale University Press, 1986.

Stevens, Robert. *Law School: Legal Education in American from the 1850s to the 1980s.* Chapel Hill: University of North Carolina Press, 1983.

Turow, Scott. *One L.* New York: Putnam's, 1977.

A Jury of Whites and Blacks, 1867. (The Bettmann Archive, Inc.)

CHAPTER 4 Juries and Community Participation in the Legal Process

Were I called upon to decide, whether the people had best be omitted in the legislative or in the judiciary department, I would say it is better to leave them out of the legislative. The execution of the laws is more important than the making of them.

Thomas Jefferson

Every culture answers, by its structure as well as by its beliefs, the question of how much and in what way the community shall participate in the legal process. The handling of conflict may be separated from the daily round of human existence and entrusted to professionals, or these functions may be widely dispersed among citizens and become a means of expressing current community beliefs and standards of behavior. What is at stake in the answer to this question of participation is the relationship of law to group life and individual autonomy.

From one point of view, of course, it is always "the people" who create conflict by their behavior and define it through their beliefs. But the fragmentation of society, the specialization of labor, and the rise of the state have contributed to such a thorough separation of the legal institution from the rest of society that law cannot be studied without asking the questions of community participation. What function does law serve in establishing or reinforcing community cohesion? What role do these group values play in determining the scope of individual liberty? Are the standards of judgment imposed by law those that reflect the values of the population as a whole? Of some special interest group? Of a deity or other source of transcendent morality? How are standards that derive from past wisdom balanced against changes in current values?

The adjudication of conflict — like the making of legislative policy — is a form of governance about which one may ask, "Who is politically sovereign?" But the depth, ambiguity, and complexity of human conflict raise still broader issues, for disputing inevitably involves challenges to a group's beliefs and values, and law authoritatively defines the relationship of the challengers to their culture.

Studying the form of community participation in law thus becomes a means to examine an important aspect of culture. In this chapter, we present materials about the jury and parallel institutions in other societies. We treat these institutional artifacts as we would pieces of broken pottery discovered at the site of an archeological dig. The goal is to learn what we can about a society from the form of legal process it created and the way this process is used. What, for example, does a comparison of the ordeal, the jury, and trial by "truth serum" or by compulsory urinalysis tell us about the origins and ultimate fate of participation? Here, as with other materials, the reader is invited, in legal philosopher Karl Llewellyn's words, to use the study of conflict and of legal institutions as "a candle to illumine the nature of society."

Sections 1–4 of this chapter focus on trial by jury. The Anglo-American legal system is unique in its use of the jury as a forum for the exploration and expression of community ethics and the deprofessionalization of law.

We begin in Section 1 with materials intended to place the jury in its historical and cultural context and to provoke speculation about whether changes in the basic values of American culture may eventually render trial by jury vestigial. The materials form a kind of time line in which the historical development of legal institutions parallels historical changes in culture and in which a recent federal case and the "trial of the future" suggest a culture of the future with which we may be less than comfortable.

Section 2 concerns the political importance of the jury in our own society and confronts the issue of popular sovereignty directly. Alexis de Tocqueville, a French lawyer and author, observed 150 years ago that in the United States the jury is essentially a political institution. He seemed to contradict this view, however, by pointing out that jury trials also instill legal culture in the minds of ordinary citizens, thus reversing, perhaps, the direction of flow of political power so that it moves from legal institutions to people rather than vice versa. Which part of Tocqueville's seemingly contradictory description of the jury is accurate today? How much of the answer to this question depends on the status of jury nullification, by which jurors can determine both law and fact in a case regardless of the judge's instructions? Readings in Section 2 ask us to estimate how much power the jury should have as an instrument of popular participation in law, and what political consequences derive from the jury's power or lack of it.

The materials in Section 3 on jury selection and jury dynamics take on added importance in view of the political role of the jury as the voice of community values. These materials help to evaluate whether changes in the U.S. jury system have contributed to its decline as an important legal institution — whether, as Hans Zeisel puts it, we are witnessing "the waning of the American jury." In the overall operation of the legal system, the jury is not very much used. Most civil cases result in out-of-court settlements or trial by judge, and more than 85 percent of criminal cases end in plea bargains rather than jury trials. Still, the jury retains a symbolic significance, and it is used in many of what seem to be the most notable and publicly significant trials. Since we seem to *want* the jury to be important as a form of public participation in law, it is essential that we examine changes in the jury system to determine whether they enhance or undercut the jury's importance and effectiveness. The issues include jury size and unanimity requirements and the selection of a jury of peers.

Finally, in the study of the jury, Section 4 presents several problems in civil disobedience and how jurors react to an attempt to engage community conscience by violating the law. To encourage an intense consideration of this problem of ethics and law, this section includes a fictionalized description of one man's challenge to nuclear power, and readers are invited to form juries to deliberate his fate and your own. Other cases presented for discussion include protests against U.S. policy in Central America, against abortion, and against nuclear arms. The section begins with Martin Luther King, Jr.'s eloquent defense of civil disobedience as a means of forging community participation into an instrument of social justice. We also present former Supreme Court Justice Abe Fortas's thoughtful views on the difference between civil disobedience and destructive disorder.

Section 5 of the chapter shifts the focus on participation from juries to other legal forms in other cultures. The cross-cultural materials deal with the Cheyenne nation, modern China, and Cuba. These materials explore alternative ways to ensure substantial public input into the handling of conflict and the operation of law.

The entire chapter raises the issue of the relationship between law and community. Public participation in legal process supports law's role as a builder of communities, a definer of cultural boundaries, and a constructive means of forging individual and group identities. But participation can also become a way to coopt popular power, just as law can become formalistic, inaccessible, and antisocial in its function. Chapter 6 presents the theoretical underpinnings of and further thought about the relationship between law and community.

1 THE JURY IN A CULTURAL CONTEXT

At its simplest level, the petit or trial jury is charged with determining facts and applying law in a particular case. The grand jury, a somewhat larger group of citizens, has the responsibility of deciding whether the prosecutor has sufficient evidence to warrant making a formal criminal accusation (and indictment) against a person. To understand the petit jury's function and its relationship to the culture that created and developed it, we must begin by examining the jury's predecessors in medieval England to discover what legitimized an apparently irrational process such as the ordeal. What changes would be required in the values of those who used the ordeal so that they would be able to consider jury trial as anything but heresy? How can we place the Lateran Council of 1215 (by which the church forbade priests to officiate at ordeals) and the *Collins* case of 1968 (in which an appeals judge overturned the use of statistical evidence in a jury trial) on a time line with ordeals, jury trials, compulsory urinalysis, and trial by injection, in order to trace the development of our cultural beliefs and assumptions?

The Ordeal as a Vehicle for Divine Intervention in Medieval Europe *William J. Tewksbury*

The ordeal is a primitive form of trial used to determine the guilt or innocence of the accused, the result being regarded as a divine or preterhuman judgment. The fundamental idea upon which the ordeal rests is that it is a device for regulating, under conditions of comparative fairness, the primitive law of force. The concept that victory would inure to the right — that divine intervention would prevail on behalf of the innocent — was a belief that was subsequently engrafted upon the concept of the ordeal. The earliest occurrences, which can be referred to as pseudo-ordeals, seem to turn on the idea of brute strength. Such was the wager of battle and other *"bilateral* ordeals" to which both sides had to submit. Only later do we see man, alleging his innocence and facing his Creator, on trial by himself.

To understand the ordeal and the use for which it was designed, one must recognize the tremendous impact that religion has on the daily lives of the people who rely on it. The usual conception of divine intervention to vindicate innocence and to punish guilt is illustrated through an occurrence which happened in 1626 in France. A master had two servants, one stupid, and the other cunning. The latter stole from the master and so framed the stupid servant that he could not justify himself. The doltish servant, allegedly guilty, was tied to a flagstaff and guarded by the accuser. In the night, the flagstaff broke, the upper part falling upon and killing the guilty cunning servant,

From William J. Tewksbury, "The Ordeal as a Vehicle for Divine Intervention," in Paul Bohanon, ed., *Law and Warfare* (Garden City, N.Y.: Natural History Press, 1967), pp. 267–70. Reprinted by permission.

leaving the innocent servant unhurt. Beliefs such as this lead to irregular judicial proceedings. One might refer to them as ordeals of chance. The innocence of a man often turned on pure luck.

I. ORDEALS BY FIRE AND HEAT

The ordeal of boiling water is important in medieval Europe and elsewhere because it combines the elements of fire and water. Water represents the deluge which was the judgment inflicted upon the wicked of old. Fire represented the fiery doom of the future — the day of judgment. This ordeal compelled the accused with his naked hand to find a small pebble within a caldron of boiling water. After the hand had been plunged into the seething caldron, it was carefully enveloped in a cloth, sealed with the signet of a judge, and three days later was unwrapped. It was at this subsequent unwrapping that the accused's guilt or innocence was announced, determined by the condition of the hand.

A related ordeal was that of the red-hot iron. Two forms of this ordeal were found in medieval Europe. The first, which can best be categorized as one of chance, is the ordeal of the red-hot ploughshares. Ploughshares are heated until they glow and are then placed at certain intervals. The accused walks blindfolded and barefooted through the prescribed course. If he escapes injury, he is acquitted. The second form of the ordeal is more widely discussed. The accused is compelled to carry a piece of hot iron for a given distance. The weight of the iron varies with the magnitude of the crime alleged. If the accused can carry the piece of iron without sustaining any burn, he is regarded as innocent.

II. ORDEALS BY WATER AND MEANS OTHER THAN A DIRECT APPEAL TO GOD

The basis of the ordeal of cold water was that water, being a pure element, will not receive into her bosom anyone stained with the crime of a false oath. Water was recognized as capable of ascertaining those things which had been injected with untruths. The result seems, today, somewhat anomalous: the guilty floated and the innocent sank.

The success of this ordeal was less than perfect. Throughout the sources on this mode of ordeal were examples of malfunctions. Witches would sink like rocks, while leading members of the community, offering themselves to the rigors of the ordeal to test their validity, would float, often not sinking at all, even with the efforts of the officiating executioner.

Some ordeals were designed for people with some type of infirmity, such as blindness, lameness, or old age. Such people had to endure less trying ordeals to determine their guilt or innocence. A person burdened by such an incapacity is placed in one scale of the balance with an equivalent weight to counterbalance him in the other scale. The accused then went before the administering official, who then addressed a customary adjuration to the ordeal of the balance. The accused ascended the balance again, and if he was lighter than before, he was acquitted. This association of lightness with innocence would seem to be contrary to the European belief that lightness is associated with the Devil, as the Devil was regarded as nothing but a spirit of air.

III. ORDEAL BY DIRECT APPEAL TO GOD

The ordeal of the cross is characterized by placing two parties, the accused and the accuser, in front of a cross with their arms uplifted. Divine service was performed, and victory was adjudged to the one who was able to maintain his arms in the upraised position for the longest period of time. If this procedure led to a stalemate, the accused was given a piece of bread or cheese over which prayers had been said. If the accused could swallow the consecrated morsel, he was acquitted. We must remember that at the time these ordeals were the vogue, the people had great faith in Christ. The criminal, conscious of his guilt, standing before God and pledging his salvation, was expected to "break" under the weight of his own conscience. The truth of the matter lies in the fact that bread or cheese is difficult to swallow when the saliva secretion in one's mouth is not functioning properly. The exorcisms which were said beforehand were subject only to the imagination of the presiding priest. The more ingenious and devising he was, the more constricted became the throat of the most hardened criminal (as well as God-fearing innocents), and, therefore, the more difficult became the function of swallowing.

It was only a slight modification of the above which resulted in the Eucharist as an ordeal. "He that eateath and drinketh unworthily eateth and drinketh damnation to himself" (I Corinthians XI). When the consecrated wafer was offered under appropriate adjuration, the guilty would not receive it; or if it were taken, immediate convulsions and speedy death would ensue.

The basis for all ordeals is that men are asking for divine help to relieve themselves of the responsibility of decision. The ordeal has as its greatest characteristics the element of certainty. Such dependence on ordeals could be had whenever man waived his own judgment and undertook to test the inscrutable ways of his Creator — i.e., the laws of Nature are to be set aside whenever man chooses to tempt his God with the promise of right and the threat of injustice to be committed in His name. This passing the buck to God was particularly prevalent when there was no evidence as to the crime or where the crime was very difficult to prove judicially. The ordeal offered a ready and satisfactory solution to the doubts of a timid judge. Man believed that God would reverse the laws of Nature to accomplish a specified object.

The ordeal was thoroughly and completely a judicial process. It seems to have been used mostly to supplement deficient evidence and amounts to nothing more than an appeal to God.

☐ Trial by jury and trial by ordeal could hardly seem less alike; yet like the opposite faces of a coin, they share the same center. The almost mythic reverence in which we hold the jury today is probably neither more nor less than the public reverence toward the ordeal in its day. Each produces, for a different society, that degree of certainty of truth and acceptability of decision necessary for the settling of disputes and the imposition of authority.

The differences between jury and ordeal are not in their function, but in the underlying cultural values of the societies that these seemingly antithetical institutions served. Medieval England looked to the judgment of God and the power of the Church. Twentieth-century America looks to rationalism, the objective consciousness, and the state. Since trial by jury is the successor to trial by ordeal, we may learn something by examining briefly a historical point of contact between them — thirteenth-century England.

The earliest juries in England were not concerned with determining guilt or innocence or civil liability, but rather with making accusations on behalf of the Crown and thereby extending its authority. At a time when the monarchy was still struggling to bring the private resolution of conflict under its own control through the extension of "law," Henry II in the Assize of Clarendon, 1166, made the jury of presentment a nationwide phenomenon, and twelve local knights or "free lawful men" of each village were charged with producing accusations of murder, theft, or arson. Having been thus accused, the defendant had to proceed to "the judgment of the water" (ordeal or trial by water).

By the first part of the thirteenth century, something a little more like jury trial as we know it began to appear in murder cases in England. Those who felt that they had been accused of murder "out of spite and hate" could purchase from the king a "writ" entitling them to a trial by twelve "recognitors" on the issue of whether the accusation was malicious. If they found it was, no ordeal was required. If the accusation was not found malicious, trial by ordeal was prescribed. This preliminary determination, not of guilt but of the good faith of the accusation, began to bring considerable revenue to the royal coffers, as it was claimed more and more as a matter of course by accused murderers seeking to avoid the ordeal.

As the procedure was developing, the Church dealt a heavy blow to the ordeal and gave the jury more room to develop. In 1215, the Fourth Lateran Council forbade the clergy to perform any religious ceremonies in connection with the ordeal. The reason for this decision is unclear, but without this religious seal of approval the mainstay of the system of determining guilt began to lose its legitimacy, and substantial confusion among the king's justices was created as to how such decisions were to be reached. In the confusion and experimentation that ensued, the jury trial began to emerge as one way of deciding issues of fact. But it was not a jury trial we would recognize today.

The central issue in using what were then called jury trials seems to have been the reluctance of the populace to accept them as a legitimate determination of guilt. Despite the increased use of juries to determine whether accusations of murder were malicious, the general attitude of most people still seemed to have been confidence in the ordeal as the judgment of God and uncertainty in the juries' verdict as the judgment of men. In fact not until 1275 did the king feel it was reasonable to impose the jury trial even on notorious felons. Up to that point people had to voluntarily accept a jury trial ("throw themselves on the country"); and some endured death by torture (being sandwiched between two boards, which were then slowly loaded with stones) rather than accept trial by jury when conviction meant forfeiture of land and chattel. What was at issue during the formative period of trial by jury was whether this institution could confer legitimacy on decisions or whether it was too inscrutable, heretical, and unfamiliar to be trusted with such an important task.

While this transformation of the mind was beginning, the early jury was at best a makeshift procedure from our point of view. It had not yet been rationalized or even settled in its procedure. In fact, it was very much like the inquisition that preceded it in making accusations (jury of presentment) or in determining the existence of taxable property (the Domesday Book of 1066). Instead of hearing evidence and making an allegedly impartial decision based on the evidence, the jury relied solely on its own knowledge of local affairs. As the king's justices traveled on circuit, they convened a jury in each village and these men were then charged with the duty of determining the guilt or innocence of the accused on the basis of whatever they knew personally or were able to find out on their own. In fact, there were often members of the accusing jury on the trial jury, and the trial was probably one of general reputation in the village. It was not until the 1500s that witnesses were even *allowed* to present information to the jury, and it was almost 1700 before the accused gained the right to compel the attendance of witnesses to help in presenting the defendant's case. The later history of trial by jury, especially in the United States, can be traced from Tocqueville's analysis and from the *Duncan* case and Horwitz excerpts, which appear on pages 371–379.

Whatever its shortcomings from the viewpoint of modern U.S. legal process, the jury did serve the purpose even then of relieving the king's justices of the responsibility of deciding issues of guilt and innocence or civil liability. In so doing, it shifted the focus, though perhaps not the reality, of authority from king to subjects, from rule of man to rule of men and ultimately rule of law. And it began to shift the justification for decisions resolving disputes from God to rational man, an equally inscrutable entity. By the 1700s, the transformation began to be layered over with the philosophy of individualism, rationalism, and what we now call due process of law. By 1954 this rationalistic jury had become so little understood, yet so sacred, that a scholarly attempt to probe its workings was met with an investigation by the Internal Security Subcommittee of the Senate Judiciary Committee and by legislation forbidding the recording of jury deliberations. Today jury deliberations are as jealously protected as in the 1950s, but calls for reducing the cost and time taken by jury trials indicate that perhaps the jury's importance is declining in American society.

Perhaps something about the function of the jury in the legal process requires this protectiveness and even mystery, lest we lose our legitimized decision-making process at the hands of objective consciousness —just as Henry II lost the ordeal in the thirteenth century at the hands of progressive religion. In any case, its symbolic role can be no less important than its practical utility.

Constitution of the United States of America, Amendments

ARTICLE III

SECTION 2. (3) The trial of all Crimes, except in Cases of Impeachment, shall be by Jury; and such Trial shall be held in the State where the said Crimes shall have been committed; but when not committed within any State, the Trial shall be at such Place or Places as the Congress may by Law have directed.

AMENDMENT VI (1791)

In all criminal prosecutions, the accused shall enjoy the right to a speedy and public trial, by an impartial jury of the State and district wherein the crime shall have been committed, which district shall have been previously ascertained by law, and to be informed of the nature and cause of the accusation; to be confronted with the witnesses against him; to have compulsory process for obtaining witnesses in his favor, and to have the Assistance of Counsel for his defence.

AMENDMENT VII (1791)

In Suits at common law, where the value in controversy shall exceed twenty dollars, the right of trial by jury shall be preserved, and no fact tried by jury, shall be otherwise re-examined in any Court of the United States, than according to the rules of the common law.

People v. Collins *66 Cal. Rptr. 497, 438 P.2d 33 (S.Ct., 1968)*

SULLIVAN, JUSTICE.

We deal here with the novel question whether evidence of mathematical probability has been properly introduced and used by the prosecution in a criminal case. While we discern no inherent incompatibility between the disciplines of law and mathematics and intend no general disapproval or disparagement of the latter as an auxiliary in the fact-finding processes of the former, we cannot uphold the technique employed in the instant case. As we explain in detail *infra,* the testimony as to mathematical probability infected the case with fatal error and distorted the jury's traditional role of determining guilt or innocence according to long-settled rules. Mathematics, a veritable sorcerer in our computerized society, while assisting the trier of fact in the search for truth, must not case a spell over him. We conclude that on the record before us defendant should not have had his guilt determined by the odds and that he is entitled to a new trial. We reverse the judgment.

A jury found defendant Malcolm Ricardo Collins and his wife defendant Janet Louise Collins guilty of second degree robbery (Pen. Code, §§ 211, 211a, 1157). Malcolm appeals from the judgment of conviction. Janet has not appealed.

On June 18, 1964, about 11:30 A.M. Mrs. Juanita Brooks, who had been shopping, was walking home along an alley in the San Pedro area of the City of Los Angeles. She was pulling behind her a wicker basket carryall containing groceries and had her purse on top of the packages. She was using a cane. As she stooped down to pick up an empty carton, she was suddenly pushed to the ground by a person whom she neither saw nor heard approach. She was stunned by the fall and felt some pain. She managed to look up and saw a young woman running from the scene. According to Mrs. Brooks the latter appeared to weigh about 145 pounds, was wearing "something dark," and had hair "between dark blonde and a light blonde," but lighter than the color of defendant Janet Collins' hair as it appeared at trial. Immediately after the incident, Mrs. Brooks discovered that her purse, containing between $35 and $40, was missing.

About the same time as the robbery, John Bass, who lived on the street at the end of the alley, was in front of his house watering his lawn. His attention was attracted by "a lot of crying and screaming" coming from the alley. As he looked in that direction, he saw a woman run out of the alley and enter a yellow automobile parked across the street from him. He was unable to give the make of the car. The car started off immediately and pulled wide around another parked vehicle so that in the narrow street it passed within six feet of Bass. The latter then saw that it was being driven by a male Negro, wearing a mustache and beard. At the trial Bass identified defendant as the driver of the yellow automobile. However, an attempt was made to impeach his identification by his admission that at the preliminary hearing he testified to an uncertain identification at the police lineup shortly after the attack on Mrs. Brooks, when defendant was beardless.

In his testimony Bass described the woman who ran from the alley as a Caucasian, slightly over five feet tall, of ordinary build, with her hair in a dark blond ponytail, and wearing dark clothing. He further testified that her ponytail was "just like" one which Janet had in a police photograph taken on June 22, 1964.

On the day of the robbery, Janet was employed as a housemaid in San Pedro. Her employer testified that she had arrived for work at 8:50 A.M. and that defendant had picked her up in a light yellow car[1] about 11:30 A.M. On that day, according to the witness, Janet was wearing her hair in a blond ponytail but lighter in color than it appeared at trial.[2]

There was evidence from which it could be inferred that defendants had ample time to drive from Janet's place of employment and participate in the robbery. Defendants testified, however, that they went directly from her employer's house to the home of friends, where they remained for several hours.

In the morning of June 22, Los Angeles Police Officer Kinsey, who was investigating the robbery, went to defendants' home. There was a yellow Lincoln automobile with an off-white top in front of the house. He talked with defendants. Janet, whose hair appeared to be a dark blonde, was wearing it in a ponytail. Malcolm did not have a beard. The officer explained to them that he was investigating a robbery specifying the time and place; that the victim had been knocked down and her purse snatched; and that the person responsible was a female Caucasian with blonde hair in a ponytail, who had left the scene in a yellow car driven by a male Negro. He requested that defendants accompany him to the police station at San Pedro and they did so. There, in response to police inquiries as to defendants' activities at the time of the robbery, Janet stated, according to Officer Kinsey, that her husband had picked her up at her place of employment at 1 P.M. and that they had then visited at the home of friends in Los Angeles. Malcolm confirmed this. Defendants were detained for an hour or two, were photographed but not booked, and were eventually released and driven home by the police.

Late in the afternoon of the same day, Officer Kinsey, while driving home from work in his own car, saw defendants riding in their yellow Lincoln. Although the transcript fails to disclose what prompted such action, Kinsey proceeded to place them under surveillance and eventually followed them home. He called for assistance and arranged to meet other police officers in the vicinity of defendants' home. Kinsey took a position in the rear of the premises. The other officers, who were in uniform and had arrived in a marked police car, approached defendants' front door. As they did so, Kinsey saw defendant Malcolm Collins run out the back door toward a rear fence and disappear behind

[1]Other witnesses variously described the car as yellow, as yellow with an off-white top, and yellow with an eggshell white top. The car was also described as being medium to large in size. Defendant drove a car at or near the times in question which was a Lincoln with a yellow body and a white top.

[2]There are inferences which may be drawn from the evidence that Janet attempted to alter the appearance of her hair after June 18. Janet denies that she cut, colored or bleached her hair at any time after June 18, and a number of witnesses supported her testimony.

a tree. Meanwhile the other officers emerged with Janet Collins whom they had placed under arrest. A search was made for Malcolm who was found in a closet of a neighboring home and also arrested. Defendants were again taken to the police station, were kept in custody for 48 hours, and were again released without any charges being made against them.

Officer Kinsey interrogated defendants separately on June 23 while they were in custody and testified to their statements over defense counsel's objections based on the decision in *Escobedo* and our first decision in *Dorado.* According to the officer, Malcolm stated that he sometimes wore a beard but that he did not wear a beard on June 18 (the day of the robbery), having shaved it off on June 2, 1964.[3] He also explained two receipts for traffic fines totalling $35 paid on June 19, which receipts had been found on his person, by saying that he used funds won in a gambling game at a labor hall. Janet, on the other hand, said that the $35 used to pay the fines had come from her earnings.[4]

On July 9, 1964, defendants were again arrested and were booked for the first time. While they were in custody and awaiting the preliminary hearing, Janet requested to talk with Officer Kinsey. There followed a lengthy conversation during the first part of which Malcolm was not present. During this time Janet expressed concern about defendant and inquired as to what the outcome would be *if* it appeared that she committed the crime and Malcolm knew nothing about it. In general she indicated a wish that defendant be released from any charges because of his prior criminal record and that if someone must be held responsible, she alone would bear the guilt. The officer told her that no assurances could be given, that if she wanted to admit responsibility disposition of the matter would be in the hands of the court and that if she committed the crime and defendant knew nothing about it the only way she could help him would be by telling the truth. Defendant was then brought into the room and participated in the rest of the conversation. The officer asked to hear defendant's version of the matter, saying that he believed defendant was at the scene. However, neither Janet nor defendant confessed or expressly made damaging admissions although constantly urged by the investigating officer to make truthful statements. On several occasions defendant denied that he knew what had gone on in the alley. On the other hand, the whole tone of the conversation evidenced a strong consciousness of guilt on the part of both defendants who appeared to be seeking the most advantageous way out. Over defense counsel's same objections based on *Escobedo* and *Dorado,* some parts of the foregoing conversation were testified to by Officer Kinsey and in addition a tape recording of the entire conversation was introduced in evidence and played to the jury.[5]

---

[3]Evidence as to defendant's beard and mustache is conflicting. Defense witnesses appeared to support defendant's claims that he had shaved his beard on June 2. There was testimony that on June 19 when defendant appeared in court to pay fines on another matter he was bearded. By June 22 the beard had been removed.

[4]The source of the $35, being essentially the same amount as the $35 to $40 reported by the victim as having been in her purse when taken from her the day before the fines were paid, was a significant factor in the prosecution's case. Other evidence disclosed that defendant and Janet were married on June 2, 1964, at which time they had only $12, a portion of which was spent on a trip to Tijuana. Since the marriage defendant had not worked, and Janet's earnings were not more than $12 a week, if that much.

[5]Included in the conversation are the following excerpts from Janet's statements:

"If I told you that he didn't know anything about it and I did it, would you cut him loose?"

"I just want him out, that's all, because I ain't never been in no trouble. I won't have to do too much [time], but he will."

"What's the most time I can do?"

"Would it be easier if I went ahead and said, if I was going to say anything, say it now instead of waiting till court time?"

Defendant indicated that he should "go and have trust in [the officer], but maybe I'd be wrong. I mean, this is a little delicate on my behalf."

At another point defendant stated: "I'm leaving it up to her."

Defendant expressed concern during the

At the seven-day trial the prosecution experienced some difficulty in establishing the identities of the perpetrators of the crime. The victim could not identify Janet and had never seen defendant. The identification by the witness Bass, who observed the girl run out of the alley and get into the automobile, was incomplete as to Janet and may have been weakened as to defendant. There was also evidence, introduced by the defense, that Janet had worn light-colored clothing on the day in question, but both the victim and Bass testified that the girl they observed had worn dark clothing.

In an apparent attempt to bolster the identifications, the prosecutor called an instructor of mathematics at a state college. Through this witness he sought to establish that, assuming the robbery was committed by a Caucasian woman with a blond ponytail who left the scene accompanied by a Negro with a beard and mustache, there was an overwhelming probability that the crime was committed by any couple answering such distinctive characteristics. The witness testified, in substance, to the "product rule," which states that the probability of the joint occurrence of a number of *mutually independent* events is equal to the product of the individual probabilities that each of the events will occur. *Without presenting any statistical evidence whatsoever in support of the probabilities for the factors selected,* the prosecutor then proceeded to have the witness *assume* probability factors for the various characteristics which he deemed to be shared by the guilty couple and all other couples answering to such distinctive characteristics.[6]

Applying the product rule to his own factors the prosecutor arrived at a probability that there was but one chance in 12 million that any couple possessed the distinctive characteristics of the defendants. Accordingly, under this theory, it was to be inferred that there could be but one chance in 12 million that defendants were innocent and that another equally distinctive couple actually committed the robbery. Expanding on what he had thus purported to suggest as a hypothesis, the prosecutor offered the completely unfounded and improper testimonial assertion that, in his opinion, the factors he had assigned were "conservative estimates" and that, in reality, "the chances of anyone else besides these defendants being there, . . . having every similarity, . . . is somewhat like one in a billion."

Objections were timely made to the mathematician's testimony on the grounds that it was immaterial, that it invaded the province of the jury, and that it was based on unfounded assumptions. The objections were "temporarily overruled" and the evidence admitted subject to a motion to strike. When that motion was made at the conclusion of the direct examination, the court denied it, stating that the testimony had been received only for the "purpose of illustrat-

conversation that any statement by Janet would not necessarily relieve him because he admittedly had been with her all that day since 11:30 A.M. The conversation closed when defendants indicated that they wished more time to think it over.

[6]Although the prosecutor insisted that the factors he used were only for illustrative purposes — to demonstrate how the probability of the occurrence of mutually independent factors affected the probability that they would occur together — he nevertheless attempted to use factors which he personally related to the distinctive characteristics of defendants. In his argument to the jury he invited the jurors to apply their own factors, and asked defense counsel to suggest what the latter would deem as reasonable. The prosecutor himself proposed the individual probabilities set out in the table below. Although the transcript of the examination of the mathematics instructor and the information volunteered by the prosecutor at that time create some uncertainty as to precisely which of the characteristics the prosecutor assigned to the individual probabilities, he restated in his argument to the jury that they should be as follows:

Characteristic	*Individual probability*
A. Partly yellow automobile	1/10
B. Man with mustache	1/4
C. Girl with ponytail	1/10
D. Girl with blonde hair	1/3
E. Negro man with beard	1/10
F. Interracial couple in car	1/1000

In his brief on appeal defendant agrees that the foregoing appeared on a table presented in the trial court.

ing the mathematical probabilities of various matters, the possibilities for [their] occurring or re-occurring."

Both defendants took the stand in their own behalf. They denied any knowledge of or participation in the crime and stated that after Malcolm called for Janet at her employer's house they went directly to a friend's house in Los Angeles where they remained for some time. According to this testimony defendants were not near the scene of the robbery when it occurred. Defendants' friend testified to a visit by them "in the middle of June" although she could not recall the precise date. Janet further testified that certain inducements were held out to her during the July 9 interrogation on condition that she confess her participation.

Defendant makes two basic contentions before us: First, that the admission in evidence of the statements made by defendants while in custody on June 23 and July 9, 1964, constitutes reversible error under the rules announced in the *Escobedo* and *Dorado* decisions; and second, that the introduction of evidence pertaining to the mathematical theory of probability and the use of the same by the prosecution during the trial was error prejudicial to defendant. We consider the latter claim first.

As we shall explain, the prosecution's introduction and use of mathematical probability statistics injected two fundamental prejudicial errors into the case: (1) The testimony itself lacked an adequate foundation both in evidence and in statistical theory; and (2) the testimony and the manner in which the prosecution used it distracted the jury from its proper and requisite function of weighing the evidence on the issue of guilt, encouraged the jurors to rely upon an engaging but logically irrelevant expert demonstration, foreclosed the possibility of an effective defense by an attorney apparently unschooled in mathematical refinements, and placed the jurors and defense counsel at a disadvantage in sifting relevant fact from inapplicable theory.

We initially consider the defects in the testimony itself. As we have indicated, the specific technique presented through the mathematician's testimony and advanced by the prosecutor to measure the probabilities in question suffered from two basic and pervasive defects — an inadequate evidentiary foundation and an inadequate proof of statistical independence. First, as to the foundation requirement, we find the record devoid of any evidence relating to any of the six individual probability factors used by the prosecutor and ascribed by him to the six characteristics as we have set them out in footnote 6, *ante*. To put it another way, the prosecution produced no evidence whatsoever showing, or from which it could be in any way inferred, that only one out of every ten cars which might have been at the scene of the robbery was partly yellow, that only one out of every four men who might have been there wore a mustache, that only one out of every ten girls who might have been there wore a ponytail, or that any of the other individual probability factors listed were even roughly accurate.

The bare, inescapable fact is that the prosecution made no attempt to offer any such evidence. Instead, through leading questions having perfunctorily elicited from the witness the response that the latter could not assign a probability factor for the characteristics involved,[7] the prosecutor himself suggested what the various probabilities should be and these became the basis of the witness' testimony (see fn. 6, *ante*). It is a curious circumstance of this adventure in proof that the prosecutor not only made his own assertions of these factors in the hope that they were "conservative" but also in later argument to the jury invited the jurors to substitute their "estimates" should they wish to do so. We can hardly conceive of a more fatal gap in the prosecution's scheme of proof. A foundation for the admissibility of the witness' testimony

[7]The prosecutor asked the mathematics instructor: "Now, let me see if you can be of some help to us with some independent factors, and you have some paper you may use. Your specialty does not equip you, I suppose, to give us some probability of such things as a yellow car as contrasted with any other kind of car, does it? . . . I appreciate the fact that you can't assign a probability for a car being yellow as contrasted to some other car, can you?" A. "No, I couldn't."

was never even attempted to be laid, let alone established. His testimony was neither made to rest on his own testimonial knowledge nor presented by proper hypothetical questions based upon valid data in the record. (See generally: 2 Wigmore on Evidence (3d ed. 1940) §§ 478, 650–652, 657, 659, 672–684; Witkin, Cal. Evidence (2d ed. 1966) § 771; McCormick on Evidence pp. 19–20; Evidence: Admission of Mathematical Probability Statistics Held Erroneous for Want of Demonstration of Validity (1967) Duke L.J. 665, 675–678, citing *People* v. *Risley* (1915) 214 N.Y. 75, 85, 108 N.E. 200; *State* v. *Sneed* (1966) 76 N.M. 349, 414, P.2d 858). In the *Sneed* case, the court reversed a conviction based on probabilistic evidence, stating: "We hold that mathematical odds are not admissible as evidence to identify a defendant in a criminal proceeding *so long as the odds are based on estimates, the validity of which have* [*sic*] *not been demonstrated.*" (Italics added.) (414 P.2d at p. 862.)

But, as we have indicated, there was another glaring defect in the prosecution's technique, namely an inadequate proof of the statistical independence of the six factors. No proof was presented that the characteristics selected were mutually independent even though the witness himself acknowledged that such condition was essential to the proper application of the "product rule" or "multiplication rule." (See Note, *supra,* Duke L.J. 665, 669–670, fn. 25.) To the extent that the traits or characteristics were not mutually independent (e.g., Negroes with beards and men with mustaches obviously represent overlapping categories), the "product rule" would inevitably yield a wholly erroneous and exaggerated result even if all of the individual components had been determined with precision. . . .

In the instant case, therefore, because of the aforementioned two defects — the inadequate evidentiary foundation and the inadequate proof of statistical independence — the technique employed by the prosecutor could only lead to wild conjecture without demonstrated relevancy to the issues presented. It acquired no redeeming quality from the prosecutor's statement that it was being used only "for illustrative purposes" since, as we shall point out, the prosecutor's subsequent utilization of the mathematical testimony was not confined within such limits.

We now turn to the second fundamental error caused by the probability testimony. Quite apart from our foregoing objections to the specific technique employed by the prosecution to estimate the probability in question, we think that the entire enterprise upon which the prosecution embarked, and which was directed to the objective of measuring the likelihood of a random couple possessing the characteristics allegedly distinguishing the robbers, was gravely misguided. At best, it might yield an estimate as to how infrequently bearded Negroes drive yellow cars in the company of blonde females with ponytails.

The prosecution's approach, however, could furnish the jury with absolutely no guidance on the crucial issue: *Of the admittedly few such couples, which one, if any, was guilty of committing this robbery?* Probability theory necessarily remains silent on that question, since no mathematical equation can prove beyond a reasonable doubt (1) that the guilty couple *in fact* possessed the characteristics described by the People's witnesses, or even (2) that only *one* couple possessing those distinctive characteristics could be found in the entire Los Angeles area.

As to the first inherent failing we observe that the prosecution's theory of probability rested on the assumption that the witnesses called by the People had conclusively established that the guilty couple possessed the precise characteristics relied upon by the prosecution. But no mathematical formula could ever establish beyond a reasonable doubt that the prosecution's witnesses correctly observed and accurately described the distinctive features which were employed to link defendants to the crime. Conceivably, for example, the guilty couple might have included a light-skinned Negress with bleached hair rather than a Caucasian blonde; or the driver of the car might have been wearing a false beard as a disguise; or the prosecution's witnesses might simply have been unreliable.

The foregoing risks of error permeate the prosecutions' circumstantial case. Traditionally, the jury weighs such risks in evaluating the credibility and probative value of trial testimony, but the likelihood of human error or of falsification obviously cannot be quantified; that likelihood must therefore be excluded from any effort to assign a *number* to the probability of guilt or innocence. Confronted with an equation which purports to yield a numerical index of probable guilt, few juries could resist the temptation to accord disproportionate weight to that index; only an exceptional juror, and indeed only a defense attorney schooled in mathematics, could successfully keep in mind the fact that the probability computed by the prosecution can represent, *at best,* the likelihood that a random couple would share the characteristics testified to by the People's witnesses — *not necessarily the characteristics of the actually guilty couple.*

As to the second inherent failing in the prosecution's approach, even assuming that the first failing could be discounted, the most a mathematical computation could *ever* yield would be a measure of the probability that a random couple would possess the distinctive features in question. In the present case, for example, the prosecution attempted to compute the probability that a random couple would include a bearded Negro, a blonde girl with a ponytail, and a partly yellow car; the prosecution urged that this probability was no more than one in 12 million. Even accepting this conclusion as arithmetically accurate, however, one still could not conclude that the Collinses were probably *the* guilty couple. On the contrary, . . . the prosecution's figures actually imply a likelihood of over 40 percent that the Collinses could be "duplicated" by at least *one other couple who might equally have committed the San Pedro robbery.* Urging that the Collinses be convicted on the basis of evidence which logically establishes no more than this seems as indefensible as arguing for the conviction of X on the ground that a witness saw either X or X's twin commit the crime.

Again, few defense attorneys, and certainly few jurors, could be expected to comprehend this basic flaw in the prosecution's analysis. Conceivably even the prosecutor erroneously believed that his equation established a high probability that *no* other bearded Negro in the Los Angeles area drove a yellow car accompanied by a ponytailed blonde. In any event, although his technique could demonstrate no such thing, he solemnly told the jury that he had supplied mathematical proof of guilt.

Sensing the novelty of that notion, the prosecutor told the jurors that the traditional idea of proof beyond a reasonable doubt represented "the most hackneyed, stereotyped, trite, misunderstood concept in criminal law." He sought to reconcile the jury to the risk that, under his "new math" approach to criminal jurisprudence, "on some rare occasion . . . an innocent person may be convicted." "Without taking that risk," the prosecution continued, "life would be intolerable . . . because . . . there would be immunity for the Collinses, for people who chose not to be employed, to go down and push old ladies down and take their money and be immune because how could we ever be sure they are the ones who did it?"

In essence this argument of the prosecutor was calculated to persuade the jury to convict defendants whether or not they were convinced of their guilt to a mortal certainty and beyond a reasonable doubt. (Pen. Code, § 1096.) Undoubtedly the jurors were unduly impressed by the mystique of the mathematical demonstration but were unable to assess its relevancy or value. Although we make no appraisal of the proper applications of mathematical techniques in the proof of facts, . . . we have strong feelings that such applications, particularly in a criminal case, must be critically examined in view of the substantial unfairness to a defendant which may result from ill conceived techniques with which the trier of fact is not technically equipped to cope. (See *State* v. *Sneed, supra,* 414 P.2d 858; Note, *supra,* Duke L.J. 665.) We feel that the technique employed in the case before us falls into the latter category.

We conclude that the court erred in admitting over defendant's objection the evidence pertaining to the mathematical theory of probabilty and in denying defendant's motion to strike such evidence. The case was apparently a close one. The jury began its deliberations at 2:46 P.M. on November 24, 1964, and retired for the night at 7:46 P.M.; the parties stipulated that a juror could be excused for illness and that a verdict could be reached by the remaining 11 jurors; the jury resumed deliberations the next morning at 8:40 A.M. and returned verdicts at 11:58 A.M. after five ballots had been taken. In the light of the closeness of the case, which as we have said was a circumstantial one, there is a reasonable likelihood that the result would have been more favorable to defendant if the prosecution had not urged the jury to render a probabilistic verdict. In any event, we think that under the circumstances the "trial by mathematics" so distorted the role of the jury and so disadvantaged counsel for the defense, as to constitute in itself a miscarriage of justice. After an examination of the entire case, including the evidence, we are of the opinion that it is reasonably probable that a result more favorable to defendant would have been reached in the absence of the above error. . . . The judgment against defendant must therefore be reversed.

In view of the foregoing conclusion, we deem it unnecessary to consider whether the admission of defendants' extrajudicial statements constitutes error under the rules announced in *Escobedo* and *Dorado.* Upon retrial, the admissibility of these or any other extrajudicial statements sought to be introduced by the prosecution must be determined in the light of the rules set forth in *Miranda* v. *State of Arizona* (1966) 384 U.S. 436, 86 S.Ct. 1602, 16 L.E.2d 694. . . . As we have pointed out, the trial herein took place between our first and second *Dorado* decisions. Although defense counsel was commendably alert in basing objections to the admission of the statements upon the decisions in *Escobedo* and *Dorado,* he of course did not have the benefit of our numerous decisions beginning with the second *Dorado* decision expounding various facets of the exclusionary rule. In the event any extrajudicial statements made by defendant are offered in evidence on retrial, the parties will have an opportunity to make a record on pertinent issues subject to prior determination by the court in the light of *Miranda* rules before such statements are received in evidence. It would be fruitless for us to essay such a task at this point when such record does not yet exist.

The judgment is reversed.

TRAYNOR, C.J., *and* PETERS, TOBRINER, MOSK *and* BURKE, JJ., *concur.*

McCOMB, JUSTICE.
I dissent. I would affirm the judgment in its entirety.

The Trial of the Future *Bernard Botein and Murray A. Gordon*

For a long time science has been deflating our notions about the infallibility of the trial process. More recently, the technicians have gone even further. There have been developed startling, effective techniques for "eavesdropping on man's unconscious," as it has been termed. If these techniques fulfill the expectations of many sober-minded men of science, the laboratory will be equpped to reveal truth much more efficiently and inexorably than the courtroom. We may reach the point where our present methods of resolving legal disputes may seem as archaic and barbaric as trial by ordeal seems to us today; and courtroom procedures as we know them may have to be scrapped.

Because we stand at the threshold of such a possibility, it should be profitable to review briefly the progress of science in the ascertainment of truth and to consider its implications for the administration of law in this country. If science can reproduce truth more reliably and effectively than our present system, we shall not be able long to defer our rendezvous with progress. The judicial test for admitting the fruits of scientific research is whether they have won general acceptance in the appropriate disci-

---

pline. Because of this stringent test various newer truth-revealing techniques have not yet won admittance to the courthouse, but they are storming its steps. . . .

Fact-finding for trial purposes today depends in large measure upon articulate, communicable testimony reflecting the recollection of witnesses. As indicated, limitations of conscious memory, even aside from the distorting factors of self-interest and partisanship, made this process painfully fallible; and its deficiencies often cannot be cured by cross-examination, that revered rectifier of purposeful fabrication or unwitting error. And many times, even when recollection is accurate, tense and frightened witnesses fail to communicate accurately to judge or jury.

Recent experience with drugs such as scopolamine and the barbiturates (sodium pentothal and sodium amytal), techniques such as hypnosis and devices such as the lie detector should be, accordingly, of profound significance in our current trial procedures. These devices suggest the eventual emergence of scientifically accepted procedures for inducing the full and truthful recollection and the relaxed narration of events. . . .

Narcoanalysis, a term loosely blanketing procedures for interrogating subjects while they are in a state of partial unconsciousness induced by drugs, is the most dramatic of the techniques mentioned. The drugs employed in narcoanalysis serve as central nervous system depressants and thereby lessen inhibitions and other blocks to disclosures. . . .

The slow and limited judicial acceptance of drug-induced revelations must be viewed in the light of similar judicial skepticism which existed and was ultimately dispelled by scientific progress leading eventually to court acceptance of fingerprint evidence, blood tests, and handwriting, X-ray and psychiatric testimony. . . .

. . . The likely timetable of judicial acceptance of drug-induced disclosures will, no doubt, reflect the observation of our outstanding authority on the law of evidence, the late Professor Wigmore: "If there is ever devised a psychological test for the evaluation of witnesses, the law will run to meet it. . . . Whenever the psychologist is ready for the courts, the courts are ready for him."

In short, recent and probable future advances in the technique of inducing revelations by narcoanalysis and the general judicial receptivity to scientifically validated evidence remove this subject from the realm of science-fiction fantasy and dictate a sober consideration of the consequences to the judicial process. . . .

As the novel methods of proof we have discussed assume greater scientific validity, serious questions must also arise as to whether findings of fact, of intention or of motive can be left, as now, to the nonscientific community of judges or juries, or whether that function will be for those whose special skills and training more particularly qualify them to appraise the materials resulting from such methods. Indeed, there would no doubt be agitation for the elimination of judge, jury and courtroom, as we know them, in favor of the more clinical precincts of the technician. . . .

More subtle than the scuttling of the traditional trial process, but probably more critical in its societal implications, would be the effect of truth-revealing techniques on rights of the individual which have long been cherished and associated with protection of his person and dignity. We shall be unable to avoid re-examining the present practice of imposing upon the claimant in a civil action the burden of proving his version by a fair preponderance of the evidence, or requiring the prosecution in a criminal case to prove the defendant guilty beyond a reasonable doubt. The trial process is usually weighted on the side of the defending party. The law places a heavy burden on the complaining party who would enlist its resources to obtain relief. This is particularly true in criminal cases, where society seeks to balance the uneven resources of government and the accused individual so as to protect him from tyrants and powerful masters who possess the means to employ the courts as instruments of oppression.

But what need will remain to such weighting and protective rules, it will be argued, if the management of litigation by the parties themselves become minimal? Constitutional and common law safeguards, such as the provisions against self-incrimination, the presumption of innocence, the right to due process, are all commonly believed to be for the protection of the innocent. Again, what need in law or logic for invoking these protections when science can reliably establish such innocence without them? . . .

It will be contended that since the end to be attained by the provisions of constitutional and common law is protection of the innocent, and since science will accomplish this so much more effectively than all of the legal doctrines laid end to end, *ergo,* this is one end that justifies the means. In such a view the presumption of innocence would be dissolved because it would become unnecessary. Likewise, a major justification for asserting the right against self-incrimination — that the innocent might become entangled in the toils of the law through his own lips — falls away. The innocent person would no longer have to hack his way through the jungle of uncertainties and technicalities which made all these legal safeguards necessary. He would be able to establish his innocence more easily and directly through science. Indeed, if the reliability of narcoanalysis is demonstrated, but it is not received as evidence, an innocent man ready to submit to the testing may be deemed to be deprived unfairly of the right to clear himself. . . .

. . . [T]he public intuitively looks to those administering justice not only to elicit truth and enforce law, but to satisfy other social and community values. Such protective rules as the privilege against self-incrimination, the presumption of innocence, and the exclusion from evidence of confidential communications between husband and wife, doctor and patient, lawyer and client, all have evolved to maintain the high value the community has set on the grandeur of the individual. Each of these principles subordinates full disclosure of the facts to some other higher social value. . . .

. . . It is . . . frequently the case that where investigatory or trial procedures for the disclosure of facts impinge upon deeply held values sustaining the integrity and the dignity of the individual, those values prevail at the expense of the facts. . . .

Each of the techniques associated with narcoanalysis involves dredging facts from the unconscious that the person interrogated might be unwilling consciously to reveal. To that extent, each of these techniques entails an invasion of his privacy, as well as his freedom of will. Each abrades the dignity of man; and such indignities can become contagious, if not epidemic. Our traditional and adversary system of litigation, though it may not prove to be the most exact medium for ascertaining truth, embodies the democratic emphasis upon respect for human dignity at every step of the way. If we do not act to anticipate, it remains for us to await — and not without anxiety — the balance finally to be struck between the service of dignity and of truth in the trial process as truth comes more surely within reach as a result of scientific validation of fact-finding through unconscious disclosures. The issue posed is, in the end, no less than an uneasy search for the character of our society of the future. For the balance finally struck between dignity and truth in our courts will be cast in the image of a society which has opted either for efficiency or for freedom.

☐ Read the following case, which is typical of cases that federal courts will be struggling with over the next five years, with three questions in mind. First, is compulsory urinalysis the kind of "trial of the future" that Botein and Gordon had in mind? Second, does the use of urine screening — however effective — amount to trial and conviction without a jury? Third, are the value issues at stake here similar to those in *Collins?*

Capua v. The City of Plainfield *643 F. Supp. 1507 (1986)*

SAROKIN, DISTRICT JUDGE

INTRODUCTION

In the face of widespread use of drugs and its intrusion into the workplace, it is tempting to turn to mass testing as a solution. The issue presented by this case is the constitutionality of such testing of current employees by governmental entities. Whether such testing may be done in the private sector or be imposed as a condition of accepting employment, even in the public sector, is not here presented. Government has a vital interest in making certain that its employees, particularly those whose impairment endangers their co-workers or the public, are free of drugs. But the question posed by this litigation challenges the means by which that laudable goal is attained, not the goal itself.

Urine testing involves one of the most private of functions, a function traditionally performed in private, and indeed, usually prohibited in public. The proposed test, in order to ensure its reliability, requires the presence of another when the specimen is created and frequently reveals information about one's health unrelated to the use of drugs. If the tests are positive, it may affect one's employment status and even result in criminal prosecution.

We would be appalled at the spectre of the police spying on employees during their free time and then reporting their activities to their employers. Drug testing is a form of surveillance, albeit a technological one. Nonetheless, it reports on a person's off-duty activities just as surely as someone had been present and watching. It is George Orwell's "Big Brother" Society come to life.

To argue that it is the only practical means of discovering drug abuse is not sufficient. We do not permit a search of every house on a block merely because there is reason to believe that *one* contains evidence of criminal activity. No prohibition more significantly distinguishes our democracy from a totalitarian government than that which bars warrantless searches and seizures. Nor can the success of massive testing justify its use. We would not condone the beatings of suspects and the admissibility of their confessions merely because a larger number of convictions resulted.

In this matter, long-time employees were coerced into testing without notice, without standards and without probable cause or reasonable suspicion. Even if such testing were justified without such individualized basis, it nonetheless, would be illegal because of the flagrant violation of plaintiffs' due process rights in this instance. Assuming a program of drug testing is warranted, before it may be implemented, its existence must be made known, its methods clearly enunciated, and its procedural and confidentiality safeguards adequately provided.

The harrassment, coercion and tactics utilized here, even if motivated by the best of intentions, should cause us all to recognize the realities of government excesses and the need for constant vigilance against intrusions into constitutional rights by its agents. If we choose to violate the rights of the innocent in order to discover and act against the guilty, then we will have transformed our country into a police state and abandoned one of the fundamental tenets of our free society. In order to win the war against drugs, we must not sacrifice the life of the Constitution in the battle.

FACTS

On May 26, 1986 all fire fighters and fire officers employed by the defendant, City of Plainfield, were ordered to submit to a surprise urinalysis test. At 7:00 A.M. on May 26, the Plainfield Fire Chief and Plainfield Director of Public Affairs and Safety entered the city fire station, secured and locked all station doors and awakened the fire fighters present on the premises. Each fire department employee was required to submit a urine sample while under the surveillance and supervision of bonded testing

---

Some citations and footnotes have been omitted.—ED.

agents employed by the city. Defendants repeated a substantially similar procedure on May 28 and June 12, 1986, until approximately all of the 103 employees of the Plainfield Fire Department were tested.

Prior to May 26, the Plainfield fire employees had no notice of defendants' intent to conduct mass urinalysis. Such urinalysis had not been provided for in the collective bargaining agreement between the fire fighters and the City. Nor was any written directive, order, departmental policy or regulation promulgated establishing the basis for such testing and prescribing appropriate standards and procedures for collecting, testing, and utilizing the information derived.

Between July 10 and July 14, 1986, sixteen firefighting personnel were advised that their respective urinalysis had proved positive for the presence of controlled dangerous substances. They were immediately terminated without pay. Those who tested positive were not informed of the particular substance found in their urine or of its concentration. Neither were they provided copies of the actual laboratory results. Written complaints were served ten days later on July 24, 1986, charging these fire fighters with numerous violations including "commission of a criminal act."

At about the same time, employees of the Plainfield Police Department were subjected to similar urine testing. On May 26, 1986, plaintiff Monica Tompkins, a communications operator for the Plainfield Police was ordered to submit a urine sample under the surveillance of a female testing agent. On July 10, Ms. Tompkins was advised by the Chief of Police that her urinalysis had been positive. As a result, Ms. Tompkins was informed that she could either resign without charges being brought or she would be immediately suspended.

Plaintiff fire fighters instituted this action on July 30, 1986, by way of an Order to Show Cause and Verified Complaint. Plaintiff Monica Tompkins filed a related action which will be considered jointly. . . .

Plaintiffs bring this action pursuant to 42 U.S.C. § 1983 seeking declaratory and injunctive relief. They seek to have the urine testing declared unconstitutional and to enjoin the City of Plainfield and its agents from further conducting standardless, department-wide urine testing in violation of the Fourth Amendment. The parties have agreed to submit the matter for a final determination on the record before the court conceding that no factual issues exist which would require a hearing.

DISCUSSION

The Fourth Amendment to the United States Constitution states:

> The right of the people to be secure in their persons, houses, papers and effects, against unreasonable searches and seizures, shall not be violated. . . .

The essential purpose of the Fourth Amendment is to "impose a standard of reasonableness upon the exercise of discretion by government officials" in order to "safeguard the privacy and security of individuals against arbitrary invasions by government officials." . . .

. . . [T]he Fourth Amendment is implicated by defendants' conduct. The threshold question then is whether urinalysis constitutes a search and seizure within the meaning of the Fourth Amendment. . . .

Having determined that urine testing constitutes a search and seizure, this court must now evaluate defendants' search under the Fourth Amendment's dictates. The fundamental command of the Fourth Amendment is that searches and seizures be "reasonable." *New Jersey* v. *TLO,* 469 U.S. 325, 105 S.Ct. 733, 743, 83 L.Ed.2d 720 (1985). . . .

. . . [T]he ultimate determination of a search's reasonableness requires a judicious balancing of the intrusiveness of the search against its promotion of a legitimate governmental interest. . . .

This Court must determine whether the intrusion occasioned by compelling members of the Plainfield Fire Department to submit to compulsory urine testing is sufficiently justified by the governmental interest in ferreting out drugs so as to be "reasonable" within the meaning of the Fourth Amendment.

Expectation of Privacy The degree of intrusion engendered by any search must be viewed in the context of the individual's legitimate expectation of privacy. . . .

Applied to the facts at hand, defendants' mass urine testing program subjected plaintiffs to a relatively high degree of bodily intrusion. As stated earlier, while urine is routinely discharged from the body, it is generally discharged and disposed of under circumstances that warrant a legitimate expectation of privacy. The act itself, totally apart from what it may reveal, is traditionally private. Facilities both at home and in places of public accommodation recognize this privacy tradition. In addition, society has generally condemned and prohibited the act in public. . . .

. . . The requirement of surveillance during urine collection forces those tested to expose parts of their anatomy to the testing official in a manner akin to strip search exposure. Body surveillance is considered essential and standard operating procedure in the administration of urine drug tests, thus heightening the intrusiveness of these searches. A urine test done under close surveillance of a government representative, regardless of how professionally or courteously conducted, is likely to be a very embarrassing and humiliating experience. . . .

Furthermore, compulsory urinalysis forces plaintiffs to divulge private, personal medical information unrelated to the government's professed interest in discovering illegal drug abuse. Advances in medical technology make it possible to uncover disorders, including epilepsy and diabetes, by analyzing chemical compounds in urine. Plaintiffs have a significant interest in safeguarding the confidentiality of such information whereas the government has no countervailing legitimate need for access to this personal medical data. The dangers of disclosure as a result of telltale urinalysis range from embarrassment to improper use of such information in job assignments, security and promotion. . . .

. . . Plainfield had not established any procedural guidelines to govern the urine testing, and in particular had not taken any precautions to vouch-safe confidentiality. Quite to the contrary, following the suspension of those fire fighters who had tested positive for drugs, the City of Plainfield publicized its actions to the media. While no individuals were identified by name, the exposure has subjected all Plainfield fire fighters to public suspicion and degradation.

There can be no doubt on this record that the members of the Plainfield Fire Department reasonably expected to be free from intrusive government urine testing while on the job. No provisions for mass urine testing were included in the collective bargaining agreement signed by the fire fighters and the City. No directive or policy statement authorizing the City of Plainfield to conduct such tests was ever written or communicated to the plaintiffs. There was absolutely no warning prior to the rude awakening on May 26, 1986, that submission to compulsory employee urine testing would become a condition of continued employment. Plaintiffs' reasonable expectations of privacy fell subject to the unbridled discretion of their government employer, contrary to the very tenet of the Fourth Amendment. . . .

The State's Interest Defendants contend that fire fighters, as public servants, have a diminished expectation of privacy, or in fact, no expectation of privacy at all with respect to job-related inquiries by the municipality. As employer, the City bears ultimate responsibility for insuring that its firefighting force is fully capable of protecting the welfare and public safety of Plainfield's citizenry. Consequently, defendants claim that their interest in the discovery and elimination of drug abuse among fire personnel overrides any privacy rights fire fighters may have.

Defendants urge the court to find that theirs was an exempted search properly within the "employment context searches of government employees" exception to the Fourth Amendment. . . .

. . . This emerging body of case law suggests that the government as employer "has the same right as any private employer to oversee its employees and investigate potential misconduct relevant to the employee's performance of his duties." *Allen* v. *City of Marietta,* 601 F.Supp. at 491.

The fundamental distinction between *City of Marietta* and this case, is that the warrantless search in *City of Marietta* was nevertheless based upon some reasonable, individualized suspicion that the employees subjected to urinalysis were under the influence of drugs while on the job. In *City of Marietta,* certain employees of the Board of Lights and Water had been observed smoking marijuana on the job. Only those employees toward whom a reasonable suspicion of drug use on the job was established were compelled to submit urine samples or resign. . . .

In each of these cases the city was able to insure the public welfare while still respecting individual employee's Fourth Amendment rights. The intrusiveness of the search was minimized because the government established an individualized basis for its need to search and carefully circumscribed the search's scope.

The City of Plainfield proceeded in its urine testing campaign without any specific information or independent knowledge that any individual fire department employee was under the influence of drugs. . . .

The Constitutional Standard The deleterious effects of drug consumption upon public safety officers' ability to properly perform their duties is undeniably an issue legitimately within the City's concern. But the merits of the City's efforts to assure that all fire fighters are free from drug induced impairments and capable to perform their public service is not at issue in this case. Rather the question to be answered is whether the means chosen by the City to achieve this laudable goal are "reasonable" within the meaning of the Fourth Amendment. This court is compelled to conclude that they are not.

As justification for undertaking the department-wide search, defendants explain that the widespread, large scale drug use in all segments of the population leads to the "reasonable and logical inference that some of those affected may ultimately be employed in a public-safety capacity." . . . Defendants contend that mass round-up urinalysis is the most efficient way to detect drug use. . . .

The invidious effect of such mass, round-up urinalysis is that it casually sweeps up the innocent with the guilty and willingly sacrifices each individual's Fourth Amendment rights in the name of some larger public interest. The City of Plainfield essentially presumed the guilt of each person tested. The burden was shifted onto each fire fighter to submit to a highly intrusive urine test in order to vindicate his or her innocence. Such an unfounded presumption of guilt is contrary to the protections against arbitrary and intrusive government interference set forth in the Constitution. Although plaintiffs' privacy and liberty interests may be diminished on the job, these interests are not extinguished and therefore must be accorded some constitutional protection. . . .

The Fourth Amendment allows defendants to demand urine of an employee only on the basis of a reasonable suspicion predicated upon specific facts and reasonable inferences drawn from those facts in light of experience. . . . The reasonable suspicion standard requires individualized suspicion, specifically directed to the person who is targeted for the search. . . .

Defendants argue that "mere suspicion" rather than "reasonable suspicion" should be the standard for urine testing of government employees given the weighty interest the state has in protecting the general public from the danger of impaired, unfit fire fighters. Concededly the state's interest is a weighty one, but the Fourth Amendment requires that it be balanced against the significant intrusion urinalysis imposes upon the individual fire fighters. . . .

The City of Plainfield['s] agents, once they possess incriminatory information concerning drug use, may not have the authority to withhold such information from prosecuting agents, even if that is their desire. More specifically, in the instant case, Plainfield charged the plaintiffs with "acts of criminal misconduct" in their formal written complaints. . . .

. . . In balancing the government's interest

in conducting the search against the intrusiveness and potential harms plaintiffs may suffer, it is clear that Plainfield defendants must meet a much higher burden of reasonableness to justify subjecting plaintiffs to potential criminal charges. For these reasons, *Shoemaker* is not controlling on the present facts.

A balancing of the state's interest against the significant invasion of privacy occasioned by the urine testing requires a determination that defendants' conduct was unreasonable and violative of the Fourth Amendment. . . .

CONCLUSION

The threat posed by the widespread use of drugs is real and the need to combat it manifest. But it is important not to permit fear and panic to overcome our fundamental principles and protections. A combination of interdiction, education, treatment and supply eradication will serve to reduce the scourge of drugs, but even a reduction in the use of drugs is not worth a reduction in our most cherished constitutional rights.

The public interest in eliminating drugs in the work place is substantial, but to invade the privacy of the innocent in order to discover the guilty establishes a dangerous precedent; one which our Constitution mandates be rejected.

For the foregoing reasons final judgment shall be entered in favor of the plaintiffs and an appropriate injunction shall issue against the defendant forthwith.

Notes and Questions

1. Tewksbury's analysis of the ordeal as a medieval legal institution reveals something about the epistemology and beliefs of medieval society. The society and its legal process are both based on a belief in divine intervention. What does trial by jury imply about the epistemology and basic beliefs of the society that spawned it? Is it significant that belief in trial by jury reached its pinnacle in Anglo-American history at the time of the Enlightenment?
2. Considering that both ordeals and jury trials provided necessary legitimacy to decisions that had to be made for society to function, why do courts today seem, as in the *Collins* case, to resist the legitimizing power of statistics, technology, and "hard" science? Does this resistance reflect at all on the values or training of lawyers and judges?
3. Trial by jury is said to involve the use of rational techniques by ordinary citizens in determining facts. Can their judgments be anything more than probabilistic? If certainty is unattainable, why might the court in *Collins* be opposed to the use of even reliable statistical evidence of guilt? What do you think the judge's opinion is of juror intelligence?
4. The mysticism involved in ordeals conducted under religious auspices concerned revelation of the divine will. What mysticism is evoked by statistics? What does the court in *Collins* protect by excluding such mysticism from the trial? Where between divine revelation and technological proof does the jury's function lie?
5. Consider the Botein and Gordon reading as a portent of things to come in trials and other legal processes aimed at certifying the "truth." What kind of society will there be when these new methods are accepted by law and the public? What values underlie your own resistance to and approval of these new methods?
6. Does the drug screening (urinalysis) struck down by Judge Sarokin in *Capua* seem to be a modern realization of Botein and Gordon's fears? Is it reasonable to view such drug screening not only as a violation of Fourth Amendment rights of privacy but also as, in essence, a technological trial without jury? How could the firefighters have overcome the evidence of drug usage provided by urinalysis if they had been charged with crimes instead of merely dismissed from their jobs?
7. In addition to drug screening through urinalysis in the public (governmental) sector, there is an increasing use of the same technological means of judging employees in the private sector. Do there seem to be any significant differences between government

and private use of compulsory urinalysis? If a person can be deprived of a job because of the results of a compulsory urinalysis, what is the effect on popular participation in the legal process?

8. Do you agree with Abbie Hoffman's claim in his book, *Steal This Urine Test* (New York: Penguin, 1987), that " drug testing is the most tangible manifestation of Big Government policies aimed at destroying civil liberties . . . [and] a ritual that has nothing to do with drug abuse and a lot to do with controlling citizens"? For cases that *approve* of drug screening, see *National Treasury Employees Union* v. *Raab,* 816 F.2d 170 (1987) and Chapter 7, "Courting Disaster," of *Steal This Urine Test.* Is it possible that the new age of trial by technology has already been ushered in?

2 THE JURY AS A POLITICAL INSTITUTION

As the previous materials imply, the function of the jury extends beyond determining the facts and applying the law in a particular case. In fact, one difficulty inherent in judging technological methods of finding the "truth" is that the jury is really asked to do much more than find factual truth. Polygraphs, truth serums, and other methods of probing the unconscious of witnesses or defendants imply that there is no necessary political content to jury decisions. The existence of such methods, moreover, might deflect us from considering how the very existence of jury trials is a political phenomenon.

In the following article, Tocqueville, writing in 1830, gives a view of the complexities of the U.S. jury system as a political institution. His view may be ambiguous, because he suggests that the jury is both an agent for extending the power and legitimacy of formal law, and a basic item of popular political sovereignty in a democracy. Inevitably a discussion of the political function of juries involves questions of the jury's power and the juror's attitude toward his or her involvement in the jury.

The *Duncan* case gives a modern view of the jury's political importance; and Horwitz then shows us how politics has shaped the jury system we have inherited from the nineteenth century. Scheflin's article discusses the issue of jury nullification, beginning with the unquestioned and unquestionable right of the jury to reach its verdict in a criminal case as a matter of conscience even when that conscience is at odds with the law. Finally, Osterman and Marshall debate whether jurors should be informed of their power of nullification, and *United States* v. *Dougherty* concerns the question of how this right of nullification ought to be treated by the trial judge.

Trial by Jury in the United States

Alexis de Tocqueville

Trial by jury, which is one of the forms of the sovereignty of the people, ought to be compared with the other laws which establish that sovereignty — Composition of the jury in the United States — Effect of trial by jury upon the national character — It educates the people — How it tends to establish the influence of the magistrates and to extend the legal spirit among the people.

Since my subject has led me to speak of the administration of justice in the United States, I will not pass over it without referring to the institution of the jury. Trial by jury may be considered in two separate points of view: as a judicial, and as a political institution. If it was my purpose to inquire how far trial by jury, especially in civil cases, ensures a good administration of justice, I admit that its utility might be contested. As the jury was first established when society was in its infancy and when courts of justice merely decided simple questions of fact, it is not an easy task to adapt it to the wants of a highly civilized community when the mutual relations of men are multiplied to a surprising extent and have assumed an enlightened and intellectual character.

My present purpose is to consider the jury as a political institution; any other course would divert me from my subject. Of trial by jury considered as a judicial institution I shall here say but little. When the English adopted trial by jury, they were a semi-barbarous people; they have since become one of the most enlightened nations of the earth, and their attachment to this institution seems to have increased with their increasing cultivation. They have emigrated and colonized every part of the habitable globe; some have formed colonies, others independent states; the mother country has maintained its monarchical constitution; many of its offspring have founded powerful republics; but everywhere they have boasted of the privilege of trial by jury. They have established it, or hastened to re-establish it, in all their settlements. A judicial institution which thus obtains the suffrages of a great people for so long a series of ages, which is zealously reproduced at every stage of civilization, in all the climates of the earth, and under every form of human government, cannot be contrary to the spirit of justice.[1]

But to leave this part of the subject. It would be a very narrow view to look upon the jury as a mere judicial institution; for however great its influence may be upon the decisions of the courts, it is still greater on the destinies of society at large. The jury is, above all, a political

---

From *Democracy in America, Volume I,* by Alexis de Tocqueville, translated by Henry Reeve, Francis Bowen, and Phillips Bradley. (Some footnotes omitted.)

---

[1]If it were our object to establish the utility of the jury as a judicial institution, many arguments might be brought forward, and among others the following:

In proportion as you introduce the jury into the business of the courts, you are enabled to diminish the number of judges, which is a great advantage. When judges are very numerous, death is perpetually thinning the ranks of the judicial functionaries and leaving places vacant for newcomers. The ambition of the magistrates is therefore continually excited, and they are naturally made dependent upon the majority or the person who nominates to vacant offices; the officers of the courts then advance as do the officers of an army. This state of things is entirely contrary to the sound administration of justice and to the intentions of the legislator. The office of a judge is made inalienable in order that he may remain independent; but of what advantage is it that his independence should be protected if he be tempted to sacrifice it of his own acccord? When judges are very numerous, many of them must necessarily be incapable; for a great magistrate is a man of no common powers: I do not know if a half-enlightened tribunal is not the worst of all combinations for attaining those ends which underlie the establishment of courts of justice. For my own part, I had rather submit the decision of a case to ignorant jurors directed by a skillful judge than to judges a majority of whom are imperfectly acquainted with jurisprudence and with the laws.

institution, and it must be regarded in this light in order to be duly appreciated.

By the jury I mean a certain number of citizens chosen by lot and invested with a temporary right of judging. Trial by jury, as applied to the repression of crime, appears to me an eminently republican element in the government, for the following reasons.

The institution of the jury may be aristocratic or democratic, according to the class from which the jurors are taken; but it always preserves its republican character, in that it places the real direction of society in the hands of the governed, or of a portion of the governed, and not in that of the government. Force is never more than a transient element of success, and after force comes the notion of right. A government able to reach its enemies only upon a field of battle would soon be destroyed. The true sanction of political laws is to be found in penal legislation; and if that sanction is wanting, the law will sooner or later lose its cogency. He who punishes the criminal is therefore the real master of society. Now, the institution of the jury raises the people itself, or at least a class of citizens, to the bench of judges. The institution of the jury consequently invests the people, or that class of citizens, with the direction of society.

In England the jury is selected from the aristocratic portion of the nation; the aristocracy makes the laws, applies the laws, and punishes infractions of the laws; everything is established upon a consistent footing, and England may with truth be said to constitute an aristocratic republic. In the United States the same system is applied to the whole people. Every American citizen is both an eligible and a legally qualified voter. The jury system as it is understood in America appears to me to be as direct and as extreme a consequence of the sovereignty of the people as universal suffrage. They are two instruments of equal power, which contribute to the supremacy of the majority. All the sovereigns who have chosen to govern by their own authority, and to direct society instead of obeying its directions, have destroyed or enfeebled the institution of the jury. The Tudor monarchs sent to prison jurors who refused to convict, and Napoleon caused them to be selected by his agents.

However clear most of these truths may seem to be, they do not command universal assent; and in France, at least, trial by jury is still but imperfectly understood. If the question arises as to the proper qualification of jurors, it is confined to a discussion of the intelligence and knowledge of the citizens who may be returned, as if the jury was merely a judicial institution. This appears to me the least important part of the subject. The jury is pre-eminently a political institution; it should be regarded as one form of the sovereignty of the people: when that sovereignty is repudiated, it must be rejected, or it must be adapted to the laws by which that sovereignty is established. The jury is that portion of the nation to which the execution of the laws is entrusted, as the legislature is that part of the nation which makes the laws; and in order that society may be governed in a fixed and uniform manner, the list of citizens qualified to serve on juries must increase and diminish with the list of electors. This I hold to be the point of view most worthy of the attention of the legislator; all that remains is merely accessory.

I am so entirely convinced that the jury is preeminently a political institution that I still consider it in this light when it is applied in civil causes. Laws are always unstable unless they are founded upon the customs of a nation: customs are the only durable and resisting power in a people. When the jury is reserved for criminal offenses, the people witness only its occasional action in particular cases; they become accustomed to do without it in the ordinary course of life, and it is considered as an instrument, but not as the only instrument, of obtaining justice.

When, on the contrary, the jury acts also on civil causes, its application is constantly visible; it affects all the interests of the community; everyone co-operates in its work: it thus penetrates into all the usages of life, it fashions the human mind to its peculiar forms, and is gradually associated with the idea of justice itself.

The institution of the jury, if confined to criminal causes, is always in danger; but when once it is introduced into civil proceedings, it defies the aggressions of time and man. If it had been as easy to remove the jury from the customs as from the laws of England, it would have perished under the Tudors; and the civil jury did in reality at that period save the liberties of England. In whatever manner the jury be applied, it cannot fail to exercise a powerful influence upon the national character; but this influence is prodigiously increased when it is introduced into civil causes. The jury, and more especially the civil jury, serves to communicate the spirit of the judges to the minds of all the citizens; and this spirit, with the habits which attend it, is the soundest preparation for free institutions. It imbues all classes with a respect for the thing judged and with the notion of right. If these two elements be removed, the love of independence becomes a mere destructive passion. It teaches men to practice equity; every man learns to judge his neighbor as he would himself be judged. And this is especially true of the jury in civil causes; for while the number of persons who have reason to apprehend a criminal prosecution is small, everyone is liable to have a lawsuit. The jury teaches every man not to recoil before the responsibility of his own actions and impresses him with that manly confidence without which no political virtue can exist. It invests each citizen with a kind of magistracy; it makes them all feel the duties which they are bound to discharge toward society and the part which they take in its government. By obliging men to turn their attention to other affairs than their own, it rubs off that private selfishness which is the rust of society.

The jury contributes powerfully to form the judgment and to increase the natural intelligence of a people; and this, in my opinion, is its greatest advantage. It may be regarded as a gratuitous public school, ever open, in which every juror learns his rights, enters into daily communication with the most learned and enlightened members of the upper classes, and becomes practically acquainted with the laws, which are brought within the reach of his capacity by the efforts of the bar, the advice of the judge, and even the passions of the parties. I think that the practical intelligence and political good sense of the Americans are mainly attributable to the long use that they have made of the jury in civil causes.

I do not know whether the jury is useful to those who have lawsuits, but I am certain it is highly beneficial to those who judge them; and I look upon it as one of the most efficacious means for the education of the people which society can employ.

What I have said applies to all nations, but the remark I am about to make is peculiar to the Americans and to democratic communities. I have already observed that in democracies the members of the legal profession and the judicial magistrates constitute the only aristocratic body which can moderate the movements of the people. This aristocracy is invested with no physical power; it exercises its conservative influence upon the minds of men; and the most abundant source of its authority is the institution of the civil jury. In criminal causes, when society is contending against a single man, the jury is apt to look upon the judge as the passive instrument of social power and to mistrust his advice. Moreover, criminal causes turn entirely upon simple facts, which common sense can readily appreciate; upon his ground the judge and the jury are equal. Such is not the case, however, in civil causes; then the judge appears as a disinterested arbiter between the conflicting passions of the parties. The jurors look up to him with confidence and listen to him with respect, for in this instance, his intellect entirely governs theirs. It is the judge who sums up the various arguments which have wearied their memory, and who guides them through the devious course of the proceedings; he points their attention to the exact question of fact that they are called upon to decide and tells them how to answer the question of law. His influence over them is almost unlimited.

If I am called upon to explain why I am but little moved by the arguments derived from the ignorance of jurors in civil causes, I reply that in these proceedings, whenever the question to be solved is not a mere question of fact, the jury has only the semblance of a judicial body. The jury only sanctions the decision of the judge; they sanction this decision by the authority of society which they represent, and he by that of reason and of law.

In England and in America the judges exercise an influence upon criminal trials that the French judges have never possessed. The reason for this difference may easily be discovered; the English and American magistrates have established their authority in civil causes and only transfer it afterwards to tribunals of another kind, where it was not first acquired. In some cases, and they are frequently the most important ones, the American judges have the right of deciding causes alone. On these occasions they are accidentally placed in the position that the French judges habitually occupy, but their moral power is much greater; they are still surrounded by the recollection of the jury, and their judgment has almost as much authority as the voice of the community represented by that institution. Their influence extends far beyond the limits of the courts; in the recreations of private life, as well as in the turmoil of public business, in public, and in the legislative assemblies, the American judge is constantly surrounded by men who are accustomed to regard his intelligence as superior to their own; and after having exercised his power in the decision of causes, he continues to influence the habits of thought, and even the characters, of those who acted with him in his official capacity.

The jury, then, which seems to restrict the rights of the judiciary, does in reality consolidate its power; and in no country are the judges so powerful as where the people share their privileges. It is especially by means of the jury in civil causes that the American magistrates imbue even the lower classes of society with the spirit of their profession. Thus the jury, which is the most energetic means of making the people rule, is also the most efficacious means of teaching it how to rule well.

Duncan v. Louisiana *391 U.S. 145 (1968)*

MR. JUSTICE WHITE *delivered the opinion of the Court.*

Appellant, Gary Duncan, was convicted of simple battery in the Twenty-fifth Judicial District Court of Louisiana. Under Louisiana law simple battery is a misdemeanor, punishable by a maximum of two years' imprisonment and a $300 fine. Appellant sought trial by jury, but because the Louisiana Constitution grants jury trials only in cases in which capital punishment or imprisonment at hard labor may be imposed, the trial judge denied the request. Appellant was convicted and sentenced to serve 60 days in the parish prison and pay a fine of $150. Appellant sought review in the Supreme Court of Louisiana, asserting that the denial of jury trial violated rights guaranteed to him by the United States Constitution. The Supreme Court, finding "[n]o error of law in the ruling complained of," denied appellant a writ of certiorari.

[A]ppellant sought review in this Court, alleging that the Sixth and Fourteenth Amendments to the United States Constitution secure the right to jury trial in state criminal prosecutions where a sentence as long as two years may be imposed. . . .

Appellant was 19 years of age when tried. While driving on Highway 23 in Plaquemines Parish on October 18, 1966, he saw two younger cousins engaged in a conversation by the side of the road with four white boys. Knowing his cousins, Negroes who had recently transferred to a formerly all-white high school, had reported the occurrence of racial incidents at the school, Duncan stopped the car, got out, and approached the six boys. At trial the white boys and a white on-looker testified, as did appellant and his cousins. The testimony was in dispute on many points, but the witnesses agreed that appellant and the white boys spoke to each other, that appellant encouraged his cousins to break off the encounter and enter his car, and that appellant was about to enter the car himself for the purpose of driving away with his cousins. The whites testified that just before getting in the car appellant slapped Herman Landry, one of the white boys, on the elbow. The Negroes testified that appellant had not slapped Landry, but had merely touched him. The trial judge concluded that the State had proved beyond a reasonable doubt that Duncan had committed simple battery, and found him guilty.

The test for determining whether a right extended by the Fifth and Sixth Amendments with respect to federal criminal proceedings is also protected against state action by the Fourteenth Amendment has been phrased in a variety of ways in the opinions of this Court. The question has been asked whether a right is among those "fundamental principles of liberty and justice which lie at the base of all our civil and political institutions,'" . . . whether it is "basic to our system of jurisprudence," and whether it is "a fundamental right, essential to a fair trial." The claim before us is that the right to trial by jury guaranteed by the Sixth Amendment meets these tests. The position of Louisiana, on the other hand, is that the Constitution imposes upon the States no duty to give a jury trial in any criminal case, regardless of the seriousness of the crime or the size of the punishment which may be imposed. Because we believe that trial by jury in criminal cases is fundamental to the American scheme of justice, we hold that the Fourteenth Amendment guarantees a right of jury trial in all criminal cases which — were they to be tried in a federal court — would come within the Sixth Amendment's guarantee. Since we consider the appeal before us to be such a case, we hold that the Constitution was violated when appellant's demand for jury trial was refused.

The history of trial by jury in criminal cases has been frequently told.[1] It is sufficient for present purposes to say that by the time our Constitution was written, jury trial in criminal cases had been in existence in England for several centuries and carried impressive credentials traced by many to Magna Carta.[2] Its preservation and proper operation as a protection against arbitrary rule were among the major objectives of the revolutionary settlement which was expressed in the Declaration and Bill of Rights of 1689. . . .

Jury trial came to America with English colonists, and received strong support from them. Royal interference with the jury trial was deeply resented. Among the resolutions adopted by the First Congress of the American Colonies (the Stamp Act Congress) on October 19, 1765 — resolutions deemed by their authors to state "the most essential rights and liberties of the colonists" — was the declaration:

> That trial by jury is the inherent and invaluable right of every British subject in these colonies.

The First Continental Congress, in the resolve of October 14, 1774, objected to trials before judges dependent upon the Crown alone for their salaries and to trials in England for alleged crimes committed in the colonies; the Congress therefore declared:

> That the respective colonies are entitled to the common law of England, and more especially to the great and inestimable privilege of being tried by their peers of the vicinage, according to the course of that law.

The Declaration of Independence stated solemn objections to the King's making "judges dependent on his will alone, for the tenure of their offices, and the amount and payment of their salaries," to his "depriving us in many cases, of the benefits of Trial by Jury," and to his

---

[1]E.g., W. Forsyth, History of Trial by Jury (1852); J. Thayer, A Preliminary Treatise on Evidence at the Common Law (1898); W. Holdsworth, History of English Law.

[2]E.g., 4 W. Blackstone, Commentaries on the Laws of England 349 (Cooley ed. 1899). Historians no longer accept this pedigree. See, e.g., 1 F. Pollock & F. Maitland, The History of English Law Before the Time of Edward I, at 173, n. 3 (2d ed. 1909).

"transporting us beyond Seas to be tried for pretended offenses." The Constitution itself, in Art. III, §2, commanded:

> The Trial of all Crimes, except in Cases of Impeachment, shall be by Jury; and such Trial shall be held in the State where the said Crimes shall have been committed.

Objections to the Constitution because of the absence of a bill of rights were met by the immediate submission and adoption of the Bill of Rights. Included was the Sixth Amendment which, among other things, provided:

> In all criminal prosecutions, the accused shall enjoy the right to a speedy and public trial, by an impartial jury of the State and district wherein the crime shall have been committed.

The constitutions adopted by the original States guaranteed jury trial. Also, the constitution of every State entering the Union thereafter in one form or another protected the right to jury trial in criminal cases.

Even such skeletal history is impressive support for considering the right to jury trial in criminal cases to be fundamental to our system of justice, an importance frequently recognized in the opinions of this Court. . . .

The guarantees of jury trial in the Federal and State Constitutions reflect a profound judgment about the way in which law should be enforced and justice administered. A right to jury trial is granted to criminal defendants in order to prevent oppression by the Government.

Those who wrote our constitutions knew from history and experience that it was necessary to protect against unfounded criminal charges brought to eliminate enemies and against judges too responsive to the voice of higher authority. The framers of the constitutions strove to create an independent judiciary but insisted upon further protection against arbitrary action. Providing an accused with the right to be tried by a jury of his peers gave him an inestimable safeguard against the corrupt or overzealous prosecutor and against the compliant, biased, or eccentric judge. If the defendant preferred the common-sense judgment of a jury to the more tutored but perhaps less sympathetic reaction of the single judge, he was to have it. Beyond this, the jury trial provisions in the Federal and State Constitutions reflect a fundamental decision about the exercise of official power — a reluctance to entrust plenary powers over the life and liberty of the citizen to one judge or to a group of judges. Fear of unchecked power, so typical of our State and Federal Governments in other respects, found expression in the criminal law in this insistence upon community participation in the determination of guilt or innocence. The deep commitment of the nation to the right of jury trial in serious criminal cases as a defense against arbitrary law enforcement qualifies for protection under the Due Process Clause of the Fourteenth Amendment, and must therefore be respected by the States.

Of course jury trial has "its weaknesses and the potential for misuse." We are aware of the long debate, especially in this century, among those who write about the administration of justice, as to the wisdom of permitting untrained laymen to determine the facts in civil and criminal proceedings. . . .[3] At the heart of the dispute have been express or implicit assertions that juries are incapable of adequately understanding evidence or determining issues of fact, and that they are unpredictable, quixotic, and little better than a roll of dice. Yet, the most recent and exhaustive study of the jury in criminal cases concluded that juries do understand the evidence and come to sound conclusions in most of the cases presented to them and that when juries differ with the result at which the judge would have arrived, it is usually because they are serving some of the very purposes for which

---

[3]A thorough summary of the arguments that have been made for and against jury trial and an extensive bibliography of the relevant literature is available at Hearings on Recording of Jury Deliberations before the Subcommittee to Investigate the Administration of the Internal Security Act of the Senate Committee on the Judiciary, 84th Cong., 1st Sess., 63–81 (1955). A more selective bibliography appears at H. Kalven, Jr. & H. Zeisel, The American Jury 4, n. 2 (1966).

they were created and for which they are now employed.

. . . In determining whether the length of the authorized prison term or the seriousness of other punishment is enough in itself to require a jury trial, we . . . refer to objective criteria, chiefly the existing laws and practices in the nation. In the federal system, petty offenses are defined as those punishable by no more than six months in prison and a $500 fine. In 49 of the 50 States crimes subject to trial without a jury, which occasionally include simple battery, are punishable by no more than one year in jail. Moreover, in the late 18th century in America crimes triable without a jury were for the most part punishable by no more than a six-month prison term, although there appear to have been exceptions to this rule. We need not, however, settle in this case the exact location of the line between petty offenses and serious crimes. It is sufficient for our purposes to hold that a crime punishable by two years in prison is, based on past and contemporary standards in this country, a serious crime and not a petty offense. Consequently, appellant was entitled to a jury trial and it was error to deny it.

The judgment below is reversed and the case is remanded for proceedings not inconsistent with this opinion.

Reversed and remanded.

The following excerpt from *The Transformation of American Law* offers a brief sketch of how the professional bar, the judges, and certain commercial interests united in the early 1800s to erode the power of juries. Each of these parties seems to have had its own independent reason for forming a coalition with the others; none described its purpose as the erosion of a jury system recently written into the Bill of Rights to secure the ratification of the Constitution. That the real effect and ideological basis of these changes remained obscure from public view at the time suggests that other proposed changes in legal structure and jury function ought to be more closely scrutinized by the public to determine whose interests such reforms actually will serve. Although brief, this section from Morton Horwitz's book provides a revealing view of the manipulation of legal institutions and rules by those seeking to consolidate their power. Moreover, Horwitz suggests that legal institutions conceived or described as a bulwark against oppression may be eroded without the consent or even the knowledge of those they are meant to protect.

Excerpt from *The Transformation of American Law* *Morton Horwitz*

It should have come as no surprise that in most cases "merchants were not fond of juries." For one of the leading measures of the growing alliance between bench and bar on the one hand and commercial interests on the other is the swiftness with which the power of the jury is curtailed after 1790.

Three parallel procedural devices were used to restrict the scope of juries. First, during the last years of the eighteenth century American lawyers vastly expanded the "special case" or "case reserved," a device designed to submit points of law to the judges while avoiding the effective intervention of a jury.

From Morton Horwitz, *The Transformation of American Law* (Cambridge, Mass.: Harvard University Press, 1977), pp. 84–85, 141–43, 154–55. (Abridged.)

A second crucial procedural change — the award of a new trial for verdicts "contrary to the weight of the evidence" — triumphed with spectacular rapidity in some American courts at the turn of the century. The award of new trials for any reason had been regarded with profound suspicion by the revolutionary generation. "The practice of granting new trials," a Virginia judge noted in 1786, "was not a favourite with the courts of England" until the elevation to the bench of Lord Mansfield, "whose habit of controlling juries does not accord with the free institutions of this country, and ought not be adopted for slight causes." Yet, not only had the new trial become a standard weapon in the judicial arsenal by the first decade of the nineteenth century; it was also expanded to allow reversal of jury verdicts contrary to the weight of the evidence, despite the protest that "not one instance . . . is to be met with" where courts had previously reevaluated a jury's assessment of conflicting testimony. In both New York and South Carolina this abrupt change of policy was first adopted in order to overturn jury verdicts against marine insurers. In Pennsylvania too the earliest grant of a new trial on the weight of evidence occurs in a commercial case.

These two important restrictions on the power of juries were part of a third more fundamental procedural change that began to be asserted at the turn of the century. The view that even in civil cases "the jury [are] the proper judges not only of the fact but of the law that [is] necessarily involved" was widely held even by conservative jurists at the end of the eighteenth century. "The jury may in all cases, where law and fact are blended together, take upon themselves the knowledge of the law . . . ," William Wyche wrote in his 1794 treatise on New York practice.

During the first decade of the nineteenth century, however, the Bar rapidly promoted the view that there existed a sharp distinction between law and fact and a correspondingly clear separation of function between judge and jury. For example, until 1807 the practice of Connecticut judges was simply to submit both law and facts to the jury, without expressing any opinion or giving them any direction on how to find their verdict. In that year, the Supreme Court of Errors enacted a rule requiring the presiding trial judge, in charging the jury, to give his opinion on every point of law involved. This institutional change ripened quickly into an elaborate procedural system for control of juries.

By 1810, it was clear that the instructions of the court, originally advisory, had become mandatory and therefore juries no longer possessed the power to determine the law. Courts and litigants quickly perceived the transformation that had occurred and soon began to articulate a new principle — that "point[s] of law . . . should . . . be . . . decided by the Court," while points of fact ought to be decided by the jury.

These procedural changes made possible a vast ideological transformation in the attitude of American jurists toward commercial law. The subjugation of juries was necessary not only to control particular verdicts but also to develop a uniform and predictable body of judge-made commercial rules.

Thus, it appears that several major changes in the attitude of judges and merchants toward commercial arbitration had begun to emerge at the beginning of the nineteenth century. First, an increasingly organized and self-conscious legal profession had become determined to oppose the antilegalism among merchants which, during the colonial period, had taken the form of resort to extralegal settlement of disputes. Second, the mercantile classes, which had found the colonial legal rules hostile to their interest began, at the end of the eighteenth century, to find that common law judges themselves were prepared to overturn anticommercial legal conceptions. Third, the development of a split in the commercial interest, first manifested in the field of marine insurance, converted a largely self-regulating merchant group into one that was made dependent on formal legal machinery. Thus, one might loosely describe the process as one of accommodation by which merchants were induced to submit to formal legal regulation in return for a major transformation of substantive legal rules governing commercial disputes. The judges' unwillingness any longer to recognize competing lawmakers is a product of an increasingly instrumental vision of law. Law is no longer merely an agency for resolving disputes; it is an active, dynamic means of social control and change. Under such conditions, there must be one undisputed and authoritative source of rules for regulating commercial life. Both the hostility of judges to arbitration and the willingness of merchants to forgo extrajudicial settlement spring from a common source: the increasingly active and solicitous attitude of courts to commercial interests. . . .

Standing beside the numerous changes in legal conceptions was an important institutional innovation that began to appear after 1830 — an increasing tendency of state legislatures to eliminate the role of the jury in assessing damages for the taking of land. It was long a commonplace that juries increased the size of damage judgments. Although there were other early instances in which legislatures eliminated the jury's role in assessing damages, it was only in connection with the building of railroads that this movement gained real force. Between 1830 and 1837 such statutes in New Jersey, New York, Ohio, and North Carolina were upheld over the objection that they violated constitutional provisions guaranteeing trial by jury. The result was that railroad companies were often allowed to take land while providing little or no compensation.

Notes and Questions

1. Horwitz's analysis of the whittling away of jury functions in early American law suggests that the merchants' economic interests combined with the judiciary's desire for exclusive control over dispute resolution to reduce popular influence on law. What light does this analysis shed on Tocqueville's description of the jury as a political institution? At the present time in history, what political, economic, or other forces might find it in their self-interest to reduce jury power still further?
2. If a weakening of jury power similar to that which Horwitz describes in commercial cases were to take place in criminal cases, would you expect the principles of the *Duncan* case to protect the jury's power?

☐ As you evaluate the following materials on jury nullification, keep Horwitz's contention in mind along with Tocqueville's warning that would-be despots seek to enfeeble the institution of the jury.

Jury Nullification — The Right to Say No *Alan Scheflin*

According to the doctrine of jury nullification, the jurors have the inherent right to set aside the instructions of the judge and to reach a verdict of acquittal based upon their own consciences, and the defendant has the right to have the jury so instructed. There was a time when "conscience" played a legally recognized and significant role in jury deliberations. . . .

In the British colonies, the role of the jury in criminal trials is exemplified by the *Zenger* case. A New York jury in 1735, at the urging of Andrew Hamilton, generally considered to be the foremost lawyer in the Colonies, gave John Peter Zenger his freedom by saying "no" to government repression of dissent. Zenger was the only printer in New York who would print material not authorized by the British mayor. He published the *New York Weekly Journal*, a news-

Alan Scheflin, "Jury Nullification—The Right to Say No," 45 *S. Cal. L. Rev.* 168 (1972), reprinted with the permission of the *Southern California Law Review*. (Footnotes omitted.)

paper designed to expose some of the corruption among government officials. All of the articles in the papers were unsigned; the only name on the paper was that of its printer, Zenger. Although a grand jury convened by the government refused to indict Zenger, he was arrested and charged by information with seditious libel. Although Zenger did not write any of the articles and it was not clear that he even agreed with their content, had the jury followed the instructions of the court they would have had to find him guilty.

Against this obstacle, Hamilton insisted that the jurors:

> . . . have the right beyond all dispute to determine both the law and the facts, and where they do not doubt of the law, they ought to do so.

He urged the jury "to see with their own eyes, to hear with their own ears, and to make use of their consciences and understanding in judging of the lives, liberties or estate of their fellow subjects." The closing words of his summation to the jury are as vital today as they were when they were uttered over 200 years ago:

> [T]he question before the Court and you gentlemen of the jury, is not of small or private concern, it is not the cause of a poor printer, nor of New York alone, which you are now trying: No! It may in its consequence, affect every freeman that lives under a British government on the main of America. It is the best cause, it is the cause of liberty; and I make no doubt but your upright conduct this day will not only entitle you to the love and esteem of your fellow citizens; but every man who prefers freedom to a life of slavery will bless and honor you as men who have baffled the attempt of tyranny; and, by an impartial and uncorrupt verdict, have laid a noble foundation for securing to ourselves, our posterity, and our neighbors that to which nature and the laws of our country have given us a right — the liberty — both of exposing and opposing arbitrary power (in these parts of the world) at least, by speaking and writing truth.

[In behavior similar to the *Zenger* case] colonial juries regularly refused to enforce the navigation acts designed by the British Parliament to channel all colonial trade through the mother country. Ships impounded by the British for violating the acts were released by colonial juries, often in open disregard of law and fact. In response to this process of jury nullification, the British established courts of vice-admiralty to handle maritime cases, including those arising from violations of the navigation acts. The leading characteristic of these courts was the absence of the jury; this resulted in great bitterness among the colonists and was one of the major grievances which ultimately culminated in the American Revolution.

In the period immediately before the Revolution, jury nullification in the broad sense had become an integral part of the American judicial system. The principle that juries could evaluate and decide questions of both fact and law was accepted by leading jurists of the period.

John Adams, writing in his Diary for February 12, 1771, noted that the jury power to nullify the judge's instructions derives from the general verdict itself, but if a judge's instructions run counter to fundamental constitutional principles

> is a juror obliged to give his verdict generally, according to his direction or even to the fact specially, and submit the law to the court? Every man, of any feeling or conscience, will answer, no. It is not only his right, but his duty, in that case to find the verdict according to his own best understanding, judgment, and conscience, though in direct opposition to the direction of the court.

Adams based this reasoning in part on the democratic principle that "the common people . . . should have as complete a control, as decisive a negative, in every judgment of a court judicature" as they have in other decisions of government. At the time of the adoption of the Constitution, this view of jury nullification prevailed. Without jury nullification, as the Founding Fathers well knew, government by judge (or through the judge by the rulers in power) became a distinct possibility and had in fact been a reality. In the *Zenger* case, two lawyers were held in contempt and ordered disbarred by the judge when they argued that he should not sit because he held his office during the King's "will and pleasure." The Court of Star Chamber was not too distant in memory for the colonists to have forgotten the many perversions perpetrated there in the name of justice and law. It was likely, therefore, that the once unchecked, unresponsive power of the judge would have been limited by the Founding Fathers through some method of public control. One method chosen was the jury function most closely guarded by the colonists: the power to say no to oppressive authority. . . .

Proper understanding of the concept of jury nullification requires it to be viewed as an exercise of discretion in the administration of law and justice. Jury discretion in this context may be a useful check on prosecutorial indiscretion. No system of law can withstand the full application of its principles untempered by considerations of justice, fairness and mercy. Every technical violation of law cannot be punished by a court structure that attempts to be just. As prosecutorial discretion weeds out many of these marginal cases, jury discretion hopefully weeds out the rest.

"Jury lawlessness," according to Dean Roscoe Pound, "is the great corrective" in the administration of law. Thus, the jury stands between the will of the state and the will of the people as the last bastion in law to avoid the barricades in the streets. To a large extent, the jury gives to the judicial system a legitimacy it would otherwise not possess. Judge control of jury verdicts would destroy that legitimacy.

A juror who is forced by the judge's instructions to convict a defendant whose conduct he applauds, or at least feels is justifiable, will lose respect for the legal system which forces him to reach such a result against the dictates of his conscience. The concept of trial by a jury of one's peers is emasculated by denying to the juror his right to act on the basis of his personal morality. For if the jury is the "conscience of the community," how can it be denied the right to function accordingly? A juror compelled to decide against his own judgment will rebel at the system which made him a traitor to himself. No system can be worthy of respect if it is based upon the necessity of forcing the compromise of a man's principles. . . .

Jessica Mitford interviewed three jurors in the *United States* v. *Spock* case after the trial's completion. She detected that they had misgivings about the unfairness of the laws which they were asked to apply. Though they all seemed to sympathize with the defendants, they were concerned, in principle, about violations of law going unpunished. Each one indicated that the conviction was necessary in light of the instructions from the judge: "I knew they were guilty when we were charged by the judge. I did not know *prior* to that time — I was in full agreement with the defendants until we were charged by the judge. That was the kiss of death!" It is reasonable to conclude that if the jury had been instructed of their power to nullify, the convictions might not have been returned. However, these jurors felt bound by the judge's instructions, even though they had previously decided the issue of guilt in favor of the defendant. If they had been told that an element of the crime was that the jury in good conscience must feel that the law was fair and was fairly applied, then they could have dispensed justice in accordance with their conscientious beliefs. Even if this jury felt guiltless because they had done what was required of them, they should not have felt comfortable about a system which may have misused them for political purposes.

If jury discretion leads to a lawless society, as some critics of nullification have argued, what does no discretion lead to? Several years ago the New York police went on "strike" on the Long Island Expressway and ticketed every motorist failing to observe any traffic regulation presently on the books. Though the police did not ticket non-violators, there was still a great outcry against their conduct. While much of the wrath was vented on the devious tactic used to get the raises, much of it was also against the lack of discretion in the enforcement of the laws. Without such discretion, the legal system becomes a mockery. But unlimited discretion in the hands of persons in power can become despotic. Accountability of such discretion to the people is the fundamental principle of democracy. It is also the underlying rationale for jury nullification.

One of the most significant principles of democracy calls for the involvement or participation of the "man in the street" in the formation of public policy. Within the framework of the judicial process, the jury has evoled as an institutional reflection of such a commitment. The "man in the street" becomes the "man in the jury box," and as such sits as the representative of the community in question. As the embodiment of the "conscience of the community" he functionally legitimizes and effectuates the authoritativeness of decisions made by and through the judicial process.

The chief distinguishing characteristic of any democratic system is effective popular control over policymakers. With reference to the judicial process this can mean only one thing: If the "man in the jury box" is to fulfill his role as the representative of the "conscience of the community," participating effectively in the making of public policy, then he must possess the power and the right to check the "misapplication" of any particular value distribution. Beyond this, he must be informed that he has such a power and the constitutional right to exercise it.

Thus, jury service is a two-way street. Community values are injected into the legal system making the application of the law responsive to the needs of the people, and participation on the jury gives the people a feeling of greater involvement in their government which further legitimizes that government. This dual aspect of the concept of the jury, flowing from its role as a political institution in a constitutional democracy, serves to keep both the government and the people in touch with each other. But should there be a divergence of sufficient magnitude, as the Founding Fathers were aware there often is, the jury can serve as a corrective with a final veto power over judicial rigidity, servility or tyranny.

In the words of Thomas Jefferson, "Were I called upon to decide, whether the people had best be omitted in the legislative or in the judiciary department, I would say it is better to leave them out of the legislative. The execution of the laws is more important than the making of them." The power of the people as a community conscience check on governmental despotism is manifested in their ability to sit on juries and limit the thrust of governmental abuse of discretion.

The jury provides an institutional mechanism for working out matters of conscience within the legal system. Jury nullification allows the community to say of a particular law that it is too oppressive or of a particular prosecution that it is too punitive or of a particular defendant that his conduct is too justified for the criminal sanction to be imposed. As William Kunstler put it,

> Unless the jury can exercise its community conscience role, our judicial system will have become so inflexible that the effect may well be a progressive radicalization of protest into channels that will threaten the very continuance of the system itself. To put it another way, the jury is . . . the safety valve that must exist if this society is to be able to accommodate itself to its own internal stresses and strains.

. . . In any politically-charged case where there is a jury acquittal, it is not always clear whether the verdict was a product of the inability of the prosecutor to prove his case beyond a reasonable doubt or rather was a demonstration that the case was so well proven that the real motive for prosecution became all too clear; stifling political dissent. Or the verdict could quite easily be a combination of deficient proof and juror outrage over governmental repression. Because of this ambiguity, and because questions of intent are vague enough to give jurors room to nullify subconsciously by honestly believing that criminal intent is not consistent with good faith resistance to seemingly unjust laws or applications of laws, any description of an acquittal as an instance of jury nullification may not be entirely accurate. . . .

Jury Instructions

CALIFORNIA

Ladies and Gentlemen of the Jury.*

It becomes my duty as judge to instruct you concerning the law applicable to this case, and it is your duty as jurors to follow the law as I shall state it to you.

The function of the jury is to try the issues of fact that are presented by the allegations in the information filed in this court and the defendant's plea of "not guilty." This duty you should perform uninfluenced by pity for the defendant or by passion or prejudice against him. . . .

You are to be governed solely by the evidence introduced in this trial and the law as stated to you by me. The law forbids you to be governed by mere sentiment, conjecture, sympathy, passion, public opinion, or public feeling. Both the People and the defendant have a right to demand and they do demand and expect, that you will conscientiously and dispassionately consider and weigh the evidence and apply the law of the case, and that you will reach a just verdict, regardless of what the consequences may be. . . .

*Excerpt from California jury instructions in criminal cases.

MARYLAND

Members of the jury†: this is a criminal case and under the Constitution and the laws of the state of Maryland in a criminal case the jury are the judges of the law as well as of the facts in the case. So that whatever I tell you about the law, while it is intended to be helpful to you in reaching a just and proper verdict in the case, it is not binding upon you as members of the jury and you may accept the law as you apprehend it to be in the case.

†Excerpt from Maryland jury instructions in criminal cases.

At Issue: Should Jurors Be Told They Can Refuse to Enforce the Law?

Should jurors disregard a law they consider unjust, and vote to acquit a defendant charged with violating it? What if the crime involves civil disobedience by a popular leader protesting an unjust law?

Steven Osterman, an associate in the New York firm of Debevoise & Plimpton, argues that these questions arise in prosecutions of members of the sanctuary movement that shelters Latin American refugees who are in this country illegally. The legal system should respond to this moral challenge, he argues, by allowing for "jury nullification," the right of jurors to nullify laws or prosecutions that violate their consciences simply by refusing to convict.

But there is a darker strain to this notion. Burke Marshall, assistant attorney general for civil rights in the Kennedy and Johnson administrations and now the John Thomas Smith Professor of Law at Yale Law School, asserts that the moral value of jury nullification is a dangerous myth.

The historical refusal of Southern juries to convict whites of racial violence is the primary example of jury nullification in our time, Marshall argues. He concludes that our system can respond to the moral challenge of nonviolent civil disobedience without nullification by juries.

Their debate begins below.

Law Must Respect Consciences *Steven D. Osterman*

Suppose Robin Hood were indicted for robbery. Should he be able to claim in court that his conduct was morally justified? If the jury agrees, should it be instructed to acquit? The questions are hardly hypothetical.

From the Boston Tea Party to King's march on Montgomery, civil disobedience is as American as America itself. It is also back. To an extent unparalleled since the civil rights and antiwar movements, persons are choosing to place the imperatives of conscience above compliance with the law — whether by aiding illegal aliens, trespassing to protest apartheid or nuclear weapons, "liberating" lab animals, or disrupting abortion clinics. Justified or not, these actions pose a major jurisprudential dilemma.

It is no answer that the law is the law and, as such, must be obeyed. If so, we could hardly lionize Gandhi, condemn the gulags, have prosecuted at Nuremberg, or celebrate the Fourth of July. Nor does it matter that punishment was accepted, even embraced, by the likes of Thoreau, Gandhi, and King.

Contemporary dissenters are defending their conduct in court, so the question remains: In a society exalting both personal moral responsibility and the moral foundation of law, how should the law respond to those who choose, out of the deepest moral conviction, to disobey it?

THE RIGHT TO REFUSE

The answer lies in reinvigorating "jury nullification" — the doctrine that defendants can insist, in appropriate cases, that jurors learn of their right to refuse to apply the law strictly where doing so would result in injustice. In

1670, a jury endured privation and imprisonment rather than convict William Penn of illegal preaching, as the judge commanded. The jury was vindicated. *Bushell's Case*, Vaughn. 135, 134 Eng. Rep. 1006 (K.B. 1670).

Along with the blow struck for religious liberty, these jurors "established the right of juries to give their verdict according to their conviction." Defense counsel Alexander Hamilton invoked the same principle in 1735 to secure the acquittal of John Peter Zenger.

Unfortunately, *Bushell's Case* has found little contemporary favor. Juries, it is argued, cannot be permitted to "nullify" a law simply because they dislike it or applaud a given act of disobedience. Generally decrying nullification as lawless and anarchic, courts consistently have rejected instructions informing jurors of their historic right to return verdicts according to conscience. *See U.S.* v. *Dougherty*, 473 F.2d 1113 (D.C. Cir. 1972).

SANCTUARY

To deny these instructions and associated evidence and argument, however, is to rob many defendants of their right to a defense. Consider the recent federal prosecution of 11 religious activists charged with offering illegal "sanctuary" to Latin American refugees. The defendants — including two priests, a minister and a nun — have never denied the charges. Instead, in the tradition of the underground railroad, they claim to have obeyed moral and religious obligations superior to the immigration laws.

Several potential defenses have been understandably barred. A "religious motivation" defense would shield not just Bishop Tutu, but Torquemada and Khomeini as well. International law, ambiguous at best, rarely vests justiciable rights in private persons.

Defendants may claim simply to have applied the 1980 Refugee Act, but relevant officials disagree. Justification is not a catch-all defense for any conduct assertedly "justified" by conscience. Nor is there any refuge in the free exercise clause. If religious fundamentalists offered "sanctuary" to abortion clinic bombers, how many in the sanctuary movement would press the same claim? Clearly, often the only defense in these cases is to inform the jury of the precedent for acquittals by conscience.

Denying nullification also ignores the normative function of juries. Why is trial-by-jury sacrosanct? Why such pains to ensure representativeness? Not because juries are the finest factfinders. In criminal trials, juries sit not just to find facts but to assess culpability. Their role is to embody the norms and reflect the collective conscience of the community. In doing so, they serve as essential safeguards against the unjust exercise of official power. *Duncan* v. *Louisiana*, 391 U.S. 145 (1968).

As Van Tilburg Clark wrote in *The Ox-Bow Incident*, "[L]aw is more than the words that put it on the books; . . . more than any man, lawyer or judge, sheriff or jailer, who may represent it. True law, the code of justice, the essence of our sensations of right and wrong, is the conscience of society." However imperfectly, we discern that conscience through representative juries.

THE HIGHEST VALUES

"Nullificiation," then, is a misnomer. When defendants claim a law is unjust, giving juries the option to temper the letter of the law to avoid injustice or chastise officialdom actually vindicates the legal system's highest values.

If the criminal law is to be more than mere words, lawyers must be allowed to instruct juries on their role, and on their right to decide as conscience dictates. With such information, Robin Hood is not just another highwayman. Without it, juries may feel forced to view the nun who shelters Salvadoran refugees as indistinguishable from the border runner who smuggles illegal aliens for profit.

And "if the law supposes that," said Mr. Bumble, "the law is a ass."

Jurors Must Respect the Law *Burke Marshall*

There is no doubt that American juries possess the raw power of "nullification" — the power to acquit someone accused of a crime even when the facts and the law, objectively looked at, say that the accused did do the unlawful act he or she was charged with.

What makes this power effective under the American Constitution is the Fifth Amendment's injunction that no person shall "be subject for the same offense to be twice put in jeopardy of life or limb." Otherwise, of course, the prosecution could appeal the jury's action, as in Canada, and a court could undo the jury's "nullification."

A LIBERAL MYTH

The connection between these undisputed constitutional facts and the tradition of civil disobedience is far from clear; indeed it is probably a liberal myth. It arises, apparently, from the cases of William Penn and John Peter Zenger during the colonial period, when juries were among the local institutions that from time to time resisted the imposition of certain rules by the Crown.

Whether those juries were protecting the "consciences" of Penn and Zenger, or making some other political statement about colonialism, is unknowable. But there is no evidence that I know of that they were creating an American tradition of jury protection of political dissent in the form of civil disobedience.

Jury nullification has a tradition in America, but the nature of that tradition is quite different from that implied by the liberal myth. Its main use in this century probably has been to protect whites from the consequences of their unlawful, often violent, racial oppression of blacks.

WHAT IS RELEVANT VIOLENCE?

These facts raise a serious problem with the notion of permitting or requiring trial judges to instruct a jury regarding its power of nullification. This notion has been rejected consistently by the few courts that have focused on it.

In what kind of case would that instruction be proper? Suppose the act of civil disobedience involves violence against person or property, contrary to the teaching of Martin Luther King, Jr.? It clearly did so in the cases of Robin Hood, the Boston Tea Party, Gandhi's movement, and many of the instances of protest cited by Steven Osterman. What is the relevance of violence in such a context?

Consider the pouring of blood on selective service records by Catholic opponents of the Vietnam war. Consider the acts of trespass against nuclear installations and the disruption of abortion clinics. What of the acts of retribution and intimidation against the civil rights workers of the 1960s in the South, who, in the minds of their opponents, were disrupting the domestic tranquility and threatening established American traditions?

Perhaps these questions can be answered in the political context: What kind of political protest justifies what methods of civil disobedience? But I do not think they can be contained easily by criteria framed in the effort at neutrality of principle that is implied in the rule of law. It is, after all, explicit in at least one strand of civil disobedience theory that legal punishment for the acts of disobedience should be accepted cheerfully and willingly, as a token of respect for law. That was the teaching of King at least, and for it he relied on Gandhi, Thoreau, and Socrates.

It does not seem to me that American law needs, or should have, the additional tool of a special instruction on jury nullification. There are plenty of other moments of discretion and judgment in the criminal system, from the decision to investigate and prosecute, through the element of reasonable doubt, to the moment of sentencing and clemency — all of which make the system pretty fair to those charged with crimes that do not fit the public perception of wrongdoing.

THE AMERICAN SOCIAL CONTRACT

Hannah Arendt brought a special American perspective to the concept of civil disobedience when she equated it with freedom of association, as contrasted with truly individualistic acts of deviation from the social and legal norms.

Civil disobedience is implied in the theory of social contract at the heart of the Constitution. And it comes into play "when a number of citizens have become convinced either that the normal channels of change no longer function, and grievances will not be heard or acted upon, or that, on the contrary, the government is about to change and has embarked upon and persists in modes of action whose legality and constitutionality are open to grave doubt."

Such times, she said, change "voluntary association into civil disobedience" and transform "dissent into resistance." Arendt's insight that the American concept of civil disobedience involves group movement — freedom of association — as well as elements of non-violence and civility, seems right to me.

Certainly it fits the examples of recent decades, as well as the abolitionist movement. If it is right, the added ingredient of jury nullification is at best a triviality; our system of law simply cannot control such resistance in the end. Perhaps that is even true of the sanctuary movement.

United States v. Dougherty et al. *473 F.2d 1113 (C.A.D.C. 1972)*

LEVENTHAL, CIRCUIT JUDGE:

Seven of the so-called "D.C. Nine" bring this joint appeal from convictions arising out of their unconsented entry into the Washington offices of the Dow Chemical Company, and their destruction of certain property therein. Appellants, along with two other defendants who subsequently entered pleas of nolo contendere, were tried before District Judge John H. Pratt and a jury on a three count indictment alleging, as to each defendant, one count of second degree burglary, 22 D.C. Code § 1801(b), and two counts of malicious destruction of property valued in excess of $100, 22 D.C. Code § 403. On February 11, 1970, after a six-day trial, the seven were each convicted of two counts of malicious destruction. The jury acquitted on the burglary charges but convicted on the lesser-included offense of unlawful entry. The sentences imposed are set forth in the margin.

Appellants urge three grounds for reversal as follows: (1) The trial judge erred in denying defendants' timely motions to dispense with counsel and represent themselves. (2) The judge erroneously refused to instruct the jury of its right to acquit appellants without regard to the law and the evidence, and refused to permit appellants to argue that issue to the jury. (3) The instructions actually given by the court coerced the jury into delivering a verdict of guilty. On the basis of defendants' first contention we reverse and remand for new trial. To provide an appropriate mandate governing the new trial, we consider the second and third contentions, and conclude that these cannot be accepted.

THE RECORD IN DISTRICT COURT

The undisputed evidence showed that on Saturday, March 22, 1969, appellants broke into the locked fourth floor Dow offices at 1030 — 15th Street, N.W., Washington, D.C., threw papers and documents about the office and into the street below, vandalized office furniture and equipment, and defaced the premises by spilling about a bloodlike substance. The prosecution proved its case through Dow employees who

Some footnotes have been omitted and the rest are renumbered.—ED.

testified as to the lack of permission and extent of damage, members of the news media who had been summoned to the scene by the appellants and who witnessed the destruction while recording it photographically, and police officers who arrested appellants on the scene. . . .

The Issue of Jury Nullification . . . [A]ppellants . . . say that the jury has a well-recognized prerogative to disregard the instructions of the court even as to matters of law, and that they accordingly have the legal right that the jury be informed of its power. We turn to this matter in order to define the nature of the new trial permitted by our mandate.

The existence of an unreviewable and unreversible power in the jury, to acquit in disregard of the instructions on the law given by the trial judge, has for many years co-existed with legal practice and precedent upholding instructions to the jury that they are required to follow the instructions of the court on all matters of law. There were different soundings in colonial days and the early days of our Republic. We are aware of the number and variety of expressions at that time from respected sources — John Adams; Alexander Hamilton; prominent judges — that jurors had a duty to find a verdict according to their own conscience, though in opposition to the direction of the court; that their power signified a right; that they were judges both of law and of fact in a criminal case, and not bound by the opinion of the court.

The rulings did not run all one way, but rather precipitated "a number of classic exchanges on the freedom and obligations of the criminal jury." This was, indeed, one of the points of clash between the contending forces staking out the direction of the government of the newly established Republic, a direction resolved in political terms by reforming but sustaining the status of the courts, without radical change. As the distrust of judges appointed and removable by the king receded, there came increasing acceptance that under a republic the protection of citizens lay not in recognizing the right of each jury to make its own law, but in following democratic processes for changing the law.

The crucial legal ruling came in *United States* v. *Battiste,* 2 Sum. 240, Fed.Cas. No. 14,545 (C.C.D.Mass. 1835). Justice Story's strong opinion supported the conception that the jury's function lay in accepting the law given to it by the court and applying that law to the facts. This considered ruling of an influential jurist won increasing acceptance in the nation. The youthful passion for independence accommodated itself to the reality that the former rebels were now in control of their own destiny, that the practical needs of stability and sound growth outweighed the abstraction of centrifugal philosophy, and that the judges in the courts, were not the colonial appointees projecting royalist patronage and influence but were themselves part and parcel of the nation's intellectual mainstream, subject to the checks of the common law tradition and professional opinion, and capable, in Roscoe Pound's words, of providing "true judicial justice" standing in contrast with the colonial experience.

The tide was turned by *Battiste,* but there were cross-currents. At mid-century the country was still influenced by the precepts of Jacksonian democracy, which spurred demands for direct selection of judges by the people through elections, and distrust of the judge-made common law which enhanced the movement for codification reform. But by the end of the century, even the most prominent state landmarks had been toppled; and the Supreme Court settled the matter for the Federal courts in *Sparf* v. *United States,* 156 U.S. 51, 102, 15 S.Ct. 273, 39 L.Ed. 343 (1895) after exhaustive review in both majority and dissenting opinions. The jury's role was respected as significant and wholesome, but it was not to be given instructions that articulated a right to do whatever it willed. The old rule survives today only as a singular relic.[1] . . .

---

[1]Wyley v. Warden, 372 F.2d 742 (4th Cir. 1967), cert. denied, 389 U.S. 863, 88 S.Ct. 121, 19 L.Ed.2d 131 (1967). In holding the provision of the Maryland Constitution consistent with the Federal Constitution,

This so-called right of jury nullification is put forward in the name of liberty and democracy, but its explicit avowal risks the ultimate logic of anarchy. This is the concern voiced by Judge Sobeloff in *United States* v. *Moylan*, 417 F.2d 1002, 1009 (4th Cir. 1969), cert. denied, 397 U.S. 910, 90 S.Ct. 908, 25 L.Ed.2d 91 (1970):

> To encourage individuals to make their own determinations as to which laws they will obey and which they will permit themselves as a matter of conscience to disobey is to invite chaos. No legal system could long survive if it gave every individual the option of disregarding with impunity any law which by his personal standard was judged morally untenable. Toleration of such conduct would not be democratic, as appellants claim, but inevitably anarchic.

The statement that avowal of the jury's prerogative runs the risk of anarchy, represents, in all likelihood, the habit of thought of philosophy and logic, rather than the prediction of the social scientist. But if the statement contains an element of hyperbole, the existence of risk and danger, of significant magnitude, cannot be gainsaid. In contrast, the advocates of jury "nullification" apparently assume that the articulation of the jury's power will not extend its use or extent, or will not do so significantly or obnoxiously. Can this assumption fairly be made? . . .

The way the jury operates may be radically altered if there is alteration in the way it is told to operate. The jury knows well enough that its prerogative is not limited to the choices articulated in the formal instructions of the court. The jury gets its understanding as to the arrangements in the legal system from more than one voice. There is the formal communication from the judge. There is the informal communication from the total culture — literature (novel, drama, film, and television); current comment (newspapers, magazines and television); conversation; and, of course, history and tradition. The totality of input generally conveys adequately enough the idea of prerogative, of freedom in an occasional case to depart from what the judge says. Even indicators that would on their face seem too weak to notice — like the fact that the judge tells the jury it must acquit (in case of reasonable doubt) but never tells the jury in so many words that it must convict — are a meaningful part of the jury's total input. Law is a system, and it is also a language, with secondary meanings that may be unrecorded yet are part of its life.

When the legal system relegates the information of the jury's prerogative to an essentially informal input, it is not being duplicitous, chargeable with chicane and intent to deceive. The limitation to informal input is, rather a governor to avoid excess: the prerogative is reserved for the exceptional case, and the judge's instruction is retained as a generally effective constraint. . . .

Rules of law or justice involve choice of values and ordering of objectives for which unanimity is unlikely in any society, or group representing the society, especially a society as diverse in cultures and interests as ours. To seek unity out of diversity, under the national motto, there must be a procedure for decision by vote of a majority or prescribed plurality — in accordance with democratic philosophy. To assign the role of mini-legislature to the various petit juries, who must hang if not unanimous, exposes criminal law and administration to paralysis, and to a deadlock that betrays rather than furthers the assumptions of viable democracy.

Moreover, to compel a juror involuntarily assigned to jury duty to assume the burdens of mini-legislator or judge, as is implicit in the doctrine of nullification, is to put untoward strains on the jury system. It is one thing for a juror to

---

Judge Sobeloff noted that "a practice may be deemed unwise, yet not be unconstitutional." He referred to the "potent and persuasive arguments . . . leveled against the wisdom of the Maryland practice," and the various jurists' analyses condemning it as "archaic, outmoded and atrocious," "unique and indefensible," an "antique constitutional thorn" in "the flesh of Maryland's body of Criminal Law.". . .

know that the law condemns, but he has a factual power of lenity. To tell him expressly of a nullification prerogative, however, is to inform him, in effect, that it is he who fashions the rule that condemns. That is an overwhelming responsibility, an extreme burden for the jurors' psyche. And it is not inappropriate to add that a juror called upon for an involuntary public service is entitled to the protection, when he takes action that he knows is right, but also knows is unpopular, either in the community at large or in his own particular grouping, that he can fairly put it to friends and neighbors that he was merely following the instructions of the court. . . .

What makes for health as an occasional medicine would be disastrous as a daily diet. The fact that there is widespread existence of the jury's prerogative, and approval of its existence as a "necessary counter to casehardened judges and arbitrary prosecutors," does not establish as an imperative that the jury must be informed by the judge of that power. On the contrary, it is pragmatically useful to structure instructions in such wise that the jury must feel strongly about the values involved in the case, so strongly that it must itself identify the case as establishing a call of high conscience, and must independently initiate and undertake an act in contravention of the established instructions. This requirement of independent jury conception confines the happening of the lawless jury to the occasional instance that does not violate, and viewed as an exception may even enhance, the over-all normative effect of the rule of law. An explicit instruction to a jury conveys an implied approval that runs the risk of degrading the legal structure requisite for true freedom, for an ordered liberty that protects against anarchy as well as tyranny. . . .

BAZELON, CHIEF JUDGE, *concurring in part and dissenting in part:*

My own view rests on the premise that nullification can and should serve an important function in the criminal process. I do not see it as a doctrine that exists only because we lack the power to punish jurors who refuse to enforce the law or to re-prosecute a defendant whose acquittal cannot be justified in the strict terms of law. The doctrine permits the jury to bring to bear on the criminal process a sense of fairness and particularized justice. The drafters of legal rules cannot anticipate and take account of every case where a defendant's conduct is "unlawful" but not blameworthy, any more than they can draw a bold line to mark the boundary between an accident and negligence. It is the jury — as spokesman for the community's sense of values — that must explore that subtle and elusive boundary.

. . . The very essence of the jury's function is its role as spokesman for the community conscience in determining whether or not blame can be imposed.

I do not see any reason to assume that jurors will make rampantly abusive use of their power. Trust in the jury is, after all, one of the cornerstones of our entire criminal jurisprudence, and if that trust is without foundation we must reexamine a great deal more than just the nullification doctrine. . . .

One often-cited abuse of the nullification power is the acquittal by bigoted juries of whites who commit crimes (lynching, for example) against blacks. That repellent practice cannot be directly arrested without jeopardizing important constitutional protections — the double jeopardy bar and the jury's power of nullification. But the revulsion and sense of shame fostered by that practice fueled the civil rights movement, which in turn made possible the enactment of major civil rights legislation. That same movement spurred on the revitalization of the equal protection clause and, in particular, the recognition of the right to be tried before a jury selected without bias. The lessons we learned from these abuses helped to create a climate in which such abuses could not so easily thrive.

Moreover, it is not only the abuses of nullification that can inform our understanding of the community's values and standards of blameworthiness. The noble uses of the power — the uses that "enhance the over-all normative effect of the rule of law" — also provide an important input to our evaluation of the substantive standards of the criminal law. The reluctance of juries to hold defendants responsible for unmistakable violations of the prohibition laws told us much about the morality of those laws and about the "criminality" of the conduct they proscribed. And the same can be said of the acquittals returned under the fugitive slave law[2] as well as contemporary gaming and liquor laws. A doctrine that can provide us with such critical insights should not be driven underground. . . .

Notes and Questions

1. Who motivates a jury to nullify the law? Is it urged on them by an articulate defense lawyer pleading the cause of liberty, or do jurors themselves decide that nullification is appropriate?
2. Why is jury nullification such a rare occurrence in modern trials? Is it the nature of the cases being tried or the nature of the crimes committed? The influence of the judge? The consciousness of the jurors?
3. How important an option is nullification if it is rarely used?
4. If the law provides that the jury can in fact disregard the judge's instructions and deliver a verdict of their own choosing without fear of any sanctions, why is there so much resistance to telling the jury its power? What effect on jury deliberations might result from telling the jurors about nullification?
5. Can you think of ways of explaining to jurors what their role in the legal process is other than the two instructions appearing on page 383?
6. Tocqueville writes that "in no country are the judges so powerful as where the people share their privileges." Does jury nullification strengthen or weaken Tocqueville's argument? What, other than jury instructions, is the source of the judge's power in the trial?
7. Under what conditions do you think a jury would consider nullification? Is nullification a matter of spontaneous outrage in a plainly political case? If an attorney were to address the issue of nullification in a summation to the jury, what sorts of things would you expect to be stressed? What kind of jurors would you want to select if you knew your case depended largely on their willingness to nullify the law in the case?
8. Would jury nullification, even if it became routine, really provide significant power to jurors? What about routine cases in which the political nature of the crime or dispute is not readily apparent? Can jury nullification change the allocation of power in the legal system or in society, or is it a superficial solution to a major denial of public participation in law?
9. Suppose a jury nullifies a law by acquitting a defendant in a plainly political case in which the defendant has the sympathy and support of the community. How does this "victory" have an effect on law and politics? What is the role of the media in effectuating the jury's actions? Is there such a thing as a social precedent even when no legal precedent results from the jury's actions?
10. The debate between Osterman and Marshall (see pages 384–387) seems to hinge on how each perceives the nature of U.S. society: Osterman sees nullification as a way to protect "progressive" political actions from the oppressive hand of government, and Marshall notes that, historically, nullification has made it possible for white racism to control jury verdicts where whites were accused of crimes against blacks. Do you think it is appropriate for the question of whether jurors should be told of their power to nullify to depend on a political assessment of society? Should the right to vote also hinge on estimates of the politics of the disenfranchised? What if the right-to-vote question arose in a society in which the prospective voters were bent on maintaining a plainly immoral system of racial slavery?

[2]H. Kalven & H. Zeisel, *supra* note 3, at 296–97. Jury nullification also provides us with crucial information about the morality of the death penalty. *See McGautha* v. *California*, 402 U.S. 183, 199, 91 S.Ct. 1454, 1463, 28 L.Ed.2d 711 (1971): In order to meet the problem of jury nullification, legislatures did not try, as before, to refine further the definition of capital homicides. Instead they adopted the method of forthrightly granting juries discretion which they had been exercising in fact. . . .

11. Judge Leventhal, in the *Dougherty* case, states that jury nullification puts "untoward strains on the jury system" and states that a juror voting his or her conscience should be able to defend an unpopular decision to friends and neighbors by claiming to be "merely following the instructions of the court." Do you agree? Should jurors be relieved of the responsibility for acting on conscience?
12. What would happen to the jury as a mechanism for expressing community values if it were possible to use the "I was just following orders" argument suggested by Judge Leventhal? Suppose an all-white jury, uninformed of its power of nullification by the judge, were to refuse to convict a white defendant plainly guilty of killing a black man; suppose further that these jurors could not be held responsible by the community at large because the jurors claimed that they were just following the judge's instructions. What is the nature of the community whose values are thus expressed? Would a process like this allow the judge to define the community, rather than allow the community to define itself as a part of legal process? What would be the eventual political consequences of such "expressions of the community"?

3 JURY SELECTION AND JURY DYNAMICS

The materials in this section focus on what constitutes a jury of one's peers and on what effects jury size and the unanimity requirement have on how a jury of one's peers deliberates. These issues are important because they affect the fairness of a jury trial from each party's point of view and because they have so much to do with whether the public perceives the jury system to be a legitimate and fair cross section of the community. But their importance is magnified considerably by the concept, developed in the previous section, that the jury is primarily a political institution. If the jury functions to articulate and apply community standards to current conflicts, including the option of nullifying a law on the books, then the composition of juries and the public perception of their legitimacy become crucial. Distortions in the representative character of juries or in the dynamics of their deliberation will become distortions in the "political" (community-defining) decisions they make. A long-term pattern of significant distortions in jury selection and dynamics will ultimately raise the question of whether the jury has been so changed as an institution that it no longer functions as a vehicle for community participation.

The next four readings concern problems of and protections for fair jury selection. Additional readings on jury dynamics follow, beginning on page 411.

Excerpts from Massachusetts Jury Selection Statute

234A M.6.L.A. § 1 et seq.

3. JUROR SERVICE

Juror service in the participating counties shall be a duty which every person who qualifies under this chapter shall perform when selected.* All persons selected for juror service on grand and trial juries shall be selected at random from the population of the judicial district in which they reside. All persons shall have equal opportunity to be considered for juror service. All persons shall serve as jurors when selected and summoned for that purpose except as hereinafter provided. No person shall be exempted or excluded from serving as a grand or trial juror because of race, color, religion, sex, national origin, economic status, or occupation. Physically handicapped persons shall serve except where the court finds such service is not feasible. The court shall strictly enforce the provisions of this section.

4. DISQUALIFICATION FROM JUROR SERVICE

As of the date of receipt of the juror summons, any citizen of the United States who is a resident of the judicial district or who lives within the judicial district more than fifty per cent of the time, whether or not he is registered to vote in any state or federal election, shall be qualified to serve as a grand or trial juror in such judicial district unless one of the following grounds for disqualification applies: —

1. Such person is under the age of eighteen years.

2. Such person is seventy years of age or older and indicates on the juror confirmation form an election not to perform juror service.

3. Such person is not able to speak and understand the English language.

4. Such person is incapable by reason of a physical or mental disability, of rendering satisfactory juror service. Any person claiming this disqualification must submit a letter from a registered physician stating the nature of the disability and the physician's opinion that such disability prevents the person from rendering satisfactory juror service. In reaching such opinion, the physician shall apply the following guideline: a person shall be capable of rendering satisfactory juror service if such person is able to perform a sedentary job requiring close attention for six hours per day, with short work breaks in the morning and afternoon sessions, for three consecutive business days. For the purposes of this section, "physician" shall include any accredited Christian Science practitioner.

5. Such person is solely responsible for the daily care of a permanently disabled person living in the same household and the performance of juror service would cause a substantial risk of injury to the health of the disabled person. Any person claiming this disqualification must submit a letter from a registered physician stating the name, address, and age of the disabled person, the nature of the daily care provided by the prospective juror, and the physician's opinion that the performance of juror service would cause a substantial risk of injury to the health of the disabled person. Any person who is regularly employed at a location other than that of his household shall not be entitled to this disqualification.

6. Such person is outside the judicial district and does not intend to return to the judicial district at any time during the following year.

7. Such person has been convicted of a felony within the past seven years or is a defendant in pending felony case or is in the custody of a correctional institution.

8. Such person has served as a grand or trial juror in any state or federal court within the

---

*The Massachusetts jury statute is representative of the revisions in statutory definition of jury obligation that are under consideration in states that have traditionally made it very easy for citizens to avoid jury service.

previous three calendar years or the person is currently scheduled to perform such service. Any person claiming this disqualification must submit a letter or certificate from the appropriate clerk of court or jury commissioner verifying such prior or pending juror service unless such service was performed or is pending in a court of the commonwealth.

Constitutional Protection of Fair Jury Selection *Stephen Arons*

For the vast majority of citizens, it is the provisions of the U.S. Constitution that guarantee a fair trial by an impartial jury of one's peers. Expensive social science tools are not available to everyone as aids in jury selection; and most defendants therefore must rely on the lawyer's skill in using constitutional standards. For those who must be content with institutional protections of fair trial such as the jury selection statutes of states, the *voir dire* questioning of prospective jurors by judge or counsel, and the protections of the Constitution, what are the prospects of getting a fair jury? More important, perhaps, what *is* a fair jury? What constitutes a jury of peers?

The phrase "jury of peers" goes back to the Magna Carta in 1215, though the significance of this pedigree is in doubt. In 1215, after all, there was little even remotely resembling trial by jury as we know it today. In fact the jury of peers represented an attempt by English barons to secure their privileges against the king's encroachment, not a notion of equality among all the populace, including those outside the nobility. Nevertheless, the concept of being tried by a jury of one's peers has become engrained in American law. The question is, what does it mean?

Does it stand for the proposition that defendants should be judged by members of their own social or economic subgroup? If so, what subgroups or communities are to be recognized as defining a person's peerage in a pluralistic society? Or does it mean that since all people are equal in a democratic republic, a jury must be a cross section of the whole society? If this is so, the problem of defining communities is still with us, for now the issue is whether a recognizable group has been excluded. Finally, perhaps we are all each other's peers by virtue of our humanity. If so, does "jury of peers" mean anything practical at all as a principle of preventing discrimination in jury selection?

The formal legal system has approached issues of jury selection according to several criteria.

RACE

Since 1880 the Supreme Court has ruled that a state cannot constitutionally exclude persons from juries solely on the basis of their race or skin color (*Strauder* v. *West Virginia,* 100 U.S. 303 [1880]). The court looked for systematic exclusion from jury rolls rather than actual absence of any race from any particular jury. The standard of racial discrimination in jury selection has thus become one of *opportunity* to serve rather than presence on a jury — that is, the method of selection of potential jurors must be racially nondiscriminatory, but presence of minority race jurors on a jury deliberating the fate of a minority race defendant is not required by the Constitution as the U.S. Supreme Court reads it.

The proof necessary to show systematic exclusion from opportunity to serve on a jury under the Fourteenth Amendment's Equal Protection Clause is difficult (*Swain* v. *Alabama,* 380 U.S. 202 [1965] and see the Federal Jury Selection Act, 28 USC 1861 *et seq.,* 1968). The demonstrated exclusions must not only be systematic, but also must be intentional (motivated by racism). Challenges to jury selection under the Sixth Amendment provision for a fair cross section of the community (see page 383) apply to issues of gender but generally not to race; and the Sixth Amendment test is easier to meet than the equal protection standard of proof. Sixth Amendment standards allow a *prime facie* (at first examination) case to be demonstrated by statistical disparities between the gender composition of jury pools and the local community, but do not require proof of intent to discriminate. (See *Duren* v. *Missouri,* 439 U.S. 357 [1979] and *Taylor* v. *Louisiana,* 419 U.S. 522 [1975].) For a case in which the Sixth Amendment was applied to racial exclusions from the jury (by means of peremptory challenges) where the Fourteenth Amendment's Equal Protection Clause was believed to be inapplicable, see *Booker* v. *Jabe,* 775 F.2d 762 (6th Cir., 1985).

In opposition to the prevailing legal doctrine, some commentators have suggested that a strong case can be made that a majority or even all jurors should be black in cases involving black defendants (see "The Case for Black Juries," 79 *Yale Law Journal* 531 [1969]). The argument is based primarily upon the absence of legitimacy a jury — and therefore the law in general — suffers when members of the black community do not see themselves reflected in actual jury composition. The ability of persons with similar life experiences to understand and credit the case of a defendant from the same community is also cited.

Peremptory challenges to empaneling jurors — in which an attorney can excuse a juror without giving a reason — may also result in juries that have no representation from any minority community. Until recently, the Supreme Court had narrowed its scope of review even further by refusing to recognize as a violation of equal protection a pattern of absence of blacks from juries when such a pattern was produced by peremptory challenges. See, for example, "Note: Peremptory Challenges and the Meaning of Jury Representation," 89 *Yale Law Journal* 1177 (1980), and Barbara Babcock, "Voir Dire: Preserving Its Wonderful Power," 27 *Stanford Law Review* 545 (1975). The U.S. Supreme Court settled the issue of racism and peremptory challenges by the prosecution in *Batson* v. *Kentucky,* reprinted in part after this article.

AGE

In *United States* v. *Guzman,* 337 F. Supp. 140 (S.D.N.Y. 1972), a United States district court interpreting the Sixth Amendment and the Federal Jury Selection Act refused to reverse the conviction of a young man for refusing induction into the armed forces. The court rejected his claim that the jury that convicted him was unconstitutionally based on systematic exclusion of 18- to 21-year-olds and "young persons" between 24 and 30. In discussing its refusal to find any constitutional flaw in the New York jury selection method that resulted in underrepresentation of young people on the jury, the court said,

> The crux of the inquiry is whether, in the source used in the selection of juries, there has been systematic or intentional exclusion of any cognizable group or class of qualified citizens. Thus, selection systems which exclude identifiable racial groups or social or economic classes are vulnerable to attack. However, perfectly proportional representation is not required, since no source list will be an exact statistical mirror of the community.
>
> If it is ascertained, however, that any cognizable group is *substantially* underrepresented in the source of names, systematic or intentional exclusion can be inferred. The test is to compare the degree of representation of a particular group to that group's percentage of the population. . . .
>
> The major problem raised by defendant's challenge is determining whether his asserted age groups are "cognizable groups." While certain racial and economic groups have been held to be "cognizable groups" for purposes of jury challenges, the cases have dealt gingerly with the methodology used to determine whether other groups are

> "cognizable." Nevertheless, various critical factors can be gleaned from the opinions.
>
> A group to be "cognizable" for present purposes must have a definite composition. That is, there must be some factor which defines and limits the group. A cognizable group is not one whose membership shifts from day to day or whose members can be arbitrarily selected. Secondly, the group must have cohesion. There must be a common thread which runs through the group, a basic similarity in attitudes or ideas or experience which is present in members of the group and which cannot be adequately represented if the group is excluded from the jury selection process. Finally, there must be a possibility that exclusion of the group will result in partiality or bias on the part of juries hearing cases in which group members are involved. That is, the group must have a community of interest which cannot be adequately protected by the rest of the populace. See "Young Adults as a Cognizable Group in Jury Selection," D. Zeigler, 76 *Michigan Law Review* 1045 (1978).

For a recent case using the *Guzman* test to find a violation of the Sixth Amendment in the systematic, nonintentional exclusion of "young adults" from jury pools, see *Barber* v. *Ponte,* 772 F.2d 987 (1st Cir., 1985).

GENDER

In *Alexander* v. *Louisiana,* 92 S.Ct. 1221 (1972), the Supreme Court quashed an indictment against a black defendant because the procedure for picking grand jurors systematically excluded members of the black community. The court refused to consider the defendant's alternative claim which was based on the systematic exclusion of women from the Grand Jury. (Louisiana Code provided that a woman could not be selected for jury duty unless she had filed a request to serve). In a concurring opinion, Justice Douglas took issue with the majority's refusal to consider the issue of sex discrimination and wrote, in part,

> The requirement that a jury reflect a cross-section of the community occurs throughout our jurisprudence: "The American tradition of trial by jury, considered in connection with either criminal or civil proceedings, necessarily comtemplates an impartial jury drawn from a cross-section of the community." (*Thiel* v. *Southern Pacific,* 328 U.S. 217, 220 [1946])
>
> This is precisely the constitutional infirmity of the Louisiana statute. For a jury list from which women have been systematically excluded is not representative of the community.
>
> It is said, however, that an all male panel drawn from the various groups within a community will be as truly representative as if women were included. The thought is that the factors which tend to influence the action of women are the same as those which influence the action of men — personality, background, economic status — and not sex.
>
> Yet it is not enough to say that women when sitting as jurors neither act nor tend to act as a class. Men likewise do not act as a class. But, if the shoe were on the other foot, who would claim that a jury was truly representative of the community if all men were intentionally and systematically excluded from the panel? The truth is that the two sexes are not fungible; a community made up exclusively of one is different from a community composed of both; the subtle interplay of influence between one and the other is among the imponderables. To insulate the courtroom from either may not in a given case make an iota of difference. Yet a flavor, a distinct quality is lost if either sex is excluded. The *exclusion of one may indeed make the jury less representative of the community than would be true if an economic or racial group were excluded.*
>
> The absolute exemption provided by Louisiana, and no other State, betrays a view of a woman's role which cannot withstand scrutiny under modern standards. We once upheld the constitutionality of a state law denying to women the right to practice law,

> solely on grounds of sex. The rationale underlying Art. 402 of the Louisiana Code is the same as that which was articulated by Justice Bradley in [1872] *Bradwell:*
>
> "Man is, or should be, woman's protector and defender. The natural and proper timidity and delicacy which belongs to the female sex evidently unfits it for many of the occupations of civil life. The constitution of the family organization, which is founded in the divine ordinance, as well as in the nature of things, indicates the domestic sphere as that which properly belongs to the domain and functions of womanhood. The harmony, not to say identity, of interests and views which belong, or should belong, to the family institution is repugnant to the idea of a woman adopting a distinct and independent career from that of her husband. . . . The paramount destiny and mission of woman are to fulfill the noble and benign offices of wife and mother. This is the law of the Creator. And the rules of civil society must be adapted to the general constitution of things, and cannot be based upon exceptional cases."
>
> Classifications based on sex are no longer insulated from judicial scrutiny by a legislative judgment that "woman's place is in the home," or that woman is by her "nature" ill-suited for a particular task. But such a judgment is precisely that which underpins the absolute exemption from jury service at issue.

Just two years later, a majority of the Court adopted Justice Douglas's views, declaring systematic exclusion of women from jury pools to be a violation of the Sixth Amendment. The decision in *Taylor* v. *Louisiana,* 419 U.S. 522 (1974) invalidated a Louisiana statute that excluded women from jury service unless they filed with the Louisiana courts a written declaration of desire to serve. The challenge was brought by a male sentenced, by an all-male jury, to death for aggravated kidnapping. In the majority opinion, Mr. Justice White held,

> Although this judgment may appear a foregone conclusion from the pattern of some of the Court's cases over the past thirty years, . . . it is nevertheless true that until today no case had squarely held that the exclusion of women from jury venires deprives a criminal defendant of his Sixth Amendment right to trial by an impartial jury drawn from a fair cross-section of the community. . . . We think it is no longer tenable to hold that women as a class may be excluded or given automatic exemptions based solely on sex. . . . If at one time it could be held that Sixth Amendment juries must be drawn from a fair cross-section of the community but that this requirement permitted the almost total exclusion of women, this is not the case today. Communities differ at different times and places. What is a fair cross-section at one time or place is not necessarily a fair cross-section at another time or a different place.

Putting this Sixth Amendment case in the same category as jury selection cases involving racial or other factors, the Court further ruled in *Taylor* that

> It should also be emphasized that in holding that petit juries must be drawn from a source fairly representative of the community, we impose no requirement that petit juries actually chosen must mirror the community and reflect the various distinctive groups in the population.

Affirming and extending the ruling on women in *Taylor,* the Court in *Duren* v. *Missouri,* 439 U.S. 357 (1979) ruled that a Missouri statute allowing women to claim an exemption from jury service by their response to a jury-selection questionnaire violated the Sixth Amendment. The case, also brought by a male defendant, held that proof of intent to discriminate on the basis of gender is not required under the Sixth Amendment, and that the requirement of showing women to have been victims of "systematic exclusion in the jury selection process" was met by defendant's "undisputed demonstration that a large discrepancy occurred not just occasionally, but in every weekly venire for a period of nearly a year . . . [indicating] . . . that the cause of the underrepresentation was systematic — i.e. inherent in the particular jury-selection process utilized." This statistical proof would presumably have been inadequate had the issue been racial exclusion forbidden by the Equal Protection Clause of the Fourteenth Amendment.

ATTITUDE AND BELIEF

In *Witherspoon* v. *Illinois,* 391 U.S. 510 (1968), the Supreme Court ruled that a jury could not constitutionally recommend a death sentence in a capital case because that jury was chosen by excluding persons who expressed conscientious or religious scruples against the death penalty. The court did not rule that a jury's determination of guilt or innocence (as opposed to sentence) would be unconstitutional if persons with scruples against the death penalty had been excluded. In its opinion, the court stated,

> If the State had excluded only those prospective jurors who stated in advance of trial that they would not even consider returning a verdict of death, it could argue that the resulting jury was simply "neutral" with respect to penalty. But when it swept from the jury all who expressed conscientious or religious scruples against capital punishment and all who opposed it in principle, the State crossed the line of neutrality. In its quest for a jury capable of imposing the death penalty, the State produced a jury uncommonly willing to condemn a man to die.

The rule therefore forbids the exclusion of a juror with scruples against the death penalty so long as those scruples would not "prevent or substantially impair the performance of his duties as a juror in accordance with his instructions and his oath." Justice Douglas, in a concurring opinion, wished to take the issue further, both as to what is a truly neutral or representative jury and as to whether persons with scruples against the death penalty could be excluded from juries determining guilt or innocence. He stated,

> My difficulty with the opinion of the Court is a narrow but important one. The Court permits a State to eliminate from juries some of those who have conscientious scruples against the death penalty; but it allows those to serve who have no scruples against it as well as those who, having such scruples, nevertheless are deemed able to determine after a finding of guilt whether the death penalty or a lesser penalty should be imposed. I fail to see or understand the constitutional dimensions of those distinctions. . . .
>
> A fair cross-section of the community may produce a jury almost certain to impose the death penalty if guilt were found; or it may produce a jury almost certain not to impose it. The conscience of the community is subject to many variables, one of which is the attitude toward the death sentence. If a particular community were overwhelmingly opposed to capital punishment, it would not be able to exercise a discretion to impose or not impose the death sentence. A jury representing the conscience of that community would do one of several things depending on the type of state law governing it: it would avoid the death penalty by recommending mercy or it would avoid it by finding guilt of a lesser offense.
>
> In such instance, why should not an accused have the benefit of that controlling principle of mercy in the community? Why should his fate be entrusted exclusively to a jury that was either enthusiastic about capital punishment or so undecided that it could exercise a discretion to impose it or not, depending on how it felt about the particular case?
>
> I see no constitutional basis for excluding those who are so opposed to capital

punishment that they would never inflict it on a defendant. Exclusion of them means the selection of jurors who are either protagonists of the death penalty or neutral concerning it. That results in a systematic exclusion of qualified groups, and the deprivation to the accused of a cross-section of the community for decision on both his guilt and his punishment.

Although the Court reverses as to penalty, it declines to reverse the verdict of guilt rendered by the same jury. It does so on the ground that petitioner has not demonstrated on this record that the jury which convicted him was "less than neutral with respect to *guilt*," because of the exclusion of all those opposed in some degree to capital punishment. The Court fails to find on this record "an unrepresentative jury on the issue of guilt." But we do not require a showing of specific prejudice when a defendant has been deprived of his right to a jury representing a cross-section of the community. We can as easily assume that the absence of those opposed to capital punishment would rob the jury of certain peculiar qualities of human nature as would the exclusion of women from juries. I would not require a specific showing of a likelihood of prejudice, for I feel that we must proceed on the assumption that in many, if not most, cases of exclusion on the basis of beliefs or attitudes some prejudice does result and many times will not be subject to precise measurement. Indeed, that prejudice "is so subtle, so intangible, that it escapes the ordinary methods of proof." In my view, that is the essence of the requirement that a jury be drawn from a cross-section of the community.

Notes and Questions

1. Which is the better place to insist on a representative cross section of the community, the rolls of names from which jurors are picked or the actual jurors on a particular jury panel? Why?
2. Should age be recognized as a factor in making up representative jury rolls or juries? Should the type of offense or the age of the defendant make any difference on this issue? What type of evidence might be offered to show that "young people" is a cognizable group under the test set forth in the *Guzman* case?
3. Instead of a representative cross section of the community, should a jury of peers be defined as one made up of people sharing the cultural or economic background of the defendant?
4. Broad participation in legal process is one of the goals to be met by using jury trials. So would it be realistic to say that, since all citizens are of equal worth, a search for a particular cross section should be abandoned? Should any juror be regarded as adequate as long as he or she has no biases about the issue and parties in the trial in question?
5. Once the courts begin identifying characteristics of the population that should not be discriminated against in juror selection, where does the process stop? Should the courts look to religious persuasion, socioeconomic status, ethnic background, language, political registration, eye color? What does your answer tell you about the fragmentation of American society? Can the jury system function in such a society? See "Note: Underrepresentation of Economic Groups on Federal Juries," *Boston University Law Review* 57 (1977): 198.
6. If attaining a representative community input into legal process is one important goal of the jury system, who should be able to challenge the composition of juries besides the defendant? An excluded juror? Should a white male defendant be able to challenge a jury from which women have been excluded? a jury from which Mexican-Americans have been excluded? See *Peters* v. *Kiff*, 407 U.S. 493 (1972), and *Taylor* v. *Louisiana*, 419 U.S. 522 (1975), for the Supreme Court's view on these issues.

7. Do you find the difference between the Supreme Court's treatment of gender discrimination under the Sixth Amendment and its treatment of racial discrimination under the Equal Protection Clause justifiable? Given the history of the United States, why should racial discrimination be made harder to prove than gender discrimination? As you examine reasoning in the following case, *Batson* v. *Kentucky,* see if it provides any clues about the difference of race and gender in jury selection.

Batson v. Kentucky *106 S.Ct. 1712 (1986)*

JUSTICE POWELL *delivered the opinion of the Court.*

This case requires us to reexamine that portion of *Swain* v. *Alabama,* 380 U.S. 202, . . . (1965), concerning the evidentiary burden placed on a criminal defendant who claims that he has been denied equal protection through the State's use of peremptory challenges to exclude members of his race from the petit jury.

Petitioner, a black man, was indicted in Kentucky on charges of second-degree burglary and receipt of stolen goods. On the first day of trial in Jefferson Circuit Court, the judge conducted *voir dire* [questioning of prospective jurors to determine their fitness to serve] examination of the venire, excused certain jurors for cause, and permitted the parties to exercise peremptory challenges. The prosecutor used his peremptory challenges to strike all four black persons on the venire, and a jury composed only of white persons was selected. Defense counsel moved to discharge the jury before it was sworn on the ground that the prosecutor's removal of the black veniremen violated petitioner's rights under the Sixth and Fourteenth Amendments to a jury drawn from a cross-section of the community, and under the Fourteenth Amendment to equal protection of the laws. Counsel requested a hearing on his motion. Without expressly ruling on the request for a hearing, the trial judge observed that the parties were entitled to use their peremptory challenges to "strike anybody they want to." The judge then denied petitioner's motion, reasoning that the cross-section requirement applies only to selection of the venire and not to selection of the petit jury itself.

The jury convicted petitioner on both counts. On appeal to the Supreme Court of Kentucky, petitioner pressed, among other claims, the argument concerning the prosecutor's use of peremptory challenges. Conceding that *Swain* v. *Alabama, supra,* apparently foreclosed an equal protection claim based solely on the prosecutor's conduct in this case, petitioner urged the court to follow decisions of other states, *People* v. *Wheeler,* . . . 583 P.2d 748 (1978); *Commonwealth* v. *Soares,* . . . 387 N.E.2d 499, cert. denied, 444 U.S. 881 . . . (1979), and to hold that such conduct violated his rights under the Sixth Amendment and Section 11 of the Kentucky Constitution to a jury drawn from a cross-section of the community. Petitioner also contended that the facts showed that the prosecutor had engaged in a "pattern" of discriminatory challenges in this case and established an equal protection violation under *Swain.*

The Supreme Court of Kentucky affirmed. In a single paragraph, the court . . . observed that it recently had reaffirmed its reliance on *Swain,* and had held that a defendant alleging lack of a fair cross-section must demonstrate systematic exclusion of a group of jurors from the venire. . . . We granted certiorari, . . . 105 S.Ct. 2111 . . . (1985), and now reverse.

In *Swain* v. *Alabama,* this Court recognized that a "State's purposeful or deliberate denial to Negroes on account of race of participation as jurors in the administration of justice violates

---

Some citations and footnotes have been omitted and footnotes are renumbered. — ED.

the Equal Protection Clause." 380 U.S., at 203–204, 85 S.Ct., at 826–27. This principle has been "consistently and repeatedly" reaffirmed, *id.*, at 204, 85 S.Ct., at 827, in numerous decisions of this Court both preceding and following *Swain.* We reaffirm the principle today.[1]

More than a century ago, the Court decided that the State denies a black defendant equal protection of the laws when it puts him on trial before a jury from which members of his race have been purposefully excluded. *Strauder* v. *West Virginia,* 10 Otto 303, 100 U.S. 303, ... That decision laid the foundation for the Court's unceasing efforts to eradicate racial discrimination in the procedures used to select the venire from which individual jurors are drawn. In *Strauder,* the Court explained that the central concern of the recently ratified Fourteenth Amendment was to put an end to governmental discrimination on account of race. . . . Exclusion of black citizens from service as jurors constitutes a primary example of the evil the Fourteenth Amendment was designed to cure.

In holding that racial discrimination in jury selection offends the Equal Protection Clause, the Court in *Strauder* recognized, however, that a defendant has no right to a "petit jury composed in whole or in part of persons of his own race." . . .

Purposeful racial discrimination in selection of the venire violates a defendant's right to equal protection because it denies him the protection that a trial by jury is intended to secure. "The very idea of a jury is a body . . . composed of the peers or equals of the person whose rights it is selected or summoned to determine; that is, of his neighbors, fellows, associates, persons having the same legal status in society as that which he holds." . . . The petit jury has occupied a central position in our system of justice by safeguarding a person accused of crime against the arbitrary exercise of power by prosecutor or judge. *Duncan* v. *Louisiana,* 391 U.S. 145, 156, . . . (1968).[2] Those on the venire must be "indifferently chosen," to secure the defendant's right under the Fourteenth Amendment to "protection of life and liberty against race or color prejudice." . . .

Racial discrimination in selection of jurors harms not only the accused whose life or liberty they are summoned to try. Competence to serve as a juror ultimately depends on an assessment of individual qualifications and ability impartially to consider evidence presented at a trial. . . . As long ago as *Strauder,* therefore, the Court recognized that by denying a person participation in jury service on account of his race, the State unconstitutionally discriminated against the excluded juror. 100 U.S., at 308; . . .

The harm from discriminatory jury selection extends beyond that inflicted on the defendant and the excluded juror to touch the entire community. Selection procedures that purposefully exclude black persons from juries undermine public confidence in the fairness of our system of justice. . . . Discrimination within the judicial system is most pernicious because it is "a stimulant to that race prejudice which is an impediment to security to [black citizens] that equal justice which the law aims to secure to all others." *Strauder, supra,* 100 U.S., at 308.

In *Strauder,* the Court invalidated a state statute that provided that only white men could serve as jurors. 100 U.S., at 305. We can be confident that no state now has such a law. The Constitution requires, however, that we look beyond the face of the statute defining juror qualifications and also consider challenged selection practices to afford "protection against action of the State through its administrative officers in effecting the prohibited discrimination." . . .

[1] . . . We agree with the State that resolution of petitioner's claim properly turns on application of equal protection principles and express no view on the merits of any of petitioner's Sixth Amendment arguments.

[2] . . . By compromising the representative quality of the jury, discriminatory selection procedures make "juries ready weapons for officials to oppress those accused individuals who by chance are numbered among unpopular or inarticulate minorities." *Akins* v. *Texas,* 325 U.S., at 408, 65 S.Ct., at 1281 (Murphy, J., dissenting).

Thus, the Court has found a denial of equal protection where the procedures implementing a neutral statute operated to exclude persons from the venire on racial grounds, and has made clear that the Constitution prohibits all forms of purposeful racial discrimination in selection of jurors. While decisions of this Court have been concerned largely with discrimination during selection of the venire, the principles announced there also forbid discrimination on account of race in selection of the petit jury. Since the Fourteenth Amendement protects an accused throughout the proceedings bringing him to justice, . . . the State may not draw up its jury lists pursuant to neutral procedures but then resort to discrimination at "other stages in the selection process." . . .

Accordingly, the component of the jury selection process at issue here, the State's privilege to strike individual jurors through peremptory challenges, is subject to the commands of the Equal Protection Clause. Although a prosecutor ordinarily is entitled to exercise permitted peremptory challenges "for any reason at all, as long as that reason is related to his view concerning the outcome" of the case to be tried, *United States* v. *Robinson,* 421 F.Supp. 467, 473 (Conn. 1976) . . . , the Equal Protection Clause forbids the prosecutor to challenge potential jurors solely on account of their race or on the assumption that black jurors as a group will be unable impartially to consider the State's case against a black defendant. . . .

A number of lower courts following the teaching of *Swain* reasoned that proof of repeated striking of blacks over a number of cases was necessary to establish a violation of the Equal Protection Clause. Since this interpretation of *Swain* has placed on defendants a crippling burden of proof, prosecutors' peremptory challenges are now largely immune from constitutional scrutiny. For reasons that follow, we reject this evidentiary formulation as inconsistent with standards that have been developed since *Swain* for assessing a prima facie case under the Equal Protection Clause.

Since the decision in *Swain,* we have explained that our cases concerning selection of the venire reflect the general equal protection principle that the "invidious quality" of governmental action claimed to be racially discriminatory "must ultimately be traced to a racially discriminatory purpose." *Washington* v. *Davis,* 426 U.S. 229, 240, 96 S.Ct. 2040, 2048, . . . (1976). As in any equal protection case, the "burden is, of course," on the defendant who alleges discriminatory selection of the venire "to prove the existence of purposeful discrimination." . . .

The standards for assessing a prima facie case in the context of discriminatory selection of the venire have been fully articulated since *Swain*. . . . These principles support our conclusion that a defendant may establish a prima facie case of purposeful discrimination in selection of the petit jury solely on evidence concerning the prosecutor's exercise of peremptory challenges at the defendant's trial. To establish such a case, the defendant first must show that he is a member of a cognizable racial group, . . . and that the prosecutor has exercised peremptory challenges to remove from the venire members of the defendant's race. Second, the defendant is entitled to rely on the fact, as to which there can be no dispute, that peremptory challenges constitute a jury selection practice that permits "those to discriminate who are of a mind to discriminate." . . . Finally, the defendant must show that these facts and any other relevant circumstances raise an inference that the prosecutor used that practice to exclude the veniremen from the petit jury on account of their race. This combination of factors in the empanelling of the petit jury, as in the selection of the venire, raises the necessary inference of purposeful discrimination. . . .

Once the defendant makes a prima facie showing, the burden shifts to the State to come forward with a neutral explanation for challenging black jurors. Though this requirement imposes a limitation in some cases on the full peremptory character of the historic challenge, we emphasize that the prosecutor's explanation need not rise to the level justifying exercise of a challenge for cause. . . . But the prosecutor may not rebut the defendant's prima facie case of discrimination by stating merely that he challenged jurors of the defendant's race on the assumption — or his intuitive judgment — that they would be partial to the defendant because of their shared race. . . . Just as the Equal Protection Clause forbids the States to exclude black persons from the venire on the assumption that blacks as a group are unqualified to serve as jurors, . . . so it forbids the States to strike black veniremen on the assumption that they will be biased in a particular case simply because the defendant is black. The core guarantee of equal protection, ensuring citizens that their State will not discriminate on account of race, would be meaningless were we to approve the exclusion of jurors on the basis of such assumptions, which arise solely from the jurors' race. Nor may the prosecutor rebut the defendant's case merely by denying that he had a discriminatory motive or "affirming his good faith in individual selections." . . . If these general assertions were accepted as rebutting a defendant's prima facie case, the Equal Protection Clause "would be but a vain and illusory requirement." . . . The prosecutor therefore must articulate a neutral explanation related to the particular case to be tried. The trial court then will have the duty to determine if the defendant has established purposeful discrimination.

The State contends that our holding will eviscerate the fair trial values served by the peremptory challenge. Conceding that the Constitution does not guarantee a right to peremptory challenges and that *Swain* did state that their use ultimately is subject to the strictures of equal protection, the State argues that the privilege of unfettered exercise of the challenge is of vital importance to the criminal justice system.

While we recognize, of course, that the peremptory challenge occupies an important position in our trial procedures, we do not agree that our decision today will undermine the contribution the challenge generally makes to the administration of justice. The reality of practice, amply reflected in many state and federal court opinions, shows that the challenge may be, and unfortunately at times has been, used to discriminate against black jurors. By requiring trial courts to be sensitive to the racially discriminatory use of peremptory challenges, our decision enforces the mandate of equal protection and furthers the ends of justice. In view of the heterogeneous population of our nation, public respect for our criminal justice system and the rule of law will be strengthened if we ensure that no citizen is disqualified from jury service because of his race. . . .

In this case, petitioner made a timely objection to the prosecutor's removal of all black persons on the venire. Because the trial court flatly rejected the objection without requiring the prosecutor to give an explanation for his action, we remand this case for further proceedings. If the trial court decides that the facts establish, prima facie, purposeful discrimination and the prosecutor does not come forward with a neutral explanation for his action, our precedents require that petitioner's conviction be reversed. . . .

It is so ordered.

JUSTICE MARSHALL, *concurring.*

I join Justice Powell's eloquent opinion for the Court, which takes a historic step toward eliminating the shameful practice of racial discrimination in the selection of juries. The Court's opinion cogently explains the pernicious nature of the racially discriminatory use of peremptory challenges, and the repugnancy of such discrimination to the Equal Protection Clause. The Court's opinion also ably demonstrates the inadequacy of any burden of proof for racially discriminatory use of peremptories that requires that "justice . . . sit supinely by" and be flouted in case after case before a remedy is available. I nonetheless write separately to express my views. The decision today will not end the racial discrimination that peremptories inject into the jury-selection process. That goal can be accomplished only by eliminating peremptory challenges entirely. . . .

Evidentiary analysis similar to that set out by the Court . . . has been adopted as a matter of state law in States including Massachusetts and California. Cases from those jurisdictions illustrate the limitations of the approach. First, defendants cannot attack the discriminatory use of peremptory challenges at all unless the challenges are so flagrant as to establish a prima facie case. This means, in those States, that where only one or two black jurors survive the challenges for cause, the prosecutor need have no compunction about striking them from the jury because of their race. See *Commonwealth* v. *Robinson,* 382 Mass. 189, 195, 415 N.E.2d 805, 809–810 (1981) (no prima facie case of discrimination where defendant is black, prospective jurors include three blacks and one Puerto Rican, and prosecutor excludes one for cause and strikes the remainder peremptorily, producing all-white jury). . . . Prosecutors are left free to discriminate against blacks in jury selection provided that they hold that discrimination to an "acceptable" level.

Second, when a defendant can establish a prima facie case, trial courts face the difficult burden of assessing prosecutors' motives. . . . Any prosecutor can easily assert facially neutral reasons for striking a juror, and trial courts are ill-equipped to second-guess those reasons. . . .

Nor is outright prevarication by prosecutors the only danger here. "[I]t is even possible that an attorney may lie to himself in an effort to convince himself that his motives are legal." . . . A prosecutor's own conscious or unconscious racism may lead him easily to the conclusion that a prospective black juror is "sullen," or "distant," a characterization that would not have come to his mind if a white juror had acted identically. A judge's own conscious or unconscious racism may lead him to accept such an explanation as well supported. As Justice Rehnquist concedes, prosecutors' peremptories are based on their "seat-of-the-pants instincts" as to how particular jurors will vote. . . .

. . . Yet "seat-of-the-pants instincts" may often be just another term for racial prejudice. Even if all parties approach the Court's mandate with the best of conscious intentions, that mandate requires them to confront and overcome their own racism on all levels — a challenge I doubt all of them can meet. It is worth remembering that "114 years after the close of the War Between the States and nearly 100 years after *Strauder,* racial and other forms of discrimination still remain a fact of life, in the administration of justice as in our society as a whole." *Rose* v. *Mitchell,* 443 U.S. 545, 558–559 . . . (1979).

The inherent potential of peremptory challenges to distort the jury process by permitting the exclusion of jurors on racial grounds should ideally lead the Court to ban them entirely from the criminal justice system. . . . Justice Goldberg, dissenting in *Swain,* emphasized that "[w]ere it necessary to make an absolute choice between the right of a defendant to have a jury chosen in conformity with the requirements of the Fourteenth Amendment and the right to challenge peremptorily, the Constitution compels a choice of the former." 380 U.S., at 244, 85 S.Ct., at 849. I believe that this case presents just such a choice, and I would resolve that choice by eliminating peremptory challenges entirely in criminal cases.

Some authors have suggested that the courts should ban prosecutors' peremptories entirely, but should zealously guard the defendant's peremptory as "essential to the fairness of trial by jury," *Lewis* v. *United States,* 146 U.S. 370, 376 (1892), . . . I would not find that an acceptable solution. . . . Our criminal justice system "requires not only freedom from any bias against the accused, but also from any prejudice against his prosecution. Between him and the state the scales are to be evenly held." . . . We can maintain that balance, not by permitting both prosecutor and defendant to engage in racial discrimination in jury selection, but by banning the use of peremptory challenges by prosecutors and by allowing the States to eliminate the defendant's peremptory as well. . . .

CHIEF JUSTICE BURGER, *joined by* JUSTICE REHNQUIST, *dissenting.*

Today the Court sets aside the peremptory challenge, a procedure which has been part of the common law for many centuries and part of our jury system for nearly 200 years. It does so on the basis of a constitutional argument that was rejected, without a single dissent, in *Swain*

v. *Alabama*, 380 U.S. 202, 85 S.Ct. 824. . . . What makes today's holding truly extraordinary is that it is based on a constitutional argument that the petitioner has *expressly* declined to raise, both in this Court and in the Supreme Court of Kentucky. . . .

Because the Court nonetheless chooses to decide this case on the equal protection grounds not presented, it may be useful to discuss this issue as well. The Court acknowledges, albeit in a footnote, the "'very old credentials'" of the peremptory challenge and "'the widely held belief that peremptory challenge is a necessary part of trial by jury.'" . . . But proper resolution of this case requires more than a nodding reference to the purpose of the challenge. Long ago it was recognized that "[t]he right of challenge is almost essential for the purpose of securing perfect fairness and impartiality in a trial." W. Forsyth, History of Trial by Jury 175 (1852). The peremptory challenge has been in use without scrutiny into its basis for nearly as long as juries have existed. . . . Permitting unexplained peremptories has long been regarded as a means to strengthen our jury system. . . . One commentator has recognized:

> The peremptory, made without giving any reason, avoids trafficking in the core of truth in most common stereotypes. . . . Common human experience, common sense, psychosociological studies, and public opinion polls tell us that it is likely that certain classes of people statistically have predispositions that would make them inappropriate jurors for particular kinds of cases. But to allow this knowledge to be expressed in the evaluative terms necessary for challenges for cause would undercut our desire for a society in which all people are judged as individuals and in which each is held reasonable and open to compromise. . . . [For example,] [a]lthough experience reveals that black males as a class can be biased against young alienated blacks who have not tried to join the middle class, to enunciate this in the concrete expression required of a challenge for cause is societally divisive. Instead we have evolved in the peremptory challenge a system that allows the covert expression of what we dare not say but know is true more often than not." Barbara Babcock, "Voir Dire: Preserving Its Wonderful Power," 27 Stan. L. Rev. 545, 553–554 (1975). . . .

A moment's reflection quickly reveals the vast differences between the racial exclusions involved in *Strauder* and the allegations before us today:

> Exclusion from the venire summons process implies that the government (usually the legislative or judicial branch) . . . has made the general determination that those excluded are unfit to try *any* case. Exercise of the peremptory challenge, by contrast, represents the discrete decision, made by one of two or more opposed *litigants* in the trial phase of our adversary system of justice, that the challenged venireperson will likely be more unfavorable to that litigant in that *particular case* than others on the same venire.
>
> Thus, excluding a particular cognizable group from all venire pools is stigmatizing and discriminatory in several interrelated ways that the peremptory challenge is not. The former singles out the excluded group, while individuals of all groups are equally subject to peremptory challenge on any basis, including their group affiliation. Further, venire-pool exclusion bespeaks *a priori* across-the-board total unfitness, while peremptory-strike exclusion merely suggests potential partiality in a particular isolated case. Exclusion from venires focuses on the inherent attributes of the excluded group and infers its *inferiority*, but the peremptory does not. To suggest that a particular race is unfit to judge in any case necessarily is racially insulting. To suggest that each race may have its own special concerns, or even may tend to favor its own, is not. . . .

In short, it is quite probable that every peremptory challenge could be objected to on the basis that, because it excluded a venireman who had some characteristic not shared by the remaining members of the venire, it constituted a "classification" subject to equal protection scrutiny. . . .

At the very least, this important decision reversing centuries of history and experience ought to be set for reargument next term.

Second-guessing the Jury *Margaret Jones*

Don Vinson was a mild-mannered professor all his professional life until late one night in 1976 when he received a telephone call that changed his life.

The call was from the New York law firm of Cravath, Swaine & Moore, which was representing IBM in a complex antitrust suit being brought by a California computer manufacturer. The lawyers who called Vinson, then a professor at the University of Southern California, said they wanted to hire him to help with IBM's defense. So eager were the lawyers to confer with the professor that they dispatched a limousine in the middle of the night to pick Vinson up.

Vinson was not, as one might think, an eminent professor of law. He was a marketing expert. But IBM's lawyers didn't want help honing the legal points of their case. They wanted someone to help them figure out what the jury was thinking.

What Vinson did was to identify the demographic and psychological traits of the 12 jury members. He then recruited six surrogate jurors who together matched the characteristics of the actual jurors. The surrogate jurors, seated throughout the courtroom, observed everything that the actual jurors observed, left the courtroom whenever the actual jurors did, and followed the same admonitions from the judge not to discuss the trial with anyone — not to discuss the lawyers, witnesses, or evidence in the case. In the evening, Vinson called each surrogate and interviewed them about their perceptions of the day's proceedings. He then relayed this information to IBM's lawyers. The lawyers used the reactions of Vinson's "shadow jury" (a term coined by an observant newspaper reporter covering the trial) as a form of feedback, tailoring their arguments accordingly. IBM won the case.

How much Vinson's shadow jury had to do with the outcome of the trial is debatable, but today the former professor is a leading entrepreneur in the profitable science of second-guessing a jury. As head of Litigation Sciences, one of the largest and wealthiest trial consulting firms in the country, Vinson works out of an office that exudes the atmosphere of his upscale law-firm clients, right down to the Audubon prints on the walls and the dark wood office furniture. His clients pay no less than $100,000 per case for Vinson's assistance in solving one of the oldest riddles in the American courtroom: predicting what takes place in a juror's mind during a trial.

The question is, is this anybody's business? Critics charge that expensive trial research such as Vinson's contributes to the cost of litigation, giving an unfair advantage to well-heeled clients who can afford it. Beyond the practical considerations, however, is a larger concern that trial consultants are interlopers in the courtroom — invading jurors' privacy and manipulating the judicial process itself. On these issues, the jury is still out. But given the recent and rapid growth of the trial consulting business, the jury may not be out for long.

Predicting what a jury is likely to do has become a multimillion-dollar industry in just the past decade; Litigation Sciences is one of a dozen firms around the country who market themselves to litigators as human behavior spe-

---

Margaret Jones is a California-based writer. Reprinted from *Student Lawyer,*

cialists. They sell the idea that verdicts are not based on a case's facts, but on the subtle predispositions and attitudes of the jurors that allow the facts to be *perceived* in a biased way. . . .

In addition to large firms that are staffed by psychologists, marketing and consumer specialists, sociologists, communications experts, anthropologists, and statisticians, there are a number of trial consultants who operate as solo practitioners. The five-year-old American Society of Trial Consultants (ASTC) lists 133 individual members with expertise in at least one social science, but they estimate there may be as many as 300 full- or part-time trial consultants in the country.

There is currently no licensing required to be a trial consultant. . . . As a result, standards for practice have not been established, and trial consultants' methods vary widely — a situation that has drawn fire from opposing lawyers. Consultants have sifted through jurors' garbage in order to draw psychological profiles; others have based their analyses on such esoteric factors as the width between a juror's eyebrows or the way a juror carries a purse. Consultants who comb jurors' communities, questioning friends and neighbors, particularly offend Sterling Norris, a deputy district attorney for Los Angeles County who has unsuccessfully sought legislation to prohibit either side of a case from gaining access to any information that cannot be learned in court.

"Here they are," Norris says of jurors, "doing their civic duty, only to have someone going behind their back to dig up information. Not only is it an invasion of privacy, but it puts pressure on jurors. They feel like *they're* the ones on trial." Norris believes that frustrated jurors who discover they are being investigated could change their mind about a verdict, just to prove they can't be second-guessed.

But many trial consultants would say that Norris's fears are unfounded. Most consultants, they say, are legitimate social scientists who are merely applying accepted research methods — the same methods that an anthropologist in New Guinea or a clinical psychologist might use to study populations or individuals — to a new venue: jury selection and trial strategy. The large-scale community survey, which is used to delineate the demographic traits of jurors most likely to be favorably or unfavorably disposed toward a case, is one example. The results of these surveys are used for both jury selection and trial tactics.

Trial consultants primarily focus their efforts on pretrial preparation. Many have developed behavior-oriented *voir dire* questions designed to ferret out less obvious prejudices of potential jurors. To gauge reactions to portions of a case presentation, such as an opening statement or a cross-examination strategy, consultants often set up a "focus group," in which eight to 10 people plus a moderator concentrate on a particular theme or issue related to the case. Credibility studies aim at analyzing how a lawyer, witness, or defendant is perceived by jurors.

Often in large corporate cases, the image of the corporation is assessed as part of pretrial preparation. Litigation Sciences, which works almost exclusively on cases involving *Fortune* 500 companies, makes corporate evaluations on the basis of a scale ranking a company on a scale of one to 10 on such qualities as corporate "goodness" or "powerfulness."

The mock trial, or trial simulation, has replaced the shadow jury as one of the most useful research tools. A complete mock trial may cost from $5,000 to $50,000 and may last from one evening to three days.

In addition to pretrial work, consultants also prepare charts, graphics, or videotapes to be used as demonstrative evidence; accompany lawyers to court during jury selection; coach lawyers and expert witnesses on communications skills; and conduct post-trial studies to evaluate the outcome.

Recently trial consultants have worked behind the scenes in a number of well-known criminal cases: for Ginny Foat, the former president of the California chapter of the National Organization for Women who was acquitted of murder charges in 1983; for Edwin Edwards, governor of Louisiana, found not guilty last May [1987] of fraud and racketeering charges; and for plaintiffs in the McMartin preschool child sexual abuse cases in Los Angeles.

But where the influence of trial consultants is fast becoming a fixture of the legal system is in the area of civil litigation, especially where one corporate giant is pitted against another. In recent years cases like *Penzoil* v. *Texaco, MCI* v. *AT&T,* and the *USFL* v. *the NFL* have all used trial consultants on both sides. In this kind of large-scale litigation, where the stakes of a single case frequently exceed the GNP of a small country, some attorneys believe that *not* hiring an outside expert to "psych out" a jury borders on negligence.

"When you're in an adversarial proceeding, you have to represent your client to the fullest extent possible" says Los Angeles lawyer Wayne McClean, a veteran of a number of tort cases against large corporations. "Let's face it: picking juries is very much a guessing game. It still is, even with a trial consultant, but at least you're reducing your risk."

But the bottom line in deciding whether to hire a consultant is not moral obligation — it's money. And the big money, admit the consultants, is in corporate civil litigation.

"Most of the cases we're involved in are cases of two haves," says Arthur Raedecke, vice president of Public Response Associates, who says their clients spend anywhere from $20,000 to $100,000 per case. Philip Johnson, of Leo Shapiro & Associates, admits that "just to get your feet wet you've got to bite off a minimum of fifteen thousand dollars," while the average tab for their services runs between $65,000 and $85,000.

Not all trial consultants work out of fancy offices or work for wealthy corporate clients. Widely regarded as trial consulting's earliest pioneer, Jay Schulman used to wear a rope belt, no socks, and sneakers to court. These days, however, Schulman tends to wear a suit, if not a three-piece suit, when he pays a call on a law firm. . . .

Schulman's first case was in 1971, when Daniel and Philip Berrigan, Catholic priests and friends of Schulman, were arrested and accused of conspiracy against the government in Harrisburg, Pennsylvania. At the time, Schulman was just leaving academia, the result of his outspoken antiwar activity. Schulman and two other academics offered their services to the defense.

"I got to Harrisburg and didn't see how seven priests and nuns and a crazy Pakistani professor were going to get a fair trial," says Schulman. The trial of the Harrisburg Seven was the first time that defense lawyers worked with social scientists to plot a strategy for jury selection. Schulman and his colleagues conducted surveys in Harrisburg, polling residents' political and religious beliefs, their trust in government, their knowledge of the indictment, and a host of other attitudes that might come into play in deciding such a case. From this information they advised the defense on which potential jurors would be most sympathetic to their clients. Schulman's methods proved successful: the case was declared a mistrial after only two jurors out of 12 were able to vote to conviction.

After the Harrisburg trial, Schulman's reputation — and knowledge of his political sympathies — propelled him into working for the defense in a number of other political trials, including Attica and Wounded Knee. During these years he lived off of personal savings; the only compensation for his trial work came from a $1,500 fund raised by some sympathetic friends.

Schulman has now worked on more than 500 jury trials, both criminal and civil. He refers to his profession as "jury work," and charges $125 an hour to corporations in civil cases and $75 an hour in criminal cases. In certain cases, Schulman says, he charges "what the traffic will bear." . . .

It is precisely the fact that the value — and the cost — of a trial consultant has gone up that troubles critics like Catholic University law professor Leroy D. Clark. He says that the presence of such nonlegal experts in the courtroom makes an already imbalanced system more so.

"There are a whole host of Supreme Court cases which say that the quality of justice should not be modulated by the defendant's resources. That's a fine statement in the ideal. However, these kinds of consultants are almost always brought in by defendants with great resources. You're not going to find them consulting in large urban areas where indigent people are on trial. The defendant who is most apt to be subject to stereotypical kinds of prejudices — minorities, the poor, the uneducated — [is] not going to have the capacity to neutralize the jury in a way that a rich defendant will with this type of resource."

[David] Island [President of the American Society of Trial Consultants] responds: "I think that to pinpoint trial consultants as having a massive effect of making jurisprudence unfair is to miss the point," he says. "You've got to be kidding yourself if you think litigation isn't exceptionally expensive and is not available in the ordinary sense to most citizens of the United States who can't afford to pay the pricetag. To go to trial is a rich person's game — no matter what side you're on."

But the image of trial consultants as just another hired gun for wealthy clients does concern Jay Schulman and a handful of his colleagues. Consequently they spend a significant portion of time doing pro bono work. Schulman's primary concerns are death-penalty cases, women's self-defense cases, and "movement" cases involving those who "like many of us, are seeking to change society," he says. Similarly, he has turned down clients for philosophical reasons, among them ex-Attorney General John Mitchell, Texas oil millionaires Bunker and Nelson Hunt, and Patty Hearst (because she was going to testify against a codefendant and Schulman's client, Wendy Yoshimura).

The National Jury Project, based in Oakland, California, was founded in 1975 by Schulman and a group of politically motivated trial consultants. It is now an independent operation, handling carefully selected criminal and civil cases.

"The majority of people now doing the work have probably made the decision to work for anyone who calls, providing they have the money it takes," says Terri Waller, a consultant with the project. "We are defense-oriented in criminal cases and won't work for the prosecutor. In civil cases the bulk of our work is plaintiff-oriented — usually the types of cases where an individual is bringing a case against a corporation." She periodically turns down monied persons and entities that do not fit the project's criteria. . . .

But Professor Clark believes there are other problems with the trial consultants in the courtroom. . . .

"What are these experts doing?" he asks. "Are they coming in and simply trying to neutralize some arbitrary prejudice against a defendant? No. They're trying to stack the jury so that people, regardless of what the facts are, are going to be biased in favor of the defendant."

Cathy Bennett disagrees that consultants engage in a form of jury rigging. She says that one out of three potential jurors does not tell the truth during jury selection out of fear of being considered biased. "It's hard to admit that you have a prejudice in front of fifty or sixty people," she says. "We all want to be seen as fair people. Many lawyers, when interviewing potential jurors about racial bias, will say, 'Have you ever had any negative experiences with black people?' It doesn't take a Rhodes scholar to know that the right answer to that question is 'no.'"

Those who object to trial consultants frequently assume that their techniques for jury selection are overwhelmingly effective. But many say that this is just not so — that for all the time and money spent, consultants have only a modest influence in the area. Elizabeth Loftus is a psychologist at the University of Washington, and has recently taught a course in law and psychology to the faculty of the Georgetown University Law Center. She says consultants may only be able to account for 9 or 10 percent of the variation in jury verdicts. "In other words," she says, "you can explain a little bit who's going to vote what way, but you probably can't account for how most of the jurors are going to behave."

"So the real question becomes one of cost-benefit tradeoff. How much is it worth to you to have that small advantage? If money is no object, you probably want whatever advantages you can get." . . .

Many lawyers, however, feel that jury selection is hallowed ground. They wouldn't consider using a jury selection expert under any circumstances. "There's no doubt that there is some skepticism among lawyers about the value of it," says Loftus. "After all, they've been selecting juries for a long time and feel that they are pretty good at it."

Leading trial lawyer Philip Corboy of Chicago does not use trial consultants for jury selection; he believes that consultants who give the impression that they know how to pick a jury are misleading their clients.

"I've been trying cases for thirty-five years and I do not know how to select jurors. Why? Because I've always got an adversary. If I could pick juries without that guy sitting there it would be a different matter."

He refers to jury selection as a process of "de-selection."

"Every juror I don't de-select, my opponent has an opportunity to kick off," Corboy says. "So what's left is a set of jurors that each of us thinks is as palatable as possible under the circumstances.". . .

"Lawyers feel that they have a great deal of control over the presentation of the case, and research shows that they usually do. But picking a jury is a real mystery. We lock them up, you don't get to talk to them, and you don't know how they're reacting. So lawyers feel much more unsure of themselves when it comes to jurors, and feel relatively confident when it comes to the case, the witnesses, and the evidence.

"So when a trial consultant comes along and offers his inventory of things he can do for you, what the lawyer is most likely to want help with is the one thing that he or she is not feeling so confident about to begin with — and that's jury selection."

He smiles.

"What it all adds up to is that it doesn't make much of a difference who's on the jury anyway. So you could go to an awful lot of contortions to pick a jury — and it's mostly just based on superstition."

Notes and Questions

1. A considerable amount of constitutional and statutory law affects how juries are selected. Moreover, there are also experts who advise lawyers about the characteristics of persons who would make good jurors from the perspective of the lawyer's client. Is all this learning and effort made irrelevant by the kind of second-guessing of juries described by Margaret Jones?
2. What effect do you think the use of shadow juries and other expensive techniques described by Jones has on the fairness of jury verdicts? On the role of the jury as expresser of community values in the formal legal system? On the public's respect for the institution of the jury? On the jurors' idea of their role and on their willingness to give up personal and work time to serve?
3. Would the widespread usage of jury simulation make jury trial useful only for the wealthy? Suppose the government used these techniques in trials of nonwealthy defendants or in "political" trials in which the defendants did not have equal resources: would these techniques make any difference, since the government's resources and power in trials are already so much greater than those of virtually all defendants?
4. Two techniques described by Jones are jury simulation and jury selection guided by social science data. Do you see any difference between the two in their effect on trials or in their appropriateness in the jury trial system?

☐ The settlement of civil cases out of court and the persistence of widespread plea bargaining in the nation's criminal courts have made trials by jury more the exception than the rule. In spite of the dwindling percentage of cases that result in jury trials, however, many critics are disturbed by the amount of time taken by impaneling the jury and by jury deliberation itself. Crowded court dockets have lent a greater urgency to these criticisms and prompted some states to reduce the size of juries or to eliminate the unanimity requirement in order to reduce the time juries take in being chosen and in deliberating. These actions raise thorny questions about the dynamics of jury deliberation, the representative character of juries, and the constitutional role of juries in the U.S. legal system.

The following three cases and two articles deal with the dynamics of jury deliberation. These readings from law and social science shed light on the direction in which the jury system seems to be moving. Taken together with the other jury materials presented, these readings may suggest that the jury is an endangered social institution.

Williams v. Florida *399 U.S. 78 (1970)*

MR. JUSTICE WHITE *delivered the opinion of the Court.*

Prior to his trial for robbery in the State of Florida, petitioner . . . filed a pretrial motion to impanel a 12-man jury instead of the six-man jury provided by Florida law in all but capital cases. That motion was denied. Petitioner was convicted as charged and was sentenced to life imprisonment. . . . The question in this case then is whether the constitutional guarantee of a trial by "jury" necessarily requires trial by exactly 12 persons, rather than some lesser number — in this case six. We hold that the 12-man panel is not a necessary ingredient of "trial by jury," and that respondent's refusal to impanel more than the six members provided for by Florida law did not violate petitioner's Sixth Amendment rights as applied to the States through the Fourteenth. . . .

The purpose of the jury trial, as we noted in *Duncan,* is to prevent oppression by the Government. . . . Given this purpose, the essential feature of a jury obviously lies in the interposition between the accused and his accuser of the commonsense judgment of a group of laymen, and in the community participation and shared responsibility that results from that group's determination of guilt or innocence. The performance of this role is not a function of the particular number of the body that makes up the jury. To be sure, the number should probably be large enough to promote group deliberation, free from outside attempts at intimidation, and to provide a fair possibility for obtaining a representative cross-section of the community. But we find little reason to think that these goals are in any meaningful sense less likely to be achieved when the jury numbers six, than when it numbers 12 — particularly if the requirement of unanimity is retained. And, certainly the reliability of the jury as a fact-finder hardly seems likely to be a function of its size.

. . . Neither currently available evidence nor theory suggest that the 12-man jury is necessarily more advantageous to the defendant than a jury composed of fewer members.

Similarly, while in theory the number of viewpoints represented on a randomly selected jury ought to increase as the size of the jury increases, in practice the difference between the 12-man and the six-man jury in terms of the cross-section of the community represented seems likely to be negligible.

Some footnotes and citations have been omitted from this case and the two that follow it.

Johnson v. Louisiana *92 S.Ct. 1620 (1972)*

MR. JUSTICE WHITE *delivered the opinion of the Court.*

Under both the Louisiana Constitution and Code of Criminal Procedure, criminal cases in which the punishment is necessarily at hard labor are tried to a jury of 12, and the vote of nine jurors is sufficient to return either a guilty or not guilty verdict. The principle question in this case is whether these provisions allowing less than unanimous verdicts in certain cases are valid under the Due Process and Equal Protection Clauses of the Fourteenth Amendment.

I

Appellant Johnson was arrested at his home on January 20, 1968. . . . Johnson pleaded not guilty, was tried on May 14, 1968, by a 12-man jury and was convicted by a nine-to-three verdict. . . .

II

Appellant argues that in order to give substance to the reasonable doubt standard which the State, by virtue of the Due Process Clause of the Fourteenth Amendment, must satisfy in criminal cases, that clause must be construed to require a unanimous jury verdict in all criminal cases. . . . Concededly, the jurors were told to convict only if convinced of guilt beyond a reasonable doubt. Nor is there any claim that, if the verdict in this case had been unanimous, the evidence would have been insufficient to support it. Appellant focuses instead on the fact that less than all jurors voted to convict and argues that, because three voted to acquit, the reasonable doubt standard has not been satisfied and his conviction is therefore infirm.

We note at the outset that this Court has never held jury unanimity to be a requisite of due process of law. . . . We can find no basis for holding that the nine jurors who voted for his conviction failed to follow their instructions concerning the need for proof beyond such a doubt or that the vote of any one of the nine failed to reflect an honest belief that guilt had been so proved. . . .

We have no grounds for believing that majority jurors, aware of their responsibility and power over the liberty of the defendant, would simply refuse to listen to arguments presented to them in favor of acquittal, terminate discussion and render a verdict. On the contrary it is far more likely that a juror presenting reasoned argument in favor of acquittal would either have his arguments answered or would carry enough other jurors with him to prevent conviction. A majority will cease discussion and outvote a minority only after reasoned discussion has ceased to have persuasive effect or to serve any other purpose — when a minority, that is, continues to insist upon acquittal without having persuasive reasons in support of its position. . . . We conclude, therefore, that, as to the nine jurors who voted to convict, the State satisfied its burden of proving guilt beyond any reasonable doubt. . . .

That rational men disagree is not in itself equivalent to a failure of proof by the State, nor does it indicate infidelity to the reasonable doubt standard. . . .

In order to "facilitate, expedite, and reduce expense in the administration of justice," *State* v. *Lewis*, 129 La. 800, 804, 56 So. 893, 894 (1911), Louisiana has permitted less serious crimes to be tried by five jurors with unanimous verdicts, more serious crimes have required the assent of nine of 12 jurors, and for the most serious crimes a unanimous verdict of 12 jurors is stipulated. In appellant's case, nine jurors rather than five or 12 were required for a verdict. We discern nothing invidious in this classification. . . .

[He] is simply challenging the judgment of the Louisiana Legislature. That body obviously intended to vary the difficulty of proving guilt with the gravity of the offense and the severity of the punishment. We remain unconvinced by anything appellant has presented that this legislative judgment was defective in any constitutional sense.

The judgment of the Supreme Court of Louisiana is therefore

Affirmed.

MR. JUSTICE STEWART, *with whom* MR. JUSTICE BRENNAN *and* MR. JUSTICE MARSHALL *join, dissenting.*

The guarantee against systematic discrimination in the selection of criminal court juries is a fundamental of the Fourteenth Amendment. . . .

The clear purpose of these decisions has been to ensure universal participation of the citizenry in the administration of criminal justice. Yet today's judgment approves the elimination of the one rule that can ensure that such participation will be meaningful — the rule requiring the assent of all jurors before a verdict of conviction or acquittal can be returned. Under today's judgment, nine jurors can simply ignore the views of their fellow panel members of a different race or class.

. . . For only a unanimous jury so selected can serve to minimize the potential bigotry of those who might convict on inadequate evidence, or acquit when evidence of guilt was clear. . . .

The requirement that the verdict of the jury be unanimous, surely as important as these other constitutional requisites, preserves the jury's function in linking law with contemporary society. It provides the simple and effective method endorsed by centuries of experience and history to combat the injuries to the fair administration of justice that can be inflicted by community passion and prejudice.

I dissent.

Apodaca et al. v. Oregon *92 S.Ct. 1628 (1972)*

[In *Apodaca* the court upheld Oregon's jury statute allowing a conviction in a felony case by a jury voting 10–2. The court refuted the claim that minority groups would be excluded from influencing verdicts when unanimity was not required.]

We also cannot accept petitioners' second assumption — that minority groups, even when they are represented on a jury, will not adequately represent the viewpoint of those groups simply because they may be outvoted in the final result. They will be present during all deliberations, and their views will be heard. We cannot assume that the majority of the jury will refuse to weigh the evidence and reach a decision upon rational grounds, just as it must now do in order to obtain unanimous verdicts, or that a majority will deprive a man of his liberty on the basis of prejudice when a minority is presenting a reasonable argument in favor of acquittal. We simply find no proof for the notion that a majority will disregard its instructions and cast its votes for guilt or innocence based on prejudice rather than the evidence.

We accordingly affirm the judgment of the Court of Appeals of Oregon.

It is so ordered.

[MR. JUSTICE DOUGLAS, *in a dissent, found faults in the majority's view of jury deliberations.*]. . .

The diminution of verdict reliability flows from the fact that nonunanimous juries need not debate and deliberate as fully as must unanimous juries. As soon as the requisite majority is attained, further consideration is not required either by Oregon or by Louisiana even though the dissident jurors might, if given the chance, be able to convince the majority. Such persuasion does in fact occasionally occur in States where the unaminous requirement applies: "In roughly one case in ten, the minority eventually succeeds in reversing an initial majority, and these may be cases of special importance."[1]. . .

It is said that there is no evidence that

[1]Kalven and Zeisel, The American Jury 490 (1966). See also The American Jury: Notes for an English Controversy, 48 Chi. Bar Rec. 195 (1967).

majority jurors will refuse to listen to dissenters whose votes are unneeded for conviction. Yet human experience teaches that polite and academic conversation is no substitute for the earnest and robust argument necessary to reach unanimity. As mentioned earlier, in Apodaca's case, whatever courtesy dialogue transpired could not have lasted more than 41 minutes. I fail to understand why the Court should lift from the States the burden of justifying so radical a departure from an accepted and applauded tradition and instead demand that these defendants document with empirical evidence what has always been thought to be too obvious for further study.

☐ The following reading is excerpted from Reid Hastie, Steven Penrod, and Nancy Pennington's extensive jury simulation study, *Inside the Jury*. The study deals with, among other things, the different dynamics occurring in juries operating on a majority rule basis and on a unanimous decision basis.

Inside the Jury: Implications for Law and Social Science

Reid Hastie, Steven Penrod, and Nancy Pennington

At the most elementary level the products of the present mock jury study are facts about the behavior and ideation of jurors. It is a truism of science and philosophy that facts must be connected to a conceptual context to become meaningful or useful. The study's findings have significance in three conceptual domains: legal policy concerning the right to trial by jury, psychological theories of group decision making, and principles to guide attorneys in winning cases at trial.

LEGAL POLICY

The research addresses two questions that interest legal professionals and policy makers concerning the effect of changing the decision rule [unanimity requirement] requirement on jury performance and the factors that facilitate or hinder proper jury decision making. Both questions relate to standards of performance that underlie the legal conceptualization of the right to trial by jury.

At an abstract level, the Supreme Court has defined the function of the jury as to create an effective deliberation process. We translated this general function into five empirically measurable characteristics of effective jury performance: representing a cross-section of the community, expressing a variety of viewpoints, performing accurate and thorough factfinding, remembering and properly applying the judge's instructions on the law, and rendering accurate or proper verdicts. The present study addresses each of these aspects of jury performance except for composition and representation. However, the individual differences found in deliberation behavior are relevant to jury composition and thus to any consideration of which classes or types of individuals ought to be included on (at least not excluded from) juries.

Decision rule affects each of the remaining characteristics of effective deliberation. Decision rule affects the counterbalancing of viewpoints during deliberation, because dissenting viewpoints, or views favored by relatively small numbers of jurors within a jury, are at a relative disadvantage in nonunanimous juries as compared to unanimous juries. Members of very small dissenting factions participate at lower rates in majority rule juries and are less satisfied

---

Abridged from pp. 227–8, 229–30, 231, 233 of *Inside the Jury* by Reid Hastie, Steven Penrod, and Nancy Pennington.

with the jury verdict when compared to small-faction members in unanimous juries.

Decision rule also affects the thoroughness of the jury's consideration of evidence and the law during deliberation, although measures of accuracy on facts and the law per se are not affected by decision rule. Nonunanimous juries discuss both evidence and law during deliberation far less thoroughly than do unanimous rule juries. However, there is no indication that juries are biased in favor of either prosecution or defense as a function of decision rule.

The effect of decision rule on verdict accuracy is not dramatic. However, even subtle signs of a decision rule effect on verdicts are important to a policy maker. . . .

. . . [An] examination of juries with equivalent starting points supports the conclusion that juries in majority decision rule conditions as compared to the unanimous rule are more likely to reach improper, first degree murder verdicts for the stimulus case. For example, five of the unanimous rule juries started deliberation with four or more jurors favoring first degree murder verdicts, but none of these juries rendered such verdicts. Under majority rules, eleven juries started with four or more jurors favoring first degree murder, and four of these juries rendered that verdict. Furthermore, the moderating influence of the longer, more thorough deliberations under the unanimous rule might have damped the sampling effects that occurred in the study and that can also occur in actual juries. . . .

Two other findings on the thoroughness of deliberation, and by implication on the jury's accuracy on the evidence and the law, favor the unanimous decision rule. First, in unanimous juries, a substantial number of important events occur during deliberation after the largest faction has reached a size of eight members. For example, a large proportion of discussion occurs during the interval between the largest faction reaching ten and the verdict being rendered. This discussion usually includes several error corrections and references to the standard of proof. Typically this is also the interval during which requests for additional instructions from the trial judge occur. Second, in juries under the unanimous decision rule, majority factions with eight members, a sufficient number to render a verdict under the eight-out-of-twelve rule, do not always prevail in the final jury verdict; these juries also hang and reverse themselves. In effect, the jury decision task is not completed even when the majority faction is quite large.

Decision rules also affect conditions at the end of deliberation. Majority rule juries finish more quickly than unanimous rule juries. Typically in majority rule juries there are small factions of holdouts, jurors who do not subscribe to the majority-rendered verdict. These holdouts express negative views of the quality of deliberation, and jurors from both majority and holdout factions have lower respect for their fellow jurors' open-mindedness and persuasiveness under the nonunanimous decision rules. These findings favor the unanimous rule.

Other findings emphasize the positive characteristics of majority rule juries. Deliberation time is shorter on the average in majority rule juries. The distribution of final verdicts does not shift dramatically from decision rule to decision rule. Deadlocked juries are also less likely to result under majority rules, and deliberation is more direct, unequivocal, and fierce.

It is up to policy makers and perhaps the voting public to assign appropriate weight to these empirical results. In our view, the unanimous rule appears preferable to majority rules because of the importance of deliberation thoroughness, expression of individual viewpoints, and protection against sampling variability effects of initial verdict preference. Furthermore, because respect for the institution of the jury is a critical condition for public acceptance of jury decisions, the lower postdeliberation evaluations of the quality of their decision by jurors in nonunanimous juries and the larger number of holdouts who reject the jury's verdict under these rules greatly diminish the usefulness of the majority rule jury as a mechanism for resolving legal disputes.

Other factors affect the quality of the jury's performance of deliberative functions. One is the counterbalancing of biases. This counterbalancing has two aspects: inclusion of a variety of viewpoints on the jury panel and expression of all viewpoints during deliberation. The issue of inclusion of viewpoints lies outside of the present study because it depends on the composition of the jury pool and the particular impanelment and selection procedures implemented at trial. But the study's focus on the contents of deliberation yields findings about the expression of views. Members of small factions express themselves less fully under majority decision rules as compared to unanimous rules. Juries that deliberate with an evidence-driven style, starting deliberations with a discussion of evidence rather than law and deferring formal voting until later in deliberation, also tend to discuss more fully and equitably. However, this latter trend is not statistically significant and deserves further study.

In their task of factfinding, juries perform efficiently and accurately. The reconstruction of the testimony and the construction of plausible narrative schemes to order, complete, and condense the trial evidence occur with thoroughness and precision. These accomplishments in jury deliberation are especially impressive when compared to the performance of even the most competent individual jurors. . . .

As for accuracy on the law, jury decision processes do not falter when confronted by abstract legal concepts, such as the beyond reasonable doubt standard, reasonable inference, and the presumption of innocence. Perhaps juries should balk at these conceptual hurdles, but on the whole they manage with an impressive display of common sense. By their actions, jurors acknowledge the impossibility of perfect conceptual clarity and accept crude, but serviceable, approximations.

The major conceptual obstacles to reaching a proper verdict arise from jurors' inability to keep the verdict categories and their elements in order. These conceptual errors do not occur because the judge's instructions are jumbled or overly complex. In fact, the contents of the instructions in the stimulus case are unusually succinct, clear, and crisp. Nonetheless, comprehension, memory, and application of the law are major problems for juries.

To avoid these failures of jury decision making, improvements are needed in the manner in which the trial judge communicates the law to the jury. Many, if not all, of these verdict errors can be avoided if the jury accurately comprehends and retains the judge's substantive instructions concerning the crime categories. Providing the jury with a written transcript, written summary, or audiotaped recording of the final charge can effectively remedy these confusions. The repetition or elaboration of specific instructions by the judge will help when the jury appears to be blocked or requests further instructions. Of course, the judge must exercise care to avoid a misleading or biasing emphasis and must not encourage the jury to depend on the Court rather than its own resources for solutions to the factfinding task. Yet concise, responsive additional instructions can facilitate error correction and productive discussion by the jury. . . .

SOCIAL SCIENCE THEORY

Social science theories of small group behavior, even those that are explicitly designated as relevant to jury decision making, are skeletal and incomplete. For example, none of the models that relate initial juror verdict preferences to jury verdicts attempts to account for information pooling during deliberation. At the same time, most hypotheses about social influence processes do not include considerations of group structure or group dynamics. [The preceding chapter] was an introduction to the . . . computer program, which provides an empirically validated theoretical account of many of the characteristics of jury behavior. The computer model synthesizes theoretical principles from social choice theory, the psychology of small group performance, and attitude change theories. In the model, individual differences in resistance to persuasion, the sizes of extant factions in the jury, and an agenda-like partitioning rule combine to predict accurately the movement of jurors from verdict faction to verdict faction. In addition, the model predicts the effects of variations in jury composition, jury impanelment procedures, jury size, and jury decision rule on the behavior of jurors during deliberation.

Given the economy of assumptions concerning individual and group decision making, the model provides an impressive match to the data from mock juries. In some cases the model predicts behavior that confounds expectations. For example, the model predicts shifts from a modal individual predeliberation verdict of manslaughter to a modal postdeliberation jury verdict of second degree murder, although none of the principles on which the model is founded explicitly prescribe such shifts. The model also identifies phenomena that can not be accounted for with existing theoretical principles. For example, factions grow at different rates under differing decision rules; however, this phenomenon was not predicted by the model.

A class of phenomena that is currently outside the model concerns the contents of discussion during deliberation. First, there is considerable inequality among jurors in the amount of participation in deliberation. This finding is consistent with the dramatic differences between the most and the least talkative participants in almost any group discussion. Higher status occupations, more education, male gender, and foreman status are associated with higher rates of participation. . . .

The Waning of the American Jury

Hans Zeisel

PEOPLE SEE AND EVALUATE THINGS DIFFERENTLY

The jury system is predicated on the insight that people see and evaluate things differently. It is one function of the jury to bring these divergent perceptions and evaluations to the trial process. If all people weighed trial evidence in the same manner, a jury of one would be as good as a jury of twelve because there would never be any disagreement among them. In fact, we know the opposite to be true, if not from observation of our community then from the performance of our juries. Two thirds of all juries find their vote split at the first ballot in a criminal case.

There is, therefore, good reason to believe that the jury, to some extent, brings into the courtroom the differences in perception that exist in the community.

It should not be difficult to see that however well or poorly twelve people may represent a widely stratified community, a six-member jury must do less well. In fact, we can measure the degree of this poorer representation with some precision. Suppose we state the question this way: assume that there is a significant minority in the community, amounting to, say, 10 per cent of the population. The minority need not be a demographic one; it may represent any minority viewpoint, although the obvious concern is for representation of demographically defined minorities. Assume then that our juries are drawn at random from the eligible population. How often will a representative of that minority be on a twelve-member and how often on a six-member jury, both drawn from the same population? The answer is that, on the average, seventy-two of every one hundred twelve-member juries, but only forty-seven of every one hundred six-member juries will have at least one minority representative.

One may argue, and I would, that we should not confront each other as majority and minority. But at this juncture of history, it is apparently not the accepted view to disregard such differences. And to force on the jury a view that is not accepted in other spheres would seem to be a rash move.

Reprinted with permission from the April 1972 *ABA Journal,* The Lawyer's Magazine, published by the American Bar Association.

A somewhat different model will help us to appraise the effect of the six-member jury in civil cases. We know from experience and from many careful studies that the values different people place on the harm done in a personal injury case are likely to diverge considerably.

The final award of a jury is very much related to these initial individual evaluations; in the end it is some kind of average. The size of the jury, therefore, matters a great deal in the determination of these awards. It can be shown that reducing the jury from twelve to six increases what one might call the "gamble" the litigants take by about 40 per cent. The term is not found in the law, but it describes a very real phenomenon — the fact that not all juries will decide a given case alike, while the litigants can have only one of these many possible jury trials. The extent of the "gamble" is easily established by asking any lawyer about to try a personal injury case two questions. What do you think will be the most likely verdict in this case? If you had to try this same case before ten different juries, what do you think their verdicts would look like? The second question will, as a rule, produce a very wide range, often from zero-verdicts (for the defendant) to considerable awards for the plaintiff. Well-established statistical analysis shows that this dispersion of verdicts for six-member juries will be about 40 per cent greater than for the twelve-member juries, hardly an "insignificant difference," as the Court called it. This is best understood by seeing the jury as a "sample" from the pool of all eligible jurors. As Gallup poll watchers, we know by now that the smaller the sample the greater the "sampling error," that is, the dispersion about the mean.

NUMBER OF HUNG JURIES MAY BE REDUCED

In addition to being less representative and increasing the "gamble," smaller juries are also likely to reduce the number of hung juries. The hung jury is an expression of respect for a strongly held dissenting view; it is one of the many noble features of our jury system. And since, on the average, not more than 5 percent of all trials end that way, it is a tolerable burden. Efficiency experts might welcome a still smaller percentage, but those concerned with the justice of our system should be wary.

The Court in *Williams* suggested that one juror against five is not worse off than two against ten, since it is the proportion that matters, not the absolute size. In support, the Court cited *The American Jury* — but in error. There on page 463 my coauthor and I said the exact opposite — that it is not the proportions that matter but the numbers: "[For a juror] to maintain his original position [of dissent] . . . it is necessary for him to have at least one ally."

There was a quick way of testing whether the Court or we are correct. I obtained a special count from the Miami circuit court of the proportion of hung juries among its felony trials before six-member juries. As expected, the proportion was 2.5 per cent, exactly one half of the 5 per cent of hung juries obtained in regular twelve-member jury trials.

But after *Williams* and the diminution of the federal jury, an even more serious potential blow [was] before the Court: the issue as to whether unanimity is essential in verdicts of criminal juries. . . .

Offhand, the unanimity requirement appears to be just another way of reducing the size of the jury; allowing ten out of twelve jurors to find a verdict would seem to be tantamount to a ten-member jury. But it is much worse. Once one sees the problem with precision, the answer is quite clear. In a twelve-member jury, in which ten are allowed to find a verdict, one or two minority dissenters can simply be disregarded. It requires a minority of at least three before the majority is forced to take note of them. In a ten-man jury that must find unanimity, even a single minority dissenter must be taken into account.

One must ask — for example, with respect to a 10 per cent minority in the population — what is the probability that there will be at least three on a twelve-member jury and at least one on a ten-member jury? The answer is that the probability of at least one minority member on a jury of ten is 65 per cent, and the probability of at least three minority members on a jury of twelve is 11 per cent.

The majority rule, aside from reducing the number of hung juries, should result in more convictions. To obtain a conviction under the unanimity rule, the prosecutor must convince the last doubting juror of the defendant's guilt. . . .

. . . By now at least nineteen of the federal district courts have reduced the size of their civil juries from twelve to six in civil cases, and the Northern District of Illinois is experimenting with six-member juries in criminal cases, albeit with consent of both sides.

One wonders what is behind this new zeal for cutting into the jury. The ostensible argument is reducing costs and delay. But the money saved by having six-member civil juries in the federal court amounts to about 2.5 per cent of the federal judicial budget and to a little more than a thousandth part of 1 per cent of the total federal budget. As to the time likely to be saved, the best estimate is three tenths of 1 per cent of the judge's working time. There is obviously more to this concerted drive at this point of time.

Unconsciously, perhaps, the motives are likely to be similar to those that went into the rewriting of the military code of procedure; not only more efficiency, but also less tolerance toward a dissenting minority. At present only about 10 percent of the defendants prosecuted for a felony are acquitted; 90 per cent either plead guilty or are found guilty after trial. Is this too small a percentage? Will the country be safer if it is 91 per cent or 92? One wonders.

By reducing the chances of effective dissent from what the judge would do, we are attacking the jury itself. If we continue to reduce the power of the jury as it stood at common law, we may soon confront the question as to why a jury at all, or why so much of it. Not that this is an improper question. Most countries never had juries, and many of those that had them do not have them any longer. To be sure, also their mode of selecting judges differs radically from ours.

My purpose is not to advocate or oppose any particular solution. It is merely to make clear that the changes imposed on our jury system are more serious than we are led to believe. They are effected, moreover, by the unobtrusive means of rule of court, instead of by the overt acts of the Congress or the state legislatures, which on second thought might consider these changes or their prevention to be their prerogative.

Notes and Questions

1. Does the court in the *Johnson* case equate having a "reasonable doubt" about guilt with "having persuasive reasons" in support of innocence? Why or why not?

2. Does the *Johnson* court reconcile its admission that the Louisiana legislature "obviously intended to vary the difficulty of proving guilt with the gravity of the offense" with its conclusion that the state's jury law does not "indicate infidelity to the reasonable doubt standard"? What questions remain?

3. In his dissent in *Apodaca,* Mr. Justice Douglas wrote,

> The late Learned Hand said that "as a litigant I should dread a lawsuit beyond almost anything else short of sickness and death." At the criminal level that dread multiplies. Any person faced with the awesome power of government is in great jeopardy, even though innocent. Facts are always elusive and often two-faced. What may appear to one to imply guilt may carry no such overtones to another. Every criminal prosecution crosses treacherous ground, for guilt is common to all men.

What significance does this statement have to the question of whether less than unanimous verdicts are constitutionally acceptable?

4. Charles Rembar, in his book *The Law of the Land* (New York: Simon & Schuster, 1980), describes the unanimity requirement as "primitive":

> . . . What was it then, this demand for unanimity? A product, I would say, of the immaturity of the law and the psyche of the time and place. It is characteristic of a

> rudimentary legal system, and it suits the medieval mind, which has no room for doubt. There is a need to deal in absolutes; there is a paralysis without them. Possibilities, probabilities, diverging views of truth — these are notions alien to these people, difficult, disturbing. A thing is so or else not so, and if it is so then everyone must know it.

Do you agree? What differences in the quality of discussion and respect for individual opinions exist between the unanimous decision and the majority decision processes? Can you find social science data or philosophical argument to support your views about this issue? Why didn't the Court consult such data or argument?

5. If six jurors are sufficient under the Constitution as in the *Williams* case, what about five? In *Ballew* v. *Georgia,* 435 U.S. 223 (1978), the Supreme Court ruled that a jury of five required by Georgia law for trial of a misdemeanor (an obscenity versus First Amendment conflict here) violated the Sixth and Fourteenth Amendment rights of defendants. The Court ruled that "the purpose and functioning of the jury in criminal trials is seriously impaired by reduction in size below six members," and that the savings of time and money to the state do not justify such an impairment.

   The Court had found some social science data that convinced a majority of the justices that reductions in size would reduce the quality of group deliberations as well as their accuracy and consistency, would benefit the prosecution in a systematic way, and would reduce the chances of adequate minority representation on the jury as Zeisel saw would be the case. Do you think the line between five and six members can be rationally explained? Should these considerations and these "new" data from the social sciences be read as a strong argument to revert to the requirement of twelve jurors? of nine? Does the legal way of discussing this issue seem at all helpful or perceptive regarding the problem involved?

6. The Hastie, Penrod, and Pennington study, *Inside the Jury,* reported significant differences between the jury dynamics of majority rule and unanimous decision juries. Should this type of information cause the Supreme Court to reevaluate its decision on the constitutionality of majority rule juries in criminal cases? Exactly what kind of jury dynamics should be encouraged by legal doctrine? What is the relationship between the "correct" jury dynamics and the theory of participation and community building on which the jury is built?

7. Although the Hastie et al. study "model" does not deal with the content of jury deliberations, it does imply that there are measurably different levels of participation for individual jurors, depending on their class status. How might a court or legislature take these facts into account in fashioning rules of trial that would affect jury dynamics? Would this knowledge be helpful to those who use shadow juries to develop trial strategies or to those social scientists who advise attorneys during jury selection?

8. In 1975, psychologist June Tapp, who had helped the defense screen prospective jurors on the issue of authoritarianism, was interviewed about her participation in the Wounded Knee trial. She was asked whether, if the government offered to hire "psycholegal technicians" to help in jury selection, she would be willing to recommend one of her own students for the job. Her answer was as follows:

> The decision to work in the public or private sector is a personal one. But the issue is not being pro or con government. Rather it is whether the hunches or fireside inductions that guide legal decision making should reflect systematic psychological findings. . . .
>
> In terms of the politics or ethics of the situation, I suppose how one feels about it depends in part about how one feels about the government and about the law generally. After all, the federal government is not a monolith, a leviathan. Also we operate in an adversary system of law. In criminal cases the government acts on behalf of the people to prosecute the accused for wrongdoing. If the adversary system is to work properly, then it's very important that both sides of the trial have equal access to information and technique.

An individual can choose, of course, whether or not to work for the government in a particular role. But if psychologists can work in governmental settings to effect policy, promote welfare, and in general try to enhance the quality of U.S. life, then it seems to me they belong *everywhere* their knowledge and skills can be used and explored.

I think of laws, and legal reforms, as forms of social experiments, and I think that behavioral scientists should be in places where they help to insure the highest possible quality of those experiments.*

Do you think defendants think of their trials as legal "experiments"? How would you have responded to the question June Tapp was asked? Do you think an expert in this area should feel any responsibility for the use to which his or her knowledge is put? Upon what kind of considerations would you base your own decision about whether to participate in jury selection if you had these skills? Should the legal system set any standards for the use of such techniques? Should these standards affect qualifications of technicians? The economics of accessibility for defendants or prosecutors or plaintiffs to these technicians? Would you recommend that such techniques be barred from the court process? Why or why not?

9. Although nearly 300,000 jury trials reportedly take place each year in the United States, this number represents a small and decreasing percentage of all the cases that could go to the jury. The materials in Section 3 suggest that the quantitative decline of the jury may be matched by a qualitative decline caused by using majority-rule juries, reduced jury size, obfuscating expert testimony, shadow juries during trials, and social science expertise in jury selection. Suppose the jury really is declining for all these reasons. How do the following two quotations help you think about the consequences and motives for this decline?

> But jury trial, at best, is the apotheosis of the amateur. Why should anyone think that twelve persons brought in from the street, selected in various ways for their lack of general ability, should have any special capacity for deciding controversies between persons?
>
> Erwin Griswold, Dean, Harvard Law School, *Report of the Dean* (1963)

> All the sovereigns who have chosen to govern by their own authority, and to direct society instead of obeying its directions, have destroyed or enfeebled the institution of the jury.
>
> Alexis de Tocqueville, *Democracy in America* (1835)

Who or what is the "sovereign" who/that "chooses" to "enfeeble" the jury in modern America? Do the earlier materials on the "Trial of the Future" and on compulsory drug screening suggest an answer? In what kind of society is Dean Griswold's statement inevitable but destructive?

---

*"The Notion of Conspiracy Is Not Tasty to Americans: Interview of June Tapp by Gordon Bermant," *Psychology Today* (May 1975), 60. Reprinted by permission of *Psychology Today.*

4 THE JURY AS CONSCIENCE, INDIVIDUAL AND COLLECTIVE: CIVIL DISOBEDIENCE IN AN AGE OF RULES

Civil disobedience presents perhaps the most revealing avenue for exploring the vitality and importance of the jury system and for uncovering citizens' attitudes toward participation in the jury process. Civil disobedience defies easy rule-oriented decision because it attempts to touch the conscience of the community with a justification for rule breaking. Civil disobedience, especially the kind presented in the following cases, also raises the question of the ordering of principles in a moral or ethical system. When, for example, if ever, can property be destroyed to preserve life? Such dilemmas require all jurors to consider not only the nature of the rule of law but the depths of conscience to which they feel they must go to fulfill the juror's role as they understand it.

Jury nullification is clearly an option where civil disobedience is on trial. In fact, when a case of civil disobedience is the basis of a possible jury nullification, all the issues of popular participation in law come to the surface in a pragmatic context. The juror will probably have to think hard about differences between his or her own views and the views of the community as the juror perceives them. Emotions in this process typically run quite deep, although they are often balanced by the inclination of some to seek refuge from personal and community ethical dilemmas in ready-made formulations of rules and authorities of formal law. Perhaps after deliberating one of the cases of civil disobedience presented here, you may be able to see the ways in which individuals either strengthen or contribute to the demise of the jury system, depending on the consciousness of law and jury role that they bring to the task of serving on a jury.

Review the readings in Section 2 on jury nullification before reading the materials here on civil disobedience. After these readings, a series of cases is presented to allow jury deliberation or class discussion on how these issues of law and conscience ought to be resolved.

While reading the first two selections on the nature of civil disobedience, keep in mind that civil disobedience is a deliberate and carefully thought-out tactic based on a clear understanding of law and morality. It has a long and largely honorable history represented in the United States most eloquently and courageously by Martin Luther King, Jr. Dr. King's "Letter from Birmingham Jail" is included to make clear the basic assumptions and attitudes that generally accompany acts of civil disobedience. Excerpts from former Associate Justice Abe Fortas's *Concerning Dissent and Civil Disobedience* indicate the complex nature and profound consequences of civil disobedience and the jury's reaction to it.

Following these civil disobedience readings are four cases that present problems in jury deliberation. The function of judgment by the community is important in any jury case, whether or not it involves civil disobedience. One explanation for this function is contained in the theories of Emile Durkheim, as represented by Kai Erikson in *Wayward Puritans* (New York: Wiley, 1966). Although jury trials are not specifically discussed in Erikson's work, his description of the role played by community judgment of deviants clearly has major implications for the functioning of juries. Take, for example, the following brief excerpts from Erikson:

> The deviant individual violates rules of conduct which the rest of the community holds in high respect; and when these people come together to express their outrage over the offense and to bear witness against the offender, they develop a tighter bond of solidarity than existed earlier. The excitement generated by the crime, in other words, quickens the tempo of interaction in the group and creates a climate in which the private sentiments of many separate persons are fused together into a common sense of morality. . . .
>
> [S]ingle encounters between the deviant and his community are only fragments of an ongoing social process. Like an article of common law, boundaries remain a meaningful point of reference only so long as they are repeatedly tested by persons on the fringes of the group and repeatedly defended by persons chosen to represent the group's inner morality.

The process by which a community defines an act as deviant provides a focus for group feeling and an opportunity for the group to discover or reaffirm its values. This process of discovery and reaffirmation is the means by which a community maintains its boundaries — the means for defining a culture or society as different from others and possessing its own unique view of human society. It is doubtful whether group cohesion can be maintained without some such boundary-maintaining process, though there is no reason to assume that the process must lead to exclusion rather than to inclusion of the deviant. Deviance may be viewed as a claim on the group leading to a change of group values to accommodate the would-be deviant. Law — especially the jury process — may be viewed as one of our society's major forms of group-process boundary definition — a participatory, group-oriented manipulation of consciousness. That such a process is often transformed into a vehicle for nonparticipatory social control does not eliminate its more democratic possibilities or design.

Excerpt from "Letter from Birmingham Jail" *Martin Luther King, Jr.*

You express a great deal of anxiety over our willingness to break laws. This is certainly a legitimate concern. Since we so diligently urge people to obey the Supreme Court's decision of 1954 outlawing segregation in the public schools, at first glance it may seem rather paradoxical for us consciously to break laws. One may well ask: "How can you advocate breaking some laws and obeying others?" The answer lies in the fact that there are two types of laws: just and unjust. I would be the first to advocate obeying just laws. One has not only a legal but a moral responsibility to obey just laws. Conversely, one has a moral responsibility to disobey unjust laws. I would agree with St. Augustine that "an unjust law is no law at all."

Now, what is the difference between the two? How does one determine whether a law is just or unjust? A just law is man-made code that squares with the moral law or the law of God. An unjust law is a code that is out of harmony with the moral law. To put it in the terms of St. Thomas Aquinas: An unjust law is a human law that is not rooted in eternal law and natural law. Any law that uplifts human personality is just. Any law that degrades human personality is unjust. All segregation statutes are unjust because segregation distorts the soul and damages the personality. It gives the segregator a false sense of superiority and the segregated a false sense of inferiority. Segregation, to use the terminology of the Jewish philosopher Martin Buber, substitutes an "I-it" relationship for an "I-thou" relationship and ends up relegating persons to the status of things. Hence segregation is not only politically, economically and sociologically unsound, it is morally wrong and sinful. Paul Tillich has said that sin is separation. Is not segregation an existential expression of man's tragic separation, his awful estrangement, his terrible sinfulness? Thus it is that I can urge men to obey the 1954 decision of the Supreme Court, for it is morally right; and I can urge them to disobey segregation ordinances, for they are morally wrong.

Let us consider a more concrete example of just and unjust laws. An unjust law is a code that a numerical or power majority group compels a minority group to obey but does not make binding on itself. This is difference made legal. By the same token, a just law is a code that a majority compels a minority to follow and that it is willing to follow itself. This is sameness made legal.

Let me give another explanation. A law is unjust if it is inflicted on a minority that, as a result of being denied the right to vote, had no part in enacting or devising the law. Who can say that the legislature of Alabama which set up that state's segregation laws was democratically elected? Throughout Alabama all sorts of devious methods are used to prevent Negroes from becoming registered voters, and there are some counties in which, even though Negroes constitute a majority of the population, not a single Negro is registered. Can any law enacted under such circumstances be considered democratically structured?

Sometimes a law is just on its face and unjust in its application. For instance, I have been arrested on a charge of parading without a permit. Now, there is nothing wrong in having an ordinance which requires a permit for a parade. But such an ordinance becomes unjust when it is used to maintain segregation and to deny citizens the First-Amendment privilege of peaceful assembly and protest.

I hope you are able to see the distinction I am trying to point out. In no sense do I advocate evading or defying the law, as would the rabid segregationist. That would lead to anarchy. One who breaks an unjust law must do so openly, lovingly, and with a willingness to accept the penalty. I submit that an individual who breaks a law

---

that conscience tells him is unjust and who willingly accepts the penalty of imprisonment in order to arouse the conscience of the community over its injustice, is in reality expressing the highest respect for law.

Of course, there is nothing new about this kind of civil disobedience. It was evidenced sublimely in the refusal of Shadrach, Meshach and Abednego to obey the laws of Nebuchadnezzar, on the ground that a higher moral law was at stake. It was practiced superbly by the early Christians, who were willing to face hungry lions and the excruciating pain of chopping blocks rather than submit to certain unjust laws of the Roman Empire. To a degree, academic freedom is a reality today because Socrates practiced civil disobedience. In our own nation, the Boston Tea Party represented a massive act of civil disobedience.

We should never forget that everything Adolf Hitler did in Germany was "legal" and everything the Hungarian freedom fighters did in Hungary was "illegal." It was "illegal" to aid and comfort a Jew in Hitler's Germany. Even so, I am sure that, had I lived in Germany at the time, I would have aided and comforted my Jewish brothers. If today I lived in a Communist country where certain principles dear to the Christian faith are suppressed, I would openly advocate disobeying that country's antireligious laws.

I must make two honest confessions to you, my Christian and Jewish brothers. First, I must confess that over the past few years I have been gravely disappointed with the white moderate. I have almost reached the regrettable conclusion that the Negro's great stumbling block in his stride toward freedom is not the White Citizen's Counciler or the Ku Klux Klanner, but the white moderate, who is more devoted to "order" than to justice; who prefers a negative peace which is the absence of justice; who constantly says: "I agree with you in the goal you seek, but I cannot agree with your methods of direct action"; who paternalistically believes he can set the timetable for another man's freedom; who lives by a mythical concept of time and who constantly advises the Negro to wait for a "more convenient season." Shallow understanding from people of good will is more frustrating than absolute misunderstanding from people of ill will. Lukewarm acceptance is much more bewildering than outright rejection.

I had hoped that the white moderate would understand that law and order exist for the purpose of establishing justice and that when they fail in this purpose they become the dangerously structured dams that block the flow of social progress. I had hoped that the white moderate would understand that the present tension in the South is a necessary phase of the transition from an obnoxious negative peace, in which the Negro passively accepted his unjust plight, to a substantive and positive peace, in which all men will respect the dignity and worth of human personality. Actually, we who engage in nonviolent direct action are not the creators of tension. We merely bring to the surface the hidden tension that is already alive. We bring it out in the open, where it can be seen and dealt with. Like a boil that can never be cured so long as it is covered up but must be opened with all its ugliness to the natural medicines of air and light, injustice must be exposed, with all the tension its exposure creates, to the light of human conscience and the air of national opinion before it can be cured.

In your statement you assert that our actions, even though peaceful, must be condemned because they precipitate violence. But is this a logical assertion? Isn't this like condemning a robbed man because his possession of money precipitated the evil act of robbery? Isn't this like condemning Socrates because his unswerving commitment to truth and his philosophical inquiries precipitated the act by the misguided populace in which they made him drink hemlock? Isn't this like condemning Jesus because his unique God-conciousness and never-ceasing devotion to God's will precipitated the evil act of crucifixion? We must come to see that, as the federal courts have consistently affirmed, it is wrong to urge an individual to cease his efforts to gain his basic constitutional rights because the quest may precipitate violence. Society must protect the robbed and punish the robber.

I had also hoped that the white moderate would reject the myth concerning time in relation to the struggle for freedom. I have just received a letter from a white brother in Texas. He writes: "All Christians know that the colored people will receive equal rights eventually, but it is possible that you are in too great a religious hurry. It has taken Christinanity almost two thousand years to accomplish what it has. The teachings of Christ take time to come to earth." Such an attitude stems from a tragic misconception of time, from the strangely irrational notion that there is something in the very flow of time that will inevitably cure all ills. Actually, time itself is neutral; it can be used either destructively or constructively. More and more I feel that the people of ill will have used time much more effectively than have the people of good will. We will have to repent in this generation not merely for the hateful words and actions of the bad people but for the appalling silence of the good people. Human progress never rolls in on wheels of inevitability; it comes through the tireless efforts of men willing to be co-workers with God, and without this hard work, time itself becomes an ally of the forces of social stagnation. We must use time creatively, in the knowledge that the time is always ripe to do right. Now is the time to make real the promise of democracy and transform our pending national elegy into a creative psalm of brotherhood. Now is the time to lift our national policy from the quicksand of racial injustice to the solid rock of human dignity.

Concerning Dissent and Civil Disobedience *Justice Abe Fortas*

A fanatic is one who redoubles his efforts when he has forgotten his ends.
— George Santayana

To break the law of the land is always serious, but it is not always wrong.
— Robert Bolt

"Is nonviolence, from your point of view, a form of direct action?" inquired Dr. Thurman. "It is not one form, it is the only form," said Gandhi.

At the beginning of this book, I said that if I had been a Negro in the South, I hope I would have disobeyed the state and local laws denying to Negroes equal access to schools, to voting rights, and to public facilities. If I had disobeyed those laws, I would have been arrested and tried and convicted. Until the Supreme Court ruled that these laws were unconstitutional, I would have been a law violator.

As it turned out, my refusal to obey those laws would have been justified by the courts. But suppose I had been wrong. Suppose the Supreme Court had decided that the laws were constitutional. Despite the deep moral conviction that motivated me — despite the fact that my violation of the discriminatory racial laws would have been in a great cause — I would have been consigned to jail, with no possible remedy except the remote prospect of a pardon.

This may seem harsh. It may seem especially harsh if we assume that I profoundly believe that the law I am violating is immoral and unconstitutional, or and if we assume that the question of its constitutionality is close. *But this is what we mean by the rule of law:* both the government and the individual must accept the result of procedures by which the courts, and ultimately the Supreme Court, decide that the law is such and such, and not so and so; that the law has or has not been violated in a particular situation, and that it is or is not constitutional; and that the individual defendant has or has not been properly convicted and sentenced.

This is the rule of law. The state, the courts, and the individual citizen are bound by a set of laws which have been adopted in a prescribed manner, and the state and the individual must accept the courts' determinations of what those rules are and mean in specific instances. *This is the rule of law,* even if the ultimate judicial decision is by the narrow margin of five to four!

The term "civil disobedience" has been used to apply to a person's refusal to obey a law which the person believes to be immoral or unconstitutional. John Milton's famous defiance of England's law requiring licensing of books by official censors is in this category. He openly announced that he would not comply with it. He assailed the censorship law as an intolerable restriction of freedom, contrary to the basic rights of Englishmen.

The phrase "civil disobedience" has been grossly misapplied in recent years. Civil disobedience, even in its broadest sense, does not apply to efforts to overthrow the government or to seize control of areas or parts of it by force, or by the use of violence to compel the government to grant a measure of autonomy to part of its population. These are programs of revolution. They are not in the same category as the programs of reformers who — like Martin Luther King — seek changes within the established order.

Revolutionists are entitled, of course, to the full benefit of constitutional protections for the *advocacy* of their program. They are even protected in the many types of *action* to bring about a fundamental change, such as the organization of associations and the solicitation of members and support at the polls. But they are not protected in the use of violence. Programs of this sort, if they are pursued, call for law enforcement by police action. They are not likely to raise issues of the subtlety of those with which I am here concerned.

This kind of violent action is in sharp contrast with the theory of civil disobedience which, even where it involves a total or partial repudiation of the principle that the individual should obey the law, does not tolerate violent methods. Thoreau presents an example of a general refusal to accept the authority of the state. Thoreau said he would pay certain taxes — for example, for roads — but not a general tax, to a government which tolerated slavery. Thoreau rejected the proposition that the individual must support all governmental activities, even those which he vigorously opposes. Thoreau asserted the right to choose which taxes he would pay; to decide for himself that this was a morally justified tax and that certain others were not. Government, he said, "can have no pure right over my person and property but what I concede to it." Thoreau's position was not far from that asserted by Joan Baez and others who refused to pay federal taxes which were used to finance the war in Vietnam. But Thoreau's position was less selective. His principle would apply to all acts of government except those which he approved.

The term "civil disobedience" has not been limited to protests in the form of refusal to obey a law because of disapproval of that particular law. It has been applied to another kind of civil disobedience. This is the violation of laws which the protestor does not challenge because of their own terms or effect. The laws themselves are not the subject of attack or protest. They are violated only as a means of protest, like carrying a picket sign. They are violated in order to publicize a protest and to bring pressure on the public or the government to accomplish purposes which have nothing to do with the law that is breached. The great exponent of this type of civil disobedience was Gandhi. He protested the British rule in India by a general program of disobedience to the laws governing ordinary civil life.

The first type, as in Milton's case — the direct refusal to obey the specific law that is the subject of protest — may sometimes be a means, even an essential means, of testing the constitutionality of the law. For example, a young man may be advised by counsel that he must refuse to report for induction in order to challenge the constitutionality of the Selective Service Act. This is very different from the kind of civil disobedience which is *not* engaged in for the purpose of testing the legality of an order within our system of government and laws, but which is practiced as a technique of warfare in a social and political conflict over other issues.

Frequently, of course, civil disobedience is prompted by both motives — by both a desire to make propaganda and to challenge the law. This is true in many instances of refusal to submit to induction. It was true in the case of Mrs. Vivian Kellems, who refused to pay withholding taxes because she thought they were unlawful and she wanted to protest the invasion of her freedom as a capitalist and citizen.

Let me first be clear about a fundamental proposition. The motive of civil disobedience, whatever its type, does not confer immunity for law violation. Especially if the civil disobedience involves violence or a breach of public order prohibited by statute or ordinance, it is the state's duty to arrest the dissident. If he is properly arrested, charged, and convicted, he should be punished by fine or imprisonment, or both, in accordance with the provisions of law, unless the law is invalid in general or as applied.

He may be motivated by the highest moral principles. He may be passionately inspired. He may, indeed, be right in the eyes of history or morality or philosophy. These are not controlling. It is the state's duty to arrest and punish those who violate the laws designed to protect private safety and public order. . . .

We are a government and a people under law. It is not merely *government* that must live under law. Each of us must live under law. Just as our form of life depends upon the government's subordination to law under the Constitution, so it also depends upon the individual's subservience to the laws duly prescribed. Both of these are essential.

Just as we expect the government to be bound by all laws, so each individual is bound by all of the laws under the Constitution. He cannot pick and choose. He cannot substitute his own judgment or passion, however noble, for the rules of law. Thoreau was an inspiring figure and a great writer; but his essay should not be read as a handbook on political science. A citizen cannot demand of his government or of other people obedience to the law, and at the same time claim a right in himself to break it by lawless conduct, free of punishment or penalty. . . .

I have no moral criticism to make of Dr. King's action in this incident [the Birmingham protests of 1961] even though it turned out to be legally unjustified. He led a peaceable demonstration. He acted in good faith. There was good, solid basis for his belief that he did not have to obey the injunction — until the Supreme Court ruled the other way. The Court disagreed with him by a vote of five to four. I was one of the dissenters. Then Dr. King, without complaint or histrionics, accepted the penalty of misjudgment. This, I submit, is action in the great tradition of social protest in a democratic society where all citizens, including protestors, are subject to the rule of law. . . .

An organized society cannot and will not long endure personal and property damage, whatever the reason, context, or occasion.

An organized society will not endure invasion of private premises or public offices, or interference with the work or activities of others if adequate facilities for protest and demonstration are otherwise available.

A democratic society should and must tolerate criticism, protest, demand for change, and organizations and demonstrations within the generally defined limits of the law to marshal support for dissent and change. It should and must make certain that facilities and protection where necessary are provided for these activities.

Protesters and change-seekers must adopt methods within the limits of the law. Despite the inability of anyone always to be certain of the line between the permissible and the forbidden, as a practical matter the lines are reasonably clear.

Violence must not be tolerated; damage to persons or property is intolerable. Any mass demonstration is dangerous, although it may be the most effective constitutional tool of dissent. But it must be kept within the limits of its permissible purpose. The functions of mass demonstrations, in the city or on the campus, are to communicate a point of view; to arouse enthusiasm and group cohesiveness among participants; to attract others to join; and to impress upon the public and the authorities the point advocated by the protesters, the urgency of their demand, and the power behind it. These functions do not include terror, riot, or pillage.

We must accept the discomforts necessarily implicit in a large, *lawful* demonstration because, in a sense, it is part of the dynamics of democracy which depends for its vitality upon the vigorous confrontation of opposing forces. But we cannot and should not endure physical assault upon person or property. This sort of assault is ultimately counter-productive. It polarizes society, and in any polarization, the minority group, although it may achieve initial, limited success, is likely to meet bitter reprisal and rejection of its demands.

In my judgment civil disobedience — the deliberate violation of law — is never justified in our nation, where the law being violated is not itself the focus or target of the protest. So long as our governments obey the mandate of the Constitution and assure facilities and protection for the powerful expression of individual and mass dissent, the disobedience of laws which are not themselves the target of the protest — the violation of law merely as a technique of demonstration — constitutes an act of rebellion, not merely of dissent.

Civil disobedience is violation of law. Any violation of law must be punished, whatever its purpose, as the theory of civil disobedience recognizes. But law violation directed not to the laws or practices that are the subject of dissent, but to unrelated laws which are disobeyed merely to dramatize dissent, may be morally as well as politically unacceptable.

At the beginning of this discussion, I presented the dilemma of obedience to law and the need that sometimes may arise to disobey profoundly immoral or unconstitutional laws. This is another kind of civil disobedience, and the only kind that, in my view, is ever truly defensible as a matter of social morality.

It is only in respect to such laws — laws that are basically offensive to fundamental values of life or the Constitution — that a moral (although not a legal) defense of law violation can possibly be urged. Anyone assuming to make the judgment that a law is in this category assumes a terrible burden. He has undertaken a fearful moral as well as legal responsibility. He should be prepared to submit to prosecution by the state for the violation of law and the imposition of punishment if he is wrong or unsuccessful. He should even admit the correctness of the state's action in seeking to enforce its laws, and he should acquiesce in the ultimate judgment of the courts.

For after all, each of us is a member of an organized society. Each of us benefits from its existence and its order. And each of us must be ready, like Socrates, to accept the verdict of its institutions if we violate their mandate and our challenge is not vindicated. . . .

☐ From among the four cases that follow, readers are asked to select one or more and form juries to deliberate the problems presented. These cases are based almost entirely on actual events. The first case, "The Trial of Sam Lovejoy," is not a traditional civil disobedience case in which a rule is willfully violated out of conviction that it is unjust. But Sam Lovejoy's actions do compel his peers to come squarely to terms with a vital public issue while simultaneously considering the relative importance of maintaining the "rule of law" as it applies to a particular case. Experiments can be done in deliberating this case both by discussing the proper jury selection standards to be applied and by varying the size or unanimity requirement to test what, if any, effect such changes have upon the experiences of the jurors and the quality of group interaction in the jury room.

The primary fictionalization in the Lovejoy case as reported here is in the judge's charge and the suggestion that the case went to the jury. In fact, a flaw in the indictment was discovered after the evidence had been presented, and the case was dismissed. An accurate indictment was never filed, and no new trial was held. The fact that the case never went to a jury was a bitter disappointment to Lovejoy. The inclusion of these materials for your deliberation is an attempt to remedy that omission.

The second case concerns students and others whose protest against CIA campus recruiting and CIA involvement in Central America resulted in charges of criminal trespass. The case is noteworthy not simply because Amy Carter and Abbie Hoffman were among the defendants, but because it used the "necessity" and international law defenses and because the jury acquitted all the defendants. In reviewing the materials on the "Carter-Hoffman" trial, consider that the defense's strategy was to ask the jurors to judge U.S. policy and practice in Central America while deliberating whether the defendants were guilty of criminal trespass.

Notice also that the reading on the necessity defense refers to cases of civil disobedience directed against doctors' offices and other places in whch elective abortions are performed. These instances of antiabortion civil disobedience have ranged from trespassing to destruction of property, and are committed by persons whose moral values are as sincerely held as those of antiwar or antinuclear protesters. Consider your own values, and those of your community, on these issues. How do they affect your views about civil disobedience in general and about the use of jury nullification?

The third and fourth cases, described only briefly, deal with protests against nuclear weaponry and actions taken to advance the sanctuary movement, in which Central and South American refugees are given sanctuary in the United States in apparent violation of law. Both cases can be researched further by consulting the articles they refer to; and jury deliberations, class discussions, or research projects can be generated based on the potential of civil disobedience to provoke intense jury deliberations and possible nullification.

Case 1: The Trial of Sam Lovejoy *Stephen Davis*

Montague, Massachusetts, lies in the green Connecticut River valley, 90 miles west of Boston. It is a beautiful township of gently rolling farmlands and majestic eastern foothills of the Berkshires. Economically Montague is spoken of as a depressed area; the small farms and light industry are slowly dying out, replaced by tract housing and high taxes and unemployment rates. Its two major villages, Montague City and Turner's Falls, look like they've been preserved intact from the Great Depression.

Early in 1973 Northeast Utilities (NU), the power combine that provides electricity to much of rural New England, made an offer to Montague its citizens didn't think they could refuse.

Stephen Davis is a veteran journalist. This article was first published, in longer form, in *The Boston Globe Magazine,* December 1, 1974. Reprinted by permission of the author.

The utility had plans for twin giant nuclear reactors to service the valley with electricity. NU proposed that the plant be built on the Montague Plains, several hundred acres of gravel, scrub oak and pine in the heart of town. The projected cost of the project was $1.52 billion, a figure almost 30 times the assessed value of the town itself. The reactors would go into operation in 1981 with a power capability of 2,300 megawatts; the Montague nuclear station would be the biggest ever built.

Local opinion toward the nuke was largely favorable. Businessmen and town boosters were delirious over the prospects of thousands of jobs, millions of dollars in new business over the years and the mammoth boost to local tax rolls the nuke would bring. An overwhelming majority of the town's 8,500 residents seemed to be in favor of the project.

But the atom has been a controversial little demon since it was first split in 1943, and opposition to the Montague nuke sprung up quickly. A group of university-oriented liberals asked that the project be built underground for safety reasons. The utility turned down the request, stating that it would cost too much and that there were no "major" safety hazards to be concerned about. The local [Franklin County] daily, the *Greenfield Recorder,* quoted NU vice-president Charles Bragg: "Even if there were significant local opposition, it wouldn't affect us."

Faced with the general attitude that the nuke was a foregone conclusion and the lack of any other direct opposition, a loose aggregation of farmers and communards formed Nuclear Objectors for a Pure Environment (NOPE). The people behind this perfectly Yankee rural acronym spent months researching the ecology of the area, the histories of existing nuclear plants and the track record of the federal Atomic Energy Commission (AEC) in monitoring and regulating them.

What the NOPEs discovered turned their stomachs with that cold tangible twist of apocalyptic fear, and they announced their unqualified opposition to the Montague project. NOPE set forth four central issues of health and safety where the Montague nuke could be hazardous.

— All existing nuclear plants exude what the AEC chooses to call "low level" radioactivity into the air. The AEC sets standards for this waste level but tends not to enforce them. Many plants exceed these levels without penalty. In his book *Low Level Radiation,* Dr. Ernest Sternglass of the University of Pittsburgh links this "low level" radioactivity with human birth defects and cancer as it gradually seeps into the local food chain.

— Controlled atomic fission is the source of generating nuclear power. If that reaction gets out of control, a reactor "melt-down" would release thousands of times more radiation than the bomb dropped on Hiroshima. The nuclear power industry and the AEC say this "melt-down" risk is minimal. But the last line of defense against any accident is the Emergency Core Cooling System, which is supposed to flood water on a "runaway" reactor. This system had been tested only six times on model reactors: the system failed all six tests.

— Reactors build solid, highly radioactive wastes with half-lives of thousands of years. Breeder reactors breed plutonium, which can be turned into bombs. The AEC admits it has yet to discover a safe disposal method for this waste. According to AEC statistics a solid waste storage facility at Hanford, Washington, had already leaked radiation 17 times in the last 20 years.

— The proposed Montague nuke would dump millions of gallons of hot, possibly contaminated water into the Connecticut River through the gravel aquifer of the Plains. Also the nuke's twin giant 550-foot cooling towers might emit enough steam to seriously affect the region's weather.

In addition to nuclear dangers, NOPE reasoned that the plant would double the town's population, reducing farmland and forest and ruining the quality of rural life. Although NOPE was a distinct minority in their own town, they were supported by many of their neighbors. The town meetings of adjacent Shutesbury, Leverett and Wendell voted overwhelmingly against the reactors.

In June 1973 the Montague selectmen issued Northeast Utilities a zoning variance to erect a 500-foot high meteorological tower on the Plains prior to construction of the nuke. The tower is required by AEC regulations to monitor meteorological conditions at a proposed site. This is where Sam Lovejoy comes in.

To an engineer the nuke tower might have been a thing of beauty; a high white aluminum-alloy rapier sporting sophisticated eco-data instruments and an Orion's Belt of relentless mercury vapor strobes visible in southern Vermont, 35 miles away.

Sam Lovejoy first saw the tower while driving home one night to his communal family's farm on Montague's Chestnut Hill. He remembers a painful thrill the first time the tower blinked at him through the dusk across the Plains.

"As soon as I saw the thing I instinctively knew it had to come down," Lovejoy said later. "It was such a heavy symbol of their arrogance, a kick in the nuts to all of us who spent our time and money battling the nuke. Now this was months before anything happened but I knew it had to go. I mean, what could be more obvious? Only at the time it wasn't so obvious that it would be *me* that would do it."

Lovejoy was 28 years old and no stranger to radical ideas. A Massachusetts native, Sam's father was a career army officer who passed away when Sam was five. Sam went to Wilbraham Academy and Amherst College, where he turned his frat brothers on to grass and convinced them to declassify their secret society into a public dorm. Sam worked on the *Amherst Student,* then edited by Marshall Bloom, the young activist who led the 1966 anti-Vietnam graduation walkout on Robert McNamara and later founded Liberation News Service. When Bloom moved the "Radical UPI" from New York to a crumbling Montague farm in 1968 Sam joined him soon after, becoming an invaluable member because he was the only communard who actually knew anything about farming.

Later Sam went to Cuba with one of the first Venceremos cane-cutting brigades made up of young Americans. He loved Cuba and the hard work but was turned off by the doctrinaire, humorless rhetoric of the SDSers [Students for a Democratic Society] who were his companions.

By the winter of 1974, months had gone by since the tower had been monitoring the valley wind currents, the NOPE campaign was stagnating due to the apathy of the townspeople and Sam Lovejoy was getting restless. The more research he did into nukes the more nervous he got.

So in the freezing and black small hours of February 22, 1974, on George Washington's birthday, a grim commando dressed in dark clothes carrying carefully muffled tools and a signed statement in his back pocket trudged through the snow-crunchy woods toward the tower. Once he reached the 8-foot chain link fence around the base of the tower, Sam looked around cautiously. Nothing happening for miles except the slight wind and the mechanical clicking of the instruments.

Sam paused a minute, listening, enjoying his own adrenaline and thinking . . . *a shame to waste this fine piece of engineering* . . . and then he went to work. With a wire cutter he sliced through the fence. The turnbuckles maintaining the tower's steel support cables required only a couple of straining turns with a heavy wrench. Once free, the cable snapped back from Sam like a monstrous, vicious whip, the tower shuddered and KKRAAAAANGAANG ANG ANG . . . went down.

Sam looked up. Through the darkness he could see that the lower 100 feet of the tower had survived and was still erect. Deciding to let sleeping towers lie, Sam collected himself, hid his tools in the brush and walked back to nearby Route 63. At three in the morning he flagged down a passing police cruiser and asked for a ride to the station. At the station house Sam lit a Kool and told the sergeant the tower was down. The sergeant had a cruiser go out and confirm that the tower was no more. Then Sam reached into his pocket and handed the sergeant this statement:

George Washington's Birthday

In the long-established tradition of challenging the constitutionality of particular events, I readily admit full responsibility for sabotaging that outrageous symbol of the future nuclear power plant, the NU meteorological tower on the Montague Plains. The Declaration of Independence rightfully legislates action ". . . whenever any form of government becomes destructive of these ends . . . of safety and happiness." The Massachusetts Bill of Rights further states, ". . . The people alone have an incontestable unalienable and indefeasible right to institute government; and to reform, alter or totally change the same, when their protection, safety, prosperity and happiness require it." With the obvious danger of a nuclear power plant, with the biological finality of atomic radiation (and other equally ominous problems), a clear duty was mine to secure for my community the welfare and safety that the government has not only refused to provide, but has conspired to destroy.

I held no malice toward the tower in itself; it was a beautiful engineering feat. Indeed I always dreamed of riding to the top to see the entire valley I am wont to love. Symbolically, however, it represented the most horrendous development this community could imagine. The very spectre of it oppressed us all.

Charles Bragg, a vice-president of N.U., said that local opposition, "wouldn't affect us. We would have to go ahead with it even if there was a protest movement mounted by the citizens of the area." When even the most learned physicists in the country continue to disagree, Prof. Inglis at UMass., for example, the citizens of the town were supposed to make a definitive judgment in a very few months on an issue that would radically alter their lives forever (or perhaps not occur at all!)! Social blackmail! Such perverse logic is a usurpation of normal human rights and cannot be tolerated.

Mr. Charles Bragg also compared the development of nuclear power plants to the western expansion of the railroads. The only possible extension of his logic is to remember the liquidation of the American Indian, and thus realize the ominous repercussions for our own fragile little community.

Characteristic of the times, though, the corporate giants not only extort us by preying on the weakness of the local citizenry, but also they degrade us with bribes. The pleasures of money magnanimously offered in the same vein as the carrot (and the stick). Here where the risks — the costs — are so devastating, the system has thrown the entire issue into the economic and political arenas. Economically for our little community, the proposed power plant budget is greater than Connecticut's entire state budget. Politically speaking, there is no democratic solution to a scientific problem. In a situation where unanimity is imperative, the opposite is true. There can be no trade-off here between money and public welfare.

The Massachusetts Bill of Rights declares, "No man, nor corporation, or association of men have any other title to obtain advantages, or particular and exclusive privileges, distinct from those of the community." And yet, are we not now only beginning to grasp how grossly the great corporations view their profit?

It was announced only recently (after much research, and then and only then admitted officially) that the relatively old Rowe nuclear reactor had not been the impeccably safe place it has been so eagerly billed by the avaricious power companies; indeed the plant had no emergency core cooling system at all until 1972! The ECCS is a rather simple water cooling idea much like a car — except it is supposed to control temperatures comparable to our sun! The AEC itself admits that all ECCS tests have been unsuccessful. The industry says that the AEC did not require one until now! What! say I.

I have been living here in Montague going on five years now, and in the valley for another five. As a farmer concerned about the organic and the natural, I find irradiated fruit, vegetables and meat to be inorganic;

and I can find no natural balance with a nuclear plant in this or any community.

There seems to be no way for our children to be born or raised safely in our community in the very near future. No children? No edible food? What will there be?

While my purpose is not to provoke fear, I believe we must act; positive action is the only option left open to us. Communities have the same rights as individuals. We must seize back control of our own community.

The nuclear energy industry and its support elements in government are practicing actively a form of despotism. They have selected the less populated rural countryside to answer the energy needs of the cities. While not denying the urban need for electrical energy (perhaps addiction is more appropriate), why cannot reactors be built near those they are intended to serve? Is it not more efficient? Or are we witnessing a corrupt balance between population and risk?

In a society only beginning to explore the philosophical implications of abortion, euthanasia and genetic manipulation, do we citizens allow the disunited and unconfident scientists to plop down heaps of high and low level radioactivity in our midst? We truly have not delved into all the repercussions of our actions, yet we seek to proliferate the construction of obviously lethal experiments in ever increasing numbers of backyards? I fear the monsters of infanticide and forced sterilization will raise their heads before this society regains its senses! Jesus begged upon the cross, "Father, forgive them; for they know not what they do."

The energy crisis, so-called, is an obvious signal for the need for immediate and nationwide introspection and re-evaluation. We must give up those false and selfish notions of individual freedom where they impinge on the freedoms necessary for a wholesome and balanced community life. We must bring to an end the greed of the corporate state. We must see that profit, as the modus operandi of our society, is defunct. The American people surely had the power to control their own lives, and I believe they still do; but today it is a question of whether they really want control. "The times, they are a' changing," but it is the task of all men to understand and control these changes.

We must remove the dangerous and sensitive issue of nuclear plant development from the economic and political arenas, and put the issue to a more prudent and judicious test. One of man's highest achievements is the principle and right of trial by jury. In any trial, indeed only one juror need voice skepticism to create a hung jury and a mistrial. The issue that faces us is more horrible even than murder, for here we speak not of one but an exponential number of grotesque deaths and mutilations. Herbert S. Denenberg, insurance commissioner of Pennsylvania, states, "It may be that no one but God could write the insurance policy we need on nuclear reactors!"

It is my firm conviction that if a jury of 12 impartial scientists was empanelled, and following normal legal procedure they were given all pertinent data and arguments: then this jury would never give a unanimous vote for deployment of nuclear reactors amongst the civilian population. Rather, I believe they would call for the complete shutdown of all commercially operated nuclear plants.

Through positive action and a sense of moral outrage, I seek to test my convictions.

Love and affection to all my fellow citizens.

Scratching his head, the sleepy, unbelieving officer read what came to be called "The Washington's Birthday Statement." The sergeant stared at the statement and then booked Sam Lovejoy. In the morning Sam was arraigned in nearby Greenfield and proudly pleaded "absolutely not guilty" to a charge of willful and malicious destruction of personal property, carrying a maximum penalty of five years in prison. Sam convinced the judge that he had turned himself in because he wanted to stand trial, and he was released without bail in his own recognizance.

The trial of Samuel H. Lovejoy began in mid-September at the Franklin County Courthouse in Greenfield, Judge Kent Smith presiding. Sam had decided to defend himself against the charge. "I wanted to show the jury the whole Sam Lovejoy," he said later, "to make this a case of humanity against property."

At the beginning of the trial the jury stared intently at Sam's striking New England features, the ungainly sports jacket just a shade too large for the man's slender frame, the rough work boots, his long hair pulled severely back and tied in a bun.

Judge Smith, as progressive and intelligent a judge as Sam could hope for in this eco-political case, was almost overly solicitous in protecting Lovejoy's rights.

"At first the judge's initial reaction to me acting as my own counsel was uptightness," Sam recalled. "At both pre-trial hearings he strongly cautioned me against the idea. And once the trial began he kept tripping me up, testing me, getting on my back with procedural trivia about my legal motions and my lack of experience." But Sam had been reading the law voraciously in the seven months since he toppled the tower. And he had two lawyers, Tom Lesser and Harvey Silverglate, behind him in the courtroom constantly passing him notes and suggestions.

Assistant District Attorney John Murphy's case for the prosecution was contained in the testimony of one major witness. Sergeant John Cade, the arresting officer, was called to the stand and asked to read the Washington's Birthday Statement and to establish the fact that Lovejoy had voluntarily turned himself in and accepted full responsibility for destruction of the tower.

Lovejoy's strategy was to prove he hadn't acted with malicious intent. As his first witness he called Dr. John Gofman. The short, grey-bearded man was sworn in and presented his credentials to the court: Director of the Lawrence-Livermore Radiation Laboratory at Stanford, co-founder with Glenn Seaborg of the AEC; discoverer of Uranium 233, inventor of the various processes of separating plutonium for producing nuclear power. Several years ago Gofman and Arthur Tamplin wrote an extraordinary AEC study of the potential hazards of nuclear power plants; the controversial report was promptly suppressed by the AEC, which had commissioned it. The two scientists subsequently published their findings as a book, *Poisoned Power.*

Gofman would be a friendly witness. Thirty years before he had helped to pry open Pandora's Box. Now, like many of his original colleagues, he wanted to shut it again for the good of humanity.

The D.A. objected before Gofman could begin to testify, stating that Gofman was in California when the tower was toppled and could present no evidence pertinent to this case.

This got Lovejoy mad. "Your honor, this witness is the key to my case. *Poisoned Power* showed me that the citizen has no recourse from the AEC or any authority in trying to keep nuclear power from coming into a community. He showed me the holocaust that the nuke could bring us. It was John Gofman who led me to the tower that night."

"Now Mr. Lovejoy," the judge asked, "did you talk to Dr. Gofman before you did anything?"

"Did I *talk* to him?" Sam exclaimed, exasperated. "I talked to George Washington and the signers of the Constitution before I did it. I talked to Thoreau when I wrote my statement. Why, your honor, don't *you* talk to Oliver Wendell Holmes when you read his books?"

The judge appeared slightly taken aback at this tirade, yet sustained the prosecution's objection. The same ruling applied to Lovejoy's other expert witness, Professor Howard Zinn of Boston University, who sought to testify on the history of civil disobedience.

After Zinn's testimony the trial was recessed for the weekend. The jury was admonished not to watch television or read the papers while they were home.

When court reconvened on Monday Sam called a succession of local character witnesses, and then put himself on the stand to testify in his own behalf. For a day and a half Sam described his farming background and the deleterious effects of pesticides, talked of his reasearch into the nukes and his reasons for destroying the tower, saying in the end that his act was for the children and their children's children. "They depend on us not to desecrate the land in the name of gross profit," he said. "I knew I had to do at least this for the children." With the testimony at a close, the judge then instructed the jury as follows:

> Ladies and gentlemen of the jury:
>
> The defendant is charged by the Commonwealth of Massachusetts with the crime of malicious destruction of property. Whoever destroys or injures the personal property of another in any manner and by any means, if such destruction or injury is willful and malicious, is guilty of malicious destruction of property.
>
> The burden of proving guilt beyond a reasonable doubt is always upon the prosecution. A reasonable doubt exists if after careful and impartial consideration of all the evidence in the case a juror is not convinced to a moral certainty that the defendant is guilty of the charge.
>
> In order to find the defendant guilty of the charge you must find that the prosecution has proven each and every element of the charge beyond a reasonable doubt. The crime of malicious destruction of property is comprised of four elements: you must find that (1) the tower was the property of Northeastern Utilities and not of the defendant, and (2) that the defendant did actually destroy or injure the tower, and (3) that the defendant acted without the permission of the rightful owner of the tower, and (4) that the injury or destruction was willfully and maliciously committed.
>
> Malice is defined as follows: if there was an intention on the part of the defendant to inflict injury upon property which was (1) not justified on any lawful ground or (2) was not palliated by the existence of any substantial mitigating circumstances, then that intention was malicious within the meaning of the law. Malice does not imply or require proof of ill will by the defendant. Malice is a state of mind which prompts the conscious violation of law to the prejudice or injury of another.
>
> You may take into account all the evidence actually presented to you in this trial. If you do not find that this evidence convinces you beyond a reasonable doubt of each and every element of the crime of malicious destruction of property as defined by me then you must find the defendant not guilty.

[As jurors, determine Lovejoy's guilt or innocence. — Ed.]

☐ The following questions deal specifically with the Lovejoy case, but they raise issues that will come up again in a slightly different form in the less-detailed cases on modern civil disobedience.

Notes and Questions

1. *Jury as a political institution:* As a juror, what was your analysis of the political context and meaning of Lovejoy's act? Did you consider this an apt case for nullification? Would a better purpose be served by Lovejoy's conviction of by his acquittal, in view of his strategy? In view of Dr. King's statements about civil disobedience?

   How much of your difference with other jurors is accounted for by your views about nuclear power? About the proper role of jurors? About the importance of maintaining the rule against destruction of property?

2. *Judicial role of juries:* How seriously did your fellow jurors take your views? Did you feel any pressure to go against your own best judgment? Did you want to explore possible difficulties with the case even after you

reached apparent agreement about how it should end? Did any people on the jury seem to refuse to face the issues? If so, how did they manifest this resistance?

What skills of persuasion or communication did you feel called on to use in the deliberations? Did any leadership structure or pattern of influence develop in your jury? What and how? How might your consciousness of your role have been influenced by the number of jurors or the vote required?

Did you feel in need of more evidence? If so, what kind and from whom?

What would have been lost if, as actually was the case, the Lovejoy trial never reached the jury? From Lovejoy's point of view? From the community's point of view? From the legal process's point of view?

3. *Jury selection:* Who would have been the ideal jurors for this trial? What kind of selection process would yield such jurors? How did your jury depend in its deliberations or verdict on who actually served on your jury? What information did you request or learn about other jurors during the deliberation, and what influence did this have on your thinking? Did any people seem to deserve more respect or carry more weight than others in the jury deliberation?

   Who are Sam Lovejoy's peers in this case? Can this question be answered by reference to his age? Lifestyle? Socioeconomic background? Race? Religion? What were the attitudes of the others jurors about the utility company? Were any peers of the corporation represented in the jury? Should there have been?

   Suppose you were working with a psychologist to help pick a jury for a trial like this? Knowing what you now do about how the discussion progressed, what kind of jurors would you have wanted to eliminate? Is your opinion on this matter at all based on the jurors' attitudes toward law in general? Toward authority? Rules? Expertise? Left to the constitutional standards for fair jury selection, how likely would Sam Lovejoy be to get a fair trial?

4. *History and future:* Is there anything about your experience in this deliberation that would make you feel more strongly or articulate your views more rationally if it were suggested that jury trials be eliminated? Replaced by ordeals? By truth serums?

Case 2: The Necessity Defense Gets a New Workout from Protesters on Both Sides of the Political Spectrum *Holly Metz*

Amy Carter and Abbie Hoffman used it successfully in Northampton, Massachusetts, this past April. So did eight anti-apartheid protesters who had been charged in 1985 with criminal trespass at the Chicago offices of the South African Consulate. And 25 Vermonters were acquitted in 1984 after using it at their trial for staging a sit-in at Senator Robert Stafford's Winsooki office in protest of U.S. involvement in Central America.

What these defendants have in common is the so-called "necessity" defense. When the necessity defense is successfully asserted, technically criminal acts are considered legal because a situation of extreme emergency nullifies the applicability of the normal rules of liability. The necessity defense argues that an offense is justifiable under three conditions: (1) the offenders believe that their actions will prevent a "clear and imminent danger" of greater harm to the community than that caused by their breach of the law; (2) the action can reasonably be expected to abate the danger (a causal

Holly Metz, "The Necessity Defense Gets a New Workout from Protesters on Both Sides of the Political Spectrum," from *Et Al.*, in *Student Lawyer*, November 1987, pp. 12–14. Reprinted by permission of the author.

relationship); (3) and lawful alternatives to the action taken are unavailable.

In the most publicized recent use of the principle, Leonard Weinglass and Tom Lesser, attorneys for Carter and thirteen other defendants (Hoffman defended himself), argued that the protesters should, because the CIA was breaking the law in Central America, be acquitted of trespass and disorderly conduct charges stemming from a 1986 protest against CIA recruitment at the University of Massachusetts.

On November 24, 1986, Hoffman, Carter, and thirteen student protesters had been charged with trespass, after occupying an administration building and demanding that the university bar recruitment of any government agency found in violation of U.S. and international law. The protesters claimed that the CIA has violated, among other laws, the 1984 Boland Amendment, which prohibited CIA operations in Nicaragua. When other activists, who had left the building, saw Hoffman and his associates being dragged and carried out by brusque state police in riot gear, they blocked police buses filled with protesters, and were then charged with disorderly conduct. Weinglass, who is perhaps best known for his 1969 defense of the Chicago Seven . . . , asked the Northampton jury: "Was this lawlessness on the part of the defendants, or were they acting to stop the lawlessness?"

The jury, after hearing one week of expert testimony from such notables as former CIA employee Ralph McGehee, ex-contra leader and recruit Edgar Chamorro, Pentagon Papers tipster Daniel Ellsberg, and former U.S. Attorney General Ramsey Clark, decided that a former president's daughter, a 50-year-old unrepentant radical and author . . . , and thirteen student protesters, were indeed trying to stop illegal CIA activities.

Media commentators balked at the verdict, criticizing the . . . district court judge for permitting the defendants to present evidence to prove their assertion of "necessity," and further, for explaining the principle and its applicability to the jury. "Judge Richard F. Connon instructed the six-member jury in a manner that gave the defense team virtually everything it wanted," a *New York Times* reporter wrote in April. When asked in an interview following the trial why he allowed the defense to be used, Judge Connon quipped, "That's the $64,000 question," then explained that there have been several cases in the state where the Supreme Judicial Court has determined that "the best constitutionally-tested method would be to allow all evidence to be put forward, and, in the end, to rule on admissibility." In some Massachusetts cases, Connon said, "it was left to the fact-finder — in this case, the jury — to decide," adding that the prosecutor in the Carter-Hoffman case "didn't object to it." The prosecution had instead argued that *Commonwealth* v. *Calderia* (the name of the case) was a clear case of trespass/disorderly conduct — nothing more.

Conservatives fumed that the defense had turned the case upside down, putting the CIA on trial and conferring legitimacy on the distinctly left-wing political perspective of the defendants.

Some of the evidence provided by expert witnesses did not address alleged CIA crimes in Nicaragua, but elsewhere. To support his contention that the CIA committed domestic, as well as international crimes, book publisher and attorney William Shattuck was allowed to present evidence about CIA infiltration of student groups during the 1960s, which had violated the First Amendment rights of the organizers. Ralph McGehee testified about training Vietnamese secret police to torture and assassinate civilians — including innocents — during the Vietnam War. A first-hand account of the CIA's recent Central American activities was provided by Chamorro, however, who said that the Nicaraguan contras had received instructions from Argentinian soldiers, hired by the CIA, on how to torture civilians.

The protesters' insistence upon calling the whole exercise "The CIA on Trial Project" unnerved conservative critics, who noted that the successful use of justification defenses in two earlier Illinois cases had justified illegal acts by leftist protesters, creating a new rule of law which essentially acted as a blueprint for those later faced with the same values conflict. (*People* v. *Jarka*, a case tried in April 1985 in the Circuit Court of Lake County, in Waukegan, Illinois, involved defendants who had been charged with mob action and resisting arrest during a protest against U.S. intervention in Central America. They were permitted to assert the necessity defense — as incorporated into the Illinois Criminal Code — and won. A month later, anti-apartheid protesters, in *Chicago* v. *Streeter*, successfully used the *Jarka* ruling as a precedent.)

The necessity defense hasn't always been used primarily by leftists. It originally was raised only in cases involving harm caused by natural forces — as in the 1853 California case of *Surocco* v. *Geary*, in which the demolition of private houses to create a firebreak was considered proper. The common-law roots of the doctrine go back to sixteenth-century England. But it has been introduced, in various forms, into the criminal codes of 22 states, as well as the Model Penal Code. . . .

Feminists have been alarmed by the number of anti-abortion demonstrators who have raised the defense when brought to trial for trespassing at abortion clinics. "As a ballpark figure, I'd say the defense was raised in about fifty cases nationwide on the district court level this year alone," says John O'Keefe, spokesperson for the Pro-Life Non-Violent Action Project, a Gaithersburg, Maryland, group whose members use civil disobedience tactics. Although stalwarts from both camps would probably disagree, O'Keefe claims that pro-lifers "are all over the political spectrum — evenly split between left and right."

Most courts have denied the defense's admissibility in abortion clinic protest cases, although in two Fairfax County, Virginia, district courts a decade ago, anti-abortion protesters were acquitted after presenting evidence that included assertions that life begins at conception. However, courts, faced with such evidence, often dismiss rather than debate the issue of when life begins — a focal point for anti-abortionists, who believe the matter was wrongly sidestepped by the U.S. Supreme Court in *Roe* v. *Wade* in 1973. Despite the *Roe* precedent protection for first-trimester abortions, clinic protesters "routinely" try to raise the defense, O'Keefe says, "*expecting* overruling and conviction."

O'Keefe admits to some bitterness about the successful assertion of the necessity defense in the Carter-Hoffman trial, although he believes that "Amy Carter's protest was laudable." Yet he can't help comparing the greater harm claimed by the student protesters, he says, with the abortions his group has tried to prevent with clinic trespass. "On that Northampton campus, no one's life is in danger. No Nicaraguans were going to be killed in western Massachusetts that day." Pro-lifers, he says, are "cynical about the court system." While abortion is legally considered a fundamental right, neither the presence of a human-created illegal harm, nor the defendant's choice of a lesser harm, can truly be established in court, explains Debbe Levin in her 1979 *University of Cincinnati Law Review* note, "Necessity as a Defense to a Charge of Criminal Trespass in an Abortion Clinic."

Even those who have attempted to raise the necessity defense in antinuclear/anti-intervention cases acknowledge that its successes — like in the Carter-Hoffman trial — are limited. "The necessity defense is generally unsuccessful because the judge doesn't permit it to be raised," says Peter Goldberger, a former professor of criminal law at Villanova University and Whittier College, who contributed material on justification defenses to the appeals brief of the Plowshares Eight, a group of Christian antinuclear activists who hammered nuclear missile nosecones at a Pennsylvania manufacturing plant in 1980. At this writing, that case is still in the courts.

"I'd rather talk about justification generally — in the whole family of criminal law defenses," Goldberger says, adding that activists must realize that precedents from common law jurisdiction are irrelevant when raising the defense in a state where there are statutory restrictions. "There is no national body of precedent and no consistent unitary body of criminal law in the United States," the Philadelphia-based attorney says. The Carter-Hoffman trial may have received much publicity, but Goldberger does not think the necessity defense will be invoked more often as a result.

Francis Boyle, the University of Illinois professor of international law who provided testimony at the Carter-Hoffman trial, agrees. "There is an informal network of lawyers working on such cases pro bono, and they already know about the defense." The question to ask is whether the Northampton victory will stir more protest, says the professor, who is on the consultative council of the Lawyers' Committee on Nuclear Policy, a New York-based national organization of attorneys and scholars concerned with nuclear-related legal issues. He believes it will, although he says there has been no shortage of groups and individuals seeking his advice and counsel in cases involving "nonviolent citizen intervention." He worked with the defense on both the *Jarka* and *Streeter* cases. Since then, Boyle had received "an average of two telephone calls a week on these type of cases."

Antinuclear Plowshares-type actions have continued to occur since the first "disarmament" attempt in 1980. This past August, in the twenty-third such action, two Christians used sledgehammers and bolt cutters on a Missouri missile silo cover. Such defendants, like those at the Carter-Hoffman trial, often attempt to raise justification defenses at their trials, and to present expert testimony on U.S. foreign policy and principles of international law, but these protesters are rarely permitted to do so. The use of nuclear weapons is illegal, they say, according to numerous treaties, and under international law, such as the 1977 addition to the 1949 Geneva Convention, that condemns the use of weapons which cannot discriminate between combatants and noncombatants.

Peter Goldberger suggests that when these defendants' alternative defenses are not allowed to go before a jury, it is for "political, not legal reasons."

What would it mean politically, if a jury acquitted antinuclear defendants using the necessity defense? Unlike the University of Massachusetts protesters, who were charged with misdemeanors, nonviolent Plowshares participants are often accused felons, facing charges including sabotage, possession of burglary tools, and destruction of national defense materials. An acquittal based on the necessity defense would justify their actions, and those of future actors under similar circumstances. And it would indicate that society looks upon such actions favorably, for "when a court applies necessity, its balancing of the harms reflects society's consensus," writes Debbe Levin. "Necessity is meant to justify action that society would clearly want to exonerate."

☐ In the summer of 1986, noted psychiatrist and Professor of Psychiatry John E. Mack was arrested for trespassing at the Nevada nuclear test site in an attempt to protest the construction and testing of nuclear weapons. In a lecture delivered at Harvard's Kirkland House on October 21, 1986, and reprinted in the *Harvard Magazine* of January–February 1987, Dr. Mack described how he came to decide to commit civil disobedience.

Case 3: Action and Academia in the Nuclear Age *John E. Mack*

There are a variety of political actions we may undertake as teachers or as concerned citizens involved in the electoral process, such as writing letters, signing petitions, marching for peace, or working for candidates whose stance on issues we support. But I write particularly about a decision I made last June to be arrested in Mercury, Nevada, at the Nuclear Test Site, in protest of U.S. testing of nuclear weapons. I would assert that the decision to commit nonviolent civil disobedience is compatible with my political analysis and consistent with traditional academic values, if not a direct outgrowth of them. . . .

Professional movements in general and the physicians' movement in particular have avoided civil disobedience or association with it until recently. I personally have had concerns that my access to subjects in doing research would be impeded, or that I would be pegged by my colleagues as undergoing some sort of midlife crisis. Psychiatrists have ways of putting one down that most people never even think of. Those people who have gone to Nevada have felt there was no alternative. Lisa Peattie spoke for all of us in her brief when she wrote that civil disobedience is "necessary to end the relative invisibility of the problem as it exists in daily life. . . . We must call attention to the grave and immediate danger posed by the nuclear arms race.". . .

So here is where I've come to. The nuclear arms race threatens academic life and freedom and everything else we cherish. Some aspects of our education may enable us to see or understand the threat more clearly than others do. Surely we need to be better informed about the nuclear arms race so that we can effectively challenge the basic tenets that have justified its perpetuation and escalation. But in addition to becoming better informed, we have the opportunity — the obligation — to do all we can to oppose this most terrible evil of our time. Each of us can do it in his or her own way. Nonviolent civil disobedience is traditionally American, but one must be prepared for the consequences. King said, "One who breaks an unjust law must do so openly, lovingly, and with a willingness to accept the penalty." For me, personally, there has been something liberating about this action. I recommend civil disobedience for your spiritual health.

☐ On January 29, 1987, Stacey Lynn Merkt began serving a 179-day prison sentence, while pregnant, at the Federal Correctional Institution in Forth Worth, Texas. On April 17, she was released and allowed to serve the remainder of her sentence under house arrest, allowed to leave home only for a daily one-hour walk, to attend Mass on Sundays, and to receive medical care. She had been convicted of 1985 charges of conspiring to transport Central American refugees in the United States. She had, in other words, been part of the sanctuary movement helping Salvadoran refugees escape from persecution and physical threats arising from war in their homeland.

In an earlier case, in 1984, Stacey Merkt was the first person in the United States to be convicted for working in the sanctuary movement, which has grown up in response to the violence in Central America. Although the jury verdict was eventually overturned on appeal, Merkt was later sentenced as a "second offender" for her actions in 1985. About her first conviction, she stated, "I don't think we're often prosecuted or persecuted for our actions. I think often we're prosecuted or persecuted for our beliefs. . . . You have to remember who your true judge is. That has always been a real centering force for me. I've not done anything wrong in the eyes of God, first of all. Nor do I believe I have done anything wrong in the eyes of the true laws that exist here. . . ."

Stacey Merkt's religiously informed reaction to the conflicts in Central America, and the law's reaction to her acts of conscience, are chronicled in the August–September 1987 issue of *Sojourner.* Before her June 1984 sentencing on the first conviction — for which she received three months' suspended sentence and two years' probation — Merkt made the statement reprinted below to U.S. District Court Judge Filemon Vela.

Case 4: The American Sanctuary Movement *Stacey Lynn Merkt*

I stand before you now because 12 persons after 17 hours finally decided that I broke the law. . . .

I wanted to give you a little bit more of a window insight of who I am and what I do. First and foremost, I have a belief in God; a God of life and a God of love and a God of people. I am a lover of life. I have a deep respect for this land, for this soil, and for all that life that she contains. I protect and nurture this earth. That's Stacey the farmer. . . . It pleases me to no end to spade and to feed and to weed and to harvest. I am the one who belongs in the field, especially as I see the connection between creation and people, between food and substances of life.

But I find myself here in the courtroom, and the reason I am here rather than in the field . . . is because I see that we have lost our connection to one another — person to person. We have lost sight of the fact that when any one of our sisters or brothers is hurting, we are hurting. I see that and I have to respond. I can't not respond. . . .

Biblical mandates ask me and command me to extend my hand and also to work for the day when my hand doesn't have to be extended any more. That is what justice is. And there is no peace when there is no justice, and there is no justice when there is no food, when there is no home, when there is no correct way to get those things. I am here to make those connections one to another. . . .

I am no celebrity and I am no martyr and I am no felon, first and foremost. I am a woman with a heart and a mind. My faith commitment connects me to people and to justice. I am a worker. You and me, we are the co-creators right now of this earth inasmuch as we accept that responsibility to work and to transform. You and me, we stand for justice and we don't take that lightly. . . .

Notes and Questions

1. Both John Mack and Stacey Lynn Merkt were found guilty — Merkt by a jury of her peers — of violating laws that had never been invalidated by any court of law. If you had been a juror in these cases, how would you have analyzed the defendants' acts of civil disobedience and the government policies against which they protested? Would your sympathy for, or antipathy to, their moral and political stances have influenced your vote on the jury? Would your feelings have influenced your reaction to a suggestion that the jury acquit the defendant in spite of the clear facts of the case?
2. Should the intensity, sincerity, or morality of the defendant's beliefs and intentions affect how the defendant is treated by the legal system? Might you have argued for the defendant's acquittal in cases like Mack's and

Merkt's even if the defendant expressed a willingness to accept punishment for the act of civil disobedience? What is the proper role and allegiance of the juror in cases such as these — to enforce the violated statute or rule? To convict the defendant, in order to further the consciousness-raising process of civil disobedience? Or to acquit the defendant if the jurors share his or her beliefs about the actions being protested?

3. Look back over the articles by King, Fortas, and Scheflin. Which provides the best guidance about the proper role of the jury as an instrument of popular participation in law? Do you think that the U.S. legal system and prevailing public attitudes about it are adequate for dealing with the kinds of government policies and individual protests represented by the civil disobedience cases in this section? Explain your answer.

5 COMMUNITY PARTICIPATION: OTHER FORMS, OTHER CULTURES

The need to relate public participation to legal process is common to all cultures, but the forms this participation takes are as varied as the cultures themselves. In some cultures, such as that of the Cheyenne nation in North America, there may be no separation of the legal institution from the rest of social life. Conflicts arise and are handled without formal legal roles, yet participation does take characteristic forms. The story of Two Twists and Red Robe is a marvelously complex and sophisticated example of conflict resolution, which represents a legal process so different from what we expect that we may at first have trouble seeing that there is any law in it at all. Yet once we do see the law in this brief story, our understanding of the uses of participation in community building is greatly increased.

Even when the legal institution is a separate one, there need not be a separation of rule making and rule application as there is in much of Western law. The Chinese divorce trial demonstrates how a wide network of participants in a legal system without a clear separation of rule making and adjudication leads to new possibilities for defining conflict and resolving it.

The Chinese divorce trial transcript is followed by a brief excerpt from the work of U.S. law professor Victor Li, which puts this one trial in the broader context of Chinese legal tradition and current practice. Li's work stresses the social role and ideological significance of public participation in formal law in socialist or populist societies.

Participation may be explicitly built into a legal system as a means of educating the populace in a revolutionary consciousness and demonstrating a commitment to popular sovereignty. The Cuban Popular Tribunals were organized around such an ideology and seem to share the dual goals that Tocqueville ascribed to American jury trials: to influence the people and to empower them. Changes that occurred in Cuba between the writing of the first and second articles highlight the importance of participation not only for the form of law but for the definition of justice.

When Two Twists Led the Cheyennes Against the Crows

Karl N. Llewellyn and E. Adamson Hoebel

Red Robe's two sons were killed by the Crows quite a while back; their father in his grief stood before his lodge in mourning and called out, "All of my horses are for those who take them." He threw the whole herd away, not keeping even one for himself to ride upon.

The Dog Soldiers went out to herd his horses together, because they simply were not going to see the old man afoot. "No one is going to take these horses," they said. Then they sent an old man to see Red Robe.

"Your sons died like men," this messenger reminded him. "They died the glorious death, not in bed sick. Why don't you take back some ponies?"

"No," Red Robe replied, "Maiyun [the Supernatural] wanted my sons to die in battle and it wants that I should be afoot awhile." Whatever they said, they could not budge him.

Finally, four soldier troops [the Elk, Bowstring, Dog, and Fox] decided to go talk to him. He had been a good man in the tribe and here he was destitute. When the camp moved, he was the last to come along. He had nothing to camp with, but just stayed in the open. This had gone on three or four months when the soldiers got together. They all came to Red Robe, but one or two did the talking for them all. "We are begging you to do what we ask you — we are not alone — see them all — every company among us is here. We still have your horses. Come in among the people."

Still he was unmoved by all their pleading. At last Two Twists, a chief of the Bowstring Soldiers, came forward. "Say yes," he implored the old man. "Say yes, and we will promise you to go to war against the Crows wherever they may be. Say yes, and I'll get revenge for you whatever the risks. If they be in breastworks, I'll drive them out."

"I accept," the bereaved old man finally answered. "I did not want to take those horses back after giving them away. It's like taking back a thing given to a friend."

"No, it is not like that to us," the soldiers all assured him.

So Red Robe came into camp. In the days which followed after, Two Twists prepared his pipe, taking it to all the soldier societies. Everyone smoked, whole troops pledging themselves to vengeance on the Crows. When all was ready the societies moved to the raid in a body. Women and children went too, for the whole tribe was on the march. Two Twists was the leader of them all.

When they had come close to the enemy, Two Twists rode about the camp accompanied by his crier, who called for the people to listen. Two Twists spoke in this vein. "Look at me now. Soon I am about to follow the two sons of Red Robe. My friends, behold me; I shall never return from this raid."

The women all came out of their lodges to gaze at him. They sang him many heartening songs of which one was this — "Only the rocks

---

lie here and never move. The human being vapors away." That night Two Twists sang the war songs of the Bowstring Soldiers.

The people were anxious to face the enemy, but the chiefs held them in. In the meantime the Crow scouts had spotted the Cheyennes and warned their camp. That night they built a breastwork of all their tipis arranged in a semicircle.

The next morning Two Twists was out in the camp again. "I sing for the last time," he cried. "People, behold me! This is my last time to walk on earth."

From all around folks brought him feathers, to help him in the thing he was to do. They tied them to his war bonnet, to his horse's mane, and to its tail.

At last the fighters went toward the Crow camp. Two Twists led them, armed only with a sabre. When they were before the enemy, he ordered his followers to hold back; he had his promise to fulfill. And so they all watched as he rode out alone toward the waiting enemy.

Straight at the tipis and into the breastwork he charged, slashing off the head of a Crow warrior as he broke through. He wheeled about, charging into the thick of them again, working havoc where his sword fell. The Crows shot, but missed and missed. Then our people saw Two Twists disappear among them in hand-to-hand struggle.

Then the Cheyennes charged into the Crows killing them on all sides. Red Robe's wife charged with an ax. Wherever she found a Crow dead or wounded she split his skull to smear the blood of the enemy upon her face and arms [pantomimed by the informant with proper gusto]. Red Robe joined in by cutting the arm from a dead Crow. He carried it into the scalp dance to scare the women with. E-E-E-E — he would hit them in the back with it; they would run screaming.

Two Twists was not killed, and from his deeds he derived the greatest honor. People said he had done his work; they would never let him do so again; he need not fulfill his vow to die. Back in camp, Two Twists sent for Red Robe and his two wives and children. He himself stripped them of their mourning rags and dressed them well. Many things were given to the women, and now Red Robe took back his horses. They, too, participated in the victory joy of the camp.

Red Robe went back to his lodge and in his turn sent for a crier to get Two Twists. Red Robe was accepting felicitations from everybody. To each person who came to greet him he gave a horse. He painted the faces of all adult comers with black charcoal — the symbol of joy in the death of the enemy. Of all his horses he kept only a few for himself, and this time he was not stopped by the soldiers.

At the end, he adopted Two Twists for his son. Two Twists was not a tribal chief then, only the leader of a soldier society; later he was made a big chief, but on that one occasion he had charge of the whole tribe. He had wanted to wear the Medicine Hat in the battle, and he had told the keeper he wished to wear it, but the keeper gave no answer. It was the keeper's wife who refused him. "You are going to war never to return. I do not think it right for us to give you the Hat. You will get it bloody; you would bring us great trouble; blood on the Hat would mean blood for all the tribe."

Notes and Questions

1. If a citizen of modern American society were to give away all his or her material possessions, do you think they would be met by the same reaction as Red Robe was? What did Red Robe hope to accomplish — consciously or subconsciously — by what he did? What does the success of his action tell us about the nature of Cheyenne culture compared to modern American society? Red Robe departed from ordinary Cheyenne custom — why wasn't he labeled a deviant?
2. Who did "the law jobs" in this story, and what were those jobs? Why did Two Twists and the others wait so long before offering to avenge Red Robe's sons' deaths? What was the function of the ritual ride around the Cheyenne camp by Two Twists? Can you say what, if any, group values were established or clarified by the actions in this story? Did this society reward those who did the law

jobs? How much and what kind of participation in conflict definition and resolution did Cheyenee culture seem to expect?

3. Would these expectations be effective in modern American culture or in any of its subgroups? How much does the ideology of individualism obstruct this kind of participation and group defining in the United States?

The following transcript of a 1972 divorce trial in Peking was recorded by Doris Brin Walker, a California lawyer and former president of the National Lawyers Guild. The trial itself is part of a long continuum of informal and formal mechanisms for conflict definition and resolution in the People's Republic of China.

The Chinese have traditionally looked down on formal legal process and law in favor of educational means of defining and controlling patterns of behavior. The trial included here comes only after the failure of many of these informal, mediating, or educational processes. All of these other methods are said to express the "mass line" in legal work by which an ideological commitment to mass participation in law is effectuated.

People's Court in China: Trial of a Divorce Case *Doris Brin Walker*

CHIEF JUDGE: Our procedure is for the parties to the case and the masses to participate and make proposals, using criticism and self-criticism. Tell us your age and nationality.

WIFE: 33 years old; Han; middle peasant family from Hopei Province; middle school education.

CHIEF JUDGE: Salary?

WIFE: 41 yen per month.

HUSBAND: 39; Han; Peking middle peasant; junior middle school.

CHIEF JUDGE: Salary?

HUSBAND: 70 yen per month.

CHIEF JUDGE: What are your reasons for seeking a divorce?

WIFE: We got acquainted through introduction by friends. Married in 1961: daughter born 1962. Had usual feelings of newly-married couple. Then I got maternal disease of irregular menses and had to stay home from work for two months. I still suffer from this illness. This led to conflicts in our sex life. At first we forgave each other, but as time passed, this was no longer possible. I myself was at fault and was often unhappy, although my husband was often quite understanding. He said that I should not become pregnant again because of this disease. Thereafter our sex life was not good. So I said this was not good for family life, and my grandmother proposed that I get a divorce and I thought this was reasonable. She told my husband that he could not sacrifice his spiritual life because I was sick. She told him that he was still in good condition and must consider future generations. For myself, I was still reluctant to get divorced, but thought I could take care of our child. Often I was very sorry, but often too sick to get up. Sometimes my husband could not suppress his sexual desires. Our Constitution says if marriage is not feasible, the couple can be separated for the sake of work and daily life.

From Doris Brin Walker, "People's Court in China: Trial of a Divorce Case," from The Guild Practitioner, Vol. 30, No. 2 and 3 (September 1973), pp. 45–53.

HUSBAND: Our problem is of long standing. She says her disease is the main problem, and she is really sick, but I do not think it is as serious as she says. The main thing is her mental feeling; the spiritual burden on her is very heavy. I think the problem can be solved, but now, since she says we should be separated, I cannot but agree.

CHIEF JUDGE: How long did you know each other before marriage?

HUSBAND: About two years. We fell in love in May, 1959. I worked in this office; she lived in the dormitory of the office building and worked on the construction team there. Later we met through an official introduction.

CHIEF JUDGE: Tell us how you felt about each other before marriage and right afterward?

WIFE: Those were the best times, but just so-so; not very bad or good. At times I thought he was quite good in some respects. Before the birth of our child, sex relations were good.

REPRESENTATIVE OF HUSBAND'S WORK UNIT: Feelings appear quite good before then.

CHIEF JUDGE: Describe conflicts and basic relations.

HUSBAND: Generally good. Busy with work. I had heavy tasks, had to travel; she handled family affairs. Until she suggested in 1968 that I suppress my sex desires. Then there was trouble. Before 1968 no big conflicts. Let her tell about conflicts.

ASSISTANT JUDGE: Has your husband stated all the main reasons?

WIFE: Yes.

CHIEF JUDGE: [reviewing husband's story] Did the misunderstandings change in character? Did they become deeper? Help us analyze the case. Your comrades know about you, but your expressions will help us to handle the contradictions according to Chairman Mao's teaching and laws. For example, when did the contradictions become very sharp?

WIFE: Sharpened after 1968. My disease was worse and I felt very bored. Quarrels could not be avoided, also misunderstandings. I was sick and he could not understand me very well.

CHIEF JUDGE: First, your sickness; second, married life no good; third, misunderstandings. Also the wife felt the husband did not show enough consideration. Right?

HUSBAND: In addition, we now have no affection; the sentiment has been broken. This has affected our work, confused our minds. After many years, I agreed to separation.

CHIEF JUDGE: How old is your child now?

HUSBAND: Ten.

CHIEF JUDGE: Have you ever talked to her about separating?

WIFE: No.

HUSBAND: No, but she knows that we quarrel.

CHIEF JUDGE: We must consider whether the situation is serious enough to warrant separation. Describe the worst quarrel.

WIFE: You say.

HUSBAND: She was to handle family affairs, but she spent her own salary and then often came to my office to find me. Often she went to the responsible leadership for help. She could not work well, due to her illness. We never cursed each other or fought. We went to comrades and finally to court for help.

CHIEF JUDGE: Your husband says you did not pay attention to family affairs; made a disturbance in his work unit, and aroused bad feelings toward him.

WIFE: Basically true.

CHIEF JUDGE: Apart from buying something for your child, you spent your own salary and made trouble. Yes?

WIFE: Yes.

CHIEF JUDGE: You did not show consideration for your wife, though she had done enough as a revolutionary partner? According to article 8 of the Marriage Law, spouses are to love, help and raise children together. When there are shortcomings, they are to be solved through criticism and self-criticism.

HUSBAND: Generally I was all right about carrying out my obligations. After she proposed separation, my feelings were hurt; then sometimes I showed insufficient consideration.

CHIEF JUDGE: What about plans for your child?

WIFE: Since kindergarten at age 4, she has been living with my husband's mother in the countryside because we are working here. I pay half her expenses for clothing and so forth.

CHIEF JUDGE: Why not tell [the] child?

WIFE: Too young; it might affect her mentally and make her unhappy. I will tell her when she is older.

CHIEF JUDGE: [to Representatives of Work Units] You know details better than we do. Leading comrades, please give us your description of the situation and your ideas.

REPRESENTATIVE OF WIFE'S WORK UNIT: We first learned of the troubles in 1969 when the wife brought bedding to sleep in our station. We asked her why. She was too shy to tell the details because I am a man, so I asked a woman comrade to talk with her and get details. We gave help, education for unity. Then she returned home, but there were frequent disputes and we tried to work with them. The situation was better, then worse, etc. As to her demand for separation, we think more work should be done before this is accepted, but her demand was urgent, so we signed approval.

REPRESENTATIVE OF WIFE'S WORK UNIT: I talked with the wife in 1969 when she came with bedding and child. I expressed my concern for the child and her view of her parents. I said there should be more self-criticism by husband and wife to see strong points of each. I pointed out her workplace was too far from the child's school and that she would arouse her husband's suspicions if she stayed at the workplace; that is not a correct way to handle conflicts.

REPRESENTATIVE OF WORK UNIT: [also from wife's unit; voiced similar views]

WIFE: The grandmother is reluctant to have the child leave her.

COMRADE: How can you as parents leave your own child if the grandmother cannot?

ASSISTANT JUDGE: [after reviewing everyone's list of the problems] If the husband shows more consideration during menses, maybe this will help solve the problems. Contradictions about sex life are not big contradictions. Perhaps a family meeting with the grandparents would help. There are no fundamental contradictions.

REPRESENTATIVE OF HUSBAND'S WORK UNIT: I have a good understanding of the husband, but don't know the wife well. My opinion now is that they have a good sentimental basis for marriage from their early years. The main contradiction is in sex life. Revolutionary comrades should keep each other, though they cannot agree on all matters. Both are responsible for situation. Why did the husband finally agree to divorce? Very painful for him. His wife came here to see the leadership and sometimes she exaggerated her husband's misdeeds. This affected her husband's colleagues and embarrassed him. That's why he agreed to separation. The wife should try harder to cure her illness and he should show more understanding. Divorce is bad for the mind of a child. How can you as parents live apart from your own child? This must influence her feelings. Try to solve contradictions through criticism and self-criticism.

HUSBAND'S FRIEND: The contradiction can be solved. She can try more for a cure and he should try to understand. [While she reviews problems, husband's left leg and foot continuously jerk up and down.] And what happens to the child if you remarry? [Leader of husband's unit repeats previous speakers.]

CHIEF JUDGE: Both parties have suffered spiritually. Under article 17 of the Marriage Law, if both sides agree to a divorce, the court will approve. You should consider this again very seriously. Are you really at a stage where you should be separated? According to Chairman Mao, there are no fundamental contradictions within the working class. I see none between you. The basis for your marriage is good. Self-criticism can find defects and make it possible to continue the marriage. As to the wife's disease, medical facilities in our country can cure many now, and they are getting better. Do you think after hearing your comrades you can make more self-criticism and reconcile? [to wife] You want a divorce, but haven't told your child. This shows a contradiction in you, that you are still uncertain. [As Chief Judge continues, husband holds his forehead.]

WIFE: You are earnest and frank. I am touched and grateful. But there is an acute struggle in my mind. If we reconcile and contradictions arise again, how will we resolve them? [Husband shows pained expression.] I must insist on my demand. This will save trouble for the leadership.

CHIEF JUDGE: Your mind is entangled with contradictions. Self-criticism will solve problems if you reconcile. Do you think all the fault is with your husband? If you reconcile and new problems arise, you can put forward certain demands on your husband. Have you really shown enough effort?

COMRADE: You may repent later if you separate now. Better reconcile — better for work and politically.

CHIEF JUDGE: What do you say? I have misgivings about a separation. You ought to be reconciled, but I see you did not criticize yourself enough or make enough demands on your husband. In the future, make more demands on yourself and show more responsibility in the family. And I say to grandparents and husband: have a family meeting. Discuss the practical problems: the wife told exaggerated stories about the husband at his work unit. He lost face and it was not good for his work. And she is afraid of future complications.

ASSISTANT JUDGE: Don't be afraid of contradictions. You will get help if they arise in the future. New unity can be reached and comrades will help.

HUSBAND'S FRIEND: Don't be afraid of future or about his attitude in future. He is a cadre with responsibilities.

CHIEF JUDGE: My final opinion is that this contradiction cannot be solved by divorce.

Others speak, mainly to wife.

CHIEF JUDGE: Tell us your final decision. [to husband] If you agree, we must grant separation. [more comments to wife]

WOMAN COMRADE: [to wife] Have faith in comrades as to future help.

WOMAN ASSISTANT JUDGE: The wife wants her husband to express his feelings.

CHIEF JUDGE: [irritated] He already has. Have faith in comrades.

ASSISTANT JUDGE: Your husband cannot be blamed for everything. In some respects your husband is quite good. He should improve.

COMRADE: Do not fear your husband will make some reprisal against you. We know his political consciousness and integrity.

COMRADE: Your husband treated you quite well despite your hot temper. Your minds are now open to each other; life will be happier.

CHIEF JUDGE: Let's hear first from the wife.

WIFE: You have been patient and given good advice. I would like to be reconciled. I will make more strict demands for help and will take more family responsibility. I withdraw my request for separation.

HUSBAND: For years I did not agree to divorce until I felt I must. Since she now agrees not to separate, I agree. All details and future plans cannot be solved here, but the basis for the future is certain now.

CHIEF JUDGE: Look to your comrades and, if necessary, to court for help. Rest for a while. Wait in another room while we study the situation.

Recess.

In absence of parties and witnesses, judges confer.

CHIEF JUDGE: There is a very acute struggle in her mind.
[Discussion among judges. Agree to reconciliation: welcome it; must work on the next stage in the relationship, including the grandmother.]

Parties return.

CHIEF JUDGE: We agree to your present view, that there is insufficient reason to separate and you now agree to reconcile. We have heard the wife's misgivings, and you must arrange for future meetings between yourselves, with your families, and within your work units. [to wife] Will you sign the minutes of the court?

Wife signs.

Husband signs.

CHIEF JUDGE: If you would like to read the minutes, you can come to court to read them and see if there are any mistakes.

Hearing concluded.

The Evolution and Development of the Chinese Legal System

Victor H. Li

TWO MODELS OF LAW

During the past twenty years, the Communist Chinese have used two separate models of law, each having its own rationale and objectives. Depending on the period, one model or the other has been dominant, but on the whole, they have existed side by side in a combination of harmony and competition.

The first model (for convenience, I will call it the "external model") is based upon the establishment of a formal, detailed, and usually written set of rules, that is, a legal code which defines permissible and impermissible conduct. A governmental organization enforces compliance with these rules, resolves ambiguities, and settles disputes. This organization in turn has regulations of its own that specify the manner in which it should operate and that provide means for members of the public to obtain redress against improper official actions. Generally, the legal system and the rules of law tend to be complicated and difficult to understand. Trained specialists are required to manage the legal bureaucracy and to act as legal advisors to the public.

This model of law is similar to and derives mainly from the Western legal concepts that were introduced into China at the beginning of this century, and reinfused into Chinese life with the adoption of Soviet legal institutions, methods and thinking after Liberation in 1949. To a lesser degree, this model also is influenced by traditional Chinese legal practices. Some of the early legalist philosophers (fachia) had similar attitudes toward the role and function of law. More important, in spite of the Confucian disdain for formal coercive law, China has had for many centuries an active and complex legal system, complete with codes, courts and the like. Thus, as part of their cultural heritage, the Communists posessed some familiarity with a formal legal system and with centralized bureaucratic government.

The adoption of the external model of law provides many advantages for the Chinese. For one thing, it makes the Chinese legal system more recognizable, and consequently more acceptable, to the West and to the Soviet Union. China's past difficulties with Western criticism of the Chinese legal system and with extraterritoriality make this an important consideration. The external model also provides a clear and rationalized system of government and administration to nation builders who are seeking clarity and rationality; and it strengthens central control. Through the establishment of legal rules and procedures, higher level authorities not only can provide guidance for lower level officials, but also can restrict the scope of their discretionary powers. Moreover, through the medium of law, the public can know when an official is acting improperly and can inform the higher level authorities through the various complaint and appeal procedures. The legal system also is an effective means of controlling the public. In addition to maintaining a degree of public order, law can be used to publicize and to enforce new social policies, as well as to monitor the implementation of and response to these policies.

The second model of law (I will call it the "internal model") is quite different. Proper modes of behavior are taught not through written laws, but rather through a lengthy and continuing educational process whereby a person first learns and then internalizes the socially accepted values and norms. Compliance is obtained not through fear of governmental punishment, but from a genuine understanding and acceptance of the proper rules of conduct. Where such self-control fails, social pressure arises spontaneously to correct and to control the deviant. The coercive power of the state is used for enforcement only in the most serious cases in which the deviant is particularly recalcitrant or depraved. Since each individual is deeply involved in the legal process, law must be simple and must be capable of being applied without the help of skilled specialists. And, since enforcement is handled to a great extent by the community at large, the role of the state in legal administration is limited and the size of the legal bureaucracy is small.

This model seems to include many traditional Chinese ideas and practices. Especially stirking is its similarity to the concept of *li* [informal norms of behavior]. Both rely heavily upon persuasion and education rather than force, and upon the use of social pressure rather than governmental power. Both also stress the importance of internalizing the rules of conduct and point out the ineffectiveness of using fear of punishment to make people behave. Indeed, if one substitutes the term "socialist morality" for "Confucian morality" and the term "comrade" for "*chun-tzu*" (gentleman), one can use some of the Chinese classics to describe this model of law.

While the traditional influences certainly are present, other factors are no less important. Communist Chinese ideology, for example, calls for the participation and involvement of the masses in all aspects of government, including law. Some degree of decision making and of sanctioning power also is granted to the masses, or at least to a local social group. Ideological commitment to the mass line is reinforced by some practical considerations. To begin with, internalization of the socially accepted values and norms is a more effective means of controlling conduct than the use of coercive force, and self-policing is much cheaper than the employment of a vast state police apparatus. . . .

Other aspects of the internal model also reflect a combination of traditional and nontraditional influences. For example, the traditional practice of having members of the community handle most dispute settlement and control most deviant conduct prepared the way for the contemporary belief that legal administration does not require the services of skilled specialists. This traditional influence is reinforced by the Communists' own experiences. In the border and the liberated areas which they occupied before 1949, there was little functional specialization in the government or in the legal system. Cadres tended to be jacks-of-all-trades. This worked fairly well since the areas were small, the societies they contained were simple, and the cadres and the masses were highly motivated by the concerns of revolution and war. In addition, almost no legal specialists were available, even if one wanted to use them. This personnel problem was not alleviated after Liberation, even though the law schools and the holdovers from the Nationalist regime provided a small supply of legally trained persons. Consequently, legal theory and practice had to be adjusted to enable generalists to operate the legal system.

There are a number of areas where the external and internal models of law conflict or, at least, pull in opposite directions. For example, the internal model stresses local initiative and decision-making power, and tolerates considerable variations in norms, methods, and results from area to area. This runs counter to the external model's desire for clarity and certainty and its emphasis on strong central government. The external model's reliance upon a professional bureaucracy and skilled specialists to administer the legal system in an efficient and rationalized manner conflicts with the internal model's commitment to simplicity and mass participation. The internal model also lacks the clear appeal procedures and channels of the external model, and must therefore find very different means to protect a person from arbitrary actions by officials or by members of his peer group.

While the two models are quite dissimilar, some of their differences are more apparent in theory than in practice. Often the two models complement each other, with the external model handling serious matters and the internal model dealing with more routine affairs. Furthermore, the existence of the external model usually does not preclude the simultaneous existence of the internal model. In general, a person does not learn what he can and cannot do by studying or even by referring to the legal codes. Most notions concerning proper and improper conduct are learned as part of the socialization process, a process whose concepts and practices greatly resemble those of the internal model.

By the same token, over a period of time the internal model tends to evolve into the external model. In the ideal internal model, general patterns of proper conduct are truly internalized so that one "knows" what to do in each case. In many instances, however, this general understanding consists of or soon turns into a list of specific precepts. These may be called *li*, rules of propriety and morality, or any other legal or nonlegal name, but in due course they come to have much the same effect as the rules of law in the external model. Both the precepts and the rules of law tell one what to do in a particular situation; failure to comply results in sure and unpleasant consequences, although in the internal model, these may be social or economic sanctions rather than forty blows of the heavy bamboo. In a similar manner, the informal style of the internal model tends to ossify and to become rigid and formalized. With continued development and refinement, the legal system increases in complexity, and legal specialists are needed more and more to operate the system. At the same time, despite the emphasis on self-policing and on community action, the legal bureaucracy tends to grow and the state comes to play a larger role in legal work. . . .

The Cuban Popular Tribunals *Jesse Berman**

INTRODUCTION

Cuba's Popular Tribunals, which have been in operation since 1964, are the embodiment of a theoretical approach to the role of a legal system in a communist society, one which, in a relatively short period of time, has undergone much profound economic, political, and social change. Dissatisfaction with conventional Western courts in Cuba was voiced early in the revolution by its leadership. In 1953, Fidel Castro, a lawyer by training, while defending himself for his abortive raid on the Moncada barracks in that same year,† argued that courts should "judge people, and not crimes," and that individuals must be judged in the context of their environment:

> When you judge a defendant for robbery, your honors, do you ask him how long he has been unemployed? Do you ask him how many children he has, which days of the week he ate and which he didn't, do you concern yourselves with his environment at all? You send him to jail without further thought.[1]

The Popular Tribunals have developed, within their sphere of competence, as an attempt to provide an alternative to the system which Castro condemned as unresponsive. This article, based in large part on personal observations and interviews made and conducted in Cuba,[2] will discuss the present day operation of the Tribunals, and evaluate their progress in light of their professed goals.

PURPOSES AND FUNCTIONS

The first Cuban Popular Tribunals were organized, in the rural areas of the provinces, on an experimental basis. . . .

The avowed, theoretical purposes of the Popular Tribunals have been outlined by Blas Roca, a member of the Central Committee of the Communist Party of Cuba *(Partido Comunista de Cuba)* and chairman *(presidente)* of the Commission for Constitutional Studies of the P.C.C.:

> [with the creation of] the Popular Tribunals, the revolutionary and socialist content of our justice is made more complete and profound, and the form, structure and organization of the courts is made more in accord with this content.
>
> The fact that the masses, in a profoundly democratic manner, choose and elect those who can be popular judges, is a decisive blow against the idea, prevalent among the people, that justice is something official, something which comes down from above, something alien to them.
>
> . . . people's justice, applied to the people, through tribunals elected by that same people.
>
> The fact that the Popular Tribunals are organized and function in the

 This article originally appeared at 69 Colum. L. Rev. xxx (1969). Reprinted by permission. Some footnotes have been omitted.

*A.B., Columbia College, 1966, J.D., Columbia Law School, 1969. Associate Appellate Counsel, Criminal Appeals Bureau. The Legal Aid Society of New York.

†The trial took place before the Cuban Revolution, under the Batista dictatorship.

[1]F. Castro, *History Will Absolve Me* (1967).

[2]Mr. Berman visited Cuba during August and September 1968, at the invitation of the University of Havana. He traveled extensively through Cuba and interviewed Cuban lawyers, law professors, law students, judges of the traditional and popular courts and administrators of several branches of the Cuban judicial system. He observed trials in the *Audiencia* [traditional and more formal legal hearing] and in a number of Popular Tribunals. While in Cuba, he was assisted by a fourth-year student in the School of Juridical Sciences of the University of Havana.

This article is based on Mr. Berman's essay which was awarded the E. B. Convers Prize for 1969 at Columbia University School of Law.

Notes on interviews conducted in Cuba for this article are on file with the author.

> neighborhood, so that neighbors and acquaintances of those being judged can attend the trials and can make these trials truly public, and that the judges sitting in these trials come from the same community in which they live and work, reinforces the idea that the justice they administer is that of the working people, the expression of the power of the working people in the socialist state.
>
> . . . to edify and consolidate the new society of socialism and communism, to educate the new man, to secure and to perfect the rules of the socialist community.

More practically speaking, the purpose of the Popular Tribunals is to encourage acceptance of the laws of a new society by making the courts, which enforce these new laws, not institutions of coercion, but familiar, popularly accepted institutions. If the people can identify with the courts, they can identify with the law they learn in those courts, and can learn to avoid voluntarily what these courts term "anti-social conduct." As Parsons has noted, "Defining an act as a crime, so long as that definition is accepted in the community, is an effective way of discouraging other people from following that example." Voluntary acceptance of new definitions, fostered by presenting these new definitions in a palatable, identifiable context, greatly lessens the need to resort to coercion for enforcement. Thus one practical function of the Popular Tribunals is to encourage voluntary compliance with the severe rationing now in force in Cuba. Illustrative of this is the fact that almost every evening's docket in a Popular Tribunal contains at least one petty black market case.

Another function of the Popular Tribunals is to introduce a revolutionary mentality into the solution of personal quarrels. The most common cases in the Havana Popular Tribunals are those involving "public disorder," often resulting from the acute housing shortage in Havana (new housing is no longer being constructed in Havana, in order to encourage migration to the rural areas, so that more labor will become available for work in agriculture). According to Rogelio Buznego, director of the Popular Tribunals for the province of Havana, this urban overcrowding results in children fighting in the streets, and their mothers defending them, creating large numbers of disputes which require peaceful settlement. This incidentally results in the fact that most litigants before the Popular Tribunals are women.

An increase in the frequency of divorces has also compounded the housing shortage, and some divorced couples are forced to remain together for months while they await separate housing. Quite naturally, numerous quarrels ensue during the interim. According to Buznego, the Popular Tribunals are often dealing with "social problems, not penal problems," because of these various environmental factors.

It must be stressed that although the Popular Tribunals do impose sanctions on litigants and on criminal defendants, these are of a relatively mild, rehabilitative nature. The essential function of the Popular Tribunals is not to settle quarrels and not to sanction, but to involve and educate the community in the day-to-day laws for their society, especially in the new laws promulgated by the revolution. . . .

THE POPULAR TRIBUNALS IN ACTION

Personnel When one attends a Popular Tribunal trial, his attention is likely to focus first on the judges. Indeed this reaction is virtually guaranteed by the sudden shout of a uniformed *miliciano* [court guard], "*¡A pie!*" (On your feet!), which announces the judges' entrance into the courtroom. The judges then seat themselves behind a simple table at the front of the room, and there are no stenographers or bailiffs to impede one's view of the proceedings. Soon other actors appear on the scene. Seated off to one side, near the front of the room, there is usually an *Asesor,* and he can be seen leaving and returning with the judges each time they retire for deliberations.

The parties themselves sit among the other members of the audience, unnoticed until their respective cases are called. Members of the local Committee for the Defense of the Revolution are certainly present, but they cannot be distinguished by an outside observer, unless they are called as witnesses and elect to identify themselves in terms of their Committee affiliation. The *miliciano* who gives the cry is always obvious, and there occasionally are regular policemen present, if they are needed as witnesses. Also among the unobtrusive actors are the "spontaneous" witnesses, some of them more camouflaged than spontaneous. These, and the regular witnesses, sit among the audience until called, either by spontaneity or by the court, to come forward.

Finally, the observer cannot ignore the audience, the residents of the *zona* [small area over which the popular tribunal has jurisdiction], who habitually pack the courtroom. In a theoretical sense, at least, the whole show is for them, and the show is not devoid of audience participation. . . .

Selection and Training [*of Judges.*] The Popular Tribunal judges are laymen. Aside from a three-week training course, their only legal experience is that which they gain while serving as Popular Tribunal judges. They are laymen, not because of any lack of professionally trained judges in Cuba (although such a shortage may exist), but because laymen are actually preferred for this position. As Blas Roca observed, the fact "that the judges sitting in these trials come from the same community in which they live and work, reinforces the idea that the justice they administer is that of the working people." Perhaps it is not unfair to say that it is deemed more important that the people know the judges, than the judges know the law.

The judges do indeed come from the community; they are among the four or five thousand residents of the *zona* over which their Tribunal has jurisdiction. They are workers, employed in various full-time jobs during the day, and they serve in the Popular Tribunals, which meet at night, without pay. Their working class background is genuine. In the Luyanó section, in Havana, for example, the judges also do all the plumbing and cleaning in the courtroom. In Havana's San Miguel del Padrón section, while I was observing a night's trials in one *zona,* a judge from a *zona* whose Tribunal was not in session that night busied himself filling a water pitcher for the judges who were sitting. While Cuba cannot yet be termed a classless society, the Popular Tribunal judges of any given *zona* appear to be relatively indistinguishable from the *acusados* [the accused], from the audience, or from the people of that *zona* in general.

How, then, are these judges selected? There is no official, written description of the whole procedure, but it appears to begin with a given number of men and, occasionally, women, being nominated by the local Party officials and by the neighborhood Committee for the Defense of the Revolution. . . .

At the close of the training session, the candidates are given an examination by the *Asesor* and he determines which six men are best qualified, based upon the exam and the inquiries made into their reputations. These six names are then submitted to the people of the *zona* for ratification, by secret ballot, evidently by majority vote. Those selected serve for an indefinite term, theoretically as long as they continue to satisfy their constituents. Since the Popular Tribunals are, at present, only four or five years old at most, it is impossible to estimate the average duration of judicial tenure. The average age for a Popular Tribunal judge in Havana seems to be in the late thirties; judges in the provinces are somewhat younger. . . .

The Spectators. Two basic concepts inherent in the Popular Tribunals are that they "function in the neighborhood, so that neighbors and acquaintances of those being judged can attend the trials and can make these trials truly public," and that the public trials "educate the new man, . . . secure the socialist laws" and "correct those who still keep the customs of the older oppressor society." These ideas may be capsulized as popular involvement and popular education. Thus, audience participation is encouraged and the residents of each *zona* show up each week in overflow crowds. When asked why they come, their answer is often simply "to see the trials."

These spectators generally pay close attention to the proceedings, reacting with "oohs" and "ahs" at appropriate intervals. One is at first tempted to conclude that the trials are seen by the people as merely entertainment, but it is perhaps more accurate to state that people come because they are interested, and overflow crowds can be observed even in *zonas* where the Popular Tribunal has been in operation for more than a year.

The ultimate in audience participation is the emergence of "spontaneous" witnesses from the audience. . . . With the audience coming almost entirely from the same neighborhood, there is nothing unusual in expecting that some of its members were, in fact, witnesses to neighborhood occurrences.

The Setting and Atmosphere in the Courtroom In cities and villages the Popular Tribunals meet in storefronts, either those belonging to the local Committee for the Defense of the Revolution or in storefronts which have been assigned exclusively to the Tribunal. The rooms are relatively small and bare, with virtually none of the trappings found in a traditional courtroom. A photograph of Che Guevara and a Cuban flag are often on the wall behind the judges, and in one *zona* the judges had a small bell which they rang at the close of each case. In another *zona* the judges personally passed out pages from old magazines during the trials, so that the spectators could fan themselves on that hot summer night.

The spectators usually sit on plain wooden benches, demonstrating great interest and involvement in the trials. Often there are not enough seats and the crowd overflows out into the street. In Camagüey, one Popular Tribunal had a small fluorescent sign outside over the doorway saying "Popular Tribunal," but that was the fanciest element of Popular Tribunal decor I ever observed. Trials of "exceptional interest" are held out of doors so that all may come and observe, as in the "wife-knifing" case, which had an audience of five thousand persons in the town of Nuevitas. Occasionally the setting differs, as when there is a mass trial, such as the educational, simultaneous, "warning" trials of several dozen habitual violators of the same minor contravention.

Procedure

Chronology of a Case. A case begins when a complaint is made to the Tribunal by an *acusador,* the combination plaintiff and complainant. There is no prosecutor and both the *acusador* and the *acusado* are virtually never represented by counsel. Consistent with revolutionary legal training in Cuba, the Popular Tribunals are not adversary proceedings; one judge conducts an investigation prior to the trial, taking depositions from all parties, witnesses, experts, and whomever else he deems appropriate. At the trial, all questioning is done by members of the court.

An offender is supposedly "brought to justice" within seven to ten days. What this probably means is that within seven to ten days after a complaint is made, one of the judges begins an investigation. When this investigation is completed, if a trial is merited it is scheduled for the next night the Tribunal is due to meet. At the trial the parties are advised of their rights, they and the witnesses are questioned once again, and, after the judges recess to deliberate, a verdict including sanctions is announced. From the date of the alleged offense through complaint, investigation and trial, an average of perhaps two months have gone by. An exception is the case of delicts against the popular economy, where a trial must be held within seven days of the alleged offense.

Appeals are usually made right after the verdict and sanctions are announced.

Rights of the Acusado. All trials in the Popular Tribunals must be public, except for cases involving "personal issues," such as a woman's honor, juvenile delinquency, or homosexuality. I did observe one juvenile case (a theft) in Havana, and it was handled privately, but in another *zona* in Havana I witnessed a woman's-honor case tried publicly, so this rule seems to be flexible.

At the start of each trial, the *Presidente* of

the Tribunal asks the parties if any of the judges is a friend or enemy of one of them. An affirmative response would require the judge to step down. Judges do not, however, have to disqualify themselves if they merely have personal knowledge of the facts of the case, as in the "pants" case, where one judge worked in the store in which the alibi was alleged to have taken place.

The *Presidente* then tells the *acusado* that he has a right to remain silent. Although after his arrest (if there was one) the *acusado* may have been held incommunicado for up to twenty-four hours, at the trial he is told that he can repudiate or modify any confession or statement made earlier. He is also informed that counsel (from a *bufete colectivo*) [law firm, serving the public] will be provided, free of charge, if he desires one. The above rights were always waived by the *acusados* in the trials I witnessed.

The parties are asked at various intervals if they are understanding the proceedings, and the response to the extent of my observations is always in the affirmative.

Appeals. All Popular Tribunal decisions are unanimous, in that there is no vote recorded and no dissenting opinions are aired publicly. The decisions are all appealable, with two types of appeal possible:

(1) An appeal of the severity of the sanction.

(2) An appeal of the verdict, essentially a motion for a new trial.

There are no grounds for appeal based on procedural errors. When the severity of a sanction is appealed, the same three judges rule on the appeal, usually on the same night as the trial. When the verdict itself has been questioned, that appeal goes to the *Asesor,* who then considers it in conjunction with two other judges from the *zona* who did not take part in the original trial. In both cases, the appeal may be requested by the parties themselves, or by the *Asesor,* in the name of justice. Appeals of severity of sanction are fairly common, as in the "clandestine bread sale" case, but appeals of the verdict itself are virtually non-existent. In the five *zonas* of the San Miguel del Padrón section, for example, there was only one such appeal in five months, out of perhaps five hundred cases. . . .

An Evaluation of the Popular Tribunals

Effectiveness. The essence of any evaluation of the Cuban Popular Tribunals must be an inquiry into how successful the Tribunals have been in effecting the ends for which they were created. . . .

As far as popular involvement is concerned, the Popular Tribunals have met with success both in theory and in practice. There is or soon will be a Popular Tribunal for every *zona* of four or five thousand persons, within walking distance of every home in the *zona.* The Tribunals meet in the evenings, when all can attend the trials, which are virtually all public. The judges are laymen from the neighborhood, and the cases deal with essentially local problems, such as housing shortages or disputes over use of a water main. Attendance is high, with the crowds actually overflowing the small courtrooms. The local residents view the Popular Tribunals as something of their own, not as a mechanism imposed on them from outside. At least some of the "spontaneous" witnesses are truly spontaneous — neighbors with personal knowledge of the case who want to offer their cooperation. The judges elicit questions and comments from the audience and explain the proceedings carefully. Most cases come to the Popular Tribunals on the complaints of local residents; the *acusadores* are policemen in only a small minority of the trials. Finally, enforcement is delegated to unpaid local people — the C.D.R. members who live in the *zona.* All of these factors, which have previously been discussed, illustrate the increased level of popular involvement, which is most apparent when compared with the traditional *Audiencia.* And despite the popular participation, there seems to be general respect for the Tribunals among the people.[3]

---

[3]C. Brinton, *Anatomy of a Revolution,* rev. & exp. ed. (New York: Vintage, 1965), pp. 180–181.

CONCLUSION

The Cuban Popular Tribunals are a considerable step forward in popular involvement in the administration of justice, at least when compared with the situation in Cuba before their inception. Although the Popular Tribunals are a revolutionary advancement when compared with the traditional Cuban *Audiencia,* they cannot be termed especially original within the realm of the socialist legal systems. However, they do appear to be considerably effective in achieving popular involvement and respect, and their decisions are for the most part just, as are their procedures, although perhaps to a lesser degree. Thus, while they have only recently come into existence, and to some extent are still in a developmental stage, the Cuban Popular Tribunals are close to being institutions which truly administer "popular justice."

The Relegalization of Cuba *Peter Irons*

. . . When I first visisted Cuba in 1980, I was unaware that the system of "people's courts," called [Popular Tribunals], had been abandoned. These courts, in which minor civil and criminal cases (with maximum sentences of six months confinement) had been tried before panels of three lay judges, had been hailed by American lawyers sympathetic to the Cuban revolution as an alternative to the legalism of the pre-revolutionary period and the oppression imposed by *Batistiano* judges. Operating informally in community centers and work places, the people's courts eschewed rules of evidence, encouraged participation by neighborhood residents who wished to comment on the facts or the character of the parties, and were designed to perform as much an educative as an adjudicatory function. As Robert Cantor wrote in 1974 in *Juris Doctor,* "the tribunals are more than courtrooms; they are also community classrooms where Cubans attempt to transform a colonial system into a real government of the people." And in another widely read article in the *Columbia Law Review,* written in 1969, Jesse Berman wrote that the "essential function of the Popular Tribunals is not to settle quarrels and not to sanction, but to involve and educate the community in the day-to-day laws of their society, especially in the new laws promulgated by the revolution." Both Cantor and Berman praised the people's courts as institutions that fairly and effectively meted out justice in an educative forum, with the egalitarian goals of the revolution uppermost in mind.

Why, then, were the people's courts dismantled in 1978 and replaced with a more formal, legalistic system remarkably similar in structure to that which existed before the revolution? On his 1980 visit to Cuba, Harold Berman (no relation to Jesse Berman) was told that "the decline of the legal profession, and general hostility to the formality and objectivity of law, left the Popular Tribunals without the kind of legal supervision that was necessary for their success." Berman differentiated the Cuban people's courts from the similar comrade's courts of the Soviet Union which he has studied and observed extensively and whose success he attributes to "a high degree of fairly sophisticated legal supervision." But this is a somewhat strange explanation of why Cuba, a country which, in contrast to the ossified bureaucracy that has long governed the Soviet Union, still exhibits a revolutionary and egalitarian fervor that is only partially subject to the miasma of state bureaucracy. Those Cuban lawyers with whom I spoke attributed the demise of the peole's courts not to heavyhanded intervention of the Cuban legal profession or any concern

---

Peter Irons, "The Relegalization of Cuba," from *ALSA Forum,* Vol. V, No. 2 (1981), edited. Reprinted by permission of American Legal Studies Association, and the author.

with legal formality (just the opposite, in fact, was true) but, rather, the growing inability of the people's courts to sustain popular involvement in their proceedings. People's court sessions as forums for the airing of community disputes soon lost their drawing power (as they generally have in the Soviet Union as well) and, consequently, their educative function declined. Like most Latin countries in both hemispheres, Cuba is an intensely disputatious country and one in which legal formality is hard to eradicate. My own impression, admittedly based on supposition, is that Fidel Castro, himself a lawyer, played a major role in the abandonment of the people's court and the revival of the structure of the prior system, which now operates within the context of revolutionary law. The differences between the pre- and post-revolutionary legal systems are those of attention to the character of the defendant and his or her willingness to adjust to the revolutionary goals of work and communal life. In this respect, the relegalization of Cuba reflects not a return to the oppressive system of the Batista era but simply an acknowledgement that the forms of legalism are adaptable to the revolutionary era.

One final question is relevant to those of us raised in the adversarial system and indoctrinated with the "due process" ideology of the Bill of Rights and the Fourteenth Amendment. Do criminal defendants in Cuba, at least in the common, run-of-the-mill cases that I observed, receive a "fair trial" in a sense that would satisfy our sense of justice? I should note two things before attempting an answer: first, on my first visit to Cuba no one in court knew that I was an American lawyer (I simply walked into court and listened to the proceedings); and second, as a former criminal defendant myself, I think I have a sensitivity to the treatment of defendants and the ordeal they endure. The trials I observed in Cuba ran the gamut of the docket of the American trial court; the charges included theft, assault, larceny, motor vehicle violations, and illegal gambling, in addition to uniquely Cuban crimes such as possession of American currency and operation of a private car for hire.

On the whole, I was impressed by what I observed of the Cuban criminal justice system. The idea of a criminal trial as a truth-seeking process in which the defendant is expected (but not required) to participate by telling the court his or her version of what happened, rather than as a contest between lawyers each seeking to color the facts by exploiting complicated rules of evidence, appeals to my sense of fairness. I was particularly struck in Cuban trials by the forthright manner in which almost every defendant and witness (the sex offender and a car thief were two exceptions) spoke up articulately and with no evident fear of the judges. Although American lawyers and laypeople make a fetish of the Fifth Amendment right against self-incrimination (a right I would defend vehemently in the context of the adversarial system), I felt in Cuba that defendants were more often helped than hindered by their almost universal waiver of the right not to testify. Harold Berman reports that 28 percent of all defendants in the Havana Provincial Court, including a large number who admit the facts of their offense, are acquitted at trial, a proportion far larger than in American courts. The trials I observed, in which about half of all defendants were acquitted, indicate that a defendant's testimony, even one technically guilty, can often sway the judges. In addition, the fact that judges have before them an *expediente* that contains not only the prosecutor's but also the defendant's evidence adds to my belief that judges presented with all relevant facts before trial are more likely than in our system to render a fair decision.

On the other hand, Americans wedded to the adversarial system are likely to question the commitment to legality of a system in which evidence of a defendant's political sympathies and social involvement is considered before a determination of guilt or innocence is made. It is a dogma of Anglo-Saxon law that the only question at trial should be "Did or did not the defendant commit the acts charged?" Permitting, and in fact encouraging, consideration of evidence extraneous to this question opens the door to reprisal against those deemed "anti-social" or "anti-revolutionary." And this is, I realize, a troubling question. But it should be equally obvious to those who have witnessed American criminal trials that the defendant's character and background affects the outcome, even in the absence of testimony about them. Given an equivalent set of facts, poor and/or black defendants are more often convicted in American courts, as the prejudices of judges and juries come into play. It is worth noting that I could observe no evidence of racism in the Cuban courts, a fact explainable not only by the government's official commitment to racial equality but also by the large number of black judges and prosecutors.

When I first visited Cuba, I expected to find a system of "people's courts" in which the educative function of law in a socialist society had replaced the repressive legalism of its colonial past. But the Cuban experiment of "law without lawyers" had, I discovered, ended at about the same time as had the Chinese experiment which it closely resembled. The reasons for the abrupt and unheralded relegalization of Cuba are difficult to uncover, since no official explanation of the shift is available. Based on my observations and conversations in Cuba, along with those of Harold Berman, it seems clear that the legal profession in Cuba, and the traditions of legalism it maintained during the period of delegalization, reasserted itself not so much because they had served their purpose during a transitional stage of the Cuban revolution. One feature of revolutionary societies in general is an initial need to cast off the forms of their pre-revolutionary pasts, in part to destroy the power of the existing *apparat* and in part to convince the people that the revolution will serve them and their needs. But revolutions become institutionalized if they last into a second generation, and the demands of system-maintenance require the imposition of legal formality.

The relegalization of Cuba (and China as well) should be viewed not as a return to the old system but as a maturing stage of socialist development. This process has brought about a revival of legal education (from a handful of students at Havana University in the mid-1970s to some two thousand today in Havana, Santiago, and Santa Clara, more than half of them women and workers); the approval of the 1976 Constitution, which includes a Bill of Rights; and the enactment of the 1979 Criminal Code, which contains significant procedural protections. These developments have come as part of balance characteristic of socialist legality: the rights of defendants are made more secure against arbitrary action, while all civil and criminal rights are subject to "the existence and objectives of the socialist state." At least from my observations in Cuban courts, this balance produces in ordinary criminal trials a measure of fairness and justice that exceeds that I have observed in American courts.

FURTHER READING

The literature on Cuban law available in English is skimpy. Perhaps the best recent overview is the section called "The Law and the Courts" in Jorge I. Dominguez, *Cuba: Order and Revolution* (Cambridge: Harvard University Press, 1978), at 249–259. Two articles in the periodical *Cuban Studies* are also worth consulting: Leonel-Antonio de la Cuesta, "The Cuban Socialist Constitution: Its Originality and Role in Institutionalization," 6 *Cuban Studies* 15 (July 1976); and Max Azicri, "The Institutionalization of the Cuban Revolution: A Review of the Literature," 9 *Cuban Studies* 2 (July 1979).

Notes and Questions

1. Jesse Berman's description of Cuban Popular Tribunals stresses their participatory and educative functions in a revolutionary society. In Irons's visit, he discovered these popular tribunals had been eliminated, but concluded this was not necessarily a negative development since the relegalized system seemed to achieve more just results than the adversarial model at work in the United States. Are you convinced that "justice" is an adequate substitute for participation? What aspect(s) of justice might be lost over the years without continuing popular participation? Do you think it is possible — given the relationship of law and culture — to revolutionize or democratize a society

without transforming its legal apparatus to reflect the new cultural values?

2. The function of deviance in setting community boundaries seems to depend in large part on the participation of nondeviants, their expressions of moral outrage and collective conscience, and their ritual observation of punishments. In modern society, what role do the print and electronic media play in engaging community participation in the process of boundary definition?
3. Li suggests that the external, formalistic model of law in China may be more suited to the predictability and rule orientation preferred by Western economic and business organizations (note the parallel implications for early U.S. legal history in Horwitz, p. 377). Does economic development in China invite a form of legal imperialism that might eventually weaken the internal model and its highly participatory character? If this happens, who would be defining the dominant values of Chinese culture?
4. What happens to individual rights in the internal model of law in China? Could you imagine adapting such a legal process to any part of life in the United States? What reactions would you expect to such a proposal?
5. In the *Duncan* case, the Court refers to jury trial as a protection against government oppression. What protects the individual against oppression by an intolerant majority bent on using participatory legal processes to enforce its values? Are there any substantive areas in which individuals or minorities ought to be protected by law from an order imposed by a majority? What does the Bill of Rights suggest about how the United States has answered this question? Should a willingness to tolerate limitations on participation in legal process depend on whether justice is being done by law, as Irons suggested about Cuban Popular Tribunals? To what extent does justice include the right of individuals to transcend social order?

Suggested Additional Readings

The American Jury System: Final Report. Annual Chief Justice Earl Warren Conference on Advocacy in the United States. New York: Roscoe Pound Trial Lawyers Association, 1977.

Bell, Derrick. *Race, Racism and American Law.* 2nd ed. Boston: Little, Brown, 1980, sections 5.12 to 5.21.

Bloomstein, Morris J. *Verdict: The Jury System.* New York: Dodd, Mead, 1972.

"Federal Grand Jury Investigation of Political Dissidents," *Harvard Civil Rights–Civil Liberties Law Review* 7 (1972): 432.

Federal Jury Selection Act, 28 USC 1861 *et seq.*

Forsyth, Walter. *History of Trial by Jury.* New York: Franklin, 1971.

Garrow, David J. *Bearing the Cross: Martin Luther King, Jr., and the Southern Christian Leadership Conference.* New York: Morrow, 1986.

Hastie, Reid, Penrod, Steven, and Pennington, Nancy. *Inside the Jury.* Cambridge, Mass.: Harvard University Press, 1983.

Kalven, Harry, Jr., and Zeisel, Hans. *The American Jury.* Boston: Little, Brown, 1966.

Kaufman, F. "The Right of Self-representation and the Power of Jury Nullification." *Case Western Reserve Law Review,* 28 (1978): 269.

Kennebeck, Edwin. *Juror Number Four: Trial of Thirteen Black Panthers as Seen from the Jury Box.* New York: Norton, 1973.

Kershen, Drew. "Jury Selection Act of 1879: Theory and Practice of Citizen Participation." *University of Illinois Law Forum* (1980): p. 707.

Palmer, Ronald. "Post-trial Interview of Jurors in the Federal Courts — A Lawyer's Dilemma." *Houston Law Review* 6 (1968): 290.

Sarat, Austin D. "Access to Justice: Citizen Participation and the American Legal Order," in Leon Lipson and Stanton Wheeler, eds., *Law and the Social Sciences.* Russell Sage, 1986.

Simon, Rita James. *The Jury System in America: A Critical Overview.* Sage Criminal Justice System Annuals, Vol. 4. New York: Russell Sage Foundation, 1975.

Subcommittee to Investigate Administration of Internal Security Act of Senate Judiciary Committee. Hearings on Recording of Jury Deliberations. 84th Cong., 1st session, 1955.

Unger, Roberto. *Law in Modern Society.* New York: Macmillan, 1976.

Van Dyke, Jon. *Jury Selection Procedures.* Cambridge, Mass.: Ballinger, 1977.

Zerman, Melvyn. *Call the Final Witness.* New York: Harper & Row, 1977.

———. *Beyond a Reasonable Doubt.* New York: Crowell, 1981.

A Nineteenth-Century Rural Court Scene. A. Wighe: *Trial by Jury.* (Museum of Art, Rhode Island School of Design. Gift of Edith Jackson Green and Ellis Jackson)

CHAPTER 5 Conflict Resolution

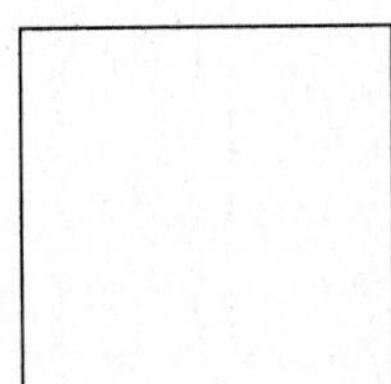

I believe that only a new legal system, based on new assumptions, will do. . . . The United States is not the only adversary society on our globe. But it is the one Americans can change. It only takes wanting to — enough. That end will be our beginning.

Anne Strick, *Injustice for All* (1977)

During the past decade there have been frequent public pronouncements about problems with law and the legal system. At the same time, in resolving disputes the use of alternatives to the formal legal system has risen dramatically. For example, currently close to five hundred programs in the United States and a growing number in Canada, Australia, and Western Europe use mediation, arbitration, facilitation, and negotiation to resolve and settle a broad range of individual and institutional disputes. What started as limited experimentation in the earlier 1970s with a few federally funded neighborhood justice centers is now characterized by many as a national movement that is altering the delivery of legal services and challenging basic norms of justice.

Although differing rationales support experimentation with alternative ways to resolve disputes, these efforts have generally stemmed from the belief that American society has become overly litigious, that too many disputes result in lawsuits, and that courts are increasingly unable to manage their overloaded dockets. Concerns have also been raised about the ways in which the legal process itself impedes access to law and justice. Some of these concerns involve a critique of the ways in which the adversarial, win-lose process leaves parties dissatisfied. Other concerns focus on dissatisfactions and unfairness resulting from the settlement of most court cases. Yet another focus has been on the ways in which law and legal process may mask or transform the original conflict.

The move away from law toward alternative ways to resolve disputes is supported by a diverse and varied constituency, including corporate executives, judges, lawyers, government officials, and community activists. It is not yet clear, however, what is motivating this interest. Does this interest signify a shift in the traditional view of social and legal reformers, which understands formal law as an essential arena where the disadvantaged can publicize their entitlement to legal rights? Does this interest reflect a move toward privatization, in which disputes will be heard and settled by private third parties instead of public officials? Who will function as these emerging private third parties? Do these developments suggest that there will be more or less popular participation in the resolution of conflict? Whose interests are advanced by the movement away from law?

This chapter is organized around three sections. The first section, "Conflict in Society and Law," examines the meaning of disputes and disputing in U.S. legal culture. The second section, "Conflict and Courts," investigates the roles courts play in resolving conflict and explores the significance and realities of the "litigation crisis" in American society. The third section, "Alternatives to the Legal System: Promise and Problems," focuses primarily on the meaning of mediation as a growing mechanism for the resolution of conflict.

As you read this chapter, think about the meaning of moving away from law. Consider these materials in the larger context of understanding how formal and informal dispute resolution processes enhance, impede, and define our understandings of the meaning of social justice itself.

---

1 CONFLICT IN SOCIETY AND LAW

> The dispute [is] a conceptual link between law and society permitting us to see courts in a much broader context.
>
> David M. Trubeck, "Studying Courts in Context," *Law and Society Review* (1980–81)

The study of law and other conflict resolution processes often ignores the investigation and analysis of conflict itself. Even though the legal system is generally thought to be the primary institution for the peaceable settlement of disputes, recently an interest has emerged in understanding the ways in which the law affects and changes the meaning of individual conflict.

Studying disputes and dispute processing is thus becoming increasingly central to sociolegal studies. As David Trubeck points out,* the study of disputes "offers the possibility of greater insight into the social relations and conflicts behind the formal structure of a lawsuit."

The following readings illustrate some differing analyses and interpretations of the meaning of disputes and disputing in American society.

*"Studying Courts in Context," *Law and Society Review,* 15, no. 3–4 (1980–81): 494.

Grievances, Claims, and Disputes: Assessing the Adversary Culture *Richard E. Miller and Austin Sarat*

DISPUTING AND THE ADVERSARY SOCIETY

The manner and rate at which disputes are generated is sometimes taken as an indicator of societal "health." This view is most characteristic of the work of historians writing after World War II. . . . They presented a picture of American society as a stable balance between conflict and calm, a society in which all disputes were resolved within a framework of consensus. Some may question the validity of that picture as a description of *any* period in American life . . . , but the experience of the last two decades has certainly undermined both the social basis upon which the balance of conflict and calm may have existed . . . and its viability as an ideology or a system of legitimizing beliefs. . . . We increasingly hear the voices of those who perceive and fear the growth of an "adversary society" . . . , a society of assertive, aggressive, rights-conscious, litigious people ready and eager to challenge each other and those in authority. . . . Images of our allegedly unprecedented assertiveness, of the ingenious ways which we have found to fight each other, flow through the popular culture, from *New Yorker* cartoons about children threatening to sue their parents for forcing them to drink their milk to palimony suits against celebrities.

There is, of course, another view of contemporary American society, a view which suggests that we are, in fact, relatively uncontentious and even passive. . . . Americans are said to be reluctant to admit that their lives are troubled and conditioned to accept circumstances and treatment which are far from ideal. . . . Since our institutions respond slowly, inefficiently, and reluctantly, we learn not to complain, not to pursue our grievances or claim our rights. Even when we do, we find that appropriate institutions do not exist. . . . As our society becomes ever more complex and expansive, it becomes easier to avoid conflict or to ignore it merely by moving on. . . .

Questions

1. What function does the widespread use of avoidance play in our adversarial legal system?
2. How do U.S. citizens become acculturated to conflict? In other words, how do they learn U.S. customs of conflict resolution? What are the institutions outside of courts that also impart the widespread social values of avoidance and confrontation?

The Emergence and Transformation of Disputes: Naming, Blaming, Claiming . . .

William L. F. Felstiner, Richard L. Abel, and Austin Sarat

I. INTRODUCTION

The sociology of law has been dominated by studies of officials and formal institutions and their work products. This agenda has shaped the way disputes are understood and portrayed. Institutions reify cases by reducing them to records; they embody disputes in a concrete form that can be studied retrospectively by attending to the words used by lay persons and officials and by examining the economic and legal context in which cases occur. . . . But disputes are not things: they are social constructs. Their shapes reflect whatever definition the observer gives to the concept. Moreover, a significant portion of any dispute exists only in the minds of the disputants.

These ideas, though certainly not novel, are important because they draw attention to a neglected topic in the sociology of law — the emergence and transformation of disputes — the way in which experiences become grievances, grievances become disputes, and disputes take various shapes, follow particular dispute processing paths, and lead to new forms of understanding. Studying the emergence and transformation of disputes means studying a social process as it occurs. It means studying the conditions under which injuries are perceived or go unnoticed and how people respond to the experience of injustice and conflict. In addition, though the study of crime and litigation rates seems to be derived from and to support the conviction that both are too high — that there is a need for more police and longer prison terms . . . that the courts are congested with "frivolous" suits . . . — the study of the emergence and transformation of disputes may lead to the judgment that *too little* conflict surfaces in our society, that *too few* wrongs are perceived, pursued, and remedied. . . .

William F. Felstiner, Richard L. Abel, and Austin Sarat, "The Emergence and Transformation of Disputes: Naming, Blaming, Claiming . . . ," from *Law and Society Review,* Volume 15:3–4. Reprinted by permission of the Law and Society Association. (Citations omitted.)

II. WHERE DISPUTES COME FROM AND HOW THEY DEVELOP

We come to the study of transformations with the belief that the antecedents of disputing are as problematic and as interesting as the disputes that may ultimately emerge. We begin by setting forth the stages in the development of disputes and the activities connecting one stage to the next. Trouble, problems, personal and social dislocation are everyday occurrences. Yet, social scientists have rarely studied the capacity of people to tolerate substantial distress and injustice. . . . We do, however, know that such "tolerance" may represent a failure to perceive that one has been injured; such failures may be self-induced or externally manipulated. Assume a population living down-wind from a nuclear test site. Some portion of that population has developed cancer as a result of the exposure and some has not. Some of those stricken know that they are sick and some do not. In order for disputes to emerge and remedial action to be taken, an unperceived injurious experience (unPIE, for short) must be transformed into a perceived injurious experience (PIE). The uninformed cancer victims must learn that they are sick. The transformation perspective directs our attention to the differential transformation of unPIEs into PIEs. It urges us to examine, in this case, differences in class, education, work situation, social networks, etc. between those who become aware of their cancer and those who do not, as well as attend to the possible manipulation of information by those responsible for the radiation.

. . . Nevertheless, in many cases it will be difficult to identify and explain transformations from unPIE to PIE. This first transformation — saying to oneself that a particular experience has been injurious — we call *naming*. Though hard to study empirically, naming may be the critical transformation; the level and kind of disputing in a society may turn more on what is initially perceived as an injury than on any later decision. . . . For instance, asbestosis only became an acknowledged "disease" *and* the basis of a claim for compensation when shipyard workers stopped taking for granted that they would have trouble breathing after ten years of installing insulation and came to view their condition as a problem.

The next step is the transformation of a perceived injurious experience into a grievance. This occurs when a person attributes an injury to the fault of another individual or social entity. By including fault within the definition of grievance, we limit the concept to injuries viewed both as violations of norms and as remediable. The definition takes the grievant's perspective: the injured person must feel wronged and believe that something might be done in response to the injury, however politically or sociologically improbable such a response might be. A grievance must be distinguished from a complaint against no one in particular (about the weather, or perhaps inflation) and from a mere wish unaccompanied by a sense of injury for which another is held responsible (I might like to be more attractive). We call the transformation from perceived injurious experience to grievance *blaming*: our diseased shipyard worker makes this transformation when he holds his employer or the manufacturer of asbestos insulation responsible for his asbestosis.

The third transformation occurs when someone with a grievance voices it to the person or entity believed to be responsible and asks for some remedy. We call this communication *claiming*. A claim is transformed into a dispute when it is rejected in whole or in part. Rejection need not be expressed by words. Delay that the claimant construes as resistance is just as much a rejection as is a compromise offer (partial rejection) or an outright refusal.

. . . We know that only a small fraction of injurious experiences ever mature into disputes. . . . Furthermore, we know that most of the attrition occurs at the early stages: experiences are not perceived as injurious; perceptions do not ripen into grievances; grievances are voiced to intimates but not to the person deemed responsible. A theory of disputing that looked only at institutions mobilized by disputants and the strategies pursued within them would be seriously deficient. It would be like constructing a theory of politics entirely on the basis of voting patterns when we know that most people do not vote in most elections. Recognizing the bias that would result, political scientists have devoted considerable effort to describing and explaining political apathy. . . . Sociologists of law need to explore the analogous phenomenon — grievance apathy.

The early stages of naming, blaming, and claiming are significant, not only because of the high attrition they reflect, but also because the range of behavior they encompass is greater than that involved in the later stages of disputes, where institutional patterns restrict the options open to disputants. Examination of this behavior will help us identify the social structure of disputing. Transformations reflect social structural variables, as well as personality traits. People do — or do not — perceive an experience as an injury, blame someone else, claim redress, or get their claims accepted because of their *social position* as well as their individual characteristics. The transformation perspective points as much to the study of social stratification as to the exploration of social psychology.

Finally, attention to naming, blaming, and claiming permits a more critical look at recent efforts to improve "access to justice." The public commitment to formal legal equality, required by the prevailing ideology of liberal legalism, has resulted in substantial efforts to equalize access at the later stages of disputing, where inequality becomes more visible and implicates official institutions; examples include the waiver of court costs, the creation of small claims courts, the movement toward informalism, and the provision of legal services. . . . Access to justice is supposed to reduce the unequal distribution of advantages in society; paradoxically it may amplify these inequalities. The ostensible goal of these reforms is to eliminate bias in the ultimate transformation: disputes into lawsuits. If, however, as we suspect, these very unequal distributions have skewed the earlier stages by which injurious experiences become disputes, then current access to justice efforts will only give additional advantages to those who have already transformed their experiences into disputes. That is, these efforts may accentuate the effects of inequality at the earlier, less visible stages, where it is harder to detect, diagnose, and correct. . . .

Questions

1. Why do only a small fraction of injurious experiences evolve into disputes?
2. What is an "unperceived injurious experience"? If a husband is not paying his ex-wife legally adequate alimony, but she doesn't consider this to be an injustice, is there a dispute? A PIE? An "unPIE"?
3. What is a dispute? Does a dispute and the disputing process necessarily involve a sense of injustice?
4. What effect do you think demographic factors, such as gender, race, and class, have on the pattern of disputing in American society?

Language, Audience, and the Transformation of Disputes

Lynn Mather and Barbara Yngvesson

I. INTRODUCTION

Our aim . . . is to suggest the usefulness of the concept "transformation of a dispute" in (1) improving our understanding of how people manage processes of disputing and (2) showing how law and other normative frameworks are articulated, imposed, circumvented, and created as people negotiate social order in their transactions with one another. We draw upon case studies of dispute processing in a variety of social, political, and economic settings and move toward developing an analytic framework for comparing cases both within a single dispute-processing institution and across different cultures. This framework should facilitate the comparison of disputes processed in institutional settings as widely different as courts, gossip networks, and broadly inclusive community arenas. Further, this framework will suggest how the processing of individual disputes is linked to larger considerations of social and political order. Specifically, we are interested in the relation between the definition and transformation of disputes, on the one hand, and the maintenance and change of legal and other normative systems, on the other.

By *dispute* we mean a particular stage of a social relationship in which conflict between two parties (individuals or groups) is asserted publicly — that is, before a third party. . . .

An assumption fundamental to our approach is that a dispute is not a static event which simply "happens," but that the structure of disputes, quarrels, and offenses includes *changes or transformations* over time. Transformations occur because participants in the disputing process have different interests in and perspectives on the dispute; participants assert these interests and perspectives in the very process of defining and shaping the object of the dispute. What a dispute is about, whether it is even a dispute or not, and whether it is properly a "legal" dispute, may be central issues for negotiation in the disputing process.

By *transformation of a dispute* we mean a change in its form or content as a result of the

Lynn Mather and Barbara Yngvesson, "Language, Audience, and the Transformation of Disputes," from *Law and Society Review*, Volume 15:3–4. Reprinted by permission of the Law and Society Association. (Footnotes and citations omitted.)

interaction and involvement of other participants in the dispute process. Transformation is continuous, beginning when one party initially perceives a grievance against another. But in this paper we do not consider those changes involved in the early definition and emergence of conflict. Instead we focus on transformation after the conflict has been brought to a third party. Note that changes in the content of a dispute may not be distinguishable from changes in the form, since the inclusion or exclusion of certain facts or issues affects the way options are articulated and solutions are perceived. . . .

At a fundamental level, the transformation of a dispute involves a process of *rephrasing* — that is, some kind of reformulation into a public discourse. Even the most rudimentary forms of disputing, such as public shouting matches which largely involve repetition and reiteration of the charges . . . , include some form of rephrasing as the dispute proceeds; Eskimo song duels involve sophisticated forms of rephrasing . . . ; and nonverbal disputing such as chest-pounding, side-slapping, club fights . . . can also be conceptualized as a way of reformulating a dispute to facilitate settlement and avoid breakdown of relations. In these examples, an audience or group of supporters acts implicitly as the third party to the dispute. As the role of third party becomes more explicit, then the rephrasing is likely to reflect a greater, or more substantive, shift in the definition of the dispute.

Narrowing is the process through which established categories for classifying events and relationships are imposed on an event or series of events, defining the subject matter of a dispute in ways which make it amenable to conventional management procedures. Narrowing is the most common process of dispute transformation, and is particularly marked when a dispute is handled by officials of a specialized tribunal, such as a court, with highly routinized ways of handling cases. . . . Note that narrowing in this sense means fixing or circumscribing a framework in which the dispute is defined, rather than simply reducing or limiting the number of issues.

Expansion, in contrast, refers to a rephrasing in terms of a framework not previously accepted by the third party. Expansion challenges established categories for classifying events and relationships by linking subjects or issues that are typically separated, thus "stretching" or changing accepted frameworks for organizing reality. Expansion does not necessarily imply the increase or magnification of issues in a dispute (although this may occur); it refers to change or development in the normative framework used to interpret the dispute. There is no neat line which clearly distinguishes narrowing from expansion, but there does seem to be something rather special about transformations which try to change the perspective through which disputes are commonly perceived. Thus we will focus on expansion with a view to identifying the strategies associated with expansion, the implications of expanded disputes for legal change, and the conditions under which disputes can be expanded.

We argue here that the expansion of individual disputes is one way that social change is linked to legal change. . . .

Language The definition of a dispute articulated by each participant is a social construct which orders "facts" and invokes "norms" in particular ways — ways that reflect the personal interest or values of the participant, or that anticipate the definitions offered by others. . . . How a relationship or dispute is phrased has significant implications for the power of competing individuals or factions with vested interests in the primacy of a particular framework.

Where there are written legal codes and an official language of disputing, language may become an even more critical variable shaping the disputing process. . . . [T]he language of law must be reckoned with in its own terms: both rulers and ruled must explicitly deal with it as a point of reference in arguing cases and in legitimizing particular courses of action. Knowledge of "the law" and skill in manipulating its language become critical resources for defining and transforming disputes. We consider the language of disputing as varying along a continuum, with everyday discourse at one end and a highly specialized "language of law" at the other; we explore the effect of variation in language on the ways in which disputes are transformed, and on the roles of participants in the disputing process.

Audience Understanding the role of the audience(s) in dispute processing is especially important in an analysis of transformation of disputes . . . [the] mobilization of a particular audience, either by the disputants or by a third party, might be a crucial strategy in the management of a dispute. . . .

Focus on language, participants, and audience helps us to explain dispute transformations and the degree to which those transformations lead to particular case outcomes, and influence order maintenance and change. These variables are by no means exhaustive; furthermore, their precise interaction cannot be specified at the present time, since transformation processes are extremely complex. Our aim in this paper is to suggest ideas for building a theory of transformation of disputes; as yet no theory enables us to predict how a given dispute is likely to be transformed.

II. NARROWING

Most disputes are transformed through some kind of narrowing — that is, through the use of established categories to organize the events and issues in dispute. Typically one thinks of narrowing in highly differentiated legal arenas where specialized legal discourse is used to transform disputes in prescribed ways. But the process is a fundamental aspect of disputing, occurring in contexts as widely diverse as the "house palavers" of the Kpelle . . . , the public shouting matches and scuffles of the Jalé . . . , and the gossip networks of North Atlantic villages. . . . In these settings, as in specialized forums, participants argue about which definition should be imposed on the events and relationships in a dispute; the question of *which* definition will be used is of considerable significance to the outcome. Whether the discourse is specialized or more general, disputes will be narrowed in ways acceptable to a third party (either to appeal *to* the third party or inflicted *by* the third party). This introduces interests beyond those of the disputants into the dispute at hand; most likely these additional interests will reflect power of the third or political interests of those connected to the third. In this way rephrasing of disputes into established categories merges with the conflict-resolving and social control activities of the third party. . . .

. . . "Zinacantecos, like many peoples, reduce . . . complex, subjective problems . . . to straightforward disagreements over something tangible, . . . that can be objectively measured and divided." Tort actions under common law epitomize this kind of transformation of disputes over injuries into disputes over money. For instance, Rosenthal's . . . study illustrates how a personal injury plaintiff describes an accident to his lawyer in terms of a broad range of medical, emotional, family, work-related, and other concerns; the lawyer then rephrases the account in terms of a dollars-and-cents description of the case. Translation into the terms of a currency, such as money or, as in the first case below, pigs, converts the complex into the straightforward; significantly, however, it also reinforces the dominance of a particular currency as the standard through which people, products, and other resources are made commensurable. . . .

The *Uprooted Seedlings Disputes* . . . involves two Chagga lineage brothers in Tanzania in a quarrel over seedlings planted along the common boundary of their coffee-banana groves. The case was brought by Elifatio, the elder and poorer of the two men, against Richard, a prosperous young clerk, for uprooting seedlings Elifatio had planted along the common border of their land. The dispute was heard by a small gathering of kinsmen and a few neighbors, one of whom was leader of the imposed legal government unit, a "ten-house cell." Richard argued that he had not uprooted Elifatio's seedlings, since the seedlings had been planted, not on Elifatio's land, but on a village (government-maintained) path which ran through Richard's own land. Thus Richard's argument shifted the substance of the dispute to the question of the boundary between the pieces of land, and to a discussion of whose land the path cut across. One of the senior men present then suggested moving to the site of the uprooted trees to hear Elifatio's wife and son say that they had seen Richard pull up the seedlings. Others agreed with this suggestion, since it would also allow examination of the path and boundary in question. Negotiation over the two conflicting definitions of the dispute continued as the entire group actually moved to the area where the plants had been.

As the discussion proceeded, the size of the group increased with the addition of kinsmen and neighbors and several white-collar workers who were daily drinking companions of Richard. Elifatio's kin tried to focus the dispute on the alleged wrong caused by Richard's actions: "He had no business taking matters into his own hands and doing the uprooting himself." . . . But supporters of Richard dominated the argument, and Richard himself succeeded in defining the normative framework through his presentation of the facts: "I don't know who planted the trees I uprooted. I uprooted them after I saw that they were planted in the land of the Government." . . . Various aspects of these issues emerged during the several hours of talk. When a lineage elder called for a compromise agreement to settle the matter, the ten-house leader openly opposed him, asserting the need for an either/or decision in the case. The ten-house leader then pronounced Richard in the right, based on a judgment about the boundary issue and ignoring the self-help issue.

Richard's success in part seems related to his ability to work out a strategy of presentation and his facility in clearly articulating his case. Beyond this, however, . . . [are] the vocal and prestigious roles of both Richard's kin and his educated, salaried friends; . . . [there are important] connections between these salaried men and the ten-house leader who decided the case. The village hearing thus provided "an opportunity for certain public collectivities to come into competitive contact, to act authoritatively, to demonstrate and to reaffirm local relationships of superordination and subordination." . . . The public which provided Richard's point of orientation and support — white-collar workers employed in the towns . . . — became the crucial audience for the Chagga leader who presided at this hearing. Had the common audience of lineage kinsmen taken precedence . . . , then the emphasis might have been on a mutually acceptable rephrasing. Instead, however, the salaried men dominated the audience and influenced the outcome of the dispute. Thus we find in nascent form the processes which are so marked in bureaucratized court contexts and which are well illustrated in the next phase of this dispute: narrowing of the dispute in accordance with the categories and interests of a particular public which may or may not share the interests of either of the disputants; and an outcome, defined by this rephrasing, which is advantageous to the public or group which imposed its classification system on the dispute.

Narrowing Through Specialized Legal Discourse In the second phase of the *Uprooted Seedlings Dispute,* Elifatio appealed the neighborhood ruling to a Primary Court on Mt. Kilimanjaro, the lowest court in the national judicial system in Tanzania. Since civil litigation would have cost a filing fee, Elifatio followed the court clerk's advice and filed a criminal complaint for malicious destruction of property, and his case was heard a week later. Elifatio had no witnesses, and Richard denied the charge that he had uprooted Elifatio's seedlings. An effort by one of the court assessors to introduce the relationship of the two men as a factor to be considered in the case failed when the Magistrate ruled that the information was irrelevant. The questions which had dominated the village proceeding — on whose property the seedlings were planted, and about the nature of the path — were not raised, and Elifatio lost his case. The general legal category of "malicious destruction of property" helped to define the normative framework for the dispute in the court hearing. Moore notes that, "once the issues are narrowed in this way, there is no need to inquire into the general situation, the background, the relationships of the parties, the motives, and the like." . . . Further, the local publics shaped the case at both the village and court levels. The individuals and the ten-house leader who supported Richard influenced the definition of the case at the neighborhood hearing; and by refusing to act as witnesses in court, they assured a definition and outcome in Richard's favor. . . .

In the Tanzanian court, a specialized legal discourse restricted the alternative frameworks available for defining events and relationships in the dispute. Here, and in the next two cases, there is one official legal language controlled by court officials or by legal specialists; proper rephrasing of a dispute in this language is essential if the dispute is to be dealt with in an official disputing forum. These forums are clearly set apart from the everyday contexts in which disputes arise and thus facilitate the imposition of an official legal idiom for disputing. To the extent, however, that the forums continue to maintain close links to a relevant public beyond the boundaries of the forum itself, the disputing idiom reinforces patterns of social order advantageous to certain community groups and less favorable to others. . . .

The *Lost Negatives Dispute* is taken from Cain's . . . research on solicitors in England, and illustrates the role of lawyers in modifying disputes so that their client's needs, as well as the requirements of the legal system, are met. Cain writes that "clients bring many issues to the solicitor, expressed and constituted in terms of a variety of everyday discourses. The lawyer translates these, and reconstitutes the issues in terms of a legal discourse which has trans-situational applicability. In this sense law is a meta-language." . . . Cain provides a clear example of translation in a case involving some lost photographic negatives of a royal family. The plaintiff was the original owner of the negatives; he gave the negatives to a woman's magazine who apparently loaned them to Smith, a director of a film company. Smith had since left the company "under a cloud," and the plaintiff was suing the company for £10,000 for the lost negatives.

Lawyer A (observed by Cain) represented the film company itself (with its remaining two directors). Lawyer A argued successfully before a court of appeal that "the company had not been formed until three days after the photographs had been given to Smith. . . . The company could not be responsible for them as it was not in existence at the time. The correct procedure would be to bring a case against Smith in person and to join the woman's magazine in the action." . . . Lawyer A thus achieved his client's outcome by "juggling the translation of people into directors. . . . The situation here was that in everyday discourse they [the remaining two directors] were not responsible, and had had nothing to do with the issue. They were being challenged, however, in terms of a legal discourse of liability, which had to be refuted *in its own terms.*" . . .

The . . . *Lost Negatives* [dispute was] . . . shaped in significant ways by the existence of a written legal code: an official, public discourse by which specific definitions of roles and relationships were legitimated. Successful management of these disputes required not simply persuasive power or a broader array of supporters, but skill in manipulating the discourse. Important questions in cases such as these, then, include: who controls the use of legal (or other official) language, who has access to the language (or to those who are skilled in using it), and to what extent is the language used responsive to the needs of disputants? . . .

. . . In . . . the preceding [case], involvement of a specialist in legal discourse was necessary to successful management of the dispute. The specialist may serve as a kind of "culture broker," translating the concerns of a disputant into the language of law; or . . . the specialist may impose his own concerns in defining the case.

Participation by legal specialists thus interjects another set of interests in the phrasing of a dispute. These interests may reflect, for example, the specialist's (whether lawyer or judge) own financial concerns, relations with colleagues on the bench or at the bar, or his own political attitudes as to goals or interests to be pursued through a particular case. The official legal language prescribes the general frameworks and definitions to be used in classifying events in a dispute, but the actual use of those categories will depend upon the intermediary legal specialists. In situations where the intermediaries and legal officials work regularly together over a period of time, they may develop their own operational meanings of the legal codes and follow their own informal procedures for processing cases. Rephrasing of disputes may then emphasize issues relevant to the informal norms and local working environment of the legal forum, rather than to the broader community or the legislative officials. Plea negotiations by criminal court regulars in American courts clearly illustrate this narrowing according to "folk legal categories" — categories which are developed by actors within the court as they process cases. . . . for example, behavior that may correspond legally to first-degree robbery will not be so labeled in plea negotiations because it is not "really" first-degree robbery in the eyes of the court.

The case of the *Drunken Burglar* . . . is drawn from research on plea bargaining in Los Angeles Superior Court, and it illustrates negotiations over the narrowing of a burglary case. The defendant had five prior burglary convictions. As the Public Defender described the case, "The guy was caught drilling a hole in the wall next to a safe in a store. There's no defense at all." . . . There was also evidence that the defendant had been drinking just before his arrest, and the Public Defender felt that "the guy's just an old drunk." . . . Bargaining over the disposition of this case centered on evaluation of the defendant's character. Based on his view of the defendant, the defense attorney tried to arrange a county jail sentence through a transfer to a particularly lenient judge, but the prosecutor would not agree. The defense attorney stated, "He figured with five priors and drilling a hole in the wall by the safe that the guy's not just an old drunk. That he's a professional burglar. I don't think so, though." . . . Thus the prosecutor insisted on a commitment to state prison based on his classification of the defendant. Finally, however, the case was transferred and the defendant pled guilty with no sentence agreement. There were two presentence investigations done on the defendant, and although both reports were unfavorable, the defense attorney had succeeded in delaying the case enough to win a lengthy county jail sentence. The judge sentenced the defendant to one year (the maximum possible) county jail with no credit for time served (which was by then about nine months).

Whether the attorneys agree on application of their folk legal categories, or whether they do not (as in the case above), it is significant to note that their classifications are determined with little direct participation from either the defendant or the victim in the dispute. Working definitions of cases in the criminal court reflect the attitudes and experience of the court regulars and the ongoing relationships among them, as well as the organizational priorities and demands of the court in terms of, for example, its limited personnel and resources. In this way, the narrowing processes of plea bargaining are often highly responsive to, and shaped by, the requirements and interests of the court itself.

Summary . . . The introduction of an official language of law increases the power of certain political interests by restricting access to the disputing forum, by defining the kinds of disputes which can be placed on the agenda of the forum (and therefore, restricting public discussions about disputes not so legitimated), and by defining the roles of the parties in very specialized ways (and thus affirming who is "relevant" to cases and who is not).

Thus, our discussion of narrowing illustrates various ways in which the disputes of individuals serve as vehicles through which others in society assert claims to power. *Which* others become central in this process may depend upon the form of discourse used and the barriers to involvement of broader publics in the disputing process.

1. Where the discourse is specialized, those who know the language will tend to control the disputing process; this control may be further reinforced by varying degrees of physical

separation of the disputing forum from the society at large.

2. Where the discourse is specialized, disputants may have less access to and influence over the disputing process than do others such as translators and representatives of interested publics. Disputes will be transformed in accordance with the relative power of those within the disputing forum.

3. Under any form of discourse, playing to a broader public becomes important for disputants and third party alike and may be a particularly useful strategy for less advantaged litigants. In addition, highly active and organized publics may capture the dispute, bypassing litigant interests to press for outcomes in accord with their own interests.

4. Where the discourse is general, the disputing process is more accessible to both disputants and publics. Under these circumstances, interests of a broad public or particular groups will constrain the ways in which litigants, supporters, and third parties can transform a dispute.

5. The more general the language and the greater the degree of audience participation, the greater the possibility that the law can be shaped by, and will be responsive to, a more broadly defined community interest. The greater the degree of inequality in the society, however, the more likely it will be that particular interests will shape dispute transformations and legal norms.

Notes and Questions

1. Why do people take their claims to court? Are some problems more appropriate for court action than others? Give some examples of disputes that are appropriate for judicial intervention and some that are not.
2. Can individuals or groups be empowered through the litigation process? Can they be disempowered? How would Yngvesson and Mather answer these questions?

☐ A number of people have suggested that lawyers, trained as adversaries, exacerbate the conflicts and disputes of their clients. The following reading discusses how lawyers "shape" the disputes of their clients.

The Transformation of Disputes by Lawyers: What the Dispute Paradigm Does and Does Not Tell Us *Carrie Menkel-Meadow*

[T]he grievant tells a story of felt or perceived wrong to a third party (the lawyer) and the lawyer transforms the dispute by imposing "categories" on "events and relationships" which redefine the subject matter of dispute in ways "which make it amenable to conventional management procedures." This process of "narrowing" disputes occurs at various stages in lawyer-client interactions and could be usefully studied empirically. First, the lawyer may begin to narrow the dispute in the initial client interview. By asking questions which derive from the lawyer's repertoire of what is likely to be legally relevant, the lawyer defines the situation from the very beginning. Rather than permitting the client to tell a story freely to define what the dispute consists of, the lawyer begins to categorize the case as a "tort," "contract," or "property" dispute so that questions may be asked for legal saliency.

Carrie Menkel-Meadow, "The Transformation of Disputes by Lawyers: What the Dispute Paradigm Does and Does Not Tell Us," from *Missouri Journal of Dispute Resolution,* 1985, pp. 31–34. Reprinted by permission.

This may narrow the context of a dispute which has more complicated fact patterns and may involve some mix of legal and non-legal categories of dispute. A classic example of such a mixed dispute is a landlord-tenant case in which relationship issues and political issues (such as in rent control areas) intermingle with strictly legal issues of rent obligation, maintenance obligation, and nuisance. Thus, during the initial contact the lawyer narrows what is "wrong" by trying to place the dispute in a legal context which the lawyer feels he can handle.

Even if the client is allowed to tell his lawyer a broader story, the lawyer will narrow or rephrase the story in his efforts to seek remediation. Beginning with an effort to negotiate with the other side, the lawyer will construct a story which is recognizable to the other lawyer so that he can demand a stock remedial solution.

Once negotiation commences the dispute is further narrowed, the issues become stylized, and statements of what is disputed become ritualized because of the very process and constraints of litigation. In negotiation, lawyers begin to demand what they will ask the court to do if the case goes to trial. Lawyers are told to plan "minimum disposition," "target," and "reservation" points that are based on an analysis of what would happen if the case went to trial. Because a court resolution of the problem will result in a binary win/loss ruling, lawyers begin to conceive of the negotiation process as simply an earlier version of court adjudication. Thus, lawyers seek to persuade each other, using many of the same principles and normative entreaties that they will use in court, that they are right and ought to prevail now, before either party suffers further monetary or temporal loss. The remedies lawyers seek from each other may be sharply limited to what they think would be possible in a court case considering the court's remedial powers. Thus, most negotiations, like most lawsuits, are converted into linear, zero-sum games about money, where money serves as the proxy for a host of other needs and potential solutions such as apologies or substitute goods. Negotiated solutions become compromises in which each side concedes something to the other to avoid the harshness of a binary solution. The compromise, which by definition forces each side to give up something, may be unnecessary and fail to meet the real needs of the parties. Consider two children disputing about a single piece of chocolate cake. The parental dispute resolver, like most lawyers, might seek the "obvious" compromise solution of cutting the cake in half, thereby eliminating a "better" solution if one child desires the cake, while the other prefers the icing.

In counseling clients lawyers may tell them what remedies are legally possible (money or an injunction) and thus preclude inquiry into alternatives which the client might prefer or which might be easier to obtain from the other party. As Engel has noted, some disputants prefer an acknowledgement that wrong has been done to them to receiving money. Once lawyers are engaged and the legal system, even if only informally, has been mobilized, the adversarial structure of problem-solving forces polarization and routinization of demands and stifles a host of possible solutions. . . .

Notes and Questions

1. How do lawyers narrow disputes? Are there other third parties who do not transform conflict? What role do therapists and other counselors play in the transformation of disputes?

2. Does American society have too much conflict or too little? How could this be measured and evaluated?

3. Nils Christie claims that legal specialists are "interested in converting the image of a case from one of conflict into one of non-conflict."* Would Mather and Yngvesson, and Menkel-Meadow agree with this conclusion?

---

*"Conflicts as Property," *British Journal of Criminology* 17 (1977): 4.

CONFLICT AND COURTS

The epidemic of litigation reflects weakness in American Society.

Marc Cannon, "Contentiousness and Burdensome Litigation," *National Forum* (1983)

American society is choking from "legal pollution"; . . . Americans, as a people, are debilitated by the malady of "hyperlexis." Five hundred years from now, when historians sift through twentieth-century artifacts, they doubtless will have as little comprehension of American legal piety as most Americans now display toward medieval religious zeal. . . . Conflict is channeled into adversary proceedings with two combatants in every legal ring; but beyond the implicit assumption that every fight and any winner is good for society, the social good is ignored. Litigation is the all-purpose remedy that American society provides to its aggrieved members. But as rights are asserted, combat is encouraged; as the rule of law binds society, legal contentiousness increases social fragmentation.

Jerold Auerbach, *Justice Without Law* (1983)

In the early 1970s, judges and government officials began to speak publicly of a growing crisis in the U.S. courts. Attorney General Griffen Bell (in the Carter administration) and many others advocated alternatives to litigation as an antidote to the overcrowding, delays, and expense involved in going to court. A widespread discussion also emerged about public dissatisfaction with the justice system and the operation of courts in American society.

The materials in this section suggest differing interpretations of the role that courts play in the resolution of conflict. The readings also reflect questions about the amount and meaning of litigiousness in American culture and about the apparent court crisis.

Courts and Conflict Resolution *Vilhelm Aubert*

Law seems to have two basic and intimately connected tasks: to solve conflicts and to foster conformity to legal rules. The conflict-solving function has left the most distinctive marks upon the structure of legal thinking and upon the occupational role of the professional jurist. . . .

Vilhelm Aubert, *Journal of Conflict Resolution,* Volume XII, No. 1, pp. 40–51, copyright 1967 by *Journal of Conflict Resolution.* Reprinted by permission of Sage Publications, Inc.

THE JUDGE AS DECISION-MAKER

Decision-making is the task around which the legal profession has developed. Lawyers have traditionally been the experts on the use of power. That is not to say that lawyers have always been among the most powerful groups in society. But insofar as they have exerted power, or served those who wielded power, they have done so in a professional capacity, as a duty towards the abstract ideals of law, and on the basis of a theoretical and technical mastery of the field.

"Power over clients" may appear to be a contradiction in terms, since a client is a person who buys services from a professional, and is free to take or leave these services at will. The term is used to suggest the ambivalence which attaches to the role of the judge, due to his dual function of settling disputes and enforcing rules. Like the private lawyer, the judge waits for somebody to take the initiative and ask for his professional opinion. A large proportion of the parties who appear before a court of law could have stayed away if they had strongly preferred to do so. In this sense they are recruited to their role in court on the basis of a choice, as is the case when an individual becomes the client of an attorney. Once they are in court, however, barring an agreement between the litigants, they have to abide by the decisions made by the judge. The decisions are binding upon these "clients." The will of the judge will be made to prevail over the will of the "clients," if necessary by the use of force.

There are other aspects of judicial decision-making to which we shall soon return. It seems appropriate, however, to emphasize the service function of the judge, since the settlement of conflicts between private individuals has played such a dominant part in shaping the law — its theory as well as the techniques of decision-making. It is inherent in the situation of the judge *vis-à-vis* his clients that his service must be different in kind from that contributed by a doctor, an architect, or an engineer. His service is a contribution, not to an individual, but to a dyadic system in conflict. The fact that a plaintiff has asked the judge for a decision establishes no particularistic relationship between plaintiff and judge. Any attempt on the part of one of the litigants to reward the judge, or any willingness on the part of the judge to receive remuneration from the winning party, would be considered wrong and a grave breach of the obligations incumbent upon him.

Not everybody who appears before a court of law has chosen to do so, or has even had the chance of opting against doing so, given that certain actions have taken place. The criminal is normally brought before the court on the initiative of the state, represented by the prosecution. In criminal cases the function of settling conflicts recedes at the expense of the task of upholding conformity with the laws. Historically, criminal law has developed from a less differentiated system with strong elements of private litigation between two parties. Even today, criminal procedure is heavily influenced by the fact that it takes place before a tribunal which is also, and predominantly, concerned with the settlement of disputes between private parties in civilian suits. This notwithstanding, the power relationship between the judge and the defendant must be classified as power over citizens, meaning a power from which there is no escape for the individual. . . .

WHY DO CLIENTS GO TO COURT? . . .

Possibly the most general reason who two conflicting parties deviate from "rational" behavior and permit a case to be settled in a court of law, with greatly increased chances of total loss for one, is the tendency to overestimate one's chances of winning. Only in a borderline case are the chances of winning 100 per cent for one of the parties.

There are some rather general reasons why people should tend to overestimate their chances to win legal suits. For one thing, the arguments favoring one's own case are much more readily available than those favoring the other party. Cognitively speaking, full insight into all the aspects of the case is lacking. The positive aspects will easily be perceptually over-represented.

Legal suits have a moral tinge. To predict loss in a courtroom would normally imply doubt concerning one's own moral right. The personal defense erected against such moral doubt will therefore tend to render factual predictions unreliable. There may even exist a need to retain one's moral aggression against the other party. Legal suits represent an area of life where it is hard for people to be completely rational, in the sense of attempting an unbiased prediction of the future based on available empirical grounds. It is, in addition — and for other reasons — an area where predictions are often "technically" difficult to make.

Notes and Questions

1. A number of commentators have observed that the judicial role is undergoing a transformation. Law professor Judith Resnick, for example, has suggested that many judges

> . . . have departed from their earlier attitudes; they have dropped the relatively disinterested pose to adopt a more active, "managerial" stance. In growing numbers, judges are not only adjudicating the merits of issues presented to them by litigants, but also are meeting with parties in chambers to encourage settlement of disputes and to supervise case preparation. Both before and after the trial, judges are playing a critical role in shaping litigation and influencing results.*

*"Managerial Judges," *Harvard Law Review,* 96 (1982): 376.

Resnick and others are concerned about the implications of "managerial judging." She claims that

> . . . As managers, judges learn more about cases much earlier than they did in the past. They negotiate with parties about the course, timing, and scope of both pretrial and postrial litigation. These managerial responsibilities give judges greater power. Yet the restraints that formerly circumscribed judicial authority are conspicuously absent. Managerial judges frequently work beyond the public view, off the record, with no obligation to provide written, reasoned opinions, and out of reach of appellate review.†

†Ibid.

Vilhelm Aubert has offered one way of understanding why people take their problems to courts. In the following reading, Marc Galanter helps advance this analysis by describing more specifically the kinds of cases most likely to be fully adjudicated rather than otherwise settled.

Reading the Landscape of Disputes: What We Know and Don't Know (and Think We Know) About Our Allegedly Contentious and Litigious Society *Marc Galanter*

Whether or not America has experienced a "litigation explosion," or is suffering from "legal pollution," or is in thrall to an "imperial judiciary," there has surely been an explosion of concern about the legal health of American society. A battery of observers has concluded that American society is over-legalized. According to these commentators, government, at our urging, tries to use law to regulate too much and in too much detail. Our courts, overwhelmed by a flood of litigation, are incapable of giving timely, inexpensive and effective relief, yet simultaneously extend their reach into areas beyond both their competence and legitimacy. A citizenry of unparalleled contentiousness exercises a hair-trigger readiness to invoke the law, asking courts to address both trifles unworthy of them and social problems beyond their grasp. In short, these observers would have us believe that we suffer from too much law, too many lawyers, courts that take on too much — and an excessive readiness to utilize all of them. As a convenient label for this whole catalog of ills, I borrow the term

Originally published in *31 UCLA L. Rev. 4,* Reprinted by permission. (Footnotes omitted.)

"hyperlexis" from one of these observers. This Article will examine one component of the hyperlexis syndrome — the alleged high rates of disputing and litigation — in the context of current research. I shall then offer a few reflections on the hyperlexis perspective.

A. THE "HYPERLEXIS" EXPLOSION

That we suffer from an excessive amount of disputing and litigation is a theme met frequently in hyperlexology. . . .

. . . Only recently the Chief Justice of the United States referred to the "litigation explosion during this generation" and reflected that:

> One reason our courts have become overburdened is that Americans are increasingly turning to the courts for relief from a range of personal distresses and anxieties. Remedies for personal wrongs that once were considered the responsibility of institutions other than the courts are now boldly asserted as legal "entitlements." The courts have been expected to fill the void created by the decline of church, family, and neighborhood unity.

That Americans litigate excessively is received wisdom among leaders of the bar. Shortly after taking office a recent president of the American Bar Association is reported to have complained that "everybody brings a lawsuit about everything these days" and vowed to "do something about the litigious society."

These learned observations are echoed and magnified in the popular press. *U.S. News and World Report* reported that:

> Americans in all walks of life are being buried under an avalanche of lawsuits.
>
> Doctors are being sued by patients. Lawyers are being sued by clients. Teachers are being sued by students. Merchants, manufacturers and all levels of government — from Washington, D.C., down to local sewer boards – are being sued by people of all sorts.
>
> The "epidemic of hair-trigger suing," as one jurist calls it, even has infected the family. Children haul their parents into court, while husbands and wives sue each other, brothers sue brothers, and friends sue friends.

Business Week observed that "[l]itigation has become America's secular religion." . . .

We should remind ourselves just how recent this perception of things is. In 1960, Charles Breitel, then a Justice of the Appellate Division of New York's Supreme Court (the state's intermediate appellate court) delivered a lecture on "The Quandary in Litigation." He commented on the paradox that "throughout the nation the courts are congested; yet it is also true that there is a decline in litigation." . . . This decline was not considered a matter for applause, as more recent discussions would lead us to expect. Indeed, a contrary view was expressed: "It is the public that is the loser in the decline of the litigation process and the litigation bar." The whole litigation complex — litigation bar, adversary system, jury, trial judiciary and appellate courts — was seen as a valuable but underutilized public resource for securing individual redress which, at the same time, made a "substantial contribution to the development of a sound body of rules of behavior."

A few years later, in 1965, a wide-ranging and authoritative discussion of the causes of court congestion did not even mention litigiousness. As recently as 1970, in his first "State of the Judiciary" address, Chief Justice Burger cataloged the problems of the courts, emphasizing funding, management, procedure, and other "supply side" matters. There was no hint that courts were the victims of runaway litigation. But by 1977, the spectre of litigiousness was fully visible. Chief Justice Burger spoke of the "inherently litigious nature of Americans" and deplored "a notion abroad in our times — especially since the 60's and early 70's which I hope will pass — that traditional litigation — because it has been successful in some public areas — is the cure-all for every problem that besets us or annoys us."

The assertion that we engage in too much disputing and litigation implies two determinations: first, ascertainment of how much we have, and, second, establishment of how much is too much. What are the data from which such determinations can be made?

Until recently there have been few attempts to measure the amount of contention and litigation. Although court statistics have been compiled for management use, they are incomplete. We have no established indicators like the Gross National Product or the rate of index crimes — indicators that are themselves fraught with all sorts of problems.

Typically the evidence cited for the litigation explosion consists of:

1. The growth in filings in federal courts;
2. The growth in size of the legal profession;
3. Accounts of monster cases (such as the AT & T and IBM antitrust cases) and the vast amounts of resources consumed in such litigation;
4. Atrocity stories — that is, citation of cases that seem grotesque, petty, or extravagant: A half-million dollar suit is filed by a woman against community officials because they forbid her to breast-feed her child at the community pool; a child sues his parents for "malparenting"; a disappointed suitor brings suit for being stood up on a date; rejected mistresses sue their former paramours; sports fans sue officials and management; and Indians claim vast tracts of land; and
5. War stories — that is, accounts of personal experience by business and other managers about how litigation impinges on their institutions, ties their hands, impairs efficiency, runs up costs, etc.

Even if these statistics and accounts establish that we have a great deal of litigation, how do we know it is too much? This evidence draws its polemical power from the implicit comparison to some better past or some more favored place. Pervading these reports is a fond recollection of a time when it wasn't so — federal courts had fewer cases, there were fewer lawyers, people with outlandish claims were properly inhibited or chastened by upright lawyers, and managers could carry out their duties without fear of being sued. In this golden pre-litigious era, problems which were not solved by sturdy self-reliance or stoic endurance were addressed by vigorous community institutions. Not only was our own past more favored but, it is often noted, other societies of comparable advancement and amenity have fewer lawyers and less litigation. Japan, in particular, is viewed as exemplary. Its few lawyers and scarce litigation are thought to betoken a state of social harmony conducive to high productivity and prosperity. . . .

C. COMPARED TO WHAT?

How can we tell whether the amount of disputing and litigation . . . is too much — or too little? In part this depends on our reading of the meaning of disputes and lawsuits — are they evils which inevitably detract from social well-being? Or do they, some of them anyway, contain the seeds of vindication, justice, even social improvement? Such judgments could be applied to any quantity of disputes. But even if individual disputes or lawsuits may be harmless or even beneficent, having too many of them may be a bad thing. But how many are too many? Are we to measure this by the capacity of courts or other institutions? But how do we know *they* are the right size? We might instead measure the value of disputing by its measurable effects, but as we shall see this a daunting and untried endeavor. As noted earlier, much of the literature expressing concern about the litigation explosion finds a standard, at least implicitly, by comparing the present situation to our own national past or to more favored lands abroad.

1. THEN AND NOW

Unfortunately for purposes of comparison, we have almost no data from earlier points in our own history that are comparable to our contemporary survey evidence. . . . But there is one kind of evidence that we can compare across time — data on the number of cases brought in the courts. By combining this with population figures we can derive a litigation rate for various populations and see if this rate has increased over time. This procedure has a number of infirmities if we are using it to estimate the disputatious or contentious character of the population. For example, are all the cases counted really disputes or contests? How comparable are the figures from time to time as recording systems change, jurisdictions are altered, etc.? Again, our rate does not reflect the portion of disputes that comes before agencies other than regular courts — administrative agencies, zoning boards, licensing bodies, small claims courts, justices of the peace, and others — whose number and identity have changed over time. Thus, our rates tell us about the use of the regular courts rather than about the entire use of official third-party dispute institutions. This is troubling because we don't know how much changes in rates reflect changes in the population of dispute institutions and the flow of traffic among them, and how much reflect changes in the tendency to litigate in the broad sense of taking disputes to governmental third parties. Nevertheless, let us see what litigation rates tell us.

Federal courts handle only a tiny fraction of all the cases filed in the United States. In 1975 there were approximately 7.27 million cases (civil, criminal, and juvenile) filed in state courts of general jurisdiction and about 160,000 in the federal district courts. There has been a dramatic rise in federal court filings in recent decades. Filings in the district courts increased from 68,135 in 1940 to 89,112 in 1960, and to 198,710 in 1980. From 1940 to 1960, the absolute rise barely kept pace with population growth, but from 1960 to 1980 there was a pronounced per capita increase in filings from 0.5 per thousand population to 0.9 per thousand.

These higher rates of filings are frequently cited as evidence of feverish litigiousness. But other evidence provides little support for the notion that these are linked with desperate congestion and crushing caseloads. David Clark's revealing analysis of federal district court activity from 1900 to 1980 shows a dramatic reduction in the duration of civil cases from about three and one-half years at the beginning of the century to 1.16 years in 1980. The number of cases terminated per judge has been steady since World War II and remains considerably lower than in the inter-war period. Not only has the increase in judges kept up with the caseload, but there has been a massive increase in the support staff. While the average number of cases terminated per judge was approximately the same in 1980 as in 1960, the total employment of the federal judiciary rose during that period from 27.7 for every million people to 65.6 per million.

However, there has been a striking growth of appeals in federal courts. The rate at which those eligible to press appeals have exercised that right has risen, especially in criminal cases. The number of appeals filed in the federal courts of appeal almost quintupled from 1960 to 1980, while the number of judges nearly doubled. Understandably, it is the Supreme Court, whose filings during this period more than doubled, and the courts of appeal, that are the provenance of much of the imagery of catastrophic overload.

Over the past century there has been a pronounced shift in the make-up of the cases being brought to regular trial courts in the United States. There has been a shift from civil to criminal in the work of these courts. On the civil side, there has been a shift from cases involving market transactions (contract, property, and debt collection) to family and tort cases.

Domestic relations cases in the five counties studied by Arthur Young, *et al.*, rose from 21.8% of filings in 1903–1904 to 49.1% in 1976–1977. In Alameda County they went from 18% in 1890 to 51.7% in 1970; in San Benito from 19.3% to 61.7%. In St. Louis, family (including estate) cases rose from 23.9% of filings in 1895 to 45.9% in 1970.

There was a comparable growth in torts as a percentage of filings. In the five counties studied by Arthur Young, *et al.*, torts were 1.2% of the filings in 1903–1904 and 12.4% in 1976–1977. In Alameda they grew from 6.0% in 1890 to 27.1% in 1970; in San Benito from 3.2% to

19.2%. In St. Louis torts went from 7.7% of filings in 1895 to 35.3% in 1970.

There was a corresponding decline in the portion of the caseload composed of commercial, contract, and property matters. In the five counties, commercial and property cases fell from 71.7% of filings in 1903–1904 to 32.3% in 1976–1977. In Alameda County contracts and property fell from 57% in 1890 to 18% in 1970; in San Benito the decline was from 58.1% to 12.3%. In St. Louis contract and property cases fell from 54.5% in 1895 to 21.4% in 1970.

Notwithstanding the differences in method among the studies from which these data are drawn, the similarity in the trends is strikingly evident. Regular civil courts in America are being called on to deal with a very different mix of matters than they formerly did. These shifts are reflected in the make-up of appellate caseloads. Studies of state supreme courts and of federal courts of appeals trace a parallel movement from business and property cases to tort, criminal law, and public law.

Not only has there been a shift in the pattern of cases coming into the courts, there have been changes in what has transpired once they are filed. The available evidence requires more detailed analysis than space or time allows, so let me confine myself to a few general observations. First, it is evident that in all these courts most cases for the entire span of time in question have been disposed of without a full adversary trial. Voluntary dismissal (presumably the result of settlement) and uncontested judgment are the most common dispositions recorded in these courts. There is no evidence to suggest an increase in the portion of cases that runs the whole course. Several studies suggest that while litigation rates have risen, there has been a decline in the per capita rate of contested cases. Similarly, there has been a decline in the per capita rate of cases eliciting written opinions from state supreme courts. . . .

There have been other changes in the character of what courts do. Less of their work is the direct, decisive resolution of individual disputes; more of it is routine administration and supervised bargaining. Courts contribute to the settlement of disputes less by imposing authoritative resolutions and more by pattern setting, by distribution of bargaining counters, and by mediation. Courts produce effects that radiate widely: Rulings on motions, imposition of sanctions, and damage awards become signals and sources of counters used for bargaining and regulation in many settings. The portion of cases that runs the whole course has declined. But for the minority of matters that runs the full course, adjudication is more protracted, more elaborate, more exhaustive, and more expensive. The process is more rational in the sense that it is free of antiquated and arbitrary formalities. Concealment is discouraged; litigants have access to more information. It is open to evidence of complicated states of facts and responsive to a wider range of argument.

If full-blown adjudication is relatively less common, absolutely there is more of it. This minority includes a growing component of large and complex cases that involve investments of immense amounts of time, exhaustive investigation and research, lavish deployment of expensive experts, and prodigious use of court resources. It also includes a growing number of what have been called "public law" or "structural" or "extended impact" cases involving public policies and institutions such as prisons, mental hospitals, or schools, in which many contending groups are locked together in an enduring relationship. In such cases the traditional format of the lawsuit is stretched in various ways and this extension of the scope of adjudication is connected with development of an expansive style of judging. Litigation on this enlarged scale also reflects the presence of larger aggregations of specialist lawyers with enduring relations to the parties, who are able to assemble factual materials, coordinate experts, and monitor performance. . . .

CONCLUSION

In the course of this quick tour of disputing and litigation in the United States, I have tried to suggest a reading of the landscape that differs radically from the "litigation explosion" reading.

This contextual reading differs in its view of the source and career of disputes and in its view of their significance. It does not view contemporary litigation as an eruption of pathological contentiousness, a dangerous and unprecedented loosening of needed restraints, or the breakdown either of a common ethos or of community regulation. Instead, I see contemporary patterns of disputing as an adaptive (but not necessarily optimal) response to a set of changing conditions. There have been great changes in the social production of injuries as a result of, among other things, the increased power and range of injury-producing machinery and substances. There has been a great increase in social knowledge about the causation of injuries and of technologies for preventing them; there has been a wide dissemination of awareness of this knowledge to an increasingly educated public. There is an enhanced sense that harmful and confining conditions could be remedied. At the same time more of the interactions in the lives of many are with remote entities over which there are few direct controls. Government is used more to regulate these remote sources of harm and to assuage previously unremedied harms. Legal remedies become available to large segments of the population who earlier had little occasion to use the law. It may be easier to mobilize social support for disputing. In the light of all these changes, the pattern of use is conservative, departing relatively little from earlier patterns.

But overshadowing the change in actual disputing patterns are changes in the symbolic aspects of the system. There is more law, and our experience of most of it is increasingly indirect and mediated. Even while most disputing leads to mediation or bargaining, rather than authoritative disposition by the courts, the courts occupy a larger portion of the symbolic universe and litigation seems omnipresent.

Is more and more visible litigation the sign and agent of the demise of community? This view of litigation as a destructive force, undermining other social institutions, strikes me as misleadingly one-sided. If litigation marks the assertion of individual will, it is also a reaching out for communal help and affirmation. If some litigation challenges accepted practice, it is an instrument for testing the quality of present consensus. It provides a forum for moving issues from the realm of unilateral power into a realm of public accountability. By permitting older clusters of practice to be challenged and new ones tested and incorporated into the constellation it helps to "create a new paradigm for the establishment of stable community life." If we relinquish the notion of community as some unchanging and all-encompassing *gemeinschaft* in favor of the multiple, partial, and emergent community that we experience in contemporary urban life, we need not regard litigation as an antagonist of community.

[*In the following numbered paragraphs, Galanter describes the most common contemporary ajudicated cases and the issues involved in their settlement.*]

(1) Perhaps the single most common type is the case where a party needs the judicial declaration — as in divorce or probate proceedings. In such cases there is typically no contest or, if there was a contest, it has been resolved by the parties before securing judicial ratification.

(2) Another very frequent kind of fully adjudicated case is one which is "cut and dried" and can be processed cheaply and routinely, as in most collection cases where the defendant frequently does not appear. In both these types the element of contest is minimal.

(3) Other cases are adjudicated because of a premium placed on having an external agency make the decision. Thus, an insurance company functionary may want to avoid responsibility for a large payout. A prosecutor may prefer that charges against the accused in an infamous crime be dismissed by the court rather than by his office.

(4) There may be value to an actor in showing some external audience (a creditor or the public) that no stone has been left unturned.

(5) Or an external decision may be sought where the case is so complex or the outcome so indeterminate that it is too unwieldy or costly to arrange a settlement.

(6) Settlement may be unappealing because the "settlement value" is insufficient. Ross describes the personal injury case in which damages are high but liability sufficiently doubtful to preclude a large settlement. Similarly, criminal defendants facing mandatory sentences may find the available bargains unattractive.

(7) Even when the bargain is acceptable in itself, it may be spurned because of the effect accepting it would have on the bargaining credibility of a player in future transactions. A litigant or lawyer may want to display his commitment and thus enhance his credibility as an adversary in future rounds of play.

(8) Finally, a party may want to adjudicate in order to affect the state of the law. Some parties — typically recurrent organizational litigants — are willing to invest in securing from a court a declaration of "good law," or avoiding a declaration of "bad law," even where such a decision costs far more than a settlement in the case at hand since such a declaration will improve the litigant's position in any future controversies.

(9) Or parties may not seek furtherance of their interests, but vindication of fundamental value commitments. This is true, for example, of the organizations which have sponsored much church-state litigation in the United States. Parties disputing about value differences rather than about interest conflicts are less likely to settle.

(10) Related to this is the special case of government bodies whose notion of "gain" is often problematic and may seek from courts authoritative interpretations of public policy — that is, redefinitions of their notion of gain.

Notes and Questions

1. Read the following observation by David Trubeck:

> We live in a strange time. High priests of our legal order are questioning the law. At ritual events and in official publications the legal elite has stopped celebrating the law and encouraging its use, and has begun to chastise the public for relying on the law and to condemn lawyers who encourage such popular vices. Where chief justices, law school deans and similar types once celebrated the Rule of Law as the core of American civilization and advocated the expansion of legal rights and legal services, some now rail against the evils of "legal pollution" and warn of the threat of a "litigation explosion."
>
> The picture that is painted is of a people in moral decline. In tones reminiscent of revival meetings, these high priests associate law with images of evil and its use with weakness and decadence. A former law school dean and president of the Legal Services Corporation calls up the foul image of "legal pollution . . . clogging the everyday affairs of all of us." The Chief Justice of the United States chastises Americans for "increasingly turning to the courts for relief from a range of personal distresses and anxieties."
>
> The nation, we are told, is threatened by the disease of hyperlexis and the litigation explosion it engenders.*

What evidences of general moral decline do you see in society today? How might they be related to overuse of the courts (if indeed they are)? What remedies do you suggest?

2. Consider the following article from the *New York Times* (March 10, 1982):

> TOKYO, March 9 — On the morning of Feb. 9, the skies were clear and the weather balmy when a Japan Air Lines DC-8 plunged into Tokyo Bay 300 yards short of the Haneda Airport runway, killing 24 people.
>
> A few days afterward, Yasumoto Takagi, president of Japan Air Lines, embarked on a sojourn of obligation that in Japan is the expected behavior of a top executive whose company is involved in such a tragedy.
>
> Mr. Takagi visited the families of most of the crash victims, apologizing profusely and paying homage on his knees before the Buddhist funeral altars in the homes of the bereaved.
>
> . . . Japan Air Lines has not yet been sued by any relatives of the passengers who died

---

*Turning Away from Law? *Michigan Law Review*, 82 (February 1984): 824. Reprinted by permission of *Michigan Law Review* and the author.

in the crash and it is unlikely that the company will be sued.

"If this had happened in the United States," James Weatherly, a spokesman for Japan Air Lines, said, "we probably would have seen a wave of million-dollar suits. But people don't sue here." . . .

"This is a nonadversarial, nonlitigious society," observed Tadashi Yamamoto, director of the Japan Center for International Exchange, a not-for-profit organization in Tokyo. "And I think that is reflected in how a misfortune like this airplane crash is handled."

The reluctance of Japanese to go to court stands in stark contrast with practices in the West, especially in the United States. International comparisons of lawsuits are imprecise. But Government figures show that in 1979 about 160,000 civil suits were filed in Japan, while the comparable total in the United States was several million.

There are about half a million lawyers in the United States, compared with just over 10,000 in Japan, which has half the population of the United States.

The lack of litigiousness in Japan is often cited as an economic advantage. The Japanese, it is said, do not spend much time, money or energy suing each other but, instead, concentrate on outproducing other nations.

That Japan is a relatively suit-free society is generally attributed to its cohesive culture, with its heritage of shunning open confrontation. . . .†

3. Galanter's exhaustive analysis suggests that the claims about our crippling litigation explosion are exaggerated and unfounded. Yet why do these claims persist? Why might some of the most influential lawyers and judges be actively promoting the view that our courts are breaking down and that our legal system is in crisis?

---

†*New York Times,* March 10, 1982. Copyright © 1982 by The New York Times Company. Reprinted by permission.

Neighborhood Justice in Capitalist Society: The Expansion of the Informal State *Richard Hofrichter*

. . . [T]he rule of law within the judicial system poses other constraints on the capacities of courts to handle effectively matters that come before them. . . . The judicial system is organized to handle certain types of disputes deemed appropriate. But the definition of appropriate keeps changing. For example, so-called small-scale or minor disputes have either been rejected by courts as nonjusticiable or relegated to small claims courts, shifted to arbitration procedures, or placed in a lesser priority on the docket. Such disputes are often described by judicial officials as "junk cases." Increasingly these types of neighborhood disputes at the level of everyday life — in contrast to those that involve loss of money or which occur among people who can handle them on their own — are becoming more disruptive to the social order. They disrupt the infrastructural stability necessary for capital accumulation. As Wolf Heydebrand explains,

> a decreased capacity for formal conflict resolution may actually increase the level of substantive conflict in the larger society. Thus, by dismissing cases or inducing settlements, courts may temporarily terminate conflicts but not ultimately resolve them. Instead, disputes are forced back into an indeterminate situation, that is, into the

---

From Richard Hofrichter, *Neighborhood Justice in Capitalist Society: The Expansion of the Informal State* (Contributions in Political Science, No. 171, Greenwood Press, Inc., Westport, CT, 1987), pp. 51–53. Copyright © 1987 by Richard Hofrichter. Reprinted with permission of author and publisher. (Citations omitted.)

> arena of conflicting socio-economic forces which had generated the dispute in the first place. . . .

As the economy sinks into deeper crisis, and as citizens use the courts to secure their rights under public programs . . . , the disputes of working-class people with the state and among themselves may proliferate. More is at stake for them. But these people are not socialized to the ways of the courts. Judicial procedures are designed for the middle and upper classes and their problems. Formal procedures and the rule of law cannot handle the particularisms brought into court by people who cannot deal with formalism. Because the court is limited by formal procedural rules, it cannot confront the roots of conflict. It cannot therefore manage with precision solutions external to legal logic, given the relations between capital expansion and social disruption which have been described. Preemptive political intervention is required, regardless of whether such disruption can be defined by specific legal offenses.

The courts are increasingly politicized. They are geared to the protection of government policy against numerous claimants (e.g., Social Security, Medicaid and affirmative action). Under those conditions they become surrogates of the state and therefore less visibly autonomous. Sometimes they must protect the working class in a time of rising entitlements and at other times they become more of a foe as the state reduces entitlements. However, this relation of claimants with the state creates a crisis of legitimacy. When courts are perceived as not resolving disputes but as protecting the state and sometimes capital (e.g., anti-trust, oil leasing decisions), dissatisfaction occurs and hegemony is undermined. People do not use courts to be treated as a social problem but in order to receive a hearing. Disorder can thus mean too many people using the courts and making claims against the state. Too much litigation from the point of view of capital is thereby a form of disorder.

Legal rules and procedures in many ways are part of the infrastructure of daily life and in that sense represent a form of hegemony. For example, people take the courts and its rules for granted, as an orderly part of their communities. . . . But increasingly, the kinds of conflicts arising in communities are more disruptive than previously. As judicial institutions become more isolated, bureaucratic, divorced from everyday life, and separated from the communities they serve, law loses legitimacy. The distinction between its reified abstractions and the culture become visible, experienced. The administrative failures of law in its implementation heighten its vulnerability and claims to legitimacy. . . .

Notes and Questions

1. The readings in this section offer different interpretations of the meaning of the increase in the use of courts by citizens. Former federal judge Simon Rifkind suggests the following:

> . . . From my vantage point as a working trial lawyer, I venture the opinion that much of today's dissatisfaction springs not from failure but from conspicuous judicial success. The courts have been displaying a spectacular performance; it enjoys a constant "Standing Room Only" attendance. The cause of complaint is that the queues are getting too long. No problem seems to be beyond the desire of the American people to entrust to the courts; many litigants are clamoring for attention.
>
> In consequence, there is a growing — and justified — apprehension that
>
> (1) Quantitatively, the courts are carrying too heavy a burden — and probably a burden beyond the capability of mitigation by merely increasing the number of judges.
>
> (2) Qualitatively, the courts are being asked to solve problems for which they are not institutionally equipped, or not as well equipped as other available agencies.*

What are Rifkind's underlying assumptions about law and society, and how do they

---

*"Are We Asking Too Much of Our Courts?" *Federal Rules Decisions,* 70 (1976): 79.

differ from those of Richard Hofrichter in the previous reading?

2. Who says that U.S. courts are overburdened and misused? How many cases should courts take? What is the right amount? How does one know which cases belong in the courtroom and which do not? Consider these questions as you read the first reading in Section 3.

3 ALTERNATIVES TO THE LEGAL SYSTEM: PROMISE AND PROBLEMS

[D]iscourage litigation. Persuade your neighbors to compromise whenever you can. Point out to them how the nominal winner is often a real loser in fees, expenses, and waste of time.

Abraham Lincoln

[O]ur system is too costly, too painful, too destructive, too inefficient for a truly civilized people.

Chief Justice Warren E. Burger, *Annual Report on the State of the Judiciary* (1982)

There must be a better way than routine court processing for handling many disputes among citizens.

Daniel McGillis, *Community Dispute Resolution Programs and Public Policy* (1986)

The past decade has seen a dramatic increase in the number of program alternatives to courts for settling disputes. The development of this movement has been prompted both by the apparent crisis in the courts (as outlined in the previous section) and by public dissatisfaction with the justice system.

Many proponents of alternative dispute resolution claim that the adversary process is inappropriate for several types of conflict, particularly those involving ongoing relationships. For example, many people feel that family problems, neighborhood disputes, and minor criminal matters are better addressed outside formal court settings, where the adversary system will not interfere with a discussion of the underlying issues in dispute.

Although alternative dispute resolution programs vary widely, most current efforts are organized around the idea that courts are inappropriate as forums for resolving many types of disputes. Some supporters of mediation programs believe that this movement will enhance the efficiency of the legal system as cases are diverted from court to informal resolution settings. Others believe that alternative dispute resolution challenges the very values and roles that U.S. legal institutions play. Whereas legal institutions are concerned with control and regulation, alternative dispute resolution, its proponents claim, is concerned with the values of peacemaking and conciliation.

The following materials focus on the differing interpretations of the dispute resolution movement in contemporary Western society. The first reading by Sally Engle Merry compares mediation in small-scale societies with American community mediation programs.

The Social Organization of Mediation in Nonindustrial Societies: Implications for Informal Community Justice in America

Sally Engle Merry

INTRODUCTION

American courts are notorious for their failure to resolve minor, interpersonal disputes quickly, effectively, and in a way that satisfies the disputing parties. The increasing urbanism, transiency, and heterogeneity of American society in the twentieth century has undermined informal dispute settlement mechanisms rooted in home, church, and community and increased the demand for other means of dealing with family, neighbor, and community disputes. However, many legal experts argue that the formality of the courts, their adherence to an adversary model, their strict rules of procedure, and their reliance on adjudication render them inappropriate for handling many kinds of interpersonal quarrels arising in ongoing social relationships. . . .

. . . The American Bar Association, the U.S. Department of Justice, the American Arbitration Association, the Institute for Mediation and Conflict Resolution, and many community groups are experimenting with the use of mediation in community-based centers to resolve minor interpersonal disputes on the assumption that this will provide a more humane, responsive, and accessible form of justice. . . . However, an examination of anthropological models of mediation suggests that community mediation in urban America, as these experiments are presently constituted, may provide a kind and quality of justice fundamentally different from that which their creators intended.

Every society develops a range of mechanisms for resolving disputes, some of which are informal, rooted in such local institutions as lineage, clan, religious association, or family, and some of which are more formal, coercive, and dependent on the political hierarchy. With the transition from small-scale, kinship-based societies to large, complex, urban social systems, disputants turn increasingly to formal rather than informal dispute resolution mechanisms. Community mediation, however, endeavors to turn the tide: to return control of certain kinds of disruptive and offensive behavior to local communities, where they can be managed through mediation, compromise, and restitution, enforced by community social sanctions and the desire of disputants to settle. It seeks to replace the formality of the court with the informality of the neighborhood, narrow considerations of legal principles with more general questions of morality and shared responsibility, win or lose outcomes with compromises, and penal sanctions of fine and imprisonment with compensation and informal social pressures. The introduction of neighborhood mediation, frequently termed citizen dispute resolution,[1] is thus part of a general

---

From "The Social Organization of Mediation in Nonindustrial Societies: Implications for Informal Community Justice in America," by Sally Engle Merry from *The Politics of Informal Justice*, edited by R. Abel. (Most footnotes and all citations omitted.)

movement toward delegalization, toward removing dispute management from the courts on the premise that substantive justice is better served outside the formal procedures of the existing legal system. . . . Clearly, the therapeutic and consensual nature of such forms of dispute resolution is attractive to a society increasingly critical of adversary adjudication and coercive sanctions. These proposed citizen dispute settlement centers appear to satisfy a happy conjunction of interests between those concerned with the quality and accessibility of justice available to the individual and those tackling problems of massive court congestion and mushrooming court costs.[2]

MEDIATION IN SMALL-SCALE SOCIETIES

Mediation is an important mode of settling disputes in societies ranging from horticultural and pastoral peoples whose political institutions are coterminous with their kinship systems to peasant villages incorporated into nation-states. Although it is difficult to evaluate the "effectiveness" of mediation in these various settings, it is possible to examine the conditions under which disputants choose mediation rather than some other process. Disputants in societies of the first type turn to mediation as an alternative to violence, feud, or warfare; those in the second choose it is preference to violence or court. . . .

The Process of Mediation Mediation is prompt. Ideally, it occurs immediately after the incident, before the disputants have time to harden their positions or, as the Waigali say, before they can "think about their ancestors" — their pride and social positions. The process is time-consuming, taking hours or days, as long as is necessary to reach a settlement. . . . Negotiations are often conducted in public forums where neighbors and kinsmen can offer opinions and condemn the behavior of unreasonable disputants. Even when the mediator is a go-between who meets with the parties privately, the wider public often knows the nature of the discussions through its kin ties to both sides.

---

[1]Community dispute settlement centers are either court based or community based. Most of the programs that have been studied are closely connected to a court, receive referrals from court clerks and judges, and rely on the threat of judicial sanction to encourage mediation. Community-based models build on local community leaders to run the programs and to serve as mediators, and they eschew any connection with the courts either as a source of cases or as a sanction against recalcitrant disputants. . . . These centers endeavor to use community social pressure to induce compliance with agreements.

[2]Citizen dispute resolution programs provide an alternative to adjudication for minor civil and criminal complaints arising from domestic, neighborhood, family, merchant-consumer, and landlord-tenant disputes in which the parties know one another. . . . Disputants air their grievances in an informal, personal, and supportive atmosphere in which a third party, usually a lay community member, simply mediates the dispute, facilitating the process by which the disputing parties collectively forge a mutually acceptable compromise solution or, in a few programs, agree to submit to arbitration. The mediation experience, ideally, is voluntary, noncoercive, more humane, and more closely tailored to the needs of individual disputants than is the court. The process is one of bargaining and negotiation, and the free-ranging discussion that fully explores feelings and perspectives usually lasts much longer than adjudication. Outcomes are generally compromises rather than zero-sum decisions and take into account the total relationship between the parties. Rules provide a framework for the discussion and are used by each side to justify its position, but they do not determine the outcome. . . . The process is not one of matching a problem to a rule but of establishing agreement between the parties about a fair or just settlement, even if this deviates from existing rules. Settlements may even create new rules. . . . The settlements are generally compensatory rather than penal, focusing on peacemaking and restitution rather than punishment. . . . They serve to reconcile the parties, diffuse hostility, and maintain relatively amicable and cooperative relationships. Mediation thus seems to be a more appropriate procedure than adjudication for resolving disrupted interpersonal relationships, since its central quality is "its capacity to reorient the parties toward each other, not by imposing rules on them, but by helping them to achieve a new and shared perception of their relationship, a perception that will redirect their attitudes and dispositions toward one another." . . .

Mediators arrange the payment of damages. Their function is usually to negotiate an outcome that will satisfy both parties through an exchange of property, the demarcation of a new boundary line, or the rendering of a public apology; vague promises of improved behavior in the future are not sufficient. Injuries such as insult, adultery, assault, and even homicide are generally perceived as reparable through gifts of cattle, sheep, or other valuables in amounts specified by custom.

The mediation process usually ends with immediate consummation of the agreement. When it is necessary to postpone the final settlement, for instance, while one disputant finds enough sheep, the assembly will often reconvene to observe the exchange. . . . In societies that lack written contracts, such an immediate exchange is the only guarantee of performance. . . . However, when debts are not paid promptly they often remain unsatisfied, offering fertile soil for future disputes. The last step in the mediation process is typically a ritual of reconciliation, whether drinking coffee together in a Lebanese village or a massive village feast financed by the loser as a public apology, as in prerevolutionary China. . . .

The Social Organization of Mediation Mediators are respected, influential community members with experience and acknowledged expertise in settling disputes. Successful settlements enhance their prestige and political prominence and often earn them some form of payment from the disputing parties. . . . Mediators often have special religious status. . . . The reputation they earn for skillful negotiation, expertise in community norms and genealogies, and fairness and impartiality brings them more cases and political influence. Mediators are not outside authorities but informal leaders of kin groups, age grades, local hamlets, or other social grouping. . . . They are usually of higher social status than the disputants. Where disputes involve members of higher social strata, outsiders are often needed. . . .

Mediators represent the norms and values of their communities, often attaining their positions by virtue of their expertise in moral issues. They advocate a settlement that accords with commonly accepted notions of justice, couched in terms of custom, virtue, and fairness, and reflecting community judgments about appropriate behavior. To flout such a settlement is to defy the moral order of the community. Mediators often deliver moral lectures to one or both disputants. Finally, they are experts in village social relationships and genealogy, bringing to the conflict a vast store of knowledge about how individuals are expected to behave toward one another in general as well as about the reputations and social identities of the particular disputants. Mediators build upon their past experience with similar cases and their knowledge of local customs regarding such disputes, manipulating these rules to justify their opinions.

The Nature of Mediated Settlements Mediated settlements are backed by coercion. Although the mediator lacks authority to impose a judgment, he is always able to exert influence and social pressure to persuade an intransigent party to accept some settlement and, often, to accept the settlement the mediator advocates. The community also exerts social pressure on disputants to settle and to abide by their agreement. Supernatural sanctions are often important as well.

Since mediators are usually powerful and influential, loss of their goodwill is itself a cause for concern. Some simply facilitate dyadic negotiations . . . , whereas others practically adjudicate, backing their decisions with armed force. . . .

The community itself exerts pressure to settle. Recalcitrant disputants become the objects of gossip and scandal. . . . Witchcraft and supernatural beliefs concerning illness also serve as a powerful incentive to restoring amicable relations. . . .

One further form of coercion and social pressure is the need to maintain peaceful relations with the other party. Terminating relations may be damaging to political, economic, or kinship transactions; threats of violence or court action raise the specter of protracted, ruinous litigation or a bloody feud. Insofar as they seek to avoid these disasters, disputing parties are coerced to settle. Nevertheless, in no case is a mediator's decision backed by institutionalized force, and parties are always free to reject mediation and face the consequences.

Mediated settlements between unequals are unequal. With few exceptions, a mediated settlement reflects the status inequalities between the disputants. Payments for homicide among the Sudanese Nuer and the Enga of New Guinea . . . depend on the social status of the dead man; Ifugao compensation varies according to the status of both plaintiff and defendant. . . .

Since a mediator lacks the ability to enforce his decisions, he must find an outcome both parties will accept. A mutually acceptable solution tends to be one in which the less powerful gives up more. . . . The greater the power of the mediator, the more leverage he has to impose a solution that disregards the inequality of the parties. The judge, at least in theory, adjudicates the legal rights of the disputants; he does not weigh their total social personalities.

COMMUNITY MEDIATION PROGRAMS IN CONTEMPORARY AMERICA

This analysis of mediation in small-scale societies has important implications for the way that process will function in urban America and for the quality of justice it can provide. First, urban American mediation is more perfunctory, more delayed, and less concrete than mediation in small-scale societies. Hearings typically occur seven to eleven days after the incident is reported. . . . This time lapse may mean that disputant positions have hardened. A large portion of referrals are made by judges, in which cases the plaintiff has already decided against seeking a consensual settlement. Experiments with delaying the hearing for a three-week "cooling-off" period support the wisdom of rapid intervention since the number of disputants appearing for these hearings drops radically. . . . Negotiations and settlements are strictly private, so that community members can neither participate in the agreement nor pressure the parties to comply, except in a few community-based programs such as the San Francisco Community Boards. Hearings in American centers last a maximum of two and a half hours and often less. . . . Although this is longer than many court trials, it does not approach the input of time and resources of mediation in small-scale societies.

Second, the enveloping social system of urban American neighborhoods is quite different from that of small-scale, nonindustrial societies. I argued earlier . . . that the efficacy of mediation depends on the existence of a cohesive, stable, morally integrated community whose powers of informal social control can be harnessed to informally achieved settlements. Yet since American centers function in large metropolitan areas, the community pressures necessary to induce disputants to accept a compromise settlement are generally absent. Disputants are rarely embedded in a close, cohesive social system where they need to maintain cooperative relationships. Even when disputants come from the same neighborhood, unless they are integrated into a unitary social structure their conflicts in one relationship do not have repercussions for others. Further, they have the option of moving away from a conflict situation rather than settling it by compromise. This is probably a frequent pattern in American society . . . , although it may carry a high cost. . . .

My own study of an urban neighborhood suggests that avoidance, or moving away, is common but is usually chosen reluctantly after a long period of conflict and the exhaustion of other alternatives. . . . Most of the disputes in this low-income, polyethnic housing project passed through a long phase of endurance, in which the disputants simply put up with barking dogs, dirty stairwells, minor thefts, and jealous, violent lovers while appealing to a variety of formal third parties — the management office, the police, and the courts. But few disputes were resolved by these third parties. Disputants rarely consulted neighborhood leaders. Efforts to mobilize community public opinion had little impact in this fragmented, diverse community whose social networks were largely restricted to each ethnic group. . . . Disputants tended to rely on violence as an alternative to formal third parties. In the long run, disputes eventually terminated only after one or both parties moved out of the project. Thus, in those segments of American society where the social structure is fragmented and the population mobile, the need to settle may be slight and the incentive to mediate and to compromise correspondingly reduced.

Nor are court-based versions of citizen dispute resolution programs organized in a way that could exploit existing patterns of informal social control. Most programs serve areas with several thousand to several million residents rather than the smaller social units whose residents may belong to a single social network. The mediator, although usually chosen from the "local community," is almost always required to be a stranger to the disputants in order to assure his impartiality. This means that he lacks the store of knowledge about personal histories and reputations and the nature of previous settlements in the local area that appears to be critical to the success of a mediator. . . . The mediator is not a person of unusual prestige, moral stature, or influence in the neighborhood but simply a resident who has had a week of training in mediation and is paid a nominal sum to hear cases occasionally on evenings and weekends.

These mediators are also unable to operate in terms of a shared moral system. They are enjoined by mediation trainers not to make moral statements or judgments and are encouraged to seek a mutually acceptable outcome, regardless of their notions of relevant laws or norms. . . . Since each center serves a large area, mediators must handle cases from a wide variety of neighborhoods with diverse norms and values. They cannot assume that they share the value system of the disputants or that the disputants themselves agree on normative standards. Nor can they be familiar with the outcomes of similar disputes settled in the disputants' neighborhoods, which could serve as precedents. Public opinion cannot reinforce a decision reached in a private session attended only be mediators and disputants. Private hearings cannot serve as arenas to raise broader issues affecting entire neighborhoods. . . . Agreements are not solemnized with the kind of public ritual that in nonindustrial societies frequently serves to solidify the commitment of the parties to support the agreement and secure public approval.

Citizen dispute resolution programs may be most effective in disputes between parties involved in an ongoing relationship they wish to preserve. Although most centers purport to deal exclusively with conflicts in "ongoing social relationships," this phrase conceals an important distinction between relationships with a long past that are terminating and those with a short history but expectations of a long future. . . . The latter is the critical variable for mediation. The willingness of a tenant to compromise with his landlord may be far greater when he plans to stay in his apartment for another ten years than that of a tenant who has been there ten years but is planning to move the following week. Similarly, a domestic conflict in which both parties wish to preserve the relationship demands different treatment from one in which they are trying to establish the terms of their separation. Where separating parties share custody of a child, however, their relations will inevitably endure, and mediation can again be appropriate. Mediators are more likely to function successfully in disputes where both parties have an incentive to settle than in those where both wish only to win.

Further, mediation depends on a community fabric that links disputants in enduring relationships important to both and provides a shared set of values within which the dispute can be discussed. In the United States, urban ethnic enclaves often possess these qualities. . . . Programs in these social settings may be able to marshal informal sanctions behind their actions by selecting influential and morally respected individuals as mediators and making hearings public.

A third implication of this cross-cultural survey of mediation is that the process may be more appropriate for concrete disputes that can be settled by a simple exchange of property than for complex, emotion-laden interpersonal hostilities arising out of tangled webs of insult and rivalry, abuse and counterabuse, love and hatred. Resolution of the latter often involves vague promises of changed behavior or avoidance. . . . It is this kind of dispute for which mediation is advocated and that judges, prosecutors, and the police feel least able to handle. . . . Yet there are indications that such cases are most resistant to long-term resolution through mediation, whereas the former result in outcomes that are easier to monitor and more likely to be viewed by disputants as satisfactory over the long run. . . . Those disputes most likely to be perceived by complainants as resolved in the long run (six to twelve months after the hearing) were landlord–tenant, harassment, and recovery of money or property; domestic or child welfare and neighborhood cases were least likely to be so perceived. . . . Ironically, the kinds of cases for which citizen dispute resolution is most often advocated thus seem resistant to mediation, whereas those in which it might be more effective are handled fairly effectively by adjudication. Programs may thus be more effective in relieving court congestion and shunting aside troublesome cases than in providing a more desirable process to those now poorly served in domestic and neighborhood disputes.

A fourth feature of mediation in small-scale societies, with critical implications for American programs, is the central role of coercion. Mediation in village and pastoral societies does not occur without coercion, but the latter takes the form of informal social pressures, fear of supernatural reprisals, and expectations of violence at the hands of the aggrieved party or the mediator, rather than that of state coercion. In American programs, the role of coercion is a recurring concern. . . . The staff and mediators of the Dade County Citizen Dispute Settlement Program, for example, see their program's "lack of teeth" as a major problem and suggest that they need subpoena power and legal enforcement of mediation agreements. . . . A persistent problem for many citizen dispute resolution programs is the high proportion of "no-shows" — disputants who fail to appear for scheduled hearings. The Florida mediators would like greater legal authority to cope with this. . . .

Moreover, the court is used to coerce disputants not only to mediate but also to settle and to abide by the outcome. In many programs, cases are continued by the court pending successful mediation so that disputants are negotiating in the shadow of the courthouse, aware that failure to agree will put them back before the judge. Mediators having difficulty persuading disputants to submit to mediation and reach an agreement threaten court action if the process stalls. The three federally funded neighborhood justice centers (NJCs) rely on the coercion implicit in referrals from police, prosecutors, or the court, which suggests that disputes not mediated will be adjudicated. . . .

Thus there are pressures within the citizen dispute resolution movement to rely more heavily on the coercive powers of the court or to demand new coercive powers for mediators in order to compensate for the absence of informal pressures. This endangers one of the primary attractions of mediation — its less coercive, more consensual process. Furthermore, this trend raises the specter of quasi-judicial entities exercising coercive powers outside the courts, controlling citizens without the legal safeguards of due process and the adversary system. . . . Such entities might become a way of expanding state intervention into the daily lives of citizens without proper regard for their legal rights. . . .

There are indications that citizen dispute resolution programs are coping with the problem of coercion through a second strategy: by producing settlements to which both parties will agree and that appear to provide a solution, yet that are essentially meaningless and unenforceable. Since a frequent measure of the success of citizen dispute resolution programs is the proportion of hearings reaching an agreement, resort to low-quality settlements is difficult to measure or evaluate. . . . Mediation programs have been criticized for their inability to deal with the underlying sources of social conflict such as social inequality, poverty, unemployment, racism, or sexism. Even in domestic disputes, however, mediation without coercion may not always produce the kinds of settlements desired. . . .

In my research on patterns of disputing in an American urban neighborhood, I found that disputants frequently appeal to the court in interpersonal disputes but use it as a sanction rather than as a forum for settling disputes. . . . It is predominantly those less capable of using violence, such as women and the elderly, who threaten or actually go to court, not because they expect to win an effective judgment (cases are often dismissed) but in order to equalize the balance. If this is the role courts are playing in domestic and neighbor disputes, mediation clearly can not provide an adequate substitute.

The criticism that mediation programs are generating meaningless settlements is supported by the facts that caseloads remain low although the programs appear to offer a much-needed service and that large numbers of cases apparently amenable to mediation continue to appear in courts. Many referrals fail to come to hearings, and the percentage of voluntary referrals is very small. In the first six months of operation, for example, the three neighborhood justice centers held 525 hearings, 86 per cent of which were declared resolved, yet this represents only 29 hearings per center per month, a surprisingly low number considering that each center serves a large metropolitan area. . . . Perhaps this low level of use simply represents public inertia or ignorance about these programs, but it is also possible that disputants perceive them as ineffective or inappropriate forums for dispute resolution and take their conflicts elsewhere.

Mediation may provide an effective tool for dispute resolution, however, if its capacities and processes are more carefully understood and its use more circumscribed. It seems most appropriate for those disputes in which both parties wish to maintain their relationship. This desire provides an incentive to settle, to seek peace rather than victory. Neighbors quarreling over a common boundary or separating spouses settling child custody, for example, must find ways of living together, and this need to settle is itself a form of pressure to agree.

The observed inequality of mediated settlements in small-scale societies raises troubling questions about the quality of justice in American mediation centers. The impact of mediation may be quite different, depending on whether the dispute is between equals or unequals. Mediated settlements perpetuate differences in social status — a characteristic with very different implications in nonindustrial ranked societies and industrialized class societies that embrace an egalitarian ideology. Conflicts between equals and between unequals both fall under the rubric of "ongoing social relationships" and may therefore be considered appropriate for mediation. Yet there are significant differences between disputes among relative equals, such as neighbors or local small merchants and regular customers, and those between relative unequals, such as a violent husband and an abused wife or a large merchant and a consumer. In disputes between unequals, the weaker party may turn to a third party to equalize the balance and seek an equitable resolution, as the powerless Cheyenne turns to an important chief. . . . To be effective, the third party must possess sufficient power to equalize the balance between the disputants. Unless mediation centers address this problem or decide to deal only with disputes between equals, they risk serving the weaker parties poorly by accommodating their demands with inadequate compensation while inhibiting their appeal to courts where they could, at least in theory, demand a legally just settlement. . . . Of course, considerable research suggests that courts also serve to perpetuate inequalities. . . .

There are some indications that disputes between unequals could become a significant proportion of the mediation caseload, although we lack information on this point from functioning programs. In the first six months of operation, the neighborhood justice centers found that almost half of their respondents were representatives of corporations or public and private organizations but that only 5 percent of complainants were. . . . In two reports on Florida programs, respondents reported satisfaction with the mediation process more often than complainants, although these studies did not tabulate the proportion of corporate representatives. . . . Thus, we must ask whether mediation serves the weaker parties better than the courts do or simply perpetuates inequalities, as it does in small-scale societies. A mode of dispute resolution whose outcomes clearly reflect the economic and political inequalities of American society may ultimately by unacceptable in a polity based on legal, if not social, equality.

CONCLUSIONS

Existing versions of mediation, particularly those programs closely connected to courts, seem to function quite differently from mediation in nonindustrial societies. These programs do not rely on informal social controls rooted in the local community. In heterogeneous urban neighborhoods where the social fabric of community is loosely woven, mediation programs turn to the threat of the court to achieve settlement. Since one inspiration for mediation was dissatisfaction with penal sanctions in interpersonal disputes, their reappearance through the back door represents a return to a mode of sanctioning that has already been judged inadequate. If disputants are impelled to try to mediat[e] before they can use the court, mediation centers may become meaningless at best and, at worst, another hurdle between the citizen and his day in court.

On the other hand, mediation has tremendous potential if it can be built on existing community structures (where these exist) rather than appended to the legal system; if it is restricted to disputes between relative equals, and if it is used only in future-oriented disputes where the parties feel a need to settle. It offers hope for resolving disputes arising from faulty communication and misunderstanding, those in which both parties wish to avoid the criminal penalties of the court, and those where an agreement involves a specific exchange rather than long-term promises of improved behavior.

Perhaps a mediation program that endeavored to build on existing social structures and mobilized informal social pressures through public hearings and the use of influential community leaders as mediators within small areas knit together through interlocking social relationships could achieve effective dispute resolution without recourse to the sanctions of the state. But in some settings, the social structure may be too diffuse and the population too transient to allow mediation to function as it does in the anthropological prototype. Mediation cannot serve as a panacea for the problems that plague the courts; nor can it, alone, reverse the trend toward the dissolution of the cohesive local community in American society.

Societies must always choose some course between the conflicting goals of order and liberty. The cumbersome, formalistic procedures of due process serve, at least ideally, to protect liberty and to preserve the rule of law against state oppression. However, the price of these procedural safeguards for the protection of individual freedom may be a certain level of disorder, of disruption or rule breaking that goes unpunished, and inefficiency in the processing of cases. The social changes of twentieth-century America have gradually loosened community control over behavior, allowing greater liberty to nonconforming, disruptive, and deviant individuals. With the dissolution of informal social controls, the perceived increase in disorder has led to heightened demands that the court restore order even in the domain of neighborhood and family conflicts. . . . From this perspective the citizen dispute resolution movement is an anomaly: It seeks to return control over nonacceptable behavior to the local community without sacrificing the greater measure of personal liberty and autonomy that the very breakdown in informal social controls have provided. Informal control mechanisms in small-scale societies produce order at the expense of individual freedom, particularly for individuals of lower rank or power. It is particularly instructive that those American settings in which mediation occurs naturally are also those where members and powerful leaders exert considerable control over their fellows. . . . If Americans are unwilling to return to a social world in which their actions can be judged and condemned by neighbors and fellow workers, mediation programs will be unable to function.

The alternative is to create institutions that appear to grant communities control over behavior yet that in reality simply provide a forum for handling disputes outside the protections of due process. . . . We still know too little about what mediation programs will do, but they contain the possibility of increasing state control over individual behavior outside the rule of law, of enhancing order at the expense of liberty.

Notes and Questions

1. Daniel McGillis, a researcher at Harvard Law School's Center for Criminal Justice, offers an interpretation that differs from those offered by preceding authors about the strengths and weaknesses of mediation programs:

> The survival and growth in numbers of dispute resolution programs suggests that they must be doing something right, especially given the routine demise of many other 1970s social programs. . . .
>
> While they have been successful in many respects, the programs have certainly failed to fulfill many of the early optimistic goals laid out for them. They were expected to reduce court caseloads in their jurisdictions, freeing up resources for the remaining cases on the docket. No demonstrable evidence exists that programs have remotely succeeded in this task. A corollary to that goal was an anticipated reduction in justice system costs (because mediation would be very cheap compared to adjudication). The courts have not been reported to be mailing checks of unexpended funds back to governmental treasuries, however. In fact, some mediation programs are quite expensive on a per-case basis. Programs have also typically failed to develop large caseloads (in comparison to comparable court caseloads). Some programs sponsored by the courts and the prosecutors' offices are exceptions to this pattern, and a few process over 10,000 cases per year. But we can probably say with some confidence after approximately ten years' experience with such programs that the American people are not eagerly beating a path to the programs' doors, although this may be due more to Americans' focus on court dispute settlement (as idealized on Perry Mason) than due to anything fundamentally wrong with dispute resolution programs.
>
> So what are the mediation programs doing right to justify the investment of scarce local and state governmental resources? The most likely achievement of the programs is that they provide a superior process for many of the types of cases that they handle. Research studies support the casual impression that people like to have their cases mediated. They typically view the process as more fair and more understandable, and they like the agreements that are achieved. Agreements are reached in approximately 80 percent of mediation sessions. Disputants consistently report that they are satisfied with the mediation process and view outcomes as fair. . . . Research on the mediation of minor civil cases in the Maine District Courts indicates that defendants in mediated cases are far more likely to pay their settlement in full than defendants in comparable court cases (70% vs. 34%, respectively).*

2. Why might mediation programs seem to have trouble attracting users? Is the size of caseload an indicator of success? What other factors should be considered in evaluating the success or failure of mediation programs?
3. Do you think it is important that people feel satisfied at the end of a case?
4. A number of states are enacting legislation that makes mediation for certain types of cases a mandatory part of the legislative process. Are there problems with this approach? What are the positive aspects of these statutes?

**Community Dispute Resolution Programs and Public Policy* (Washington, D. C.: U.S. Department of Justice, National Institute of Justice, 1986), pp. 13–14.

As mediation programs proliferate in contemporary society, a number of concerns are being raised about their significance for women and their relationship to the formal legal system. The following materials address some of this discussion.

Mediation from a Feminist Perspective: Promise and Problems

Janet Rifkin

INTRODUCTION

The interest in alternative dispute resolution is intensifying in this country and others as well. Programs offering mediation, arbitration, negotiation and conciliation services are proliferating throughout the United States, Canada, Australia and Western Europe. These programs may be court-related or community-based. In either case, the overt justifications for mediation programs are similar. Mediating conflict as a substitute for litigating disputes has been justified by two basic rationales: First, the formal court system is not suited to handle the range and number of disputes being brought to it. Second, the adversary process itself is not suited to resolve interpersonal disputes.

While mediation is flourishing, concern about the theory and practice of "informal" justice is also increasing. Most of the criticisms focus on the manipulative potential of informal systems such as mediation. For example, critics suggest the bureaucratic logic that supports state legality is as much a part of the process in informal and non-bureaucratic settings as it is in the formal court of law. Critics also suggest that the state, faced with fiscal crisis, achieves spending cuts by resorting to informalization, accompanied by appeals to popular participation, consensual social life, and the struggle against bureaucracy. Others argue that mediation fosters the privatization of life — the cult of the personal — and denies the existence of irreconcilable structural conflicts between classes or between citizen and state. Finally, critics claim that mediation is detrimental to the interests of women, who, being less empowered, need both the formal legal system and aggressive legal representation to protect existing rights and pursue new legal safeguards.

Although these criticisms remain, the debate about mediation lacks a careful questioning of law and alternative dispute programs from a feminist perspective. For the most part, mediation's critics predicate their questions on the traditional view of law that litigation leads to social change and that the "lawsuit" is *the* appropriate and most effective vehicle for challenging unfair social practices, for protecting individuals, and for delineating new areas of guaranteed "rights."

This dominant view leaves unchallenged the patriarchal paradigm of law as hierarchy, combat, and adversarialness; and, therefore, generates only a certain kind of questioning of mediation. This viewpoint has not asked whether and in what way alternative dispute resolution reflects a feminist analysis of law and conflict resolution, and whether in theory and practice mediation challenges or reinforces gender inequality in contemporary society.

My intention in this discussion is to articulate some of the questions basic to an understanding of the relationship between law, mediation and feminist inquiry. As one commentator noted:

> [O]bjective epistemology is the law of law. It ensures that the law will most reinforce existing distributions of power when it most

---

Janet Rifkin, "Mediation from a Feminist Perspective: Promise and Problems," from *Law and Inequality: A Journal of Theory and Practice,* Volume II, February 1984, No. 1. (Footnotes omitted.)

> closely adheres to its own highest ideal of fairness. . . . Such law not only reflects a society in which men rule women; it rules in a male way. The rule form which unites scientific knowledge with state control in its conception of what law is, institutionalizes the objective as jurisprudence.

What is not yet clearly developed is how mediation in theory reflects "a new jurisprudence, a new relation between life and law." Further, what is not yet known is whether in practice, mediating disputes reflects feminist jurisprudential differences from the male ideology of law or whether mediating simply reinforces the "objective epistemology" of law.

I. MEDIATION IN THEORY: FEMINIST PEDAGOGY AND THE STUDY OF LAW

Social structures supporting the pedagogy practiced in traditional American law schools conflict with the social structures espoused as the basis of mediation. In traditional legal pedagogy, the case book is the emblem of the authoritative character of the law and the "Socratic Method" mirrors and reinforces the structure of authority. Traditional legal pedagogy is hierarchical with a vengeance. It trains students to reject an analysis of social reality as it is subjectively experienced, and instead requires them to internalize a series of abstract rules. Traditional legal pedagogy is deeply wedded to a patriarchal conception of law. This wedding is characterized by hierarchy, adversarialness, linearity, and rationality, a paradigm in which reason is synonymous with rule and the ideal of the reasonable man is the fundamental frame of reference for making decisions. Whereas formal law reinforces the dominance of hierarchy and rationality supporting traditional ideas of public and private, mediation challenges these notions. By explicitly asking different kinds of questions, by supporting dialogue and by challenging the authority of "objective epistemology" implicit in the law and in legal teaching, a new pedagogy emerges which is essential to a new way of thinking about law. This new pedagogical approach, in a mediation course, places the emphasis on the female concerns of responsibility and justice. These concerns contrast with the concerns for individual rights that are characteristic of the male pedagogy dominant in law school and most other academic settings.

The study of mediation thus introduces and, indeed, requires a feminist pedagogy, a feminist pedagogy fundamentally different from traditional legal pedagogy. "[F]eminist method is consciousness raising: the collective critical reconstitution of the meaning of women's social experience as women live through it."

Legal pedagogy involves a learning process in which "facts, issues, principles, reasoning and laws are learned without specific reference to behavior or experience; where students are required to think in legal terms and to articulate problems and issues in the language of the law." Legal pedagogy reflects the power relationships which feminist theory challenges. The study of mediation from a feminist perspective focuses on questions which are antithetical to traditional legal study: Is liberal law and the rationalistic linear mode of thinking, of which law study is a part, in some fundamental way male and distinguishable from female contextual thinking? Do women have a distinct moral language emphasizing concern for others, responsibility, care, and obligation as distinguished from male morality, which focuses on abstract notions of individual rights? Do female and male engenderment generate different modes of thinking and discourse and is it useful to distinguish between them?

These questions not only exist outside the framework of traditional legal teaching but also represent a challenge to the way of thinking that supports the operation of law in this society. Theoretically, at least, the study of mediation challenges traditional pedagogy. This challenge and mediation's emphasis on the female concerns of responsibility and justice necessitate framing questions from a feminist perspective.

II. MEDIATION IN PRACTICE: PROMISE AND PROBLEMS

Mediation in practice operates as a process of discussion, clarification, and compromise aided by third party facilitators. It is a process in which the third party has no state-enforced power. A third party's power lies in the ability to persuade the parties to reach a voluntary settlement. It involves the creation of consensus between the parties in which the parties are brought together in an atmosphere of confidentiality to discover shared social and moral values as a means of coming to an agreement.

In mediation, the focus is not on formal and substantive rights. The emphasis is on the process by which the individual parties are encouraged to work out their own solution in a spirit of compromise. The intervention of a mediator turns the initial dyad of a dispute into a triadic interaction of some kind. However, the disputing parties retain their ability to decide whether or not to agree and accept proposals for an outcome irrespective of the source of the proposals.

The following chart highlights some of the main contrasts between adjudication and the practice of mediation.

Adjudication	*Mediation*
public	private
formal	informal
strict evidentiary rules	no formal parameters — conversationalist
coercive	voluntary
emphasis on conflict of interest, value dissensus	emphasis on areas of agreement, points in common
win/lose — combative	compromise — conciliatory
decision oriented	agreement oriented
rule oriented	person oriented
professional decision maker	community lay volunteers
representation by lawyer	direct participation

Although the mediator is a neutral intervenor with no self-interest, a mediator does become a negotiator. In that role the mediator inevitably brings to the process, deliberately or not, certain ideas, knowledge, and assumptions. What a mediator can do is also affected by the particular context and the parties' expectations of mediation.

The question of a mediator's technique brings us back to the issue of whether the methodology is premised on the same view of objectivity inherent in legal ideology. If neutrality, an important feature of being a mediator, masks the same "objectivist" paradigm of law, then mediation, like legalism, reinforces the ideology fundamental to the state as male and further institutionalizes male power. . . . The rhetoric of mediation rejects the "objectivist epistemology" of the law. Theoretically, in mediation precedents, rules, and a legalized conception of facts are not only irrelevant but constrain the mediator's job of helping the parties to reorient their perception of the problem to the extent that an agreement can be reached. The legal rights of the parties are not central to the discussion which takes place in mediation. Again, in theory, the lack of focus in mediation on abstract legal rights contrasts with the emphasis on them in legal proceedings.

These differences, however, are clearer in theory than in practice. . . .

. . . Numerous questions emerge from actually mediated disputes:

1. Does the mediation process substitute another form of "objectivist" manipulation of conflict?

2. Does the mediation process really shift the focus of the dispute from an abstract notion of right to the more female concerns of care, responsibility, and concern for others?

3. Does mediation involve a new definition of justice?

4. What is the measure of whether these things or others are happening in mediation? What kinds of questions need to be asked of the participants in particular and of the process in general?

5. Does mediation of a conflict alter the power relationship between the parties? Does it redistribute that power or does it perpetuate a relationship of unequality?

6. Does mediation, by requiring participation and decision making by the parties, offer a better forum for resolving problems in situations where traditionally women have been particularly victimized?

Notes and Questions

1. Mediation has been criticized by women's groups and by others concerned about issues relating to family violence. The following excerpt reflects one perspective on this issue:

   It is not a coincidence that, just when the state legislatures are passing strong laws with respect to battery, marital property and child support enforcement, and when the U.S. Congress and U.S. Supreme Court are acting for the first time in history on family law issues, there is a movement to exclude these issues from the courts. It is no coincidence that, as battered women are gaining increased access to the courts through pro se civil procedures or increased arrests, there is a movement that would exclude these cases from the jurisdiction of the civil and criminal courts. Nor is it a coincidence that, as standards and enforcement are beginning to be developed by the legal system in the areas of child and spousal support, mediation, which would offer no enforcement, is being encouraged.

   Only the legal system has the power to remove the batterer from the home, to arrest when necessary, to enforce the terms of any decree if a new assault occurs, to discover hidden assets, to prevent dissipation of assets, and to enforce support orders. Only the legislatures and courts can create, develop, expand and enforce women's rights. Mediation offers no protection, no deterrence, no enforcement, and no opportunity to expand women's rights.

   At a time when women are making significant progress on family law issues in the courts and legislatures on both the state and federal levels, after years of inactivity by these bodies, a dispute resolution approach that is private and not required to be consistent with the law is being advocated. This approach defeats the progress of women's rights, and therefore must be rejected forcefully.*

2. Consider the following comment by Lisa Lerman.

   Abuse cases can be successfully resolved (that is, the violence can be stopped) in a number of different fora. Sometimes legal action designed to prevent violence or to rehabilitate the offender is more effective than directly punitive action, especially if the parties want to maintain their relationship. Action in civil court may be less threatening, and therefore more accessible to victims of abuse. On the other hand, some abuses will not respond seriously to any civil action but are effectively intimidated by criminal charges.

   Although ambivalent about working with a legal system which is often unreceptive to feminist values and priorities, battered women's advocates have moved toward a loose consensus that law enforcement is valuable. They agree that remedies are more likely to be effective if they lay clear responsibility for the violence on the abusive party, let him know that serious consequences will flow from repeated violence, and follow through on that threat when further violence occurs. Remedies are believed to be most effective if the system provides assistance and protection to the women during and after the legal proceedings and tailors its remedies to the needs of the victims on a case-by-case basis. Finally, the battered women's movement favors remedies which focus on abuse as the primary issue, and address other problems, such as visitation and property issues, in the context of avoiding continued abuse.

   Measured against these criteria, mediation emerges as perhaps the weakest of available formal legal remedies.†

3. How does this perspective differ from that offered in the previous reading by Rifkin?

4. Would the perspective be appropriate for "wife-battery" cases discussed in Chapter 1? What are the important concerns to consider in developing your answer? How would Lerman, Woods, and Rifkin respond?

---

*Laurie Woods, "Mediation: A Backlash to Women's Progress on Family Law Issues," *Clearinghouse Review*, Summer 1985, p. 436. Reprinted by permission.

†"Mediation of Wife-Abuse Cases: The Adverse Impact of Informal Dispute Resolution on Women," *Harvard Women's Law Journal* 7(1984). Copied with permission. Copyright © by the *Harvard Women's Law Journal*.

☐ Consider the following discussion of the principles of mediation and of a mediated case. Is it consistent with any of the feminist perspectives discussed in the preceding material?

Mediation: Some Keys to the Process *Margaret L. Shaw*

The process of mediation involves the management of conflict and negotiation between parties. The key to effective management of conflict negotiation lies in the way the mediator defines and frames the issues in dispute and sets an agenda for the parties to consider those issues. Yet it is precisely these steps that are most often neglected by practicing mediators.

Our temptation, as mediators, is to engage in a premature search for solutions. Once the parties have committed themselves to the mediation process and once they have expressed their major areas of agreement and disagreement, we will then proceed to gather information and discuss possible solutions and hope, by the end of the process, to avoid an impasse on any specific item. We carry our ribbon in our pockets, in anticipation of tying up our package of agreements in a neat bow — and often we can do so.

To ensure that the mediation process is effective we must, as mediators, focus clearly on an intermediate step between the parties' statement of the problem and the search for solutions, even before further information gathering. This step involves, first, the mediator's taking an active role to define and frame the issues, for the way in which the issues are framed will shape both further discussion of the matters in dispute and the possible range of solutions. In addition, the mediator must take an active role to set the agenda for discussion. Thoughtful ordering of the issues can help assure positive momentum to the entire mediation process. Both roles are critical to successful mediation.

DEFINING AND FRAMING ISSUES

What is the role of the mediator in defining and framing issues? What is an issue in mediation?

To arrive at clear answers to these questions, consider [this] case[:]

Case Example: Smith and Spruce John Smith is a senior in college and lives next door to Janet Spruce, age sixty-seven. Smith complains that Spruce's dog howls constantly, day and night, thereby preventing him from studying. He is seriously concerned that his inability to study will result in poor grades and, consequently, denial of admission to medical school. He says that Spruce mistreats and has no control over the dog. Two weeks ago, at 3:30 a.m., Smith heard the dog howling and called Spruce to complain. Spruce's teenage daughter, Susan, answered the phone and told Smith to "go to hell." Spruce was recently widowed. She purchased the dog for protection. This is the first dog she has ever owned. Susan, her "adopted daughter," is a high school senior who lives in the house. Although most of her time is spent at school during the day, she studies at home at night.

How would a mediator define and frame the issues in this case? In this case example, many people identify as one of the issues the difficulties caused to Spruce by her recent widowhood. While Spruce's loss may be a factor in her need for protection, it is simply not an issue capable of being addressed in the mediation process. Mediation can only address those issues whose resolution can be achieved by the participation or cooperation of both parties.

Margaret L. Shaw, "Divorce Mediation: Some Keys to the Process," from *Legal and Family Perspectives in Divorce Mediation,* edited by J. A. Lemmon, printed in *Mediation Quarterly,* No. 9, September 1985.

Suppose the mediator, having heard this statement of the problem by Smith and Spruce, said, "Let's talk about the issue of the howling dog." Consider the course of the discussion that is likely to ensue: "My dog does not howl." "Your dog has barked endlessly day and night for weeks." "None of the other neighbors have complained." "If you don't shoot that dog, I will." "Why don't you find some other place to live if you don't like it."

Characterizing the issue as "the howling dog" presents two major problems. The first is that the mediator has adopted the issue as framed by one of the parties. The issue so framed assumes a judgment that the dog howls. This leads clearly and inevitably to an offensive-defensive debate between Smith and Spruce.

A mediator who simply accepts the statement of the problem in the terms used by one or the other of the parties is locked into that person's perceptions of the dispute, perceptions that are a large part of the reason the parties have reached a stalemate and sought outside help. A principal opportunity afforded by mediation is the mediator's ability to perceive the dispute in a different way from the parties and thereby to help them discuss and resolve the dispute effectively.

The second major problem with framing the issue as "the howling dog" (or indeed even as "the dog") is a more subtle one. Even if the characterization of the dog as howling is eliminated, the discussion that ensues will focus on the dog's behavior. How often has the dog barked in the past? During what hours? How loud? Have other neighbors been bothered?

Mediation is not a search for the truth. While the truth or falsity of the facts the parties bring may be relevant to a court proceeding, they are not what the issues are all about in mediation.

What if Smith is right that the dog is loud, noisy, beyond Spruce's control, and disturbing to the neighborhood? Perhaps the solution is indeed for Spruce to get rid of the dog. If it is established that the dog's barking is in fact not constant and that none of the other neighbors have complained, then Spruce's position that Smith should "put up or shut up" becomes more persuasive.

Consider the difference in the discussion that would ensue with respect to both the matters in dispute and the possible range of solutions if the mediator characterized the issues as "Smith's study time" and "Spruce's protection." The process would unfold very differently. Is Smith's need for quiet time greatest at night? Is the daughter home at night to offer some protection to Spruce? Would Spruce be willing to take her dog to obedience school in exchange for Smith's studying in the library several nights a week for a defined period?

What distinguishes mediation from other kinds of dispute resolution, including court proceedings, is that it is a process through which individual needs are accommodated by a search for solutions acceptable to both parties. While the facts may have impact on the workability of proposed solutions, they are not relevant to the way in which the mediator frames the issues. What is most relevant are the needs, interest, priorities, and concerns of the parties.

This principle is well illustrated by the often-told story (that has its origins in the work of Mary Parker Follett). Two men were studying across the table from one another in the library. After they had been working for some time, one of the men got up and threw open the window next to the table. As soon as he sat down and became engrossed again in his work, the second man got up and quietly closed the window. A few minutes later he looked up and saw that the first man had opened the window again. He sprang out of his chair and closed it. A librarian, observing these events, came over and asked the first man why he wanted the window open. The man replied that the room was stuffy and he was falling asleep. The librarian then turned to the second man, who said that he was just getting over the flu, and the open window was creating a draft on his neck. Without another word, she left the room and opened a window in the adjoining room, thus satisfying both men. This simple solution was made possible by framing the issue in terms of the needs and interests of the parties.

A useful definition of an issue in mediation, then, is that it is an element of the dispute that expresses the needs or interests of the parties and the resolution of which involves the participation or cooperation of both parties.

Notes and Questions

1. Does mediation reflect a particular set of cultural beliefs about conflict and rationality? Steven Weiss notes that

> One of the goals of mediation is to reach an agreement that is reasonable to all parties. "Being reasonable" is often a culture-bound determination. Differences in the use of reason/logic in the mediation context may often lead to confusion and the perception that the thinking of another participant is rigid at one extreme or random at the other. Before concluding that a disputant is being unrealistic it is important to consider the possibility of cultural differences in reason/logic.*

*National Institute of Dispute Resolution Forum, 1986.

There are many rationales currently being offered in support of mediation and other alternative dispute resolution programs. Many proponents of this new field come from the legal profession. The following article suggests a different, perhaps opposing, rationale for dispute resolution programs.

The Social Agenda of Dispute Resolution *Raymond Shonholtz*

The dispute resolution field can become one of two things. It can become an adjunct to the existing justice system, or it can fulfill its promise as a new way for people of all colors and cultures to use skills built on the values of harmony and peace. This broader approach would model practical, participatory, non-binding forms of dispute settlement which can be used successfully by corporations, prisons, schools, churches, community organizations, and other institutions.

Each time the discussion moves away from the social promise inherent in conciliation, one enters the debate over issues of control and certification, and the role of the legal and "non-legal" communities in conflict resolution. From a social and policy perspective, peace-making is unequivocally a civic responsibility and as such should be taught in our schools and communities and valued as a means of resolving differences. The failure to make conciliation the foundation of dispute resolution means that the movement will be overwhelmed by the presently stronger legal institutions, which are primarily concerned with control and regulation, rather than with conciliation.

Meeting the challenge ahead needs the imagination and skills of the legal profession, as well as others, because conciliation has no "natural home" in the organization of modern American life. Institutional pressures favor existing structures, and few conciliation programs are connected to any public entities familiar with managing citizen-sponsored and -controlled conflict resolution, especially when service providers are trained volunteers.

Adopting conciliation as the premise for all dispute resolution policy requires re-thinking

Raymond Shonholtz, "The Social Agenda of Dispute Resolution," from *The Prospectus of Summer 1982,* published bi-annually by the Community Board Center for Policy and Training. Reprinted by permission.

how we teach conciliation values and skills and how they are subsequently modelled in society. As a diverse and divided society, it would be prudent for us to commit substantial resources to developing and promoting this skill and creating a social expectancy concerning its use. This decision needs to be the starting point if we are to make real changes or advance from the parochial concerns that currently plague the "professionalization" of dispute resolution.

Notes and Questions

1. What are some of the problems associated with the professionalization of the dispute resolution field?
2. Are the values underlying legal practice in conflict with the conciliation approach outlined in Shonholtz?
3. Are there limits to the use and value of conciliation as a mechanism for resolving social conflict?

CONCLUSION

The readings in this chapter illustrate the range of questions being asked about the rise of informal dispute resolution. Clearly, no consensus exists about its value or its meaning for American society. Although a number of research studies have explored mediation and its effects on disputants, more research needs to be undertaken that investigates the processes themselves and furthers understanding of their implications for contemporary social life.

These readings suggest differing, occasionally contradictory interpretations of the dispute resolution movement in modern society. Some observers have focused on the political agenda underlying the support for mediation, which is seen as furthering and consolidating the reach of the justice system. Others have focused on the opportunities that mediation and other alternative processes offer for individual participation in settling conflict. In this view, individuals benefit from these processes, more satisfied than they are with the process and outcomes of formal court proceedings. Still others, concerned with the threat of war and rising national and international tensions, argue that mediation promises a new paradigm for the settlement of conflict in which the likelihood of peaceable, cooperative outcomes is greatly enhanced. Finally, there are some who claim that the dispute resolution field reflects an approach to conflict based on traditionally female concerns emphasizing the value of relationships, which are in contrast with traditionally male concerns focusing on rights and responsibilities.*

All these explanations are relevant to the understanding of alternative dispute resolution. Although one cannot be certain what institutional mechanisms for conflict resolution will develop in the future, it is apparent that the current alternative dispute resolution movement is becoming an essential feature of contemporary legal and social culture.

---

*See *In a Different Voice: Psychological Theory and Women's Development* (Cambridge, Mass.: Harvard University Press, 1982).

Suggested Additional Readings

Abel, Richard. *The Politics of Informal Justice.* Vols. 1 and 2. New York: Academic Press, 1982.

Auerbach, Jerold. *Justice Without Law: Resolving Disputes Without Lawyers.* New York: Oxford University Press, 1983.

Azar, Edward E., and Burton, John W. *International Conflict Resolution: Theory and Practice.* Boulder, Colo.: Lynne Rienner, 1982.

Davis, Albie. *Community Mediation in Massachusetts: A Decade of Development: 1975–1985.* Salem, Mass.: Administrative Office of the District Court, 1986.

Fisher, Roger, and Ury, William. *Getting to Yes,* New York: Penguin Books, 1982.

Folberg, Jay, and Taylor, Allison. *Mediation: A Comprehensive Guide to Resolving Conflicts Without Litigation.* San Francisco, Jossey-Bass, 1985.

Gilligan, Carol. *In a Different Voice: Psychological Theory and Women's Development.* Cambridge, Mass.: Harvard University Press, 1982.

Goldberg, Stephen, Green, Eric, and Sander, Frank E. A. *Dispute Resolution.* Boston: Little, Brown, 1985.

Gulliver, P. H. *Disputes and Negotiations: A Cross Cultural Perspective.* New York: Academic Press, 1979.

Harrington, Christine. *Shadow Justice.* Westport, Conn.: Greenwood Press, 1985.

Hofrichter, Richard. *Neighborhood Justice in Capitalist Society.* Westport, Conn.: Greenwood Press, 1987.

Moore, Christopher W. *The Mediation Process: Practical Strategies for Resolving Conflict.* San Francisco: Jossey-Bass, 1986.

Nader, Laura. *No Access to Law: Alternatives to the American Judicial System.* New York: Academic Press, 1980.

Dutch Lawyer in His Study. (Harvard Law Art Collection)

CHAPTER 6 Images of Law

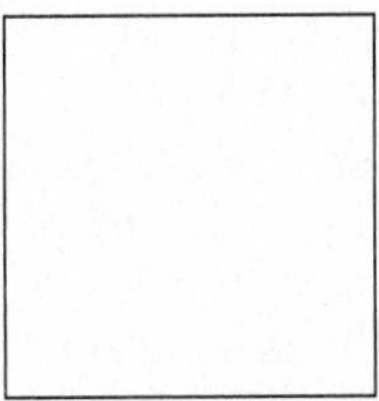

[W]henever any Form of Government becomes destructive of these ends, it is the Right of the People to alter or to abolish it. . . . [E]xperience hath shown, that mankind are more disposed to suffer, while evils are sufferable, than to right themselves by abolishing the forms to which they are accustomed. But when a long train of abuses and usurpations, pursuing invariably the same Object evinces a design to reduce them under absolute Despotism, it is their right, it is their duty, to throw off such Government.

The Declaration of Independence (1776)

An injunction duly issuing out of a court of general jurisdiction with equity powers, upon pleadings properly invoking its action, and served upon persons made parties therein and within the jurisdiction, must be obeyed by them, however erroneous the action of the court may be. . . . [A]nd until its decision is reversed for error by orderly review, either by itself or by a higher court, its orders based on its decision are to be respected, and disobedience of them is contempt of its lawful authority, to be punished.

Howat v. Kansas (42 S.Ct. 277, 280–281, '

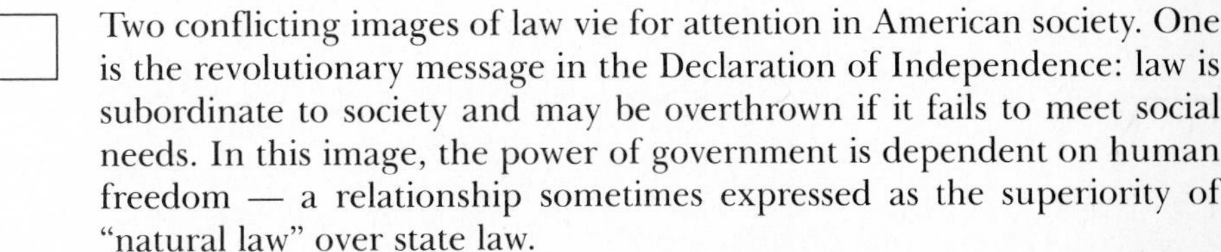

Two conflicting images of law vie for attention in American society. One is the revolutionary message in the Declaration of Independence: law is subordinate to society and may be overthrown if it fails to meet social needs. In this image, the power of government is dependent on human freedom — a relationship sometimes expressed as the superiority of "natural law" over state law.

The other image of law is one of established power, of constituted government with its rules and procedures, as in the *Howat* case quoted above. In this case the state of Kansas enjoined 150 members of the

United Mine Workers of America from striking against a coal company. When the miners struck anyway, they were sentenced to one-year jail terms for violating the injunction. Their appeals argued that the Kansas statute on which the injunction was based violated the federal Constitution. The U.S. Supreme Court refused to consider this argument, on the grounds that the miners should have appealed the injunction itself instead of first violating it and then appealing their convictions. This decision puts forth the image that human freedom depends on law, a relationship often explicitly stated on courthouse buildings as, for example, "Obedience to the law is liberty."

Perhaps every legal system that has begun with political revolution is characterized by this conflict of images. On the one hand, people feel the need to justify the revolution itself, as an attack on established law. On the other hand, when the revolution has succeeded in establishing a new government, people feel the need to justify its authority. Images that serve to justify the overthrow of law are replaced by images to support the imposition of new law. Yet the revolutionary images cannot be completely forgotten, because the new government has a history. So the contradictory images exist simultaneously.

Generally, government presents these contradictory images separately, to insulate each from the canceling effect of the other. For example, in contemporary terms, the image of obedience to authority is used for such purposes as justifying health and safety regulations, while the image of freedom is used for justifying the *absence* of regulations on corporate investment decisions.

The two contradictory images are usually presented separately in popular culture, too. Heroes who "do justice" when "the system" fails portray one image, while the other image is portrayed by villains who cause injustice when they "take the law into their own hands."

This chapter seeks to bring these contradictory images together. The variety of perspectives — psychological, anthropological, historical, economic, and literary — provide an awareness of the conflict itself, and are used to explore the ways in which the contradictory images invoke different political values and different understandings of human nature.

Running at 55 *David Lenson*

The tiny Libertarian Party, one of the only political organizations in recent history to introduce even a single idea into a presidential election, is back again this year. . . . They've decided to campaign against the 55 mile-per-hour speed limit. . . .

. . . In many parts of the nation hatred of 55 has reached a flashpoint, and whoever can harness the political energy when it finally explodes is going to do some accelerating themselves.

Fifty-five is a more complex issue than it seems. It means different things to different people. Timid drivers are almost alone in supporting it, even though the statistics that claim to show its beneficial effect on highway safety are unconvincing. Everybody else dislikes it, even (and maybe especially) law-abiding citizens, because it makes criminals of us all. You see, we *have* to speed. Not only are the Interstates built for 75 or so, they are too soporific and ill-banked for 55. Many trucks cannot use their highest and most fuel-efficient gears till 60 or 65, and therefore they are in effect forced to speed.

Add to this the fact that the pace of traffic remains around 65, so that legal cars are dangerously slow. Deciding how fast to go therefore involves a choice between safe driving and obeying the law. Most of us choose safety, and get tickets.

How the law was originally imposed probably accounts for some of its unpopularity. There was no research, no debate, no vote, no nothing. Nixon just decreed it, supposedly in response to the gasoline shortages of the fall of 1973. . . .

The way we accepted the law, falling into line like slow-moving sheep, seems like an eternal discredit to our pride. At first it was 50 miles-per-hour! But the New Jersey Turnpike and some other toll roads refused to co-operate, so a "compromise" was made. I remember my first drive from Massachusetts to New York at 50. It seemed to take days. It was so slow it was almost relaxing. It was like driving under water. And now, while Germans screech along the Autobahn at 120, once-proud American drivers are international laughingstocks, slowpokes, tortugas. . . .

Most of these objections are shared, in one form or another, by people of all political persuasions. So why is this junk law still on the books after almost 13 unlucky years? In my judgment, 55 isn't intended to save lives or gas. It was imposed *for its own sake,* just to restrict individual liberty. The gas crisis, which was created by the oil companies as an excuse to raise prices, gave the politicians an opportunity to crack down on the ordinary citizen. It was "unpatriotic" to object. Recently, mass police crackdowns have once again been instituted in the name of "stopping drunken driving," and what decent person can object to that? But government in fact doesn't care how many people, guilty or innocent, are killed. If they did, they wouldn't allow auto manufacturers to market today's Reynolds-wrap slopbuckets; if they did, they wouldn't be subsidizing tobacco companies; if they did, they wouldn't have fired all the air traffic controllers; if they did, they wouldn't declare wars and deploy nuclear weapons. No, gang, you know in your heart that the reason 55 has been left in place all these years is that it gives the government, through the medium of the police, an excuse to hassle *anybody.* And that is why they will not let it go.

Once a law is a law it's The Law. . . . Whether it is a just law, whether it is "for our own good," and whether we obey it or not is truly of no concern to lawmakers. A law is an instrument for population control. Period. And control is something that politicians, those who live on power, can never surrender.

The Libertarians have once again done us a service by raising these questions about the ba-

---

sis of government and law. Most of their ideas come straight out of Henry David Thoreau's "Civil Disobedience." They . . . are the true Conservatives, in that there is something they actually want to conserve: the Constitutional guarantees of individual freedom. I part company with them and with Thoreau over the question of "corporate freedom," whatever that means. Government *could* be used as a tool against the direct dictatorship of multinational corporations, though you wouldn't know that from studying the last six years' history. It's hard to give up that old, slightly Utopian notion that someday government could be enlisted in the cause of common sense. . . .

Notes and Questions

1. How does Lenson determine that safety and legality are opposite choices? What is the relationship between the laws of physics and traffic laws?
2. Lenson suggests that patriotism will prevent people from voicing their objections to laws. Do you agree? Does this tendency strengthen or weaken the society?
3. Do you agree that Lenson's examples show government doesn't care how many people are killed?
4. Lenson distinguishes between individual freedom and corporate freedom. Is this logical?

☐ Lenson's argument against the speed limit helps us to see that even an apparently simple law can involve deep complexities of legal theory, where images of freedom are pitted against images of social control. In other words, even the most ordinary laws may provoke value questions and political debate, and may reveal economic conflict.

In some areas of law, the image of freedom is dominant; in others, the image of obedience is. But the dominance is never complete. The opposing image is always available, sometimes just beneath the surface of consciousness, sometimes rising into overt challenge. When a law is challenged in court, the image of freedom may predominate in the determination of the particular legal issue, but the image of obedience to authority will almost always dominate any question of the court's power to decide legal issues. In other words, no matter which image is used to justify any particular decision, the court's power to make such decisions will be explained in terms of the image of obedience.

Sometimes a court will express the revolutionary image of law, as in the following example:

> [S]overeign power in our government belongs to the people, and the government of the United States and the government of the several states are but the machinery for expounding or expressing the will of the sovereign power.*

But, as the Supreme Court indicated in the *Howat* case, the hierarchy of judicial power generally claims the right to be respected even when it is wrong.

In the history of America, the two images of law have been thrown against each other repeatedly, most vividly in times of social crisis and

---

**Cherokee Nation* v. *So. Kans. Ry. Co.*, D.C. 33 F 900, 906 (1888).

struggle. Martin Luther King and the 1963 Easter civil rights demonstration in Birmingham, Alabama, are a famous example of the images in conflict, and of the typical reaction of courts to any direct challenge to the authority of the legal system itself. Here is how that case happened:

> The salient facts can be stated very briefly. Petitioners are Negro ministers who sought to express their concern about racial discrimination in Birmingham, Alabama, by holding peaceful protest demonstrations in that city on Good Friday and Easter Sunday 1963. For obvious reasons, it was important for the significance of the demonstrations that they be held on those particular dates. A representative of petitioners' organizations went to the City Hall and asked "to see the person or persons in charge to issue permits, permits for parading, picketing, and demonstrating." She was directed to Public Safety Commissioner Conner, who denied her request for a permit in terms that left no doubt that petitioners were not going to be issued a permit under any circumstances. "He said, 'No you will not get a permit in Birmingham, Alabama to picket. I will picket you over to the City Jail.' and he repeated that twice." A second, telegraphic request was also summarily denied, in a telegram signed by "Eugene 'Bull' Connor."†

The City of Birmingham obtained a state court injunction *ex parte* (without an adversary hearing), ordering the ministers and others to refrain from any demonstration without a permit. The ministers, continuing with their plans, issued a statement challenging the court's action. In it, they put forth an image of the state's law being subject to a higher law, a law of justice and morality. They argued that this higher law justified their refusal to obey government authority. Notice how they tried to integrate the revolutionary image of a higher law into the image of the Constitution as established authority:

> This is raw tyranny under the guise of maintaining law and order. We cannot in all good conscience obey such an injunction which is an unjust, undemocratic and unconstitutional misuse of the legal process.
>
> We do this not out of any disrespect for the law but out of the highest respect for *the* law. This is not an attempt to evade or defy the law or engage in chaotic anarchy. Just as in all good conscience we cannot obey unjust laws, neither can we respect the unjust use of the courts.
>
> We believe in a system of law based on justice and morality.‡

The demonstrations were held as planned on Easter weekend. On Monday, the Alabama court held the demonstrators, including Reverend King, in contempt. The ministers initiated a series of appeals, but their argument was rejected at every step. The case eventually reached

---

†*Walker* v. *Birmingham,* 87 S.Ct. 1824, 1834 (Warren dissenting) (1967).

‡87 S.Ct. at 1833.

the Supreme Court of the United States. The Court agreed with the ministers that the Birmingham parade ordinance and injunction "unquestionably raised substantial constitutional issues." Nevertheless, the Court ruled against the civil rights marchers, following the *Howat* principle that constituted legal authorities and their injunctions may not be ignored even if they are unconstitutional:

> [P]recedents clearly put the petitioners on notice that they could not bypass orderly review of the injunction before disobeying it. . . . This Court cannot hold that the petitioners were constitutionally free to ignore all the procedures of the law and carry their battle to the streets. One may sympathize with the petitioners' impatient commitment to their cause. But respect for judicial process is a small price to pay for the civilizing hand of law, which alone can give abiding meaning to constitutional freedom.§

This chapter explores the relationship between law and freedom; it raises issues about the relationship between state and society, about political economy and ideology, and about power and values. The purpose of the chapter is to show that law coexists with resistance to law, that authority exists in the context of struggle, that force and violence are as much a part of law as they are a negation of law. Ultimately, the chapter aims for a dialogue that goes beyond simple debate between two contradictory images.

---

§87 S.Ct. at 1832.

1 RULES AND REASONS

> The true system, the real system, is our present construction of systematic thought itself, rationality itself. . . . If a revolution destroys a systematic government, but the systematic patterns of thought that produced that government are left intact, then those patterns will repeat themselves in the succeeding government.
>
> Robert M. Pirsig, *Zen and the Art of Motorcycle Maintenance* (1974)

Legalism is the philosophy that obedience to rules is the basis of social order; it is the belief that logic is superior to experience as a basis for conflict resolution and justice. Legalism teaches that the enforcement of rational principles by governmental authorities is the essence of freedom.

Like every belief system, legalism is effective only to the extent that it is rooted in the minds of the masses of people who make up society. A major purpose of legal texts is to defend and deepen this root, to justify the supremacy of rules over ordinary life by making the rules appear ordinary and natural.

A common instance of this function is the "reasonable person" rule used by courts to define the limits of legally acceptable behavior. The "reasonable person" is a logical abstraction, a fictional being used (as in the following example) to subordinate human judgment to legal rules:

> . . . [W]e believe that plaintiff was contributorily negligent as a matter of law. The fact that plaintiff subjectively did not consider his actions dangerous is not the issue. . . . The issue is would a reasonable prudent person anticipate the danger of using his foot to dislodge a clog in an area where there were moving parts of the machine which would cause serious injury.
>
> . . . Plaintiff asserts that there was an issue of fact as to "[w]hat effect the custom of the community had on the standard of care when all the witnesses testified it was the common custom in the community to do what plaintiff did." Several witnesses testified by deposition that it was customary in the community to use one's foot to kick loose and unstop the machine when it became clogged.
>
> As stated in *Wills v. Paul* . . . ". . . In determining whether the particular acts of a plaintiff constitute negligence, the test is not the frequency with which other men commit such acts but whether the plaintiff at the time of the occurrence, used that degree of care which an ordinarily careful person would have used for his own safety under like circumstances. . . ."
>
> "We find it difficult to accept a philosophy which asserts that negligent and careless conduct by frequent repetition in a community converts it into a non-negligent conduct . . ." *Ferguson v. Lounsberry*. . . . Custom in and of itself is not conclusive. It must meet the standard of ordinary care.*

The real people involved in the *Cox* case (a man working for his father) suffered real injury (loss of a foot in a machine), but were denied compensation from the equipment-manufacturing corporation (a fictional, legal "person"), on the ground that they did not behave as a fictional, "reasonable prudent person," despite the fact that witnesses (other real people) testified that their behavior was customary practice. The decision substitutes legal ordinariness for real ordinariness. From the claimants' viewpoint, the decision violates their experience. From the viewpoint of the corporation, the decision enhances the predictability of the corporation's potential liability for damages. This pattern can be traced back to what Morton Horwitz describes as the "transformation of American law" in favor of commercial interests.

**Karl Cox, Jr. v. Karl Cox v. J. I. Case Company,* 89 N.M. 555, 555 P.2d 378 (1976).

The danger of legalism is that such a strong emphasis on rules obscures the fact that the rules are socially created, embodying political choices and value judgments. If the social basis of legality is obscured, one's perception of society itself becomes clouded, and human relations become dominated by abstractions.

The readings in this section emphasize the difference between existential and legal realities, whether defined in terms of "care," "freedom," "truth," or "justice."

The Law Is Terror Put into Words

Peter d'Errico

We are living in a time of changing consciousness about the meaning and function of authority. Law, which is often taken to be the backbone of authority structures in society, has come increasingly under scrutiny, both for its role in maintaining oppressive social conditions and for the exceeding narrowness of legalism as a world-view.

In a sense, we no longer believe in our system of legal rules the way we used to. We are beginning to see through the facade of a "government of laws" to the people who animate that system. And further, we are coming to understand that legalism is as much an obscuring veil as a clarifying lens for approaching social problems. Law and legal thinking are as frequently the cause of social trouble as the means of resolving it. Thus, as Addison Mueller [law professor] has noted, in our "free-enterprise" economy, "freedom of contract" is the consumer's losing card (*Contracts of Frustration,* 78 *Yale L.J.* 576 [1969]).

This skepticism and criticism about law is part of the decline of legalism in our culture. The decline, however, is not a simple matter. It is beset with resistance and contradiction. For example, even as the evidence becomes more and more clear that prison is a dysfunctional, self-defeating, self-perpetuating social institution, the force of the state is called again and again into action against the victims of that institution.

In an overall way, these contradictions are forcing us to realize that our justice system is only another social institution, subject to all the ills that befall any other institution: bureaucracy, preoccupation with its own maintenance and expansion, depersonalization of those whom it is supposed to serve, etc. Disenchantment with laws as the basis for authority in social and personal life is now so pervasive that we are at a crisis in the history of law itself. . . .

The central purpose of law school education . . . is socialization into the legal profession. This process is the antithesis of free and open-ended inquiry into the nature and function of law. That is why the contracts teacher, for example, cannot pause to consider the basic injustice of "freedom of contract" in a monopolistic economic system. To do so would not only take time away from the job of teaching how to manipulate legal doctrine, it would positively disrupt the socialization process itself. That is, criticism of basic legal forms and processes is incompatible with the inculcation of allegiance to the framework of legalism as a way of thinking and acting.

This incompatibility is especially significant in the first year of law school. It is there that so many idealistic young people, eager to "help others" and "change society," first encounter the full force of legalism and come to grapple with its peculiar and surprising ability to step aside from every question of substance and value con-

---

flict. Questions about social history, or economics, or psychology, or even of philosophy, are admitted into the classroom only to the extent that they do not distract from the main task. That task is learning how to sidestep all such questions in the parsing of doctrine and, thus, in the exercise of legal power.

Law students are taught to seek and use power, rather than truth. And as a way of persuading them to give up any persistent pursuit of the latter, they are encouraged to think of the "justice" they can accomplish when they have acquired power. The first year is complete when the students can no longer separate "justice" from "law," and when all critical consciousness has been engulfed by positivism and social relativism.

WE ARE AUTHORITY ADDICTS

Daily life under legalism is permeated in all its aspects by a belief in authority, and an accompanying tension between authoritative descriptions of the world and our own individual perceptions of life. We are authority addicts, hooked on rules. As Judith Shklar [legal historian] has noted, the institutional and personal levels of commitment to legalism form a social continuum: "At one end of the scale of legalistic values and institutions stand its most highly articulate and refined expressions, the courts of law and the rules they follow; at the other end is the personal morality of all those men and women who think of goodness as obedience to the rules that properly define their duties and rights" (*Legalism* [1964] p. 3).

At every moment, even to the level of how and when to eat, smile, sleep, talk, touch and move, and beyond this to the level of how and what we are supposed to think, fantasy and dream, there are rules. Life for most people seems to be a project of obedience, of duty and responsibility to authority. Constantly there is the struggle to fit ourselves into someone else's dream, someone else's definition of reality. And with this struggle, as part of it and in turn perpetuating it, goes a fear of letting go of authority as well as attempts to impose our authority on others, preoccupation with what others think, feelings of isolation from others and the world, and fear that we will not exist if we do not define ourselves, label our relationships and categorize ourselves and each other.

David Cooper [psychiatrist], studying such phenomena in *The Death of the Family* (1971), writes:

> If, then, we wish to find the most basic level of understanding of repression in society, we have to see it as a collectively reinforced and institutionally formalized panic about going mad, about the invasion of the outer by the inner and of the inner by the outer, about the loss of the illusion of "self." The Law is terror put into words (p. 33).

Under legalism, we are constantly trying to control ourselves and each other within limits laid down by authority, all the time not seeing any alternative to this positivistic world, accepting it as necessary and inevitable. In law school, one learns to put the terror into words and to conceal its true nature. The heart of law school training is the refinement into positivism of a pre-existing allegiance to authority, the inchoate legalism acquired by the ordinary person in school and family.

The vaunted "case method" is nothing more than a frank recognition that authority is what counts; what is important to the lawyer is what has been held to be important.

The law student learns that *finding* the law regarding some particular social or economic conflict is more important than *understanding* the conflict. The student is trained to manipulate the language of a judge's opinion, and to exclude . . . consideration of . . . social, political, historical, and other factors and forces involved in the case. . . .

The verbal framework and apparatus for the exercise of power which is thus created in law school becomes reality for the lawyer; the legal system takes primacy over the effects it has on real people in real social situations. Witness Edward H. Levi [law professor], discussing "The Nature of Judicial Reasoning":

> Perhaps it should be said that the effect of . . . (a legal decision) so far as the judge or lawyer is concerned is primarily on the fabric of the law. The lawyer's or the judge's function may be sufficiently self-delimited so as to exclude from the realm of their professional competence the larger social consequences. . . . For the judge or lawyer the relevant effects are upon the web of the law, the administration of law, and the respect for law (*Law and Philosophy,* Hook, ed. [1964] p. 264).

The result of this process, as legalism continues to build on itself, is an increasing separation between the concerns of law and the concerns of justice. Law becomes preoccupied with preserving itself and the social order with which it is identified. The concern of justice, in contrast, remains the achievement of social *wholeness* rather than simple order.

Charles Silberman, in his powerful critique of the 1971 Association of American Law Schools curriculum study report, "Training for the Public Professions of the Law," pointed out this divergence between the concern for social order and a concern for justice. Noting that the words "justice" and "injustice" do not appear in the AALS report, Silberman called for the "depoliticalization" of law school, saying that law school is

> politicized through its commitment to the status quo. . . . The point is that where gross injustice exists, the pursuit of justice may involve the exacerbation of social conflict, not its resolution. It is precisely this commitment to conflict resolution rather than to justice that creates the lawyer's bias for the status quo. . . .

The concept of a person's "rights," for example, is basic to legalism. It is one of the most powerful formulations in gaining and sustaining popular support for the operation of the legal system.

The common understanding of this concept is that law takes the side of the people against governmental or other systematic injustice. This uncritical view is elaborated upon in law school and throughout the legal system. Actually, however, once one understands that the central concern of legalism is with the maintenance of its own power system, one sees that the law only *appears* to take the side of the people. In fact, the real concern of legalism in its recognition of popular claims of right (civil rights, etc.) is *to preserve the basic governmental framework in which the claims arise.*

The concept of civil rights has meaning only in the context of an over-arching system of legal power against which the civil rights are supposed to protect. Ending the system of power would also end the need for civil rights. But it is precisely here that one sees the impossibility of ending the oppression by means of civil rights law. In the end, this analysis points to the concept of personal "rights" as being a technique for depersonalizing people. We are taught to respect the rights of others, and in doing so we focus on the abstract bundle of rules and regulations which have been set up by judges and other officials to govern the behavior of people. In this focus, we miss the actual reality of the others as whole, real individuals. We end up, in short, respecting the law rather than people; and this, for legalism, is the essential aim.

Due process is another sacred cow. Legalism would have us regard this notion as the key to freedom under law, the means by which fairness and regularity are incorporated into legal decision-making. In reality, due process is the attempt of the system to insure that claim and counterclaim, freedom and grievance, both occur only within the existing legal universe and in its terms.

Every due process decision is thus only a further elaboration of the pre-existing legalist mazeway. People confront the claim of law to control social life, and the law responds; whatever the legal response to the confrontation, the law is concerned with itself first and foremost. The basic due process problem, as far as legalism is concerned, is only to preserve the apparatus of official legal control, even when the framework of that control must bend to meet the demands and needs of the people whose lives the officials govern. In a critical view, due process is essentially a technique for co-opting social change forces that threaten, or appear to threaten, official control of society.

In my own experience in practice — in an urban ghetto, on an Indian reservation, and in a middle class college community — I found again and again that people were able to see through law and legal processes in ways I had been taught to close my eyes to. When their vision was rebuffed by law, it became the basis for a deep cynicism about legal process. I saw, moreover, that even when lawyers succeeded in legalism's own game — the creation of a new rule, or the vindication of an old one — that we didn't really win anything, because legalism wasn't dealing with the roots of problems, but only with their surface appearances.

And it is not only "radical" law or legal services practice which generates such insight and skepticism. I found many traditional lawyers in conventional practices who were well aware that the law was not reaching their clients' real problems: economic, familial, psychological, and so on. These lawyers were sometimes deeply troubled by this awareness, and yet they remained unable even to articulate their experience. Locked into the mazeway of legalism in their education, and bereft of any critical viewpoint, they seemed resigned to a life of legal routine.

I have come to regard legalism as a defunct social ideology. Capable at one time of unleashing tremendous productive social forces, legalism is now only a source of confusion and contradiction. Far from uniting America into a coherent and just society, traditional ideas of law foster division and give the stamp of approval to inequality.

ONE LEGACY OF LEGAL REALISM

If "authority" is needed for this iconoclastic view of legalism, one need only look back to the last major jurisprudential shakeup in American history, legal realism. Karl Llewellyn, one of the most profound thinkers and observers in the realist movement, commenting on "the place and treatment of concepts," wrote (in *A Realistic Jurisprudence — The Next Step, Col. L. Rev.* 453 [1930]) ". . . categories and concepts, once formulated and once they have entered into thought processes, tend to take on an appearance of solidity, reality and inherent value which has no foundation in experience." In a time like the present, when belief in the central myths, or explanations of reality, around which our social life has been organized is breaking down, it becomes especially important to go beyond superficial exploration of social phenomena to an examination of concepts. The legal realist movement opened the door to new ways of thinking about the law, ways colored by non- or even anti-legalist perspectives. . . .

Professional legal education is an example of what Paulo Freire [a Brazilian educator] calls "the banking concept of education":

> Education thus becomes an act of depositing, in which the students are the depositories and the teacher is the depositor. Instead of communicating, the teacher issues communiques and makes deposits which the students patiently receive, memorize, and repeat. This is the "banking" concept of education, in which the scope of action allowed to the students extends only as far as receiving, filing, and storing the deposits. They do, it is true, have the opportunity to become collectors or cataloguers of the things they store (*Pedagogy of the Oppressed* [1974] p. 58).

At first, the law teacher "owns" the law and the students seek to possess this as a piece of property, something worth having. Later, the property having been conveyed, the students enter into the status of co-owners, taking upon themselves the role of guardian of this property which they have acquired and which will support them as a means of earning a living. . . .

In legal studies, on the other hand, at least in its humanistic, self-developmental mode, . . . the existing cultural framework of legalism is viewed not as a limit but as a challenge in an ontological and historical process of people becoming more fully human. . . .

Notes and Questions

1. Do you agree that there is widespread disenchantment with law? What current examples of this can you find? What examples of belief in law can you find?
2. What are the sources of disenchantment or belief? Does the mass media tend in either direction in presenting legal issues?
3. David Cooper (quoted in this reading) comments on "the loss of the illusion of 'self'." What relationship do you see between self-control and legal control? How might the images of law be seen as illusions?
4. This reading discusses how law students are taught to exercise power. What similarities or contrasts do you find between this process and your own education?

In Death's Grey Land *Philip Caputo*

The typewriters in the quonset hut began to click promptly at eight o'clock, when the legal clerks came in to begin another routine day of typing up routine reports. The red light on the electric coffee pot glowed and the electric fans on the clerks' desks stirred the warm, dense air. Having slept undisturbed for eight hours, as they did every night, and breakfasted on bacon and eggs, as they did every morning except when the division HQ mess served pancakes, the clerks were happy, healthy-looking boys. They appeared slightly bored by their dull work, but were content in the knowledge that their rear-echelon jobs gave them what their contemporaries in the line companies lacked: a future.

Sitting in one corner of the hut with my defense counsel, Lieutenant Jim Rader, I looked at the clerks and wished I were one of them. How pleasant it would be to have a future again. A crowd of witnesses milled around outside: marines and Vietnamese villagers, the latter looking utterly bewildered by the courtroom drama in which they would soon play their assigned roles. One of the clerks muttered a curse as a fan blew some papers off his desk. The artificial gust blew against the wall behind him, rustling the pages of his short-timer's calendar. . . . All the dates had been crossed off except today's, the 30th, the day on which Lance Corporal Crowe was tried on two counts of premeditated murder.

I was to appear as a witness for the prosecution. There was an absurdity in that, as I was to be tried on the same charges by the same prosecutor the following morning. But then, the fact that we had been charged in the first place was absurd. They had taught us to kill and had told us to kill, and now they were going to court-martial us for killing.

A bound sheaf of papers as thick as a small-town phone book and entitled "Investigating Officer's Report" sat on Rader's desk. It was the product of five months' labor on the part of various military lawyers, and the two top forms — DD457 and DD458 — contained the charges against me: ". . . in that First Lieutenant Philip J. Caputo . . . did murder with premeditation Le Dung, a citizen of the Republic of Vietnam. In that First Lieutenant Philip J. Caputo . . . did murder with premeditation Le Du . . ." There was a third charge, resulting from my panicked attempt to deny that I had tried to cover up the killings: "In that First Lieutenant Philip J. Caputo . . . did subscribe under lawful oath a false statement in substance as follows: 'I did not tell them to stick by their statements,' which statements he did not then believe to be true."

There was a lot of other stuff — statements by witnesses, inquiry reports, and so forth — but one square on form DD-457 was conspicuously blank. It was the square labeled EXPLANATORY OR EXTENUATING CIRCUMSTANCES ARE SUBMITTED HEREWITH. Early in the investigation, I wondered why the investigating officer had not submitted any explanatory or extenuating circumstances. Later, after I had time to think

things over, I drew my own conclusion: the explanatory or extenuating circumstance was the war. The killings had occurred in war. They had occurred, moreover, in a war whose sole aim was to kill Viet Cong, a war in which those ordered to do the killing often could not distinguish the Viet Cong from civilians, a war in which civilians in "free-fire zones" were killed every day by weapons far more terrible than pistols or shotguns. The deaths of Le Dung and Le Du could not be divorced from the nature and conduct of the war. They were an inevitable product of the war. As I had come to see it, America could not intervene in a people's war without killing some of the people. But to raise those points in explanation or extenuation would be to raise a host of ambiguous moral questions. It could even raise the question of the morality of American intervention in Vietnam; or, as one officer told me, "It would open a real can of worms." Therefore, the five men in the patrol and I were to be tried as common criminals, much as if we had murdered two people in the course of a bank robbery during peacetime. If we were found guilty, the Marine Corps' institutional conscience would be clear. Six criminals, who, of course, did not represent the majority of America's fine fighting sons, had been brought to justice. Case closed. If we were found innocent, the Marine Corps could say, "Justice has taken its course, and in a court-martial conducted according to the facts and the rules of evidence, no crime was found to have been committed." Case closed again. Either way, the military won.

"I was talking to your old skipper outside," Rader said. "He told me you seemed nervous."

"Well, how the hell do you expect me to feel? By tomorrow night, I could be on my way to Portsmouth for life." Portsmouth, the U.S. Naval prison, is a penal institution that was said to combine the worst aspects of Marine boot camp and medieval dungeon. Nevertheless, a life sentence there was better than the alternative — execution by firing squad. That possibility had been hanging over our heads until only a few weeks before, when it was ruled that our case would be tried as noncapital. We were not to be shot if found guilty. A boon!

"Look, I don't want you thinking that way," Rader said. "I'm confident about what the outcome'll be. Even if you're convicted, we'll appeal. All the way up to the President if we have to." . . .

"Well, I don't break, Jim. That's one thing I'm not going to do. I broke once and I'm never going to break again."

"Hell, when did you ever break?"

"That night. The night I sent those guys out there. I just cracked. I couldn't take it anymore. I was frustrated as hell and scared. If I hadn't broken, I would've never sent those guys out."

"Oh, that. We've been over that a dozen times. No drama, okay? This is the real world. We've been over that, over and over. You told them to capture those Vietnamese and to kill them if they had to. You didn't order an assassination. That's what you'll say on the stand and you'll say it because it's the truth."

Rader and I had argued the point before. We had argued it from the day that he was appointed my defense counsel. That had been in February, after several villagers from Giao-Tri lodged a complaint with their village chief, who went to the district chief, a Vietnamese Army colonel, who took the matter to the American military authorities in Danang. Two young men from Giao-Tri, both civilians, had been assassinated by a marine patrol. The investigation got under way. The battalion was meanwhile establishing new permanent positions forward of the old front line. The Viet Cong protested the intrusion into their territory with land mines, infiltrators, mortars, and snipers. My platoon lost several more men, including Jones, who was seriously wounded by a booby trap. The other two platoons suffered about sixteen casualties between them, and C Company became so shorthanded that Neal had to make riflemen out of the mortar crews attached to the company, leaving no one to man the eighty-ones.

It was in this depressing atmosphere of steady losses that the five marines and I were called to battalion HQ to be questioned about what came to be known as "the incident at Giao-Tri."

Most of the particulars of that long and complicated inquiry have faded from memory.

What remains most vividly is the mind-paralyzing terror that came over me when the investigating officer told me I was under suspicion of murder. *Murder.* The word exploded in my ears like a mortar shell. *Murder.* But they were Viet Cong, I told the IO, a hearty lawyer-colonel from the division legal section. At least one of them was. No, he said, they did not appear to be VC. That had been confirmed by the village police chief and the village chief. *Murder.* I knew we had done something wrong, but the idea of homicide had never occurred to me. Bewildered and frightened, I answered the colonel's questions as best as I could, but when he asked, "Did you tell your men to stick to their statements?" I blurted out "No!"

Accompanied by his reporter, a lance corporal who had tapped out my answers on a transcript machine, the colonel left a few minutes later with his papers, case books, and machine, all the paraphernalia from the tidy world of Division HQ, the world of laws, which are so easy to obey when you eat well, sleep well, and do not have to face the daily menace of death.

I was badly shaken afterward, so badly I thought I was going to break in two. It was not only the specter of a murder charge that tormented me; it was my own sense of guilt. Lying in a tent at HQ, I saw that boy's eyes again, and the accusation in their lifeless stare. Perhaps we had committed homicide without realizing it, in much the same way McKenna had. Perhaps the war had awakened something evil in us, some dark, malicious power that allowed us to kill without feeling. Well, I could drop the "perhaps" in my own case. Something evil had been in me that night. It was true that I had ordered the patrol to capture the two men if at all possible, but it was also true that I had wanted them dead. There was murder in my heart, and, in some way, through tone of voice, a gesture, or a stress on *kill* rather than *capture,* I had transmitted my inner violence to the men. They saw in my overly aggressive manner a sanction to vent their own brutal impulses. I lay there remembering the euphoria we had felt afterward, the way we had laughed, and then the sudden awakening to guilt. And yet, I could not conceive of the act as one of premeditated murder. It had not been committed in a vacuum. It was a direct result of the war. The thing we had done was a result of what the war had done to us.

At some point in this self-examination, I realized I had lied to the investigating officer. Walking over to the adjutant's tent, I called the colonel and said I wanted to amend my statement and to exercise my right to counsel. He returned to battalion HQ with Rader, a tall redhead in his late twenties.

"Sir, I said, "that part in my statement where I said that I didn't tell the men to stick by their statements? Well, that isn't true. I wasn't thinking straight. I'd like it deleted and replaced with the truth."

Sorry, he said, that statement had been made under oath. It could not be deleted. That was the law. If I wished to say something else, fine, but the original statement would remain in the record. The colonel smiled, quite pleased with himself and the inexorable logic of his precious law. He had me on another charge. I made another statement.

Afterward, Rader and I had the first of our many long interviews. He asked me to describe everything that had happened that night.

"All right," I said. "but before I do, I want you to read this. I wrote it while I was waiting for you and the colonel to get here."

I handed him a turgid essay on front-line conditions. In a guerrilla war, it read, the line between legitimate and illegitimate killing is blurred. The policies of free-fire zones, in which a soldier is permitted to shoot at any human target, armed or unarmed, and body counts further confuse the fighting man's moral senses. My patrol had gone out thinking they were going after enemy soldiers. As for me, I had indeed been in an agitated state of mind and my ability to make clear judgments had been faulty, but I had been in Vietnam for eleven months. . . .

Rader crumpled up my literary ramblings and said, "This is all irrelevant, Phil."

"Why? It seems relevant to me."

"It won't to a court-martial."

"But *why*? We didn't kill those guys in Los Angeles, for Christ's sake."

Rader replied with a lecture on the facts of

life. I cannot remember exactly what he said, but it was from him that I got the first indication that the war could not be used to explain the killings, because it raised too many embarrassing questions. We were indeed going to be charged as if we had killed both men on the streets of Los Angeles. The case was to be tried strictly on the facts: who said what to whom; what was done and who did it. A detective story. The facts, Rader said, are what he wanted. He did not want philosophy.

"Did you order your men to assassinate the two Vietnamese?" he asked.

"No."

"Did you say they were to capture them, or to shoot first and ask questions later?"

"No. They were supposed to capture them, kill them if they had to. But the thing is, I must have given them the impression that I wouldn't mind if they just killed them. Jim, I wasn't right in the head that night . . ."

"Don't try temporary insanity. There's a legal definition for that, and unless you were bouncing off walls, you won't fit it."

"I'm not saying I was crazy. What I'm saying is that I was worn-out as hell. And scared. Goddamnit, I admit it. I was scared that one of those damned mines was going to get me if I didn't do something. You've got to realize what it's like out there, never knowing from one minute to the next if you're going to get blown sky-high."

"Look, a court-martial isn't going to care what it's like out there. You've got to realize that. This isn't a novel, so drop the dramatics. Nothing would've happened if those villagers hadn't complained. But they did and that started an investigation. Now the machine's in gear and it won't stop until it's run its course. Now, did anyone else hear you brief the patrol?"

"Yeah, Sergeant Coffell and the platoon sergeant were there."

"So, in other words, you gave orders to capture if possible, kill if necessary, or words to that effect. That's what you said, and there are two witnesses who'll corroborate you. Right?"

"That's what I said. I'm not sure if I completely meant it. I had this feeling that night . . . a sort of violent feeling . . ."

"Feelings aren't admissible evidence. I'm not worried about your psyche. The important thing is whether or not you ordered your men to commit an assassination."

"Damnit, Jim. It keeps coming back to the war. I wouldn't have sent those guys out there and they would never have done what they did if it hadn't been for this war. It's a stinking war and some of the stink rubs off on you after a while."

"Will you please drop that. If you ordered an assassination, tell me now. You can plead guilty and I'll try to get you a light sentence — say, ten to twenty in Portsmouth."

"I'll tell you this. I'll have a helluva time living with myself if those guys get convicted and I get off."

"Do you want to plead guilty to murder?"

"No,"

"Why?"

"Because it wasn't murder. Whatever it was, it wasn't murder. And if it was murder, then half the Vietnamese killed in this war have been murdered."

"No. You don't want to plead guilty because you're innocent as charged. You did not order an assassination."

"All right. I'm innocent."

"So, what we have is this: you gave orders to a patrol to capture two Viet Cong suspects who were to be killed only if necessary. That's a lawful order in combat. And there are two NCOs who'll support you on that, right?"

"You're the boss. Whatever you say. Just get me out of this mess."

"Don't give me that 'you're the boss' routine. Are those the facts or aren't they?"

"Yes, those are the facts."

And so I learned about the wide gulf that divides the facts from the truth. Rader and I had a dozen similar conferences over the next five months. "Preparing testimony," it was called. With each session, my admiration for Rader's legal skills increased. He prepared my case with the hardminded pragmatisim of a battalion commander preparing an attack on an enemy-held hill. In time, he almost had me convinced that on the night of the killings, First Lieutenant Philip Caputo, in a lucid state of mind, issued a clear, legitimate order that was flagrantly disobeyed by the men under his command. I was fascinated by the testimony that was produced by our Socratic dialogues. Rader had it all written on yellow legal tablets, and I observed that not one word of it was perjured. There were qualifying phrases here and there — "to the best of my recollection," "if I recall correctly," "words to that effect" — but there wasn't a single lie in it. And yet it wasn't the truth. Conversely, the attorneys for the enlisted men had them convinced that they were all good, God-fearing soldiers who had been obeying orders, as all good soldiers must, orders issued by a vicious killer-officer. And that was neither a lie nor the truth. The prosecution had meanwhile marshaled facts to support its argument that five criminal marines, following the unlawful orders of their criminal platoon leader, had cold-bloodedly murdered two civilians whom they then tried to claim as confirmed Viet Cong to collect the reward their captain had offered for enemy dead, a reprehensible policy not at all in keeping with the traditions of the U.S. Marine Corps. And that was neither a lie nor the truth. None of this testimony, none of these "facts" amounted to the truth. The truth was a synthesis of all three points of view: the war in general and U.S. military policies in particular were ultimately to blame for the deaths of Le Du and Le Dung. That was the truth and it was that truth which the whole proceeding was designed to conceal. . . .

I was called sometime in the late afternoon. Crowe, sitting at the defendant's table, looked very small. I confess I don't remember a word of what I said on the stand. I only recall sitting there for a long time under direct and cross-examination, looking at the six-man court as I had been instructed to do and parroting the testimony I had rehearsed a hundred times. I must have sounded like Jack Armstrong, all-American boy. Later, during a recess, I heard the prosecutor congratulating Rader. "Your client did very well on the stand today, Mister Rader." I felt pleased with myself. I was good for something. I was a good witness.

The trial dragged on to its conclusion. In my tent awaiting the verdict, I felt in limbo, neither a free man nor a prisoner. I could not help thinking about the consequences of a guilty verdict in my own case. I would go to jail for the rest of my life. Everything good I had done in my life would be rendered meaningless. It would count for nothing.

I already regarded myself as a casualty of the war, a moral casualty, and like all serious casualties, I felt detached from everything. . . . I had declared a truce between me and the Viet Cong, signed a personal armistice, and all I asked for now was a chance to live for myself on my terms. I had no argument with the Viet Cong. It wasn't the VC who were threatening to rob me of my liberty, but the United States government, in whose service I had enlisted. Well, I was through with that. I was finished with governments and their abstract causes, and I would never again allow myself to fall under the charms and spells of political witch doctors like John F. Kennedy. The important thing was to get through this insane predicament with some degree of dignity. I would not break. I would endure and accept whatever happened with grace. For enduring seemed to me an act of penance, an inadequate one to be sure, but I felt the need to atone in some way for the deaths I had caused. . . .

Rader walked into the tent in the early evening. "Phil," he said, "they've come in with a verdict on Crowe. Not guilty on all counts."

I sat up and lit a cigarette, not sure what to think. "Well, I'm happy for him. He's got a wife and kids. But how does that make it look for us?"

"Well, I think it looks good. Just hang loose until tomorrow. You go up at oh-nine-hundred."

Curiously, I slept very well that night. Maybe it was my sense of fatalism. Worrying could do no good. Whatever was going to happen, I could do nothing about it. The next morning, . . . [t]he same crowd of witnesses milled around outside. Captain Neal was there. He looked worn and old. I went out and offered him a cigar. Smoking it, his eyes fixed on the ground, he shook his head and said, "We lost half the company. I hope they realize that. We'd lost half the company then."

At a quarter to nine, Rader called me back inside.

"Here's the situation. The general is thinking of dropping all charges against the rest of you because Crowe was acquitted. In your own case, you'd have to plead guilty to the third charge and accept a letter of reprimand from the general. What do you want to do?

"You mean if I plead guilty to charge three, there's no court-martial?"

"Unless you want one."

"Of course I don't want one. Okay, I'm guilty."

"All right," Rader said ebulliently, "wait here. I'll let them know and get back to you."

I paced nervously for fifteen or twenty minutes. It looked as if my instincts had been right: the higher-ups wanted this case off their backs as much as I wanted it off mine. Wild thoughts filled my head. I would atone in some way to the families of Le Du and Le Dung. When the war was over, I would go back to Giao-Tri and . . . and what? I didn't know.

Rader returned grinning. "Congratulations," he said, pumping my hand. "The charges have been dropped. The general's going to put a letter of reprimand in your jacket, but hell, all that'll do is hurt your chances for promotion to captain. You're a free man. I also heard that the adjutant's cutting orders for you. You'll be going home in a week, ten days at most. It's all over."

Notes and Questions

1. In this reading, Caputo refers to the "tidy world . . . of laws." How does this image relate to the conflicting imagery of law discussed in the introduction to this chapter?
2. One point Caputo makes is that not all killing is murder. In both military and civilian law, some killings are justified, others are excused. A soldier can be killed for refusing to kill the enemy. Is there any logic that explains these different legal categories for killing?
3. Caputo describes how he learned about "the wide gulf that divides the facts from the truth." What are the implications of this gulf for the warring images of freedom and obedience?
4. Do you think Caputo regards himself as a casualty of the law as well as "a casualty of the war"? Are there any casualties of law in this episode?

The Plague *Albert Camus*

"To make things simpler, Rieux, let me begin by saying I had plague already, long before I came to this town and encountered it here. Which is tantamount to saying I'm like everybody else. Only there are some people who don't know it, or feel at ease in that condition; others know and want to get out of it. Personally, I've always wanted to get out of it.

"When I was young I lived with the idea of my innocence; that is to say, with no idea at all. I'm not the self-tormenting kind of person, and I made a suitable start in life. I brought off everything I set my hand to, I moved at ease in the field of the intellect, I got on excellently with women, and if I had occasional qualms, they passed as lightly as they came. Then one day I started thinking. And now — . . .

"When I was seventeen my father asked me to come to hear him speak in court. There was a big case on at the assizes, and probably he

---

Albert Camus (1913–1960), a French writer, can be described as a humanist existentialist, in that his works deal with the interwoven themes of life's absurdity and human courage. He was awarded the Nobel Prize for Literature in 1957.

thought I'd see him to his best advantage. Also I suspect he hoped I'd be duly impressed by the pomp and ceremony of the law and encouraged to take up his profession. I could tell he was keen on my going, and the prospect of seeing a side of my father's character so different from that we saw at home appealed to me. Those were absolutely the only reasons I had for going to the trial. What happened in a court had always seemed to me as natural, as much in the order of things, as a military parade on the Fourteenth of July or a school speech day. My notions on the subject were purely abstract, and I'd never given it serious thought.

"The only picture I carried away with me of that day's proceedings was a picture of the criminal. I have little doubt he was guilty — of what crime is no great matter. That little man of about thirty, with sparse, sandy hair, seemed so eager to confess everything, so genuinely horrified at what he'd done and what was going to be done with him, that after a few minutes I had eyes for nothing and nobody else. He looked like a yellow owl scared blind by too much light. His tie was slightly awry, he kept biting his nails, those of one hand only, his right . . . I needn't go on, need I? You've understood — he was a living human being.

"As for me, it came on me suddenly, in a flash of understanding; until then I'd thought of him only under his commonplace official designation, as 'the defendant.' And though I can't say I quite forgot my father, something seemed to grip my vitals at that moment and riveted all my attention on the little man in the dock. I hardly heard what was being said; I only knew that they were set on killing that living man, and an uprush of some elemental instinct, like a wave, had swept me to his side. And I did not really wake up until my father rose to address the court.

"In his red gown he was another man, no longer genial or good-natured; his mouth spewed out long, turgid phrases like an endless stream of snakes. I realized he was clamoring for the prisoner's death, telling the jury that they owed it to society to find him guilty; he went so far as to demand that the man should have his head cut off. Not exactly in those words, I admit. 'He must pay the supreme penalty,' was the formula. But the difference, really, was slight, and the result the same. He had the head he asked for. Only of course it wasn't he who did the actual job. I, who saw the whole business through to its conclusion, felt a far closer, far more terrifying intimacy with that wretched man than my father can ever have felt. Nevertheless, it fell to him, in the course of his duties, to be present at what's politely termed the prisoner's last moments, but what would be better called murder in its most despicable form.

"From that day on . . . I took a horrified interest in legal proceedings, death sentences, executions, and I realized with dismay that my father must have often witnessed those brutal murders — on the days when, as I'd noticed without guessing what it meant, he rose very early in the morning. I remembered he used to wind his alarm-clock on those occasions, to make sure. . . .

"I came to grips with poverty when I was eighteen, after an easy life till then. I tried all sorts of jobs, and I didn't do too badly. But my real interest in life was the death penalty; I wanted to square accounts with that poor blind owl in the dock. So I became an agitator, as they say. I didn't want to be pestiferous, that's all. To my mind the social order around me was based on the death sentence, and by fighting the established order I'd be fighting against murder. That was my view, others had told me so, and I still think that this belief of mine was substantially true. I joined forces with a group of people I then liked, and indeed have never ceased to like. I spent many years in close cooperation with them, and there's not a country in Europe in whose struggles I haven't played a part. But that's another story.

"Needless to say, I knew that we, too, on occasion, passed sentences of death. But I was told that these few deaths were inevitable for the building up of a new world in which murder would cease to be. That also was true up to a point — and maybe I'm not capable of standing fast where that order of truths is concerned. Whatever the explanation, I hesitated. But then

I remembered that miserable owl in the dock and it enabled me to keep on. Until the day when I was present at an execution — it was in Hungary — and exactly the same dazed horror that I'd experienced as a youngster made everything reel before my eyes.

"Have you ever seen a man shot by a firing-squad? No, of course not; the spectators are hand-picked and it's like a private party, you need an invitation. The result is that you've gleaned your ideas about it from books and pictures. A post, a blindfolded man, some soldiers in the offing. But the real thing isn't a bit like that. Do you know that the firing-squad stands only a yard and a half from the condemned man? Do you know that if the victim took two steps forward his chest would touch the rifles? Do you know that, at this short range, the soldiers concentrate their fire on the region of the heart and their big bullets make a hole into which you could thrust your fist? No, you didn't know all that; those are things that are never spoken of. For the plague-stricken their peace of mind is more important than a human life. Decent folks must be allowed to sleep easy o' nights, mustn't they? Really it would be shockingly bad taste to linger on such details, that's common knowledge. But personally I've never been able to sleep well since then. The bad taste remained in my mouth and I've kept lingering on the details, brooding over them.

"And thus I came to understand that I, anyhow, had had plague through all those long years in which, paradoxically enough, I'd believed with all my soul that I was fighting it. I learned that I had had an indirect hand in the deaths of thousands of people; that I'd even brought about their deaths by approving of acts and principles which could only end that way. Others did not seem embarrassed by such thoughts, or anyhow never voiced them of their own accord. But I was different; what I'd come to know stuck in my gorge. I was with them and yet I was alone. When I spoke of these matters they told me not to be so squeamish; I should remember what great issues were at stake. And they advanced arguments, often quite impressive ones, to make me swallow what none the less I couldn't bring myself to stomach. I replied that the most eminent of the plague-stricken, the men who wear red robes, also have excellent arguments to justify what they do, and once I admitted the arguments of necessity and *force majeure* put forward by the less eminent, I couldn't reject those of the eminent. To which they retorted that the surest way of playing the game of the red robes was to leave to them the monopoly of the death penalty. My reply to this was that if you gave in once, there was no reason for not continuing to give in. It seems to me that history has borne me out; today there's a sort of competition who will kill the most. They're all mad over murder and they couldn't stop killing men even if they wanted to.

"In any case, my concern was not with arguments. It was with the poor owl; with that foul procedure whereby dirty mouths stinking of plague told a fettered man that he was going to die, and scientifically arranged things so that he should die, after nights and nights of mental torture while he waited to be murdered in cold blood. My concern was with that hole in a man's chest. And I told myself that meanwhile, so far anyhow as I was concerned, nothing in the world would induce me to accept any argument that justified such butcheries. Yes, I chose to be blindly obstinate, pending the day when I could see my way more clearly.

"I'm still of the same mind. For many years I've been ashamed, mortally ashamed, of having been, even with the best intentions, even at many removes, a murderer in my turn. As time went on I merely learned that even those who were better than the rest could not keep themselves nowadays from killing or letting others kill, because such is the logic by which they live; and that we can't stir a finger in this world without the risk of bringing death to somebody. . . .

"Yes, Rieux, it's a wearying business, being plague-stricken. But it's still more wearying to refuse to be it. That's why everybody in the world today looks so tired; everyone is more or less sick of plague. But that is also why some of us, those who want to get the plague out of their systems, feel such desperate weariness, a weariness from which nothing remains to set us free except death.

"Pending that release, I know I have no place in the world of today; once I'd definitely refused to kill, I doomed myself to an exile that can never end. I leave it to others to make history. I know, too, that I'm not qualified to pass judgment on those others. There's something lacking in my mental make-up, and its lack prevents me from being a rational murderer. So it's a deficiency, not a superiority. But as things are, I'm willing to be as I am; I've learned modesty. All I can maintain is that on this earth there are pestilences and there are victims, and it's up to us, so far as possible, not to join forces with the pestilences. That may sound simple to the point of childishness; I can't judge if it's simple, but I know it's true. You see, I'd heard such quantities of arguments, which very nearly turned my head, and turned other people's heads enough to make them approve of murder; and I'd come to realize that all our troubles spring from our failure to use plain, clean-cut language. So I resolved always to speak — and to act — quite clearly, as this was the only way of setting myself on the right track. That's why I say there are pestilences and there are victims; no more than that. If, by making that statement, I, too, become a carrier of the plague-germ, at least I don't do it willfully. I try, in short, to be an innocent murderer. You see, I've no great ambitions.

"I grant we should add a third category: that of the true healers. But it's a fact one doesn't come across many of them, and anyhow it must be a hard vocation. That's why I decided to take, in every predicament, the victims' side, so as to reduce the damage done. Among them I can at least try to discover how one attains to the third category; in other words, to peace."

Notes and Questions

1. What does Camus's character mean when he says that "the social order around me was based on the death sentence"? What does he mean by the "plague"?
2. Why does the character say his refusal to kill is "a deficiency, not a superiority"?
3. How might Camus respond to John Lennon's song, "Working-Class Hero," which says that there is room at the top for those who learn to smile as they kill?
4. What similar images of the law can you find in the readings by Caputo and Camus?
5. Contrast Camus's philosophy with this quote from the U.S. Supreme Court:

   > [T]he very concept of ordered liberty precludes allowing every person to make his own standards on matters of conduct in which society as a whole has important interests. Thus, if the Amish asserted their claims because of their subjective evaluation and rejection of the contemporary secular values accepted by the majority, much as Thoreau rejected the social values of his time and isolated himself at Walden Pond, their claims would not rest on a religious basis. Thoreau's choice was philosophical and personal rather than religious, and such belief does not rise to the demands of the Religion Clauses.*

   What image is here presented of the relationship between law and religion? Between law and philosophy?

**Wisconsin* v. *Yoder*, 406 U.S. 205, 215–216 (1971).

Virginian Liberators *John T. Noonan, Jr.*

THE LEGAL STRUCTURE OF PRE-REVOLUTIONARY SLAVERY

On the eve of the Revolution, slavery in Virginia did not exist as a relationship of brute power. A social institution, it was given its shape by a hundred assumptions and omissions, intentions and neglects, customs and conventions. Law formed a part of these multiple pressures and, although far from the whole institution, was essential to it. The statutes on the control of slaves provided not a set of detailed instructions which the slaves meticulously obeyed but a message primarily directed at the white community. The statutes defining the legal status of slaves determined the dispositions to be made at a slave's birth and at a master's death. Slavery was not a transient condition: the law gave it immortality. Control statutes and status statutes together were indispensable to the creation and maintenance of the institution.

The statutes on control were designed on the model of a criminal code regulating public behavior. No slave was to leave his or her owner's plantation without a pass. No slave was to carry a club, staff, or other weapon. No slave was to own a horse, hog, or cow. No slave was to run away and lie out, hiding and lurking in swamps, woods, or other obscure places. No slave was to resist his or her owner administering correction. No slave was to lift his or her hand in opposition to a Christian, provided the Christian was not a Negro, mulatto, or Indian. No slave was to attempt to rape (the possibility of successful rape was not contemplated) a white woman. No slave was to prepare or administer medicine. No slave was to meet with four or more other slaves. No slave was to attend a religious service except with his or her "white family." The statutes were accompanied by provisions, specifying punishments for their violation, ranging from whipping to castration to death. . . .

The statutes, the legislature prescribed, were to be read aloud at the door of each parish church twice a year, on the first sermon Sundays in March and September, so that the slaves could make no pretense of ignorance if they disobeyed. . . .

The pedagogy of the statutes pointed to the slaves as creatures who must be coerced, upon whom it was right to exercise force. The statutes measured the amount of violence that masters might employ. The owner's boisterous passions were to be modeled to the community's norm. Violence on the slaves was authorized and rationalized by being put in the form of a rule. Punishments were set as though each penalty had been measured to the act prohibited. The model of this approach was an act of 1723 whose ostensible purpose was to put slave witnesses "under greater obligation to tell the truth." If their testimony was shown to be false, not by "due proof," but merely by "pregnant circumstances," then

> every such offender shall, without further trial, be ordered by said court to have one ear nailed to the pillory, and there to stand for the space of one hour, and then the said ear to be cut off; and thereafter, the other ear nailed in like manner, and cut off, at the expiration of one other hour; and moreover to order every such offender thirty-nine lashes, well laid on, on his or her bare back, at the common whipping-post.

Sadistic in its precision of detail, this statute appeared to focus on the witnesses. It was to be read to them before they gave testimony, in the only case in which they could give testimony — the trial of another black. . . . Directed to read it to black witnesses, the judge was reminded of their unreliability, their subjection, their amenability to physical threats. Compelled to bring these brutal threats into the actual conduct of his court, he was instructed in the act of administering justice.

A selection adapted from "Virginian Liberators" from *Persons and Masks of the Law* by John T. Noonan, Jr.

The communication made by the statute to the judge in the paradigm case of a trial was the communication transmitted by other control laws to sheriffs, deputy sheriffs, constables, prosecutors, county courts, and owners. More powerful in intensity than the standards mumblingly communicated to the slaves was the clear word brought to the masters: the community is with you in your exercise of domination.

"Without force, the alienability of the title to the human capital of blacks would have been worthless," write [Robert Williams] Fogel and [Stanley L.] Engerman, stressing in their fundamental reevaluation of Southern slavery that the plantation system required a judicious blending of economic incentive with coercion. But what made it possible for slavery to continue for more than a generation? Without acceptance of the rule that the slaves could be transferred by their owners and by the testaments of their owners, neither force nor economic incentive could have maintained the system. To regulate birth and overcome death, and incidentally to determine the transmission and distribution of slaves, a special world had to be created in which rules had a force, a magic, of their own. This second function of the law of slavery depended on a mass of concepts, decisions, and statutes, whose exact application to human beings required the industry and imagination of lawyers.

"Slaves," said the index to the first laws of Virginia, "See Negroes." From the beginning of the colony, "slave" and "Negro" were terms of art indicating a special legal status. The content of these terms was largely given by the popular understanding of what a slave or Negro was. From the beginning, Africans were distinguished from Europeans by complexion, physiognomy, customs, language, and treatment. Lawyers did not single-handedly determine their definition. Yet when it came to the key questions posed by death and birth, answers could not be given by popular perception. What happened to an African when the one for whom he worked died? What happened to a child born of an African? Answers to these questions issued from the use of concepts and rules which, even before they were written up as a code, had the character of law. Africans in Virginia, having arrived by means of purchase, were viewed as *property.*

"For the better settling and preservation of estates within this dominion" — so their desire for immortality was confessed — the Burgesses in 1705 decreed that plantation slaves "shall be held, taken, and adjudged to be real estate (and not chattels)." The object of the statute was to secure the perpetuity of ownership in plantations, insuring that slaves would descend with the land they worked. Designation of plantation slaves as real estate dramatized the triumph of landed proprietorship over death. The dead owner's slave was not cast into a state of nature. The slave was to pass "to the heirs and widows of persons departing this life, according to the manner and custom of land of inheritance held in fee simple." Slaves in the possession of merchants and factors were exempted from the operation of the statute and were to be held "as personal estate in the same condition as they should have been, if this act had never been made." Whether real estate or personal estate, slaves were property, subject to all the rules by which the rights of the dead were imparted to their spouses or to their descendants.

Overcoming the death of the master, determining the status of the offspring, the legislators and courts of Virginia presented a doctrine on the morality of slavery. They taught that it was good. In the pedagogy of the law, slaves were identified with the soil — the literal foundation of prosperity in the colony — or, generically, with property. As long as the teaching of the lawgivers was accepted, slavery could not be criticized without aspersion on the goodness of wealth itself. . . .

Locke's notion that a purpose of government was to protect property could justify all measures taken to secure the stability of the slaveholder's domain. The masters' ties of commerce, marriage, and kindred, so often intertwined with the masters' property arrangements, and dependent upon them, confirmed the position of the slaves. Property was the most comprehensive and most necessary of social categories. Catalogued within it, slaves fell within a classification which announced that it was right and good to maintain their enslavement.

The concept of property performed a further function. It put the slaves at a distance from the world of men and women. "Slave" and "Negro" functioned in the same way, but neither term by itself carried a primary meaning suggesting the non-human. "Property" obliterated every anthropoid feature of the slave. Consistently inculcating this description, the statutes assured the owning class that they did not need to attend to the person of the slave in any conveyance, lease, mortgage, or devise [transfer by will] they cared to make of their human possessions.

Addresses of the property statutes were only in an incidental way the slaves themselves. In theory, as real estate or personal estate, they could not be addressed at all. Definition as property determined their physical location, their employment, their sexual opportunities, and their familial relationships whenever they were made the object of sale, lease, mortgage, foreclosure, gift, bequest, intestacy, or entailment. They could not, however, apply this law to themselves. If they grasped the general idea that they and their children were always at the direction of another, they had deciphered the message of the law for themselves.

The law treating slaves as property conflicted with the control statutes which treated the slaves as responsible, triable, teachable human beings. . . .

Inconsistency was not fatal to the dominant message communicated to the trustees and executors, lawyers and judges, auctioneers and sheriffs who had to manage the transfer of particular persons when ownership in them passed, and to the testators and heirs, donors and donees, buyers and sellers, mortgagors and creditors, who wanted to know the terms upon which ownership in particular persons could be conveyed. To all those interested in the disposition and distribution of slaves, the message communicated was single: individuals do not have to be looked at when a conveyance is made. . . .

Between 1705, when the definition of plantation slaves as real estate was enacted, and the Revolution, legislators and lawyers argued how far the metaphor of real estate should be pressed. Lenders wanting the largest tangible assets of the plantations as collateral wished that the slaves be as freely transmissible as other forms of personal property. Owners seeking credit had a corresponding need for slaves to be readily disposable. Against these interests ran the dynastic desire of the planters to have the slaves descend with the land to their families in perpetuity. . . .

Virginian lawyers of the eighteenth century, even when they were revolutionaries, it might be supposed, were so imprisoned by traditional legal assumptions about slavery that they had no choice but to ratify the legal institution. However universalist their proclamations of liberty, they lacked, it might be imagined, a concept which would correspond in law to what they announced as ideology. Suppositions of this sort would be mistaken. Only a dozen years old, new but already popular and prestigious, the *Commentaries on the Laws of England,* by the Professor of the Laws of England at Oxford [Sir William Blackstone], provided both a legal critique of slavery and a concept on which to base a law of universal liberty. . . .

In retrospect, [Thomas] Jefferson recalled two reasons for refusing to make the laws afresh with Blackstone as a basis. First, new laws would have to be "systematical." . . . Second, the result would be to "render property uncertain."

The first reason could not have been controlling. The old law was not systematized. Why should the new have been? . . .

The key difficulty is focused on in Jefferson's "render property uncertain." The property which would have been made most fundamentally uncertain was property in slaves. John Quincy Adams accurately described the committee's dilemma: If they had started afresh, "they must have restored slavery after having abolished it; they must have assumed to themselves all the odium of establishing it as a positive institution, directly in face of all the principles they had proclaimed."

Slavery, nonetheless, had to be dealt with. . . . Jefferson did the text on the control laws. The bill was reported to the legislature in 1779. Managed by James Madison, it was adopted without substantial alteration in 1785. . . .

Jefferson discarded the detail which had made the old control laws exact and hideous and substituted a simple scheme of elegant generality. Instead of specifically proscribing meetings of groups of slaves, the practice of medicine by slaves, hiding out by runaway slaves, and the lifting of a slave's hand in opposition to a white Christian, he prohibited "riots, routs, and unlawful assemblies, and seditious speeches." Instead of specifically designating thirty-nine lashes, castration, or death as sanction, he made each crime punishable by whipping at the discretion of a justice of the peace. The statute on false testimony of slaves disappeared. The new provision on seditious speeches was a far broader control of the use of language. Milder but more comprehensive, functionally the new statute did not differ from the colonial grotesquerie it replaced. Its message to the white community — the message of the legislature, the message drafted by Jefferson and approved by Jefferson, [Edmund] Pendleton, and [George] Wythe* — was: We are with you in the use of measured force.

The opening clause of the new legislation parodied the revolutionaries' statement on the inalienable liberty of human beings. "Be it enacted by the General Assembly," the committee bill said, "that no persons shall henceforth be slaves within this commonwealth, except such as were so on the first day of this present session of the Assembly, and the descendants of the females of them." This was not unlike saying, "Be it enacted that no persons shall henceforth be convicts within this commonwealth except such as are already convicted and those subsequently found guilty by process of law." No one was born a hereditary slave in Virginia unless he was the descendant of a female slave. Still, the provision was not wholly innocuous or tautological: it banned the importation of slaves. But the ban on imports, increasing the value of slaves already within the commonwealth and to be born within it, did not touch the institution. The new statute proclaimed the lawfulness of slavery in Virginia, provided for its perpetuation, and left the slaves the option of "locking up their faculties" or providing the slaves of the next generation. . . .

The [work of] Wythe and Jefferson . . . may be measured not only against the principles of Blackstone but against the work of Edmund Burke, who in 1780 drafted and in 1792 proposed a code for the amelioration of the conditions of slavery in the British colonies. . . .

The difference between Burke's draft and the Virginians' statutes is this: accepting the slaves as human beings, Burke worked toward their enjoyment of human liberties; Jefferson and Wythe treated the slaves as human beings for the purposes of the control laws; they proposed no law by which their enjoyment of human liberties was recognized. . . .

For that decision they were responsible — that is, it must be recognized that they as human beings performed the acts by which slavery was continued as a legal institution. They chose to participate in the system. With their own hands they put on the masks of the law and imposed them on others.

THE VIRGINIA PARADOX

. . . In 1768, in *Blackwell* v. *Wilkinson,* Wythe had argued that the real nature of a slave was "personalty." In 1770 he had won *Howell* v. *Netherland* by standing on the power of the legislature to cancel freedom. In 1792, in *Turpin* v. *Turpin,* he had ruled that slaves passed by will "as if they were chattels." In 1798, in *Fowler* v. *Saunders,* he had declared that a transfer of slaves was like a

*Both Pendleton and Wythe were lawyers. Pendleton was First Judge, the Virginia Court of Appeals, and Wythe was Chancellor of the Commonwealth of Virginia. — Ed.

transfer of a quadruped or kitchen utensil. As a lawyer and as a judge, he had not challenged the power of legislatures and judges to suppress a birthright. . . .

The split between the ideals of the American Revolution and the maintenance of slavery was evident to contemporaries like [St. George] Tucker [a professor and judge]; it has now been comprehensively explored by David Brion Davis, who has probed with particular sensitivity Jefferson's "uncertain commitment" to universal liberty. The liberators were divided, knew they were divided, and were able to function because they entered a universe with distinctive rules.

Jefferson did not apply his reproach to Wythe. Wythe did not apply it to himself. . . . He took the legal universe to be self-contained. When he entered that special world, he accepted the masks of the law — they were the law's creations, not his. He did not see it as his fault that these fictions effected the distribution of slaves and the perpetuation of slavery. . . .

The Virginia paradox was this: Wythe believed that human beings are by nature free. He believed that the legislature is not omnipotent over nature. He believed that the legislature can enslave human beings. Rule-centered, he perceived with sharpness the injustice of an unjust rule; he did not perceive the injustice of removing human beings from consideration as persons. The Virginia paradox is the legal paradox, generally.

At least half of the property cases before the Chancellor involved the disposition of slaves. He could not have compassion for each of them as a person and still be a judge. His role in a slave system necessitated the use of masks. If he acted at all in his judicial office, those he disposed of had to fall within an appropriate subdivision of property. He needed to suppress humanity in the objects he transferred. He had to impress upon them the mask of property. The operation was not wholly external. . . . He could not pay attention to his torment. He had to act with apathy. He had to suppress humanity in himself. He had to put on himself the mask of the court.

When one reads of the earnest efforts of young eighteenth-century lawyers to master Roman law, one could weep at their futility — what possible relevance had the learning of fifth-century Byzantium to the affairs of America? Tears would be misplaced. Learning the Roman law was far from ineffective indoctrination in the fiction-making power of a legal system. Citation of Roman law, as Wythe cited it in *Turpin* v. *Turpin,* was not mere harmless display of erudition; it was active evocation of the magic of the law. Roman law could make a horse a consul and did make a horse a priest; it could and did extinguish a person's past; and if it did these "impossible" things, it could and did unmake persons. Legal education has often been education in the making and unmaking of persons. Wythe was a superb teacher.

The essential was that no exceptions be permitted to break the spell. The control statutes, modeled on criminal law, had judges' options, sheriffs' options, prosecutors' options, owners' options. No one had options under the property concept, save the owner who had the option, following a prescribed ritual, to end the spell altogether and make his slave free. If emancipation was not granted, the property concept was absolute and all-enveloping for purposes of distribution and perpetuation. . . .

George Wythe is the first of all the lawyers of the United States who from 1775 to 1865, North and South, kept slavery in existence. He is first not in that he caused the others to follow him, but in that, as professor of law, as legislator, as Chancellor of the Commonwealth of Virginia, he taught the others. His pupils followed in his path. Jefferson wanted to end the evil of slavery. So did Henry Clay, James Monroe, and John Marshall. Deploring the evil, they overcame their objections to it as Speaker, President, and Chief Justice, respectively, and sustained the system, accepting the power of the law to convert persons into personalty. They could believe in the natural law of freedom, and champion emancipation, and enforce slavery, so long as the legal universe was a special world with its own rules.

Like Wythe himself, they personally owned slaves. Their acceptance of the masks of the law did not blind them to the personalities of those they knew domestically. Sally Hemings, for example, his wife's half-sister and his slave, was a person Thomas Jefferson responded to when on an April day in Paris he spent two hundred francs on "clothes for Sally." Yet when he died her ownership moved under the property clauses of his will and her eventual fate had to depend on the claims of Jefferson's creditors not consuming the estate. The masks he had accepted, constructed, sustained, permitted him to distribute Sally Hemings in a fashion that would have been impossible if in the act of transmission he had to confront another living person. At the critical moments the masks of the law covered the faces of the slaves. Only an act of violence could shatter the concealing forms.

Slavery survived in Virginia after the Revolution not as an act of brute power and not as a discredited social habit, a colonial vestige repudiated by an enlightened ideology. It survived as a full-blown social institution with the control mechanisms and metaphors for transfer and distribution of the colonial regime intact. As an institution its survival was assured by the cataloguing power, the rule-making capacity, the indifference to persons of — the law? That is to depersonalize those responsible; better say — the lawyers. Without their professional craftsmanship, without their management of metaphor, without their loyalty to the system, the enslavement by words more comprehensive than any shackles could not have been forged.

Notes and Questions

1. What image of law do you think the Virginia legislature saw when it required the slave laws to be read in churches? What image did it want the people to see?
2. Noonan says that the message of the slave laws to the masters was "the community is with you." Why would the masters need to hear this message?
3. What social institutions besides slavery can you think of where personal domination is supported by law? Does managerial control of employees fall into this category? teachers' control of students? parents' control of children? husbands' of wives? In each of these situations, what image does the law uphold about the relationship between the dominant person(s) and the society?
4. What significance do you find in the following facts? George Wythe had emancipated his mulatto slave, Michael Brown, and his housekeeper, Lydia Brodnax, and had prepared a will leaving property and stock in trust to support them. The rest of his estate was to go to his grandnephew, George Wythe Swinney. Apparently unhappy with this arrangement, Swinney poisoned both Wythe and Brown. Wythe lived long enough to disinherit Swinney, but Swinney could not be successfully prosecuted for murder. The reason: the chief witness, Lydia Brodnax, was prevented from testifying by the application of a Virginia law that permitted blacks to testify only against blacks.

2 STATE AND SOCIETY

> Law reflects but in no sense determines the moral worth of a society. . . . The better the society, the less law there will be. In Heaven, there will be no law, and the lion will lie down with the lamb. . . . The worse the society, the more law there will be. In Hell, there will be nothing but law, and due process will be meticulously observed.
>
> Grant Gilmore, "The Age of Anxiety," *Yale Law Journal* (1975)

The nation-state can be viewed as a system of vertical power relations, a hierarchy of authority, in which rules are passed down from the top to various levels for implementation. This structure is typical of Anglo-European societies, as seen historically in the feudal lord–vassal relationship or in the contemporary relationships of boss–employee, master–servant, leader–follower. The defining characteristic of power in this system is that it is based on institutional roles. This characteristic is brought out by the military adage "Salute the uniform, not the person." It is also displayed in the familiar notion of "a government of rules and not of persons."

In contrast, a system of horizontal power relations displays authority collectively, in circular, rather than pyramidal, form. Leaders arise for a particular task and return to the group when that task is completed. This structure is typical of traditional American Indian societies and of many indigenous peoples around the world. The defining characteristic of authority in this system is that it attaches to persons rather than to institutional roles. The horizontal concept of power implies that it is socially destructive for one person to have institutionalized control over others.

The readings in this section focus on anthropological, historical, and contemporary organizational aspects of the difference between vertical and horizontal authority structures.

The Rule of Law versus the Order of Custom *Stanley Diamond*

The lowest police employee of the civilized state has more "authority" than all the organs of gentilism combined. But the mightiest prince and the greatest statesman or general of civilization may look with envy on the spontaneous and undisputed esteem that was the privilege of the least gentile sachem. The one stands in the middle of society, the other is forced to assume a position outside and above it.

— [Friedrich] Engels

. . . We live in a law-ridden society; law has cannibalized the institutions which it presumably reinforces or with which it interacts. . . . [W]e are encouraged to assume that legal behavior is the measure of moral behavior. . . . Efforts to legislate conscience by an external political power are the antithesis of custom: customary behavior comprises precisely those aspects of social behavior which are traditional, moral and religious — in short, conventional and nonlegal. Put another way, custom *is* social morality. The relation between custom and law is basically one of contradiction, not continuity.

. . . William Seagle writes:

> The dispute whether primitive societies have law or custom, is not merely a dispute over words. Only confusion can result from treating them as interchangeable phenomena. If custom is spontaneous and automatic, law is the product of organized force. . . .

Thus, law is symptomatic of the emergence of the state. . . . Custom — spontaneous, traditional, personal, commonly known, corporate, relatively unchanging — is the modality of primitive society; law is the instrument of civilization, of political society sanctioned by organized force, presumably above society at large and buttressing a new set of social interests. Law and custom both involve the regulation of behavior but their characters are entirely distinct. . . .

Published by permission of Transaction Publishers, from *In Search of the Primitive*, by Stanley Diamond.

(Abridged and footnotes omitted.)

ARCHAIC LAW AND LOCAL CUSTOM

The simple dichotomy between primitive society and civilization does not illustrate the passage from the customary to the legal order. The most critical and revealing period in the evolution of law is that of archaic societies, the local segments of which are the cultures most often studied by anthropologists. More precisely, the earlier phases of these societies, which I call proto-states, represent a transition from the primitive kinship-based communities to the class-structured polity. In such polities, law and custom exist side by side; this gives us the opportunity to examine their connections, distinctions and differential relationship to the society at large. The customary behavior typical of the local groups — joint families, clans, villages — maintains most of its force; the Vietnamese, for example, still say: "The customs of the village are stronger than the law of the emperor." Simultaneously, the civil power, comprising bureaucracy and sovereign, the dominant emerging class, issues a series of edicts that have the double purpose of confiscating "surplus" goods and labor for the support of those not directly engaged in production, while attempting to deflect the loyalties of the local groups to the center.

These archaic societies are the great historical watershed; it is here that Sir Henry Maine and Paul Vinogradoff [legal historians] located the passage from status to contract, from the kinship to the territorial principle, from extended familial controls to public law. For our understanding of the law, we need not be concerned with the important distinctions among archaic societies, or with the precise language or emphases of those scholars who have recognized their centrality. The significant point is that they are transitional. Particularly in their early phase, they are the agencies that transmute customary forms of order into legal sanction. . . . The following example from the archaic proto-state of Dahomey, prior to the French conquest in 1892, will make this process clear.

Traditionally in Dahomey, each person was said to have three "best" friends, in descending order of intimacy and importance. This transitional institution, . . . of the same species as blood brotherhood, reinforced the extended family structure, which continued to exist in the early state, but was being thrown into question as a result of the political and economic demands made by the emerging civil power. So for example, the best friend . . . of a man charged with a civil crime could be seized by the king's police in his stead. However, these traditional friendships were so socially critical, so deeply held, so symbolically significant that the person charged, whether or not he had actually committed a civil breach, would be expected to turn himself in rather than implicate a friend in his punishment. Whether or not he did so, the custom of friendship was given a legal edge and converted by the civil power into a means of enforcing its will. This example . . . has the virtue of explicitly revealing the contradiction between law and custom. But there are other examples in which the law appears as a reinforcement of customary procedure.

In eleventh-century Russia, for instance, Article 1 of the codified law states:

> If a man kills a man . . . the brother is to avenge his brother; the son, his father; or the father, his son; and the son of the brother (of the murdered man) or the son of his sister, their respective uncle. If there is no avenger (the murderer) pays 40 grivna wergeld. . . .

Similarly, circa A.D. 700, the law of the Visigoths states: "Whoever shall have killed a man, whether he committed a homicide intending to or not intending to . . . let him be handed over into the potestas of the parents or next of kin of the deceased. . . ." In these instances, a custom has been codified by an external agency, thus assuming legal force, with its punitive character sharpened. Such confirmation is both the intimation of legal control and the antecedent of institutional change beyond the wish or conception of the family. . . .

[Sydney P.] Simpson and [Julius] Stone [law and society scholars] explain this apparent reinforcement of custom by the civil power as follows:

> Turning then to the role of law in the emergent political society . . . it is true that political institutions, independent of the kin and the supernatural, had risen to power; yet these institutions were young, weak and untried. Their encroachment on the old allegiance was perforce wary and hesitating. Social cohesion still seemed based on nonpolitical elements, and these elements were therefore protected. . . .

Ultimately, local groups have maintained their autonomy when their traditional economies were indispensable to the functioning of the entire society. They could be hedged around by restrictions, harassed by law or as we have seen, they could be "legally" confirmed in their customary usage. But so long as the central power depended on them for support, in the absence of any alternative mode or source of production, their integrity could be substantially preserved. . . .

As the state develops, according to Maine, "the individual is steadily substituted for the family as the unit of which civil laws take account." And in R. von Jhering's [scholar of Roman law] words, "The progress of law consists in the destruction of every natural tie, in a continued process of separation and isolation." . . . The legal stipulation that spouses may not testify against each other appears as one of the last formal acknowledgements of familial integrity and the exception that proves the historical case. Clearly, the nuclear family in contemporary, urban civilization, although bound by legal obligations, has minimal autonomy; obviously, the means of education, subsistence and self-defense are outside the family's competence. It is in this sense that, given the absence of mediating institutions having a clearly defined independent authority, the historical tendency of all state structures vis-à-vis the individual may be designated as totalitarian. Indeed, the state creates the disaffiliated individual whose bearings thus become bureaucratic or collective; the juridical "person," who may even be a corporation doing business, is merely the legal reflection of a social process. If "totalization" is the state process, totalitarianism cannot be confined to a particular political ideology but is, so to speak, the ideology, explicit or not, of political society.

This étatist tendency has its origins in archaic society. We can observe it with unusual clarity in the proto-states of sub-Saharan Africa. In East Africa, pastoralists, competing for land, and in West Africa, militaristic clans, catalyzed by the Arab, and later, the European trade, notably in slaves, conquered horticulturalists, thereby providing the major occasions for the growth of civil power. . . . [W]e can reconstruct through chronicles extending back for centuries and by means of contemporary field work, the structure of early state controls. . . .

In such societies, [anthropologist R. S.] Rattray tells us, referring to Ashanti:

> the small state was ever confronted with the kindred organization which was always insidiously undermining its authority by placing certain persons outside its jurisdiction. It could only hold its own, therefore, by throwing out an ever-widening circle to embrace those loyalties which were lost to it owing to the workings of the old tribal organization which has survived everywhere. . . .

Concerning the Islamized Nupe of the Nigerian Middle Belt, [anthropologist S. F.] Nadel saw "a much more subtle development and a deeper kind of antagonism [than interstate warfare], namely, the almost eternal antagonism of developed State versus that raw material of the Community which, always and everywhere, must form the nourishing soil from which alone the state can grow." And Engels refers to the "irreconcilable opposition of gentile society to the state."

I have documented this conflict in detail in a study of the Dahomean proto-state. There, as elsewhere, it is apparent that the contradictory transition from customs to specified laws . . . is by no means the major source of law. Whether the law arises latently in confirmation of previous usage or through the transformation of some aspect of custom which the law itself may have provoked, as in the ambiguous example of the "best friend," neither circumstance brings us to the heart of the matter. For we learn, by studying intermediate societies, that the laws so typical of them are unprecedented. . . . They arise in opposition to the customary order of the antecedent kin or kin-equivalent groups; they represent a new set of social goals pursued by a new and unanticipated power in society. These goals can be reduced to a single complex imperative: the imposition of the census-tax-conscription system. The territorial thrust of the early state, along with its vertical social entrenchment, demanded conscription of labor, the mustering of an army, the levying of taxes and tribute, the maintenance of a bureaucracy and the assessment of the extent, location and numbers of the population being subjected. These were the major direct or indirect occasions for the development of civil law.

The primary purpose of a census is indicative. Census figures provide the basis on which taxes are apportioned among conquered districts and on which tribute in labor is exacted from kin units. The census is also essential for conscripting men into the army. . . .

The census figures represented the potential power of the state and were carefully guarded; perhaps they were the first state secret. The act and intent of the census turned persons into ciphers and abstractions; people did all they could to avoid being counted. Suspicion persists; even in the United States the authorities during the period of census taking find it necessary to assert that census information will not be used to tax or otherwise penalize the individual and in fact, to do so is said to be against the law.

The double meanings of certain critical terms in common English use — "custom," "duty" and "court," reveal this conflict between local usage and the census-tax-conscription system of the early state. We have been speaking of custom as traditional or conventional nonlegal behavior, but custom also refers to a tax routinely payable to the state for the transportation of goods across territorial borders. . . .

Fiscal or legal coercion and political imposition were not the purpose of . . . ancestral ceremonies which ritually reenacted reciprocal bonds. The customs of the sovereign were laws, the ceremonies of the kin groups were customs.

Similarly, the term *duty* implies a moral obligation on the one hand and a tax on the other. . . . [T]he paradox inherent in the term becomes more obvious as we examine archaic civilizations.

The term *court* is analogously ambivalent. On the one hand, it refers to the residence or entourage of the sovereign; on the other, to a place where civil justice is dispensed, but at their root the functions fuse. The prototypical juridical institution was, in fact, the court of the sovereign where legislation was instituted, for which no precedent or formal analogue existed on the local level. . . .

Clearly, the function of the court was not primarily the establishment of order. In primitive societies, as in the traditional sectors of proto-states, there already existed built-in mechanisms for the resolution of conflict. Generally speaking (as Max Gluckman, among others, has shown), in such societies conflicts generated by the ordinary functioning of social institutions were resolved as part of the customary ritual cycle integral to the institutions themselves. With regard to more specific breaches, we recall Rattray's observation on the Ashanti: "Corporate responsibility for every act was an established principle which survived even the advent of . . . the administration of public justice." That is to say the kin unit was the juridical unit, just as it was the economic and social unit. Furthermore,

> Causes which give rise to the greater part of present "civil" actions were practically nonexistent. Inheritance, ownership of moveable and nonmoveable property, status of individuals, rules of behavior and morality were matters inevitably settled by the customary law, with which everyone was familiar from childhood, and litigation regarding such matters was . . . almost inconceivable. Individual contract, moreover, from the very nature of the community with which we are concerned, was also unknown, thus removing another possible, fruitful source of litigation.

. . . In the census-tax-conscription system, every conceivable occasion was utilized for the creation of law in support of bureaucracy and sovereign. We observe no abstract principle, no impartial justice, no *precedent,* only the spontaneous opportunism of a new class designing the edifice of its power. It should be re-emphasized, however, that in certain instances . . . analogues . . . existed on the local level, but no formal or functional precedents. Civil taxation, for example, can be rationalized in the context of reciprocal gift-giving in the localities . . . , similarly, corvée labor is a political analogue of local cooperative work groups. But such evolutionary and dialectical relationships are most important for their distinctions.

[Legal historian William] Stubbs writes about the Norman kings that "it was mainly for the sake of the profits that early justice was administered at all." [Captain Sir Richard] Burton relates that at Whydah in Dahomey in the event of a financial dispute, the Yevogan, the leading bureaucrat in the district, sat in judgment. For his services, he appropriated half the merchandise involved, in the name of the king and another quarter for various lesser officials. The remainder presumably went to the winning contestant in the judicial duel. Among the Ashanti, the central authority relied on the proceeds of litigation as a fruitful means for replenishing a depleted treasury. Litigation, Rattray notes, came actually to be encouraged.

Tolls were an important source of revenue. In Ashanti, the king had all the roads guarded; all traders were detained until inquiries were made about them, whereupon they were allowed to pass on payment of gold dust. [Explorer] W. Bosman writes that in early eighteenth century Whydah, "in proportion to his country, the king's revenue is very large, of which I believe, he hath above one thousand collectors who dispose themselves throughout the whole land in all market roads and passages, in order to gather the king's toll which amounts to an incredible sum, for there is nothing so mean sold in the whole kingdom that the king hath no toll for it. . . ."

The punishment for the theft of property designated as the king's was summary execution by kangaroo courts organized on the spot by the king's agents. . . .

In [legal historian Frederic William] Maitland's words, "the king has a peace that devours all others." If in these proto-states, the sovereign power is not yet fully effective, it nonetheless strives to that monopoly of force which characterizes the mature state.

The purpose and abundance of laws inevitably provoked breaches. The civil authority, in fact, continually probed for breaches and frequently manufactured them. . . .

Thus, rape was invented as a civil crime. If rape had occurred in the traditional joint-family villages . . . , the wrong could have been dealt with by composition (the ritualized giving of goods to the injured party), ritual purification, ridicule and, perhaps for repeated transgressions, banishment; the customary machinery would have gone into effect automatically, probably on the initiative of the family of the aggressor. Such examples as this only sharpen the point that in early states crimes seem to have been invented to suit the laws. The latent purpose of the law was punishment in the service and profit of the state, not prevention or the protection of persons, not the healing of the breach. . . .

. . . For [another] example, civil protection of the market place or highway was certainly not necessary to the degree implied in the archaic edicts at the time they were issued. Joint-family markets and village trails were not ordinarily dangerous places, if we are to believe the reports of the earliest chroniclers as well as those of more contemporary observers. More significantly if trouble had developed, the family, clan or village was capable of dealing with it. But, in an evolving state, the presence of the king's men would itself be a primary cause of disruption. Indeed, as [M.] Quénum, a descendant of Dahomean commoners, informs us the soldiers were referred to as bandits and predators who victimized many people. Sometimes their forays were confined to a compound, where someone, whether man, woman, or child, resided who had spoken badly of the sovereign or whom the king suspected. . . .

As the integrity of the local groups declined, a process which . . . must have taken generations or even centuries, conditions doubtless developed which served as an ex post facto rationalization for edicts already in effect. In this sense, laws became self-fulfilling prophecies. Crime and the laws which served it were, then, covariants of the evolving state. . . .

The intention of the civil power is epitomized in the sanctions against homicide and suicide; indeed, they were among the very first civil laws. Just as the sovereign is said to own the land, intimating the mature right of eminent domain, so the individual is ultimately conceived as the chattel of the state. In Dahomey, persons were conceived as *les choses due monarque* [property of the monarch]. Eminent domain in persons and property, even where projected as a fiction, is the cardinal prerequisite of the census-tax-conscription system. We recall that Maine designated the individual the unit of which the civil law steadily takes account. [Legal historian William] Seagle stated the matter as follows: "By undermining the kinship bond, they [the early civil authorities] made it easier to deal with individuals, and the isolation of the individual is a basic precondition for the growth of law."

Homicide, then, was regarded as an offense against the state. In Rattray's words, "The blow which struck down the dead man would thus appear to have been regarded as aimed also at the . . . central authority." In Ashanti, homicide was punishable by death in its most horrible form as customarily defined, in Dahomey, by death or conscription into the army. . . .

Traditionally, murder in a joint-family village was a tort — a private, remediable wrong — which could stimulate a blood feud, not to be confused with the *lex talionis* [law of revenge], until redress, though not necessarily injury in kind, was achieved. But a breach was most often settled by composition. As [anthropologist] Paul Radin put it: "The theory of an eye for an eye . . . never really held for primitive people. . . . Rather it was replacement for loss with damages." And this is echoed by [anthropologist J. G.] Peristiany: "they claim restitution or private damages and not social retribution." In any case, the family was fully involved. "The family was a corporation," said Rattray, and "it is not easy to grasp what must have been the effect . . . of untold generations of thinking and acting . . . in relation to one's group. The Ashanti's idea of what we term moral responsibility for his actions must surely have been more developed than in peoples where individualism is the order of the day." This more or less typical anthropological observation makes it clear that the law against homicide was not a "progressive" step. . . . "Anti-social conduct [is] exceptional in small kinship groups," writes [anthropologist] Margery Perham of the Igbo. Crimes of violence were rare, Richard Burton reported of Dahomey, and "murder virtually unknown."

Acts of violence, of course, must be distinguished from crimes of violence. The incidence, occasion for, and character of violence in primitive societies is a subject of the utmost importance. But the question here has to do with crimes in which violence is used as a means to an end, such as the theft of property. In contemporary societies, unpremeditated acts of personal violence that have no ulterior motive, so-called crimes of passion, may not be penalized or carry minor degrees of guilt, that is, their status as legally defined crimes is ambiguous. This would certainly seem to reflect a historically profound distinction between crime and certain types of violence; in primitive societies violence tends to be personally structured, nondissociative and thereby self-limiting. As with other crimes defined by civil law, crimes of violence may have increased as the social autonomy, economic communalism and reciprocity of the kin units weakened. . . .

The law against suicide, a capital offense, was the apotheosis of political absurdity. The individual, it was assumed, had no right to take his own life; that was the sole prerogative of the state, whose property he was conceived to be. The fanatical nature of the civil legislature in claiming sole prerogative to the lives of its subjects is conclusively revealed among the Ashanti, where, if the suicide was a murderer, "the central authority refused to be cheated thus and the long arm of the law followed the suicide to the grave from which, if his kinsmen should have dared to bury him, he was dragged to stand trial." This contrasts remarkably, if logically, with the behavior of the more primitively structured Igbo, as reported by Victor Uchendu, an anthropologist who is himself an Igbo:

> Homicide is an offense against *ala* — the earth deity. If a villager is involved, the murderer is expected to hang himself, after which . . . daughters of the village perform the rite of . . . sweeping away the ashes of murder. If the murderer has fled, his extended family must also flee, and the property of all is subject to raids. When the murderer is eventually caught, he is required to hang himself to enable the [daughters of the village] to perform their rites. It is important to realize that the village has no power to impose capital punishment. In fact, no social group or institution has this power. Everything affecting the life of the villager is regulated by custom. The life of the individual is highly respected; it is protected by the earth-goddess. The villagers can bring social pressure, but the murderer must hang himself.

It can hardly be argued that the purpose of the civil sanction against suicide was to diminish its incidence or to propagate a superior moral consciousness. Dare we say, as with other crimes, that attempts at suicide increased as society became more thoroughly politicized? The law against suicide reveals, in the extreme, the whole meaning and intent of civil law at its origins. In the proto-state, the quintessential struggle was over the lives and labor of the people, who, still moving in a joint family context, were nonetheless conceived to be *les choses du monarque.*

LAW AND DISORDER

If revolutions are the acute, episodic signs of civilizational discontent, the rule of law, from Sumer or Akkad to New York or Moscow, has been the chronic symptom of the disorder of institutions. [Anthropologist] E. B. Tylor stated: "A constitutional government, whether called republic or kingdom, is an arrangement by which the nation governs itself by means of the machinery of a military despotism."

The generalization lacks nuance, but we can accept it if we bear in mind what seems to be Tylor's point of reference: "Among the lessons to be learnt from the life of rude tribes is how society can go without the policeman to keep order." When he alludes to constitutional government, Tylor was not distinguishing its ultimate sanction from that of any other form of the state: all political society is based on repressive organized force. In this he was accurate. For pharaohs and presidents alike have always made a public claim to represent the common interest, indeed to incarnate the common good. Only a Plato or a Machiavelli in search of political harmony, or a Marx in search of political truth, has been able to penetrate this myth of the identity between ruler and ruled, of equality under the law. The tradition of Plato and Machiavelli commends the use of the "royal" or "noble lie," while that of Marx exposes and rejects the power structure (ultimately the state) that propagates so false a political consciousness. On this issue, I follow Marx. . . .

The legal order, which Plato idealized, is as Tylor maintained and Marx understood, synonymous with the power of the state. "The state," writes Paul Vinogradoff, "has assumed the monopoly of political co-ordination. It is the state which rules, makes laws and eventually enforces them by coercion. Such a state did not exist in ancient times. The commonwealth was not centered in one sovereign body towering immeasurably above single individuals and meting out to everyone his portion of right." And Engels, reflecting on the origins of the state, asserts: "The right of the state to existence was founded on the preservation of order in the interior and the protection against the barbarians outside, but this order was worse than the most disgusting disorder, and the barbarians against whom the state pretended to protect its citizens were hailed by them as saviors." Moreover, "The state created a public power of coercion that did no longer coincide with the old self-organized and (self) armed population." Finally, in a passage that epitomizes the West's awareness of itself, Engels writes:

> The state, then, is by no means a power forced on society at a certain stage of evolution. It is the confession that this society has become hopelessly divided against itself, has estranged itself in irreconcilable contradictions which it is powerless to banish. In order that these contradictions, these classes with conflicting economic interests may not annihilate themselves and society in a useless struggle, a power becomes necessary that stands apparently above society and has the function of keeping down the conflicts and maintaining "order." And this power, the outgrowth of society, but assuming supremacy over it and becoming more and more divorced from it, is the state. . . .

In a word, the state is the alienated form of society. . . .

THE RESPONSE TO CIVIL LAW

. . . Finally, we are led to ask, as did Nadel about the Nupe:

> What did the tax-paying law-abiding citizen receive in return for allegiance to king and nobility? Was extortion, bribery, brutal force, the only aspect under which the state revealed itself to the populace? The people were to receive, theoretically, on the whole, one thing: security — protection against external and internal enemies, and general security for carrying out the daily work,

> holding markets, using the roads. We have seen what protection and security meant in reality. At their best, they represented something very unequal and very unstable. This situation must have led to much tension and change within the system and to frequent attempts to procure better safeguards for civil rights.

The struggle for civil rights, then, is a response to the imposition of civil law. . . .

Procedure is the individual's last line of defense in contemporary civilization, wherein all other associations to which he may belong have become subordinate to the state. The elaboration of procedure is a unique if fragile feature of more fully evolved states, in compensation, so to speak, for the radical isolation of the individual; procedure permits the individual to hold the line, while working toward associations designed to replace the state. In the proto-states, the harshness of rudimentary procedure was countered by the role of the kinship units which, as we recall, retained a significant measure of functional socio-economic autonomy and, therefore, of local political cohesion. But "law has its origin in the pathology of social relations and functions only when there are frequent disturbances of the social equilibrium." Law arises in the breach of a prior customary order and increases in force with the conflicts that divide political societies internally and among themselves. Law and order is the historical illusion; law versus order is the historical reality. . . .

Notes and Questions

1. In considering Diamond's analysis of the relationship between law and custom, note the rejection of custom in the *Cox* case discussed in the introduction to Section 1 of this chapter.
2. Diamond says that custom is definite and known, whereas law is vague and uncertain. What does he mean? Consider the following court opinion:

> [The Naturalization Law provides] that the court must "be satisfied that" the applicant . . . "has behaved as a man of a good moral character, attached to the principles of the constitution of the United States, and well disposed to the good order and happiness of the same." It is of course true that repeated and deliberate violation of any ordinance indicates the absence, *pro tanto*, of that obedience to the will of the community that is the duty of all citizens. That would be true, for example, of those regulations now common that provide waste baskets for litter which one must use so as not to clog the pavement or the roadway. A purist may indeed argue that, if clean streets are a part of the "good order" of a city, when anyone deliberately and persistently refuses to use such baskets, it proves that he is not "well disposed to the good order" of the city. However, such a rigid interpretation of the words seems to us unduly to enlarge their proper scope. Like any other statute, this one is to be read with its purposes in mind, which are to admit as citizens only those who are in general accord with the basic principles of the community. Disregard of parking regulations, even when repeated as often as this was, is not inimical to its "good order," so construed. . . .
>
> We should of course yield to the text, when the text is plain, but "good order" is a word of vague content: particularly when used as an alternate to "good moral character." If it be answered that this bases our construction on our personal judgment of the public importance of the conduct involved, we agree. Not infrequently a legislature means to leave to the judges the appraisal of some of the values at stake. For example, those rights, criminal and civil, that are measured by what is "reasonable," really grant to courts such a "legislative" power, although we call the issues questions of fact. They require of the judges the compromise that they think in accord with the general purposes of the measure as the community would understand it. We are of course aware of the resulting uncertainties involved in such an interpretation; but the alternative would be specifically to provide for each situation that can arise, a substitute utterly impractical in operation. We can say no more than that we think it plain that this statute did not mean to make naturalization

> depend upon obedience to such a regulation as that before us. . . . In the case at bar we hold that disobedience to the parking regulations of a great city, even though repeated and deliberate, does not show a disposition contrary to the "good order" of the United States; and was a permissible delegation of power.*

3. Vine Deloria, Jr., has contrasted the "two concepts of community" that differentiate American Indian tribal culture from Anglo-European civilization. Compare his description of contemporary American society with Diamond's analysis of the economic basis of law:

> Today the land is dotted with towns, cities, suburbs, and the like. Yet very few of these political subdivisions are in fact communities. They are rather transitory locations for the temporary existence of wage earners. People come and go as the economics of the situation demand. They join churches and change churches as their business and economic successes dictate. . . . People may live side by side for years having in common only their property boundaries and their status as property taxpayers. . . . Today many of the Indian tribes are undergoing profound changes with respect to their traditional solidarity. . . . Massive economic development programs on the reservations have caused population shifts that have tended to break down traditional living groups and to cause severe strain in the old clan structure.†

4. Diamond discusses how the administration of justice served as a source of revenue for the early nation-state. Compare his analysis with the following remarks by Adam Smith on "the expense of justice":

> . . . In the Tartar governments of Asia, in the governments of Europe which were founded by the German and Scythian nations who overturned the Roman empire, the administration of justice was a considerable source of revenue, both to the sovereign and to all the lesser chiefs or lords who exercised under him any particular jurisdiction, either over some particular tribe or clan, or over some particular territory or district. Originally both the sovereign and the inferior chiefs used to exercise this jurisdiction in their own persons. Afterwards they universally found it convenient to delegate it to some substitute, bailiff, or judge. This substitute, however, was still obliged to account to his principal or constituent for the profits of the jurisdiction. Whoever reads the instructions which were given to the judges of the circuit in the time of Henry II will see clearly that those judges were a sort of itinerant factors, sent round the country for the purpose of levying certain branches of the king's revenue. In those days the administration of justice not only afforded a certain revenue to the sovereign, but to procure this revenue seems to have been one of the principal advantages which he proposed to obtain by the administration of justice.
>
> This scheme of making the administration of justice subservient to the purposes of revenue could scarce fail to be productive of several very gross abuses. The person who applied for justice with a large present in his hand was likely to get something more than justice; while he who applied for it with a small one was likely to get something less. Justice too might frequently be delayed, in order that this present might be repeated. The amercement, besides, of the person complained of, might frequently suggest a very strong reason for finding him in the wrong, even when he had not really been so. That such abuses were far from being uncommon, the ancient history of every country in Europe bears witness.‡

5. Consider the relations today between "developed" nations and "underdeveloped" nations, between "multinational" corporations and their "host" countries. Do

---

**Yin-Shing Woo* v. *United States,* 288 F2d 434, 435 (1961).

†Vine Deloria, Jr., *God Is Red* (New York: Delta, 1973), pp. 221–22.

‡Adam Smith, *An Inquiry into the Nature and Causes of the Wealth of Nations,* 4th ed., vol. 2 (Dublin: Colles, Moncrieffe, et al., 1785), pp. 230–231.

you think these relations involve a rearrangement of customary social structures by powerful groups competing for legal control? What different images of law and society are involved in these situations? The following report by a German duke visiting Africa before World War I may help you respond to these questions:

> Ruanda is certainly the most interesting country in the German East African Protectorate — in fact, in all Central Africa — chiefly on account of its ethnographical and geographical position. Its interest is further increased by the fact that it is one of the last negro kingdoms governed autocratically by a sovereign sultan, for German supremacy is only recognized to a very limited extent.
>
> Added to this, it is a land flowing with milk and honey, . . . a land which offers the brightest of prospects to the white settler. . . .
>
> To anyone with an intimate knowledge of African affairs it seemed a sheer impossibility that so powerful a sovereign, the ruler over some one and a half million people, would voluntarily submit to the new regime and agree to enter upon no undertakings within his vast, thickly populated, and unexplored realms except by permission of the European Resident.
>
> To compel him to do so would have meant bloody wars and an enormous sacrifice of human life as the inevitable consequence. The sudden change of existing conditions, too, would have involved a heavy pecuniary sacrifice, as the government would have found it necessary, with such a large population, to appoint a relatively large number of European officials. As such measures would have proved impracticable, complete anarchy would have followed.
>
> So the country was therefore allowed to retain its traditional organization, and the sultan was given full jurisdiction over his fellow-people, under control of the Resident, who was to suppress cruelty as far as possible. In one word, the government does not acknowledge the Sultan as a sovereign lord, but fully recognizes his authority as chief of his clan. Kindred tribes, non-resident in Ruanda, are therefore not subject to the Sultan's jurisdiction, but are under the administration of the Resident.
>
> The fundamental principle is the same with all Residents. It is desired to strengthen and enrich the Sultan and persons in authority, and to increase thereby their interest in the continuance of German rule, so that the desire for revolt shall die away, as the consequence of a rebellion would be a dwindling of their revenues. At the same time, by steadily controlling and directing the Sultan and using his powers, civilizing influences would be introduced. Thus by degrees, and almost imperceptibly to the people and to the Sultan himself, he eventually becomes nothing less than the executive instrument of the Resident. . . .
>
> Similarly to their sovereign ruler, the chiefs are descended from various distinguished families or clans. These clans hold land, pay taxes to the Sultan, are keen to avenge the bloodshed of kinsmen, and possess a totem — some object of adoration, which usually takes the shape of an animal or plant. . . .
>
> From what I have written it will easily be seen that the greater part of Ruanda is eminently adapted for colonization by white men, . . . and that there is a splendid opening here for the establishment of business on a vast scale. . . .
>
> When we took our leave of the Sultan, at early dawn on the 12th of August, it was with a certain amount of satisfaction. We had been afforded an insight into the court life of a negro prince and favored with a display of his power such as no one had ever experienced previously or would probably ever experience again. When the illimitable power of this Sultan has receded before European influence, and when busy throngs of traders encroach upon the haughty aloofness of this most aristocratic of all negro tribes and the white man's herds graze in its pastures, then we shall be able to appreciate to the full the value of our remarkable experience.§

---

§Duke Adolphus Frederick of Mecklenburg, "A Land of Giants and Pygmies," in *In the Heart of Africa* (London: Cassell, 1912).

6. Farley Mowat, naturalist and historian, has written about life among some of the Eskimo people in Canada. Their social order, he asserts, is based on principles that diverge widely from the legal order of the Canadian state. In a sense, one might say that the Eskimo law is not based on "principles" at all, but rather on concrete, existential experience stretching over many generations. Compare Mowat's description of Eskimo society with Diamond's contrast between "customary law" and "civilized law":

   [T]here are deviations from law, and there are crimes in the land; for no race of men can be free of these things. But there are also certain forces which the People control and which in turn direct the actions of men, and these forces keep the law-breaking within narrow bounds. To understand these forces is to realize why the Ihalmiut have no need of our laws to maintain the security of their way of life.

   There is absolutely no internal organization to hold authority over the People. No one man, or body of men, holds power in any other sense than the magical. There is no council of elders, no policeman. There are no assemblies of government and, in the strictest sense, the Ihalmiut may be said to live in an anarchistic state, for they do not even have an inflexible code of laws.

   Yet the People exist in amity together, and the secret of this is the secret of co-operative endeavor, limited only by the powers of human will and endurance. It is not blind obedience or obedience dictated by fear. Rather it is intelligent obedience to a simple code that makes sense to those who must live by its rules. . . .

   . . . Should a man continuously disregard the Law of Life, then little by little he finds himself isolated and shut off from the community. There can be no more powerful punishment . . . in a world where man must work closely with man in order to live. . . . The law does not call for an eye for an eye. If possible the breaker of law is brought back to become an asset to the camps. His defection is tacitly forgotten, and to all intents and purposes it never happened at all.‖

7. In thinking further about the contemporary significance of the difference between custom and law, consider the following remarks of Jane Jacobs:

   The first thing to understand is that the public peace — the sidewalk and street peace — of cities is not kept primarily by the police, necessary as police are. It is kept primarily by an intricate, almost unconscious, network of voluntary controls and standards among the people themselves, and enforced by the people themselves. In some city areas — older public housing projects and streets with very high population turnover are often conspicuous examples — the keeping of public sidewalk law and order is left almost entirely to the police and special guards. Such places are jungles. No amount of police can enforce civilization where the normal, casual enforcement of it has broken down. . . .

   An incident at . . . , a public housing project in New York illustrates this point. A tenants' group . . . put up three Christmas trees. The chief tree, so cumbersome it was a problem to transport, erect, and trim, went into the project's . . . landscaped central mall and promenade. The other two trees, each less than six feet tall and easy to carry, went on two small fringe plots at the outer corners of the project where it abuts a busy avenue and lively cross streets of the old city. The first night, the large tree and all its trimmings were stolen. The two smaller trees remained intact, lights, ornaments and all, until they were taken down at New Year's. "The place where the tree was stolen, which is *theoretically* the most safe and sheltered place in the project, is the same place that is unsafe for people too, especially children," says a social worker. . . . "People are no safer in that mall than the Christmas tree. On the other hand, the place where the other trees were safe,

‖From Farley Mowat, *People of the Deer* (Boston: Little, Brown, 1951), pp. 176–178.

where the project is just one corner out of four, happened to be safe for people."#

Jacobs says that city planners, architects, politicians, real estate developers, bankers, and others who make decisions about the building and rebuilding of cities often act from false ideas about how communities work. These false ideas center on making things look good rather than on making things really good as places for people to live. Jacobs believes that community life consists of people watching out for each other, and that people do this unless the environment they live in prevents or obstructs them. The basic problem, she maintains, is to understand and provide for the complexity of healthy social relations. She says, for example, that no amount of law enforcement can take the place of a living network of relations among people.

What qualities do living relations have that law does not? Can you see how law enforcement might actually damage a living network of people's lives? What other forces might damage a network of human relations?

#From Jane Jacobs, *The Death and Life of Great American Cities* (New York: Random House, 1961), pp. 31–32, 34.

The Organizational Revolution *Frederick C. Thayer*

We must sweep away the conventional baggage of what we know as "politics" and "economics." Our system of representative government is designed only to preserve *hierarchy*, and our economic system is based upon the ideal of *competition*. Yet neither hierarchy nor competition has a place in our future, for both compel us to repress ourselves and each other. The organizational revolution is an attempt to end repression, and the alienation that accompanies it. . . .

When the organizational revolution has run its course, and when societies have been transformed as they must be if we are to survive, the world of organizations will be one of innumerable small face-to-face groups characterized by openness, trust, and intensive interpersonal relations. . . .

This entire book argues for a *different* way of looking at the world in which we live, and especially at the organizations (nation-states, universities, public agencies, corporations, and whatever) which dominate the world's activity. The initial premise, which may seem extremely disorienting at first glance, is that formal organizations as we think of them either *do not exist* or are *dysfunctional*. The most useful work is accomplished only through *other* processes for which we now have no accepted explanation or theory. To put it simply, we do not yet know *how* we do useful work. When we discover an explanation or theory — and this book is an attempt to suggest how we might begin — we will apply the same organizational principles to all social structures, from families to corporations to nation-states. All distinctions between public and private, national and international will be erased as we learn that democracy cannot exist anywhere unless it exists everywhere — though in ways we cannot yet completely understand, predict in detail, or design. The reader must be willing to assume that an intellectual leap is at least possible, and that a revised view of the world might conform more closely both to how useful things *are done and how they should be* done.

Frederick Thayer, after service in the United States National Security Council, began formal study of organization theory and structure. He is now a professor of organization theory, whose work focuses primarily on the implications of hierarchical and participatory structures in contemporary societies.

The change we seek is, first and foremost, *a different way of seeing things as they are today.* Much of the organizational revolution is invisible because we cannot see it within the intellectual frameworks we use. Thus, change must begin in a way we usually do not think of as change, because everything remains the same except the way we look at it. Later change will follow, of course, but only after this first step. As a starting point for understanding the nature of the intellectual leap, the world of organizations provides two research and operational approaches which seldom are directly compared. . . .

HIERARCHICAL SPAN OF CONTROL VERSUS THE SMALL GROUP

In formal organizations, no principle of management remains more significant than "span of control," i.e., the number of subordinates one supervisor can effectively manage. The superior-subordinate relationship is vertical. The superior must evaluate subordinates, moreover, on a periodic basis (often through the use of "efficiency reports"), a system which gives the superior massive leverage, in that his evaluations of subordinates determine who is promoted and who is fired. The precise ratio of subordinates to superiors has never been scientifically determined, but management literature recommends spans of control between three and nine subordinates in most environments, four being considered most desirable. At lower levels of routinized work, spans of control can expand, so it is thought, to about thirty.

Turn quickly now to different research, based upon small-group processes which do not include superior-subordinate relationships. The small group is conventionally defined as one in which each member must receive an impression or perception of each other member that is distinct enough to enable the member to react or give some opinion of each of the others — and to recall later one or more impressions of each of the others. Research into the processes of "action-taking groups" (where decisions are made), subcommittees in legislative bodies which do the toughest detailed work (both in Western and non-Western cultures), experiments with various-sized groups of youngsters, and the observations, of, for example, sociologist Georg Simmel and bureaucratic commentator C. Northcote Parkinson all reach the same conclusion: *the size of effective small groups is precisely the same as that prescribed for vertical spans of control.* It is possible to be almost mystical about the problem of "numbers," in that some of our current organizational problems may be traceable to the shift from "hunting" to "agricultural" societies many centuries ago, and our social hierarchies seem to date from that shift. When people hunted together in bands, their languages seldom had words for numbers over five, which is still the most desirable size for an effective small group. While common sense would seem to dictate that there can be no "magic" number, five appears so often in so many environmental situations as to carry persuasion with it.

These results come from research shaped by two theories which, by definition, determine the researchers' interpretations of those results. Only the theories and the interpretations differ, *not the results themselves.* Which theory conforms to organizational reality? Do groups produce effective outcomes because one individual is armed with authority to direct the work of four subordinates, or because five individuals interact in a non-hierarchical process in which no individual is "boss" of the others? Even two "classical" theorists of administration, Chester Barnard and Lyndall Urwick, were reluctant to use the vertical pattern to describe their experiences. Barnard acknowledged hierarchy on grounds that it was forced upon organizations from without, thus implying it was unnatural, and Urwick surrounded his views on spans of control with explicit caveats which interpreters often overlook. Both seem to have distorted their observations to make them fit conventional wisdom.

Is it possible that the effective conduct of social business occurs *in spite* of hierarchy, not because of it? This should not be too startling a question. Theorists have admitted for years that a principal objective of any permanent organization is its own survival — a finding which holds for corporations, nation-states, and public agencies. Many organizations, in other words, spend their time exacerbating the problems they supposedly want to solve. This is why welfare agencies behave in ways which perpetuate poverty instead of removing it, and why the Federal Bureau of Investigation pours money and people into the Communist party. To ensure survival ("boundary maintenance" in the jargon of administration, "security" in that of the nation-state), hierarchical leaders direct a competitive struggle for resources (corporations for markets, universities and public agencies for funds, armies for territory). This requires that organizational members be kept under strict discipline, through the dispensing of rewards and punishments. This is why organizations use the military stereotype for selecting leaders, searching for "decisive," "hard-nosed," "tough-minded" executives who can "ruthlessly" cut away "deadwood" in the name of effectiveness. Organizations select those who excel at repressing others, place them in positions they cannot handle because reality does not correspond to the theory, and thus operationalize the "Peter Principle." The error lies not in those who select leaders, nor in the leaders themselves, but in the conventional wisdom that both use. The vertical theory, then, explains only how we create problems; in solving them, we use another theory, yet to be articulated in detail, that has the effect of eliminating the typical formal organization as an agent of social purpose. . . .

THE "WITHERING AWAY" OF ORGANIZATIONS

"Withering away" may be a frightening phrase, but no other will quite do. A reanalysis of past trends and an assessment of current ones make it possible to view all effective social interaction through horizontal, rather than vertical, lenses. Conventional organization theory concentrates on the permanent formal organization. But we have entered an era of interdependence in which autonomous organizations, including nation-states, can do little of importance alone, unless one considers the disciplining of employees an achievement. Everything useful is done in cooperation with other organizations and individuals, and in most cases these broader relationships cannot be twisted into superior-subordinate patterns. . . .

That we do not have thousands of documented examples is due to the conventional organizational assumption that the only important actions are those of authoritative decision-makers. We condemn committees as the worst form of organization, failing to note that in so doing we imply that individuals should act only in total isolation from one another — never, never together. Yet just the opposite is true: nothing of any significance can be, or should be, done alone. Committees were one of the first responses to the need to bring people together in groups. They deserve an honored place in the history of organizations, even if we have done our best to ensure they do not work. . . .

A [committee process which crosses organizational boundaries] is likely to be effective only when the committee chairman's role is one of facilitation — *not* one of personal responsibility for, and authority over, outcomes. This suggests a law for such processes, which turns conventional wisdom inside out: *The effectiveness of group processes is inversely proportional to the amount of formal decision authority assigned to chairmen; the less the authority assigned an individual chairman, the more likely an effective outcome.* This does not imply that chairmen cannot be or should not be responsible for outcomes; they can be, indeed, and they should be, but the same can be said for all other members. The individualistic perspective thus gives way to a collective one which assumes that each individual makes, or can make, a unique contribution to the small-group outcome. . . . [T]here are and can be no exceptions to this law — not for presidents, governors, generals, or university presidents. Achieving effective outcomes requires *collective responsibility,* and further requires that we pay attention to the number of individuals involved in each group — something for which the literature on span of control and small groups provides broad guidelines. If a problem requires the involvement of many individuals from many organizations, we must create enough groups to keep each one small enough to be effective. Groups can then be linked together through overlapping memberships. The skills required of chairmen, of those holding overlapping memberships, and indeed of all members are not the skills of giving and carrying out orders. . . .

CITIZEN PARTICIPATION AND THE "CHARRETTE"

Participation disorients many of the elite managers who dominate organizational systems. It means they must face demands from lower-class citizens whose capabilities they have denigrated for years. When this occurs, the elites argue that involvement is dangerous because the outsiders are not well enough educated to deal with the expert professionals who make day-to-day decisions. For other elites who face demands from affluent suburbanites and sophisticated college students, the same arguments do not apply. In these cases, the elites insist that they are the only ones with legal authority to make decisions. Both arguments make them uncomfortable. Either they must stress their own inherent superiority or tell citizens that what happens to them or their children is none of their business, even if those citizens are, by conventional wisdom's own standards, as qualified as the professionals. Having no consistent argument to advance, the elites feel trapped within a theory from which they see no escape. Meanwhile, the trend toward involvement has advanced far beyond the "maximum feasible participation" of the 1960's, which turned into an old-fashioned power struggle; those in authority defined participation as something that would destroy them, and those on the outside did indeed seek control. Only after intense discomfort on all sides has it become clear that the issue is not a *transfer* of authority but a *sharing* of it. This shift has not been a noisy one, but it is revolutionary, and it is happening in countless organizations. Here is one black principal's description of how he manages an elementary school:

> . . . The secret . . . is not to get upset about the power struggle. The old-line principals are fighting like mad because the parents want some power. You see, I don't care, quite frankly. I really don't. . . . There are certain decisions that have to be made. I can share the decision-making process with all the people who want power. I would do it anyway. I want to know what the parents feel. I feel it's essential that teachers tell me how they feel. . . . The PTA president recently came in and told me she had just hired someone. I said, "Fine, who did you hire?" Well, the thing is she can't hire anybody. But she had somebody she wanted me to hire, and it was a good person . . . an aide . . . and we needed one. The old-line principals would have got uptight and started a long discussion about how you can't hire her, how dare you, and all of this kind of thing. But the new-style principal has to share all this power. . . . You have all these various elements to deal with, and you have to get them to cooperate with one another, and you have to share power with them. Everyone is jealous of what everyone else is doing, and you've got to move and circulate and get the whole thing working. If you're going to be uptight about power, then you're going to be in trouble. . . .

The "charrette" is the best example we have yet. A word used to describe horse-drawn carts which carried prisoners to the guillotine, and also the carts used later to gather up the plans the Beaux Arts architectural students submitted for the annual Paris competition, "charrette" has acquired a new meaning for school and other forms of community planning. In contemporary settings, the charrette is a process vehicle (without wheels), systematically constructed to collect and sort out as many ideas as possible generated by individuals directly interested in a given project. . . .

The only known way to begin is to assemble in one place, say a large auditorium or arena, people whose perspectives encompass the major conflicts within a community. These may include ghetto residents, policemen and police chiefs, elected and appointed public officials, professional civil servants, affluent suburbanites, businessmen, and others. All they have in common when they begin is a temporary agreement that there is a problem to be solved, that they want to explore it, and that they will bring in professional process-facilitators. If the process survives an initial period of intense hostility, subcommittees are formed, consultants are attached to each one, and interaction is continued. Each group is structured to include persons whose interests are diametrically opposed. Periodic progress is reported to the entire body, or to the steering committee, so that conflicts between subcommittees can be worked out. Individuals move back and forth between groups until they find the one of greatest concern to them, or until they decide to leave. . . .

Regrettably, even those who shout the loudest in praise of charrettes assume that such processes are, and must remain, temporary undertakings. Once an agreed plan is developed, the assumption is that the charrette should be disbanded and the "official" government should get on with implementation. In Toronto, where the city's director of education has predicted that "never gain will the Board of Education build a neighbourhood school without the active involvement and participation of the neighbourhood residents," there is no evidence that charrette supporters see the process as a quasi-official addition to the formal structure of government. Yet it seems obvious that no plan ever can be implemented precisely as written, and that changes in a plan should be "fed back" and worked out with those who developed it in the first place. Therefore the charrette which is abandoned at this early stage can become only another temporarily satisfying "experience" which, over time, leads to long-term disillusion. Once again, the problem is in the way we look at things. If we can visualize a charrette sound enough and strong enough to develop a workable plan, we ought to be able to regard it as an ongoing process which sees things through. To get to that point, however, we will first have to examine our theories of political government. . . .

We commonly assume that participative processes would add substantially to the cost of government, if only because of the extra time required. But it can be argued that before long all of us will recognize that participative decisions can be uniquely "cost effective" — to use a favorite phrase of recent years. One of the major problems in the United States is that a great many decisions are made solely to overcome the unintended consequences of earlier decisions; i.e., only when an attempt is made to implement certain decisions is it discovered that something prevents their being implemented, something the decision-makers did not know when they decided what to do. Most of the time, the unintended consequences affect individuals and groups who were not consulted before decisions were made. There could be no better way of discovering as many such problems as possible than to include in decision processes those individuals most likely to be affected by them. Although this would slow down the processes, it would produce more effective decisions which, because hidden consequences had been discovered in advance, would become cost effective through *cost avoidance*. . . .

To suggest that citizenship itself consists, or should consist, of an individual's involvement in decision processes — and to add that the governance of organizations is best visualized as a series of group processes in which no individual is identified as "in charge" of any process — is to begin to come to grips with the enormity of the intellectual obstacles which inhibit the full flowering of the organizational revolution. People everywhere are trying to make organizations more attractive to those who work in them, to remove the alienation which affects all of us, and to behave in more humane fashion toward each other. That they have yet to succeed is because none of us completely understands how much change is needed in the way we look at things. The unfortunate probability is that the fundamental causes of our alienation from our work and from each other are deeply imbedded in our theories of political government and economic activity. . . .

There will be plenty to do in the future for those we now term leaders, but not the traditional function of issuing orders. They will feel disoriented and threatened for a time, until it is clear to them that this revolution seeks not merely to overthrow them in favor of other elites, but to transform *relationships* between individuals and groups so that none dominates others. This revolution cannot be understood as a threat, only as an opportunity. The first step toward a livable future is to understand how our conventional theories of politics and economics stand in the way of attaining it.

Notes and Questions

1. How do you think the military model of organization came to dominate people's ideas about social structure? Do you find it significant that Thayer's own work background includes years of experience in high levels of the federal government and military?
2. A common rationale for hierarchy is that it is the only way to organize large groups of people. But might not the opposite be true: the more people there are, the *less* likely it is that they can all be organized into a single chain of command?
3. What could a move away from vertical and toward horizontal organization imply for schools, prisons, and other institutions? As you think about this, consider the images and attitudes expressed by the Supreme Court of California in the following decision:

> Petitioner complains that the prison authorities did not return to him legal information that he had copied from books in the prison law library, and alleges he was informed by a member of the staff that "any information" copied from such books and taken to his cell "would be considered contraband and confiscated."
>
> . . . Director of Corrections rule . . . D2602 . . . declares in relevant part that "No inmate shall assist or receive assistance from another in the preparation of legal documents. Any brief or petition not pertaining to his own case found in the possession of an inmate shall be confiscated." The latter is . . . a reasonable exercise of the statutory authority of the Director of Corrections over the "supervision, management, and control" of the state prisons, for such trafficking in writs may well tend to result in unhealthy or dangerous inmate relationships and create substantial custodial problems.*

What do you think the court means by saying that mutual assistance in legal research might be "unhealthy"? And how could such cooperation be "dangerous"?

**In Re Schoengarth,* 425 P.2d 200, 206–207 (1967).

3 DOLLARS AND DEMOCRACY

> You talk of prisons and police and legalities, the perfect illusions behind which a prosperous power structure can operate while observing . . . that it is above its own laws.
>
> Frank Herbert, *God Emperor of Dune* (1981)

The relationship between law and wealth has been a topic of perennial debate in U.S. history. The debate has surfaced in a variety of forms, ranging from the earliest discussions about how to finance the federal government to more recent controversies about property and income taxes.

One of the commonest forms of this debate focuses on the relationships between property, poverty, and crime. Both critics and supporters of economic inequality recognize that such relationships exist, but differ on their implications. At the core of this debate is a deep philosophical argument about the meaning of freedom.

From one perspective, economic inequality is an outgrowth of the free development of human differences. Crime is viewed as a threat to the accumulations of property that are a desirable and inevitable consequence of this freedom. In this view, the central purpose of government is to provide a legal framework whereby freedom to accumulate individual wealth will be protected. To the extent that democracy tends toward the equalization of wealth, this perspective will call for mechanisms of law to counteract this tendency.

From another perspective, all human beings have equal rights to the necessities of life, and economic inequality is an outgrowth of the denial of freedom by legal privilege. Crime is seen as a response to this legalized inequality. In this view, the central purpose of government is to provide a legal framework whereby political freedom (democracy) may be extended to the economy. To the extent that law promotes individual accumulation of wealth, this perspective calls for political activity to change the law.

The readings in this section provide a basis for discussing the political economy of law.

Address to the Prisoners in the Cook County Jail *Clarence Darrow*

If I looked at jails and crimes and prisoners in the way the ordinary person does, I should not speak on this subject to you. The reason I talk to you on the question of crime, its cause and cure, is that I really do not in the least believe in crime. There is no such thing as a crime as the word is generally understood. I do not believe there is any sort of distinction between the real moral conditions of the people in and out of jail. One is just as good as the other. The people here can no more help being here than the people outside can avoid being outside. I do not believe that people are in jail because they deserve to be. They are in jail simply because they cannot avoid it on account of circumstances which are entirely beyond their control and for which they are in no way responsible.

I suppose a great many people on the outside would say I was doing you harm if they should hear what I say to you this afternoon, but you cannot be hurt a great deal anyway, so it will not matter. Good people outside would say that I was really teaching you things that were calculated to injure society, but it's worth while now and then to hear something different from what you ordinarily get from preachers and the like. These will tell you that you should be good and then you will get rich and be happy. Of course we know that people do not get rich by being good, and that is the reason why so many of you people try to get rich some other way, only you do not understand how to do it quite as well as the fellow outside.

There are people who think that everything in this world is an accident. But really there is no such thing as an accident. A great many folks admit that many of the people in jail ought not to be there, and many who are outside ought to be in. I think none of them ought to be here. There ought to be no jails; and if it were not for the fact that the people on the outside are so grasping and heartless in their dealings with the people on the inside, there would be no such institutions as jails.

I do not want you to believe that I think all you people here are angels. I do not think that. You are people of all kinds, all of you doing the best you can — and that is evidently not very well. You are people of all kinds and conditions and under all circumstances. In one sense everybody is equally good and equally bad. We all do the best we can under the circumstances. But as to the exact things for which you are sent here, some of you are guilty and did the particular act because you needed the money. Some of you did it because you are in the habit of doing it, and some of you because you are born to it, and it comes to be as natural as it does, for instance, for me to be good.

Most of you probably have nothing against me, and most of you would treat me the same way as any other person would, probably better than some of the people on the outside would treat me, because you think I believe in you and they know *I* do not believe in them. While you would not have the least thing against me in the world, you might pick my pockets. I do not think all of you would, but I think some of you would. You would not have anything against me, but that's your profession, a few of you. Some of the rest of you, if my doors were unlocked, might come in if you saw anything you wanted — not out of any malice to me, but because that is your trade. There is no doubt there are quite a number of people in this jail who would pick my pockets. And still I know this — that when I get outside pretty nearly everybody picks my pockets. There may be some of you who would hold up a man on the street, if you did not happen to have something else to do,

---

Clarence Seward Darrow (1857–1938), a social reformer as well as a criminal lawyer, is remembered today for his defense in the landmark Scopes trial in 1925. He defended John Scopes, who was being tried for teaching evolution theory in a Tennessee public school, which was against state law; Scopes was convicted, but released on a technicality. The well-known opposing counsel was the statesman William Jennings Bryan.

and needed the money; but when I want to light my house or my office the gas company holds me up. They charge me one dollar for something that is worth twenty-five cents. Still all these people are good people; they are pillars of society and support the churches, and they are respectable.

When I ride on the streetcars I am held up — I pay five cents for a ride that is worth two and a half cents, simply because a body of men have bribed the city council and the legislature, so that all the rest of us have to pay tribute to them.

If I do not want to fall into the clutches of the gas trust and choose to burn oil instead of gas, then good Mr. Rockefeller holds me up, and he uses a certain portion of his money to build universities and support churches which are engaged in telling us how to be good.

Some of you are here for obtaining property under false pretenses — yet I pick up a great Sunday paper and read the advertisements of a merchant prince — "Shirtwaists for 39 cents, marked down from $3.00."

When I read the advertisements in the paper I see they are all lies. When I want to get out and find a place to stand anywhere on the face of the earth, I find that it has all been taken up long ago before I came here, and before you came here, and somebody says, "Get off, swim into the lake, fly into the air; go anywhere, but get off." That is because these people have the police and they have the jails and the judges and the lawyers and the soldiers and all the rest of them to take care of the earth and drive everybody off that comes in their way.

A great many people will tell you that all this is true, but that it does not excuse you. These facts do not excuse some fellow who reaches into my pocket and takes out a five-dollar bill. The fact that the gas company bribes the members of the legislature from year to year, and fixes the law, so that all you people are compelled to be "fleeced" whenever you deal with them; the fact that the streetcar companies and the gas companies have control of the streets; and the fact that the landlords own all the earth — this, they say, has nothing to do with you.

Let us see whether there is any connection between the crimes of the respectable classes and your presence in the jail. . . .

The reformers who tell you to be good and you will be happy, and the people on the outside who have property to protect — they think that the only way to do it is by building jails and locking you up in cells on weekdays and praying for you Sundays.

I think that all of this has nothing whatever to do with right conduct. I think it is very easily seen what has to do with right conduct. Some so-called criminals — and I will use this word because it is handy, it means nothing to me — I speak of the criminals who get caught as distinguished from the criminals who catch them — some of these so-called criminals are in jail for their first offenses, but nine tenths of you are in jail because you did not have a good lawyer and, of course, you did not have a good lawyer because you did not have enough money to pay a good lawyer. There is no very great danger of a rich man going to jail.

Some of you may be here for the first time. If we would open the doors and let you out, and leave the laws as they are today, some of you would be back tomorrow. This is about as good a place as you can get anyway. There are many people here who are so in the habit of coming that they would not know where else to go. There are people who are born with the tendency to break into jail every chance they get, and they cannot avoid it. You cannot figure out your life and see why it was, but still there is a reason for it; and if we were all wise and knew all the facts, we could figure it out.

In the first place, there are a good many more people who go to jail in the wintertime than in summer. Why is this? Is it because people are more wicked in winter? No, it is because the coal trust begins to get in its grip in the winter. A few gentlemen take possession of the coal, and unless the people will pay seven or eight dollars a ton for something that is worth three dollars, they will have to freeze. Then there is nothing to do but to break into jail, and so there are many more in jail in the winter than in summer. It costs more for gas in the winter because the nights are longer, and people go to jail to save gas bills. The jails are electric-lighted. You may not know it, but these economic laws are working all the time, whether we know it or do not know it.

There are more people who go to jail in hard times than in good times — few people, comparatively, go to jail except when they are hard up. They go to jail because they have no other place to go. They may not know why, but it is true all the same. People are not more wicked in hard times. That is not the reason. The fact is true all over the world that in hard times more people go to jail than in good times, and in winter more people go to jail than in summer. Of course it is pretty hard times for people who go to jail at any time. The people who go to jail are almost always poor people — people who have no other place to live, first and last. When times are hard, then you find large numbers of people who go to jail who would not otherwise be in jail.

Long ago, Mr. Buckle, who was a great philosopher and historian, collected facts, and he showed that the number of people who are arrested increased just as the price of food increased. When they put up the price of gas ten cents a thousand, I do not know who will go to jail, but I do know that a certain number of people will go. When the meat combine raises the price of beef, I do not know who is going to jail, but I know that a large number of people are bound to go. Whenever the Standard Oil Company raises the price of oil I know that a certain number of girls who are seamstresses, and who work night after night long hours for somebody else, will be compelled to go out on the streets and ply another trade, and I know that Mr. Rockefeller and his associates are responsible and not the poor girls in the jails.

First and last, people are sent to jail because they are poor. Sometimes, as I say, you may not need money at the particular time, but you wish to have thrifty forehanded habits, and do not always wait until you are in absolute want. Some of you people are perhaps plying the trade, the profession, which is called burglary. No man in his right senses will go into a strange house in the dead of night and prowl around with a dark lantern through unfamiliar rooms and take chances of his life, if he has plenty of the good things of the world in his own home. You would not take any such chances as that. If a man had clothes in his clothes-press and beefsteak in his pantry and money in the bank, he would not navigate around nights in houses where he knows nothing about the premises whatever. It always requires experience and education for this profession, and people who fit themselves for it are no more to blame than I am for being a lawyer. A man would not hold up another man on the street if he had plenty of money in his own pocket. He might do it if he had one dollar or two dollars, but he wouldn't if he had as much money as Mr. Rockefeller has. Mr. Rockefeller has a great deal better hold-up game than that.

The more that is taken from the poor by the rich, who have the chance to take it, the more poor people there are who are compelled to resort to these means for a livelihood. They may not understand it, they may not think so at once, but after all they are driven into that line of employment.

There is a bill before the legislature of this state to punish kidnaping children with death. We have wise members of the legislature. They know the gas trust when they see it and they always see it — they can furnish light enough to be seen; and this legislature thinks it is going to stop kidnaping children by making a law punishing kidnapers of children with death. I don't believe in kidnaping children, but the legislature is all wrong. Kidnaping children is not a crime, it is a profession. It has been developed with the times. It has been developed with our modern industrial conditions. There are many ways of making money — many new ways that our ancestors knew nothing about. Our ancestors knew nothing about a billion-dollar trust, and here comes some poor fellow who has no other trade and he discovers the profession of kidnaping children.

This crime is born, not because people are

bad; people don't kidnap other people's children because they want the children or because they are devilish, but because they see a chance to get some money out of it. You cannot cure this crime by passing a law punishing by death kidnapers of children. There is one way to cure it. There is one way to cure all these offenses, and that is to give the people a chance to live. There is no other way, and there never was any other way since the world began; and the world is so blind and stupid that it will not see. If every man and woman and child in the world had a chance to make a decent, fair, honest living, there would be no jails and no lawyers and no courts. There might be some persons here or there with some peculiar formation of their brain, like Rockefeller, who would do these things simply to be doing them; but they would be very, very few, and those should be sent to a hospital and treated, and not sent to jail; and they would entirely disappear in the second generation, or at least in the third generation.

I am not talking pure theory. I will just give you two or three illustrations.

The English people once punished criminals by sending them away. They would load them on a ship and export them to Australia. England was owned by lords and nobles and rich people. They owned the whole earth over there, and the other people had to stay in the streets. They could not get a decent living. They used to take their criminals and send them to Australia — I mean the class of criminals who got caught. When these criminals got over there, and nobody else had come, they had the whole continent to run over, and so they could raise sheep and furnish their own meat, which is easier than stealing it. These criminals then became decent, respectable people because they had a chance to live. They did not commit any crimes. They were just like the English people who sent them there, only better. And in the second generation the descendants of those criminals were as good and respectable a class of people as there were on the face of the earth, and then they began building churches and jails themselves.

A portion of this country was settled in the same way, landing prisoners down on the southern coast; but when they got here and had a whole continent to run over and plenty of chances to make a living, they became respectable citizens, making their own living just like any other citizen in the world. But finally the descendants of the English aristocracy who sent the people over to Australia found out they were getting rich, and so they went over to get possession of the earth as they always do, and they organized land syndicates and got control of the land and ores, and then they had just as many criminals in Australia as they did in England. It was not because the world had grown bad; it was because the earth had been taken away from the people.

Some of you people have lived in the country. It's prettier than it is here. And if you have ever lived on a farm you understand that if you put a lot of cattle in a field, when the pasture is short they will jump over the fence; but put them in a good field where there is plenty of pasture, and they will be law-abiding cattle to the end of time. The human animal is just like the rest of the animals, only a little more so. The same thing that governs in the one governs in the other.

Everybody makes his living along the lines of least resistance. A wise man who comes into a country early sees a great undeveloped land. For instance, our rich men twenty-five years ago saw that Chicago was small and knew a lot of people would come here and settle, and they readily saw that if they had all the land around here it would be worth a good deal, so they grabbed the land. You cannot be a landlord because somebody has got it all. You must find some other calling. In England and Ireland and Scotland less than five per cent own all the land there is, and the people are bound to stay there on any kind of terms the landlords give. They must live the best they can, so they develop all these various professions — burglary, picking pockets, and the like.

Again, people find all sorts of ways of getting rich. These are diseases like everything else. You look at people getting rich, organizing trusts and making a million dollars, and somebody gets the disease and he starts out. He catches it just as a man catches the mumps or the measles; he is not to blame, it is in the air. You will find men speculating beyond their means, because the mania of money-getting is taking possession of them. It is simply a disease — nothing more, nothing less. You cannot avoid catching it; but the fellows who have control of the earth have the advantage of you. See what the law is: when these men get control of things, they make the laws. They do not make the laws to protect anybody; courts are not instruments of justice. When your case gets into court it will make little difference whether you are guilty or innocent, but it's better if you have a smart lawyer. And you cannot have a smart lawyer unless you have money. First and last it's a question of money. Those men who own the earth make the laws to protect what they have. They fix up a sort of fence or pen around what they have, and they fix the law so the fellow on the outside cannot get in. The laws are really organized for the protection of the men who rule the world. They were never organized or enforced to do justice. We have no system for doing justice, not the slightest in the world. . . .

The people who are on the outside, who are running banks and building churches and making jails, they have no time to examine 600 or 700 prisoners each year to see whether they are guilty or innocent. If the courts were organized to promote justice the people would elect somebody to defend all these criminals, somebody as smart as the prosecutor — and give him as many detectives and as many assistants to help, and pay as much money to defend you as to prosecute you. We have a very able man for state's attorney, and he has many assistants, detectives, and policemen without end, and judges to hear the cases — everything handy.

Most all of our criminal code consists in offenses against property. People are sent to jail because they have committed a crime against property. It is of very little consequence whether one hundred people more or less go to jail who ought not to go — you must protect property, because in this world property is of more importance than anything else.

How is it done? These people who have property fix it so they can protect what they have. When somebody commits a crime it does not follow that he has done something that is morally wrong. The man on the outside who has committed no crime may have done something. For instance: to take all the coal in the United States and raise the price two dollars or three dollars when there is no need of it, and thus kill thousands of babies and send thousands of people to the poorhouse and tens of thousands to jail, as is done every year in the United States — this is a greater crime than all the people in our jails ever committed; but the law does not punish it. Why? Because the fellows who control the earth make the laws. If you and I had the making of the laws, the first thing we would do would be to punish the fellow who gets control of the earth. Nature put this coal in the ground for me as well as for them and nature made the prairies up here to raise wheat for me as well as for them, and then the great railroad companies came along and fenced it up.

Most all of the crimes for which we are punished are property crimes. There are a few personal crimes, like murder — but they are very few. The crimes committed are mostly those against property. If this punishment is right the criminals must have a lot of property. How much money is there in this crowd? And yet you are all here for crimes against property. The people up and down the Lake Shore have not committed crime: still they have so much property they don't know what to do with it. It is perfectly plain why these people have not committed crimes against property: they make the laws and therefore do not need to break them. And in order for you to get some property you are obliged to break the rules of the game. I don't know but what some of you may have had a very nice chance to get rich by carrying a hod for one dollar a day, twelve hours. Instead of taking that nice, easy profession, you are a burglar. If you had been given a chance to be a banker you would rather follow that. Some of you may have had a chance to work as a switchman on a railroad where you know, according to statistics, that you cannot live and keep all your limbs more than seven years, and you can get fifty dollars or seventy-five dollars a month for taking your lives in your hands; and instead of taking that lucrative position you chose to be a sneak thief, or something like that. Some of you made that sort of choice. I don't know which I would take if I was reduced to this choice. I have an easier choice.

I will guarantee to take from this jail, or any jail in the world, five hundred men who have been the worst criminals and lawbreakers who ever got into jail, and I will go down to our lowest streets and take five hundred of the most abandoned prostitutes, and go out somewhere where there is plenty of land, and will give them a chance to make a living, and they will be as good people as the average in the community.

There is a remedy for the sort of condition we see here. The world never finds it out, or when it does find it out it does not enforce it. . . .

And this has been the history of the world. It's easy to see how to do away with what we call crime. It is not so easy to do it. I will tell you how to do it. It can be done by giving the people a chance to live — by destroying special privileges. So long as big criminals can get the coal fields, so long as the big criminals have control of the city council and get the public streets for streetcars and gas rights — this is bound to send thousands of poor people to jail. So long as men are allowed to monopolize all the earth, and compel others to live on such terms as these men see fit to make, then you are bound to get into jail.

The only way in the world to abolish crime and criminals is to abolish the big ones and the little ones together. Make fair conditions of life. Give men a chance to live. Abolish the right of private ownership of land, abolish monopoly, make the world partners in production, partners in the good things of life. Nobody would steal if he could get something of his own some easier way. Nobody will commit burglary when he has a house full. No girl will go out on the streets when she has a comfortable place at home. The man who owns a sweatshop or a department store may not be to blame himself for the conditions of his girls, but when he pays them five dollars, three dollars, and two dollars a week, I wonder where he thinks they will get the rest of their money to live. The only way to cure these conditions is by equality. There should be no jails. They do not accomplish what they pretend to accomplish. If you would wipe them out there would be no more criminals than now. They terrorize nobody. They are a blot upon any civilization, and a jail is an evidence of the lack of charity of the people on the outside who make the jails and fill them with the victims of their greed.

Notes and Questions

1. Do you think these images of law should have been given to prisoners? In the introduction to the lecture, which he had printed in pamphlet form and sold for 5 cents, Darrow wrote:

   > Realizing the force of the suggestion that the truth should not be spoken to all people, I have caused these remarks to be printed on rather good paper and in a somewhat expensive form. In this way the truth does not become cheap and vulgar, and is only placed before those whose intelligence and affluence will prevent their being influenced by it.

   It was said that one of the prisoners in the audience commented that the speech was "too radical." What might Darrow have said that this remark showed about that prisoner?
2. If Darrow thinks that jails are the invention of the ruling class, how can he say that some people are "born with the tendency to break into jail"?
3. Does Darrow assume that the basic motivation of all people is to get rich? Why does he view the drive for wealth as a basic social problem? What are the implications of the fact that the law protects and even encourages the accumulation of wealth?
4. Clarence Darrow (see footnote, page 554) abandoned a lucrative career in corporate law to represent Eugene Debs and other workers in the 1894 Pullman strike. He was a strong opponent of the death penalty. Why do you suppose that Darrow's images of law

are not more widely known in America, especially since his reputation as a criminal defense lawyer is almost legendary? (How do you suppose Darrow would answer this question?)

5. Does it seem reasonable to you to think of kidnapping and theft as ways of surviving in a capitalist economy?
6. What do you think people's main aim in life would be if "every man and woman and child in the world had a chance to make a decent, fair, honest living"?
7. Emma Goldman, 1869–1940, became famous as an anarchist and feminist in America, and was imprisoned several times on such charges as inciting to riot, advocating birth control, and obstructing the draft. As you think further about what Darrow said to the prisoners, consider Goldman's remarks on law, order, and crime:

> Order derived through submission and maintained by terror is not much of a safe guaranty; yet that is the only "order" that governments have ever maintained. True social harmony grows naturally out of solidarity of interests. In a society where those who always work never have anything, while those who never work enjoy everything, solidarity of interests is non-existent; hence social harmony is but a myth. The only way organized authority meets this grave situation is by extending still greater privileges to those who have already monopolized the earth, and by still further enslaving the disinherited masses. Thus the entire arsenal of government — laws, police, soldiers, the courts, legislatures, prisons — is strenuously engaged in "harmonizing" the most antagonistic elements in society. . . .
>
> Crime is naught but misdirected energy. So long as every institution of today, economic, political, social, and moral, conspires to misdirect human energy into wrong channels; so long as most people are out of place doing the things they hate to do, living a life they loathe to live, crime will be inevitable, and all the laws on the statutes can only increase, but never do away with, crime.*

*Alix Schulman, ed., *Red Emma Speaks* (New York: Vintage, 1972), p. 57.

Alexander Hamilton and the Leviathan State *Vernon Louis Parrington*

. . . Alexander Hamilton . . . originated and directed the main polices of the Federalist group, and brought them to successful issue. . . . The jealousies and rivalries that obstructed the creation of a centralized Federal government found no sympathy with him. He was annoyed beyond all patience with the dissensions of local home rule. . . . For town-meeting democracies and agrarian legislatures he had frank contempt. The American village and farmer he never knew and never understood; his America was the America of landed gentlemen and wealthy merchants and prosperous professional men. . . . And it was in association with this group of conservative representatives of business and society that he took his place as directing head in the work of reorganizing the loose confederation into a strong and cohesive union. When that work was accomplished his influence was commanding, and for a dozen years he directed the major policies of the Federalist party. His strategic position as Secretary of the Treasury enabled him to stamp his principles . . . deeply upon the national economy. . . . Capitalism with its credit system, its banks and debt-funding and money manipulation, was wholly congenial to his masterful temperament. He read Adam Smith with eagerness and *The Wealth of Nations* was a source book for many of his state papers. To create in America an English system of finance, and an English system of industrialism, seemed to him the surest means to the great end he had in view; a centralizing capitalism would be more than a match for a decentralizing agrarianism, and the power of the state would augment with the increase of liquid wealth. . . .

. . . [T]here was nothing in the history of political *laissez faire* as it had developed in America, that justified the principle to Hamilton. It had culminated in agrarianism with legislative majorities riding down all obstacles, denying the validity of any check upon its will, constitutional, legal or ethical. The property interests of the minority had been rendered insecure. There had been altogether too much *laissez faire;* what was needed was sharp control of legislative majorities; the will of the majority must be held within due metes and bounds. . . . Hamilton deduced the guiding principle that has since been followed, namely, that governmental interference with economic laws is desirable when it aids business, but intolerable and unsound when it aims at business regulation or control, or when it assists agriculture or labor. . . .

Accepting self-interest as the main-spring of human ambition, Hamilton accepted equally the principle of class domination. From his reading of history he discovered that the strong overcome the weak, and as they grasp power they coalesce into a master group. This master group will dominate, he believed, not only to further its interests, but to prevent the spread of anarchy which threatens every society split into factions and at the mercy of rival ambitions. In early days the master group was a military order, later it became a landed aristocracy, in modern times it is commercial; but always its power rests on property. "That power which holds the purse-strings absolutely, must rule," he stated unequivocally. The economic masters of society of necessity become the political masters. . . .

Such are the fundamental principles which lie at the base of Hamilton's philosophy. He was in accord with John Adams and James Madison and Noah Webster, in asserting the economic basis of government, with its corollary of the class struggle. He not only accepted the rule of property as inevitable, but as desirable. As an aristocrat he deliberately allied himself with the wealthy. That men divide into the rich and the poor, the wise and the foolish, he regarded as a commonplace too evident to require argument. The explanation is to be sought in human nature and human capacities. For the common people, about whom Jefferson concerned himself . . . , he felt only contempt. Their virtues and capacities he had no faith in. "I am not much attached to the *majesty of the multitude,*" he said during the debate over the Constitution. . . . His notorious comment — . . . "The people! — the people is a great beast!" — was characteristically frank. . . . [N]othing was plainer to his logic than the proposition that if the people possessed the capacity to rule, their weight of numbers would give them easy mastery; whereas their yielding to the domination of the gifted few proves their incapacity. . . . The people are easily deceived and turned aside from their purpose; like children they are diverted by toys; but if they become unruly they must be punished. Too much is at stake in government for them to be permitted to muddle policies. . . .

In certain of his principles Hamilton was a follower of Hobbes.* His philosophy conducted logically to the leviathan state, highly centralized, coercive, efficient. But he was no idealist to exalt the state as the divine repository of authority, an enduring entity apart from the individual citizen and above him. He regarded the state as a highly useful instrument, which in the name of law and order would serve the interests of the powerful, and restrain the turbulence of the disinherited. For in every government founded on coercion rather than good will, the perennial unrest of those who are coerced is a grave menace; in the end the exploited will turn fiercely upon the exploiters. In such governments, therefore, self-interest requires that social unrest shall be covered with opprobium and put down by the police power; and the sufficient

*Thomas Hobbes, seventeenth-century English philosopher, was the author of the theory of absolute sovereign power; his major work, *Leviathan*, was published in 1651. — Ed.

test of a strong state lies in its ability to protect the privileges of the minority against the anarchy of the majority. In his eloquent declamation against anarchy Hamilton was a conspicuous disciple of the law and order school. From the grave difficulties of post-Revolutionary times with their agrarian programs, he created a partisan argument for a leviathan state, which fell upon willing ears; and in the Constitutional convention, which, more than any other man, he was instrumental in assembling, he was the outstanding advocate of the coercive state. . . .

. . . In developing his policies as Secretary of the Treasury he applied his favorite principle, that government and property must join in a close working alliance. The new government would remain weak and ineffective so long as it was hostile to capital; but let it show itself friendly to capital, and capital would make haste to uphold the hands of government. Confidence was necessary to both, and it was a plant of slow growth, sensitive to cold winds. The key to the problem lay in the public finance, and the key to a strong system of finance lay in a great national bank. This, Hamilton's dearest project, was inspired by the example of the Bank of England. No other institution would so surely link the great merchants to government, he pointed out, for by being made partners in the undertaking they would share both the responsibility and the profits. It was notorious that during the Revolution men of wealth had forced down the continental currency for speculative purposes; was it not as certain that they would support an issue in which they were interested? The private resources of wealthy citizens would thus become an asset of government, for the bank would link "the interest of the State in an intimate connection with those of the rich individuals belonging to it." . . .

. . . If the material power and splendor of the state be the great end of statesmanship — as Hamilton believed — no just complaint can be lodged against such a policy; but if the well-being of the individual citizen be the chief end — as Jefferson maintained — a very different judgment must be returned.

Although the fame of Hamilton has been most closely associated with the principle of constitutional centralization, his truer significance is to be found in his relation to the early developments of our modern capitalistic order. In his understanding of credit finance and the factory economy, he grasped the meaning of the economic revolution which was to transform America from an agrarian to an industrial country; and in urging the government to further such development, he blazed the path that America has since followed. . . .

Notes and Questions

1. Hamilton called for the rich to have a controlling hand in government, on the grounds that the masses are only motivated by self-interest rather than by the common good. Does this argument make sense to you? Does Hamilton provide any evidence that the wealthy are not self-interested? Is this argument consistent with his belief that human nature is "beastly"?
2. In thinking about the relationship between democratic government and wealth, and in particular about Hamilton's promotion of the national debt, consider the following comments by Henry Carter Adams, historian and political economist:

> When a . . . government desires to borrow money it must divest itself for the time being of all sovereign powers, and come before its subjects as a private corporation. It must bargain with those who have money to lend, and satisfy them as to questions of payment and security. . . . The broad theory of constitutional liberty is that the people have the right to govern themselves; but the historical fact is that, in the attempt to realize this theory, the actual control of public affairs has fallen into the hands of those who possess property. It follows from this that when property-owners lend to the government, they lend to a corporation controlled by themselves.*

---

*Henry Carter Adams, *Public Debts: An Essay in the Science of Finance* (New York: D. Appleton, 1887), pp. 7, 9.

3. Parrington says that Scottish economist Adam Smith's *Wealth of Nations* was a "source book" for Hamilton. With this in mind, read the following comments by Smith about the relationship between property and law:

   . . . Wherever there is great property, there is great inequality. For one very rich man, there must be at least five hundred poor, and the affluence of the few supposes the indigence of the many. The affluence of the rich excites the indignation of the poor, who are often both driven by want, and prompted by envy, to invade his possessions. It is only under the shelter of the civil magistrate that the owner of that valuable property, which is acquired by the labor of many years, or perhaps of many successive generations, can sleep a single night in security. He is at all times surrounded by unknown enemies, whom, though he never provoked, he can never appease, and from whose injustice he can be protected only by the powerful arm of the civil magistrate continually held up to chastise it. The acquisition of valuable and extensive property, therefore, necessarily requires the establishment of civil government. Where there is no property, or at least none that exceeds the value of two or three days labor, civil government is not so necessary. . . .

   . . . The rich, in particular, are necessarily interested to support that order of things, which can alone secure them in the possession of their own advantages. Men of inferior wealth combine to defend those of superior wealth in the possession of their property, in order that men of superior wealth may combine to defend them in the possession of theirs. All the inferior shepherds and herdsmen feel that the security of their own herds and flocks depends upon the security of those of the great shepherd or herdsmen; that the maintenance of their lesser authority depends upon that of his greater authority, and that upon their subordination to him depends his power of keeping their inferiors in subordination to them. They constitute a sort of little nobility, who feel themselves interested to defend the property and to support the authority of their own little sovereign, in order that he may be able to defend their property and to support their authority. Civil government, so far as it is instituted for the security of property, is in reality instituted for the defense of the rich against the poor, or of those who have some property against those who have none at all.†

4. What similarities do you find between the events set in motion by the federalists in the United States and the processes of the "proto-states" analyzed in "The Rule of Law versus the Order of Custom" (in Section 2 of this chapter)?

5. What does Thayer's study of hierarchy (in Section 2 of this chapter) imply for an understanding of Hamilton's influence on the United States?

6. According to Parrington, Hamilton wanted to protect the "property interests of the minority" from the actions of the "legislative majorities." Compare this with the following analysis of the meaning of "minority rights" protected by the U.S. Constitution:

   The nation's Founding Fathers were acutely aware of the latent contradiction in the democratic form of government, as indeed were most political thinkers in the late eighteenth and early nineteenth centuries. They recognized the possibility that the propertyless majority might, once it had the vote, attempt to turn its nominal sovereignty into real power and thereby jeopardize the security of property, which they regarded as the very foundation of civilized society. They therefore devised the famous system of checks and balances, the purpose of which was to make it as difficult as possible for the existing system of property relations to be subverted. American capitalism later developed in a context of numerous and often bitter struggles among various groups and segments of the moneyed classes — which had never been united, as in Europe, by a common struggle against feudal power. For these and other reasons, the governmental institutions which have taken shape in the United States have been heavily weighted

†Adam Smith, *An Inquiry into the Nature and Causes of the Wealth of Nations*, 4th ed., vol. 2 (Dublin: Colles, Moncrieffe, et al., 1785), pp. 224–225, 229.

on the side of protecting the rights and privileges of minorities: the property-owning minority as a whole against the people, and various groups of property-owners against each other.‡

7. Parrington says that in Hamilton's view "the economic masters of society of necessity become the political masters." In this regard, consider the following comment by Karl Marx:

> The ideas of the ruling class are in every epoch the ruling ideas: i.e., the class, which is the ruling material force of society, is at the same time its ruling intellectual force. The class which has the means of material production at its disposal has control at the same time over the means of mental production, so that thereby, generally speaking, the ideas of those who lack the means of mental production are subject to it. The ruling ideas are nothing more than the ideal expression of the dominant material relationships, the dominant material relationships grasped as ideas; hence of the relationships which make the one class the ruling one, therefore, the ideas of its dominance. The individuals composing the ruling class possess among other things consciousness, and therefore think. In so far, therefore, as they rule as a class and determine the extent and compass of an epoch, it is self-evident that they do this in their whole range, hence among other things rule also as thinkers, as producers of ideas, and regulate the production and distribution of the ideas of their age: thus their ideas are the ruling ideas of the epoch.§

‡Paul A. Baran and Paul M. Sweezy, *Monopoly Capital* (New York: Modern Reader, 1966), pp. 157–158.

§Karl Marx, "German Ideology," trans. by T. B. Bottomore (1845), in Erich Fromm, ed., *Marx's Concept of Man* (New York: Ungar, 1966), pp. 212–213.

4 VALUES AND VIOLENCE

> . . . I agonized, initially not only for myself, but for the Court. Parenthetically, in doing so publicly, I disobeyed one suggestion Hugo Black made to me when I first came here. He said, "Harry, never display agony in public, in an opinion. Never display agony. Never say that this is an agonizing, difficult decision. Always write it as though it's clear as crystal."
>
> Justice Harry A. Blackmun, "Interview," *New York Times Magazine* (February 20, 1983)

By the beginning of the nineteenth century, the practice of public punishment (pillory, stocks, and so on) and the use of prisoners in public works (the chain gang) were dying out. Similarly, public executions were increasingly seen as problematic, as repeating or exceeding the savagery of the crime at which they were directed. But this does not mean that the law was no longer involved with punishment. On the contrary, as French philosopher Michel Foucault has pointed out, punishment became "the most hidden part of the penal process. . . . As a result, justice no longer takes public responsibility for the violence that is bound up with its practice. If it too strikes, if it too kills, it is not as a glorification of its strength, but as an element of itself that it is obliged to tolerate, that it finds difficult to account for."*

By the end of the nineteenth century, the institutions of incarceration, which had been developed as alternatives to public punishment, were themselves the targets of criticism. Investigators saw filth, corruption, and brutality behind the prison walls, and noted no reduction of crime outside. But the result of these findings was neither a return to public punishment nor an abandonment of incarceration. Instead, the findings became the basis for recommending more prisons and more guards.

The problem of punishment is the problem of law enforcement generally: the use of *force* to sustain *law*. Law presents itself as the embodiment of reason, but it depends on violence for its efficacy. What is seen in this puzzle is that law does not banish force and violence, but organizes it as a state monopoly. Attempts to regulate or ban the sale of firearms to the public are an example of this. Looking at law as a system of rules tends to obscure this view of law as the social organization of violence. Both aspects are present.

The readings in this section focus on lawful violence, providing a context in which the values and value conflicts underlying law en*force*ment may be examined.

**Discipline and Punish: The Birth of the Prison* (New York: Vintage, 1979), p. 9.

The Violence of Legal Acts *Robert M. Cover*

Legal interpretation takes place in a field of pain and death. This is true in several senses. Legal interpretive acts signal and occasion the imposition of violence upon others: A judge articulates her understanding of a text, and as a result, somebody loses his freedom, his property, his children, even his life. Interpretations in law also constitute justifications for violence which has already occurred or which is about to occur. When interpreters have finished their work, they frequently leave behind victims whose lives have been torn apart by these organized, social practices of violence. Neither legal interpretation nor the violence it occasions may be properly understood apart from one another. . . .

The deliberate infliction of pain . . . we call torture. The interrogation that is part of torture, [Elaine] Scarry* points out, is rarely designed to elicit information. More commonly, the torturer's interrogation is designed to demonstrate the end of the normative world of the victim — the end of what the victim values, the end of the bonds that constitute the community in which the values are grounded. Scarry thus concludes that "in compelling confession, the

Reprinted by permission of The Yale Law Journal Company and Fred B. Rothman & Company from *The Yale Law Journal Company*, Vol. 95, p. 1601. Some footnotes have been omitted and the rest are renumbered.

*Author of *The Body in Pain* (1985), an analysis of pain. — ED.

torturers compel the prisoner to record and objectify the fact that intense pain is world-destroying." That is why torturers almost always require betrayal — a demonstration that the victim's intangible normative world has been crushed by the material reality of pain and its extension, fear. . . .

. . . But the relationship between legal interpretation and the infliction of pain remains operative even in the most routine of legal acts. The act of sentencing a convicted defendant is among these most routine of acts performed by judges.[1] Yet it is immensely revealing of the way in which interpretation is distinctively shaped by violence. First, examine the event from the perspective of the defendant. The defendant's world is threatened. But he sits, usually quietly, as if engaged in a civil discourse. If convicted, the defendant customarily walks — escorted — to prolonged confinement, usually without significant disturbance to the civil appearance of the event. It is, of course, grotesque to assume that the civil facade is "voluntary" except in the sense that it represents the defendant's autonomous recognition of the overwhelming array of violence ranged against him, and of the hopelessness of resistance or outcry. . . .

If I have exhibited some sense of sympathy for the victims of this violence it is misleading. Very often the balance of terror in this regard is just as I would want it. But I do not wish us to pretend that we talk our prisoners into jail. The "interpretations" or "conversations" that are the preconditions for violent incarceration are themselves implements of violence. To obscure this fact is precisely analogous to ignoring the background screams or visible instruments of torture in an inquisitor's interrogation. The experience of the prisoner is, from the outset, an experience of being violently dominated, and it is colored from the beginning by the fear of being violently treated.

The violence of the act of sentencing is most obvious when observed from the defendant's perspective. Therefore, any account which seeks to downplay the violence or elevate the interpretive character or meaning of the event within a community of shared values will tend to ignore the prisoner or defendant and focus upon the judge and the judicial interpretive act. Beginning with broad interpretive categories such as "blame" or "punishment," meaning is created for the event which justifies the judge to herself and to others with respect to her role in the acts of violence. I do not wish to downplay the significance of such ideological functions of law. But the function of ideology is much more significant in justifying an order to those who principally benefit from it and who must defend it than it is in hiding the nature of the order from those who are its victims. . . .

. . . The best known study and theory of social codes and their role in overcoming normal inhibitions against inflicting pain through violence is Milgram's *Obedience to Authority.* In the Milgram experiments, subjects administered what they thought were actually painful electric shocks to persons who they thought were the experimental subjects. This was done under the direction or orders of supposed experimenters. The true experimental subjects — those who administered the shocks — showed a disturbingly high level of compliance with authority figures despite the apparent pain evinced by the false experimental subjects. From the results of his experiment, Milgram has formulated a theory that . . . relies heavily on the distinction he draws between acting in an "autonomous" state and acting in an "agentic" state. Milgram posits the evolution of a human disposition to act "agentically" within hierarchies. . . .

[1]I have used the criminal law for examples throughout this essay for a simple reason. The violence of the criminal law is relatively direct. If my argument is not persuasive in this context, it will be less persuasive in most other contexts. I would be prepared to argue that all law which concerns property, its use and its protection, has a similarly violent base. But in many, perhaps most, highly visible legal transactions concerning property rights, that violent foundation is not immediately at issue. My argument does not, I believe, require that every interpretive event in law have the kind of direct violent impact on participants that a criminal trial has. It is enough that it is the case that where people care passionately about outcomes and are prepared to act on their concern, the law officials of the nation state are usually willing and able to use either criminal or violent civil sanctions to control behavior.

The judge in imposing a sentence normally takes for granted the role structure which might be analogized to the "transmission" of the engine of justice. The judge's interpretive authorization of the "proper" sentence can be carried out as a deed only because of these others; a bond between word and deed obtains only because a system of social cooperation exists. That system guarantees the judge massive amounts of force — the conditions of effective domination — if necessary. It guarantees — or is supposed to — a relatively faithful adherence to the word of the judge in the deeds carried out against the prisoner. . . .

We have done something strange in our system. We have rigidly separated the act of interpretation — of understanding what ought to be done — from the carrying out of this "ought to be done" through violence. At the same time we have, at least in the criminal law, rigidly linked the carrying out of judicial orders to the act of judicial interpretation by relatively inflexible hierarchies of judicial utterances and firm obligations on the part of penal officials to heed them. Judges are both separated from, and inextricably linked to, the acts they authorize. . . .

. . . Judges, officials, resisters, martyrs, wardens, convicts, may or may not share common texts; they may or may not share a common vocabulary, a common cultural store of gestures and rituals; they may or may not share a common philosophical framework. There will be in the immense human panorama a continuum of degrees of commonality in all of the above. But as long as legal interpretation is constitutive of violent behavior as well as meaning, as long as people are committed to using or resisting the social organizations of violence in making their interpretations real, there will always be a tragic limit to the common meaning that can be achieved.

The perpetrator and victim of organized violence will undergo achingly disparate significant experiences. For the perpetrator, the pain and fear are remote, unreal, and largely unshared. They are, therefore, almost never made a part of the interpretive artifact, such as the judicial opinion. On the other hand, for those who impose the violence the justification is important, real and carefully cultivated. Conversely, for the victim, the justification for the violence recedes in reality and significance in proportion to the overwhelming reality of the pain and fear that is suffered.

Between the idea and the reality of common meaning falls the shadow of the violence of law, itself.

Notes and Questions

1. In thinking about Cover's analysis of the violence of legal acts, consider the following comment on the link between punishment and social values:

> . . . The social values which are given the protection of the law, the rules which are enforced by the political power of the state because they are embodied in the criminal code, are those which are deemed desirable by those social groups within the state who have the power to make law. This fact is not so easy to discern when we confine our observations to democratic states, but in other forms of political organization it is obvious. The class distinctions in the criminal law — different penalties for masters and slaves, for nobles and commoners, for instance — furnish good illustrations. Fundamentally, then, the aim of all punishment is the protection of those social values which the dominant social group of a state regard as good for "society."
>
> The multiplicity of theories of punishment and the confusion of thinking they have produced seems to be due to a confusion of ends with means. The *means* to secure the protection of "society" have varied greatly because the law-enforcing powers of different societies have chosen those means which they believed to be at a given time most likely to secure obedience to their law. These beliefs are in turn dependent on tradition, the level of knowledge, and the nature of social and economic institutions and conditions. The sanguinary punishments and tortures of old are no evidence of blood-thirstiness or sadism on the part of those who used them. They rather testify to the fact that those

who designed them could conceive of no better, that is more efficient, way of securing protection for the social values which they treasured. The character of punishments, then, is inextricably associated with and dependent on the cultural values of the state that employs them.*

2. Compare Cover's concept of law as "the social organization of violence" with d'Errico's "The Law Is Terror Put into Words" (in Section 1 of this chapter). What similarities and differences do you see in their perspectives?
3. Cover suggests that "all law which concerns property . . . has a . . . violent base." Would Clarence Darrow agree? Alexander Hamilton? Stanley Diamond? Albert Camus?
4. Cover views the hierarchic role structure of the legal system as the "'transmission' of the engine of justice," saying that this system "guarantees . . . faithful adherence to the word of the judge." What is the relation between this view and Thayer's analysis of hierarchy? Does Diamond's argument about procedure or d'Errico's perspective on due process contradict Cover's view?

*Georg Rusche and Otto Kirchheimer, *Punishment and Social Structure* (New York: Columbia University Press, 1939), pp. v–vi.

A Model, Clockwork-Orange Prison *Phil Stanford*

Jessup, Md.: The Patuxent Institution for Defective Delinquents is widely considered a "model rehabilitative prison" and a showplace of enlightened penology. At Patuxent (named for a nearby river), inmates are called patients, which means that they are here not to be punished but to be cured. Patuxent's director, Dr. Harold M. Boslow, a properly benign gentleman with a soft pink face, swept-back white hair and glasses that slide down his nose, is a psychiatrist. Two of the three associate directors are behavioral scientists, and for a prison population of about 400, there are more than 40 psychiatrists, psychologists and social workers on the staff. To use a phrase I heard there frequently in interviews, Patuxent is more a "therapeutic community" than a prison.

In one of Patuxent's many brochures, Dr. Boslow describes the institution this way: "Dealing with nonpsychotic patients, it combines the functions of a mental hospital and a penal institution." To a visitor, the second function is immediately apparent. Patuxent is surrounded by a 30-foot chain-link fence fronted with a sheet of slick plastic "climb-proofing" and with barbed wire along the top. The guards in the towers carry high-powered rifles, and all the windows on the two main buildings in the compound come equipped with steel bars.

Under Maryland's Defective Delinquency Law, convicted lawbreakers who appear by their records to have a compulsive criminal nature can be referred to Patuxent for a psychiatric evaluation. The trial judge, the prosecuting attorney, or even the defense lawyer may request the diagnosis after sentencing. (The men referred, it might be emphasized, are all legally sane, or as Dr. Boslow puts it, "nonpsychotic." If they were judged insane, they would go to the state hospital.) Once a person has been diagnosed as a "defective delinquent," he may be formally committed to Patuxent by a civil court — or, if not, returned to the penitentiary to complete his sentence. If he is committed to Patuxent, which happens 85 per cent of the time, he will receive treatment for his condition. When he is well, he can leave.

From the first, Patuxent has had the enthusiastic support of America's liberal psychiatric establishment, which has long seen crime as a social and emotional problem. . . .

Phil Stanford, "A Model, Clockwork-Orange Prison," *The New York Times Magazine*, September 17, 1972.

Dr. Karl Menninger, perhaps the country's most honored psychiatrist, thinks Patuxent is a "great idea." . . .

Dr. Thomas Szasz, professor of psychiatry at New York's Upstate Medical Center, sees it somewhat differently. Szasz, an author who is critical of nearly everything about institutional psychiatry today, says Patuxent is a "concentration camp." "Patuxent," he told me, "is worse than the way they use mental institutions in Russia, except that when they haul someone off over there everyone here gets upset. It reminds me of the Biblical proverb of the mote in the eye." In Patuxent Szasz sees merely a further extension of psychiatry's already abused power to "define and rule." . . .

On the third Thursday of every month, the Patuxent Institution Board of Review meets in a basement room of the administration building. It is a very ordinary, utilitarian room, and in the middle of it there is a long conference table. The seven members of the board sit around three sides of the table. The patient, when he is summoned, sits at the other end. Over a year, every one of the 400 or so patients at Patuxent will get a hearing, and depending on his progress toward responsible citizenship, as indicated by his disciplinary record, achievements in a vocational program and in psychotherapy, the board may vote to release him or bind him over for another year. . . .

Dr. Boslow explains that Patuxent "is designed to identify dangerous offenders, retain and treat them." Of the 425 patients currently at Patuxent, 305 have been committed and the other 120 are waiting to be diagnosed. A recent breakdown of patients' crimes shows murder (4), second-degree murder (18), assault with intent to murder (43), robbery (35), robbery with a deadly weapon (87). There are a number of convictions for sex offenses, including rape (45), attempted rape (14), statutory rape (2), perverted practices (29), indecent exposure (4), and attempted perversion (1). The list also includes breaking and entering (9), housebreaking (14), rogue and vagabond (2), petty larceny (3), car theft (10), forgery (2) and writing bad checks (2).

Dr. Arthur Kandel, who was my guide for most of my visits, anticipates the question. . . . Kandel explains that 78 per cent of the patients are in for crimes involving violence. The others were examined and found to be "potentially violent." A patient's criminal record is of course important to the psychiatrist making a diagnosis, but it is only one consideration. "Our focus here is on behavior," says Kandel, "and we are not that concerned with the concept of guilt or innocence." What all patients committed to Patuxent have in common is that all of them have been diagnosed as "defective delinquents."

Under Maryland's unique statute, a defective delinquent is "an individual who, by the demonstration of persistent, aggravated, antisocial or criminal behavior, evidences a propensity toward criminal activity, and who is found to have either such intellectual or emotional unbalance, or both, as to clearly demonstrate an actual danger to society so as to require such confinement and treatment, when appropriate, as to make it reasonably safe for society to terminate the confinement and treatment."

As the Patuxent staff interprets the law, this means a very particular type of criminal. The brochures stress that certain lawbreakers, such as a professional gunman, wouldn't qualify. Dr. Kandel explained why. "The professional gunman," he said, "ordinarily has chosen this as a way of earning a living, and in most other respects you won't tell him apart from any other human being. He may very well have a wife and kids that he's devoted to. He'll probably pay his taxes reasonably well. He'll probably live in a decent neighborhood, in a decent home. You know, it's just that he picks this peculiar way of earning a living. Now a professional gunman, for example, doesn't act on impulse or he wouldn't be a professional. Whereas our people, by and large, one of their characteristics is they're very impulsive. The professional gunman can delay frustration, he can tolerate delay, he can plan. And if he plans a hit at this time and this place and it doesn't pan out, so he retracts and makes new plans and goes ahead again."

A defective delinquent, to use psychiatric language, is someone afflicted with a behavioral problem called an antisocial disorder. Until recently the official term was sociopath, and before that it was psychopath, but both terms have been dropped from the official nomenclature of the American Psychiatric Association. Perhaps the best description of a defective delinquent comes from Dr. Guttmacher, who played ... an important role in getting Patuxent started. In a 1965 court case (when it was still fashionable to refer to a defective delinquent as a sociopath), Guttmacher was asked to describe the symptoms, which he did at some length:

"My own feeling is that probably the most basic thing is their inability to make any strong identifications with other people, and by that I mean they don't become a real member of the group. They are not team players; they don't have strong loyalties toward their country, toward their family, toward anyone. Their affectionate relationships are very shallow. They become involved in numerous affairs with women, frequently with multiple marriages. . . .

"Then there is this underlying hostility which manifests itself in many ways. As I said before, there is, in a sense, a war with society, and they get great satisfaction in seeing what they can get away with in their acting out against society. They are an extremely restless group of people. . . . They normally have not the success in school which their intelligence would indicate they might have. . . . They very frequently become dropouts. They frequently have conflict with teachers because part of their pattern is to be in conflict with authority figures. . . . They can't take criticism with any degree of equanimity, so that their work records are almost universally very fugitive. They rarely stick to anything for any great length of time. They are basically hedonistic, and they must satisfy their needs as rapidly as they possibly can and at the expense of others."

Interestingly enough, elsewhere in his testimony Guttmacher referred to a defective delinquent as "a rebel without a cause." Robert Lindner, who was another of the founding fathers of Patuxent, must have been very surprised when the character James Dean played in the movie version of his book became the antihero of a generation. Lindner wanted to cure him. . . .

At Patuxent a patient enters what the professional staff calls a "therapeutic milieu." That means it is a total environment, every part of which — including group psychotherapy, vocational therapy and a programed system of incentives — is intended to work toward the patient's rehabilitation and prepare him to return to society.

Patients are expected to attend weekly group-therapy sessions, where (to quote from another of Patuxent's brochures) "they are made aware of their distorted perceptions, feelings and attitudes, and the part these distortions play in developing their antisocial behavior pattern."

The core of the program is the "graded-tier" system, which "provides rewards for socially acceptable behavior." There are four levels to the system, and a new patient must start on the lowest and work his way up. "As he moves upward in the tier system, a patient gains more privileges, but also more obligations and responsibilities. . . . The rewards reinforce the positive aspects of his behavior." Fourth-level patients, for example, can stay up as late as they want, third-level patients must be in bed by 11:30 and second-level patients by 11. Only fourth-level men get to have Sunday afternoon picnics on the prison lawn with members of their families or other approved guests. Fourth-level day rooms have pool tables, but third-level day rooms have only Ping-Pong tables. Most important, to be eligible for parole a patient must have reached the third or fourth level. "It works," Dr. Croce told me, "because that's the way life itself is set up."

Dr. Kandel, helpful and talkative as usual, says the institution has also tried a number of drug programs with Johns Hopkins, the University of Maryland and the National Institute of Mental Health. "We have ongoing research with all of these agencies in terms of drugs that are coming out that may be effective as behavioral controls in terms of impulsivity," he said. "They use all the usual psychotropic drugs." Johns Hopkins, he said, was currently doing a great deal of research with Dilantin, on the theory that in some of the patients "the electrical transmissions of the brain are messed up." He says, sweat getting volunteers because all of these programs pay volunteers." Kandel recalls that once Patuxent started an aversive therapy program using electroshock. "But we caught so much flak we had to drop it before we could even get going."

"Our experience," says Dr. Boslow, who has been Patuxent's director since it began, "has confirmed the fact that all human beings are essentially alike, that all people can be treated and helped, provided they want to be. I don't believe in punishment. I don't think in those terms. I think that people who commit crimes should be treated until they are capable of going out into society again."

That, in outline, is Patuxent's treatment program. The only thing that remains is perhaps to underscore what Dr. Boslow has already stated — that once a patient is committed to Patuxent, he must stay until he is cured. One of Patuxent's unique features as a prison — another one borrowed from practice at mental institutions — is the indeterminate sentence. To get out, a patient must meet the approval of the institution's Board of Review, which is responsible only to itself. Failing that, he can try a recommitment hearing, to which he is entitled every three years. . . .

According to figures released by the institution, 38 per cent of all patients are now serving beyond their original sentences. Of those who were sentenced to terms of five years or less, 75 per cent are, as they might see it, overdue. Dr. Boslow acknowledges that Patuxent has been under fire lately, particularly for its indeterminate sentence. "What they don't understand," he says, "is that it is necessary for therapeutic reasons." In one of his pamphlets, Dr. Boslow writes that "there is a long history of disbelief in the efficacy of psychotherapy with persons having strong antisocial tendencies." At first, many defective delinquents won't even admit that they're sick. The indeterminate sentence is simply "a mechanism for making them realize that they need help," he explains. "That's why the indeterminate sentence is so important. It's a means of attracting their attention to the fact that they need to make some changes to get out." . . .

The patients, who have staged four publicized disturbances this year, including a 60-man sit-in in August, may have another viewpoint. But they are not the only non-psychiatrists who have failed to appreciate Patuxent's therapeutic approach to criminal behavior. Lawyers are a source of constant complaints. Patients' lawyers are not allowed to be present during psychiatric examinations, although they argue that the information gathered there, including facts about crimes for which the patient was never charged, is used against the patient at his commitment trial. Lawyers are also excluded from the Board of Review because they would "interfere with the therapeutic program."

One of the most irritating of these lawyers to the staff (Dr. Kandel calls him "a kooky young lawyer trying to make a name for himself") is Julian Tepper, head of the National Law Office of the Legal Aid and Defender Service in Washington, D. C. On behalf of 13 patients, Tepper in 1971 brought suit in Maryland court (*McCray et al.* v. *Patuxent*) on a lengthy list of complaints.

During the trial several patients complained of being locked up for long periods of time in totally dark cells. Besides the regular four tiers of cells that are part of Patuxent's "graded-tier system," there are two separate rows where patients who misbehave are frequently sent. Some of these cells are smaller and can be closed with a heavy steel door. Critics of Patuxent often refer to them as "punishment" or "solitary confinement."

When Dr. Kandel was called to the witness stand, he explained this misunderstanding to the court. There are some people who respond favorably to positive reinforcement, as for example, the graded-tier system, he said. "There are also people who don't respond and need [to devote] a certain period of time to what is known as negative reinforcers." Patuxent's negative-reinforcement program included "deprivation schedules" and perhaps a certain amount of "sensory deprivation," which is probably what the patients referred to when they said there wasn't any light in their cells.

To judge from comments by the Patuxent

administrators, the McCray case was an even more traumatic episode than the U.S. Supreme Court decision (*McNeil* v. *Patuxent*) this summer.

In *McCray,* Patuxent was ordered to establish a written disciplinary code, to limit the time patients could be put in "negative-reinforcement" cells and to allow access to the press. In June the Supreme Court told Patuxent to release noncommitted patients whose terms had expired. These "noncooperatives," as they are called, had refused to let a psychiatrist interview them for their precommitment diagnosis. Patuxent has released about 10 of these patients since the decision. There are at present about 60 to 70 "noncooperatives" at Patuxent. The ruling, of course, does not affect the more than 305 patients already committed. . . .

This summer Patuxent received a couple days of publicity in the Baltimore and Washington papers when the courts ordered the release of a 29-year-old patient, Grover Miller, who had already served more than eight years for breaking a window. The exact charge was "malicious destruction of property." Miller's disciplinary record, which the institution let me see, showed page after page of entries saying, "refused medication" and "refused meals," but nothing that indicated violent or even unruly behavior. . . .

When I approached Dr. Kandel, he took a look at the record and said that Miller was "probably one of those marginal cases." Running an institution such as Patuxent is no simple matter, he acknowledged. Administering the indeterminate sentence was perhaps the most difficult problem of all. "They say to you, 'How do you know I'm going to foul up if you don't give me the chance to get out there and foul up?' It's not an easy thing to handle," said Kandel. . . .

When Roosevelt Murray came to Patuxent in 1958, a skinny 17-year-old kid from the black part of Baltimore, it became apparent to the professional staff that he was a defective delinquent. Tests showed a decided potential for violence. A psychiatrist who interviewed him diagnosed the problem as a "Sociopathic Disorder — Antisocial (with affinity for auto theft)," and on Oct. 11, 1961, Murray was committed to Patuxent, just as his four-year sentence for unauthorized use of a motor vehicle was about to expire. He has never really gotten used to the idea.

Murray, 31, a starchy 5-foot-8 or so, sits glaring across the conference table, at everyone in general, but particularly at. Dr. Boslow. He is in handcuffs and a guard waits by the door. Clearly no one is taking any chances. Not long ago Murray slugged his social worker. He is also charged with stabbing another social worker, whom, as Dr. Boslow explained later, "he didn't even know."

"You know why you're here," says Dr. Boslow. "Tell us what you want to tell us."

"I want to tell you that you have no right to be holding me," begins Murray at somewhere near a shout. "I want to say, for all the damn good it will do me, that I want to get out of here, man. That's what I want to tell you."

The board listens to approximately two minutes of this tirade before it decides to ask Murray about his behavior. "Mr. Murray," asks the sociologist Olive Quinn in a conciliatory voice, "why don't you behave some way so we feel we can let you out?"

In truth, as the file shows, Murray has always been a problem at Patuxent. In 1962 he made his first appearance before the Board of Review. The record says he appeared hostile and spoke belligerently to the board. "I don't like the idea of my time being up and me still being here," he had said. In 1963 Dr. Boslow interviewed Murray at length for a psychiatric evaluation. Toward the end of the session, Murray apparently lost control of his emotions. "Murray launched into a hostile attack on the United States and said he wanted to go to Russia," Dr. Boslow wrote in his report. "At this point he seemed very angry, paranoid and disturbed." In 1965 at his recommitment hearing, Murray lashed out again. After the judge finished reading a list of Murray's disciplinary infractions at Patuxent, Murray was said to have turned over the table he was sitting at and shouted, "This is the unfairest court I've ever seen." The newspaper account says he threatened Dr. Boslow.

Murray's ample disciplinary record, which begins with entries for smoking, throwing a bag out the window and fighting with another inmate, shows a similar progression toward violence. The board asks about the recent incidents which are mentioned on the mimeographed sheet. Someone asks Murray why he stabbed a social worker. "Because I wanted to get out of this place any way possible," he shouts.

QUINN (sweetly): And did you think the proper way to get out of here was to kill a social worker?

MURRAY (loudly, pleadingly): You're killing me, aren't you? You people don't realize what you did to me in my 14 years here. You know that Roosevelt Murray never stabbed anyone before he came here.

I don't like what you're doing to me here. If you had any decency you'd let me go free. Why don't you send me to the pen? Does it make any sense to hold me here when you can see it isn't doing me any good?

BOSLOW (after a pause): Is there anything else?

MURRAY: Yes. I'd like to know why you postponed my hearing three times. I think it was a deliberate attempt to harass me and provoke me into actions you could use to keep me here. I'd like to know why.

(No answer.)

MURRAY: Don't you have the decency to do things right?

BOSLOW: Don't you have the decency to do things right?

Murray is led out shouting: "You're not a man, you're an animal. Let me out. If you just take these handcuffs off me, I'll show you man to man."

After the meeting I ask Dr. Kandel about Murray. "Well, you saw for yourself," he says. "He's a very violent man."

Isn't it possible, I suggest, that Murray is really angry at the institution for keeping him beyond his sentence, just as he said?

"It's a matter of projection," Kandel says. "Many of these people like to blame anything instead of what really bothers them. That's part of their problem."

I ask why Murray was put in Patuxent in the first place, since Patuxent is for dangerous and violent criminals.

"It's true," Kandel says, "that Murray came here for something relatively minor, like stealing a car or something. But when he came here we examined him and judged him to be potentially violent. Events have proved us right." . . .

"What do you think holds society together?" Boslow asks, suddenly intense. Before I can say I don't know he answers himself. "Love," he says. "It's love."

I'm not sure, I tell him.

"Yes," says Dr. Boslow, "it is. Love in its broadest sense, which includes the need for the regard and esteem of one's fellow men. Without this mutual need our society would fall apart. For example, what do you think causes a man to walk into a machine-gun nest?"

I don't know. I really don't.

"It's love," Dr. Boslow says, wondering perhaps what it is that makes me so slow to see this very basic equation of our civilization.

Notes and Questions

1. What is the function of calling inmates "patients"? Is this a "mask" in Noonan's terms (see "Virginian Liberators")?
2. Is the Patuxent Institution part of the "social organization of violence" in Cover's terms? How would d'Errico and Darrow view Patuxent?
3. Stanford says that Patuxent is referred to as a "therapeutic community." Does Patuxent fit any definition of community discussed in this chapter (for example, in the excerpts by Jane Jacobs, Farley Mowat, Stanley Diamond, and Vine Deloria, Jr.)?
4. Compare Dr. Boslow's comments about "love" with the following account of how Nazi Dr. Mengele once explained why he killed Jewish women together with their children at Auschwitz:

   Orli had told me once how Mengele explained to her why he killed Jewish women together with their children. "When a Jewish child is born, or when a woman comes to the camp with a child already," he had explained, "I don't know what to do with the child. I can't set the child free because there are no longer any Jews who live in freedom. I can't let the child stay in the camp because there are no facilities in the camp that would enable the child to develop normally. It would not be humanitarian to send a child to the ovens without permitting the mother to be there to witness the child's death. That is why I send the mother and the child to the gas ovens together."

Imagine that cynical criminal justifying his hideous crimes in the name of humanitarianism, making a mockery of the tenderest of all feelings, a mother's love for her children.*

*Sara Nomberg-Przytyk, *Auschwitz,* trans. by Roslyn Hirsch (Chapel Hill: University of North Carolina Press, 1985), p. 69.

McNeil v. Director, Patuxent Institution *92 S. Ct. 2083 (1972)*

MR. JUSTICE MARSHALL *delivered the opinion of the Court.*

Edward McNeil was convicted of two assaults in 1966, and sentenced to five years' imprisonment. Instead of committing him to prison, the sentencing court referred him to the Patuxent Institution for examination, to determine whether he should be committed to that institution for an indeterminate term under Maryland's Defective Delinquency Law. Md. Code Ann., Art 31B. No such determination has yet been made, his sentence has expired, and his confinement continues. The State contends that he has refused to cooperate with the examining psychiatrists, that they have been unable to make any valid assessment of his condition, and that consequently he may be confined indefinitely until he cooperates and the institution has succeeded in making its evaluation. He claims that when his sentence expired, the State lost its power to hold him, and that his continued detention violates his rights under the Fourteenth Amendment. We agree.

I

The Maryland Defective Delinquency Law provides that a person convicted of any felony, or certain misdemeanors, may be committed to the Patuxent Institution for an indeterminate period, if it is judicially determined that he is a "defective delinquent." . . .

Defective delinquency proceedings are ordinarily instituted immediately after conviction and sentencing; they may also be instituted after the defendant has served part of his prison term. In either event, the process begins with a court order committing the prisoner to Patuxent for a psychiatric examination. The institution is required to submit its report to the court within a fixed period of time. If the report recommends commitment, then a hearing must be promptly held, with a jury trial if requested by the prisoner, to determine whether he should be committed as a defective delinquent. If he is so committed, then the commitment operates to suspend the prison sentence previously imposed.

In *Murel* v. *Baltimore City Criminal Court* . . . , several prisoners who had been committed as defective delinquents sought to challenge various aspects of the criteria and procedures that resulted in their commitment. . . .

But Edward McNeil presents a much more stark and simple claim. He has never been committed as a defective delinquent, and thus he has no cause to challenge the criteria and procedures that control a defective delinquency hearing. His confinement rests wholly on the order committing him for examination, in preparation for such a commitment hearing. That order was made, not on the basis of an adversary hearing, but on the basis of an *ex parte* judicial determination that there was "reasonable cause to believe that the defendant may be a defective delinquent." Petitioner does not challenge in this Court the power of the sentencing court to issue such an order in the first instance, but he contends that the State's power to hold him on the basis of that order has expired. He filed a petition for state post-conviction relief on this ground. . . .

II

The State of Maryland asserts the power to confine petitioner indefinitely, without ever obtaining a judicial determination that such confinement is warranted. It advances several distinct arguments in support of that claim.

A. First, the State contends that petitioner has been committed merely for observation, and that a commitment for observation need not be surrounded by the procedural safeguards (such as an adversary hearing) that are appropriate for a final determination of defective delinquency. Were the commitment for observation limited in duration to a brief period, the argument might have some force. But petitioner has been committed "for observation" for six years, and on the State's theory of his confinement there is no reason to believe it likely that he will ever be released. A confinement which is in fact indeterminate cannot rest on procedures designed to authorize a brief period of observation.

We recently rejected a similar argument in *Jackson* v. *Indiana*. . . .

B. A second argument advanced by the State relies on the claim that petitioner himself prevented the State from holding a hearing on his condition. The State contends that, by refusing to talk to the psychiatrists, petitioner has prevented them from evaluating him, and made it impossible for the State to go forward with evidence at a hearing. Thus, it is argued, his continued confinement is analogous to civil contempt; he can terminate the confinement and bring about a hearing at any time by talking to the examining psychiatrists, and the State has the power to induce his cooperation by confining him.

Petitioner claims that he has a right under the Fifth Amendment to withhold cooperation, a claim we need not consider here. But putting that claim to one side, there is nevertheless a fatal flaw in the State's argument. For if confinement is to rest on a theory of civil contempt, then due process requires a hearing to determine whether petitioner has in fact behaved in a manner that amounts to contempt. At such a hearing it could be ascertained whether petitioner's conduct is willful, or whether it is a manifestation of mental illness, for which he cannot fairly be held responsible. . . .

Moreover, a hearing would provide the appropriate forum for resolution of petitioner's Fifth Amendment claim. Finally, if the petitioner's confinement were explicitly premised on a finding of contempt, then it would be appropriate to consider what limitations the Due Process Clause places on the contempt power. The precise contours of that power need not be traced here. . . . The contempt analogy cannot justify the State's failure to provide a hearing of any kind.

C. Finally, the State suggests that petitioner is probably a defective delinquent, because most noncooperators are. Hence, it is argued, his confinement rests not only on the purposes of observation, and of penalizing contempt, but also on the underlying purposes of the Defective Delinquency Law. But that argument proves too much. For if the Patuxent staff was prepared to conclude, on the basis of petitioner's silence and their observations of him over the years, that petitioner is a defective delinquent, then it is not true that he has prevented them from evaluating him. On that theory, they have long been ready to make their report to the Court, and the hearing on defective delinquency could have gone forward.

III

Petitioner is presently confined in Patuxent without any lawful authority to support that confinement. . . . Accordingly, he is entitled to be released. The judgement below is reversed, and the mandate shall issue forthwith.

Reversed.

Notes and Questions

1. In his article on Patuxent, Phil Stanford refers to the *McNeil* case as "traumatic" to the administrators of the institution. Why do you think they might feel it to be so?
2. Does the decision in *McNeil* completely prevent Patuxent from holding someone who refuses to cooperate with the doctors beyond the sentence expiration date? How might such continued incarceration be permitted by law?
3. Is the *McNeil* case an example that supports d'Errico's assertion (in "The Law Is Terror") that due process is an extension of "the legalist mazeway"?
4. How do you think prisoner rights cases would be affected if judges were required to spend time in prison?

Cracking the Safe *Chuang Tzu*

For security against robbers who snatch purses,
rifle luggage, and crack safes,
One might fasten all property with ropes, lock
it up with locks, bolt it with bolts.
This (for property owners) is elementary good
sense,
But when a strong thief comes along he picks
up the whole lot,
Puts it on his back, and goes on his way with
only one fear;
That ropes, locks, and bolts may give way.
Thus what the world calls good business is only
a way
To gather up the loot, pack it, make it secure
In one convenient load for the more
enterprising thieves.
Who is there, among those called smart,
Who does not spend his time amassing loot
For a bigger robber than himself?

In the land of Khi, from village to village,
You could hear cocks crowing, dogs barking.

Fishermen cast their nets
Ploughmen ploughed the wide fields,
Everything was neatly marked out
By boundary lines. For five hundred square
miles
There were temples for ancestors, altars
For field-gods and corn-spirits.
Every canton, county, and district
Was run according to the laws and statutes —
Until one morning the Attorney General, Tien
Khang Tzu,
Did away with the King and took over the
whole state.
Was he content to steal the land? No,
He also took over the laws and statutes at the
same time,
And all the lawyers with them, not to mention
the police.
They all formed part of the same package.
Of course, people called Khang Tzu a robber,
But they left him alone
To live as happy as the Patriarchs.
No small state would say a word against him,
No large state would make a move in his
direction,

Chuang Tzu, a Taoist philosopher, lived toward the end of the classic period of Chinese philosophy (550–250 B.C.). His work is noted for its humor and literary subtlety, and represents a flourishing of mystical social criticism, linking concern for cosmic balance with ordinary, everyday existence: the "way of Tao." The following poem is based on an interpretive reading of this ancient philosopher by Thomas Merton (1915–1968), a Trappist monk best known for his contemplative integration of Western and Eastern religions.

So for twelve generations that state of Khi
Belonged to his family. No one interfered
With his inalienable rights.

The invention
Of weights and measures
Makes robbery easier.
Signing contracts, setting seals,
Makes robbery more sure.
Teaching love and duty
Provides a fitting language
With which to prove that robbery
Is really for the general good.
A poor man must swing
For stealing a belt buckle
But if a rich man steals a whole state
He is acclaimed
As statesman of the year.

Hence if you want to hear the very best
 speeches
On love, duty, justice, etc.,
Listen to statesmen.
But when the creek dries up
Nothing grows in the valley.
When the mound is levelled
The hollow next to it is filled.
And when the statesmen and lawyers
And preachers of duty disappear
There are no more robberies either
And the world is at peace.

Moral: the more you pile up ethical principles
And duties and obligations
To bring everyone in line
The more you gather loot
For a thief like Khang.
By ethical argument
And moral principle
The greatest crimes are eventually shown
To have been necessary, and, in fact,
A signal benefit
To mankind.

Notes and Questions

1. Thomas Merton commented on the meaning of this poem by Chuang Tzu as follows:

 > The more "the good" is objectively analyzed, the more it is treated as something to be attained by special virtuous techniques, the less real it becomes. As it becomes less real, it recedes further into the distance of abstraction, futurity, unattainability. The more, therefore, one concentrates on the means to be used to attain it. And as the end becomes more remote and more difficult, the means become more elaborate and complex, until finally the mere study of the means becomes so demanding that all one's effort must be concentrated on this, and the end is forgotten.*

 If we substitute "justice" or "life, liberty and the pursuit of happiness" for "the good," what does this statement say about law?

2. Chuang Tzu says that "A poor man must swing/For stealing a belt buckle/But if a rich man steals a whole state/He is acclaimed/As statesman of the year." Can you think of examples to support this assertion?

---

*Thomas Merton, "A Study of Chuang Tzu," in *The Way of Chuang Tzu,* p. 23.

CONCLUSION

> From the doctrine of the unity of the [legal] text we need to move to doctrines of the unity of life, from linguistics to metaphysics and more crudely from questions of how we live to questions of what we live.
>
> Peter Goodrich, *Reading the Law* (1986)

The purpose of law is to rationalize social relations, to subject human conduct to the governance of rules. This purpose is celebrated as "the rule of law." The presumption is that it is good to follow rules and bad to act without reference to rules. As Tocqueville wrote about lawyers, "they are less afraid of tyranny than of arbitrary power." And as Llewellyn wrote about precedent, "To know the law is helpful, even when the law is bad."

The philosophy of human nature that underlies this perspective is that human conduct is basically rational (capable of conforming to rules) and motivated by the logic of self-interest (therefore susceptible to reward and punishment). Wrongful behavior (whether tort [wrong act for which civil suit may be brought] or crime) is the result either of an intentional violation of the rules in pursuit of self-interest, or of an incapacity to be rational (whether or not in pursuit of self-interest). In the first case, the function of law is to increase self-interest in obedience by applying penalties to violations. In the second case, law functions by removing the irrational actor from the general social population.

The philosophy of the rule of law denies that chance or fate plays any primary role and asserts that the function of law is to provide a stable context for working out competing individual intentions. In this sense, the rule of law involves a certain kind of utopian faith. First, there is a faith in the ability of rulemakers to design a set of rules broad enough to encompass the full range of human interactions, yet narrow enough to be applied in particular conflicts; flexible enough to permit change, yet rigid enough to permit predictability of consequences. Second, there is faith in the ability of reason itself to adequately guide behavior, in a social context in which chance and fate do seem to play a part, and in which human emotion is a motivational and valuational element of life.

The questions that arise when one examines the contradictions involved in the theory and practice of the rule of law are ultimately metaphysical problems, issues about human nature, the nature of society, the meaning of life. Politics, insofar as it deals with these same issues, impinges on law, and presents alternative conceptions both of the rules that ought to be enforced and of the methods of enforcement. Economics, insofar as it involves systems of behavior motivation and control, also is implicated in any discussion of law. History and anthropology are two other dimensions of activity and analysis ultimately intertwined with the metaphysical issues presented by this analysis of the rule of law. History presents the possibility of seeing the development of rules and rule systems in a society, while anthropology allows cross-cultural comparison and contrast.

Probably no field of inquiry is wholly irrelevant to an understanding of law, once one sees what the deepest issues are. Law is almost always involved with issues of self and other, and often involved with issues of life and death. It is not surprising, therefore, that the meaning of life and death and of human relations is at the center of an interdisciplinary study of law. To raise these deep questions is not to obscure the day-to-day significance of law, but to illuminate it. To the extent that this illumination challenges some of the fundamental faiths that support the rule of law, one might become afraid that the result will be anarchy, lawlessness. This fear is a basic part of the will to believe in the rule of law, "even when the law is bad." But if your commitment is to human freedom, based on self-knowledge and self-respect and on knowledge of and respect for others, then you must walk through this fear.

We are in the presence of nihilism — a failure or refusal of faith. But this need not result in cynicism — the view that power is all that matters, the acceptance of the "emperor's new clothes." Legal studies offers the possibility of open discussion about the values involved in the rule of law. This discussion counteracts cynicism and despair about law and social conflict by beginning a renewed search for the truth of our social being and the wellsprings of human action and relations. Legal studies denies that law is simply a set of rules and authorities to be obeyed, and asserts instead that the conditions under which rules and authorities can be obeyed must be the topic of discussion.

Our faith can be in the capacity of human beings to create social order and freedom. Our questioning of the rule of law can be a powerful positive force, affirming our desire to create modes of social organization that are adequate to the multicultural, global society of Earth.

Suggested Additional Readings

Acosta, Oscar Zeta. *The Autobiography of a Brown Buffalo.* San Francisco: Straight Arrow Books, 1972.

Bankowski, Zenon, and Mungham, Geoff. *Images of Law.* London: Routledge & Kegan Paul, 1976.

Berman, Harold J. *Law and Revolution.* Cambridge, Mass.: Harvard University Press, 1983.

Bloch, Marc. *Feudal Society.* Trans. by L. Manyon. Chicago: University of Chicago Press, 1961.

Boyer, Richard O., and Morais, Herbert M. *Labor's Untold Story.* New York: United Electrical, Radio, and Machine Workers, 1955.

Braverman, Harry. *Labor and Monopoly Capital.* New York: Monthly Review Press, 1974.

Brinton, Maurice. *The Irrational in Politics.* Montreal: Black Rose Books, 1974.

Brown, Dee. *Bury My Heart at Wounded Knee.* New York: Bantam, 1970.

Carter, Forrest. *The Education of Little Tree.* Albuquerque: University of New Mexico Press, 1986.

Deloria, Vine, Jr. *God is Red.* New York: Dell, 1973.

Douglass, James W. *Resistance and Contemplation.* New York: Dell, 1972.

Ellison, Ralph. *The Invisible Man.* New York: New American Library, 1952.

Engels, Frederick. *The Origin of the Family, Private Property, and the State.* Trans. by Alec West. New York: International Publishers, 1973.

Foucault, Michel. *Discipline and Punish.* New York: Vintage, 1979.

Freire, Paulo. *Pedagogy of the Oppressed.* Trans. by Myra Bergman Ramos. New York: Seabury Press, 1973.

Goldman, Emma. *Living My Life.* 2 vols. New York: Dover Publications, 1970.

Goodrich, Peter. *Reading the Law.* Oxford, England: Blackwell, 1986.

Haudenosaunee. *Basic Call to Consciousness.* Mohawk Nation: Akwesasne Notes, 1978.

Horwitz, Morton J. *The Transformation of American Law, 1780–1860.* Cambridge, Mass.: Harvard University Press, 1977.

Kinoy, Arthur. *Rights on Trial.* Cambridge, Mass.: Harvard University Press, 1983.

Koestler, Arthur. *Darkness at Noon.* Trans. by Daphne Hardy. New York: Bantam, 1966.

Lame Deer, John (Fire), and Erdoes, Richard. *Lame Deer, Seeker of Visions.* New York: Simon & Schuster, 1972.

Lao Tzu. *The Way of Life According to Lao Tzu.* Trans. by Witter Bynner. New York: Capricorn Books, 1962.

Larner, Christina. *Witchcraft and Religion.* Oxford, England: Blackwell, 1985.

LeGuin, Ursula. *The Dispossessed.* New York: Avon Books, 1974.

———. *Always Coming Home.* New York: Harper & Row, 1985.

MacPherson, C. B. *The Political Theory of Possessive Individualism.* Oxford, England: Oxford University Press, 1962.

Malcolm X and Haley, Alex. *The Autobiography of Malcolm X.* New York: Grove Press, 1965.

Nomberg-Przytyk, Sara. *Auschwitz.* Trans. by Roslyn Hirsch. Chapel Hill: University of North Carolina Press, 1985.

Orwell, George. *1984.* New York: New American Library, 1961.

Polanyi, Karl. *The Great Transformation.* Boston: Beacon Press, 1957.

Quinney, Richard. *Critique of Legal Order.* Boston: Little, Brown, 1974.

Reich, Wilhelm. *The Mass Psychology of Fascism.* Trans. by Vincent Carfagno. New York: Farrar, Straus & Giroux, 1970.

Rowbotham, Sheila. *Woman's Consciousness, Man's World.* New York: Penguin, 1973.

Sandoz, Mari. *Cheyenne Autumn.* New York: Avon Books, 1953.

Shklar, Judith. *Legalism.* Cambridge, Mass.: Harvard University Press, 1964.

Skillen, Anthony. *Ruling Illusions: Philosophy and the Social Order.* Hassocks, England: Harvester Press, 1977.

Smedley, Agnes. *Daughter of Earth.* Old Westbury, N.Y.: Feminist Press, 1973.

Strauss, Gerald. *Law, Resistance, and the State.* Princeton, N.J.: Princeton University Press, 1986.

Thompson, E. P. *Whigs and Hunters.* New York: Pantheon Books, 1975.

Unger, Roberto. *Knowledge and Politics.* New York: Free Press, 1975.

Waters, Frank. *The Man Who Killed the Deer.* Chicago: Swallow, 1942.

Weinstein, James. *The Corporate Ideal in the Liberal State.* Boston: Beacon Press, 1968.

Woodward, Bob, and Armstrong, Scott. *The Brethren.* New York: Simon & Schuster, 1979.

Zaretsky, Eli. *Capitalism, the Family, and Personal Life.* New York: Harper & Row, 1976.

Zola, Émile. *Germinal.* Trans. by Havelock Ellis. New York: Nonesuch Press, 1942.

Index